THE STORY OF
Human
Development

W9-BFA-538

DEBRA POOLE

AMYE WARREN

NARINA NUÑEZ

PEARSON

Prentice
Hall

Upper Saddle River, New Jersey 07458

Library of Congress Cataloging-in-Publication Data

Poole, Debra A.

The story of human development / Debra A. Poole, Narina Nuñez, Amye Warren. —1st ed.

p. cm.

Includes bibliographical references and index.

ISBN 0-13-030752-1

1. Developmental psychology.   2. Developmental biology.   I. Nunez, Narina.   II. Title.

BF713.P66 2007

155—dc22   2006025086

Editorial Director: Leah Jewell
Executive Editor: Jeff Marshall
Editorial Assistant: Jennifer Puma
Senior Media Editor: Brian Hyland
Supplements Editor: Richard Virginia
Assessment Editor: Kerri Scott
Director of Marketing: Brandy Dawson
Senior Marketing Manager: Jeanette Moyer
Assistant Marketing Manager: Billy Grieco
Marketing Assistant: Laura Kennedy
Editor in Chief, Development: Rochelle Diogenes
Senior Development Editors: Susanna Lesan/Leslie Carr
Managing Editor (Production): Maureen Richardson

Production Liaison: Randy Pettit
Prepress and Manufacturing Manager: Nick Sklitsis
Prepress and Manufacturing Buyer: Sherry Lewis
Creative Design Director: Leslie Osher
Interior and Cover Design: Ilze Lemesis
Cover Illustration/Photo: Getty Images
Image Rights and Permissions Manager: Zina Arabia
Image Researcher: Diane Austin
Image Permission Coordinator: Annette Linder
Text Permission Specialist: The Permissions Group
Composition/Full-Service Project Management: Preparé Inc.
Printer/Binder: RR Donnelly & Sons
Cover Printer: Phoenix Color Corp.

To our parents, Gina and Bob, Jo and John, and Hilda and Aalejo

Credits and acknowledgments borrowed from other sources and reproduced, with permission, in this textbook appear on appropriate page within text (or on page C-1).

Pearson Prentice Hall™ is a trademark of Pearson Education, Inc.
Pearson® is a registered trademark of Pearson plc
Prentice Hall® is a registered trademark of Pearson Education, Inc.

Pearson Education, Ltd.
Pearson Education Australia PTY, Limited
Pearson Education Singapore, Pte., Ltd.
Pearson Education North Asia Ltd.
Pearson Education, Canada, Ltd.

Pearson Educación de Mexico, S.A. de C.V.
Pearson Education–Japan
Pearson Education Malaysia, Pte., Ltd.
Pearson Education, Upper Saddle River, New Jersey

10 9 8 7 6 5 4 3 2 1
ISBN-10:   0-13-240857-0
ISBN-13: 978-0-13-240857-8

Contents

CHAPTER 1 Introduction to Human Development

CHAPTER 2 Heredity and Environment

CHAPTER 3 Prenatal Development and Birth

CHAPTER 4 Profile of the First Three Years

CHAPTER 5 Pathways through the First Three Years

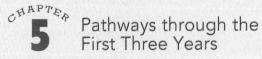

CHAPTER
6   Profile of Early Childhood

CHAPTER
7   Pathways through
Early Childhood

CHAPTER 10 Profile of Adolescence

CHAPTER 11 Pathways through Adolescence

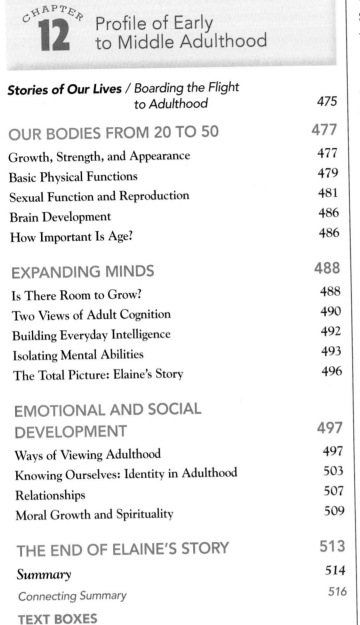

CHAPTER 15 Pathways through Middle to Late Adulthood

Epilogue: The End of Life

Preface

It is impossible to turn on the television without seeing a camera pointed at someone's life. Millions of viewers tune in each week to watch nannies tame naughty children, young adults vie for a shot at the career of their choice, and people of all ages struggle to survive. We are fascinated by stories of other people's lives, perhaps because these stories help us understand who we are ("I look just like her"), who we might become ("I could do *that*"), and how to live ("He insulted his team and got fired"). Although the preferred medium for telling stories has shifted from fireside chats to books and, now, to television and the Internet, stories about real life are as captivating as ever.

The science of human development answers questions about life that cannot be answered by watching the individual lives around us. For example, all children have annoying behaviors, but research that has followed children into adulthood can tell us which behaviors have little consequence for later adjustment and which to nip in the bud. Human development researchers can tell you why love feels the way it feels, what the characteristics of long-lasting relationships are, and why you are not alone if you're thinking of changing jobs. They can also tell you how to prevent some of the obvious signs of aging and how to increase your chances of being healthy and vigorous in the years to come. The science of development has written the ultimate reality show—the story of our lives.

We wrote this book because we wanted to share the wonder of development and how research on development can improve our lives. Before we had gotten very far, however, we found that we had to design an organization for our book that was different from the organization of existing books. The traditional human development textbook divides topics into three categories, first talking about physical development, then cognitive development, and then emotional and social development. But this approach, which made sense when the science of development was young, doesn't convey what we know about development today. As you'll read in Chapter 9, for example, physical abuse threatens children's development by changing the way they attend to and interpret information, which affects their learning in school and how they get along with peers. Now that scientists have monitored the brains of abused children, tracked their academic progress, and looked at their social relationships, it isn't clear whether the topic of abuse should appear under physical, cognitive, or social development. *The problem is that a whole person develops—not fragmented parts.*

Because traditional textbooks have been forced by their organization to talk about bits and pieces of individuals, generations of students have passed through human development classes without learning much about how children and adults actually behave in their everyday lives. We realized this when we began receiving phone calls from parents, social workers, attorneys, and teachers who had questions about an array of practical issues ranging from children's sexual behavior and sibling fights to the reliability of autobiographical memories. During this time, we found ourselves turning to popular sources—not the textbooks we had assigned for class—to answer our own questions about rearing children, managing work and family life, and helping elderly parents. When we decided to write a human development textbook, we knew that we wanted to help students use scientific findings to inform their everyday lives and give them concrete skills they could use in their professional lives.

The philosophy of our book is to convey how a whole person develops in different environmental contexts. We organized information about each age bracket in a new way to accomplish this goal but retained a chronological approach that does not require instructors to reconfigure lecture notes. After you look over the major features of this approach in the following list, we invite you to turn to the remarks we wrote for instructors and to some helpful suggestions for students.

TWO-CHAPTER PAIRS

After three preliminary chapters lay out the history, methods, approaches, and genetic and environmental underpinnings of development, we discuss each period of life in a set of two chapters. The first chapter in each pair describes what a typical individual is like by summarizing the physical, cognitive, emotional, and social changes of that age bracket (for example, "Profile of Middle and Late Childhood"). Then a second chapter explains how individuals develop in different environmental contexts (for example, "Pathways through Middle and Late Childhood"). For instance, after learning how children usually develop between 6 and 12 years of age in Chapter 8, you'll read how abuse experiences alter the path of development in Chapter 9, when you also explore individual differences and the impact of different environmental contexts, such as different family structures and types of school.

TWO-PAGE CONNECTING SUMMARIES

We tie related chapters together with a summary that eliminates divisions between physical, cognitive, emotional, and social development. We put the whole person back together on the left side of each summary by describing the major changes that occur during the early, middle, and later years of that age bracket; on the right side we describe some contexts that influence the path development takes. This organization conveys the philosophy of our text—the whole person developing in context.

REVISITING DEVELOPMENTAL PRINCIPLES

Four guiding principles of development are introduced in Chapter 1:

- ▶ Development is the joint product of nature and nurture.
- ▶ Physical, cognitive, and socioemotional development are interrelated.
- ▶ Developmental outcomes vary over time and contexts.
- ▶ Development is characterized by continuity and discontinuity.

These principles thread through the text by appearing in a featured topic at the end of each two-chapter part (for example, "Revisiting Developmental Principles: Are the First Years of Life the Most Important Years?" or "Revisiting Developmental Principles: Do Parents Matter?"). By showing how scientists use general principles of development to think about complex issues, we prepare students to analyze new issues that will arise during the course of their personal and professional lives.

STORIES OF OUR LIVES

Each chapter opens with a true story that illustrates a central theme in the material that follows. Examples throughout the text are about real people (although often we changed names to protect people's privacy and sometimes spliced interviews or observations of several people into a single example).

DON'T BE FOOLED!, SOLUTIONS, AND INNOVATIONS TEXT BOXES

Everyone needs critical thinking skills to avoid jumping to the wrong conclusions. We use these skills whenever we spot that a "fact" in a magazine is implausible, realize that a study described as a controlled experiment is not a controlled experiment, and understand that a short-term solution for unwanted behavior may lead to long-term problems. Periodic *Don't Be Fooled!* features build critical thinking skills by focusing on individual issues that have special relevance for human development research. Two other text box features provide a look at day-to-day life, both now and in the future. *Solutions* features provide practical advice for solving life problems and *Innovations* features explain contributions from cutting-edge technologies and research.

FOR INSTRUCTORS

Recent advances in genetics, neuroscience, and methodologies for studying complex behavior in everyday settings have transformed the way scientists think about development. We wrote this textbook partly to launch a new generation of books that better represents the science of development, but we also wrote this book to try to solve the problems you face as you strive to make a lasting influence on students—an influence that will help students solve problems in their personal and professional lives for years to come. The philosophy of our book, therefore, involves five overarching goals: provide a contemporary approach to development, engage students and help them learn, promote critical thinking, build practical knowledge, and package information to give instructors maximum flexibility to customize their classes.

PROVIDE A CONTEMPORARY APPROACH TO DEVELOPMENT

A solid understanding of physical, cognitive, emotional, and social development includes an understanding of how these facets of an individual interrelate. Our "whole person developing in context" approach helps students better understand how people behave and grow during each period of life. At the end of the first chapter in each two-chapter pair ("Profile of. . ."), students have a sense of what a typical individual is like from the beginning to the end of that age bracket. Then the second chapter ("Pathways through. . .") looks at variations in development by exploring how life pathways are affected by individual differences and variations across environments and cultures. New information about genetics, neuroscience, and cultural influences are integrated throughout the text.

ENGAGE STUDENTS AND HELP THEM LEARN

Students often say that textbooks don't hold their interest. The major problem is that authors are pressured to cover every topic and mention every study, which has turned textbooks into encyclopedias. Paragraphs in most books are lists of findings with no overarching story, no plot, and—at the end of the chapter—no final point.

What is the solution? People love real-life stories, and our long-term memory system evolved to recall stories. Over time, details of a story are lost and the general point, what memory researchers call the "gist," remains. We usually don't remember much about narratives that don't tell a story, even after a few minutes. Moreover, our memory system is designed to store information that re-

peats over time, because these things are usually more important than one-shot events. In a story, people are introduced, drift in and out of plots and subplots, and have their relationships wrapped up by the end of the book. Once we thought about our own love of stories and our students' love of reality programming, we knew that we wanted to write *The Story of Human Development*.

Of course, we couldn't literally write our textbook as a story. But we could set a theme for each chapter with a real-life story and illustrate subthemes with stories about real people. Then, instead of introducing material once and then dropping it, we made sure that important concepts appear multiple times throughout the text in different contexts, with more information added each time. Finally, we wove the entire text together with a plot. This plot is composed of the four principles of human development that appear periodically in the "Revisiting Developmental Principles" feature. Here students will explore how basic developmental principles help us understand complex issues, such as "Are the first years of life the most important years?" and "How do you build a resilient teen?" By learning to think like a developmentalist, students will build an approach to analyzing problems that will help them deal with new issues in their later personal and professional lives. These principles are an important component of our next goal: to promote critical thinking.

PROMOTE CRITICAL THINKING

Years ago, Carole Wade and Carol Tavris started a revolution by integrating critical thinking into introductory-level psychology texts. Students need the next step when they enroll in a human development class: a set of concepts that will help them think critically about developmental research and change over time. These are concepts that help them spot when a "fact" in a magazine is implausible, realize that a study described as a controlled experiment is really correlational, and understand that a short-term solution for unwanted behavior may lead to long-term problems. Students will learn about these and other issues in *Don't Be Fooled!* text boxes that discuss engaging debates, such as the controversy about "spoiling" babies and claims that male and female sexualities are both wildly different and surprisingly similar.

BUILD PRACTICAL KNOWLEDGE

It is possible to read an entire developmental textbook and not have a feel for how children of various ages behave or what is developmental about the chapters on adulthood. To address these problems, we help students appreciate the applications of course content by relating basic information about physical, cognitive, emotional, and social development to practical issues. Throughout the text, questions that are important to parents, health and mental health professionals, and educators are answered as students explore topics such as toilet training, how to promote healthy eating, how to teach for long-term retention, how to build strong bones, and dozens of other useful issues. In addition, *Solutions* features provide in-depth discussions of how to solve important problems throughout the life span.

GIVE INSTRUCTORS MAXIMUM FLEXIBILITY TO CUSTOMIZE CLASSES

The organization and features of our text allow you to select one textbook and customize it for classes of various sizes and purposes. The 15-chapter format plus epilogue fits easily into a semester and gives you the opportunity to choose from a wide array of topics when you are planning how to use the class time associated with each reading assignment. But because our text covers the same foundational topics as other texts, there is no need to revamp lectures to transition from another book.

Our two-chapter organization with frequent connections between age brackets lends itself to three major approaches to planning lectures:

1. *Chronological lectures* focus on developmental milestones during the age period currently assigned. For example, students who are reading about the preschool period might hear a lecture that discusses the behavioral implications of early brain development.

2. *Topical lectures* focus on specific topics related to the age period assigned for that week. For example, a lecture on health and safety during the preschool period might discuss accidental injuries and lead poisoning.

3. *The matrix approach* is a topical approach to lectures with a life span perspective. For example, a lecture on peer relations in middle to late childhood might include information about the early correlates of peer status as well as the long-term implications of early rejection. By bringing a life span perspective to every topic, this approach encourages students to think about continuities and discontinuities between early and later development.

Our text includes study features that help students master basic terms, concepts, and developmental milestones on their own, including definitions of vocabulary words, key terms in the margins, periodic *Memory Makers* questions, and summaries that revisit important information. These features, plus a study guide and review tests on the companion Web site, help every student succeed (see *For Students*). The engaging, storytelling narrative and clear goals of the text free you to use class time for various purposes depending on your students' backgrounds and professional plans. You can spend some or all of your class time helping students master basic material from the book, but you can also instruct students to master basic material on their own to free class time for discussions and presentation, films and guest speakers, or activities that place more emphasis on the critical thinking skills that are emphasized by our *Revisiting Developmental Principles* and *Don't Be Fooled!* features. A number of support materials are available to help you customize your course.

Instructor Supplements:

▸ **Instructor's Resource Manual.** Prepared by Nicholas P. Murray, Ph.D., of East Carolina University, the Instructor's Resource Manual includes key learning objectives, self-contained class lectures and activities for each chapter, discussion ideas, and an annotated list of additional resources, including *LivePsych!* animations, the *Observations* videos accompanying the text, the Association for Psychological Science (APS) reader *Current Directions in Developmental Psychology*, Web sites, and other outside resources such as texts, journals, and video clips. All resources are organized by chapter section in an effort to better focus content and ease the process of lecture preparation for instructors. The Instructor's Resource Manual will be available as a print item or for download via the Prentice Hall eCatalog or the MyDevelopmentLab platform. [ISBN 978-0-13-175725-7]

▶ **PowerPoint Lecture Slides with Classroom Response System Questions**. These slides are not only intended to be the basis for class lectures but also for class discussions. The incorporation of the CRS questions into each chapter slide show facilitates the use of "clickers"—small hardware devices similar to remote controls, which process student responses to questions and display results in real time. CRS questions are a great means to engage students in learning and precipitate contemplation of text concepts. The slides, created by Jayne P. Bowers of Central Carolina Technical College, also feature prominent figures and tables from the text. The PowerPoint Lecture Slides with Classroom Response System Questions will be available for download via the Prentice Hall eCatalog or the MyDevelopmentLab platform. [ISBN 978-0-13-175718-9]

▶ **Test Item File with TestGen Software.** Authored by Jeannette W. Murphey, Ph.D., of Meridian Community College, this test item file contains approximately 300 to 400 high-quality questions per chapter, including multiple-choice, short answer, and essay items. The items are coded as factual, conceptual, or applied and are given difficulty ratings to help instructors create a balanced test. The test item file also includes a two-page Total Assessment Guide (TAG) that lists all of the test questions in an easy to reference grid. The latest version of TestGen allows instructors to easily create tests for in-class delivery. [TIF ISBN 978-0-13-158214-9 and TestGen ISBN 978-0-13-230115-2]

▶ **MyDevelopmentLab** is the easy-to-use adaptive assessment tool that allows instructors to assess student performance and adapt course content without investing additional time or resources. The student side of this feature, described under Student Supplements, builds a customized study plan for students and draws on multiple learning and tutorial opportunities to help them master the content. The instructor's side of MyDevelopmentLab allows instructors to adjust course content based on class results and organizes instructor resources by section, providing the freedom and flexibility to use these supplementary materials in a variety of ways. Special thanks to Chrisanne Christensen of Southern Arkansas University for creating the MyDevelopmentLab content and for guiding the project from inception to completion. MyDevelopmentLab is available as a stand-alone product [ISBN 978-0-13-223958-5] or is built-in as part of a Blackboard cartridge [ISBN 978-0-13-230117-6] or WebCT e-pack. [ISBN 978-0-13-243557-4]

▶ *Prentice Hall Lecture Launcher Video for Developmental Psychology.* Adopters can receive this new video that includes short clips covering all major topics in introductory psychology. The videos have been carefully selected from the *Films for Humanities and Sciences* library and edited to provide brief and compelling video content for enhancing your lectures. Contact your local representative for a full list of video clips on this tape.

▶ *Prentice Hall is pleased to present Developmental Psychology Videos in a Cultural Landscape.*

▶ **Virtual Child!** *A Web-based program designed to be used by undergraduate students in child and life span development courses.* This interactive simulation offers students the opportunity to act as a parent and raise a virtual child. By making decisions about specific scenarios, **students raise their child from birth to age 17 and see how their own decisions and parenting actions affect their child over time.** At each age, students are given feedback about the various milestones their child has attained. As in real life, certain "unplanned" events may randomly be presented for students. Key stages of the child's development will include personalized feedback.

The Virtual Child ISBN: 978-0-13-175165-1

The Virtual Child is also available as part of MyDevelopmentLab.

► *Instructor's Resource CD-ROM.* The Instructor's Resource CD (978-0-13-243559-8) has instructor materials like the Test Item File, PowerPoints, and the Instructor's Manual. [ISBN 978-0-13-243559-8]

► **SafariX WebBooks.** This new *Pearson Choice* offers students an online subscription at a 50 percent savings. With the SafariX WebBook, students can search the text, make notes online, print out reading assignments that incorporate lecture notes, and bookmark important passages. Ask your Prentice Hall representative for details or visit **www.safarix.com**.

► **OneSearch Guide with ResearchNavigator™.** This guide gives students a quick introduction to con-  ducting research on the Web and introduces Research Navigator™. Research Navigator helps students find, cite, and conduct research with three exclusive databases: EBSCO's ContentSelect Academic Journal Database; *The New York Times* Search by Subject Archive; and Best of the Web Link Library. Available when packaged with a new text for college adoptions; ask your Prentice Hall representative for ordering information.

► *Twenty Studies That Revolutionized Child Psychology* by **Wallace E. Dixon, Jr.** Presenting the seminal research studies that have shaped modern developmental psychology, this brief text provides an overview of the environment that gave rise to each study, its experimental design, its findings, and its impact on current thinking in the discipline.

► *Human Development in Multicultural Context: A Book of Readings.* Written by Michele A. Paludi, this compilation of readings highlights cultural influences in developmental psychology.

► *The Psychology Major: Careers and Strategies for Success.* Written by Eric Landrum (Idaho State University), Stephen Davis (Emporia State University), and Terri Landrum (Idaho State University), this 160-page paperback provides valuable information on career options available to psychology majors, tips for improving academic performance, and a guide to the APA style of research reporting.

Student Supplements:

► *Student Study Guide.* The Student Study Guide for this first edition elevates the notion of study guidance to a new level. Beginning with a candid message from Deb Poole, the narration throughout the "guided review" sections provides students with a new degree of insight into their own learning practices. The Student Study Guide follows the conversational tone of the text, making it among the most reader-friendly and comprehensive printed student supplements available. By the end of the story, students should not only have a firm grasp of material but also the process by which they have reached that point of understanding.

The Student Study Guide's features include chapter highlights, key terms and concepts, comprehensive guided progress tests with multiple-choice, fill-in-the-blank, matching, short answer, and essay questions, and a fun study activity for each chapter. Each chapter also contains two "exit tests" that encourage students to self-assess once all review activities have been completed. The Student Study Guide was prepared by Wendy Bartkus of Adams State College; author Deb Poole assisted with editorial duties and was heavily involved in the organization of content. [ISBN 978-0-13-230105-3]

► *MyDevelopmentLab* is the easy-to-use adaptive assessment tool that provides students with a robust self-assessment. It contains varied question types and builds a customized study plan based on the results of that self-assessment. The customized study plan draws on multiple learning and tutorial opportunities that help students master the content. [ISBN 978-0-13-230118-3]

► *Companion Website at* www.prenhall.com/poole This online study guide provides students with chapter overview and review material as well as practice tests.

▶ *Prentice Hall's Observations in Developmental Psychology CD.* [ISBN 978-0-13-243560-4] Packaged with every new text, this CD-ROM brings to life more than 30 key concepts discussed in the narrative of the text, and offers additional extended videos that coincide with each part in the text to allow students to see real children in action. Students get to view each video twice: once with an introduction to the concept being illustrated and again with commentary describing what is taking place at crucial points in the video. Whether your course has an observation component or not, this CD-ROM provides your students the opportunity to see children in action.

▶ *Current Directions in Developmental Psychology: Readings from the Association for Psychological Science.* This new and exciting reader includes over 20 articles that have been carefully selected for the undergraduate audience, and taken from the very accessible journal, *Current Directions in Psychological Science.* These timely, cutting-edge articles allow instructors to bring their students real-world perspective about today's most current and pressing issues in psychology.

▶ **MyPearson Store**

FOR STUDENTS

You are about to be introduced to one of the most exciting fields of study—the field of human development. The ideas you will encounter in this book may help you understand the people in your life better, but what you will be learning may also reveal some secrets of your own life and help you predict—and possibly even change—your future.

We titled our book *The Story of Human Development* because our goal was to give you an engaging narrative that will hold your interest and make it easy to learn. No matter how appealing a textbook is, however, the amount of information in each chapter is still more than most people can remember by sitting down and reading through a single time. The good news is that researchers have figured

out a lot about how your memory works and what you can do to be more successful in college. Because we have a special interest in memory, every feature of this book—from the overall narrative to the artwork and learning aids—was designed to help you succeed. The following suggestions are ways to get better results from your study time.

▶ *Don't jump right in.* The worst way to read a textbook chapter is to start at the beginning and read to the end. The problem with this straightforward approach is that your brain has no idea what to expect before you begin, so it doesn't know which information is most important or how to organize information. A better way to start is to read the *Table of Contents* and then turn to the *Summary* to get an overview of the entire chapter. (It is not a bad idea to turn to some other activity or sleep on what you've learned at this point.)

▶ *Use pictures and figures to your advantage.* Perhaps at your next sitting, start reading the chapter from front to back, stopping to look at pictures and figures that illustrate findings. Because your brain is especially good at remembering pictures, looking at these items will improve memory, cut down on your study time over the long run, and help you retrieve important concepts when you are taking a test.

▶ *Divide your reading time into several sessions.* Instead of reading through an entire chapter in a single session, try breaking up your study time into several 30- to 40-minute sessions. This will prevent material you have just read from interfering with memories of material you have recently learned.

▶ *Use the built-in learning aids.* Pay special attention to bolded *key terms* and read each *table* that summarizes information or provides examples. Periodically, a footnote at the bottom of the page will define a vocabulary word in case you are unfamiliar with that word. By stopping to answer questions in the *Memory Makers* boxes after each section of a chapter, you can determine whether you are thinking deeply about what you are reading or need to slow down.

▶ *Reread the summary.* It is time to reread the summary after you've read the entire chapter. Now you've seen major material at least three times—when you first read the summary, when you read the chapter, and when you reread the summary. (You've encountered material in tables, figures, and Memory Maker boxes three or four times.) Because repetition strengthens memories, you probably know many of the major terms and concepts at this point. But it's unlikely that you will remember everything. Now you are ready for the final steps that build long-lasting memories.

▶ *Review key terms and revisit unfamiliar information.* A good way to start mastering the material is to work through the *list of key terms* at the end of the chapter, defining each one and coming up with an example of each term or thinking about why each term is important. After you've reread sections of the chapter that explain unfamiliar terms, you are ready to use the study guide.

▶ *Work through your study guide.* It is a mistake to turn to a study guide before you have carefully read a chapter because study guides lack the supportive narratives that build understanding. But although a study guide is not designed to introduce you to the material, it is designed to strengthen memories and identify gaps in your knowledge so you will spend the majority of your review time learning unfamiliar information.

▶ *Use practice quizzes on the companion Website to test your knowledge.*

Of course, if you have other strategies for learning that work well for you, by all means keep using them. But if you've ever felt you could be getting better results from your reading and studying time, we encourage you to try the steps that have helped many of our students improve their test performance.

But enough about studying—a story awaits. Our warmest welcome to *The Story of Human Development*.

Debra Poole
Amye Warren
Narina Nuñez

ACKNOWLEDGMENTS

Taking on a textbook project ensures that one will spend many hours pestering researchers for in-press articles, asking librarians to track down information, and soliciting advice and support from a large team of people who help in so many ways, small and big, behind the scenes. We asked some researchers for more than others during the past years. Chuck Nelson and Sid Segalowitz patiently explained, and then re-explained, recent neuroscience findings and supplied photos and figures, while numerous others sent information ranging from SPSS printouts and standardized tests to laboratory photos and suggested stories. We send special thanks for providing these types of materials to Larry Fenson, Jeff Kellogg, Carolyn Rovee-Collier, Jodie Plumert, Steve Reznick, Suzanne Gaskins, Sharon Bradley Johnson, Carl Johnson, Larissa Niec, Bob Bjork, Alan Baddeley, Renée Babcock, Kerri Laguna, Lucy Brown, Helen Fisher, Elaine Hatfield, Rose Zacks, and PRO-ED, Inc. Much of the artwork in this book reflects more than just a single scientific contribution. For example, the famous photographs illustrating infant vision that Tony Young provided represent 40 years of research by his wife, Davida Teller. We are humbled by the body of knowledge we drew upon to write this book and by the people who generated that knowledge. We hope the dozens of other scientists who answered e-mail questions and sent article reprints will also accept our thanks. It is their collegiality that makes the field of human development so rewarding.

Although we wrote from three universities, Central Michigan University libraries bore the brunt of the traffic involved in researching this book. The Park Library building is a beautiful place to work on a book, a place where library staff invite you into their offices and gladly spend hours researching mysterious inconsistencies in research materials. From a copy of Mark Twain's autobiography in the Clarke Historical Library to a large array of databases and services, there was never a source that was unavailable or a question we couldn't get answered.

We consulted with many colleagues at our universities about topics outside our specialties. Terry Beehr was a valuable resource on work issues and retirement, Susan Jacob lent her expertise in school psychology ethics and law, Rich Metzger provided insightful ideas and resources on cognitive and physical aging, Sharon Bradley-Johnson was a frequent resource on norm-referenced tests and disabilities, and Carl Johnson provided up-to-date information on infant sleep. Many others tolerated us popping into their offices with questions, and we hope these individuals enjoy spotting their contributions in the final result. Encouraging words from Pete Koper, who looked at an early draft, came at just the right time and will always be remembered.

Several students provided much-appreciated research services. Regan Murray, Matthew Beehr, and Jenny Denver tracked down information for several chapters, and Lin Nelson suggested several topics covered in the book, provided the inspiration for two of the text boxes, and pitched in during the final months to help with the references. Throughout this process, office professional Barb Houghton kept information flowing speedily between authors and the production staff. Her knowledge of how to keep things running smoothly is unsurpassed.

Jennifer Gilliland and Jeff Marshall, our editors, did an outstanding job coordinating the team at Prentice Hall who turned our rough ideas into a bound book, but they also contributed many creative ideas. Leslie Carr's and Susanna Lesan's development assistance provided the sentence-by-sentence editing that creates the final "read" of a book, and Leslie Carr also lent us hours of advice and support during photo selection and the production of special features. The hours we spent on the phone with our editors were some of the most enjoyable hours we invested in the book. Other key players who share credit for the feel of the book are managing editor Maureen Richardson, production editor Caterina Melara, designer Ilze Lemesis, and photo researcher Diane Austin. We leaned heavily on production liaison Randy Pettit, who was much appreciated for being our "buck stops here-I'm answering your question" guy, and are also indebted to the energetic marketing team who worked under the direction of Jeanette Moyer.

   We owe special thanks to two groups of people. First, the reviewers listed below took their task seriously and contributed hundreds of suggestions that directed the content of the book. Finally, our families receive

heartfelt thanks for delaying publication of the book with activities that made life worth living and challenges that helped us grow. Prentice Hall knew they were contracting with an author team that puts family life first, and we hope we have honored their trust and our families with the result.

REVIEWERS

Cheryl Anagnopoulos–Black Hills State University

Jonathan Bates–Hunter College, Medgar Evers College, CUNY

Jack Bauer–Northern Arizona University

Dan Bellack–Trident Technical College

Rafael Bejarano–Henderson State University

Kathleen Bergquist–University of Nevada at Las Vegas

Anne Bomba–University of Mississippi

Tanya Boone–California State University at Bakersfield

Michelle Boyer–Middle Tennessee State University

Jerry Bruce–Sam Houston State University

Janine P. Buckner–Seton Hall University

Kate Byerwalter–Grand Rapids Community College

Robert Cameron–Fairmont State University

Toni Campbell–San José State University

Elaine Cassel–Lord Fairfax Community College

Mary Conroy–San José Community College

Dianna Cooper–Purdue University, University of Indianapolis

Nate Cottle–University of North Texas

Diane Daniels–University of North Carolina at Charlotte

Michelle R. Dunlap–Connecticut College

Rebecca Eaton–University of Alabama at Huntsville

Jenni Fauchier–Metropolitian Community College

Diane Feibel–University of Cincinnati

Krista Forrest–University of Nebraska at Kearney

Maria Fracasso–Towson University

Donna Goetz–Elmhurst College

Nicole Guajardo–Christopher Newport University

Michael Hall–Iowa Western Community College

Sharon Hiett–University of Central Florida

Susan Horton–Mesa Community College

Tasha Howe–Humboldt State University

Kathleen Hulbert–University of Massachusetts at Lowell

Ann Jirkovsky–Bellarmine University

Cindy Kamilar–Pikes Peak Community College

Jeff Kellogg–Marian College

Joan Kuchner–Stony Brook University

Martha Langhirt–Columbus State Community College

Corliss Anne Littlefield–Morgan Community College

Pamelyn M. MacDonald–Washburn University

J. Elizabeth Miller–Northern Illinois University

Ronald L. Mullis–Florida State University

Sadie Oats–Pitt Community College

Joe Price–San Diego State University

Janice Rank–Portland Community College

Robert Rycek–University of Nebraska at Kearney

Susan Savage-Stevens–University of Maryland

Mary Ellet Shehadeh–The College of St. Scholastica

Peggy Skinner–South Plains College

Joan Thomas Spiegel–Los Angeles Harbor College

Isabel Trombetti–Community College of Rhode Island

About the Authors

Debra Poole received her bachelor's degree from the University of Connecticut and her Ph.D. in developmental psychology from the University of Iowa. She began her career at Beloit College in Wisconsin and then relocated with her family to Central Michigan University (CMU), where she is a professor in the Department of Psychology. Deb's commitment to teaching introductory psychology and developmental psychology courses earned her CMU's Teacher of the Year and Honors Professor of the Year awards. She is also a recipient of CMU's President's Award for Outstanding Research and Creative Activity for her work on the social policy implications of cognitive development. Deb's interests range from gender differences to the heritability concept, but she is best known as an expert on children's eyewitness testimony, false memories, and techniques for interviewing children. She drafted the forensic interviewing protocol that is used in Michigan for the Governor's Task Force on Children's Justice, using recommendations from her book with Michael Lamb, *Investigative Interviews of Children: A Guide for Helping Professionals* (1998), as the model. Poole has received a Governor's Award from the Family Independence Agency for public service to the state of Michigan and Fellow status in the Association for Psychological Science. When she is not teaching, writing, or analyzing evidence for criminal cases, Deb enjoys her close-knit neighborhood in Mt. Pleasant, a small town in central Michigan, and looks forward to stories from her two grown children.

Amye Warren attended the Georgia Institute of Technology as a National Merit Scholar for her bachelor's degree and stayed to earn a doctoral degree in applied and experimental psychology with concentrations in developmental and cognitive psychology. She then began her career-long position in the Psychology Department at the University of Tennessee at Chattanooga (UTC), where she holds the Patricia Draper Obear Distinguished Teaching Professorship. Amye enjoys teaching courses in child development, language, memory, aging, and research methods, and she loves to motivate graduate students in her practicum on teaching psychology. She has won several teaching and advising honors over the course of more than 20 years at UTC, including the University of Tennessee National Alumni Association Outstanding Teacher Award. She has published numerous articles on children's language and memory development, the abilities of children as witnesses in the legal system, proper and improper techniques for interviewing child witnesses, and the relation between early language development and later reading abilities. Currently, Warren serves as co-director on a grant from the U.S. Department of Education involving the implementation of a statewide training program for early childhood educators who work with young children at risk for later school difficulties. Amye lives with her husband and son in Chattanooga, Tennessee, where they plan frequent outings to zoos, museums, and aquariums.

Narina Nuñez earned her bachelor's degree from the State University of New York at Cortland and a Ph.D. in developmental psychology from Cornell University. She then joined the psychology faculty at the University of Wyoming where she currently serves as chair of the department with a joint appointment in the Department of Criminal Justice. Narina teaches courses on behavioral disorders of childhood and child maltreatment, but her favorite course—which she has taught more than 30 times—is adolescent development. Her research on children has included studies of the impact of maltreatment on development, how jurors perceive children and adolescents, and whether modifications in interviewing techniques can improve children's testimony. Narina serves on the editorial board of the journal *Child Maltreatment*, and she recently received the George Duke Humphrey Outstanding Faculty Award from her university. Narina lives with her husband and youngest son in Laramie, Wyoming, and is fortunate to have her grown daughter living nearby in Denver, Colorado. The family frequently enjoys the outdoor activities of the Rocky Mountain area.

CHAPTER ONE

Introduction to Human Development

Stories of Our Lives
Reminiscences

"No one perspective is sufficient for knowing all that one wishes to understand about anything."

Min Weifang

Principle #3: Developmental Outcomes Change over Time and Contexts

Principle #4: Development Is Characterized by Continuity and Discontinuity

Summary

TEXT BOXES

DON'T BE FOOLED! *How Media Reports Misrepresent Research: A Lesson from the Breast-Feeding Controversy*

INNOVATIONS *Brain Science: The New Frontier*

We would like to introduce you to the field of human development by first introducing ourselves. We are mothers, developmental psychologists, and longtime friends. One fall morning, while we were planning this book, conversation turned to our childhoods. You may have asked your friends some of the same types of questions we did, including "What was your family like?" and "What do you think helped make you the person you are today?" Here are some highlights from our talk.

Deb's family life was colored by the culture of her maternal grandparents, Quinta and Barnebino, who immigrated to the United States from northern Italy. Her childhood was filled with lively conversation, and Deb grew up to be an independent, talkative adult. When we each picked an event that had shaped our lives, Deb described a birth defect that prevented her from walking until she was 2 years old. She had surgery, frequent medical checkups, and was cared for by a nurse while her mother was ill. As a child, Deb preferred quiet activities and was always miserable when teachers organized races and softball games during recess.

Narina's family immigrated more recently. Her father, Aalejo, grew up in Puerto Rico; he met her mother, Hilda, in Germany after World War II. Narina moved frequently with her military family and was immersed in German, English, and Spanish. When we asked about a significant childhood event, Narina paused and said, "I remember the first time I realized that people didn't like Puerto Ricans." Narina's story began in the second grade, when her family, newly stationed in New York City, was looking for an apartment. Time and time again, her dark-skinned father was turned away. It was not until the third grade, when Narina was taunted by children in school, that she realized what discrimination was.

Many generations in the United States left Amye's family with no single ethnic identity. The event she first mentioned as shaping her family's values was economic: "My parents were born in 1928," she said quietly, "before the crash." During the Great Depression of the 1930s, Amye's family made do in rural Georgia. Her father's family lived on a farm, and her mother's father, a barber, accepted chickens and other goods for his services. Like many parents who lived through the depression, John Roy and Vera Jo emphasized education, hard work, and economic independence for their three children. Amye identified strongly with her father, an engineer, and she attended the Georgia Institute of Technology.

Your own life is influenced by the same types of factors that sculpted our three lives: the biological events that left their marks, the neighborhoods and families in which you lived, and the historical events that colored your values. This book is the story of how these and other factors influence human development. This book is the story of our lives.

WHY DO SOME PEOPLE rebound easily from trauma whereas others develop emotional problems? At what age do children develop gender and ethnic identities? What individual differences mold our values and career choices? If you have asked any of these questions—or found yourself thinking about the events that have shaped your life—you will enjoy learning about human development. In this chapter, you will read about the field of human development, including some ways researchers study development and some theoretical perspectives (points of view) they use to organize their findings. Finally, you will learn four principles of development that thread through all of the ages and variations you will encounter in this course.

What Is the Field of Human Development?

The field of **human development** is the scientific study of patterns of change and stability that occur as we move from conception to death. People who study development are interested in describing how individuals change over the course of their lives, explaining why these changes occur, and understanding individual differences in life courses.

One reason people are interested in development is that they want to understand themselves. For example, Sal may never know whether he would have been happier if his brother had never been born, but a review of research on the characteristics of only children and children with siblings might encourage Sal to

human development The scientific study of patterns of change and stability that occur as we move from conception to death.

stop blaming his brother for his problems. People also use information about development to handle the challenges of life. For example, research on aging helps people distinguish between normal forgetfulness and the early signs of Alzheimer's disease. Finally, society relies on developmental science to help us cope with social problems. For example, many laws—from those that determine children's role in legal proceedings to those that regulate driving privileges—are informed by developmental research.

To help you understand what the field of human development is today, it is useful if we first describe where it came from. Then we will outline four ideas that have shaped its basic character.

The Historical Backdrop

If you had questions about your troubled teenager in 1800, you could not speak with a local child psychologist or family specialist. Although mathematics, physics, and biology already had long histories, it would be another 100 years before the field of human development would begin to form. Instead, you might have turned to a religious leader, a physician, or the writings of famous philosophers for information about the nature of children and how to raise them. The answers you received would have represented one of three popular ideas about human nature:

▶ During the Middle Ages*, the religious notion of original sin led people to believe that children were inherently bad and that harsh discipline and moral training were needed to purge them of evil.

▶ In the seventeenth century, the English philosopher and physician John Locke (1632–1704) proposed a less gloomy possibility: We are born **tabula rasa**, a blank slate, and experiences "write" on this slate to help form our talents and personalities. According to this view, we are all products of our environments, and changing negative influences in our environments is the best way to change the course of development.

▶ In the late eighteenth century, the French philosopher Jean-Jacques Rousseau (1712–1778) rejected Locke's position in favor of an even more attractive view of humanity. Rousseau proposed the *doctrine of innate goodness*: Humans are born basically good, so the goal of raising children is to protect them from the corrupting influences of society.

People became more interested in debating these ideas by the mid-1800s, when several historical changes gave children a more prominent role in society (Kessen, 1965). One important factor was advances in understanding nutrition and disease. Many infants never survived their first years of life when Locke and Rousseau were writing, so the typical citizen during these eras had relatively little interest in young children. During the nineteenth century, however, medical discoveries provided hope that children might benefit from careful handling, and materials for parents, such as Holt's *The Care and Feeding of Children* (1894), became popular.

---

*Middle Ages: The period from the end of the Roman Empire to the Renaissance, about A.D. 450 through the mid-fifteenth century.

tabula rasa A blank slate. Used by philosopher John Locke to convey his idea that children are neither good nor bad at birth; rather, they are the product of their subsequent experiences.

In the past, many children worked physically demanding and dangerous jobs. These boys were employed in a Georgia cotton mill in the early 1900s, before economic and social changes defined childhood as a time that is best spent playing, studying, and helping the family by pitching in closer to home.

The industrial revolution also helped usher in the study of human development by highlighting differences between children and adults. Children worked alongside adults from a young age in farming communities, and they continued to do adult work when jobs first shifted to mines and factories. Initially, few people were concerned about the long hours and dangerous working conditions that children were enduring. For example, only two out of 28 physicians who were surveyed in 1833 considered a 12-hour workday excessive for children (Lomax, Kagan, & Rosenkrantz, 1978). Over time, social reformers and educators called for more humane conditions, and they were backed by labor unions that were fearful of job competition from children. Throughout the 1800s and early 1900s, legislation passed in Britain and the United States set children apart from adults and emphasized childhood as a distinct developmental period.

Once medical and economic advances had drawn attention to children, Charles Darwin's theory of evolution provided the justification for studying them scientifically (Darwin, 1859; Dixon & Lerner, 1999). Briefly, the theory of evolution proposed that new species emerge through a gradual process directed by *natural selection*. Natural selection occurs when organisms that are better adapted to their environments survive in greater numbers, thereby passing their traits on to the next generation. The concept of evolution stresses the history of an organism and the role of the environment in shaping physical traits and behavior. This focus on change and development sparked the idea that children were a "natural museum" of adaptive traits that might help us understand the history of our species (Kessen, 1965, p. 115).

By the early 1900s, school attendance laws had created a need for professional educators, clinics had been established to deal with the problems children were having in school and with the law, and a "child study" movement was well under way (Sears, 1975). Interest in adolescence and adulthood soon followed. G. Stanley Hall (1844–1924), who is widely regarded as the founder of developmental psychology, is also considered the father of the scientific study of adolescence for his two-volume set entitled *Adolescence* (1904). Another of his works, *Senescence: The*

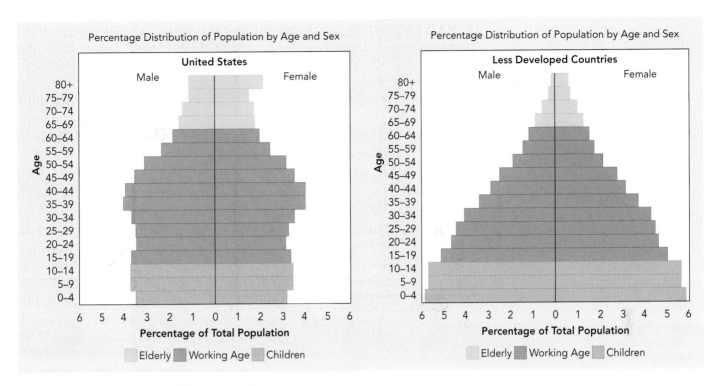

FIGURE 1.1 The squaring of the pyramid.

Family size shrinks and life expectancy increases as countries become industrialized. As a result, the age profile of a population changes from the pyramid we still find in less developed countries to the square shape of the current U.S. population. The "squaring of the pyramid" has dramatically increased interest in aging.

SOURCE: McDevitt & Rowe (2002).

Second Half of Life (1922), marked the beginning of the psychology of aging. In the years that followed, interest in aging increased due to a phenomenon called the *squaring of the pyramid*. As Figure 1.1 illustrates, this phrase refers to a demographic* change from few older individuals to the current pattern in industrialized countries, in which elderly people are a significant proportion of the population.

Today, the field of human development reflects its past. People look to the field for clues about human nature, but they also hope to find answers to practical issues, including questions about how to raise children, when (and how much) teenagers should work, and what we can do to preserve our physical and mental functions as we age. In less than a century, the study of human development has evolved into a varied and exciting field that has a set of characteristics you will read about next.

The Field of Human Development Today

Four characteristics describe the field of human development today: It is interdisciplinary, it studies change across the life span, it is concerned with typical and atypical development, and it relies on scientific evidence.

---

*demographic: Describing characteristics of human populations, such as size and vital statistics. The field of study is called *demography*, and people who work in this field are *demographers*.

life span approach to development An approach to studying development that emphasizes the potential for change that exists throughout life.

normative approach to development An approach to understanding development that describes average or typical development at various ages. Results are often summarized in charts that are called *developmental norms*.

TABLE 1.1   Major Periods of the Life Span

Prenatal period	conception to birth
Infancy and toddlerhood	birth to 3 years
Early childhood	3 to 6 years
Middle childhood	6 to 12 years
Adolescence	12 to about 20 years
Early adulthood	20 to 40 years
Middle adulthood	40 to 65 years
Late adulthood	65 years and older

HUMAN DEVELOPMENT IS INTERDISCIPLINARY. Scientists who study development may be trained in biology, psychology, sociology, anthropology, or a number of other disciplines, including integrative fields such as family studies. In addition, many applied fields—including medicine, education, and social services—make practical use of new findings and work with researchers to identify issues for future study. Currently, people whose jobs involve developmental issues need a broad education that prepares them to work with many types of professionals. For example, a psychologist who works in the schools may need to consult with a physician about a birth defect that is making it difficult for 8-year-old Brent to speak clearly, make a referral to a speech pathologist, and help Brent's teacher deal with classmates who are teasing him.

HUMAN DEVELOPMENT STUDIES CHANGE ACROSS THE LIFE SPAN. There are two approaches to thinking about the changes involved in the journey from childhood to our later years. According to the *traditional approach to development*, change is most rapid during infancy and declines sharply as people approach adulthood. Then, after years of stability, the declines associated with aging begin. Authors who take this perspective often believe that early life events are particularly important for shaping adult interests and abilities. In contrast, the **life span approach to development** emphasizes the potential for change that exists throughout our lives. Today, both approaches include research that is primarily focused on one of the age periods described in Table 1.1 and some that analyzes trends across periods.

HUMAN DEVELOPMENT IS CONCERNED WITH TYPICAL AND ATYPICAL DEVELOPMENT. When should children talk? At what age does the adolescent growth spurt usually occur? How often does the typical married couple have sex? The **normative approach to development** indulges our curiosity about other people by summarizing data from large numbers of individuals. These findings are often reported in tables, called *developmental norms*, that present average scores for various age groups. (The most frequently reported "average" is the mean, which is simply the sum of scores divided by the number of scores.) Developmental norms describe such things as physical changes across the life span and the average age at which people achieve various developmental milestones, such as walking or speaking 50 different words.

Norms are useful reference guides, but it is easy to misinterpret the meaning of average scores. Misunderstandings occur because many traits, including height and IQ scores, are distributed throughout a population in a roughly *bell-shaped distribution* such as the one in Figure 1.2 (Fenson, 2002). As you can see, a bell-shaped distribution is one in which many individuals cluster around the mean, with fewer people having extremely high or low scores. The distribution in Figure 1.2 reports the number of words 2-year-olds have spoken (including sound effects like "uh oh" and "mooo"). It is rather remarkable that the average 2-year-old knows 312 different words and sounds. But this information scared Dawn and Carl, whose 2-year-old daughter, Lexie, knows only 100 words. Parents with children like Lexie should be reminded that about 50 percent of children use fewer words than the mean on a table of norms. Moreover, most of these

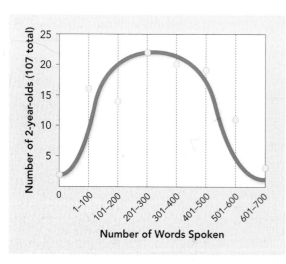

FIGURE 1.2 A bell-shaped distribution.

Many traits are distributed in a bell shape, with most individuals clustering around the average score and few having very high or very low scores. This graph reports the mean number of different words that 2-year-olds have spoken (as reported by their parents). Most children who are below average are normal children who are developing just fine.

SOURCE: Fenson (2002).

slower talkers are perfectly normal children who will later be indistinguishable from their peers.

Differences among individuals represent two types of variation. *Quantitative differences* reflect differences in the *amount* of some characteristic. For example, the developmental processes that produced 6-foot, 2-inch Matt are the same as those that produced 5-foot, 6-inch Justin. Both men are well within the normal range and their height difference has no particular implication for their health. *Qualitative differences* occur when different developmental processes place people into different categories. If no one can understand Lexie's words except her parents, for example, then she may have a condition that distinguishes her from other children, such as a hearing loss. The study of human development uses information on normal and abnormal development to distinguish between differences that have no important implications for development and differences that put people at risk for later problems.

HUMAN DEVELOPMENT RELIES ON SCIENTIFIC EVIDENCE. Experts learn about human development by observing natural phenomena, conducting experiments, and publishing their results so others can evaluate their methods. In other words, human development is a science just as biology and chemistry are sciences.

Over the years, scientific findings have corrected many wrong ideas about development, such as the notion that masturbation will lead to mental disease (Tissot, 1758) and John B. Watson's (1928) warning that mothers should never hug or kiss their children. (You will be reading more about Watson later in this chapter.) Even so, the public has recently lost some confidence in the scientific process. Instead of viewing science as totally objective, scholars now warn the public that science is a human activity, one that is influenced by investigators' biases and social trends. In addition, the flip-flop nature of advice about development (sleep with your children, never sleep with your children, sleep with your children) leads many people to think that "scientific" findings are no more reliable than old-fashioned common sense.

If the scientific process is subject to errors and biases, why should we base the study of human development on scientific methods? The answer is that unlike ideas based on authority ("A famous philosopher said") or intuition ("I can tell"), scientific ideas *progress*. In other words, the scientific process encourages us to consider opposing ideas, specifies what observations might prove us wrong, and eventually leads to progress that improves our understanding of the world.

The history of ideas about mothers is a good example of the value of a scientific perspective. Mothers have been blamed for causing a wide range of problems in their children, from behavior disorders and juvenile delinquency to schizophrenia and autism. One analysis of articles published between 1970 and 1982 found that mothers were blamed for 72 different kinds of problems, including tantrums, the inability to deal with color blindness, and "koro" (a feeling of penile shrinkage and fear of death) (Caplan & Hall-McCorquodale, 1985). Of course, we now know that unresponsive parenting does not cause schizophrenia or autism and that various biological and cultural factors play a role in other disturbances that used to be blamed on dear old mom (Meltzer, 2000; Wing, 1997).

Once the power of mothers was called into question, scientists began looking at development in new ways. They discovered that parenting is not just a one-way street but also that *children* alter the parenting styles of their mothers and fathers (Lerner et al., 1995). They also found that neighborhoods and peers affect the directions we take in life (Rose et al., 2003). Although some mothers may have regretted not being the only influence in their children's lives, most sighed with relief when they were told to stop shouldering all the blame for their

There is more in this picture than a mother who is providing a stimulating reading activity for her son. There is also a child whose enthusiasm prompts his mother to keep reading—long after she is tired of the subject matter. Research findings have led scientists to stop focusing on how parents influence children and to look instead at how parents and children influence each other.

children's failings. In other words, a scientific perspective encouraged people to consider alternative explanations, which led to a more complete view of development. In our next section, you will be looking at the methods scientists use to gather data and at the scientific process in general.

〉〉〉 MEMORY MAKERS 〈〈〈

1. The field of human development is best described as the _D_.
   (a) study of child development
   (b) practical application of medical and behavioral findings to improve our lives
   (c) systematic collection of data on normal and abnormal behavior
   (d) scientific study of patterns of change and stability that occur as we move from conception to death

2. _A_ proposed that we are born *tabula rasa*, that is, _____.
   (a) Locke; a blank slate   (b) Locke; with original sin
   (c) Rousseau; a blank slate   (d) Rousseau; with original sin

3. Dr. Gesell collects data on when children first roll over, crawl, and walk. He is taking a _C_ approach to the study of human development.

   (a) multivariate   (b) qualitative   (c) normative   (d) idiographic

[1-d (the field of human development relies on scientific methods to study change and stability across the life span); 2-a (philosopher John Locke proposed that we are like a blank slate; experiences "write" on us to form our talents and personalities); 3-c (the normative approach is interested in describing typical characteristics or accomplishments at various age)]

Research Methods

Investigators rarely talk about their lives but—truth be known—the work of science can be deadly dull. Developmental researchers spend hours soothing uncooperative infants, watching videotapes, and waiting for adults who forgot their appointments. Few investigators endure these tasks to confirm what they believed all along. On the contrary, scientists are motivated by the twists and turns of research—the surprising finding, the peculiar observation, or the new technology that promises to open a door that has been locked for centuries. To search for the unexpected, developmental scientists use a variety of methods to collect information and look for patterns in the results.

Collecting Information

The scientific process begins when developmental researchers collect information about people's characteristics, life events, or behavior. The target characteristics, events, or behaviors are the **variables** in a study. Variables can be anything that has more than one value, such as a person's weight, the number of accidents, and so forth. For example, studies on the impact of moving on children's adjustment have looked at two variables: how often children have moved and the number of behavior problems they have (Adam, 2004). (As you probably predicted, children who have moved more often have more behavior problems.) Scientists use a variety of ways of gathering information about the variables they are interested in, including observations, self-reports, archival data, and results from tests and automated recording devices.

WATCHING AND DESCRIBING. There are three broad categories of observational methods. In **naturalistic observation**, researchers watch people in real-world settings such as shopping malls, day care centers, and schools. The goal of

variables Characteristics, events, or behaviors that take more than one value, such as weight, number of hospitalizations, and so forth. The factors scientists manipulate or measure when they conduct a study are the *variables* in the study.

naturalistic observation Observation in real-world settings that does not interfere with or influence people's ongoing activities.

naturalistic observation is to collect information without interfering with or influencing people's behavior. In **participant observation**, researchers observe while participating in a group's ongoing activities. Participant observation is most helpful when we know very little about a group or the group's activities are not public (Jorgensen, 1989). For example, anthropology professor Cathy Small (aka "Rebekah Nathan") took a leave of absence to attend college and live in a residence hall in order to observe and describe today's college culture. Her book, *My Freshman Year*, is a fascinating account of how students spend time and their views of the college experience (Nathan, 2005). This book is an **ethnography**, an in-depth description of a group's daily life. Ethnographies give us a window into life in other cultures, including other societies' approaches to child rearing, family relationships, and transitions to adulthood.

Structured observation is a useful approach when researchers need more control over the situation or want to observe behavior that is unlikely to occur spontaneously. For structured observation, researchers create specific situations and observe people's reactions. Arranging for children to work together on a school project in order to record their conversations is an example of structured observation (Menn & Ratner, 2000).

SELF-REPORTS. The easiest way to get information about what people do, know, and believe is to ask them. Researchers collect **self-reports**—people's descriptions of their own life events, behaviors, feelings, or attitudes—in a variety of ways.

In a *diary study*, people record behavior or feelings during specified time periods. In one study, for example, parents made an entry in a log whenever their children were watching television. This information agreed well with video records and was more accurate than simply asking parents how much time their children spent watching television (Anderson et al., 1985). Today, diaries are used to study infant sleep, the relationship between daily events and mood, and numerous other topics (Barr et al., 2005; Hankin, Fraley, & Abela, 2005).

Interviews are verbal conversations conducted in person or on the phone. Interviewing skills are an important part of training for many professions because people's answers are affected by the interviewer's behavior and the way questions are phrased. For example, young children provide more accurate information when interviewers make open-ended requests, such as "Tell me what happened," rather than ask misleading questions, such as "He was wearing a hat, wasn't he?" (Dickinson, Poole, & Laimon, 2005).

A *questionnaire* is a list of questions that people read and answer. Questionnaires are less flexible than interviews because the researcher cannot clarify ambiguous questions or add new questions to follow up on unexpected answers. But it is relatively inexpensive and quick to administer questionnaires, which is one reason they are a popular research tool (Groves et al., 2004).

ARCHIVAL DATA. Self-reports do have their drawbacks. People often give researchers inaccurate information because their memories fail or they are embarrassed to tell the truth. For example, parents are unreliable sources of information about which vaccinations their children have had and when their children first

participant observation
Observation by a researcher who is actively participating in a group's activities.

ethnography An in-depth description of a group's daily activities, generally developed by participant observation.

structured observation
Observations of behavior in situations or settings that are created by the investigator.

self-reports People's descriptions of their own life events, behaviors, feelings, or attitudes. Self-reports include diary records and responses to interviews and questionnaires.

Asking people to keep a diary of their television viewing leads to more accurate data about their viewing habits than simply asking them how much television they watch.

showed psychiatric symptoms (Angold et al., 1996; Lee et al., 1999). In cases in which self-reports are likely to be inaccurate, researchers sometimes look up information in existing records. **Archival data** include such things as school files, medical records, and police reports. Although you might assume that archival data are always more accurate than self-reports, some types of archival data are notoriously subject to bias (Hurst, 1995). For example, ambiguity about the definition of hate crimes (crimes motivated by prejudice) makes it difficult to interpret published crime statistics (Nolan et al., 2004).

TESTS AND OTHER MEASURES. Standardized tests (discussed in Chapter 5) require people to answer questions or perform a series of tasks. The word *standardized* means that researchers have already summarized data from a large number of people who have taken these tests, so any individual's score can be compared against others of his or her age.

Computers or other machines that record responses are also common ways to collect information about people's abilities, decisions, and even their brain activity. Recording devices eliminate the errors human observers make but are not without problems of their own. For example, one study found that adults who felt less competent with computers scored lower than their peers on a computerized memory test, and older participants were more likely than younger participants to be "computer anxious" (Laguna & Babcock, 2000). This study raises the possibility that age differences in memory might be exaggerated when investigators use equipment that intimidates one age group more than another.

It is not uncommon for researchers to use several methods of collecting information in a single study. For example, Cathy Small supplemented her observations of campus life with information she obtained by conducting one-on-one interviews, analyzing answers to questions she posted in women's bathrooms, recording her own activities in a diary, and getting permission to look at attendance records for a large lecture class (which is a type of archival data).

Designing Research

Once researchers have decided which variables they want to study, it is time to choose a research design. Research designs specify who will be studied, when data will be collected, and how the research team will interact with participants. Researchers choose different research designs depending on their goals. Three basic approaches are case studies, correlational studies, and experiments. Developmental research designs include age as a variable in order to study developmental change.

CASE STUDIES: DESCRIBING INDIVIDUALS. Many scholars (including Charles Darwin) wrote descriptions of their own children's development that came to be called "baby biographies" (Lomax et al., 1978). Each of these biographies was a **case study**: an in-depth study of a particular person.

One early case study of atypical development involved a girl known as Isabelle, who was discovered in 1938 at the age of $6\frac{1}{2}$ years. Born illegitimately to a deaf-mute mother, Isabelle was raised in a dark room and had no chance to develop verbal speech (Mason, 1942). Despite delayed physical and social development, her subsequent recovery was remarkable, and she reached a normal educational level by the age of $8\frac{1}{2}$ years. Although outcomes as favorable as this are not typical of isolated children, data from Isabelle and other severely deprived children argue against the idea that individuals never recover from a lack of attention during their early years. Today, case studies remain popular for exploring

archival data Information in existing records such as school files, police reports, and government documents.

case study An in-depth study of a particular person.

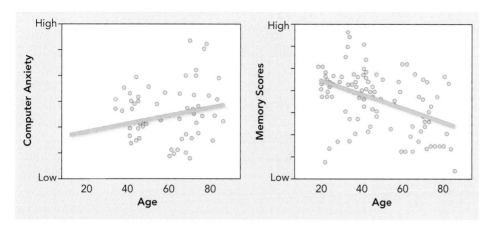

FIGURE 1.3 Correlation coefficients.

Correlation coefficients report the direction and strength of a relationship between two variables. On these graphs, lines passing through actual data make the relationships more obvious. On the left is the +.32 correlation between age and computer anxiety: As age increases, computer anxiety also increases. On the right is the −.44 correlation between age and memory for recently presented information: As age increases, memory decreases. Correlations of this magnitude are common in human development research.

SOURCE: Laguna & Babcock (2000).

unusual circumstances, such as peculiar behaviors produced by brain injury (Colvin, Funnell, & Gazzaniga, 2005).

CORRELATIONAL STUDIES: LOOKING FOR RELATIONSHIPS. One goal of science is to discover relationships between events. A **correlational study** looks for a relationship between *naturally occurring variables*—physical traits, behaviors, and attitudes as these things naturally exist in the world. In this book, you will read about many relationships that have been investigated using correlational studies, such as the relationship between alcohol use during pregnancy and children's intelligence (in Chapter 3) and the relationship between how frequently parents monitor their teenagers' whereabouts and teenagers' grades (in Chapter 10).

Scientists determine whether there is a relationship between two variables by computing a **correlation coefficient**. A correlation coefficient is just a number that indicates how well you can predict the value of one variable if you know the value of the other variable. To provide information about the *direction* and *strength* of the relationship, correlation coefficients range from −1.0 to +1.0. The sign (either positive or negative) tells you the direction of the relationship. A positive correlation (+) means that as scores on one variable increase, scores on the other variable also increase. For example, we mentioned the positive correlation between age and computer anxiety (as age increases, fear of computers increases). A negative (−) correlation means that scores on one variable *decrease* as scores on the other variable increase. For example, there is a negative correlation between age and some types of memory (as age increases, memory scores decrease).

The size of a correlation coefficient, regardless of it being positive or negative, tells you the strength of the relationship. A correlation of 0.0 indicates there is no relationship between the variables. The strongest relationships are *perfect* correlations (either +1.0 or −1.0). If a correlation is perfect, you can predict someone's score on one variable without error if you know his or her score on the other variable. In actual studies, correlation coefficients usually range from weak correlations, such

correlational study A study that looks for a relationship between *naturally occuring variables*—physical traits, behaviors, and attitudes as these things naturally exist in the world.

correlation coefficient A statistic that describes the strength and direction of the relationship between two variables.

as −.12 or +.12, to strong correlations, such as −.84 or +.84. To show you what correlational data look like, we plotted data from a study mentioned earlier that looked at relationships between age, computer anxiety, and memory (Laguna & Babcock, 2000). Figure 1.3 shows you the actual relationship between age and computer anxiety (a positive correlation) and the actual relationship between age and memory for information presented on a computer (a negative correlation).

Correlations tell you whether two variables are related, but they cannot tell you *why* those variables are related. For example, we know that people who dislike computers perform more poorly than other people on computerized memory tests. It is possible that computer anxiety *causes* poor performance (because anxiety lowers performance). But other explanations are possible as well. Memory problems might cause computer anxiety (because people with poor memories hate complicated equipment). Alternatively, another variable, such as poor health, might raise anxiety *and* cause memory problems. In this case there is a **third variable problem**, a problem that occurs when a variable other than the two in question is responsible for the relationship. Because it is always possible that some "third variable" is responsible for correlational findings, correlations *cannot tell us about cause and effect*. As you will read next, the best way to determine what is *causing* a relationship is to design an experiment.

EXPERIMENTS: FINDING CAUSES. The goal of an experiment is to determine cause-effect relationships—in other words, to figure out what causes something to occur. To accomplish this, researchers manipulate one variable at a time, trying to hold all other variables constant. In simple terms, an **experiment** is a research method for discovering cause-effect relationships by manipulating one variable to discover its effect on another variable.

To design an experiment, researchers begin by formulating a *hypothesis* (a prediction) about a specific casual relationship. For example, some developmental psychologists who were working in the 1990s became fascinated by bizarre events that preschool children had reported during interviews about suspected sexual abuse, including claims of being pierced with knives (when there was no physical evidence) and having peanut butter licked off their bodies at school. Because most of these interviews contained highly leading questions, people began to suspect that children were more likely than adults to go along with suggestions embedded in questions ("Some of the kids told me that things happened with knives.") (Ceci & Bruck, 1995, p. 116). To test the hypothesis that misleading questions might actually *cause* false reports, researchers brought children into the laboratory to talk about events. Some children were assigned to be interviewed with open-ended questions ("What happened?") whereas others were interviewed with highly suggestive questions ("He touched you, didn't he?"). In study after study, children exposed to suggestive questions reported more false events than children who experienced more neutral interviews (Poole & Lamb, 1998). As you will read in Chapter 6, results from these experiments have helped us understand more about children's memory and how to investigate crimes against children.

Unlike correlational studies, experiments have two *types* of variables. The **independent variable** is the variable researchers control when they create groups or conditions. In interviewing studies, the type of interview (neutral or misleading) is the independent variable. The **dependent variable** is the variable researchers *measure*, for example, the accuracy of children's event descriptions. (An easy way to remember these terms is to think, "report accuracy is *dependent upon* the type of interview, so report accuracy is the dependent variable.")

third variable problem The problem that exists when two variables are correlated because they are both associated with a third variable, not because one causes the other. The possibility of unmeasured "third variables" makes it impossible to make causal influences from a single correlation coefficient.

experiment A research method for discovering cause–effect relationships that involves manipulating one variable to discover its effect on another variable.

independent variable The variable a researcher manipulates in an experiment. Independent variables consist of two or more groups or conditions.

dependent variable The variable a researcher measures in an experiment to determine the influence of the independent (manipulated) variable.

It is difficult to design a perfect experiment, so we generally have greater confidence in results that have been repeated, or *replicated*, in many different experiments. Any individual study might have influences that have gone undetected. For example, some of the things children report during interviewing experiments could reflect things they have heard from other children who have already participated (Principe & Ceci, 2002). Another problem exists when results fail to generalize to other situations or individuals. For instance, studies conducted at university day care centers often test children who are used to participating in studies. These children may be more relaxed and more likely to act silly than the typical child who is interviewed about an alleged crime. The best experiments successfully control any variables that might distort results and reveal cause–effect relationships as these relationships exist in the real world.

Scientists communicate findings from case studies, correlational studies, and experiments by publishing their results in professional journals (magazines containing articles that have been reviewed and accepted by experts in the field). The general public usually learns about these findings from newspapers and mass-circulation magazines, such as *Newsweek*, *Time*, and other familiar titles. Unfortunately, the information presented in popular sources is not nearly as detailed as what is reported in scientific journals. Because newspapers and magazines are pressured to give the public clear-cut answers, it is common for journalists to draw causal conclusions from correlational studies. Even more troublesome, journalists sometimes describe correlational studies *as if they were* controlled experiments. When this occurs, even sophisticated readers may find it difficult to think critically about the results. For an example of these problems, read our first *Don't Be Fooled!* feature on scientific findings in the popular media.

DON'T BE FOOLED

Research results described in newspaper and magazine articles often present correlational studies as if they were controlled experiments. Remember that correlational studies only document a relationship; they *cannot* identify the *cause* of the relationship.

HOW MEDIA REPORTS MISREPRESENT RESEARCH: A LESSON FROM THE BREAST-FEEDING CONTROVERSY

One of the earliest decisions parents make is also one of the most difficult: Should baby be breast-fed or bottle fed? For some, breast-feeding is a child's birthright; for others, it is a highly personal choice. In the United States, the public casts a split ballot, with 70 percent of new mothers breast-feeding their infants (Centers for Disease Control and Prevention, 2005e).

A controversy about breast-feeding erupted in 1992, when a team of investigators published a follow-up study of premature babies who had been fed either breast milk or formula during their early weeks of life (Lucas et al., 1992). At 7 to 8 years of age, children who had received breast milk scored 8 points higher than formula-fed children on an intelligence test. Around the world, newspapers and magazines were quick to announce that a substance in breast milk promoted good mental development.

Breast Milk for Premature Babies Tied to Higher Intelligence Scores

By TERESA L. WAITE
Published: March 4, 1992

Children fed breast milk as premature infants scored significantly higher on intelligence tests than children also born prematurely who had not received their mothers' milk, a study has found.

The results, reported recently in The Lancet, a British medical journal, were called significant, even after taking into account other possible explanations, for example that mothers who provided breast milk tended to be better educated and from higher-income families.

The study adds weight to growing evidence that breast milk may be superior to formula...

strongly suggests that human milk might have factors important to brain development," said Dr. Alan Lucas, who conducted the study with four colleagues. A Biological Explanation

Dr. Lucas, who is head of infant and child nutrition at the Medical Research Council's Dunn Nutrition Unit in Cambridge, said it was biologically plausible that breast milk could influence intelligence, since it contains essential long-chain fats and hormones that are not found in formula and that are important to the the developing brain's structure.

The scientists studied 300 premature...

intelligence tests when they were 8 years old than children who had not received their mothers' milk.

Since the infants received milk by tube, the scientists were able to study the influence of breast milk apart from the bonding process of breast-feeding, which could in itself affect development. Even after excluding the 35 infants who were breast-fed once they were sent home, the intellectual advantage remained the same for those who received their mothers' milk.

The researchers also took in...

A Study Links I.Q. and Breast-Feeding

Published: May 8, 2002

The longer infants are breast-fed higher they are likely to score on intelligence tests as adults, a Danish study said today.

I.Q. tests administered to more than 3,000 Danes born from 1959 to 1961 showed that being breast-fed for up to nine months conferred a

long-lasting intellectual benefit.

The study appears in this week's issue of The Journal of the American Medical Association.

Those who were breast-fed less than one month as infants scored a mean of 99.4 on an I.Q. test, with progressively higher scores correlating to the longer

duration of breast-feeding. Those breast-fed from seven to nine months scored a mean 106 on the test. Those breast-fed longer than nine months showed a dip in mean score, to 104.

A score above 100 is more than 50 percent of people achieve; 25 percent score above 110.

The media frenzy generated by this article included a flurry of commentaries in professional journals. Critics were quick to point out that the study was *not* a controlled experiment because mothers had not been *assigned* to feeding conditions. Instead, mothers *decided* whether or not to provide breast milk to the hospital and, therefore, the design was correlational. It is well known that mothers who choose to breast-feed are different than those who use formula: On average, they are older, better educated, less likely to smoke during pregnancy, and more likely to provide a stimulating home environment (Horwood & Fergusson, 1998). Therefore, the 8-point advantage among breast-fed children could have been due to any number of factors. In one critique, three physicians analyzed 40 studies published from 1929 to 2001. Only two studies evaluated full-term infants and met a set of basic research standards, such as controlling for parents' economic status and using observers who were unaware of the children's feeding status. Of these two studies, one concluded that breast-feeding promotes intelligence; the other did not (Jain, Concato, & Leventhal, 2002).

Did the media misrepresent Lucas and colleagues' findings? Not entirely. Many articles, such as one from *The Washington Post* ("Children's higher IQ is linked to breast milk," 1992), cautioned readers that "the study is not definitive proof." Nonetheless, 35 reports failed to mention that the results were based on premature babies and might not apply to most infants (Lucas & Cole, 1992). Also, most reports lacked enough detail for readers to know whether the study was experimental or correlational. The lesson for consumers is obvious: Media announcements draw our attention to new research, but they cannot substitute for reading the scientific article.

The effect of formula feeding on mental development remains an unsolved issue. One study of adults born before 1961 also found a difference in IQ scores between breast-fed and bottle-fed groups, but formula was less nutritionally complete 30 years ago (Mortensen et al., 2002). Another study of mostly full-term babies found no effect of early feeding after mother's intelligence and parenting skills were taken into account (Jacobson, Chiodo, & Jacobson, 1999). Furthermore, recent studies have found that relationships between infant feeding choices and intelligence disappear as children age (Anderson, Johnstone, & Remley, 1999; Malloy & Bernendes, 1998; Wigg et al., 1998). This finding suggests that social and environmental factors have a large impact on cognitive development after infancy.

Was the media wrong to advocate breast-feeding? Not at all. Breast-fed babies enjoy a host of health advantages, including lower rates of infection and fewer allergic reactions (Uauy & Peirano, 1999). Still, it is misleading to peddle higher IQs as a reason to breast-feed. What can we learn from the breast-feeding controversy? First, a study with two or more groups is *not always* a controlled experiment. Second, it is unwise to base important life decisions on a report in the popular media. When you want to make an informed decision, it pays to read original research from a variety of authors and sources.

RESEARCH DESIGNS FOR STUDYING DEVELOPMENT. In order to study developmental change, researchers must take age and the passage of time into account. The three major designs for developmental research are illustrated in Figure 1.4: cross-sectional studies, longitudinal studies, and cross-sequential studies.

In a **cross-sectional study**, researchers test people from several different age groups at one point in time. For example, a cross-sectional study of well-being across adulthood might involve asking 25-year-olds, 45-year-olds, and 65-year-olds to rate how happy they are.

Cross-sectional studies provide information about different age groups but not about the stability of *individuals'* behavior over time. Thus, a cross-sectional study of happiness can tell us that 65-year-olds are as happy as 25-year-olds, but this information does not tell us whether each individual tends to maintain a particular level of happiness. Also, each age group represents a different *cohort*—a group of people born at a particular time—so we cannot be sure that the patterns we observe are due *only* to age. For example, consider the relationship between problem-solving skill and age. Scores on tests that require people to analyze visual patterns have been increasing steadily over time, possibly because more recent generations have been exposed to more complicated visual environments through experiences with computer screens, video games, and so forth (Neisser, 1997). Therefore, comparing the problem-solving abilities of older people against computer-game-addicted adults could lead us to attribute performance differences to aging that are really just a function of cultural experiences. Researchers use the term **cohort effects** to refer to differences between age groups that result from cultural changes.

cross-sectional study A research design in which investigators test individuals from several different age groups at one point in time.

cohort effects Systematic differences between age groups that are due to cultural changes over time.

	Age Groups Studied		
	1980	**1990**	**2000**
Cross-sectional Study	20-year-olds 30-year-olds 40-year-olds		
Longitudinal Study	20-year-olds ⟶	Same individuals as 30-year-olds ⟶	Same individuals as 40-year-olds
Cross-sequential Study	20-year-olds ⟶	Same individuals as 30-year-olds	
	30-year-olds ⟶	Same individuals as 40-year-olds	
	40-year-olds ⟶	Same individuals as 50-year-olds	

FIGURE 1.4 Developmental research designs.

To conduct a cross-sectional study, researchers collect data at one point in time from different age groups. For a longitudinal study, they observe a single group of individuals over time. These strategies can be combined in a cross-sequential study by starting with two or more age groups and following them longitudinally. Comparing people of the same age across samples provides information about cohort (group) effects in the cross-sequential design.

Findings from developmental studies are influenced by the social circumstances of the cohorts that are compared or followed over time. For example, the intellectual skills and social behaviors that were emphasized in a typical classroom in the 1950s are different from the skills and behaviors that are valued today.

longitudinal study A research design in which investigators follow a group of individuals over a period of time.

cross-sequential study A combination of cross-sectional and longitudinal designs, in which several age groups are identified at one point in time and then retested at regular intervals.

A **longitudinal study** observes or tests the same individuals over a period of time. This research strategy provides information about patterns of stability and change in development. For example, a longitudinal study would tell us whether everyone tends to maintain their level of happiness over time or whether some individuals report decreased happiness as they age while others report increased happiness. This type of study would also allow us to look at how early events relate to later outcomes, so we can look at which characteristics in young adulthood predicted happiness later in life. This information provides a richer picture of development than the one provided by a cross-sectional study.

But longitudinal research also has its limitations. When only a single cohort (age group) is followed, changes that appear to be developmental may actually be due to historical events. For example, a study of happiness that began in the late 1960s would compare young adults during an optimistic time with middle adults during the economic recession that arrived about 20 years later. In this case, both age and social circumstances have influenced results. Another problem is that it is difficult to keep track of participants over the years. Often, the people who drop out of longitudinal studies are less educated and differ in other important ways from those who remain, making the data from older ages less representative of people as a whole. Finally, repeated exposures to testing procedures or the questions used in the study provide practice that may camouflage developmental change.

The limitations of cross-sectional and longitudinal research have led some investigators to use combined techniques called *sequential designs* (Schaie, 1965, 1996). As shown in Figure 1.4, investigators begin a **cross-sequential study** by designing a cross-sectional study but then retesting groups at regular intervals. This method creates a series of separate longitudinal designs, each involving a different cohort of people. By comparing data across selected groups, investigators can rule out the possibility that a particular time in history or systematic dropout produced the observed changes over time. Of course, even cross-sequential studies provide no guarantee that results will represent people from other times and places.

The Professional Responsibilities of Human Development Researchers

It is time-consuming and often frustrating to conduct research, but investigators are rewarded by knowing that their findings may be used to improve people's lives. As you will read in later chapters, developmental research has been used to plan reading instruction, help couples cope with the challenges of marriage, and design homes for the elderly. Concern for human welfare also influences the process of planning research. Investigators strive to protect the safety and dignity of the people they study by following recommendations that committees and professional groups have developed for preventing research participants from being exploited or harmed. Ethical guidelines address two general topics: standards for the ethical treatment of people who participate in research and guidelines for communicating findings with other professionals and the general public.

STANDARDS FOR CONDUCTING RESEARCH. Public awareness of the need to oversee research reached new levels in May 1997, when President Clinton apologized to the families of men who were involved in a project to study the progression of untreated syphilis. The study began in 1932, when hundreds of poor,

African American men believed that the United States Public Health Service had offered them free medical treatment for "bad blood" (a local term for syphilis, anemia, and fatigue). But instead of receiving treatment, scientists merely observed the men's health—even after penicillin was identified as an effective treatment (Love, Thomson, & Royal, 1999).

To prevent such abuses, universities and centers that receive funds from the federal government are required to have *institutional review boards (IRBs)* that approve projects to ensure that research procedures follow accepted practice. When investigators plan to deceive participants or use procedures that might cause physical discomfort or psychological harm, they must first convince their IRB that the potential benefits of the project justify these risks. In addition to policies established by the federal government, many professional organizations publish guidelines that apply to their members who conduct research.

Ethics guidelines are not black and white. Most researchers agree that people should not be denied an effective medical treatment that others receive just for the sake of an experiment, but many situations are more ambiguous. For example, is it ethical to ask children to lie in order to study the development of lying? Under what circumstances should people who are legally responsible for relatives with Alzheimer's disease be allowed to enroll their family members in studies? Although there will never be unanimous agreement about such cases, ethical guidelines agree that investigators should not use coercive procedures to recruit volunteers and that they should get informed consent from participants, protect them from unnecessary harm or discomfort, compensate them fully and equally for participation, and guarantee their confidentiality. These responsibilities are reviewed in Table 1.2.

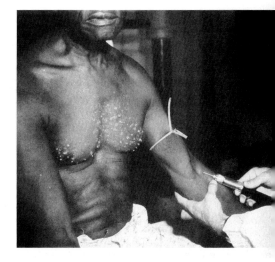

The men in the Tuskegee study of untreated syphilis, which began in 1932, thought they were receiving treatment for "bad blood." Instead, their health was merely observed, even after penicillin became available to treat the disease. This study could not be conducted today due to legislation that requires investigators to seek approval to conduct each research project from an institutional review board (IRB).

TABLE 1.2 The Professional Responsibilities of Human Development Researchers

Standards for the Ethical Treatment of Individuals Who Participate in Research

Do not use coercive procedures to recruit volunteers. Investigators should not offer excessive or inappropriate incentives to recruit participants. Incentives for children should not exceed the range of incentives children normally experience.

Solicit informed consent from research participants. Investigators should explain the procedures of the study, and any foreseeable risks, discomforts, and benefits, in language that participants will understand. When the participant is a minor, a parent or legal guardian must provide written consent, and children must give oral assent if they are old enough to do so.

Protect participants from unnecessary harm or discomfort. Investigators should choose the least stressful procedures possible, and risks should be reasonable in relation to anticipated benefits. Investigators do not deceive participants about significant aspects of the study that would affect their willingness to participate.

Compensate participants fully and equally for their participation. Participants must be explicitly informed that they have the right to withdraw from the study at any time without penalty. Researchers should monitor children's behavior and withdraw them from the study if they become unduly distressed.

Guarantee participants' confidentiality. Investigators should remove identifying information from data that will be processed by individuals other than the investigator. Participants' identities should be concealed in all reports of the results.

Guidelines for Communicating Findings

Be careful when reporting results to avoid misinterpretations. Investigators realize that a broad audience might read their reports. Therefore, they try to clarify the limitations of their results to avoid misinterpretation.

Share data with other investigators. Investigators do not withhold their data from other professionals who want to verify their conclusions.

Provide only those services that are justified by one's training and experience. Investigators realize the limitations of their knowledge. They are responsible for understanding the professional standards that apply in the various contexts in which they work.

SOURCES: American Psychological Association (2002); Committee on Ethical Guidelines for Forensic Psychologists (1991); Society for Research in Child Development (2005); U.S. Department of Health and Human Services (2005).

GUIDELINES FOR COMMUNICATING FINDINGS. Standards for conducting research ask investigators to communicate information about their results accurately and fairly. Specifically, the guidelines in Table 1.2 direct them to try to anticipate possible misinterpretations of their results, to share data with other investigators, and to provide only those services that are justified by their training and experience. For example, a researcher who has looked at the effects of breast-feeding on later development should emphasize that results from high-risk children may not be relevant to the general population, should share their data set with people who want to reanalyze it, and should not provide counseling to new parents unless they are licensed to provide such services. Many investigators also acknowledge how their assumptions about development may have influenced their conclusions because—as you will read next—there are many different ideas about the fundamental nature of development.

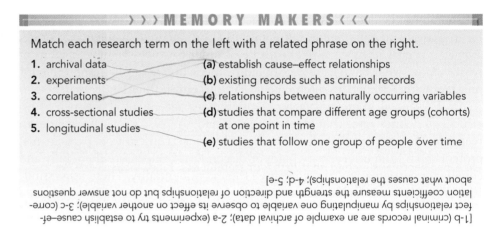

>>> MEMORY MAKERS <<<

Match each research term on the left with a related phrase on the right.

1. archival data
2. experiments
3. correlations
4. cross-sectional studies
5. longitudinal studies

(a) establish cause–effect relationships
(b) existing records such as criminal records
(c) relationships between naturally occurring variables
(d) studies that compare different age groups (cohorts) at one point in time
(e) studies that follow one group of people over time

[1-b (criminal records are an example of archival data); 2-a (experiments try to establish cause–effect relationships by manipulating one variable to observe its effect on another variable); 3-c (correlation coefficients measure the strength and direction of relationships but do not answer questions about what causes the relationship); 4-d; 5-e]

Theoretical Perspectives

Once researchers become interested in a topic, how do they decide which behaviors to focus on, which way to collect data, and how to interpret their findings? When little is known about a topic, the first step is usually to collect as much information as possible. For example, scientists who first studied children's memory simply compared how well children of various ages remembered specific types of information compared to adults. After results accumulate, researchers try to make sense of their findings by designing a theory. A **theory** is a set of concepts that organizes and explains data. All theories—such as Darwin's theory of evolution and Einstein's theory of relativity—are ideas about the rules that underlie patterns in nature. We never directly observe these rules but only the patterns themselves and, therefore, we can never prove that a theory is correct. No matter how many results are consistent with a theory, there is always the chance we will eventually make an observation that is not predicted by the theory. When this occurs, we are supposed to revise or discard the theory. In practice, though, people often resist abandoning familiar ideas. Consequently, theories tend to linger until new perspectives offer more satisfying explanations (Valenstein, 1998).

If we can never be certain that a theory is correct, why are theories so important? One reason is that theories help generate ideas. Once a theory has been proposed, scientists generate hypotheses (predictions) from the theory about relationships that have not been explored yet, and these hypotheses suggest new studies and unconventional ways of looking at evidence. For example, a theory of

theory A set of concepts that organizes and explains data. Theories generate hypotheses (predictions) that can be tested.

memory development called fuzzy trace theory predicted some circumstances that lead *false* memories to endure longer than *true* memories (Brainerd & Mojardin, 1998; Brainerd & Poole, 1997). Theories also have a practical function: Without theories, we could never make predictions unless the situations we were interested in exactly matched a study that had already been conducted (Brainerd, Reyna, & Poole, 2000). For example, memory theories allow experts to analyze eyewitness reports even though the features of any specific crime, such as the length of time since the event, do not exactly match those of any memory experiment. Because theories specify the *range* of situations in which we are likely to observe specific phenomena, we can apply our knowledge to real-world problems in education, medicine, and the law.

Theories of human development are organized into approaches or *perspectives*, with each perspective representing a group of theories that share common guiding assumptions about the nature of development. These assumptions go by a variety of names, including "worldviews," "metatheories," and "**metamodels**" (Ford & Lerner, 1992). Often metamodels grip people's imaginations long after the specific theories they gave rise to have been discarded. Thus even if you have not read about Freud, Watson, or some of the other theorists in this chapter, their ideas have had such a widespread influence that some of your assumptions about development may have been influenced by their work.

We invite you to think about theoretical perspectives in human development by recording your opinions as you read this section. After a review of each perspective is a chart that lists four statements. Place a check in the box to the left of each statement if you agree—or mostly agree—with the statement. At the end of this section, we will tell you how a large group of college students responded so that you can compare your views to theirs.

The Psychodynamic Perspective

The **psychodynamic perspective** focuses on the underlying biological and psychological forces that motivate behavior and development. The term *dynamic* conveys the idea of biological energies that are channeled in various ways. As nature propels us through developmental stages, individual experiences combine with biological needs to determine our adult personalities. It is impossible to be more specific about dynamic theories as a group because individual theories emphasize different types of motivating forces. Therefore, let's begin by describing the earliest and most famous of these theories: Freud's *psychoanalytic theory*.

FREUD'S PSYCHOANALYTIC THEORY. Austrian physician Sigmund Freud (1856–1939) was trained in medicine (specifically, neurology) at the University of Vienna. He became especially interested in *hysteria*, a disorder in which physical symptoms, such as paralysis and blindness, have no medical cause. In the first psychoanalytic monograph, physician Joseph Breuer and Freud (1893–95/1955) put forth a brilliant yet controversial idea: If the patients they treated consciously (knowingly) tried to stop their symptoms but could not, then the source of their problems must be unconscious (beyond conscious awareness) (Westen & Gabbard, 1999).

Psychoanalysis is simultaneously a theory of development, a theory of psychological disorders, and an approach to treating those disorders. Because psychoanalytic therapy is a frequent target of jokes in cartoons and movies, the general public is most familiar with Freud's "talking cure." Briefly, Freud believed that emotional events are sometimes kept out of conscious awareness but manifest themselves as anxiety or other troubling behavior. By encouraging clients to talk

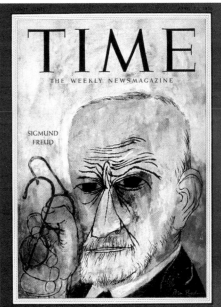

Sigmund Freud is a "cultural icon," a person so famous that his name will continue to live on. His face is also one of the most widely recognized in history. Here is Freud himself, next to one of the numerous caricatures that have been drawn of the first psychoanalyst.

metamodels Guiding assumptions about the nature of development that characterize various theoretical perspectives.

psychodynamic perspective A group of theories, inspired by Sigmund Freud and his followers, that emphasizes how biological forces and developmental experiences combine to produce behavior and personality.

about and understand their pasts, Freud thought that therapists (analysts) could reduce these unwanted symptoms. Today, the idea that unconscious mental activity contributes to behavior is one of the most widely accepted of Freud's ideas.

The central concept of psychoanalytic theory is the importance of sexuality as a basic motivation or drive. But sexuality did not mean just sexual intercourse to Freud. Reproduction involves courtship, protection of the female throughout pregnancy, and child rearing and, therefore, a broad range of behaviors associated with intimacy was described in sexual terms (Baldwin, 1980). Freud used the term *libido* to refer to sexual energy, and later he wrote that aggressive impulses were a second instinctual drive. According to Freud, the major task of children's socialization is to control their sexual and aggressive drives by channeling them into socially acceptable behaviors.

Freud proposed that the focus of libidinal energy shifted from one body area to another as individuals matured, causing them to progress through the universal *psychosexual stages* that are outlined in Table 1.3 (Freud, 1905/1953). For example, babies focus on their mouths during the *oral stage*, but their focus shifts to the anus as they become capable of being toilet trained. Throughout development, the way parents handle their children's sexual and aggressive drives helps shape their offsprings' personalities and psychological well-being. According to Freud, too little or too much gratification can prevent a child from moving on to the next stage of development. For example, a child who was overwhelmed by strict toilet training in the anal phase might grow up to become the typical "anal character": an orderly, stubborn individual who wants the world to be clear-cut and neat (P. H. Miller, 2002).

TABLE 1.3	Freud's Stages of Psychosexual Development	
Stage	**Approximate Age**	**Developmental Events**
Oral	Birth to 1 year	Infants meet their needs though sucking. They begin to define themselves by seeing how their actions affect their mothers. Attachment to their mothers is the foundation for later social relationships.
Anal	1–3 years	The need for toilet training requires children to control biological urges, placing them in conflict with adult society. Children learn to earn praise from adults and develop the concept that things have value.
Phallic	3–5 years	The genitals become the focus of erotic pleasure. Opposite-sex parents become love objects and children identify with their same-sex parent.
Latency	5 years to puberty	Sexual issues become less important as children turn their attention to school and play.
Genital	Puberty through adulthood	Sexual impulses reappear and attention turns to the opposite sex. Relationship patterns from earlier years may influence mate choices.

anal alter ego (handwritten note in margin)

Freud viewed the personality as having three components that take shape during the first three psychosexual stages (Freud, 1923–25/1961, 1932–36/1964). The *id*, which is present at birth, includes as our basic desires, such as sexual and aggressive forces, that seek immediate gratification. But needs cannot always be met immediately. Faced with this reality, the child begins to develop an *ego*, which is the rational part of personality that inhibits drives in order to achieve long-term goals. The final structure, the *superego*, refers to societal morals and values that begin to form our conscience at around 4 years of age. In sum, your id screams for gratification ("I want to rip that toy away from my baby brother!"), your superego scolds you ("No taking things from the baby"), and your ego acts as the go-between to satisfy your impulses in ways your parents would approve of ("I'll see if he'll trade this toy for the one I want").

According to Freud, boys and girls do not follow identical paths to adulthood. During the phallic stage (around 3–4 years of age), a boy falls in love with his mother but fears his father will retaliate, possibly even by cutting off his penis! To resolve the fear of castration, a boy identifies with his father ("I am my father") and, in the process, develops a superego that embodies all his father's values and standards. (This process is called the *Oedipus complex*, after the Greek myth about a son who kills his father and marries his mother.) A girl undergoes a similar set of events but, lacking a penis, has less to fear and less motivation to develop a superego. As a result, Freud said, females forever lack the moral and legal sense of a male.

Psychoanalysis is often criticized for being nothing more than the unscientific musings of a brilliant but arrogant physician. Freud has also been accused of forming ideas first, then pressuring patients to produce memories that confirm his theory (Kihlstrom, 1998). Critics have also pointed out that psychoanalytic concepts are so loosely defined that is it impossible to design research to disprove the theory (Thomas, 2005). In addition, psychoanalytic ideas about female development have long been unpopular. For example, one critic called the idea that females feel inadequate for not having a penis his "most outlandish" concept (Westen & Gabbard, 1999, p. 61), while another concluded that "the only mind he [Freud] laid bare for us was his own" (Crews, 1985, pp. 32–33).

Despite these criticisms, the metamodels that underlie psychoanalysis have emerged over and over again in different clothing. In one survey, 39 percent of clinical psychologists checked "psychodynamic" as one of their guiding perspectives (Poole et al., 1995), and the idea that early experiences influence later development is one of the most popular metamodels in developmental science.

ERIKSON'S PSYCHOSOCIAL THEORY. German-born psychoanalyst Erik Erikson (1902–1994) received his training in Vienna and was analyzed by Freud's daughter, Anna. Following the path of many analysts who lived in Europe during the rise of Hitler in the 1930s, Erikson emigrated to the United States where he subsequently held a variety of university positions.

Erikson began his career working with troubled children from middle-class families, but he also based his theory on studies of poor children, university students, and child-rearing strategies in other cultures (Coles, 1970). Unlike Freud, Erikson placed development in a social rather than sexual context by emphasizing how peer groups, schools, and cultural values influence development. To Erikson, the bodily changes individuals experience as they develop force them to face a series of social challenges, and his theory is, therefore, a *psychosocial theory* of development. Erikson expanded Freud's views by emphasizing the development of healthy personalities and proposing a life span theory (Erikson, 1950, 1959).

Erikson's eight stages of psychosocial development are described in Figure 1.5. According to this model, new challenges arise as we grow older, but issues from the past are not dealt with and put aside forever. As a result, most of us develop a basic sense of trust during the first stage of childhood, and we develop feelings of autonomy (competence and independence) during the second stage, but throughout our lives there will always be times when we mistrust others and doubt our abilities. Erikson liked to depict his theory as shown in Figure 1.5 to emphasize that each developmental challenge exists in some form before its critical time arrives and that people confront the challenges of the next stage regardless of whether or not they have adequately mastered the current stage.

Erikson's writings captured the imaginations of scholars around the world. Like Freud, though, he left it to others to design systematic tests of his views.

FIGURE 1.5 Erikson's model of life span development.

Erik Erikson encouraged developmentalists to think about change throughout the life span. He depicted eight stages of psychosocial development as a matrix to remind us that the challenges we associate with particular ages often exist (to some degree) earlier and later as well.

SOURCE: Adapted from Erikson (1950).

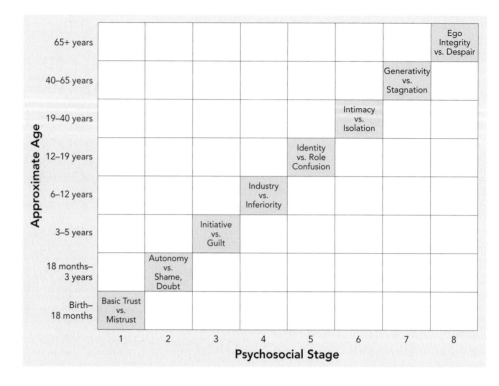

Researchers who ignored Erikson's warnings that "a chart is only a tool to think with" (Erikson, 1950, p. 270) have sometimes complained that the psychological issues in his theory do not occur at the same time in people from different circumstances and cultures (Pearlin, 1982). Nonetheless, many professionals have found Erikson's stages to be useful springboards for thinking about developmental tasks across the life span. If we discard the details of Freud's and Erikson's theories, we are left with a set of familiar-sounding assumptions that form the core of the psychodynamic perspective. Count how many of these assumptions you support:

Ideas from the Psychodynamic Perspective

❏ **how to study development**	A good way to understand people is to ask them to talk about their lives.
❏ **the nature of developmental change**	The early years of life play a critical role in later development.
❏ **child-rearing advice**	Satisfy children's needs at each stage of development but don't overindulge them.
❏ **description of a healthy adult**	The hallmarks of a healthy person are the ability to love and the ability to work.

The Learning Perspective

Freudian theory fueled clinicians' interest in analyzing people's descriptions of their experiences, but it was the **learning perspective** that dominated research psychology from the 1920s until well into the 1960s. This perspective is both a philosophy of *how* to study development and a viewpoint about *why* change occurs over time. The learning perspective grew out of a movement called *behaviorism*, which advocated the study of observable events and behaviors rather than unverifiable mental processes. As its name implies, the learning perspective proposed that developmental change occurs as the result of **learning**—relatively

learning perspective A theoretical perspective that focuses on how people learn by describing observable relationships between environmental events and behavior.

learning Relatively permanent changes in behavior that result from experience.

permanent changes in behavior that result from experience. Two approaches to learning theory are traditional behaviorism and social learning theory.

THE EARLY BEHAVIORISTS. In 1913, psychologist John B. Watson (1878–1958) published a paper entitled "Psychology as a Behaviorist Views It" (Watson, 1913). In this and subsequent writings, Watson argued that psychology should describe connections between observable stimuli in the environment (such as the smell of pie floating through the back window) and the organism's responses (such as running into the house). In Watson's words, "Now, what can we observe? We can observe behavior—what the organism does or says" (Watson, 1924/66, p. 6). Soon **behaviorism**—the movement to focus on the observable phenomenon rather than the underlying mental events that intrigued Freud—was a dominant force in American psychology.

Watson's emphasis on environmental stimuli and responses grew out of the work of a Russian physiologist, Ivan Pavlov (1849–1936). Pavlov discovered that dogs would salivate to the sight of the laboratory assistants who gave them food. The finding that responses such as salivating could transfer from existing stimuli (food) to new stimuli (the sight of laboratory assistants) came to be called *classical conditioning*. Watson later proposed that emotional reactions and other behaviors arose through paired environmental events (such as "bee + sting" leading to "sight of a bee → fear"). In a famous demonstration, Watson and a colleague, Rosalie Rayner (1920), taught an 11-month-old boy named Albert to fear a rat by repeatedly making a loud noise whenever Albert reached for the animal. Five days later, Albert acted afraid of the rat, and his fear generalized to other furry objects, including a rabbit and a sealskin coat.

Armed with the concept of classical conditioning, Watson claimed that most of the differences in how people behave result from differences in their past experiences rather than hereditary differences. In one of the most memorable quotes in all of psychology, Watson announced that he would "feel perfectly confident in the ultimately favorable outcome of careful upbringing of a healthy, well-formed baby born of a long line of crooks, murderers and thieves, and prostitutes. Who has any evidence to the contrary?" (Watson, 1924/66, p. 103). Watson continued:

> I should like to go one step further now and say, "Give me a dozen healthy infants, well-formed, and my own specified world to bring them up in and I'll guarantee to take any one at random and train him to become any type of specialist I might select—doctor, lawyer, artist, merchant-chief and, yes, even beggar-man and thief, regardless of this talents, penchants, tendencies, abilities, vocations, and race of his ancestors . . . Please note that when this experiment is made I am to be allowed to specify the way the children are to be brought up and the type of world they have to live in. (p. 104)

What strained the public's imagination was not Watson's claim that children learned from their environments but his belief that complex behaviors could be learned through classical conditioning. It was one thing to believe that a baby could be made to fear a rat, but what is the stimulus for tossing cereal off a high chair tray or saying, "I do mySELF"? How, through classical conditioning, do children learn to tie their shoes?

Behaviorist B. F. (Burrhus Frederick) Skinner (1904–1990) tried to explain these more complex behaviors by proposing another form of learning called *operant conditioning*. Whereas classical conditioning deals with the stimuli that

The story of Little Albert has acquired a life of its own. Years after John Watson and Rosalie Rayner (1920) conditioned Albert to fear a rat, many textbooks greatly exaggerated his fear of animals and white objects. In fact, most of the tested objects Albert feared were *not* white, and Albert was not very afraid. Ten days after Watson and Rayner conditioned Albert to fear the rat and bolstered training with an additional conditioning trial, the baby merely crawled away from the rat (Harris, 1979).

behaviorism A movement in psychology that encouraged scientists to study the relationship between observable events and observable behavior, especially as described by the principles of conditioning.

social learning theory An aspect of the learning perspective that emphasizes how individuals learn through imitation (also called **modeling**).

modeling (also called **imitation** and **observational learning**) The processes involved in observing and copying other people's behavior.

come *before* responses, operant conditioning deals with the consequences that *follow* responses. For example, we may never know what prompted a child to first say a swear word, yet we know the child will say it again if adults laugh. Thus, the basic principles of operant conditioning are simple: If a behavior is followed by reinforcement, the probability of that behavior occurring again increases; if a behavior is followed by punishment, the probability of that behavior occurring again decreases (Skinner, 1969). According to Skinner, it is the *consequences* of our actions that create individual differences (Skinner, 1957, 1969, 1974).

Focusing on classical and operant conditioning shifts attention from the biological forces that direct development to the behavior of parents and other significant caretakers. When a child is misbehaving, learning theorists ask, "What consequences in the environment support this misbehavior?" For example, a father who says "No" when his children ask for more candy but gives in after they whine for an hour will probably have children who whine a lot (because they have been reinforced for doing so).

Many practical applications were inspired by the work of the early behaviorists. *Behavior modification* programs use conditioning techniques to change problem behavior in classrooms and nursing homes, and learning principles are an essential part of therapies for reducing unwanted fears (such as the fear of flying) and unwanted behaviors (such as smoking). Yet despite its popularity, the learning approach has some limitations. The most frequent complaint is that this perspective underestimates the role of heredity in accounting for individual differences and developmental change. In reality, learning principles are tempered by the existence of *constraints on learning*, which are genetically determined limitations on the learning process (Hinde & Stevenson-Hinde, 1973). For example, the fact that many humans fear snakes and spiders but rarely fear electrical appliances suggests that we are genetically "prepared" to learn some associations quickly, others not so quickly, and some not at all (Bijou & Baer, 1961; Seligman, 1970). And as we'll discuss next, the biggest dissatisfaction with traditional learning approaches is that humans are complicated creatures who learn in numerous ways—not only by directly experiencing the consequences of their own behavior.

SOCIAL LEARNING THEORY. It is enough work minding an active 3-year-old without a house full of relatives like Aunt Emma, who just flicked the door lock in front of Jake. One thoughtless moment and now Jake knows how to escape! And then there is Uncle Bill, lighting a cigarette, and the teen brigade, kissing in the living room. On days like this one, you want to put blinders on your kids.

Social learning theory is an aspect of the learning perspective that emphasizes how individuals learn through **modeling** (also called **imitation** and **observational learning**)—the processes involved in observing and copying other people's behavior. The classic study of observational learning in children is the "Bobo" doll study by

The Bobo doll is the most famous toy in developmental science. Albert Bandura used films of grown-ups punching the doll to demonstrate that children learn by watching what other people do. His research explains why it usually doesn't work to tell children, "Do as I say, not as I do."

psychologist Albert Bandura (1965), a prominent social learning theorist. In this study, children between 3 and 6 years of age watched a film while they waited for their turn in the "surprise playroom." In that film, an adult approached a life-sized Bobo doll and ordered him to "Clear the way!" After glaring at the unresponsive doll, the adult proceeded to punch the doll while making distinctive comments such as "Sockeroo . . . stay down!" Some of the children saw no consequences from this behavior, whereas others watched the adult being rewarded with a snack or smacked with a rolled-up magazine. After the children were left alone with the Bobo doll, assistants recorded how many behaviors from the film the little ones spontaneously mimicked. Even when the model's behavior was not followed by positive consequences, many children acted out what they had seen, demonstrating that children do not have to see reinforcement—or be reinforced themselves—in order to learn a complex series of behaviors.

Social learning theorists emphasize that human behavior is influenced by higher-order cognitive (mental) processes, including predictions about our own likelihood of success if we imitate a particular person's behavior. Instead of mindlessly imitating, people tend to imitate models they view as similar to themselves and those who are powerful and successful (Bandura, 1977). Therefore, Bandura calls his approach a *social-cognitive theory of learning* (Bandura, 1999). Experts who endorse the learning perspective have shown that the idea of modeling, when combined with the principles of classical and operant conditioning, can help us toilet train children, reduce bullying on playgrounds, and encourage nursing home residents to act more independently. How many of the following ideas from the learning perspective do you endorse?

Ideas from the Learning Perspective

❏ how to study development	The best way to learn about development is to study it scientifically by making observations that can be repeated and verified.
❏ the nature of developmental change	Most development is the result of small changes from experiences that accumulate over time.
❏ child-rearing advice	Adults should decide how they want children to behave and give them consistent feedback about their actions.
❏ description of a healthy adult	Healthy adults have acquired behaviors that make them successful in their environments.

The Evolutionary Perspective

The perspective that emphasizes how a species' genetic endowment regulates behavior, learning, and development is the **evolutionary perspective**. This perspective traces its roots to Darwinian theory and the idea that members of a species share physical and behavioral traits that helped their ancestors adapt to their environments. Two traditions from this perspective that have influenced thinking about human development are ethology and evolutionary psychology.

Ethology. **Ethology** is the study of animal behavior. Ethologists are especially interested in behavior as it occurs in natural habitats and, therefore, they often observe organisms in the field. But in addition to describing behavior, ethologists also

evolutionary perspective A theoretical perspective that asks how patterns of growth and behavior reflect a species' adaptation to past environments.

ethology The study of animal behavior, especially in natural habitats.

The father of modern ethology, Konrad Lorenz, takes his goslings for a stroll. Through a process called *imprinting*, some species of goslings form an attachment to the first thing they see that moves.

conduct experiments to test hypotheses about the stimuli that control or influence animal behavior. In Chapter 13, for example, we'll look at research that has determined which brain chemicals cause some mammals to bond to their partners.

One of the founding fathers of ethology is zoologist Konrad Lorenz (1903–1989), a scientist who received a Nobel prize in 1973 for exploring behavior in nonhuman species. Many of us recognize Lorenz from a widely reproduced picture of goslings following him about his garden. This picture illustrates *imprinting*—a type of learning in which exposure to a specific type of stimulus during a specific period of life leads to a predictable behavior. For example, Lorenz documented that some birds follow the first nurturing figure they encounter, which for fortunate goslings is usually a mother bird. Lorenz used the term *critical periods* to refer to times in development when specific experiences must be encountered for development to proceed normally. When later research showed that early imprinting is not always permanent, a less restrictive concept of **sensitive periods** gained popularity. Sensitive periods are times in development when certain experiences produce *stronger* effects than at other times. Lorenz learned that experiences during sensitive periods not only influenced immediate responses, such as following, but also sometimes even later responses, such as sexual behavior. For example, a jackdaw bird that was raised by a neighbor once courted Lorenz by trying to put crushed worms into his mouth, illustrating an alarming lack of jackdaw dating savvy (Crain, 2005).

An influential theorist who applied ethological concepts to human development was the British psychoanalyst John Bowlby (1907–1990). Bowlby argued that human infants need to stay close to a protective adult in order to survive. But because babies are unable to follow or cling, they rely on crying and smiling to encourage adults to care for them. Adults, in turn, are biologically predisposed to respond to these signals, leading to two-way interactions that promote emotional bonds between infants and parents (Bowlby, 1969–1980). In the years that followed, psychologists who continued this way of thinking about human behavior launched a field called evolutionary psychology.

EVOLUTIONARY PSYCHOLOGY. Evolutionary psychology is the most recent framework to apply Darwin's ideas to human behavior. Evolutionary psychologists try to identify the blueprint for human behavior by searching for and explaining the common features in human cultures around the world (Buss, 2004, 2005).

The evolutionary analysis of mating choices is the clearest example of this approach to thinking about human behavior. According to evolutionary psychologists (Buss, 1994, 2004), men and women adopt different sexual strategies to achieve reproductive "success," which in Darwinian terms means one thing: passing one's genes on to the next generation. Because women bear the burden of pregnancy and nursing, successful mothers increase their children's chances of surviving by attracting a mate who will provide physical resources. In contrast, men's reproductive success increases with the number of sexual encounters they have with healthy, fertile partners. These realities, evolutionary psychologists say, explain why women are sexually choosy and prefer older, rich men, whereas men crave variety and prefer young, beautiful women.

sensitive periods Times in development when specific experiences produce stronger effects than at other times.

According to evolutionary psychologists, people around the world agree that these women are beautiful because each has features associated with health. Evolutionary approaches assume that "beautiful" features predict the ability to reproduce. Still, there is no consensus about which facial features signal "gorgeous!"

We can also protect our genetic legacy by promoting the well-being of relatives who, to one extent or another, share our genes. Consequently, family relationships are also subject to an evolutionary analysis. For example, the famous quip "I am prepared to lay down my life for more than 2 brothers or more than 8 first cousins" computes how many relatives you must help to pass on more of your genes than you would pass on by helping yourself (Haldane, reported in Hamilton, 1971, p. 42).

To avoid a common misunderstanding about evolutionary analyses, it is important to mention that not all outcomes of natural selection are adaptive (that is, help the organism survive) (Buss et al., 1998). *By-products* of evolutionary processes have no functional value but occur as side effects, so to speak. For example, a belly button is a side effect of the umbilical cord; it has no adaptive function of its own. Another product of evolution is noise or *random effects*, which are characteristics like hair swirls that are carried along from generation to generation merely because there are no negative consequences for the organism. Analyzing which characteristics are adaptive and which fall into other categories is part of the fun of an evolutionary analysis.

Supporters of evolutionary analyses believe the approach generates novel hypotheses about development that can be systematically tested, including some we will explore in later chapters (Bjorklund & Blasi, 2005; Ketelaar & Ellis, 2000). In a one-two punch, critics claim this approach oversimplifies human behavior and downplays variability across historical times, cultures, and contexts. Evolutionary explanations have been described as mere stories that follow a predictable plot: identify a behavior, propose how the behavior increases reproductive success, assume a genetic basis for the behavior, and then infer that natural selection built the behavior because of its advantages (Gould, 1991). Often, investigators make no effort to pit the hypothesis that particular strategies are genetically transmitted against the hypothesis that these strategies have been learned. Moreover, critics argue that because evolutionary explanations can account for everything after the fact (known as *post hoc* reasoning), it is impossible to prove them wrong.

Despite controversy about the value of the evolutionary perspective, scientists have found it difficult to avoid speculating about the evolutionary bases of behavior. For instance, the tendency of children to act younger when a new baby arrives—a behavior Freud called "regression"—might be a biologically prepared tactic that helps them compete for parental attention (Trivers, 1974). Moreover, the emergence of guilt during the preschool years might be an adaptation that protects new siblings from harm at the hands of jealous brothers or sisters (Kagan, 1998). In recent years, nearly every aspect of our lives—from the timing of puberty to how we distribute wealth in our wills—has been viewed through the lens of natural selection (Surbey, 1998). Find out if you agree with some ideas from the evolutionary perspective by reacting to the following statements:

Ideas from the Evolutionary Perspective

❏ how to study development	We can understand a behavior by asking how it helped us survive in the environment in which it evolved.
❏ the nature of developmental change	Each stage of development represents adaptations to circumstances at that point in the life span.
❏ child-rearing advice	People behave in ways that promote the spread of their own genes, and family members do not have identical genes. As a result, it is natural for some sibling rivalry and power struggles between parents and children to exist.
❏ description of a healthy adult	Desirable attributes are those that help organisms survive and reproduce in their respective environments.

The Cognitive Perspective

Ursula was at that age when children ask endless questions and parents listen with only half an ear. One day she walked up to her father and asked, "Daddy, how do we know?" "At first I started to say, 'Ursula, how do we know *what?*'" he later told a friend of ours. "But then I realized—that was the question."

Ursula was pondering the central question of the **cognitive perspective**, the perspective that looks at how mental processes, such as perception, memory, and reasoning, change as we age. The word *cognitive* comes from the Latin word *cognito*, meaning "to have ideas in mind." This perspective describes how we acquire knowledge and use it to solve problems, make decisions, and guide behavior—in other words, how we think. Two influential cognitive traditions are Piaget's cognitive developmental theory and the information processing approach.

PIAGET'S COGNITIVE DEVELOPMENTAL THEORY. Jean Piaget (1896–1980), who was born in a small town in Switzerland, showed unusual intellectual talent as a young boy. He published an article at the age of 10, did research on mollusks in high school, and experienced an intellectual crisis at age 15 when he realized that philosophical ideas lacked a scientific foundation. Although Piaget earned a doctorate in the natural sciences, he decided to study children's mental development as a vehicle for answering questions about the nature of knowledge (Brainerd, 1978; Ginsburg & Opper, 1988).

While working in a laboratory that was developing an intelligence test, Piaget became intrigued by the regularity of children's mistakes. In other words, children did not simply know less than adults, they seemed to think about the world in an entirely different way. To study children's knowledge in a way that

cognitive perspective A theoretical perspective that analyzes how we think, that is, how we acquire knowledge and use it to solve problems, make decisions, and guide behavior.

would not limit the types of answers they gave, Piaget developed a clinical method in which he posed problems to children, often by asking questions about objects they could handle. To explore number concepts, for example, Piaget placed six candies in front of one 4-year-old and said that they were for a friend, Roger. He then told the child, "Put as many sweets here as there are there. Those . . . are for Roger. You are to take as many as he has." After the child made a row of candies, Piaget asked, "Are they the same?" (Piaget, 1952, p. 75). By collecting children's answers to questions about various situations, Piaget developed a theory about how their understanding of the world changes as they grow.

Piaget argued that children actively construct their understanding of the world by interacting with it during daily activities. Unlike the gradual, incremental learning that learning theorists emphasized, Piaget thought that children experience *qualitative* changes in their representations of the world as their knowledge grows. At first these representations, called *schemes*, are physical routines for acting on objects in the world, such as grasping or tasting. (Schemes are also called *schemas* or *schemata*, which are plural forms of *schema*.) Then, as children develop, they begin to represent information as mental images or symbols, and schemes increasingly become mental events. For example, toddlers' schemes about objects include the fact that things fall to the ground when they are dropped, so their delight at a helium balloon is a symptom of how they think about their world. Development occurs when children confront new knowledge that conflicts with their existing understanding of the world, which forces them to revise their schemes (Piaget, 1936/52).

Piaget recognized that change is a continuous process, with no sudden reorganization that transforms children's thinking in all areas of reasoning. Nonetheless, he found it useful to distinguish between the different stages of development, outlined in Table 1.4, that we will describe in more detail throughout this book. As children progress through these stages, they change from infants who do not have mental symbols to adults who have the capacity for abstract, scientific reasoning.

Piaget's writings began to have a major impact in the United States in the 1960s, when dissatisfaction with the learning perspective opened the window for other views to take hold. Many scholars see him as the leading historical figure in developmental psychology. Developmental psychologist John Flavell (1980, p. 1) expressed the field's appreciation when he said, "We owe him a host of insightful concepts of enduring power and fascination . . . we owe him a vast conceptual framework that has highlighted key issues and problems in human cognitive development . . . we owe him the present field of cognitive development."

TABLE 1.4	Piaget's Stages of Cognitive Development	
Stage	**Approximate Age**	**Developmental Events**
Sensorimotor	Birth to 2 years	Infants' knowledge of the world is tied to their senses and physical actions. At the end of this period, children develop mental representations. For example, at the beginning of this stage baby Josh could only think about his mother if he was seeing, touching, or feeling her; at the end of this stage, he could think about his mother even when she was in another room.
Preoperational	2–7 years	Children's thinking focuses on one aspect of a problem or situation and is often illogical. For example, Sarah believes that her mother can see anything she can see, no matter where her mother is.
Concrete operational	7–12 years	Children begin to apply logical operations to concrete objects—objects that are present or can be represented mentally. For example, Danny can sort objects by length and understands basic concepts, such as the concept of number.
Formal operational	12 years on	Adolescents and adults can understand abstract concepts and hypothetical situations, and they can generate possibilities. For example, Nicole can plan an experiment to determine the best amount of fertilizer and water to use on miniature roses.

information processing approach
An approach to studying thinking that analyzes how our brains manipulate information during the processes of perception, attention, memory storage and retrieval, and decision making.

Piaget has been called one of the two unquestioned geniuses in the field of psychology (the other is Freud) (Lerner, 2002). Yet he never took a single course in psychology!

But Piaget's ideas have their limitations. It is true that, by and large, children respond to Piaget's questions the way he predicted they would. What troubled cognitive psychologists, however, were Piaget's explanations of *why* children responded this way (Siegal, 1997). Hundreds of studies have documented that children understand more than Piaget gave them credit for, leaving researchers scrambling to explain why, exactly, children fail to answer his questions accurately (Wellman & Gelman, 1998). On the flip side of this problem, adults do not perform nearly as well as Piaget predicted they should. We leave the details of these puzzles—and the fascinating studies they fostered—for later chapters. For now, we turn to the approach many researchers adopted to resolve these problems: information processing.

THE INFORMATION PROCESSING APPROACH. In the middle-to-late 1950s, growing excitement with emerging computer technologies prompted many psychologists to view humans as information processing devices, like computers, that took in information, transformed it, and acted upon it to produce output. The **information processing approach** analyzes how our brains manipulate information as we attend to our world, remember information, and make decisions.

By the late 1960s, developmental psychology had jumped onto the information processing bandwagon, asking questions such as, "How is the human organism programmed to make sense out of the world?" and "What would an information-processing system require in order to exhibit the same behavior as the child?" (Klahr & Wallace, 1976). Information processing research ranges from small-scale studies of how people solve particular types of problems to ambitious efforts to model the overall "architecture" of human cognitive systems. Proposed systems are often represented graphically, as in Figure 1.6, or as computer programs that try to reproduce human behavior. Information processing psychologists compare the performance of children and adults across a wide variety of tasks to learn how changes in attention, memory, language, and mental strategies account for age differences across the life span.

FIGURE 1.6 Information processing models.

Information processing researchers often represent cognitive systems as boxes to depict how information flows from one system to the next. In this example of a memory model, some of the information detected by your sensory systems is transferred to a working memory system that contains the information you are actively thinking about in any given moment. Long-term memory is your permanent storehouse of knowledge and learned routines. This is one of many possible models.

SOURCE: Inspired by Baddeley (2000).

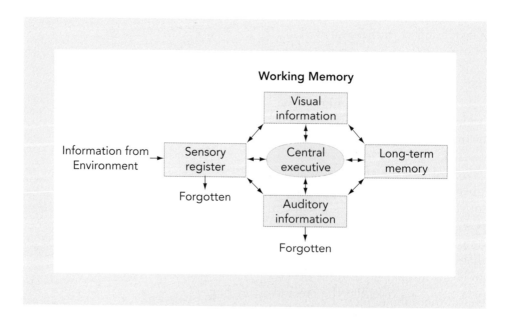

The scientific community has given the information processing approach high marks for practicality. For example, viewing students as information processors helps teachers identify the strategies students need to solve problems and which limitations underlie learning disabilities (Thomas, 2005). As with all perspectives, though, this one cannot answer every question about human development. Critics have complained that the approach has produced only sketchy explanations of *why* underlying mental processes change over time and generally ignores social and emotional development. For professionals in applied fields, both Piaget's theory and the information processing approach are annoyingly silent on clinical issues, including child-rearing advice and standards of health. Nonetheless, we propose some practical statements that are consistent with current findings from the cognitive perspective:

Ideas from the Cognitive Perspective

❏ **how to study development**	To understand development, we need to study changes in the underlying cognitive processes that help people make sense of their world.
❏ **the nature of developmental change**	Development consists of gradual changes, such as acquiring knowledge, and rapid changes, such as shifting from one preferred strategy to another.
❏ **child-rearing advice**	Children learn best when they are given a stimulating environment to explore.
❏ **description of a healthy adult**	A competent adult can choose which cognitive strategy is most appropriate for various situations.

The Contextual Perspective

Developmental theory has always grappled with the fact that children develop in very different social and cultural *contexts*, that is, environments that include different material objects, relationships between people, and beliefs that guide actions. One child grows up in Sub-Saharan Africa and another in Paris; one grows up as an only child in Arkansas and another in a family of ten children in Texas. The **contextual perspective** is an approach to development that considers how environments influence development and how, in turn, people influence their environments. Although many theoretical approaches talk about cultural influences, theorists who embrace contextual approaches place supreme importance on the interactions between people and contexts. Examples of this perspective are Vygotsky's sociocultural theory and Bronfenbrenner's bioecological theory.

VYGOTSKY'S SOCIOCULTURAL THEORY. There are many parallels between the lives of Lev Vygotsky (1896–1934) and Jean Piaget. Both were born in the same year, were intellectually precocious boys, and read widely from a broad range of disciplines. Remarkably, both were known as child psychologists despite the fact that neither one had formal training in that field. Unlike Piaget, however, Vygotsky's contributions were cut short when he died of tuberculosis at the age of 37.

Vygotsky and his colleagues constructed their views during the social upheaval that followed the Russian revolution. They were influenced by the values

contextual perspective An approach to development that looks at mutual influences between children and their environments.

According to Lev Vygotsky (shown below), children learn more when older children or adults help them accomplish tasks that are a little too difficult for them to accomplish on their own.

zone of proximal development
In Vygotsky's sociocultural theory, the distance between what children can currently do and their potential when they collaborate with more competent individuals.

of socialism* and wanted to develop an approach to psychology that emphasized how people could serve society by sharing and cooperating. They also wanted to use their field to help solve practical problems of the time, including massive illiteracy in Soviet society. Vygotsky's major theme—education through cooperation—follows naturally from this background.

Vygotsky believed that the way to understand children was to study the child participating in an event in context (P. H. Miller, 2002). For Vygotsky, development is a social process because the social context defines children's experiences and, in turn, children affect their contexts (Vygotsky, 1962). For example, a mother who is helping her young daughter, Kayla, put together her first wooden puzzle may start by placing pieces in the right orientation. As Kayla gets better at putting the puzzle together, her mother will challenge her by leaving the pieces wherever they fall after the puzzle is turned upside down. Vygotsky argued that cultural values and skills are transmitted by older children or adults who help a child achieve a level of competence that is just beyond their current level (Vygotsky, 1978). The distance between what children know how to do now and what they are able to learn when they interact with more competent individuals is what he called the **zone of proximal development**.

Vygotsky's ideas have had an enormous impact. His approach for studying change in individual children as it is actually occurring is used by information processing theorists (Siegler, 2006), and his cry for contextualism has encouraged scores of scientists to investigate cross-cultural differences in child rearing, the dynamics of parent-child interactions, and the role of schools in transmitting culture. But unlike prominent theorists like Piaget, Vygotsky did not leave us with many specific tasks for studying children. He also did not explain how various factors in individual children's lives combine to determine their development (Thomas, 2005). It was Bronfenbrenner's bioecological theory that drew attention to these factors.

BRONFENBRENNER'S BIOECOLOGICAL THEORY. Because research psychologists generally observe people in the laboratory, Uri Bronfenbrenner (1917–2005) once criticized developmental psychology for being the "science of the strange behavior of children in strange situations with strange adults for the briefest possible periods of time" (1977, p. 513). His *bioecological theory* is a framework for returning children—and the scientists who study them—back into the world at large.

Bronfenbrenner's bioecological theory places organisms into five ecological levels that interact with one another, just as ecological systems in nature do (Bronfenbrenner, 1979, 1999). As shown in Figure 1.7, individuals are in the center of the system, along with the biologically based traits that influence their behavior. The next level, the *microsystem*, involves the settings closest to them, including families, schools, health-care services, and church groups. The *mesosystem* involves relationships among microsystems, such as connections between school and health-care services. The *exosystem* involves social settings that individuals do not interact with directly but that impact their immediate environments. For example, the closing of a local business may eliminate jobs and force parents to work farther from home, which affects children by changing their

---

*socialism: An economic system of collective ownership.

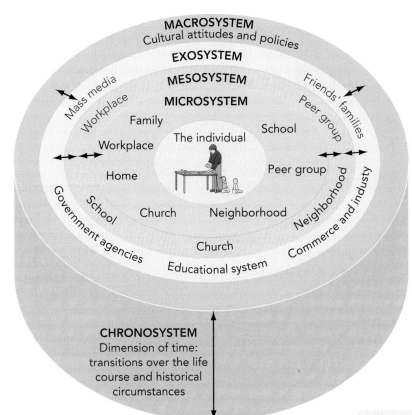

FIGURE 1.7 Bronfenbrenner's bioecological theory.

Bronfenbrenner's bioecological theory considers all levels of the developmental system, from biological forces within the individual to the broadest social contexts. The two biologically unique children in this picture are affected by the microsystems they interact with on a daily basis, relationships between microsystems (the mesosystem), factors such as parents' jobs and friends' families (which compose the exosystem), and cultural attitudes and policies (the macrosystem). All of these systems are changing over time, which is represented by the chronosystem.

SOURCES: Bronfenbrenner & Morris (2000); Cole & Cole (1989); Lerner (2002).

child-care arrangements. The *macrosystem* is the broader culture we live in, including belief systems and tools. The *chronosystem* involves changes over time in all of these systems.

Bronfenbrenner frequently used a longitudinal study of children who grew up in different economic circumstances to illustrate the importance of considering multiple ecological levels (Bronfenbrenner & Ceci, 1994; Bronfenbrenner & Morris, 1998). This study looked at the number of behavior problems children had as a function of their families' socioeconomic status and how responsive their mothers were (Drillien, 1957, 1964). Figure 1.8 presents the results collected when the children were 4 years old. On average, poor children had more behavior problems than children who were raised in more fortunate circumstances. What is interesting, though, is how mothers' behavior buffered children against the negative effects of social class. As you can see in Figure 1.8, social class was important *only* when children had unresponsive mothers. In other words, the effect of social class *varied* depending on the quality of parenting. This result is an *interaction*, a situation in which the impact of one variable changes depending on the level of another variable. Interactions can be hard to visualize but, as Bronfenbrenner explained, "In ecological research, the principal main effects are likely to be interactions" (1979, p. 38).

In contextual models, changes in one part of the system have implications for other parts of the system. Because these models are interested in interactions between individuals and ecological levels,

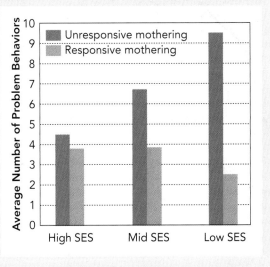

FIGURE 1.8 Interactions in developmental research.

Interactions occur when the impact of a variable is not the same in all contexts. This study shows the relationship between socioeconomic status (SES) and the number of problem behaviors that low-birth-weight children have at age 4, broken down by how responsive mothers are to their children. Notice that low-socioeconomic status (SES) is associated with high levels of problem behavior only when mothers are not responsive.

SOURCE: Bronfenbrenner & Ceci (1994).

as well as relationships among ecological levels, they are often called "ecological systems" models. If this approach sounds complicated to you, you are not alone. Even scientists find this perspective vague and lacking in specific predictions. But despite these problems, the contextual perspective has encouraged more sophisticated research by showing how important it is to compare people from different social contexts and cultures. Consider whether or not you agree with this selection of contextual values:

Ideas from the Contextual Perspective

❏ **how to study development**	Development can only be understood by studying all of the contexts that influence growth and change, including biological differences, family contexts, neighborhoods, and generational influences.
❏ **the nature of developmental change**	Change occurs when people repeatedly experience more complex activities or interactions with other individuals.
❏ **child-rearing advice**	Parents should provide environments that invite children to explore, and they should participate in activities with their children.
❏ **description of a healthy adult**	People are healthy when their psychological and social functioning fit the demands of particular settings.

Thinking about Theoretical Perspectives

The theoretical perspectives you just read about have different significance to different people. Some professionals identify strongly with a particular approach and rarely think about other approaches, whereas others draw ideas from a variety of perspectives. For example, an educational researcher who wanted to improve algebra instruction might rely on Piaget's theory to decide which age group to study, consult the information processing approach for ideas about how to classify children's mistakes, and use learning principles to motivate students. Researchers who borrow ideas from a number of different perspectives have an *eclectic* theoretical orientation*. It is extremely common for scientists to integrate different perspectives. For example, Robert Siegler, whose work you will read about in Chapter 8, draws ideas from Piaget, Vygotsky, information processing, and the principles of evolution to understand cognitive development (Siegler & Alibali, 2005).

Throughout this book, you will encounter ideas from all of the perspectives we have outlined. Will you enjoy this eclectic presentation? One way to predict the answer is to count up how many checkmarks you put beside statements in the boxes following each perspective. When we asked a group of students to do just that, the psychodynamic perspective attracted the most support, with 89 percent of students endorsing three or four of the listed ideas. The learning and cognitive perspectives came in a close second and third, with support from 81 and 80 percent of the students, respectively. The majority of students (66 percent) also

---

*eclectic: Combining elements from a variety of sources or systems.

endorsed three or four ideas from the evolutionary perspective. Looking across perspectives, 75 percent of the students agreed with at least two statements from each perspective. If you did, too, we think you will enjoy looking at topics from a number of perspectives.

Recently, some commentators have suggested that developmental theories will become unnecessary as the *neuroscience revolution* increasingly helps us explain developmental phenomena in terms of underlying biological changes in the brain. Neuroscientists study the brain by mapping which brain regions are involved in performing tasks, determining how brain chemicals direct behavior, and tracing how the brain develops throughout our lives. When scientists understand the cellular mechanisms that underlie behavior, will biologists and neuroscientists write all of the books on human development? To explore this question, turn to our first *Innovations* feature entitled "Brain Science: The New Frontier."

INNOVATIONS

Scientists who study behavior across the life span are joining hands with neuroscientists to understand more about normal and abnormal development. Their findings will help us identify children who are at risk for future problems, treat developmental and mental disorders, and age more successfully.

BRAIN SCIENCE: THE NEW FRONTIER

Charles Nelson, working in a windowless room, attaches over 100 electrodes to baby Jessica's head while her mother distracts her with finger games. A scientist who studies the brain, Nelson is one of thousands of investigators participating in what has been called the "Ultimate Moon Walk"—the neuroscience revolution (Brennan, 1999). As one author marveled, "The science is elegant, the scientists dismayingly young, and the pace of discovery absolutely staggering" (Jamison, 1995, p. 196).

Neuroscience is an interdisciplinary venture that attracts biologists, chemists, psychologists, and computer scientists who want to understand the basic brain functions that underlie behavior. Recent advances in neuroscience were made possible by technological advances, including the development of new brain-imaging techniques—procedures for taking snapshots of brain activity while volunteers react to stimuli or perform tasks. One promising technique is functional magnetic resonance imaging (fMRI), a procedure that detects brain activity by measuring changes in the level of oxygen in different parts of the brain. But because fMRI is impractical for wiggling babies like Jessica, research on development in the early years relies on techniques like event-related potentials (ERP). With ERP, electrodes resting on the scalp measure the electrical activity generated by groups of neurons.

Is neuroscience the end of the road for theories of human development? Will "mind science" eventually become only "brain science"? These questions illustrate a fear of *reductionism*, the belief that complicated phenomena will be reduced to chains of neural events (Miller & Keller, 2002). In fact, most behavioral scientists are not at all threatened

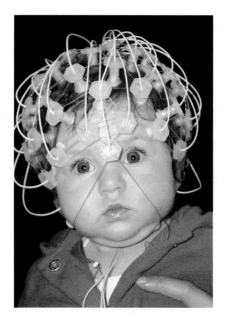

by advances in neuroscience. "One could stare forever and a day at subjects' neuronal goings on without being able to work out what they believe and desire," explained philosopher Frank Jackson (1999, p. 840). Scientists agree that the complex events that developmental researchers study—whether abandonment in infancy or parental discipline—are not in danger of being reduced to neural events any time soon (de Jong, 2002).

Today, the prevailing view is that neuroscience and developmental theory enrich each other. Behavioral research gives neuroscientists road maps that tell them where to look for developmental changes in the brain. For example, research on the behavior of drug-exposed infants suggests what parts of the brain may be harmed when mothers take cocaine during pregnancy. And when there are competing ideas about development, many scientists lay their money on the ones supported by neurological findings. For example, the claim that adults could describe events that occurred during early infancy was challenged when neuroscientists found that the brain areas responsible for such memories are not well developed during the first year of life. The potential benefits from the collaboration between behavioral research and neuroscience include healthier children, better treatments for emotional disorders, and a higher quality of life for the elderly. In Charles Nelson's dreams, behavioral and brain studies will someday achieve a new view of development that "illuminates the whole individual" (March 13, 2000).

> > > **MEMORY MAKERS** < < <

Three friends are sharing stories about their lives. Which theoretical perspective would best apply to each of the following observations, and why?

1. "I chew on pencils because my mom weaned me when I was only 6 months old."
2. "I'll lend money to my brother but not to my cousin."
3. "I don't understand why my preschooler cannot solve simple subtraction problems."
4. "I learned a lot about cars because my dad always showed me how to do repairs that were a little harder than the ones I could do by myself."
5. "I imitate my brother because good things always seem to be happening to him."

[1. the psychodynamic perspective, particularly Freudian psychoanalysis (overindulging or underindulging children's needs influences their subsequent behavior and personality); 2. the evolutionary perspective, particularly evolutionary psychology (we are more likely to help people who share more of our genes); 3. the cognitive perspective, particularly Piaget's theory (children make errors when their mental frameworks—their schemes—are flawed or incomplete); 4. the contextual perspective, particularly Vygotsky's sociocultural theory (people learn from social encounters with more experienced individuals); 5. the learning perspective, particularly social learning theory (people learn by imitating other people, especially people they admire)]

Four Principles of Human Development

All developmentalists watch human behavior, so it is not surprising that different accounts of development agree on some general principles. Four principles of development are accepted by most scientists regardless of which topics they study or which theoretical approaches guide their work. These principles are valuable because many of the problems you will face in life are problems that have not yet been studied systematically. For example, no one can tell you with certainty which job offer you should accept or how your child will be affected by an electronic innovation that doesn't exist today. Whenever you cannot look up answers to questions, these principles can guide your thinking and help you make important decisions. Beginning with Chapter 5, a featured topic at the end of each two-chapter section will illustrate how the following four principles help us to understand complicated developmental issues.

Principle #1: Development Is the Joint Product of Nature and Nurture

The **nature–nurture controversy** is the debate about whether our behavior is primarily due to heredity (nature) or the environment (nurture). In other words, are we mainly a product of our genes or our experiences? Your preference to think about one or the other will influence which theoretical approach appeals to you more. For instance, people who like to think about heredity tend to be drawn to the evolutionary perspective, whereas people who like to think about environmental influences tend to be drawn to the learning perspective. But scholars from both theoretical perspectives agree that it is impossible to separate these influences. As you will learn in later chapters, your genetic endowment influences which environments you approach, and your environment influences gene expression by turning individual genes on and off. As theorists Donald Ford and Richard Lerner (1992, p. 64) explained, "The proper question one should ask is 'how?' that is, 'how do nature and nurture interrelate to provide a basis for behavior?'"

Principle #2: Physical, Cognitive, and Socioemotional Development Are Interrelated

It is convenient to divide development into three general topics: physical development (bodily changes, including brain development and motor control), cognitive development (changes in attention, memory, and thought processes), and socioemotional development (social and emotional behavior, including such things as peer relationships and emotional attachments). But there is a problem with sorting topics into these categories: Whole individuals develop, not fragmented parts. For example, social skills influence people's involvement in group activities, which contributes to their physical and cognitive growth. Currently, cutting-edge research on development often spans these three areas of development (Rothbart, 2004b).

In this book, we try to help you see these interrelationships by organizing the chapters that cover infancy through older adulthood into two-chapter sections. In the first chapter of each section, you will read what a typical person in that age bracket is like by learning about the physical, cognitive, emotional, and social developments that occur at that age. After this "profile of development," the next chapter explores differences by describing the contexts in which people live. We call these the "pathways" chapters to emphasize how people's journeys through life depend on their health, personalities, social circumstances, family structures, and other factors. Instead of forcing topics such as child abuse, marriage, and caring for an elderly parent into "physical," "cognitive," or "socioemotional" development, pathways chapters let us present topics as they exist in real life—as issues that affect the whole individual.

nature–nurture controversy The debate about whether development is directed primarily by heredity or the environment.

Principle #3: Developmental Outcomes Change over Time and Contexts

Developmental science tries to explain how influences at one point in life relate to who you become at a later point in life. For example, students have asked us how their lives have been affected by a medical trauma they experienced at birth or the fact that they reached puberty earlier than their peers. It is difficult to answer these questions because relationships between influences and outcomes change as a function of when we sample behavior and the environment in which people grow. In other words, *time* and *context* are critical concepts for the study of human development.

Consider an example. Several longitudinal studies have studied infants who experienced oxygen deprivation at birth, which is a condition called *perinatal anoxia*. (*Perinatal* means "the period around childbirth" and *anoxia* refers to a lack of oxygen.) Perinatal anoxia occurs for a variety of reasons and is often present in infants who have other risk factors. Therefore, no single conclusion will be true for all infants. Nonetheless, some patterns emerge. One is that problems at one age may not be present at another. For example, anoxic infants score lower than other infants on a test of cognitive functioning at 3 years of age, but these two groups score the same on most cognitive measures at age 7 (Corah et al., 1965; Graham et al., 1962). The diminishing effect of an influence over time is called a **washout effect**, and such effects are common among children who have experienced mild trauma. On the other hand, problems that are not visible at 3 years of age can appear later in development. For example, anoxic and nonanoxic groups are equally socially adjusted at age 3, but by age 7 the anoxic group shows delays in social skills. Years later, this birth complication also significantly increases the risk of schizophrenia (Zornberg, Buka, & Tsuan, 2000). Scientists use the term **sleeper effect** to describe an effect that cannot be detected early in development (because it is "sleeping") but later becomes obvious. To complicate things further, mild biological trauma can have no long-term consequences for children who are reared in stimulating environments even though these same experiences put children raised in poverty at risk (Anderson, Northam, et al., 2001). If the effects of some environmental influences disappear with time (washout effects) while others appear with time (sleeper effects), we need to observe multiple areas of functioning, at multiple ages, for children reared in multiple environments, before we can know the consequences of an experience.

Principle #4: Development Is Characterized by Continuity and Discontinuity

The autobiographical sketches at the beginning of this chapter illustrate a popular pastime: searching people's histories to speculate about the origins of their present behavior. This activity illustrates a belief in *continuity* or *connectedness*, the idea that current functions are built on previous functions. There are two implications to this idea. First, development is often seen as gradual and incremental in the connected worldview. Even radical changes in behavior, such as the negativity of the "terrible twos," are viewed as part of a chain of developmental

washout effect When a condition or event has an effect on development at one point in time but not at a later point in time (the effect "washes out").

sleeper effect When a condition or event that has no detectable effect at one point in development begins to have consequences later in development.

events that has actually been occurring for some time. Second, the idea of connectedness encourages belief in the stability of traits over time and is, therefore, part of a tradition that emphasizes the early years of life. For example, Watson (1928, p. 3) alarmed more than a few parents when he asked, "But once a child's character has been spoiled by bad handling which can be done in a few days, who can say that the damage is ever repaired?" As we will explain in later chapters, belief in the importance of early development is one of the most enduring themes in developmental psychology and also one of the most frequently challenged.

In contrast, some scientists emphasize *discontinuity*: the appearance of new behavior that does not build on prior behaviors and experiences. Some discontinuities have a biological basis, such as the intense interest in sex that appears during puberty. Other times, discontinuities stem from changes in our environments, such as going to college, historical events (including inventions, such as computers, that transform how we spend our time), and personal experiences (such as illnesses).

There is evidence for both continuity and discontinuity (Kagan, 1994). Some characteristics, such as a general tendency to be social and outgoing, are remarkably consistent across development (McCrae & Costa; 2003). But for the most part, stability is observed more frequently when the time between observations is short and people's environments have remained the same. Over long periods or when environments have changed, discontinuity is common. Thus, the question is not, "Is development characterized by continuity or discontinuity?" but rather, "*When* is development characterized by continuity or discontinuity?" If you have ever wondered whether you will be attracted to the same type of person 20 years from now, you have asked about continuity and discontinuity in your own development.

The four principles of development show us that answers to questions about development are rarely simple. As psychologist Jerome Kagan quipped (1998, p. 24), "The mammalian brain was not constructed to make scientific research easy."

﹥﹥﹥ MEMORY MAKERS ﹤﹤﹤

1. Heredity is to nature as the way we are raised is to _____.
2. Physical, _____, and socioemotional development influence one another.
3. The opposite of a washout effect is a _____ effect.
4. Development is characterized by continuity and _____.

[1. nurture; 2. cognitive; 3. sleeper; 4. discontinuity]

Our brains may not have been constructed for the convenience of scientists, but they certainly were designed to amaze, delight, and bedazzle. In the next chapter, you will learn about two fundamental influences that have affected you since the beginning of your life: heredity and the environment. Together, we will explore why these forces, and the remarkable connections between them, ensure that you are the only "you" who will ever exist.

⟩ ⟩ ⟩ SUMMARY ⟨ ⟨ ⟨

What Is the Field of Human Development?

1. Three historical factors—medical advances, the industrial revolution, and Darwin's theory of evolution—changed the relationship between children and society and paved the way for the systematic study of development to emerge.

2. Today, the field of **human development** is an interdisciplinary science that describes change and stability from conception to death, including typical and atypical development.

Research Methods

3. Investigators use many methods to collect information about development, including **naturalistic**, **participant**, and **structured observations**, **self-reports**, **archival data**, standardized tests, and mechanical recording devices.

4. Developmental researchers use different research designs to answer different types of questions. Descriptions of individuals, called **case studies**, are useful for documenting rare conditions or circumstances. **Correlational** studies tell us whether there is a relationship between variables, but they cannot tell us *why* the variables are related (that is, if one variable causes the other). **Experiments** test hypotheses about causal relationships by manipulating one variable to observe its effect on another variable. Investigators use developmental research designs to study change over time, including **cross-sectional studies** (comparisons of individuals from two or more age groups at one point in time), **longitudinal studies** (which follow a group of individuals as they develop), and **cross-sequential studies** (in which several age groups are identified and retested over time).

5. Ethical guidelines for conducting research discuss the rights of research participants (including the right to withdraw from the study and to understand foreseeable risks and benefits from their participation) and professional standards for communicating findings (including the need to present findings in ways that minimize misinterpretations of the findings).

Theoretical Perspectives

6. Theories are sets of concepts that organize and explain data. Theoretical perspectives are groups of theories that share common **metamodels**—fundamental assumptions about the nature of development. For example, the **psychodynamic perspective** describes the unconscious forces that motivate behavior. Traditional psychoanalysis focuses on how sexual energy shifts from one body area to another as individuals develop, leading them to face different conflicts with parents. Erikson's psychosocial theory emphasizes how individuals face different social challenges throughout the life span.

7. The early **behaviorists** emphasized how learning occurs through classical and operant conditioning. **Social learning theories** emphasize how cognitive processes influence what individuals will **imitate**.

8. The **evolutionary perspective** explains how specific behaviors helped individuals adapt to their ancestral environments. **Ethologists** focus on cross-species comparisons, such as the similarity between the human attachment response and infant–parent bonding in other animals. Evolutionary psychologists focus on explaining similarities in behavior across human cultures.

9. The **cognitive perspective** describes the mental processes involved in thinking. Piaget's theory of cognitive development says that children are active agents who periodically reorganize their mental structures to fit new information. The **information processing approach** describes the processes involved in completing a task, including attention, memory, language, and strategy selection.

10. The **contextual perspective** encourages researchers to look at how broader cultural factors influence development. Vygotsky's sociocultural theory views learning as a social activity in which children gain skills by interacting with more competent mentors. Bronfenbrenner's bioecological theory describes how individuals are influenced by events outside their immediate families.

11. Most scientists use concepts from a variety of theoretical perspectives and, therefore, have an *eclectic* theoretical orientation.

Four Principles of Human Development

12. Change across the life span is the joint product of **nature (heredity) and nurture (environment)**. Scientists are interested in how genes and environments interact to determine behavior.

13. Physical, cognitive, and socioemotional development are interrelated. To understand why individuals develop in particular ways, we need to consider how changes in all three areas of functioning contribute to behavior.

14. The effects of biological and environmental influences change over time and contexts. **Washout effects** occur when influences become less important over time; **sleeper effects** occur when factors that have no noticeable effects immediately show an effect later in development.

15. Development is characterized by continuity and discontinuity. We observe continuity when current behavior builds on prior development and early behavior predicts later behavior. We observe discontinuity when current behavior differs substantially from prior behavior. Human development researchers are interested in which circumstances foster continuity versus discontinuity.

>>> KEY TERMS <<<

human development (p. 4)
tabula rasa (p. 5)
life span approach to development (p. 8)
normative approach to development (p. 8)
variables (p. 10)
naturalistic observation (p. 10)
participant observation (p. 11)
ethnography (p. 11)
structured observation (p. 11)
self-reports (p. 11)
archival data (p. 12)
case study (p. 12)
correlational study (p. 13)
correlational coefficient (p. 13)
third variable problem (p. 14)
experiment (p. 14)
independent variable (p. 14)
dependent variable (p. 14)
cross-sectional study (p. 17)
cohort effects (p. 17)

longitudinal study (p. 18)
cross-sequential study (p. 18)
theory (p. 20)
metamodels (p. 21)
psychodynamic perspective (p. 21)
learning perspective (p. 24)
learning (p. 24)
behaviorism (p. 25)
social learning theory (p. 26)
modeling (p. 26)
evolutionary perspective (p. 27)
ethology (p. 27)
sensitive periods (p. 28)
cognitive perspective (p. 30)
information processing approach (p. 32)
contextual perspective (p. 33)
zone of proximal development (p. 34)
nature–nurture controversy (p. 39)
washout effect (p. 40)
sleeper effect (p. 40)

Heredity and Environment

Stories of Our Lives
Seeing Double

> "Biology gives you a brain. Life turns it into a mind."
>
> Jeffrey Eugenides

Summary

When Tamara Rabi began attending Hofstra University on Long Island, New York, she noticed that strangers were smiling and saying, "Hi." "I was like, why are these people waving at me?" she later told *Latina* magazine (O'Connor, 2003). Then, at her twentieth birthday party, Justin Latorre told her she looked just like a friend of his, Adriana Scott. There were other eerie coincidences: The two women shared the same birthday, were born in Mexico, and were both adopted.

When Justin arranged for Tamara and Adriana to exchange instant messages, Adriana's mother realized she would have to tell her daughter the story: Years earlier, when Mr. and Mrs. Scott had picked her up from Guadalajara, problems with the adoption process forced them to leave her twin sister behind. After Adriana sent Tamara her picture, both women knew their lives were changing forever (Gootman, 2003):

"The picture came up and our jaws dropped," said Christie Lothrop, 19, one of Tamara's suitemates. "We didn't know what to do."

The twins agreed to meet the following Sunday in a McDonald's parking lot near Hofstra, a world away from the Guadalajara hospital where they had last been together. Tamara brought two friends; Adriana, a junior at nearby Adelphi University, brought one.

On the way, each twin panicked and suggested turning around. The friends would not have it. Identical twins separated at birth find one another on Long Island and then chicken out of their reunion? Forget about it.

Soon they were face-to-face, sisters who had grown up as only children. "I'm just standing there looking at her," Adriana recalled. "It was a shock. I saw me."

The group went somewhere for lunch, where the twins sat side by side nibbling at chicken fajitas as their friends ogled at the similarities in their expressions, their gestures and how both rested for a few minutes midmeal, then resumed eating . . .

The following weeks were a whirl of breathless e-mail, eye-popping surprises and constant retellings to anyone who would listen, which meant everyone. The twins paraded each other through their respective campuses, and to their part-time jobs. A Hofstra student interviewed Tamara for a class assignment, and a senior communications major asked to do his final project on the twins . . .

They have discovered that as children, they occasionally had the same haunting nightmare in which a loud sound fades into softness and then gets loud again, and that they both love dancing and started lessons when they were young.

When Adriana told Tamara about an audition for Entertainment Tonite, a D. J. company looking for dancers to help energize parties, they decided to go together. At the audition Wednesday night, the twins danced side by side, their ponytails swinging in sync as they followed the choreographer, Dayton A. Mealing.

Afterward, they told him their story. "I would have freaked," he proclaimed. "Awesome." (p. A1)

But the twins are not completely alike. Tamara loves Chinese food; Adriana does not. Adriana is shy; Tamara is more outgoing. Tamara has a birthmark near her right eyebrow; Adriana does not. And despite the fact that they grew up so close to one another, their childhood worlds were different: Adriana was raised as a Catholic in the suburbs while Tamara was raised as a Jew in Manhattan. Blending their worlds will take time. As Tamara explained, "We're not at the sister relationship yet, but I see us being close friends, then best friends, and then sisters, able to tell each other anything, and always there for each other" (O'Connor, 2003).

***

THE WOMEN IN OUR OPENING story are *reunited twins*: identical twins who grew up in separate households and found one another as adults. The world watches twins like Tamara and Adriana closely, searching for clues to one of the most interesting mysteries in the world: How do our genes (nature) and environments (nurture) create who we are?

In this chapter, you will learn the basic concepts you will need to follow the dance of nature and nurture throughout the life span. Here you will read about the characteristics that make human beings unique, the nature of our genetic blueprints, and how genetic and environmental influences interact to produce the interesting differences between us. The stories that frame these issues will take you around the globe—into the lives of other American twins, to a Japanese nursery school, and even into the inner workings of your brain.

What Is a Human Being?

It sounds ridiculous to ask what a human being is; we are what we are. But to understand what is unique about human life histories, we have to consider what we could be but are not. What makes us different from dogs, monkeys, or chimpanzees?

Biologists classify living things into groups, including a kingdom, class, order, family, genus, and species. Humans share the order primates with apes (chimpanzees, gibbons, gorillas, and orangutans), monkeys, lemurs, and tarsiers. Humans and apes also share the same superfamily. But humans are the only living members of a genus called *Homo*—a genus that consists of one living species, *Homo sapiens*. *Homo sapiens* is Latin for "wise human being," and developing that wisdom requires an unusual course of development.

Compared to other primates, our offspring are large for the size of their mothers. And despite the fact that our babies grow rapidly, their physical functions mature very slowly. Human infants have been described as "ridiculously . . . helpless," barely rolling over at an age when infant chimpanzees are playing with their friends (Low, 1998, p. 132). And unlike chimpanzees and other primates, who wean their young when teeth appear, humans wean their infants early, several years before molars erupt (Harvey, Martin, & Clutton-Brock, 1987). But the most obvious difference between humans and other animals is our extended childhood, a time when we depend heavily on our parents for food, protection, and guidance (Montagu, 1989). No other primate takes more than a decade to mature, but humans reach maturity only after 18 to 25 years. As one team of scientists explained, "No creature spends more time dependent on others for its very existence than a human baby, and no creature takes on the burden of that dependence so long and so readily as a human adult" (Gopnik, Meltzoff, & Kuhl, 2001, p. 158).

Most species survive because they are adapted for particular environments. Some butterflies, for example, sport colors that help them blend into local foliage, which reduces their chances of being seen and eaten. As humans, however, we survive because our flexible brains help us adapt to a wide *variety* of environments—from the arctic tundra to southern Manhattan. The cost of this flexibility is a long childhood, a time when each of us masters at least one complex language, acquires problem-solving skills no other species can rival, and (with varying degrees of success) learns to act differently around our parents, friends, and bosses (Surbey, 1998). To acquire these abilities, we rely on brains that are large for our size. But our brains contain no structures that are not found in other primate brains. Human uniqueness lies in the greater volume of our brains (especially in areas responsible for complex thought) and our extended period of rapid cognitive development (Johnson, 1998; McKinney, 1998).

The human life span is also an oddity. Small organisms tend to reach sexual maturity young, reproduce often, and die young. Larger animals, who are less likely to be killed by predators, can afford a more leisurely existence. But our maximum life span—about 120 years—is longer than we would expect from our size. By comparison, the life span of a chimpanzee—who averages 60 kg (132 lb) for an adult male—is only about 53 years (Falk, 2000).

So what is a human being? We are an animal who is born big, grows fast, weans early, matures late, and lives long (Low, 1998). We are highly intelligent,

Homo sapiens Latin for "wise human being" and the name of the human species.

Humans have large and fast-growing brains that allow us to adapt to an impressive array of environments.

heredity The genetic mechanisms by which parents pass traits on to their children.

highly social animals with large brains that allow us to reflect on the meaning of our own existence. One of the greatest wonders of the world is the development of our bodies and minds—development guided by a set of genetic instructions that distinguishes us from all other organisms.

The Genetic Blueprint

People have always known that children resemble their parents, yet it was only during the last century that scientists pieced together the mysteries of reproduction and genetics to explain those resemblances. During the 17th century, *preformation* was a popular view of reproduction. This theory said that future generations were nested inside one another, like the Russian dolls in the left panel of Figure 2.1. After the discovery of sperm cells, some preformationists claimed that immature organisms were housed in the heads of these cells, as illustrated by a famous drawing in the right panel of this figure (Pinto-Correia, 1999). In the late 19th century, some physicians believed that a sufficient *number* of sperm cells had to enter the female sex cell to trigger normal development. (Of course, this idea violated a basic principle of reproduction: that one female reproductive cell + one male reproductive cell = one embryo) (Martensen & Jones, 1997).

An understanding of **heredity**—the genetic mechanisms by which parents pass traits on to their children—developed gradually over the course of about a hundred years. Early experiments led scientists to propose the concept of a "gene"—a biological unit with instructions for creating a trait. Later, in a series of discoveries that are among the most exciting in the history of science, the structure of these units was unveiled. A good place to start the story of these discoveries is in the 1800s, in the gardens of Gregor Mendel.

Mendel's Discovery

Gregor Johann Mendel (1822–1884), the son of poor peasants from central Europe, joined a monastery* at the age of 21. Monastery leaders encouraged scientific as well as religious study, and Mendel was sent to study mathematics and science at the University of Vienna to prepare for a teaching career.

FIGURE 2.1 The theory of preformation.

Preformation, an early theory of reproduction, said that future generations were nested inside one another like the Russian dolls on the left. After scientists discovered sperm cells, preformationists drew tiny organisms inside male reproductive cells, as shown on the right.

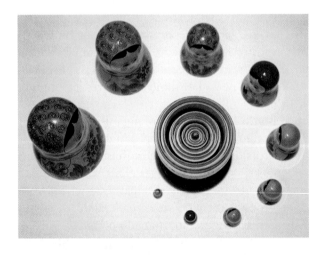

*monastery: A place for people under religious vows, such as monks.

In his gardens, Mendel did experiments with pea plants, studying the inheritance of physical traits such as the color of seeds and the shape of the pods (Orel, 1996).

In Mendel's time, scientists assumed that heredity involved a mixture of genetic information, similar to mixing different colors of paint together. Mendel's experiments were important because they showed that information was inherited in discrete (individual) units that do not blend together. In one experiment, for example, he crossbred pea plants that produced yellow seeds with pea plants that produced green seeds. Instead of producing yellowish-green seeds, seeds from the resulting plants were yellow. When this generation of plants was crossed, the next generation had both yellow *and* green seeds, with a ratio of about three yellow-seed plants to one green-seed plant. From these results, Mendel formulated a number of basic genetic principles.

Mendel found that traits could be "hidden" for a generation or more and then reappear in subsequent generations. His findings suggested that traits were transmitted by units, now called **genes**, that come in pairs. Genes produce variety because they come in different forms called **alleles**. During the creation of male and female reproductive cells, gene pairs separate (*segregate*) randomly, so that each member of the pair appears with equal frequency in the resulting cells. Individuals then receive one of the genes they need to complete each pair from their father and one from their mother. In Figure 2.2, Mendel's results for seed color are related to albinism, a condition in which people lack the pigment that gives skin its color.

Our genetic makeup cannot always be predicted by our physical appearance. Look again at Figure 2.2. Some people with normal pigmentation have two normal alleles, but others have one normal allele and one allele for albinism. Therefore, we need to distinguish between our actual physical and biochemical characteristics, which are our **phenotypes**, and our underlying genetic codes, which are our **genotypes**.

Normal skin pigmentation is the result of a **dominant allele**. Dominance occurs when one allele masks the influence of another allele. As you can see in Figure 2.2, albinism is transmitted by a **recessive allele**, one that is not expressed

genes Segments of DNA molecules that are the functional units of heredity.

alleles Alternative forms of single genes. For example, a parent may carry an allele for normal skin pigmentation and an allele for albinism, the absence of pigment.

phenotype An organism's actual physical and biochemical characteristics, which are the result of an underlying genetic code (*genotype*) interacting with the environment.

genotype An organism's genetic makeup.

dominant allele An allele (form of a gene) that masks the influence of other alleles and is, therefore, expressed.

recessive allele An allele (form of a gene) that is not expressed unless both alleles in a pair are recessive.

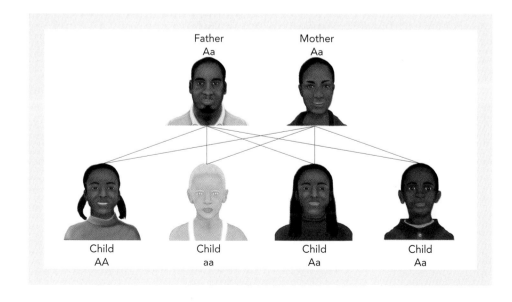

FIGURE 2.2 Genetic transmission of albinism.

People with albinism lack the pigment that normally colors our skin, hair, and eyes. Albinism is inherited as a recessive disorder, so two carrier parents will average three normal children for every child who has albinism. Some children with normal pigmentation have two normal alleles, whereas others have one normal allele and one allele for albinism. A = normal allele, a = allele for albinism.

TABLE 2.1	Examples of Recessive and Dominant Traits

Trait	Description
Recessive Traits	
Albinism	Pigment is absent in the hair, skin, and eyes. This disorder affects all races.
Green color blindness	A form of color blindness caused by an absence of medium-wavelength color pigment in the green color receptors. This condition is more common among males than females because it is X-linked.
Cystic fibrosis	Affected individuals produce an abnormal amount of mucus in the lungs and digestive system. Bacteria in this mucus causes recurrent infections and lung damage.
Hemophilia A	A blood coagulation problem in which affected individuals bruise easily, have prolonged bleeding after an injury, and often suffer from joint pain. This is an X-linked disorder.
Phenylketonuria	An enzyme deficiency that prevents victims from metabolizing the amino acid phenylalanine, a substance that is especially abundant in high-protein foods. Treatment to prevent mental retardation consists of a special diet to restrict the intake of phenylalanine.
Dominant Traits	
Congenital stationary night blindness	A term used to describe many types of night blindness that have different patterns of genetic transmission. One type that is transmitted as a dominant trait is a nonprogressive condition in which individuals have normal daytime vision in the center of the retina but impaired night vision.
Brachydactyly, Type C	Fingers and toes are abnormally short in individuals with otherwise normal growth.
Huntington disease	A progressive neurological disorder that usually produces symptoms between 30 and 40 years of age. The condition causes dementia, personality change, and early death.
Marfan syndrome	A condition characterized by tall stature and extremely long arms and legs. There are many associated features, such as crowded teeth and a high arched palate. Premature death can occur from heart abnormalities.

SOURCES: Klug et al. (2006); Online Mendelian Inheritance in Man (2005).

unless both alleles are recessive. Mendel's principles of discrete traits, random segregation, and dominance/recessiveness explain the 3:1 ratio of traits in the children of parents who carry two different alleles. Some traits that are produced by dominant and recessive genes are listed in Table 2.1.

Mendel's work was largely ignored during his lifetime. Then, in the early twentieth century, two scientists noticed that threadlike substances in the nuclei of cells segregated randomly into two sets when cells divided to form female or male reproductive cells. Because this behavior seemed to provide a physical basis for crossbreeding findings, they proposed that these threads were the source of hereditary information. Subsequent research unraveled the structure of the genetic code and found many exceptions to Mendel's principles.

The Genetic Code

Your genetic blueprint is made up of molecules of deoxyribonucleic acid, or **DNA**. The existence of DNA was discovered in the 1860s by a Swiss chemist, but it was not until 1944 that a classic paper in molecular genetics set the stage for proving that DNA was the foundation of genetic information. Then, in 1953, James Watson and Francis Crick described the structure of DNA in a two-page paper that earned them a Nobel prize (Watson, 1999).

As Watson and Crick proposed, each DNA molecule looks like the twisted ladder in Figure 2.3. The rungs of the ladder are made up of four types of chemical units called *bases*. These four bases, abbreviated A (adenine), T (thymine), G (guanine), and C (cytosine), are the alphabet that spells out genetic instructions. Notice that each rung of a DNA molecule contains two bases linked together. This pairing of bases is specific: Adenine always bonds with thymine, and guanine always bonds with cytosine. DNA molecules duplicate themselves by unzipping, coming apart at the middle and picking up free-floating bases, thereby creating two identical DNA molecules.

The functional units of heredity—genes—are specific segments of a DNA molecule that range from less than a thousand bases to several million bases in length. *Structural genes* produce traits by directing the production of proteins, and these segments of DNA determine your eye color, the texture of your hair, and so forth. But some traits are designed to be expressed only at specific times in development or only under specific environmental circumstances. For example, many people stop producing an enzyme that digests milk sugar after infancy, and women stop menstruating when they lose too much weight. These examples illustrate that circumstances can turn genes on and off during the course of development. One way genes are controlled is through **regulatory sequences** (sometimes called **genetic switches**), which are segments of DNA that influence when and where other genes are expressed. The mechanisms that regulate gene action are the building blocks of development (Carroll, 2005). These mechanisms determine such things as when we should grow taller and at what ages our brains should "clean house" by eliminating unnecessary connections between neurons.

A single DNA molecule, tightly coiled with protein, is the building block for a chromosome. **Chromosomes** are structures in the nucleus of each cell that define individual species. Humans have 23 pairs of chromosomes: 22 matching pairs called *autosomes* and a 23d pair called the *sex chromosomes*. Females are typically XX, meaning they have two X chromosomes for the 23d pair, whereas males are typically XY. Chromosomes within a cell can be

American blues musician Johnny Winter and his younger brother, Edgar were both affected by albinism. Their talent and inherited condition earned them the title, "the white boys of the blues."

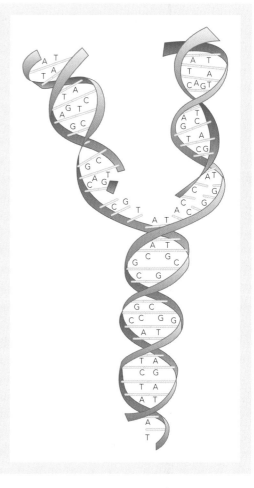

FIGURE 2.3 The structure and duplication of DNA.

DNA is built like a ladder with each rung composed of a pair of bases. DNA molecules duplicate themselves by separating in the middle and picking up free-floating bases. One of the most exciting riddles in science is to explain how the complexities of biological life originate from such a simple structure.

DNA Deozyribonucleic acid, a molecule that contains the genetic code.

regulatory sequences (sometimes called **genetic switches**) Segments of DNA that influence when and where other genes are expressed.

chromosomes Threadlike structures in the nuclei of cells, constructed from DNA, that contain the genetic code. Humans typically have 46 chromosomes arranged in 23 pairs.

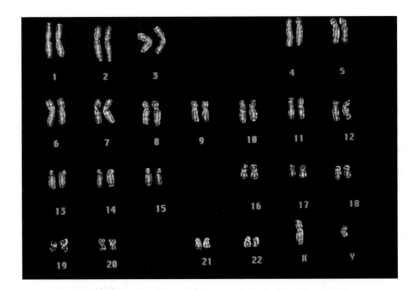

FIGURE 2.4 A karyotype.

A karyotype is a picture of an individual's chromosomes that are arranged in a standard sequence. This karyotype shows the 23 chromosome pairs from a human male.

photographed and arranged in order by pairs, creating a *karyotype*, such as the one in Figure 2.4, that reveals whether you are XX (female) or XY (male). Look at Figure 2.5 to help you visualize genes as a segment of a single DNA molecule that coils to form a chromosome.

Unless you are one of the rare exceptions, you inherited 46 chromosomes from your parents—23 from your mother and 23 from your father. The reproductive cells from your parents, called **gametes**, were produced by *meiosis*, a process of cell division that reduces the number of chromosomes from 46 to 23. Meiosis begins when each

gametes Reproductive cells. A new organism is produced when gametes from a male and a female combine.

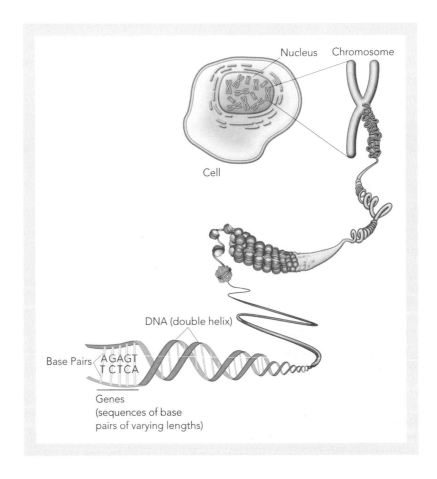

FIGURE 2.5 The building blocks of life.

Genes are segments of a single DNA molecule. This molecule coils to form a chromosome.

chromosome makes a copy of itself. Pairs of chromosomes then divide, forming cells that each contain one chromosome from the original pair. Human female reproductive cells do not undergo the final division that halves the number of chromosomes until fertilization (the moment the male and female reproductive cells join). Hence, human females have *oocytes* prior to fertilization ("eggs" with the full number of chromosomes) rather than *ova* (cells with half the number of chromosomes). The male reproductive cells, like those in other species, are *spermatozoa* that carry the reduced number of chromosomes. In Chapter 3, you'll explore the fascinating events that follow the joining of male and female gametes.

Some Patterns of Hereditary Transmission

To honor Mendel for proposing the concept of dominant and recessive alleles, traits that are produced in this fashion are said to follow Mendelian transmission. But if you think about how your physical traits relate to those of your parents, you will probably have difficulty fitting some of your features into this simple system of dominant and recessive traits. In fact, many traits are produced through one of many *non*-Mendelian patterns of transmission, including the ones you will read about next.

PARTIAL DOMINANCE AND CODOMINANCE. Crossing red snapdragons with white snapdragons results in some plants with pink flowers. This illustrates incomplete or *partial dominance*, a situation that occurs when two alleles produce an intermediate trait. It is relatively rare in humans to find cases in which the phenotype is intermediate. One example is Tay-Sachs disease, a condition associated mostly with Jews of Eastern European ancestry. Babies who inherit two recessive alleles do not metabolize fatty substances called *lipids* normally, causing gradual destruction of their central nervous systems followed by death during the first 1 to 3 years. Adults who carry one abnormal allele do not suffer from the disease but actually have only about half of the enzyme activity (the process that removes excess lipids from the body) that normal adults have (Klug, Cummings, & Spencer, 2006).

Codominance occurs when each combination of alleles results in a distinctly different phenotype. For example, your blood type is determined not by two alleles, as in Mendel's examples, but by three. These three alleles, combined in pairs of two, produce four distinct phenotypes: types A, B, AB, and O.

POLYGENIC INHERITANCE. Traits that are determined by many genes are said to be transmitted by **polygenic inheritance**. Eye color and intelligence, for instance, are believed to be influenced by more than one gene. Many traits that are important in agriculture, such as milk production and the oil content of seeds, also result from the combined influence of many alleles. For these traits, each individual allele either adds to the quantity of the trait or not, and the total of these "additive" alleles determines what quantity of the trait is expressed. Thus, your height was partly the result of an additive genetic process, with the food you ate as a child determining how your genes were expressed.

X-LINKED AND SEX-INFLUENCED INHERITANCE. Pairs of chromosomes provide people with a biological backup system: If one copy of a gene is flawed, in most cases the corresponding gene on the other chromosome is normal and dominant. Because females have two X chromosomes for the 23d pair, they have the

polygenic inheritance When trait inheritance is determined by more than one gene.

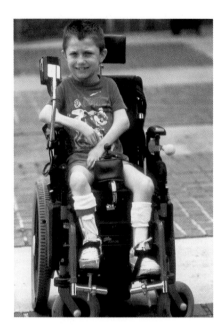

This boy has muscular dystrophy, a group of genetic diseases that cause the skeletal muscles to gradually weaken. Boys are more likely to have muscular dystrophy because the most common forms are inherited in an X-linked, recessive pattern.

X-linked traits Traits transmitted on the X chromosome. Such traits are more likely to be expressed in males than in females because females have a second X chromosome that often carries a dominant version of the trait.

sex-influenced inheritance When the expression of a trait is influenced by individual hormone levels and is, therefore, expressed differently in males than in females.

genetic imprinting (also called **genomic** or **parental imprinting**) When expression of a trait depends on whether it was inherited from the mother or the father.

human genome The entire set of genes that defines our species.

mutations Changes in genes that occur due to spontaneous internal processes or environmental influences.

usual protection of a backup gene on their sex chromosomes. Males, however, have one X and one Y chromosome. There are some corresponding regions between X and Y chromosomes, but Y chromosomes are smaller and contain little genetic information. Because genes that appear only on the X chromosome will be expressed in males, males exhibit these **X-linked traits** more frequently than females. Examples of X-linked traits are some forms of color blindness, muscular dystrophy (a disorder that causes muscle degeneration), and hemophilia (a blood clotting abnormality that causes life-threatening bleeding).

Some *autosomal traits* (traits that are *not* coded on the sex chromosomes) show different patterns of expression in males and females. In **sex-influenced inheritance**, expression of a trait is influenced by individual hormone levels. A well-known example is male pattern baldness, the type of baldness that causes hair loss on the top of the scalp. A well-guarded secret is that some women are also affected by this pattern of hair loss, although they usually show it to a lesser extent than males do.

GENETIC IMPRINTING. The rules that govern gene expression are usually the same regardless of which side of the family contributed a specific gene. However, in the case of **genetic imprinting** (also called **genomic** or **parental imprinting**), genes retain a chemical "imprint" that marks where they originated, and the expression of these traits depends on whether you inherited the trait from your mother or your father. For example, two distinct disorders arise from the deletion of a chromosome region of the 15th pair (Soejima & Wagstaff, 2005). If only the maternal chromosome is normal, a condition called Prader-Willi syndrome is present. This condition is associated with mental retardation, obesity, and a characteristic facial appearance that includes almond-shaped eyes. In contrast, Angelman syndrome results when only the paternal chromosome is normal, causing mental retardation and a collection of other abnormalities, including inappropriate laughter and little or no speech (Chatkupt, Antonowicz, & Johnson, 1995). Due to imprinting, genetic instructions from *just* a mother or father do not contain the necessary information to produce an offspring. The presence of imprinted genes is one reason scientists cannot produce a human embryo using reproductive cells from two mothers or two fathers (da Rocha & Ferguson-Smith, 2004).

MUTATIONS. The entire set of genes that defines our species—the **human genome**—is not merely shuffled when each couple reproduces. Instead, every species experiences **mutations**, which are changes in the genetic code. Each species has an average rate of spontaneous mutations due to internal chemical processes, but mutations can also be caused by environmental factors such as exposure to radiation and certain chemicals. Mutations can occur at the level of single genes or chromosomes. Chromosomal mutations involve changes either in the number of chromosomes or the arrangement of segments of chromosomes. (You will read about some common disorders that arise from these errors of nature in Chapter 3.)

EXTRANUCLEAR INHERITANCE. Cells house some DNA in a structure outside the nucleus called the mitochondria. *Mitochondrial DNA (mtDNA)*, which is inherited only from the mother, encodes several important gene processes. A number of serious disorders can be transmitted from mother to child through mtDNA, causing deafness, blindness, seizures, and other medical problems. One hypothesis of why aging occurs is that mtDNA mutations across the life span lead to a loss of mitochondrial function (Wallace, 2005).

The Human Genome

Few scientific efforts have captured the public's imagination like the **Human Genome Project**, an international undertaking to map the human genetic code. The project, which began in 1990, was a 13-year effort coordinated by the U.S. Department of Energy and the National Institutes of Health. The goals of the project were staggering: to sequence the 3 billion bases that make up human DNA, make the data available to the public, and address the ethical, legal, and social issues that arose from the project.

Rival teams published a rough draft of the human genome in 2001, when reports appeared simultaneously in *Science* and *Nature* (International Human Genome Sequencing Consortium, 2001; Venter et al., 2001). Media reports dubbed the event one of biology's "Big Moments," ranking in importance with Darwin's work on evolution, Mendel's discovery of the laws of genetics, and Watson and Crick's discovery of the double helical structure of DNA (Angier, 2001). The project was officially completed in 2003, but information is still being released.

One of the most startling findings was the size of the genome. Your parents were taught that humans had about 100,000 genes, but the majority of newer estimates were under 30,000 (Human Genome Project Information, 2004). Because the lowly fruit fly has 13,601 genes, scientists scrambled to explain how humans could be so complex with so few genes. Some scientists argued that lower counts resulted from flawed techniques, but most were comfortable with the lower number. After all, small changes that code for a few more proteins can create a much more complex organism, and changes in a few regulatory sequences can have a dramatic effect on when and where genes are used during development. As developmental biologist Sean Carroll (2005) explained, the *size* of a genome is not nearly as important as what genes are *doing*.

Spokespersons for the Human Genome Project claim it will reap fantastic benefits, including new gene therapies and drug treatments, procedures to detect vulnerabilities to disease, and improved technologies for solving crimes from DNA evidence. But critics worry that knowledge of the genetic tendencies of a person or a fetus will outstrip society's ability to use the findings safely and equitably. Will people with genetic predispositions to disease be denied health insurance? Will those who are more susceptible to workplace toxins be fired? Will parents abort fetuses who do not meet their biological standards? As ethicist George Annas remarked, "The right not to know is going to be as important as the right to know" (Shapiro, 2000, p. 38). To confront these and other issues, about 3 to 5 percent of the annual project budget was earmarked for ethical, legal, and social issues programs.

Excitement about the Human Genome Project was also tempered by the realization that people are more than just their genes. One scientist from the project, Eric Lander, called the database a mere "parts list." "If I gave you the parts list for the Boeing 777," Lander explained, "I don't think you could screw it together and you certainly wouldn't understand why it flew" (Roberts, 2000, p. 38).

Human Genome Project An international effort to map the human genetic code. The project was officially completed in 2003.

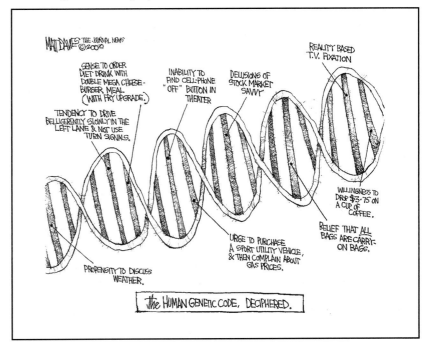

The HUMAN GENETIC CODE, DECIPHERED.

Over and over again, research has shown that sequences of genetic material will never define an individual because the environment interacts with genetic information. It is here, in contact between genes and environments, that the real wonder of development occurs.

> > > **MEMORY MAKERS** < < <

1. Compared to most other species, humans are ____.

   (a) born mature and have a short childhood and short life for their size
   (b) born mature and have a long childhood and long life for their size
   (c) born immature and have a short childhood and long life for their size
   (d) born immature and have a long childhood and long life for their size

2. Fill in the blanks with the following words:
   Mendelian, non-Mendelian, genome, chromosomes, genes, recessive
   The basic units of heredity, _genes_ are actually segments of one of the 46 _chrom_ that make up the human _genome._ Traits that are either dominant or _recess_ are examples of _Men_ inheritance. Polygenic inheritance and X-linkage are examples of _non_ inheritance.

[1-d (Humans are born unusually immature and require care from parents for an extended period of time. Compared to other primates, our life span of about 120 years is long). 2-genes, DNA, chromosomes, genome, recessive, Mendelian, non-Mendelian]

How Genes and the Environment Interact

Even before people had any real understanding of genetic mechanisms, many believed that our physical makeup single-handedly determined our successes, failures, and status in society. This idea—which is called *biological determinism*—was widely accepted during the 19th and early 20th centuries (Gould, 1996). But the more scientists learned about genetics, the more they were awed by the ability of organisms to respond to changes in their environments. Soon it became clear that there were subtle and varied interactions between genes and environments. In fact, the way in which genetic tendencies come to be expressed—or not expressed—is at the heart of the principle of nature versus nurture discussed in the previous chapter. As research psychologist Robert Plomin explained, "Some of the most interesting questions for genetic research involve the environment and some of the most interesting questions for environmental research involve genetics" (1994, p. 40). As we noted at the start of this chapter, nowhere are these questions more likely to spring to mind than when we enter the fascinating world of identical twins.

Lessons from Twin and Adoption Studies

A picture in a women's magazine shows two adorable babies, identical girls, with pink barrettes and matching gingham dresses. The image invites you to marvel at their nearly identical features. Then you find the target of this full-page ad: The babies hold different spoons, one ornate,* the other simple. Above the angelic faces are the words, "nurture individuality" (Oneida advertisement, 2001).

---

*ornate: Excessively detailed, showy.

Advertisers know that identical twins catch readers' attention. But this promotion is especially interesting because it asks us to think about how different these babies will be as adults. When twins are reared together, their differences remind us that genes are just the blueprint—not the realization—of development. Despite their genetic similarities, identical twins are not two for the price of one but two very different individuals.

How different *are* genetically identical people? When a major physical defect occurs in one identical twin, the other twin is affected less than half of the time. And just like other siblings, identical twins often suffer from different diseases and make different lifestyle choices that influence how heavy they are and how rapidly they appear to age. Even conjoined (Siamese) twins, who are attached for life, show distinctly different personalities and interests (Segal, 1999). This was true for Lori and Reba Schappell, a set of conjoined twins that developmental psychologist Nancy Segal interviewed for her book about twins. Reba, the smaller of the two, is paralyzed from the waist down from birth defects. A singer, she received the L.A. Music Award for best new country artist in 1997. Lori, her extroverted twin, has worked as a clerk and nurse receptionist. As Segal (1999, p. 304) explained, "Lori likes to watch television, Reba does not; Lori loves to shop, Reba does not, Lori craves sweets, Reba does not . . . When I asked the twins to list some similarities, Lori replied, 'We have the same last name and we love each other.'"

Studies of twins who grew up together offer a picture of just how difficult it is to tease out the relationship between genes and the environment. Do parents encourage individuality and, by doing so, exaggerate their children's differences? Do genes contribute to similarities in complex behaviors, such as attitudes or consumer choices? To answer these questions, investigators use a group of research designs, called *adoption studies*, in which they evaluate people reared by parents who are not biologically related to them. This solves a nagging problem that exists with most identical twin pairs: that the parents who contributed their genes also created the environments in which they lived. In other words, when twins are raised by their own parents, either parental genes *or* parental environments might have produced the similarities in their behavior. This is why adopted twins such as Tamara and Adriana in our opening story provide scientists with such a valuable opportunity for research.

Some of the most intriguing adoption data are from studies of identical twins reared apart. The most famous case, the "Jim twins," is of a pair of identical brothers who were reared in different adoptive homes in Ohio. Soon after Jim Springer phoned his brother Jim Lewis in 1979 after a 39-year separation, the two became the first pair of such twins to be tested by Thomas Bouchard and his colleagues, launching the Minnesota Study of Twins Reared Apart. Journalists loved the Jim twins, and the resulting media coverage focused on a long list of their amazing similarities. Despite decades of separation, the two brothers were almost as alike as the same person tested twice on intelligence, personality, heart rate, and brain waves. But what dominated newspaper and

Famous reunited bothers, the "Jim" twins, were among the initial twins studied for the *Minnesota Study of Twins Reared Apart.*

monozygotic twins Twins produced from one fertilized egg that divides between the first and fourteenth postfertilization day, commonly called identical twins.

dizygotic twins Twins produced from two fertilized eggs, commonly called fraternal twins.

environment Nonheritable influences. The environment includes biological influences, such as exposure to diseases, as well as social influences.

magazine articles were examples of their idiosyncratic* similarities: Each twin had had a dog named Toy as a child, married a first wife named Linda and a second wife named Betty. Both had a son with the same name (but spelled differently), had worked part time as sheriff's deputies, smoked Salems, and left love notes to their wives around the house.

Amusing descriptions of twins reared apart prompted immediate criticism. Many commentators pointed out that any two *unrelated* people who spent hours comparing the details of their lives would surely find numerous similarities. For example, the women in our opening story had both lost fathers to cancer by the time they were college students, yet these were *adoptive* fathers, so this coincidence has no genetic significance. Before we jump to the conclusion that genes produce every similarity, we need to consider data from comparison groups to determine whether identical twins are more similar than pairs of people who do not share the same degree of genetic relatedness.

One way to accomplish this is to compare identical and fraternal twins. *Identical twins*, also called **monozygotic twins**, form from a single fertilized egg that splits early in development (*mono* means "one," and *zygote* is the early cell mass that is forming). Thus, these twins share 100 percent of their genes (ignoring mutations that occur after early cell divisions). In contrast, *fraternal twins*, also called **dizygotic twins**, form from two fertilized eggs (*di* means "two"). Fraternal twin pairs can be either the same sex or different sexes, and they are no more genetically similar than siblings who were carried by their mother at different times. (Same-sex pairs share 50 percent of their genes, on average.) When the similarity between identical twins is greater than the similarity between fraternal twins, scientists conclude that genes play a role in development. This logic led to the discovery that many behavioral characteristics are at least partly sculpted by genes, including a number of personality traits (such as the tendency to be outgoing and emotional stability), many forms of mental illness (including schizophrenia and depression), and even the tendency to develop addictions to tobacco and other drugs (Plomin et al., 2003).

But the **environment** *does* matter. For example, the educational level of biological *and* adoptive parents is associated with scores on IQ tests (Capron & Duyme, 1991; Neiss & Rowe, 2000), and social scientists agree that families influence people's values, religious orientations, and political beliefs. Results from countless studies have shown that genes and environments work *together* to direct development (Bouchard, 2004; Plomin et al., 2003). As developmental psychologist Howard Gardner explained, researchers continuously grapple with two mysteries, "The fact that identical twins reared apart are almost as alike as those that are reared together, and the fact that identical twins still turn out to be quite different from one another" (1998, p. 20).

Gene–Environment Relationships

Genes and environments do not throw independent contributions into the developmental pot. Instead, heredity and environments influence each other in specific ways. Here we explain two examples of the interplay between nature and nurture: how environments and genes work together to produce traits and gene–environment correlations. Don't let these complicated-sounding ideas

---

*idiosyncratic: A characteristic or behavior peculiar to an individual.

discourage you: As you read on, you will notice that the underlying principles are simple concepts you have already noticed just by watching the plants, pets, and people in your world.

But before we begin, it is important to explain what scientists mean by the term *environment*. Being cuddled as a baby and read to as a toddler are environmental influences, but so are diet and exposure to disease. Environment, then, refers to a huge range of *nongenetic* influences, including biological ones. Consider the impact of being poor. Poverty contributes to malnutrition and a host of other medical problems associated with crowding and inadequate medical care, but it also leads to nonmedical problems, such as fewer educational opportunities. A broad definition of *environment* encompasses all of the risk factors that make up this complex social problem. Throughout this book, the term *environment* refers to all of the influences that affect us in our homes and communities.

HOW ENVIRONMENTS AND GENES WORK TOGETHER.

It is not uncommon for genetically influenced traits to produce different outcomes in different environments. For example, the evening primrose produces red flowers when grown at 23° centigrade but white flowers when grown at 18° centigrade (Klug et al., 2006). Temperature, humidity, and nutrition are just a few of the environmental factors that influence individual phenotypes.

In humans as in primroses, genes do not dictate a single result. Many mechanisms—including the ability of regulatory sequences to switch genes on or off as needed—provide biological flexibility. These mechanisms help people change their physiology when they move to high elevations, adjust to climates of varying temperatures, and reproduce more often when food is plentiful than when they are starving. Organisms also have *epigenomes*, chemicals that mark genes for increased or decreased activity levels. Shortly after birth, these chemicals begin to change, sometimes randomly and sometimes due to environmental events, so even identical twins have chromosomes that look increasingly different the longer they have lived in different environments (Fraga et al., 2005). In other words, the environment influences the *expression* of our genetic code: The term *hereditary* does not always mean "inevitable."

One condition that illustrates environmental influences on how traits take shape is phenylketonuria, or PKU for short. PKU, which is caused by a recessive gene, affects about 1 in 15,000 newborns (National Institutes of Health, 2000). Individuals with PKU cannot metabolize the amino acid phenylalanine, which is abundant in high-protein foods. If children with PKU eat a normal diet, phenylalanine levels rise in their blood, causing permanent mental retardation before their first birthdays. But newborns with PKU who are kept on a low-phenylalanine diet achieve intelligence test scores that are within normal range. In this way, the food children eat determines how their potential for intelligence is expressed.

The environment also influences traits we all share. Consider height. As we mentioned earlier, height is probably transmitted by a number of genes in an additive manner. The shuffling of genes produces variability among the children in each family, but on average children with two very short parents will be shorter than children with two tall parents. We are so accustomed to thinking of height as inherited that it is easy to underestimate the extent to which nutrition contributes to our final stature. Remarkably, one study of second-generation Japanese American males found they were over five inches taller than their predicted height would have been had they had been reared in Japan (Greulich, 1957)! Similarly, the average height of Japanese children increased rapidly between 1945

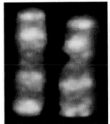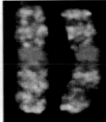

Chromosome 1 from 3-year-old identical twins (left) looks more similar than the same chromosome in 50-year-old twins (right). Random events and environmentally induced changes modify our genetic code, so even identical twins are different individuals.

Fraga et al. (2005). Epigenetic differences arise during the lifetime of monozygotic twins. *Proceedings of the National Academy of Sciences, 102,* 10604–10609.

and 1960, as the country recovered from a food shortage (Murata, 2000). Clearly, adequate food changes the way our genetic potential for height is expressed.

Often, relationships between genes and the environment are not apparent until later in development. Consider schizophrenia, a class of conditions involving problems in perception, thinking, and mood that usually appear in late adolescence or early adulthood. A person's risk of developing schizophrenia is three times higher if both parents have the diagnosis than if only one parent does, and people are more likely to develop symptoms if an identical twin has the disorder rather than a fraternal twin. These findings are strong evidence that schizophrenia has a genetic basis. Mysteriously, though, your risk of developing schizophrenia is less than 50 percent *even if* your identical twin has the disorder, suggesting that environmental factors are involved in triggering the disease. The risk of schizophrenia also shows interesting fluctuations, including higher rates among people born during the winter. Based on these findings, scientists think that schizophrenia is produced when genetically vulnerable people confront environmental factors that interfere with normal brain development. Although the triggering events are not yet known, some possibilities include physical trauma during birth, an unidentified virus (which pregnant women are more likely to "catch" during the winter), and maternal nutritional deficiencies (which are also more common during winter months) (Cantor-Graae, Ismail, & McNeil, 2000; McGrath, 1999; Mednick, Huttunen, & Machón, 1994).

Down syndrome is one of the most frequent examples of the relationship between nature and nurture. Children with Down syndrome either have an extra chromosome from the 21st pair or an extra portion of this chromosome, resulting in mental retardation and a distinctive appearance that includes a thick tongue, round face, and a fold of skin in the upper eyelid that gives them a distinctive appearance. Years ago, Down syndrome children were often institutionalized and viewed as unable to care for themselves. As medical advances helped increase their life expectancy and more parents began rearing them at home, it became clear that stimulating environments produced better mental functioning than anyone had expected was possible. Today, most Down syndrome children test in the mild to moderately retarded range, and many learn to read, write, and provide basic care for themselves.

The concept of *reaction range* is often used to explain how Down syndrome children develop differently in different environments. Reaction range implies that genes set the lower and upper limits for a trait while the quality of the environment determines where a person will fall within this range. For example, genes might determine the lowest level of intelligence an individual will achieve as well as the highest level that is possible if the individual is raised in a stimulating environment.

But gene–environment interactions can be more complicated than this. To illustrate, Figure 2.6 plots how different plants grow at three different elevations. Notice that some plants grow best in one environment whereas others grow best in another environment. According to biologists, this idea of **norms of reaction** (specific outcomes from specific genotype–environment pairs) captures the complexity of gene–environment relationships (Lewontin, 2000). Norms of reaction help us realize that a specific environment may not be best for everyone. For example, a quiet child who likes to read may be happier than his spirited, athletic brother if their parents are intolerant of noisy activity, but the spirited brother may be the happier sibling if the family is highly involved in sports.

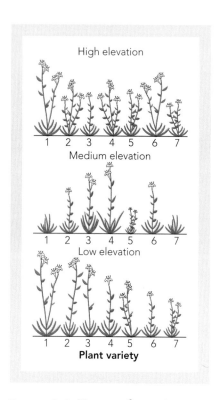

FIGURE 2.6 Norms of reaction.

A single genotype often produces different phenotypes in different environments, and the environment that is best for one individual may not be best for another. Some varieties of this plant grow best at low elevations, for example, whereas others grow best at higher elevations. *Norms of reaction* describe how individuals with different genetic makeups develop in different environments.

SOURCE: Adapted from Lewontin (2000); Griffiths et al. (1996).

norms of reaction The idea that genetically influenced traits develop differently in different environments.

Of course, not all traits are heavily influenced by the environment. Try as you might, exercising babies will only encourage walking a little earlier than they would have walked without a dedicated effort. The term **canalization** describes how difficult it is to throw development off its expected track. Traits that are highly canalized tend to develop normally across a broad range of environments. These traits, like walking, require unusual, severe, or persistent environmental extremes to alter their expression. Other traits, such as musical talent, develop more fully in enriched environments. Generally, behaviors that are necessary for survival, such as those involved in getting around and communicating, are more highly canalized than behaviors that are not related to reproductive fitness, such as musical talent (Bruer, 1999). It is, therefore, meaningless to ask, "Does experience influence development?" Rather, the question is, "What experiences, at what points in development, influence what outcomes?"

GENE–ENVIRONMENT CORRELATIONS. Social scientists cheered when they finally had evidence that environments influence genetic regulation. But it was another matter altogether when geneticist C. D. Darlington (1953) suggested that *genes* influence environments. Although many people thought this idea was preposterous back in the 1950s, most eventually accepted Darlington's basic premise (Plomin et al., 2001). Today, scientists know it is difficult to determine when genes and environments are influencing human behavior because genes and environments tend to be correlated. In other words, it is often difficult to tell where a genetic influence ends and an environmental influence begins.

It is easy to understand **gene–environment (G–E) correlations** (also called genotype–enviroment correlations) if you think back to someone like Sally, a high school student one of us once knew. Sally's entire family was successful and attractive, and Sally was pretty, perky, and extremely social. She loved to talk, laughed easily, and always seemed comfortable around other people. Whenever it was time to stand up in front of the class or lead a group, Sally made it seem easy. We never resented Sally, though, because she knew when to poke fun at herself, she made others feel good about themselves, and she never acted self-consciously. Everyone remembers a Sally in their lives because we all wanted to BE Sally.

Was Sally's personality a gift from heredity or the environment? There are three reasons why it is difficult to tell. One is that Sally's parents made a home environment that was consistent with their genetically influenced talents. Because her parents were also social and successful, they frequently had friends over and provided an intellectually stimulating household. Sally may have inherited "social" genes, but she may have been social simply because she had so many opportunities to watch her parents operating happily and comfortably in social situations. *Passive gene–environment correlation* refers to the fact that most children share both genes and environments with parents who encourage their own talents and avoid their own weaknesses. For example, children who are poor readers due to an inherited perceptual problem are more likely to have a parent who is also a poor reader (Willcutt et al., 2003). These children may not be read to as often as other children, therefore creating a correlation between genes and experiences that hinders the development of reading.

Sometimes the relationship between a genetic trait and an environmental influence is a reactive one. It is easy for attractive people like Sally to grow up self-confident because attractive, easygoing people tend to receive positive feedback from other people. For example, attractive children are viewed by adults as

canalization The extent to which a trait develops normally across a range of environments. Highly canalized traits are difficult to deflect from their expected tracks.

gene–environment (G–E) correlations (also called genotype–enviroment correlation). Ways in which genetic mechanisms influence individuals' environments and experiences.

niche-picking The tendency of individuals to choose activities and environments that match their personalities and interests.

smarter and better behaved than less attractive children (Lerner & Lerner, 1977; Serketich & Dumas, 1997), and even preschool children prefer to play with more attractive schoolmates (Dion, 1973). This second type of gene–environment correlation, *reactive gene–environment correlation*, describes how children with different genetic makeups elicit different reactions from their environments. This type of correlation also has a dark side, such as when children with irritable dispositions cause peers to reject them.

When Darlington suggested that genes create environments, he was especially interested in a third type of correlation. "In this world no two individuals have to put up with the same environment," he explained. "We have a choice" (1953, p. 302). Sally's love of people led her to choose activities in which she would develop her social skills, including drama and dance. By choosing situations in which she had to confront any fears she might have had of public attention, Sally widened the difference between her ease and the growing discomfort of shyer students who avoided the spotlight. *Active gene–environment correlation* means that people select environments that are consistent with their genetic preferences. As we grow older, we have more input into how we use our free time, whom we choose as friends, and even how we spend our workdays. Playing off the word *niche*, which is a place or activity that best suits a person, developmental psychologists use the term **niche-picking** to describe this tendency to choose activities, friends, and places that suit our interests and abilities (Campos, Frankel, & Camras, 2004; Scarr & McCartney, 1983).

Gene–environment correlations can lead us to question traditional interpretations of developmental findings. Consider drug use during adolescence, which is a behavior that is influenced by the behavior of our friends (Spooner, 1999). An environmental analysis says that peers encourage drug use because they model it and actively encourage unconventional behavior. But there may be other pathways to drug use. For example, family conflict could alienate teens from adult norms and lead them to seek out unconventional friends (Brook, Brook, & Whiteman, 1999; Brook, Whiteman, & Finch, 1998). Taking gene–environment correlations into account suggests yet another possibility: Some adolescents may have genetically based personality traits, such as a tendency to be irresponsible, that contribute to family con-

People are influenced by their friends, but they also choose friends who suit their personalities and interests. By choosing their activities, individuals help construct their own environments.

flict *and* draw them to peers who use drugs. If this is true, then *some* of the relationship between family conflict, friends' behavior, and teen behavior gets chalked up to the influence of genes—not to the influence of the environment.

Given passive, reactive, and active gene–environment correlations, it is no easy task to separate the effects of genes from the effects of environments. In fact, once these forces collide in the human brain, it may be impossible to do so.

How Genes and the Environment Build a Brain

As we mentioned in Chapter 1, scientists who study behavior are joining forces with scientists who study the brain to create a more complete picture of why people develop the way they do. Throughout this book, you will read about the major changes that take place in the brain as people pass through various phases of life, changes that explain why children are so distractible, some teenagers are so irresponsible, and some grandparents are so forgetful. Here we provide an overview of how genes and the environment join forces to shape the brain throughout life.

Your brain is built from two types of cells. **Glial cells** (from the Greek word for "glue") have the less glamorous job of providing brain cells with nutrients, insulating cells, and removing cellular waste. The stars of the brain are communication specialists called **neurons**—billions of microscopic cells designed to receive and send signals. These cells make it possible for you to balance on a skateboard, remember a chess play, and plan tomorrow's dinner. Neurons vary in size and shape depending on their function, but typical neurons consist of dendrites (rootlike fibers that receive messages from other neurons), a cell body, and a trunklike axon that sends messages to other neurons or to muscle and gland cells. (Some neurons lack an axon and communicate only with adjacent neurons.)

Early in development, the brain and spinal cord begin to form when the mass of fetal cells flattens, folds, and seals, forming a neural tube during the process of **neurulation**. Inside this tube, **neurogenesis**, the forming of new neurons, begins when cells that are precursors* to neurons and glial cells form by rapid cell division. Massive production of new neurons begins about the fifth week after fertilization and peaks about 3 to 4 months after fertilization. Because the majority of brain cells are produced before a child is born, and the resulting brain will contain an estimated 100 billion cells, the rate of neurogenesis during midpregnancy is staggering—several hundred thousand new nerve cells each minute (Brown, Keynes, & Lumsden, 2001; Nelson, Thomas, & de Haan, 2006).

Although neurogenesis determines the number of brain cells a child will have, the organization of those cells is determined by a process called **neural migration**. After production, immature cells migrate outward to their final locations. In the most advanced part of the brain, the cerebral cortex, the first cells to migrate occupy the closest position, with newcomers migrating to higher layers. Neurogenesis and neural migration are influenced by a variety of environmental *insults* (conditions that damage the brain). For example, the number and organization of cells in the cerebral cortex are abnormal when mothers drink alcohol during pregnancy. In severe cases, babies born to alcoholic mothers have large gaps in their brains because there are so few neurons to fill in, and the neurons in some brain regions are disorganized, as if they did not know where to stop when they were migrating (Guerri, Pascual, & Renau-Piqueras, 2001).

But neural production and migration do not produce a finished product. As illustrated in Figure 2.7, the brain of a newborn lacks the extensive network of connections that supports thinking in older children and adults. The interesting

---

*precursor: Something that precedes another.

glial cells Cells in the nervous system that insulate neurons, provide them with nutrients, and remove cellular waste.

neurons Cells in the nervous system that are designed to receive and send information.

neurulation The process of forming the neural tube, which will become the brain and spinal cord.

neurogenesis The production of neurons in the brain.

neural migration The migration of neurons from the location where they are produced to their final locations in the brain.

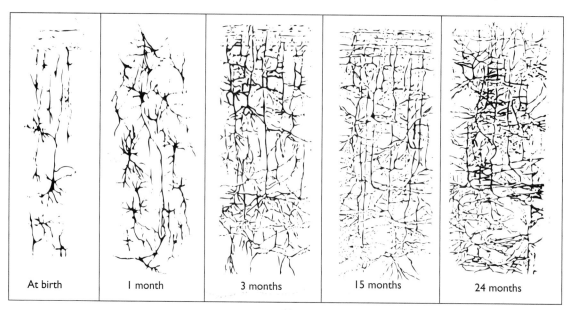

| At birth | 1 month | 3 months | 15 months | 24 months |

FIGURE 2.7 Synaptogenesis.

During the early years of life, new dendrites and synapses—points of communication between neurons—grow furiously, adding complexity to the wiring diagram of the brain. The structure of the brain continually changes as some connections are strengthened and others eliminated.

synaptogenesis The process of developing interconnections between neurons.

synaptic pruning The elimination of synaptic connections. The synaptic pruning that occurs throughout childhood is essential for intellectual growth.

neural plasticity The brain's ability to change from experience.

part of brain development is **synaptogenesis**, the gradual process of developing interconnections (*synpases*) between neurons. Immature neurons begin to mature after they reach their final destination where developing axons and dendrites allow them to connect to other neurons. Beginning only weeks after neurogenesis starts, synaptogenesis occurs at a startling pace and tapers off in different brain regions about 1 to 3 years after birth (Huttenlocher, 1999; Johnson, 1999).

Early synaptogenesis is a genetically controlled—and rather haphazard—process. The brain produces many more synapses (points of communication) between one neuron and another than it needs, and it is not very selective in producing these connections. This sloppy beginning produces an infant with limited cognitive abilities, but one with remarkable flexibility. A young mind is a world of possibility because the final sculpting of the brain is directed not by genes but by experiences.

Consider two toddlers, one raised in a small town in Illinois, another in a city in the People's Republic of China. The first, who is the son of a music professor, listens to Mozart each morning, his ears flooded with hissing from the "s" sound in his parents' quietly spoken English. The second toddler, a little girl, hears her grandparents speaking Mandarin, a language in which changes in voice frequency signal changes in meaning. All of these children's experiences—what they hear, feel, see, and touch—stimulate networks of neurons. Synapses that are activated by particular experiences, such as the sound of classical music, undergo changes that make them more permanent.

Between early childhood and adolescence, these children will lose *billions* of synapses per day in a process called **synaptic pruning**, which is the elimination of unnecessary synaptic connections. This process has been called *neural Darwinism*, a type of survival of the fittest in which activated interconnections beat out weaker neighbors for a place in the brain. In the process, they will gradually trade some **neural plasticity**—the ability of their brains to change with experience—for a less flexible brain that processes information more quickly and efficiently. Like a gardener attacking an unshapely hedge, the environment shapes the wiring diagram of the human brain. For example, our music-loving toddler may grow up to have *absolute pitch*, an unusual ability to identify tones that children usually retain only with years of musical experience (Takeuchi & Hulse, 1993). But unless his parents relocate to China during his childhood, our little musician will never learn to speak Mandarin without an accent.

The slow process of selecting synapses is accompanied by another important event: **myelination**. Myelin is a fatty substance that coats the axons of most neurons in the adult brain, speeding signal transmission and insulating fibers to prevent interference from neighboring cells. Neurons begin to develop myelin sheaths about the ninth month after conception, but myelin is still forming at age 20 and, in some brain areas, well into adulthood (Sowell et al., 2003). Following the general pattern for brain development, more primitive brain regions complete myelination before areas that support more advanced abilities do. The environment leaves few neural processes untouched, and myelination is no exception. For example, the fat content of a child's diet affects myelination, so malnourishment can slow this aspect of brain development (Nelson, 2000). Myelination is the reason many pediatricians recommend that children drink whole milk until age 2, after which parents can shift to low-fat or skim milk.

Scientists used to believe we were born with all of the neurons we would ever have. Now they know that new neurons continue to be produced in some brain regions even during adulthood (Curtis et al., 2005) and that new connections develop throughout our lives. As with all brain processes, our lifelong flexibility follows a "use it or lose it" principle, with environmental stimulation increasing function and deterioration occurring during times of extreme stress, illness, or when environments fail to stimulate us mentally (Kolb & Whishaw, 1998; McEwen, 1999).

So here we have the intersection of genes and environment in the human brain, as illustrated in Figure 2.8: a sequence consisting of neurulation, neurogenesis, synaptogenesis, myelination, synaptic pruning, and, finally, the formation of new connections throughout the course of our lives (Nelson et al., 2006). If Figure 2.8 seems complicated, just think about James Kalat's friendly version of the "assembly manual"

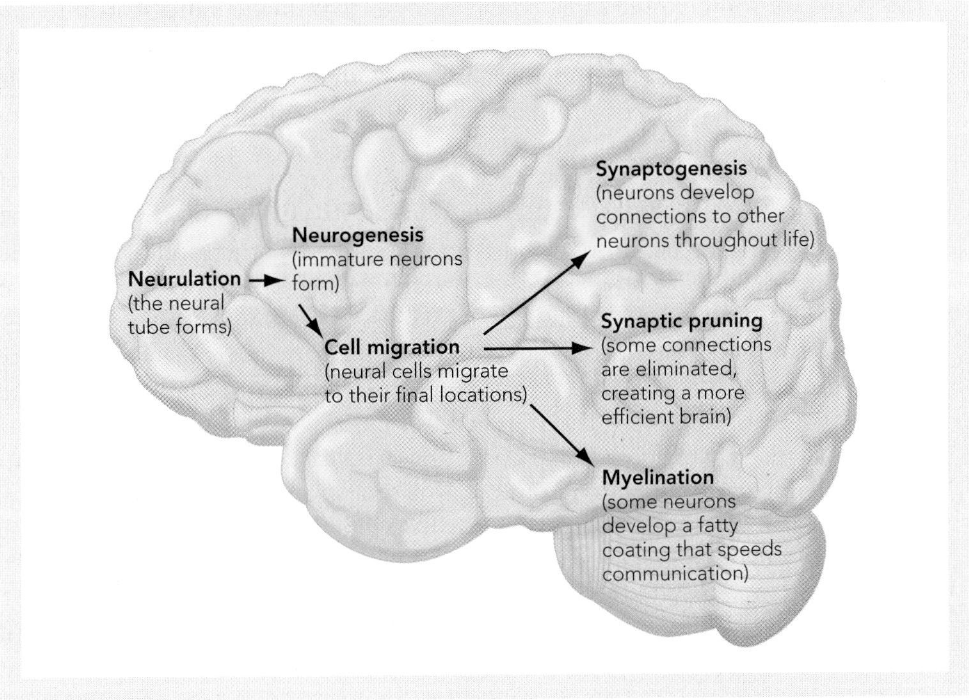

myelination The production of a fatty substance around axons to insulate fibers and speed transmission.

FIGURE 2.8 The major mechanisms of brain development.

A new brain begins to form when tissues fold to produce the neural tube during the process of *neurulation. Neurogenesis* (the production of neurons) begins and immature neurons migrate to their final locations. There they develop dendrites and axons to communicate with other neurons through the process of *synaptogenesis.* Later, *synaptic pruning* will periodically eliminate some connections while preserving others. Even before birth, the axons of some neurons are developing a fatty layer of insulation through the process of *myelination,* a process that continues well into adulthood.

for a brain: "Put these axons here and those dendrites there, and then wait to see what happens. Keep the connections that work the best, throw away the others, and then make new ones similar to the ones that you kept. Later, if those connections aren't working well, discard them and try new ones" (Kalat, 2004, p. 107). As Kalat and many other scientists have concluded, it takes a lifetime to build a brain.

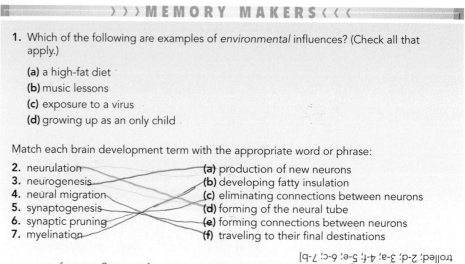

>>> MEMORY MAKERS <<<

1. Which of the following are examples of *environmental* influences? (Check all that apply.)

   (a) a high-fat diet
   (b) music lessons
   (c) exposure to a virus
   (d) growing up as an only child

Match each brain development term with the appropriate word or phrase:

2. neurulation
3. neurogenesis
4. neural migration
5. synaptogenesis
6. synaptic pruning
7. myelination

(a) production of new neurons
(b) developing fatty insulation
(c) eliminating connections between neurons
(d) forming of the neural tube
(e) forming connections between neurons
(f) traveling to their final destinations

[1-all of these examples are environmental influences because they are not genetically controlled; 2-d; 3-a; 4-f; 5-e; 6-c; 7-b]

Genetic and Environmental Diversity

The 3 billion base pairs in the human genome provide endless variety. As geneticist Dean Hamer explained, "There are more possible human DNA sequences than there are people who have ever walked the Earth, or who ever will be born before our solar system disappears" (1997, p. 111). Add a limitless number of cultures to this basic recipe and you know why every person is unique. Throughout this book, we will be using some common terms that divide individuals into different categories, including racial terms (such as Caucasian and African American), ethnic terms (such as Hispanic), and terms that describe people's economic circumstances (such as poor versus middle class). As you'll learn next, these terms are prevalent yet sometimes controversial.

Two Ways of Thinking about Genetic Diversity

One goal of developmental research is to determine whether findings from one group of people hold for other groups. For example, height and weight norms that represent all children in the United States will be misleading for Korean adoptees, who tend to be smaller. To study such differences, scientists frequently categorize people into *races* such as whites, blacks, and East Asians (or Caucasoid, Negroid, and Asian) (Rushton, 1996; Rushton & Rushton, 2003). The concept of race assumes that people who look similar come from families who have spent many generations living and intermarrying in particular parts of the world and, therefore, they will share more genes than people from unrelated groups. Although the three-race system is familiar to most of us, the number of races that have been proposed ranges from two to somewhere in the hundreds (Brace, 1964).

The notion that there are distinct races had almost complete support until the late 1930s, when some scholars began to challenge the concept (Lieberman,

1997; Lieberman & Jackson, 1995). Genetic differences among the races seemed apparent, but were these differences only skin deep? By the 1970s, two camps had formed that continue to debate today. On the one hand are scientists who believe that "race" has no biological reality (Brace, 1996; Lewontin, 1972). On the other hand are forensic anthropologists, psychologists, and other professionals who believe that racial terms capture meaningful differences between populations (Edwards, 2003).

The easiest way to understand why there is controversy about racial terms is by looking at Figure 2.9. These maps show the distributions of two features associated with being called "black" in the United States: skin color and hair texture. Each map plots *clines*, which are changes in the frequency of a trait across a geographic area. For example, the frequency of dark skin is low in northern Europe, intermediate in the Mediterranean region, and high in Africa. If we traced these maps onto plastic sheets and laid them over one another, boundary lines for the two features would not reveal a sharp division between "blacks" in Africa and "whites" in Europe. Adding maps for other traits, such as the ABO blood system, would only muddy the picture further. Because individual traits are adaptations to particular environmental pressures that do not share geographic boundaries (Lieberman & Jackson, 1995), scientists who criticize the race concept have concluded that "there are no races, there are only clines" (Livingstone, 1962, p. 279). These scientists believe it is misleading to classify people into racial groups on the basis of facial characteristics or other arbitrary features. Instead, they encourage researchers who are interested in diversity to study the implications of *individual* traits that may be adaptive in specific environments.

Scholars who defend the race concept say it is overly simplistic to think about diversity only in terms of individual traits. Although it is true that knowing someone's skin color may not tell us with much certainty what his or her blood type is, certain traits *do* tend to be correlated. For instance, a dark-skinned person is more likely than a light-skinned person to have curly hair, the trait for hemophilia, and many other traits. When researchers use statistical techniques that look for associations among traits, clusters of traits emerge that correspond to traditional racial terms. Moreover, most people can be accurately classified into a single race on the basis of a cluster of identifying traits (Edwards, 2003).

Why does it matter whether races exist or not? If racial categories are meaningless, then researchers should not divide their data according to race and physicians should not take race into account when treating illness. On the other hand, if traits are distributed in meaningful ways across racial categories, then scientists should continue to compare results from different racial groups. Heart disease is one of many conditions that illustrate the danger *and* the benefit of racial categories. African Americans respond poorly to some drugs for heart disease, so these drugs have warnings that explain racial differences in effectiveness. But many African American men, like Decarlo, did *not* inherit the gene associated with a poor drug response. If Decarlo's doctor thinks of him as a black patient—and, therefore, prescribes a less effective drug than the one she would prescribe to an Asian patient—she will not provide him with the best care. But across all of her patients, Decarlo's doctor will make more beneficial

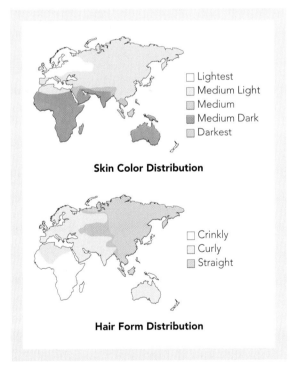

Skin Color Distribution

☐ Lightest
☐ Medium Light
☐ Medium
■ Medium Dark
☐ Darkest

☐ Crinkly
☐ Curly
■ Straight

Hair Form Distribution

FIGURE 2.9 Human diversity: How traits are distributed.

These maps show how skin color and hair texture vary across Africa and Europe. If you overlapped these maps, you would not find a clear dividing line between people whom American culture considers "black" or "white." Human diversity is continuous and racial terms vary from culture to culture.

SOURCE: Brace (1964).

decisions if she prescribes different drugs to dark-skinned and light-skinned peoples. As one commentator explained, "Ideally, we would all have our genomes sequenced before swallowing so much as an aspirin. Yet until that is technically feasible, we can expect racial classifications to play an increasing part in health care" (Leroi, 2005).

Thus, there are two ways to take genetic diversity into account when designing research and discussing the findings: One is to look at the impact of *individual* traits; another is to categorize people into broad groups that can then be compared. Both approaches have their supporters. For example, scientists who analyze blood prefer to think of human variation as *clinal* (consisting of continuous change that cannot be captured by racial categories), whereas forensic specialists who identify decomposed bodies from skeletal features tend to support the race concept (because they can categorize people fairly accurately) (Gill, 2005).

Racial terms will continue to be controversial because they are socially defined. For instance, people who are only one-eighth African descent may be called "black" in the United States, but they will be called one of half a dozen or more terms in Brazil. Those with brown or black hair, tan skin, a nose that is not narrow, and lips that are not thin may be *morena*: people who, if Brazilians were forced to divide their categories into whites versus blacks, would be a kind of white (Fish, 1995). Moreover, racial groupings often correlate with important environmental factors, such as economic status. As long as racial categories correlate with social circumstances, differences between racial groups will be a complicated mixture of biological and environmental differences.

The Cultural Landscape

All species, including humans, develop in a specific habitat such as a rain forest, plain, or desert. Humans also develop in a specific culture. **Culture** refers to such things as the technology, art, morals, laws, customs, and beliefs of a society—in short, "the sum total of human creations" (Stark, 2004, p. 39). Unlike the term *environment*, which includes diseases and other biological influences, culture refers to features of the environment that are socially created. Anthropologists have tried to capture the essence of culture by calling it a "design for living" (Kluckhohn, 1951) and "the total way of life of a people" (Geertz, 1973). When scientists say that the environment sculpts the human brain as it develops, they mean that the brain is influenced by biological influences in the environment, such as nutrition, *and* by the socially constructed landscape of culture.

Unlike other species, our actions are often directed not by stimuli themselves but by the *meaning* of those stimuli in our culture. For example, our reaction to a neighbor's kiss is very different if we live in a society where only lovers kiss than if we live where friends of both sexes peck each other's cheeks. Because humans are symbol users, it is pointless to ask what a human being is apart from culture. As anthropologist Clifford Geertz (1973, p. 46) explained, culture is an "essential condition" of human existence.

People who are familiar with only a single culture often assume that everyone thinks about life the same way they do. These individuals are likely to be frustrated in unfamiliar environments because they interpret the meaning of other people's behavior in terms of their own cultural standards. As people learn more about other cultures, they come to understand that culture influences every aspect of their lives. For example, a clock cannot determine when someone is "late" because culture determines how we think about time and appointments. Similarly, no rule

culture Features of the environment that are learned, including the technology, art, morals, laws, customs, and beliefs of individual societies.

book can specify when privacy has been invaded because culture determines our rules for interpersonal space and our right to use objects that are lying around. Culture influences the nature of your daily activities, the way you interpret behavior, and even how you trade time and favors with other people.

Scientists often use two types of terms to describe groups of people who share a number of cultural influences: ethnic terms and terms that describe people's socioeconomic status. Throughout this book, we will be using these terms to contrast groups of people who have had different experiences as they developed. After introducing these terms, we will explain how culture influences basic assumptions about the nature of development.

ETHNICITY. Problems with the concept of race have led to alternative ways of thinking about human diversity. One concept, ethnicity, was first used by sociologists to describe waves of immigrant populations into and around the United States during the Great Depression (Marable, 2000). **Ethnicity** refers to the self-definition of groups based on a common history, nationality, or culture. Ethnic groups feel that similarities bind their members together and separate them from other groups (Lieberman & Jackson, 1995; Stark, 2004). For example, whenever families take pride in their Polish or Korean heritage, they are focusing on their ethnic roots.

The U.S. census categorizes people by racial terms (such as "American Indian or Alaska Native," "Asian," and "white") *and* ethnic terms. The category "Hispanic or Latino" refers to ethnicity because people in this category can be of any race. Unlike race, the concept of ethnicity recognizes that biological *and* cultural differences distinguish populations. Ethnic identities are fluid over time, reflecting how people think about themselves and external political forces (Nagel, 1994). Furthermore, an increasing number of individuals are identifying themselves in terms of more than one ethnic tradition.

Studying the effects of culture and ethnicity on development can be tricky simply because preferences for various ethnic terms change over time. For instance, many people who are considered Hispanic or Latino by the Census Bureau identify themselves as Mexican American, Cuban American, and so forth. Some of these people dislike the broader terms "Hispanic" and "Latino" because these are terms the dominant culture used to lump together groups that historically have not identified strongly with one another. If they had to choose, some people prefer the term "Latino" over "Hispanic" because they view "Latino" as recognizing the diversity of Latin American countries. However, the term "Hispanic" has gained more acceptance and was preferred by the majority of registered Latino voters in one survey (Granados, 2000).

Comparing ethnic groups helps scientists evaluate how the environment influences development. For example, Hispanic infants tend to be healthier than one might predict based on their higher poverty rate. Even with poor prenatal care, the infant mortality rate in one Mexican American sample was less than half the rate for poor African American women (James, 1993), and Hispanics have a rate of low birth weight that is similar to that

ethnicity Membership in a group defined by a common history, nationality, or culture. For example, Korean and Hispanic are ethnic terms.

During the summer, hundreds of ethnic festivals in the United States celebrate the food, music, and traditions that have blended to create American life. These Scottish dancers are pointing their toes for an audience in Colorado.

of whites (Fuentes-Afflick, Hessol, & Pérez-Stable, 1999). It is still unclear which cultural differences protect Hispanic women and their babies, but studies have identified a number of interesting possibilities, including diets that are higher in calcium, folate, protein, vitamin A, and ascorbic acid (Fuentes-Afflick & Lurie, 1997). Because scientists cannot conduct experiments that stress human fetuses, cultural variation in lifestyle helps us test hypotheses about the impact of various environmental factors on development.

SOCIOECONOMIC STATUS. Another aspect of culture, as the previous example of Hispanic infants suggests, is **socioeconomic status (SES)**. Compared to high SES families, low SES families are less educated, have less prestigious jobs, and have lower incomes. As you will learn in later chapters, low SES is associated with many developmental problems, including high infant mortality rates, poor school achievement, and a higher rate of behavioral problems (Gottfried et al., 2003; Zigler & Finn-Stevenson, 1999). Partly because so many outcomes are associated with SES, it is one of the most frequently studied environmental variables.

Like culture, SES is another concept that is difficult to define (Duncan & Magnuson, 2003). An adult can have little formal education yet earn a great deal of money, or have a lot of education and be unemployed. Researchers, therefore, define SES in different ways depending on the topics they are studying, sometimes focusing on education, other times on income, and other times taking direct measures of factors they believe are important for development. When studying children, one alternative to SES classifications is to use one of the HOME inventories (Home Observation for Measurement of the Environment). These are checklists that describe the types of learning materials in a child's home, the degree of parental involvement, and other direct family influences (Bradley, Caldwell, & Corwyn, 2003).

CULTURAL ASSUMPTIONS ABOUT DEVELOPMENT. Culture not only influences our development, but it also influences our *views* about development. For example, it seems obvious to European Americans that infants are born helpless and, therefore, the goal of child rearing is to foster independence. Japanese parents, however, are likely to think that infants are separate, strong-willed organisms who need to be drawn into interdependent relations with others (Caudill & Weinstein, 1969; Shimizo & Levine, 2001). These different assumptions have profound influences on parents' child-care decisions. For example, most European Americans set up nurseries for their babies and encourage them to sleep through the night by themselves. Their attitudes about parent–infant relationships are illustrated by magazine articles with titles such as *Winning Bedtime Battles* (Ganske, 2001). Japanese parents, in contrast, prefer sleeping with their babies (Wolf et al., 1996), which is a decision shared by some cultural groups in the United States. As one Appalachian mother explained, "How can you expect to hold on to them later in life if you begin their lives by pushing them away?" (Abbott, 1992, p. 60).

Of course, parents in the United States tend not to fret about how they will hold on to their children later in life. Americans emphasize the *individualist* values of independence, unique solutions to problems, and personal happiness more than *collectivist* values that focus on the welfare of the group. Some features of these two value systems are listed in Table 2.2. In adolescence, these traditions create a humorous difference between cultures. In the United States, a harsh punishment for teenagers is to "ground" them (prevent them from leaving the house)—as if forcing children to be with their family is the most terrible fate imaginable! In Japan,

socioeconomic status (SES) A measure of economic status. Low SES is associated with low incomes, less formal education, and less prestigious occupations.

TABLE 2.2 Individualist Versus Collectivist Values

	Individualist	Collectivist
The self	The self is defined as independent and separate from the group.	The self is defined in terms of one's relationship to the group.
Parental responsibility	Parents encourage skills that promote autonomy.	Parents protect and care for children and teach them their responsibilities within the group.
The primary goal of socialization	Interactions with adults and peers develop children's unique talents and encourage individuality.	Interactions with adults and peers teach children to fit harmoniously into a group and promote the goals of the group.
Achievement	Differences in achievement are largely due to individual differences in talent.	Differences in achievement result from differences in training and effort.
Social decision making	Individuals' attitudes and feelings are important determinants of their behavior.	The well-being of the group and group norms are important determinants of behavior.

however, angry parents might threaten to ban a child from the family (although no one thinks they are being serious) (Hajime Otani, personal communication, April 26, 2000). (Perhaps if teenagers just switched households, everyone might like their punishment.)

One research team (Tobin, Wu, & Davidson, 1989) conducted a revealing study of how cultural values influence child rearing. This team videotaped preschoolers in Japan and the United States during the course of a day, including examples of misbehavior and its consequences. Then Japanese and American adults watched the tapes. Americans were shocked that the affluent Japanese had 30 preschoolers to one teacher in a single classroom. The Japanese, in contrast, felt that American classes were "sad and underpopulated." As one Japanese adult remarked, "I wonder how you teach a child to become a member of a group in a class that small?" (p. 38). Responses to misbehavior were also quite different. Some Americans thought that a Japanese boy, Hiroki, misbehaved because he was smart and bored. In contrast, the Japanese thought that Hiroki had not learned to be dependent, possibly because he did not have a mother in the home. The Japanese also disapproved of how the American teachers promoted individualism. For instance, one respondent said that the practice of asking children about their feelings was inappropriate, because it was "too heavy, too adultlike" for small children (p. 53).

Japanese attitudes about preschool are clearly connected to the core values in Japanese business: *wa*, the Japanese word for group harmony, and

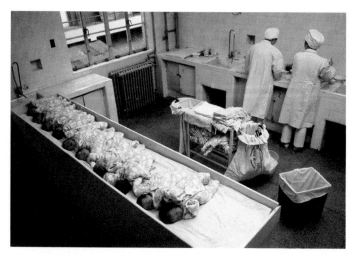

Teaching children to get along with the group (collectivism) or fend for themselves (individualism) starts early. The babies in the photo above are waiting to be bathed in a hospital in Shanghai, which is in the People's Republic of China. Throughout life, adults will encourage these children to develop a strong sense of connection to their families and communities.

doryoku, the ability to persevere in the face of hardship (Cole, 1999). In both school and business, Japanese people are often uncomfortable putting individual needs above those of the group, and they attribute success to effort and careful training. In contrast, many people in the United States celebrate differences between individuals and emphasize how individual talent contributes to success. As you will read in Chapter 9, these core cultural values influence educational practices and contribute to differences between countries in mathematics performance.

But culture is not absolute. Even within a single society, values and practices vary from family to family. In one study of infant sleep practices, 17 percent of Japanese parents did not sleep with their children, while 43 percent of white parents in the United States sometimes did (Wolf et al., 1996). Also, the individualist–collectivist dimension is only one of many dimensions that describe cultural values. Finally, it is misleading to categorize specific cultures into one category or the other. All societies have collectivist and individualist features because everyone must develop a sense of self that involves both relationships with others (as child, parent, employee, and so forth) and a sense of their own uniqueness. This is why Chinese adults, like Americans, value individual responsibility and success (Mascolo & Li, 2004).

It is important for professionals who work with people from other cultures to take their values and beliefs into account. For example, one nurse we heard about thought that a female patient was hallucinating after the woman mentioned speaking to her dead mother, and social workers sometimes misinterpret marks from folk medical cures as evidence of abuse (Hansen, 1998). To avoid such misunderstandings, ethics guidelines now state that professionals have an obligation to learn about cultural differences that might affect their work (American Psychological Association, 2002; American Psychological Association Council of Representatives, 2002). And all professionals, regardless of their discipline, must work to avoid **ethnocentrism**—the assumption that their own culture and traditions are superior to those of other groups.

ethnocentrism The belief that one's ethnic group is superior to other groups.

But being tolerant of different cultural practices does not mean that professionals must accept all cultural practices regardless of their effects on people. For an example of conflict between cultural traditions and modern ethics, turn to *Solutions*, "Parental Investment and Gender."

⟩⟩⟩ MEMORY MAKERS ⟨⟨⟨

1. If you wanted to know how parental education and income influence development, you would probably use a measure of:

   (a) ethnicity   (b) socioeconomic status (SES)
   (c) race   (d) clines

2. ___ terms define a group on the basis of a common history, nationality, or culture.

   (a) Racial   (b) Ethnic
   (c) Socioecononic (SES) (d) National

3. People who argue *against* the race concept believe that human diversity is better represented by (ethnic terms; <u>clines</u>). People who defend the race concept say that racial categories can be useful because (<u>traits are often associated</u>; racial concepts are the same all over the world).

[1-b (the concept of SES considers such things as parental education and income); 2-b ("Hispanic" is an ethnic term because an Hispanic individual can be of any race); 3. People who argue against the race concept believe that human diversity is best captured by looking at clines, which are changes in the probability of specific traits across a geographic region. People who defend the race concept say that racial categories are useful because traits are often associated, so knowing someone's racial category can provide information about the probability he or she has other traits, such as a positive response to a particular medication.]

PARENTAL INVESTMENT AND GENDER

Some cultures lead parents to invest more resources in raising boys or girls, depending on which gender will have greater economic security and opportunities. This preferential trend can be overcome when government policies help every adult enjoy economic opportunities and fair treatment.

It's a boy! It's a girl! Around the world, "What is it?" is the first question many of us ask about a new arrival. The influence of culture on development is never more obvious than when we watch parents' reactions to the answer. Depending on where you were born, your sex influenced the name you received, the toys you played with and—in some cases—even your chances of survival.

Parents do not always greet male and female children with equal enthusiasm. In traditional China, for example, males were valued more highly because they helped with farming and cared for aging parents. Females, in contrast, were barred from many agricultural activities and joined their husbands' families after marriage, which meant they were no longer around to assist as their parents grew old. Peasant couples felt

Mukogodo girls (top) are often better cared for and healthier than boys (bottom). Mothers breast-feed daughters longer and take them for medical care more often.

behavioral genetics The field that studies how much nature and nurture contribute to individual differences in human behavior.

they had to have at least one son because they raised their daughters for another family (Secondi, 2002).

One of the consequences of this preference for male children is a disturbing imbalance in the ratio of males to females. An alarming trend was found after the People's Republic of China instituted a one-child policy in 1979 to avert future food shortages. The normal sex ratio at birth is about 105 boys to 100 girls, but the number of infant boys per 100 girls in China rose to 114 between 1982 and 1989. As Greenhalgh and Li concluded, "Little girls are being eliminated from Chinese society—at close to 1.2 billion, the largest society on earth—on a massive scale" (1995, p. 391). Selectively killing or abandoning children who are an economic burden is a frequent practice. Prior to 1930, the Inuit (Canadian and North Alaskan Eskimos) may have killed 21 percent of their female infants, and it was estimated in 1998 that 10,000 female fetuses were aborted every year in India as a consequence of prenatal tests that determine sex (Dube, Dube, & Bhatnagar, 1999; Smith & Smith, 1994).

But females are not always the ones targeted for abortions, *infanticide* (the killing of newborns), and abandonment. When circumstances give females better economic opportunities, parental investment shifts accordingly. For example, favoritism toward daughters occurs among the Mukugodo, a sheep and goat herding people of central Kenya. Mukugodo males have difficulty finding wives because they have neither wealth nor power compared to neighboring groups. But because men from other groups are allowed to have as many wives as they can afford, all Mukugodo women find husbands and wives are in short supply (Cronk, 1995). Although there is no evidence that the Mukugodo practice infanticide, males suffer from "selective neglect," a pattern of behavior in which they are nursed for shorter periods of time than girls, taken to medical clinics less often, and offered less healthy food. Parental investment favoring girls has also been documented in other cultures, including the Kanjar of Pakistan, where usual gender roles are reversed and women dominate public affairs (Cronk, 1995).

How can society protect everyone's right to live and thrive? When countries work to equalize the economic and reproductive chances of males and females, parental attitudes change accordingly. As women gained rights in the People's Republic of China, more young people began expressing a desire for a daughter to provide comfort during their elderly years (Greenhalgh & Li, 1995). Cross-cultural research on parenting shows that seemingly personal decisions, such as those involved in reproducing and parenting, often reflect environmental realities.

Measuring Genetic and Environmental Influences on Behavior

So far in this chapter we've looked at the mechanisms that mold traits and behaviors: genes and the environment. Teasing out the relative contributions of these influences to who we become is the work of **behavioral genetics**, the field that studies *how much* nature and nurture contribute to individual differences in behavior. For example, a behavioral geneticist might wonder whether Adriana and Tamara were talented dancers because their genes produced similarly coordinated bodies or because television and their New York upbringings had filled their lives with music and dancing. Unfortunately, scientists cannot answer questions like this one about specific individuals because the abilities and personalities of any one person are always the result of interactions between an underlying genetic code and environmental opportunities. However, the field of behavioral genetics can analyze how genetic and environmental influences affect individual differences among a *group* of people, using a concept called *heritability*.

Heritability

There are many strategies for estimating the relative contribution of genes and the environment, including two described earlier in this chapter: comparing the similarity between identical (monozygotic) and fraternal (dizygotic) twin pairs, and considering whether adopted children most resemble the parents who raised them or their biological parents. Another strategy is to compare the degree of similarity between children and their biological siblings versus their adoptive siblings (Plomin et al., 2001).

Using data from these comparisons, behavioral geneticists estimate the degree to which genes and environments contribute to observable traits by calculating a statistic called **heritability (h^2)**. For any particular trait, heritability is simply a number that tells us whether none of the variability we observe within a specific group is due to genetic factors, all of the variability is due to genetic factors, or something in between. Consider height, a trait that works well for explaining heritability because it is so easy to visualize. Figure 2.10 shows two groups of teenagers. *Variability* refers to the degree of individual differences; obviously, Group A is more variable than Group B. For any particular trait, heritability (h^2) is simply the *proportion* of the total variability in a population that is due to genetic factors. In other words, heritability = variability due to genetics / total variability. The formula for h^2 tells us five things about heritability (Poole, 1995):

1. ***Heritability must range between 0.0 and 1.0.*** A value of 0 means that none of the variability we observe is due to genetic factors, whereas 1.0 means that all

heritability (h^2) For a particular trait, heritability is the proportion of observed variability among individuals in a group that is attributed to genetic variability. Heritability estimates range from 0 (no influence of genetic variability) to 1.0 (all of the observed variability is due to genetic variability).

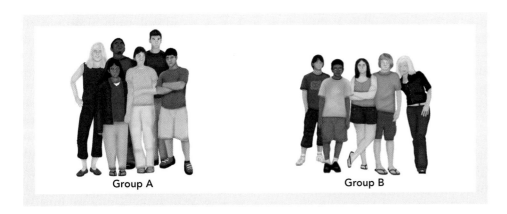

FIGURE 2.10 What is heritability?

Like all groups of teenagers, the ones in this diagram show variability in their height, hair color, and even their personalities. But not all groups are alike. For example, the heights of teenagers in group A are more *variable* than those in group B. Heritability is a statistic that estimates *how much* of the variability we observe within a particular group is due to genetic factors.

of the variability is due to genetic factors. In practice, h^2 usually falls between these two extremes. For example, the heritability of height ranges between .68 and .93, depending on the population (Silventoinen et al., 2003).

2. *Unless a trait is caused only by genes or only by the environment, the size of the heritability statistic is not fixed.* Rather, the size of h^2 depends on the amount of genetic and environmental variability in the population. Consider intelligence. A group of college students who were all raised in an affluent neighborhood by very similar parents has experienced little environmental variability. In this case, the proportion of variability in intelligence that is due to genetic factors should be large (because there is so little variability due to the environment). In contrast, if we looked at a group of college students who came from low SES families that differed widely, the size of the heritability statistic should be lower (because more of their individual differences are due to environmental differences). This is exactly what happens: The contribution of genes to individual differences in intelligence is substantial in affluent families and smaller in poor families (Turkheimer et al., 2003).

3. *Heritability does not apply to individuals.* A heritability of .65 for intelligence means that 65 percent of the variability in a population is due to genetic factors; it does not mean that 65 percent of *your* IQ score is due to genetic factors. Because genes and environments work together to produce traits, it is not possible to say that some fixed proportion of someone's height, weight, or musical talent is due to genetics.

4. *Heritability cannot tell us why two populations differ.* For example, Group A in Figure 2.10 is taller on average than Group B is. But even though the heritability of height is about .75, we cannot say that the difference between these groups is due to heredity because their childhood diets could have been different.

5. *Heritability does not tell us how much behavior might change in a new environment.* Imagine that the students in Group B each give birth to a pair of identical twins that we separated into two genetically identical groups (by placing one twin from each pair in one group and the second in another group). We then raise the first group on a high-protein, dairy-rich American diet and the second on a low-calorie diet of rice and vegetables. Despite the fact that height is highly heritable, the difference in height between these two groups would be due to the environment (because the groups are genetically the same). Even when heritability is high, we have no idea how people might have turned out had they been raised in another environment.

Heated arguments about the usefulness of heritability research often focus on racial issues. For example, IQ scores show fairly high heritability (somewhere between .5 and .8), and African Americans achieve lower average scores on traditional intelligence tests than white Americans do. In a classic paper from 1969, psychologist Arthur Jensen wrote that society probably could not do much to boost the scholastic achievement of African Americans because most of the variability in IQ scores was hereditary. Critics countered that heritability results were irrelevant to this issue because heritability tells us nothing about *why* there are differences between groups. Nonetheless, over two decades later, Richard Herrnstein and Charles Murray used the heritability of IQ to make a similar argument in a controversial book entitled *The Bell Curve* (Herrnstein & Murray, 1994).

(You will hear more about this issue in Chapter 9 when you read about intelligence testing.)

As a person who is likely to read about this sort of controversy in the press, it is important for you to remember that "genes contribute to X" does *not* mean "the environment is irrelevant." As noted biologist Richard Lewontin explained, "The organism does not compute itself from its genes. Any computer that did as poor a job of computation as an organism does from its genetic 'program' would be immediately thrown into the trash and its manufacturer would be sued by the purchaser" (2000, p. 17). Lewontin is referring to the fact that the environment influences gene expression, so your genetic code does not dictate a specific result.

But as long as we keep the limits of the heritability concept in mind, it is fascinating to ask which traits are heritable. Table 2.3 lists some examples. Notice that heritability hovers around .50 for a wide variety of psychological traits (Bouchard, 2004). This means that even when there is a genetic component to individual differences, about half of the variability in many behaviors is due to the environment.

In summary, heritability does not reveal the origins of our individual quirks and behaviors, why there are differences between groups of people, or what might be done to alter behavior. As a result, some scientists believe that heritability research is too fraught with limitations to have much value (Baumrind, 1993). Others argue that behavioral genetics helps us avoid the problems that arise when we assume that behavior stems *only* from the environment (Pinker, 2002; Scarr, 1993). For example, the tendency to blame mothers for their children's problems, which you read about in Chapter 1, prevented scientists from recognizing the biological origins of autism and schizophrenia. Regardless of how useful heritability estimates are, it is clear that behavioral genetics has generated some novel ways of thinking about development. As you will read next, this way of thinking can even help you understand your own family.

TABLE 2.3	The Heritability of Selected Traits
Trait	**Heritability**
Body weight	.70
Blood pressure	.50
Cognitive test scores	
Verbal	.57
Spatial	.71
Speed	.53
Memory	.43
Personality measures	
Agreeableness	.42
Conscientiousness	.49
Extroversion	.54
Psychiatric illnesses	
Schizophrenia	.80
Major depression	.37
Antisocial behavior	.41

SOURCES: Bouchard (2004); Plomin et al. (2001).

Why Are Siblings So Different?

Listen to how Nancy, age 10, and her brother Carl, age 6, summed up their relationship for a study of siblings (Dunn & Plomin, 1990, p. 88):

Nancy: Well, he's nice to me . . . I think I'd be very lonely without Carl. I play with him a lot and he thinks up lots of ideas and it's very exciting. He comes and meets me at the gate after school and I think that's very friendly . . . He's very kind . . . Don't really know what I'd do without a brother.

Carl: She's pretty disgusting and we don't talk to each other much. I don't really know much about her.

Interviewer: What is it you particularly like about her?

Carl: Nothing. Sometimes when I do something wrong she tells me off quite cruelly.

It is obvious that siblings look different and have different talents. But due to their unique personalities, they also have different perceptions of their parents and their relationships with each other (Hur & Bouchard, 1995). How could children raised in the same family be so different?

Genetics plays an important role in making siblings as different as they are similar. Same-sex siblings share only 50 percent of their genes, on average, which allows plenty of room for individuality to complicate family life. Moreover, many traits are determined by multiple genes, and unique combinations of genes produce unexpected results. For example, *emergenic* traits, such as beauty, are traits that arise when particular combinations of genes occur together, so these traits emerge from the whole rather than the sum of the parts. This phenomenon, which is illustrated in Figure 2.11, explains why some traits, though genetic, do not tend to run in families. A wide variety of traits may be emergenic, including leadership, artistic ability, and even genius (Lykken, Tellegen, & Bouchard, 1992).

Some researchers suspect that specific combinations of genes underlie the eerie similarities that often occur among identical twin pairs who were separated at birth. For instance, when one pair of male twins was reunited as adults, they discovered they both used Vademecum toothpaste, Canoe shaving lotion, Vitalis hair tonic, and Lucky Strike cigarettes. A second pair of female twins both entered the water backwards, but only up to their knees (Lykken et al., 1992). If unique combinations of genes were responsible for these similarities, if would be highly unlikely that any siblings who were *not* identical twins would share such specific and peculiar traits.

Siblings not only have different genes, but they also have different environments. Of course, children who are reared together live in the same house, spend time with the same parents, and go to the same schools. These influences, which are called *shared family environment*, should make them similar. But they also have *nonshared environmental influences*, such as different friends and different treatment by parents, which should make them different.

Researchers have developed techniques that separate the environmental portion of the heritability equation into these shared and nonshared components. Much of this research has found that the environmental influences that affect development the most are *not* shared by siblings (Bouchard & McGue, 2003; Hetherington, Reiss, & Plomin, 1994; Plomin et al., 2001). For example, in Chapter 9 you'll read how peers have a profound influence on school-age

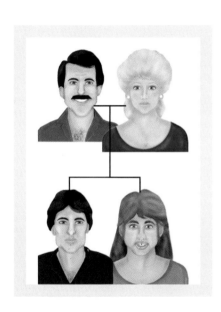

FIGURE 2.11 Genetic traits that may not run in families.

Some traits, like beauty, cannot be predicted by the sum of the parts. In these drawings, the features of two handsome actors were randomly rearranged. Notice how the impact of a particular feature depends on its context. Traits that result from particular combinations of genes are called *emergenic* because they "emerge" from the whole configuration.

SOURCE: Adapted from Lykken et al. (1992).

children's development. The finding that nonshared environment is so influential is surprising because it suggests that routine experiences at home—that is, those that are shared by everyone in the family—do not matter very much. Others, however, have proposed that nonshared experiences play only a modest role in making us who we are (Turkheimer & Waldron, 2000). The truth is probably somewhere in between: Nonshared experiences could matter a lot in some environments and not much in others. For example, well-adjusted parents may treat easy and difficult children in similar ways, so differences in how parents treat their children are not very important in these households. But depressed parents are overwhelmed by their difficult children and parent them less effectively. In these families, parental behavior could create important nonshared differences (Asbury et al., 2003). Currently, scientists are moving beyond asking "how much" the environment matters and asking more specific and interesting questions, such as which experiences matter in which environments and for which types of children.

So why are siblings different? The answer is a familiar one: nature and nurture. Each of us has a unique configuration of genes and unique, nonshared environmental influences. We can inhabit the same address, but we can never live the same lives.

Concluding that genes and the environment are both important just sounds like common sense. Still, it can be difficult to study nature and nurture. To understand why, turn to the next *Don't Be Fooled!* feature entitled "Eugenics and the Shame of Pellagra."

>>> MEMORY MAKERS <<<

1. The heritability of a personality trait called *agreeableness* is about .42. This means that_____.

   (a) 42 percent of *your* degree of agreeableness is due to genetics
   (b) your personality would be basically the same if you were reared in a different environment
   (c) 42 percent of the variability in agreeableness in the population studied was due to genetics
   (d) all of the above

2. The history of pellagra illustrates_____.

   (a) how rapidly society adjusts to new scientific findings
   (b) environmental "blindness"
   (c) how difficult it is to identify diseases caused by slow-acting viruses
   (d) how harmful genes tend to congregate in low-income groups

3. The best answer to the question, "Why are siblings so different?" is_____.

   (a) different genes
   (b) different environments
   (c) different genes and different environments

[1-c (heritability does not refer to a particular individual and does not tell us how people would have developed if they had grown up in a different environment); 2-b (people rejected evidence that pellagra was a nutritional deficiency disease); 3-c (siblings share only 50 percent of their genes, but they also grow up in different environments because they choose they differ-ent activities, have different friends, and are treated differently by parents and other people)]

DON'T BE FOOLED

Traits such as poor health and mental slowness can be passed down from generation to generation *without* being genetically transmitted. Take care not to assume that traits are genetically determined just because family members appear to be similar.

EUGENICS AND THE SHAME OF PELLAGRA

Many societies have wealthy people who own property and poor people who take care of their houses, gardens, and businesses. Why are individuals divided between upper and lower socioeconomic classes?

Centuries ago, inequality was explained on religious grounds. Kings and queens were said to rule by "divine right," and peasants were encouraged to accept their place in society as the natural order of the world. When science became a major authority in policy debates, the concept of genetic transmission came to be used as an explanation for inequality.

By the turn of the 20th century, advocates of what was called the "eugenics" movement believed that poverty and its consequences—including low IQ, lack of energy, and criminality—were largely due to unfavorable genes (Davenport, 1910; Galton 1883). The term *eugenics* refers to the idea that we can improve human populations by breeding "superior" individuals, much as animals are selectively bred for horse racing and agricultural purposes. Although eugenics was popular, a focus on genes made it difficult for people to notice environmental influences. One of the most striking examples of this "environmental blindness" is the tragedy of pellagra.

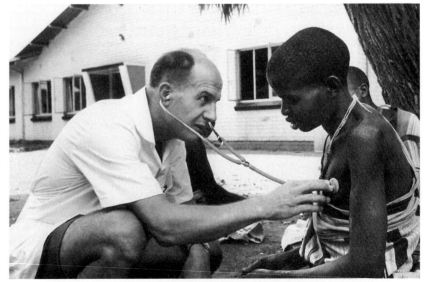

This doctor is examining an African woman who is suffering from pellagra. Pellagra is common wherever people eat large quantities of corn or other foods that are deficient in niacin.

Pellagra may have been the most widespread nutritional disease ever recorded in the history of the United States (Park et al., 2000). Sweeping most heavily over the southern part of the country in the early 1890s, pellagra was common wherever corn was the major source of energy. The disease produced a cluster of symptoms that became known as the four D's: diarrhea, dermatitis (a skin rash), dementia, and death (Crabb, 1992). In addition to skin and mental disorders, pellagra also lowered resistance to infectious and parasitic diseases, including malaria, tuberculosis, and hookworm.

Two hypotheses developed to explain these symptoms (Chase, 1975; Roe, 1973). Some scientists believed that pellagra was caused by spoiled corn or an unknown microbe. Others, including the director of the Eugenics Record Office, believed it was a genetic disease among people of inferior breeding stock. Both groups were wrong. Proof that pellagra was caused by malnutrition was gathered by Joseph Goldberger, a scientist appointed by the U.S. Public Health Service to head a task force in 1914.

Joseph Goldberger noticed that institutions filled with the poor never had pellagrous employees, as one would expect if pellagra were infectious. Convinced that the disease was caused by poor nutrition, Goldberger cured pellagra in an orphanage by feeding children milk, eggs, meat, beans, and oatmeal. Then, in a highly controversial demonstration, he induced pellagra in a group of healthy white prison inmates in exchange for pardons (Goldberger & Wheeler, 1920). Despite these findings, a privately funded commission concluded that pellagra was an infectious disease caused by poor sanitation. Anxious to set aside this hypothesis once and for all, Goldberger, along with his wife and several associates, took injections, ate, and inhaled blood, feces, urine, nasal secretions, and skin scrapings from pellagrous patients to prove that the disease was not transmitted by infection (Etheridge, 1972).

Goldberger's findings were minimized when another commission concluded that pellagra was a hereditary disease. Tragically, pellagra continued to afflict the poor for decades after the riddle of its cause had been solved. During the long period between Goldberger's discoveries and the start of public health measures, pellagra killed an estimated 600,000 people (Crabb, 1992). Eventually, vitamin B_3 (niacin) was identified as the agent that prevented pellagra and, in 1938, bakers began voluntarily to enrich white bread with high-vitamin yeast (a natural source of niacin). Decades later, the disease was largely eliminated (Park et al., 2000).

The history of pellagra shows us that traits that are *not* transmitted genetically can cluster in families and appear to be passed down from generation to generation. Today, the best scientists keep an open mind and consider many possible causes for social problems.

The special bond between Tamara and Adriana, the reunited twins from our opening story, is only partly due to biology. They know they once shared a mother, a womb, and even a moment of conception. But these things are not enough to make them feel like sisters. "I definitely believe that we will eventually become sisters in the true sense of the word," Adriana speculated, "once we have a chance to share experiences and find more in common" (O'Connor, 2003). In the next chapter, we look at the months before birth that the twins shared, as well as those early months during which they were separated, so that you can explore the first influences that shaped their lives.

>>> SUMMARY <<<

What Is a Human Being?

1. Humans belong to a social species called *Homo sapiens*, which is Latin for "wise human being." Compared to other primate species, human beings grow fast, wean early, mature late, and live long. Our large brain volume (especially in areas responsible for complex thought) and our prolonged childhood produce language and problem-solving skills that are unsurpassed in the animal kingdom.

The Genetic Blueprint

2. **Heredity** refers to the mechanisms by which parents pass traits on to their children. Gregor Mendel's results showed that traits are transmitted by units, now called **genes**, that come in pairs. Mendel proposed that genes segregate randomly during the production of reproductive cells so that a mother and father each contribute one-half of the genes that define their child. The transmission patterns Mendel observed suggested that some genes were either **dominant** or **recessive**.

3. We now know that the functional units of heredity, genes, are segments of DNA molecules. **DNA** molecules make up the 46 **chromosomes**, arranged into 23 pairs, that define human beings. The reproductive cells, called **gametes**, are produced when cells with 46 chromosomes split during meiosis to form cells that have 23 chromosomes.

4. There are many exceptions to Mendel's principle of dominance/recessiveness. Examples include partial dominance, codominance, **polygenic inheritance**, **X-linkage**, **sex-influenced inheritance**, **genetic imprinting**, extra-nuclear inheritance, and mutations.

5. The **Human Genome Project** was an international effort to map the 3 billion bases that make up human DNA. Ethical, legal, and social issues programs focused on topics such as the ethics of genetic testing.

How Genes and the Environment Interact

6. Genes do not single-handedly direct development. In fact, even identical (**monozygotic**) twins are unique individuals with different talents and interests. Studies of twins and people reared in adoptive homes prove that genes *and* the environment influence development.

7. Environments influence how genes are expressed because many genes produce different outcomes in different environments. Genes influence the environment through **gene–environment (G–E) correlations**, including passive G–E correlation (the fact that parents contribute genetically to their children but also construct their children's environments), reactive G–E correlation (the fact that people with different genotypes elicit different reactions from others), and active G–E correlation (the fact that people choose environments consistent with their genetically influenced talents and interests).

8. The joint influence of genes and environments is especially evident in the developing brain. Environmental events influence all stages of neurological development, including **neurulation**, **neurogenesis**, **neural migration**, **synaptogenesis**, **synaptic pruning**, and **myelination**.

Genetic and Environmental Diversity

9. Racial terms divide people by obvious physical differences, and these terms vary from culture to culture. Some scientists believe that racial terms do not identify biologically distinct groups and, therefore, they prefer to think of biological variability in terms of *clines* (changes in the frequencies of specific traits across geographic regions).

10. **Culture** refers to learned features of the environment, including the technology, art, morals, laws, customs, and beliefs of individual societies. **Ethnic** terms define groups based on a common history, nationality, or culture. **Socioeconomic status (SES)** defines people on the basis of factors such as income, education, and job prestige. Different cultures have different beliefs about the nature of development and what characteristics are most desirable in an adult.

Measuring Genetic and Environmental Influences on Behavior

11. The field of **behavioral genetics** uses data from twin and adoption studies to measure genetic and environmental influences on traits, such as height, personality, and intelligence. A statistic, **heritability (h^2)**, indicates the proportion of variability among individuals in a group that is due to genetic variability. The value of heritability varies from population to population and does not reveal why there are differences between groups.

12. One reason siblings are different is that they share only 50 percent of their genes on average. Some traits also emerge from the configuration of many genes, and these traits, though genetic, do not tend to run in families. Siblings also have *nonshared* environmental influences, such as different friends and different perceptions of their families.

>>>KEY TERMS<<<

Homo sapiens   (p. 47)
heredity   (p. 48)
genes   (p. 49)
alleles   (p. 49)
phenotype   (p. 49)
genotype   (p. 49)
dominant allele   (p. 49)
recessive allele   (p. 49)
DNA   (p. 51)
regulatory sequences (sometimes called
genetic switches)   (p. 51)
chromosomes   (p. 51)
gametes   (p. 52)
polygenic inheritance   (p. 53)
X-linked traits   (p. 54)
sex-influenced inheritance   (p. 54)
genetic imprinting (also called genomic
or parental imprinting)   (p. 54)
human genome   (p. 54)
mutations   (p. 54)
Human Genome Project   (p. 55)
monozygotic twins   (p. 58)

dizygotic twins   (p. 58)
environment   (p. 58)
norms of reaction   (p. 60)
canalization   (p. 61)
gene–environment (G–E) correlations   (p. 61)
niche-picking   (p. 62)
glial cells   (p. 63)
neurons   (p. 63)
neurulation   (p. 63)
neurogenesis   (p. 63)
neural migration   (p. 63)
synaptogenesis   (p. 64)
synaptic pruning   (p. 64)
neural plasticity   (p. 64)
myelination   (p. 65)
culture   (p. 68)
ethnicity   (p. 69)
socioeconomic status (SES)   (p. 70)
ethnocentrism   (p. 72)
behavioral genetics   (p. 74)
heritability (h^2)   (p. 75)

Prenatal Development and Birth

Stories of Our Lives

The Miracle of Birth

Midwife Penny Armstrong knew that every birth is a unique experience. Yet she was still surprised when she attended her first birth in an Amish community in Lancaster County, Pennsylvania. Only a few weeks after she joined Stephen Kaufman's medical practice, Penny heard that Enos and Katie's baby was ready to be born.

Enos was taking 2-year-old Johnny to his aunt's house by horse and carriage when Penny arrived at the cottage. The expectant mother, Katie, was applying lacquer to a rocking chair. Katie stopped to stretch her back with the concentrated look of a woman having a labor contraction. "Is it pretty strong?" Penny asked. "Yes, I believe it is," replied Katie. "And I haven't put that plastic thing on the bed yet." Here is the story as Penny told it to her friend, Sheryl Feldman (Armstrong & Feldman, 1986):

> "Before we make the bed, let's see how dilated you are." I was thinking that this woman couldn't be too far along since she was running around like she was getting ready for her first date.

Every Night & every Morn
Some to Misery are Born
Every Morn & every Night
Some are Born to sweet delight
Some are Born to sweet delight
Some are Born to Endless Night

William Blake

Wrong. Nine centimeters.

"Where's that plastic sheet?" I said. "Looks to me like you're about to have a baby."

She chattered her way off to the linen closet and back. "Oh, I'm so excited," she said. "I can hardly wait. Every night when I go to bed, I say to Enos, 'Maybe tonight I'll have the baby. Maybe by tomorrow morning it will be lying right here between us.' And then in the morning when I wake up, I'm so disappointed because it didn't happen and I've been thinking I would have to wait all the way until the next night before there was even a chance again. I never even thought I could have it during the day. Enos keeps telling me not to be so impatient. He says he has to remind me that he believes the baby really will be born."

She stopped again for another contraction, and as soon as it passed she went back to spreading out the plastic sheet over the mattress cover. I was supposed to be helping her, but I had trouble concentrating. I kept staring. The woman was nine centimeters dilated and she was bustling about furiously.

We finished making up the bed; then she thought maybe she'd change from her dress into a gown. Next thing I knew, she'd hopped into the bed. Her face was flushed and she was ready to push.

Stephen's office was only a quarter of a mile away. I'd put a call in to him on my radio as soon as I checked Katie that first time, and he pulled in just as she was getting serious about pushing her baby out. Enos followed right behind him. He went to Katie's side and grabbed her hand.

The three of us attended quietly. A couple of times Katie said it hurt and she called her husband's name, and he got closer to her and held her so she could push more easily.

The baby, a boy, popped out as if he were on his way to the outfield to catch a long fly. I put him on the bed at Katie's side, and she curled herself around him.

"Oh," she said, "look at him. Look at our new baby. Oh, I wonder what Johnny will think."

Enos stroked her head and said, "So now you have your baby." (pp. 59–60)

NOT ALL BIRTHS LEFT PENNY ARMSTRONG as euphoric as the one in our opening story did, yet she was always amazed by the women of Lancaster County. Social support, trained birth attendants, and close emergency care made birthing a welcomed event that was integrated into the daily fabric of family life.

But examples of uncomplicated deliveries are only half the story of human birth. The truth is that reproduction has always been a dangerous gamble (Harrison, 1985). According to church records from Europe, 1 in 14 married women died in childbirth during the nineteenth century, some from delivery problems and others from disease. Because fewer than 2 percent of motherless babies survived until 5 years of age, these deaths were virtual death sentences for newborns (Högberg & Broström, 1985).

Today, safe birthing conditions are not evenly distributed around the world. About 20 mothers die for every 100,000 live births in industrialized countries, compared to 440 in developing countries (World Health Organization, UNICEF, & United Nations Population Fund, 2004). Infant mortality (death) rates show similar patterns. Many organizations use the risk of dying before age 5 as an indicator of children's overall risk because this rate reflects a variety of factors, including mothers' health and the quality of health care. As you can see in Figure 3.1,

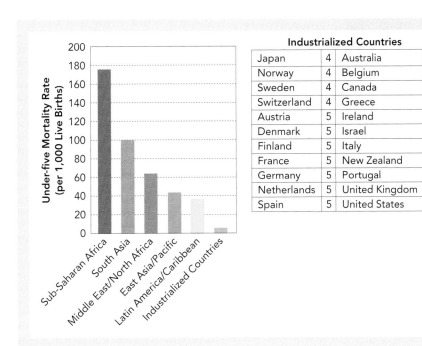

Industrialized Countries

Japan	4	Australia	6
Norway	4	Belgium	6
Sweden	4	Canada	6
Switzerland	4	Greece	6
Austria	5	Ireland	6
Denmark	5	Israel	6
Finland	5	Italy	6
France	5	New Zealand	6
Germany	5	Portugal	6
Netherlands	5	United Kingdom	6
Spain	5	United States	8

FIGURE 3.1 The under 5 mortality rate.

Children in developing countries have less chance of surviving to 5 years of age than those who are born in wealthier countries. The United States has a higher mortality rate than many industrialized countries, possibly due to the lack of free prenatal and postnatal health care.

SOURCE: UNICEF (2001).

early childhood mortality rates are 29 times higher in Sub-Saharan Africa than in wealthier countries.

Parents in industrialized countries have a buffet of options for monitoring pregnancy and giving birth, from low-intervention home births like Katie's to births in high-tech medical centers. But regardless of their choices, everyone hopes for the same outcome: a healthy newborn. In this chapter, you will read about development in the womb, birthing practices, and some of the problems that can occur, including genetic errors, environmental influences that threaten early development, and the challenges of labor and delivery. Then you will revisit the principles of development from Chapter 1 when you explore our featured topic for Part 1: "What Is the Long-Term Impact of Early Biological Trauma?"

Our story in this chapter begins with the *prenatal* period (the time before birth) and includes the routine events and common problems that occur during the *perinatal* period (from a few months before birth to 1 month after birth). As you read, look for examples of how the gifts and challenges you received during these periods might have influenced your *postnatal* development (development after birth).

Starting a New Life

For most of human history, the process of reproduction was mysterious and shrouded from view. To explain how new life began, some Australian Aborigines and Trobriand Islanders described a supernatural cause—the entry of a spirit child into a woman (McClain, 1982). Peasants from an Egyptian village believed that babies formed when a man's seed mixed with menstrual blood from a woman (Morsy, 1982). Other cultures thought that repeated sexual acts were necessary to nourish a baby, so fathers in these societies felt they were contributing throughout pregnancy to their babies' welfare (Beckerman & Valentine, 2002). Now that we know how new life begins, we also know that the real story of early development is just as marvelous as these traditional explanations were.

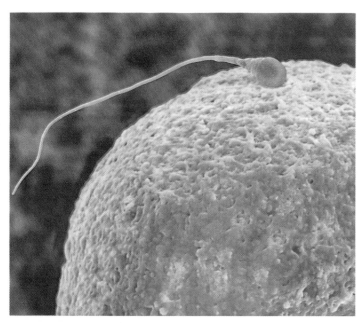

Tiny size gives a sperm cell (spermatozoon) the speed it needs to beat out the competition. This lucky winner will penetrate the egg, triggering an electrochemical signal that prevents others from entering. As DNA from mother and father merge, two cells will become one.

Fertilization

An individual starts to form when the male and female reproductive cells (gametes) combine to form a single cell called a **zygote**. This process is often called *conception*, but biologists prefer the term **fertilization**. (The term *conception* is less precise because it has sometimes been used to describe implantation into the uterine wall.) Recall from Chapter 2 that normal human gametes contain only 23 chromosomes, so the newly formed zygote has the 46 chromosomes that define an individual.

The male reproductive cells, *spermatozoa*, are produced inside the scrotal sac of the testes. After sexual maturity, human males produce spermatozoa at an astonishing rate of about 300 million a day. These cells typically survive inside the male for up to 4 days with new spermatozoa continually replacing existing supplies. During orgasm, over 300 million tadpole-like spermatozoa mix with fluid and are expelled through the *urethra*. Spermatozoa are produced throughout the male life span, although the quantity of production declines with age.

Females are born with their lifetime supply of potential *oocytes* (1–2 million) housed in *follicles* inside their ovaries. The first meiotic division occurs in the developing ovary before a baby girl is born, but then the process of meiosis stops until sexual maturity. After maturity, one oocyte completes development about every 28 days, traveling to the surface of the ovary and erupting from its follicle during ovulation. As shown in Figure 3.2, the newly released oocyte is trapped by the funnel-shaped end of a fallopian tube, where it begins a $6\frac{1}{2}$-day journey to the uterus (Carlson, 1999). Meanwhile, the follicle produces hormones that prepare the uterine lining for implantation. If implantation does not occur, the follicle stops producing hormones and the uterine lining is shed.

The male and female gametes are an odd couple, with vastly different sizes that are explained by their functions. A spermatozoon is a "lean racing vehicle" (Vaughan, 1996, p. 27). About 1/600 of an inch from head to tail and one of the smallest cells in the body, it is perfectly shaped for wiggling through mucus to deliver DNA to the oocyte. But unlike the tiny spermatozoon, each oocyte must be packed with material to nourish a fertilized cell. Therefore, oocytes measure about 1/175 inch in diameter—visible to the eye and the largest cell in the body.

Ovulation usually occurs about 2 weeks from the first day of a woman's menstrual cycle. It is difficult to predict exactly when a woman's fertile days will be because the timing of ovulation varies, especially in teenagers who

FIGURE 3.2 Ovulation.

After an oocyte is released from an ovary during ovulation, it begins its journey through the fallopian tube to the uterus. A zygote may form if it meets with a sperm cell on the way.

zygote A one-celled organism formed by the union of the male and female reproductive cells (gametes).

fertilization The process by which sperm and egg fuse to form the first cell of a new individual (also called **conception**).

CHAPTER 3 ★ PRENATAL DEVELOPMENT AND BIRTH **89**

often have irregular menstrual cycles. Even though oocytes survive only for 1 day after ovulation, the window of opportunity for fertilization is wider because spermatozoa deposited before ovulation can survive in the female reproductive track for several days (Carlson, 1999; Moore & Persaud, 2003). Therefore, most pregnancies result from intercourse 2 days before ovulation through the day of ovulation.

When reproductive cells collide, digestive enzymes from the tip of the sperm dissolve the outer layer of the egg. Once a spermatozoon enters the oocyte, an electrochemical signal immediately blocks others from entering. There is no "moment of fertilization" but rather a process lasting several hours as the last meiotic division occurs and maternal and paternal chromosomes intermingle (O'Rahilly & Müller, 2001). The resulting zygote then begins its journey of 3 or 4 days down the fallopian tube to the uterus.

Prenatal Development

The time from fertilization until birth is the *gestational period.* This period averages 38 weeks, with most women delivering their babies some time earlier or later than their predicted due dates. Much to the confusion of parents, however, medical professionals often describe pregnancy as a 40-week affair because they date pregnancy from an event that is usually known: the start of a woman's last menstrual period. In this chapter, we adopt the perspective most parents take by reporting developmental milestones in terms of time since fertilization.

The gestational period is divided into three stages: the **germinal period** (the first 2 weeks after fertilization), the **embryonic period** (from the beginning of the third week after fertilization through the eighth week), and the **fetal period** (from the beginning of the ninth week after fertilization until birth). Corresponding to these terms, the potential life that began as a single-cell zygote is called an **embryo** 2 weeks after fertilization and a **fetus** from 8 weeks after fertilization until birth.

THE GERMINAL PERIOD (THE FIRST 2 WEEKS AFTER FERTILIZA-TION). The zygote undergoes its first cell division within a day after fertilization. Three days later, the developing organism is a small, hollow ball of 32 cells called a blastocyst. A cluster of cells that develops inside the blastocyst will develop into a human body, while the outside layer becomes supporting structures for gestation. An *amniotic sac* and its outer layer, the *chorion,* surround the embryo and fill with fluid to provide a protected environment for growth, as shown in Figure 3.3. Part of the chorion develops into the **placenta,** a fleshy disk of tissue that provides oxygen, delivers nutrients, and removes waste products. The placenta separates the maternal and embryonic bloodstreams, keeping the two circulatory systems separate but transferring substances back and forth to sustain the life of the embryo. The *umbilical cord* is a lifeline that connects the embryo to the placenta.

Eight days after fertilization the mass of cells starts attaching (implanting) to the lining of the uterus, establishing a supply of nourishment from the mother's blood system. Only lucky survivors—as few as 20 to 30 percent of ovulations—complete the journey from ovulation to fertilization and implantation (Tong, Meagher, & Vollenhoven, 2002).

germinal period The first 2 weeks of development after fertilization.

embryonic period Prenatal development from the beginning of the third week through the eighth week.

fetal period Prenatal development from the beginning of the ninth week until birth.

embryo The developing organism from 2 weeks after fertilization through the eighth week.

fetus The developing organism from the beginning of the ninth week after fertilization until birth.

placenta A fleshy disk of cells that keeps the mother's bloodstream separate from the bloodstream of the developing embryo. The placenta sustains the life of the embryo by transferring oxygen and nutrients, removing waste products, and after the initial months of gestation, secreting hormones that sustain the pregnancy.

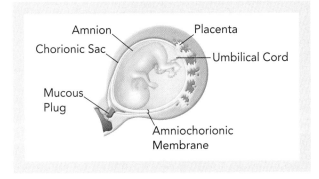

FIGURE 3.3 Supportive structures for growth.

Early in pregnancy, the outer layer of the blastocyst develops into structures that nourish and protect the developing fetus. The umbilical cord connects the fetus and mother through the placenta, a fleshy disk where materials are exchanged between the two blood systems. An inner amniotic sac and outer chorionic sac enclose the developing fetus.

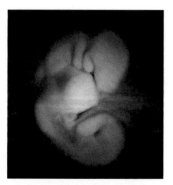

4 weeks after fertilization

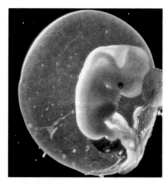

6 weeks after fertilization

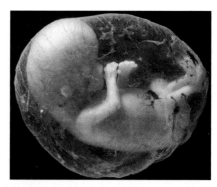

8 weeks after fertilization

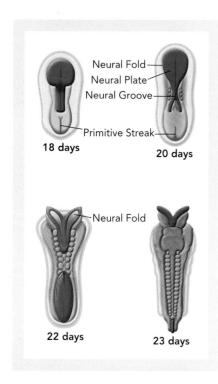

FIGURE 3.4 How the neural tube forms.

The neural tube forms when the primitive neural plate thickens, folds, and fuses. Cells trapped inside the tube will develop into the central nervous system.

neural tube defects Defects caused by failure of the neural tube to close completely. Fusion failure at the top of the tube causes an absence of brain tissue called anencephaly; fusion failure farther down causes spina bifida, in which parts of the spinal cord develop outside the vertebrae.

THE PERIOD OF THE EMBRYO (THE BEGINNING OF THE THIRD WEEK THROUGH THE EIGHTH WEEK). We still tease our friends Leah and Joel for not telling us as soon as Leah got pregnant. Cautious couples like this one know that the first 3 months of pregnancy, which is called the first *trimester*, is a vulnerable time. About 20 percent of embryos are expelled from the uterus when pregnancy ends naturally due to a *spontaneous abortion*, also called a *miscarriage*. Most of these failed pregnancies are the result of a defective embryo, and about half show chromosomal abnormalities (Wynbrandt & Ludman, 2000).

Two cell layers that construct a body have already formed by the beginning of the embryonic period. The *ectoderm* will develop into the outer layer of skin and contribute to the nervous system and sense organs, while the *endoderm* will develop into the digestive system, associated glands, and respiratory system (O'Rahilly & Müller, 2001). About 13 days after fertilization, a small group of cells forms a third layer, the *mesoderm*, between these layers, creating a vertical groove in the center of the oval-shaped embryo. The growing mesoderm releases a chemical, flipping genetic switches in cells of the ectoderm and causing them to differentiate into a *neural plate* that will soon become the brain and spinal cord. Figure 3.4 illustrates how the neural plate gradually folds up and fuses between 18 and 24 days of age, first connecting in the center, then connecting outward toward the head and tail to form a *neural tube*. By 28 days of age the tiny embryo has a peculiar looking head, body, and spinal cord.

Sometimes the neural tube fails to close normally, resulting in **neural tube defects**. A fatal condition called *anencephaly* results when the tube fails to fuse at the top and most of the brain never develops. This condition, due to an error that occurs less than 24 days after conception, is present in about 1 in 8,000 births. A more common defect is *spina bifida*, a condition in which part of the spinal cord develops outside of the vertebrae that should be protecting it. Spina bifida, which occurs in about 1 in 2,000 births, causes a range of problems that can include motor deficits, problems with bowel and bladder control, and learning difficulties (March of Dimes, 2005).

One condition that increases the risk of neural tube defects is a deficiency of the B-complex vitamin **folic acid** or **folate** (Charles et al., 2005). (Folic acid is the synthetic form of folate, but both forms function the same once they are absorbed by the body.) Women at risk for having a child with a neural tube defect can reduce this risk more than 70 percent simply by taking a multiple vitamin each day (Kalter, 2000). But because half of all pregnancies are not detected in time for women to benefit from supplements, many countries fortify flours and cereal with folic acid to reduce the occurrence of defects. The risk of neural tube defects is also greater when the mother is obese, has poorly controlled diabetes, or takes some types of medication for epilepsy (Duncan et al., 2001; Hendricks et al., 2001).

Four key processes organize embryonic cells into a body (Vaughan, 1996):

▶ *Folding.* Like the Japanese art of paper folding, cells at critical locations in tissue cause sheets to bend, causing complex shapes to emerge from fairly simple transitions. For example, the face begins to appear about 26 days after fertilization when a series of folds collapse and fuse. Cleft lips and cleft palates are birth defects that result from fusion failures after folding. Folding also forms the heart, which begins as a straight tube.

▶ *Cell instruction.* All cells in the body carry the same set of genes, so how do individual cells know where they are and what function they should perform? One way is through chemical signals that tell cells where they are relative to other cells in the body. Some medicines that cause birth defects disrupt these chemical signals, blocking the communication system that defines the embryo's shape. Through different mechanisms of cell instruction, the basic shape of a human is in place by the end of the eighth week, when cells are already performing highly specialized jobs.

▶ *Cell death.* Body structures fine-tune themselves by killing off cells. For example, mass suicide of cell clusters at particular points in development eliminates tissue between the fingers and toes, freeing them for independent movement. Cell death also occurs during early development in parts of the nose and the brain.

▶ *Cell migration.* As you read in Chapter 2, some cells reorganize themselves by traveling through a process called *cell migration*. For instance, early cell migration in the brain is critical for normal development.

By folding, cell instruction, cell death, and cell migration, the basic design of a human being is in place during the earliest weeks of development. Miraculously, by the end of the embryonic period the heart has already been beating for about a month. Still, the embryo needs the achievements of the next developmental period before it will be ready to survive outside the womb.

THE PERIOD OF THE FETUS (THE BEGINNING OF THE NINTH WEEK UNTIL BIRTH). By the beginning of the ninth week after fertilization, the single-cell zygote has developed into a fetus that is about 1.6 inches long (4 centimeters) and distinctively human in shape. Bone development now speeds up and finishing touches, such as fingernails and toenails, begin to form. Movement starts to occur about 6 weeks after fertilization, but in the fourth month of pregnancy parents are finally rewarded by *quickening*, the first kicks mothers can feel. Although this term sounds odd today, the word *quick* used to be a synonym for being alive, and many cultures have considered quickening an important event that defined the beginning of a new life (Vaughan, 1996).

During the period of the fetus, anxious parents are most concerned about reaching one important hurdle: the age of viability. **Viability**, which is the ability to survive outside the womb with expert care, is not reached by all fetuses at the same age. Instead, the probability of surviving outside the womb gradually increases from 24 percent at 23 weeks' gestation to more than 90 percent at 28 weeks (Hack & Fanaroff, 2000; Louis et al., 2004). These figures continue to change as new technologies are invented. Currently, the age of viability is said to

folic acid (or **folate**) A B-complex vitamin. Folic acid is the synthetic form of folate, but both forms function the same once they are absorbed by the body. Women deficient in folic acid have a higher risk of delivering children with neural tube defects.

viability The ability of a fetus to survive outside the uterus with expert care. The chance of survival is low at 22 weeks and increases with increasing gestational age.

Six months after fertilization, the fetus has been moving for months and can hear different sounds. The protected environment of mother's womb provides the best conditions for fine-tuning the lungs, brain, and other body structures.

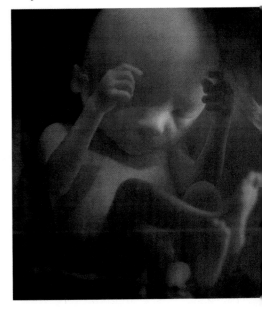

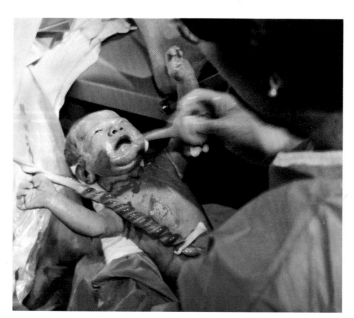

Nine months of waiting end when the squirmy newcomer clears lungs with a first beautiful cry. The umbilical cord will be cut as soon as this newborn is pink and ready to be cleaned up.

be 22 weeks after fertilization because it is rare for a younger fetus to survive, but the chances of survival improve significantly when fetuses reach 3 pounds by 28 weeks (Markestad et al., 2005; Moore & Persaud, 2003).

Important changes occur throughout the last months of gestation. By 26 weeks, a detergent-like molecule called *surfactant* is produced that helps the lungs inflate and reduces the chance the fetus will die of respiratory problems if it is born early. During the last 2 months, the fetus's immune system receives antibodies from the mother's bloodstream that will protect the baby for months after birth, and fat is stored that will help the baby regulate its temperature. The final product of 9 months of development, as shown on the left is a beautiful newborn.

Fetuses are active and experiencing the world throughout this period of pregnancy. Taste buds form by 13 weeks, when fetuses begin to swallow amniotic fluid, and they are exposed to various tastes depending on the foods their mothers eat. This activity is important because substances in amniotic fluid give them a nutritional boost and help the stomach and intestinal tissue mature (Klurfeld, 1999). Most fetuses begin hearing by the sixth month of pregnancy and can distinguish sounds of different frequencies during the last trimester (Joseph, 2000). As a result, they are exposed to the sounds of their mother's heartbeat and environmental sounds that pass through the abdominal wall and uterus, including the sound of their mother's voice (Sohmer et al., 2001).

Fetuses are also learning by the last trimester. One way to test early learning is the *habituation procedure*, a technique that relies on the tendency organisms have to respond to novel stimuli but *habituate*, or stop responding, when stimulation becomes routine. Habituation is an early form of learning that helps us ignore irrelevant background stimuli, such as the ticking of clocks, so we focus on significant events. In one experiment, researchers measured the movements of third-trimester fetuses when a tone was sounded, then waited until the fetuses

TABLE 3.1	Prenatal Development
[1 month]	The embryo is about 1/2 inch long (1 cm) and weighs just a few grams. The heart began beating about the twenty-fifth day after fertilization. The head is clearly visible and the neural tube almost closed, but the embryo looks more like a tadpole than a human. Arm and leg buds are barely visible, but you can see folds called "gill arches" that will fuse to form a face.
[3 months]	About 4 inches long (10 cm), the fetus has tooth buds, the beginning of soft nails, and inner ears that are beginning to form. The genitalia are clearly male or female. The fetus swallows amniotic fluid and can respond to pressure on the skin.
[6 months]	The fetus, which is starting to pack on fat, still measures in at only about 11–14 inches (27–36 cm). Lungs begin to make surfactant and can breathe air. Eyes are partially open and have eyelashes.
[9 months]	The average newborn is between 6 and 9 pounds and about 20 inches long (50 cm). Most have lost their lanugo hair but are still covered with vernix caseosa. The face and head may be beautiful and round or scrunched and odd-looking with bluish pink skin.

SOURCES: Carlson (1999); Clinical Reference Systems (2000); Moore & Persaud (2003).

became bored with (habituated to) the tone. Fetuses increased their body movements after the tone was changed, which proved they were storing information about sounds (Shalidullah & Hepper, 1994). Another way to test early learning is to give newborns a nipple that turns on sounds when they suck. Remarkably, they work harder to listen to their mother's voice than an unfamiliar voice, and they would rather hear a story their mother read during the last 6 weeks of pregnancy than an unfamiliar story (DeCasper & Spence, 1986). Clearly, the right mix of novelty and familiarity delighted you even before you were born.

Brain Development

Parents would recognize a familiar activity if they could see inside the womb during the last month of pregnancy: their fetus's eyes moving rapidly back and forth with muscles twitching. Their little one is enjoying REM (rapid eye movement) sleep, the same stage of sleep in which children and adults dream. At this stage of pregnancy, the fetus is probably sleeping about 95 percent of the time and spending about 60 percent of its sleep time in REM sleep (Vaughan, 1996).

How does a single-cell zygote change in just a few months into an organism with sleep–wake cycles that senses, moves, and probably even dreams? The answer is by building a brain at an astonishing rate of speed. To understand how the wormlike brain of the 3-week-old embryo shown in Figure 3.5 turns into the recognizable brain of a 38-week-old fetus, let's place the steps of brain development from Chapter 2 on a developmental time line. The first stage is *neurulation*, the process of forming the neural tube between 18 and 24 days after fertilization. Development begins in earnest with *neurogenesis*, the rapid creation of immature neurons. Neurogenesis peaks about 6 to 7 weeks after fertilization and is largely complete by 4 months' gestation.

But immature neurons do not stay where they are born. Instead they migrate outward, hopping a ride on cells that provide long tentacles. In the outer layer of the brain, immature neurons detach themselves from these tentacles when they reach their destinations, with late comers assuming positions in the outermost layer. Cell migration is complete by about 6 months' gestation, yet the brain is still not fully formed.

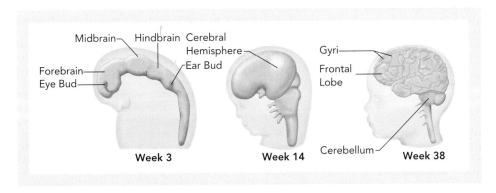

FIGURE 3.5 Brain development.

In only 9 months, a young brain forms as neural cells rapidly divide, migrate to their respective locations in the brain, and begin to interconnect. Ridges (gyri) on the brain of a normal 38-week-old fetus form when the surface area of the brain tissue grows too large to fit in the skull without folding.

The final stages of brain growth involve *synaptogenesis* and *myelination*. Recall from Chapter 2 that synaptogenesis is the development of connections between neurons. All brain regions overproduce synapses during the early years and then prune unnecessary connections, but the timing of overproduction and pruning is different in different brain regions. Synaptogenesis will not reach peak densities in brain centers that control problem solving and reasoning until over a year after birth. Myelination, the development of fatty insulation on axons, is also incomplete during the fetal period. A large number of developmental abnormalities are caused by interruptions in these two basic processes. For example, genetic disorders, nutritional deficiencies, and extremely low birth weight can interfere with myelination, causing neurological symptoms such as seizures and mental retardation (Nelson, 2000).

Although *structural* development of the brain is impressive at birth, *functional* development is not. As you will learn in later chapters, years of experience are necessary to direct the forming of new connections and the elimination of others, and these experiences will dramatically change how the brain handles information as children mature.

Becoming Male or Female

The process of becoming male or female begins when we inherit a set of sex chromosomes from our parents. But sexual differentiation occurs in steps, so our physical appearance does not always follow from our chromosomes. At various points along the way, genetic disorders and environmental events can steer development away from its expected path.

All embryos begin with tissue that can differentiate into *either* male or female forms. Females are nature's default* sex, which means that the embryo will develop a female form unless a particular set of events triggers masculinization. Embryos with male and female chromosomes develop similarly for the first few weeks. Then, about 6 weeks after fertilization, the Y chromosome directs synthesis of a protein that prompts reproductive tissue to form into testes (the male sex glands). When there is no Y chromosome, a week later this tissue starts to differentiate into ovaries (the female sex glands). Once formed, the *gonads* (testes or ovaries) produce hormones that further direct the process of sexual differentiation.

In males, the testes synthesize *testosterone*, one of a group of hormones called *androgens*. Testosterone causes the male reproductive tract to develop while another hormone causes the female reproductive system to disappear. In females, the ovaries begin producing the hormones *estrogen* and *progesterone*, causing the male system to degenerate while the female system develops. Figure 3.6 shows the similar appearance of males and females at the second to third months of pregnancy, with structures developing into male or female forms during subsequent months.

Although testosterone is called the "male" hormone and estrogen and progesterone the "female" hormones, all three hormones can be produced in the testes, ovaries, and adrenal glands. Males and females have different amounts of these hormones, but individuals of the same sex also produce hormones in varying amounts. Because sexual characteristics are influenced by hormone levels before and after birth, the concept of "sex" is actually somewhat continuous.

---

*default: The state that will occur unless something happens to override it.

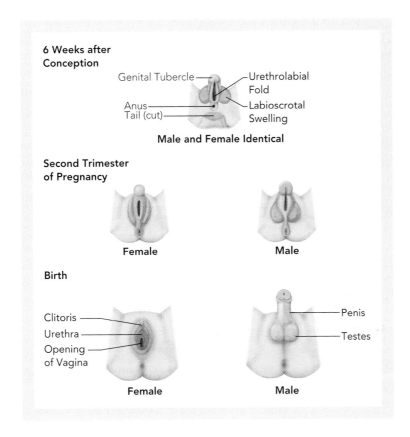

FIGURE 3.6 Sexual differentiation.

Male and female embryos have undifferentiated gonadal tissue that gradually develops into male and female genitals. The process of sexual differentiation is complex, and biological errors at various points along the way can produce intermediate forms.

SOURCE: Adapted from Money & Ehrhardt (1972).

About 1 out of every 4,500 newborns is considered *intersexed* because their genitalia do not look typically male or female (Renshaw, 1999). For example, chromosomal males with androgen insensitivity may be born looking female because they lack the ability to react normally to testosterone. These individuals do not have internal female reproductive organs but develop female contours and generally live as females. Another condition is *congenital adrenal hyperplasia*, a set of disorders in which people do not produce adequate amounts of a necessary enzyme. Genetic females with the condition secrete a substance that masculinizes their genitals, producing effects that range from an enlarged clitoris to a penis with empty scrotum. Although some of these babies escape detection and are reared as boys, most are surgically corrected and reared as girls.

Sharing a Womb

Every August in Twinsburg, Ohio, people rub their eyes and stare at the crowd that is gathering in town. What seems to be an epidemic of double vision is actually the Twins Days festival, an event that draws thousands of people for the world's largest annual gathering of twins. Pictures from the popular "Most Look-A-Like" contest are in high demand, perhaps because these images challenge our cultural obsession with individuality.

About two-thirds of all twin sets are dizygotic (two fertilized eggs) twins, commonly called *fraternal twins*. As you read in Chapter 2, members of these pairs can be either the same sex or different sexes, and they are no more genetically similar than siblings who were carried by their mother at different times. The attention-getting pairs are the monozygotic twins (from one fertilized egg) who began life as a single cell that divided between the first and fourteenth day after fertilization into two genetically identical cell masses (hence, the name *identical twins*). In rare occasions, this process repeats more than once to produce identical triplets, quadruplets or, in the case of the famous Dionne sisters, quintuplets.

Identical twinning occurs at similar rates across ethnic groups (about 1 in 250 births), but rates of fraternal twinning are variable. Before the use of fertility drugs and other reproductive technologies (which has increased the rate of dizygotic twinning), African Americans boasted the highest rate of dizygotic twinning (about 1 in 63 births), followed by people of European descent (about 1 in 125 births) and Asians (about 1 in 330 births) (Segal, 1999).

The excitement that surrounds a multiple birth is often tempered by challenges. Any pregnancy with more than one fetus is a high-risk pregnancy due to an increased risk of prematurity, low birth weight, and other threatening conditions. In fact, perinatal mortality rates are four times higher for twins and six times higher for triplets than for singletons (The ESHRE Capri Workshop Group, 2000). Consequently, it is not surprising that there is concern about the increase in multiple births caused by new reproductive technologies. More and more often, the simple desire to have a child turns into a web of choices that will forever change the lives of parents and the new lives they create. We will review reproductive options in Chapter 13 when we discuss some high-tech options for starting a family.

>>> MEMORY MAKERS <<<

1. Which is the correct order of the prenatal periods?

   (a) period of the embryo, period of the fetus, germinal period
   (b) period of the fetus, period of the embryo, germinal period
   (c) germinal period, period of the embryo, period of the fetus
   (d) germinal period, period of the fetus, period of the embryo

2. Neural tube defects are associated with a ____ deficiency.
   (a) vitamin A   (b) protein   (c) iron   (d) folic acid

3. The ability to survive outside the womb with expert care is called _____.
   (a) the default   (b) the fetal period   (c) viability   (d) the perinatal period

[1-c (the germinal period lasts for the first 2 weeks, followed by the period for the embryo for the next 6 weeks and the period of the fetus for the last 30 weeks or until birth); 2-d; 3-c]

Problems During Prenatal Development

About 2 to 3 percent of newborns have an identified birth defect, with additional children receiving diagnoses as they grow (Ericson, 1999). *Birth defects* include structural abnormalities, such as a malformed heart, and medical conditions from inherited diseases, infections, injuries, or other causes. Table 3.2 lists some of the leading categories of defects and the proportion of children who are affected by each condition.

Most of the time, the cause of a birth defect is unknown (Centers for Disease Control and Prevention, 2005c). Nonetheless, scientists are learning more each year about the genetic and environmental events that can produce defects, including some you will read about next.

TABLE 3.2	Leading Categories of Birth Defects
Birth Defects	**Estimated Rate of Occurrence**
Structural/metabolic	
Heart and circulation	1 in 115 births
Muscles and skeleton	1 in 130 births
Club foot	1 in 735 births
Cleft lip/palate	1 in 930 births
Genital and urinary tract	1 in 135 births
Nervous system and eye	1 in 235 births
Anencephaly	1 in 8,000 births
Spina bifida	1 in 2,000 births
Chromosomal syndromes	1 in 600 births
Down syndrome	1 in 900 births
Respiratory tract	1 in 900 births
Metabolic disorders	1 in 3,500 births
PKU	1 in 12,000 births
Other	
Rh disease	1 in 1,400 births
Fetal alcohol syndrome	1 in 1,000 births

SOURCE: March of Dimes Perinatal Data Center (2000).

Genetic and Chromosomal Abnormalities

The genetic diversity introduced by random mutations helps a species survive by increasing the chance that some of its members will be able to cope with environmental changes. But genetic changes are more often neutral or harmful rather than helpful. Nature's love of diversity primarily benefits species, not the individuals who compose a species. This unsettling reality raises an interesting question: If most genetic changes are harmful, why do undesirable traits stay in a population's gene pool for more than one or two generations? Wouldn't affected individuals die out or fail to reproduce? The reason there are so many errors of nature will be clear if we look at some common categories of disorders.

AUTOSOMAL DOMINANT CONDITIONS. Some damaging conditions persist from generation to generation because their negative effects do not show up until people have already reproduced. This is the case with *Huntington disease* (also called *Huntington's chorea*), a condition that causes gradual neural degeneration and, eventually, death. Individuals with Huntington disease typically do not develop symptoms until about age 40, when many have already passed the harmful gene on to their children.

Huntington disease is one of many *autosomal dominant conditions*, conditions caused by a dominant gene on any of the 22 autosomal chromosome pairs. (Recall from Chapter 2 that the 23d pair is the sex chromosomes; the others are autosomes.) Such genes are the known or suspected cause of more than two thousand genetic disorders (Wynbrandt & Ludman, 2000). But not all of these conditions persist due to late-developing symptoms. Some autosomal dominant conditions do not produce noticeable symptoms in every carrier (that is, every

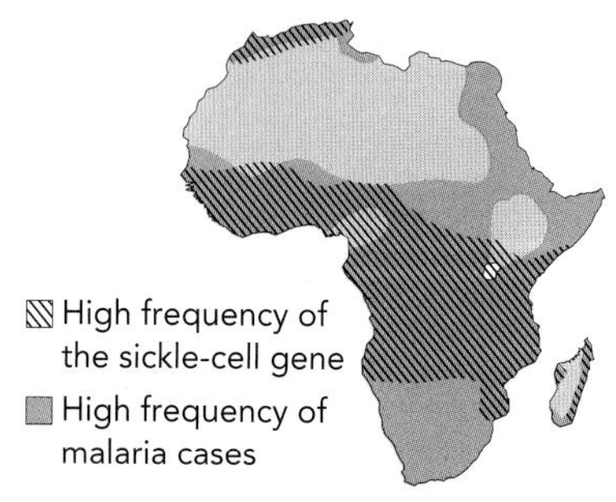

FIGURE 3.7 Why are African Americans more likely to have sickle-cell anemia?

People who inherit one allele for sickle-cell disease are more likely to survive where malaria is a threat than those who inherit two normal or two sickle-cell alleles. As a result, there is a high frequency of the sickle-cell allele in locations where malaria is common—and a high frequency among families whose ancestors came from these regions. Sickle-cell disease illustrates why genes that cause harmful conditions sometimes occur with surprising frequency.

SOURCE: Adapted from encarta.msn http://encarta.msn.com/Sickle-Cell_Anemia.html Retrieved March 28, 2006.

fragile X syndrome The most frequent inherited cause of mental retardation. This syndrome results from an abnormal number of copies of three bases of genetic code on the X chromosome.

person who has the harmful gene) whereas other conditions, including a common type of dwarfism, persist because spontaneous mutations produce new cases (Gilbert, 2000).

AUTOSOMAL RECESSIVE CONDITIONS. Some harmful alleles do not get selected out of the population because they are recessive. This is the case with *autosomal recessive conditions*, conditions caused by recessive alleles on one of the autosomal chromosome pairs. If you are Caucasian, for example, you have a 1 in 29 chance of carrying the trait for *cystic fibrosis*, a common genetic disorder that occurs in 1 in 3,300 Caucasian births. (Cystic fibrosis is rare among native Africans and Asians.) Children with cystic fibrosis produce an abnormal amount of sticky mucus that interferes with normal functioning of the lungs and digestive system. If a healthy carrier conceives a child with another healthy carrier, each of their children has a 25 percent chance of developing the disease and a 50 percent chance of being a healthy carrier.

One reason there are ethnic differences in rates of genetic disorders is that individuals from specific groups married among themselves in the past, so mutations tended to remain within the group. This is why Tay-Sachs disease, a condition mentioned in Chapter 2, used to be found primarily among Jews of Eastern European ancestry (who favored marrying other Jews). In the United States, about 1 in every 25 individuals of Jewish descent is a carrier.

Some recessive conditions occur more frequently in particular ethnic groups because people who have only one abnormal allele are more likely to survive where past generations lived. A good example is sickle-cell anemia. This disorder has a high frequency among African Americans in the United States, with 1 in 12 carrying the trait and 1 in 625 live births suffering from the syndrome. Individuals with the syndrome have red blood cells that collapse (sickle) under conditions of low oxygen, causing pain and organ damage when defective blood cells clog small blood vessels. But sickling interrupts the life cycle of the organism that causes malaria, and one allele for sickle-cell anemia does not cause a full-blown case of the disease. As a result, the sickle cell trait helps people survive throughout parts of Africa and adjacent regions where malaria is a major health risk (Figure 3.7). It is possible that other disorders are as prevalent as they are because it was once beneficial to be a carrier. For instance, there is speculation that carriers of cystic fibrosis might have been resistant to typhoid fever (Online Mendelian Inheritance in Man, 2005).

X-LINKED CONDITIONS. As you read in Chapter 2, X-linked conditions (also called sex-linked disorders) are associated with genes residing on the X chromosome. X-linked traits can be dominant or recessive (although most are recessive), but some do not clearly fit either pattern. Recall that females are unlikely to inherit abnormal genes on both of their X chromosomes, so they are less likely than males are to suffer from one of the approximately 350 X-linked disorders (Wynbrandt & Ludman, 2000). A well-known example is hemophilia, a condition in which one of the factors involved in blood clotting is deficient and individuals experience excessive bleeding. The most common form, Hemophilia A, is present in about 1 in 10,000 male births. This disease persists because mild forms do not hinder reproduction, female carriers are unaffected, and up to a third of cases arise through new mutations.

FRAGILE X SYNDROME. The most common inherited form of mental retardation is **fragile X syndrome**. This syndrome occurs in 1 out of every 1,250 male births and accounts for 4 to 8 percent of mental retardation among males.

(The condition is half as common among females.) Fragile X syndrome is caused by a mutation in a gene on the X chromosome that contains repeated copies of a *trinucleotide*, which is a set of three bases of genetic code. Most people have 6–54 copies of this repeat; individuals with 55–200 copies have a "premutation" and generally show no abnormalities. If these premutations expand into longer sequences during production of the mother's reproductive cells, the gene can be inactivated. Unlike most Down syndrome cases, fragile X syndrome is an *inherited* disorder because the fragile site is present on the *parent's* X chromosome, as shown in Figure 3.8.

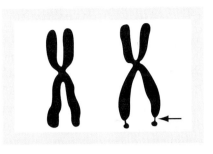

FIGURE 3.8 Fragile X syndrome.

Unlike the normal chromosome on the left, the chromosome on the right has a "gap" region near the bottom that is associated with fragile X syndrome.

SOURCE: Klug, Cummings, & Spencer (2006).

CHROMOSOMAL ABNORMALITIES. About 1 in 200 newborns has a **chromosomal abnormality**, which is an abnormality in the arrangement of the chromosomes rather than a particular gene. Half of these cases show no negative consequences, whereas the other half show one of many syndromes. Chromosomal abnormalities are present in about half of all spontaneously aborted fetuses and 12 percent of mentally retarded children (Wynbrandt & Ludman, 2000).

Down syndrome (also called "trisomy 21") illustrates three mechanisms that produce chromosomal syndromes. As we mentioned in Chapter 2, most people with this syndrome have mental retardation in the mild to moderate range, and many have medical complications such as heart abnormalities and hearing loss (Holland et al., 2000). The syndrome occurs in about 1 in 800 live births through one of the following means:

▶ In most cases, an error during production of a reproductive cell results in two copies of chromosome 21. When this cell combines with a normal reproductive cell during fertilization, the resulting zygote has three copies of chromosome 21 rather than two. (The extra chromosome comes from the mother in 95 percent of cases and the father in 5 percent of cases.) The probability of this type of error increases dramatically after a mother passes her thirty-fifth birthday.

▶ In a small percentage of cases, the error occurs during a cell division *after* fertilization, resulting in a condition, *mosaicism*, in which only some of the embryo's cells are affected.

▶ Other cases are inherited. Parents who contribute to the inherited form are normal themselves because genetic material from their chromosome 21 is merely shifted to another location, so they have the correct genetic material across all of their chromosomes. During production of their reproductive cells, some cells receive additional genetic material that is then passed on to their children.

Some chromosomal disorders involve major deviations in the sex chromosomes. For example, girls with *Turner syndrome* are born with only a single X chromosome. These girls have a short stature, a webbed neck, infertility, and an increased rate of learning disabilities. *Klinefelter syndrome* is restricted to males and is caused by an extra X chromosome, resulting in an XXY pattern instead of the expected XY. This condition may be unrecognized until puberty, when a failure to masculinize produces small testes, sparse body hair, and infertility. Most boys with Klinefelter syndrome fall into the normal range of intelligence, but many have language and reading impairments (Sandberg & Barrick, 1995).

This boy who competed in the Special Olympics was born with Down syndrome, a condition caused when a child inherits three copies of chromosome 21.

chromosomal abnormality An abnormality caused by the loss of chromosomal material, duplication of chromosomal material, or the transfer of chromosomal material from one location to another. Down syndrome is an example.

Down syndrome A condition characterized by a distinctive physical appearance and moderate to severe mental retardation, often accompanied by defects that produce medical complications. It is caused by an extra copy or portion of chromosome 21; also called **trisomy 21**.

genetic counseling Evaluation and counseling by a genetic care provider or other professional to calculate the risk of bearing a child with a genetic defect, provide prevention information, or diagnose a genetic condition.

Genetic Counseling

When Deb decided to start her family, she worried that her baby might also be born with a malformed hip and spine. After a trip to a medical library and a call to a genetic counseling program, she knew the probability that a baby would have her birth defect and what tests she should ask for after the birth.

Some people seek **genetic counseling** to calculate their risk of bearing a child with a genetic defect or to diagnose genetic conditions. During a genetics consultation, genetic care providers explore the reason for the consultation and the client's understanding of genetics. If necessary, they evaluate the client's medical and family history, conduct a physical examination, and order tests to detect genetic abnormalities. If the consultation is primarily for pregnancy planning, a provider will discuss the course of high-risk conditions and describe reproductive options. Table 3.3 summarizes some of the common reasons for seeking a genetics consultation.

TABLE 3.3   Who Should Have a Genetics Consultation?

Common Reasons for a Preconception/Prenatal Genetics Consultation:

+ Mother will be 35 years or older at delivery
+ Abnormal results from a fetal ultrasound
+ Personal or family history of a known or suspected genetic disorder, birth defect, or chromosomal abnormality
+ Mother has a medical condition known or suspected to affect fetal development
+ Two or more pregnancy losses
+ Close biological relationship of parents
+ Ethnic predisposition to certain genetic disorders

Common Reasons for a Pediatric Genetics Consultation:

+ Abnormal newborn screening results
+ One or more major malformations in any organ system
+ Abnormalities in growth
+ Mental retardation or developmental delay
+ Blindness or deafness
+ Presence of a known or suspected genetic disorder or chromosomal abnormality
+ Family history of a known or suspected genetic disorder, birth defect, or chromosomal abnormality

SOURCES: Adapted from GeneTests, a medical information service funded by the National Library of Medicine of the National Institutes of Health and the Maternal & Child Health Bureau of the Health Resources and Services Administration. Copyright 2001. **www.genetests.org**

Environmental Risks

The placenta is a magical organ. It provides nutrition and oxygen to the developing embryo, transfers waste products back to the mother's bloodstream, produces hormones, and modifies the mother's immune response to protect the embryo from attack and rejection. But despite this impressive list of talents, the placenta does not fully protect an embryo or fetus from drugs and other environmental hazards.

Efforts to protect developing embryos increased in the early 1960s, after the drug thalidomide caused a horrifying tragedy. This sedative and treatment for morning sickness was thought to be so harmless that it was available in some locations without a prescription. By the time the effect of thalidomide on developing babies was discovered, the drug had produced devastating birth defects in more than 12,000 infants, including misshapen limbs and defects of the heart, lungs, and kidneys (Kagan & Gall, 1998; Neiger, 2000; Thalidomide Victims Association of Canada, 2005). Over the years, new medical problems arose. As one thalidomider explained, "We're deteriorating in ways we were never warned of by doctors or scientists or persons who developed artificial limbs to make us look like everybody else" (U.S. Food and Drug Administration, 2001).

Tragedies like this one occur because it is surprisingly difficult to predict the effects of a drug on developing humans. One challenge is that experiments with animals produce both false negatives (failures to detect problems that exist in humans) and false positives (defects in animals that do not appear in humans). For example, thalidomide did not cause limb defects in most experiments with nonprimate animals (Bertollini, Pagano, & Mastroiacovo, 1993). But it is also difficult to identify harmful drugs because some conditions triggered by drug exposure do not show up until adulthood, long after drug studies have ended. One example is a synthetic estrogen called DES, which was administered to millions of pregnant women in the United States and Europe by physicians who believed it prevented miscarriages. Years later, the drug was linked to cancer of the vagina and cervix in young women who had been exposed in utero (in the womb) and to noncancerous growths on the testicles of men (Centers for Disease Control and Prevention, 2006a; Hatch, Palmer, & Titus-Ernstoff, 1998; Travis, 1999).

Shortly after the thalidomide tragedy, experts organized worldwide cooperation among birth-defect tracking systems so that rare defects would be spotted more quickly. But this was not the end of the thalidomide story. The drug is still used to treat leprosy and it is a promising treatment for numerous other diseases (Kyriakou et al., 2005; Neiger, 2000). As a result, there is ongoing debate about how to balance the benefits of the drug against the risks to developing fetuses. Threats from agents that both destroy and improve lives are the major force behind *teratology*: the study of environmental agents that cause malformations.

teratogen Any nongenetic agent that produces birth defects at exposures that commonly occur; derived from the Greek word *teras*, meaning "monster" or "marvel."

UNDERSTANDING TERATOGENS. A **teratogen** is any nongenetic agent that produces birth defects at exposures that commonly occur. (The term is derived from the Greek word *teras*, meaning "monster" or "marvel.") Teratogens include drugs and environmental chemicals, diseases, X rays, harmful diets, and conditions such as advanced maternal age.

There are many mistaken ideas about teratogens. For example, one of our students announced that her nephew had not suffered from his mother's alcohol use during pregnancy because the 1-year-old boy was "normal." Another student told us that cocaine use was not harmful during pregnancy because he had seen some children of cocaine users and "they were fine." In fact, it is dangerous to base your own behavior on these types of reports because the influence of a teratogen varies with the following factors:

1. *The timing of exposure.* Specific teratogens damage specific parts of the body. As a result, teratogens usually do the most harm when exposure occurs while the systems they affect are rapidly developing. As you can see in Figure 3.9, the first 8 weeks of gestation are an especially vulnerable time because most parts of the body take shape during this early period. Due to timing effects, two sisters who use the same drug during pregnancy may produce one normal and one malformed child if one mother used the drug outside the "sensitive period." Thus, the lack of birth defects in some children is not proof that a drug is safe.

2. *Maternal and fetal genes and conditions.* Even when mothers are exposed to teratogens during the same weeks of pregnancy, it is typical for only some of their infants to develop birth defects. The impact of a teratogen is influenced by a mother's physical condition, including her weight, nutritional status, and health.

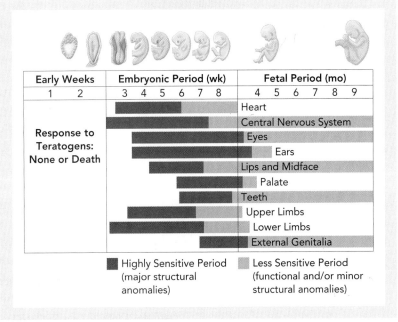

FIGURE 3.9 Sensitive periods for exposure to teratogens.

Adapted from Carlson (1999); Moore & Persaud (2003).

fetal alcohol syndrome (FAS)
A condition characterized by facial deformities, growth retardation, and central nervous system impairment that is caused by exposure to alcohol during gestation. Disruptions to the developing brain can lead to poor coordination, attentional problems, and mental retardation.

Also, genetic factors protect some embryos and fetuses from harm. Due to differences in the timing of exposure and these other factors, only about 20 percent of fetuses exposed to thalidomide during the first trimester developed malformations.

3. ***Length and intensity of exposure.*** Even minimal exposure to a teratogen can have devastating effects if exposure occurs during a sensitive period of development. For example, Randy, the thalidomider quoted earlier, suffered through 32 operations to correct birth defects caused by the two times his mother took the drug. Nonetheless, teratogens are more *likely* to cause harm at high doses or when exposure occurs over long periods of time.

4. ***Time since birth.*** The impact of a teratogen may not be clear at birth or even 1 year later. For example, the brain areas responsible for planning and strategy use develop late and, therefore, damage to these regions may not be evident until age 10 or older.

Because it is so difficult to predict the effect of a teratogen, the best course of action is to avoid unnecessary drugs and chemical exposure during pregnancy. To determine whether a particular substance is safe to use during pregnancy, your best source of information is research on large and diverse samples—not casual observations from friends. Such research has identified a number of factors that increase risk to developing babies, including some we will discuss next.

ALCOHOL. Physicians became seriously concerned about the effect of alcohol on developing fetuses over 30 years ago, when a research team published case reports of babies who were born full term but small (Jones et al., 1973). Among these babies were eight children whose mothers had all consumed alcohol during pregnancy. Suspiciously, these children had similar physical deformities, including

Children can be born with deformities when mothers drink alcohol during pregnancy. This child has the facial characteristics associated with fetal alcohol syndrome, including a small head, a flat nasal bridge, and eye folds.

small heads, low nasal bridges, thin upper lips, and eye folds. Gradually, hundreds of cases accumulated to support the new diagnosis: **fetal alcohol syndrome (FAS)** (Armstrong, 1998). Currently, about 1 to 3 infants per 1,000 is born with FAS (Barr & Streissguth, 2001).

Children with FAS have distinctive facial features that include a thin upper lip and eye folds, growth retardation, and central nervous system impairments. Alcohol kills neurons in the developing brain and prevents new neurons from migrating normally, which prevents brain structures from forming properly (Lewis, 1985; Streissguth & Connor, 2001). The resulting brain abnormalities cause a wide variety of problems, including poor coordination, attentional difficulties, speech and language delays, low IQ, and problems with daily living due to poor judgment (National Center on Birth Defects and Developmental Disabilities, 2005).

The term *fetal alcohol effect* (FAE) is sometimes used to describe children who do not have the obvious facial features associated with FAS. But children with FAE are not qualitatively different from children who meet the criteria for FAS (Sampson et al., 2000), so FAS and related disorders are sometimes referred to as "fetal alcohol spectrum disorders" or "alcohol-related birth defects" (Riley & McGee, 2005). When children with milder impairments are included in statistics, estimates of how many children are impaired from alcohol increase to 1 to 3 per 300 live births. Because animal and human studies have failed to find a level of alcohol use that is totally safe, health organizations advise women to avoid alcohol altogether during pregnancy.

OTHER DRUGS. Many legal drugs are unsafe to use during pregnancy. For example, women who smoke cigarettes are more likely to have premature and low-birth-weight babies, and these infants face a higher risk of sudden infant death syndrome, a disorder in which infants stop breathing and die (Chong, Yip, & Karlberg, 2004; Haustein, 1999). Many prescription drugs are also unsafe. For example, mothers' use of antibiotic drugs from the tetracycline family are associated with stained teeth in children, a drug for manic depression is associated with heart defects, and some antiepileptic drugs cause growth retardation and spina bifida.

Many illegal drugs also harm developing children. For example, mothers who are addicted to heroin deliver babies who are also addicted, and these infants suffer from irritability and tremors that may persist for up to 3 months (Fabris et al., 1998). Prenatal exposure to marijuana is associated with delayed growth before birth, attentional problems during the school years, and an increase in behavior problems (Goldschmidt, Day, & Richardson, 2000; Hurd et al., 2005; Walker, Rosenberg, & Balaban-Gil, 1999).

In Chapter 1 you learned that some early influences wash out over time whereas others show sleeper (delayed) effects. The fact that children grow out of some problems and grow into others has made it difficult to pin down the effects of cocaine. Dire predictions about an epidemic of highly impaired "crack" babies were modified once it became clear that many children recover from mild neurological damage (Koren et al., 1998). Still, cocaine is associated with impaired fetal growth and numerous congenital malformations, including urinary tract and cardiac malformations (Chiriboga, 1998; Inciardi, Surratt, & Saum, 1997). There are also small differences between cocaine-exposed and nonexposed children on IQ tests (Lester, LaGasse, & Seifer, 1998) and larger differences in behavior. As they grow, fetally exposed children have attentional problems and difficulty managing impulses and frustration, especially in challenging situations that place limits on their behavior (Harvey & Kosofsky, 1998; Stanwood & Levitt, 2001). This is why exposed babies may seem perfectly normal while they are toddlers at home and yet seem out of control in preschool, when they are expected to sit for longer periods and follow directions.

Health professionals want to warn the public about the dangers of drugs without creating negative attitudes that will lead parents and teachers to give up on children who have a history of prenatal exposure. Alan Leshner, former director of the National Institute on Drug Abuse, explained the challenge in the following way (Leshner, 1998):

> We need to think about a strategy for rolling out to the public—and to health care providers, child welfare workers, teachers, etc.—the truth, including the truth about the complexity of the problem and the unpredictability of who is or who will be affected and who will not. It is also important for the public to realize that there are many kids who will have serious problems. And we need to explain all this without inadvertently stigmatizing large numbers of children, many of whom may be, at most, minimally affected. (p. xvii)

COMMON ENVIRONMENTAL HAZARDS. Routine activities can inadvertently expose a fetus to danger. Expectant parents should be aware of all of the following dangers:

▶ **Radiation.** Medical procedures involving radiation, such as diagnostic X rays, increase the risk of birth defects and cancer. Women should always inform their health care professional if there is a chance they might be pregnant.

▶ *Heavy metals in fish.* Women of childbearing age should follow recommendations about eating fish to reduce their consumption of mercury and PCBs, two industrial chemicals that have been found in waterways. At high doses, mercury causes severe brain damage, cerebral palsy, and blindness (Harada, 1995); at lower does, it is associated with language delays and problems with fine-motor skills (Needleman & Bellinger, 1994). Because mercury becomes more concentrated higher in the food chain, pregnant women should avoid eating large predatory fishes such as shark and swordfish. PCBs were banned in the 1970s when it became clear that these chemicals caused neurological problems, but women in some locations are still advised to limit their consumption of lake fish.

▶ *Lead.* Blood levels of lead are elevated in women who drink contaminated water or engage in activities that expose them to lead-based products, such as sanding old paint. Prenatal lead exposure has been linked to neurological impairments and numerous structural abnormalities.

▶ *Unsafe chemicals.* Prospective mothers *and* fathers need to limit their exposure to unsafe environmental chemicals. For instance, there is an increase in neonatal deaths and congenital abnormalities among the children of men who have been exposed to certain pesticides, vapors from some industrial chemicals, and lead (Kristensen et al., 1993; Rupa et al., 1991; Vinceti et al., 2001). Because acceptable levels of exposure are unknown for most of the chemicals in our environment, the safest course of action is for everyone to be cautious about chemical exposure.

MATERNAL DISEASES AND CONDITIONS. A number of infectious diseases can harm a developing fetus. A well-known danger, *rubella* (German measles), causes eye, ear, cardiac, and brain abnormalities in the developing fetus that vary as a function of timing during pregnancy (Alger, 2000). For example, cardiac problems and deafness are most common for exposure prior to 10 weeks' gestation, deafness between 11 and 16 weeks, and growth retardation later in pregnancy (Miller, Cradock-Watson, & Pollack, 1982). Immunizing young women against rubella is the best protection against these problems.

Sexually transmitted diseases (STDs), which you will read about in Chapter 11, also endanger developing babies. For example, *chlamydia* is a common cause of neonatal eye disease, and *syphilis* can cause premature labor, fetal death, and neonatal infection (Centers for Disease Control and Prevention, 2005i). Most of the children with human immunodeficiency virus (HIV) infection were infected before birth or during the birth process (Hueppchen, Anderson, & Fox, 2000). Because there are no inoculations to prevent most STDs, responsible sexual behavior is the only way to prevent complications.

Infectious diseases can also be transmitted from mother to fetus by seemingly harmless activities. For instance, *toxoplasmosis*, which is caused by a common parasite, can be acquired by changing cat litter or gardening in contaminated soil. The risks from toxoplasmosis include miscarriage and mental retardation when infection occurs early in pregnancy, and eye, ear, and neurological abnormalities later in pregnancy (Stray-Pedersen, 2000). *Listeria monocytogenes*, a common food-borne pathogen, causes miscarriage and stillbirth. Pregnant women should protect themselves from this danger by washing raw vegetables, thoroughly heating sandwich meats, and staying away from soft cheeses such as Brie (Woteki, 2001).

Numerous medical conditions also increase the risk of miscarriage and fetal abnormalities. One is *Rh factor incompatibility*, which is present in about 10 percent of pregnancies (Klug et al., 2006). Some mothers have blood that does not contain a protein called Rh factor, so they are Rh– (R-H-negative). When blood cells from an Rh+ (R-H-positive) fetus commingle with hers, the mother's immune system builds up antibodies to fight the foreign protein. Commingling usually occurs at birth and, therefore, the first child is usually unaffected. Subsequent fetuses may develop **Rh disease**, which can cause anemia, brain damage, and even death. An injection given after each birth prevents antibody formation.

Maternal diabetes also complicates pregnancy by increasing the risk of prematurity, congenital defects, infant brain damage, and infant death. Diabetic mothers are also more likely to develop *preeclampsia*, a condition that complicates 3 to 7 percent of all pregnancies (Lockwood & Paidas, 2000). Preeclampsia is associated with high blood pressure, swelling, and protein in the urine. Progression to the severe form (*eclampsia*) can cause serious complications, including brain damage in mothers and growth retardation in their infants.

The probability of an uncomplicated pregnancy and delivery also varies with the age of the mother. Adolescent mothers experience more pregnancy-induced high blood pressure and die at a higher rate than older mothers, and their infants are more likely to be small and premature. But adolescents are also more likely than other mothers to be single, poor, and to receive inadequate prenatal care, and these characteristics are all associated with higher rates of pregnancy complications. Current evidence suggests that health status, rather than age, explains the poor outcomes of many adolescent pregnancies (East & Felice, 1996; Rossiter et al., 1985; Shawky & Milaat, 2001).

Advanced age is also a risk factor. Older mothers have an increased chance of conceiving a Down syndrome child or one with a mitochondrial DNA disorder (a disorder from DNA outside the cell nucleus). Older mothers are also more likely than younger mothers to have complications associated with hypertension and diabetes, and delivery complications are more pronounced for mothers who deliver their first infant after the age of 39 (Chan & Lao, 1999; Scholz, Haas, & Petru, 1999). But most medical complications are treatable, so most older mothers deliver healthy infants (Abu-Heija, Jallad, & Abukteish, 2000).

EATING FOR TWO. Numerous nutritional deficiencies have consequences for mothers and their developing babies. The following examples illustrate the problems that can occur when a mother's diet is inadequate:

▶ *Folic acid.* As described earlier, folic acid deficiency has been linked to neural tube defects and may also play a role in heart defects and rates of Down syndrome (Botto et al., 1999; Moyers & Bailey, 2001).

▶ *Iodine.* Iodine deficiency is the most common preventable cause of mental deficits worldwide (Worthington-Roberts, 2000). Insufficient iodine intake in the third trimester leads to cretinism, a condition characterized by dwarfism and other abnormalities that include poor muscular coordination. In some remote regions, as much as 5 percent of the population is afflicted with this preventable disorder (Anderson,

Rh disease A condition produced when antibodies from an Rh– mother, whose blood lacks a protein called Rh factor, attacks the blood system of an Rh+ infant. Because commingling of blood is necessary to trigger antibody production, the mother's first child is usually unaffected. An injection given after childbirth prevents antibody production.

Eating for two is harder than it looks! Pregnant women need to eat a variety of nutritious foods, but they also need to avoid foods that might contain heavy metals (such as large fish) or organisms that cause disease (such as soft cheeses and cold sandwich meats). A prepregnancy visit with a doctor or midwife is a good time to talk about how to eat well and keep baby safe.

Anderson, & Glanze, 1998). (Salt is supplemented with iodine because rural communities cannot provide salt for themselves and are forced to import it.)

▸ *Iron.* Iron deficiency anemia is a serious condition that increases the risk of premature delivery.

▸ *Zinc.* Low zinc levels are associated with low birth weight and small head circumference.

Unfortunately, over 50 percent of low-income women consume less than 70 percent of the recommended amounts of six critical nutrients during their pregnancies (Block & Abrams, 1993). A simple solution is to start taking multiple vitamins at the time of fertilization to reduce the risk of cleft palate, limb reductions, and other defects (Werler et al., 1999). But high doses of some nutrients are also risky. For example, excessive iron interferes with zinc absorption, and too much vitamin A causes birth defects. Therefore, mothers-to-be should always consult with a medical professional *before* choosing supplements or making dramatic changes to their diet.

As you can see, prospective parents need a lot of knowledge to keep their future children safe and healthy. Review your understanding of pregnancy risks by explaining the ABCs of pregnancy that appear in Table 3.4.

Prenatal Care

The concept of prenatal clinics was born in the 1800s, when pregnant women in Dublin had to visit a physician before giving birth in a hospital. Overcrowded conditions prompted some expectant mothers to register well before their due dates. The physicians who examined them recommended bed rest to those who were showing signs of preeclampsia, such as headaches and swelling. Unexpectedly, rates of eclampsia declined, and the concept of prenatal clinics was born (Bernstein et al., 2000). As medical knowledge grew, prenatal care expanded to include a wide range of assessment procedures that help protect babies.

THE GOALS OF PRENATAL CARE. When it comes to prenatal care, the sooner, the better. Most women know they should visit a doctor when they are pregnant, but medical advice *before* pregnancy is also important. Health professionals educate parents about the effects of drugs, identify preexisting medical conditions and screen for domestic violence, and encourage immunization and good nutrition. After a woman becomes pregnant, a schedule of 9 to 14 visits provides continued monitoring of the mother and developing baby (Bernstein et al., 2000).

In the United States, 83 percent of mothers begin prenatal care in the first trimester, 13 percent in the second trimester, and 4 percent in the third semester or not at all (March of Dimes Perinatal Data Center, 2005). As shown in Figure 3.10, African American, Native American, and Hispanic women more often receive inadequate care than Caucasian or Asian/Pacific Islander women. Because no federal program guarantees care for all pregnant women in the United States, economic factors are largely responsible for these ethnic differences in care. Unfortunately, it is women who cannot afford prenatal care, including teenagers, unmarried mothers, and recent immigrants, who are at highest risk for nutritional

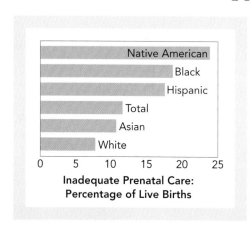

FIGURE 3.10 Ethnic differences in prenatal care.

The adequacy of the care a mother receives prenatally can be placed into four categories (inadequate, intermediate, adequate, and adequate plus) based on factors such as the timing of prenatal care and the number of prenatal doctor visits. In the United States, Native American mothers are almost 2½ times as likely as white mothers to receive inadequate care. African American, Hispanic, and Asian mothers are also less likely than white mothers to start prenatal care early and receive the recommended number of visits.

SOURCE: Adapted from the March of Dimes (2002).

TABLE 3.4   The ABCs of Pregnancy

A   *Avoid exposure to toxic substances and chemicals*, such as cleaning solvents, lead and mercury, some insecticides, and paint.

B   *Be sure to see a doctor* and get prenatal care as soon as you think you're pregnant.

C   *Cigarette smoking* during pregnancy can result in low-birth-weight babies. It has been associated with infertility, miscarriages, tubal pregnancies, infant mortality, and childhood morbidity. If you smoke, you should try to quit.

D   *Drink extra fluids* (water is best) throughout pregnancy to help your body keep up with the increases in your blood volume. A good way to know you're drinking enough fluid is when your urine looks like almost-clear water or is very light yellow.

E   *Eat healthy foods* to get the nutrients you and your unborn baby need.

F   Take *folic acid* as prescribed by your doctor both before pregnancy and during the first few months of pregnancy.

G   *Genetic testing* should be done appropriately. If there have been problems with pregnancies or birth defects in your family, report these to your doctor.

H   *Hand washing* is important throughout the day, especially after handling raw meat or using the bathroom. This can help prevent the spread of many bacteria and viruses that cause infection.

I   Take *iron* as prescribed by your doctor to reduce the risk of anemia later in pregnancy.

J   *Join a support group* for parents to be, or join a class on parenting or childbirth.

K   *Know your limits.* Let your physician know if you experience pain of any kind, strong cramps, uterine contractions at 20-minute intervals, vaginal bleeding, leaking of amniotic fluid, dizziness, fainting, shortness of breath, rapid beating of the heart, constant nausea or vomiting, trouble walking, swelling of joints, or if your baby has decreased activity.

L   *Legal drugs such as alcohol are important issues* for pregnant women. Eliminate or limit your use of legal drugs.

M   *Medical conditions* such as diabetes, epilepsy, and high blood pressure should be treated and kept under control. Discuss with your doctor all medications, prescribed and over the counter, that you are taking, including herbs and vitamins.

N   *Now is the time to baby-proof* your home.

O   *Over-the-counter cough and cold remedies* may contain alcohol or other ingredients that should be avoided during pregnancy.

P   *Physical activity* during pregnancy can benefit you and your baby. But always check with your doctor before beginning any kind of exercise, especially during pregnancy.

Q   *Queasiness*, stomach upset, and morning sickness are common during pregnancy. Eating five or six small meals a day instead of three large ones may make you feel better.

R   *Rodents* may carry a virus that can cause severe abnormalities or loss of the pregnancy. Avoid all contact with rodents, including pet hamsters and guinea pigs, and with their urine, droppings, and nesting materials throughout pregnancy.

S   *Saunas*, hot tubs, and steam rooms should be avoided while you are pregnant.

T   *Toxoplasmosis* is an infection caused by a parasite that can seriously harm an unborn baby. Avoid eating undercooked meat and handling cat litter, and be sure to wear gloves when gardening.

U   *Uterus size increases* during the first trimester, which makes you feel the need to *urinate more often.* If you experienced burning along with frequency of urination, be sure to tell your doctor.

V   *Vaccinations* are an important concern for pregnant women. Get needed vaccines before pregnancy. The Centers for Disease Control has clear guidelines for the use of vaccines during pregnancy.

W   *Being overweight or underweight* during pregnancy may cause problems. Try to get within 15 pounds of your ideal weight before pregnancy.

X   *Avoid X rays.* If you must have dental or diagnostic tests, tell your dentist or physician that you are pregnant so that extra care will be taken.

Y   Your baby loves you, and *you should show your baby that you love him or her too.* Give your baby a healthy environment to live in while you are pregnant.

Z   *Get your ZZZZZZZ's . . .* Be sure to get plenty of rest. Rest on your side as often as possible, especially on your left side as this provides the best circulation to your baby and helps reduce swelling.

SOURCE: Adapted from the National Center on Birth Defects and Developmental Disabilities (2005b).

deficiencies and medical complications. In contrast, women in many industrialized countries, including Belgium, Denmark, France, Germany, Ireland, Netherlands, Norway, Spain, Switzerland, Great Britain, and Israel, receive government-supported care. This is one reason why the United States has the highest infant mortality rate among the industrialized nations listed earlier in Figure 3.1.

FETAL ASSESSMENT. On refrigerators around the country, the traditional newborn hospital picture has been replaced with an earlier image: an ultrasound picture of the uterus, placenta, and fetus. **Ultrasonography** has been called the "greatest leap forward" in obstetrics in this generation (Beischer, Mackay, & Colditz, 1997, p. 116). During this painless procedure, a technician beams high-frequency sound waves at the mother's abdomen while a unit that analyzes reflected waves produces a two-dimensional picture (a *sonogram*). Ultrasound can determine whether a fetus is alive or dead, improve estimates of gestational age, identify whether the position of the placenta will interfere with delivery, and reveal malformations (Enkin et al., 2000).

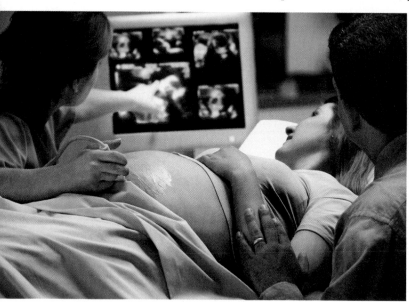

This couple is looking at an ultrasound image of their baby as a medical professional passes a wand over the mother's abdomen. If they are like most parents, they need some explanation to interpret what they are seeing.

Locating the fetus with ultrasound is an essential part of **amniocentesis**, a procedure in which a fine needle is passed through the mother's abdominal wall to draw off a sample of amniotic fluid. Fetal cells in the fluid provide information about genetic disorders, and substances in the fluid can suggest the presence of spina bifida and diagnose lung maturity. When amniocentesis is performed between 14 and 16 weeks' gestation, the miscarriage rate associated with the procedure is about 0.5 to 1 percent (Alfirevic, Sundberg, & Brigham, 2003; Wilson, 2000). **Chorionic villus sampling** can be used to collect fetal cells from the membrane surrounding the fetus as early as 8 to 13 weeks, but the risk of miscarriage or malformation is higher than when amniocentesis is conducted after 14 weeks (Alfirevic, Gosden, & Neilson, 2000).

Ultrasound techniques, amniocentesis, and chorionic villus sampling are three of many techniques that are used to evaluate the fetus. A simple procedure is a maternal blood test to determine levels of *alphafetoprotein*, a protein that is elevated when neural tube defects are present and low when the fetus has Down syndrome. Suggestive findings must be confirmed by ultrasonography or amniocentesis. This test can be useful for women under age 35 because this group does not usually elect amniocentesis, yet they produce 80 percent of Down syndrome babies because they give birth more frequently than older women.

Of course, screening and diagnostic procedures are only valuable if the information gathered will influence decisions or treatment. Some mothers decline testing for Down syndrome because they would continue their pregnancy regardless of the result. Others, however, want to know if their fetus is affected so they can terminate pregnancy or prepare for their special needs baby. As new procedures have been developed for diagnosing and correcting problems in utero, the ethical issues surrounding fetal assessment have taken on more importance. To explore these issues further, turn to our next *Innovations* feature, "Repairing Mother Nature."

ultrasonography The use of high-frequency sound waves to produce a two-dimensional picture (a sonogram) of an embryo or fetus.

amniocentesis A procedure in which a fine needle is passed through the mother's abdominal wall to draw off a sample of amniotic fluid. Fetal cells in the fluid provide material for genetic testing, and substances in the fluid predict lung development and other conditions.

chorionic villus sampling A procedure for collecting fetal cells from the chorion, a membrane surrounding the fetus.

INNOVATIONS

Each day, scientists come one step closer to correcting numerous hereditary and later-acquired conditions. Advances in fetal surgery, gene therapy, and stem cell therapy offer hope for millions of patients and their families.

REPAIRING MOTHER NATURE

The numerous problems that can arise during early development have motivated scientists to try to correct nature's errors by any means possible. Some of the newest solutions—including fetal surgery, gene therapy, and cell therapy—border on science fiction.

FETAL SURGERY. Few photographs are as captivating as the picture of Sarah Marie Switzer's arm, barely the size of a finger, extending out of her mother's uterus. Doctors at Vanderbilt University operated on Sarah Marie in utero to treat her spina bifida, a neural tube defect in which part of the spinal cord fails to close properly. Shortly after the photo was taken, Sarah was repackaged in her mother's womb to grow for 2 more months, after which she checked into the world (for the second time) at $4\frac{1}{2}$ pounds.

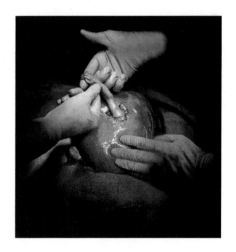

In the 1960s, transfusions for fetuses threatened by Rh disease sparked interest in fetal surgery, and later advances in ultrasound and other technologies increased the success of in utero procedures. But it is not always clear when treating a fetus before birth reaps benefits that outweigh the risks (Casper, 1998; Chervenak, McCullough, & Birnbach, 2004). For example, early surgery for spina bifida can reduce the severity of the defect by protecting neural tissue from injury, but procedures increase the chance of low amniotic fluid, premature delivery, and uterine rupture (Senior, 1999). Nevertheless, some parents and doctors accept these risks because the consequences of spina bifida, including paralysis, incontinence, and sexual dysfunction, can be devastating.

Today, fetal surgery includes a wide variety of procedures, from nutritional feeding in utero to procedures that clear airway obstructions. As the field has developed, open surgeries have gradually been replaced by less invasive procedures using fiber-optic techniques—jokingly called Fetendo—that require only small incisions in the uterus (Harrison, 2004). But despite improved technology, new procedures do not always benefit babies, and the long-term risks are not always known (Harrison et al., 2003).

GENE THERAPY. On September 14, 1990, 4-year-old Ashanti DeSilva became the first patient to undergo federally approved gene therapy (Anderson, 1995). Ashanti inherited a defective gene from each parent that prevented her from producing an enzyme her body needed for normal immune system function. Without this enzyme, Ashanti was vulnerable to infections, making simple childhood pleasures, like a birthday party, unacceptably dangerous.

Years later, Ashanti was healthy and active. A team from the National Institutes of Health removed white blood cells from her body, inserted normal copies of the defective gene, and placed the engineered cells into her circulation. Gene therapies such as this one offer hope for victims of more than 4,000 conditions that result from damage to a single gene (Anderson, 1995).

Optimism about gene therapy gave way to criticism when 18-year-old Jesse Gelsinger died in 1999 while participating in a gene therapy trial for an inherited liver disorder. Despite repeated claims of cures, the goals of gene therapy have been difficult to achieve (Anderson, 1998; Rosenberg & Schechter, 2000). The human body has spent thousands of years learning to protect itself from hazards—including onslaughts by foreign DNA. As a result, investigators need to develop more effective ways to deliver genetic material that will not be rejected by the body, control the level of expression of new genes, and produce evidence that treatment does not have unanticipated side effects (Nathwani, Davidoff, & Linch, 2005). Although some scientists believe the risks are low, others worry that new genes may trigger cancer or, even worse, find their way into reproductive cells and be passed on to the next generation. Because new genes might not turn on and off appropriately, the effects could be devastating to a developing fetus (Garber, 2000).

Setbacks in the laboratory have not deterred scientists such as Kathy High and her colleagues at the University of Pennsylvania. They hope their research on hemophilia, an inherited bleeding disorder, will end the suffering that is caused when painful bleeding breaks down joints (Margaritis et al., 2004). Hemophilia is an excellent candidate for gene therapy because researchers need to produce only 5 percent of the normal production of blood-clotting factor to achieve a cure, and success or failure can be determined by a simple blood test (Garber, 2000). Research is also under way to use gene therapy to correct numerous other disorders, including cystic fibrosis and various cancers.

STEM CELL THERAPY. Fans of Michael J. Fox were stunned in 1998 by the announcement that he had Parkinson's disease, a disorder that causes patients to lose voluntary control of movement. Parkinson's disease causes dopamine-producing neurons in the brain to die, which prevents some neurons from communicating with each another. Currently, the popular star of movies and television is supporting efforts to cure Parkinson's—a cure that might involve a type of treatment called *cell therapy*.

With cell therapy, damaged tissue or organs are repaired by transplanting healthy cells. The process sounds easy but is actually ridden with challenges. Cells for transplantation must first be harvested; then they must integrate with existing cells, avoid detection by the immune system, and renew themselves. Early work with Parkinson's disease involved grafting neurons from aborted fetuses, and these efforts proved that cell transplantation was effective. But for ethical and practical reasons, fetal neurons will probably never be available to treat a disease that afflicts over 1 million people in the United States alone (Barinaga, 2000).

Hope for such patients may lie in research with *stem cells*. Stem cells are a type of cell that can be coaxed to turn into a number of different cell types. Cells from embryos are the most versatile, but there are ethical concerns about harvesting cells from aborted fetuses or infants conceived specifically to harvest umbilical stem cells for ill siblings. Adult stem cells sidestep moral issues, and new findings have proven that adult stem cells are more abundant and flexible than scientists once believed (Prentice, 2004; Vogel, 2000). For example, stem cells harvested from the nose are currently being used to treat patients with spinal cord injuries, and scientists hope that cell transplantation may prove useful for treating diabetes and numerous other diseases.

With new advances in fetal surgery, gene therapy, and stem cell therapy being announced each week, the future never looked more hopeful for children born with structural and biochemical disorders. One commentator summed up the mounting excitement when he quipped, "The whole field has a gold-rush aura" (Marshall, 2000, p. 1420).

Michael J. Fox's battle with Parkinson's disease has increased public support for research that could lead to a cure. Parkinson's disease kills cells in the brain that produce dopamine, a chemical involved in muscle control and movement.

>>>**MEMORY MAKERS**<<<

Match each term on the left with the correct phrase on the right:

1. fragile X syndrome
2. Turner syndrome
3. hemophilia A
4. cystic fibrosis
5. amniocentesis

(a) a sex chromosome abnormality
(b) the most common inherited form of mental retardation
(c) a procedure for obtaining fetal cells for genetic analysis
(d) a condition of the lungs and digestive system
(e) an X-linked condition

6. Timing of exposure, length of exposure, and amount of exposure are three of the many factors that influence the effect a _____ will have on a developing embryo or fetus.

   (a) zygote   **(b)** blastocyst   **(c)** teratogen   **(d)** mesoderm

[1-b; 2-a; 3-e; 4-d; 5-c; 6-c]

Birthing

In our opening story, Katie and Enos were eager for signs that labor was about to begin. Three weeks before the onset of labor, their fetus's head dropped toward Katie's pelvis during an event called *lightening*. Katie suddenly felt more pressure in her pelvic region and mild uterine *contractures*. These sensations were not labor contractions but only the occasional, painless activity of the uterus that occurs throughout late pregnancy. Because only 5 percent of babies are born on their expected due date and the onset of labor is usually gradual, it is not uncommon for parents to experience one or more false alarms before true labor begins.

Fetuses with severe brain deformities led scientists to suspect that babies were involved in timing their own births. *Anencephalic* infants lack part of the brain and are usually born well past their expected due dates, suggesting that missing brain structures were involved in initiating birth. Subsequent studies proved that the brains of mature fetuses trigger hormonal events that prompt the mother's body to switch from prelabor contractures to labor contractions (Nathanielsz, 1996).

The processes that initiate labor can falter for a variety of reasons, causing early delivery or prolonged pregnancy. Premature babies have more medical problems than full-term babies do, but delivery after 40 weeks is also dangerous because the placenta deteriorates and it is difficult to birth a larger skull. For these reasons, physicians often induce labor within 2 weeks after the expected due date.

Stages of Childbirth

Childbirth stories vary widely, from routine deliveries like Katie's to the occasional baby-in-a-bathroom. But despite some variability in the details, all births progress in a sequence of four stages.

During the first stage of labor, uterine contractions occur every 5 to 15 minutes and become more regular. These contractions force the fetus against the cervix, thinning it and *dilating* (expanding) the opening into the birth canal. The purpose of this stage of labor is to dilate the cervix to 10 centimeters so the baby's head can pass through, as shown in Figure 3.11. As Katie's story illustrates, the mother is usually relatively comfortable during the early part of this stage and may even enjoy making final preparations for birth. As labor progresses, contractions become longer, stronger, and occur closer together. Once the cervix has dilated to 8–9 centimeters, the phase called *transition* begins, signaling the transition between the first and second stages of labor. First-stage labor typically lasts

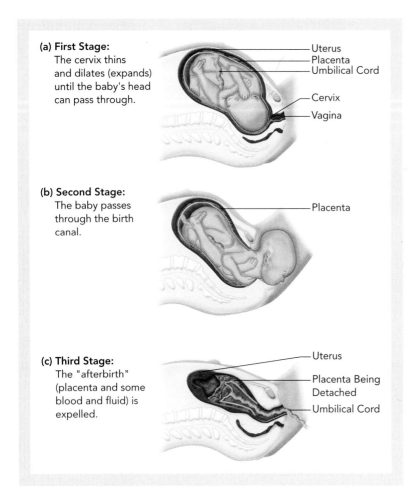

(a) First Stage:
The cervix thins
and dilates (expands)
until the baby's head
can pass through.

Uterus
Placenta
Umbilical Cord
Cervix
Vagina

(b) Second Stage:
The baby passes
through the birth
canal.

Placenta

(c) Third Stage:
The "afterbirth"
(placenta and some
blood and fluid) is
expelled.

Uterus
Placenta Being
Detached
Umbilical Cord

FIGURE 3.11 Stages of childbirth.

Most of the work of delivering a baby occurs during the first and second stages of childbirth. The placenta is delivered during the third stage, and the mother is monitored to detect any immediate medical complications during the fourth.

prenatal (antenatal) classes
Classes that prepare parents for the experience of childbirth. Common topics include the stages of labor and techniques for managing pain.

12 hours or more for a woman's first delivery, with the amniotic sac rupturing anytime between the onset of labor and transition.

The second stage of labor begins once the cervix has fully expanded. Now the mother bears down on her contractions to push the baby through the birth canal. This process typically lasts about $1\frac{1}{2}$ to 2 hours for a first delivery, with subsequent babies arriving more quickly. If the baby shows signs of distress or little progress is being made, the doctor may grasp the baby's head with tongs called *forceps* or apply suction to help extract the baby. The baby is usually born over the course of several contractions with the scalp appearing first, then a head, and then the shoulders and body.

Uterine contractions expel the placenta during the third stage of childbirth, usually within 10 minutes of the baby's arrival. Some experts consider the 2 to 4 hours after birth a fourth stage when the mother is monitored for medical complications, such as excessive bleeding and fluctuating blood pressure.

Birthing in Industrialized Countries

Modern birthing practices in industrialized countries include both natural childbirth and a technology-oriented approach that provides additional options for initiating birth, reducing pain, monitoring the fetus, and speeding delivery. In practice, these two approaches to childbirth exist along a continuum, with individual mothers planning their ideal birthing experience and deciding how much assistance they want nearby should complications arise. Both natural and technology-oriented approaches encourage preparation for childbirth, social support by fathers or other partners, and medically trained birthing attendants.

Preparation for childbirth usually begins by the third trimester of pregnancy, when mothers and fathers or other birthing coaches attend classes to prepare for the birth, decide where they want to give birth, and choose who will be part of the team that attends the birth. After discussing these early decisions, we will describe some of the technologies that are available for hospital deliveries.

PREPARING FOR CHILDBIRTH. Mothers and their support persons attend **prenatal classes** (also called *antenatal* classes) to learn about the stages of labor and receive information about options for medication and medical assistance during delivery. Prenatal educators also give families practical health advice and teach women relaxation and breathing techniques that will help them experience less pain throughout labor and delivery. There are a number of specific philosophies for managing discomfort during labor, including an approach designed by physician Grantly Dick-Read (an early advocate of natural childbirth), Lamaze, and Bradley methods (Anderson et al., 1998). Today, most prenatal educators teach techniques from a variety of methods (Enkin et al., 2000).

Choosing one or more support persons is an important part of childbirth preparation. During the delivery, support persons help the mother focus on breathing techniques, provide backrubs, and serve as a cheering section to help keep her energy and spirits up if she begins to tire. The presence of a support person reduces the need for medication and is associated with slightly shorter labor and a lower incidence of birth complications (Hodnett, 2000). Babies' fathers and friends of the mother are the most frequent labor coaches, but these individuals are not always the best assistants. Lay people lack training, and fathers are emotionally involved in the birth and have their own needs for support. One alternative is a **doula**, a person who is trained to serve as a labor coach. In clinical trials, doula-supported mothers had shorter and less difficult labors, fewer delivery complications, and showed less depression after birth than women who received support only from the father (Scott, Klaus, & Klaus, 1999).

Women can choose a physician or **midwife** as their primary medical professional. Midwives and nurse midwives are trained to assist women who are not experiencing serious complications by providing a more personal and less technological approach to childbirth. Industrialized countries that favor midwives as attendants for healthy women have favorable outcomes, with lower perinatal mortality rates and lower cesarean rates than countries in which women receive care primarily from obstetricians (Enkin et al., 2000).

One of the most controversial decisions is whether to give birth at home, in a birthing center, or in a hospital. Home births are safe for uncomplicated deliveries, but complications sometimes arise unexpectedly. For example, the maternal death rate in Sweden was only 10 per 10,000 births for hospital deliveries between 1961 and 1965, but it was 450 per 10,000 for women who opted for home birth—even though transfer to the hospital was possible in the event of a complication (Högberg & Joelsson, 1985). Due to data such as these, most experts recommend birthing settings that combine a family-friendly atmosphere with the safety of emergency medical care. A birthing center offers a homier atmosphere than a hospital and some medical equipment but is not equipped to offer some types of anesthesia or surgical procedures (Spitzer, 1995).

BIRTHING TECHNOLOGIES. Hospital deliveries frequently involve four practices that are not part of a natural delivery: inducing (initiating) labor that does not begin spontaneously, fetal monitoring, cesarean deliveries, and anesthesia to control pain. As with most medical services, all of these procedures have benefits and risks.

Labor is induced in about 20 percent of deliveries by breaking the amniotic sac or administering medication (Glantz & Guzick, 2004). Induced labor often starts more abruptly and must be closely monitored. As a result, mothers who do not go into labor on their own have less freedom to walk about and may find it more difficult to control pain through breathing and other techniques. Some medical conditions require induction, but birthing statistics suggest that labor is also induced for the convenience of scheduling deliveries to avoid weekends and holidays (National Statistics, 2001; New Jersey Department of Health and Senior Services, 2005).

doula A lay person who is trained to serve as a labor coach.

midwife A medical professional who provides birthing assistance to mothers who do not have serious illness or complications.

There has long been concern that anesthesia (drugs to reduce pain) will influence infant behavior and increase the need for a surgical delivery by slowing down labor. Currently, a popular choice for vaginal deliveries is one of several procedures that administer medication to the spinal cord, including spinal anesthesia (in which medication is injected directly into the cerebrospinal fluid), epidural anesthesia (in which medication is injected just outside the spinal canal), and combined spinal-epidural anesthesia. Unlike older evaluations, recent studies have found no differences in health or behavior between medicated and unmedicated babies (King, 1997; Vendola et al., 2001) and no evidence that administering regional anesthesia early in labor is more risky than waiting (Wong et al., 2005). In addition, surgery rates are comparable for women who receive regional anesthesia and those who do not, possibly because newer procedures for managing labor allow more time in second-stage labor before performing a surgical delivery (Russell, 2000).

Most of the criticism about hospital practice focuses on **fetal monitoring** and its impact on cesarean (surgical) delivery rates. During fetal monitoring, the fetus's heart rate is continuously monitored by strapping a unit across the mother's abdomen or attaching an electrode to the scalp of the unborn child. Experts who oppose aggressive monitoring of low-risk deliveries believe that fetal monitoring has dramatically increased the rate of surgical deliveries because doctors overreact to normal changes in fetal heart rate (Paneth, Bommarito, & Stricker, 1993; Rosen & Dickinson, 1993). They also point out that rates of infant death and cerebral palsy are not reduced in low-risk pregnancies when labor is electronically monitored, although there might be a small decrease in seizures (Dodman & Natale, 2004; Feinstein, 2000; Thacker, Stroup, & Chang, 2001). These disappointing results stem from the fact that most infant brain damage occurs before delivery, including the majority of cases of cerebral palsy (Pschirrer & Yeomans, 2000). Fetal monitoring is most beneficial when the mother or fetus has a condition that increases the chance of fetal death or brain damage (Liston et al., 2002).

The practice of removing the baby through a surgical incision in the mother's abdomen is called a **cesarean section (C-section)**. Cesarean sections are performed when labor fails to progress, the baby is in a position that complicates delivery, there is more than one fetus, or there are signs of fetal distress. Although general anesthesia is necessary in some cases, regional anesthesia allows mothers to participate in their births and lowers the risk of medical complications (Hawkins et al., 1997).

Rates for C-sections have been rising over the years. In the United States, only 5.5 percent of births were surgical deliveries in 1970 compared to 29 percent in 2004 (Centers for Disease Control and Prevention, 1993b; Hamilton et al., 2005). One concern is that doctors are performing a large number of cesarean sections to avoid lawsuits by parents who might claim that their babies' medical problems could have been avoided. It is difficult to set goals for what the cesarean rate should be, but there is no evidence that infant health improved when rates passed 15 percent (Centers for Disease Control and Prevention, 1993b).

Birthing in Developing Countries

In developing countries, inadequate nutrition, infectious diseases, and a lack of trained birth attendants make childbirth a dangerous event. According to the World Health Organization, only 53 percent of deliveries in developing countries are attended by a health professional, and only 40 percent take place in a hospital

fetal monitoring Continuous monitoring of fetal heart rate either externally (by strapping a unit across the mother's abdomen) or internally (by attaching an electrode to the scalp of the fetus).

cesarean section (C-section) Surgery to remove a fetus through an incision in the mother's abdomen.

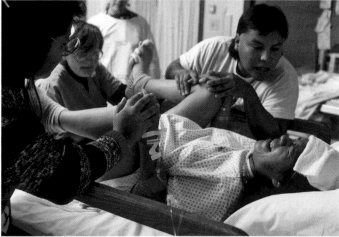

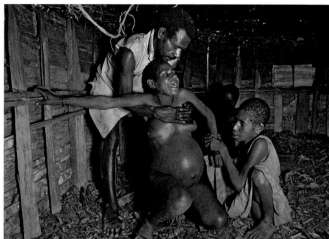

Different cultures have different ideas about who should attend a birth, how the mother should be positioned, and whether it is good or bad to make loud noises during the effort. Here an Arizona mother (left) delivers her baby in a comprehensive care facility. Another mother in Papua, New Guinea (right), hopes an upright position will help the baby arrive sooner.

or health center. About 15 percent of women who become pregnant experience life-threatening complications that require emergency care, leading to high maternal and infant mortality rates. To address these problems, the World Health Organization, World Bank, United Nations Population Fund, and UNICEF launched the Safe Motherhood Initiative in 1987, which is an ongoing effort to make childbirth safer worldwide (Rosenfield, 1997).

The presence of a medically trained attendant during childbirth is the most effective way to protect new mothers and their infants. For example, increasing access to skilled attendants was a key factor that reduced maternal deaths by 80 percent in Tunisia between 1971 and 1994 (The World Bank Group, 2001). Today, increasing the supply of midwives is a major component of international efforts to improve the health of women and children.

›››MEMORY MAKERS‹‹‹

1. During the first stage of childbirth, the _____.

(a) baby rotates to a head-up position
(b) baby is pushed out of the birth canal
(c) placenta is delivered
(d) cervix thins and dilates to 10 centimeters

2. A doula is trained to _____.

(a) serve as the primary medical professional for childbirth
(b) serve as a labor coach
(c) administer anesthesia during childbirth
(d) evaluate the newborn infant

3. A major component of international efforts to improve the health of women and children in nonindustrialized countries is _____.

(a) encouraging more hospital deliveries
(b) increasing the rate of cesarean sections
(c) increasing the use of fetal monitoring
(d) increasing the supply of widwives

[1-d; 2-b; 3-d]

premature (preterm) infants
Infants born 3 or more weeks before their due dates.

low birth weight A birth weight of less than 2,500 grams (5.5 pounds).

small-for-gestational-age Birth weight less than 90 percent of what infants born the same gestational age weigh.

Fragile Newborns

Jason Michael Waldmann, Jr., weighed only 1.2 pounds when he was born in Atlantic City. With fused eyes and thin skin that easily tore, the fragile newborn was not yet ready to live outside the womb. Immediately, the son born during Laurie and Jason Sr.'s twenty-fifth week of pregnancy was attached to a set of space-age machines that would keep his heart beating and lungs breathing. While medical staff placed intravenous lines into veins the width of a hair, all his parents could do was deliver breast milk to the hospital and wait (Funderburg, 2000).

In the next chapter, we'll describe what life is like when a typical newborn arrives after a full-term pregnancy. But that discussion doesn't apply to parents whose babies are born too early or too small. For information about what the future might hold, these parents look to studies that have evaluated other newborns like Jason. This information helps them understand the medical complications they face, how their children's early births might affect them in the future, and how they can be better parents to their high-risk baby.

Prematurity and Low Birth Weight

Length of gestation and birth weight are the most important predictors of infants' health and survival (Mathews, MacDorman, & Menacker, 2002). Babies born 3 or more weeks before their due dates are called **premature** or **preterm**. Some of these "preemies" are healthy and can be discharged from the hospital without special care, but others have serious medical problems. In the United States, about 6 to 9 percent of newborns arrive prematurely, yet these babies account for 70 percent of perinatal deaths and half of the babies who suffer from long-term neurological problems (Gibbs, 2001).

Some of the medical problems that cause premature delivery are a detached placenta, a low-placed placenta, premature rupture of the membranes, and a cervix that dilates too soon. Prematurity is also more likely when mothers carry more than one fetus, use cocaine, or are infected with harmful pathogens* (Goyal et al., 2004). For example, mothers who carry the sexually transmitted bacterium *Ureaplasma urealyticum* are 14 times more likely to deliver early (Roush, 1996). But not all causes of prematurity are exotic. Common gum disease is also associated with a fourfold increase in premature deliveries (Jeffcoat et al., 2001; Scannapieco, Bush, & Paju, 2003). When a mother's body (and possibly the fetus's body) detects invading pathogens, it produces substances that disrupt the delicate hormonal and immunological changes that maintain pregnancy (Hirsch & Wang, 2005).

The most vulnerable neonates have **low birth weight** (less than 2,500 grams or 5.5 pounds). Among this group, *very low-birth-weight infants*, who arrive weighing less than 1,500 grams (3.3 pounds), are especially likely to have medical complications. Some babies, like Jason, are small only because they were born too early, but about one-third of low-birth-weight babies are smaller than expected for their age. These **small-for-gestational-age** (also called small-for-date) babies weigh less than 90 percent of all babies born at the same age. Many of these babies have growth retardation due to poor maternal nutrition, maternal medical conditions, drug use, multiple fetuses, or other factors. Figure 3.12 illustrates prenatal growth in normal infants compared to infants whose mothers smoked, had poor nutrition, or carried twins.

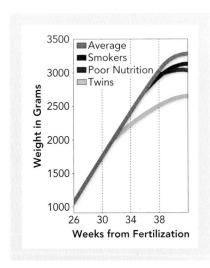

FIGURE 3.12 Fetal growth during the last trimester.

Fetuses who share space with a sibling, or whose mothers are undernourished or use nicotine, fall behind in growth during the weeks before birth.

SOURCE: Moore & Persaud (2003).

---

*pathogens: Microorganisms that cause disease.

Because their vital organs are underdeveloped, the mortality rate of very low-birth-weight babies is 100 times higher than the rate for babies born 2,500 grams or more (Mathews et al., 2002). Medical ethicist John Lantos (2001) explains the "cascade of life-threatening events" these small babies face:

> Tiny preemies can't control their body temperature, can't breathe, and can't maintain an appropriate blood pressure. They need to have their temperature and blood pressure and oxygen levels and glucose levels constantly monitored and kept neither too high nor too low. If that works, and they make it through the first crucial hours, then they begin to have other needs. They need intravenous nutrition for weeks or sometimes for months before they can eat on their own. They need monitoring of their livers and their kidneys, their lungs, brains, and bowels. Their immune systems are underdeveloped, so they need a sterile environment, but they are still at high risk for overwhelming infections. What they really need is an artificial womb, so we try to build one with our medical Tinkertoys. The result is something that works much better than nothing but much worse than the real thing. Most preemies live and do well. Some die. Worst of all, some end up somewhere in between. (p. B13)

Low-birth-weight babies face a daunting number of medical problems. The most common threat is *respiratory distress syndrome*, which is a consequence of immature lungs. Another condition is caused by a bacterial infection that destroys part of the intestines. Fluctuating oxygen levels can lead to scarring of the retina and blindness (McColm & Fleck, 2001), while fragile blood vessels in the brain can bleed, producing long-term neurological symptoms (Edgren, 1999). Early birth also exposes the developing brain to trauma from low oxygen levels, stress hormones, and medications. Collectively, these problems contribute to numerous neurological problems, including abnormal brain cell organization and cell loss in areas responsible for motor functions and storing new memories (Perlman, 2001; Skranes et al., 1997, 1998).

LIFE AFTER A DIFFICULT START. Medical advances have improved the chances that babies like Jason will survive, but a substantial portion suffer from long-term problems (Doyle & Anderson, 2005; Hack et al., 2005). Among those who survive a birth at 25 weeks' gestation, between 16 and 71 percent (depending on the sample) experience chronic lung disease and 12 to 35 percent experience severe disabilities such as cerebral palsy, blindness, and deafness (Hack & Fanaroff, 2000).

Very low birth weight also puts children at risk for cognitive disorders. Individuals with a history of very low birth weight are more likely to repeat a grade and are less likely to enroll in college, even after cases with subnormal IQ are eliminated from samples (Hack et al., 2002). In three studies conducted eight years after birth, very low-birth-weight children averaged 10 points lower on IQ tests than children born at term and were three times as likely to have scores indicating mental deficiency (Rose & Feldman, 2000). In addition to academic problems, children born small are also more likely than other children to have attentional and behavioral problems (Litt et al., 2005). The differences between the very low-birth-weight children and children born at term increase over time, which means that low-birth-weight children do not outgrow their problems (Taylor et al., 2000). Similarly, small-for-gestational-age children also have higher rates of academic problems (Hollo et al., 2002).

Compared to very low-birth-weight children, low-birth-weight children often do remarkably well. Children who are only moderately premature have cognitive scores by age 19 that are similar to those of other children (Tideman, 2000). Academic problems are more pronounced, however. One study that compared children born between 1,500 and 2,500 grams and term children found small differences in reading skill at age 11 and larger differences for mathematics achievement. Nonetheless, mothers' education contributed more to explaining academic achievement than low birth weight did (Breslau, Johnson, & Lucia, 2001).

PARENTING A HIGH-RISK BABY. Parenting a preterm infant has been described as "more work and less fun" (Goldberg & DiVitto, 1983, p. 107). Preterm infants sometimes lack the physical features adults find cute and appealing, and they are often irritable and difficult to soothe. The good news is that, after a year or so, the emotional bonds between child and parents are the same for preterm and term babies (Goldberg & Divitto, 1995).

Forty years ago, hospitals limited contact between parents and premature babies because they worried about infections. Then, in the 1970s, an experiment proved it was safe for parents to help care for their newborns (Barnett et al., 1970). Later, a trial program in Colombia showed that small but healthy babies did well when they were released to mothers who agreed to use *kangaroo care*, a type of care in which parents keep babies in close physical contact (Anderson, Marks, & Wahlberg, 1986). These findings prompted interest in how stimulation helps high-risk newborns develop.

Scientists have discovered that premature babies are very responsive to stimulation. They seek contact with a stuffed bear that "breathes" (through a hose attached to an internal bladder), and babies who have "breathing" bears show more quiet sleep and less crying (Thoman et al., 1995). Infant researcher Tiffany Field (1998, 2000) discovered that preterm infants who receive light massages gain weight faster and are released from the hospital sooner than nonmassaged infants. Even tiny infants are sensitive to the effects of their own behavior. For example, infants who receive 15 minutes of rocking and heartbeat sounds each hour whenever they have been inactive for 90 seconds show more normal reflexes than infants who receive stimulation that is not dependent on their own behavior (Barnard & Bee, 1983).

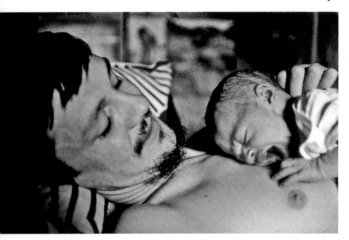

This father is helping his premature baby thrive by providing "kangaroo care," skin-to-skin contact that provides just the right amount of stimulation without overwhelming his baby.

If preterm infants benefit from sensitive caretaking in the hospital, can a supportive environment prevent cognitive deficiencies later in life? In one study, low-birth-weight children had relatively more problems in urban settings, largely due to maternal smoking and other risks associated with social class (Breslau & Chilcoat, 2000). Apparently, early biological trauma makes it harder for children to handle the risks that accumulate in less privileged environments. But even high-cost interventions sometimes produce only modest benefits for low-birth-weight children, so experts agree that *preventing* low birth weight is the best way to produce dramatic improvements in children's lives (Baumeister & Bacharach, 2000).

Prematurity and Public Policy

There is no doubt that high-tech medicine keeps low-birth-weight babies alive (Cifuentes et al., 2002). But in a moving letter to a pediatric journal, one parent complained that families are not informed about the risks and costs of treatment.

"These tiny babies are not viable," the parent argued. " . . . There's a huge cost involved and parents need to be told what that is before they agree" ("A parent speaks out," 2002, p. 249). That cost, for example, reached half a million dollars for the first 8 weeks of treating Jason Waldmann, Jr. (Funderburg, 2000).

It is not easy to decide how much medical intervention is appropriate for unhealthy newborns. Some adults believe that every child should be given a chance to survive, regardless of the cost or the subsequent level of disability. But when parents believe in limiting care, their decisions are complicated by the fact that long-term outcomes are usually unknown. Even extreme cases, such as a child born at 280 grams (0.62 pound), may have a chance of developing well (Muraskas et al., 1992). To add to their uncertainty, parents and health professionals have to choose a course of action immediately, even though the impact of new interventions may not be known for decades (American Academy of Pediatrics Committee on Fetus and Newborn, 2002). These uncertainties are another reason why efforts to prevent prematurity and low birth weight are so important.

The information in this chapter proves that reproductive choices are always choices that involve weighing risks, from the risk of passing a genetic condition on to your child to the risk that early medical treatment will benefit your child over the long run. Throughout this book, you will read about many developmental risks and ways to avoid risk. To help you think about risks that might affect your own life, turn to our next *Don't Be Fooled!* feature entitled "Those Slippery Risk Statistics."

Published statistics are sometimes wildly off target. Before becoming scared by what you read, think about whether the information is reasonable. When you are trying to evaluate your own risk, seek information from reputable sources based on samples that match your age, ethnicity, and other relevant characteristics.

THOSE SLIPPERY RISK STATISTICS

A warning light went off in sociologist Joel Best's head as he read a dissertation proposal, a plan for research that would satisfy final requirements for a student's doctoral degree. The proposal began with a "grabber," a statistic to catch the reader's attention. The following quotation, reproduced from a professional journal, opened the first paragraph: "Every year since 1950, the number of American children gunned down has doubled."

Best nominated this quotation "the worst social statistic ever" in his book, *Damned Lies and Statistics: Untangling Numbers from Media, Politicians, and Activists* (2001, p. 1). As Best explained:

Just for the sake of argument, let's assume that the "number of American children gunned down" in 1950 was one. If the number doubled each year, there must have been two children gunned down in 1951, four in 1952, eight in 1953, and so on. By 1960, the number would have

The risks of pregnancy and childbirth vary widely as a function of individual genetic makeups, how people live, and the medical care they receive. These women from India are taking an important step to protect themselves and their babies by attending a health education program where they are receiving information about safe childbirth practices and childcare after birth.

been 1,024. By 1965, it would have been 32,768 (in 1965, the FBI identified only 9,960 criminal homicides in the entire country, including adult as well as child victims) . . . Another milestone would have been passed in 1987, when the number of gunned-down American children (137 billion) would have surpassed the best estimates for the total human population throughout history (110 billion). By 1995, when the article was published, the annual number of victims would have been over *35 trillion*—a really big number, of a magnitude you rarely encounter outside of economics or astronomy.

Thus my nomination: estimating the number of American child gunshot victims in 1995 at 35 trillion must be as far off—as hilariously, wildly wrong—as a social statistic can be. (pp. 2–3)

Where did this statistic come from? The author of the quoted article had inadvertently reworded a statement from the well-known advocacy group, the Children's Defense Fund. The original statement had read, "The number of American children killed each year by guns has doubled since 1950."

Questionable statistics are often picked up by authors and passed on as fact—enough examples to fill Joel Best's book. Many of these statistics deal with important issues in human development, such as the characteristics of teenagers who commit suicide, the number of children who are abducted by strangers, and the changing nature of the workforce. These figures influence how we prioritize social programs, how we raise our children, and which lifestyle choices we make. Unfortunately, most unreliable statistics are not so easy to spot, and most are not the product of a simple rewording error. For example, some confusing numbers come from poorly worded survey questions or when researchers use questionable assumptions to "adjust" events they believe are underreported.

We decided to caution you about the slippery slope of social statistics due to our own difficulty collecting risk statistics for this text. For example, reputable sources report rates of occurrence of spina bifida ranging from 1 in 2,000 to about 1 in 4,800—over a twofold difference. Different numbers between samples are due to random error plus variability from factors that correlate with spina bifida, such as graphic location. Whenever we were confronted with these types of discrepancies, we selected rates from current sources that included large samples, generally choosing geographically representative samples from the United States.

But sometimes our job was not so simple. For example, to show some medical intervention in childbirth is justified, we wanted to know the proportion of women who die when births are not assisted by modern medical technology. We knew that mortality rates were higher in hospitals than in home deliveries until almost 1940 (due to higher infection rates), so we needed estimates that either predated the transition to hospital births or that represented current data from rural settings (O'Mara, 1999). The Swedish study reported at the start of this chapter, based on rural settings in the 19th century, provided one example.

Next we selected an alarming quote from four United Nations agencies: "In some developing countries, one woman in 10 dies from a pregnancy-related cause over the course of her child-bearing years" (World Health Organization, United Nations Population Fund, United Nations Children's Fund, World Bank, 2001). Reading further revealed that one-third of these deaths stemmed from complications due to unsafe abortions. Clearly, this statistic was not an estimate of the risk of childbirth, so we deleted it. But we noticed that eliminating one-third of these deaths yielded a lifetime mortality rate from childbirth of 7 percent, which is remarkably close to data from the Swedish study. If we had not read further, we might have joined the ranks of other people who misreported an alarming statistic.

The solution to slippery statistics is to take a thoughtful approach when you read. As Joel Best concluded, "Every statistic has flaws. The issue is whether a particular statistic's flaws are severe enough to damage its usefulness" (p. 167). Before you become alarmed by a risk statistic, ask how the event of interest was defined and think critically about whether the statistic makes sense given the other information you know. Finally, when you are trying to evaluate your own risk, seek information from reputable sources based on samples that match your age, ethnicity, and other relevant characteristics.

⟩ ⟩ ⟩ MEMORY MAKERS ⟨ ⟨ ⟨

Choose the correct word to complete each sentence:

1. Premature babies are born [3, 5] or more weeks before their due dates.
2. Low-birth-weight babies weigh less than [1,500 grams (3.3 pounds); 2,500 grams (5.5 pounds)].
3. A baby who weighs less than 90 percent of babies born at the same gestational age is called [very low birth weight; small for gestational age].
4. Preterm infants who receive light massages and rocking [show signs of stress from overstimulation; gain weight faster].

[1–3; 2–2,500 grams (5.5 pounds); 3–small for gestational age; 4–gain weight faster]

Revisiting Developmental Principles: What Is the Long-Term Impact of Early Biological Trauma?

It is natural for people who plan to be parents some day to feel somewhat frightened after reading about prenatal development and birth. So much can go wrong! If you had this reaction—or if you experienced some early biological trauma in your own life—you may be interested in hearing more about the long-term consequences of early biological risk. After reviewing what scientists mean by "biological risk," we will show you how the four principles of development from Chapter 1 can help you understand why it is difficult to predict how any individual baby will develop years down the road.

Biological risk includes harmful biological events that occur during the prenatal, perinatal, and postnatal periods. *Prenatal risks* include genetic conditions, such as chromosomal disorders and exposure to teratogens. *Perinatal risks* include oxygen deprivation during birth (anoxia), low birth weight, and other events from about 7 months' gestation to 1 month after birth. *Postnatal risks* include problems from infections, accidents, and nutritional deficiencies after birth. Because most genetic conditions cannot be prevented, research on biological risk focuses on problems that are not due to inherited disorders.

An early study that explored the significance of early biological events, the Collaborative Perinatal Project, tracked the outcomes of 53,000 pregnancies by monitoring births and evaluating children at 4 and 8 months of age, during early childhood, and again at the beginning of the school years (Kopp & Krakow, 1983). The most interesting finding was that health at birth was a poor predictor of long-term mental development. Instead, the most consistent predictor of mental retardation during the school years was mothers' education (which is highly correlated with family income). This was the first of many projects to show that low social class predicts negative outcomes better than early biological risk.

biological risk The risk of developmental problems stemming from harmful biological events during the prenatal, perinatal, and postnatal periods.

Identical conclusions were drawn from a study conducted on the island of Kauai in Hawaii. Researchers described the outcomes of 1,000 pregnancies among a group of primarily low SES women by studying their children until they were 18 years old. The team was especially interested in relationships between biological risk factors, stressful environments, and developmental outcomes. Except for major handicapping conditions, such as severe mental retardation, environmental conditions were the strongest predictors of outcomes. Furthermore, developmental problems were most frequent among children who had experienced severe perinatal stress *and* adverse environments (Bierman et al., 1965; Werner, Bierman, & French, 1971). Subsequent research confirmed that young brains often recover from mild to moderate trauma early in development (Nelson, 2000).

But severe or multiple risks *are* associated with later developmental problems. Let's turn to some principles that help scientists and medical professionals think about which children are most likely to rebound from early stresses to their bodies and brains.

Developmental Principles and Early Risk

What have scientists learned about the long-term development of high-risk infants? The four developmental principles from Chapter 1 are a useful way to organize their findings.

1. *Development is the joint product of nature and nurture.* The most perplexing conclusion is that risks such as birth complications produce different outcomes in different children (Shonkoff & Marshall, 2000). The fact that development is influenced by nature *and* nurture helps explain this finding. On the "nature" side of the equation, it is clear that genetic factors make some children more resistant to biological insults than other children. On the "nurture" side, the impact of many biological events is modified by environmental conditions. As one expert team explained, "A premature infant who struggles through multiple medical complications and is discharged from the neonatal intensive care unit to a nurturing home with excellent social supports is likely to do well developmentally; another baby with an identical medical history who is reared in an unstable environment by an isolated, disorganized, and highly stressed single parent is likely to have a host of developmental disabilities" (Shonkoff & Marshall, 2000, p. 36). Many studies have found that biological risk *and* family functioning predict later outcomes, but family functioning is often more important than birth complications for predicting later adjustment (Laucht et al., 2000).

2. *Physical, cognitive, and socioemotional development are interrelated.* Research on biological risk also illustrates how various aspects of development are interrelated. For example, alcohol exposure before birth causes physical changes in the brain, but these changes produce cognitive deficits, including attentional problems, that interfere with children's ability to interact socially with peers. In other words, children who have deficits associated with early biological trauma often have problems in multiple areas of development.

3. *Developmental outcomes vary over time and contexts.* It is hard to describe the effects of specific biological risks because outcomes vary across time and contexts. Like the cocaine-exposed children mentioned earlier in this chapter, young children may appear to have escaped damage from early trauma yet be very different from their peers during adolescence, when adults expect them to assume more responsibility. But even among these adolescents, there may be striking differences in how well adjusted individuals are depending on the environments in which they were reared. In one study, for example, boys who survived life-threatening birth complications showed higher rates of violent behavior at 6 and 17 years of age, but only when their parents faced challenges such as young parental age or low-paying jobs (Arseneault et al., 2002). In response to the question of whether early developmental delay predicts poor adjustment later in development, child development researchers James Garbarino and Barbara Ganzel concluded, "It would seem that it depends on the family and community environment in which the child is growing up" (2000, p. 78). As explained in Chapter 1, interactions between risk factors and family environments are common (Boyce & Ellis, 2005).

4. Development is characterized by continuity and discontinuity. Research on cocaine-exposed infants is a good example of this principle. These children often maintain their general intellectual functioning over time, which illustrates continuity. But discontinuities occur when some show problems in high-level skills later in development, such as reasoning about social situations ("Is Willie teasing me or threatening me?").

In sum, the best advice for parents of high-risk children is to provide a stimulating environment for growth and to expect their children to succeed, but also to be ready to offer new types of support as their children develop and confront new challenges.

Thinking Realistically about Risk

As medical care has improved, families have come to expect that every child will be perfectly formed. As a result, some experts believe that parents are becoming more intolerant of imperfections and unnecessarily concerned about risks. For example, the staff at one prenatal counseling service discovered that women were being advised to terminate pregnancies because they had taken medications, even though the medications they had ingested had no known teratogenic action. The words of a mother who sought a second opinion from the counseling center illustrate how the desire to avoid any chance of malformations can lead to a tragic loss of life (Koren, Bologa, & Pastuszak, 1993):

> Last December, I sought your help regarding a couple of tranquilizers I had taken within the first few weeks of my pregnancy. The prescribing doctor and a well-respected obstetrician had suggested that I abort the pregnancy. As a result of your advice [not to terminate the pregnancy], my husband and I are the ecstatic parents of a beautiful, healthy baby girl. I cannot thank you enough. The work you are doing is a wonderful necessity. (p. 321)

Exaggerated concern about early biological trauma can also lead teachers and health professionals to assume that affected children are unlikely to benefit from instruction or treatment. But as you just read, the accurate message is that many risks interact with environmental circumstances to determine the course of development. Therefore, scientists have shifted the emphasis from biological risk to **developmental risk**. Developmental risk is a broader term that includes risk from potentially harmful biological events *and* risks from harmful family and community influences. The chapters to come will describe the many factors that contribute to developmental risk and the influences that keep some at-risk children on positive developmental pathways.

In 1989, Madeline Mann became the smallest baby ever to survive after she was born weighing only 280 grams. Fourteen years later, she was a small but intelligent teenager who scored in the top 20 percent on an academic achievement test. Mann illustrates the ability some children have to rebound from early biological trauma, but medical experts fear that publicity about her case will give false hope to parents of other extremely small newborns.

developmental risk The risk of developmental problems stemming from harmful biological events or environmental factors during the prenatal, perinatal, and postnatal periods.

Like Katie and Enos's new baby, each of us was once a miracle of birth. You were dealt a unique selection of potentials and challenges, some contributed by nature and others determined by your family's behaviors and life circumstances.

But the bundle in a blanket that was once you was only a bundle of possibilities; the most interesting part of your story was yet to unfold. What parts of you were deeply canalized and what parts could have unfolded differently? How is your future determined or limited by the potentials and challenges that were present at birth? Developmentalists do not have the full answers to these questions, but they have generated a body of knowledge about the developmental course you traveled to get where you are today. In Part 2, we continue the story of human development from the moment of birth through the first 3 years of life. This is a time when infants exhaust and delight us, when the drama of birth is overshadowed by the rapid developments that turn babies into children, and when caretakers see the early flickers of individuality.

>>> SUMMARY <<<

Starting a New Life

1. A new individual begins to form when the male and female reproductive cells combine during **fertilization** to form a single cell called a **zygote**. The zygote then begins a journey of 3 to 4 days down the fallopian tube to the uterus.

2. Prenatal development is a sequence of three continuous periods. During the **germinal period** (the first 2 weeks after fertilization), rapidly dividing cells form layers and attach to the uterine lining, establishing a supply of nourishment from the mother. During the **period of the embryo** (the beginning of the third week through the eighth week), major organs differentiate through processes that include folding, cell instruction, cell migration, and cell death. During the **period of the fetus** (the beginning of the ninth week until birth), further development occurs that will enable the **fetus** to live outside the uterus.

3. Brain development is a lifelong process that begins with neurulation, the closing of the neural tube about 24 to 26 days after fertilization. The production of immature neurons is followed by cell migration, a process that is largely completed by 6 months after fertilization. Processes that will continue after birth include the interconnection of cells (synaptogenesis), the elimination of excess connections (synaptic pruning), and the insulation of axons with a fatty substance that speeds signal transmission (myelination).

4. All embryos have tissue that can differentiate into male or female forms. Male genitals typically develop when the Y chromosome triggers production of the testes about 6 weeks after fertilization; the ovaries develop in the absence of a Y chromosome. Once formed, the male and female gonads produce hormones that direct the process of sexual differentiation.

5. Twins result from two fertilized eggs (dizygotic twins) or one egg that divides between 1 and 14 days after fertilization (monozygotic twins). Multiple births are associated with higher rates of birth complications.

Problems during Prenatal Development

6. Birth defects caused by defective genes stay in the population when the problems they cause do not appear until after individuals reproduce, when mutations cause new cases, when symptoms are mild, and when individuals who are carriers have a survival advantage in particular environments. About 1 in every 200 babies has a chromosomal abnormality, but half of these experience no negative consequences.

7. Individuals seek **genetic counseling** to calculate the risk of bearing a child with a genetic defect and to diagnose genetic conditions.

8. **Teratogens** are agents that produce alterations or malformations in offspring at exposures that commonly occur. Alcohol and many other drugs have teratogenic effects, as do some dietary deficiencies and excesses, environmental toxins, and numerous diseases and medical disorders.

9. Prepregnancy care educates parents about the effects of drugs, identifies preexisting medical conditions and domestic violence, and encourages immunization and adequate nutrition. Medical professionals use several technologies to monitor fetal growth and development. **Ultrasonography** produces a two-dimensional picture of the fetus by beaming high-frequency sound waves. **Amniocentesis** is the process of collecting fetal cells for genetic analysis through a thin needle inserted through the mother's abdomen. When samples of fetal cells are desired early in pregnancy, they can be collected from the membrane surrounding the fetus using a procedure called **chorionic villus sampling**.

Birthing

10. Childbirth occurs in four continuous stages. During the first stage of labor, uterine contractions become regular and force the fetus against the cervix, thinning it and expanding the opening into the birth canal. The mother bears down on contractions during the second stage of labor to push the baby through the birth canal. Uterine contractions expel the **placenta** during the third stage. The 2 to 4 hours immediately after birth is a fourth stage when the mother is monitored for medical complications.

11. Parents face many birthing decisions, beginning with the selection of a childbirth education class. During birthing, mothers can be attended by their partner or a trained labor coach called a **doula**, and the primary medical attendant can be a physician, a nurse midwife, or a **midwife**. Parents must also decide on a home delivery, a birthing center, or a hospital birth. A birthing center offers a homier atmosphere than a hospital and some medical equipment but is not equipped to offer some types of anesthesia or surgical procedures.

12. Increasing the supply of health providers with midwifery skills is a key component of international efforts to improve the health of women and children.

Fragile Newborns

13. Length of gestation and birth weight are the most important predictors of infant health and survival. **Low-birth-weight** babies (under 2,500 grams) and **small-for-gestational-age** babies have higher rates of neurological problems than normal-birth-weight babies do. Years later, children who were very low birth weight (under 1,500 grams) have more attentional, behavioral, and academic problems.

14. There is no consensus about how much medical attention to give to babies who are born very early or very small. Decisions are complicated by the fact that long-term outcomes for individual cases are generally unknown.

Revisiting Developmental Principles: What Is the Long-Term Impact of Early Biological Trauma?

15. The four principles of human development help organize findings on long-term outcomes after early biological trauma: (a) biological events (nature) and later environments (nurture) both contribute to development; (b) interruptions in one area of development, such as cognitive functioning, influence other areas of development, such as social functioning; (c) time and context are important because outcomes vary across developmental periods and environments; and (d) these principles combine to create both continuities and discontinuities, so children are more likely to show stability over time for some developmental outcomes than for others.

16. Because positive outcomes are more likely when children are raised in stimulating environments, researchers have shifted the emphasis from **biological risk** to **developmental risk**, which is a broader term that includes risk from harmful biological events *and* risk from harmful family and community influences.

>>>KEY TERMS<<<

zygote (p. 88)
fertilization (p. 88)
germinal period (p. 89)
embryonic period (p. 89)
fetal period (p. 89)
embryo (p. 89)
fetus (p. 89)
placenta (p. 89)
neural tube defects (p. 90)
folic acid or folate (p. 91)
viability (p. 91)
fragile X syndrome (p. 98)
chromosomal abnormality (p. 99)
Down syndrome (p. 99)
genetic counseling (p. 100)
teratogen (p. 101)

fetal alcohol syndrome (FAS) (p. 102)
Rh disease (p. 105)
ultrasonography (p. 108)
amniocentesis (p. 108)
chorionic villus sampling (p. 108)
prenatal (antenatal) classes (p. 112)
doula (p. 113)
midwife (p. 113)
fetal monitoring (p. 114)
cesarean section (C-section) (p. 114)
premature (preterm) infants (p. 116)
low birth weight (p. 116)
small-for-gestational-age (p. 116)
biological risk (p. 121)
developmental risk (p. 123)

CHAPTER FOUR

Profile of the First Three Years

Stories of Our Lives
The Silent Victims of AIDS

> "A new baby is the beginning of all things—wonder, hope, a dream of possibilities."
>
> Eda Le Shan

"I Do MySELF!"

Attachment: Balancing Intimacy and Autonomy

Summary

TEXT BOX

SOLUTIONS
 What Babies Need: Studies of Orphanage-Reared Infants

Around the world, the majority of babies enjoy the nearly constant attention that is the result of being close to mother or an older sister throughout the day. These lucky babies have a team of family members who are working to provide each other with food, clothing, and love. But in every generation, some babies lose their parents due to war and disease. In the past, most orphaned children were caught by the safety net of an extended family and reared by relatives. In today's Africa, however, the size of the AIDS epidemic is flooding communities with orphans, as illustrated by the following stories of two grandmothers (Masland & Nordland, 2000):

Josephine Ssenyonga, 69, lives on a small farm in the Rakai district of Uganda, where AIDS has been cutting through the population like a malevolent scythe for 14 years: 32 percent of the under-15 population, a total of 75,000 children, have been orphaned in Rakai. Of the four daughters and nine sons Ssenyonga raised, 11 are dead. Her son Joseph left her with eight children; Francis left four; Peter left three. "At first there were 22, living in that small hut over there," she says. "My children did not leave me any means to look after these young ones. All they had was sold to help treat them." Overwhelmed, she took the children to the hut one day. "I told them to shut the door so we could all starve to death inside and join the others," Ssenyonga says. She changed her mind when a daughter returned home to help, and World Vision provided a three-room house for them all.

Bernadette Nakayima, 70, lives in Uganda's Masaka district, where 110,000 of the 342,000 children are orphans. Nakayima lost every one of her 11 children to AIDS. "All these left me with 35 grandchildren to look after," she says. "I was a woman struck with sorrow beyond tears." But she is not alone: one out of every four families in Uganda is now caring for an AIDS orphan. (p. 43)

In sub-Saharan Africa, projections estimate that the number of children who have lost one or both parents to the "slim disease" could reach 18 million by 2010 (Joint United Nations Programme on HIV/AIDS, 2004). The scope of the crisis is partly due to the large number of AIDS deaths, but the number of orphans is also due to cultural values. "Most Africans like to have big families," Emma Guest explained in her book, *Children of AIDS* (2001, p. 10). "It offers status and acts as an insurance policy; your children will look after you in old age. Consequently, when African parents die, they leave lots of orphans. Ugandan women, for instance, had an average of seven children in 1998, and Zambian women had an average of five or six."

A small percentage of Africa's orphans are transferred to institutions, where child care workers struggle to give them reassurance and love. But there are simply too many babies and children to recreate a typical family environment. As a result, a generation of children is being raised without the simple joy of knowing that they can be held. As a social worker in one orphanage explained to Emma Guest (2001):

"You see how when you come, they all stick up their hands to be picked up? Sometimes you'll have three children around you. How do you pick up three children?" asks Frances. "You keep them around you like a hen, you know, just hold them like that. But sometimes that's not enough for them. They want to be picked up." (p. 93)

BABIES NEED TO BE PICKED up and held. But what else do babies need? Every day, millions of parents ask that question. To know what it takes to raise healthy human infants, it helps to understand what they can do and when they can do it. For example, when babies are too young to recognize their mothers and fathers, they are not upset if a nurse or babysitter cares for them instead. But once they become better at remembering people and objects from one day to the next, the security of a familiar environment helps them explore and learn. Thus, one of the goals of studying infants is to describe how development unfolds in typical environments, that is, to answer the question, "What can babies do?" A second goal is to describe the environmental factors that support these unfolding abilities, that is, to answer the question, "What do babies need?"

We have organized this discussion of the first three years of life around these two questions. By describing what infants and toddlers can do at various points in development—and the conditions that keep them healthy enough to do it—we explain what babies need to grow physically, cognitively, and emotionally. Let's continue our story where we left off in the last chapter with a new baby who has just entered the world.

The Newborn

Most newborns, or **neonates**, have already had 9 months of development. Nonetheless, the first 4 weeks of life are a special time, called the **neonatal period**, when they must adjust to life on the outside—a life that suddenly has days and nights, warmth and cold, hunger and contentment.

neonates Newborn babies.

neonatal period The first 4 weeks after birth.

Apgar score A score given to newborns at 1 and 5 minutes after birth to indicate their general condition.

Initial Appearance

A group of newborns is usually an odd-looking assortment. At birth they are coated with a white substance called *vernix* that protected their skin during pregnancy, and some have temporary patches of fine hair, called *lanugo*, that gives them a monkey-like appearance.

Most full-term babies weigh between 5.5 and 10 pounds (2.5 to 4.5 kilograms) and measure between 18 and 22 inches long (46 to 56 centimeters). But no matter what size they are, all newborns look out of proportion with large heads that are one-fourth the length of their bodies.

It is not unusual for newborns to have wrinkled, blotchy skin and any number of newborn rashes or birthmarks. There is no reason to be concerned about "stork bites," the little pink patches that often decorate light-skinned babies, or *Mongolian spots*, the bruiselike birthmarks that appear on the backs and buttocks of some darker-skinned babies. Many newborns have elongated heads that will round out over time, a sign that unfused skull bones shifted while passing through the birth canal, and these babies often look like battered prizefighters compared to babies who were surgically delivered. But despite these differences, all healthy babies come equipped with a set of "cuteness" features that signals youth and helplessness to adults: a round face with a receding chin, large forehead, and big eyes (Alley, 1981; Gross, 1997).

Both male and female infants have been exposed to their mother's hormones, which can cause their breasts to enlarge temporarily and even cause a pink discharge from a baby girl's vagina. Newborns breathe irregularly and have cold hands and feet while their bodies adjust to taking over functions their mothers' bodies used to provide. But variability from baby to baby makes it is difficult to know when to be alarmed and when to take things in stride. As a result, even experienced parents rely on health professionals to conduct a thorough evaluation of their newborn.

Early Evaluations

Hospital stays are short for uncomplicated births, so medical personnel work quickly after a hospital birth to evaluate newborns and coordinate *postpartum* (after birth) parent education. At 1 minute and again at 5 minutes after birth, an attendant records an **Apgar score** to indicate the newborn's general condition. Table 4.1 explains how babies receive a 0, 1, or 2 for each of five characteristics. About nine in ten babies in the United States receive a score of 8 to 10, but few receive perfect scores because hands and feet are typically blue after birth. Newborns with low scores may receive oxygen, fluids, and medication to strengthen their heartbeat, followed by transfer to a special-care nursery if more attention is necessary (Shelov, 2004). For a home birth, a midwife can perform the initial newborn evaluation and schedule postpartum visits to check on mother and baby. It is recommended that babies born at home be seen by a pediatrician for a more thorough evaluation within a week of birth.

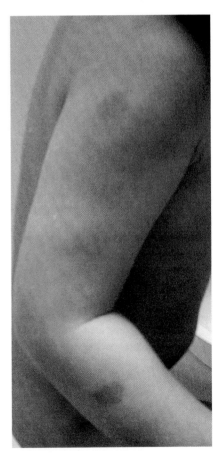

Slate-blue Mongolian spots look like bruises but are harmless birthmarks that decorate the majority of dark-skinned infants.

TABLE 4.1	Apgar Scores		
		SCORE	
Sign	0	1	2
Heart rate	Absent	Less than 100 beats per minute	More than 100 beats per minute
Breathing	Absent	Slow, irregular; weak cry	Good; strong cry
Muscle tone	Limp	Some flexing of arms and legs	Active motion
Reflex*	Absent	Grimace	Grimace and cough or sneeze
Color	Blue or pale	Body pink; hands and feet blue	Completely pink

*Reflex judged by placing a catheter or bulb syringe in the infant's nose and watching the response.

SOURCE: Adapted from Shelov (2004).

In some countries, newborns receive medicine in their eyes to prevent infections and a vitamin K injection to prevent excessive bleeding. Shortly after birth, medical attendants look for problems with respiration, heart function, and neuromuscular problems. They also look for minor defects that raise concerns about abnormalities in systems that develop at the same gestational time. For example, low-set ears may occur along with kidney problems, and an umbilical cord with one rather than two arteries alerts medical personnel to look for heart and skeletal problems (Seidel, Rosenstein, & Pathak, 2001).

Newborns are routinely evaluated for conditions that are common, easy to detect, and treatable. For example, all newborns have extra red blood cells that produce the chemical *bilirubin*, and babies whose immature livers have trouble processing this chemical develop a yellow cast to their skin. This condition, called *jaundice*, affects over half of all newborns. Because severe jaundice can cause hearing loss and brain damage, babies with high bilirubin levels may be placed under special lights to help their bodies remove the bilirubin collecting in their skin (Ross, 2003).

Hospitals also perform a blood test to screen for **phenylketonuria (PKU)**, a condition we mentioned in Chapter 2 that affects about 1 out of every 15,000 newborns (National Institutes of Health, 2000). Babies with this condition lack normal levels of an enzyme needed to metabolize phenylalanine, an amino acid that is abundant in milk and other high-protein foods. Children with PKU experience a buildup of phenylalanine that causes widespread brain damage (Hörster, Surtees, & Hoffmann, 2005), making PKU the most common biochemical cause of mental retardation (Diamond, 2001). If blood tests detect the condition, the infant is placed on a special diet to prevent developmental problems. All states in the United States also test for hypothyroidism, a condition in which too little hormone production from the thyroid gland can threaten brain development. Local policies determine which other tests newborns will receive (Seidel et al., 2001).

New parents can order optional tests to screen for dozens of other rare disorders (Black, 2005). These so-called *orphan diseases* receive little attention because

phenylketonuria (PKU) A condition in which individuals lack normal levels of an enzyme needed to metabolize phenylalanine, an amino acid that is present in large quantities in high-protein foods. Mental retardation is prevented by placing affected children on a special diet.

each one affects so few individuals. (In the United States, a condition is considered an orphan disease if it affects fewer than 200,000 individuals.) Collectively, though, the economic cost of delaying treatment is high, and undetected cases often lead to severe disability and even death. Supplementary screening for these diseases will undoubtedly become more common as new technologies make screening more affordable.

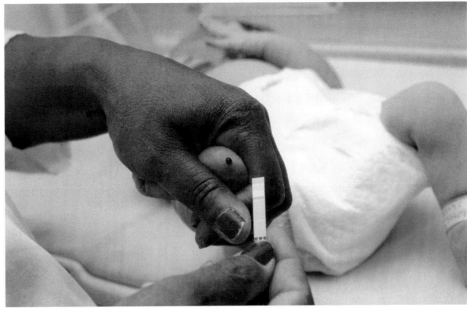

A single drop of blood from this newborn can reveal whether he has phenylketonuria (PKU) or one of dozens of other inherited disorders.

Early evaluations also include assessments of behavior and nervous system function (Daily & Ellison, 2005). One procedure is the Neonatal Behavioral Assessment Scale (NBAS), a 20- to 30-minute evaluation developed by well-known pediatrician and book author T. Berry Brazelton. The NBAS measures babies' responses to human and nonhuman stimuli as they move through various states, from deep sleep to fussing and crying. Evaluators assess visual, social, and motor activity, scoring the infant's best performance on each item (Brazelton, 1992). Scores do not correlate highly with later development among low-risk babies, partly because infants tend to recover from minor difficulties (Lasky et al., 1981). Among low-birth-weight babies, however, scores do predict childhood behavioral problems (Ohgi et al., 2003).

Falling in Love with a Newborn

Some people assume that any behavior that is critical for a species to survive, such as investing in newborns, must be directed by genes. But even in species such as the lowly rat, parenting is not strictly preprogrammed. When rat pups born to outgoing mothers and pups born to reserved mothers are raised by mothers with the opposite dispositions, the pups' future behavior is influenced: Rats raised by relaxed mothers are strongly maternal and less affected by stress, regardless of the behavior of their biological mothers (Francis et al., 1999). For rats and humans alike, genes do not single-handedly direct parenting behavior.

One idea about parenting that originated from animal research is the idea that mothers must have close physical contact with their babies shortly after birth in order to develop the strong emotional attachment that will lead them to provide the best care. The roots of this *maternal bonding hypothesis* were planted in the 1960s, when strong criticism developed over the medicalization of childbirth, especially the frequent use of anesthesia, forceps, and cesarean sections. At that time, babies were usually separated from their mothers after birth and cared for by nurses. In a popular book, physicians Marshall Klaus and John Kennell (1976) expressed concern that these practices might undermine mothers' feelings for their infants. Because goat mothers reject unfamiliar newborns unless they have spent time together during a sensitive period, Klaus and Kennell thought there might also be a sensitive period for human mothers to attach to their infants after birth. Subsequently, many parenting failures were blamed on inadequate "bonding," including increased rates of child abuse (O'Connor et al., 1980).

The maternal bonding hypothesis helped promote many positive changes, including the introduction of birthing rooms where mothers could labor, deliver, and spend time with their newborns in a comfortable atmosphere. But the hypothesis also led mothers who were separated from their babies after birth to worry about their feelings and parenting skills. As you might have guessed, research failed to support the idea that there is a specific, limited time when human parents and infants must be in continuous contact for love to form (Eyer, 1992; Maestripieri, 2001). Instead, human emotional attachment and parenting skills are acquired gradually and are constantly changing. As the American Academy of Pediatrics concluded, "Bonding has no time limit" (Shelov, 2004, p. 33).

Rather than relying on genes, human parents learn parenting behaviors from family members, friends, and other social contacts. These people provide information, moral support, and welcomed relief from the daily chores of caring for baby. As a result, parents who have strong social networks have more nurturant* parenting styles and lower rates of abusive behavior than isolated parents. Strong social networks increase parenting satisfaction and competence across all races and economic levels, and the benefits of social support are especially evident among teenage mothers (Osofsky & Thompson, 2000).

Social support is important for new parents because it is exhausting to care for an infant. To understand why, let's look at the behavior of a typical newborn.

Talents and Limitations

As mentioned in Chapter 2, human newborns are immature compared to the newborns of other primate species. Nevertheless, they arrive with an interesting collection of skills. It is easier to make sense of their talents and limitations if we consider that most cultures strap newborns onto a mother (or a sibling or grandparent) for most of the day. As you will learn in this chapter, newborns' perceptual abilities are more than sufficient to see faces close up, hear voices, and react to changes in support as mothers move. Similarly, their internal organs function well enough for someone who will be breast-fed for many months and in contact with adults who provide constant warmth and stimulation. As one pediatrician explained, "There is no such thing as a baby; there is a baby and someone" (Small, 1998, p. 35).

THE COMPETENT NEWBORN. Scientists used to think newborns were helpless, unable to perceive most of their environment and unable to make sense of what they did perceive. William James, who is often called the "father of modern psychology," summed up this view when he said that a baby experiences the world as "one great blooming, buzzing confusion" (1890, Vol. 1, p. 488). Why would scientists assume that babies are so confused? Consider the visual system, which is a major source of information for the new arrival. The image of the world that projects on the inner surface of the eye is strikingly different from the outside world: It is upside down, two dimensional, and curved, with a hole in the middle where the optic nerve leaves the eye to carry information to the brain. Clearly, scientists thought, it must take years of learning before an infant could interpret this distorted image.

---

*nurturant: Providing physical and emotional care.

An alternative position was offered by J. J. Gibson (1979), a psychologist who advanced an *ecological approach* to perceptual development. Gibson argued that perceptual systems evolved to detect "perceptual invariants" in our environment, which are relationships that remain unchanged in the ever-changing flow of sensory information. For instance, you don't need to touch a cup to know that the handle is part of the cup because the handle and container maintain their relationship to each other as images move across your retina. In other words, the basic structure of the environment is "out there," waiting to be picked up (Hockberg, 1979; Slater, 2000). As researchers learned how to test infant perception, the idea caught on that babies might be born with organized perceptual systems that grasp such information.

Today, scientists know that even newborns perceive a great deal of information. They enjoy looking at objects that are about 8 to 15 inches in front of them and are attracted to movement, which is perfect for watching the face of the person holding them (Nelson & Horowitz, 1987). Although they see little at a distance (Figure 4.1), their vision improves rapidly during the next few months (Dannemiller, 2001). Newborns' color vision is also poor but quickly develops. Initially they perceive red more easily than other colors and react only to large patches of extremely saturated color (Adams & Courage, 1998; Adams, Courage, & Mercer, 1994).

Hearing is relatively well developed at birth. Newborns hear most of the speech in conversations near them and love human voices, especially the silly "goo-GEE-gaa" speech adults use with babies. Newborns also prefer music over noise (Butterfield & Siperstein, 1972), can turn toward the direction of a sound (Morrongiello et al., 1994), and can recognize their mothers' voices (Kisilevsky et al., 2003).

Babies also arrive with the ability to smell, taste, and feel. They quickly learn to prefer their mothers' smell (Rattaz, Goubet, & Bullinger, 2005) and respond with different facial expressions to sweet, sour, and bitter substances (Bergamasco & Beraldo, 1990). Newborns love to be touched and react to changes in temperature and pressure. Physicians used to think they did not feel pain the way adults do, but new evidence has prompted medical organizations to recommend medication for newborns who have painful procedures such as circumcision* (American College of Obstetrics and Gynecology, 2001). The vestibular system, including mechanisms in the inner ear that register motion and maintain balance, is especially well developed. In fact, vestibular stimulation, such as light bouncing from carrying an infant, is the most effective way to soothe crying babies during their first few months (Hunziker & Barr, 1986).

It's fun to move and touch an infant because stimulation triggers some reflexes that are present at birth or shortly afterwards. **Reflexes** are involuntary, unlearned movements that occur in response to specific stimuli. Approach reflexes help babies take in what they need to survive. For example, *rooting* is the behavior of turning toward a stroke on the cheek, which helps babies find a breast for nursing. Avoidance reflexes, such as eye blinks and sneezing, protect them from harmful substances. Other reflexes are *vestigial*, meaning they probably had a purpose in

---

*circumcision: A surgical procedure that removes the foreskin of the penis.

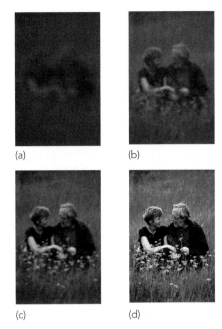

(a) (b) (c) (d)

FIGURE 4.1 Infant vision.

These photographs show a man and woman as they might appear to a newborn who is many feet away from the couple (a), a 3-month-old (b), a 6-month-old (c), and an adult (d). Newborns like it when people and toys are close to their faces because they see little at a distance, but their vision improves rapidly.

SOURCE: Provided by Tony Young and Davida Teller.

reflexes Involuntary, unlearned movements that occur in response to specific stimuli.

TABLE 4.2   Some Newborn Reflexes

Reflex	Stimulation and response	Developmental course
Babinski	Stroke infant's foot from toe to heel; toes fan out and foot twists in.	Disappears by about 1 year.
Moro	Hold infant horizontally and drop head slightly or make a loud noise. Infant arches back, extends legs, and flings out arms before bringing them back toward the center of the body, as if trying to grab onto something.	Disappears by 3 to 6 months.
Palmar grasp	Press a finger against the infant's palm; infant grasps tightly.	Weakens after a few hours and fades completely after 3 to 4 months.
Rooting	Touch infant's cheek near the mouth; infant turns head and may start sucking.	Usually disappears by 3 to 6 months.
Walking	Hold infant upright and place bare feet on a surface; infant lifts one foot, then the other.	Seems to disappear at 1 to 3 months, when body weight begins to exceed strength, then reappears between 11 and 16 months.
Sucking	Put finger in infant's mouth; infant sucks.	Strongest in the first 3 to 5 months but continues throughout infancy.
Swimming	Put infant face down in water; infant makes swimming motions.	Disappears at 3 to 6 months.
Tonic neck	Put infant on back; infant assumes "fencing" pose with fists, one arm extended, and head turned to one side.	Disappears at 4 months.

SOURCES: Anderson et al. (1998); Fogel & Melson (1988); Kagan & Gall (1998).

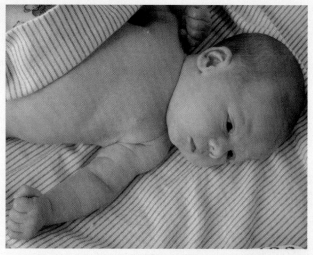

Tonic Neck Reflex

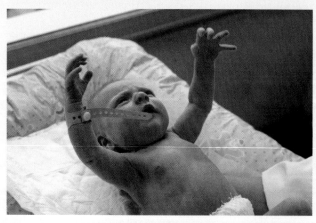

Moro Reflex

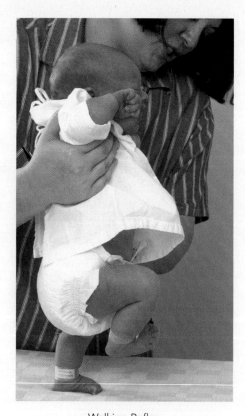

Walking Reflex

the history of the species but serve no useful purpose today. For example, babies respond to loud sounds or the sudden loss of support by swinging their arms out and bringing them together again. This *Moro reflex* may have helped nonhuman primates hang onto their mothers' fur. Table 4.2 describes some of the 27 major infant reflexes.

Some reflexes fade as higher brain centers develop, so their disappearance is a sign that the nervous system is developing normally. This means that older infants gradually lose some abilities younger infants have, such as swimming behavior. In fact, there is cause for concern if some reflexes do not disappear on schedule or if there are missing or abnormal reflexes.

THE IMMATURE NEWBORN. Despite their talents, the basic body systems of a baby are still immature. Newborns have little body fat and a high ratio of skin surface to body volume, so they use a lot of energy keeping warm in cool weather. They also cannot shiver and sweat, so they are uncomfortable in very hot weather. Cold babies fuss to generate heat, whereas overly warm babies try to stretch out to lose heat. During the first weeks of life, the ability of their kidneys to concentrate urine gradually improves, breathing becomes more regular, and blood pressure stabilizes.

Human life is patterned by physiological cycles (often called *biological rhythms*) that occur in a periodic fashion. The daily sleep-wake cycle parallels the rising and setting of the sun, and shorter cycles occur throughout the day as individuals transition through different levels of arousal. Changes in arousal from deep sleep to crying produce the various **infant states** that are described in Table 4.3. Infants are affected by the activity around them, but early state changes are primarily influenced by a complicated set of internal processes. Thus, parents adjust to newborns more than newborns adjust to parents.

Newborns spend about 18 hours a day sleeping, with about 50 percent of this time in rapid eye movement (REM) sleep (also called "dreaming" or "active" sleep) (Anders, Goodlin-Jones, & Sadeh, 2000). (In comparison, adults spend only about 20 percent of their sleep time in REM sleep.) This should make them easy to care for, but unfortunately wakeful periods interrupt sleep every few hours throughout the day and night. It takes newborns about a month

infant states Changes in consciousness from deep sleep to alert behavior, fussing, and crying.

TABLE 4.3	Infant States
State	**Description**
Quiet sleep	Eyes are closed and breathing is slow and regular. The infant may startle occasionally, sigh, or move the mouth rhythmically.
Active sleep	Eyes are closed and respiration is uneven. Rapid eye movements occur. The infant may smile, frown, grimace, suck, or sigh.
Sleep–wake transition	The infant shows behaviors of both wakefulness and sleep, sometimes with fussing sounds. Eyes are unfocused and may be opening or closing slowly.
Nonalert waking	Eyes are open but unfocused, and motor activity may range from low to high.
Alert	Eyes are open and attentive or scanning. Motor activity is low in the newborn, but the older infant may be active.
Fussing and crying	Fussing sounds or crying occur intermittently or continuously.

SOURCE: Adapted from Thoman (2001).

to "get their days and nights straightened out," and even then parents will have to wake one or more times at night to feed them. Thus, newborns are around-the-clock jobs: They want to nurse every 2 to 3 hours but will feed more often if given the chance. Anthropologists have observed babies nursing every 13 minutes among the !Kung San, a hunter-gatherer culture who permit unrestricted feeding (Small, 1998).

Few babies would survive if they continued to wake the family without even giving a tired parent a smile for the effort. (As you will read later, babies develop social smiles around 4 to 6 weeks of age.) But due to the developments you will read about next, life quickly changes.

>>>**MEMORY MAKERS**<<<

1. *Neonate* is another word for ____.

    (a) a premature baby   (b) a mother's first infant
    (c) an unhealthy newborn   (d) a newborn

2. An Apgar score ranges from 0 to ___ to indicate ___.

    (a) 10; the overall physical health of a newborn
    (b) 20; the overall physical health of a newborn
    (c) 10; the quality of the relationship between a mother and her infant
    (d) 20; the quality of the relationship between a mother and her infant

3. Infants who test positive for phenylketonuria (PKU) are treated by ___ to prevent ___.

    (a) special lights; the buildup of bilirubin in their blood
    (b) a special diet; the buildup of bilirubin in their blood
    (c) special lights; brain damage from phenylalanine
    (d) a special diet; brain damage from phenylalanine

4. Changes in arousal from deep sleep to crying are called infant ____.

    (a) repertoires   (b) states   (c) sleep phases   (d) arousal patterns

[1-d; 2-a; 3-d; 4-b]

Physical Development

Early physical development is so rapid that it is hard to keep the family Web site up to date. Due to **maturation**—the genetically determined unfolding of physical and behavioral changes over time—babies' motor skills improve each day, and they are increasingly alert and engaged with their environments.

Two principles guide early physical development. One is **cephalocaudal development**, which literally means "from head to tail." Growth is more rapid at the top at first and gradually moves downward. Motor control follows this same pattern, which is why infants gain control of muscles in the head and neck first, followed by control of muscles in the trunk and legs. The second principle is **proximodistal development**, meaning "from near to far." Bones and muscles develop near the center of the body first, followed by structures farther out. Motor control follows this pattern as well, with infants gaining control of their trunks

maturation The genetically determined unfolding of physical and behavioral changes over time.

cephalocaudal development A pattern in which growth and development start at the head and proceed downward.

proximodistal development A pattern in which growth and development begin in the center of the body and radiate outward.

before their arms, hands, and, finally, fingers. The genetic program for maturation determines how babies grow, gain motor control, perceive the world, and continue building their brains.

Body Growth

The fastest rate of growth after birth occurs during the first year, when the average infant adds 9.8 inches (25 centimeters) of height. Growth slows to 4.8 additional inches (12 centimeters) during the second year and 3.1 inches (8 centimeters) during the third. The average change in height per year then gradually declines until the growth spurt of puberty occurs during the teenage years. Body weight follows a similar pattern. Newborns typically lose weight during the first week of life, while they are getting accustomed to eating and their mothers' milk supply is becoming established, but afterward they add weight quickly (Gabbard, 2004).

The best estimate of physical maturity is *skeletal maturity*, also called "bone age." As shown on an X ray, soft cartilage gradually converts to bone as children develop. Maturity rates vary from child to child as a function of their internal biological clocks, with diet and health influencing the pace of development. It is typical for children who are ill or malnourished to stop growing temporarily and then experience catch-up growth when conditions improve. The period of catch-up growth can be as short as several months (for children who experience an acute illness) or as long as many years (when growth retardation is caused by ongoing environmental challenges) (Adair, 1999; Paerregaard et al., 1990).

Motor Control

Newborns have been described as "prisoners of the forces of gravity" who cannot even raise their own heads (Clearfield & Thelen, 2001, p. 253). Yet in just one year they come to sit, crawl, walk, and pull apart anything breakable with busy and curious hands.

MOTOR MILESTONES. In addition to reflexes, newborns show repetitive motions, like rhythmic leg kicking and arm waving, that are called *spontaneous movements*. If you watch a newborn, you will notice that spontaneous movements occupy as much as 40 percent of their waking behavior. The frequency of spontaneous movements peaks between 6 and 10 months of age, then declines as goal-directed behavior develops. These voluntary actions, called *rudimentary movements*, are involved in controlling posture, motion, and manipulating objects. Rudimentary movements, which coexist with reflexes and spontaneous movements, develop in a predictable fashion and are the foundation for all later movement skills (Gabbard, 2004).

Health professionals use checklists of various motor skills to evaluate development. *Gross motor skills* include feats such as rolling over, walking, and other movements that require large muscles. *Fine motor skills* include grasping objects, tracing lines, and other movements directed by smaller muscles. Fine motor skills are especially challenging. For example, the simple task of touching each finger to the thumb is not passed until around 3 years of age (Gabbard, 2004). Gross and fine motor skills that emerge according to a predictable timetable are called **motor milestones**.

motor milestones Gross and fine motor behaviors that emerge according to a predictable timetable.

TABLE 4.4 Motor Milestones	
Milestone	**Age range in which most children master the skill***
Rolls from back to stomach	4–7 months
Grasps a small object off a flat surface	4–7 months
Crawls on hands and knees	7–10 months
Sits with enough balance and support to free hands for an activity such as pat-a-cake	10–11 months
Drinks from cup held with both hands, with assistance	11 months–1 year, 3 months
Walks up stairs, both feet on each step	1 year, 6 months–2 years
Builds a four-block tower	1 year, 6 months–2 years
Walks well and rarely falls	1–2 years
Turns doorknob to open door	2 years–2 years, 6 months
Runs well	2–3 years
Scribbles with crayon	2–3 years

SOURCE: Brigance (1991).

*The age when children master skills varies so widely across samples that test authors are reluctant to report averages for individual skills. Albert Brigance developed this list by reviewing a number of published sources. His age ranges are only guidelines, and many normally developing children master one or more of these skills after the listed age range.

Movement is a coordinated system in which one action depends on many muscle groups. Consider the simple act of reaching for an object, which infants accomplish around 4 months of age. Reaching requires head and trunk control to provide a stable posture; otherwise the act of reaching would move the head and interrupt vision and balance. Infants, therefore, develop in a predictable order—first holding the head up, then the head and chest, then rolling and sitting—partly because they must have control of the muscles for early emerging skills before later emerging skills can be mastered. Table 4.4 lists the approximate ages of emergence of basic movements that develop as young infants turn into toddlers who can run, jump, and color a picture. There is cause for concern if a child is severely delayed in multiple areas of functioning, but the rate of early motor development does not predict later intelligence for most children (Bee et al., 1982).

Children love to practice emerging skills over and over again, only to lose interest once they master a behavior. Different cultures react differently to these early efforts. In cultures that emphasize independence, parents often provide practice opportunities as soon as infants express an interest. Thus, parents in the United States plop cereal on a high-chair tray and watch with delight while babies try to pick up the pieces, even though most of the snack ends up on the floor. In other cultures, parents believe that adults should help children as part of their responsibility for training them to do things properly (Chao, 1994). For example, a visiting professor from the People's Republic of China told us how astonished she was to see toddlers smearing food on their faces and walking down stairs by themselves. This child care specialist thought it was foolish to let children try activities they obviously couldn't accomplish correctly or safely. Some children in China, she told us, are fed until they are 2 or 3 years old, and many cultures see little point in encouraging young preschoolers to dress themselves or drink from a cup (Valdivia, 1999).

EXPLAINING MOTOR DEVELOPMENT. Scientists used to think that reflexes had to disappear before voluntary movement could develop, so they assumed that motor progress depended only on genetically programmed maturation. After studies failed to support this assumption, researchers scrambled to propose other explanations for motor development.

Currently, motor development is thought to involve both maturation, as physical size and strength increase, and babies' active experimentation. Consider the differences between two babies, Gabriel and Hannah. Gabriel was active and made large, powerful movements with his arms. In contrast, Hannah's movements were small and slow. Before they could successfully reach for objects, Gabriel had to move more slowly and less forcefully. Hannah, in turn, had to extend her arms more. Gradually, each baby stopped making unsuccessful movements but retained a smaller set of actions that accomplished their goals, so their movements became less random, more consistent, and more successful (Thelen et al., 2001).

Perceptual Development

Latisha thought everything her son did was beautiful while her husband, Randy, was more of a worrywart. Should the baby's eyes be drifting off in two directions like that? Why did he stare so long at the lights? Research on infant perception helps child care experts answer these questions and choose the best course of action for children who have perceptual problems.

VISUAL PERCEPTION. There are numerous differences between the visual systems of infants and adults. At birth, cells in the interior surface of the eye are immature and not densely packed, and visual pathways in the brain are not fully developed. But despite a slow beginning, visual processing "starts with a vengeance" at birth (Karmiloff-Smith, 1996, p. 10). By 4 to 6 months, acuity has improved to about 20/55, meaning infants can see something from a distance of 20 feet that adults can see from 55 feet, and acuity is nearly adultlike (20/30) by 1 year (Hoffman et al., 2003).

The study of infant perception burst open when Robert Fantz developed the **visual preference method**, the quick and reliable technique for testing infants. Fantz realized that infants explore the world early in life, so any preference they have to look at one stimulus rather than another means they detect a difference. As you can see in Figure 4.2, one of Fantz's early findings was that infants as young as 5 days old look longer at patterns than at colored disks (Fantz, 1963; Kellman & Banks, 1998). Other studies discovered they prefer red, blue, yellow, and green over colors such as violet and blue-green, which may account for why these colors are popular choices for toys (Bornstein, 1975). Infants also prefer figures that have many elements at the top, so they love to look at faces (Turati, 2004).

A clever way to study infants' reactions to depth cues is Gibson and Walk's (1960) visual cliff. As shown in Figure 4.3, a visual cliff is built by placing a transparent material across a shallow platform and a sharp drop-off. Younger babies show a *decreased* heart rate when they are placed over the deep side, which indicates they notice the difference between the two sides but are not yet afraid (Campos, Langer, & Krowitz, 1970). In contrast, crawling 6- to 14-month-old babies will not cross the deep side to get to their mothers—even when mothers encourage them to do so—indicating they recognize the drop-off and are scared. In many studies, babies with crawling experience were more likely to fear the deep side, suggesting that feedback from motor experience increases fear of heights (Berthenthal & Campos, 1984).

Early visual experience is important for normal perceptual development. For example, babies born with congenital cataracts (cloudy lenses) cannot see patterns until they have had corrective surgery, and at 9 months their acuity is still at newborn levels (Mauer & Lewis, 2001). Similarly, babies with crossed eyes may

visual preference method A method of determining what infants can discriminate by measuring whether they look longer at one of two visual stimuli.

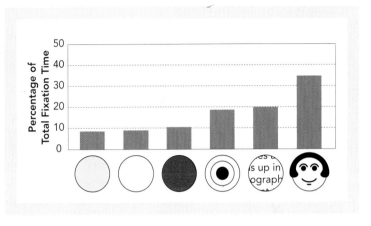

FIGURE 4.2 The visual preference method.
- -
To measure infants' visual preferences, Robert Fantz (1963) showed them patterns and recorded how long they looked at each one. (Later studies presented two stimuli at once to see which one infants chose.) These results, from a study of 2- to 6-month-olds, show that infants enjoy exploring patterns.

SOURCE: From *Life Spam Development, 7E* by John E. Santrock. Reprinted with permission of the McGraw-Hill Companies.

FIGURE 4.3 The visual cliff.
- -
Gibson and Walk used a man-made "cliff" like this one for their research on infant depth perception. Despite feeling the glass and seeing Mother's encouragement, this infant doesn't want to cross.

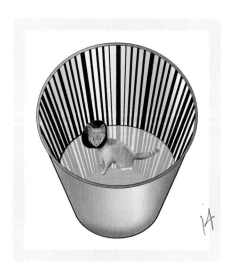

FIGURE 4.4 Experience and perceptual development.

When kittens were raised in the dark except for time they spent in this "vertical" world, they showed decreased neural activity for horizontal lines. (Other kittens raised in a "horizontal" world had difficulty perceiving vertical lines.) This famous experiment proved that exposure to patterns is critical for the visual system to develop normally.

SOURCE: Blakemore & Cooper (1970).

not develop normal depth perception unless they are surgically corrected within a year of developing the condition (Ing & Okino, 2002).

There is other evidence that experience is important for normal perceptual development. In an early study, kittens were exposed to light only when they were in a chamber of vertical or horizontal stripes, as shown in Figure 4.4. Cuffs on the kittens' neck prevented them from seeing anything except the stripes. At 5 months of age, kittens exposed to vertical lines acted blind when a rod was shaken horizontally, whereas their "vertical" siblings ran and played with it. This "blindness" had a neurological basis: Cells in their visual cortex did not respond to the orientation the kittens ignored (Blakemore & Cooper, 1970). These findings show that some exposure to light and patterns is a necessity for normal visual development. Neuroscientists use the term **experience-expectant brain development** to describe growth that occurs in response to stimulation that is normally available in human environments, such as light and visual patterns.

SOUND AND SPEECH PERCEPTION. Newborns turn their eyes toward a source of sound and make some discriminations between sounds of different pitches. The ability to tell where sounds are coming from improves until about age 3, and the ability to discriminate sounds continues to improve well past the preschool years.

Infants are biologically equipped to process speech as a special category of sound. To see what speech "looks" like, glance at the visual image produced when someone says "Rice University" (the left panel of Figure 4.5). Notice that there are no clear pauses between individual sounds within a word. This "speech chain" is made up of *phonemes*, units of sound that are "psychologically real" (Slobin, 1979). For example, "b" and "p" are two different phonemes in English because these sounds cannot be interchanged without changing meaning ("bad" is not the same word as "pad"). The pictures of these phonemes in the right panel of Figure 4.5 show that [ba] is "voiced," which means that the time between release of a burst of air and the onset of vocal fold pulsing is very short. A longer voice onset

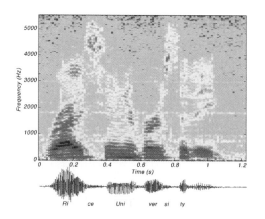

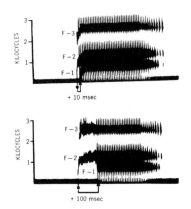

FIGURE 4.5 What speech looks like.

On the left you can see the sound frequencies produced when someone says "Rice University." Research with infants proves that humans are biologically equipped to break this complicated signal into individual units of speech called *phonemes*. For example, when infants hear syllables that are electronically produced to fall in between [ba] and [pa] (right panel), they perceive the initial sound as one phoneme or the other rather than many separate sounds—just as you do.

time produces the "unvoiced" phoneme [pà]. (You can feel the vibration from a voiced sound by putting your hand on your throat while saying "ba ba ba ba.") Voicing is one of many features that distinguish pairs of phonemes.

Speech, like color, is perceived *categorically*, which means we divide a signal that changes continuously into a small set of categories. For example, when voice onset time is varied gradually from short to long, adults clearly hear only two or three categories (depending on their native language). Infants also perceive speech sounds categorically. In a famous study, 1- and 4-month-old infants sucked a nipple that turned on a recording of electronically produced speech (Eimas et al., 1971). After infants tired of a stimulus, experimenters changed the sound by a fixed amount. Surprisingly, infants sucked faster when the stimulus change crossed a boundary adults perceive, demonstrating that infants are equipped to perceive the basic building blocks of human language. Subsequent studies showed that infants who are better at discriminating speech sounds at 6 months of age are more advanced in language development at 2 years (Tsao, Liu, & Kuhl, 2004). And as we'll discuss in Chapter 6, speech perception later plays an important role in learning to read.

Brain Development and Early Milestones

Brain and behavior are involved in an intricate dance throughout the life span: Brain development precedes the appearance of new behavior, but increasingly complex behavior also prompts further brain development. To understand how the brain changes during each of the periods described in this book, it is helpful to start by looking at the basic structures of an adult brain in Figure 4.6.

If you look down at the top of the brain, you can spot the left and right cerebral hemispheres (*cerebrum* is the Latin word for "brain"), which are connected by the *corpus callosum*. Underneath protective membranes and blood vessels is the outermost layer, the *cerebral cortex*, which is where most mental processing takes place. (In Latin, *cortex* means "bark"; hence, the cerebral cortex is the "bark on the brain.") The brain is divided into four major lobes, but it is the frontmost region that makes humans so unique. Of special interest to psychologists is one part of these lobes, the *prefrontal cortex*, which coordinates brain functions to solve complex problems and plan for the future. This structure, which continues to develop until adulthood, takes up to 25 percent of the human cortex but only 15 percent in chimpanzees and 7 percent in dogs (Diamond, 2001).

Beneath the cortex are *subcortical* structures that are active when you remember new facts, make quick decisions to approach or withdraw from a situation, and form new habits (such as learning to reach for a key on an unfamiliar keyboard). Below these regions are the "lower" brain regions, a term that describes their physical location and the fact that these areas look similar in less complex animals. At the top of the spinal cord is the *brainstem* (which controls a wide variety of very basic functions including breathing and heart rate,

experience-expectant brain development Changes in the brain that require stimulation available in virtually all human environments, such as visual patterns.

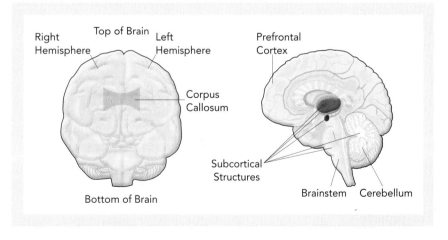

FIGURE 4.6 The brain.

- -

These basic structures of the adult brain are already differentiated at birth. On the left are the two hemispheres of the outer layer, the cortex, connected inside the brain by the corpus callosum. On the right, the brain is turned and cut in half to reveal the subcortical structures, including structures inside the brain and the "lower" brain regions that lie below.

swallowing, and regulating arousal and sleep). The *cerebellum*, meaning "little brain," perches near the brainstem (providing a sense of balance and coordinating muscles for smooth motor movements, among other functions).

Because these structures are already in place at birth, development during the first years of life consists of continuing the processes you read about in Chapter 2: building more connections, pruning unnecessary or unused connections, and myelinating neurons. A so-called **brain spurt** occurs between 6 months after fertilization and 18 months postnatal. This is a roughly 2-year period of rapid synaptogenesis when brain areas—at somewhat different times—reach their peak number of interconnections between neurons (Nelson et al., 2006). Let's look at how emerging behaviors relate to these neurological events.

THE FIRST YEAR. A developmental psychologist we know liked to tease her husband by telling him that Ruby, their daughter, would be a different baby altogether once she was 3 months old. "Just wait and see," our friend reminded him frequently. "Soon she'll be a lot more interesting." The day Ruby turned 3 months old, she woke up and laid in her crib singing long vowel sounds, such as "EEEEE!" Nonchalantly, our friend turned to her husband and said, "I told you."

There's a welcomed developmental leap around 3 months of age, when babies begin sleeping for longer stretches of time, making cooing sounds, and generally acting more responsive. At this time, cortical centers start sending signals to the brainstem that inhibit motor neurons, which is why the palmar grasp reflex, described in Table 4.2, begins to disappear. The cortical visual system is myelinating furiously at this time, which improves visual processing, and a brain area that is critical for storing new facts is also growing rapidly. These changes explain why the ability to remember faces and objects improves around 3 months of age (Herschkowitz, 2000; Pascalis et al., 1998).

This set of neurological changes brings an often inconvenient behavioral change: Infants become afraid of strangers at about 7 months of age, when brain structures that support memory are increasingly linked to areas that determine the emotional significance of events. Now babies experience a discrepancy between "mother" versus "this isn't mother," and they can attach an emotional response to "not mother" (Herschkowitz, 2000). But babies are increasingly fun to play with between 7 and 10 months of age because they more often act on, and emotionally react to, information in *working* memory (what they are thinking about right now). For example, it is easy to make babies laugh by establishing a pattern of hand motions and sounds, then changing the pattern suddenly with an expression of delight.

THE SECOND YEAR. Increased myelination during the second year improves the efficiency of communication between various parts of the brain. As neural teamwork develops, children increasingly use the left and right sides of their brains for different purposes, so they develop a dominant eye and a preference to use one hand for drawing. These preferences reflect **brain lateralization**, the specialization of the left and right cerebral hemispheres for different tasks. Lateralization is present to some extent at birth but sharpens noticeably during the early years. Due to brain lateralization, most 3- to 4-year-olds show a preference to use one hand over the other, although this preference may not stabilize until 6 years of age (Bryden, Pryde, & Roy, 2000).

THE THIRD YEAR. The brain centers that coordinate planning and other higher cognitive functions myelinate late and are among the last to build synapses and prune neurons. The immaturity of a 2-year-old's prefrontal cortex is striking.

brain spurt The period of rapid synaptogenesis that occurs between 6 months after fertilization and 18 months postnatal.

brain lateralization The tendency for the left and right cerebral hemispheres to be specialized for different tasks.

As we'll talk about shortly, the typical 2-year-old is easily distracted, has difficulty inhibiting responses, and cannot get over a disappointment by thinking about the future. Clever adults learn to live with these behaviors by designing child-friendly environments, avoiding too much excitement, and using healthy doses of distraction when children fall apart at the seams. Eventually, children outgrow these limitations caused by their immature brains.

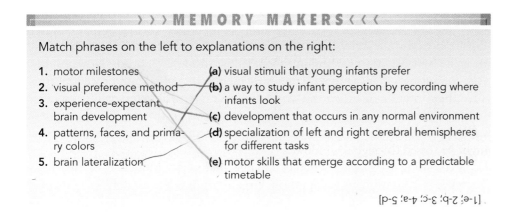

> > > **MEMORY MAKERS** < < <

Match phrases on the left to explanations on the right:

1. motor milestones
2. visual preference method
3. experience-expectant brain development
4. patterns, faces, and primary colors
5. brain lateralization

(a) visual stimuli that young infants prefer
(b) a way to study infant perception by recording where infants look
(c) development that occurs in any normal environment
(d) specialization of left and right cerebral hemispheres for different tasks
(e) motor skills that emerge according to a predictable timetable

[1-e; 2-b; 3-c; 4-a; 5-d]

Cognitive Development

In the 1960s, the computer revolution and the development of video recorders gave scientists new ways to think about the mind and new tools for recording its products (Gopnik et al., 2001). Suddenly it was fashionable to ask questions about the minds of infants, and the ideas of one brilliant scientist, long ignored by Americans, became the most influential ideas in the field of human development. That scientist was Jean Piaget.

Piaget's Theory

Two competing ideas were popular when Piaget began writing. One, which won the hearts of European psychologists, said that the basic components of human intelligence were *innate* (inborn). The other, which came to dominate American psychology, said that infants were blank slates, totally dependent on experience to build a functioning mind, piece by tiny piece. Piaget's assumption was strikingly novel: Perhaps biology equips children with mechanisms for learning that help them *construct* their understanding of the world. Knowledge doesn't have to be present at birth, nor does experience simply write the facts of the world onto passive creatures. Instead, Piaget said that infants *actively direct* their own development through the processes you will read about next (Brainerd, 1978).

HOW KNOWLEDGE DEVELOPS. Piaget believed that a universal plan for learning causes predictable changes in thinking as individuals develop. Children do not just know less than adults, Piaget said. Instead, their ideas about people and objects are *qualitatively* different from adults' ideas. To capture these shifts in thinking, Piaget proposed that development follows a sequence of stages. At each stage, thinking is guided by a set of organized cognitive structures, which are ways of interpreting events and interacting with the world.

Piaget formulated his ideas from extensive observations that he and his wife made of their three children, Jacqueline, Lucienne, and Laurent. Because of their thoroughness, Piaget's descriptions of behavior have withstood the test of time; that is, children generally behave exactly as he said they would. But Piaget wasn't content just to describe behavior. Instead, he wanted a theory that would specify the mental rules that produced these behaviors.

As described in Chapter 1, Piaget proposed that the basic unit of cognition is a **scheme** (also called a *schema*), a psychological structure that contains the knowledge, rules, and strategies children use to understand and explore the world. During the first 2 years of life, intelligence is dominated by *sensorimotor* schemes, which are action patterns such as reaching, grasping, or tasting. When children transition from infancy to early childhood, they shift from knowing the world through physical action to thinking about things inside their heads. Now children have *cognitive schemes*, which are mental symbols (thoughts) and procedures that guide their interactions with the world. For example, children develop a scheme that balls are round, soft objects that bounce back when thrown into furniture or walls. As a result, the first golf ball they grab becomes a dangerous object that might be tossed through a window.

According to Piaget, schemes change under the influence of two basic processes: organization and adaptation. **Organization** is the tendency to integrate schemes into more complex systems. For example, newborns have schemes for sucking, looking, and grasping that are not yet organized, but these schemes eventually become coordinated into more complicated behaviors that involve seeing, reaching, and bringing an object into the mouth.

Children also learn to adapt (adjust) to new situations. **Adaptation** involves two processes: assimilation and accommodation. **Assimilation** occurs when infants fit new information into an existing scheme. For example, they might assimilate the first peach they see into their looking-grasping-sucking scheme by reaching for it and putting it into the mouth, just as they do with most food and small toys. But periodically, incoming information is so incompatible with existing schemes that psychological structures have to change through the process of **accommodation**. For example, infants discover that fuzzy objects like blankets and cotton balls do not lend themselves to the looking-grasping-sucking scheme ("Yuck!"), so older infants soon learn to finger fuzzy things instead of mouthing them. (In fact, reactions to cotton balls are so predictable that recording what infants do with a cotton ball is an item on a mental development test we will describe in Chapter 5.) Throughout life, the need to accommodate our schemes in the face of new experiences leads us to develop increasingly complex cognitive structures (Piaget, 1936/52).

As daily experiences prompt children to absorb new knowledge and modify existing schemes, they move through the four stages of cognitive development mentioned in Chapter 1. Children reach these stages at somewhat different ages, but all children go through the stages in the same order because the accomplishments of the early stages are foundations for more complicated cognitive structures.

THE SENSORIMOTOR STAGE. From birth until about 2 years, children are in the **sensorimotor stage**. The journey through this stage is clear if you watch parents trying to keep their infants safe. When babies start to crawl, parents simply grab nasty objects, like dog chews, out of their hands. Soon parents learn to offer a safe item as trade for the item they want to snatch, otherwise babies will wail in frustration. Still, it is easy to watch crawling babies because they are not yet looking into every cupboard or opening every box. A few months after

scheme A psychological structure that contains the knowledge, rules, and strategies children use to understand and explore the world.

organization The tendency to integrate psychological structures (schemes) into more complex systems.

adaptation In Piaget's theory of cognitive development, the ability to adapt to the environment by integrating new experiences into existing schemes (assimilation) and modifying existing schemes to reflect discrepant experiences (accommodation).

assimilation In Piaget's theory of cognitive development, integrating a new experience into an existing scheme or way of understanding the world.

accommodation In Piaget's theory of cognitive development, modifying a scheme, or way of understanding the world, to adjust to a new experience.

sensorimotor stage The stage in Piaget's theory, from birth until approximately 2 years of age, when infants coordinate sensory systems, learn to keep mental representations of objects in mind, and begin to think through the results of actions before performing them.

their first birthdays, however, babies develop a clear sense that interesting things are hidden everywhere, and now parents cannot take their eyes off them for a minute.

What accounts for this interesting transformation in babies' behavior? According to Piaget, the most important characteristic of the sensorimotor stage is a change from knowing the world by sensing and acting (hence, the name *sensorimotor* stage) to the ability to manipulate mental symbols (in other words, the shift from *sensorimotor* to *cognitive* schemes). Babies who wail when you snatch an item away from them have developed what Piaget called **object permanence**, which is the idea that objects continue to exist even when we are not directly experiencing them. According to Piaget, object permanence develops in the following way (Piaget, 1954):

▶ *"Out of sight, out of mind" (birth to 4 months).* Young infants act as if things they cannot see do not exist. For example, they make no attempt to find an object when they drop it or an adult hides the object under a blanket.

▶ *Beginning of object permanence (4 to 8 months).* Object permanence begins to develop when infants search for objects that are partially hidden.

▶ *Object permanence emerges (around 8 months).* Older infants will remove a blanket to retrieve an attractive toy they just saw hidden. But if the adult hides an object under one blanket (side A) several times and then shifts and hides it under another blanket (side B), infants look for the object where they found it the first time. This well-known phenomenon is called the **A-not-B error** because infants look in the first location, A, rather than the second location, B.

▶ *Retrieving objects after a visible move (12 to 18 months).* Shortly after their first birthdays, most infants will search for objects in the last place they saw them—provided they saw the hiding. Still, they cannot always find objects if the hiding was concealed from them, which happens when an adult moves objects from one location to another inside closed hands.

▶ *Retrieving objects after a concealed move (18 to 24 months).* Now infants can find hidden objects even if some of the shifts were concealed from them, showing a more mature ability to think about things inside their head.

As infants develop through the sensorimotor stage, they move from primitive reflexes to more flexible behavior, become better at manipulating mental symbols, and begin to think through the results of behavior before they act. Once these achievements are in place, children are curious and poking into everything because they are not limited to thinking about what is in front of them. Now parents "childproof" the house with special latches because their little ones are interested in the measuring cups they saw in the drawer yesterday and what's behind the bushes outside. By 2 years old, when children are relying on mental symbols to think, they have moved into the *preoperational stage*, which you will read about in Chapter 6. For now, turn to Table 4.5 to review the landmarks of the sensorimotor period.

object permanence The ability to understand that objects continue to exist in space and time even when they are not currently being perceived.

A-not-B error The tendency infants have to search for objects where they found them earlier (A) rather than their current location (B).

This baby has the concept of object permanence because she realizes her toy hasn't disappeared just because it was covered. She probably enjoys playing pee-a-boo and looking into cupboards.

WELL, WE THOUGHT WE HAD CHILD-PROOFED THE HOUSE... BUT DANG IF ONE DIDN'T GET IN ANYWAY...

Dave Coverly/Creators Syndicate

TABLE 4.5 Sensorimotor Development

Substage	Competencies and examples from Piaget's diaries
1. Birth to 1 month	Experience is already modifying reflexive behaviors. Infants begin to perceive the difference between objects and show an early form of recognition memory.
	During the second day . . . Laurent again begins to make sucking-movements between meals . . . His lips open and close as if to receive a real nippleful but without having an object. (Piaget, 1952, pp. 25-26)
2. 1–4 months	Infants try to rediscover behaviors that led to interesting events, and habits develop when these efforts are successful. They begin to anticipate events, are interested in moderately novel events, and can imitate behaviors that are similar to their existing schemes.
	Lucienne spontaneously uttered the sound raa, but did not react at once when I reproduced it. [three days later], however, when I made a prolonged aa, she twice uttered a similar sound, although she had previously been silent for a quarter of an hour. (Piaget, 1951, p. 10)
3. 4–8 months	Infants are showing more interest in the environment and are beginning to have an object concept.
	Lucienne is busy scratching a powder box placed next to her on her left, but abandons that game when she sees me appear on her right. She drops the box and plays with me for a moment, babbles, etc. Then she suddenly stops looking at me and turns at once in the correct position to grasp the box; obviously she does not doubt that this will be at her disposal in the very place where she used it before. (Piaget, 1954, p. 25)
4. 8–12 months	Infants pursue goals, begin to imitate novel actions, and have a good concept of objects. However, they cannot track a complex series of object displacement.
	Jacqueline is seated on a mattress without anything to disturb or distract her (no coverlets, etc.). I take her parrot from her hands and hide it twice in succession under the mattress, on her left, in A. Both times Jacqueline looks for the object immediately and grabs it. (Piaget, 1954, p. 51)
5. 12–18 months	Infants now try new ways to achieve goals, imitate difficult actions, and track complex series of object displacements.
	She [Jacqueline] watched me with interest when I touched my forehead with my forefinger. She then put her right forefinger on her left eye, moved it over her eyebrow, then rubbed the left side of her forehead with the back of her hand, as if she were looking for something else. (Piaget, 1951, p. 56)
6. 18–24 months	This stage brings the beginning of thought. Infants imitate models who are not present and track object displacements that are not visible.
	At 1;4(3) Jacqueline had a visit from a little boy of 1;6 whom she used to see from time to time, and who, in the course of the afternoon, got into a terrible temper. He screamed as he tried to get out of a playpen and pushed it backward, stamping his feet. Jacqueline stood watching him in amazement, never having witnessed such a scene before. The next day, she herself screamed in her playpen and tried to move it, stamping her foot lightly several times in succession. (Piaget, 1951, p. 63)

NOTE: Numbers refer to age in years, months, and days, respectively.

SOURCE: Ginsburg & Opper (1988).

TESTING PIAGET'S THEORY. Piaget's writings challenged a generation of scholars to try to prove him wrong. These scientists knew that sensitive testing procedures had revealed unexpectedly good perceptual abilities early in life, so naturally they wondered whether new procedures would reveal an early understanding of concepts such as object permanence.

A clever way to tap into babies' minds is the *violation-of-expectation paradigm*, a procedure for observing how infants react to tricks that violate basic physical principles (Baillargeon, 2004). In an early study, for example, 5-month-olds watched an object disappear behind a screen. Then, when the object should have emerged on the other side, a different object appeared. Instead of accepting this slight of hand, infants searched the display for the original object, suggesting they could think about an object that was not actually present (Moore, Borton, & Darby, 1978).

Contrary to what Piaget said, there is other evidence that young infants hold information in mind when it is not in view. For example, they solve the A-not-B problem more often when they have not reached repeatedly to one side (Schutte & Spencer, 2002; Spencer, Smith, & Thelen, 2001; Thelen et al., 2001), yet even 2- and 4-year-olds make errors if they have just seen an object hidden in one location several times (Spencer & Schutte, 2004). These results suggest that difficulty inhibiting previous responses and previous mental representations—rather than a lack of object knowledge—might account for infants' illogical behavior toward objects.

But Piaget was not entirely wrong. Studies of infant behavior are an amusing mixture of unexpected successes and mysterious failures. For example, when a hand deposits objects, such as keys, near a cloth that is moved to cover them, some infants look for the objects under the cloth. But when a hand with an object slides under the cloth and emerges empty, infants also look in the last place they saw the objects: the experimenter's hand, which is now empty (Moore & Melt-zoff, 1999). This finding suggests that Piaget was right when he said that infants lack a mature understanding of objects. As one research team explained, "The baby lives in a universe that is profoundly different from our own. For us, it seems absolutely obvious that the keys must be under the cloth no matter how they're put there—where else could they be? But this is not only not obvious to the baby; it's something that has to be painstakingly learned" (Gopnik et al., 2001, p. 73).

After years of claiming that Piaget was wildly off target, scientists now acknowledge that his fundamental premise—that infants do not understand the world the way adults do—was right all along. But exactly what infants come into the world assuming and what they must learn is hotly debated. Research psychologists who lean toward *nativism* believe the mind arrives with a great deal of understanding about the world (that is, that most basic ideas are *innate*). For example, Elizabeth Spelke believes that skills such as reading and mathematics are built on a foundation of *core knowledge systems* that emerge very early (Spelke, 2000; Wood & Spelke, 2005). Core knowledge might include a basic grasp of objects, the ability to represent number for small quantities, and some understanding of how one event can cause another. On the other hand, scientists who support *empiricism* believe that experiences help construct such ideas. These individuals believe it is inappropriate to assume infants understand things the way an adult does on the basis of where they look or how surprised they act. As Marshall Haith argued, "A person can regard an event as odd without knowing why" (1998, p. 177).

Regardless of what infants know, all developmentalists now see them as "little scientists" who constantly test their environments. Like scientists, infants and children sometimes ignore facts that do not fit their expectations of the world and other times update their views of the world. And infants, like scientists, get enormous pleasure from figuring things out. Because development is less abrupt than Piaget anticipated, some scientists believe that young children get better at figuring things out due to improvements in basic cognitive processes, such as changes in attention and memory, that help them manipulate mental information more efficiently as they grow. Studying the development of these separate processes is the goal of the information processing approach.

attention The process of focusing on particular information in the environment.

discrepancy principle The idea that individuals pay more attention to information that differs somewhat—but not too much—from their existing schemes.

Information Processing

At a community playground, a young mother was keeping her eye on Emma, a little girl about 2 years old. Soon Emma approached the bench her mother was sitting on, hunched over a bit, and rubbed her hands together as if she where holding them under water. "Are you washing your hands?" her mother guessed as Emma smiled and quietly nodded "Yes." Since her last birthday, many developments have taken place in Emma's attention, memory, and ability to form concepts that have led to a dramatic increase in "pretend" (symbolic) play. Cognitive psychologists think of these skills as part of an information processing system that selects, stores, and manipulates information.

ATTENTION. You are always bombarded with more sights and sounds than your mind can handle, so you pay attention to some things and ignore others. **Attention** is the process of focusing on particular information in your environment. Because it takes years before children can effectively coordinate what they see and hear (attention) with what they are doing (action), they often focus on information that will not help them achieve their goals. Thus, food slips off spoons when they suddenly turn toward a sound, and they often ask questions but fail to listen to the answer.

Interesting developments start in the crib. Between 1 and 3 months of age, visual attention becomes "sticky" as babies seem to get caught by interesting events. This phenomenon occurs when visual pathways to the brain are developing but a specific pathway that is responsible for shifting visual focus is less mature (Rothbart & Posner, 2001). This temporary phase is useful because it causes babies to stare at faces, which helps caregivers bond with their youngsters.

Infants develop a strong preference to look at novel events between 4 and 6 months. Novelty is so engaging that most parents switch at this age from rocking cranky babies to distracting them with something interesting. What is "interesting" tends to follow the **discrepancy principle**, meaning that babies pay more attention to information that differs somewhat—but not too much—from their existing schemes. As a result, 8-month-olds who are familiar with adult faces are excited by pictures of infants but not butterflies, whereas 2-year-olds, who are familiar with all kinds of faces, are excited by butterflies. As developmental psychologist Jerome Kagan explained, "The mind grows at the edge where the expected does not occur or is moderately transformed" (Kagan, 1994, p. 39). The idea that children are most interested in things that are moderately novel is a fundamental educational principle.

Even small children rely on prior learning to direct their attention. For example, 30- to 48-month-olds look at and away from the television about 150 times per hour, but their attentional shifts are far from random (Anderson & Levin, 1976). Instead, children quickly learn to monitor sound-track features, like children's voices, which tell them when something interesting is appearing on the screen (Anderson et al., 1981). By age 3, children have favorite programs, sing commercial jingles, and ask parents for toys they have seen advertised.

But even though young children can be mesmerized by something interesting, toddlers have short attention spans when they are not caught up in an activity. Thus, it is difficult for adults to keep them entertained long enough to accomplish anything. Toddlers not only have problems *staying* on task, but they also have difficulty *leaving* tasks that have captured their interest (especially if you are trying to herd them to a less appealing activity). As their ability to hold things in memory gradually improves, children's attention spans also improve.

MEMORY. What we call "memory" is really a collection of related abilities that rely on different neural pathways. *Sensory memory* briefly holds large amounts of perceptual information, typically for less than 1 second. *Short-term memory* holds the information we are thinking about right now, which is usually limited to about four to seven "chunks" of information at any one time (Cowan, Chen, & Rouder, 2004; Miller, 1956). A related concept is **working memory**, which includes short-term memory and the processes that operate on information in short-term memory. When you add a set of numbers, for example, you have to keep numbers in mind *while* you are adding. Working memory is the entire system that holds information while you work with it, so this form of memory is critical for reasoning and problem solving (Baddeley, 2000; Handley et al., 2004).

Young infants do not hold information in working memory for very long. To study *how* long, psychologists Bena Schwartz and Steven Reznick (1999) arranged for 9-month-olds to view a playful adult who appeared in one of two windows. After their mothers spun them around in a chair, an assistant recorded where the babies looked to determine whether they remembered the adult's location. Surprisingly, only 67 percent of the infants looked to the correct location after only a *10-second* delay. With increasing age, babies maintain information in mind for longer periods of time and also hold *more* information in mind. A popular rule of thumb is that children can report back about one item in a list for every year of their age. This rule overestimates the performance of school-aged children, but nonetheless it is helpful to know that 2-year-olds may hold only two pieces of verbal information in mind at any given time (Dempster, 1981). This explains why it is best to give young children one instruction at a time ("put the blocks away") rather than several at once ("put the blocks away, drink your juice, and pick out a nighttime story").

Research on how children learn focuses on **long-term memory**, the system that records experiences for hours, weeks, or years. Infant expert Carolyn Rovee-Collier and her colleagues rely on operant conditioning to test the early emergence of long-term memory. After tying a ribbon around babies' ankles and attaching the other end of the ribbon to a mobile, the team waits for babies to discover that kicking makes the mobile move. Then the babies are put back in the crib after various lengths of time to observe whether or not they kick, indicating they remember the relationship between kicking and the interesting movement of the mobile. (Older infants and toddlers are tested by teaching them to press a lever that moves a train around a track.) As Figure 4.7 shows, the amount of time infants retain these learned responses increases regularly from 2 through 18 months of age (Rovee-Collier, Hayne, & Colombo, 2001).

Another way infants show long-term memory is by imitating actions after a delay. Even 6-month-olds can imitate actions they saw 24 hours earlier, but recall becomes more reliable during the second year of life (Barr, Dowden, & Hayne, 1996; Bauer, 2005). For example, children from 13 to 20 months often reenact three-part actions—such as putting a wooden block in one half of a barrel, putting the two barrel halves together, and shaking the barrel—up to 12 months after they performed or saw the actions. In other words, *be careful, because if toddlers are watching you, they are learning!* (Bauer et al., 2000).

working memory A memory store for holding and manipulating the mental information individuals are thinking about at any particular time.

long-term memory A memory store that records experiences for hours, weeks, or years.

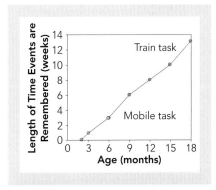

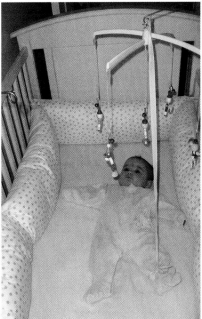

FIGURE 4.7 The development of long-term memory.

Children remember interesting experiences for longer periods of time as they grow. Below, a young infant learns that kicking makes a mobile move. The graph above shows the length of time infants remembered making a mobile or a train move.

SOURCE: Adapted from Rovee-Collier, Hayne, & Colombo (2001).

infantile amnesia The phenomenon that older children and adults typically have no memories of events that occurred before 2 to 3 years of age.

executive processes The processes involved in monitoring and controlling individuals' attention and behavior, planning, and performing multiple tasks at once.

inhibition Process that decreases the probability of neural activity. Cognitive inhibition reduces interference from distracting events, suppresses irrelevant items in memory, and blocks previous responses from occurring again.

We also know that young children remember the past because they talk about it as soon as they have words to speak. Children as young as 14 months refer to past events (Reese, 1999), and 21- to 36-month-olds chatter about the past even when they think that no one is around to hear (Nelson, 1988). But unlike some types of learning, these *autobiographical memories* do not "survive the transition" into later years (Bauer & Wewerka, 1995). In one study of memory for frightening medical procedures, no children who were 2 years old at the time of a procedure described it when they were 3 to 13 years of age, whereas two-thirds of the children who were 4 years old did (Quas et al., 1999). Memory experts use the term **infantile amnesia** to describe the fact that adults typically have no memories for things that happened before ages 2 to 3.

If young children remember moving mobiles and adults' actions, why do they fail to retain autobiographical memories? One possibility is that autobiographical memories cannot be stored until children develop a sense of self, which emerges around 2 years of age. A sense of self allows children to do more than just remember an event—it allows them to remember that "this is happening to *me*" (Howe, 2000, 2003; Howe & Courage, 1993). Once a sense of self is in place, other mechanisms gradually help children store more memories as they grow (Peterson, 2002). For example, brain areas that connect different features of events mature (Newcombe et al., 2000), and growing language skills help children consolidate memories by talking about their experiences (Fivush & Nelson, 2004; Simcock & Hayne, 2002).

INHIBITION AND EXECUTIVE PROCESSES. Some of the most striking changes during the early years stem from changes in **executive processes**, the mental events involved in controlling our attention, planning, and performing multiple tasks at once. Executive processes help you put your socks on before your shoes and pull your hand back after you remember the pan is still hot. An important component of executive processes is **inhibition**, the mechanism that *decreases* the probability of neural activity. Cognitive inhibition keeps your attention from being sidetracked by unimportant events and blocks previous responses from occurring again. Inhibitory processes keep us from being distracted by irrelevant information, help us respond flexibly when situations change, and allow us to hide our true feelings in social interactions.

In the early years, the ability *not to respond* is not very strong. For instance, when children are told to press one of two keys that matches a picture, 2-year-olds often press the key that is *on the same side* as the picture even if it does not match. A transition occurs at about 30 months of age, when toddlers perform accurately regardless of where the key appears (Gerardi-Caulton, 2000). Because the brain regions that control this type of behavioral inhibition are not mature until adulthood, children often fail tasks that seem very simple to adults.

Immature executive processes produce an interesting phenomenon during the third year of life: Young children can know a rule, yet not be able to act on it. For example, if you show 2- and 3-year-olds pictures of common objects, such as tools and items of clothing, they can easily answer questions like "Is this something you *work* with or something you can *wear*?" Yet children under 3 will find it virtually impossible to sort those pictures into two piles using a simple rule ("put tools—something you work with—by this picture of a tool; put clothes—something you wear—by this picture of clothes"), *even if you frequently remind them of the sorting rule* (Zelazo & Reznick, 1991). Unfortunately, giving a 2-year-old a rule is a bit like giving a cat a curfew.

The "terrible twos" is a popular description of children knowing what adults want but failing to inhibit what *they* want. Instead of assuming that toddlers are just being stubborn, knowledge of development can help you be more patient. As Diamond (2001) explained, "Infants and young children. . . sometimes do the wrong thing even though they know what they should do and are trying to do it. Their attention is sometimes so captured by the desired goal object that they either cannot inhibit responding. . . or cannot override the strong tendency to go straight to that goal" (p. 463).

Language Development

Infants are communication specialists who survive by coaxing others to work for them. "The baby has a role to play in keeping the care coming," and babies set themselves to the task from the moment they are born (Gibson & Pick, 2000, p. 52).

EARLY COMMUNICATION. As we mentioned earlier, newborns discriminate the basic sounds of human language, recognize their mothers' voices, and detect some characteristics of their native language. They are also calmed by human voices and elicit a great deal of speech from the adults around them (Gibson & Pick, 2000).

As summarized in Table 4.6, by 1 to 2 months of age infants are smiling when people speak to them, and by about 2 to 3 months of age they begin to "coo," making long, "sing-song-y" vowel sounds like "ooooo" and "eeeeee."

Between 3 and 7 months they respond differently to friendly and angry tones, and they produce their first laughs around 4 months. Infants babble between 6 and 8 months, producing single-syllable streams like "ba ba ba" and "ga ga ga." By 8 to 12 months this babbling acquires the up-and-down intonation of sentences, so babies already sound as if they are having a conversation. During this time, infants gradually lose some ability to discriminate features of speech that are irrelevant in their native language. For example, earlier we mentioned that the difference between "b" and "p" is a feature called *voicing.* Thai speakers recognize a third phoneme that does not exist in English (one with a very long voice-onset time), but infants in English-speaking environments gradually lose the ability to distinguish this sound (Kuhl, 2001). As perception changes, babbling begins to reflect babies' native tongues, so Japanese babies babble like Japanese babies and Russian babies babble like Russian babies.

Around their first birthdays, babies all over the world produce their first words, some a little earlier and some a little later than this average age. How do they learn these words? Their first hurdle is to break speech into words. To infants, all conversations sound the way foreign languages

TABLE 4.6	Milestones of Early Language Development
Newborn	Turns head toward sounds
	Prefers mother's voice to a stranger's
	Discriminates many speech sounds
1–3 months	Smiles and coos (e.g., "ooo") when spoken to
	Laughs
3–7 months	Responds differently to different intonations (e.g., friendly, angry)
	Makes some single syllable sounds (e.g., "ba," "ga")
	Takes turns in language interactions
7–12 months	Babbles (repeats syllables such as "bababa")
	Responds to name
	Responds to "no"
12–18 months	Points and follows the pointing of others
	Says single words
18–24 months	Combines two words
	Produces 200 words on average by 2 years
24–36 months	Continues to learn new words at a rapid pace
	Speaks increasingly longer phrases and sentences
	Adds words and endings to words that signal new grammatical relationships, such as "s" for plural, "ed" for past tense, and prepositions

SOURCES: Adapted from Sachs (2001) and Tager-Flusberg (2001).

ihaveadreamthatonedaythisnationwillriseupandliveoutthetruemeaningofitscreedweholdthesetruth
stobeselfevidentthatallmenarecreatedequalihaveadreamthatonedayontheredhillsofgeorgiathesons
offormerslavesandthesonsofformerslaveownerswillbeabletositdowntogetheratatableofbrotherhoo
dihaveadreamthatonedayeventhestateofmississippiadesertstatessweltteringwiththeheatofinjusticean
doppressionwillbetransformedintoanoasisoffreedomandjusticeihaveadreamthatmyfourchildrenwil
lonedayliveinanationwheretheywillnotbejudgedbythecolotoftheirskinbutbythecontentoftheirchara
cter.

FIGURE 4.8 The word segmentation problem.

Words sound like one continuous stream to young babies, as illustrated by this famous
passage. The frequency of sound combinations is one clue that helps babies break this
stream of speech into individual units that have meaning.

SOURCE: "I Have a Dream" by Martin Luther King, Jr., delivered on the steps at the Lincoln Memorial in
Washington, D.C. on August 28, 1963.

do to you—a stream of gibberish like the famous paragraph that is printed continuously in Figure 4.8. Infants need strategies for breaking this flow into words. By $7\frac{1}{2}$ months they start using stress patterns ("Do you want the BALL?") as a clue for separating words (Jusczyk, 2002), and they zero in on highly familiar words like their names (Bortfeld et al., 2005). Another strategy is to keep track of how often sounds repeat. For example, language expert Jenny Saffran and her colleagues (Saffran, 2003; Saffran, Aslin, & Newport, 1996) repeated 2 minutes of artificial speech to babies that consisted of four words in random order: "pabiku," "tibudo," "golatu," and "daropi." Later, 8-month-olds listened longer to combinations that had not occurred as frequently, such as "pigola," showing they kept track of how often specific combinations had occurred. But repetition isn't the whole story. Babies who hear "ga ti ga" also react as if similar patterns, such as "wo fe wo," are familiar, so they also form general rules about patterns (Marcus, 2000). In other words, infants are born with sophisticated strategies for learning their language.

Once they begin to use words, the pace of children's vocabulary growth is astounding. Most start out slowly, gaining only 8 to 11 new words each month (Benedict, 1979), and then have a "word spurt" once their vocabulary size reaches about 50 words (Fenson et al., 1994). As we will discuss more in a later chapter, children have working vocabularies of between 8,000 and 14,000 words by 6 years of age, which means they learn about 5 to 8 new words per day after the age of 1 year (Carey, 1978). Children can learn rapidly because they sometimes assign meaning to a word the first time they hear it through a process called **fast mapping**. Fast mapping occurs when children quickly link, or map, a word onto concepts they already know. But because these early attempts at meaning are often incomplete, children sometimes use words too broadly or too narrowly. As a result, it is not uncommon for toddlers to call almost any animal a "doggie" or to deny that bathing suits or pajamas are "clothes."

Children start putting two words together about 7 months after they say their first words (Reich, 1986). These multiple-word utterances mark the emergence of **syntax**, the rules for arranging words and other meaningful units (such as "s" and "ed") in sentences. Early sentences are **telegraphic** because they lack function words like prepositions and articles ("Daddy book"), the very words people used to omit from telegrams to save money ("Train station 6:00"). As children's knowledge of syntactic (grammatical) rules expands, they frequently apply rules in situations where the rules don't apply. Thus, children charmingly apply the plural "s" to create words such as "mouses" or "teeths," and the regular past tense "ed" to create words such as "goed" or "putted." This behavior, which is called **overregularization**, shows that children are developing hypotheses about language rules. But it takes years to learn the syntactic rules of a language, which is why 3-year-olds do not understand long or complicated sentences.

When toddlers start chattering in earnest, what do they talk about? From the time language begins, they talk about their desires, perceptions, and emotions. As a result, *want*, *no*, and *sad* are among their earliest words. By their third birthdays,

fast mapping The process of assigning meaning to a new word by quickly linking the word onto concepts that are already known.

syntax The rules for combining words and other meaningful units (such as "s" and "ed").

telegraphic speech Early word combinations that lack prepositions, articles, and other function words.

overregularization The use of a linguistic rule in a situation in which it doesn't apply, such as when children say "mouses" or "I putted it away."

children talk about differences in other people's desires, perceptions, and emotions. As one 2-year-old explained weeks after a disappointing dessert, "You know what, Mommy, pineapple is yummy for you, but it's yucky for me" (Gopnik et al., 2001, p. 43). It is easy for adults to be fooled by such eloquence* and think children know more about language than they really do. In fact, important developments are yet to come in all areas of language development. For example, it will be years before this 2-year-old can pronounce all of the sounds of English or understand the social uses of language, such as how to ask politely and how to tell a good story.

Children's remarkable ability to learn language without special instruction continues for many years. In the past, language experts thought there was a *critical period* for language acquisition because people who learn a second language close to or after puberty typically do not develop pronunciation or grammatical skill equal to those who learned earlier (Lenneberg, 1967). But newer data do not support the idea that a window for learning closes at any particular time. Instead, mastery of a second language seems to decline gradually throughout life (Hakuta, Bialystok, & Wiley, 2003; Wiley, Bialystok, & Hakuta, 2005; Yeni-Komshian, Flege, & Liu, 2000).

HOW LANGUAGE DEVELOPS. Many species communicate, but other animals produce only a small number of sounds or gestures that carry specific meanings. Amid all the excitement about chimpanzees and gorillas using sign language, the best-kept secret is how little they actually learn. Even a well-trained chimp produces utterances like, "Give orange me give eat orange me eat orange give me eat orange give me you." As cognitive psychologist Steven Pinker (1994) remarked, "What impresses one the most about chimpanzee signing is that, fundamentally, deep down, chimps just don't 'get it'" (p. 340). Zoologist E. O. Wilson cast a similar vote when he said that animal communication was "repetitious to the point of inanity" (Pinker, 1994, p. 340). In contrast, humans combine meaningless phonemes to produce an infinite number of utterances. How do we accomplish this incredible feat?

The early behaviorists believed that language was learned the same way other behaviors were learned—by imitation and reinforcement (Skinner, 1957). In contrast, linguists* argued that imitation and reinforcement *do not* direct language learning, even though these mechanisms might be involved in some minor way. To argue their point, they mentioned that parents generally reinforce children when the *meaning* of what they say is correct, even when children say something the wrong way ("Doggy goed splash!", "That's right, he did."). Furthermore, language does seem to be a special type of behavior because infants move in synchrony with voices but not other sounds (Condon & Sander, 1974).

The linguistic approach was spearheaded by Noam Chomsky, a theorist who proposed that babies are born with a **language acquisition device (LAD)**. The LAD is a hypothetical mental structure that houses basic assumptions about language and strategies for learning language (Chomsky, 1957, 1965). These things might include inborn strategies for breaking the language stream into units, an understanding that nouns and verbs are separate classes of words, and a set of rules that specifies how these classes of words might be combined. According to Chomsky, children's task is to listen to the language around them and figure out which rules are important in their particular language. To do this, they use learning

language acquisition device (LAD) A hypothetical mental structure, including innate assumptions about the nature of language, that allows children to learn language.

---

*eloquence: Powerful, persuasive speech.

*linguist: A person who studies the structure of human languages.

child-directed speech The speech older children and adults use with young children, which is often simpler and more predictable than speech directed at adults.

Gua (16 months) and Donald (18 1/2 months) as they looked waiting for bedtime. The attempt to rear the pair together was not a success for Donald or Gua: Donald was not developing as he should with Gua as his playmate, and Gua failed to adjust to captivity after the Ape and the Child study ended and died shortly afterward. All young depend on the early experiences members of their species usually provide to grow up well adjusted.

SOURCE: Kellogg & Kellogg (1933/1967).

Archives of the History of American Psychology–The University of Akron.

strategies that are uniquely suited for decoding language (Slobin, 1979). At any point in time, knowledge is represented as working hypotheses about the structure of language. The linguistic approach explains the regularity of language acquisition across cultures and the fact that children say things they have never heard ("Daddy comed! Daddy comed!").

Many contemporary views of language development recognize that multiple factors influence language development. As Pinker explained, "There has to be something innate—otherwise house cats would learn language the same way that children do. But a whole language can't be innate" (Monastersky, 2001, p. A15). One example of this line of thinking is the *social interaction* approach. According to this perspective, language emerges out of the functions it serves in social contexts and, therefore, children develop more mature ways of communicating as they develop more sophisticated ways of relating to others (Bohannon & Bonvillian, 2001). For example, children who are experiencing a vocabulary spurt generally initiate interactions about activities that interest them, which prompts their mothers to provide reflections and feedback ("Are you putting the baby bear to bed too?") (Bloom & Tinker, 2001). In this way, children are actively involved in directing their own learning. The social interaction approach is part of a broader movement to study cognitive development in the real-life social situations where most human learning occurs.

Social Interaction and Cognitive Development

Psychologist Winthrop Kellogg and his wife Luella wanted to know what chimpanzees were capable of learning. To find out, the spunky couple adopted $7\frac{1}{2}$-month-old Gua, a chimp, and reared her for 9 months with their own son, Donald. The Kelloggs treated Gua exactly as children were treated in 1931, including dressing her in stylish clothing and building her a chimp-sized "walker." Gua and Donald, who was $2\frac{1}{2}$ months older, were splendid playmates. In fact, Gua outshined her brother on many tasks, including using a spoon and flicking light switches (Kellogg & Kellogg, 1933/1967). But Donald was the superior imitator. Before long, Donald was biting walls, chimp-barking in the presence of food, and generally proving to be a bit of a disappointment to his parents. Whereas the average 19-month-old produces more than 50 words, Donald spoke only three when Gua was shipped away. Writer Judith Harris (1998) summed up this demonstration perfectly when she quipped, "The Kelloggs had tried to train an ape to be a human. Instead, it seemed that Gua was training their son to be an ape" (p. 100).

There is no doubt that children learn new behaviors from social interactions. What is less obvious is that older children and adults also alter their behavior when they interact with children. One frequently studied example is the language addressed to children, which is called adult–child or **child-directed speech**. In many cultures, adults talk to babies using a high-pitched, singsongy, and slow style that exaggerates vowel sounds. Adults are rewarded for these efforts because babies prefer such speech. Child-directed speech was once called *motherese*, but research has shown that fathers, grandmothers, and even older children talk differently to young children than they do to one another (Shatz

& Gelman, 1973; Shute & Wheldall, 1999, 2001). Long after baby talk ends, adults continue to provide youngsters with clues to meaning by synchronizing words and actions, talking about the here and now, and using short, error-free utterances (Gogate, Bahrick, & Watson, 2000; Reich, 1986).

Older siblings and adults use many techniques to help infants and toddlers learn, including drawing their attention to objects, controlling frustration by providing assistance, and demonstrating solutions to problems (Stone, 1998). As we mentioned in Chapter 1, many developmentalists have been influenced by Vygotsky's idea that older children and adults help younger children learn by bridging the gap between what children can do themselves and what they are capable of doing with assistance—a distance that Vygotsky called the *zone of proximal development*. Later, Vygotsky's theory inspired developmentalists to adopt the **scaffolding** metaphor to describe this process: Just as a scaffold is a temporary structure that helps people construct a building, the behavior of others acts as temporary support that enables children to build new skills (de Vries, 2005).

Does child-directed speech and scaffolding actually enhance development? Not always. Children learn basic survival skills across a wide range of environments, so infants learn to speak in cultures that do not use infant-directed speech just as they learn to walk without special instruction. But patterns of social interaction do predict less universal behaviors. In one study, for example, mothers who offered objects, demonstrated, and pointed more than other mothers had toddlers who scored higher on a test of infant development (Stevens et al., 1998). Because learning is often a social activity, psychologists and educators now view healthy social and emotional development as a critical foundation for learning.

scaffolding The process whereby competent mentors encourage development by providing clues, prompting, or modeling a skill.

>>> **MEMORY MAKERS** <<<

Which word or phrase in each pair best describes the sensorimotor stage of cognitive development?

1. (a) infants passively absorb new knowledge *or*
   (b) infants actively direct their own learning

2. (a) infants develop object permanence *or*
   (b) infants think logically about objects

3. (a) infants switch attention easily *or*
   (b) infants make the A-not-B error

4. (a) newborns have mental representations *or*
   (b) newborns develop mental representations

5. "Sticky" vision, novelty preference, and the discrepancy principle are concepts that explain how infants _____.
   (a) direct their attention   (b) remember new information   (c) learn new skills

6. Children's early sentences are called ___ because they lack function words.
   (a) telegraphic   (b) generalized   (c) truncated   (d) syntactic

7. Vygotsky used the term ___ to describe how older children and adults help younger children learn by assisting with tasks that are a little too hard for children to complete on their own.
   (a) overregularization   (b) scaffolding
   (c) child-directed speech   (d) task construction

[1-b; 2-a; 3-b; 4-b; 5-a; 6-a; 7-b]

Emotional and Social Development

If emotional reactions and social skills are part of our personalities, babies seem to become different babies altogether every few months. Newborn Bret, for example, cried each day between 4 and 6 o'clock, for no apparent reason. In a few short months his irritable personality gave way to smiling, laughter, and delight at anything new. Then frustration joined his repertoire of emotions during the time when 2-year-olds like "No!" more than any other word. By his third birthday, Bret had discovered how to get what he wanted from his parents by acting cute instead of demanding. It is remarkable that the basic emotional tools we use to navigate our social environments—from excitement and joy to jealousy and guilt—emerge during the first 2 to 3 years of our lives.

Early Emotional Expression

Emotional life begins at birth, when young infants' faces signal disgust, distress, and interest (Snow, 1998). But early expressions are not yet linked to specific emotions because newborns smile during sleep and when they are merely contented. Social smiling—the ability to smile predictably at other people—appears at about 4 to 6 weeks of age, and joyful expressions and laughter arrive at around 3 months.

Anger, surprise, and sad but noncrying expressions join infants' list of faces at about 3 to 4 months of age. Then, at around 6 to 7 months, fear suddenly becomes a fact of life as the memory abilities that support more complex thinking emerge. Most infants this age start to show *stranger anxiety* by fretting or crying when unfamiliar adults approach, and by 8 to 9 months they show *separation anxiety* when a familiar caregiver leaves. The intensity of these reactions typically increases for about 4 months and then tapers off. Subtle behaviors that signal shame, shyness, embarrassment, and guilt appear at around 2 years of age.

Figure 4.9 illustrates two viewpoints on these developments. According to the traditional view, *basic emotions* like happiness and fear appear early whereas *nonbasic emotions*, like jealousy, guilt, or pride, require a level of interpersonal awareness that is not available until the second year of life. An alternative view is that nonbasic emotions also emerge early but in a form that does not require a sophisticated level of social awareness (Draghi-Lorenz, Reddy, & Costall, 2001). For example, infants younger than 1 year old sometimes act jealous when their mothers hold other babies, but they probably are not thinking about whether their mother will have time to read them a book later in the day. Complicated emotions emerge gradually, so the "guilt" or "jealousy" of an infant does not have the richness of meaning these emotions have to a 3-year-old.

What causes new emotional expressions to appear? Emotions are linked to cognition and social interactions, so toddlers begin to feel self-conscious and guilty as they

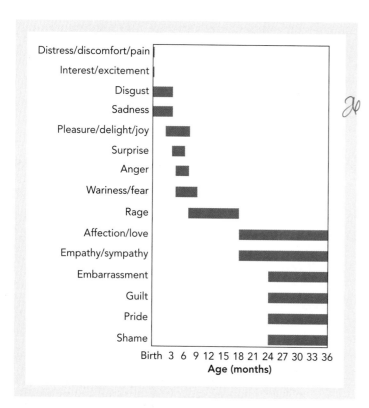

FIGURE 4.9 Emotional expression during the first 3 years.

Most infants clearly show emotions at the ages indicated by the bars. Some emotion theorists believe that complex emotions, such as embarrassment and guilt, can be observed in younger infants.

SOURCE: Adapted from Snow (1998).

begin to think more complexly about themselves and other people. At all ages, our emotional and social lives are tightly connected.

social referencing A strategy for deciding how to react by watching how other people are reacting.

Early Social Interactions

We are all familiar with the rhythm of social interaction, as illustrated in this essay on the fine art of flirting (Gopnik et al., 2001):

> Flirting is largely a matter of timing. If you look around at a party, you can tell who's flirting just by looking at them, without even hearing a word. What you see is the way two people time their gestures so they're in sync with each other and with nobody else in the crowded room. She brushes her hair off her face, and he puts his hands in his pocket; she leans forward eagerly and talks, and he leans back sympathetically and listens. (p. 31)

Social rhythm begins even before children can speak. Babies flirt by 3 months of age, cooing in response to goofy talk from adults and smiling in response to smiles, creating "an intricate dance, a kind of wordless conversation, a silly love song, pillow talk. It's sheer heaven" (Gopnik et al., 2001, p. 31). Infants create rhythmic "dialogues" with adults by alternating short vocalizations with "switching" pauses that invite the other person to take a turn. These routines are more than just amusement: They are the foundation for human interaction. Taking turns is well established by the end of the first year, and 4-month-olds who coordinate their behavior with an adult later score higher on tests of cognitive development than less responsive infants do (Jaffe et al., 2001; Warren & McCloskey, 1997).

WATCHING THE WORLD TOGETHER. Coordinated "dialogues" are followed by another important accomplishment: *joint visual attention.* The simple act of looking where adults look helps infants learn language by telling them which objects are under discussion. For example, when an experimenter told 16- to 19-month-olds the names of unfamiliar objects, learning occurred only when both of them were looking at the target object, that is, when there was joint visual attention (Baldwin, 1991).

Ten-month-olds look in the general direction in which adults are looking, but 12- to 18-month-olds become skilled at looking *exactly* where adults are looking. This new stage of joint attention begins at the same time pointing does. At 6 to 9 months, babies often look at the pointing hand rather than the target, but by 12 months they direct their visual attention quickly and accurately. Pointing has been called the "royal road from pre-verbal communication into spoken language" because babies who point earlier have better speech comprehension months later (Butterworth, 1998, p. 171). Once babies are signaling other people to look at objects and events, "Daaa?" or simply "That?" is a favorite word, often said dozens of times a day.

Children also consult people's facial expressions for emotional information that will help them choose their own reactions. This behavior, called **social referencing**, occurs especially often when children are in unfamiliar situations. In one demonstration, for example, volunteer mothers placed an attractive toy on the "deep" side of a visual cliff, not unlike the one you saw in Figure 4.5, while their infants watched from the shallow side. When their mothers looked happy, 14 out of 19 babies crossed onto the deep side, whereas none of the babies who watched a fearful mother did (Sorce et al., 2000). Social referencing may explain why some fearful toddlers become more relaxed over time if they are reared by calm, relaxed caregivers.

This toddler is looking exactly where her mother is pointing. Once accurate joint attention emerges between 12 and 18 months, children's vocabularies expand rapidly because they can map what they are seeing onto what people are saying. As a result, this little one will be chatting away furiously within a few months.

PLAYING WITH FRIENDS. Children's developing social interactions often involve other children. Babies as young as 2 months stare at other babies, and by 6 to 9 months they vocalize and smile at each other. By the second year, infants change their behavior depending on the age of their social partners (Brownell, 1990), and their social behavior becomes better coordinated and is maintained for longer periods of time.

Young toddlers generally engage in *parallel play* (playing close to other children but without interaction) (Howes & Matheson, 1992; Parten, 1932). By 13-15 months most also show *complementary and reciprocal play*, a type of play in which each partner's actions reverse the other person's actions. These young-sters chase and are chased, or peek and say boo after their partner peeks and says boo. Play becomes more gamelike between 18 and 24 months of age. Now children frequently give and take back or exchange verbal turns, but they still rarely cooperate.

It is exciting when youngsters start to incorporate symbols into their play. During the first stage of this pretend play, called *cooperative social pretend play*, children show nonliteral exchanges, such as passing a miniature cup to some-one holding a miniature pitcher. This type of interaction is observed in over half of 30- to 35-month-olds (Howes & Tonyan, 1999). Now children are more likely to imitate each other's behavior or initiate a social interaction by doing something related to the ongoing activity. (Pretend play is what Emma was doing when she pretended to wash her hands near her mother.) This type of play is part of a collection of symbolic behavior that starts by the second year of life and is in "full swing" by 24 months (Lillard & Witherington, 2004), in-cluding pointing and using other gestures to communicate (Iverson & Goldin-Meadow, 2005). But although children have the *potential* for interesting interactions with others, 2- and 3-year-olds are not mature enough to cooper-ate for long periods.

Toddlers are very social creatures who often bid annoyingly for attention from adults whenever a playmate can't be found. But there is not a direct relation-ship between the feedback we give them ("Not now, honey") and their behavior ("I said, 'Not NOW!'"). Their frequent lack of desire to please us makes sense if we consider that young children are experimenting with a fascinating new discovery: the realization that other people have desires that don't match their own.

"I Do MySELF!"

A light goes on in the minds of toddlers during the last half of their second year: Suddenly, the world is organized around "me" versus "you." But developing a con-cept of self is more gradual than it seems. By 4 months infants react differently to mirror images of themselves than to images of an adult who is mimicking their behavior, and by 9 months they increasingly try to engage those adults in social interactions, indicating they know the difference between their reflections and those of other people (Rochat & Striano, 2002). But the gold standard of self-recognition is how children react during a procedure known as the "rouge" task. If you put a spot of red rouge on babies' faces and place them in front of a mirror, at 18 months old some of them will touch *themselves* rather than their mirror images. These self-aware toddlers also act with self-consciousness in front of the mirror, smiling shyly or touching themselves in adorable displays of budding awareness (Howe & Courage, 1993).

There are other signs that 18 months is a landmark time for children's emerging sense of self. Early pointing involves pointing at objects or other people, but around 18 months children begin pointing at themselves, indicating "me." Driven more by maturation than the environment, about 75 percent of children show self-recognition at the end of the second year, but other children develop more slowly (Howe, 2000).

As soon as the world is categorized into "me" and "you," toddlers show glimmers of a wide range of social judgments and emotions. Two-year-olds can make inferences about other people's feelings, so they sometimes soothe people who are sad. They also begin applying the categories of "good" and "bad" to their own actions. For instance, they push food on the floor and look at their fathers with anticipation, knowing they violated a rule, and they may fret about things that are "bad," such as broken toys or small flaws on their high-chair tray (Kagan, 1998).

Unfortunately, these early glimmers of moral behavior don't translate into perfect behavior. Toddlers are still learning, still testing. They can know that an action is wrong without knowing what will happen if they do it anyway. So they experiment. They reach slowly for a vase while looking at their mothers and smiling, or they refuse to put on their clothes. Apparently, it is one thing to know that other people have different desires than you do but another thing altogether to know when differences will create conflict. "The child is a budding psychologist, we parents are the laboratory rats," one team of psychologists explained. "It may be some comfort to know that these toddlers don't really want to drive us crazy, they just want to understand how we work" (Gopnik et al., 2001, p. 38). Their intense interest in us began months earlier, with a process psychologists call "attachment."

Attachment: Balancing Intimacy and Autonomy

One riddle of life is how to strike a balance between our need for intimacy and our desire for autonomy (independence). According to some theorists, this challenge is the first significant conflict that children confront. Others go one step further and assume our adult personalities and relationships are influenced by how we managed this early conflict. The developmental theorists you will read about next believed that healthy emotional attachments early in life help children meet their needs for intimacy and autonomy throughout life.

FREUD'S ACCOUNT OF INFANT ATTACHMENT.
Freud's psychoanalytic theory assumes that personality starts to form as soon as infants interact with their mothers. In the *oral stage*, from birth through 18 months, infants achieve pleasure primarily from sucking and biting, said Freud. Because infants' strongest need is to take in food, Freud assumed they developed bonds to the mothers who satisfy this need.

Baby rhesus monkeys prefer the contact comfort of a soft mother over the hard wire mother that feeds them. Human babies also bond to the people who hold and cuddle them.

There are many challenges to the idea that attachment develops to the person who feeds an infant. The most famous blow came from primatologist Harry Harlow, who worked at the University of Wisconsin in the 1950s. When Harlow and his associates separated baby monkeys from their mothers and reared them on bottles, they found that the babies developed strong attachments to the pads that lined their cage bottoms (Harlow, 1959). The distress the monkeys showed when the pads were removed for cleaning led Harlow to conduct a clever experiment. He raised baby monkeys in cages with two surrogate* "mothers." Half of the infants were fed by a stiff wire mother while the other infants were fed by a similar mother covered with cloth. Regardless of who fed the monkeys, they clung to the cloth mother most of the time and ran to her for comfort when they were frightened (Harlow & Zimmermann, 1959). These studies have been widely cited as evidence that contact comfort, rather than food, is the primary basis for infant emotional attachment.

ERIKSON ON TRUST AND AUTONOMY. Erik Erikson's psychodynamic theory reframed Freud's ideas. It is not feeding itself that influences infants, Erikson said, but rather their general sense of whether they will be cared for consistently. During his first psychosocial stage, **basic trust versus mistrust**, infants with responsive parents develop basic trust in the world, which promotes later exploration and independence, whereas those with unresponsive parents become mistrustful. But it is not healthy to be entirely trusting, so individual cultures value trust to varying degrees. For example, a baby in some cultures is fed at the earliest whimper, whereas in others he is "forced to cry 'please' for his meals until he literally gets blue in the face" (Erikson, 1959, p. 57). The mouth, then, is "the territory where the infant first meets his future tribe or nation"—a baby's first exposure to the values of his social group (Coles, 1970, p. 69).

It annoyed Erikson when people thought of concepts such as trust as "achievements" that occur at particular points in time because people confront trust issues throughout their lives (Erikson, 1959). Still, he described infancy as a special time when assumptions about trust are forged most easily. Between 18 months and 3 years of age, Erikson said that children entered a second stage of **autonomy versus shame and doubt**, when their biggest emotional challenge is to develop a sense of autonomy or independence. Now that children are potty training and learning to feed themselves, they are responsive to feedback about their successes and failures. Erikson thought that parents who do not set boundaries will fail to develop their children's sense of safety, whereas those who expect too much will leave their children feeling defeated.

THE ETHOLOGICAL APPROACH TO ATTACHMENT. Psychiatrist John Bowlby's interest in attachment began when he worked in a home for troubled boys. In an article entitled, "Forty-four Juvenile Thieves: Their Characters and Home Life," Bowlby (1944) argued that major disruptions in mother–child relationships were a frequent reality in the lives of delinquent boys. After writing a monograph on orphaned infants, Bowlby developed two convictions: that infants' early relationships with a mother or substitute caretaker were critical, and that Freud's account of why babies attached to their caregivers did not fit the facts. "But if this theory did not seem to me to fit the facts," Bowlby (1980) asked, ". . .what was the alternative?" (p. 650).

In his answer, Bowlby proposed that infants are biologically driven to maintain closeness to their mothers in order to survive. Through daily interactions, infants learn about their primary caretaker's accessibility and responsiveness, and

basic trust versus mistrust The first stage of Erik Erikson's psychosocial theory, when sensitive caregiving gives infants from birth to 18 months of age a basic sense of trust in the world. Unresponsive or unpredictable caregiving leads infants to be mistrustful.

autonomy versus shame and doubt The second stage of Erik Erikson's psychosocial theory, when children from 18 months to 3 years of age react to feedback about their successes and failures by developing confidence in their abilities (autonomy) or feeling shame and doubt.

---

*surrogate: A substitute.

through these interactions they develop mental representations of one or more attachment figures and themselves.

Mary Ainsworth, an influential colleague of Bowlby's, described one of the most important consequences of attachment (Ainsworth & Marvin, 1995). Guided by ideas from her graduate school mentor, Ainsworth noticed that infants all over the world use attachment figures as secure bases for exploration. In other words, infants need parents to survive, but they also need to venture into the environment in order to learn and develop. Infants make decisions to explore or play it safe based on their evaluation of the environment and their caretaker's past behavior. For example, toddlers playing in an empty playground scurry happily away from their mothers, but they act clingy when unfamiliar children are near. Thus, the attachment bond is more than just an emotional system: It is a system that promotes cognitive development by giving children the sense of safety they need to learn. As Bowlby (1988) later explained, "All of us, from cradle to grave, are happiest when life is organized as a series of excursions, long or short, from the secure base provided by our attachment figure(s)" (p. 62).

Ainsworth created a way to classify infants by watching their attachment and exploration behaviors (Ainsworth et al., 1978). Her procedure, called the **Strange Situation**, begins when a parent and infant are introduced to an unfamiliar room. After a brief adjustment period, a stranger enters and plays with the infant for 1 minute. The infant's behavior is then observed at three points: while the parent leaves the room and returns, while the infant is left alone briefly, and when the infant is rejoined by the stranger and the parent.

Ainsworth described three attachment classifications (Ainsworth et al., 1978):

1. *Secure infants* use their mothers as a base for exploration. These infants show signs of missing mothers who are leaving the room and greet her when she returns. Once secure infants are comforted, they actively explore their environment.

2. *Insecure avoidant infants* do not react when mother leaves and avoid her when she returns. They stiffen when they are picked up and seem more interested in toys than their mother.

3. *Insecure ambivalent (or resistant) infants* are either fussy or passive. These infants are distressed when their mother leaves but are not easily comforted when she returns. Insecure ambivalent infants do not explore much and often act inconsistently, alternating requests for contact with signs of anger or rejection.

Other researchers subsequently added a fourth category to describe most of the 15 percent of infants who do not fit into the first three groups (Main & Solomon, 1990). These *disorganized infants* seem confused and disoriented, as if they cannot decide how to respond to their mother's comings and goings, and some appear fearful of the parent (Solomon & George, 1999).

What accounts for individual differences in attachment styles? According to attachment theory, parental behavior is critical. Mothers of securely attached infants respond promptly, affectionately, and appropriately to their babies' signals. Mothers of avoidant infants are rejecting, and mothers of ambivalent infants are inconsistent. Disorganized infants have troubled mother–infant interactions including, in some cases, maltreatment.

Attachment theorists believe the emotional foundation of secure attachment forecasts favorable adjustment later in life. As Bowlby (1982) explained, "A young child's experience of an encouraging, supportive and co-operative mother, and a little later father, gives him a sense of worth, a belief in the helpfulness of others, and

Strange Situation A sequence of events staged in the laboratory to measure infants' attachment behaviors.

Infants form attachments to all of the important people in their lives.

a favourable model on which to build future relationships" (p. 378). In sum, attachment theory contains four main ideas: (1) Infants in all cultures become attached to one or more caregivers, (2) secure attachment is typical and desirable, (3) maternal sensitivity is the major cause of secure attachment, and (4) attachment security predicts emotional and social competence throughout life (van IJzendoorn & Sagi, 1999). These cornerstones of attachment theory prompted an immediate and enthusiastic response from the field of human development: "Let the research begin."

EVALUATING ATTACHMENT THEORY. The idea that a 30-minute interaction might capture the relationship between a mother and child, and predict the quality of later relationships, seemed implausible to critics of attachment theory. Some argued that early behaviors solve particular developmental problems that are unrelated to similar behaviors later in life (Kagan, 1998). For example, proximity to the mother during the toddler years promotes survival by protecting the child from physical dangers, such as falling into fires, but there is no logical reason why this early behavior should predict a person's later behavior in romantic relationships, where another developmental issue (reproduction) is at stake.

One critic of attachment theory, Jerome Kagan (1998), believes that behavior in the Strange Situation reflects normal variations in child-rearing practice and temperamental differences. For example, children who are dropped off at a day care center each day may not fuss when mother leaves because they are accustomed to the routine—not because they are insecurely attached. The Strange Situation may also be measuring individual differences in *temperament*, which are biologically based differences in how children react to stimulation and change. For example, some babies are irritable and fearful in any new situation, so these babies fuss more when strangers approach and are categorized as insecurely attached. But many of these babies have sensitive, predictable mothers, so it is unfair to blame mothers for their children's later difficulties.

How have the four major ideas of attachment theory held up under scrutiny? As with most theories of behavior, this one has some strengths and limitations:

▶ The hypotheses that infants across cultures become attached to caregivers, and that secure attachment is typical and desirable, are well supported. In samples ranging from the Israeli kibbutzim (where infants sleep away from their parents) to the Efé in Africa (where babies nurse from several adult females), secure attachment is the most common pattern and the one adults consider ideal (van IJzendoorn & Sagi, 1999).

▶ The central premise of attachment theory—that sensitive parenting promotes secure attachment—has not received consistent support (de Wolff & van IJzendoorn, 1997). In one study of West African mothers and infants, traditional measures of maternal sensitivity failed to predict infant security (although frightening behavior, such as rough handling and approaching aggressively, did) (True, Pisani, & Oumar, 2001). But a review of parenting interventions did find that promoting sensitive parenting can reduce symptoms of disorganized attachment (Bakermans-Kranenburg, van IJzendoorn, & Juffer, 2005). These results suggest that caregiver behavior sometimes matters but that most of the variation we see among parents doesn't matter very much.

▶ The idea that attachment security relates to later social competence also has limited support. Secure attachment predicts harmonious relationships between mothers and infants during the early years but not always later in development. Regarding other relationships, early attachment predicts functioning in intimate relationships better than nonintimate relationships, so secure attachment predicts the quality of close friendships better than the quality of children's relationships with other peers (Schneider, Atkinson, & Tardif, 2001).

Supporters of attachment theory are not upset by some conflicting results. As Mary Ainsworth explained, many factors influence how children respond in situations that do not involve close ties, and no one ever claimed that the attachment system single-handedly directs the course of development (Ainsworth & Marvin, 1995). It is best to think of attachment as the beginning in a long chain of events that influence children, any of which might cause discrepancies between early emotional functioning and later adjustment. Therefore, attachment research is a wonderful reminder that the environment matters but that it is rare for any single influence to matter a lot.

Of course, most attachment studies look at children who at least have a mother. But what happens to children whose environments are not like typical human environments? Will behavioral developments occur normally, but later? Are some abilities spared while others are thrown off course? To explore these questions, turn to our *Solutions* feature, "What Babies Need: Studies of Orphanage-Reared Infants."

Studies of infants reared in orphanages help us understand what babies need to develop normal mental skills and social behavior. In addition to adequate food and medical care, environments for babies should be stimulating, provide opportunities for them to experience the effects of their own actions, and allow them to bond emotionally with specific caregivers.

WHAT BABIES NEED: STUDIES OF ORPHANAGE-REARED INFANTS

Child advocates have long feared that raising babies in orphanages would prevent them from forming secure emotional attachments. More recently, the discovery that environmental stimulation is necessary for normal perceptual development raised concern about whether the quality of life in orphanages was sufficient to promote normal mental development. By the early 1990s, the fall of a communist regime in Romania had given scientists the opportunity to look at these issues.

The tragedy began during the regime of dictator Nicolai Ceauçescu. Determined to increase Romania's population, Ceauçescu instituted policies to penalize small families and ban birth control and most abortions. Due to harsh economic conditions, many parents were unable to provide for their children, and more than 600 state institutions were filled with 142,000 abandoned children by the time Ceauçescu was overthrown (Children's Health Care Collaborative Study Group, 1992; Hunt, 1991). As illustrated by the following report, some children lived in circumstances that rarely exist in a modern industrialized country:

> Children were sometimes two in a crib, and all wore sweaters and knitted caps in their beds to keep them warm. In that dirty, foul-smelling orphanage there were no pictures, no heating ovens, no outside play equipment, and it was there that we saw a child who had pulled out hunks of her own hair, another . . . who rocked back and forth hitting his head against the metal bars of his crib, and at least three . . . children who shrank from my hand when I extended it toward them . . . [In the] worst orphanage I saw, 2- and 3-year-olds sat on plastic potties placed on small individual chairs four times a day for a half-hour each time. And the amazing thing was that they did just sit. (Ames, 1990, in Castle et al., 1999, p. 426)

After reports like this one became known, representatives from aid organizations and private citizens quickly flocked to Romania. Many families brought children back to the United Kingdom, Canada, and the United States where they were later enrolled in studies to track their progress.

Personal stories in the mass media told of disturbed, unmanageable children who taxed their parents' limits. But scientific reports painted a more complicated picture of how early deprivation influenced later development. For example, the scatter plot in Figure 4.10 shows the relationship between cognitive development scores for one group of children and the ages when they joined their adoptive households (Rutter et al., 2004). Notice that the lowest scores are from children who had spent the longest time in institutional care. Still, a striking feature of these data is how variable they are: Every group, regardless of age at time of adoption, had children at and above the expected average of 100 and children below that average. Despite some disturbing outcomes, many of these orphans demonstrated remarkable *resilience*, the ability to rebound from challenging conditions. (You will read more about resilience in Chapter 11.) Still, a significant number of institutionally raised children *are* markedly inattentive and fail to show preferences for specific caregivers or friends (Roy, Rutter, & Pickles, 2004).

What is it about institutional care that hinders development? To answer this question, developmental psychologist Megan Gunnar (2001) reviewed studies of children in several countries who had experienced three levels of privation. Children who experienced "global privation" did not have their basic health and nutritional needs met, nor did they have adequate stimulation or the opportunity to form meaningful relationships. Other children had been housed in institutions that met their medical needs but not their needs for stimulation and relationships. Finally, some institutions provided adequate physical caregiving and stimulation, but staff changes prevented children from forming long-term relationships.

The results tell an important story. First, it is not enough to meet infants' medical needs; humans need psychological stimulation to develop normally. Children reared with inadequate stimulation experience devastating developmental delays and are listless and passive. According to Gunnar, these findings suggest that the motivation to act requires "response-contingent" stimulation, that is, stimulation in which children experience the effects of their own behavior on objects and people. Second, environments that provide sufficient stimulation but deprive children of opportunities to develop consistent social relationships often produce children who have problems with higher-level skills, such as regulating attention and inhibiting inappropriate behavior. For example, one study found that 16-year-olds who were reared in orphanages that did not provide opportunities to form long-term relationships often had clinically significant problems with concentration (Hodges & Tizard, 1989).

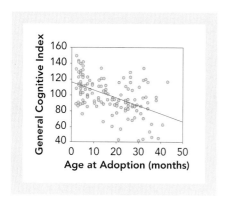

Figure 4.10 The mental development of Romanian adoptees.

At 6 years old, children who spent the most time in an orphanage before being adopted by families in the United Kingdom scored lower than other adoptees on a test of cognitive development. But it is hard to predict how any *individual* child will develop because there are children with high and low scores in every group.

Source: Rutter, O'Connor, and the English and Romanian Adoptees (ERA) Study Team (2004).

In sum, stimulation that is adequate for sensory and motor development may not be enough to support the development of higher-level skills, such as responding appropriately to social cues and boundaries. Unlike general intelligence, these advanced functions are impaired by short-term deprivation and show less recovery after children are transferred into stimulating environments. What is it about consistent child–adult relationships that promotes normal development? The answer is not yet known. It is possible that caregiver changes trigger stress hormones that interfere with normal brain development. But it is also possible that humans simply need relationships where "persons, more so than the functions they serve, emerge as the salient elements over time" (Gunnar, 2001, p. 626).

⟩⟩⟩ MEMORY MAKERS ⟨⟨⟨

1. Match each emotion with the age when it typically emerges: social smiles _A_, laughter _b_, fear of strangers _C_, embarrassment and guilt _D_.

   (a) 4 to 6 weeks
   (b) 3 months
   (c) 6 to 7 months
   (d) 2 years

2. Young Max was wary of the neighbor's Saint Bernard and looked at his mother. When his mother smiled, Max walked toward the dog. This interaction illustrates _D_.

   (a) the discrepancy principle   (b) nurturant behavior
   (c) infant states   (d) social referencing

3. The _____ Situation is a procedure for measuring infants' patterns of attachment; the most common type of attachment behavior is ____ attachment.

   (a) Strange; secure   (b) Strange; insecure avoidant
   (c) Surrogate; secure   (d) Surrogate; insecure avoidant

[1. a (3 months), b (4 to 6 weeks), c (6 to 7 months), d (2 years); 2-d; 3-a].

What do studies of infant development tell us about what babies need? All babies, including the AIDS orphans in our opening story, depend on adults to meet their basic needs for food, warmth, and protection. Vulnerable brain regions, such as areas that control visual processing, need experience-expectant stimulation, such as adequate light and exposure to patterns. Babies also need stimulation through movement and the opportunity to move, and they need to experience the feedback that results from their own actions. They want the rich social environment most humans enjoy, filled with the sounds of language and the rhythm of social interaction.

Most orphans receive the stimulation they need to sit, walk, and master the basics of their language. But in crowded households like those in our opening story, babies may not experience the predictable social interactions that help them build emotional connections to other people and a sense of mastery over their world. If their living conditions fail to improve, many of these children will have difficulties regulating their emotions and responding appropriately to other people's behavior. In other words, some of these environments are falling below what babies need.

Studies of orphaned babies raise many questions. If some stimulation is necessary for normal growth, is more even better? How do infants develop in environments with difference resources and priorities? These are some of the issues you will read about in our next chapter.

>>> S U M M A R Y <<<

The Newborn

1. Newborns (also called **neonates**) usually weigh between 5.5 and 10 pounds (2.5 to 4.5 kilograms) and measure between 18 and 22 inches long (46 to 56 centimeters). Many have irregular breathing, cold hands and feet, and temporary side effects from maternal hormones while they adjust to life outside the womb.

2. In hospitals, medical personnel assign **Apgar scores** to indicate a newborn's general condition, conduct early physical evaluations, screen for medical conditions such as jaundice and **phenylketonuria (PKU)**, and test newborn behavior.

3. Parent-infant bonding is an ongoing process that has no strict time limit. Compared to isolated parents, parents with social contacts have more nurturant parenting styles and lower rates of abusive behavior.

4. Newborns are amazingly competent and surprisingly immature. Their vision is relatively poor but their hearing, touch, and vestibular systems are more developed. For the first few months, basic body systems are still immature and a daily sleep–wake cycle is not yet established.

Physical Development

5. Early development follows a **cephalocaudal** pattern (from head to tail) and a **proximodistal** pattern (from the trunk of the body outward). Changes in height and weight occur rapidly in the first year and less rapidly during the second and third years.

6. During the first year, many newborn reflexes disappear and spontaneous movements peak between 6 and 10 months. Rudimentary movements are voluntary movements for locomotion and manipulating objects. Rudimentary movements that appear in a predictable sequence are called the **motor milestones**. Early motor development is influenced by physical maturation and experience.

7. Perceptual development is rapid during the first year. Color perception is good by 2 to 3 months, and visual acuity is excellent by 12 months but continues to improve for many years. Children are born with the ability to process basic speech sounds, but the ability to discriminate and localize sounds continues to develop for several years.

8. During the first year, some reflexes disappear as higher brain centers begin to mature. Around 7 months of age, when infants become afraid of strangers, the brain structures that support memory are developing more connections to structures that determine the emotional significance of events. **Brain lateralization**, the specialization of the left and right cerebral hemispheres for different tasks, is present to some extent at birth but continues to develop during the second year. During the third year, young children still have difficulty following rules because the brain centers responsible for **executive processes** (the mental processes involved in such things as planning and problem solving) are still immature.

Cognitive Development

9. Piaget believed that children progress through stages of cognitive development that represent qualitatively different ways of viewing the world. During the **sensorimotor stage** (the first two years), children learn to coordinate sensory systems and keep mental representations in mind. Infants and toddlers know more than Piaget predicted, but he correctly assumed that small children do not always understand the world the way adults do.

10. The information processing approach looks at how behavior is influenced by basic mental processes such as attention, memory, and executive processes. With increasing age, infants and toddlers hold more information in working memory and recall information after longer periods of time, but young children have difficulty inhibiting irrelevant responses and using rules to guide their behavior.

11. Language development begins with cooing, babbling, first words, and early two-word phrases. A language explosion occurs after children start to combine words, yet it will be many years before they have mastered their native language. Behavioral approaches to language development treat language as just another form of learning, whereas linguistic approaches focus on language-specific abilities and learning strategies.

12. Older children and adults assist development during social interactions by drawing children's attention to objects, helping maintain their attention, and demonstrating solutions to problems.

Emotional and Social Development

13. Young children express anger, surprise, sadness, and joy during the first year; shame, embarrassment, and guilt appear at around 2 years of age. Some scientists believe that complex emotions appear later because they require a more advanced sense of interpersonal awareness; others believe that complex emotions are present earlier but in a less sophisticated form.

14. Infants participate in social dialogues that involve turn-taking behavior. At the end of the first year they show accurate joint visual attention and, through a process called **social referencing**, use other people's emotional reactions to guide their own reactions.

15. At about 18 months of age, children point to themselves rather than their mirror images when they notice red spots on their noses, and they point to "me" and "you." As soon as they have a concept of self, children begin to anticipate the feelings and reactions of other people.

16. There is no evidence for the psychoanalytic assumption that infants develop emotional attachments primarily to the individual who provides their food. Erik Erikson emphasized that the first 18 months are the stage of **basic trust versus mistrust**, when infants develop a general sense of whether they will be cared for consistently. Then, between 18 months and 3 years, children's biggest emotional challenge is to develop a sense of autonomy during the stage of **autonomy versus shame and doubt**. The ethological approach says that infants who are securely attached to a mother or other attachment figure will use their caregiver as a secure base for exploration. Secure attachment is the most common attachment pattern and the pattern most often associated with successful intimate relationships.

>>> KEY TERMS <<<

neonates (p. 129)
neonatal period (p. 129)
Apgar score (p. 129)
phenylketonuria (PKU) (p. 130)
reflexes (p. 133)
infant states (p. 135)
maturation (p. 136)
cephalocaudal development (p. 136)
proximodistal development (p. 136)
motor milestones (p. 137)
visual preference method (p. 139)
experience-expectant brain development (p. 141)
brain spurt (p. 142)
brain lateralization (p. 142)
scheme (p. 144)
organization (p. 144)
adaptation (p. 144)
assimilation (p. 144)
accommodation (p. 144)
sensorimotor stage (p. 144)

object permanence (p. 145)
A-not-B error (p. 145)
attention (p. 148)
discrepancy principle (p. 148)
working memory (p. 149)
long-term memory (p. 149)
infantile amnesia (p. 150)
executive processes (p. 150)
inhibition (p. 150)
fast mapping (p. 152)
syntax (p. 152)
telegraphic speech (p. 152)
overregularization (p. 152)
language acquisition device (LAD) (p. 153)
child-directed speech (p. 154)
scaffolding (p. 155)
social referencing (p. 157)
basic trust versus mistrust (p. 160)
autonomy versus shame and doubt (p. 160)
Strange Situation (p. 161)

MILESTONES of the first three years

Newborn to 1 Year Helpless newborns transform into babies with individual likes, dislikes, and personalities.

- Babies begin to smile at people by 4- to 6-weeks of age, and around 3 months they laugh and coo delightfully, and some are rewarding their caregivers by sleeping through the night.

- Most babies sit unsupported and handle toys by 7 months, so it is easier to amuse them than it was a few months earlier. They become afraid of strangers as brain structures that support memory and emotion develop.

- They show object permanence about 8 months of age by removing a blanket to retrieve a toy.

- Then, around 12 months, babies look where other people are pointing and many learn to say their first words.

1 to 2 Years The physical changes that occur in the brain during the first 2 years are reflected in babies' growing mental abilities.

- In the second year, toddlers start putting words together into simple phrases ("Candy gone").

- By 18 months, they show self-awareness by recognizing themselves in mirrors.

- Armed with a new ability to think about relationships between themselves and others, by the end of the second year they begin to show shame, shyness, embarrassment, and guilt.

- As their interest in mastering the social world is blossoming, so is their interest in mastering their environments. Two-year-olds want to feed themselves and mimic what adults around them are doing.

2 to 3 Years Children demand more independence by the third year of life.

- They learn to run well and scribble with a crayon.

- Over half of 30- to 35-month olds show cooperative social pretend play, a type of play that involves exchanges such as passing a miniature cup to someone holding a miniature pitcher.

- At this time, children begin chatting about their own and other people's desires, perceptions, and emotions.

- Because the brain centers that control complicated thinking and planning are still very immature, young children are easily distracted and have difficulty following rules.

Are the first years of life

Preview: The first three years in CONTEXT

Bringing up Baby

Babies are completely dependent on caregivers to provide adequate food and protect them from preventable diseases and injuries. Their chances of surviving and thriving depend on numerous factors you will read about in the next chapter—from early feeding to the medical care they receive and the safety of their homes.

Raising the Toddler and Young Child

Children's behavior is influenced by how consistently adults in their lives set limits, the type of discipline their families rely on, and how much emotional support and stimulation are available at home and in day care.

Individual Differences

Children are a diverse group that includes some infants and toddlers who are easy to care for and others who have difficulty adjusting to change. As they grow, their dispositions and talents are modified by the people around them. Children who live with easygoing caregivers tend to become more easygoing themselves over time.

Environmental Influences and Early Development

Children who live in environments that are rich in language and stimulating experiences tend to have large vocabularies and many things to talk about with others. Poverty and abuse threaten children's development, but programs that assist at-risk children and their families can help keep development on course.

In this next chapter you'll learn how developmental principles explain the pathways individuals take through the first three years when we consider the question:

Are the first years of life the most important years?

the most important years?

Pathways through the First Three Years

Stories of Our Lives
The Quest for a Better Baby

{ "Scientists and cribs, and the children in them, belong together." **}**

Alison Gopnik, Andrew Meltzoff, and Patricia Kuhl.

Summary

EXT BOXES

DON'T BE FOOLED!
When Short-Term Solutions Lead to Long-Term Problems

SOLUTIONS *What Babies Want*

Parents have always looked to experts to answer their childrearing questions. To their dismay, though, they often hear two points of view: the belief that experience directs development and the belief that genes do. Consider the routine task of toilet training, which is an issue every parent faces. Early in the 20th century, John Watson, the flamboyant "father of behaviorism," stood on one side of the issue. Learning guided development, Watson said, so parents should mold their babies' behavior as early as possible (Cairns & Ornstein, 1979). On the other hand, physician Arnold Gesell thought it was fruitless to train infants; one "simply had to wait until the cells of the nervous system 'ripened'" (McGraw, 1981, p. xvi). As a result of the disagreement between Watson and Gesell, parents read radically different advice: Watson recommended using conditioning principles to start toilet training as young as 3 weeks of age, whereas Gesell told parents to wait until their children were old enough to learn quickly.

Developmental researcher Myrtle McGraw stepped smack into the middle of this nature–nurture debate when she wrote *Growth: A Study of Johnny and Jimmy* (1935). McGraw observed twin boys in a laboratory

5 days a week to explore when training would start to influence development. For almost 2 years, Johnny was encouraged to explore the limits of his physical abilities while brother Jimmy received routine care. Years later, McGraw (1985) recalled this remarkable story:

> In every activity throughout the first year of Johnny's special exercise or practice we took the lead from the infant's behavior, the signals of behavioral change, to select appropriate challenges and practice of the emerging new activity. For example, when he first began to make creeping movements we provided inclines of different steepness which he could climb up and down. But when it came to standing and trying to step we were, at first, puzzled as to how to prepare the favorable challenge for equilibrium and stepping. The idea of ball-bearing roller skates was suggested. We all laughed, thinking it ridiculous. But we did just that. We had a pair of ball-bearing skates custom-made and attached to the soles of a pair of shoes that fitted him.
>
> I don't recall just how the thought of a tricycle first arose, but we were familiar with Raven's report of teaching a chimpanzee to ride a tricycle. So we bought a tricycle suitable for Johnny's size and fastened the soles of his shoes to the pedals. Johnny was first exposed to the roller skates and the tricycle on the same day, just about three days before his first birthday.
>
> Of course we never had the slightest idea of getting that baby to learn to roller skate; we just wanted to see how his growing neuromotor system adjusted to an unfamiliar situation. We certainly took it for granted that he would learn to manipulate the tricycle, with his feet tied to the pedals, long before he would be able to perform well on skates. We were in for an inexplicable surprise. Within 2 months, at the age of 14 months, Johnny was performing amazingly well on skates, and not only on flat surfaces. He was able to coast down a slightly inclined hallway—and did so with glee. During that same 2 months on the tricycle he knew what he wanted to do, and by shaking his body forward and backward he tried to get the vehicle to move. If we attempted to give him the sensation of the vehicle moving by giving the rear wheel a little push, he would take his hand and try to start it but never with enough force.
>
> I knew that this baby would learn to ride that tricycle some day, and I was determined to find out when and how. So for 7 months, twice a day, 5 days a week, we hitched his feet to the pedals and tried to lure him forward. But during those 7 months no appreciable improvement was manifest.
>
> Then one day when he was 19 months of age, I stepped into the laboratory after his feet had been tied to the pedals and Johnny looked up at me as if he had discovered a law of the universe. He had just realized that it was the pressure of his leg on the pedal that started the vehicle to move. There is no way to describe the emotional communication and delight shared by me and the baby at that moment! The recollection of it is just as vivid today as it was on its occurrence. Within 10 days Johnny had mastered the tricycle, but he never manifested the delight of the accomplishment as much as he did when he skated when only 14 months old. (pp. 166–167)

Journalists loved McGraw's skating baby. At first they hailed Johnny's feats as evidence that special opportunities improve skill. Then, when Johnny's advantage faded because Jimmy caught up, they told the public that early experiences didn't count (Dalton & Bergenn, 1995). McGraw, meanwhile, acknowledged the importance of heredity *and* experience. "Like most controversial issues, the truth is somewhere between the extreme claims," McGraw concluded.

2

"The development of children is not merely a matter of waiting for the nerves to grow; nor can one take any child and make anything they want to out of him merely by controlling the environment in which he shall live" (McGraw, cited in Dalton & Bergenn, 1995, p. 111). Training makes a better baby, McGraw said, but only when the baby is ready.

THE DESIRE TO RAISE A BETTER BABY has outlasted the memory of Myrtle McGraw's skating wonder. Since the events in our opening story, news stories have periodically claimed that special experiences will make an Einstein out of little Shawn and Shawna. For example, a 1965 article in *McCall's* magazine invited parents to "Train Your Baby to Be a Genius," and in the late 1970s the Better Baby Institute began teaching parents how to raise their babies' intelligence by starting academic instruction in the crib (Spitz, 1986; Tuhy, 1984). More recently, parents have been told that playing classical music will boost their baby's mathematical abilities, and books like *How to Give Your Baby Encyclopedic Knowledge* (Doman, Doman, & Aisen, 2001) are still available, still showing pictures of parents flashing cards at tots in diapers. All this pressure has left parents with a nagging question: Am I providing what my child needs to have the best beginning in life?

In this chapter, we look at how the typical development described in Chapter 4 unfolds when infants' environments provide different opportunities and risks. You will read how daily care affects their well-being, how developmental paths can be altered by poverty and maltreatment, and how professionals evaluate individual differences. Finally, you will revisit the four principles of development from Chapter 1 for this part's featured topic: Are the first years of life the most important years?

Bringing up Baby

What do parents worry about? A parent education program staffed by pediatric psychologists,* social workers, and nurses collected data to answer this question. For $2\frac{1}{2}$ years, staff members kept records of the questions parents asked during call-in hours and walk-in appointments (Mesibov, Schoeder, & Wesson, 1977). As you can see in Figure 5.1, parents of 1- to 5-year-olds accounted for the majority of questions, with 2- to 3-year-olds appearing to be especially good at perplexing their mothers and fathers. Surprisingly, most of the parents' questions centered on routine issues. Across all age groups, they complained the most about negative behavior (crying, whining, and tantrums), followed by toilet training, school problems, developmental delays, and sleep problems. In other words, parents worry most about the daily details of bringing up baby.

3

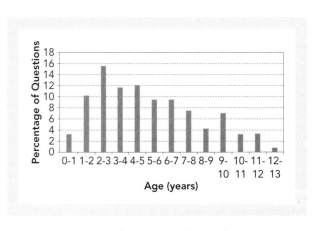

FIGURE 5.1 Parental concerns about their children.

Parents of 2- to 3-year-olds made the most calls to a parent help line. Across all age groups, the most frequent questions involved complaints about negative behaviors, such as whining and refusing to cooperate with parents' requests.

SOURCE: Adapted from Mesibov, Schroeder, & Wesson (1977).

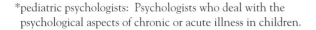

*pediatric psychologists: Psychologists who deal with the psychological aspects of chronic or acute illness in children.

Two-year-olds don't make it easy to catch planes. Uncooperative behavior is one of the most frequent complaints parents have about their young children.

A taste of celery is familiarizing this baby with raw vegetables. But once she can bite off a piece, she may choke on this healthy-looking snack. Small cooked peas or little cubes of cooked carrots are a better choice—and fun to try to pick up!

Feeding

Caregivers provide food at meals, but they also transmit attitudes about food and a food culture. The patterns they establish during the early years usually continue into the school years, when food choices have a profound impact on children's health.

BREAST-FEEDING. One of the first choices parents make is whether to breast-feed or formula-feed their babies. In general, breast milk is the healthier choice. The recipe for human milk is species specific, so its major ingredients—sugar, digestible protein, and fat—are perfectly balanced. Formula does not provide enzymes and antibodies that fight disease, and formula-fed infants are more likely than breast-fed babies to develop allergies later in life (Obihara et al., 2005). For all of these reasons, health organizations advise mothers in industrialized countries to breast-feed for 1 year, or longer if mothers and their babies desire (American Academy of Pediatrics Work Group on Breast-feeding, 1997; James, Dobson, & the American Dietetic Association, 2005).

Breast-feeding is a matter of life or death in parts of the world where contaminated water or poverty threatens survival. The United Nations (2001) estimates that as many as 10 percent of the deaths of children less than 5 years of age could be prevented by a modest increase in breast-feeding rates worldwide. It is dangerous to substitute formula for breast milk in developing countries because the water used to wash bottles and mix formula is often unclean, and poor families sometimes stretch their food budgets by diluting formula. The World Health Organization (2000–2004) recommends breast-feeding for at least the first 2 years in high-risk regions to reduce episodes of diarrhea and prevent respiratory and ear infections, pneumonia, meningitis, and many other diseases (Bahl et al., 2005).

In addition to protecting babies' health, breast-feeding also benefits mothers and families. Nursing helps mothers regain their prepregnancy shape, improves bone remineralization (which reduces hip fractures later in life), and provides some protection against breast and ovarian cancer. Families who breast-feed also enjoy lower feeding costs, spend fewer days caring for sick children, and find it less inconvenient to feed newborns the 8 to 12 times a day they require (American Academy of Pediatrics Work Group on Breast-feeding, 1997). Nursing also helps families space their children by suppressing (though not always eliminating) ovulation (Ngianga-Bakwin & Stones, 2005).

But there are circumstances when formula feeding is a better choice. Health professionals recommend formula when mothers have active tuberculosis or take medications that can harm their infants, when infants have conditions requiring special diets, or when mothers' milk has been contaminated by environmental chemicals (Massart et al., 2005). Formula feeding may also be more practical for mothers who work outside the home. Parents who wean their babies from breast-feeding before age 1 should switch to iron-enriched formula rather than cow's milk.

BUILDING HEALTHY FOOD HABITS. Babies deplete their inborn mineral reserves by 5 to 6 months old, about the same time they stop reflexively pushing food out of their mouths with their tongues. Now is the time to add strained foods to their diets. It is best to start with foods that few babies are allergic to (such as rice cereal) before adding foods that are more likely to trigger reactions (such as wheat products). Some foods should be avoided altogether early in life. For example, honey is dangerous for infants because it can contain bacterial spores that cause a disease called *infant botulism*. Unlike older children and adults, babies' less acidic digestive system cannot kill these spores (Shelov, 2004).

Mealtime with a toddler can be fun or the beginning of food struggles. Growth slows after the first year and toddlers grow intermittently, so their interest in food naturally waxes and wanes. As a result, it is not unusual for children to skip a meal or to eat only a few tablespoons of food at a sitting. Instead of selecting a balanced diet at every meal, young children often go in streaks, eating mostly one type of food for a day or so before switching to another.

Many children develop **food neophobia**—a fear of new foods—by 18 to 24 months. This occurrence turns delightful diners into picky eaters who reject many foods, including some familiar ones. It is useful for frustrated caregivers to remember that food neophobia is adaptive because toddlers explore a world where many plants are poisonous, so it is best if they gradually learn what to eat by watching other people. Adults promote "learned safety" when they repeatedly expose toddlers to foods in a relaxed environment where adults are enjoying their own food (Johnson, 2002). Young children may need to see a highly suspicious food a dozen times or more before they finally accept it, but in the long run children in South America eat chili peppers and Japanese children eat sushi (as do children in other countries if they are exposed to these foods).

Worried family members sometimes react to picky eating by coaxing, bribing children with sweets, and generally creating the impression that food is a playing field for struggles over control. All this fussing is unnecessary, though, because children will eventually eat a variety of foods if they are surrounded by healthy choices. A few practices can minimize mealtime battles:

▶ *Serve a reasonable amount.* It is a good rule of thumb to start out with about 1 tablespoon of each food for every year of age and feed toddlers four to six mini-meals a day (Kleihman & American Academy of Pediatrics Committee on Nutrition, 1998).

▶ *Avoid "competing" foods.* Fussy tots are more likely to eat foods they avoid when controversial items are served alone instead of paired with foods they prefer.

▶ *Do not use food as a reward.* It is never too early to teach children that we eat because we are hungry—not because we want to feel special or loved. To avoid conveying the wrong attitude about food, avoid using "junk" food as a reward for good behavior or eating. In one demonstration, children who were pressured to eat a specific food by bribing them with sweets actually liked the food *less* afterward, proving that food rewards produce short-term gains that are counterproductive in the long run (Johnson, 2002). Many early feeding problems can be prevented by following the simple recommendations in Table 5.1.

MALNUTRITION. Picky eating is not an issue for millions of infants who lack adequate food. Tragically, malnutrition affects almost one-third of the children in developing countries (UNICEF, 2006). A leading cause of childhood deaths in these countries is **protein-energy malnutrition (PEM)**, a condition in which the intake of energy or protein is too low to sustain the body. One form of PEM, *marasmus*, often develops when infants are weaned between 6 months and 1 year old and too little food prompts the body to break down its own tissues for calories. Children with this condition lose body fat and muscle, causing a thin, wasted

food neophobia A fear of new foods, used to describe the tendency young children have to avoid unfamiliar foods.

protein-energy malnutrition (PEM) A type of malnutrition that occurs when the intake of energy or protein is too low to sustain the body.

TABLE 5.1   Tips for Feeding Infants and Toddlers

Infant feeding	Breast-feed for the first 1 to 2 years if you can. Parents who choose not to breast-feed or want to supplement breast-feeding should select an iron-fortified infant formula for baby's first year.
Starting solids	Begin offering strained foods at 6 months. Introduce foods one at a time, allowing a few days before introducing a new food to check for tolerance. Start with low-allergy foods like rice cereal before moving on to vegetables, fruits, and meat. Do not add honey to food or prepare baby food from products that contain large amounts of salt or sugar.
Food competition	Some children will eat less than they should if adults do not make sure they are getting an adequate share. Put children's food in their own dish and encourage children who are underweight or sick to eat.
Portion sizes	Start each meal for 2- to 3-year-olds with small portions. Sample portion sizes are 2 to 3 tablespoons (or a few pieces) of vegetables, 1 to 2 ounces of meat, and 1/2 cup to 1 cup of cereal. Provide more if children finish their servings and are interested.
Food safety	Avoid giving toddlers foods that are round, hard, or do not dissolve in saliva. Hot dogs, grapes, raw vegetables, and nuts are choking risks. Supervise children while they eat so you can intervene if necessary. Avoid eating in the car where you cannot assist them quickly.
Repeated exposure	Do not be discouraged about offering foods that children have not accepted in the past. Continue to present a variety of foods without pressure or comments that label their preferences, such as "Val doesn't like broccoli."
Relaxed atmosphere	Do not bribe children to eat by offering sweets or other low-nutrition foods, and do not use food as a reward for good behavior.

Sources: Kleinman & American Academy of Pediatrics Committee on Nutrition (1998); World Health Organization (1998).

This child has *kwashiorkor,* a common form of malnutrition caused by insufficient protein. Notice the characteristic swollen abdomen.

appearance. Another form of PEM, *kwashiorkor,* occurs when children's diets are low in protein (Müller & Krawinkel, 2005). This condition often develops after children have been weaned from breast-feeding between 1 and 3 years of age. As their bodies are forced to break down their own protein, faces, abdomens, and legs swell with water, causing a characteristically bloated stomach.

Even nonpoor children can be malnourished. In one study, 6 percent of 1- to 5-year-olds from nonpoor families were deficient in folate (a B vitamin), 25 percent were deficient in iron, and over 33 percent were deficient in zinc (Bellamy, 1998). These substances are *micronutrients,* vitamins or minerals that are needed in small amounts to sustain life processes such as hormone production, growth, and immune system functioning. Micronutrient deficiencies have a negative effect on brain growth and cognitive functioning (Castejon et al., 2004). For example, iron deficiency during infancy is associated with a 10- to 12-point reduction in scores on a test of infant development (Georgieff & Rao, 2001), and a lack of zinc increases emotional behavior and impairs children's ability to learn (Bhatnager & Tanega, 2001). Toddlers can develop micronutrient deficiencies when they are offered so many bottles of milk that they are too full to eat fruits and vegetables.

Do malnourished children recover once their diets are corrected? The answer depends on the type, extent, and duration of their dietary problems. Iodine, selenium, folate, and vitamin A play important roles in early brain processes, and later supplementation may not fully correct problems caused by early and severe deficiencies (Georgieff & Rao, 2001). On the other hand, humans evolved in harsh environments where food shortages were common, so brain development generally recovers from short-term malnutrition as long as environmental stimulation is adequate (Guesry, 1998).

FAILURE TO THRIVE. Sometimes babies don't grow as they should. This perplexing problem is known as *failure to thrive* (also called *growth deficiency*), a condition in which children do not grow as expected for their age, gender, and family history (Bogner & Rafal, 2005). In the past, pediatricians used the term *nonorganic failure to thrive* to imply that slow growth was mostly due to emotional problems or troubled parent–child interactions. (*Nonorganic* means "not physical.") Today, experts know that a combination of biological and caregiving issues can contribute to growth failure (Drotar & Robinson, 2000).

Growth-deficient children often have medical conditions, but growth problems are also more likely to occur when families have inaccurate beliefs about children's nutritional needs. Delayed growth is associated with introducing solid foods too early or simply providing the baby with too little food. Some cases develop in the second half of the first year when caregivers fail to adjust to children's increasing independence, as in the following example (Birch, 1999):

> Candy, a good-tempered, easygoing infant of 11 months, was described by her mother as "into everything." Candy's mother felt overwhelmed by the new need to monitor Candy and seemed unaware of the possibility of "child-proofing" the environment. Instead, she kept Candy almost continuously in a walker, which allowed her to travel around the apartment but not to touch anything. Candy's mother was very controlling of feelings, chastising Candy for using her left hand or getting food on her dress. She fed Candy in the walker and actually appeared relieved when, as usually happened, Candy propelled herself away from the tense, uncongenial feeding interaction. Candy's mother was unable to adapt to Candy's need to explore and to have more control of her feeding. Candy, rather than engage in protracted power struggles or submit, chose to avoid both mother and food. (p. 402)

Treatment for children like Candy involves a medical evaluation to rule out physical problems along with education to teach parents how to make mealtimes more enjoyable. Parent education can help adults understand more about other infant behaviors as well, including two you will read about next.

Crying and Sleeping

Whenever babies cry, adults have an overwhelming urge to make the crying stop. Crying serves babies well because it draws adults closer and prompts them to act, which reduces the risk of starvation, hypothermia,* and danger from predators. But crying that doesn't stop with attention is costly and risky. Concerns about infant crying and sleeping cost the British National Health Service about 65 million pounds in a single year (St. James-Roberts, 2001), and about 20 percent of United States parents discuss crying with their health care provider (Johnson & Johnson, 2001). Excessive crying also contributes to maternal depression (Papousek & von Hofacker, 1998) and precedes many episodes of child abuse (Reijneveld et al., 2004). Fortunately, a little basic information about crying and sleeping can ease some of the stress that fussy infants cause.

---

*hypothermia: Abnormally low body temperature.

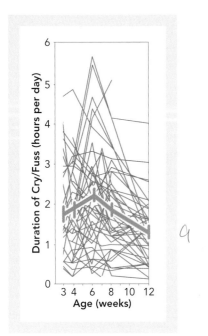

FIGURE 5.2 Crying across the first 12 weeks.

It is normal for young infants to cry many hours each day, with their crying time divided into many bouts. Here you can see the total number of hours each day that 50 infants fussed or cried. The thick, dark bar is the average across all infants. Notice that the total duration of crying usually peaks around 6 weeks of age.

SOURCE: Barr (1990).

UNEXPLAINED INFANT CRYING. Some babies who cry persistently have health conditions that improve with treatment. For the vast majority, however, crying bouts are a normal developmental phenomenon. Crying that bothers parents differs in three ways from routine crying: Babies with *unexplained crying* cry longer and louder during each bout, are difficult to console, and tend to cry during particular times of the day (usually late afternoon or evening). This behavior, though bothersome, is just at the upper end of the distribution of normal infant crying, and there is no evidence that cranky babies grow up to be irritable or demanding children (Barr, St. James-Roberts, & Keefe, 2001).

Unexplained crying is sometimes called *colic*, a term that implies digestive discomfort, but digestive problems account for only a small percentage of unexplained crying. Experts now believe that central nervous system immaturity is the primary cause of unexplained crying because developmental trends in crying are predictable, unrelated to later medical conditions, and similar across cultures. As one physician explained, crying "*is something normal infants do, rather than a condition they have*" (Barr, 2001, p. 89, as in original). Compared to other babies, infants with unexplained crying simply have difficulty soothing themselves and are less responsive to soothing stimuli.

Every baby is a little different, but infant crying and fussing typically increase around 2 weeks of age, peak around 6 weeks (as shown in Figure 5.2), then gradually decline until 4 months. The obvious improvement around 3 months corresponds to the development of a daily (circadian) rhythm for physiological functions, resulting in more regular sleep–wake cycles. This developmental trend is found even among the !Kung San, a culture where adults carry their infants almost continuously and typically respond to cries within 10 seconds. Among this hunting and gathering group, the duration of crying bouts is significantly less than in Western cultures but the *pattern* of crying is the same.

Around the world, babies who cry for no apparent reason during the day often want one thing: more stimulation. Many fussy babies are bored babies who respond to swaddling (tight wrapping in a blanket), music, and other forms of increased stimulation. Parents who know these tricks often ask themselves if satisfying baby with more attention will eventually produce a demanding baby. To explore this question, turn to our next *Don't Be Fooled!* discussion, "When Short-Term Solutions Lead to Long-Term Problems."

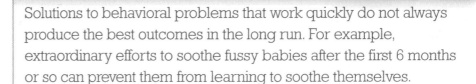

Solutions to behavioral problems that work quickly do not always produce the best outcomes in the long run. For example, extraordinary efforts to soothe fussy babies after the first 6 months or so can prevent them from learning to soothe themselves.

WHEN SHORT-TERM SOLUTIONS LEAD TO LONG-TERM PROBLEMS

Run to a crying baby—or not? That's the question for millions of people each day. Over the years, advice on this issue has sounded like night and day, as illustrated by the following suggestions:

You will have a strong desire to pick up the baby, find out what is causing him to cry, and make him happy. This is a perfectly normal and natural desire, probably an inborn behavior pattern that helped the species survive. Wait and see what happens when you exercise this natural tendency! You are sure to find someone saying, "uh, uh, don't pick up that baby. You'll spoil it". . . . The advice not to pick up your crying baby, in effect, says, "Your baby will be better off being unhappy than if you pick him up and make him happy." If you look at it this way, the recommendation will seem as foolish as it is—Lee Salk, M.D.

Crying as such very shortly becomes conditioned. The child quickly learns that it can control the responses of nurses, parents and attendants by the cry, and uses it as a weapon thereafter—J. B. Watson.

Will attending to babies make them happier children or manipulative schemers? To answer this question, developmental researchers Silvia Bell and Mary Ainsworth (1972) recorded how often infants cried during their first year and how long their mothers waited to respond. Because mothers who responded quickly had infants who cried less than other infants months later, Bell and Ainsworth concluded that prompt responding produces contented babies. But the story doesn't end here.

Supporters of the evolutionary perspective welcomed this study because they believe that infants are designed to be carried by parents who respond quickly to their needs. But behavior analysts, who believe that reinforcement should *increase* crying, were eager to find fault with the study's methods (Gewirtz & Boyd, 1977). Ultimately, the debate boiled down to one issue: Could other investigators replicate Bell and Ainsworth's findings?

Two researchers set out to do just that. They recorded interactions between mother–infant pairs every 3 weeks for 9 months and compared two correlations: the correlation between mothers' responsiveness and the frequency of their infants' crying months later (to determine if mothers' behavior was associated with later crying), and the correlation between early crying and mothers' responsiveness months later (to determine whether early infant crying was associated with mothers' behavior) (Hubbard & van IJzendoorn, 1991). Because the correlations were equivalent, there was no evidence that prompt service produced less fussy babies.

Why did results from these two studies differ? Ainsworth and Bell suggested one possibility. "There was no mother in our sample who rushed anxiously to intervene whenever her baby cried," they explained (1977, p. 1213). Ainsworth and Bell's responsive mothers were *selective* mothers who ignored minor fussing but responded before their babies could "get all worked up and out of control" (p. 1213). In contrast, other mothers in their study ignored their babies as much as 97 percent of the time. Ainsworth and Bell may have detected an effect of mothers' behavior because their sample included such extreme behavior. Together, results from these studies suggest that *sensitive responding*—responding quickly to serious problems but giving babies a chance to work out minor difficulties themselves—may be what works the best (van den Boom, 2001).

Today, representatives from the evolutionary and learning theory perspectives have shaken hands on the spoiling issue. Because crying is strongly programmed to ensure survival, withdrawing attention from a baby during the first 3 months of life does not reduce crying (Hubbard & van IJzendoorn, 1991). But babies can start to learn how to calm themselves after 3 to 5 months of age. At this time, parents who use extraordinary means to settle babies, such as taking them on car rides or nursing satisfied babies to sleep, tend to have toddlers who have trouble self-soothing (Barr et al., 2001). In other words, heroic methods offer short-term relief but tend to cause long-term problems. Being responsive—without being intrusive—is the best balance for caregivers and babies alike.

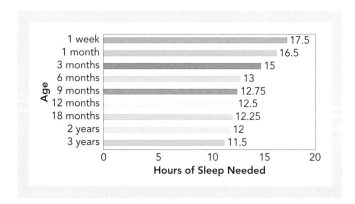

FIGURE 5.3 How much sleep do infants and toddlers need?

The average number of hours young children sleep declines steadily from birth to 3 years of age. Still, the average 3-year-old needs over 11 hours of sleep each day.

SOURCE: Mindell & Dahl (1998).

sudden infant death syndrome (SIDS) A label for the unexplained death of a sleeping infant less than 1 year of age. SIDS occurs most often between 2 and 4 months.

All babies are safest sleeping on their backs, the position associated with the lowest risk of death from SIDS. Safe sleeping practices are especially important for vulnerable infants, including premature babies and those with heart conditions.

ADJUSTING TO DAY AND NIGHT. Parents are very interested in keeping babies alert and happy during the day and sleepy at night. Unfortunately, these goals are not very important to babies. Still, infants make remarkable progress during the first year in terms of when they sleep, how long they sleep, and how safely they sleep.

Figure 5.3 shows the average number of hours children sleep from 1 week through 3 years of age. While the amount of sleep is declining, the duration and organization of sleep are also changing. Gradually, the percentage of time infants spend in REM sleep decreases, from 50 percent at birth to 25 percent at 2 to 3 years. And whereas newborns drift into REM sleep immediately or soon after sleep begins, by 2 to 3 months the order of sleep stages has shifted to a more mature pattern, with non-REM sleep preceding REM sleep (Roffwarg et al., 1966; Shelov, 2004).

During the early months, infants' cycles of wakefulness and sleep are more dependent on cycles of hunger than cycles of light (Goodlin-Jones, Burnham, & Anders, 2000). At about 3 months of age, the internal clock that regulates daily rhythms begins to function, creating a pattern to cycles of activity, crying, and body temperature. But as you will read next, the neurological changes that help some babies start to sleep through the night have a serious consequence: the threat of sudden death.

SUDDEN INFANT DEATH SYNDROME. Sudden infant death syndrome (SIDS) is a label for the unexplained death of a sleeping infant less than 1 year of age. SIDS occurs most often between 2 and 4 months of age and is more common among infants with risk factors such as prematurity and low birth weight. Nonetheless, SIDS strikes unpredictably and can affect families from all walks of life (Daley, 2004).

An early clue about factors that contribute to SIDS came from cross-cultural comparisons. Asian families, who worry about babies suffocating, prefer to place them to sleep on their backs (that is, in the *supine* position). In contrast, American families, who worry about babies spitting up and choking, used to place babies on their stomachs (in the *prone* position) (Jobe, 2001). Because SIDS rates were much lower in Asian populations, a national "Back-to-Sleep" campaign was launched in 1994 to promote placing infants on their backs. Within a few years, the rate of SIDS dropped almost 50 percent (Malloy & Freeman, 2000). As a bonus, positioning babies on their backs also lowered the frequency of fevers, stuffy noses, and ear infections (Hunt et al., 2003).

Although the cause of SIDS remains elusive, most authorities agree that three factors are involved in many SIDS cases (Alexander & Radisch, 2005; Brouillette & Nixon, 2001):

▶ *Biological vulnerabilities.* Abnormalities in brain areas that control respiration, heart rate, and neuromuscular functioning prevent some infants from arousing during sleep or maintaining normal physiological functions (Hunt, 2005). Prematurity, low birth weight, maternal smoking and drug use, and being male are factors that increase the risk of biological failures during sleep.

▶ *Developmental factors.* Changes in the control of sleeping and waking, breathing, and other basic processes destabilize infants' systems between 2 and 4 months of age, when the brain centers responsible for voluntary movement cause defensive reflexes to disappear. At this age, infants are less capable than younger or older infants of clearing blocked airways or rousing themselves from sleep.

▶ *Environmental factors.* Finally, environmental challenges sometimes overwhelm immature bodies. Babies are harder to arouse when they are in the prone sleeping position, when the air temperature is high, and when they sleep without interruptions in their own room (Groswasser et al., 2001; Mao et al., 2004; Sullivan & Barlow, 2001). There is also overwhelming evidence that SIDS is associated with unsafe sleeping environments, including soft bedding, daytime sleeping on sofas, and the use of pillows or comforters that can block babies' faces (Brouillette & Nixon, 2001). Other threats, such as infection, may be involved in some deaths.

Infants of African American mothers, unmarried mothers, and mothers who received limited prenatal care are more likely than other infants to die of SIDS. These groups have more biological risks, but their caregivers are also less likely to place them in the supine position (Paris, Remler, & Daling, 2001). To do a better job of preventing SIDS, some hospitals have stopped using the side sleep position for newborns to reduce the chance that parents will model this riskier position after they return home (Hein & Pettit, 2001).

Any adult who watches a baby should know the SIDS prevention tips listed in Table 5.2. But it is possible to overdo these recommendations. Babies who spend too much time on their backs sometimes develop flat heads (which has created a market for special helmets to correct this harmless flaw), and these babies often sit and crawl later than other babies (Davis et al., 1998). To respond to these concerns, the American Academy of Pediatrics suggests repositioning babies' heads periodically and giving them supervised exercise time on their stomachs.

TABLE 5.2 Tips for Reducing the Risk of Sudden Infant Death Syndrome

* Place the baby on the back to sleep at night and naptime.
* Use a firm mattress in a safety-approved crib.
* Eliminate fluffy, loose bedding from the baby's sleep area.
* Keep the baby's face clear of coverings.
* Be careful not to overheat the baby.
* Don't allow anyone to smoke around the baby.
* Educate babysitters, day care providers, grandparents, and everyone who cares for the baby about SIDS risks.

SOURCE: First Candle/SIDS Alliance (2006).

GETTING TO SLEEP AND STAYING ASLEEP. Most child-care books say that babies sleep "through the night" by 3 months old, but the full story is not so optimistic. Babies usually wake briefly at the end of each 3- to 4-hour sleep cycle, although some are better than others at soothing themselves back to sleep. Child-care books report endless reasons why babies are likely to wake at night: At 7 to 8 months old when separation anxiety appears, whenever baby is cutting a tooth, and between 12 to 15 months when active dreaming disrupts sleep (Shelov, 2004). It is no wonder that over 20 percent of parents say their young children have problems settling down at night or staying asleep throughout the night (Mindell & Dahl, 1998). These complaints are related. About 70 percent of 1-year-olds go back to sleep on their own after a nighttime awakening; the other 30 percent cry. In contrast to *self-soothers*, *signalers* rely on adults to soothe them to sleep, both initially and whenever they awake (Goodlin-Jones et al., 2000).

Four interventions have been tested to help babies who are at least 4 to 6 months of age sleep better:

▶ *Extinction*, the most rapid approach, involves putting the child to bed at a designated time and not returning—even if the child cries. Although "crying it out" is effective, many parents are too distressed by the procedure to follow through with this advice.

▶ *Graduated extinction* involves returning periodically to reassure the child, with progressively longer waits before checking.

▶ *Scheduled awakening* is an odd alternative for parents who don't like to let baby cry. For this technique, parents arouse infants shortly before they would usually wake, with a gradual elimination of scheduled awakenings.

▶ *Positive bedtime routines* can be added to any approach. This involves helping children "wind down" before bedtime by lowering lights and avoiding stimulating activities. Routines such as reading stories are effective ways to help a tired child transition into sleep by providing a clear clue that says "bedtime—time to settle down." Young children also transition more easily when bedtime occurs at the same time and place each day so they come to associate time of day and environmental cues with calming behavior.

Unfortunately, none of these approaches completely eliminates nighttime waking in all infants (Johnson, 1991; Mindell, 1999; Rickert & Johnson, 1988). The fuss and trouble have led some pediatricians to reassure parents that it is okay to return to that time-worn standby: sleeping with the baby. Cosleeping is so widespread around the world that it is difficult to criticize the practice as long as parents take reasonable safety precautions. Pediatrician Ronald Barr echoed the sentiments of many experts when he said that "the concept of an optimal caregiving style for crying, poor sleeping or feeding, or for other behaviors, is a misassumption. One of the benefits of cross cultural studies is offering choices" (High, 2001, p. 253). To look into how most of the world reduces parent–infant conflict, turn to our *Solutions* feature, "What Babies Want."

Babies enjoy the security and stimulation they receive when they are carried during the day and lie in close proximity to a parent at night. As long as the baby is sleeping in a safe location, parents do not need to worry about spoiling their baby by providing the type of care most parents around the world provide.

WHAT BABIES WANT

Meredith Small is fascinated by parents. "Parents in some cultures refuse to speak much to their babies, thinking such activity will produce a high-strung, selfish, obnoxious adult," she explains. "The Gusii women of Africa, for example, hold babies close, answer their cries with soothing mumbles and offer a breast, but they do not chat . . . In contrast, Western cultures are devoted to verbal stimulation" (Small, 1997, p. 503). The differences between cultures are too numerous to list. Dutch parents advocate discipline and regularity; American parents celebrate independent flexibility. Western parents find it odd when an African child cares for her baby brother; African parents are troubled when an American baby cries in his crib.

Small became aware of these differences when she entered the new field of *ethnopediatrics*, a cross-disciplinary group of anthropologists, child development researchers, and pediatricians who study how parenting styles influence infant health. Ethopediatrics recognizes cultural variability while emphasizing some almost universal regularities. As Small wrote in one of her books (1998, p. xii), "I discovered that babies in other cultures lead lives very different from those I was used to seeing and hearing about here in the United States. Babies in some other societies, I learned, are carried in slings all day, sleep with their parents in the same bed, and are often integrated into the social fabric early on. I also heard that in other cultures, babies do not cry very often and never develop colic. This was an entirely different view of raising children than the one espoused by Dr. Spock."

The assumption of ethnopediatrics is that babies are "designed" for close relationships with caregivers. For example, babies cry not only when they are hungry but also when they are disconnected from stimulation. Around the world, the common practice of strapping babies to caregivers provides almost continuous movement that minimizes long crying bouts. Similarly, breast-feeding works as an effective contraceptive only when babies feed frequently, even at night, which is encouraged in most societies by allowing the baby in bed with parents.

These insights explain why parenting often feels like a battleground: Parenting values in industrialized countries often conflict with the biology of babies who were not designed to feed on schedule, sleep alone, or spend hours each day separated from motion. But this analysis has created another battleground: Parents who are tired of fighting are reverting to time-worn customs, only to be criticized by people who disapprove of nursing 2-year-olds and bed-sharing 4-year-olds. As Small observed, "Everyone feels it is his or her duty to correct the obviously 'wrong' ways of other parents" (1998, p. 214). Nowhere is this new battle more evident than in debates about the "family bed."

In many cultures, parents and children sleep in the same room, although not always in the same bed. Advocates claim that family sleeping (cosleeping) promotes breast-feeding and gives everyone a good night's sleep. Sharing a room at night is also associated with less time spent in deep stages of sleep, when sudden infant death is more likely to occur (Mosko, Richard, & McKenna, 1997).

Skeptics counter that sharing the bed is risky because babies can be trapped in bedcovers or smothered by a turning parent (Carroll-Pankurst & Mortimer, 2001). Moreover, there is no clear evidence that bed sharing protects babies against SIDS (American Academy of Pediatrics Task Force on Sudden Infant Death Syndrome, 2005). Until more evidence is available, a safe compromise for parents who want their babies close is to keep them nearby but on their own sleeping surface.

Meanwhile, parents like this father, who Small (1998) saw walking with his 3-year-old in a sling, remind us of what babies want:

> He admitted, embarrassed, that he and his wife always carried this boy: "He just wanted to be carried from the moment he was born, even after he could walk." The father apologized, as if it were a psychological defect, a pathology. With his arm resting lightly on his father's shoulder, the boy also looked at me, not the least bit embarrassed, simply happy to be where he was. "Yes, of course he wants to be carried, that's how he's designed," I answered, offering him reassurance from a perfect stranger that he was doing

Around the world, many parents carry their children as they go about their day-to-day chores.

a great job. To me, they looked like people from another culture where no one is ashamed about maintaining the parent–infant bond, where independence is not an issue, not a goal. To carry a child that size must surely be hard work, but the parents had responded to the child's needs and their own intuition that this was okay. Even though carrying a toddler all the time is unacceptable in this culture, and though surely these parents must put up with an endless stream of comments from others, even strangers, the little boy looked perfectly content to me.

Jumping back on my bike, I pedaled away and thought once again about how many decisions there are that parents can and must make, so many subtle ways to interact with children that affect both the welfare of the baby and the tenor of family life. And as I took a quick glance backward, the father shifted the boy to his other hip, smiled at his son, and continued his slow and dedicated voyage through parenthood. (pp. 231–232)

Preventing Medical Problems

Modern medicine has taught us how to handle infants' daily cycles of sleeping, waking, and crying; it has also given us a sense of security that if babies get sick, a doctor will make them better again. But even today, the process of treating disease and injury is sometimes unsuccessful. This is why the key to good health is to prevent problems before they occur.

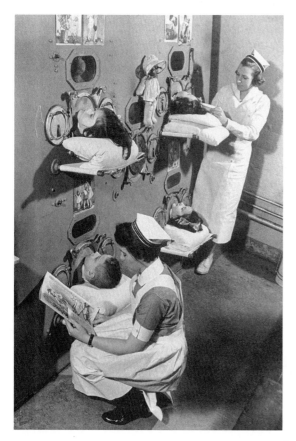

During the 1940s and early 1950s, nurses cared for rooms full of children who were forced to live in "iron lungs" after polio weakened the muscles that control breathing. Polio became virtually nonexistent in the United States after a vaccine was invented to prevent the disease.

IMMUNIZATION. Tremendous progress has been made to reduce the rate of infectious disease. For example, until the 1920s diphtheria killed over 10,000 people every year in the United States; now, it is rare for physicians to treat a case. Similarly, polio paralyzed thousands of children in the 1950s, but the Centers for Disease Control and Prevention (2006d) believes that, like smallpox, this disease will soon be part of history. These diseases are less of a threat today due to better sanitation, better nutrition (which helps people's immune systems fend off disease), and *immunization*, a medical procedure that trains the body to detect and fight disease.

Children can be immunized against a dozen or so major killers, including diphtheria, tetanus, and whooping cough. The shots they receive, called *vaccines*, work by injecting weakened or killed pathogens into their bloodstreams, which prompts their bodies to produce antibodies that fight the disease. These antibodies then remain in the body and allow children to fight off diseases before they get sick.

A movement against immunization gains supporters whenever fear of disease is low. Spokespeople for this movement claim that vaccines have not been responsible for the decline in childhood diseases and that harmful side effects outweigh the benefits. However, these claims are based on misunderstandings. It is true that improvements in public health helped rein in diseases, but immunization also played a major role. To illustrate the benefits of vaccinating, Figure 5.4 plots the number of measles cases in the United States between 1950 and 1990. Rates of most diseases rise and fall over time, which can lead to faulty conclusions when short time intervals are analyzed. Still, it is clear that the vaccine preceded a large drop in the number of cases. Other supportive data come from periods when hysteria about side effects led to decreased immunization. For example, vaccination rates dropped from 80 to 20 percent among infants in Japan after rumors spread that the whooping cough vaccination was unsafe. Shortly afterwards, Japan had a major epidemic involving more than 13,000 cases and 41 deaths. The number of new cases dropped sharply again after the introduction of a new vaccine (Centers for Disease Control and Prevention, National Immunization Program, 2002).

The Japanese epidemic illustrates why we continue to immunize even when disease rates are low: If we stopped immunizing, rates would increase. Immunization is not risk free, but the risks of not being immunized far outweigh the risks of side effects. Consult Table 5.3 to compare these risks for yourself.

OTITIS MEDIA. Babies frequently have earaches because the ear tube that drains fluid is shorter and more horizontal in infancy, making it easier for germs to reach the middle ear. **Acute otitis media (AOM)** is an ear infection in which fluid accumulates behind the eardrum causing fever, pain, and temporary hearing loss. AOM is the most frequently diagnosed disease in childhood, affecting about 85 percent of children by 3 years of age (Carson-DeWitt, 2001). Most parents, therefore, learn to recognize its symptoms: fever, tugging at the ear, and fussing from discomfort.

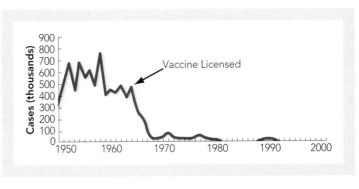

FIGURE 5.4 Measles cases in the Unites States, 1950–2001.

The number of measles cases shows year-to-year fluctuations with a sharp decline after a vaccine was licensed. Findings for measles and other diseases demonstrate that improved sanitation did not single-handedly cause the drop in disease rates.

SOURCE: Centers for Disease Control and Prevention, National Immunization Program (2005).

acute otitis media (AOM) An ear infection in which fluid accumulates behind the eardrum causing fever, pain, and temporary hearing loss. AOM is the most frequently diagnosed disease in childhood.

TABLE 5.3	Risk from Disease Versus Risk from Vaccines
Disease	**Vaccines and their potential side effects**

Measles
    Pneumonia: 1 in 20
    Encephalitis: 1 in 2,000
    Death: 1 in 3,000
	MMR
	    Encephalitis or severe allergic reaction:
	        1 in 1,000,000

Mumps Encephalitis: 1 in 300	

Rubella
    Congenital Rubella
        Syndrome: 1 in 4
        (if women become
        infected during
        pregnancy)	

Diphtheria
    Death: 1 in 20
	DTP
	    Continuous crying, then full recovery: 1 in 100
	    Convulsions or shock, then full recovery: 1 in 1,750
	    Acute encephalopathy: 0 to 10.5 in 1,000,000

Tetanus Death: 3 in 100	Death: none proven

Pertussis
    Pneumonia: 1 in 8
    Encephalitis: 1 in 20
    Death: 1 in 200	

Note: Encephalitis is an inflammation of the brain that can cause neurological damage. Congenital rubella syndrome is a collection of birth defects, often including heart abnormalities and hearing loss, due to German measles.

SOURCE: Centers for Disease Control and Prevention, National Immunization Program (2002).

In about half of AOM cases, fluid persists in the ear for up to a month after treatment, with mild to moderate hearing loss occurring during some of this time (Monobe et al., 2003; Ravicz, Rosowski, & Merchant, 2004). Because fluid muffles speech sounds, infants with a history of AOM produce sounds that are less speechlike and sometimes have problems discriminating speech sounds, especially in noisy environments. They also score lower on a variety of language measures at 3 to 5 years, including articulation and vocabulary (Rvachew et al., 1999). Generally, though, AOM has no long-term effects because the amount of language input in cognitively stimulating homes is more than sufficient to keep them on course (McCormick et al., 2001). These results suggest that children with a history of AOM will benefit from dedicated time for talking, reading, and singing to fine-tune their language skills before they attend school.

Recently, there has been increased concern that routine use of antibiotics to treat AOM is spurring the development of antibiotic-resistant bacteria. To balance the risks involved in over- and undermedicating children, some physicians give parents a prescription but ask them not to fill it unless their children's symptoms worsen within 48 hours. Armed with this "prescription pad safety net," less than one-third of parents administer medication (Siegel et al., 2003).

PREVENTING INJURIES. Young children are accidents waiting to happen, as illustrated by the chilling stories nurse Marietta Stanton (Stanton & Therolf, 1990) tells about her family. A 9-month-old at a family picnic, handed a chip by a little boy, almost choked to death silently while adults stood nearby. (Choking babies cannot cry.) Marietta's brother and sister played "church" with candles and set the house on fire. Her own daughter, at only 7 or 8 months of age, hung onto her crib rail, bounced, and catapulted over the side! At one social gathering, every parent Marietta interviewed knew the common types of childhood accidents, yet *everyone* also admitted that their child had had at least one injury requiring medical treatment.

In industrialized countries, unintentional injuries are the leading cause of death between 1 and 4 years of age (Hoyert, Kung, & Smith, 2005). Many experts prefer not to use the term *accident* because this word suggests that injuries are unpredictable and unavoidable. In fact, many injuries can be prevented by adequate supervision and a few simple precautions.

There are many developmental reasons why the first years of life are dangerous. Take choking. At birth, babies have a high larynx* that lets air pass from the nose to the lungs without involving the mouth and throat. The larynx descends into a lower position about 3 months of age, providing space that allows the tongue to make a wider range of sounds. Now food and drinks pass over the opening of the trachea, creating a constant risk that something will fall into the lungs. The benefits of language outweigh the inevitable deaths from choking, but the fact remains that breathing and chewing at the same time is a complicated maneuver for humans and, especially, young children (Pinker, 1994). This is why it is important to avoid serving young children foods that are associated with choking, such as peanuts and hot dog chunks.

Caregivers often fail to take simple precautions to prevent injuries. In one survey, for example, only 32 percent of infants were restrained in rear-facing safety

---

*larynx: The part of the respiratory tract that contains the vocal cords.

seats, the recommended seats for children less than 1 year old (National Highway Traffic Safety Administration, 2003). Climbing and exploring should also be carefully supervised when children become more independent from 2 to 4 years of age, because toddlers often strike objects head first when they fall (Matheny, 1988). Also, young children are not mature enough to restrain their behavior, so they often dart across roads when balls go astray or they see a familiar person on the other side.

To make the world safer for children, manufacturers follow standards for designing toys and equipment to prevent unnecessary injuries. Physical spaces, such the distance between crib bars, are small to prevent little heads from getting jammed, strings on toys are short enough to prevent strangulation, and items intended for children less than 3 years old are large enough to prevent swallowing. Adults need to complete the job of making environments safe by following the basic safety guidelines summarized in Table 5.4.

You know this little boy is loved because he is properly restrained in a rear-facing infant seat. Babies less than 1 year and less than 20 pounds should be placed in the back of the car, facing the rear. After age 1, toddlers over 20 pounds should be moved to a forward facing seat in the back of the car, where they cannot be injured if an air bag deploys.

TABLE 5.4   Safety Tips for Infants and Toddlers

1. Buy a crib that meets current safety standards, with slats no more than $2\frac{3}{8}$ inches apart and a mattress that leaves no more than a two-finger gap around all edges.

2. Check the house for risky products such as plastic bags, items with sharp edges or corners, and window blinds with cords that can wind around the neck.

3. Check for product recalls. Web sites for the Consumer Product Safety Commission (**www.cpsc.gov**) and the National Safe Kids Campaign (**www.safekids.org**) provide recall lists and other valuable safety announcements.

4. Buy age-appropriate toys. Keep floors and tables free from small objects like buttons and coins. Toys or parts of toys that fit into a cylinder that is $1\frac{1}{4}$ inches wide and $2\frac{1}{4}$ inches long are not recommended for children less than 3 years.

5. Lock up household cleaners, medicines, and vitamins and remove poisonous houseplants. Ask for child-resistant packaging when you fill prescriptions. Keep ipecac syrup/activated charcoal locked away for a poison emergency and post the phone number for a toll-free poison hot line (U.S.: 1-800-222-1222).

6. Never leave children unattended near bathtubs, sinks, or buckets that contain water.

7. Set your water heater at 120 degrees Fahrenheit or lower to prevent burns.

8. Cover electrical outlets and teach children not to touch outlets.

9. Never leave children unattended in a car. In one year alone, at least 30 children died in the United States from overheating in cars.

10. Restrain children properly in motor vehicles. Place infants in rear-facing car seats and remember that the back seat of a vehicle is always the safest location. Children older than 1 year who weigh between 20 to 40 pounds should ride in a forward-facing child seat for as long as their shoulders are below the seat strap slots. Children who outgrow their seats should use a booster seat until the lap and shoulder harnesses fit properly.

11. Take an infant CPR course at your local hospital so you can respond effectively in an emergency.

SOURCES: Adapted from the National Center for Injury Prevention and Control (2006), the National Safe Kids Campaign (2006), and the U.S. Consumer Product Safety Commission (2006).

>>> MEMORY MAKERS <<<

1. The World Health Organization recommends breast-feeding in developing countries for the first _____ of life.

   (a) 3 months   **(b)** 6 months   **(c)** 1 year   **(d)** 2 years

2. Unexplained infant crying is usually due to _____.

   (a) medical conditions   **(b)** poor parenting practices

   (c) stomachaches   **(d)** central nervous system immaturity

3. To prevent SIDS (sudden infant death syndrome), infants should be placed ___ to sleep, which is the ___ position.

   (a) on their backs; prone   **(b)** on their stomachs; prone

   (c) on their backs; supine   **(d)** on their backs; prone

[1-d; 2-d; 3-c]

Raising the Toddler and Young Child

Shortly after children become better at soothing themselves back to sleep and entertaining themselves a bit, a new challenge appears: Toddlers want to do what they want to do. Around the world, adults start teaching acceptable behavior as soon as children are old enough to bite, reach for eyeglasses, and yank a tempting hunk of hair. Studies of parent–child interactions are fascinating accounts of how typical parents accomplish this task.

Life with a Young Child

Why is it tiring to take care of children? In a revealing example, developmental psychologist George Holden (1983) watched mother–child pairs in the supermarket while a tape recorder captured conversations near the cart. The children, all about $2\frac{1}{2}$ years old, requested objects, called for attention, or engaged in troublesome behavior (such as standing up in the cart or reaching for objects) about once every 1.3 minutes! There is nothing unique about a supermarket: 2- to 4-year-olds at home average about one unpleasant behavior every 1.5 minutes (Chamberlain & Patterson, 1985).

Although boys and girls acted similarly in the supermarket study, boys are generally more challenging than girls in less confining situations because they comply with parental demands less often (Kalb & Loeber, 2003) and are somewhat more aggressive. But as with all sex differences, both groups include children who are easy to manage and some who frequently try everyone's patience. And in both sexes, the frequency of aggressive behavior peaks at around 2 years of age and then gradually declines (Chamberlain & Patterson, 1985). Read on to learn how adults respond to outbursts and what works best.

Effective Teaching Strategies

How do most parents cope with toddlers' demands? In the supermarket study, mothers responded almost once per minute. Sometimes they consented (14 percent of the time) but more often they refused with a reason (32 percent), used *power assertion* by saying "No!" or physically intervening (25 percent), ignored the child (15 percent), diverted the child's attention (7 percent), merely acknowledged the child (6 percent), or bribed the child to be good (1 percent).

How did toddlers respond to these strategies? Children complied about 69 percent of the time with their mother's requests, which confirmed the typical finding that toddlers obey adults only about half the time (Londerville & Main, 1981). Also consistent with other studies, diverting children's attention or giving them a reason were the most effective strategies (Putnam, Spritz, & Stifter, 2002). Finally, mothers who prevented unpleasant interactions by talking to their children or occupying them with food or toys experienced fewer unpleasant interactions.

Scientists have also evaluated different control strategies by asking parents to act in particular ways. In one clever study, mothers of 18- to 32-month-olds were instructed to talk on the phone to elicit the inevitable interruptions from their little ones. Each mother either (a) reprimanded the child ("Don't interrupt me!") 100 percent of the time for interrupting, (b) reprimanded 50 percent of the time and ignored the child the other 50 percent of the time, (c) reprimanded 50 percent of the time and gave them positive attention 50 percent of the time, or (d) responded to each interruption with both a reprimand and attention ("Don't interrupt me; yes, I like your tower" or "Yes, I like your tower; don't interrupt me"). The children behaved similarly in all conditions *except one*: When mothers acted inconsistently by reprimanding some of the time and giving positive attention other times, toddlers demanded attention more frequently and showed the most negative emotions. As the research team concluded, "Clear positive feedback for inappropriate demands is a type of inconsistent discipline that can cause normal toddlers to become 'terrible twos'" (Acker & O'Leary, 1996, p. 703).

Toddlers are sure to interrupt when a parent is on the phone. This little girl is probably thinking, "What are you doing? Pay attention to ME!" In a year or so, she can learn that quietly putting a hand on her mother's arm is another way to say, "I'd like a turn to talk."

Spanking

One foolproof way to start a disagreement is to ask a group of college students how they feel about spanking. In our experience, the class will immediately start a heated debate, with sides largely determined by how individuals were raised. The world also casts a split vote. In 1979, Sweden was the first country to ban corporal (physical) punishment, but ten other countries (Austria, Croatia, Cyrpus, Denmark, Finland, Germany, Israel, Italy, Latvia, and Norway) have followed suit with laws designed to change public attitudes about spanking (Gershoff, 2002). In the United States, parents weigh in on the opposing side: In one survey, 67 percent of the parents of 2- to 3-year-olds reported spanking their children (Wissow, 2001).

Despite continued debate, most researchers agree that three conclusions sum up the evidence on physical punishment:

▶ *Physical punishment can have negative effects on children.* Physical punishment increases immediate compliance but can impair children's ability to regulate their own behavior, especially when it is the primary form of discipline. In a summary of 88 different studies, Gershoff (2002) found that physical punishment was associated with an increase in aggression, delinquent behavior, and depression.

▶ *Mild swats are not usually harmful.* There is no evidence that occasional mild swats to toddlers produce long-term negative outcomes. Still, researchers and pediatricians do not support spanking because it puts children at risk for abuse and does not teach them what they should be doing (Baumrind, Larzelere, & Cowan, 2002; Kazdin & Benjet, 2003).

▶ *The effects of spanking depend on one's culture.* Children who live in neighborhoods that oppose spanking have a different experience when they are spanked than children who believe their parents discipline them out of love.

For example, African Americans are more supportive of physical discipline than European Americans are, and studies of African Americans have not found consistent associations between physical punishment and child outcomes (Whaley, 2000). These results show that debates about parenting behavior must take the cultural meaning of parental behavior into account.

When all is said and done, it is still the case that spanking—though not harmful in some contexts—does a poor job of improving children's behavior (Holden, 2002). Consider the fact that parents report using physical punishment more often when children are being aggressive than for any other behavior problem, which often amounts to hitting children for hitting (Gershoff, 2002). Physical punishment also does not teach children to use words to resolve conflicts, nor does it help them learn strategies for waiting patiently, distracting themselves, or regulating their behavior in other ways. In other words, excessive reliance on spanking is another example of a short-term solution that may cause long-term problems.

Fathers and Tots

Most research on parenting focuses on mothers because mothers typically provide the most direct care. But times have changed, and questions about children's interactions with their parents are now often questions about fathers and children.

Families define "fatherhood" in various ways. For example, fathers from more than a dozen cultures in South America believe in *partible paternity*—the ability of multiple fathers to share paternity. Adults in these cultures believe that a fetus grows by adding semen, so women who have sex with multiple partners during pregnancy bear children with multiple fathers. This social arrangement works like an insurance policy: Children with multiple fathers are more than twice as likely as children with one father to survive, and fathers who share paternity know their children will be cared for if they no longer can (McDonald, 1999).

But you don't have to travel to South America to find different definitions of fatherhood. In the United States, historical trends have created two pictures of how men participate in their children's lives. One is a trend for more involvement. Now that many women are in the workforce and divorce is common, about one in five preschoolers receives more care from a father than from any other provider (U.S. Census Bureau, 2004), and over a million children live with a single father (Fields, 2003). Greater father involvement has prompted studies to look at how men respond to and care for young children. The flip side of father involvement is a rise in the number of homes without fathers: Currently, about 23 percent of children in the United States live with a single mother. This situation has led scientists to wonder what fathers contribute to children's development (Tamis-Lemonda & Cabrera, 1999). Research on these issues suggests four conclusions:

▶ *Fathers are competent parents.* Fathers are responsive to infant cues, such as distress signals and mouth movements, and they adjust their behavior accordingly. As a result, fathers and infants regulate each other's behavior during interactions just as mothers and infants do (Lamb, 2000). Fathers and mothers are also equally successful in carrying out routine tasks like feeding, even though some fathers worry about their level of skill (Parke, 1995).

▶ *Father and mothers behave differently around young children.* Especially when mothers are nearby, fathers spend more time in play than in routine caregiving. Generally, they initiate more activities that arouse children whereas mothers are more calming and prefer to read or engage in joint interactions with toys. But these differences are not universal, and fathers' behavior looks like mothers' behavior when fathers are primary caregivers (Parke, 2004). Accordingly, infants of highly involved fathers interact similarly with their mothers and fathers (Frascarolo, 2004).

 ▶ *Interactions with fathers are important.* Children are influenced by all of their interactions; therefore, their fathers' behavior is important. For example, the children of fathers who are affectionate, responsive, and teaching oriented are more likely than other children to score well on tests of cognitive and language development (Black, Dubowitz, & Starr, 1999; Shannon et al., 2002).

▶ *Fathers' contributions benefit the family.* Fathers buffer children from the effects of poverty and improve the quality of mothering by lowering family stress (Lamb, 1998).

Most fathers are competent caregivers who enrich their children's lives.

It is clear that competent fathers improve children's lives. But as one research team commented, "Children do not benefit from the mere presence of fathers" (Black et al., 1999). A father's absence is not always associated with developmental problems because extended family members often take over supportive roles. Even more surprising, young children who are raised without a father display the same gender-role behaviors as other children do, indicating that early gender-role development moves along nicely without an immediate role model (Stevens et al., 2002). These studies illustrate that any single component of a child's environment is just that—one part of a larger system of relationships that determines health and well-being.

Early Day Care

If fathers are important to children, but not indispensable, how important is constant care by a mother? What is the impact of putting a baby in day care while mother works outside the home? The answer to these questions isn't obvious. For most of human history, babies lived in close contact with their mothers for the first 2 years of life. Therefore, it wouldn't be surprising if day care interfered with attachment or if switching back and forth from day care to home caused some stress reactions. On the other hand, babies usually lived in bands of interrelated families that included aunts, grandparents, and other adults. In these cultures, infants were routinely passed off to helpers or strapped to an older sibling while mothers did chores. When we think of it this way, day care looks like another form of shared child rearing that humans have enjoyed for generations (Lamb, 2000). Which mental picture—baby with mother or baby with the band—helps us understand the effects of day care?

The National Institute of Child Health and Human Development (NICHD) Study of Early Child Care was designed to answer this question by enrolling 1,364 families when infants were 1 month old, including some mothers

In many cultures, it is common for older siblings or other relatives to help with the baby while parents get some work done. This Kurdish girl from Turkey will bring a fussing or crying baby back to her mother.

who planned to work outside the home and others who did not. The large sample size allowed investigators to control for family characteristics when they compared children in nonparental care with children reared exclusively at home. There have been three major results from this and similar other studies:

▶ Day care generally does not affect infants' attachment security toward their mothers. However, infants in low-quality child care whose mothers are low in sensitivity are less likely to be securely attached (NICHD Early Child Care Research Network, 1997).

▶ The effect of day care on cognitive development depends on how the quality of out-of-home care compares to what children would have experienced at home (NICHD Center for Research for Mothers & Children, 2000; NICHD Early Child Care Research Network, 2001, 2003). In general, children from low-socioeconomic families benefit from high-quality day care, whereas outcomes for other children are variable (NICHD Early Child Care Research Network & Duncan, 2003). For example, married couples' children who spend more than 30 hours in day care during the first year of life score lower on tests of cognitive development than comparable children who have experienced no out-of-home care or fewer hours of care (Brooks-Gunn, Han, & Waldfogel, 2002).

▶ Children who spend a lot of time in nonparental care are more disobedient and aggressive than their home-reared peers during the transition to kindergarten, but the difference between groups is not large (NICHD Early Child Care Research Network, 2003). The stability of out-of-home care may be more important than the amount of time children spend in out-of-home care, so behavioral problems are primarily associated with unstable child-care arrangements (Love, Harrison, & Sagi-Schwartz, 2003).

Overall, the effects of day care are small. One reason for this finding is that working parents provide a lot of one-on-one time during their nonworking hours. Logs of the daily experiences of children in high-quality care versus home-reared children show that both groups experience equal amounts of stimulation, basic care, and attention (Ahnert, Rickert, & Lamb, 2000). Because children generally spend more time with their parents than in day care, the quality of parental care is still the best predictor of child outcomes (NICHD Early Child Care Research Network, 2002). But this is not the case in understaffed facilities where children must compete for attention. In the NICHD study, day care quality had modest effects on children's cognitive and language scores, although the effects of quality tend to wash out over time as other factors overshadow the influence of early care (Scarr, 1997).

In sum, it does not seem to matter much whether young children are with their mothers all of the time ("baby with mother") or separated from mothers part of the time ("baby with the band"). Instead, it is the quality and consistency of children's relationships that drives development. To promote high-quality care, the National Association for the Education of Young Children publishes standards for developmentally appropriate infant and toddler child care that are summarized in Table 5.5. These standards say that children should have the opportunity to form relationships with qualified, stable caregivers who provide individual attention, a safe environment with a daily schedule that provides a balance of quiet and active play, and a caregiving philosophy that encourages parental involvement and communication between parents and other caregivers.

> **TABLE 5.5** Features of Quality Child Care for Infants and Toddlers

Feature	Description
Interactions	Caregivers interact frequently with individual children, show affection by holding and talking to them, and are sensitive to overstimulation and boredom. Staff turnover is low and caregivers have primary responsibility for particular children, so children form meaningful relationships. There is 1 caregiver for every 3 infants from birth to 12 months, 1 per 3 to 5 children age 12 to 24 months, and one per 4 to 6 children for 2-year-olds.
Curriculum	Caregivers create environments that are developmentally appropriate so children are not always being told "no." Thoughtful equipment and play materials are available, such as lightweight, washable toys for infants and pull toys and picture books for toddlers. The daily schedule provides a balance of activities, including quiet and active play.
Relationships	There is good communication between caregivers and parents with a system for sharing information about children's daily experiences. Parents are welcomed visitors.
Staff qualifications	Caregivers have training in child development, injury prevention, and first aid. They have good communication skills, enjoy working with children, and are interested in learning about new findings in their field.
Physical environment	Indoor and outdoor environments are clean, safe, and spacious with building materials that maintain acceptable levels of noise. There is room for children to play alone or in small groups, always under adult supervision.
Health, safety, licensing	The program is licensed to operate by the appropriate local or state and agencies. Optional accreditation by organizations such as the National Association for the Education of Young Children or the National Association for Family Child Care is evidence that the program meets a set of high standards.

SOURCE: National Association for the Education of Young Children (1998).

Regardless of how babies and toddlers are raised, every group contains an interesting mix of boys and girls with different personalities and patterns of development. We turn next to these differences that influence our pathways through the first 3 years.

> > > **MEMORY MAKERS** < < <

1. In the supermarket study, the strategies for dealing with toddlers' demands that worked the best were ___ and ___.
   (a) diverting their attention; giving a reason (b) saying a stern, "No!"; ignoring them
   (c) bribing them; saying a stern, "No!" (d) ignoring them; bribing them

2. Experts do not recommend mild spanking because (pick all that apply).
   (a) it is always harmful to children's long-term development.
   (b) it does not teach children what they *should* be doing.
   (c) it can escalate into abuse.
   (d) it decreases immediate compliance.

3. Which of the following words capture the characteristics of out-of-home care that best predict children's development? quality, consistency, location, frequency

[1-a; 2-b and c. (Mild swats have no long-term consequences for children's development, especially in cultural settings where this practice is associated with good parenting. Physical punishment usually *increases* compliance shortly afterward, which is why it is a popular practice.) 3-quality and consistency.]

Individual Differences

Humans are always slicing life into categories. Instead of just watching the interesting differences among children, we like to decide where each one "fits" in a set of descriptive boxes. Two of the earliest questions we ask are "Is it a boy or a girl?" and "Is he (or she) an easy baby?" A few months later, we find it hard not to compare one child's rate of development with the development of other children we have known. How boring life would be without the individual differences that begin with the first breath of life!

Our Gendered Selves

Over 30 years ago, researchers asked first-time mothers to "describe your baby as you would to a close friend or relative" (Rubin, Provenzano, & Luria, 1974). Despite the fact that boys and girls had the same average birth weight, length, and Apgar scores, parents saw their children through pink and blue lenses: Boys were more often described as "big" and girls as "little," "beautiful," and "cute." Over 20 years later, parents still rated their girls as weaker, more delicate, and more feminine (Karraker, Vogel, & Lake, 1995). Although it's not clear why identity is so intertwined with gender, there is no doubt that the process of establishing a gender identity begins remarkably early.

EARLY SEX DIFFERENCES. Contrary to the stereotype of boys as the strong, tough sex, males are actually more vulnerable than females during the first year. Boys have a higher infant mortality rate because their single X chromosome makes them more prone to hereditary abnormalities (Klug et al., 2006; Lary & Paulozzi, 2001), and they are more negatively affected than girls to drug exposure in utero (Moe & Slinning, 2002). On the other hand, girls are physically and neurologically more advanced. Even when only healthy neonates are considered, females score higher than males on measures of how easily and predictably they transition between states of arousal (Lundqvist & Sabel, 2000), and they potty train sooner. The early vulnerability of males helps explain why more boys than girls die of SIDS.

But some differences confirm our stereotypes about the sexes. Newborn boys weigh a little more and have larger hearts and lungs than girls. Boys also have less fat at birth, and this difference between the sexes increases throughout infancy (Tanner, 1990). Infant boys are the more active sex, and as toddlers and preschoolers they engage in more rough-and-tumble play. Girls, however, are the more precocious communicators: They point earlier than boys and are quicker to produce words (Butterworth, 1998). In one study, females had spoken about 90 unique words by 16 months whereas boys averaged only 30 (Fenson et al., 1994). Even in infancy, girls are better at discriminating facial expressions (McClure, 2000). As toddlers, they comply more often than boys when mothers make a request, and they show more guilt when there is a mishap (Kochanska, Coy, & Murray, 2001; Kochanska et al., 2002).

Parents' perceptions of their children are influenced by sex-role stereotypes, so it is not surprising that their perceptions are often unreliable. For example, boys and girls achieve motor milestones at about the same time, yet mothers overestimate their boys' abilities and underestimate their girls'. In a telling demonstration, researchers asked mothers of 11-month-olds to estimate the steepest slope their babies could crawl down without falling, using an apparatus shown in Figure 5.5

FIGURE 5.5 Mother's predictions for boys versus girls.

Stereotypes about boys and girls influence mothers' predictions of their children's motor abilities. Despite the fact that boys and girls are equally skilled at crawling down a sloped walkway like this one, mothers overestimate the angle their sons can manage and underestimate the slope their daughters can manage.

SOURCE: Mondschein, Adolph, & Tamis-LeMonda (2000).

(Mondschein, Adolph, & Tamis-LeMonda, 2000). There were no sex differences when children actually performed the task, but mothers consistently expected there to be. The results were dramatic: On average, the mothers expected their daughters to fail when the probability of success was 100 percent, and they expected sons to succeed when the probability of success was 0 percent. The message is clear: Parents have different expectations for boys and girls, but you need to watch children if you want to know how they actually behave.

Observations of boys and girls prove they are more similar than different. Regarding activity levels, for example, the average difference between groups is only .2 of a standard deviation (a measure of how variables scores are), a difference that is illustrated in Figure 5.6. Clearly, many girls are wiggling more than many boys, so knowing a baby's sex tells us very little about how fast we'll have to run to keep up.

GENDER IDENTITY. Newborns can be classified as male or female based on their chromosomal profiles, their responsiveness to hormones, or their external anatomy (Kessler, 1998). But our biological sex is just part of what we mean by gender. Each of us also develops a **gender identity**, which is our fundamental sense of being male or female. As we learn the conventions of our culture, we also acquire **gender-role behaviors**, which are behaviors consistent with cultural norms for how males and females should act. By adolescence or young adulthood, most of us have adopted a **sexual orientation**, which is a preference to interact sexually with opposite-sexed partners, same-sexed partners, or both sexes.

These layers of our gendered selves begin to emerge very early. Children start to label themselves and other people as male or female around 18 months of age, the same time they begin to look longer at pictures of toys that are associated with their gender (Serbin et al., 2001). From 2 to 3 years, children who are more advanced about labeling their gender also have more knowledge about gender-role behaviors. These knowledgeable children readily classify objects as male or female and begin to prefer same-sex peers (Fogel, 2001). By 3 years, most children identify themselves and others as male or female, show gender-based toy preferences, and have already begun to act differently with same-sex versus opposite-sex peers.

OTHER GENDER PATHS. In cases of **gender dysphoria**, a child's gender identity does not correspond to his or her physical appearance, so a normal-looking male will feel as if he is a female trapped in a male body, and vice versa. The mean age of referral for children with gender dysphoria is 6 or 7 years old, but parents and teachers say that dissatisfaction is evident much earlier. Outcomes are variable: Some children continue to feel dysphoric as they grow, and most of these children are later attracted to their own sex, but in some cases dysphoric feelings lessen or disappear (Zucker & Bradley, 2000).

Some scientists study *intersexed* individuals to try to understand how someone's gender identity can be inconsistent with their physical appearance. (Recall from Chapter 3 that intersexed babies are born with nonstandard genitals due to conditions that influence early hormone exposure or response to hormones.) Doctors used to recommend surgery for these babies, usually as early as possible. Typically this involves removing tissue from the enlarged clitoris of a girl and reassigning boys with extremely small penises to the female gender. For a feature

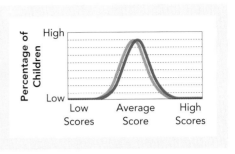

FIGURE 5.6 Much ado about small sex differences.

The means of these bell-shaped curves differ by .2 standard deviations, the average difference in activity level between infant boys and girls. Most sex differences tell us very little about how individual boys or girls will act.

Despite all the stereotypes about boys and girls, both sexes start out exploring the world with an amazing lack of fear.

gender identity Our fundamental sense of being male or female.

gender-role behaviors Behaviors consistent with cultural norms for how males and females should act.

sexual orientation The preference to interact sexually with opposite-sex partners, same-sex partners, or both sexes.

gender dysphoria A condition in which an individual's gender identity does not match his or her biological sex.

story in *Johns Hopkins Magazine*, physician William Reiner described the case that led him to rethink his beliefs about early surgery—a 7-year-old whose situation, in Reiner's words, "just about tore everybody's guts out" (para. 3):

> Like most of the other children in the study, Kayla had been castrated and was being raised as a girl. But she was not a happy child. Small and aggressive, she had gotten into a number of fights with her classmates. Rather than the dolls her parents gave her, she played with cars and trucks, and she had insisted that her schoolmates call her by the biblical boy's name she had chosen for herself. Eventually she had refused to go to school altogether.
>
> Reiner gave Kayla a battery of psychological tests and found that she came out overwhelmingly male on measurements of gender-typical behaviors and self-concept. He told Kayla's parents what he had observed. After some reflection, the parents decided that their child ought to know that she had been born a boy. They asked Reiner if he would tell her.
>
> So the next day, Reiner explained to Kayla that she had been born a boy who had no penis, so her doctors and parents had decided to raise her as a girl.
>
> "His eyes opened about as wide as eyes could open," recalls Reiner. "He climbed into my lap and wrapped his arms around me and stayed like that."
>
> As Reiner cradled the child in his arms, he felt as though an enormous weight had been lifted, and he himself was overcome with emotion. The child remained in his arms without moving for half an hour. (Hendricks, 2000, para. 8-12)

Reiner is part of a growing number of physicians who believe that some children are born with a male or a female gender identity and remain that way regardless of how they are reared. Patients like Kayla, who declare themselves to be boys after years of being reared as girls, suggest that the brain may be biased toward a gender identity by prenatal hormone exposure. This view is a dramatic shift from previous thinking, which held that infants were blank slates whose identity was molded by early experiences.

Intersex is caused by a variety of conditions that expose fetuses to abnormal hormonal environments. Therefore, the success of early reassignments varies. In two follow-up studies of 34 patients like Kayla, 22 had reassigned themselves as males (Hendricks, 2000), yet almost all patients in another group were content with the gender in which they were raised (Wisniewski et al., 2000). But even a few discontented patients is too many for the intersex community, which is against unnecessary surgery before individuals are old enough to provide informed consent. In the future, it may be possible to determine which identity is more likely to be successful based on a child's condition or results from diagnostic tests. For the time being, experts admit that we do not know the full story of how gender identity is constructed during our earliest years.

Early Personalities

Adults come in cheerful and cranky varieties with many possibilities in between. This is also true of babies. Some are generally happy, react positively to new situations, and calm themselves quickly. Others are irritable and slow to recover from troubling events. When we talk about the "personality" of infants, we are usually talking about **temperament**: individuals' characteristic moods, ways of reacting to situations, and styles of self-regulation.

TEMPERAMENTAL DIFFERENCES. The most famous study of temperament is the New York Longitudinal Study, which was launched in 1956 by psychiatrists Alexander Thomas and Stella Chess (Thomas, Chess, & Birch, 1968).

temperament Individuals' characteristic moods, ways of reacting to situations, and styles of self-regulation.

Eighty-five families agreed to let these researchers study 141 of their children from early infancy through adulthood. The results led Thomas and Chess to propose nine dimensions of infant temperament, including activity level, rhythmicity (how regular infants were in body functions such as sleeping and eating), and intensity of reactions. Because certain traits tended to cluster together, Thomas and Chess proposed that many children fall into one of the following temperamental categories:

▶ *Difficult children* (10 percent of the sample) had irregular biological functions, responded negatively to new stimuli and changes in the environment, and had intense reactions to events. Though slow to adapt, these children were indistinguishable from other children in nonchallenging environments. But whenever life inflicted new demands on them, such as a transition to nursery school, their irritable patterns reappeared.

▶ *Easy children* (40 percent of the sample) established regular routines, were cheerful, and were unusually positive in the face of new situations.

▶ *Slow-to-warm-up children* (15 percent of the sample) reacted to new foods, people, and events by turning away and fussing. Their negative reactions were mild, though, and they acted like other children once they had adjusted to a new situation.

Thomas and Chess found that children who were difficult during their early years had higher rates of behavior problems later on than easy children, slow-to-warm-up children, or the 35 percent of children who did not fit a single category. Other studies have confirmed that some children are at risk for troublesome behavior. For example, difficult temperament is associated with higher rates of doctor visits, accidents, and sleep disturbances (Carey, 1985).

But data on the relationship between difficult temperament and later problems have often been inconsistent. One problem researchers encountered was measuring some of Thomas and Chess's dimensions. For example, infants who were rhythmic in bowel habits were not always rhythmic in sleeping, and those who reacted intensely in one situation did not necessarily react that way in another (Rothbart, 2004a; Rothbart, Ahadi, & Evans, 2000; Rothbart, Chew, & Gartstein, 2001). To address problems such as this one, some investigators have tried to identify dimensions of temperament that reliably capture infants' behavioral styles. One result, the Infant Behavior Questionnaire, yields scores on dimensions that have frequently emerged from these studies: activity level, smiling and laughter, fear, distress at limitations (frustration), soothability, and attentional persistence (Gartstein & Rothbart, 2003; Rothbart & Mauro, 1990).

"Oh, he's cute, all right, but he's got the temperament of a car alarm."

If your parents have talked about your baby behavior, you might be wondering whether these early traits are stable. The answer is yes and no. Consider the difference between *inhibited* and *uninhibited* temperaments. Inhibited children act distressed in unfamiliar situations whereas uninhibited children are sociable and spontaneous. Infants who respond with a lot of motor activity and distress to stimulation (about 20 percent of European American infants) are most likely to be inhibited in the second year, whereas those who show minimal distress (about 40 percent) tend to become uninhibited. But the heritability of inhibited temperament is only about .50, which means that heredity *and* environment contribute to this reaction pattern (Robinson et al., 1992). It is not surprising, then, that longitudinal studies have found both stability and change. For example, inhibited children who spend time in nonparental care are more likely than those reared solely by parents to change classifications (Fox et al., 2001). Day care experiences might foster an easygoing approach to life by giving children more exposure to unfamiliar situations, or perhaps parents who use day care are less protective. In either case the take-home message is clear: Temperament has biological underpinnings, but we cannot understand the long-term implications of temperament without looking at the interactions between children and parents.

TEMPERAMENT AND PARENTING. Bobby, a typical slow-to-warm-up child, reacted at 6 months to carrots by stopping dead in his tracks and letting them dribble out of his mouth. His parents immediately decided that he didn't like carrots and never gave them to him again. Unfortunately, most encounters with food followed this pattern, so by age 10 Bobby ate little more than hamburgers, applesauce, and boiled eggs. Similarly, when he backed away from children on the playground at 2 years old, his parents concluded that he didn't need such a noisy environment. Subsequent play opportunities consisted of a few family members who met at his home. Perhaps as a result of his parents' decisions, Bobby excelled in solo activities during childhood but avoided group sports and social organizations (Thomas et al., 1968).

 What would Bobby have been like if his parents had given him a chance to warm up to the world? We'll never know. But studies of childhood styles and parenting strategies have shown that different combinations produce different outcomes. Thomas and Chess used the term *goodness of fit* to describe parents' ability to adapt to their infants and infants' abilities to compensate for deficiencies in their parents. Goodness of fit describes the dynamics of parent–child relationships, something that changes over time as infants, parents, and their social contexts change (Seifer, 2000).

Developmental psychologist Kenneth Rubin and his colleagues reported a striking example of how parents affect the stability of children's temperament (Rubin, Burgess, & Hastings, 2002). They observed toddlers in potentially frightening situations involving an unfamiliar woman, a clown, and a robot that spewed smoke. Then they watched the children interact with peers when they were 4 years old. As you might have predicted, toddlers who didn't approach unfamiliar people or objects tended to become preschoolers who watched from afar. But results were more interesting when mothers' behavior was taken into account. The correlations between early and later inhibition were strong for children whose mothers were intrusive, overprotecting, or prone to make negative comments ("That's not right—let me do that") but not for children whose mothers were relaxed and positive. The ability of parents to help bring inhibited children out of their shells is one example of how adults can gently nudge children onto new behavioral paths (Fox et al., 2005).

CULTURAL VALUES. Before you begin wishing that your parents had pushed you to be a bit less inhibited (or perhaps a bit more inhibited!), keep in mind that culture plays a role in how we evaluate temperament. In North America, for example, uninhibited children are considered better adjusted than inhibited children, but being reserved is highly valued in Chinese society. Perhaps as a result, North American mothers who are accepting and encouraging tend to have uninhibited children, whereas Chinese mothers who are accepting and encouraging tend to have inhibited children. Apparently, warm, encouraging parents lead children to adopt their culture's valued behavioral style (Chen et al., 1998). Because assumptions about how children should act do not always cross cultural boundaries, the American Psychological Association encourages professionals to become familiar with the values and practices of the people they advise (American Psychological Association, 2002).

This Hmong mother comes from a southeast Asian culture that values sharing and cooperation. Her baby's inhibited manner will make it easy to fit in with the group, so she will do little to encourage more rambunctious behavior.

Evaluating a Child's Development

Andrew was born without complications and had an unremarkable first year: He sat up at 6 months, crept at 8 months, and walked at 12 months. His mother nonetheless became concerned about his developmental progress at a neighborhood play group. Compared to some of the other toddlers, Andrew had difficulty coloring and finishing other activities that involved fine motor coordination. After a pediatrician referred him for an evaluation, an examiner tested him at 36 months using a developmental assessment called the *Bayley Scales of Infant Development* (Bayley, 1993).

Andrew's mother had noticed something many parents notice: that Andrew was farther ahead in some areas of development than in others. Parents also worry when children stop making progress or lose a skill. Sometimes everything is perfectly normal, but other times these events flag an underlying medical or developmental problem. How do professionals tell the difference? Before we answer this question, we'll explain why some patterns of development that cause concern are actually perfectly normal. Then we'll describe how professionals evaluate a child's development.

DETERMINING WHAT IS TYPICAL (AND WHAT IS NOT). It's tempting to think of development as a steady journey, one in which infants gradually get better at navigating motor skills, language, and social interactions. But the reality is less predictable. Rather than simply adding a skill or two each day, development occurs in fits and starts, with rapid change following times of relative stability. And instead of always heading in one direction, children sometimes take two steps forward and one step back. Finally, infants and toddlers learn some skills quickly even though they are virtually incapable of learning other skills that do not seem more difficult. It's no wonder parents sometimes worry whether their children are developing on schedule.

Physical growth is a good example of sudden leaps in development. Young children can appear to stay the same height for days or months, then show measurable growth over a 24-hour period (Lampl, Veldhuis, & Johnson, 1992; Lampl et al., 1998). Both gradual and sudden changes are perfectly normal in many areas of development, including motor development and language learning.

Development plays another interesting trick: Children may seem to regress or lose progress when they first learn a new skill. For example, crawling babies who have learned not to plunge headfirst down a steep incline will nonetheless plunge down the incline when they first learn to walk. What looks like an unexpected bout of baby stupidity is really a lack of transfer from one skill to a new, more advanced skill (Adolph, 1997, 2000). This is why caregivers who trust a baby in a specific situation, such as at the top of stairs, may have an accident on their hands when the baby gets older. Other developmental advances also produce regressive-looking behavior. For example, a child who shares may suddenly become a toy snatcher after the concept of "mine" appears.

Finally, it is difficult to predict how easily children will learn one skill by considering how quickly they have learned others. Infants quickly learn behaviors that promote survival but have difficulty learning actions that are unnecessary (Rovee-Collier, 1996). For example, premature babies quickly learn body movements that bring them closer to a "breathing" bear (perhaps because proximity to others can ensure survival), yet these same preemies have difficulty kicking their feet to make a mobile move. Early development is so individual and complicated that even Myrtle McGraw didn't predict that Johnny would skate before he would ride a tricycle! To quantify these complexities, developmental professionals rely on special tests to evaluate children.

NORM-REFERENCED TESTS. It is hard to evaluate children by watching them in their natural environments because specific events that might reveal their strengths and weaknesses are unlikely to occur. For example, you would never know whether Andrew avoided puzzles because he has difficulty holding the pieces or because he just isn't interested in puzzles. This is why professionals rely on **norm-referenced tests** (also called *standardized tests*) to assess children's skills. Norm-referenced tests have been administered to large samples of children so the performance of individual children can be compared against children as a whole.

One of the most widely used norm-referenced tests is the one Andrew took: the *Bayley Scales of Infant Development* (Bayley, 1993). The goal of the Bayley is to describe development from 1 month through 42 months of age by sampling abilities that are typically present at a given age. For a recent version, the Bayley-III, examiners directly assess infants' cognitive, language, and motor development. For example, they watch how infants use their hands with toys and how they respond to the examiner. In addition, caregivers fill out a questionnaire to describe their infant's typical behaviors, such as their feeding and sleeping habits.

How did Andrew perform on the Bayley? Splendidly. He scored well above average on both mental and motor development, and the examiner reassured his mother that the difference between these scores was typical of 37 percent of children (Bayley, 1993).

Although the Bayley is useful for describing where a baby is *right now*, early versions could not predict how most children would do in the future. Like many infant tests, the Bayley lacked **predictive validity** (Bradley-Johnson, 2001), the ability to predict later behavior, skills, or academic achievement. (Longitudinal data are not yet available for the Bayley-III.) In fact, there is virtually no relationship between scores before 2 years of age on most infant tests and later IQ scores; after age 2, the relationship between performance and later IQ gradually

norm-referenced tests Tests that have been administered to large and representative samples of children so the performance of individual children can be compared against the performance of children as a whole.

predictive validity The ability of tests to predict later behaviors, skills, or academic achievement.

increases. The reason early performance is not very predictive is that descriptive tests measure sensorimotor skills that have little in common with the language and problem-solving tasks that populate tests for older children. As education professor Linda Siegel (1981) explained, "The infant grasping a dangling ring and putting it in his or her mouth is engaging in a different kind of behavior than a 5-year-old pointing out the similarities between an apple and a banana" (p. 545).

But performance in the first year of life does predict later intelligence when tasks tap basic information processing skills. For instance, infants who later score well on intelligence tests get bored by (habituate to) a repeated stimulus more rapidly, spend more time looking at novel rather than familiar pictures, and prefer looking at a picture of an object they recently felt with their hands (Rose & Feldman, 1995). One thing these tasks have in common is speed of processing. "Short-looking" infants need to view a picture for only about 10 seconds before they will prefer a novel one, whereas "long-looking" infants need about 40 seconds. There are more long-looking babies among preterm infants, so speed of processing may be one reason why high-risk babies often grow up to have poorer memories and IQ scores than term babies do (Rose & Feldman, 2000; Sigman, Cohen, & Beckwith, 1997).

To improve predictive validity, the recent edition of the Bayley Scales incorporated more items that measure habituation and novelty preference (Bayley, 2006). Other investigators have started from scratch and developed new tests by selecting items specifically to predict language and school-related skills. Figure 5.7 illustrates some of the attention and communication items in one 20- to 30-minute assessment procedure called the Cognitive Abilities Scale-2 (CAS-2). Scores on this test correlate with intelligence test scores 5 years later, even for children who are only 1 year old (Clemmer, Klifman, & Bradley-Johnson, 1992; Johnson & Bradley-Johnson, 2002).

Examiner places a cloth on the table . . .

puts an actractive toy on the cloth . . .

and records whether the baby pulls the cloth to retrieve the toy.

Explanation

Nearly all 10-month-olds solve this problem; success is predictive of later vocabulary and IQ scores.

Examiner records whether the baby looks at a black and white face . . .

follows the picture . . .

and prefers to look at novel picture.

Explanation

Early attention and a preference for novel information correlate with later intelligence test scores.

FIGURE 5.7 Sample Items from the Cognitive Abilities Scale-2 (CAS-2)

SOURCE: Bradley-Johnson & Johnson (2001).

>>> MEMORY MAKERS <<<

Match each term on the left with an explanation on the right:

1. gender identity
2. gender-role behaviors
3. sexual orientation
4. gender dysphoria

(a) preferences about the sex we prefer to interact with sexually
(b) when one's gender identity does not match one's appearance
(c) behaviors consistent with cultural norms for how males and females should act
(d) our fundamental sense of being male or female

5. Activity level, fear, and soothability are three dimensions of infant _____.

(a) gender identity
(b) temperament
(c) states
(d) cognitive performance

6. A test that has been administered to a large number of children so the performance of individual children can be compared against children as a whole is called a _____ or _____ test.

(a) developmental; structured
(b) developmental; standardized
(c) norm-referenced; standardized
(d) norm-referenced; structured

[1-d; 2-c; 3-a; 4-b; 5-b; 6-c]

Environmental Influences and Early Development

Worldwide, about 1 out of every 12 children dies before the age of 5 years. Tragically, almost all of these deaths are preventable. In developing countries, 7 out of 10 childhood deaths are due to only five causes: acute respiratory infection, diarrhea, measles, malaria, and malnutrition (United Nations, 2001).

The keys to protecting the world's children include access to safe food and water, education for parents, and improved health care. In developing countries, infants and toddlers need resources that most children in developed countries already enjoy, including adequate protein and calories, vitamin A supplementation (which reduces the incidence of measles and diarrhea), and inoculations to prevent disease. Other needs vary with the location. For example, insecticide-treated bed nets can reduce childhood death rates by 35 percent in malarial zones (World Health Organization, 1997).

But survival is only the first step. Infants and toddlers also need healthy, stimulating environments to develop the skills they need to benefit from education and community life a few years down the line. Regardless of where they live, this goal is threatened when children come into the world challenged by poverty and maltreatment.

Poverty

Children who live in central Africa and southern Asia are more likely than those in other parts of the world to face the challenges of low family incomes and inadequate public services. But poverty is not restricted to these regions. More than 1 out of 10 children live in poverty in some of the richest countries in the world, including the United States, Canada, the United Kingdom, and Germany (UNICEF, 2000).

Family SES (socioeconomic status) is correlated with developmental outcomes because poverty is associated with numerous direct risks, including biological trauma, few learning opportunities in the home, and unresponsive parent–child interactions. Let's look at each of these problems in turn.

POVERTY AND BIOLOGICAL TRAUMA. Low-income infants are especially likely to be exposed to malnutrition, disease, and, in some locations, toxic substances (such as lead) that concentrate in low-cost housing. The impact of biological trauma can span several generations. For example, female rats that are fed protein-deficient diets have small offspring that show attentional problems and hypersensitivity to noise. But when the diets of malnourished rats are corrected during pregnancy, their offspring still show learning deficits. Humans also show intergenerational effects. For example, lead in mothers' bones can elevate lead levels in their fetuses and cause abnormalities (Chuang, Schwartz, Gonzales-Cossio et al., 2001; Raymond et al., 2002). These findings illustrate why efforts to reduce biological risk may not show immediate results.

POVERTY AND LEARNING OPPORTUNITIES. Poverty also limits children's access to material goods and enriching events. One way to describe a child's closest environment is the **Home Observation for Measurement of the Environment (HOME)**, a procedure in which a trained interviewer visits the home and evaluates a list of characteristics including parental responsiveness (such as whether the parent touched the child), learning stimulation (including how many books the child has), and miscellaneous stimulation (such as whether the child's play environment is free of hazards). Even before 3 years of age, poor children have less stimulating environments than nonpoor children, with parents who are less likely to respond to their speech, less likely to hug them, and less likely to provide interesting activities. Higher scores on the HOME are associated with more advanced motor, cognitive, and social development (Bradley et al., 2001; Bradley, Caldwell, & Corwyn, 2003; Leventhal, Martin, & Brooks-Gunn, 2004).

There is evidence that economic well-being directly affects children's development. In one study, investigators evaluated over a thousand families and their children when the children were 1 to 36 months old. Figure 5.8 presents some of their results. Notice that the lowest scores came from children in families that had experienced declining incomes. But changes in economic circumstances affected HOME scores, which in turn predicted school readiness, language development, and positive social behavior (Dearing, McCartney, & Taylor, 2001). The fact that cognitive development sometimes responds to changes in family circumstances shows that correlations between income and development are not due solely to biological differences between poor and nonpoor children, such as the consequences of low birth weight or other biological factors associated with poverty.

Other studies have also found that as much as 50 percent of the relationship between income and cognitive development is due to the home environment

Home Observation for Measurement of the Environment (HOME) An inventory for measuring the quality of a child's home environment by direct observation and an interview with the child's primary caregiver.

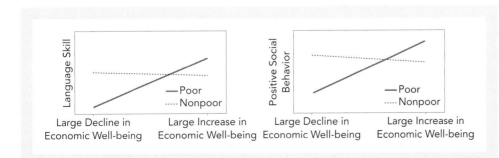

FIGURE 5.8 Changes in families' income can influence children's development.

In nonpoor families, language and social behavior scores at 36 months do not change much when families' income changes. But in poor families, economic gains are associated with improved cognitive and social functioning.

SOURCE: Adapted from Dearing, McCartney, & Taylor (2001).

social reproduction The tendency for children to grow up to occupy the same social class level their parents occupy.

child maltreatment Actions (or failures to act) by caregivers that put children at risk of harm. Maltreatment includes physical abuse, sexual abuse, neglect, and emotional abuse.

(Duncan & Brooks-Gunn, 2000). Sociologists use the term **social reproduction** to describe the tendency for children to "inherit" their parents' social class through nonbiological means (Farkas & Beron, 2001). One way this works is through the knowledge and skills parents pass on from one generation to the next. For example, adults with professional jobs provide an average of over 2,000 words of language input to their young children per hour, compared to about 1,200 words for working-class adults and 600 words for poor adults (Hart & Risley, 1995). Poor parents sometimes provide less stimulation because they have less education, but other times they are simply overwhelmed by the challenges of their environments.

POVERTY AND PARENTAL RESPONSIVENESS. Poverty increases stress on parents, many of whom are single mothers. For example, 28 percent of the poor mothers in one sample reported being depressed, compared to only 17 percent of nonpoor mothers (Liaw & Brooks-Gunn, 1994).

Depression affects how mothers act toward their babies. As we saw in the last chapter, most infants and mothers synchronize their behavior, with mothers regulating their actions to keep infants appropriately stimulated. In contrast, depressed mothers are less responsive and predictable (Milgrom, Westley, & Gemmill, 2004). These mothers alternate withdrawn behavior with intrusive actions, such as poking or tickling, that do not help their babies learn to regulate their own behavior. They also imitate their babies less often than nondepressed mothers do, show fewer responses to their infants' behavior, and play fewer games (Field et al., 1990, 2003). Because infants need to experience their behavior producing predictable effects on the environment, they learn more from nondepressed but unfamiliar mothers than they do from interactions with their own depressed mothers (Kaplan et al., 2002).

Maternal depression is a risk factor regardless of a family's income. In fact, quality of maternal caregiving is one of the best predictors of early cognitive and social competence (NICHD Early Child Care Research Network, 2002). Still, economic hardship places infants at higher risk for being raised by a parent who suffers from depression (Petterson & Albers, 2001).

Child Maltreatment

Toddlers are like mirrors that reflect the world. A little girl who watches her mother install picture hooks will soon be hammering away with her blocks while a boy with a new sister may try to push a diaper onto the stomach of the helpless baby. Some images children reflect are disturbing, as in this example of a 32-month-old who was observed at preschool (Main & George, 1985):

> [He] tried to take the hand of the crying other child, and when she resisted, he slapped her on the arm with his open hand. He then turned away from her to look at the ground and began vocalizing very strongly. "Cut it out! CUT IT OUT!" each time saying it a little faster and louder. He patted her, but when she became disturbed by his patting, he retreated, "hissing at her and baring his teeth." He then began patting her on the back again, his patting became beating, and he continued beating her despite her screams. (p. 410)

As you might have guessed, this little boy had been physically abused. Because young children place huge demands on adults, they are often the victims of **child maltreatment**: actions or oversights by caregivers that harm children or put them at immediate risk of harm. There are four major categories of maltreatment (Cicchetti, Toth, & Maughan, 2000):

▶ *physical abuse* causes bodily injury that is not accidental.

▶ *neglect* is the failure to provide minimum care and supervision, including the failure to provide necessary medical services.

▶ *sexual abuse* involves attempted or actual sexual contact between the caregiver and the child.

▶ *emotional maltreatment* is a persistent failure to fulfill a child's emotional needs.

In the United States, over 900,000 cases of abuse and neglect come to the attention of child protection agencies each year, or about 12 for every 1,000 children. Children 3 years old and younger are more likely than older children to be maltreated, and this vulnerable group also experiences the majority of deaths from abuse (United States Department of Health and Human Services, 2005). Of course, actual maltreatment rates are unknown because most cases are never detected.

THE ECOLOGY OF ABUSE AND NEGLECT. Children with difficult temperaments and physical disabilities are more likely to be abused than those who make fewer demands on their caregivers. But characteristics of parents and communities—not characteristics of children—explain most of the variability in maltreatment rates (Ammerman, 1991; Kolko, 2002). Abusive parents are more likely to be young, poor, socially isolated, and living in neighborhoods that lack social resources. They often have unrealistic expectations about children, place their needs above their children's, and discipline inconsistently. Females are more likely than males to abuse, probably because they spend more time with children, but the risk of abuse skyrockets when a man in the household is not the child's biological father. For example, the probability that a baby will be beaten to death is a hundred times greater at the hands of a stepfather than a biological father (Daly & Wilson, 2000). Using the framework of Bronfenbrenner's bioecological model, which you read about in Chapter 1, Table 5.6 summarizes the major risk factors for abuse and neglect at three levels of a child's ecological system.

Babies are especially vulnerable when they are shaken or thrown violently. These actions cause a number of injuries, including retinal and brain hemorrhages, that are called **shaken baby syndrome**. Shaken babies have a high mortality rate, and survivors often suffer from subtle neurological disorders or seizures (American Academy of Pediatrics Committee on Child Abuse and Neglect, 1993; Barlow et al., 2004). Inappropriate play can cause shaken baby syndrome, but the usual cause is a caregiver who became frustrated by relentless crying.

Maltreatment rates can be reduced by giving high-risk caregivers information about parenting, social support, and encouragement to expand

shaken baby syndrome Retinal and neurological injuries caused by shaking a baby or violently throwing him or her against a surface.

TABLE 5.6	Risk Factors for Child Maltreatment
Microsystem	Adults are more likely to abuse if they were severely disciplined or abused as children (although only about 30 percent of children who are physically abused become abusers themselves). Other family risk factors are drug and alcohol abuse; parental depression or poor impulse control; anger, conflict, or violence in the home; inconsistent child-rearing practices; unrealistic expectations about children's behavior; and the presence of a stepfather.
Exosystem	Community risks include high unemployment and poverty rates, neighborhood violence, and isolation from extended family and informal social networks.
Macrosystem	Cultural beliefs and values that promote maltreatment include endorsement of physical punishment and racism that blocks families' access to financial opportunities and social resources.

SOURCES: Cicchetti, Toth, & Maughan (2000); Kolko, (2002).

This social worker is helping a young mother gain the knowledge and resources she needs to provide a safe, stimulating home for her child. Home visitation programs make a difference in children's lives when there are clear program goals and mothers have a chance to develop relationships with highly trained staff members.

their social networks. In one demonstration project, mothers who were mostly teenaged, unmarried, and low income were visited by a nurse before and for 2 years after the birth of their first child. During these visits, nurses focused on a broad range of health and lifestyle issues that are part of the ecology of abuse and neglect. Only 4 percent of the unmarried teens who received nurse visits abused their children compared to 19 percent of comparison mothers, and the children of nurse-visited mothers had fewer medical visits for injuries. In addition to saving lives, intervention programs for high-risk families also save the government money, proving that prevention has widespread social benefits (Olds et al., 1998).

CONSEQUENCES OF ABUSE AND NEGLECT. Child abuse and neglect have a negative impact on many aspects of development. The sad boy described earlier ("Cut it out! CUT IT OUT!") illustrates that abused toddlers often have problems with relationships. Compared to their nonabused peers, these children are withdrawn, aggressive, and less likely to be securely attached to their primary caregivers. Infants and toddlers who are exposed to violence have problems controlling their emotions, are less responsive to environmental events, and show abnormalities in their self-concepts. For example, some abused toddlers react negatively to mirror images of themselves and are not very persistent when situations call for a bit of problem solving, as if they do not believe they can succeed (Kaufman & Henrich, 2000).

Maltreatment can also influence how children cope with stress. All newborns have highly reactive stress systems that release stress hormones whenever they are upset. Later in the first year of life, most babies no longer show large hormone fluctuations when they are fussing because they have learned to communicate displeasure without becoming physiologically distressed—if they anticipate the problem will be fixed (Gunnar & Donzella, 2002). In a wonderful example, 9-month-olds who had a sensitive, responsive babysitter did not show stress reactions when they were separated from their mothers, whereas infants who were left with a babysitter who ignored them unless they cried acted distressed (Gunnar et al., 1992). Through the stress-response system, young children's bodies can record their caregiving histories.

Programs for Families and Children

The recipe for raising infants sounds simple: They need responsive and continuous relationships with caregivers who have the knowledge and means (including financial resources and social support) to protect and stimulate them. But as the examples you will read about next illustrate, some attempts to educate parents or stimulate their children have had no long-term benefits, and others have actually harmed them. This is why **evaluation research**—research that assesses the impact of intervention programs—is a critical component of efforts to help children at risk.

SUCCESSFUL INTERVENTIONS. Earlier we described a nurse-visitation program that decreased rates of child abuse and unintentional injuries. Successful home visitation programs tend to have several characteristics: Visits are made at least two to three times per month and last for over a year, home visitors are highly trained and have a low turnover rate (so clients develop relationships with staff members), and the programs have clearly specified goals

evaluation research Research to evaluate the effectiveness of programs or interventions.

(Brooks-Gunn, 2001). When efforts are less comprehensive, parental behavior often changes too little or too slowly to have a positive influence on children (St. Pierre & Layzer, 1998).

Interventions that deliver services directly to children have had more success than parent training programs. Still, the value of services during the first 3 years of life is hotly debated because benefits tend to fade after programs end. For example, the Infant Health and Development Project (IHDP) was a costly intervention that attempted to reduce the negative consequences of low birth weight by combining home visits during the first year with childhood education from 1 to 3 years. Each site operated a full-day child development center that exceeded state licensing requirements, and staff members worked with parents to coordinate educational activities in the center and at home. Figure 5.9 shows the impact of the program on children's IQ scores at 36 months. Clearly, the program was effective in leveling the playing field for children with less-educated mothers, but it did nothing for children from low-risk homes, proving that more is not always better when infants and toddlers are already in stimulating environments (Ramey et al., 2002).

Was the IHDP a resounding success for high-risk children? The data in Figure 5.9 say "yes" but critics say "no." The reason is that differences between intervention and control groups were no longer significant at age 5. Unfortunately, the cognitive benefits of most interventions gradually decline after interventions cease because development is not complete by 3 years of age (Blair & Wahlsten, 2002). For children who spend every day in environments challenged by poverty, quick (or not-so-quick) fixes during infancy are just not enough. As education professor Dale Farran (2000) concluded from her review of intervention programs, "A developmental focus that covers the first 12 to 15 years of life would be a good start" (p. 542).

ENRICHING THE ENRICHED. Figure 5.9 shows that expensive programs may not benefit children who are already in stimulating environments. Yet college-educated parents are the ones who most often seek enriching activities. Baby swim classes, toddler gymnastics, and music lessons for stick bangers are an ever-present reality in dual-career communities. Are enrichment activities anything more than harmless excuses to socialize?

The answer depends on the type of activity. At each stage of development, children's abilities are limited by their muscle strength, neurological development, and interests. For example, infant swim classes are fun and popular, but they do not "drown-proof" babies (American Academy of Pediatrics Committee on Sports Medicine and Fitness & Committee on Injury and Poison Prevention, 2000). Moreover, excessive swallowing of pool water can lead to water intoxication, a potentially fatal condition that occurs when immature kidneys cannot maintain blood salt levels. Another example is infant "walkers," seats on wheels that were pulled from store shelves after numerous children had fallen down stairs. Unexpectedly, infant walkers were associated with later—not earlier—sitting, crawling, and walking (Siegel & Burton, 1999).

Because some interventions and enrichment programs do not produce positive outcomes, child advocates embrace the notion of an "experimenting society": a society in which we put ideas to the test with sound evaluation research (Campbell, 1987; Meisels & Shonkoff, 2000). Like McGraw's experiment with roller-skating babies, mentioned at the beginning of this chapter, people will always

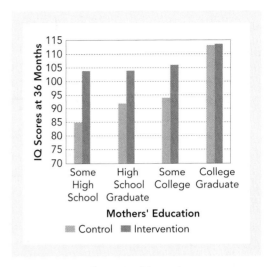

FIGURE 5.9 Infant Health and Development Program.

The Infant Health and Development Program improved the IQ scores of children whose mothers did not graduate from college. But even extensive, well-planned interventions have little effect on children who are already in safe, stimulating environments.

SOURCE: Ramey et al. (2002).

Swim time is fun for parents and babies, but it is dangerous for babies to swallow too much pool water and "lessons" will not drown-proof an infant or toddler. Early experiences do not always make baby safer, happier, or more competent.

have new ideas about how to make a better baby. An experimenting society is the only way we can be sure we are actually improving children's lives.

>>> **M E M O R Y   M A K E R S** <<<

1. The HOME is a procedure for _____.

   (a) measuring the use of physical punishment in the home.
   (b) measuring characteristics of a child's home environment.
   (c) measuring parental income and education.

2. Which of the following is *not* a characteristic of depressed mothers?

   (a) They alternate withdrawn behavior with poking and tickling.
   (b) They imitate their babies less often than nondepressed mothers.
   (c) They are more likely to respond to their infants' behavior.

3. Physical abuse, neglect, sexual abuse, and emotional maltreatment are collectively called _____.

   (a) child maltreatment   (b) status offenses
   (c) parenting failure   (d) early childhood parenting risk

[1-b; 2-c; 3-a]

Revisiting Developmental Principles: Are the First Years of Life the Most Important Years?

Scholars have long subscribed to **infant determinism**, the belief that early events influence the rest of our lives. A belief in infant determinism can be found in Roman texts and was firmly established by the 18th century. But it was not until recently that society had a modern explanation for why the early years might be the most important years: Neuroscientific evidence, some people claimed, proved that they were.

During the 1990s, dozens of Web sites and conferences sprang up to explain why new research on brain development tells us what is best for babies. There were only three problems with this information: It wasn't new, it wasn't accurate, and it didn't tell us how to raise babies. Soon neuroscientists, psychologists, and educators were publishing rebuttals to explain why well-known principles of development are still our best guides for understanding the earliest years of life. After describing the new infant determinism, we'll explain what experts have to say about the role the first years of life play in the rest of our lives.

The New Infant Determinism

People who embrace infant determinism have often made three claims to "prove" that early events stamp our brains for life (Bruer, 1999).

1. ***The synaptic density myth.*** Most synapses form during infancy, and environmental stimulation causes synapses to form. Therefore, early experiences fix intelligence and personality for life.

The facts: As you read in Chapter 2, initial synapse formation is under genetic—not environmental—control. Furthermore, the number of synapses does *not* determine intelligence. For example, people with cognitive challenges due to fragile X syndrome have an unusually high number of synapses (perhaps because

infant determinism The belief that early events influence the rest of our lives.

normal synapse elimination fails to occur), and adults have *fewer* synapses than children, not more.

2. **The critical period myth.** There is a critical period for stimulation during the first years of life. Therefore, infants and toddlers who are understimulated will never catch up.

The facts: Infant determinists often use examples from perceptual development to illustrate critical periods. For example, a study of kittens raised in a "horizontal" environment, which you read about in Chapter 4, is sometimes cited as evidence of a critical period for visual development. But as you learned, visual development is guided by *experience-expectant brain development*, a type of development that occurs normally as long as infants receive the stimulation that exists in virtually all human environments. In contrast, learning new words and appreciating music are guided by **experience-dependent brain development**, those changes that occur throughout life as a function of experience. Experience-expectant processes help us develop behavior that is common to all members of our species, whereas experience-dependent processes help us adapt to our *unique* environments. Unlike some aspects of visual development, experience-dependent brain development is not limited to specific periods.

3. **The early enrichment myth.** Because the most rapid synapse formation occurs during the first few years, stimulation during those years matters more than later stimulation does.

The facts: This claim is easy to dismantle. There is no evidence that merely bombarding infants with heavy doses of stimulation creates superbabies—or that early learning is especially enduring. If these things were true, the impact of early cognitive interventions would not diminish once interventions ceased. As Stella Chess explained, "A child is nothing like a racing car . . . Souping up babies doesn't work" (Chess & Whitbread, 1978, p. 15).

Experts worry about the frightening message that infant determinists send to parents. For instance, one article warned that "every lullaby, every giggle and peek-a-boo, triggers a cracking along his neural pathways, laying the groundwork for what could someday be a love of art or a talent for soccer" (Kantrowitz, 1997, p. 7). What do the neuroscientists say about all this crackling and zapping? Neuroscientist Charles Nelson (1999) wrote,

> I am sorry to say that there is little evidence to support the view espoused by the popular press. Yes, the first few years of life are important, but so are the next few years and the next few years after that. Prenatal development is important, as are genes, environments, parents, and peers. When one looks at the myriad factors that correlate with positive developmental outcomes, one is hard pressed to point to only the first 3 years of life as holding all the cards. (p. 235)

Developmental Principles Revisited: Are the First Years of Life the Most Important Years?

Neuroscience findings confirm why the general principles from Chapter 1 are still our best guides for understanding the magical early years.

1. **Development is the joint product of nature and nurture.** The concepts of experience-expectant development (development that occurs as long as an individual is exposed to a typical human environment) and experience-dependent development (development that requires specific types of experiences) help us understand how nature and nurture direct development. As mentioned at the beginning of the chapter, Jimmy caught up to Johnny because basic motor functions

experience-dependent brain development Changes that occur in the brain when we adapt to specific environments, such as when we learn vocabulary words or how to ride a bicycle. (In contrast, *experience-expectant brain development* involves changes that occur when we acquire universal skills, such as vision or locomotion. Experience-expectant brain development occurs as long as basic stimulation is adequate.)

and other necessary skills develop normally as long as stimulation is adequate. As neuroscientist Steve Petersen explained, "At a minimum, development really wants to happen" (Bruer, 1999, p. 188). But nurture *is* important for skills that differ across different environments, such as acquiring a large vocabulary or using chopsticks.

2. ***Physical, cognitive, and socioemotional development are interrelated.*** When the environment falls below nature's expectations, physical, cognitive, and socioemotional development are all affected. For example, maltreatment affects self concepts and stress reactions, not just interpersonal relationships.

3. ***Developmental outcomes vary over time and contexts.*** Within the broad range of normal environments, the future of most children is not determined by 3 years because behavior changes over time and contexts. For example, some behaviors, like unexplained infant crying, are associated with specific developmental periods; others, like a difficult temperament, can be modified by supportive environments.

4. ***Development is characterized by continuity and discontinuity.*** Some early characteristics tend to survive into later life. For example, infants who score highly on cognitive tests rarely fall below average later in development, and those with delightful temperaments tend to stay delightful. In general, positive traits demonstrate a high degree of stability from one developmental period to another (Kohlberg, LaCrosse, & Ricks, 1972). In contrast, some cranky babies outgrow their problems with time, demonstrating discontinuity. The degree of stability in development depends on what is measured, when it is measured, and how infants are raised. The adult does not always reside in the baby.

The most amazing thing about a group of 3-year-olds is just how . . . *human* they already are. They run, talk, and socialize; they feel joy, sadness, and jealousy. They want things and don't easily forget what they want. Yet if you watch a group of active 3-year-olds playing, you can hardly believe these same children will soon be sitting in school and learning to read. How they travel the rest of their preschool years is the topic of the next two chapters of our story.

⟩⟩⟩ SUMMARY ⟨⟨⟨

Bringing up Baby

1. Breast-feeding for the first 1 to 2 years reduces the chances of malnutrition, allergic reactions, and disease. When children begin eating a variety of foods, it is best to repeatedly expose them to nutritious foods without bribing them to eat. **Protein-energy malnutrition (PEM)** and micronutrient deficiencies are common problems that have widespread effects on children's development.

2. Unexplained infant crying is a normal consequence of central nervous system immaturity. All children wake one or more times during the night, but those who have learned to self-soothe are better at getting themselves back to sleep.

3. Early medical problems can be minimized by immunizing children against childhood diseases, staying alert for signs

of chronic **otitis media** (middle ear infections), and following safety guidelines to prevent unintentional injuries.

Raising the Toddler and Young Child

4. Toddlers are challenging because they frequently bid for attention but obey adults only about half of the time.

5. Pairing consistent feedback with age-appropriate explanations is the best way to reduce conflict between young children and their caregivers.

6. Children who experience corporal (physical) punishment tend to have increased behavior problems later in development. Still, there is no evidence that occasional mild swats are harmful in the absence of other risk factors.

7. Fathers are competent caregivers who can buffer children from the negative effects of poverty.

8. Children in high-risk environments benefit from high-quality day care, but children in understaffed facilities do not score as highly as expected on developmental assessments. High-quality day care provides trained staff, good child-to-staff-ratios, and activities that promote development.

Individual Differences

9. Boys have more medical problems early in life than girls, are slower to mature, reach some language milestones later, and are more active. By 3 years of age, children label themselves male or female and have begun to acquire gender-consistent toy preferences. Studies of inter-sexed children suggest that hormone exposure in utero plays a role in determining our **gender identities**.

10. Children's **temperaments** are their characteristic moods and ways of reacting to situations. Temperament is biologically based but can be modified by the environment.

11. As they are developing, children alternate between times of slow and rapid progress, appear to lose skills they previously acquired, and learn some tasks much more quickly than others. **Norm-referenced tests** help professionals evaluate their progress by comparing their abilities to those of other children.

Environmental Influences and Early Development

12. Poor children are more likely than other children to be exposed to biological trauma, to live in homes that provide fewer learning opportunities, and to have depressed, unresponsive caregivers.

13. **Child maltreatment** includes physical abuse, sexual abuse, neglect, and emotional maltreatment. Abusive caregivers often have unrealistic expectations about children and lack the social networks that buffer them from stress. Maltreatment can have negative effects on children's relationships, emotional regulation, self-concepts, and reactions to stress.

14. Intervention programs show the greatest benefits for children who have the most need. Efforts that push children to develop skills too early—such as baby swim classes that submerge infants—can expose them to physical risks.

Revisiting Developmental Principles: Are the First Years of Life the Most Important Years?

15. There is no evidence for the belief that the number of synapses a child develops due to experiences during the first years of life determines lifelong intelligence.

16. The four principles of development from Chapter 1 are our best guides for understanding the first 3 years. Early brain development includes genetically programmed growth that occurs across all human environments (illustrating the role of nature) and environmental-specific growth (illustrating the role of nurture). All aspects of development—physical, cognitive, and socioemotional—are affected when environments fall below a minimum standard. Developmental outcomes change over time and contexts, so there is both continuity and discontinuity between early and later behavior.

>>>KEY TERMS<<<

food neophobia   (p. 175)
protein-energy malnutrition (PEM)   (p. 175)
sudden infant death syndrome (SIDS)   (p. 180)
acute otitis media (AOM)   (p. 185)
gender identity   (p. 195)
gender-role behaviors   (p. 195)
sexual orientation   (p. 195)
gender dysphoria   (p. 195)
temperament   (p. 196)
norm-referenced tests   (p. 200)

predictive validity   (p. 200)
Home Observation for Measurement of the Environment (HOME)   (p. 203)
social reproduction   (p. 204)
child maltreatment   (p. 204)
shaken baby syndrome   (p. 205)
evaluation research   (p. 206)
infant determinism   (p. 208)
experience-dependent brain development   (p. 209)

CHAPTER SIX

Profile of Early Childhood

Stories of Our Lives
Dangerous Misunderstandings

> "Why, a 4-year-old child could understand this . . . . run out and find me a 4-year-old child."
>
> Groucho Marx

It is not unusual for conversations with young children to contain embarrassing truths and obvious mistakes. For example, 5-year-old Robyn told Grandma that her father swore yesterday, which was true, but she also said she had visited a pumpkin patch with Mrs. Hall's class when, in fact, she'd actually gone with another teacher. Errors like this one are usually insignificant. But when children witness crimes, investigators may rely on their testimonies to determine important matters, such as who participated in a murder or whether sexual abuse occurred. Problems can arise when people fail to talk to young witnesses in ways that encourage accurate explanations of events. Sometimes adults ignore children's comments because they believe that preschoolers should not be be taken seriously, while other times they take children's comments too literally and everyone overreacts.

Communication failures between children and adults can have disastrous results, as in the case of Margaret Kelly Michaels. Michaels, a 26-year-old teacher, was convicted of sexually abusing children at a nursery school in New Jersey. Prosecutors claimed she had raped and assaulted children over a 7-month period with knives, forks, and Lego

Kelly Michaels was convicted of molesting 20 children after numerous 3- to 5-year-old children made bizarre reports of abuse during highly misleading interviews. She was released from prison after an appeals court reversed her conviction. Michaels's case is one of many day care abuse cases that led scientists to study how young children are influenced by suggestions from adults.

blocks—even though none of the staff had noticed anything odd. Developmental psychologists Stephen Ceci and Maggie Bruck (1995) later summarized her story:

> The first suspicion that Kelly Michaels abused her charges occurred 4 days after she had left the Wee Care Nursery School to accept a better paying position elsewhere. At the time, a 4-year-old former student of Michaels was having his temperature taken rectally at his pediatrician's office when he said to the nurse, "That's what my teacher does to me at school." When asked to explain, he replied, "Her takes my temperature." That afternoon, the child's mother notified the state's child protective agency.
>
> Two days later, the child was brought to the prosecutor's office, where he inserted his finger into the rectum of an anatomical doll and told the assistant prosecutor that two other boys also had their temperature taken. . . . Over the next 2 months, a number of professionals interviewed the children and their families to determine the extent to which the abuse occurred. . . . On the basis of the testimony provided by 19 child witnesses, Kelly Michaels was convicted of 115 counts of sexual abuse against 20 three- to five-year-old children. Sentenced to serve 47 years in prison, Michaels was released on bail after 5 years as a result of the appeals court of New Jersey reversing her conviction (*State v. Michaels*, 1993). The prosecution appealed that decision to the Supreme Court of New Jersey; their appeal was denied (*State v. Michaels*, 1994). The court ruled that if the prosecution decided to retry the case, they must first hold a pretrial taint hearing and show that despite improper interviewing techniques, the statements and testimony of the child witnesses are sufficiently reliable to admit them as witnesses at trial. In December, 1994, the prosecution dropped all charges against Michaels. (pp. 12–13)

This case is one of a number of day care cases in the 1980s and 1990s that shared several features: The children never reported abuse until they were questioned by adults, allegations gradually escalated to include events that were clearly impossible, and forensic tests of objects mentioned by the children failed to produce any physical evidence (Rosenthal, 1995). Scientists, fascinated by the possibility that children's memories might have been influenced by adults, designed laboratory studies that proved that suggestive conversations could generate false reports. In turn, findings from these studies were used to construct guidelines for investigating crimes involving young witnesses. In the process, society gained a new appreciation for how important it is to try to understand children.

WHY WOULD JURORS believe bizarre, impossible tales like the ones in our opening story? In similar cases, jurors said they thought *something* must have happened for so many children to provide such detailed, graphic testimony. Why, they wondered, would youngsters who had no motivation to lie tell stories that were clearly unbelievable?

The answer is that there are two sides to preschoolers. Their competent side remembers small details, ponders complex issues like fairness, and worries about living up to adults' standards. On a good day, young children are so verbal and thoughtful that it is tempting to believe everything they say. But there is another side. This side of preschoolers has a short attention span, memory limitations, and an inability to predict the consequences of their actions. In this chapter you will read about the developmental strengths and limitations of 3- to 6-year-olds—children on the exciting journey between the toddler years and middle childhood.

At the end of this chapter, we will revisit children in the courtroom to explain why preschoolers sometimes say the most startling things.

Taking Charge of Their Bodies

Young children are curious and eager to learn, yet most societies wait until they are about 6 years old before starting formal education. There are good reasons to wait. Preschoolers are still acquiring the motor skills they need to dress themselves, eat neatly without supervision, and manipulate paper and pencil. Their eyes aren't ready for long periods of close work, and they need a healthy balance of active play and frequent rests (Gallahue & Ozmun, 2006). During this developmental period, one of their most important jobs is to master their bodies.

Growth

Preschoolers experience slow, steady growth that gradually changes their appearance. The average 3-year-old weighs only 31 pounds (14 kilograms), but most gain 14 additional pounds (6.4 kilograms) by 6 years, or about 4 to 5 pounds (1.8 to 2.3 kilograms) per year. During this time they also grow almost 8 inches (20 centimeters), or 2.6 inches (6.8 centimeters) per year. As they get taller, children lose baby fat and look sleeker. This normal trend to "thin out" is clear from the **body mass index (BMI)** values in Figure 6.1. BMI is a measure of how heavy someone is adjusted for height (which is calculated by dividing weight in kilograms by height in meters square). Notice that the average value dips between 2 and 6 years, then gradually increases. While BMI is falling, children's spines straighten and their pot bellies disappear, creating a more grown-up appearance.

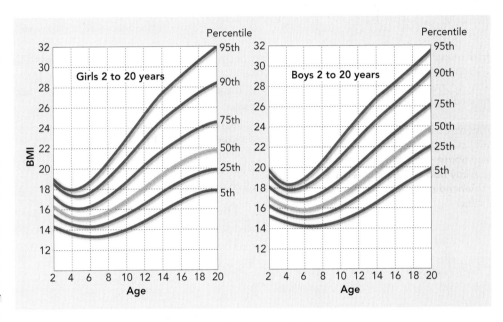

FIGURE 6.1 Age-related changes in body mass index.

Body mass index is a measure of whether a child's weight is healthy for his or her height. The average BMI declines between 2 and 6 years of age, when children develop a straighter, leaner appearance.

SOURCE: Centers for Disease Control and Prevention (2000).

Health professionals measure children's heights and weights to identify growth patterns that may signal medical or caregiving problems. For example, developmental norms helped child protection workers argue that 3-year-old Jerad should be removed from his home. Jerad, who had grown to 120 pounds, received needed medical tests and a change in diet after he was transferred into a foster home, where he soon lost 50 pounds (Associated Press State and Local Wire, 2002).

As children are growing taller, skeletal changes also help them look more mature. Arms and legs become slender and the head, though growing, gets proportionately smaller for the length of the body. Slowly the face looks less baby-like as the lower jaw becomes more pronounced. Permanent teeth do not begin

body mass index (BMI) A formula for determining how heavy someone is adjusted for height. BMI is calculated by dividing weight in kilograms by the square of height in meters (weight ÷ height^2), or [(weight (lb) ÷ height (inches)^2 × 703].

erupting until 6 or 7 years, though, so the dental changes that define an adult face are still many years away.

Motor Control

It is fun to watch preschoolers learn to tie shoes and put on coats, but pressure to perform too early can make them frustrated and unhappy. Information about normal motor development helps parents, teachers, and baby-sitters set realistic expectations.

FUNDAMENTAL MOTOR SKILLS. Preschoolers are still developing their basic coordination and balance skills. For example, the simple act of walking does not show a mature movement pattern until 4 to 5 years of age. Similarly, children first walk down steps by moving one foot to a step and shifting the other foot to the same step, but the mature pattern (one foot per step without support) is also delayed until 4 to 5 years, about a year after children learn to go up with confidence (Gabbard, 2004).

Table 6.1 lists some fundamental motor skills and the ages when children have the potential to execute these skills with ease. When looking at charts like this one, remember that motor skills are not learned in an all-or-none fashion. Instead, children gradually learn to adapt to changing circumstances, so minor changes in an activity may influence success. For instance, a child who can knock pinecones off a wall with small stones might still have difficulty throwing large objects to another person (Gallahue & Ozmun, 2006). Because it takes practice to adjust to different situations, and environments emphasize different skills, ability in any one activity is not a good predictor of a child's overall progress (Cermak & Larkin, 2002).

TABLE 6.1	The Development of Motor Skill	
Movement Pattern	**Ability**	**Approximate Age at Onset**
Dynamic balance	Walks a 1-inch (2.5-cm) straight line	3 years
	Performs basic forward roll	3–4 years
Hopping	Hops up to 3 times on preferred foot	3 years
	Hops from 4 to 6 times on same foot	4 years
Skipping	One-footed skip	4 years
Running	Efficient and refined run	4–5 years
Static balance	Balances on one foot for 3 to 5 seconds	5 years
Catching	Basket catch using the body	3 years
	Mature catching pattern*	6 years
Jumping	Jumps for distance (about 3 ft/1 m)	5 years
	Mature jumping pattern*	6 years

* Age indicates that children have the developmental potential to be at the mature stage, but whether or not they are will depend on the task and environment.

Adapted from Gallahue & Ozmun (2006).

MANIPULATION AND WRITING. About 30 to 60 percent of an older child's school day is spent in fine motor activities (mostly writing), which is why early manipulation skills lay the groundwork for future academic success (McHale & Cermak, 1992). Finger dexterity and speed improve rapidly during the preschool years, with slower improvements continuing into the school years. For example, 3-year-olds can oppose each finger to the thumb in turn, but performance on this simple skill improves until age 8.

Most children can hold a writing tool by 18 months of age, and by $4\frac{1}{2}$ to 6 years they show a variety of holding grips. Writing follows the principle of *proximodistal* order described in Chapter 4, with movements in the shoulders and arms occurring earlier than movements in the wrists and fingers. As children mature, their hands move closer to the end of the writing tool, giving them more control. As a result of control progressing outward from the trunk, infants who can only scribble grow into 3-year-olds who can use a crayon to make lines. Most 4-year-olds can copy a circle, and a year later they learn to copy a square. By 5 years many children print their first names, although most 6-year-olds still cannot print small letters or space letters properly.

As mentioned in Chapter 5, most people have a dominant cerebral hemisphere, a side of the brain that is better at coordinating fine motor actions. Signs of brain lateralization appear even before birth (Hepper, Wells, & Lynch, 2005), but cerebral dominance emerges more clearly during the preschool years. Most children favor one hand by the time they are 3 or 4 years old, when 75 percent select their right hand. Hand preference stabilizes around age 6, when 90 percent of children are clearly right-handed. There is a higher percentage of left-handers among children with motor, language, or general cognitive dysfunctions, and boys are more likely both to be left-handed and to have these dysfunctions. Nonetheless, the majority of lefties are perfectly normal.

Boys lag behind girls in fine motor skills as a result of slower neurological development. But for both sexes, handwriting is a complicated feat that many children practice before they have the motor control to handle writing tools efficiently. Preschoolers who spend a lot of time drawing before they have established stability in their hands or a dominant hand sometimes lock into inefficient gripping styles by the start of school (Benbow, 2002). This interesting finding shows that early practice does not always produce better ability in the end.

DEVELOPMENTAL COORDINATION DISORDER. Some parents wait longer for basic motor skills to emerge, as in this case report from a team of occupational therapists* (May-Benson, Ingolia, & Koomar, 2002):

> Jennifer's mother describes that she and her husband have always been "on duty" from when Jennifer awakens until she goes to sleep at night. Since she was an infant, Jennifer has required assistance in meeting her needs. Due to Jennifer's limited stamina and endurance for motor activities, her parents pushed Jennifer in a stroller for a much longer period than other children. As her mother describes it, "Everything was more of an effort." (p. 145)

Jennifer has **developmental coordination disorder**, a condition in which motor clumsiness impairs daily activities (Cermak & Larkin, 2002). Motor problems, which affect about 6 percent of children, can have far-reaching effects on adjustment. Children with motor difficulties explore less on play equipment and have fewer social interactions than their peers. They are also less popular, partly because movement difficulties interfere with play but also because they often have problems with anxiety and social skills (Cermak, Gubbay, & Larkin, 2002). And because many children with motor or language problems have trouble in both areas, motor development problems are associated with later academic difficulties (Estil & Whiting, 2002). For these reasons, normal motor development is a sign that a child's overall development is on track.

ORGANIZED SPORTS. In the past, most parents minded the farm while youngsters played unsupervised in small, mixed-age groups. Then, as organized sports became popular, parents began encouraging children to participate at younger

---

*occupational therapists: Health and rehabilitation professionals who teach self-help and creative activities so that people will regain or develop skills that are important for independent functioning and self-satisfaction.

developmental coordination disorder A condition in which motor clumsiness significantly impairs daily self-help skills or achievement.

Young children love short periods of organized activity intermixed with plenty of time for free play.

and younger ages. Although children need exercise and contact with peers to grow socially, it is important that parents and coaches keep the developmental needs of preschoolers in mind. The American Academy of Pediatrics (AAP) published the following recommendations to help families and sports organizers adjust athletic activities to match young children's abilities (AAP Committee on Sports Medicine and Fitness & Committee on School Health, 2001):

▶ ***Do not rush children.*** Basic skills such as throwing and kicking do not always develop sooner simply because children practice them at an earlier age. Teaching skills before children are ready to learn produces frustration rather than long-term success.

▶ ***Do not overstructure young children's time.*** Preschoolers have short attention spans, so exercise sessions should be short, playful, and focused on a variety of movement skills. Structured activities should be limited to 15 to 20 minutes combined with 30 minutes of free play.

▶ ***Emphasize hands-on learning.*** Young children learn best when verbal instructions are combined with physical demonstrations.

▶ ***Consult a health professional.*** Pediatricians can help parents decide if their child has a medical condition that might affect participation. Health professionals can also evaluate the fit between particular activities and an individual child's level of maturation.

It is possible for adults to be too involved in children's play. As the American Academy of Pediatrics explained, "Tournaments, all-star teams, most valuable player awards, trophies, and award banquets are by-products of adult influences. Despite good intentions, increased involvement of adults does not necessarily enhance the child athlete's enjoyment. The familiar image of parents imploring their 5-year-old to 'catch the ball,' 'kick the ball,' or 'run faster' is a reminder of how adult encouragement can have discouraging effects" (AAP Commitee on Sports Medicine and Fitness & Committee on School Health, 2001, pp. 1459–1460).

How can families know when an activity is safe and fun? Children do not hide their feelings very well, signs of distress—or 10 children running in 10 different directions—are warnings that an activity is developmentally inappropriate. Children's interests and abilities vary, though, so decisions about joining a sport should be made on a child-by-child basis.

Brain Development

Brain development and behavioral development go hand-in-hand, with both showing rapid changes early in life. By 2 years of age the average brain is already about 75 percent of its adult weight, and this increases to 90 percent by age 5 (Tanner, 1990).

As we mentioned in Chapter 2, early brain growth is rapid because the infant brain overproduces neurons and synapses. Then, as synapses are pruned, the brain becomes more efficient and better tuned to the environment. By 3 years, significant pruning has already occurred in regions responsible for vision, auditory perception, and language. In the prefrontal cortex, which handles higher cognitive functions such as solving problems, pruning is just beginning and will continue throughout middle childhood and early adolescence (Nelson et al., 2006). This slow maturation of higher brain centers contributes to many of the cognitive limitations you will read about later in this chapter.

If excess neurons and synapses are gradually eliminated, why does brain size increase? One reason is increased myelination. Brain volume grows as axons develop the fatty coating that speeds information transmission. Because some regions myelinate earlier than others, skills emerge in a predictable order. For example, fibers that link the cerebellum (an area responsible for balance and motor movements) to the cerebral cortex complete myelination during the preschool years, when children begin to throw balls, hop, and participate in simple outdoor games (Tanner, 1990). But the speed of neural conduction improves for pathways involved in individual finger movement until age 10, suggesting that these fibers take longer to myelinate (Gordon, 2001). The brain also adds volume as axons mature and neurons develop more dendrites (the branches that reach out to receive messages from other neurons). Finally, supportive structures for neural tissue, such as glial cells and blood vessels, also increase.

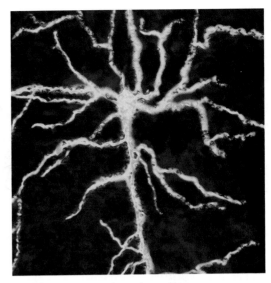

FIGURE 6.2 Dendritic branching.

A typical pyramidal cell in the brain is a tree-like structure with branches and thorn-like spines. Many conditions that produce cognitive deficits are associated with abnormal branching, including thinner branches and fewer spines.

Brain growth has a profound effect on behavior and cognitive development. For example, about 80 percent of neurons in the brain are pyramidal cells like the one in Figure 6.2. The dendrites of these cells have tiny thorn-like "spines" that contain most of the receptors the cells need to communicate with other cells. Children with some forms of mental retardation have a variety of cellular abnormalities, including thinner dendrites and fewer spines. Because brain-cell abnormalities produce differences in brain volume, smaller brain volumes are found in many conditions that are associated with cognitive deficits, including fetal alcohol syndrome (Riley & McGee, 2005). Even among typically developing children, brain size accounts for about 20 percent of the variance in IQ scores between the ages of 5 and 17 years (Reiss et al., 1996).

Growth spurts occur at different times in different parts of the brain. Development is rapid between 3 and 6 years in the left hemisphere, the half of the brain that houses most language skills. While language is blossoming, recordings of electrical activity reveal only slow growth in the right hemisphere. Because the right hemisphere supports spatial processing, preschoolers cannot be trusted to explore away from home without getting lost, and their drawings are usually amusing (Thatcher, Walker, & Giudice, 1987). Growth spurts are also seen during the preschool years in the corpus callosum, the band of fibers that connects the two hemispheres, and in circuits involved in planning and maintaining attention to a task (Thompson et al., 2000). Due to their immature brains, 3-year-olds manage best in unstructured environments whereas 6-year-olds are ready for more organized activities. Some of the changes caused by a maturing body and brain are subtle, including the changes in perceptual skills you will read about next.

> > > **MEMORY MAKERS** < < <

1. Between 2 and 6 years, BMI should (a) increase (b) decrease (c) stay the same.

2. Hand preference stabilizes around ___ years of age. (a) 3 (b) 6 (c) 8

3. A good rule of thumb for organized sports for preschoolers is ___ minutes of structured activity followed by ___ minutes of free play.

    (a) 2 to 4; 10   **(b)** 15 to 20; 30   **(c)** 30; 30   **(d)** 45; 15

4. During early childhood, brain growth is rapid in the ____ hemisphere, the hemisphere that houses most ____ skills.

    (a) left; language   **(b)** left; spatial   **(c)** right; language   **(d)** right; spatial

[1-b; 2-b; 3-b; 4-a]

Perceptual Development

Three-year-old Malcolm is riveted to the TV, watching a cartoon. When a boring commercial comes on, he jumps up, runs over to his father, and chatters furiously. From watching Malcolm's behavior, you might think his perceptual skills are adult-like—but they are not. Preschoolers are still acquiring the visual and auditory skills they will need to become good readers and writers down the road.

During the preschool years, the most important perceptual changes lie at the crossroads of physical and cognitive development. Physical maturation continues to refine basic abilities, but perceptual development increasingly involves changes in what children attend to and how they interpret information from the environment (Bornstein & Arterberry, 1999).

Vision

Compared to the rapid changes that took place during Malcolm's infancy, visual development is slow during his preschool years. Much like the lag in fine motor skills at this age, the finer aspects of vision also take many years to develop. Malcolm's *grated acuity* (the smallest black and white stripes he can detect) will not reach adult levels until he is between 4 and 6 years old (Skoczenski & Norcia, 2002). *Contrast sensitivity* (the smallest difference in brightness he can detect between an object and the background) will take even longer to mature. Depending upon the test of visual perception, Malcolm will not have the constrast sensitivity of an adult until he is between 6 to 15 years old. Preschoolers see more poorly than adults due to immaturities throughout the visual system. For example, individual cells in the retinas (the back surface of the eyes) are less densely packed during early childhood, and synaptic densities farther down the visual pathway will not prune to adult levels until 11 years of age (Mauer & Lewis, 2001).

Children should have their vision checked by 3 years and again at 5, with additional checkups every other year (American Optometric Association, 2006a). Early exams are important because some problems, like *amblyopia*, are difficult to correct if treatment is delayed. Amblyopia is a condition in which children's brains begin to ignore information from one eye due to acuity differences or misaligned eyes. One screening program diagnosed 5 percent of preschool and kindergarten children with amblyopia, and another 7 percent needed eyeglasses (Preslan & Novak, 1998).

Hearing

Hearing also experiences some fine-tuning throughout early and middle childhood. Children's ability to detect high notes becomes adult-like by 6 years of age, but there is continued improvement for low notes until age 10 (Werner & Marean, 1996).

If you have ever tried to get a child's attention, you know that it often goes something like this: "Malcolm, do you want some carrots to snack on? Malcolm? Malcolm, I'm talking to you . . . DO YOU WANT CARROTS?" Picking up sound in a quiet room is not the same as picking up sound in the midst of a noisy family. Compared to adults, children need a bigger difference in loudness between background noise and a signal before they react. This difference decreases during the preschool years and stabilizes around 15 years of age (Schneider & Trehub, 1992).

Because we are used to children ignoring us, it is not uncommon for a child's hearing loss to go unnoticed. In one study, over half of the children with a hearing loss in both ears were not diagnosed until they were between 2 and 11 years (Walch et al., 2000), and the average identification age was 6 years for a group with mild loss (Finckh-Krämer, Spormann-Lagodzinski, & Gross, 2000). Infant tests would detect most of the 3 in 1,000 babies who are born with hearing loss, but follow-up testing is necessary to detect problems that develop later. This is why the American Academy of Audiology (2005) recommends yearly tests for all children who have a family history of hearing impairment.

This little girl is enjoying her hearing test. Yearly tests for preschoolers with a family history of hearing loss will detect problems that appear after infancy.

When Information Conflicts

The world is buzzing with stimulation, and our perceptual systems act like filters that choose what is important. When information conflicts, children's choices sometimes differ from adults', often in amusing ways. For instance, toddlers rely more than adults on visual cues to maintain balance. To illustrate, one research team hung a small, floorless room inside a room, then stood 13- to 16-month-olds on a mat and moved the floorless room toward them. Because visual cues indicated they were falling forward, many toddlers compensated and fell backward (Lee & Aronson, 1974). The adult pattern of using visual information and information from receptors in the muscles, joints, and inner ear does not emerge until 4 to 6 years (Shumway-Cook & Woollacott, 1985).

Children often rely on information from one modality (such as vision, hearing, and so forth) and ignore other information. What captures their attention depends upon the situation (Napolitano & Sloutsky, 2004). For example, it is confusing when adults smile while expressing disapproval with their voices because children sometimes rely on facial expressions to judge emotions (Heyman, 1996; Lewkowicz, 1988). In social situations, both children and adults appreciate consistent information.

Perceptual Learning

You are probably aware of what we will call the "shopping phenomenon." There is a common object, say, backpacks for laptop computers, that you have seen a hundred times. But you never paid attention to them until you decided to buy one. Perhaps you stop at the campus bookstore, write down some brand names, and visit some Web sites. You check measurements, look for storage features, and compare materials. Suddenly, as you walk around campus, you start distinguishing regular backpacks from computer backpacks. You see a clever cell-phone pocket and an ugly zipper. You find one in violet and think, "That's odd, I've never seen a violet one before." Suddenly, you can't stop noticing backpacks.

You experience **perceptual learning** whenever experience leads you to attend to, process, or interpret perceptual information differently. Perceptual learning is important because you can't process everything in the environment, so you learn to notice information that serves a purpose. Of course, you were always able to *see* backpacks, but you had no reason to discriminate one from the other until you needed one.

People learn to detect complicated relationships when they experience perceptual learning. To appreciate what children face when they are learning to

perceptual learning The process by which people learn to attend to, process, or interpret perceptual information.

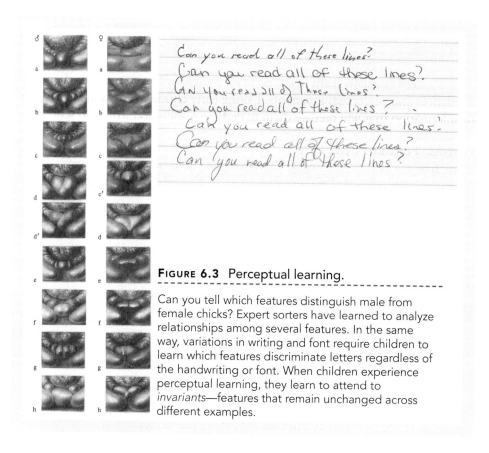

FIGURE 6.3 Perceptual learning.

Can you tell which features distinguish male from female chicks? Expert sorters have learned to analyze relationships among several features. In the same way, variations in writing and font require children to learn which features discriminate letters regardless of the handwriting or font. When children experience perceptual learning, they learn to attend to *invariants*—features that remain unchanged across different examples.

affordances Fits between characteristics of the environment and opportunities for action. For example, chairs afford sitting and balls afford throwing.

perceptual invariants Features that remain the same in the changing flow of perceptual information. These features help us distinguish one object from another.

discriminate letters and numbers, consider the diagrams in Figure 6.3. On the left is an agricultural skill: learning to sort male and female chicks. Look down the columns and try to figure out how expert sorters tell the difference. We can't do this task, but we know that some sorters are accurate 99.5 percent of the time (Gibson, 1969). Now consider the task on the right side: learning to read handwriting even though individuals form letters so differently. When children begin to read, letters are as mysterious to them as chicks are to you. Eventually, though, they learn this task with remarkable efficiency.

What is learned when perceptual learning occurs? First, people learn **affordances**. An affordance is a fit between a characteristic of the environment and an opportunity for action. Affordances include physical aspects of the environment, such as the fact that chairs afford sitting, and events, such as the fact that birthday parties afford playing. When children perceive an affordance, they perceive a fit between the environment and their own abilities and limitations. Thus children who are learning to ride a tricycle discover that a flat surface affords biking, but a steeply slanted driveway does not.

In addition to noticing affordances, children also learn to extract **perceptual invariants** from sensory information. Invariants are features that remain the same in the ever-changing flow of information. Invariants make objects meaningful and help us distinguish some objects from others. For example, children learn to recognize balls for bouncing because these types of balls have some invariant properties. Nevertheless, a 3-year-old might throw the first round paper weight she sees through a window, hoping it will bounce. After this unfortunate event, she will become more choosey (if her parents are lucky), and hard objects will be excluded from her throw-and-bounce routine. Soon she learns to attend to the look and feel of round objects because these features distinguish objects that afford bouncing from those that do not.

Children gradually learn to attend to meaningful information when they learn affordances and perceptual invariants. During early childhood, this includes learning information that will prepare them to become readers and writers in school.

VISUAL PERCEPTUAL LEARNING. Reading readiness starts when toddlers realize that books can be read. At this stage they hold books (often upside down) and turn pages, talking as if they were reading. Next they learn that writing says something but they don't know what. Then, during the preschool years, many children begin naming letters and printing their names.

Because letters and numbers come in different sizes and fonts, children have to learn their invariant features. Initially they perceive letters and their mirror images as the same, perhaps because objects in the real world are the same regardless of their orientations. But b is not the same as p, and u is not the same as o, so children gradually learn that orientation and breaks in lines are important. Compared to older children, young children are much more likely to say that a shape is "the same" as its mirror image, to miss reversed letters when they are asked to mark which letters in a line of print are "backward," and to print letters and numbers backward (Gibson et al., 1962; Jordan & Jordan, 1990).

In sum, literacy begins when children learn which visual features differentiate letters. But as important as this ability is, it is a speech-perception skill that best predicts which children will take to reading like ducks to water.

PHONOLOGICAL AWARENESS. Awareness of speech sounds is important for early reading because the English writing system associates letters, such as p and b, with *phonemes*. Phonemes are abstract units, not individual sounds. For instance, you can prove that the p in *pit* is not exactly the same as the p in *split* by putting a small piece of paper in front of your lips while saying these words. (Notice the puff of air when you say *pit* but not *split*.) Nonetheless, these two sounds are members of one phoneme in English because you interpret words the same even when these sounds are interchanged. In other words, phonemes are *psychological* rather than physical segments of speech (Rayner et al., 2001).

The abstract nature of phonemes is one reason why the relationship between letters and sounds is not obvious to children. As a result, one of the most important reading skills is **phonological awareness (phonemic awareness)**: knowledge of the sound structure of spoken words. Children demonstrate phonological awareness when they decide whether two words rhyme or start with the same sound. They also demonstrate phonological awareness when they respond to questions like "Say a little bit of 'pat'" by saying "p." Children who do well on these types of tasks are better early readers than children who are less aware of speech sounds (Anthony & Lonigan, 2004; Fox & Routh, 1984; Routh & Fox, 1984). Since phonological knowledge grows through exposure to language activities, adults help prepare children for school whenever they provide engaging language activities, such as rhyming songs and silly stories that play with sounds.

phonological awareness (phonemic awareness) Knowledge of the sound structure of spoken words. Children demonstrate phonological awareness when they decide if two words rhyme or start with the same sound.

Music prepares children for reading when rhyming songs encourage them to attend to language sounds and rhythms.

> > > **MEMORY MAKERS** < < <

1. Which of the following conclusions best captures the nature of visual development during the preschool years?

   (a) Most children temporarily experience a worsening of their vision.

   (b) Vision is adult-like by 4 years of age.

   (c) Basic visual skills are intact by 3 years, but refinements occur until 6 years of age.

   (d) Basic visual skills are intact by 3 years, but refinements occur for at least another decade.

2. Preschool children need a bigger difference in loudness between a signal and background noise before they will react. This difference declines during childhood and stabilizes around ___ years.

   (a) 4   (b) 6   (c) 8   (d) 15

3. When experience leads you to attend to, process, or interpret perceptual information differently, you have experienced _____.

   (a) perceptual learning   (b) sensory enhancement

   (c) affordance learning   (d) Gestalt reorganization

4. Which of the following is an especially good predictor of early reading skills?

   (a) 20/20 vision

   (b) a tendency to attend to visual information when information is presented in two modalities

   (c) a tendency to attend to auditory information when information is presented in two modalities

   (d) phonological awareness

[1-d; 2-d; 3-a; 4-d]

Cognitive Development

Around the world, adults change their expectations for what children should contribute to family life once they reach 6 to 7 years of age (Rogoff et al., 1975). In hunting and gathering societies, children begin to hunt and gather; in agricultural societies, they have greater responsibility for tending animals. In industrialized countries, 6-year-olds are considered "teachable" (Sameroff & Haith, 1996, p. 5). The idea that children do not have common sense and rationality until they are 6 or 7 has a name: *the 5 to 7 year shift* (White, 1965).

Why do adults say that preschoolers lack common sense? The person who ignited interest in this question was Jean Piaget, so his theory is the best place to begin exploring this question.

Piaget's Theory of Preoperational Thought

Preschoolers are in a developmental stage that Piaget called "preoperational." According to Piaget, 2- to 7-year-olds are busy thinkers, but they think illogically. It is easy to understand what this means if we look at the types of behavior Piaget actually observed.

THOSE ILLOGICAL PRESCHOOLERS. Young children often give baffling answers to questions that seem straightforward. For example, Piaget showed young children sticks of various lengths and asked them to pick the smallest one. Then he said, "Now try to put first the smallest, then one a little bit bigger, then another a little bit bigger, and so on" (Piaget, 1952). Instead of making a neat row of sticks of increasing length for this *seriation* task, some children laid out the sticks in random order, ordered only a few sticks correctly, or created two piles by placing little ones and big ones together. Still others produced the arrangement shown in Figure 6.4: They carefully laid out the tops of the sticks but failed to notice that the bottoms were haphazardly arranged.

Task	Materials	Request or Question	Preoperational Response
Seriation	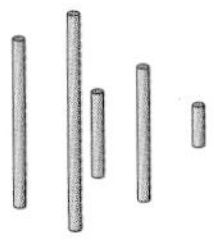	Now try to put first the smallest, then one a little bit bigger, then another a little bit bigger, and so on.	
Class Inclusion		Are there more horses or animals?	"More horses."
Appearance-Reality		What animal is this?	"A cat."
Perspective-Taking	Doll sits here 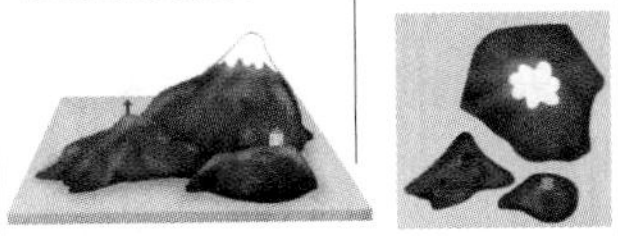 Child sits here	What does Dolly see? 	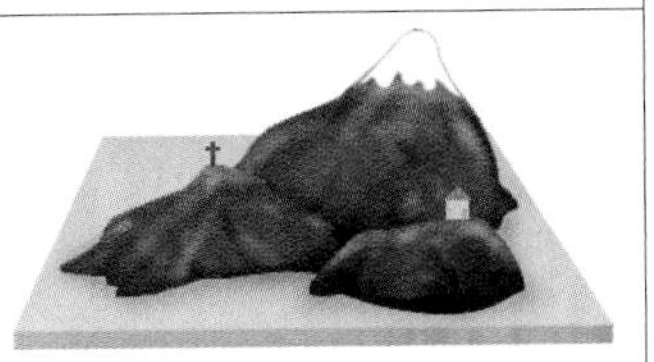

For his *class inclusion* task, Piaget showed children sets of objects like the five horses and two cows in Figure 6.4. After asking them to count the horses, the cows, and the animals, Piaget asked, "Are there more horses or more animals in this picture?" Surprisingly, many preschoolers answered, "More horses," and they didn't change their answer when they were asked to recount the sets (Inhelder & Piaget, 1964).

The next example of illogical thinking in Figure 6.4 is an *appearance-reality* task. For one version of this task, Piaget showed children a small dog and asked them what type of animal it was. They said it was a dog. Then he covered the dog's head with a mask that looked like a cat's face and repeated the question. This time children said it was a cat (Piaget, 1968).

The last panel in Figure 6.4 illustrates a *perspective-taking* problem. Piaget said he would place a doll at various locations and the game was to decide what things looked like from the doll's position. As he moved the doll, Piaget asked which photograph matched the doll's perspective. Typically, preschoolers could not select the correct photograph when it differed from what *they* were seeing. Instead, they continued to select the picture that matched their own perspective (Piaget & Inhelder, 1956).

What accounts for these puzzling responses? Piaget believed that young children lack *mental operations*. Operations are like actions except they are performed on *mental symbols* rather than actual objects. The ability to manipulate mental representations helps older children and adults think logically. For example, you can add mentally and also subtract, so you have a mental operation called *reversibility*. Piaget proposed that children in the **preoperational stage** are illogical because they lack a set of fundamental abilities that are necessary for performing mental operations (hence, the name "*preoperational*," meaning "*before* mental operations"). Specifically, Piaget said that preoperational thought is characterized by the following tendencies:

▶ Young children's thinking is *centered*, which means they focus on one aspect of a problem at a time. For example, they do not conceptualize horses as a set while, at the same time, viewing horses as part of a larger set called "animals." Instead, preoperational children focus on what is perceptually in front of them: horses versus cows.

FIGURE 6.4 Piaget's tasks.

Young children who are in the preoperational stage of cognitive development respond illogically to these Piagetian problems. Their performance sometimes improves when stimulus materials are familiar or questions are reworded.

preoperational stage Piaget's second stage of cognitive development (roughly from 2 to 7 years), when children are illogical because their thinking is centered (focused on only one aspect of a problem), appearance-bound (focused on what is perceptually obvious), static (considering only the current state of affairs), and irreversible (not capable of reversing a prior change).

▶ Young children's reality is *appearance-bound.* Just as they must learn to notice perceptual invariants, they must also learn to notice cognitive invariants. One invariant is *identity,* the idea that essential characteristics of people and objects do not change when surface features change. After all, Mom in a Halloween costume is still Mom. When young children center, however, they sometimes focus on appearances rather than the cognitive invariants that define reality. In the appearance-reality task, this leads them to make decisions based on what the dog looks like at a particular point in time rather than what the dog really is.

▶ Young children's thinking is *static,* which means they base decisions on the current state of affairs rather than focusing on transformations. For example, the fact that the animal was a dog just a minute ago does not influence their decision because they do not consider what it was a minute ago.

▶ Young children's thinking is *irreversible* because they lack the ability to mentally reverse operations. For example, an adult would mentally remove the mask from the dog, but young children do not.

▶ Finally, the most important characteristic of preoperational thought is **egocentrism**. Egocentric people are unaware that other people have perceptions, ideas, or feelings that are different from their own. In the perspective-taking task, for instance, children respond as if everyone sees what they see. Considering other people's point of view requires individuals to (a) think about multiple pieces of information and (b) realize that views change when circumstances change. But these are exactly the mental gymnastics that preschoolers cannot manage. Egocentric behavior is often funny, as when children point to a book and shout to their father, who is in another room, "Daddy, what is *this?*"

In sum, Piaget's explanation for the 5 to 7 year shift boils down to a few key concepts: Young children reason illogically because their thinking is centered, focused on appearances, static, and irreversible. These limitations produce an egocentric child who fails to take other people's perspectives into account. Piaget's descriptions are satisfying because they capture children's responses to the tasks in Figure 6.4 so well. But theorists were vexed by a problem: Children often answer correctly when Piaget's tasks are changed slightly. Let's turn to what these unexpected successes tell us about the minds of preschoolers.

UPDATING PIAGET'S THEORY. A few examples illustrate that preschoolers know a good deal more than Piaget predicted. Consider the question, "Are there more horses or animals?" When class inclusion questions like this one are worded more explicitly, young children are remarkably good at answering. In one study, for instance, 5-year-olds correctly answered questions such as, "Here is a pile of blocks. Who would have more toys to play with, someone who owned the blue blocks or someone who owned *the pile?*" (Markman & Seibert, 1976). In addition to knowing something about sets of objects, it is also clear that preschoolers are not entirely egocentric. For example, they change their speech depending upon the needs of their listeners (Shatz & Gelman, 1973) and sometimes perform well on perspective-taking tasks that involve familiar objects (Borke, 1975).

Why, then, do preschoolers perform poorly on standard Piagetian tasks? One reason is that Piaget's questions violate basic rules of language and conversation (Siegal, 1997). For example, the class inclusion task asks children to compare objects at two different levels ("Are there more horses or more animals?"), which is virtually unheard of in normal conversation. Indeed, even adults are sometimes confused by these questions (Winer & Falkner, 1984). When faced with such situations, children may respond to what they think the *intent* of a question is, rather

egocentrism A tendency to see things from one's own perspective. Egocentric people are unaware of other people's perceptions, ideas, or feelings.

than what the question literally asks. Also, Piaget's tasks often involve situations and materials, such as shapeless mountains, that are unfamiliar to young children.

Researchers who have modified Piaget's tasks have converged on two conclusions: Children show many mental competencies earlier than Piaget thought, and older children and even adults sometimes fail his problems (especially when tasks are unfamiliar). Does this mean that Piaget was wrong about preschoolers? Not entirely. Despite the fact that children sometimes take multiple dimensions into account and act in nonegocentric ways, the fact remains that—typically— they don't (Haith & Sameroff, 1996). Instead, young children frequently focus on one part of a situation and ignore other information, especially when situations are cognitively challenging. Difficult tasks require children to sit for long periods, remember a lot of information, or ignore social cues suggesting they should answer in particular ways. Children also act illogically when materials are unfamiliar or distracting features capture their attention. Piaget's description of preoperational thought as centered, focused on appearances, static, irreversible, and egocentric can be viewed as "characteristic ways of thinking": ways of reasoning and responding that influence performance in many situations. Due to characteristic ways of thinking, 2-year-olds generally respond differently than 5-year-olds, and 5-year-olds respond differently than 10-year-olds. But it is also the case that young children sometimes perform better than expected and that errors are not entirely absent in older children or even adults (Siegler & Alibali, 2005).

Information Processing

In his later writings, Piaget began exploring concepts that departed from "classic Piaget" (P. H. Miller, 2002, p. 88). For example, he talked about how children develop strategies for solving problems, and he started to view development as more continuous and less stage-like. At the time of his death, the field of cognitive development had already moved in these directions. Intrigued by the fact that children's performance varied across situations, investigators began using information processing analyses to understand their patterns of successes and failures.

According to the information processing approach, young children have a limited ability to work with mental information due to neurological immaturity and sparse knowledge about the world. As they grow, they execute basic mental processes more efficiently and are able to hold more information in mind. At each developmental period, characteristic ways of thinking are the result of processing limitations in the mental systems involved in attending, remembering, and reasoning about information.

PAYING ATTENTION. It is obvious that children do not pay attention very well. But the term *attention* actually covers several different skills. *Focused attention*, also called concentration, is the ability to maintain attention over time. *Attentional switching* is the ability to shift focus, such as when a child who is watching television suddenly realizes that Sparky is barking to be let into the house. Because ability on one task does not always predict performance on others, psychologists consider different attentional processes to be relatively distinct skills (Dunbar, Hill, & Lewis, 2001). Still, as a group these skills develop noticeably with age.

The attention span of a 2-year-old is quite short—and that of a 4-year-old is not much longer. To illustrate, Figure 6.5 shows

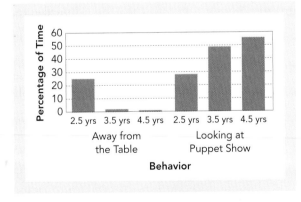

FIGURE 6.5 Age-related changes in attention.

The amount of time children spent away from the table during a 10-minute videotape of a puppet show decreased dramatically from 2 to 4 years. Correspondingly, the amount of time they spent looking at the videotape increased.

SOURCE: Data from Ruff et al. (1998).

how $2\frac{1}{2}$-, $3\frac{1}{2}$-, and $4\frac{1}{2}$-year-olds behave when asked to watch a 10-minute videotape of a puppet show (Ruff, Capozzoli, & Weissberg, 1998). Notice that 2-year-olds find it hard to even stay near the activity: This age group spends 25 percent of the time roaming around the room. Four-year-olds almost never leave the table, but their attention wanders even if they don't: They are almost as likely to not be looking at the screen as they are to be looking at it.

Preschool children also have a hard time with tasks that require them to be organized about switching the focus of their attention. Consider what happened when experimental psychologist Elaine Vurpillot (1968) asked 3- to 9-year-olds whether houses, like the ones in Figure 6.6, were the same or different. Young children tended to look randomly at the windows and made decisions without looking at some, so they often concluded that different houses were the same. In contrast, children 6 years and older used a more organized and thorough approach, one in which they looked at more window pairs when the houses were identical.

If children's attentional skills are still immature, why do parents often brag that their young sons and daughters have amazing powers of concentration? One reason is that children act more maturely when they are engaged in interesting, familiar activities. As we mentioned in Chapter 4, for example, even preschoolers know that certain sounds on television signal something interesting, so they know when to look up to catch important information. This skill helps them learn a lot from shows such as *Sesame Street* even if they are playing with toys while they watch (Pezdek & Hartman,

Eye Movements from a 5-year-old

Eye Movements from a 6-1/2-year-old

FIGURE 6.6 The development of visual scanning.

Elaine Vurpillot recorded children's eye movements as they judged whether two houses (like the ones on the left) were the same or different. Eye movements from a 5-year-old and $6\frac{1}{2}$-year-old show where these two children looked before saying a pair of houses was "the same." As you can see, children 6 years and older use a much more systematic approach.

1983). Of course, sophisticated behavior in front of a television is the product of hundreds of viewing hours, but these experiences do not make children act maturely in less familiar situations. And as you'll read next, their lack of maturity is also evident when you test what they *remember* about novel experiences.

REMEMBERING. After a memory expert lectured about the court case described in our opening story, someone in the audience asked the following question:

> A child I know was visiting the circus with his parents when a trapeze artist missed a catch and fell. Cries swept through the crowd, the performance was stopped, and the tent was cleared. Remarkably, this child has no memory of the event. Isn't this proof that she blocked the experience from memory because it was so traumatic?

"Not necessarily," the presenter answered. Memory researchers know many reasons why a child might not remember an event like this one. After reviewing some basic information about memory development, we'll revisit this day at the circus to explore these reasons.

As you read in Chapter 4, young children can hold only a few pieces of information in mind at a time. For example, the average 2-year-old can only repeat 2 numbers from a short list (that is, has a "memory span" of 2), whereas 6-year-olds remember an average of 4.5 and adults remember about 7. Children find it especially challenging to remember information while completing an action, which is why kindergarten teachers give them daily practice with three-part requests, such as "Go back to your desk, put your name on a piece of paper, and draw a picture of your favorite rainy day." Four developmental changes help children hold more information in working memory as they grow (Schneider & Pressley, 1997):

Most young children have trouble playing attention when they are not very interested in what's being said.

▶ **An expanding knowledge base.** Familiar information is generally easier to remember, which is why you are more likely to remember the name "Justin" than the name "Sivaram" after a brief introduction. One reason young children have difficulty keeping information in working memory is that most information is not very familiar to them.

▶ **Increased speed of processing.** Older children and adults name items, recognize faces, and name faces faster than younger children do. As processing speed increases, children hold more information in working memory because they can load more new items into memory before the older items are forgotten (Hitch, Towse, & Hutton 2001).

▶ **Improved inhibition and resistance to interference.** In Chapter 4 we mentioned that children are not very good at inhibiting a previous response (such as reaching to the left after they have just reached to the right). Deficiencies in inhibition also influence mental life. For example, when preschoolers recall lists of words, their responses often contain numerous unpresented words (Harnishfeger & Bjorklund, 1993, 1994). As minds mature, improved inhibition and resistance to interference frees up mental "space" for children to remember what they need to remember.

▶ **Better use of memory strategies.** Adults often use memory aids, such as repeating grocery lists to themselves while they are shopping. But this strategy of repeating information, which is called *rehearsal*, is not something young children tend to do. In an early study, for example, only 10 percent of kindergarten children spontaneously named objects they were trying to remember, whereas 85 percent of fifth-grade children did (Flavell, Beach, & Chinsky, 1966).

Appreciating the value of memory strategies is one component of **metamemory**: our awareness of and knowledge about memory (DeMarie et al., 2004). You demonstrate good metamemory skill when you make a list because you know you are likely to forget something, or when you associate "Sivaram" with "sieve" and "ram" to remember this name. In contrast, young children are not very knowledgeable about the limits of their memory and not very aware of factors that influence memory. In fact, their beliefs about memory are "wildly inconsistent with reality" because they often think they can remember large amounts of material and do not know that some things are easier to remember

metamemory Knowledge about memory. Metamemory includes such things as knowing how much information you can learn in a specific amount of time and which of two lists will be easier to learn.

episodic memories Memories of events that are stored as specific episodes by including information about the context in which the events occurred.

semantic memories Memories for general knowledge, like the meaning of words and facts about the world.

than others (Schneider & Pressley, 1997, p. 320). For instance, when experimenters displayed picture cards from each of three categories and asked children how the cards might be learned in a few minutes, only 35 percent of kindergarten children mentioned any type of categorization strategy, whereas 80 percent of fifth-grade children did (Kreutzer, Leonard, & Flavell, 1975).

Improvements in working memory have important consequences for behavior. Children who can hold more in mind are better at many tasks, from understanding stories to planning drawings. It makes sense, then, that intelligence correlates with memory span: Children with low IQs have smaller memory spans than average children do, and gifted children have larger than average spans, especially in content areas in which they excel (Schneider & Pressley, 1997).

As children grow, they also experience improvements in long-term memory—the relatively permanent reservoir of knowledge that allows you to remember what you did yesterday or this time last year. But you do not have a single long-term memory system. Instead, long-term memory is like a library that has different types of media, each with different characteristics and different rates of development.

Episodic memories are associated with a particular time, place, or circumstance. For example, information about where you went yesterday is retained by your episodic memory (Rajah & McIntosh, 2005). These memories have different degrees of detail. *Verbatim memory traces* correspond to the surface form of experiences, or what literally happened. When you attend a baseball game, for example, you might store a memory of drinking a Pepsi™. But you also store *gist memory traces*. Gist refers to patterns and meaning, such as the fact that you went to a baseball game and drank something (Brainerd & Reyna, 2004). The detailed context provided by verbatim memories helps us remember how we learned something, such as the fact that Mike told us a particular joke at the game rather than Matt. The ability to identify the source of our memories, which is a skill called *source monitoring*, is not very developed during the preschool years. Thus young children sometimes integrate information they dreamt about, heard, or saw in a book into stories about their own lives (Poole & Lindsay, 2001, 2002).

When children learn the meaning of new words or facts, like "a triceratops is a meat-eating dinosaur," they add information to their **semantic memories**, their storehouse of words and basic information about the world. Young children are semantic memory sponges who rapidly soak up general information about people, objects, and activities in their world. They have a special talent for developing *script memories*, which are memories for the typical features of repeated experiences (such as what usually happens when you go to a restaurant). Thus you might have difficulty getting 4-year-olds to talk about a *particular* visit to McDonald's (which

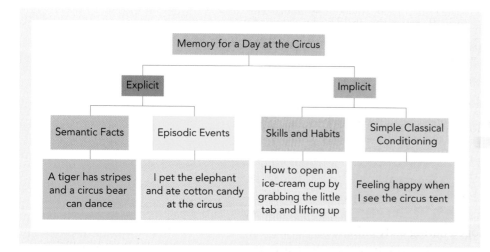

FIGURE 6.7 Long-term memory for a day at the circus.

The different long-term memory systems shown here record different types of information and have different patterns of development. Preschoolers easily store general knowledge about the world but have more difficulty retrieving memories of specific incidents. And while there are large age differences in explicit memory, age differences in implicit memory are, at best, small.

is an episodic memory), but they can rattle on with enthusiasm about what *usually* happens when their families go out for a burger (a semantic memory) (Hudson, Fivush, & Kuebli, 1992).

As shown in Figure 6.7, semantic and episodic memories are **explicit memories**. We represent these memories as words or mental pictures that come to mind readily, and this type of knowledge transfers easily to new situations. In contrast, conditioned responses, habits, and learned procedures are **implicit memories**. You rely on implicit memories when you react with fear to a dog because you have been bitten in the past (which is a conditioned response) or put together a familiar puzzle (which is a learned procedure). In these cases, your reactions are rapid and automatic. Implicit memories are not voluntarily called to mind, and this type of learning tends to be tightly associated with specific learning environments. Unlike tests of explicit memories, which show large age differences, tests of implicit memories show only small or no age differences (Hayes & Hennessy, 1996; Thomas & Nelson, 2001; Vinter & Perruchet, 2002).

What is memorable to adults is not always what is memorable to children. Therefore, it is hard to predict what this 4-year-old will remember from his exciting birthday party.

This basic "architecture" of long-term memory is intact early in development. As a result, children's recall is influenced by the same factors that influence yours: They are most likely to remember information that is important to them, that maps onto what they already know about the world, or that they encounter more than once.

Going back to the circus, why didn't the child remember that a trapeze artist fell? There are many possibilities, but it is likely that the visit was novel and exciting. Circuses are filled with bizarre events, like a dog riding a tiger, and highly memorable events, like eating cotton candy. Because the child had no script for what *should* happen at the circus, the fall was probably not very distinctive or meaningful. It makes sense that a child who just saw a man put a sword down his throat might have trouble realizing that the fall injured someone, especially when the roar from the crowd was so similar after these two events. Often, children who are thrown into unfamiliar situations remember peculiar details that have meaning to them, such as the size of a clown's shoes, rather than the events adults consider important.

Are children unaffected by events they cannot describe at a later time? Not necessarily. Even though this little girl didn't seem to remember the circus, she may still be *afraid* of the circus because different memory systems control these two behaviors: The ability to describe a specific event relies on episodic memory, a form of memory that is not very developed during early childhood, but associating a situation with fear relies on the implicit memory system, which *is* well developed. Thus even though children do not recall many *specific* experiences, they are still influenced by trips to the zoo, the thousand stories they are read, and the special feeling they get from being tucked in at night.)

Improvements in attention and memory during the preschool years are just part of the cognitive developments that pave the way for school-readiness. As illustrated by the next topics, some developments during the preschool years

explicit memories Memories represented as words or mental pictures. Semantic and episodic memories are explicit memories.

implicit memories Conditioned responses, habits, and learned procedures that can influence behavior without being voluntarily called to mind.

symbolic artifacts Objects or printed symbols that represent something else, such as models and maps.

dual representation The ability to mentally represent a model as an object in its own right and, at the same time, as a symbol that stands for something else.

FIGURE 6.8 Becoming symbol-minded.

This young boy is treating a tiny chair as if it were the full-size chair he saw just minutes earlier. Two-year-olds also fail to appreciate the relationship between a model of a room and the room itself. As a result, they act as if they do not know where a toy is hidden in a room even though they know where a similar toy is hidden in the model. These behaviors occur because children under 3 years lack *dual representation*: the ability to think about something as an object *and* as a symbol of something else at the same time. Some 3-year-olds are still confused by symbols, and it takes years before children fully understand maps and other symbolic artifacts.

Adapted from DeLoache (2005).

involve how children *reason* about information that is right in front of them or in their minds. Reasoning is a form of higher-order thinking that calls upon a range of cognitive skills, of which attention and memory are just pieces.

BECOMING SYMBOL-MINDED. Infants and toddlers are terrific symbol users: They gesture to be picked up, learn language easily, and engage in symbolic play with dolls, swords, and anything they can fashion to imitate their parents. But understanding **symbolic artifacts**—objects or printed symbols that represent something else—is a gradual process. Almost half of toddlers between 18 and 30 months of age will try to sit on tiny chairs or force their feet into tiny cars if they have recently been playing with a full-sized chair and child-sized car. These *scale errors* occur because most children less than 3 years lack **dual representation**: the ability to mentally represent a model as an object and, at the same time, as a symbol that stands for something else (Figure 6.8). Confused toddlers are amazingly persistent. For example, one little girl who was filmed by developmental psychologist Judy De-Loache even tried to cram her foot into a tiny car by taking off her shoe (DeLoache, 2005)!

The concept of symbolic artifacts starts to click in children's minds around 3 years of age, when they understand that symbols represent something else. To illustrate this achievement, DeLoache (1995) shows children a scale model of a room that matches a full-sized room nearby. As each child watches, an experimenter hides a miniature toy near a piece of little furniture while saying, "Watch! I'm hiding Little Snoopy here. I'm going to hide Big Snoopy in the same place in his big room!" (Figure 6.8). Then the experimenter asks the child to find Big Snoopy. A child who understands that the scale model represents the big room will quickly retrieve it.

There are dramatic differences in the performance of $2\frac{1}{2}$-year-olds and 3-year-olds on this task: Fewer than 20 percent of the younger children find Big Snoopy, whereas over 75 percent of the older children do. But the younger children are not uninterested in the game. In fact, they happily search for the toy, and nearly all of them retrieve the miniature toy (proving they have not forgotten where it was). What they seem to lack is *representational insight*: an understanding that the scale model *stands for* the room (DeLoache, Miller, & Rosengren, 1997).

Children do not lack representational insight one day and wake up with errorless performance the next. Even children older than 3 years sometimes show symbolic "ignorance," and it will be years before most children fully grasp the concept of maps and other models. Preschoolers understand symbols better when the physical similarity between the symbol and what it stands for is strong or adults clearly explain the relationship between the two. And as you will read next, this emerging ability to consider two aspects of reality at once also helps them understand other people.

THEORY OF MIND. Parents encourage children to think about mental states ("How do you think it makes Sandy feel when you grab her toy?"), and they believe their little ones are ready for school when they can consider other people's feelings. Understanding mental events is so central to our lives that scientists have been eager to learn when children develop a

theory of mind, in other words, when children understand that other people have thoughts, desires, and intentions.

Children know that people are agents who convey intentions by the end of infancy. As world-renowned biologist Svante Paabo explained, "For the first ten months you can't tell the difference between chimps and humans. Then the human children realize that behind your eyes is something that they can direct. That there are other people like me" (Shute, 2003, p. 63). There is a lot of evidence that infants appreciate the difference between people and objects. They are upset by a motionless person but not by a still, inanimate object (Adamson & Frick, 2003), and they look where people are looking (Butterworth, 2000). Most 2-year-olds predict that a story character will choose an activity the character likes rather than one they prefer themselves (Wellman & Woolley, 1990), and by 3 years children start to use a variety of mental verbs, including "think," "remember," and "pretend" (Wellman, 1992).

But preschoolers do not always think logically about mental life. For example, try showing a 5-year-old a candy box and asking her what is inside. She will probably say "Candy." Then say "Surprise!" and show her crayons. Next, explain that someone else will be coming into the room and ask, "What will *he* think is inside the box?" A typical 5-year-old will say, "Candy!", with a great deal of delight about the deception. But a typical 3-year-old will simply say, "Crayons." This game, which tests children's understanding that people can have inaccurate mental representations, is a **false-belief problem.** Children perform above chance on a variety of false-belief tasks around 4 to 5 years of age. Moreover, this accomplishment occurs around the world, in North American countries, hunter-gatherer societies in Africa, and even among Peruvian Indians (Callaghan et al., 2005; Wellman, Cross, & Watson, 2001).

Preschoolers often fail false-belief problems because they have difficulty thinking about several possibilities at once—especially when their thinking is pulled by reasoning biases that are common to all age groups. For example, children and adults alike are prone to think that other people know what *they* know, although this "curse of knowledge" declines with age (Birch, 2005).

Adults can encourage children to be more sensitive to other people's thoughts and feelings. Parents who talk frequently about mental states ("He wants ___" or "She knows what's going to happen") have children who are better than age-mates at answering questions about mental states (Ruffman, Slade, & Crowe, 2002). So even though preschoolers do not spend a lot of time thinking about thinking, it helps them to discuss television shows and stories with adults who comment on the mental layer of everyday events.

COGNITIVE FLEXIBILITY. Look at the four cards in the left panel of Figure 6.9. Pick two cards that are the same in some way. Now pick two cards that are the same, but in a different way. Let's try another one. Look at the pictures in the right panel. Pick two cards that are the same in some way. Now pick two cards that are the same, but in a different way. Easy, right? Not for preschoolers.

When researchers Sophie Jacques and Philip Zelazo (2001) showed children how to pick pairs from cards like those on the left side of Figure 6.9, 85 percent of the 2-year-olds, 22 percent of the 3-year-olds, and 12 percent of the 4-year-olds were mystified by this problem. Moreover, children who passed

theory of mind One's grasp of mental concepts, including one's understanding that other people have thoughts, desires, and intentions.

false-belief problem A test of whether people can set aside what they know to appreciate that other people may have different beliefs.

Parents can encourage their children to consider other people's feelings by talking about people's thoughts, desires, and emotional reactions.

Figure 6.9 Cognitive flexibility.

Most 3-year-olds understand abstract dimensions, such as color and shape, and can pick two cards that are alike in some way from the cards on the left. But it will be years before they can flexibly shift their focus from one abstract dimension to the next. Once 5-year-olds choose two cards that are alike in some way from the cards on the right, they often fail when asked to find a pair that is alike in a *different* way.

Source: Jacques & Zelazo (2001).

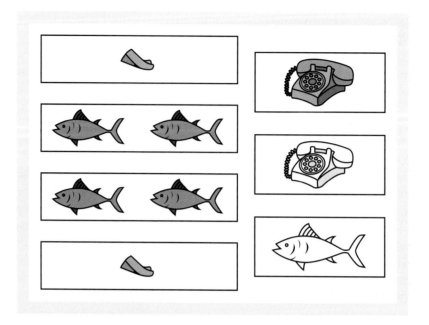

this easy task were often challenged by the cards on the right. After selecting their first pair, 4-year-olds found another pair only a third of the time, and 5-year-olds found a correct second pair only half of the time.

The cards in Figure 6.9 measure abstraction and cognitive flexibility, two abilities that are part of *executive processing* (a concept you read about in Chapter 4). Jacques and Zelazo's results show that 3-year-olds have problems with abstraction: They find pairs when cards match perfectly but not when they have to detect an abstract dimension, such as color only or shape only. Older children detect one dimension but have difficulty shifting their focus to a second dimension. Perhaps this is why card games like UNO, in which players try to match either the number or color of the last card in the pile, delight children. And perhaps this is also why adults are sometimes exasperated by how inflexible preschool children's thinking can be.

Language Development

One reason children gradually become better at remembering the past is that growing language skills help them reinforce memories by talking about the past. And more so than younger children, older children talk to themselves to keep track of what they need to do next ("Mom said pick two, pick two"). The biggest advances in language occur during the preschool years, when children transform themselves from novice talkers into eager conversationalists.

Learning to speak clearly. Some preschoolers need a parent or sibling to translate their garbled-sounding speech. Pronunciation errors usually follow some predictable rules. For example, it is difficult to produce groups of consonants at the beginning of words, so *string* might be pronounced "tring", or *stop* might be "top" (De Villiers & De Villiers, 1978). Children also substitute easy sounds for sounds that are harder to pronounce (saying "wabbit" for *rabbit*) (Hoff, 2001).

About one in 20 preschoolers goes through a brief period when they hesitate between words or repeat syllables or words. These problems, which are more common among boys, occur more often when children are upset, tired, or just talking faster than they are thinking (Shelov, 2004). It is hard to identify children who are merely in a temporary phase because those who eventually outgrow this phase and those with persistent stuttering show similar language skills (Watkins, Yairi, & Ambrose, 1999). Children should be evaluated by a speech and language professional if problems persist for more than a few months or interfere significantly with communication. Meanwhile, it is best if adults ignore early stuttering and set a relaxed tone for conversation by speaking slowly (Jones & Ryan, 2001).

VOCABULARY AND SYNTAX. Typical first graders can choose the definition of over 10,000 words (Anglin, 1993). But their remarkable ability to understand language can mislead adults into thinking they know all of the short, common words. In fact, young children can be confused about words that seem easy—even when they use those words in their own speech.

Interest in preschoolers' vocabularies increased in the early 1990s, when court cases like the one in our opening story suggested that children misunderstood many of the questions lawyers asked. This problem prompted language experts to write guidelines that help adults understand **semantic development**: children's developing understanding of word meanings (Walker, 1999). These categories of words are especially likely to be misunderstood:

▶ *Prepositions.* Young children are still learning the meaning of prepositions, such as *in* and *before*. For example, 3-year-olds sometimes use *in* to mean "between," 4-year-olds confuse *above* and *below*, and many 6-year-olds misinterpret *before* and *after*.

▶ *Temporal words.* Preschoolers sometimes use *yesterday* to refer to any time in the past, not the day before the current day.

▶ *Kinship terms.* Words like *aunt* and *uncle* are especially baffling because relationships vary depending on who is speaking. For example, a female sibling is a sister, but she could also be someone's aunt and a mother. Because it takes time to sort out these terms, preschoolers make amusing comments like "Is Uncle Bonnie coming?"

Young children's understanding of *syntax*—the rules for combining words and meaningful units like *s*—is also incomplete. Their use of pronouns is especially confusing to adults. For example, one 4-year-old described a series of pictures involving a girl and a woman on a plane in the following way: " . . . she's (i.e., a girl) sitting on the seat airplane . . . she's (i.e., a woman) giving something to a girl, now she's (i.e., the woman) looking at a book . . . now she's putting the thing up high" (Wigglesworth, 1990, p. 119). Even 6- and 8-year-olds sometimes use pronouns ambiguously, although they often correct themselves. Miscommunications between children and adults are common because young children are still mastering dozens of language details, including when to use a pronoun and when to use a name instead.

BECOMING A GOOD CONVERSATIONAL PARTNER. A psycholinguist who wanted to order wine at a banquet approached the waiter and said, "Excuse me, but would you tell me what the entrée is?" The baffled waiter hesitated, then slowly answered, "Well, it's the course that comes after the salad but before the dessert" (Keysar & Henly, 2002, p. 207).

This story is funny because adults usually understand ambiguous questions. We also monitor cultural norms that regulate how we are expected to speak in different situations, and we take the needs of our listeners into account. These skills are part of **pragmatics**: the uses of language in social contexts. (The term *pragmatic* means "related to practical affairs.") But long after children have acquired the vocabulary and syntax to tell a good story, they are still learning how to

semantic development The part of language development that deals with understanding word meanings.

pragmatics The social uses of language, such as how to take turns at appropriate times, how to interpret intended meanings, and how to modify one's speech for different listeners.

use language appropriately. While they are learning, children often amuse and embarrass us because they so frequently violate norms for socially appropriate conversation.

Just as children fail to think flexibly on reasoning tasks, they also have difficulty thinking up multiple meanings and selecting one that matches a speaker's intention. This is why 6-year-old Ruby still answers the phone and responds to, "Is your mother home?" by saying, "Yes," but without going to get her mother. It is not until age 6 or older when children reliably separate the literal meaning of a statement from its intended meaning. But once they grasp the contrast, they may find it unbearably funny to ignore intentions. For example, a child might respond to, "Can you pass the salt" by keeping his hands in his lap and saying, "Yes . . . ha ha ha ha ha!"

Children are also learning that *how* they say something is as important as *what* they say. Human language is rich with meaning—we change how we talk depending upon the formality of a situation, whether we have higher or lower status than our conversational partner, and whether our request is small or large. Children grasp politeness adjustments early because parents insist on it, as in the following example (Becker, 1988):

> **Mother:** I beg your pardon?
> **Child:** What?
> **Mother:** Are you ordering me to do it?
> **Child:** Mmm, I don't know, Momma.
> **Mother:** Can't you say, "Mommy, would you please make me some?" (p. 178)

With experience, children become more sensitive to social situations and learn more ways to phrase requests. By 5 years they soften a request the second time they make it and realize they should be more polite when an adult is busy (Warren & McCloskey, 1997). But they still have difficulty keeping a conversation on topic, recognizing when they need to ask for clarification, and anticipating natural breaks in conversation that help people take turns smoothly. It is important to help children learn these skills because people like socially competent children better than their less competent peers (Bryant, 2001). Lack of social grace is charming in young children but, all too soon, the charm wears off.

Putting It All Together: Self-Regulation

Young children frequently misbehave due to limitations in **self-regulation**: the skills involved in monitoring and controlling their thoughts, emotions, and behavior. But there are large differences in the extent to which individual children obey verbal commands and control their behavior. To illustrate, consider how two 4-year-olds, Jacob and Janelle, acted when an adult, Maria, tested their self-control (McCabe, Cunnington, & Brooks-Gunn, 2004):

> Maria gives Jacob the following instructions: "I have a present for you. But I need to wrap it first so it will be a surprise. You need to help me. Try not to look so that I can wrap your surprise for you. I'll let you know when I'm ready to give you the present. OK? Try not to look!" Maria then walks behind Jacob. Standing about 5 feet from him, she crinkles the wrapping paper noisily so as to attract Jacob's attention. Almost immediately Jacob turns around to look at Maria. "Are you done yet?" he asks. Maria reminds him that the rule of the

self-regulation The skills involved in monitoring and controlling one's thoughts, emotions, and behavior.

game is to not look. Jacob turns back. Five seconds later, as Maria continues to make wrapping noises, Jacob turns around again. He grins slyly at Maria. "Remember, no looking," says Maria. Jacob ignores this reminder and continues to watch Maria until, after 60 seconds, she hands him a wrapped gift. (p. 340)

Unlike Jacob, Janelle fingered her shoelaces to distract herself during the Gift Wrap task, and she did not peek until Maria announced, "I'm done." Later, when Jacob and Janelle sat together for a second round of testing, Janelle pushed Jacob's face and reminded him, "No looking!"

Self-regulation improves dramatically during the preschool years. Three- and 4-year-olds find it extremely difficult to substitute a response adults want for another that is "pulling" them. For instance, if you ask children to say "day" when they see a card with the moon and stars but "night" when they see the sun, 30 percent of 3-year-olds and young 4-year-olds cannot follow these instructions even after a series of practice trials. Older children learn the task, but their performance steadily improves between $4\frac{1}{2}$ and 7 years (Gerstadt, Hong, & Diamond, 1994). During this time, children also become better at waiting for a reward, finding pairs that match in different ways, and thinking about other people's mental states. Many developments improve their ability to regulate thoughts and behavior, including improvements in working memory (which helps them keep track of what they are supposed to be doing), inhibition (which helps them suppress a preferred response), language (which helps them stay on task by talking to themselves), and the ability to think about more complicated systems of rules (which helps them keep track of how rules change in different situations). Turn to Table 6.2 for a review of these developments.

Children like Jacob, who have poor self-regulation skills, are more likely than children like Janelle to have poor self-control many years later (Raffaelli, Crockett, & Shen, 2005; Rothbart, Ellis, & Posner, 2005). Because self-control predicts behavioral and peer problems later in life, it is important to help children learn strategies for regulating their behavior. In the next chapter, we will explain some ways parents and teachers can help.

Most preschoolers want to be good, but it will be many years before this girl develops self control.

TABLE 6.2   Information Processing Expands during the Preschool Years

Skill	Explanation	Developmental Trends
Attention	Attention involves many abilities, including the ability to focus on some things while ignoring others and the ability to shift the focus of one's attention.	Children younger than 6 years have difficulty focusing their attention on information selected by adults. By age 6 they are more organized in shifting their attentional focus, so they are more accurate at deciding whether two pictures are the same or different.
Working memory	The ability to hold information, such as a list of instructions, in mind for short periods of time.	The amount of information children hold in mind increases from 3 to 6 years of age.
Long-term memory	The relatively permanent reservoir that includes two types of information: (1) explicit memories (memories of specific events are held in episodic memory; general knowledge is held in semantic memory) and (2) implicit memories (conditioned responses, habits, and learned routines).	Episodic memory matures more gradually than other forms of long-term memory. Young children rapidly add information to semantic memory and also form implicit memories without difficulty, but they often have difficulty recalling specific episodes or events. The ability to recall specific events improves from 3 to 6 years of age, but even 6-year-olds sometimes remember information without remembering *where* they learned it.
Understanding symbols	Children must learn that *symbolic artifacts*—objects or printed symbols that represent something else—are objects but are also symbols.	*Dual representation*—the ability to mentally represent a model as an object and, at the same time, as a symbol of something else–emerges about 3 years of age. Nevertheless, children only gradually come to understand maps and other types of symbolic materials.
Theory of mind	Children's ability to think about other people's thoughts and mental states.	Children begin to realize that other people have thoughts that are different than their own around 4 to 5 years of age. But even after they grasp this concept, young children frequently view situations from their own perspective.
Cognitive flexibility	The ability to shift one's mental focus. Children demonstrate cognitive flexibility when they can identify one abstract dimension in a set of cards ("all of the red ones") and then shift their thoughts to a second abstract dimension ("all of the ones with two pictures").	Preschoolers frequently fail tasks that ask them to think about one aspect of a situation and then shift to a second. For example, when pictures on cards vary along more than one dimension, such as color, shape, and number, 5-year-olds fail about half the time if you ask them to find cards that match some way and then ask them to find cards that match a different way.

>>>**MEMORY MAKERS**<<<

1. Which of the following is NOT one of the terms Piaget used to describe preoperational thought?

   (a) centered　　　　　　(b) appearance-bound　　　　(c) static
   (d) flexible　　　　　　 (e) irreversible　　　　　　　(f) egocentric

2. An expanding knowledge base, faster speed of processing, and improved resistance to interference are explanations for why children can _____ as they mature.

   (a) speak more clearly
   (b) hold more information in working memory
   (c) remember more events that occurred a long time ago
   (d) predict other people's thoughts more accurately

3. Children perform above chance on a variety of theory of mind tasks around ___ years of age.

   (a) 1 to 2　　　　(b) 2 to 3　　　　(c) 3 to 4　　　　(d) 4 to 5

4. Semantics involves understanding ____; pragmatics involves understanding ___.

   (a) the sound system of a language; word meanings
   (b) word meanings; the sound system of a language
   (c) word meanings; the social uses of language
   (d) the social uses of language; word meanings

[1-d; 2-b; 3-d; 4-c]

Emotional and Social Development

Preschoolers are at an interesting juncture—too old to hang onto adults every minute but too young to run off with age-mates. Around the globe, most little ones solve this dilemma by watching older children play. As they gain independence, children gradually spend more time interacting with peers, and by 6 years many have best friends and sometimes even enemies.

Erik Erikson observed that young children are focused on "making": They interrupt, build elaborate towers, pursue goals, and compete in their broadening social worlds (P. H. Miller, 2002). Unlike 2-year-olds, who run through the house destroying things along the way, older children have an expanded sense of self and a developing conscience. By age 4 they are in Erikson's stage of **initiative versus guilt** (which spans ages 3 to 6), when they compare themselves to others and want to master what other people have mastered. The reactions they receive determine whether they feel worthy or bogged down by guilt because their behavior seems inadequate. As Erikson described, "Being firmly convinced that he *is* a person, the child must now find out *what kind* of a person he is going to be" (1959, p. 74). Increasingly, children explore who they will be by experiencing the joys and frustrations that come from living and playing with people whose goals are not always the same as their own.

Children's Emotional Worlds

Preschoolers display the full range of human emotions—from joy and sadness to jealousy and guilt—and they display them often. According to one estimate, young children express emotion over 200 times a day (Stein, 2002). But what causes emotional reactions? As adults we feel emotional when an event changes

initiative versus guilt Erikson's third stage of psychosocial development, from roughly 3 to 6 years of age, when children compare themselves to others and want to master what other people have mastered. During this stage, the feedback they receive determines whether they feel worthy or bogged down by guilt because their behavior seems inadequate.

the likelihood that we will attain a personally significant goal. We are stirred when we have just achieved a goal, failed to achieve a goal, or perceived an event that changes the probability of reaching a goal. We are angry when someone blocks our goal, sad when we lose what we cannot replace, and happy when we achieve something meaningful to us.

According to developmental psychologist Nancy Stein, preschoolers use the same causal schemes that we do to understand, evaluate, and react to events. Stein and her colleagues (Stein, 2002) studied emotional development by asking children to describe the event in their lives that made them or a friend the most happy, sad, angry, or afraid. Remarkably, children's stories were similar regardless of their ages. Even 3-year-olds reported what started the event, how their goal was interrupted by the event, who was to blame, how they felt, what they preferred, and how they reacted to success or failure. The complexity of their emotional worlds is illustrated by this 3-year-old's report of her angry friend:

> **Adult:** *Pretend that Rachel's really, really mad. What would make her feel that way?*
> **Child:** If somebody wouldn't let her talk. If they said, "No! Wait 'til I'm finished!" and it was going to be until, and they said that they were going to talk until, until clean-up time.
> **Adult:** *And that would make her mad, if someone didn't let her talk until clean-up time—*
> **Child:** MMMMM! (Shakes head vigorously with a yes.) And she would go like MMMMM! "You never let me talk! You always talk."
> **Adult:** *Well, what would she be thinking about if someone wasn't going to let her talk?*
> **Child:** She would want to punch him, but she wouldn't. She really wouldn't.
> **Adult:** *She wouldn't? What would she do?*
> **Child:** She would tell the teachers because it made her feel bad.
> **Adult:** *Because it made her feed bad, huh? And what would telling the teachers accomplish?*
> **Child:** The teachers would say, "Take turns. You could, um, tell half of it, and Rachel could tell half of what she wants to say. And you could tell half of it, and she could tell half of it. And you could tell half of it, and she could tell half of it." If they didn't let her, she could, I think she would tell the teachers that they kept on doing it. That's what I think she'd do, that's what she always do, lah lah lah lah! Just like my every, just like my every, just like every of my friends. (p. 254)

Notice that even this 3-year-old knew what made her friend mad, what her friend's strategy for solving the problem was, and what her friend would do if her first strategy failed.

How well do children remember emotional experiences? To answer this question, Stein's team asked 3- to 6-year-olds to describe the time when they felt their most intense emotion and then reinterviewed them 10 years later. Ninety percent of the children who had chosen a fearful event, such as a hospital visit, recalled that event years later, and 76 percent remembered events that had made them angry, such as a time a parent had lied. So even though children often fail to remember events selected by adults, it is not uncommon for memories of personally significant events to survive many years later.

In sum, the emotional lives of children and adults differ primarily in terms of what individuals are emotional about and how well they control outward expressions of emotion. As Stein (2002, pp. 260–261) explained, "the themes in children's lives are different because the goals they pursue are often different from those of adults"—not because there are fundamental differences in what triggers an emotion. Therefore, one key to understanding children is to realize that their goals are as important to them as our adult goals are to us.

Concepts of Themselves and Other People

You just read that children often remember meaningful information even though they frequently forget things that are important to adults. Children's understanding of themselves and others also depends upon the situation. During the preschool years, each little body houses a sensitive, socially insightful child along with an insensitive, egocentric one.

THE SELF IN TIME. When Piaget's daughter, Jacqueline, was 35 months old, she looked at herself in a photograph and said, "It's Jacqueline." Puzzled that she hadn't said, "It's me," Piaget asked, "Is it you or not?" Jacqueline replied, "Yes, it's me, but what has the Jacqueline in the photo got on her head?" (Piaget, 1951, p. 225).

It is curious that Piaget's daughter referred to herself as "Jacqueline." As we saw in Chapter 4, pronoun use and self-recognition emerge between 18 and 24 months, when children begin to pass the "rouge" test. Why, then, didn't Jacqueline seem to fully recognize herself? Piaget's answer was that preschoolers do not have a mature sense of individual identity.

Cognitive psychologist Daniel Povinelli (2001) set out to investigate Piaget's claim. He arranged for preschoolers to play with an adult who patted each child on the head several times. Unbeknownst to the children, on the last pat a large sticker was placed on their heads. Only 3 minutes later, each child watched the events on videotape, including footage showing the sticker. Surprisingly, none of the 2-year-olds and only 25 percent of the 3-year-olds reached up to search for the sticker. In contrast, 75 percent of the 4-year-olds removed the sticker within seconds of seeing it. The 4-year-olds, Povinelli explained, "seemed to have an immediate and intuitive grasp of the connection between the delayed video images and their present state" (p. 78).

In a related study, an assistant showed children photographs of themselves. While pointing to the sticker, the assistant asked, "Who is that?", "What is that?", and "Where is that sticker right now?" Even after prompting, only 13 percent of the young 3-year-olds reached for the sticker. But when they were given a mirror, 85 percent of the nonresponders reached up to their heads. Apparently, 3-year-olds need to see immediate feedback between their movement and movement in an image before they can mentally connect themselves to their image. But there was another interesting finding: As in Piaget's example, the 3-year-olds often used their proper names instead of saying "me," whereas older children almost never responded this way. The peculiar viewpoint of 3-year-olds was captured by one child who said, "It's Jennifer," but then added, "Why is she wearing my shirt?" (Povinelli, 2001, p. 81).

Do these results mean that young children live only in the here and now? No. Preschoolers often talk about past events and anticipate future events. But just as they have difficulty imagining several possibilities at once, they also have difficulty thinking about themselves at different points in time. In other words, preschoolers are still developing a **temporally extended self**, a rich view of the self that connects information about oneself over time (Moore & Lemon, 2001). Passing the landmark "rouge task" is just the first step toward self-understanding, a step when toddlers conceptualize themselves in terms of their current physical

temporally extended self A rich view of the self that connects information about the self over time.

"Grammie, tell me again about when I was a baby!" By 4 or 5 years, children love to hear about things they did when they were younger—and they start to talk about what they will be when they grow up. Now they have a richer view of themselves that goes backward and forward in time.

and mental states. A second transition occurs around 4 to 5 years of age, the same time children develop the ability to pick pairs of cards that are similar in different ways. With the ability to hold multiple representations in mind, children can now organize their past, present, and future selves into a richer concept of "me."

DESCRIPTIONS OF THEMSELVES AND OTHER PEOPLE. If you ask a preschooler to describe herself, she will probably mention physical traits, like size and hair color, or activities she enjoys, like coloring or playing school. Compared to her 8-year-old brother, who says that he is smart, funny, or has other psychological traits, she thinks in more concrete terms. And unlike her teenage sister, who is constantly comparing herself to other people, our preschooler is not yet preoccupied with how she stacks up to her peers (Fivush, 2001; Shantz, 1975).

Young children differ from older children in another interesting way: They frequently overestimate what they know and what they can do, even when they have just failed at a task (Plumert, 1995; Schneider, 1998). And compared to adults, who view traits as stable over time, they are more likely to believe that people's characteristics will change in a positive direction. For example, 40 percent of the kindergarteners through second graders in one study thought that people could overcome traits like missing a finger or being extremely small (Lockhart, Chang, & Story, 2002). Scientists speculate that this *youthful optimism* helps children learn. As one research team explained, "If children believed that their failure to ride a bike, tie their shoes, or correctly tell a good joke after repeated tries was due to something fixed and unchangeable within themselves, they would probably quickly give up and fail to develop mastery in these areas" (Lockhart et al., 2002, p. 1409).

Despite their limitations, preschoolers have an uncanny ability to notice socially relevant traits in other people. For example, even 3-year-olds notice skin color and other markers of racial categories, and by 4 years they have an emerging ethnic awareness. In fact, when 4-year-olds sort photographs into piles, they classify more often by race/ethnicity than by sex, age, or facial expression (Bernstein et al., 2000). For a discussion of preschoolers and race, turn to our next *Solutions* feature, "Racism in the Private Spaces of Children."

Young children notice racial differences and pick up racial attitudes from adults. Caregivers can help them treat everyone with respect by talking about discrimination when children make hurtful comments. Fun activities that teach children about different cultures help them feel relaxed and comfortable around people who are not exactly like themselves.

RACISM IN THE PRIVATE SPACES OF CHILDREN

At the start of nap time, 3-year-old Carla picked up her cot and moved it to the other side of the classroom. When her teacher asked what she was doing, Carla pointed to Nicole, a 4-year-old African American child on a cot nearby. "I can't sleep next to one," she said. The stunned teacher ordered Carla to return to her place and not to use "hurting words" (Van Ausdale & Feagin, 2001, p. 1). When Carla's parents arrived at the day care for a meeting, the European American father and European American/Asian mother were baffled by Carla's behavior. Then a light went off in the father's head: Carla might have picked up her attitude from her playmate Teresa's dad.

Because preschool children are often egocentric and socially unaware, child specialists have long assumed they accept other children without question. When little ones *did* blurt out slurs, adults thought they were merely mimicking adults, without any real understanding of their actions. Is this view of childhood innocence and unquestioned acceptance accurate?

No, concluded sociologists Debra Van Ausdale and her coauthor, Joe Feagin, in *The First R: How Children Learn Race and Racism* (2001). During nearly a year of fieldwork in urban preschools, Van Ausdale frequently heard children questioning their ethnicities, excluding other children from activities because of ethnic stereotypes, and concealing their racial attitudes from teachers. She thinks the widespread belief that young children cannot have negative stereotypes is an *adult-centric view*, one in which adults interpret behavior according to how they *think* children behave, rather than how children *actually* behave. Carla's comment, for example, didn't simply imitate something she had heard; she applied what she had learned to a novel and personal interaction. As Van Ausdale and Feagin explained, "This is not the thoughtless blunder of a sleepy child" (p. 2).

Nor, said Van Ausdale, were the dozens of other racially motivated interactions she observed. For example, one child repeatedly worried that her tan meant she would not be "white" anymore, and other children argued over what color their faces were. Some of the teachers reacted with hostility to these findings. One said that young children did not have the cognitive tools to understand race; another questioned whether Van Ausdale was making up the anecdotes. Supportive teachers wondered what was wrong with the school, as if they were responsible for ideas that pervaded the children's social world.

Why were the teachers so distressed? Apparently, they were shocked by Van Ausdale's stories because children generally conceal their racial teasing. As Van Ausdale and Feagin explained, "These three-, four-, and five-year-olds were proficient at maintaining private spaces more or less free from adult intervention, and this facilitated their experimentation with racial and ethnic concepts and issues. Despite the teachers' best efforts, children

Even preschoolers are very aware of physical differences. They are less likely to exclude children who look different from themselves when adults talk openly about skin color, disabilities, and culture.

managed to create places for their activities removed from the prying eyes of adults" (p. 167). Van Ausdale, on the other hand, observed without comment or correction, so the children ignored her. From this special vantage point, their play revealed knowledge of many sensitive issues—knowledge that was hidden as soon as a teacher approached.

These findings illustrate why we understand children better when we study them with multiple methodologies—including observing their daily activities. Van Ausdale's observations also explain why it is never too soon to address racism. Instead of ignoring racist teasing or insults, these behaviors provide "teachable moments": times when adults can talk about differences, prejudices, and discrimination. Teachers can also plan activities that introduce children to ethnic relations. For example, one diversity program reduced how often children sorted picture cards on the basis of race rather than other features (Bernstein et al., 2000). As one child summed up at the end of this program, "Like we're all different, but the same" (p. 189).

Moral Development

Children become aware of behavioral standards—that is, how they should speak and act—by their third birthdays, and adults around the world expect them to have reasonable control over their behavior by their seventh birthdays. The transition from irresponsible 2-year-old to school-aged child is rapid. Children start comparing their performance to standards as early as 3 to 4 years old, when they act distressed if they do not live up to expectations. Unlike 2-year-olds, who are usually oblivious to the quality of their work, older preschoolers care about the value of what they make. In one study, for example, 3- and 4-year-olds were asked to build an airplane that was too challenging to finish. Many of these children stopped playing after failing and made comments such as, "I want to try it again," and "I could do it now" (Nolan, 1979, described in Kagan, 1994). By 6 years children appreciate how their actions contributed to misdeeds, such as missing cookies and broken vases, and these older children worry more than younger children about the consequences of their misbehavior.

Moral development follows the same pattern we find with cognitive development: Young children appear to be immature, concrete thinkers when we ask them to reflect on hypothetical or unfamiliar situations, but they often surprise us with their understanding of meaningful events. Findings by Piaget and others provide more examples of these two sides of the preschooler.

premoral stage A stage of moral development when children show little concern about rules. In Piagetian theory, this stage lasts from birth to about 5 years.

morality of constraint A stage of moral development when children respect rules but see them as absolute and unchangeable. In Piagetian theory, this type of thinking is most common between the ages of 5 and 7 years.

morality of cooperation A stage of moral development when people understand that social rules are arbitrary agreements that can be changed. In Piagetian theory, this type of thinking can begin as early as 7 years but is more common by 10 or 11 years.

PIAGET'S STAGES OF MORAL DEVELOPMENT. Children can be destructive, so adults usually get serious about teaching them socially appropriate behavior by the time they are 3 years old. During the next few years, advances in moral development alter how children conceptualize rules and how they reason about moral issues.

Piaget proposed that cognitive development directs children through three stages of moral development. In the **premoral stage** (from birth through age 5 or so), children show little concern about rules. For example, they often play with the pieces of a game without trying to follow a fixed set of procedures. Children who have just learned to follow rules typically adopt a **morality of constraint** in which they respect rules but see them as unchangeable. Friends who have learned different rules often fight at this stage because each child believes there is only one way to play. Children progress into a **morality of cooperation** when they understand that rules are arbitrary agreements people can change. These types of morality refer to ways of thinking about an issue rather than distinct stages, so it is difficult to assign firm age brackets to each one. In fact, individual children often show both types of thinking. Nonetheless, a morality of constraint is common between 5 and 7 years, whereas a morality of cooperation is typical around 10 or 11 years. The period from 7 to 10 years is a transitional time when children gradually think in more sophisticated ways about fairness and responsibility.

Piaget used the following stories to evaluate children's reasoning about moral transgressions (Piaget, 1965/1977):

> Story A: A little boy who is called John is in his room. He is called to dinner. He goes into the dining room. But behind the door there was a chair, and on the chair there was a tray with fifteen cups on it. John couldn't have known that there was all this behind the door. He goes in, the door knocks against the tray, bang go the fifteen cups and they all get broken!
>
> Story B: Once there was a little boy whose name was Henry. One day when his mother was out he tried to get some jam out of the cupboard. He climbed up on to a chair and stretched out his arm. But the jam was too high up and he couldn't reach it and have any. But while he was trying to get it he knocked over a cup. The cup fell down and broke. (p. 122)

After reading these stories, Piaget asked questions about the boys. Here is a typical response from a 6-year-old (Piaget, 1965/1997):

> **Adult:** Is one of the boys naughtier than the other?
> **Child:** The first is because he knocked over twelve cups.
> **Adult:** If you were the daddy, which one would you punish most?
> **Child:** The one who broke twelve cups.
> **Adult:** Why did he break them?
> **Child:** The door shut too hard and knocked them. He didn't do it on purpose.
> (pp. 124–125)

In contrast, older children answered as this 9-year-old did (Piaget, 1965/1997):

> **Child:** Well, the one who broke them as he was coming in isn't naughty, 'cos he didn't know there was any cups. The other one wanted to take the jam and caught his arm on a cup. (p. 129)

These comments show that young children focus on concrete results: It is bad to break cups, so whoever broke more cups is naughtier. According to Piaget, children who reason from the vantage point of a morality of constraint focus more on the *consequences* of actions than the *intentions* of the characters.

When other investigators read these stories to children from Western industrialized countries, their results confirmed Piaget's stages. But other studies suggested that Piaget's findings do not always generalize to other cultures or situations. Individuals in some cultures do not become more flexible about rules as they grow older (Havighurst & Neugarten, 1955), and children consider intentions more often than Piaget claimed when stories are rewritten so that one of the characters clearly intended the misdeed (Armsby, 1971). As in many other situations, children's attention is captured by information that is important to them, so some tasks do not reveal their understanding of complicated issues. Still, children who have developed a theory of mind are somewhat aware that ethical judgments should include information about people's intentions. As they grow, intentions also become important for thinking about lying.

UNDERSTANDING WHAT A LIE IS. Eight-year-old Michael mistakenly gave the wrong street directions. Did he tell a lie? In one study, 90 percent of 5-year-olds and 69 percent of 8-year-olds said that mistaken children told a lie (Peterson, Peterson & Seeto, 1983). Apparently, children start out believing that a lie is any false statement and only gradually come to consider *intent*, in other words, whether or not the speaker knows that the statement is false. But how early children take intent into account depends upon the situation. For example, one research team told children that a bear had *not* seen mold on some bread. When they asked whether the bear "lied or made a mistake" when he said the bread was okay to eat, many of the 3-year-olds and over half of the 4- and 5-year-olds responded that the bear was simply mistaken (Siegal & Peterson, 1996).

Children's *actions* also reveal a good understanding of deception. In one study, 3 percent of 3-year-olds and 75 percent of 4-year-olds lied to experimenters about whether they had broken a rule (Fen, Weixin, & Wenjing, 2005), and parents who kept diaries said that their 4-year-olds lied an average of 5 times per week (Stouthamer-Loeber, 1987). Studies like these provide even more support for the conclusion that children show more understanding when they are tested in meaningful settings that have real emotional implications. As one team of researchers wisely noted, "Children are, after all, members of the human race" (Ceci, Leichtman, & Putnick, 1992, p. 7). The human ability to trick other people illustrates our next topic: children's fascination with social interactions.

Social Relationships

Children are highly attuned to their social worlds. By 18 months they interact differently with same-aged peers than with 24-month-olds (Brownell, 1990), and a few years later they joke differently with children and mothers by reserving most of their disgusting comments for other children (Dunn, 1996). Relationships play a central role in children's stories about what makes them sad, angry, or happy (Dunn & Hughes, 1998). Family members are frequent topics of emotional conversations, but children increasingly test their social skills with friends, imaginary companions, and siblings.

©2003 Charles Rodrigues/Creators Syndacate.

" . . . Aw, don't be a killjoy, Charlie, get in Bobby's MRI."

PLAY AND EARLY FRIENDSHIPS. Children's play changes noticeably during the preschool years. Recall from Chapter 4 that over half of 30- to 35-month-olds show *cooperative social pretend play,* a type of play that involves symbolic actions such as filling and passing a miniature cup. After their third birthdays, growing symbolic and language skills support more advanced play. In *complex social pretend play,* children plan and negotiate sequences of symbolic interactions, such as planning a tea party for stuffed bears ("This bear, it's his birthday and he invited this bear to come for tea"). Now children periodically step out of the "script" to change the plan or correct a player. Nearly half of all children engage in this type of play by 43 to 47 months, or just before their fourth birthdays (Howes & Tonyan, 1999).

Relationships progress into friendships when children prefer the company of specific children and express enjoyment about being with them (Howes & Phillipsen, 1992). Stable friendships form as early as 2 years, and by age 3 children who have stable peer groups can discuss who their friends are. Children start engaging in complex pretend play at different ages, though, so they also show individual differences in the quantity and quality of their friendships. Importantly, these differences predict later social behavior. Preschoolers who engage in complex play at a younger age are more socially competent during middle childhood than children who are slow to develop peer relationships. What's more, children who have close friendships at age 4 tend to report supportive friendships at age 9 (Howes, Hamilton, & Phillipsen, 1998).

Friendship enriches children's lives in the following ways (Howes & Tonyan, 1999):

▶ *Friends provide support and intimacy.* For example, day care providers know which children are friends and use this knowledge to help children separate from parents by giving children someone else to be near. By age 4, children disclose more information about themselves to friends than nonfriends.

▶ *Interactions with friends help children master social interactions.* Preschoolers play more elaborate games with friends than nonfriends, and children who stay with stable peer groups during their early years are more socially competent than those who have not had a chance to stay with a group. These findings suggest that friends provide opportunities to learn about getting along with others that are not readily available with less familiar peers.

▶ *Friends help children learn about people who are not like themselves.* The younger children are, the more likely they are to develop cross-gender and cross-ethnic friendships.

While children are playing, they are also constructing mental representations of how people might behave and how, in return, *they* might act. Some children bring this internal process out into the world in the form of imaginary companions.

IMAGINARY COMPANIONS. A 4-year-old we'll call Trevor had a friend named Fake Tom. Fake Tom wore Velcro shoes and rode a horse named Wacko. Trevor also had a horse named Wacko, so the two of them could ride together (Gleason, 2002).

Fake Tom and Wacko are unusual because they are invisible friends. Preschoolers often invent *imaginary companions* or personify objects, such as calling a cloth diaper "Raggie" or saying that a stuffed bear pretends to be a kitty. In the survey that produced these examples, parents said that 21 percent of their 4-year-olds had imaginary friends and another 21 percent had personified objects (Gleason, 2002). The frequency of imaginary friends challenges the old-fashioned notion that preschoolers are concrete, inflexible thinkers (Carlson & Taylor, 2005). Instead, their social lives can be perceptive, inventive, and—sometimes—altogether comical.

Why do some children invent imaginary friends? They are not inventing perfect companions because children often say their imaginary friends are difficult and even frightening (Taylor, 1999). There is also no evidence that most children use imaginary friends to compensate for social awkwardness. Actually, it is the children who have the most active imaginations who perform best on measures of social understanding (Taylor & Carlson, 1997). Finally, children with imaginary companions do not differ from other children in having friends, and they do not have less positive reactions to preschool, so there is no evidence that these children fantasize to escape from social stress (Gleason, Sebanc, & Hartup, 2000).

Who, then, are these children with a roomful of people the rest of us cannot see? Children with invisible friends are more often firstborn or only children who spend more time alone, so home environments contribute to this phenomenon. Nonetheless, we know that aloneness is not the entire story because many children with invisible friends occupy other places in their families. The truth is that scientists are not sure why children create these relationships, although they do know that children interact differently with personified objects than with invisible people. Children nurture stuffed toys and pieces of fabric, which provides opportunities to act out cognitive schemes related to caregiving. In contrast, children with invisible companions act out schemes for "friend": They recreate activities, dialogue, and even conflicts that are typical of friendships but not relationships with parents. Because imaginary companions appear when children are expanding their understanding of relationships, fantasy relationships may be a way to experiment with or practice new social knowledge (Gleason, 2002).

SPARRING WITH SIBLINGS. Darcy was just a preschooler when her baby sister, Raven, was born. At first their mother encouraged Darcy to hold her sister, which Darcy loved. As the months passed and Raven gained weight, however, her mother decided that Raven was too heavy for Darcy to carry safely. Nevertheless, Darcy would not stop picking up "her" baby. "Darcy, you are going to drop the baby," her mother pleaded. "Darcy, put Raven down." Then, one day, the three were in the living room when the kitchen phone rang. The mother left for a few minutes, but when she returned the living room was empty and laughter was streaming from a back bedroom. The mother cried furiously, "Darcy, how many times have I told you not to carry your sister!" "I didn't carry her," Darcy replied smugly. "I rolled her."

The only predictable thing about sibling relationships is how unpredictable they are. Some children show an increase in behavior problems when a new baby arrives whereas others join the majority of children who act more maturely (Dunn, Kendrick, & MacNamee, 1981). As time passes, some siblings develop loving and cooperative relationships while others are ripped apart by hostility and rivalry. The factors that influence these outcomes are too numerous to list. Children's gender and temperaments, their age differences, and the behavior of their parents are some of the factors that predict the quality of sibling behavior. For example, toddlers are less bothered by the appearance of a new baby than older preschoolers are, and same-sex children who are close in age are more likely to become both companions and rivals. The quality of a sibling relationship is determined by many issues, including whether a pair has contrasting personalities (which predisposes them to conflict) or compatible temperaments (Munn & Dunn, 1989).

Sibling relationships are more conflict-ridden than friendships are, and children say they are more likely to seek help from friends than from siblings (Gleason, 2002). Unlike friends, siblings are a captive audience that will not go away simply because people do not get along—and they often do not get along. In fact, young children average as many as seven conflicts per hour (Dunn & Munn, 1986; Ross et al., 1994). But positive and negative interactions are not opposite sides of the coin. Brothers and sisters interweave spats with friendly behavior, so conflict does not necessarily mean lack of affection (Lempers & Clark-Lempers, 1992).

Most siblings have a great deal of affection for each other, even if they also have frequent spats. It looks as if the bond between these brothers is off to a good start.

How do sibling conflicts usually end? It depends on whether or not adults are structuring the situation. When Ram and Ross (2001) asked siblings to divide a set of toys with a parent nearby, 90 percent quickly succeeded. Under their parents' eyes, these children used problem-solving strategies, such as proposing trades or taking turns picking, the majority of the time. And even when the youngest sibling was only 4 years old, children rarely threatened to withdraw, insulted their sibling, or grabbed toys. But these results are not typical of how children behave at home. One study found that the most common outcome of disagreements at home was no resolution. Furthermore, preschool siblings who fought at home compromised only 5 percent of the time and reconciled by comforting or apologizing only 2 percent of the time (Siddiqui & Ross, 1999). Together, this pair of studies shows that preschoolers are capable of negotiating disputes, but they usually don't.

Conflict gives children a chance to practice skills that are essential for social development, including brainstorming, negotiation, and problem solving. This is why child care experts advise adults to let children work out minor squabbles on their own or with as little help as possible (Siddiqui & Ross, 1999; Vandell & Bailey, 1992). And if mental health professionals have learned anything about managing siblings, it is that the entire ecology of families sets the stage for positive relationships. Warm relationships are associated with parents who are warm and responsive to their children. Also, parents who maintain their own relationships with discussion and problem-solving sessions witness fewer jealous reactions among their children than parents who have poor communication skills (Volling, McElwain, & Miller, 2002).

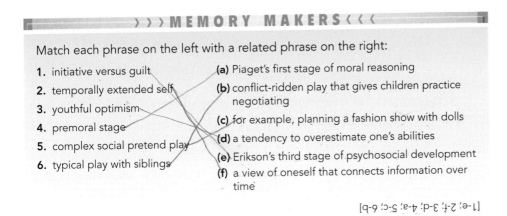

>>> **MEMORY MAKERS** <<<

Match each phrase on the left with a related phrase on the right:

1. initiative versus guilt
2. temporally extended self
3. youthful optimism
4. premoral stage
5. complex social pretend play
6. typical play with siblings

(a) Piaget's first stage of moral reasoning
(b) conflict-ridden play that gives children practice negotiating
(c) for example, planning a fashion show with dolls
(d) a tendency to overestimate one's abilities
(e) Erikson's third stage of psychosocial development
(f) a view of oneself that connects information over time

[1-e; 2-f; 3-d; 4-a; 5-c; 6-b]

Understanding Preschoolers

Early in this chapter, we promised to revisit the Kelly Michaels's case to answer an intriguing question: Why would preschool children tell bizarre stories about their nursery school teacher? Although we can never know exactly what happened in an actual case, researchers have pieced together an answer by exposing children to influences that are typical of cases such as the one involving Kelly Michaels.

Numerous studies have found that young children are highly reliable *and* highly unreliable witnesses, depending upon the circumstances. Young children are accurate sources of information when they understand events, have the vocabulary to describe their experiences, and are not misled by confusing questions or conversations. In one experiment, for example, every 3-year-old accurately said

"No" when interviewers asked if a man they had played with 3 months ago had put something yucky in their mouths or pushed their tummies (Poole & Lindsay, 2001). Children's descriptions of what *did* happen were brief, though, largely because young chidren forget details, have trouble holding information in working memory, and have not learned how to tell a "good" story.

Children's testimonies collect errors when adults press them for details by asking lots of specific questions. There are many reasons why misunderstandings blossom when untrained interviewers talk to children (Ceci & Bruck, 1995; Poole & Lamb, 1998):

1. *Children try to answer most questions.* Children believe they should be cooperative in conversation and take turns, so they often answer questions even when they have to guess. In one study, for example, interviewers asked a difficult question about a research assistant: "What does the man do for a living, what is his job?" Instead of saying, "I don't know," many children replied by saying things like "basketball coach" (Poole & White, 1993). Young children are especially poor at answering questions that only require a "yes" or "no" answer, probably because it is so easy to say "yes" or "no" without really thinking about the answer (Brady et al., 1999).

2. *Children do not always understand interviewers' questions.* For example, a child who was injured 2 months ago might say "Yes" to the question, "Did she hurt you yesterday?" because he thinks that "yesterday" means "any time in the past" (Walker, 1999).

3. *Young children have limited attention spans and difficulty keeping the topic of conversation in mind.* For these reasons, preschoolers have trouble staying focused and sometimes interject silly or unrelated comments (Poole & Lindsay, 2001). This tendency to drift off topic is one reason why allegations of abuse sometimes expand over time to include multiple people, locations, and events as children start talking about one event and then drift into talking about unrelated events.

4. *Interviewers often misunderstand children's speech and feed back information the children did not report.* This is more than a minor problem. One analysis of 68 sexual abuse interviews found 140 instances in which the interviewer misinterpreted the child. Many of these errors involved important information, like which person the child was talking about, and the children agreed with the interviewers' mistakes one-third of the time (Roberts & Lamb, 1999).

Policy groups have published recommendations for talking to children that minimize misunderstandings due to these problems, including five key tips in Table 6.3. But careful interviewing will not solve the problems that occur when young witnesses have picked up false information *before* an interview simply by hearing people talk. As we mentioned earlier in this chapter, preschoolers are not very good at remembering *where* they learned information, so they sometimes describe events they only heard about as if they have actually witnessed those events. In one study, for example, children who never saw someone ruin a treasure map or break a special rock during a pretend "archeological dig" reported these events as often as children who actually witnessed these events—simply because they shared a classroom with children who had experienced leading questions about the dig ("How did Dr. Diggs break the rock . . . did he step on it or did he drop it?") (Principe & Ceci, 2002). As the research team suggested, young

TABLE 6.3 Top Five Tips for Talking to Preschoolers

Principle	Techniques
1. Start conversations with an open-ended prompt.	Use open-ended prompts that let children choose what they remember. Open-ended prompts are comments such as, "What happened at the zoo?" or "Tell me everything that you and Kyle did today." Avoid questions that can be answered with a "yes" or "no" response, such as "Did you see a tiger?"
2. Encourage children to describe events in their own words.	When children stop talking, encourage them with simple prompts, such as "Then what happened?", "Tell me more," or "What else?"
3. Avoid misleading questions.	When children stop providing new information, ask questions about information they have already mentioned. For example, you might say, "You said something about a rock—tell me what happened with the rock." Avoid misleading questions, which are questions that add information children haven't reported. For example, "Did he hurt you with the rock?" is a misleading question.
4. Repeat the topic of the conversation frequently.	Young children often get distracted and begin speaking about different events than the one you think they are describing. It helps to repeat the topic in your prompt. For example, you might say, "Tell me about the rock that *you and Kyle played with today.*"
5. Do not assume that children are using words the way you would.	Preschoolers often lack the vocabulary words to describe events accurately. For example, they may say "uncle" when they mean "aunt" or "potato" instead of "tomato." Double-check important facts by asking follow-up questions, such as, "Does Kyle's uncle have another name?" or "What did the rock look like?"

children sometimes "see" with their ears! Similarly, when the 3-year-olds we mentioned earlier heard a story about a man putting something yucky in their mouths or pushing their tummies, 37 percent falsely said "yes" to questions about these events.

Research on young children's eyewitness testimony illustrates many of the developmental trends described in this chapter. Preschoolers are highly verbal, fast at learning meaningful information, and eager to show other people what they know. As a result, they often perform with remarkable maturity when they understand what is expected of them. On the flip side, they do not appreciate the consequences of their testimony and will try to respond even when adults are taxing their cognitive abilities with lengthy interviews and complicated questions. This is why there is no answer to the question "Are young children reliable witnesses?" Instead, the appropriate question is, "Under *what circumstances* are young children reliable witnesses?"

Preschool children entertain us with their unexpected insights and enthusiasm for life. But while they are flexing their physical, cognitive, and emotional muscles, their unpredictable behavior can be exasperating. The key to enjoying young children is to arm yourself with a heavy dose of wisdom, including knowledge about common problems and how the environment steers development toward positive outcomes. In the next chapter, we address these issues by turning to practical matters, including children's health, parenting issues, and early school experiences.

>>> SUMMARY <<<

Taking Charge of Their Bodies

1. Growth slows during the preschool years, when children add about 5 pounds (2.3 kilograms) and 2.6 inches (6.8 centimeters) of height per year. As **body mass index (BMI)** falls, children start to look sleeker and more mature.

2. Motor development is gradual. A mature walking pattern does not emerge until about 4 to 5 years, and most 6-year-olds still cannot print small letters or space letters properly. Sports activities should accommodate children's limited skills, stamina, and attention spans. Children with **developmental coordination disorder** develop self-help skills more slowly than their peers.

3. Brain development is uneven during early childhood. Pathways that support large motor skills mature earlier than those that support fine motor skills, and language areas experience a growth spurt before areas that support spatial processing do.

Perceptual Development

4. Basic visual abilities are fine-tuned between 3 and 6 years. Preschoolers should have a complete vision examination at 3 years and another at 5 years.

5. The ability to detect sounds in a noisy environment gradually improves until age 15. Children with a family history of hearing loss should have yearly hearing tests.

6. Young children often focus on information from one modality, such as visual or auditory information, more so than adults. As a result, they perform better when information from different modalities is consistent.

7. Through the process of **perceptual learning**, children gradually recognize **affordances** (fits between characteristics of the environment and opportunities for action) and **perceptual invariants** (features that distinguish objects from one another). Experiences with letters and language games help children learn the features of written language and the phonemes that letters represent.

Cognitive Development

8. Piaget said that children in the **preoperational stage** are illogical because their thinking is centered (focused on only one aspect of a situation at a time), appearance-bound (focused on physical appearances rather than underlying realities), static (focused on the current state of affairs), irreversible (ignoring reversible transformations), and **egocentric** (focused on their own perspective). Because children often perform well beyond Piaget's expected levels with familiar materials and questions, scientists view Piaget's descriptions as *characteristic ways of thinking* rather than absolutes.

9. During the preschool years, children become better at attending to what is important, enjoy improvements in working memory, and experience a growing knowledge base in long-term memory. They start to understand symbolic artifacts around age 3, and by age 4 to 5 a developing **theory of mind** helps them appreciate that other people can have different thoughts than their own. Cognitive flexibility grows after age 4, so children become better at tasks that ask them to follow one rule but then shift to a different rule.

10. Children pronounce most of the sounds in their language by the end of the preschool period, but their knowledge of **semantics** (word meanings) and syntax (rules for combining meaningful units) are still incomplete. Preschoolers often say inappropriate things because they are still learning about language **pragmatics** (the social uses of language).

11. Between 3 and 6 years of age, children show dramatic improvements in **self-regulation**: the skills involved in monitoring and controlling their thoughts, emotions, and behavior.

Emotional and Social Development

12. Young children's stories about emotional events are surprisingly similar to adults', and they sometimes remember emotional experiences for years. Children and adults have different goals but react with the same emotions when goals are blocked.

13. Toddlers see themselves in terms of their current state, but 4- to 5-year-olds begin to organize their past, present, and future selves into a richer concept of "me." But this concept is not always realistic or complex. Preschoolers are overly optimistic about their skills and futures, and their descriptions of people tend to focus on concrete characteristics, such as gender and race.

14. Children gradually progress from having little interest in rules (the premoral stage) to viewing rules as fixed and unchangeable (a **morality of constraint**). It is not until about 10 or 11 years that they consistently conceptualize social rules as arbitrary agreements (a **morality of cooperation**). Studies of lying show that children display a more sophisticated understanding of social interactions when they are tested in meaningful settings that have real emotional implications.

15. Nearly half of all children show *complex social pretend play* by their fourth birthdays. Friendships provide support and intimacy, teach children how to master social interactions, and expose children to people who are different from themselves. Some children act out their growing relationship schemes by inventing imaginary companions, and many children practice their negotiation skills with siblings.

Understanding Preschoolers

16. Preschoolers are reliable witnesses when they understand target events and have the words to describe their experiences. However, limitations in attention, language, and memory contribute to false reports when children are exposed to inappropriate interviewing or misleading information.

>>>KEY TERMS<<<

body mass index (BMI)   (p. 215)
developmental coordination disorder   (p. 217)
perceptual learning   (p. 221)
affordances   (p. 222)
perceptual invariants   (p. 222)
phonological awareness (phonemic awareness)   (p. 223)
preoperational stage   (p. 225)
egocentrism   (p. 226)
metamemory   (p. 229)
episodic memories   (p. 230)
semantic memories   (p. 230)
explicit memories   (p. 231)
implicit memories   (p. 231)

symbolic artifacts   (p. 232)
dual representation   (p. 232)
theory of mind   (p. 233)
false-belief problem   (p. 233)
semantic development   (p. 235)
pragmatics   (p. 235)
self-regulation   (p. 236)
initiative versus guilt   (p. 239)
temporally extended self   (p. 241)
premoral stage   (p. 244)
morality of constraint   (p. 244)
morality of cooperation   (p. 244)

MILESTONES of early childhood

3 to 4 Years Young preschoolers love to practice their growing motor and language skills.

- Three-year-olds can scribble with a crayon, and most show a preference to use one hand over the other.
- Language skills are developing rapidly, but preschoolers often misinterpret words and fail to explain things clearly.
- Young children have short attention spans and find it difficult to inhibit inappropriate responses.
- Even young children enjoy playing with other children, and nearly half engage in complex social pretend play (such as playing house or super heroes) by their fourth birthdays.

4 to 5 Years Children become more agile and are increasingly aware of other people's thoughts and feelings.

- Now they learn to skip and run well, and by 5 years many can print their first names.
- Throughout early childhood, children are preoperational thinkers who often focus on one aspect of a situation at a time and reason illogically.
- Between 4 and 5 years of age, children realize that other people can have false beliefs and ideas that are different from their own.
- As social awareness grows, children become interested in playing games with rules, although they often treat rules as unchangeable.

5 to 6 Years Expanding bodies and minds prepare children for the demands of school.

- Children start to become interested in dancing and playing sports as the skills needed to balance well and catch a ball mature.
- The abilities to pay attention and follow rules improve markedly by 6 years, so older preschoolers can enjoy more structured activities.
- As they begin to reflect on language, children become fascinated by rhyming games and learn that letters stand for language sounds.
- Preschoolers experience the same emotions adults do when goals are achieved or blocked. Their emotional lives are often revealed when they play and fight with siblings, friends, and imaginary friends.

What are the effects of

Preview: Early childhood in CONTEXT

Creating Safe and Healthy Environments

Preschool children are not mature enough to avoid unsafe situations or to know what is best for their health. As a result, the characteristics of their families and communities influence

their rates of unintentional injury, their chances of being exposed to toxic chemicals, and the quality of their early nutrition.

Boy-land, Girl-land

Children can be rigid about gender roles as they are learning about the differences between males and females. Around the world, boys and girls segregate into same-sexed play groups during the preschool period. Both sexes enjoy active play, but boys engage in more rough-and-tumble play.

Preschool Experiences

Different preschools place different degrees of emphasis on individual exploration, social activities, and direct instruction to build academic skills. Quality preschools improve the health of at-risk preschoolers and increase their chances of academic success.

Different Children— Different Problems

It is not unusual for preschool children to wet at night, have sleeping problems, or embarrass adults with their sexual curiosity. Some children have more serious behavioral issues, such as intense anxiety or acting-out behavior. Attention deficit hyperactivity disorder and autism spectrum disorders can also show up at this age.

Children across Cultures and Family Contexts

Every culture has its own set of assumptions about how children learn and how adults should interact with young children. In general, children are more likely to comply with adult rules when they have warm relationships with caregivers who clearly explain rules and enforce rules consistently.

In this next chapter, you'll learn how developmental principles explain the pathways individuals take through early childhood when we consider the question:

What are the effects of growing up with television?

growing up with television?

CHAPTER SEVEN

Pathways through Early Childhood

Stories of Our Lives

A Good Heart

In many societies, adults recruit children as young as 4 or 5 years old to help care for babies and toddlers, and these young children are expected to put their siblings' needs above their own. For example, traditional Hopi communities socialized children to value a "good heart," one in which there is no unhappiness, envy, or bad feelings toward other people—including one's brothers and sisters. When selfish behavior reared its head, family members used shame to instill a deep desire to conform to the group's moral values. The following story illustrates how memorable these early lessons could be (Eggan, 1997):

> "My mother had a good deal of trouble with me but I think she enjoyed it. She had none at all with my brother Henry, who was two years younger than I, and I think that the unbroken monotony of his goodness and truthfulness and obedience would have been a burden to her but for the relief and variety which I furnished in the other direction."
>
> Mark Twain

My younger sister ___ was born when I was about four of five, I guess. I used to watch my father's and mother's relatives fuss over her. She didn't look like much to me. I couldn't see why people wanted to go to so much trouble over a wrinkled little thing like that baby. I guess I didn't like babies as well as most girls did . . . But I had to care for her pretty soon anyway. She got fat and was hard to carry around on my back, for I was pretty little myself. First I had to watch her and joggle the cradle board when she cried. She got too big and wiggled too much and then my mother said to me, "She is *your sister*—take her out in the plaza in your shawl."

She made my back ache. Once I left her and ran off to play with the others for a while. I intended to go right back, but I didn't go so soon, I guess. Someone

257

found her. I got punished for this. My mother's brother said: "You should not have a sister to help you out when you get older. What can a woman do without her sisters? You are not one of us to leave your sister alone to die. If harm had come to her you would never have a clan, no relatives at all. No one would ever help you out or take care of you. Now you have another chance. You owe her more from now on. This is the worst thing that any of my sister's children has ever done. You are going to eat by yourself until you are fit to be one of us." That is what he said. That is the way he talked on and on and on. When meal time came they put a plate of food beside me and said, "Here is your food; eat your food." It was a long time they did this way. It seemed a long time before they looked at me. They were all sad and quiet. They put a pan beside me at meal time and said nothing—nothing at all, not even to scold me. My older sister carried ____ now, I didn't try to go near her. But I looked at my sisters and thought, "I need you—I will help you if you will help me." I would rather have been beaten...I was so ashamed all the time. Wherever I went people got sad [i.e., quiet]. After a while [in about ten days as her mother remembered it] they seemed to forget it and I ate with people again. During those awful days Tuvaye [a mother's sister] sometimes touched my head sadly, while I was being punished, I mean. Once or twice she gave me something to eat. But she didn't say much to me. Even she and my grandfather were ashamed and in sorrow over this awful thing I had done.

Sometimes now I dream I leave my children alone in the fields and I wake up in a cold sweat. Sometimes I dream I am alone in the desert place with no water and no one to help me. Then I think of this punishment when I dream this way. It was the worst thing I ever did. It was the worst thing that ever happened to me. No one ever mentioned it to me afterward but ____ [older male sibling], the mean one. I would hang my head with shame. Finally, my father told him sharply that he would be punished if he ever mentioned this to me again. I was about six when this happened, I think. (pp. 346–347)

This woman was 40 when she told her story to anthropologist Dorothy Eggan, yet she cried when she spoke.

FAMILIES AROUND THE WORLD interact differently with youngsters and expect them to make different contributions to family life. For example, parents in industrialized countries sometimes wait until children are about 12 years old before asking them to watch younger children, but it is not unusual for parents in traditional cultures to expect some help as soon as there is a new baby to entertain. In these societies, even preschoolers readily accept the responsibilities described in our opening story. In Polynesia, for instance, mothers teach 3- and 4-year-olds to feed and distract babies, and "the young child becomes upset if caregivers do not give him *his* crying baby. The young child takes his job seriously and learns the baby's likes, dislikes, and habits" (Martini & Kirkpatrick, 1992, p. 211).

But regardless of whether families expect preschoolers to help with chores or just enjoy themselves, all cultures start the task of *socializing* children—that is, teaching them the preferred behaviors, customs, and values of their society—between 3 and 6 years. Each community's child-rearing practices determine how safe and healthy children will be and what skills they will learn. As each child's temperament and talents intersect with the opportunities, risks, and lessons provided by his or her culture, millions of pathways are forged through early childhood.

Creating Safe and Healthy Environments

The risk of death declines sharply once children survive the first years of life. But there are still many threats to their safety and health. Let's continue our visit with early childhood by looking at three things preschoolers need to thrive: protection from injuries, protection from harmful substances in the environment, and healthy food habits.

Unintentional Injuries

As you can see in Figure 7.1, unintentional injuries claim the lives of more children in industrialized countries than any other cause of death (Hoyert et al., 2005). But the risk of serious injury varies depending upon where children live. In one analysis of 11 countries, the United States had the second highest childhood death rate from injuries—2.5 times the rate in England and Wales (Fingerhut, Cox, & Warner, 1998). U.S. children have a higher risk than children in many industrialized countries of dying from motor vehicle crashes, drowning, fire, and a host of other dangers.

Car and truck crashes account for the majority of injuries in the United States, killing an average of 4 children and causing more than 600 injuries *each day* (NCIPC, 2005). Sadly, nearly 50 percent of children who are killed in collisions were unrestrained by a seat belt or child-approved car seat, and many others were improperly restrained (NCIPC, 2006). A common mistake is transporting preschoolers without a booster seat. Seat belts do not fit properly until children are 4′ 9″ tall, so children who have outgrown their infant seats should be placed in a booster seat that accommodates a seat belt. Also, children under 12 should never ride in the front seat because the force from some passenger-side airbags can harm small bodies.

Even children who escape serious injuries usually experience some bumps and bruises during the preschool years. In records from one day care center, only 11 percent of children were injury-free during a 42-month period, and the remaining children averaged 11 accidents apiece. Most of these mishaps involved bruises from falls and collisions, with head trauma occurring in 73 percent of these incidents (Elardo, Solomons, & Snider, 1987). It is comforting to know that mild head injuries early in life rarely affect memory or attention, and problems that do occur usually disappear after 6 to 12 months (Satz, 2001).

Three broad factors are associated with the risk of unintentional injuries:

▶ *Family factors.* Families differ widely in how vigilant they are about keeping hazards out of the home and monitoring dangerous activities (Gulotta & Finney, 2000). Adults contribute to injuries when they relax safety standards as children grow or assume that children who know safety rules will make responsible choices. Later-born children are injured more often than firstborns not only because busy parents provide less supervision but also because households with older children are not well adapted to younger children's needs. Injury rates also increase whenever family stress decreases supervision, so injuries are more frequent when there is marital conflict, a lack of rules, few adults per child, or chronic illness in a family member (Matheny, 1988).

▶ *Characteristics of the child.* A child who logged 71 injuries in the day care study probably met the profile of a frequently injured preschooler: busy, curious, and impulsive. Children with a history of injuries tend to be less flexible in controlling

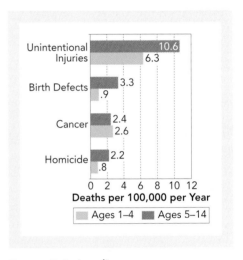

FIGURE 7.1 Leading causes of death.

Unintentional injury is the leading killer of children throughout the industrialized world. Preschool children are especially vulnerable when caregivers fail to restrain them properly in vehicles or provide inadequate supervision around pools and other hazards.

SOURCE: Hoyert et al. (2005).

Most preschoolers can't be trusted not to bolt into traffic without looking, especially if they are particularly impulsive.

the focus of their attention and less capable of inhibiting inappropriate responses. To illustrate these limitations, one research team taught preschoolers a computer game in which a frog switched hiding places whenever a border appeared or disappeared on the screen. Children who responded slowly to changes in hiding places were less likely to look at traffic when they crossed roads, possibly because they were so captured by their thoughts that they failed to consider what was happening around them (Dunbar, Hill, & Lewis, 2001).

▶ *Characteristics of the environment.* The easiest way to prevent childhood injuries is to legislate safer behavior and child-friendly products. Laws requiring car seats and standards for pool fences, flame-retardant sleepwear, childproof medication bottles, and numerous other products have dramatically lowered injury rates. In contrast, programs that teach preschool children safety rules are not very effective, largely because young children are not capable of following rules consistently (Garbarino, 1988). To learn how household products combine with other factors to endanger children, turn to our special feature on fire entitled, "Snap, Crackle, Pop: The Allure of Fire."

Children start many of the fires that cause damage and death. Adults can decrease the risk of fire play by not allowing young children to light matches or turn on stoves (which makes them feel safe around fire), locking up matches and lighters, and educating all children about fire danger.

SNAP, CRACKLE, POP: THE ALLURE OF FIRE

One of our children set her room on fire. Twice. The first time was unsettling, but the second dashed any fantasies we had that such things never happen to "good" parents. After reviewing some facts about fire safety, we will revisit the smoldering room to tell you how the fire started and what it taught us about keeping children safe.

Children are fascinated by fire. It moves, changes, and reacts to slight movements in the air. "Children do not become bored with fire," cautions the National Association of State Fire Marshals (NASFM, 2000, p. 22). Consequently, interest in fire is nearly universal. Over half of all children play with fire by the time they finish elementary school, and fire play is the leading cause of fire deaths among preschoolers. In one study, more fires were started by 4-year-olds than any other age group, and over 50 percent of fires were started by children between the ages of 4 and 9 years (NASFM, 2000).

A number of factors increase the risk of fire play. One is early exposure to fire. Children who are allowed to light candles or participate in cooking believe they can put out small flames and feel safe playing with fire (Grolnick et al., 1990). Adults add to the problem when they believe their preschoolers are too young to need fire education and when they store matches and lighters in unlocked drawers. These lapses of judgment—combined with children's curiosity—are the recipe for danger.

Most fires are started by children from well-functioning families who have no history of behavior problems. In these cases, arson prevention specialists focus on educating the family. Children from chaotic family environments need more aggressive interventions. In one evaluation, only 1 percent of young fire setters who had no observable family problems repeated the behavior, compared to 8 percent of children who had one or more family problems (Cole et al., 1986).

Our experience with a smoldering bedroom illustrates how family issues contribute to accidents. The parents in our story had recently divorced, so the teenager involved (we'll call her Amanda) had just moved into a smaller house. To ease the transition, Amanda's mother decided to renovate the bedrooms, leaving Amanda's in

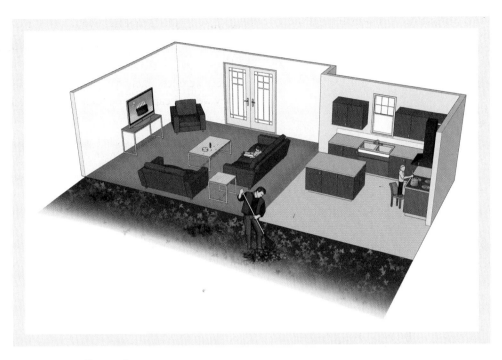

FIGURE 7.2 Fire safety.

Can you find four factors associated with fire play in this picture? (Turn to page 262 for the answers.)

shambles while the walls were being repaired. And because everyone in the family now shared a bathroom, Amanda had to get ready for school in the midst of her bedroom clutter. Stressed by the move and separated from her usual routine, Amanda laid a plugged-in curling iron on her carpet. Luckily, her mother walked into the room just as the carpet ignited. But then she made a dangerous mistake: She thought her daughter's carelessness would never happen again. A few weeks later, the carpet was smoldering again.

The frazzled mother in this story learned two important lessons. First, it is not unusual for children to be so distracted that they fail to think about their actions. Second, accidents often recur unless the environment is changed to prevent them. This is why frequent strolls to look for hazards should be part of every household routine, and why parents should increase supervision during stressful family times. Happily, the mother in our story strolled often, so she saved the room—and probably the house—a second time. Now the family put Amanda's room in order and set new rules for using electrical devices. To find out if Amanda's story has made you more aware of fire danger, try to find four risks for fire play in Figure 7.2.

Environmental Pollution

Many threats to health and safety are invisible. Particles from improperly ventilated wood stoves, pesticides, and mercury from fish are some of the hidden hazards children encounter. In addition, some children are poisoned by chemicals in herbal supplements, imported candy, and folk remedies (Lynch & Braithwaite, 2005). For example, an orange powder used by the Hmong (an ethnic group originally from Laos*) contains lead and arsenic, and some Chinese medications labeled "herbal"

---

*Laos: A landlocked country between Vietnam and Thailand.

lead poisoning Damage to the brain, nerves, and other body systems caused by swallowing or inhaling lead.

Answers to Figure 7.2:

1. The parent is not supervising the children.

2. A child is watching someone light candles on television, which may increase curiosity about fire.

3. A child who is too young to be cooking independently is using the top burners of the stove.

4. There is a lighter on the living room table that needs to be kept out of the children's reach.

FIGURE 7.3 Sources of lead in central New Orleans.

- -

These three-dimensional surface plots of the inner city of New Orleans compare levels of lead in children's blood to soil lead levels and the percentage of older houses. Notice that peaks for soil lead provide the best match to blood levels. The major cause of contaminated soil in urban areas is lead from gas fumes that has deposited near highways and high-traffic intersections.

SOURCES: Mielke H. W. (1999). Lead in the inner cities. *American Scientist, 87*(1), 62–73.

contain potentially lethal heavy metals. Children are especially vulnerable to these hazards because they absorb nutrients and excrete toxic substances differently than adults. For example, the bodily mechanisms that transport calcium respond similarly to lead, so lead is readily absorbed and deposited in rapidly growing bones. As a result, an adult may absorb only 10 percent of the lead they ingest whereas a 2-year-old may absorb 50 percent (Etzel, Balk, & American Academy of Pediatrics Committee on Environmental Health, 1999).

Lead poisoning is one of most common pediatric health problems in industrialized countries (Tong, von Schirnding, & Prapamontol, 2000). Once it enters the brain, lead causes neuronal death, interferes with neural communication, and hinders myelin production (Lidsky & Schneider, 2003). As a result, children who have been exposed to lead have lower IQ scores, learning difficulties, and attentional and behavioral deficits. They are also more hyperactive than their peers, less willing to follow directions, and more aggressive. Because lead damages nearly all body systems, exposure is also associated with high blood pressure, impaired hearing, and slowed growth (Smith, 2001).

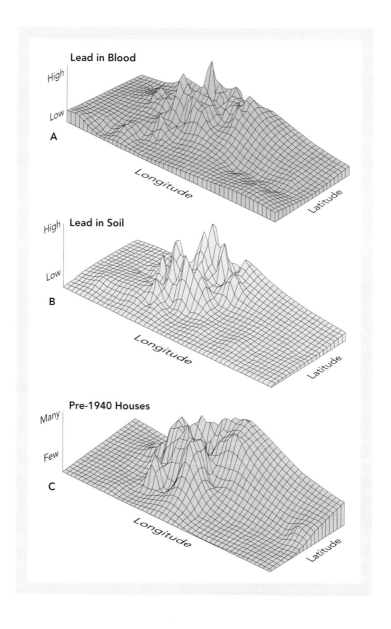

How do children come in contact with lead? A well-known source is lead-based paint, which is present in over 80 percent of houses built before 1978. (Leaded house paint was outlawed in the United States that year.) Children ingest lead by eating paint chips, rubbing their hands over painted railings, and inhaling airborne lead when parents sand woodwork. But visible paint is *not* the biggest danger. Over 50 percent of young children in the inner cities of New Orleans and Philadelphia have lead levels in their blood that are above current guidelines, yet in Manhattan, where most apartments contain lead-based paint, only 6 percent do. What accounts for this difference?

Howard Mielke, a biologist and geographer, has the answer. Mielke plotted children's lead levels across central New Orleans against soil levels and housing age. Notice in Figure 7.3 how well the distribution of soil levels matches the distribution of blood levels. Other data have confirmed that soil contamination from leaded gas (which was banned in 1986) is the major cause of lead poisoning in urban areas (Laidlaw et al., 2005; Mielke, 1999). Mielke's results suggest that lead poisoning is infrequent in Manhattan because there are few yards, so children are less likely to transfer lead into their bodies by playing in contaminated soil and putting their hands into their mouths. His results also explain why his 2-year-old daughter had a high blood level of lead: Her licensed day care home was several hundred yards from a freeway.

Mostly due to residue from leaded gas and paint, about 2 percent of preschool children have high blood levels of lead. But rates are higher in many locations (Centers for Disease Control and Prevention, 2005d). In Ohio counties, for example, the percentage of children with high levels ranges from 1 percent to 27 percent. Poor children and ethnic minorities usually have the highest levels because cheaper housing tends to be closer to high traffic areas, and children who are deficient in calcium absorb lead more readily (Wright et al., 2003).

Knowledge is the best defense against lead poisoning. **Primary prevention** involves protecting children from exposure by following the guidelines in Table 7.1, including painting over leaded paint and teaching children to wash their hands after

primary prevention Efforts to prevent a hazard from occurring.

TABLE 7.1 Preventing Lead Poisoning

Risk Factor	Prevention Strategy
Leaded house paint	Put a coat of primer and unleaded paint over the old paint. Keep children away during renovations of homes built before 1978, ventilate well, and clean up all dust.
Soil	Plant bushes next to older homes with painted exterior walls. This will keep children out of contaminated soil. Soil near older housing or major highways should be tested for lead. Place an artificial surface such as decking over contaminated soil in high-traffic areas and ground cover or grass over other areas. Replace sand in sandboxes, especially if children have dug down to the soil. Teach children to wash their hands after they come in from outdoors, before each meal, and at bedtime.
Water	Have water tested. If plumbing contains lead, use only water from the cold-water tap for drinking and cooking, and run the water for several seconds before using.
Work and hobbies	If your work or hobbies expose you to lead, change clothes and shower before entering areas of the home where children play.
Imported cans, pottery, candy, herbal remedies, and cosmetics	Some imported products contain lead. Although there is no comprehensive list of products to avoid, warnings are posted by the Centers for Disease Control at **www.cdc.gov**.

SOURCES: Centers for Disease Control and Prevention (2003a); Etzel, Balk, & American Academy of Pediatrics Committee on Environmental Health (1999); Smith (2001).

secondary prevention Efforts to respond to the first symptoms of a hazard, so the problem will not become worse.

food insecurity Fear of not having access to safe, nutritious food.

they come indoors from playing. When screening identifies an exposed child, **secondary prevention** focuses on removing sources of lead, which allows blood levels to gradually decline. (Children with extremely high levels can be treated with a chemical that helps their bodies excrete lead at a faster rate.) The success of these efforts varies depending upon the amount and timing of exposure. IQ scores gradually increase after children are removed from short-term, low-level exposure, but early or heavy exposure can cause permanent neurological damage (Soong et al., 1999).

Nutrition and Health

You read about malnutrition in developing countries in Chapter 5. Here we focus on malnutrition in industrialized countries, where the portrait of poverty looks very different.

FOOD INSECURITY. The United States is one of the richest countries in the world, yet 8 percent of its children suffer from hunger or nutritionally inadequate food (Kleinman et al., 1998). About 12 percent of households experience **food insecurity**, a situation that exists when people worry about having access to safe, nutritious food because food has been scarce in the past, even if they are not currently hungry (Carlson, Andrews, & Bickel, 1999; Kaiser et al., 2002).

Unlike malnutrition in developing countries, where hungry children are underweight, food insecurity in industrialized countries is associated with obesity. To understand why, let's look at how children develop food-related behaviors. Prior to 3 years, food intake is not much influenced by how much food children are served. But children learn eating habits by mimicking the people around them, so by age 5 they eat more when adults offer them more (Rolls, Engell, & Birch, 2000) and learn to prefer foods that are served frequently (Birch, 1990). In poor families, everyone learns to eat when food is available rather than when they are hungry, which can disrupt their ability to monitor internal cues for hunger and fullness (Hood et al., 2000). Poor families also stop purchasing fruit, vegetables, and meat when budgets are tights, so their children have fewer opportunities to learn to accept nutritious foods. Then, when money is available, low-income families often provide sugary treats. As a result of a feast-or-famine environment, poor children have difficulty regulating the quantity and quality of what they eat. And because food cultures are long-lasting, unhealthy patterns often survive for generations, influencing families that never experienced food shortages.

As processed food has become more popular, an increasing percentage of children are suffering from being overweight. Currently, about 6 percent of Caucasian 4- and 5-year-olds are overweight (BMI equal to or greater than the 95th percentile), compared to 10 percent of African American and 13 percent of Mexican American preschoolers (Fitzgibbon et al., 2002). Moreover, about 32 percent of children enrolled in Head Start, a preschool program for low-income families, are overweight (Hernandez et al., 1998).

MISCONCEPTIONS ABOUT WEIGHT. Physician Anjali Jain and her colleagues (2001) wondered why low-income parents didn't change their eating habits after their children started gaining too much weight. To explore this issue, they interviewed mothers of preschoolers who had BMIs at or above the 90th percentile for their age. Each mother answered a series of questions about food and weight, including "What causes a child to be overweight?" and "Tell me what you can do to keep your child from becoming too heavy." These mothers frequently expressed three misunderstandings about weight control:

► *Misunderstanding 1: You can't define "overweight" by children's rank on a growth chart.* Many low-income mothers did not accept the practice of using growth charts to classify children. As one mother explained, "They [health professionals] always go by these charts, and I don't think that's accurate because when is there ever an average child, or the right height, and the right weight child? I've never seen it" (p. 1141). As a result of this attitude, many mothers who accurately recognized their own weight problem didn't believe their *children* were overweight. Instead, these mothers defended their children's size by saying they were solid, muscular, or big-boned.

► *Misunderstanding 2: People aren't overweight until their activities are limited or they are teased about their weight.* In general, these mothers didn't realize their children could be harmed by their weight. As one mother said, "If he wasn't playing right or he was short of breath, that would be concerning" (p. 1141). But the truth is that overweight children are at higher risk for numerous weight-related problems, including early puberty, diabetes, and social discrimination that can lead to depression (University of Michigan Health System, 2003).

► *Misunderstanding 3: You can't control children's weight because weight is determined by heredity.* As one mother explained, "When you got a fat gene, you got a fat gene, and there's nothing you can do about it" (p. 1142). In fact, only 30 to 50 percent of the variability in weight within a population is attributed to genetic variability; the remaining variability is due to patterns of eating and exercise (Pérusse & Bouchard, 1999).

Lack of knowledge about weight control made it difficult for these low-income mothers to manage their children's weight. For example, they felt proud when they could provide unhealthy treats and said it would be starving a child to say "no" when he or she wanted to eat. Other studies have confirmed that at least half of low-income parents with overweight children are unconcerned about their weight (Rich et al., 2005). But attitudes and habits *can* be changed. For example, one group of low-income children gained weight more slowly after their schools introduced a program that encouraged their parents to serve more fruits and vegetables (Fitzgibbon et al., 2005).

EARLY NUTRITION AND HEALTH. Children who have plenty of food can still develop vitamin and mineral deficiencies if their diets contain too much processed, sugary food. Today's 2- to 5-year-olds consume an average of 15 teaspoons of added sugar *per day*, equaling 16 percent of their total energy intake (Kranz & Siega-Riz, 2002). What are children eating that has so much sugar? According to the U.S. Department of Agriculture, 51 percent of preschoolers eat cookies over a 2-day period, 53 percent drink soft drinks, and 23 percent eat non-chocolate candy (Smiciklas-Wright et al., 2002).

The most common consequence of too many treats is tooth decay. When protein in saliva mixes with sugar, a sticky coating called *plaque* deposits on teeth and provides a breeding ground for the bacteria that cause decay. In one inner-city sample, 67 percent of preschoolers had signs of decay, averaging over six decayed surfaces per child (Nainar & Crall, 1997). Dental problems can affect the whole family by increasing financial strain and causing children pain and sleepless nights (Acs & Ng, 2002).

Good dental health begins as soon as teeth erupt. Caregivers need to wipe babies' teeth and gums with a cloth after meals and begin brushing their teeth by 2 years. Between 2 and 3 years, all children should visit their dentist. Early checkups should be pleasant events that build positive attitudes about dental health.

For example, one dentist we know merely touches the lips of reluctant 3-year-olds before sending them off with a bag of surprises. These children are usually happy to open their mouths on the next visit, when they join the ranks of preschoolers who enjoy their twice-yearly checks.

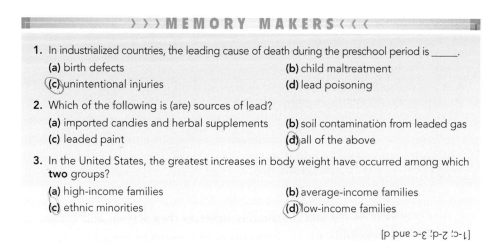

>>> MEMORY MAKERS <<<

1. In industrialized countries, the leading cause of death during the preschool period is _____.
   (a) birth defects
   (b) child maltreatment
   (c) unintentional injuries
   (d) lead poisoning

2. Which of the following is (are) sources of lead?
   (a) imported candies and herbal supplements
   (b) soil contamination from leaded gas
   (c) leaded paint
   (d) all of the above

3. In the United States, the greatest increases in body weight have occurred among which **two** groups?
   (a) high-income families
   (b) average-income families
   (c) ethnic minorities
   (d) low-income families

[1-c; 2-d; 3-c and d]

Different Children—Different Problems

Even in the healthiest environments, some children have more problems behaving and settling into routines than other children do. Many preschoolers have toileting and sleeping difficulties, and it is common for sexual curiosity to cause caregivers some embarrassment. In addition, a minority of children have special conditions that influence their ability to cope with stress, learn, and follow rules.

Toileting

Children are ready for toilet training when they understand and use words for elimination (such as "potty," "poop," and "pee"), want to imitate and please adults, and can stay dry for at least 2 hours at a time. Most children achieve these skills between 22 to 30 months of age, with boys lagging a few months behind girls (Schum et al., 2002). Individual children vary by as much as a year, though, so many 3-year-olds are still completing toilet training. Indeed, many of today's parents are enduring some criticism for toilet training later than earlier generations did (Blum, Taubman, & Nemeth, 2004): Currently, only half of young children achieve daytime dryness by $3\frac{1}{2}$ years and nighttime dryness (most of the time) by 4 years (Jansson et al., 2005).

Figure 7.4 reports the percentage of children who experience frequent bed-wetting, which is a condition called **nocturnal enuresis** (wetting at night, from the Greek *enourein*, meaning "to void urine"). Notice that one out of five 4-year-olds and more than one out of ten 6-year-olds wet often at night. These problems are usually temporary, though, with 92 percent of bed-wetting 6-year-olds achieving dry nights within a few years.

Despite the fact that children cannot control nighttime "accidents," about 20 to 36 percent of parents say they have punished children for bed-wetting. What should they do instead? Once medical conditions have been ruled out, pediatricians recommend only simple lifestyle changes for children under 6 or 7 years of age: Remove caffeinated soft drinks and chocolate from their diets (because caffeine increases urine production) and increase fluid consumption

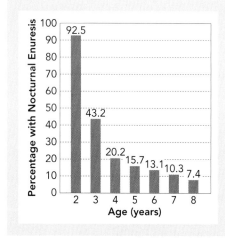

FIGURE 7.4 Nocturnal enuresis.

The percentage of children who wet the bed at night declines with age, but more than one out of ten 6-year-olds still wet the bed. Most children eventually outgrow this problem.

SOURCE: Jalkut, Lerman, & Churchill (2001).

nocturnal enuresis The loss of bladder control during sleep.

early in the day (because children with enuresis tend to drink most of their fluids at the end of the day). Around 7 years—when children want to stay overnight with friends or relatives—some families explore treatment options. The "pad and bell" system is a popular approach in which a pad sounds an alarm whenever it detects a few drops of urine. Through conditioning, most children learn to inhibit voiding, finish in the bathroom and, eventually, stop nighttime wetting altogether (Butler, 2004; Jalkut, Lerman, & Churchill, 2001).

Sleepless Nights

Sleep patterns gradually change throughout childhood and adolescence. Preschoolers need about 10 to 12 hours of sleep per night and spend more time than their older brothers and sisters in a deep stage of sleep called delta sleep. Young children enter delta sleep about 1 to 3 hours after dozing off and sometimes experience **partial arousals** when they transition out of this stage. Partial arousals include behaviors such as talking in their sleep, sleepwalking, and a frightening phenomenon called **night terrors**. Children who are experiencing a night terror appear awake and desperately upset as they scream and thrash in bed. As Table 7.2 explains, night terrors occur in a different stage of sleep than nightmares do and are accompanied by different behaviors. The frequency of all types of partial arousals declines during adolescence, when the amount of delta sleep drops off dramatically (Mindell & Dahl, 1998).

Few parents are totally satisfied with their preschoolers' bedtime habits. Young children generally resist going to bed and often pop up like jack-

partial arousals Behaviors such as talking, sleepwalking, or night terrors that occur during the transition out of deep (delta) sleep.

night terrors A type of partial arousal in which children scream, thrash about, and act incoherently.

TABLE 7.2	How to Tell a Child's Nightmare from a Night Terror	
	Nightmare	**Night Terror**
What it is	A scary dream followed by complete awakening.	A partial arousal from very deep sleep.
When you become aware of it	After it's over, when children wake up and tell you.	During the terror itself, as they scream and thrash.
When it happens	In the second half of the night, when dreaming is most intense.	Usually 1 to 4 hours after falling asleep, during a transition from deep sleep.
What children do	Cry and act fearful after waking.	Thrash and cry with sweating and a racing heart. Confusion disappears when they awake.
Children's responsiveness	After waking, children are aware of your presence and feel reassured.	Children are not very aware of others and may push them away.
How they return to sleep	May have trouble falling back to sleep because they are afraid.	Falls back to sleep rapidly, without fully awakening.
What they remember about it	Often remember the dream and may talk about it.	No memory of a dream or of their behavior.

SOURCE: Adapted from Ferber (1985); Pagel (2000).

"I know sex is no longer a taboo subject. I just don't feel like discussing it all the time, that's all."

in-the-boxes looking for company in the middle of the night. General negativity often improves when parents establish and stick to a bedtime routine (Bates et al., 2002). The time-honored bedtime story helps children relax and compensates them for the loss of fun associated with going to bed. As with infants, it is best to let children fall asleep by themselves instead of staying with them until the magic moment. Finally, it is best not to punish poor sleepers who misbehave during the day by sending them to their rooms because rooms can become associated with fear and isolation. Instead, rooms for sleep-resistant children should be pleasant but boring places that are associated with sleeping.

Sexual Curiosity

A mother once contacted a friend of ours for advice. Her daughter (we'll call her Mia) had been playing at a neighbor's house when she was discovered lying on top of her playmate. "Is something wrong with my daughter?" the embarrassed mother asked. While the psychologist was asking questions to explore whether Mia might have learned this behavior from someone else, she discovered that Mia and her mother had recently discussed "where babies come from." Like many young children, Mia didn't know what behavior would upset adults.

It is normal for children to be curious about body parts. Infants touch their genitals just as they explore their ears and toes, and some children later learn to stimulate themselves by rocking against objects or balled-up blankets. When fine motor skills improve, some even discover masturbation. This behavior is so common that adults have long been advised to take it in stride (Martinson, 1994). As they grow, children become interested in looking at other people's bodies and sometimes explore with same-sex and opposite-sex playmates. Largely because children learn to conceal behavior that adults disapprove of, overt expressions of sexual curiosity usually decline by the school years (Chess & Hassibi, 1986).

How common is "playing doctor"? One way to answer this question is to ask parents to report what they have observed. Some typical findings appear in Table 7.3. While looking at these results, remember that sexual behavior varies across families and cultural contexts. In general, parents who are nonchalant about nudity report more childhood sexual behavior than do parents who are more reserved (Larsson, Svedin, & Friedrich, 2000).

Experts recommend honest answers when children ask about sex—

TABLE 7.3 Percentage of Parents Who Saw Various Sexual Behaviors from Their 3- to 6-Year-Olds during the Past 6 Months		
	Parents of Girls	Parents of Boys
Does not want to appear naked	10	18
Walks around indoors without clothes	20	28
Talks about sex	18	17
Uses sex words	21	17
Tries to look at people undressing	39	30
Shows genitals to children	17	28
Plays "doctor-games"	20	22
Touches own genitals	35	39
Masturbates with hand	15	14
Draws genitals	6	8

SOURCE: Adapted from Larsson & Svedin (2002).

but without launching into scientific discussions. For instance, a 4-year-old who asks where babies come from will probably be satisfied to know they grow in a special place inside his mommy. Because preschoolers often blurt out new knowledge without regard for etiquette, there is no point in providing information they will not understand. When children want more detailed discussions, it is useful to talk about cultural standards for sexual behavior along with biological facts. For example, it will not make children guilty to explain that some behaviors are private or reserved for adults. And when two children are discovered exploring together, it is helpful to mention that everyone has a right to tell other people not to touch their bodies.

Developmental Psychopathology

Behavior problems during early childhood range from minor quirks, such as fussy eating, to serious offenses, such as repeated aggression against playmates. But these behaviors are not simply early versions of the same problems in an adult. For example, a 3-year-old who refuses most foods is not acting the same as a real estate agent who starves herself to be thin. **Developmental psychopathology** is the field that views problem behaviors from a developmental perspective. Developmental psychopathologists try to determine which problems are short-lived and which have long-term consequences. Their findings help answer the question, "Should I ignore this behavior or should I do something about it?" These scientists also study the causes of unwanted behavior and work to develop effective treatments. Here we explore some problems that can have long-lasting implications for development: internalizing behavior, externalizing behavior, attention deficit hyperactivity disorder, and autistic spectrum disorders.

INTERNALIZING AND EXTERNALIZING BEHAVIORS. Although most temperamental differences between children have no significance for adjustment during adolescence and adulthood, children with extreme behavior are sometimes at risk for later problems. Two clusters of behaviors that are easy to spot are internalizing and externalizing behaviors. Children with **internalizing behaviors** are unusually withdrawn and anxious. These children seem sad and shy, often complain of stomachaches, and are nervous or tense. Children who show only one or two internalizing problems, such as a reluctance to meet new people or a fear of going to new places, are not at high risk for similar problems as they develop. For example, only a quarter of children who are persistently shy during early childhood have anxiety problems as teenagers (Prior et al., 2000). However, children with many internalizing problems are three times as likely as other children to have similar problems as adolescents (Mesman & Koot, 2001).

Children with **externalizing behaviors** are boisterous and aggressive. These children have temper tantrums, are more disobedient than most children, and are prone to irritability and jealousy. But because it is so common for preschoolers to "act out," it can be hard to decide when naughty behavior is excessive (NICHD Early Child Care Research Network, 2004). One team of investigators looked for benchmarks by asking parents to give orders to their 2- to 5-year-olds, then counting the number of times children complied. As you can see in Figure 7.5, normal 2-year-olds listen to their parents less than 30 percent of the time. There is a big improvement around 4 years, when children begin to listen over 70 percent of the time (Brumfield & Roberts, 1998). Unlike children who are not perceived to be a nuisance, those who are referred to mental health clinics show a large number of noncompliant, negative behaviors, such as lying repeatedly and hitting, and their

developmental psychopathology The field that studies problem behavior from a developmental perspective.

internalizing behaviors A cluster of behaviors that includes sadness, shyness, anxiety, and physical complaints.

externalizing behaviors A cluster of behaviors that includes disobedience, temper tantrums, irritability, and jealousy.

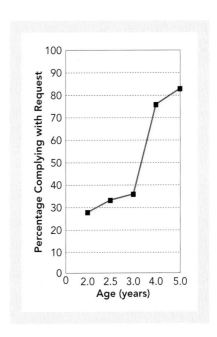

FIGURE 7.5 Preschooler compliance.

Preschoolers are not very cooperative, although their behavior improves with age. In this study, 2-year-olds complied less than 30 percent of the time when parents made a request, but this value jumped to about 80 percent by age 5.

SOURCE: Adapted from Brumfield & Roberts (1998).

attention deficit hyperactivity disorder (ADHD) A condition associated with age-inappropriate patterns of inattention and impulsivity, often with hyperactivity.

behavior does not improve much over time. In fact, children with significant externalizing symptoms at 3 years of age are five times more likely than other children to have externalizing problems later in development (Mesman & Koot, 2001). Children are especially likely to have continued problems when their parents use ineffective strategies to control behavior (such as not following through with threats) and there is a great deal of family stress (Campbell, Shaw, & Gilliom, 2000).

ATTENTION DEFICIT HYPERACTIVITY DISORDER. Sometimes a child's behavior problems are the result of a more broad-based inability to regulate attention and stay on task. One of the most frequent mental health diagnoses in childhood, **attention deficit hyperactivity disorder (ADHD)**, captures these problems. Descriptions of children with ADHD sound like descriptions of younger children: They have a hard time following rules, create disturbances at mealtimes or bedtimes, and are fidgety and disruptive. Over the years, clinicians have shifted their emphasis from focusing on activity level as the defining feature of ADHD to focusing on attentional problems and, recently, poor impulse control. Because a variety of behavior problems is involved, clinicians now view ADHD as a family of disorders that includes several subtypes, including children who have poorly controlled attention, children who are primarily hyperactive and impulsive, and a combined type (Campbell, 2000).

About 3 to 7 percent of children meet the criteria for ADHD, with four times as many boys as girls receiving the diagnosis (American Psychiatric Association, 2000). Symptoms are present during early childhood, but concern often develops when children begin school and their inability to sit and pay attention for periods of time makes some children stand out. There is no clear line between normal and abnormal behavior, however. As a result, critics have argued ADHD is a cultural phenomenon in which normal behavior is now being called a disability (Stolzer, 2005). To counter this claim, ADHD researchers have pointed out that rates of the condition are similar in the United States and other countries, which indicates that ADHD is not culture specific (Rohde et al., 2005). Also, adults who were diagnosed with ADHD as children have poorer occupational outcomes and more relationship problems than peers, suggesting that ADHD is not just a label for spunky children (Barkley et al., 2002). Clinicians who treat ADHD do not see a conflict between these two views. Instead, they emphasize that ADHD behaviors are maladaptive even if they are not uncommon.

What causes ADHD? Many symptoms, such as difficulties filtering out irrelevant information and organizing ideas, describe problems with executive functioning (Sonuga-Barke et al., 2002). It makes sense, then, that events that affect brain development are associated with ADHD (Bush, Valera, & Seidman, 2005). Among the contributing factors are a family history of ADHD (Faraone et al., 2005), exposure to harmful chemicals or heavy metals such as lead (Weiss & Landrigan, 2000), and brain damage from accidents or abuse (Herskovits et al., 1999). But ineffective parenting increases behavior problems, so children are more likely to receive a diagnosis of ADHD if their families have poor child management strategies (Cunningham & Boyle, 2002).

ADHD is often treated with prescription medications, including a stimulant called methylphenidate (Ritalin) (Johnson, Safranek, & Friemoth, 2005). Although it seems odd to give active children a stimulant, Ritalin works by increasing levels of the neurotransmitter *dopamine*. This neurotransmitter, which is involved in feelings of pleasure and motivation, decreases children's distractibility by decreasing the "background firing" rate of neurons (Gottlieb, 2001). Children do not become psychologically or physically addicted to the medication because it does not produce a sudden "high." Instead, Ritalin helps children stay interested in tasks that would otherwise not be very appealing. But drugs alone are not a solution to all of the problems associated with ADHD. School-aged children on medication often show improved behavior without improved academic performance, and drugs cannot teach them how to manage their own behavior. Experts, therefore, recommend a multifaceted approach to treating ADHD that includes academic services, psychological interventions that focus on behavior, and parent effectiveness training (Hechtman, Abikoff, & Jensen, 2005).

AUTISM SPECTRUM DISORDERS. Frankie was a good baby who laid quietly in his crib—too quietly, his parents worried. When they picked him up, Frankie stiffened and arched his back. He also avoided eye contact, refused to cuddle, and was unresponsive to affection. As Frankie's younger siblings developed into curious toddlers, Frankie's problems became more obvious. He never developed language and was extremely upset whenever his parents changed his routine. He also made bizarre, repetitive motions with his hands and would sit for hours staring at a revolving fan. By 5 years, when Frankie still did not play with other children, it became clear that he would never experience a normal childhood (Graziano, 2002).

Autistic behavior ranges from subtle problems, such as difficulties interpreting people's intentions and nonverbal cues, to severe sensory, language, and cognitive delays.

Frankie is a textbook case of **autistic disorder (autism)**. Autistic disorder is present early in life but is usually diagnosed by $2\frac{1}{2}$ to 5 years of age, when the following impairments become obvious (American Psychiatric Association, 2000; Goin-Kochel & Myers, 2005):

▷ *Marked impairments in social interaction.* Children with autistic disorder lack normal interested in social contact, do not seek or enjoy affection, and seem aloof and alone.

▷ *Deficits in language development and imaginative activity.* These children often fail to develop language or show a range of language abnormalities. For example, they may repeat phrases or fail to use the pronouns "I" and "you" appropriately. Nonverbal communication, such as eye-to-eye gaze and gesturing, is often impaired. Also, children with autistic disorder lack imaginative play, such as pretending to cook.

▷ *Restricted scope of activities and interests.* Children with autistic disorder are often obsessed with sameness and show rigid, repetitive behavior. They are drawn to small details and may be mesmerized by objects. For example, they may rock back and forth or stare at the pattern in carpeting for hours.

These characteristics are present to some degree in all of the children who experience a lifetime of autistic aloneness. But behavior varies greatly. Mental retardation is present in about 75 percent of cases, yet some children have above-average IQ scores. Some children injure themselves; others do not. Some have astounding abilities to memorize specific types of information, such as bus schedules or musical scores; others show no remarkable skills. Due to this variability in behavior, scientists consider *autism* an "umbrella" term that describes several biological conditions associated with social deficits and peculiar patterns of attention (Graziano, 2002; Hrdlicka et al., 2005).

Autistic disorder and other conditions that involve autistic features are collectively called *autism spectrum disorders*. These disorders include (1) autistic disorder; (2) cases that show some—but not all—of the features of autistic disorder; and (3) a condition called *Asperger syndrome*. Children with Asperger syndrome have restricted interests and trouble navigating social interactions

autistic disorder (autism) A condition characterized by marked impairments in social interactions, deficits in language and imaginative activity, and a restricted scope of interests.

without language delays or general cognitive deficits (American Psychiatric Association, 2000). The causes of autism spectrum disorders are currently unknown. There is evidence that genetic factors contribute (Philippi et al., 2005; Wassink et al., 2005), but viruses, heavy metals, or other environmental factors may also be involved in triggering abnormal brain development (Fido & Al-Saad, 2005; Libbey et al., 2005).

Some scientists hope that research into the genes that contribute to internalizing and externalizing problems, ADHD, and autism spectrum disorders will suggest ways to reduce the number of children who develop these conditions. Others worry that this knowledge—together with new reproductive technologies—will be used to eliminate the genetic variation that produces these conditions. To understand why some people are concerned about tampering with nature, turn to this chapter's *Don't Be Fooled!* feature entitled, "Raise Your Glass to Our Different (and Difficult) Children."

DON'T BE FOOLED

Traits that are harmful in one environment may be valuable in another. It is risky to try to eliminate every bothersome trait because diversity helps species survive and flourish when situations change.

RAISE YOUR GLASS TO OUR DIFFERENT (AND DIFFICULT) CHILDREN

Are we going to control life? I think so. We all know how imperfect we are. Why not make ourselves a little better suited for survival? That's what we'll do. We'll make ourselves a little better—James Watson

Any attempt to shape the world and modify human personality in order to create a self-chosen pattern of life involves many unknown consequences. Human destiny is bound to remain a gamble, because at some unpredictable time and in some unforeseeable manner nature will strike back—René Dubos

While riding in the car one day, 15-year-old Joshua asked his mother, "What's all the fuss about cloning? What could be wrong with picking our good traits and getting rid of the bad ones?" Josh had been hearing about two controversial technologies: *cloning* and *germ-line gene therapy*. With cloning, scientists would make a genetic replica of an individual by harvesting DNA and placing it into a cell that develops into an embryo. With germ-line gene therapy, genes in an individual's sex cells would be altered. Unlike gene therapy, which places new genes into nonsex cells, modifications in germ-line gene therapy could be passed onto subsequent generations. These technologies could someday be used to make "designer children"—offspring with specific physical or behavioral traits. Although neither technology is currently used for humans, there is tremendous concern about the ethics of these procedures.

The opening quotes illustrate two views on this issue. Biologist James Watson, who unraveled the structure of DNA with Francis Crick, presents one side: We are imperfect, so why not use science to make ourselves a little better? The reason, according to environmentalist René Dubois, is that efforts to design a better human could backfire if a trait that *seems* undesirable is not undesirable in all environments. To understand his point, consider

Spunky children can be irritating, but some of these children grow up to explore the planet, rescue lives, and contribute to society by pursuing seemingly impossible dreams.

psychiatrist Marten deVries's (1984) work with infants in Kenya. DeVries identified babies who had extremely "difficult" or "easy" temperaments and then located some of the infants after a massive drought. To his surprise, only 17 percent of the babies with difficult temperaments had died compared to 71 percent of the easy babies. DeVries speculated that negative temperaments may be "attention-getting" temperaments—personalities that help children cope under hostile conditions by eliciting more resources from parents. In other words, preschoolers who are demanding and aggressive might be better equipped to fend for themselves when the going gets rough. In the same fashion, societies composed only of easygoing, cooperative people would be less able to cope with challenges than those that contained a range of talents and personalities.

But what about conditions that can kill you or disabilities like autistic disorder? What could be wrong with eliminating the genes that cause these conditions?

To answer this question, recall the discussion of sickle cell anemia from Chapter 2. The gene that produces sickle-cell anemia when people inherit two copies also protects people from malaria, which is why the disease is more common among ethnic groups whose ancestors lived in malarial zones. Because some of the genes that cause illness might give people a survival advantage under specific circumstances, scientists are cautious about voting traits out of existence. In the same fashion, families with an autistic relative have an unusually high frequency of engineers and computer specialists, suggesting that the cognitive style associated with autism spectrum disorders contributes to innovation and discovery (Wheelwright & Baron-Cohen, 2001).

In conclusion, diversity helps humans conquer a complicated and ever-changing world. Stamping ourselves only from a few molds could restrict our potential and even our ability to survive. But in the final analysis, people like Josh are the best reason to be cautious about designer children. Like a minority of children, Josh was a cranky infant and a demanding preschooler. Parents who were allowed to select the dispositions of their young might choose an easier path. But they could miss so much. Today, Josh is a successful, adventurous man who hunts, fishes, and dives shipwrecks. Both he and his easygoing sister have treasured places in their family and important contributions to make to the world.

So let's raise our glasses and toast to the different (and difficult) children of the world. They help us adapt to environmental challenges and show us a world of possibilities and potentials. If we eliminated strong-willed or active children, who would dive shipwrecks?

>>> MEMORY MAKERS <<<

Match terms on the left to related words on the right:

1. night terrors
2. partial arousals
3. nocturnal enuresis
4. developmental psychopathology
5. internalizing behavior
6. externalizing behavior
7. ADHD
8. autism

(a) screaming and thrashing in one's sleep
(b) unusually aggressive or disobedient behavior
(c) sleepwalking and talking in one's sleep
(d) shyness, sadness, and anxiety
(e) frequent wetting at night
(f) deficits in social interaction, language, and imagination
(g) problems with attention and impulse control
(h) analyses of childhood behavior problems from a developmental perspective

[1-a; 2-c; 3-e; 4-h; 5-d; 6-b; 7-g; 8-f]

Boy-land, Girl-land

A research assistant brings 4- and 5-year-olds into a room to watch cartoons. But there is a catch: Only one child can watch at a time because the cartoons appear through a movie-viewer eyepiece. Also, at least two other children must help to run the movie, one to operate the lights and another to turn a crank. Can young children cooperate? Will anyone get a chance to watch cartoons?

The answer to both of these questions is "yes." In one study, each child averaged about 1 minute of viewing time during a 12-minute session (Charlesworth & Dzur, 1987). But boys and girls used different strategies to get a turn. As Figure 7.6 illustrates, the boys frequently pushed, pulled, and hit—yet they were not being hostile. In fact, they enjoyed their roughhousing, laughed more than the girls, and cooperated as much as the girls. Unlike the boys, the girls relied on verbal strategies to work out roles: They were 10 times as likely as the boys to show concern for another child and twice as likely to order another child to do something.

The division of the world into "boy-land" and "girl-land" is one of the most fascinating events on the planet. Around the world, children identify themselves as male or female by 3 years of age and begin segregating into same-sex play groups well before 6 years. And as you will read next, young children are "gender detectives" who actively search for information about what it means to be male or female (Martin & Ruble, 2004).

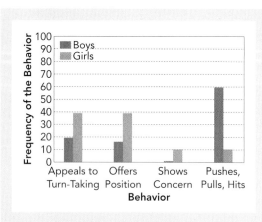

FIGURE 7.6 How boys and girls cooperate.

Boys and girls use different strategies to try to get other children to do what they want. The preschoolers in this study were filmed as they worked out which two children would run a projector so a third could watch cartoons. Girls relied mostly on verbal strategies to get a turn whereas boys used more physical approaches.

SOURCE: Charlesworth & Dzur (1987).

Learning about Gender

One preschooler said that his pediatrician, Jane, was a boy (a decision he made after he decided that doctors were men). His mom corrected him by explaining, "No, Dr. Jane is a girl. She has girl hair and wears skirts." Without hesitation he countered, "Well, she was a boy but turned into a girl."

This little boy was confused about what made someone male or female. The first step toward understanding gender occurs around 2 to 3 years, when children show *gender identity* by labeling themselves and others as boys or girls. Next they grasp *gender stability*, which is the idea that boys grow up to be men and girls grow up to be women. Children express gender stability around 3 to 4 years when they talk about growing up to become mommies or daddies. But at this point, some youngsters still base gender decisions on superficial cues, such as what people are wearing or their occupations, rather than biological sex. As children gain genital knowledge, they develop **gender constancy** (also called **sex-category constancy**): the understanding that gender is a permanent distinction based on one's genitals (Bem, 1989). Children usually achieve gender constancy by 5 years, although individual children learn the biological basics of gender at different ages (Golombok & Fivush, 1994).

Children can be painfully inflexible about gender while they are trying to make sense of the world. For instance, little Lin would wear only pink or purple clothing after she first realized that blue and red items were hand-me-downs from her older brother. This little tyke was not concerned that the clothes were used; she was concerned that the clothes were for boys. Her rejection of anything associated with the opposite sex has been called the "hot potato" effect. To illustrate this phenomenon, one research team asked children to rate how much they liked sex-

gender constancy (sex-category constancy) An awareness that gender is a permanent characteristic based on one's genitals.

neutral toys after an adult had said nothing about gender, labeled them as toys for children of the same sex, or labeled them as toys for the opposite sex. The children gave lower ratings to toys they thought were for the opposite sex—dropping them, so to speak, like a hot potato (Martin, Eisenbud, & Rose, 1995). It is common for children to become increasingly rigid about gender stereotypes up to about 4 to 6 years of age and then show a marked increase in flexibility about 2 years later (Gelman, Taylor, & Nguyern, 2004; Trautner, Gervai, & Németh, 2003).

Why do boys and girls act differently and monitor gender labels? To answer these questions, scientists have observed children in other cultures, measured the hormone levels of pregnant women, and watched how youngsters from other primate species behave.

Sex Differences

Differences between boys and girls emerge early. On average, young boys are taller than girls and weigh a bit more (Ogden et al., 2002). Boys are better at throwing something at a target, whereas girls are generally better at tasks that rely on fine motor skills, such as putting small pegs into holes. In the cognitive domain, boys copy large Lego models faster than girls while girls read earlier (Hyde & Linn, 1988; Kimura, 1999). Sex differences in physique and basic skills are minimal, though, so boys and girls are still more alike than they are different during the preschool years.

The most obvious differences between the sexes involve play preferences and social behavior. Young boys show more interest in cars and balls whereas their sisters are more likely to play with dolls. Play style differences are most noticeable when preschoolers interact in groups. Like the young of many species, human children play-fight, chase, and jump on each other, but males engage in relatively more of this **rough-and-tumble play** (Humphreys & Smith, 1987; Smith, 2005). To capture these differences, one research team watched $4^{1}/_{2}$-year-olds as they played in a room containing a trampoline, a beach ball, and a BoBo doll like the one pictured in Chapter 1. The girls spent more time than the boys on the trampoline, proving they enjoy active play. But they almost never threw themselves on top of others or burst into mock fights, which the boys frequently did (Maccoby, 1988). Consistent with these findings, boys suggest more physical aggression than girls when they are asked to describe how they might enter a peer group or take turns (Walker, Irving, & Berthelsen, 2002). Due to different styles of interacting, it is not surprising that boys got to watch cartoons more than three times as long as girls when the sexes participated together in the cartoon-viewing situation described earlier (Charlesworth & La Freniere, 1983). Of course, boys and girls do sometimes play together successfully, but they often separate when they have many playmates to choose from (Fabes, Martin, & Hanish, 2003; Maccoby, 1988).

Why are males more physical and less nurturant than females?

rough-and-tumble play A type of play that involves chasing, pushing, and play fighting.

Girls enjoy active play just as boys do, but boys are more likely to engage in rough-and-tumble play, a type of play that involves good-natured poking and wrestling.

gender typing (also called **sex typing**) The process of adopting behaviors and preferences that are associated with males or females.

Why do children so often adopt the interests and preferences associated with their own gender? These questions ask about **gender typing** (also called **sex typing**): the process of adopting behaviors and preferences that society associates with males or females.

Explanations of Gender Typing

The assumption that biology alone directs boys and girls to act differently came under attack when cultural anthropologists repeatedly found that different societies associate different traits with men and women. For example, typical gender roles are reversed among Kanjar families in Pakistan, where women provide most of the income and dominate their families' public affairs (Cronk, 1993). Faced with such evidence, psychologists began viewing gender typing as an interactive process that requires a handful of biology, a handful of cognitive activity, and a handful of culture-based social learning.

BIOLOGICAL APPROACHES. The hormones that regulate the process of sexual differentiation described in Chapter 3 provide one of the links between genetic sex and sex-typed behavior (Hines, 2004). During gestation, hormones that occur in greater quantities in males (androgens) and those that control the female reproductive cycle (estrogens and progesterone) enter the brain, where they influence cell death, dendritic growth, and synapse formation (Arnold & Gorski, 1984; Matsumoto, 1991). For example, testosterone (an androgen) is present in higher levels in males from the 8th through the 24th week of gestation and during the first 6 months of infancy (Smail et al., 1981). In animal experiments, female rats who receive a single dose of testosterone at birth show more male-typical sexual behavior during adulthood, such as mounting, and testosterone influences the amount of rough-and-tumble play that rats and monkeys display (Hines et al., 2002).

Among humans, girls' interest in sex-typical toys was related in one study to their mothers' testosterone levels during pregnancy but *not* to whether they had older brothers or adult males in the household (Hines et al., 2002). One way hormones might influence toy preferences is by influencing preferences for movement and certain forms. For example, boys as young as 18 months prefer to look at photographs of vehicles rather than dolls, whereas the reverse is true for girls—and veret monkeys show the same sex differences in toy preference that humans do (Alexander & Hines, 2002; Serbin et al., 2001). Prenatal hormones may be responsible for many sex differences in the brain, including different patterns of activation in the amygdala (an area responsible for interpreting emotional information) and the hippocampus (an area responsible for encoding memories) (Giedd et al., 1996, 1997; Thomas et al., 2001).

But gender researchers caution us not to blame every sex difference on the brain. Some neurological differences between

Children learn what it means to be male or female by watching the people around them. When this house was built by an all-women crew, the little girls in the neighborhood probably couldn't wait to swing a hammer of their own.

males and females are not clearly related to behavioral differences (Allen et al., 1991; Bell & Variend, 1985), and it is not always known whether brain differences lead to behavioral differences or vice versa. Finally, gender-typed behaviors vary from culture to culture, so something other than biological differences must also contribute to the interesting differences between boys and girls. To handle the gaps left by a strictly biological approach, gender researchers have looked for other reasons why children queue up so early into separate lines.

COGNITIVE APPROACHES. Children who possess more gender knowledge than their peers engage in more sex-segregated play and are less flexible about gendered activities (Levy, Barth, & Zimmerman, 1998; Martin, Ruble, & Szkrybalo, 2002). These findings support a cognitive approach to sex differences, one that analyzes how knowledge about what it means to be a boy or a girl promotes gender-typed behavior (Martin & Ruble, 2004).

A perspective called *gender schema theory* views emerging gender knowledge as the gradual accumulation of information about what it means to be male or female in a particular culture. According to this approach, internal knowledge schemes become organized in increasingly complex ways as children develop. For example, if we tell you that the tenants in the next-door apartment are male, you will probably make certain assumptions about what they look like, what activities they might like, and so forth. Children develop these expectations as they learn what occupations males and females assume, what chores they do at home, and numerous other details about typical behavior. Gender schema theory assumes that gender is a powerful motivator because humans have an innate tendency to organize the world according to categories and a strong need to belong to specific social groups (Martin et al., 2002).

Gender representations are important because people are more likely to pay attention to and remember information that is consistent with their schemes. Therefore, a boy and a girl who spend a day in the same preschool classroom will leave at 3:00 with different memories because each child chooses different activities and finds different information interesting. When a boy tells his father about the trucks in a story while a girl describes a snack she'd like to make at home, each child is actively structuring interactions with his or her world.

SOCIALIZATION APPROACHES. There is no doubt that cultural experiences can exaggerate or minimize gender differences. Consider the Yanomamö Indians of South America, who have a reputation as fierce fighters who frequently spar with neighboring villagers. Yanomamö boys play-fight with bows and arrows so realistically that they often injure each other, and parents support this activity because it prepares their boys for physical competition. As a result, Yanomamö boys experience very different encouragement than boys who grow up in cultures that actively discourage fighting. Expectations for girls also vary around the world. In general, girls are socialized to be less obedient and more aggressive in societies where women inherit property and influence political decisions, whereas passive behavior is valued wherever men control resources (Geary, 1999).

There's no mystery whether this is a little girl or a little boy. Gender-typed interests and behaviors are clearly in place in early childhood.

Socialization approaches account for these variations by assuming that many gender-typed behaviors are learned. One learning mechanism is *differential reinforcement*, the tendency of parents and peers to reinforce gender-conforming behavior and ignore or disapprove of gender-conflicting behavior. For example, American parents encourage girls to play with dolls and discourage them from acting competitively, but they discourage boys from playing house and staying near adults (Marmion & Lundberg-Love, 2004). In general, adults are more likely to discourage males from acting feminine than they are to discourage girls from acting masculine (Golombok & Fivush, 1994; Killen et al., 2005).

Another mechanism is *observational learning* (also known as *modeling*), the process of learning by watching others that we mentioned in Chapter 1. Children notice differences between people and soon pay more attention to models who are similar to themselves. A model of gender development called *social cognitive theory* (Bussey & Bandura, 1999) assumes that children learn gender roles by explicit feedback from their parents and through observational learning. This model says that children cast their mental net widely, combining observations from home with what they experience in school and from the media.

PUTTING IT ALL TOGETHER. So why do boys and girls act differently, choose different toys, and pay attention to gender labels? There is no simple answer because multiple forces shape gender-role behavior. Biological factors influence body and brain, but behavior is also molded by internal representations of gender, differential reinforcement, and observational learning. Cognitive and socialization theorists acknowledge biological factors and, conversely, biological researchers freely admit that hormones do not single-handedly direct behavior.

As scientists began to appreciate how biology and learning interacted, it became difficult for them to maintain a distinction between the term *sex*—which they had tried to reserve for biological differences—and *gender*—which implies social constructions of what is masculine and feminine. As a result, some authors now use terms like *sex differences* and *gender differences* interchangeably (Golombok & Fivush, 1994). By doing so, they recognize that nature and nurture always walk hand in hand.

›››MEMORY MAKERS‹‹‹

1. Which is the correct order for the emergence of gender knowledge?
   (a) gender constancy, gender stability, gender identity
   (b) gender identity, gender stability, gender constancy
   (c) gender stability, gender identity, gender constancy

2. The process of adopting the behaviors and preferences society associates with males and females is called _____.

   (a) gender identity   (b) gender stability
   (c) gender awareness   (d) gender typing

Match each explanation of gender typing with the focus of that view:

3. biological approaches   (a) reinforcement, punishment, and observational learning
4. cognitive approaches   (b) sex hormones
5. socialization approaches   (c) gender knowledge

[1-b; 2-d; 3-b, 4-c; 5-a]

Children across Cultures and Family Contexts

If you ask two people the same question about raising children, you will probably get two different answers. These differences mean that at a family level, each child is likely to grow up in a very different environment—and environmental differences are even more striking at a cultural level. Here is what two friends said when we asked them to explain how they handled day-to-day issues like sleeping, discipline, and teaching children to relate to adults:

Children around the world often keep their distance from adults, with older children keeping an eye on younger brothers and systers.

Sandy: I didn't want my children to cry, so I rocked them at night; played lullabies. Abby is 8 years old and I still lie next to her until she falls asleep. I have no issue with co-sleeping. I have my kids call my friends by their first names. I want them to treat them like a relative, like an aunt or uncle, someone they can call when they need help. I know Nicole would say I'm more permissive than she is, but I don't think so. I say "no" more often, and I use a lot more punishing sentences. I'll say something like, "I've had it up to here! I told you twice not to do that, so stop it!" She says more textbook things to my kids, like, "I like it when you help your mom, so let's clear the dishes for her." I mean, you just can't pull that off with your own kids . . . [laugh] . . . that talk lasts for about 6 months.

Nicole: It's fine to rock babies to sleep, but there comes a time when children need to soothe themselves because you can't have someone rock you to sleep for the rest of your life. I don't care what my friends think, when children get older I think it is important for them to say "yes Ma'am" and "no Ma'am" as a sign of respect. I don't believe in letting little things slide, because little things turn into big things.

How do different strategies for handling day-to-day issues influence children's behavior? One way to find out is to study children who are being reared in cultures where ideas about children are very different from our own.

Culture and Children's Behavior

As you read in our opening story, cultural differences create differences in how children behave and when they assume various responsibilities. One cultural psychologist, Suzanne Gaskins, studied the importance of culture by observing children in a traditional Mayan village. At her field site in Yucatan, Mexico, teenage boys and men earn a living in distant fields or by leaving the village for cash jobs. Meanwhile, women, girls, and young children spend their time in family compounds, where mothers are busy cooking, tending to gardens, sewing, and collecting firewood. In this setting, Gaskins (2000) found three cultural beliefs that organize Mayan children's activities:

▶ *The primacy of adult work.* Mayan families have a clear understanding that adult work must get done and that children should contribute to household work as much as possible and not interrupt adults. Adults rarely speak to young children except to tell them what to do or explain how to do something, and they do not encourage play or believe that play is necessary for children to develop normally. Instead, play is welcomed only because it allows adults to get their work done and indicates that children are in good health.

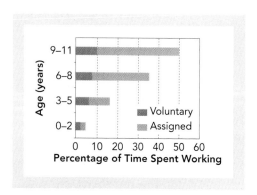

FIGURE 7.7 Children's life in a Mayan village.

Cultural values influence how children spend their time. Mayan parents believe that even young children shouldn't interrupt work and should help with daily household chores. As a result, young Mayan children spend a significant amount of time making contributions to the family.

SOURCE: Adapted from Gaskins (2000).

▶ *The importance of learning by watching.* Because Mayan parents believe that development unfolds by itself, they do not structure activities to promote development. They also believe that children learn best by watching rather than direct instruction.

▶ *The independence of child motivation.* Adults expect children to entertain themselves and give them a great deal of independence over their moment-to-moment activities. Parents do little to interfere with when or what children eat or how much they sleep, and young children rarely ask adults to find something for them to do.

Typical Mayan 2-year-olds attempt basic maintenance behaviors, such as dressing and feeding, by themselves, and most 5- and 6-year-olds are responsible for almost all of these necessary activities. Mayan children spend a great deal of time watching others, and by 3 years they can usually report where members of the household are and what they are doing. But despite their interest in the social environment, these children rarely initiate conversation with adults. They also spend relatively little time in pretend play. Instead, most of their play time is spent manipulating objects or engaging in large motor activities such as running. Finally, work is important. By 6 years children are expected to run errands, accompany older siblings beyond the compound to complete chores, and take care of younger brothers and sisters, so they spend a significant amount of time helping the family (Figure 7.7). Because these activities are highly valued, even 3- to 5-year-olds volunteer to do 40 percent of the work they do.

The expectation that even young children should do household work is typical of many societies. But even in a single community, individual families differ in the extent to which they expect productive activity from preschoolers. Striking differences across families and cultures raise an interesting question: What aspects of parents' early behavior continue to matter years later, when children have grown into adults? As you will read next, parenting research exploded after a seminal study of Boston kindergartners found some unexpected answers to this question.

A Lesson from Boston Kindergarteners

In the 1950s, three investigators wondered how routine parenting decisions—such as when to toilet train children, how strict to be about messes, and how to deal with children's sexual behavior—influenced children (Sears, Maccoby, & Levin, 1957). To explore this issue, they studied 379 kindergartners and their families by rating each mother on nearly 150 child-rearing practices.

A striking feature of some parents was their reliance on punishment. When Sears and his colleagues correlated this parenting practice with children's behavior, they found that mothers who punished for aggressive behavior had more aggressive children, those who punished for wetting had bed-wetting children, and those who punished dependent children for acting clingy and helpless ended up with more dependent children. But parents who ignored unwanted behavior also had children who continued that behavior. Based on these findings, the investigators concluded that effective parents put restrictions on children and use positive techniques to socialize them, such as redirecting their attention or working with them on acceptable activities.

To find out whether early parenting behavior made a difference years later, a different team studied a subset of these children after 25 and 36 years, when they were 30 and 41 years old (Franz, McClelland, & Weinberger, 1991; McClelland et al., 1978). Amazingly, the number of significant correlations between early child-rearing practices and adult outcomes was only slightly higher than what would be expected by chance. In other words, self-reliance and genuine concern for others were not determined by specific early practices such as the duration of breast-feeding, how children were toilet-trained, or bedtime routines. But parents' enduring feelings toward their children did predict future adjustment. Children who had warm, affectionate parents generally grew up to be socially accomplished people who reported better relationships, more work achievements, and greater psychological well-being.

Data from the Boston kindergarteners suggest that minor differences in how Sandy and Nicole parent probably will not influence how successful their children will be. Alas, development is too complicated for most early decisions to matter over the long run. Still, some types of parents are more likely to have children who grow up to be self-reliant, self-controlled, and contented. Capturing the key features of what these parents do is the goal of research on parenting styles.

Parenting Styles and Children's Behavior

Psychologist Diana Baumrind's research on parenting styles launched decades of research to describe how parents steer children in desired directions. Studies by Baumrind and others have identified some key dimensions of parenting, investigated how these dimensions influence children's behavior, and led to helpful suggestions for modifying children's behavior.

CLASSIFYING PARENTING STYLES. In an early study, Baumrind (1967) identified three distinct parenting styles:

▶ **Authoritarian parents** set high standards for their children and expect them to obey without question. (The word *authoritarian* means "expecting unquestioned obedience.") These parents provide few explanations for their rules, show relatively little affection, and do not encourage children to express their own views. Compared to other parents, authoritarian parents are less nurturant and involved with their children.

▶ **Permissive parents** demand little from their children and do little to train them to be more independent. Research that followed Baumrind's study suggested the need to distinguish between two subtypes of permissive parents. *Democratic-indulgent* parents are loving parents who rarely restrict children's behavior unless there is serious danger. These are tolerant people who often go along with children's wishes. In contrast, *rejecting-neglecting* parents are too disinterested or overwhelmed by life to attend to parenting details. Unlike democratic-indulgent parents, these parents are unaware of what their children are interested in or what they are doing.

▶ **Authoritative parents** have high standards for their children but—unlike authoritarian parents—they create households that are supportive and nurturant in addition to being firm. (The word *authoritative* means "asserting authority.") These parents set standards and have high expectations for their children, but they explain the reasons for rules and are excellent communicators who clearly tell children what they expect from them.

Baumrind found that different types of parents tended to have different types of preschoolers (Baumrind, 1967, 1971; Baumrind & Black, 1967). Specifically,

authoritarian parents Parents who set high standards and expect their children to obey without question.

permissive parents Parents who demand little from their children and do little to train them to be more independent.

authoritative parents Supportive, nurturant parents who set standards, have high expectations, and explain the reasons for rules and restrictions.

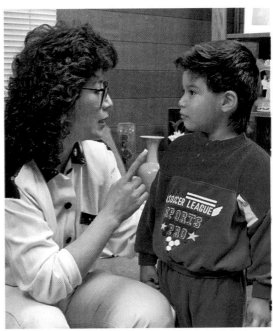

Even young children like to be told why they should act the way grown-ups want them to act. Children who hear explanations from adults are more likely to use rules to regulate their own behavior as they grow.

induction A strategy for correcting children that involves modeling empathy while explaining how children's behavior affects themselves or other people.

power assertion A strategy for controlling children that appeals to one's status and right to set the rules. Power assertion often involves demands, threats, and punishments.

the children of authoritarian parents were obedient but unhappy. When stressed, some of these children became hostile while others regressed and acted like younger children. The children of permissive parents tended to be unhappy children who lacked self-control and self-reliance. In contrast, authoritative parents had children who were adjusted, well-behaved, and independent. The loving but firm control from authoritative parents encouraged children to develop self-help skills and to communicate clearly with others.

An important component of authoritative parenting is **induction,** a strategy in which parents show empathy while explaining to their children how behavior affects themselves or other people ("You never throw pencils because you could hurt someone's eye.") Induction helps children internalize moral standards so they will want to act appropriately even when no one is watching (Hoffman & Saltzstein, 1967; Olejnik, 1980). In contrast, parents who use **power assertion** expect children to listen because an authority figure is in charge, so these parents often control children by threats and punishments ("Do what I said or I'll . . . "). This highly controlling approach can produce children who show poor self-regulation because they do not have an internal set of values and general rules to guide actions and decisions (Houck & Lecuyer-Maus, 2004; Kochanska, Padavich, & Koenig, 1996).

EVALUATING PARENTING STYLES. Many people welcomed Baumrind's research because she helped parents learn how to strike a balance between encouraging freedom and promoting responsibility (Baumrind, 1966). Although she did not claim that authoritative parenting was always the optimal parenting strategy, many investigators nonetheless set out to test how this parenting style fared in other cultural settings.

Many cross-cultural studies have also found benefits from authoritative parenting. For example, an analysis of African American caregivers found that authoritative parents experience the fewest behavior problems from their 3- to 6-year-olds (Querido, Warner, & Eyberg, 2002), and this style also predicted better school performance in a sample of second-generation Chinese adolescents (Chao, 2001). The components of authoritative parenting—including warmth and explicit teaching of social skills—were also associated with adjustment in a group of ethnically and socioeconomically diverse families in Tennessee and Indiana (Pettit, Bates, & Dodge, 1997).

But is authoritative parenting always the best way to parent? This question has no simple answer. The concept of authoritative parenting combines characteristics that Western cultures value, and in Western samples certain parenting customs tend to occur together. For example, authoritative parents are loving, consistent, and unlikely to resort to severe punishment. In contrast, traditional Chinese culture values obedience and respect for parents. Thus Asian parents often score authoritarian on parenting-style scales even though they are generally loving and consistent. Because Baumrind's categories fail to capture the typical styles of Chinese parents, some studies have found no or only weak benefits of authoritative parenting among Asian families (Chen, Dong, & Zhou, 1997; Kim, 1996).

What can we conclude about parenting styles? There is support for the value of authoritative parenting, but many parents have characteristics from more than one style. As a result, some psychologists prefer to summarize findings on parent–child interactions by focusing on four specific practices that promote adjustment:

▶ *Parenting that is culturally consistent.* Generally, the most well-adjusted children come from parents who conform to their culture's idea of how a parent should act (Harris, 1998). One reason for this finding is that children are influenced by what a parental behavior means in their culture. For example, painful inoculations prove that parents care dearly for their children, so these procedures do not produce aggressive, uncaring adults. Also, culturally deviant parenting is often extreme parenting that is either overly restrictive or neglectful.

▶ *Warm and responsive parenting.* Children are more likely to imitate adults' behaviors and moral standards when they enjoy their time with adults and sense that adults enjoy them (Kochanska & Aksan, 2004).

▶ *Setting of consistent limits.* Parents who enforce reasonable limits with consistent feedback give children a sense of security and mold their behavior in desired directions (Cornell, 2004; Frick, Christian, & Wooton, 1999).

▶ *Inductive parenting.* Explanations ("It hurts Snowball when you pull his tail") help children understand *why* they should act in particular ways, which makes them more likely to act appropriately in new situations. For example, when parents take the time to explain that tail pulling harms cats, their children are more likely to grow up believing it is wrong to harm animals.

In addition to these general findings, parenting experts have compiled some concrete suggestions for how to consistently enforce rules and expectations. Let's turn to some of their useful advice.

Improving Interactions Between Parents and Young Children

As you can see in any episode of the hit show *Super Nanny*, preschoolers are often frustrated because they lack control over their lives. Caregivers who do not have strategies for handling outbursts get worn down, which leads them to discipline inconsistently. Children then sense the opportunity to take control and bad behavior escalates.

Around the world, people use a number of techniques to direct young children's behavior, including yelling, physical punishment, withdrawing love by expressing disapproval and—as our opening story illustrates—inducing guilt. But as research on parenting styles has revealed, these techniques are not equally effective. For example, we mentioned in Chapter 5 that physical punishment can escalate into abuse and does not teach children what they should be doing. Similarly, yelling usually doesn't help children build new habits quickly, such as hanging up coats or taking their plates off the table. What is a parent to do? Experts provide two types of assistance: helpful strategies you will read about next and one-on-one interventions for parents who are experiencing severe problems managing their children.

TIPS FOR HELPING PRESCHOOLERS BEHAVE. The best way to handle misbehavior is to prevent it before it occurs. Young children can figure out what is expected of them more quickly when caregivers reinforce them for good behavior, teach them to express themselves with words, model appropriate behavior ("I'm sorry I interrupted you, Sammy, I thought you were finished talking"), and avoid putting children in situations that tax their limited ability to attend and sit still. These and other helpful suggestions for living with preschoolers are summarized in Table 7.4.

TABLE 7.4   Dealing with the Angry Child

Catch the child being good. Tell the child what behaviors please you. A sensitive adult will find many opportunities during the day to make comments such as, "I like the way you come in for dinner without being reminded."

Provide physical outlets and other alternatives. It is important for children to have opportunities for physical exercise and movement, both at home and at school.

Manipulate the surroundings. Aggressive behavior can be encouraged by placing children in tempting situations. Plan the surroundings so that misbehavior is less apt to happen. Sometimes rules and regulations, as well as physical space, may be too confining.

Use closeness and touching. Move physically closer to the child to curb his or her angry impulse.

Appeal directly to the child. Tell the child how you feel and ask for consideration. For example, you may gain a child's cooperation by saying, "I know that noise you're making doesn't usually bother me, but today I've got a headache, so could you find something else you'd enjoy doing?"

Use physical restraint. Occasionally a child may lose control so completely that he has to be physically restrained or removed from the scene to prevent him from hurting himself or others. In such situations, an adult cannot afford to lose his or her temper, and unfriendly remarks by other children should not be tolerated.

Say "No!" Limits should be clearly explained and enforced. Children should be free to function within those limits.

Teach children to express themselves verbally. Talking helps a child have control and reduces acting out behavior. Encourage the child to say, for example, "I don't like your taking my pencil. I don't feel like sharing just now." Remind them by saying, "Use your words."

Model appropriate behavior. Parents and teachers should be aware of the powerful influence of their actions on a child's or group's behavior.

SOURCE: Adapted from a *Plain Talk Series* pamphlet originally published by the U.S. Department of Health and Human Services (1978, reprinted 1985, 1992). Publication No. (ADM) 92-0781.

A few minutes of time-out gives everyone a chance to calm down.

time-out A procedure for punishing children by making them sit alone in a quiet, unstimulating place for a few minutes.

But even in the most child-friendly environment, most preschoolers will occasionally show aggressive or destructive behavior that requires a sterner response. One approach to convey disapproval without yelling is **time-out**, a procedure that involves making children sit alone in a quiet, unstimulating place for a few minutes. Time-out functions as a punishment because children temporarily lose access to interesting people and toys (Readdick & Chapman, 2001). Unlike hitting or yelling, however, this strategy gives angry children a chance to settle down on their own, which helps them learn self-regulation. When time-out is over, adults should explain how children might act the next time disappointment rears its ugly head.

TREATMENTS FOR OVERWHELMED PARENTS. Some parents seek professional help when life with their preschooler has gotten out of control. After Sheryl enrolled in parenting therapy, for example, she and her son David were filmed in a small room containing a table, chairs, and a selection of toys. During this initial observation session, David ran aimlessly from object to object, throwing chairs and swearing at his mother while Sheryl sat passively. Students who later watched this tape were flabbergasted that a mother would shrink away from a 5-year-old child.

About half of child referrals to mental health centers involve children like David who show externalizing behavior (Wells & Forehand, 1985). An effective way to alter this type of behavior is the therapy Sheryl experienced: Parent–Child Interaction Therapy (PCIT). PCIT is an intervention for parents of 2- to 6-year-old children with behavioral and emotional problems. The two components of the program are based on the finding that children need parental nurturance and limit-setting to learn age-appropriate behavior. For this reason, therapy is structured into two parts. During *Child-Directed Interaction*, parents learn to interact positively with children by choosing strategies that do not trigger negative behavior (as described later). Once children are enjoying time with their parents, training progresses to *Parent-Directed Interaction*. During this phase, parents learn to issue clear commands and enforce a consistent time-out procedure when their children disobey (Herschell & McNeil, 2005; Niec et al., 2005).

Sheryl met frequently with a therapist who explained why the skills she would be learning were important. Then Sheryl and her therapist role-played until Sheryl was comfortable trying new behaviors. Next, Sheryl and her son worked in a quiet room while the therapist watched through a one-way mirror and gave Sheryl suggestions via an electronic "bug" in her ear, as in the following example (Herschell et al., 2002):

By working with her daughter on an enjoyable activity, this mother is developing her child's desire to spend time with her and please her. Interventions such as Parent-Child Interaction Therapy teach parents a set of skills that come naturally to this mother, including how to express interest by describing their children's behavior.

> **Parent** (to child): You're building a house.
>
> **Therapist:** Good behavioral description. That shows him you're interested in what he's doing.
>
> **Parent** (to child): It looks like the house is going to be tall and strong.
>
> **Therapist:** Good information description. He likes your attention.
>
> **Parent** (to child): Good job, Aaron!
>
> **Therapist:** Nice praise.
>
> **Parent** (to child): You're making that house nice and strong.
>
> **Therapist:** Great *labeled* praise! It's good to tell him exactly what you like. (p. 19)

Table 7.5 describes the specific skills Sheryl practiced. After therapy, Sheryl was a more confident parent who was no longer at the mercy of her son. Research has found that PCIT is an effective way to reduce behavioral problems in young children (McNeil et al., 1999; Schuhmann et al., 1998), and the benefits generalize to other children in the family (Brestan et al., 1997).

Parent–child therapy does a lot more than just make home lives more pleasant. By learning to control his outbursts and listen to simple directions, David will be better prepared for the important transitions you'll read about next: adjusting to preschool and kindergarten.

TABLE 7.5   Sample Parenting Skills from Parent–Child Interaction Therapy

Child-Directed Interaction Skills	Examples
The PRIDE Skills: Praise	"Great job sitting in your seat."
Reflection	Child: "I maded a heart." Parent: "Yes, a big heart."
Imitation	Child: (picks up blocks and begins building a tower) Parent: (picking up blocks) "I'm going to build a tower just like you."
Description of behavior	Child: (squishing down Play-Doh) Parent: "You're making that Play-Doh flatter and flatter."
Enthusiasm	Child: (finishes a drawing) Parent: (smiles and speaks in an animated voice) "What a beautiful picture you've drawn!"

Parent-Directed Interaction Skills	Characteristics
Giving effective commands	✦ simple ✦ given one at a time ✦ specific, not vague
Determining whether compliance or noncompliance has occurred	It is noncompliance if: ✦ the child is doing something slightly different than told ✦ the child is ignoring the command ✦ the child complies and then undoes the requested action

Applying appropriate consequences
    After compliance
 	
    After noncompliance
	✦ give praise and include an explanation of why it is good that the child obeyed
	✦ give full attention to the child (show enthusiasm, appreciation, use positive touch)
	✦ initiate the time-out procedure
	✦ ignore all extraneous child behavior
	✦ Child-Directed Interaction skills are initiated after time-out is completed to calm both the parent and the child.

SOURCE: Adapted from Herschell et al. (2002).

>>> **MEMORY MAKERS** <<<

1. Which member of each pair describes the cultural beliefs Mayan children experience?
   (a) speak often to children or speak infrequently to children
   (b) let children watch to learn or explicitly teach children skills
   (c) protect children from adult work or expect young children to contribute
   (d) let children direct their activities or structure children's time

2. Match each parenting style with a description:
   (a) authoritarian   (D) parents who rarely restrict children's behavior
   (b) permissive   (E) unaffectionate parents who expect children to obey
   (c) authoritative   (F) nurturant parents with high standards who discuss reasons for rules

3. Which of the following skills are taught during Parent–Child Interaction Therapy (PCIT)?
   (a) how to ignore aggressive behavior
   (b) how to interact without triggering negative behavior
   (c) how to issue clear commands and enforce a time-out procedure
   (d) b and c   (e) all of the above

[1. speak infrequently to children, let children watch to learn, expect young children to contribute, and let children direct their activities; 2. a-E, b-D, c-F; 3-d]

Preschool Experiences

Most states in the United States require children to enroll in school by the time they are 6 or 7 years old, so younger children have long been called "preschoolers." However, only a quarter of children ages 3 and older who are not yet in kindergarten are cared for solely by their parents (Mulligan, Brimhall, & West, 2005), and many families rely on preschools to meet their day care needs. Thus early education is "pre" school only in the sense that it is voluntary rather than compulsory and because extensive instruction in reading and writing does not usually start until children are 6 years old.

The demand for preschools increased after the 1960s, when women with young children began joining the labor force in larger numbers. Like the differences that exist from family to family, the preschools that rose to meet this demand represent different philosophies about what is best for young children.

Preschool Curricula

Because different schools emphasize different types of activities, parents and foster parents often visit a number of preschools before deciding where to send their children. Here is a description of a typical morning in one preschool:

> A class of 4- and 5-year-olds had a successful cookie sale after a week of excited baking and sign making. "Now it's time to decide how we want to spend our money," Paul reminded the children as they met in their morning circle. He asked the children to make suggestions and listed their ideas on the flip chart. "I want a Barbie house," suggested Aurelia. "I want a remote control car," shouted Ignatio. The list went on. Tessa quietly suggested, "I think that we should give the money to some poor children." Several children nodded. Many suggested, "I think that we should go on a trip with that money." When the list was full, Paul reviewed their ideas. Then he asked, "Would it be OK if we use our money to buy a Barbie house for Aurelia?" His question prompted much animated discussion about why that use of the money wasn't "right." After 20 minutes of discussion, Paul told the children, "I think that we need more time to work on this decision. Think about it some more and tomorrow we'll talk about it again and see if we can decide on one idea with which everyone can agree." (Driscoll & Nagel, 2002, p. 185)

Paul has a particular philosophy about education that helps him structure his classroom. After comparing some approaches to preschool education, we'll revisit Paul's classroom to talk about the activity he chose and how it reflects his view of preschool education.

TYPES OF PRESCHOOL. Three of the most popular philosophies of preschool education are the Montessori approach, teacher-directed preschool, and child-centered instruction. Each approach focuses on different goals and uses different types of activities to accomplish their goals.

This little girl is learning about patterns in a Montessori preschool by making a design with colored shapes. In a few years, experiences like this one may help her understand the patterns involved in mathematical concepts.

Maria Montessori is the best-known name in early childhood education. Born in 1870, this remarkable woman became Italy's first female physician when she was 26 years old. A passionate advocate for disadvantaged children, Montessori was especially interested in developing programs for children with special needs. In 1907 she opened a Children's House ("Casa dei Bambini") to provide education for poor children in Rome, and by 1913 she was famous for her novel educational ideas (Crain, 2005).

The daily routine in a **Montessori preschool** reflects several key assumptions. One is the idea that children are biologically primed to enjoy specific tasks at specific times in development. For example, preschoolers have a strong desire for order because they are noticing regularities in the world, which is why they love plugging wooden blocks into shape boards and are distressed when routines change. In Montessori schools, *directresses* (teachers) take advantage of this characteristic by structuring an orderly environment and providing appropriate activities.

Children in a Montessori class are free to select activities and work on them individually. A directress rarely needs to interfere with their learning because the materials are designed to provide feedback. For example, when a child who is sorting wooden cylinders into holes puts a small cylinder into a big hole, the last cylinder will not fit and the child's own curiosity will motivate her to correct her mistake. Montessori classrooms are quiet places where children work on practical tasks, such as gardening or fastening buttons, with directresses introducing them to increasingly complex activities.

In contrast, a **teacher-directed preschool** provides children with direct instruction in letters, numbers, and other academic skills. This philosophy stems from the desire to help unprepared children begin school with the same knowledge that other children have. To accomplish this goal, teachers control the learning process by presenting academic materials and reinforcing children with praise and other rewards. The materials in teacher-directed preschools look like simplified versions of elementary school materials, complete with flash cards, books, and work sheets. Because teachers deliberately instruct children in specific skills, these programs are often called *didactic-academic preschools*. (The word *didactic*, meaning "intending to instruct," is from the Greek word for "to teach.")

Another approach, the **child-centered preschool**, is based on Piaget's belief that children construct knowledge by interacting with their environment. Some child-centered programs also incorporate Vygotsky's view that children learn best when they work with more competent peers or adults, so learning in these schools is a combination of individual exploration and social activities. Teachers in child-centered classrooms encourage children to learn by playing with materials that challenge their current level of understanding. For example, water play with floating and sinking materials provides lessons in physics, while group games teach children cooperation. Unlike didactic-academic preschools, child-centered preschools do not emphasize instruction in basic academic skills. But unlike Montessori preschools, these programs do encourage group activities. These three preschool philosophies are compared in Table 7.6.

What philosophy was Paul relying on when he asked children how they wanted to spend their bake-sale money? Paul was using a type of child-centered approach that is called *constructivist*, in honor of Piaget's belief that children construct reality by engaging in socially meaningful activities. Paul's class learned literacy skills by using picture recipe cards, chemistry by mixing and baking, and math by counting their money. Later they explored moral issues when Paul asked them how they wanted to spend their money. With a simple activity, this group of

Montessori preschool An approach to preschool education in which children are allowed to choose from a number of skill-building activities.

teacher-directed preschool Preschool that emphasizes teacher-directed instruction in basic academic skills, such as letters and numbers.

child-centered preschool Preschool in which children learn by playing with everyday objects and participating in meaningful projects and interactions with other children.

TABLE 7.6   Three Approaches to Preschool Education

	Montessori	Teacher-Directed	Child-Centered
Theoretical influences	The importance of maturation and sensitive periods	Principles of learning through repetition and reinforcement	Piaget's and Vygotsky's developmental theories
Assumptions	Children learn best when they control their own learning in an orderly environment. They show great concentration when they interact with objects that appeal to their interests.	Young children learn the same way older children do, only more slowly. They will learn more quickly in school if they arrive with a good vocabulary and a basic knowledge of letters and numbers.	Children construct their understanding of the world through interactions with objects and people. They learn better through real-world activities than by formal instruction.
Classroom materials	Tasks and materials engage children's attention and provide feedback for mistakes. Large tying frames, sandpaper letters to trace with a finger, and a scraper to peel carrots are some of the materials preschoolers enjoy.	Children use flash cards and other printed materials, including books and work sheets, to learn academic skills.	Children play with meaningful objects such as cooking materials, weighing and measuring items, and paints for mixing.
Classroom atmosphere	Children select their own activities and work individually.	A teacher, working with a small group of children, asks questions and provides feedback and encouragement.	Children play individually or in groups. Learning often occurs through socially meaningful activities such as recording the lunch count or preparing a snack.

SOURCES: Crain (2005); Driscoll & Nagel (2002); Epstein, Schweinhart, & McAdoo (1996).

children learned that one person's wishes might not be best for the group as a whole. Paul's approach helped his class work on many skills while they also developed pride in their work, which motivated them to learn in the future.

EVALUATING PRESCHOOL CURRICULA. Each educational philosophy is a response to specific challenges and goals. Maria Montessori was especially interested in children who were cognitively delayed, so her approach focuses on allowing all students to progress at their own rates. Although there is no evidence that the lack of pressure in a Montessori classroom slows development (Epstein, Schweinhart, & McAdoo, 1996), there is concern about the limited social interaction in these classrooms. For example, one evaluation found that preschoolers from Montessori schools were less skilled at resolving conflict than children from constructivist classrooms (deVries & Goncu, 1990).

There is heated debate about the merits of teacher-directed versus child-centered approaches. Supporters of teacher-directed learning argue that academic instruction levels the playing field by putting academically unprepared children on equal footing with other children by the start of school. But there is a risk that forcing children to learn with drills and work sheets will undermine their motivation to learn (Stipek & Greene, 2001). Furthermore, children from highly teacher-directed programs are more likely than those from child-centered programs to exhibit stress behaviors, such as stuttering and destroying work sheets (Burts et al., 1990). In some studies, academically oriented programs have shown no advantages over less structured preschool programs, even when academic outcomes were measured (Stipek, 2001). But children do not pick up academic skills merely by playing (Mayer, 2004), so most early childhood educators believe that preschools should guide learning in an environment that is adapted to young children's needs.

developmentally appropriate practice Educational practices that recognize and accommodate children's developmental levels and interests. An appropriate curriculum promotes development of the whole child by considering physical, emotional, social, and cognitive needs.

DEVELOPMENTALLY APPROPRIATE PRACTICE. The term **developmentally appropriate practice** refers to a curriculum based on knowledge of early child development. Appropriate practice promotes growth of the whole child by considering physical, emotional, social, and cognitive needs. Activities engage children in learning by appealing to their natural curiosity while avoiding unproductive conflict and frustration (Driscoll & Nagel, 2002).

Table 7.7 compares appropriate and inappropriate practices as described by the National Association for the Education of Young Children (NAEYC, 1997). These principles recognize that the physical and cognitive needs of young children are different from those of older children, that it is important to develop cognitive *and* social skills, and that a key goal of early education is to develop positive attitudes toward learning. According to the NAEYC, young children construct their understanding of concepts but also benefit from direct teaching; they like to make choices but also need a clear understanding of boundaries.

TABLE 7.7 Examples of Developmentally Appropriate Versus Inappropriate Practice

Focus	Appropriate Practice	Inappropriate Practice
Learning materials	Activities (such as setting the snack table) are concrete and relevant to children's lives.	Materials are primarily books, work sheets, and pencils or crayons. Each activity focuses on a narrow range of concepts.
Motivation to learn	Emphasizing a narrow range of skills with excessive drill and practice can threaten children's motivation to learn. Instead, teachers motivate children by planning interesting, meaningful activities.	Teachers drill children in letters, numbers, and other basic skills. They believe their task is to correct errors and make sure children know the right answers. They try to motivate children by rewarding them with stickers or praising them in front of the group.
Physical development	Young children are more fatigued by long periods of sitting than by running, jumping, or bicycling. Therefore, teachers emphasize active rather than passive activities.	Children sit for long periods of "seat work." Physical activity is seen as a "break" that reduces the time available for academic instruction.
Individual differences	Individual differences are expected. Therefore, teachers design activities that accommodate a range of abilities, and children have some discretion to opt out of specific activities.	All children are expected to participate in the same activities and are evaluated against group norms.
Educating the whole child	Teachers realize that social, emotional, and cognitive development are interrelated. Therefore, they create an emotionally safe environment, and they provide children with opportunities to develop their social skills by working together.	Teachers focus on a narrow set of cognitive goals and try to instill appropriate social behavior by lecturing, demanding, or punishing.
Preventing behavior problems	Teachers limit overexposure to highly stimulating or frightening activities, such as highly arousing television programs or parties.	Teachers are not sensitive to signs of overstimulation, so they punish children for misbehavior or encourage them to release pent-up energy in an uncontrolled activity.

SOURCE: NAEYC (1997).

Adults follow developmentally appropriate practice when they establish a safe environment that recognizes the abilities and limitations of young children.

Research that has attempted to classify classrooms as developmentally appropriate versus inappropriate have yielded mixed results. Developmentally appropriate practice is associated with fewer stress reactions and greater creativity but does not have a consistent benefit on literacy (prereading, reading, or writing) skills (Van Horn et al., 2005). The failure to find an overwhelming advantage of one preschool approach versus another suggests that we need to consider what works best for specific types of children rather than trying to find a single "winner."

CULTURE AND PRESCHOOL. The following took place in a preschool in Japan:

> The classroom at the Wakaba Preschool fills with the noise of 40 four-year-olds preparing for lunch. They talk animatedly as they put away their reading materials and wash their hands. With no direction from the teacher, they scrub down their desks and place them in groups of four. An aide staggers in with heavy plastic bins filled with food. The children give a cheer: "It's McDonalds!" The teacher plays a chord on the piano. The children scramble to their seats while a representative from each group fetches a paper bag containing the group's food. Each child spreads out a cloth napkin from home for a place mat, and places a hamburger carefully in the middle, with a drink at the top right corner . . . The teacher plays a chord and the children close their eyes, hands pressed together in prayer. "We will keep our feet together, we will sit up straight, we will eat everything," they say in unison. Then, "Itadakimasu—I gratefully take this food." (Holloway, 2000, p. 1)

The Wakaba Preschool is an example of a *role-oriented* school, one of several types of schools that exist in Japan. Role-oriented schools strive to help children meet the demands of particular situations by emphasizing conformity and discipline. In contrast, *relationship-oriented* preschools place high value on teaching children to enjoy group activities by focusing on group celebrations and forming friendships, whereas *child-oriented preschools* have few group activities and no direct instruction. Instead, the play-like atmosphere of child-oriented preschools replicates the

These Japanese children are not very concerned about staying in their own space while they nap at preschool. In every country, different preschools emphasize somewhat different goals, yet every preschool—regardless of its educational philosophy—has to accommodate the developmental needs of young children

warmth and dependence that characterize mother–child relations in Japan. Throughout Japan, educators worry about balancing the need for collective life with a desire to promote individual expression, but different programs tip the balance in different directions (Holloway, 2000). Thus preschools in Japan—like preschool programs everywhere—reflect tensions between competing cultural values.

After visiting 32 preschools and child care centers, early childhood educator Susan Holloway (2000) concluded that preschool practices always reflect cultural values. Even within a single country, diversity is the rule because different social classes and ethnic groups have different child-rearing goals.

Early Childhood Intervention Programs

The most widely studied preschools are government-funded interventions for needy children. One ambitious project, *Head Start*, was designed to reduce the difference in school achievement between low-income children and their peers. Starting as a 6- to 8-week summer intervention before kindergarten, Head Start has evolved into a program that now serves over 900,000 children per year from birth through age 5 (Head Start Bureau, 2006). In addition to the educational program, children enrolled in Head Start receive physical and dental exams, inoculations, and nutritious meals. Their parents receive information about child development and volunteer in classrooms, and staff members assess families' needs and link families to community resources (Zigler & Styfco, 1993).

Evaluations of Head Start have proven that early interventions help at-risk preschoolers. An early analysis of over 200 studies found that Head Start improved immunization rates, overall health, and socioemotional adjustment (McKey et al., 1985). In other studies, participation in Head Start was associated with better school adjustment and a lower risk of being retained in a grade or requiring special education services during the elementary school years (Lazar & Darlington, 1982; Ramey & Ramey, 1998). Compared to siblings who did not attend the program, Head Start children also grew up to complete more schooling and were less likely to be charged with a crime (Garces, Thomas, & Currie, 2002). Cost–benefit analyses have shown that quality early childhood education programs save taxpayers dollars in the long run by reducing funds spent on school services, welfare payments, and costs associated with delinquency (Barnett, 1998; Meier, 2003).

As with most early intervention programs, the cognitive gains associated with Head Start begin to fade after children leave the program. The diminishing impact of Head Start over time has led critics to argue against expanding such programs. To counter, advocates of early interventions explain that it is "magical thinking" to expect that time-limited programs will eliminate the devastating effects of poverty (Brooks-Gunn, 2003). As an alternative, they suggest studying variations in program quality to identify characteristics of the most effective interventions. Hundreds of such studies have collectively identified four components of successful early childhood interventions (Zigler & Styfco, 1993):

▶ *Addressing the "whole" child.* Programs that address multiple needs produce greater benefits than programs that are narrowly focused on increasing IQ scores. Effective programs address health issues and nutrition, and provide emotionally supportive atmospheres that motivate children to learn. These programs also help families provide more secure environments for their children.

▶ *Parental involvement.* The most effective programs involve parents. Parent involvement increases the "dose" of an intervention by bringing classroom strategies into the home and affecting siblings who are not directly served by the program.

▶ *Quality staffing.* Quality programs have good child-to-staff ratios and teachers who are trained in early childhood development.

▶ *Continued intervention.* There are no quick fixes for poverty. Therefore, positive impacts are more likely to be maintained when services extend past the early years of life.

Starting Kindergarten

Kindergarten helps children transition between the relaxed atmosphere of home and the demands of school. While learning some academic basics, such as numbers and letters, children are also learning how to sit quietly in a group, how to finish an assignment without talking to friends, and how to follow rules and routines.

Each year, about 10 percent of U.S. parents delay their children's entrance into kindergarten. Some parents hold back children who have birthdays near the cutoff date so their sons and daughters will not be the youngest members of the class. Other times school districts advise parents to wait after their children have failed a screening test that measures basic language and coordination skills that are helpful for participating in classroom activities. The practice of holding children out of school, which is called **redshirting**, produces nearly a 2-year age spread in some classes (Stipek, 2002).

Educators who support delayed entry claim that students need to reach a threshold of skills before they are prepared to benefit from school. According to this view, cognitive and emotional readiness is largely determined by maturation, and some children are biologically ready at an earlier age. From this perspective, redshirting is a "gift of time" that allows children to build the necessary competencies for academic success.

Educators who oppose delayed entry do not believe in the "readiness" concept because children show different competencies across different facets of development. They also argue that experience promotes learning better than maturation alone, which is why it makes no sense to delay education for children who are already lagging behind their peers.

Does delayed entry help children achieve? One strategy for answering this question is to compare children of different ages who are in the same grade and children who are the same age but in different grades. The first comparison evaluates how maturation influences school success, whereas the second looks at how an extra year of school influences children of comparable age. Such studies have not found that delaying school entry produces any particular benefits (Stipek, 2002). There is a small advantage to being older in the younger grades, but the benefit diminishes with time. Also, there is no evidence that older children learn more than their younger counterparts. Across a variety of skills, children acquire more knowledge from a year of schooling than they do from a year at home (Crone & Whitehurst, 1999). Even among low-income children, those who are a bit younger than their peers are not academically disadvantaged over the long run (Stipek & Byler, 2001).

Should school districts use individual evaluations to decide when children are ready to begin school? Unfortunately, so-called "readiness" tests do not reliably predict which children will benefit from another year because many of the items (such as the ability to identify colors and to count) do not tap qualities that

redshirting Delaying a child's entrance into kindergarten. (This term, borrowed from collegiate sports, refers to the red jerseys athletes wear when they are kept out of varsity competition for a year.)

are highly predictive of school success, such as emotional adjustment and self-regulation (Blair, 2002; National Association of Early Childhood Specialists in State Departments of Education 2000). These qualities are difficult to measure because children's social behavior changes so much across contexts and is unstable over time (La Paro & Pianta 2000). One expert echoed the feelings of many early childhood educators when she concluded that "the appropriate policy question . . . is not what children need to know or be able to do when they get to school, but what schools need to do to meet the social and educational needs of the children who walk through their doors" (Stipek, 2002, p. 13).

Research on kindergarten entry does not mean that parents and school systems should be inflexible about kindergarten eligibility dates. Some children might benefit from being held back, especially if they have an extra year of high-quality preschool. But research does not support redshirting as a routine practice, especially when test scores are the primary means of making decisions. What the research does support is the *ready school movement*—the movement to build school programs that accommodate the normal diversity that exists among young children.

>))) **MEMORY MAKERS** (((

Match each preschool philosophy with some of its core features:

1. Montessori preschool   **(a)** individual exploration and social activities
2. didactic-academic preschool   **(b)** free selection of activities designed to provide feedback
3. child-centered preschool   **(c)** instruction in basic academic skills

4. Which descriptions best describe developmentally appropriate practice? (Pick all that apply.)

    (a) Children have free reign to play and do as they please.

    (b) Cognitive skills are emphasized more than social skills so that children will be prepared for school.

    (c) Teachers strike a balance between giving children choices and establishing boundaries.

    (d) The environment appeals to children's natural curiosity while avoiding unnecessary frustration.

[1-b; 2-c; 3-a; 4-c and d]

Revisiting Developmental Principles: What Are the Effects of Growing up with Television?

If you approached a group of 7-year-olds in 1945 and asked, "What's a television?", you could be virtually certain they would not know (Liebert, Sprafkin, & Davidson, 1982). By 1980, the average household had a television set on 5 to 6 hours a day, and many children were spending more time watching television than going to school. As Figure 7.8 reports, 1-year-olds now average an hour of viewing each day, and that number creeps up to over 4 hours by age 6. Is television a mind-deadening drug or a harmless helper for busy adults? What are the effects of parking a growing child in front of an electronic world?

Scientists began asking these questions the minute television invaded their homes. One of their worries has been that children will imitate what they see on television. There is reason for concern. Studies have consistently found high rates of violence in television programming, especially in programs targeted to children (Wilson et al., 2002), and programs also depict explicit and unrealistic sexual content (Brown, Steele, & Walsh-Childers, 2002; Larson, 2001a). For example, one analysis found that two-thirds of the programs in the 1999–2000 season had sexual references, and sexual intercourse was suggested or depicted in one out of every 10 programs (Kunkel et al., 2001).

Numerous studies have found that children who watch more television violence act more aggressively. In general, the relationship between television viewing early in childhood and later aggression is stronger than the relationship between early aggression and later preferences for violent programs. These findings suggest that the relationship between watching violence and acting violent is not simply due to the fact that aggressive children prefer aggressive shows. Moreover, violent programming increases aggressive behavior among children who are randomly assigned to watch violent shows. But not all children are equally prone to imitate aggressive behavior. On average, boys are more affected than girls by violent programming, although all children are less likely to be affected as time goes on, especially when their cultures are highly disapproving of aggressive behavior (Anderson et al., 2003; Browne & Hamilton-Giachritsis, 2005).

In addition to concerns about the *content* of television, scientists worry that the *medium* of television harms children by taking them away from productive activities. According to this view, television viewing is associated with poor school achievement and obesity because it is passive entertainment (Williams et al., 1982). One study actually found that television lulls children into such a relaxed state that their calorie consumption drops *below* their usual resting state, thereby justifying the term *couch potato* (Klesges, Shelton, & Klesges, 1993).

Concerns about dangerous content and lost opportunities have led the American Academy of Pediatrics Committee on Public Education (1999) to recommend

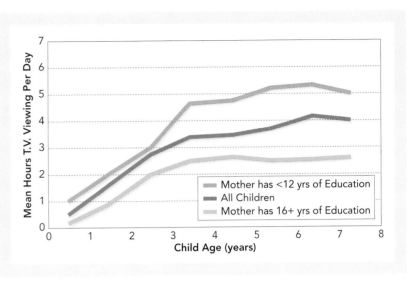

FIGURE 7.8 Television viewing by age.

For good or for bad, television is a major influence on development. By age 6, the average child is tuning in over 4 hours per day.

SOURCE: Certain & Kahn (2002).

A little television viewing won't hurt, but children who watch too much are at risk for obesity, poor achievement in school, and behavior problems.

that children limit their time with entertainment media (television, video games, and the Internet) to 2 hours per day. Taken out of context, some parents have interpreted this advice to mean that any television at all is bad. But there is no evidence to support such an extreme reaction. In one study, children who performed the best in school averaged 10 hours of TV viewing per week—*more* than their less successful peers (Williams et al., 1982). If television is such a bad influence, why are there so many well-adjusted children who watch TV? The answer to this question is a little clearer if we think about the general principles of development that were introduced in Chapter 1.

1. **Development is the joint product of nature and nurture.** Because biology and environment interact, children's temperaments and existing behaviors lead them to react differently to television programming. For example, children who are usually aggressive react more strongly to violent content, and viewing violence has larger effects on arousal for boys. As one group of experts explained, "TV violence has a large effect on a small percentage of youngsters and a small but significant effect on a large percentage of youngsters" (Liebert et al., 1982, p. 100).

2. **Physical, cognitive, and socioemotional development are interrelated.** Environmental influences rarely impact a single area of development. This is also true of television. For example, preschoolers improve their letter-word, number, and vocabulary skills when they watch educational programs, which increases their chances of feeling good about their performance in kindergarten. In turn, children with better vocabulary skills are more likely to select more informative programs, which sets the stage for further cognitive growth. In this way, cognitive skills, self-concept, and motivation are all impacted by the type of programming children view (Wright et al., 2001). In one study, preschoolers who watched a lot of informational programming became teenagers who read more books and had better perceptions of their academic competence, even after family backgrounds were taken into account (Anderson et al., 2001). Such findings explain why a moderate amount of television is associated with positive outcomes in some studies.

3. **Developmental outcomes vary over time and contexts.** Most social influences produce different outcomes depending upon when and where those outcomes are measured. For example, watching violent programming increases the likelihood that children will act aggressively (Anderson et al., 2003), but results are more consistent when there is a short time between viewing violence and measuring outcomes. One study found no relationship between viewing during the preschool years and adolescent aggression, probably because behavior that society discourages is not very stable over time (Anderson et al., 2001). This explanation is bolstered by data from different communities. For example, investigators detected no relationship between viewing violence and acting violently among children raised on a kibbutz* in Israel, although there was a relationship among Israeli children raised in the suburbs (Huesmann & Eron, 1986). In other words, the effects of television violence are not constant across time or cultures.

4. **Development is characterized by continuity and discontinuity.** The Israeli studies suggest that families and communities influence whether early aggression will survive into the later years. It makes sense that 4-year-olds who imitate fighting on television will be aggressive 10 years later if their community

---

*kibbutz: A communal farm in Israel.

encourages boys to be aggressive (showing continuity over time). Yet other boys may outgrow early aggressiveness because their play-fighting is quickly stopped by adults (showing discontinuity).

What should we conclude about the impact of television? Television affects children in different ways depending on their personalities, their family environments, and the type of shows they watch. Educational television helps children prepare for school even though heavy viewing of general programming hinders success. Furthermore, the impact of television depends upon what children would be experiencing if they were not watching television. As developmental psychologist Daniel Anderson and his colleagues concluded, "The medium is *not* the message: The message is" (2001, p. viii).

Erik Erikson once said that preschoolers intrude "into other bodies by physical attack . . . into other people's ears and minds by aggressive talking . . . into space by vigorous locomotion . . . into the unknown by consuming curiosity" (Erikson, 1959, p. 76). His description matches our own experiences. Preschoolers are delightful, funny, and sometimes exhausting. Due to varied temperaments and environments, they leave this developmental period with a range of competencies and challenges. But the life they are walking into is more complicated than what their life at home and preschool has been. Over the next few years, formal schooling and peer relationships will act like magnifying glasses, making individual differences seem twice as large as they appeared to be when children were young. Ready or not, each child will continue his or her journey into the next chapter of the story of human development.

>>> SUMMARY <<<

Creating Safe and Healthy Environments

1. Unintentional injuries claim more children's lives in industrialized countries than any other cause. Characteristics of the family, the child, and the physical environment all contribute to accidental injuries.

2. Children are more vulnerable than adults to many environmental pollutants. **Lead poisoning** interferes with normal neurological development, leading to lower IQs, attentional difficulties, and behavior problems. Children contact lead from many sources, including leaded paint, soil contaminated by leaded gasoline, and imported foods and herbal remedies.

3. Children in families that have experienced food shortages are at risk for obesity because they have trouble regulating their eating and are not familiar with a variety of nutritious foods. Many parents fail to take responsibility for their children's weight because they do not understand how early eating habits and childhood weight contribute to later obesity. Too much sugar in a child's diet replaces foods that contain needed nutrients and causes tooth decay.

Different Children—Different Problems

4. Many 3-year-olds are still completing toilet training, and some children wet at night throughout the preschool years. Most wetting problems are largely due to physical immaturity, but caffeinated drinks and low fluid intake during the day can make the problem worse.

5. Sleep problems are common during the preschool period. Some children experience **partial arousals**, such as sleepwalking and **night terrors**, when they transition out of delta sleep. Because inadequate sleep is associated with behavior problems, children who have sleeping difficulties should be kept on a regular sleep schedule that includes an enjoyable bedtime routine.

6. Adults should answer children's questions about sex simply yet honestly, and conversations about sex should mention cultural standards for sexual behavior.

7. **Developmental psychopathology** is the study of problem behavior from a developmental perspective. Three common behavioral patterns are **internalizing behavior** (a pattern of behavior that includes sadness, shyness, and

physical complaints), **externalizing behavior** (a pattern of behavior that includes temper tantrums, disobedience, and irritability), and **attention deficit hyperactivity disorder** (ADHD, a condition associated with poorly controlled attention and impulsivity). Children with **autistic disorder** have impaired social relationships, language disturbances, and a restricted range of interests.

Boy-land, Girl-land

8. Children ages 2 to 3 years demonstrate **gender identity** by calling themselves and others boys or girls. By 3 or 4 years children indicate **gender stability** by talking about "girls growing up to be mommies" and "boys growing up to be daddies." By age 5 most children have acquired **gender constancy**: an understanding that genitals define one's sex, not what people wear or how they act. Preschool children segregate early into same-sex play groups and tend to be rigid about gender issues.

9. The largest gender differences early in life involve play preferences and social behavior. Boys engage in more rough-and-tumble play and use physical strategies to resolve conflicts, whereas girls rely more on verbal strategies to control resources.

10. **Gender typing** is the process of acquiring behaviors and preferences that are associated with males or females. Scientists explain gender typing in terms of biological factors (especially how sex hormones influence early brain development), cognitive factors (such as how gender knowledge influences attention, memory, and gender-role behavior), and socialization (especially the role of reinforcement and observational learning).

Children across Cultures and Family Contexts

11. Children who have warm and affectionate mothers or fathers tend to grow up to be socially accomplished people who report good relationships with significant others, more work achievements, and better psychological well-being.

12. **Authoritarian parents** are low in nurturance and expect children to obey without question. **Permissive parents** set few demands and rarely restrict children's behavior. **Authoritative parents** set firm limits and clearly communicate the reasons for rules. The loving but firm control from authoritative parents encourages children to develop self-help skills and to communicate clearly with others. Across many cultures, successful children have parents who conform to community standards for how parents should act, convey reasons why children should act in particular ways, and set reasonable and consistent limits.

13. A popular alternative to physical punishment is **time-out**, when adults isolate children briefly and explain how to handle themselves better in the future.

14. Programs like Parent–Child Interaction Therapy (PCIT) teach parents how to spend pleasurable time with their children and enforce consequences for naughty behavior.

Preschool Experiences

15. **Montessori preschools** encourage children to choose activities from materials that provide corrective feedback. **Teacher-directed (didactic-academic) preschools** emphasize group instruction in academic skills, and **child-centered preschools** encourage children to work individually and with peers on meaningful projects. Early childhood educators support **developmentally appropriate curricula**—practices that consider the physical, emotional, social, and cognitive needs of young children. Every country has competing models of preschool education because every society struggles to balance competing cultural values.

16. High-quality preschool intervention programs reduce the achievement gap between children from low-income families and their more advantaged peers. Successful interventions provide a wide range of services, involve parents, have good child-to-staff ratios and trained personnel, and extend services past the early years of life.

17. Because screening tests do not reliably predict which children will succeed in kindergarten, most educators do not support the practice of holding children out of school for an extra year.

Revisiting Developmental Principles: What Are the Effects of Growing up with Television?

18. The effects of television are best understood by considering the four principles of development outlined in Chapter 1. First, nature *and* nurture are important because violent programming has more impact on children who are prone to be aggressive. Second, programming influences multiple areas of development, including cognitive skills, self-concept, and motivation. As a result, educational programming helps prepare children for school. Third, outcomes vary over time and contexts, so the impact of television is not the same at every age and in every environment. Finally, children are more likely to continue to act out aggressive behavior they see on television (that is, to show *continuity* in aggressive behavior) when their families and communities do little to inhibit violent behavior.

>>>KEY TERMS<<<

lead poisoning   (p. 262)
primary prevention   (p. 263)
secondary prevention   (p. 264)
food insecurity   (p. 264)
nocturnal enuresis   (p. 266)
partial arousals   (p. 267)
night terrors   (p. 267)
developmental psychopathology   (p. 269)
internalizing behaviors   (p. 269)
externalizing behaviors   (p. 269)
attention deficit hyperactivity disorder (ADHD)   (p. 270)
autistic disorder (autism)   (p. 271)
gender constancy (sex-category constancy)   (p. 274)

rough-and-tumble play   (p. 275)
gender typing (also called sex typing)   (p. 276)
authoritarian parents   (p. 281)
permissive parents   (p. 281)
authoritative parents   (p. 281)
induction   (p. 282)
power assertion   (p. 282)
time-out   (p. 284)
Montessori preschool   (p. 288)
teacher-directed preschool   (p. 288)
child-centered preschool   (p. 288)
developmentally appropriate practice   (p. 290)
redshirting   (p. 293)

CHAPTER EIGHT

Profile of Middle and Late Childhood

Stories of Our Lives

Becoming Clever

Middle to late childhood is the time for exploring neighborhoods, joining clubs, and opening lemonade stands. In the movies, it is also the time for plotting and scheming. From *The Parent Trap* to *Spy Kids*, children are manipulating divorced parents, solving mysteries, and generally upstaging adults. Children from 6 to 12 years love these movies because they are in the process of developing the kind of cleverness, cunning, and street smarts their heroes exhibit. Children think more strategically as they grow and, if we may say so, develop some psychological insight. At home and in their neighborhoods, they use these skills to figure out how to get other people to act in ways that benefit themselves. As you will see, this sort of cleverness is quite an accomplishment. It requires that the child formulate a goal, figure out a strategy for achieving it and, finally, put a plan into action.

Some school-aged children rival the feats that sell movies. One of the most impressive examples of how clever this age group can be is the story of how Frederick Douglass, a father of the civil rights movement, learned to

> "Childhood lasts all through life. It returns to animate broad sections of adult life . . . Poets will help us to find this living childhood within us, this permanent, durable immobile world."
>
> Gaston Bachelard

Frederick Douglass's ability to trick other children into teaching him to read and write forecast a life of social activism and brilliant writing. School-aged children appreciate tales of childhood cunning because they are becoming more skilled at manipulating their own social worlds.

read. Douglass, who was born in 1817, escaped from slavery and worked to abolish slavery in the United States. His tale began when he was sold to the Auld family of Baltimore at the age of 8 years. Mrs. Auld decided to teach Frederick to read, but Mr. Auld overheard them and put a stop to the lessons. Teaching Frederick would make him unmanageable, Mr. Auld explained; there would be no keeping him a slave. As Douglass (1989) later wrote, "I now understood what had been to me a most perplexing difficulty—to wit, the white man's power to enslave the black man. . . . From that moment, I understood the pathway from slavery to freedom" (p. 36). Douglass continued:

> The plan which I adopted, and the one by which I was most successful, was that of making friends of all the little white boys whom I met in the street. As many of these as I could, I converted into teachers. With their kindly aid, obtained at different times and in different places, I finally succeeded in learning to read. When I was sent on errands, I always took my book with me, and by doing one part of my errand quickly, I found time to get a lesson before my return. I used also to carry bread with me, enough of which was always in the house, and to which I was always welcome; for I was much better off in this regard than many of the poor white children in our neighborhood. This bread I used to bestow upon the hungry little urchins, who, in return, would give me that more valuable bread of knowledge. (pp. 40–41)

By the time he was 12, Douglass was an avid reader who wanted to learn to write:

> The idea as to how I might learn to write was suggested to me by being in Durgin and Bailey's ship-yard, and frequently seeing the ship carpenters, after hewing, and getting a piece of timber ready for use, write on the timber the name of that part of the ship for which it was intended. When a piece of timber was intended for the larboard side, it would be marked thus—"L." When a piece was for the starboard side, it would be marked thus—"S." . . . I immediately commenced copying them, and in a short time was able to make the four letters named. After that, when I met with any boy who I knew could write, I would tell him I could write as well as he. The next word would be, "I don't believe you. Let me see you try it." I would then make the letters which I had been so fortunate as to learn, and ask him to beat that. In this way I got a good many lessons in writing, which it is quite possible I should never have gotten in any other way. (p. 45)

Years later, Douglass edited a weekly paper called the *North Star*, became an influential friend of President Abraham Lincoln, and earned a place as one of the most famous men in history. In life as in fiction, the future begins when boys and girls venture into their neighborhoods to exercise the curiosity and cleverness that can change the world.

IN OUR OPENING STORY, Frederick Douglass's drive to read and write blossomed between 8 and 12 years, a time when children are broadening their minds through books, honing their ability to influence others, and deepening their understanding of themselves. Douglass's clever strategies for learning how to read and write are not a story about early childhood because younger minds do not weave elaborate plans that exploit human weaknesses. By late childhood, however, children have a desire for freedom from adult control and some skills to earn that freedom. The physical, mental, and emotional changes that fuel this exciting transformation are the topics of this chapter.

Physical Development

It is fun to notice family similarities, such as a dad and his children facing the ocean in bathing suits, sporting three identical pairs of legs, or a son with long fingers, just like his mom. It is also surprising how often children differ from their parents in size, shape, and physical skills. Some of these differences are due to the genetic differences between parents and their children; others are due to differences in their rearing environments. For example, improvements in health and nutrition have produced a gradual increase in height and shoe size in many countries, creating a *secular trend* that has added almost 4 inches (10 centimeters) to the average height of adults during the 20th century (Beard & Blaser, 2002).

But modern life does not guarantee that every child will reach his or her physical potential. Today's children spend more time than earlier generations participating in competitive sports and staring at television and computer screens, which put them at risk of some types of injuries and perceptual problems. Because parents might not look for conditions that are not part of their family history, it is important to monitor children's physical development so problems will be detected as soon as possible.

Growth and Movement Skills

Home videos of 6-year-olds in ballet class or on the soccer field are always entertaining. Hands flail, feet trip, and it is a rare occasion when everyone is dancing or running in the same direction. By 12, however, many children are competent dancers and ballplayers, and some are even training for the Olympics. In 6 short years, growth and exercise build children's strength, stamina, and grace.

BODY SIZE AND PROPORTIONS. For sentimental reasons, the utility closet in one of our homes has never been painted: It contains penciled growth-marks placed there by the previous owners. Lines labeled "Eric," "Lauren," and "Molly" show how irregular growth is. For example, Eric grew 2 inches (5.1 cm) between $8\frac{1}{2}$ and 9 years and then slowed to 1.25 inches (3.2 cm) between 9 and 10. While Eric was growing, his body was laying down new bone in spongy *growth plates*, layers of cells near the ends of his thigh, leg, and other long bones. When growth rates are averaged across children, periods of slow and rapid change average out, creating smooth growth norms like those in Figure 8.1 (Centers for Disease Control and Prevention, 2000).

On average, children add just over 2 inches of height and $7\frac{1}{2}$ pounds of weight each year during middle childhood. They enter middle childhood standing about 3 feet 9 inches tall (115 cm) and leave it at age 12 having grown to about 4 feet 10 inches for boys (149 cm) and 4 feet 11 inches for girls (151 cm). Genes, nutrition, and disease all influence growth, however, so it is difficult to predict a child's final size. It is not uncommon for a boy who is smaller than most of his peers to become an average-size teenager, and some girls who tower over their friends grow to be smaller-than-average adults.

Visit any fifth-, sixth-, or seventh-grade class and you'll see the evidence that males

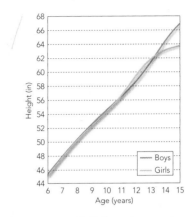

FIGURE 8.1 Childhood growth.

Girls experience their preadolescent growth spurt earlier than boys do. As a result, classrooms of 11- and 12-year-olds are an odd-looking mix of tall females and younger-looking males. Happily for boys, this situation reverses in a year or so.

SOURCE: Centers for Disease Control and Prevention (2000).

Many children have Olympic dreams, but few stick with their sport.

and females have different growth patterns. Girls experience the rapid growth that forecasts puberty earlier and surpass boys in height, weight, and general physical maturity around 11 years of age. Then, $2\frac{1}{2}$ years later, boys overtake the girls again.

Physical development affects people's perceptions of boys and girls differently. Many adults believe that tall boys are more popular during childhood and experience more social success after they grow up, whereas height is not such an issue for girls (Voss, 1999; Young & French, 1998). Indeed, concern about the social adjustment of short boys is so common that parents sometimes mention size as a reason they kept their sons out of kindergarten for an extra year. But studies do not support parents' fears. Short girls score like their peers on measures of adjustment, and short boys also express positive feelings about themselves (Sandberg, Brooke, & Campos, 1994). It is true that small boys are often teased about height, but this does not cause them to be rejected or to have poorer social adjustment as adults (Gilmour & Skuse, 1999; Sandberg, 1999; Zimet et al., 1999).

A minority of short children suffer from a *growth-hormone (GH) deficiency*, and these children can receive hormone treatments to help them grow. But normal-GH children who receive hormone treatments do not surpass their predicted adult size, so doctors advise parents of short but healthy children to accept their children's stature (Lanes & Gunczler, 1998). Instead of worrying about height, parents and teachers can foster a positive self-image by helping children participate in activities that suit their bodies.

Short or tall, all children undergo predictable changes in body proportions as they age. The facial changes that transform adorable kindergarteners into mischievous-looking middle schoolers are especially striking. Between 6 and 12 years, the lower face lengthens and broadens while 20 primary ("baby") teeth are gradually replaced by permanent teeth. Third graders look like works in progress, with teeth that seem too big for their mouths. It is not until late childhood when all of their facial features come into balance again. Information about growth helps forensic specialists "age" children's photographs, which assists in finding children who have been missing for years. As one imaging artist explained, "All the significant change is going to take place from underneath the eye . . . The eyes and ears are pretty much like fingerprints. We don't have to alter those" (Hudson, 2003, para. 3). Age progression photographs, like the one in Figure 8.2, illustrate these developmental changes.

PHYSICAL ABILITIES. The strength and stamina children gain as they grow allow them to gradually enjoy longer bike rides and hikes. Beginning around 7 years, children enter a phase of motor development they will refine for the rest of their lives. Recall from Chapter 6 that preschoolers are developing fundamental skills such as throwing, catching, and running up and down hills. These activities delight young children because they enjoy shifting their bodies to adapt to different situations. School-aged children transition into the *specialized movement phase*. Now they start refining and combining skills for use in more demanding situations. For example, hopping and jumping give way to elaborate jump-rope routines or artful moves on a basketball court (Gallahue & Ozmun, 2006).

Because children build physical skills by experimenting with their bodies, it is best if they participate in a wide variety of activities (American Academy of Pediatrics, Committee on Sports Medicine and Fitness 2000b). Seven- to 10-year-olds tend to have a lot of interests and go through phases, preferring baseball

FIGURE 8.2 Predicting physical development.

Body proportions, including facial features, change in predictable ways as children grow. On the left is a picture of 8-year-old Cherrie Mahan, who was reported missing after she stepped off a school bus. On the right, an age progression photograph shows what she might look like as a 23-year-old woman.

one season and losing interest in the sport the next. By 11 or 12 years, it is natural for children to become passionate about activities that suit their talents. Now some shorter children are begging to go to gymnastics camp while the taller ones are focused on basketball. For a variety of reasons, both mental and physical, older children have stronger preferences about what they like to do and are more active in planning their activities than are younger children.

KEEPING SPORTS FUN. Children's expanding abilities in middle childhood are not without risks. Parents and coaches need to be aware that children's bodies respond to heat and exertion differently from adults, so it is dangerous to assume that children can do what adults are comfortable doing. Heat-related illness is an example. Children produce relatively more heat during physical activities, sweat less than adults, and overheat easily. Their tolerance for exercise declines markedly when temperatures exceed 95° F (35° C), and they are vulnerable to heat exhaustion. Heat exhaustion occurs when body temperature rises, causing dizziness, weakness, nausea and vomiting, and muscle aches. Severe cases can progress to heatstroke, a life-threatening condition that damages internal organs. The American Academy of Pediatrics, Committee on Sports Medicine and Fitness, (2000a) recommends the following practices to prevent heat-related illness:

▶ Reduce the intensity of physical activity whenever air temperature and humidity are high.

▶ Give children time to adapt to changes in outdoor temperature and humidity. They may need 8 to 10 exposures to a hotter climate (lasting 30 to 45 minutes each) to lower their risk of heat-related illness.

▶ Children may not realize when they need to drink. Adults should supervise periodic drinking during hot weather.

▶ Dress children in lightweight, light-colored clothing to reduce heat absorption.

Children are also more prone to growth-related injuries as they become more interested in competition. For example, flexibility declines during growth spurts because bone growth temporarily outstrips muscle and tendon growth. Reduced flexibility and overuse can cause painful conditions such as "swimmer's shoulder," an ache that afflicts as many as two-thirds of adult competitive swimmers (Wetzler et al., 2002). To prevent injuries, it is important for young athletes to stretch before practices and competitions.

Power lifting is also a concern. Heavy loads can injure growth plates in the bones, leading to reduced growth. Consequently, the American Academy of Pediatrics, Committee on Sports Medicine and Fitness (2001), recommends delaying maximal lifts until children are grown. However, even elite child athletes show no evidence of growth complications from supervised running, gymnastics, or weight training (American Academy of Pediatrics, Committee on Sports Medicine and Fitness, 2000b; Damsgaard et al., 2000).

Although most children do not experience medical complications from involvement in sports, it is best if they do not shift into specialized training too early.

Knowledgeable families know that keeping their distance and letting children have fun is the key to building a lifelong interest in sports.

Older athletes who participated in a variety of sports during childhood perform more consistently, experience fewer injuries, and maintain their interest in sports longer than athletes who specialized at a young age (American Academy of Pediatrics, 2000b). While they are exploring their interests, children will enjoy sports more if they are not overly pressured about their performance. For example, one study found that men who were encouraged to exercise as children had less active lifestyles than men who were rarely nagged by adults (Taylor et al., 1999). As with eating habits, exercise habits develop best when children are surrounded by healthy role models. Children who see adults smiling as they go to the gym and stretching before a run will grow up assuming that exercise is fun.

Perceiving the World

Do you remember Malcolm, the preschooler in Chapter 6 who was so engrossed by the television set that he did not hear his mother talking? Although Malcolm's perceptual systems were well developed by 6 years, some slow-maturing functions will continue to mature. As we mentioned earlier, his ability to detect low-frequency sounds will improve until age 10, and his ability to pick out sounds in a noisy environment will improve until age 15 (Schneider & Trehub, 1992).

Malcolm's visual system is also changing. One ability that matures rather late is *dynamic visual acuity*: the ability to focus on a moving object long enough to interpret details. Children experience an improvement in this skill around 6 years of age and reach an adult level of performance around age 15 (Gabbard, 2004; Schrauf, Wist, & Ehrenstein, 1999). This means that Malcolm's eye movements will gradually become smoother as he tracks moving objects (Haishi & Kokubun, 1995). Because children with a history of preterm birth are at risk for eye movement abnormalities, many of these children perform poorly on tasks that involve moving stimuli (Langaas et al., 1998).

Malcolm's parents wear glasses, so there is a good chance he will also need corrective lenses sometime during the school years. Figure 8.3 illustrates two common visual problems. Children with *myopia* (commonly called nearsightedness) see near objects clearly but distant objects appear blurred. Myopia occurs when the eye is too long or the cornea too steeply curved, causing the eye to focus images in front of the retina (where the cells that detect light are located). Myopia usually develops during childhood when growth changes the shape of the eye. Although heredity predisposes children to nearsightedness, this condition is more common among people who spend a lot of time reading, watching television, and looking at computer screens.

A less common problem is *hyperopia* (also called farsightedness). Children with this problem focus images behind their retina due to a short eyeball or too little curvature. Children under 6 years tend to be hyperopic, but less than 10 percent of school-aged children remain farsighted as they grow (Zadnik et al., 2003). Regular vision exams are important because school exams do not always detect hyperopia and children rarely tell anyone when they have difficulty seeing. Two other common problems are *astigmatism* and *eye coordination problems*. Children with astigmatism have eyes with an irregular surface that creates problems focusing at a variety of distances. Children with eye coordination problems have problems moving their eyes together, which makes it difficult for their brains to fuse images from the two eyes. These four common problems are reviewed in Figure 8.3.

Some children are experiencing a relatively new problem: visual strain from too much computer time, causing blurred vision, dry eyes, headaches, and fatigue. Children's eyes tend to lock into a viewing distance when they sit too long in a particular position, and visual strain is compounded by poor lighting and workstations designed for adults. Young children are especially vulnerable to eye strain because they have limited self-awareness and will continue enjoyable activities to the point of near exhaustion. The American Optometric Association (1997) recommends three practices to prevent fatigue:

▸ *Enforce limits on the amount of time a child continuously uses a computer.* A 10-minute break every hour will minimize focusing problems.

▸ *Check the height and arrangement of the computer.* The best viewing angle is slightly downward, so children work best at low tables that allow their feet to touch the floor. (They can also sit comfortably on a higher chair with a footstool supporting their feet.)

▸ *Check for glare on the computer screen.* The optimal lighting level for computer use is about half the level normally found in a classroom.

Brain Development

The most remarkable changes during middle and late childhood unfold inside the brain. Here genetically controlled growth and everyday experiences gradually reshape the mind, expanding children's potential and producing more interesting personalities.

BUILDING THE BRAIN. Some aspects of brain development add volume to structures that already exist. During middle childhood, continued myelination of motor pathways improves fine motor coordination up to age 10, and higher brain centers continue to myelinate for at least another decade (Nelson, 2004). Also, branching of dendrites and thickening axons add volume to some brain regions.

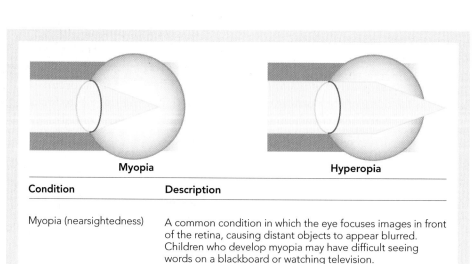

Condition	Description
Myopia (nearsightedness)	A common condition in which the eye focuses images in front of the retina, causing distant objects to appear blurred. Children who develop myopia may have difficult seeing words on a blackboard or watching television.
Hyperopia (farsightedness)	A condition typical of younger children that often (but not always) disappears with age. Near objects appear blurred for children with hyperopia because images reach the retina before they converge into focus.
Astigmatism	A condition in which the front surface of the eye has an irregular shape. Individuals with astigmatism may experience blurring at a variety of distances.
Eye Coordination Problems	Children with eye coordination problems have trouble keeping their eyes in proper alignment so the brain can fuse the two images together. Due to eye strain, these children may avoid activities requiring close work such as reading, cover one eye with their hands, or skip lines while reading.

FIGURE 8.3 Common visual problems.

Visual problems are uncomfortable and interfere with children's ability to learn. Because children rarely draw attention to the fact that they are having trouble seeing, periodic exams are important to screen for these four conditions.

SOURCE: American Optometric Association (2006b).

For example, there is rapid growth of structures involved in language and understanding spatial relationships between 6 and 15 years (Thompson et al., 2000), and areas that are critical for decision making do not reach mature size until 11 to 12 years (Giedd et al., 1999). The effect of these changes is evident in any piano studio: Six-year-olds slowly stab keys and often fail to notice repeated patterns while their older brothers and sisters move fingers swiftly and quickly become bored of simple songs.

While some brain regions are growing, others are shrinking by as much as 50 percent as synapses are pruned during development (Thompson et al., 2000). Myelination and neural pruning work together to make information transfer more efficient, which improves children's working memory and their ability to prepare for a response. Brain circuits also reorganize as new connections integrate brain regions into loops that can accomplish more difficult tasks (Luna & Sweeney, 2004). For example, children who bike into an unfamiliar area must keep the goal of getting back home in mind, attend to and remember spatial information, and successfully reverse their route to find their way home. This task is too challenging for most 7-year-olds, but 12-year-olds rarely get lost because the brain networks that keep information in mind for future use are more developed at this age. Thus, brain development during childhood consists of increased volume, tissue loss in some regions, and the integration of widely distributed brain regions.

By age 8, children can lay still long enough for scientists to study their brains with functional magnetic resonance imagery (fMRI), a technology you read about in Chapter 1. The results from brain-imaging studies are forcing scientists to rethink neurological development. As you learned in Chapter 6, neuroscientists have long assumed that cortical maturation was the primary reason why children are able to inhibit impulsive behavior as they grow. It is true that children act more responsibly as their frontal lobes mature (Rosso et al., 2004), but changes in other brain regions are important as well. The integration of widely distributed brain functions supports these exciting advances, including connections to so-called lower regions. Two of these lower regions are the thalamus, which sends sensory information to the cortex, and the cerebellum, which is involved in movement and attention.

Developmental psychologist Beatriz Luna and her associates (2001) developed an ingenious method for recording how distant brain regions start to cooperate during middle to late childhood. As illustrated in Figure 8.4, 8- to 30-year-olds looked at a dot followed by a light that appeared to the left or right. A green dot told the volunteers to follow their natural tendency to look at the light. Conversely, a red dot instructed them to look away from the light. Luna's team recorded neural activity in 15 brain regions to learn what parts of the brain are active as children become better at inhibiting the tendency to look at the light. The results were fascinating: Children and adolescents showed less activation than adults in six brain regions, proving that the ability to suppress behavior develops as broadly distributed brain circuits develop.

Immature connections between distant brain regions make it difficult for children in middle childhood to stay prepared to suppress responses. In simple terms, even children who have the best of intentions sometimes have difficulty controlling their behavior, especially when they are tired or distracted. Scientists call this ability to inhibit a dominant response in order to make another response **effortful control** (Rothbart & Rueda, 2005). Effortful control is an important component of *self-regulation*, a collection of abilities that help children control their thoughts and behavior (Banfield et al., 2004). Effortful control improves markedly between 2 and 4 years, and then improves even further during the school years. As effortful control develops, children find it easier to walk away from reinforcing situations and easier to approach situations that might involve punishment. For instance, a child with good effortful control can walk away from a ripe melon in the neighbor's garden yet confess that he mistakenly stepped on a plant.

By late childhood, children's brains have matured enough to build their spatial and planning skills. Now they explore farther from home—and usually get back without help.

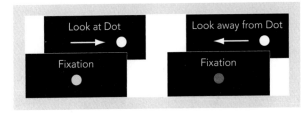

FIGURE 8.4 The development of effortful control.

Beatriz Luna and her colleagues imaged the brains of 8- to 30-year-olds while they looked at—or tried not to look at—flashes of light. A green light told them to look at the next flash of the light, whereas a red light told them to look away from the next flash of light. The research team found that children have difficulty preparing to suppress a dominant response because connections between distant brain regions are immature.

SOURCE: Luna et al. (2001).

effortful control The ability to inhibit a dominant response in order to perform another response. Effortful control develops gradually during middle childhood as distant brain regions become integrated into functional circuits.

Children who have good effortful control tend to be happier than poorly controlled children because they can direct their attention away from the negative feelings produced by the immediate situation. Children with good self-control are also less aggressive than their peers and show greater empathy for other people (Rothbart & Posner, 2001, 2006). Of course, all children feel tempted to strike out when they are angry, and everyone sometimes speaks without thinking. But children who develop good effortful control can inhibit these tendencies more often than not and consider the consequences of their actions. As children's brains mature, adults do not have to monitor them so closely and family life is more relaxed.

GAINS BRING LOSSES TOO. As you read in Chapter 2, *neural plasticity* refers to the brain's ability to change in response to experiences. During middle and late childhood, the brain's ability to rewire itself after damage or injury declines as connections develop. This loss of neural plasticity (flexibility) is especially apparent for language functions. Adults who suffer damage to language centers in their left hemispheres often experience permanent communication difficulties, but similar damage between 1 and 5 years often produces few or no impairments. Middle to late childhood is a transitional period when the ability of the brain to recover from injury gradually diminishes (Bates et al., 2001; Hertz-Pannier et al., 2002; Vargha-Khadem, Isaacs, & Muter, 1994).

But early injuries do not always produce the mildest damage. For example, injury to the frontal lobes during adulthood may have little impact on intelligence test scores, whereas the same injury during infancy or childhood often harms general intelligence. Because brain development is complicated, the type of injury, its location, and the timing of injury during development all influence whether children or adults are more affected by trauma (de Haan & Johnson, 2003).

Brain development sets the stage for other kinds of development. Not only do brain developments produce improved effortful control in middle childhood, as discussed earlier, but the child's general reasoning and thinking abilities show striking improvement as well. These developments expand the range of concepts children can learn and allow people like Frederick Douglass (from our opening story) to outwit other children using the cognitive tools you will read about next.

>>> **M E M O R Y   M A K E R S** <<<

1. Which member of each pair is better advice during the school years? Why?

   (a) (1) treat all short children with hormones OR (2) treat low-GH children
   (b) (1) participate in a range of physical activities OR (2) focus on one sport for best results
   (c) (1) do not encourage drinking during sports OR (2) supervise drinking
   (d) (1) reduce room light for computer use OR (2) increase room light for computer use

2. Which of the following describes brain development during middle and late childhood?

   (a) increased volume
   (b) the integration of widely distributed brain regions
   (c) tissue loss in some regions
   (d) a and b
   (e) all of the above

[1a-2 (normal GH children do not benefit), 1b-1 (abilities and interests are still developing), 1c-2 (children do not always know when they need to drink and may get heatstroke), 1d-1 (reduce light to reduce glare on the screen); 2-e]

Cognitive Development

Children's growing mental abilities can tax adults' abilities to respond to some of their thoughts and questions. For example, one troubled mother was giving her 7-year-old daughter, Becky, a cup of water before bedtime when Becky said, "Mommy, sometimes I think you are going to put poison in the water so you can live your own life" (Ames & Haber, 1985, p. 124). Shocked and hurt, the mother called her husband to finish putting Becky to bed. In a letter to the Gesell Institute of Human Development, the mother asked,

> Was I wrong? One minute I think I should have passed it over as her just being seven. But the next minute I think even a seven-year-old is old enough to try not to hurt others with what they say.
>
> Becky did cry when I left and said she didn't mean it, but I was too hurt to stay and hear her prayers or kiss good night a child who could accuse me of murder.

Dr. Louise Bates Ames responded, "I'd say that you did make too much of the whole thing. . . . Children at seven have enough trouble within themselves with their violent thoughts without having adults take them seriously" (Ames & Haber, 1985, pp. 124–125). Becky's question illustrates the mismatch between two developmental trends that occur in middle childhood: Cognitive development prompted her to think about frightening possibilities, but social development was not advanced enough for her to anticipate the effect her words might have on her mother. After reviewing some of the developments that lead to interchanges like this one, we will revisit Becky, her mother, and Dr. Ames's useful advice.

Piaget's Theory of Middle Childhood

In Chapter 6 you learned about the stage of *preoperational thought*, a period when children's thinking is often illogical. Their answers take an interesting turn around 7 years, when children gradually become less confused by the appearance of materials and the wording of questions. Piaget used the term **concrete operational thought** to describe this third stage of cognitive development. Concrete operational thought describes children's thinking until age 12 or so, when the last of Piaget's stages appears.

CONCRETE OPERATIONAL THOUGHT. School-aged children often think logically and flexibly about the world—as long as they are thinking about things they can see or touch (hence, the term *concrete* operations). When problems involve abstract concepts, however, concrete operational children struggle. For example, Antoine is a typical 8-year-old who understands that his class earned money collecting cans, so it was fair when they voted to spend the money on fish for their aquarium. But Antoine is unlikely to fully grasp the *concept* his teacher has been trying to explain, which is that adults pay taxes and also vote for the people who decide how their money will be spent. Piaget and his colleagues arrived at this distinction between concrete and abstract thought by watching how children solve a variety of problems, including two you will read about next: *conservation of number* and the *pendulum problem* (Inhelder & Sinclair, 1969).

Briefly, children *conserve* when they realize that some physical quantities remain the same even after people make objects look a bit different. For example, boys and girls in middle childhood know that a row of five black chips and a row of five white chips have the same number of chips no matter how the chips are arranged, but preschool children do not. To illustrate, Piaget placed six candies on a table in front of children and said they belonged to his friend,

concrete operational thought
A mode of thinking, lasting roughly from 7 to 12 years of age, when children begin to think more logically and flexibly about concrete materials (materials they can see and touch). Concrete operational children have difficulty handling abstract concepts, that is, reasoning about possibilities that do not physically exist.

FIGURE 8.5 Conservation.

Children conserve quantities when they know that basic properties of objects have not changed even though the position or shape of the objects has changed. Children conserve number first, followed by weight and then volume.

Conservation of Number (typically mastered by age 6)	"Does one of us have more candy?"	Tester moves the candies in one row. "Are there as many here as here?"
Conservation of Weight (typically mastered by 9 or 10 years)	"Do these clay balls weigh the same?"	Tester flattens one of the balls. "Will the scale still balance or will one side be heavier?"
Conservation of Volume (typically mastered by 11 or 12 years)	"Are they exactly the same?"	She pours hers like this. "Do you both have the same amount now?"

Roger. Then he said, "Put as many sweets here as there are there. Those . . . are for Roger. You are to take as many as he has." Some preoperational children built a row of seven or more tightly packed candies. When Piaget asked if the two rows had the same number of candies, they said, "Yes," while pointing to the length of the rows (Piaget, 1952, p. 75). Because many of these children could count, Piaget knew that children could learn counting routines without understanding the concept of number.

More advanced children constructed two equivalent sets, as shown in Figure 8.5, but they still did not understand the concept of number. When Piaget closed up one of the sets and asked if the rows had the same number, these children also said, "No." Remarkably, the fact that the candies were equivalent a minute ago did not influence their answers, even though no candies had been added or removed.

Children who fail conservation of number are still in the stage of *preoperational thought*. These children center on irrelevant dimensions (such as the length of a row) and fail to mentally reverse the movement of the candies. Children reach the stage of concrete operations when they realize the rows are equivalent even *after* the experimenter changes the length of one of the rows. Most children grasp conservation of number around age 6, but it may be years before they conserve for other types of quantities, such as the amount of liquid in a glass. As you can see in Figure 8.5, children usually understand conservation of weight around 9 or 10 years and conservation of volume a year or two later. Piaget used the phrase *horizontal decalage* (*décalage* is French for "time lag") to describe the fact that children grasp conservation at different rates for different types of quantities.

Concrete operational children also pass other Piagetian tasks that you read about in Chapter 6, such as ordering sticks from smallest to largest, and they can detect simple logical inconsistencies. In one study, for example, experimenters read children two stories, including one that had sentences such as, "Peter is eating an apple, and not only that, Peter is not eating an apple." Children under

6 years *remembered* the inconsistent statements yet showed no ability to pick out which story was "silly." In contrast, the concrete operational children easily spotted the inconsistent remarks (Ruffman, 1999).

What is behind the development of concrete operations? Piaget thought that children's minds expanded when they confronted discrepancies between what they believe and what they observe. To test this idea, he tried to nudge children into higher stages of thinking with carefully planned activities. To his surprise, however, learning experiences were ineffective if the children's existing schemes limited what they were ready to comprehend. For example, no amount of effort counting chips in the two rows on a conservation task will change the answers of a child who is not ready to understand the concept. As a result, Piaget concluded that there were limits to the role of environmental influences because both experience and physical maturation promote development.

LIMITATIONS OF CONCRETE OPERATIONAL THOUGHT. School-aged children reason more cleverly and logically than preschoolers—but they do not think like adults. Piaget's pendulum problem, which is illustrated in Figure 8.6, illustrates the type of situation that confuses the concrete operational child. For this problem, a tester takes a weight on a string and shows the child how to change the length of the string, the amount of weight, the height the weight is released from, and the force on the weight as it is released. The tester then asks the child to figure out which of these factors, individually or in combination, determines the number of swings the pendulum makes in a fixed amount of time (Inhelder & Piaget, 1958). How well do children of various ages solve this problem?

It is comical to watch preoperational children play with the strings and the weights: They have no overall plan, record their results inconsistently, and come to conclusions that are not justified by the results. For example, one 6-year-old told Piaget, "You have to take off all the weights and let the string go all by itself" while pushing the string with his finger (Inhelder & Piaget, 1958, p. 69). Concrete operational children do better because they investigate a number of options and occasionally find the solution. Often, though, their behavior looks like that of a 10-year-old boy Piaget interviewed. As illustrated in Figure 8.6, this boy varied the length of the string and correctly concluded that the pendulum swung slower when the string was longer. Then he put a 100-gram weight on a medium-length string and compared the results to a 50-gram weight on a short string. This time he inaccurately concluded that a heavy weight makes the pendulum swing slowly. (In fact, the speed of the pendulum is determined only by the length of the string.) If this 10-year-old had approached the problem scientifically, as an older child might, he would have imagined all possible combinations of variables and tested them systematically. Still, this child is on course developmentally because scientific thinking is not typical during middle childhood.

From watching children experiment with scientific problems like this one, Piaget concluded that concrete operational thinking is *reality bound*: Children apply logical operations to concrete materials but flounder when tasks require them to envision possibilities (such as possible combinations of string lengths and weights). It is only in the next stage of cognitive development, discussed in Chapter 10, when they will be able to systematically test hypotheses.

COGNITIVE DEVELOPMENT AROUND THE WORLD. When Piaget started observing children, he thought that all children developed cognitive skills in the same order and at much the same rate, regardless of their experiences. However, it

Instructions:
The child saw strings of varying lengths and a set of weights. The tester showed him how to hook weights onto the strings to determine how fast the pendulum would swing.

Comparison 1:
The child tested several string lengths with one weight and correctly concluded, "It goes slower when it's longer."

Comparison 2:
The child then compared a 100-gram weight on a medium-length string with a 50-gram weight on a short string. He mistakenly concluded that a heavier weight makes the pendulum swing slowly.

FIGURE 8.6 The pendulum problem.

Concrete operational children cannot figure out what causes an event by systematically testing one possibility at a time. When asked to figure out what makes a pendulum swing rapidly or slowly, this 10-year-old boy paired particular weights with particular string lengths. Because he failed to isolate the influence of each of these factors alone, he erroneously concluded that a heavy weight makes the pendulum swing slowly. (In fact, it is the length of the string that is important.)

This child is learning to visualize how several patterns come together to form one. As a result, she will probably solve certain types of spatial problems better than a child who lacks her weaving experience.

soon became clear that culture plays a role in cognitive development. Depending on the task, children who experience Western-style schooling sometimes pass conservation tasks at a younger age than their nonschooled counterparts, sometimes at the same age, and sometimes at a later age. After cross-cultural findings became available, Piaget acknowledged that performance on his tasks could be influenced by differences in children's environments (Rogoff & Chavajay, 1995).

In general, studies have found that children perform more competently when they handle familiar materials or reason about familiar information. For example, Zinacantec children from Mexico solve a particular spatial problem earlier than their counterparts in Los Angeles: The Zinacantec children are better at predicting which pattern of cloth will result from an arrangement of colored threads on a loom (Maynard & Greenfield, 2003). Yet even children with very different learning histories perform similarly when they answer questions about information they share. For example, Mexican Indian children show the same understanding of kinship terms (such as "uncle" and "great-grandmother") regardless of whether they attend school or not (Rogoff, 2003).

Cross-cultural research supports the conclusion that there is a universal timetable for cognitive growth and a role for experience to alter that timetable. Children around the world master object permanence and conservation, and all children go through a phase of nonconservation before they conserve. When children in middle to late childhood respond differently across cultures, familiarity with the test materials or the testing environment is often the cause rather than fundamental differences in how they think (Cole, 1990; Poortinga & van de Vijver, 2004).

EVALUATING PIAGET'S THEORY. Piaget said that cognitive growth occurs when new mental operations (mental actions) allow children to reason in new ways. As we have said before, scientists have praised Piaget for describing children's behavior so accurately, and many have agreed that school-aged children overcome centered, static, and irreversible thinking. But as you read in Chapter 6, many cognitive psychologists doubt that development is driven by logical operations. If groups of 7- and 11-year-olds are both in the concrete operational period, why do 7-year-olds play simple games whereas 11-year-olds learn chess and are capable of outwitting their friends? And why does children's behavior vary so much across tasks?

To answer these questions, many scientists have adopted an *information processing approach*. As described in Chapter 6, this approach assumes that children reason illogically when the demands of a problem outstrip their ability to pay attention to relevant information, remember it, and ignore distractions that come along while they are figuring out a problem. The information processing approach explains why young children act more maturely when the processing demands of a task are light, yet even adults get frustrated and impatient when task demands are heavy or material is unfamiliar. For example, even college students are more likely to add numbers incorrectly on a statistics exam when they are distracted by students leaving the room or they are still thinking about an earlier question that stumped them.

Information Processing

What makes typical 11- and 12-year-olds so much more inventive than their younger brothers and sisters? As you will see, the developments you read about in Chapter 6 continue throughout the school years, producing a more efficient—and clever—mind.

SPEED OF PROCESSING INCREASES. Children process mental information more quickly as they grow (Demetriou et al., 2002; Luna et al., 2004). Scientists assume that basic neurological changes, such as increased myelination and synaptic pruning, explain this trend. In one study, for example, children and teenagers were tested on four tasks, such as deciding whether letters matched or pressing different buttons for arrows that pointed in different directions. As shown in the left panel of Figure 8.7, the greatest improvement in processing speed occurs in middle childhood—between 6 and 12 years. But even 12-year-olds still process information about 50 percent slower than adults, so additional improvements are yet to come (Hale, 1990).

WORKING MEMORY EXPANDS. Short-term and working memory increase throughout middle childhood. *Short-term span* refers to the number of items people can hold passively in memory, such as when you repeat a list you have just

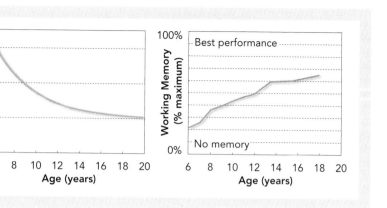

FIGURE 8.7 The development of processing speed and working memory.

Processing speed and working memory improve with age. The left panel shows how long it takes children to complete simple mental tasks compared to adults. As speed of processing improves, working memory also improves. For the memory task reported in the right panel (listening span), individuals filled in the last word of sentences and tried to remember the growing list of last words. Notice the large improvement in memory from 6 to 8 years of age.

SOURCES: Fry & Hale (1996); Siegel (1994).

heard. Six-year-olds typically repeat about four items, whereas the average adult can repeat about seven. *Working memory span* describes the number of items people can hold in memory while they perform mental operations. In one study, for example, people listened to sentences that were missing final words. While they completed the sentences, they also tried to remember the growing list of missing words. As the right panel of Figure 8.7 shows, performance on this task increases from 6 to 18 years, with faster improvement occurring during the early years (Siegel, 1994).

The ability to remember information while you are thinking about something else is critical for solving problems and finishing tasks after a distraction. For example, young children who try to complete several chores ("Put these shoes back in your room and bring me your trash and your laundry") often forget the second assignment while they are completing the first. Improved working memory is a major reason why older children have a better chance of completing all three. And because they can hold more information in mind, older children are better than younger children at reasoning through a problem, so they are less likely to pick up the wrong puzzle piece twice or lose track of what ingredient they should add next when they are helping to bake cupcakes. The relationship between working memory and reasoning holds across age groups (older children hold more information in mind and also reason better) and within age groups (children of the same age who have large working memories tend to reason better than their peers) (Fry & Hale, 2000).

Why does memory improve during the school years? Three important changes make it easier for older children to hold onto ideas:

▶ ***Older children make better use of memory strategies.*** When preschoolers try to remember black-and-white patterns, their performance is influenced by how similar the patterns look. By age 8, however, children are not very affected by visual similarity because they tend to think in words ("That one has a blob at the bottom") (Pickering, 2001). The shift from remembering visual information to talking to oneself means that older children can use a wider variety of memory strategies. One that appears early in the school years, **rehearsal**, involves repeating information over and over again. Children also use **organization**, such as clustering information into groups of related items ("all of my outside chores" and "all of my inside chores"). Later they discover the power of **elaboration**, which is expanding on an idea by forming a mental image or creating a story to help them remember. As their *metamemory* (knowledge about memory) improves, children are more likely to realize when memory strategies are necessary and they become more efficient at using these strategies.

▶ *Older children have more knowledge that helps them remember.* Knowledge helps people organize information into meaningful patterns, which reduces the burden on limited memory resources. In fact, children sometimes remember better than adults when they know more about the to-be-remembered information. In a famous example, cognitive psychologist Michelene Chi (1978) asked chess players in the third through eighth grades to remember the arrangement of chess pieces on boards and then compared their performance to adults who only had a passing familiarity with chess. The adults remembered longer lists of numbers, but the children with more knowledge of chess outperformed them on the chessboard task.

▶ *Older children process information faster.* Faster processing speed, as discussed earlier, means that children can store more items before early items in a list have faded, and they can perform operations on these items quickly. As Frederick Douglass grew older, for example, he could plot his strategy for learning to read by thinking, "I'll take some bread with me, then I'll work fast, then I'll find Sammie, who is always hungry by noon . . . no, Jack lives closer." The process is a lot like juggling balls—the faster you move, the more balls you can juggle.

▶ *Older children have better cognitive inhibition.* Improved ability to suppress or stop a thought has widespread effects on cognitive development. Inhibition helps children's working memory by keeping irrelevant information from popping into mind, which in turn improves their problem-solving skills.

The ability to keep more information in mind gives older children the ability to think about several strategies at once and pick the best one. And as you will read next, this ability to choose between several strategies is an important part of problem solving throughout life.

STRATEGIES DEVELOP. Many people assume that cognitive development looks like the staircase in the left panel of Figure 8.8. According to this view, children march along using one form of thinking until a reorganization pops them into a new and better way of thinking. But dozens of experiments have suggested that this figure does not do a good job of describing development. Videotapes of children solving problems reveal that individual children generally use a variety of strategies at any given time, including some that are typical of earlier stages of learning. For example, school-aged children sometimes solve simple addition problems (4 + 2) by retrieving the memorized answer (6), but other times they count on their fingers from 1, count from the smaller number (2, 3, 4, 5, 6), or use another strategy. Most children use a variety of strategies even on sets of identical problems. In other words, children do not stick with a particular strategy until

rehearsal A strategy for remembering that involves mentally repeating items over and over again.

organization A strategy for remembering that involves clustering items into related groups, such as remembering all animals together and all flowers together.

elaboration A strategy for remembering that involves using information from existing knowledge to give meaning to to-be-remembered information. For example, making a mental picture of items on a grocery list and relating a new word to one that is already familiar are examples of elaboration.

Who is helping whom? Children who have extensive computer knowledge may remember procedures and shortcuts better than the average adult.

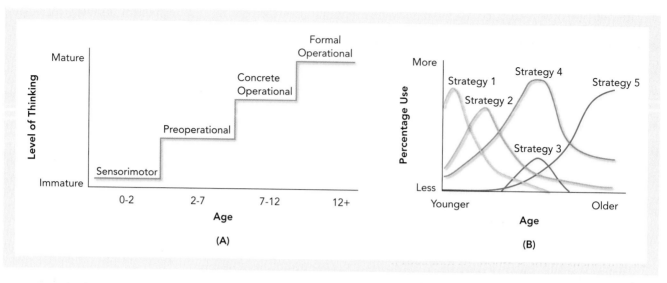

FIGURE 8.8 Overlapping waves theory.

Many people assume that children use a particular strategy to solve problems until they learn a better one, as shown in (a). In reality, cognitive development looks like the overlapping waves in (b). This diagram shows that children use a variety of strategies at any given age, with the probability of using specific strategies changing as children mature and learn.

overlapping waves theory A theory that says that children and adults typically use a variety of strategies to solve problems. People retain multiple strategies as they mature, but the probability they will use any given strategy changes as they gain knowledge and experience.

they have learned a better one. Instead, what changes with development is the *probability* of using specific strategies: First graders are more likely than third graders to count on their fingers from 1, but third graders are more likely to retrieve the answer from memory. This means that development looks more like the diagram in the right panel of Figure 8.8: as overlapping waves, with multiple strategies coexisting at each developmental period. The idea that individuals use a number of different strategies at each developmental period is called **overlapping waves theory** (Siegler, 1996; Siegler & Alibali, 2005).

Overlapping waves theory also describes how adults solve problems. For example, college students at Northern Colorado University retrieved the answer to simple arithmetic problems only 72 percent of the time, and students at Carleton University (in Canada) did so only 71 percent of the time (Geary & Wiley, 1991; LeFevre, Sadesky, & Bisanz, 1996). What did they do on other trials? A little bit of this and a little bit of that—including counting on their fingers! So don't be worried if you catch yourself problem solving like an 8-year-old. According to the father of overlapping waves theory, psychologist Robert Siegler, variable strategy use is a "basic property of human thought" (1996, p. 13).

Why do people of all ages alternate between brilliance and stupidity? One possibility is that learning several ways of doing things allows you to solve easy problems with simple but efficient strategies while giving you the option of using more complicated strategies for difficult problems. In other words, having a variety of strategies helps you adapt to changing circumstances. The benefit of this variability outweighs the fact that neither children nor adults always use the best possible strategy (Siegler, 1996). And as you will read next, inconsistent performance is never more obvious than when children open their mouths to share their thoughts with the world.

Language Development

School-aged children talk so fast and furiously that it is easy to forget they are still learning language. But even 12-year-old children are still picking up new words, improving their understanding of sentence structures, and learning to explain things clearly. And because the language children experience at home, school, and in books influences their rates of development, individual differences grow as time passes.

SOUNDS AND WORDS. Children master most language sounds by the time they start school, yet it is not unusual for them to be flustered by some challenging ones. During the early school years, many children struggle with pronouncing the "th" in "thin," the "sh" in "shed," and the "r" in "rainy." A few years later, they are still improving their ability to produce long words and complicated sound sequences. During this time, it is easy to delight them with tongue teasers like "She sells shells by the seashore" (Hoff, 2001).

School-aged children know so many words that it is difficult to measure the size of their vocabularies. Developmental psychologist Jeremy Anglin (1993) tackled this task by sampling one word from every two pages of a dictionary and selecting a subset of words that some children might know. Assistants read each word and a set of possible definitions to students in the first, third, and fifth grades. By multiplying the children's scores by 595, Anglin estimated the vocabulary sizes shown in Figure 8.9. Amazingly, the average child added 9,000 words between the first and third grades and another 20,000 words between the third and fifth grades!

Are children really learning 20,000 new words in 2 years? Probably not. Anglin's list included totally new words and many words that contained familiar parts. The greatest increase in knowledge occurred for "derived words," words created by adding an ending onto a root word, such as "sad + ness" for "sadness" and "preach + er" for "preacher." Because children's ability to understand these words increased sharply around 8 years of age, Anglin concluded that there are large increases after this age in children's ability to figure out what new words mean by drawing on existing knowledge.

Even though some 10-year-olds have a vocabulary of 40,000 words, they are still confused by many words that seem simple to adults. This became more apparent when children's involvement in the legal system prompted investigators to explore how well children understand what attorneys and judges tell them about courtroom procedures. In one study, for example, investigators showed children a drawing of a courtroom and asked them to explain 16 legal terms. In a group of 9- to 11-year-olds, fewer than 25 out of 40 knew what a "witness" or "lawyer" was, and few 6- to 8-year-olds could explain even basic information about the words *court, guilty,* and *promise* (Maunsell, Smith, & Stevenson, 2000). In response to the question, "What is the jury and what do they do?", children under 7 in an earlier study gave answers like "It sparkles on your finger" (because they assumed the assistant had said "jewelry"), and even 30 percent of the 12-year-olds said they just did not know (Warren-Leubecker et al., 1989).

UNDERSTANDING DIFFICULT SENTENCES. Children are also confused by difficult rules for combining words. One challenge is figuring out pronouns. For example, consider the following sentences:

When he came home, John made dinner.

He made dinner when John came home.

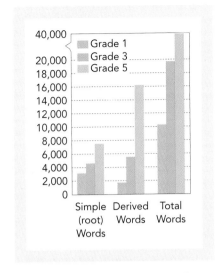

FIGURE 8.9 Vocabulary growth.

Children's vocabularies grow quickly during the school years. The largest increase in knowledge occurs for "derived words": words made up of multiple meaning units (sad + ness + sadness). Notice the sharp increase after the third grade in children's ability to infer the meaning of new words.

SOURCE: Anglin (1993).

"He" can refer to John in the first sentence but not in the second. Why? Few people can explain the rule, but "John" links backward to a pronoun only when the pronoun is in a subordinate clause. If you are confused by this explanation, you won't be surprised to learn that children often fail to link pronouns correctly to people's names. Consider what happened when a group of 6-year-olds saw a picture of Mama Bear with her hand on her own stomach, looking at Goldilocks. When the tester said, "This is Mama Bear; this is Goldilocks. Is Mama Bear touching *her?*", many children said, "yes" (Chien & Wexler, 1990). Even by middle childhood, children do not interpret pronouns in difficult sentences the way adults do (Wigglesworth, 1990), and it also takes time for them to master long sentences, negatives ("Did you not see a woman in the video?"), and tag questions ("You broke it, didn't you?") (Walker, 1999).

METALINGUISTIC AWARENESS. "Did you hear the joke about the skunk? Never mind, it stinks," Daniel shouted before dashing onto the playground. Teachers call these jokes "third-grade humor"—a surefire sign that language awareness is blossoming (Pan & Gleason, 2001).

Metalinguistic awareness is the ability to reflect on language as an object. During the school years, growing skills on this front produce increasingly mature language play. Long before they start school, children show evidence of metalinguistic awareness by experimenting with nonsense words and word sounds. Then, between the first and third grades, they are mesmerized by riddles that play on sounds or double meanings. Metalinguistic awareness develops gradually, though, so children often miss the point of double meanings during everyday conversations. This is why a child who is watering plants and the carpet at the same time might think he's being complimented when his father snickers, "Good job." In contrast, an older child will realize his father's sarcastic intent and stop pouring. As children grow, they are more likely to appreciate puns, irony, and metaphor—all signs of their growing ability to consider and compare multiple representations (Ely, 2001).

COMMUNICATING CLEARLY. Another cognitive skill that develops markedly during middle and late childhood is the ability to tell stories and give directions that other people will understand. Transcripts from a classic study by John Flavell (1975) illustrate how puzzling young children's explanations can be. Experimenters taught children in the second and eighth grades a game and then asked them to explain it to a blindfolded adult. See if you can understand what the game is from this second grader's explanation to a blindfolded adult:

> "You put that thing in the cup and then you pour it out and you move your pig up and then you put it back in and then you move your pig up again. And when you put it in there sometimes you can't move it up." (p. 96)

Now read how an eighth grader explained the game:

> "The items in this game are a cup, a block with four—three different colors on it—black, blue and red—two pigs, one's white, one's brown, and there's a long board with seven—fourteen squares on it. Uh, the colors are red, blue, and white. Uh, first thing that you do on beginning the game is one person—he picks up the two pigs one in each hand and, uh, shuffles them under the take. Then he lets the other person pick which pig he has with, uh, the pigs inside his fist so the person can't see it. Then, uh, they put them on the first squares which are both red and . . . (etc.)" (p. 98)

Flavell found that the older children used a larger number of different words to describe the game, provided more details, and made fewer ambiguous comments. Older children's explanations are less ambiguous because they can keep multiple per-

metalinguistic awareness The ability to reflect on language as an object. Children show metalinguistic awareness when they appreciate nonliteral uses of language, such as when they understand puns or use sarcasm (saying "Nice catch" to someone who has just dropped a ball).

spectives in mind and have more "verbal machinery" for crafting their explanations, including more vocabulary words and a better understanding of how to use pronouns.

This growing ability to communicate clearly is found throughout the world, regardless of the language children speak. In a study conducted in Hong Kong, China, for example, children told stories to a puppet about a series of pictures that illustrated various activities such as "washing the car." Adults read each story and determined whether the child clearly explained that a character in later pictures was the same person who had appeared earlier in the story. Five-year-olds made it clear who they were talking about only 38 percent of the time, whereas 12-year-olds were clear 84 percent of the time (Wong & Johnston, 2004).

As they move through middle childhood, children also become better at sticking to the topic of a conversation and adjusting their speech for different social situations. For example, by 10 years they can hint that they want something, ask nicely, or issue a demand (Pedlow, Sanson, & Wales, 2004). And by this age, children dislike people who make inappropriate requests, such as "Give me your pencil" (Becker, 1986; Place & Becker, 1991).

Cognitive Development and Education

Educators need two professional "hats" to think about how children learn. First is the hat of a developmentalist: This hat helps them consider how children differ from adults. Second is the hat of a cognitive psychologist: This hat helps them remember that children are, after all, human. The basic architecture of a child's mind is the same as an adult's, so many factors that help or hurt your learning also help or hurt children's learning. To explain how children learn, we will start with the hat of a developmentalist and look at how educators structure lessons to adjust to children's needs. Then we will describe some general principles of teaching that work for students of all ages.

MODIFYING LESSONS FOR CHILDREN. Piaget was reluctant to give advice to teachers (Evans, 1973), but many education experts agree that his findings support the following instructional practices (Brainerd, 1978; Thomas, 2005):

▶ *Avoid presenting material that is far above the child's level of understanding.* Children learn concepts gradually and in a fixed sequence. For example, they learn to place objects in one-to-one correspondence before they master conservation of number, and a child who does not conserve number (as you saw in Figure 8.5) cannot understand subtraction. The best instruction helps children who already understand a concept bridge to the next level of understanding.

▶ *Do not rush learning; repetition is good.* Children master concepts best when they have time to apply those concepts to a variety of materials and situations. For example, children who are just starting to make juice from cans will learn to follow written instructions better if they practice reading instructions on a number of different brands.

▶ *Use concrete demonstrations to convey information.* There are many ways to bring lessons alive for children. For example, they can learn about democracy by electing a class president or explore gravity by dropping balls of different sizes. Effective instruction helps children understand the relationship between activities and the concepts these activities represent (Mayer, 2004).

▶ *Arrange activities so that children will discover inconsistencies between what they currently believe and the concept you want them to learn.* For example, one teacher illustrates negative numbers by using a model building that has several floors "below zero" (Bransford, Brown, & Cocking, 1999). Her children learn the conventions of writing addition and subtraction problems by observing where miniature people end up when they enter the elevator and ride a specific number of floors ($4 - 6 = -2$). But the elevator model is limited because students only see that −5 is *lower* than −2, so they may not realize that −5 is *less* than −2. Once children grasp negative numbers, the teacher switches to activities involving money to help children understand the concept of negative numbers.

Piaget emphasized that children in middle childhood are active learners who are not ready to learn well from verbal instruction alone. Because children lack many concepts that new learning builds upon, it is important for adults to take their cognitive level into account.

BUILDING REAL-WORLD COMPETENCE. Even with the best instruction, children and adults alike sometimes fail to use what they have learned. For example, the 11-year-old who earned 100 percent on all of his fractions quizzes may still ask his mother a dozen questions when he first tries to cut a cookie recipe in half. This behavior is common because people of all ages often fail to transfer what they know to new situations, especially if they are used to using their knowledge only in one context (Bransford et al., 1999; Woll, 2002).

There is no point in being frustrated when children seem to know less than they should. Instead, adults can create learning opportunities that help children apply their knowledge more broadly. In general, students are more likely to transfer knowledge to the real world when material is learned to a high level of mastery, they truly understand the new concept, they have time to connect the concept to information they already know, the concept is related to real life, and they have had practice applying the concept in a variety of contexts. For example, children who can use fractions in their daily lives have probably had a lot of experience solving fractions (mastery), have had hands-on experience dividing food or treats among classmates (conceptual understanding), have been given time to solve new problems on their own (time to make connections), have had experience with cooking or other real-life applications (motivation), and have had opportunities to use fractions in a variety of situations (dividing earnings from a lemonade stand, building a model house, and so forth). The experiences that help children transfer learning to new situations are reviewed in Table 8.1.

Children who use mathematical concepts to shop, cook, or play games develop the deep, enduring knowledge that helps them transfer what they have learned in school to real life situations.

The instructional practices that feel comfortable to students are not always the ones that help them learn the best. Consider Lynn and Terry, two teachers who have very different classroom styles. Lynn is organized and structured. She chooses activities that help her students learn quickly, such as spending large blocks of time on a topic and using sequences of similar examples. Her students can easily predict what she will ask on tests and they think she is fair. In contrast, Terry is less predictable. She uses examples that are not very similar and she often revisits material covered earlier in the week. The organization of her handouts does not match how she presented the material, and her students score lower than Lynn's students on initial tests. Who is the better teacher, Lynn or Terry?

Surprisingly, Terry may be. Terry's teaching methods introduce **desirable difficulties**: instructional conditions that make initial learning more difficult but

desirable difficulties Instructional conditions that make initial learning more difficult but improve long-term memory and transfer of learning to new situations.

TABLE 8.1 Experiences That Help Children Transfer Learning to New Situations

Highly Effective Learning Experiences	Explanation
Children learn material to a high level of mastery.	Incomplete knowledge is unlikely to transfer to new situations. For example, children who have only a little experience with a computer skill are not likely to transfer what they know to new problems.
Learning experiences build children's conceptual understanding and not just factual knowledge.	Children memorize facts quickly, but they are more likely to use their knowledge when they learn with understanding. For example, students who memorize what veins and arteries are may not be able to figure out what properties an artificial artery would need to have. Students who understand the different *functions* of veins and arteries can solve this problem.
Children are given time to make connections between what they are learning and what they already know, and they are encouraged to do so.	Children cannot organize knowledge when learning is rushed. For example, it takes children up to 15 seconds to relate information from words and pictures, so they fail to mentally connect information when information is presented quickly.
Children participate in activities that motivate them to learn.	Children like activities that have practical consequences and those that are challenging but not too difficult. For example, one first-grade class was so motivated to write books for other children that teachers had to tell them they could not leave recess to work on them.
Children apply new concepts in a variety of contexts.	New knowledge will tend to be linked to a specific context if children only use that knowledge in one situation. For example, children who learn about distance-rate-time problems from examples about boat trips may not transfer the concepts to examples about rockets.

SOURCE: Bransford et al. (1999).

improve long-term memory and transfer of learning. Desirable difficulties slow learning by introducing features that encourage children to build connections between information, which produces longer-lasting, more flexible knowledge (Bjork, 1994, 1999, 2006). For example, it may seem a little confusing when a teacher uses three dissimilar examples of a verb, but students who hear more types of verbs will remember the concept better. Terry introduces desirable difficulties by not presenting information about nouns and verbs in the same order each time she covers grammar. She seems less organized than Lynn, but her students are less likely to simply memorize without understanding. Terry also gives her students more frequent tests. Students learn more quickly when class time is devoted to studying rather than sacrificing time for tests, but they remember more over the long run when study times are interrupted with progressively more difficult tests. Using a variety of examples, organizing information in different ways, and testing frequently are all ways to introduce desirable difficulties.

In sum, it takes time to build conceptual understanding. Teachers who value rapid learning and performance on immediate memory tests may deny their students the challenges that help them learn. Throughout middle childhood and beyond, children understand new concepts gradually as they gain experience using their knowledge in a variety of settings.

>>> MEMORY MAKERS <<<

Fill in each blank with an appropriate term from the following list: desirable difficulties, metalinguistic awareness, conservation of number, concrete operational, overlapping waves, working memory

1. According to Piaget's theory, children have reached the stage of concrete operations when they pass _____ tasks. *conservation of number*

2. School-aged children who fail the pendulum problem are probably in the stage of _____ thought. *concrete operational*

3. Increased processing speed, strategy use, and more knowledge are all reasons why _____ increases during the school years. *working memory*

4. The theory that says that individual children use a variety of strategies at any given age is called _____ theory. *overlapping waves*

5. The ability to reflect on language as an object is _____ *metaling*

6. Learning features that slow initial learning in order to build longer-lasting knowledge are called _____. *desirable d*

[1-conservation of number; 2-concrete operational; 3-working memory; 4-overlapping waves; 5-metalinguistic awareness; 6-desirable difficulties]

Emotional and Social Development

According to Erik Erikson, children from 6 years of age until puberty are in the phase of **industry versus inferiority**: They have only a few short years to learn what they need to become productive adults, so they are intrigued by the world of knowledge and work. Children want to master the technologies of their cultures, and they monitor how successful they are. During this stage, emotional and social development are as important as cognitive development is. When children succeed, Erikson said, they develop a sense of mastery and competence; when they fail, they feel inadequate and inferior (Erikson, 1950; Lerner, 2002).

Frederick Douglass's drive to read and write—which you read about in our opening story—illustrates how important mastery is to children. During the school years, children begin comparing themselves to other people, so their sense of themselves and their relationships become more complicated. This is why Douglass was in agony over being a slave, was planning his escape, and was skillfully manipulating people to achieve his goal. Of course, Douglass was an exceptional child. But as you will read next, learning to cope with a more complicated emotional life is an important part of middle childhood for nearly everyone.

Children's Emotional Lives

The emotional reactions of a 12-year-old are quite different from those of a 6-year-old. Compared to their older brothers and sisters, 6-year-olds do not hold many thoughts in mind at once, are not very concerned about other people's feelings, and do not tend to dwell on what happened yesterday. So when 6-year-old

industry versus inferiority
Erikson's fourth stage of psychosocial development, from roughly 6 years of age to puberty, when children are intrigued with the world of knowledge and work, try to master the technologies of their cultures, and monitor the success of their efforts. Children who succeed develop a sense of mastery and competence; those who fail feel inadequate and inferior.

Nicolas and his sister Hannah fought bitterly over the last piece of cake, Nicolas cried uncontrollably but perked up as soon as his mother gave him half a piece. In contrast, 12-year-old Hannah was happy to have some cake yet annoyed at her brother at the same time. She also worried that she had acted immaturely, so she volunteered to wash the dishes to redeem herself. As you will read next, 12-year-olds are more likely than younger children to feel multiple emotions at the same time, more likely to connect emotional reactions with their concepts of themselves, and more likely to use emotions to guide their behavior.

UNDERSTANDING AND EXPRESSING EMOTIONS. Preschoolers are often elated one moment and miserable the next. But by the school years, children maintain their thoughts and feelings for longer periods of time. Now they brood about disappointments for days or weeks, hold grudges, and eagerly anticipate future events. It is harder to distract older children from the issue of the day, though, so adults need to handle emotional situations sincerely and thoughtfully. As one college-aged daughter reminded her mother, "I remember how MAD I was that you wouldn't let me have a trampoline when I was 8 (laugh) . . . I was mad at you *for years* about that!"

In addition to holding onto emotional states for longer periods of times, children's emotional lives change in three other ways as they mature:

▶ *They come to recognize simultaneous emotions.* Young children tend to focus on one thing at a time, so they fail to realize that positive and negative emotions can occur together. As cognitive skills develop, however, children realize they can be happy and sad at the same time, but for different reasons ("I was happy I got to keep the puppy but sad my bike broke"). Then, by late childhood, they recognize multiple emotions toward the same event ("I was happy that I got a present but mad that it wasn't what I wanted") (Harter, 1999, p. 52).

▶ *They develop self-conscious emotions.* Pride, shame, and guilt are complicated feelings that involve comparing oneself to external standards and thinking about other people's reactions. Preschoolers sometimes express self-conscious emotions, but the ability to explain these emotions does not appear until middle to late childhood. In one study, for example, assistants asked children what "proud" and "ashamed" meant. The 4- and 5-year-olds knew that "proud" was a good feeling and "ashamed" was not, but they had no real understanding of these terms. Six- and 7-year-olds explained without mentioning anyone ("You're proud when something good happens like you ran a race"). In contrast, many 8- and 9-year-olds mentioned how meeting or failing to meet standards influenced themselves and others. As one child said, "I was proud of myself for getting straight As on my report card; I was real happy and my parents were happy for me too" (Harter, 1999, p. 101).

▶ *They come to understand that people may not show their true feelings.* By the early school years, children understand that outward expressions and underlying feelings are not always the same. **Cultural display rules** are social conventions for expressing feelings, such as the rule that you should act happy even when you receive a gift you don't like. Most 6-year-olds are aware of display rules, but knowledge and reasoning about these rules increase between 6 and 11 years. Compared to 6-year-olds, for example, 9-year-olds more frequently say that a child who is sad about a present would look happy to avoid hurting someone's feelings (Jones, Abbey, & Cumberland, 1998). Throughout childhood, cultural differences emerge as children adopt their groups' preferred ways of handling difficult situations

cultural display rules Social conventions for expressing feelings, such as the rule that we should act happy about receiving a gift we do not want.

Due to their growing knowledge of cultural display rules, school-aged children sometimes try to conceal their real feelings—but they don't always succeed. Is this girl really happy about her present or is she just posing for the camera?

(Cole, Bruschi, & Tamang, 2002). There are individual differences as well. As early as the preschool years, children with good effortful control are better at putting on a socially appropriate face (Kieras et al., 2005).

Child psychologists describe the period from 8 to 11 years as time of relative calm. Children at this age have some insights that help them get along with others but do not dwell on their emotional lives the way teenagers do. During middle childhood, children view emotions as side effects of efforts to master the world, not things that are especially interesting in their own right. As a result, 8-year-olds usually get bored if you ask them to sit and talk about their feelings, whereas 12-year-olds may bore *you* with details of how they reacted to their day.

FEARS AND WORRIES. Fears and worries change as children learn more about the world. Babies fear loud noises, separation from loved ones, and fearful expressions on adults' faces that indicate something is wrong. Preschoolers fear what is strange, the unknown, and the imaginary. A dark bedroom, swift movements from an unfamiliar dog, and the possibility of monsters unsettle most little ones. As they move into the school years, children fear immediate danger less often. Now fearful stimuli are increasingly abstract as children spend more time worrying about what other people think about them.

One study evaluated the fears of 7- to 18-year-olds on two occasions 3 years apart (Gullone & King, 1997). The most common fears at all ages involved death and danger-related events (being hit by a car, serious illness, etc.), although children also reported fear of the unknown (darkness, strangers, etc.), failure and criticism (failing a test, making mistakes), specific animals (bees, snakes, etc.), and a variety of psychological stressors and medical issues (having no friends, having to go to a hospital). Replicating many studies, children reported fewer fears as they grew, and girls were more fearful than boys at all ages. But psychological stressors and medical fears were an exception to the general finding that fear subsides with age. Fear of such things as losing friends and having to talk in front of a class increased after age 10, when children become more concerned about fitting in with the crowd.

In summary, all children fear death and danger, and after age 10 they spend more time than before worrying about how they fit into their social environments. Because most fears are short-lived, there is usually no need to worry about a child's fears. However, some unusually fearful children are at risk for developing anxiety disorders, and many of these children show problems by middle childhood. For example, the average age at which children develop irrational fears of specific things or situations, which are called *phobias*, is 6 to 8 years (Vasey & Ollendick, 2000). Children who are afraid of taking tests, medical checkups, or other situations may become worse if adults act anxiously themselves or allow them to avoid specific situations. Instead, it is good for children to learn that people control anxiety by distracting themselves and facing small challenges ("Go ahead into your flute lesson—you'll be fine").

EMOTIONAL INTELLIGENCE. Most people distinguish between "book smarts" and "street smarts." Street-smart individuals can "read" people well and skillfully influence other people's behavior. (Frederick Douglass, for example, used street smarts to gain book smarts.) After psychologist and journalist Daniel Goleman published a book on this topic in 1995, popular culture quickly latched onto the term **emotional intelligence (EI)** to describe the skills that help people manage their emotions and respond to other people's emotional needs.

Although people like the concept of EI, there is no agreement about what EI actually is. Some theorists view EI as a trait that is relatively stable across situations. For others, EI is a set of skills that develops as a result of past experiences. Finally, EI may not be anything concrete at all but merely the name for a field of study that explores emotionally relevant cognitions and behaviors (Zeidner et al., 2003). Despite a lack of consensus, however, there is surprising overlap in the skills people mention when they talk about EI. According to one model (Mayer, Salovey, & Caruso, 2000), EI is best defined by the abilities to:

▶ **Accurately perceive and express feelings.** Emotionally intelligent children and adults are in touch with their own emotional states and good at detecting other people's emotional states.

▶ **Use emotional information to inform thoughts and opinions.** Emotionally intelligent people use emotional information to help them attend to what is important and to think about things from a different perspective.

▶ **Understand the causes and consequences of emotions.** Emotionally intelligent people can interpret the significance of a situation for everyone involved. For example, 12-year-old Hannah understood that the fight over cake might make her mother less tolerant of her for the rest of the night.

▶ **Manage emotions.** Emotionally intelligent people react to emotional information in constructive ways. They consider possible reactions and act in ways that promote positive feelings. For example, Hannah avoided her brother for the rest of the evening to avoid another fight.

Emotional intelligence helps people maintain friendships during the school years, avoid unnecessary risks during adolescence, and achieve relationship and job success as adults (Hubbard & Dearing, 2004; Kunnanatt, 2004; Trinidad et al., 2004). But some children fail to develop these skills on their own. To help, many schools are building social skills training into their curricula. For example, a program called PATHS (Promoting Alternative Thinking Strategies) provides teachers with prepared units that help them discuss self-control (how to "stop and think"), feelings and relationships (including emotional vocabulary and how our behavior influences other people's emotions), and interpersonal problem solving (how to identify the problem, generate solutions, and plan a course of action). The PATHS program improves social problem solving, reduces misbehavior, and promotes a better classroom atmosphere (Greenberg & Kusché, 2006). Similar programs have also produced increases in prosocial behavior that can last for years (Topping, Holmes, & Bremner, 2000).

emotional intelligence Skills that help people manage their emotions and respond to other people's emotional needs.

Emotional intelligence helps children control their own emotions, console friends, and work through disputes.

Learning about Themselves

If you ask children to write descriptions of themselves, you will probably get responses like these (Montemayor & Eisen, 1977):

[9-year-old boy] My name is Bruce C. I have brown eyes. I have brown hair. I have brown eyebrows. . . . I LOVE! Sports. I have seven people in my family. I have great! eye site. I have lots! of friends. I live on 1923 Pinecrest Dr.

[11-year-old girl] My name is A. I'm a human being. I'm a girl. I'm a truthful person. I'm not pretty. I do so-so in my studies. I'm a very good cellist. I'm a very good pianist . . . I try to be helpful. I'm always ready to be friends with anybody. Mostly I'm good but I lose my temper. (pp. 317–318)

As you can see, children's descriptions become more complicated over time. Older children form generalizations ("I'm a truthful person"), hold multiple pieces of information in mind, and are more likely than younger children to contrast their appearances and abilities with those of other children. More complex thinking produces three major changes in children's concepts of themselves (Harter, 2003; Thompson, 1999). First, children pay more attention to abilities and personality traits as they age. Preschoolers describe themselves by mentioning concrete attributes, such as physical characteristics, possessions, and activities they enjoy. In contrast, older children describe themselves in terms of trait-like competencies and qualities, such as "smart" or "bossy."

A second change is that children distinguish among various domains* of competency as they grow, such as skill in math versus writing and behavior in different settings. Gradually they begin to form a coherent picture of themselves that includes opposing information, so they know they can be smart *and* dumb (depending on the subject), coordinated *and* uncoordinated. Developmental psychologist Susan Harter and her colleagues found that 8-eight-year-olds usually mentioned opposing traits in different domains, such as academic versus social ("You could say something really smart in school but be really dumb with your friends, acting like a jerk") (Harter, 1999, p. 50). Children from 9 to 10 years gave more examples within the same domain. For example, they mentioned being smart in one subject in school but dumb in another. By 11 to 12 years, self-descriptions became even more differentiated, so children could talk about how they understood one part of science but not another.

Finally, self-esteem declines for many children between the first and third grades. The term **self-esteem** refers to global evaluation of oneself, such as whether one is generally a worthwhile and competent individual. Self-esteem drops as children begin to compare themselves to peers, schools provide feedback on their academic abilities, and parents become more critical than they were a few years ago (Abe & Izard, 1999). Unlike self-esteem, **self-concept** refers to self-evaluations of specific competencies, such as math ability or physical appearance.

self-esteem Individuals' global (overall) evaluation of their self-worth.

self concept Individuals' evaluation of their worth in specific domains, such as physical appearance, academic ability, or social skill.

*domains: Spheres of knowledge or activity.

Self-concepts vary across domains, improving for some characteristics and declining for others. Regarding appearance, for example, Figure 8.10 shows that boys and girls rank themselves comparably in the third grade, but girls' self-concepts begin a steep decline shortly afterwards. Around age 8, children start developing strategies for preserving self-worth, such as valuing domains where they can succeed (Cole et al., 2001).

People who work with children are often troubled by downturns in self-esteem. During the 1980s, a popular school of thought held that low self-esteem was behind numerous social woes, including underachievement, teen pregnancy, and child abuse (Branden, 1984). There were two assumptions behind this self-esteem movement. Because self-esteem is correlated with intelligence, popularity, and other positive characteristics, some professionals thought that raising self-esteem would lead children to do better in school and act more responsibly. They also believed that the way to raise self-esteem was to give children positive feedback, most often in the form of frequent praise. By the late 1990s, however, both assumptions were challenged by the following evidence (Baumeister et al., 2003):

▶ **Self-esteem is not strongly related to positive attributes.** It is true that people with high self-esteem also tend to rate themselves highly on physical attractiveness, intelligence, and other desirable characteristics. But high ratings are by-products of self-esteem, not a cause of it. For instance, there is not a strong relationship between self-esteem and attractiveness when attractiveness is measured by having peers rate photographs of people.

▶ **There is little evidence that low self-esteem causes undesirable behavior.** A team of Norwegian investigators found that doing well in sixth grade was associated with higher self-esteem the next year, but high self-esteem in the sixth grade was associated with *lower* academic achievement in the seventh grade (Skaalvik & Hagtvet, 1990). These and other findings suggest that doing well promotes high self-esteem, not the reverse.

▶ **Efforts to promote desirable behavior by increasing self-esteem have generally failed.** Programs that make people feel good about themselves without having to work often remove the motivation to work (Baumeister et al., 2003).

Under the weight of these findings, scientists have concluded that achievement and success with peers lead to high self-esteem. Therefore, experts advise adults to promote positive self-concepts by helping children learn what they need to succeed (DeRosier & Marcus, 2005). People of all ages feel good about themselves when they contribute to family and community life, master new tasks, and have good interactions with friends. Furthermore, children develop a sense of **self-efficacy**—the belief that they have the skill to achieve specific goals—by putting forth effort and doing well (Bandura, 1995). Adults foster persistence when they set developmentally appropriate goals, encourage children to work through difficulties, and avoid excessive, meaningless praise that dilutes the value of hard-earned praise. To read more about praise, turn to the next *Solutions* feature entitled "Praising Children: Is Mississippi Almost the Capital of Spain?"

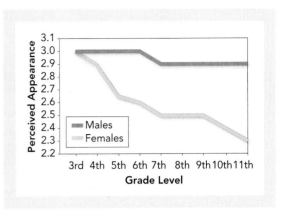

FIGURE 8.10 Children's perceptions of their physical appearance.

In the third grade, boys and girls are equally satisfied with their physical appearance, but girls' ratings drop steeply during the school years. Girls who base their self-worth on perceptions of physical appearance are more likely than their peers to suffer from low self-esteem and depression.

SOURCE: Harter (1999).

Children develop a sense of self-efficacy—the belief that they have the skill to achieve goals—by putting forth effort and doing well.

self-efficacy The belief that one has the skill to achieve specific goals. (*Efficacy* means "having the power to produce a desired effect.")

How can we raise motivated children? Praise is motivating when it is truthful, leads children to attribute success to factors they can control, and communicates reasonable expectations. "That is the best job you've done cleaning your room this month!" is more motivating than saying, "Thank you for trying!" to a child who didn't work very hard.

Praising Children: Is Mississippi Almost the Capital of Spain?

Children like it when you tell them they are wonderful—don't they? After listening to her son talk about school, writer Melissa Fay Greene (2000) decided that the answer is, "Not always":

> "You act just like most of my teachers," my son Lee complained during fifth grade, when I went in weekly to read novels to his class. "You never tell a kid he's wrong. You say, 'Who knows the capital of Spain' and someone says, 'Mississippi' and you say, 'Almost!'" Lee's favorite teacher, by contrast, would say bluntly, "No. Wrong," and call on the next arm-waving kid. She is the only teacher Lee has ever had like that. She was his favorite. (p. 80)

College students feel the same way Lee did—they want the truth, even though it might be painful at first. For example, one professor told her class that everyone would see a lot of comments on their paper drafts. "The amount of red won't show how you rank against other students," she said. "This is about how *you* can become better." Many of her students were upset by this process, but they flocked to thank her at the end of the semester. As one student explained, "Other teachers never spend any time with us, but you cared."

In the past, praise was considered emotional money in the bank, a direct route to higher self-esteem and a reservoir of good feelings that children draw upon to get them through hard times and disappointments. One teacher education student was actually told, "There's no need to ever to tell a child he or she has given a wrong answer. You should say, 'That's the right answer, but to a different question'" (Greene, 2000). As appealing as such a positive approach is, there's just one problem with having a perpetual cheering section: According to recent research, it doesn't work.

Praise starts to backfire around the third grade, when children realize that effort and ability influence performance. At this age, praise for performance that doesn't warrant praise conveys the message that adults must not have been expecting very much. For example, when 4- through 12-year-olds saw a videotape of students solving a problem, younger children believed the praised students had higher ability, whereas older students thought the reverse (perhaps because they assumed the adult was trying to motivate less capable students) (Barker & Graham, 1987).

Another reason praise does not always work is that it can interfere with **intrinsic motivation**, our internal drive to engage in a behavior. Suppose you are part of a cleanup day at your local park. You and your friends spend the day picking up litter, pruning bushes, and planting flowers. As you are admiring your work at the end of the day, someone comes along and says they will pay you $20 to do the same thing next weekend at

intrinsic motivation The desire to do something because you want to, not because you are encouraged or forced to.

another park. Would you feel as motivated if you were working for pay? Probably not. Praise can backfire in a similar way. In one demonstration, adults praised a group of children for drinking a novel yogurt drink while others were praised for unrelated behavior. Both groups liked the new beverage equally well at the beginning of the study, but children who were praised liked it less by the end (Birch, Marlin, & Rotter, 1984). Apparently, rewards can sabotage intrinsic motivation.

There are also risks from overemphasizing how much talent children have. Young children sometimes perform better when adults tell them they are capable, but praising older children's ability can lead them to think that effort is unimportant. For example, fifth graders who were praised for ability ("You must be smart at these problems") were less persistent in the face of failure than peers who had been praised for effort ("You must have worked hard on these problems") (Mueller & Dweck, 1998). Conversely, an overemphasis on effort can lead children to assume they lack ability (Henderlong & Lepper, 2002). It is no wonder why East Asian cultures have long assumed that frequent praise can harm a child's character (Salili, 1996). Often, pride from accomplishment is the reward children crave the most.

Should adults unplug the praise dispenser? Not entirely. Praise encourages achievement when it is sincere, leads children to attribute performance to factors they can control, and communicates reasonable expectations (Henderlong & Lepper, 2002). Adults provide this type of feedback when they say, "This is the best picture of the three—I can tell you worked harder on this picture." However, constant praise can make children overly self-conscious and interfere with learning. Ultimately, even the most naive 8-year-old will figure out that Mississippi isn't close to Spain.

Moral Development

Many adults assume that children are uninterested in moral issues. Surely, they think, a fourth or sixth grader is too young to care about courage or whether someone has made the right choice. But adults who know that children don't dwell on such things sometimes underestimate children's interest in moral discussions. Child psychiatrist Robert Coles learned this lesson when he taught a unit on the founding of America to a fourth-grade class. As you might expect, some children were paying attention while others were clearly bored. "I want to unite them in passionate interest," Coles said, "and so I resort to stories, show pictures, use maps. Suddenly a girl does my work for me with this question: 'In those boats [that brought the first settlers here], do you think the people were happy to be there?'" (Coles, 1997, pp. 117–120).

Falling back on his psychiatric training, Coles asked, "What do you all think?" The girl responded, "I was wondering if the Pilgrims, once they were aboard the ships, and once they were out to sea, if they thought to themselves: we did the best thing, we made the right decision."

"Now the class caught fire," Coles recalled. One girl explained, "When you do something you know is right to do, you feel glad that you made the right choice, and you're going to be happy, even if the result is a lot of pain and trouble." There was a flurry of hands as children competed to talk about how people live their values. They talked about how the Pilgrims must have been scared yet happy to be seeking religious freedom. They talked about the meaning of "courage" and whether faith was demonstrated by beliefs or actions. Coles was amazed. "An elementary school child shows a capacity for probing moral analysis," he later wrote.

Even though children lack the type of abstract thinking needed to fully understand the logic of science experiments or systems of government, they can be remarkably insightful about real-life situations that relate to their own concerns about getting along with others. For example, young children are fascinated by fairness and are more than willing to argue about basic moral principles. As Coles concluded, "This is the time for growth of the moral imagination" (p. 98).

THINKING ABOUT FAIRNESS. School-aged children love to shout, "No fair," but their perceptions of fairness are linked to their expectations about cooperation and sharing. In one family, where children are expected to help care for their younger brothers and sisters, it is fair to ask them to give up a day of play if their mother is busy; in another, a mother who leaves her toddler with an older sibling is being unfair. Yet despite some differences in *how* people cooperate, the *expectation* that people will cooperate with others and be fair is universal. The importance of moral obligation is clear by how early children attend to what is fair. For instance, one father we know was so tired of his children fighting over who had more pistachio nuts that he sorted them one by one into bowls, only to watch his children argue about who had the plumpest nuts.

Children's ideas about fairness change as growing mental powers advance their moral reasoning. Recall from Chapter 6 that school-aged children typically have a *morality of constraint* when they begin school. At this stage of life, children respect rules but tend to see them as absolute. As a result, the young school-aged child usually feels strongly about treating everyone the same—regardless of the circumstances. For example, when researchers ask children to distribute money a class has earned, kindergarteners want to give everyone the same amount—even if some of the children had worked harder or others were poor. Children become more flexible after they develop a *morality of cooperation* during middle to late childhood (generally by the age of 10 or 11). They still often vote to distribute earnings equally (McGillicuddy-De Lisi, Watkins, & Vinchur, 1994), but now they sometimes take circumstances into account and give some people more than others (Sigelman & Waitzman, 1991). These older children also understand that rules can be altered when people agree to do so, and they enjoy debating principles. We will revisit moral reasoning in Chapter 10 when we consider Lawrence Kohlberg's famous theory.

ENCOURAGING SHARING AND COOPERATION. It is one thing to ask children how to distribute resources but quite another to watch how they actually do it. Consider the following interaction, which was recorded by one of psychologist William Damon's graduate students in a pizza parlor. The story began as a waiter delivered pizza to seven children in hockey uniforms (Damon, 1988):

> **Child 1:** Heh, there's eight pieces here. What about the extra piece?
>
> **Child 2:** The guy who's the oldest should get it. How old are you?
>
> **Child 1:** Nine.
>
> **Child 3:** I'm nine and a quarter.
>
> **Child 1:** My birthday's coming up this summer. I'm—I'll be ten in one, two months.
>
> **Child 2 (to Child 4):** How old are you?
>
> **Child 4:** Eleven, and I'll be twelve next month.
>
> **Child 2:** Well, I'm twelve, so I'll get the extra piece.
>
> **Child 1:** What about giving it to the one with the small piece?

Child 4: Well who's got the smallest piece?

Child 1: I've got the smallest piece—look at it!

Child 2: C'mom, let's cut it. The oldest kids will get one piece and the kid with the smallest piece will get one piece. (p. 44)

After some debate, Child 3 jumped up and began picking cheese off the extra piece, which prompted other children to start grabbing hunks. Why is this interaction so typical of middle childhood? Unlike preschoolers, the children did not grab at the beginning; instead, they searched for a *principle* to justify their actions. But they were not lacking in self-interest because they suggested principles that served themselves. (Child 2 was the oldest, and Child 1 had the smallest piece.) In the end, though, the dilemma was resolved by grabbing, not by a democratic process. In other words, children have the potential for unselfish behavior, yet they still often disappoint adults.

What distinguishes children who comfort, help, and share from those who are less concerned about other people? Prosocial children (those who are likely to help) tend to be competent, advanced in moral reasoning, and good at imagining themselves in other people's shoes. Their parents model prosocial behavior, talk about the influence of one person's behavior on another's, and include children in helping activities without forcing them to participate (Eisenberg & Valiente, 2002). Even the most kind and generous child is sometimes heartless and selfish, however. Altruism is more likely to shine through when children are happy, pleased with themselves, and helping someone they like or someone who has helped them (Eisenberg & Mussen, 1989).

During the early school years, children enjoy doing something practical for people they know. After the first or second grade, their ability to feel other people's pain is less tied to their own experiences, and they feel empathy about broad situations such as poverty. This is why older children are more enthusiastic about community projects that benefit distant people who are grappling with unfamiliar circumstances. For example, in the aftermath of the tsunami disaster in December 2004, 8-year-old twins Themio and George Pallis delivered $5,660 to an aid organization that helped children affected by the tsunami. These special brothers were among the tens of thousands of children worldwide who worked for money and collected donations to benefit children abroad ("American Students Respond," 2005). School-aged children's growing ability to feel for others also means they are better friends, which influences how they play with each other.

Peers and Play

Over 25 years ago, psychologists made two fascinating discoveries about the importance of peer interactions. First, troubled relationships with peers predict a host of adjustment problems during adolescence and young adulthood. For example, children who are rejected by their peers are at risk for delinquency and dropping out of high school, and they are overrepresented in adult psychiatric populations, military bad-conduct discharges, and adult suicides (Kelly & Hansen, 1987). Second, children are sometimes more accurate than teachers or mental health workers at predicting which children in a classroom will have troubled lives (Kohlberg et al., 1972). Apparently, adults focus on behavior that worries adults, such as shyness or nervousness, rather than behavior that bothers other children, such as acting hostile or making irrelevant comments. These discoveries sparked curiosity about how children form good relationships and why some children fail.

Many children raised money for tsunami victims after the December, 2004 disaster. Natural disasters are frightening to children but, as you can see from their faces, they take pride in helping others.

THE IMPORTANCE OF FRIENDSHIP. One way to find out what friendship means to children is simply to ask, "What is a best friend?" or "What do you expect from a best friend?" Children's answers evolve from an early focus on concrete attributes to a focus on abstract qualities. At 7 or 8 years, children say that friends are those who live nearby, play with them, and have interesting toys. By 10 or 11 years they mention shared values, and they expect loyalty and mutual support from a friend. After the age of 11, friendship is cemented by similar interests and the exchange of thoughts and feelings (Rubin et al., 1999). For example, 11-year-old Angela said that a friend was "someone who likes to do the stuff I want to do. When they sleep over we stay up late and talk about school all night." As the basis for friendship deepens, children demonstrate more knowledge about their friends, so older children know more than younger children about their friends' likes, dislikes, and typical emotional responses (Diaz & Berndt, 1982). The sample responses in Table 8.2 illustrate these developments.

Children, like adults, tend to be attracted to people who are similar to themselves (Dunn, 2004b). One reason friends tend to resemble one another is that neighborhood families often share economic, ethnic, and educational circumstances. Also, observable characteristics are important to children, so they naturally gravitate to peers who are the same sex and age as themselves. As concepts of friendship develop, similarity among friends increases. By late childhood, friends tend to share personality traits, such as shyness, and they are more

TABLE 8.2 The Development of Friendship

Age	Interview responses	Characteristics of friendship
5 years	Do you have lots of friends? *Chris, Amy, Paula, Bart, and Kevin.* How did you get so many friends? *I got them when I moved into this class.* Are all of your friends in this class? *Yes.* Who's your best friend in your class? *Amy.* Why is Amy your best friend? *I like her. I knew her in . . . Head Start and I knew her before I came to school.* How did you meet Amy? *We sat on the bus, we played together . . .* How do you make a friend? *You say, "Hi, what's your name," and that's all.*	Preschool children have loosely structured networks of play partners. They consider many children friends and often choose best friends based on physical proximity.
8 years	Who's your best friend? *Shelly.* Why is Shelly your best friend? *Because she helps me when I'm getting beaten up, she cheers me up when I'm sad, and she shares . . .* What makes Shelley so special? *I've known her longer, I sit next to her and got to know her better . . .* How come you like Shelly better than anyone else? *She's done the most for me. She never disagrees, she never eats in front of me, she never walks away when I'm crying, and she helps me on my homework.*	School-aged children are more choosy about playmates. Now they describe friendship as an enduring relationship in which people share and help one another. Girls have more close friends than boys do, but boys have larger social networks.
11 years	Who's your best friend? *Carol, but she lives far away.* Why is Carol your best friend? *She's not snobby or bratty, so we like to play together.* Could you and Carol ever stop being friends? *Maybe, but we don't let silly little things break up our friendship . . .* What is a good friend like? *A person who's not snobby and plays what you want to play. Someone who does what both of you want to do . . .* What do good friends do? *They help you with your problems, they help you meet new people, they play with you, they stay with you, and they do lots of things.*	By late childhood, it is important for friends to share interests and values. Friends are intimate, trusting partners who share their problems and concerns. Now children's peer groups have distinctive cultures involving nicknames, styles of dress, and unspoken rules for how members are expected to behave toward one another.

SOURCES: Berndt (1996); Dunn (2004b); Rubin et al. (1999); interview responses from Damon (1977, pp. 155–163).

alike than nonfriends in popularity and academic achievement (Chen et al., 2005; Hartup, 1996).

Most children have one or more best friends and, by late childhood, are part of a **peer group** that includes children who do not necessarily consider each other best friends. Peer groups tend to be organized in a hierarchical fashion, one in which some children have more power than others and roles govern how children interact with one another as leaders and followers (Rubin et al., 1999). If you observe these groups, you will notice that members convey shared values by dressing alike, using nicknames, and assuming a special vocabulary that identifies them as a group. Creative children some-times form clubs or invent secret activities that emphasize their special connection to each other. For instance, these chil-dren might make up a word that means "my parents are listening" or agree to wear similar clothes.

By late childhood, most children want to look and act like others in their peer group.

Children, like the rest of us, act differently with friends (Newcomb & Bagwell, 1995):

▶ *Interactions among friends are punctuated with talking, smiling, and laughter.* This atmosphere provides emotional support and helps children cope with stress. In fact, older children say they get more companionship and intimacy from friends than they do from their parents or siblings (Underwood & Hurley, 1999).

▶ *Children work to resolve disputes with friends in ways that will preserve the relationship.* This does not mean that friends avoid conflict; indeed, children frequently have disputes with their friends. But compared to interactions with nonfriends, children are more likely to empathize with friends, assume some responsibility for misunderstandings, and negotiate solutions both parties can accept. In fact, it is with friends that children begin to learn these skills.

▶ *The familiarity fostered by friendship encourages children to work together as a team.* One study found that pairs of 10-year-old friends who wrote stories to ac-company a science unit repeated more of their partner's comments than nonfriends did, spent twice as much time talking about the project, and wrote better stories. Eleven-year-olds in another study solved a higher percentage of difficult scientific problems when they were friends, even though they disagreed more often with one another (Zajac & Hartup, 1997).

These findings show that friendship gives children a chance to practice social skills that are not emphasized in other types of relationships (Hartup, 1996). For example, interactions with adults provide fewer opportunities to compromise or cooperate with someone who does not already know the an-swer. Similarly, siblings will continue to be siblings even if children act like monsters, so there is little reason to practice one's best behavior with them. Among friends, though, children are motivated to put their best foot forward, swallow their pride occasionally, and enjoy the gift of creating and exploring among equals.

peer group A social unit, often consisting of leaders and followers, that generates shared values and standards of behavior.

PEER STATUS. Even in elementary school, children have no trouble identifying who is "in" and who is not. In fact, social status—what psychologists call *peer status*—is so important that many of us remember school cliques dozens of years later.

One way scientists map social relationships is to ask children to list the peers they like and dislike. These nominations tend to place children into one of five status groups (Cillessen & Mayeux, 2004):

▶ *Popular children* receive many positive nominations and few negative nominations.

▶ *Rejected children* receive many negative nominations and few positive nominations.

▶ *Neglected children* receive few positive or negative nominations.

▶ *Controversial children* receive many positive nominations but also many negative nominations.

▶ *Average children* do not receive an extreme number of positive or negative nominations.

Across studies, about 11 percent of children are popular, 13 percent are rejected, 9 percent are neglected, 7 percent are controversial, and 60 percent are average.

In an early study to compare these groups, developmental psychologist Kenneth Dodge (1983) brought unacquainted second-grade boys together for eight play sessions. Boys who became unpopular (rejected or neglected) tended to act inappropriately by standing on tables or disrupting activities in other ways. These boys were not shy, but continual rebuffs from their peers eventually caused them to withdraw. Dodge described these children as "moving frequently from peer to peer in search of a play partner, but failing to find one" (p. 1396). Rejected boys were also more aggressive than boys who were simply neglected. In contrast, popular boys did not initiate interactions frequently, but when they did they were cooperative, able to play well with others, and good at maintaining interactions with social conversation. Controversial boys were even more overtly friendly than popular boys, but they often made aggressive comments, annoying sounds, and were generally unpredictable.

Why do some children have trouble fitting in? Before answering, we need to mention that all children find it remarkably difficult to infiltrate peer activities. Popular second and third graders are rejected or ignored over 25 percent of the time they approach peers, and children rarely do anything to put other children at ease (Putallaz & Wasserman, 1990). Socially skilled children learn they will not be immediately accepted, so they adopt strategies to increase their chances of success. These children often hang back at first to observe what is going on and then act in ways that mimic the group's behavior before trying to become involved. In other words, popular children blend in while they figure out the norms of the group rather than drawing attention to themselves. Other children have trouble entering a group because they do not perceive the ongoing activity and fail to make relevant contributions. Children's success at entering a group is such a powerful predictor of future popularity that one researcher was able to correctly predict a child's peer status simply by analyzing only 5 minutes of their group entry behavior recorded 4 months earlier (Putallaz, 1983).

Aggression increases the chances of rejection but mainly when hostility is not offset by socially appropriate behavior. Rejected children who are not aggressive are often immature or withdrawn (Rubin et al., 1999). Because they seem to lack the social antennae necessary to pick up on the behavior of their peers,

popular children Children who receive many positive nominations and few negative nominations when their peers indicate whom they like and dislike. (See *rejected, neglected,* and *controversial* children.)

rejected children Children who receive many negative nominations and few positive nominations when their peers indicate whom they like and dislike. (See *popular, neglected,* and *controversial* children.)

neglected children Children who receive few positive *or* negative nominations when their peers indicate whom they like and dislike. (See *popular, rejected,* and *controversial* children.)

controversial children Children who receive many positive nominations but also many negative nominations when their peers indicate whom they like and dislike. (See *popular, rejected,* and *neglected* children.)

rejected children tend to recreate their unpleasant status over and over again (Coie & Kupersmidt, 1983). It is not surprising that rejected children want to avoid school, score lower than other status groups on measures of school achievement (Buhs & Ladd, 2001), and are more likely than other children to have problems with the law 7 years later (Morison & Masten, 1991). In contrast, children who are viewed by their peers as sociable leaders later score better than other groups on numerous outcomes, including academic achievement, job performance, and social competence. Table 8.3 summarizes the characteristics and consequences of peer status categories.

TABLE 8.3   Peer Status

Status	Number of Peer Nominations		Behavioral Profile	Developmental Implications
	LIKE	DISLIKE		
Popular	High	Low	✦ Highly sociable and with good social problem-solving skills ✦ Score well on measures of academic achievement and intellectual ability ✦ Can be assertive but are not especially aggressive ✦ Willing to offer emotional support to others	Popular children have optimistic futures. They tend to be bright and socially-skilled, so they perform well in school and have rewarding relationships.
Rejected	Low	High	✦ May be overly aggressive or withdrawn ✦ Have difficulty perceiving a group's ongoing activity and making a relevant contribution ✦ Often score lower than average on tests of cognitive ability	Rejected children are at risk for negative outcomes. They are more likely than other children to do poorly in school, drop out of school, abuse drugs or alcohol, and commit crimes. Aggressive-rejected children are more likely than nonaggressive children to remain rejected over time.
Neglected	Low	Low	✦ Less aggressive and sociable than average children ✦ Not very familiar to their classmates because they are not very sociable	Neglected children do not act much differently than average children, and many change their peer status after they move into a new environment. Loneliness is a persistent problem for some of these children.
Controversial	High	High	✦ Show behaviors typical of popular *and* rejected children ✦ Are disruptive and sometimes aggressive but compensate by being sociable ✦ Score higher on tests of cognitive ability than rejected children	Controversial children are at risk for lower grades in later school years and teenage pregnancy.

SOURCES: Cillessen et al. (1992); Newcomb, Bukowski, & Pattee (1993); Rubin et al. (1999); Underwood, Kupersmidt, & Coie (1996); Wentzel (2003).

Hostility is a fact of life during middle and late childhood, so it helps if children have had some practice thinking of better ways to handle themselves when tempers flare.

Psychologists recommend starting interventions for rejected children early, before they develop reputations that will be difficult to change. Successful programs teach children the skills their popular classmates use, such as how to comment on ongoing play, how to ask questions in a neutral tone, and how to deal with anger (Conduct Problems Prevention Research Group, 2004; Mize & Ladd, 1990). All of these skills help prevent an unsettling side of peer interactions: hostile behavior toward other children.

HOSTILE BEHAVIOR. As you probably remember from your own childhood years, it is not uncommon for children to say mean things to each other and act cruelly. Aggressive behavior is especially likely to occur during the middle school years, when the blending of children from different schools threatens the stability of peer groups. In one midwestern middle school, for example, 80 percent of the students said they had participated in teasing, name-calling, threatening, physical aggression, and ridiculing of peers during the previous 30 days (Asidao, Vion, & Espelage, 1999). And in a Los Angeles middle school, 46 percent of sixth graders reported experiencing some type of peer harassment in a single 4-day period (Nishina & Juvonen, 2005). After middle school, as friendship networks stabilize again, aggression decreases but remains a disturbing reality for many children (Pellegrini & Long, 2002).

Even when children are not battling it out on the playground, it is extremely common for them to have *mutual antipathies*, that is, to dislike children who dislike them. Not surprisingly, the more popular a child is, the fewer people he or she mutually dislikes. A survey of 8-year-olds found that 32 percent of popular children, 70 percent of average children, and 95 percent of socially rejected children had mutual animosities toward another child. Children who report a lot of antipathies are more likely to be viewed as aggressive and socially inept by their peers, and they are more likely to describe themselves as a "bully"—a child who is repeatedly cruel to other children (Abecassis et al., 2002). To read what we can do to help bullies and their victims, turn to our next *Innovations* feature entitled "Bullying: The Dark Side of Peer Relations."

INNOVATIONS

One way to improve children's lives is to translate research findings on the nature and causes of problem behavior into interventions that help prevent problem behavior. Research on bullying behavior in school and the parenting characteristics associated with prosocial behavior have helped experts design school-based interventions that reduce the amount of bullying behavior children experience.

BULLYING: THE DARK SIDE OF PEER RELATIONS

// My name is Jeff Williams," the man told police officers after he arrived at a California high school. "Apparently my son did this" (Roth, 2001, para. 34).

Jeff and his son, Andy, had moved to Santana, California, from Maryland only a year earlier. Soon Jeff was being teased at school for his accent and clothes. Still, his father was unaware that anything was seriously wrong until March 5, 2001, when the 15-year-old took a .22-caliber handgun from his father's gun cabinet and killed two students in a fit of revenge. "It was just too much," Mr. Williams said about the physical assaults against his son (Roth, 2001, para. 2). Prosecutors disagreed. According to other students, Andy had experienced only the usual taunting the students had all come to accept—nothing that would explain away his actions. A jury agreed, and Andy was sentenced as an adult to 50 years to life in prison.

A stream of school shootings has forever changed how society views bullying. In the past, adults considered peer aggression an unpleasant but harmless side of childhood. The stereotype of a bully was a tall, strong boy who used physical force to intimidate boys who could not retaliate. Ironically, bullies often received as much sympathy as their victims because adults assumed they were suffering from poor home lives and low self-esteem. As research on bullying accumulated, though, none of these stereotypes has survived.

The "big-sad-boy" stereotype has been replaced by a more complicated picture of bullying. Researchers have found that an alarming percentage of children engage in bullying—including girls (Putallaz & Bierman, 2004). Moreover, bullies use a range of strategies to intimidate peers, not just physical aggression. Finally, there is not a straightforward relationship between poor self-esteem and aggression, and bullying is far from harmless (Bushman & Baumeister, 1998). The following findings have helped experts design recommendations and school-based interventions to help prevent bullying behavior.

★ **There is a bullying continuum.** It is not easy to identify bullies and victims because children bully to varying degrees, and many bullies are also victims (Rigby, 2005; Unnever, 2005). Studies have found that teachers can identify bullies only about 50 percent of the time and can pinpoint victims only about 10 percent of the time (Paulk et al., 1999). For this reason, interventions that treat only children referred for help will miss students who need help. More successful are programs with "all school" approaches that discuss bullying with the entire student body (Smith, Pepler, & Rigby, 2004).

★ **There is physical and relational bullying.** Some bullies use physical force and threats of violence. However, other bullies engage in relational victimization in which the bullied children are treated as outcasts and deprived of friendship. Relational victimization includes such behaviors as spreading rumors to encourage other children not to associate with a child, excluding the target child from important social gatherings, and threatening to stop associating with a friend who won't comply with demands. Boys are more likely to be victims of physical abuse, whereas some (but not all) studies have found more relational victimization among girls (Crick, Casas, & Nelson, 2002; Pepler et al., 2004). Like physically abused children, those who experience relational victimization are also at risk for depression and future rejection by peers, so efforts to reduce bullying behavior must address all behavior that threatens children's need to affiliate with others (Crick et al., 2002; Eisenberg & Aalsma, 2005).

★ **Victims are not all alike.** Some victims of bullying are anxious children who are out of step with their peers' clothing, physical appearance, or interests (Asidao, Vion, & Espelage, 1999). Other victims are irritable, hot-tempered children who provoke their peers. Instead of walking away from taunts or making a humorous comeback, these children become upset, perhaps bracing for a fight. Because aggressive victims often come from homes where they see violence modeled through physical abuse and parental conflict, bullies and victims alike benefit from programs that teach effective ways to handle peer problems (Schwartz et al., 1997).

★ **Bullying has long-term effects.** At least 9 to 10 percent of children are repeatedly teased or attacked by peers (Kochenderfer & Ladd, 1996). These children are more likely than their peers to be anxious, depressed, lonely, and unhappy in school. In fact, almost 10 percent of children say they have stayed home from school because of bullying (Slee, 1994).

Parents and schools have a role to play in preventing bullying. Bullying tends to become worse when parents are overly permissive about hostile behavior ("boys will be boys") or not very involved in their children's lives. When asked questions such as "Does your father help with your plans for the future?" and "Does your mother take an interest in your schoolwork?" the bullies in one study were more likely than other children to answer "No" (Flouri & Buchanan, 2003). In addition to monitoring their children's behavior, parents should encourage them to spend time with peers who have good social skills, because peer groups who engage in illegal or antisocial behavior can undermine the benefits of supportive parenting (Chen et al., 2005). Finally, school staff can build a safer school climate by acknowledging good behavior ("Thank you, Jeff, for picking up Leon's hat") instead of only noticing misbehavior (Flannery et al., 2003).

Some schools have experienced 30 to 70 percent reductions in bullying after they adopted innovative programs that enforce rules against aggressive behavior, increase supervision during lunchtime and recess, involve parents in handling complaints, and make efforts to establish atmospheres of warmth and concern for students (Olweus Bullying Prevention Program, 2005; Spivak & Prothrow-Stith, 2001). No one knows whether school-based programs can prevent tragedies like the one in Santana, California. What we do know is that bullying does not disappear on its own as children mature. Instead, everyone who touches children's lives has a critical role to play in making their communities safer places to live.

>>> MEMORY MAKERS <<<

1. Which of the following is a self-conscious emotion?
   (a) anger   (b) sadness   (c) shame   (d) happiness

2. A child who acts happy when he receives a disappointing gift is using _____.
   (a) simultaneous emotions   (b) industry
   (c) a cultural display rule   (d) self-efficacy

3. Your global evaluation of yourself is your _____.
   (a) self-esteem   (b) self-concept   (c) self-efficacy   (d) none of these

4. When a group of children is engaged in an activity, virtually *all* rejected children act _____.

   (a) shyly   (b) aggressively
   (c) superior to other children   (d) inappropriately

[1-c (shame involves comparing your behavior against a standard); 2-c; 3-a (self-concept is how you feel about yourself in a particular domain, such as talent in sports or math); 4-d (many—but not all—rejected children act aggressively; most are "out of sync" with the behavioral norms of their peers]

Becky's Story

Remember Becky, the 7-year-old who said, "Mommy, sometimes I think you are going to put poison in the water so you can live your own life"? Becky was just beginning her fascinating journey into middle childhood. Like many youngsters, she was starting to think about possibilities, so she was fearful about personal safety and death. Her thinking was self-centered and concrete, though, so she didn't realize how her words would hurt her mother. And unlike her mother, who would remember this episode for years to come, by morning Becky was probably absorbed with other thoughts.

What does our summary of cognitive and socioemotional development lead us to predict for Becky's future? Over the next few years, she will experience increases in working memory and a growing network of connections between the brain centers that regulate attention, problem solving, and emotion. These changes will help her think about her ideas and how they affect other people simultaneously, so she will be better able to anticipate her effect on others.

We think that Becky will have wonderful friendships because her misery at hurting her mother's feelings demonstrates the empathy she needs to maintain relationships. Soon she will be testing out more of her personal thoughts with friends rather than parents. Still, she will probably reserve the most stinging barbs for Mom and Dad because she is not afraid these relationships will end. Becky's mother can help her daughter cope with her perplexing new thoughts by taking such incidents in stride and talking about her concerns. Comments about murderous mothers are wonderful opportunities to talk about safety, family love, and the power of words.

We started this chapter with a story about Frederick Douglass to show the remarkable potential that lies within every child. Douglass made the most out of the changes that occur between 6 and 12 years of age. When he ventured into the world, he overcame enormous obstacles to learn to read and write, persisted in striving for his long-term goals, and showed the sort of clever insight into human nature that enabled him to get along with and manipulate his peers. Lives like his remind us that the roots of greatness are sprouting during childhood. However, individual lives do not unfold in a vacuum. All children are influenced by their environments, including the characteristics of their families, their neighborhoods, and their cultures. These influences are the focus of our next chapter.

>>> SUMMARY <<<

Physical Development

1. Children grow about 2 inches and $7\frac{1}{2}$ pounds per year during middle to late childhood. Those who are unusually short due to a growth-hormone (GH) deficiency can receive hormone treatments, but there is no evidence that normal-GH children benefit from treatment. School-aged children are in a final stage of motor development when they combine skills to master more demanding activities. It is best if children participate in a wide range of physical activities to build their skills.

2. School-aged children gradually become better at picking out sounds from noisy environments and focusing on moving objects. Regular vision exams are needed to detect visual problems such as myopia (blurring of distant objects, often called nearsightedness) and hyperopia (blurring of near objects, also called farsightedness). Children who spend a lot of time looking at computer screens benefit from working on low tables and having room lights that dim to reduce glare.

3. The brain is gradually remodeled during middle and late childhood. Changes include increased volume in some regions as neurons continue to myelinate and develop dendrites, tissue loss from synaptic pruning, and the integration of widely distributed brain regions. These changes improve **effortful control**, the ability to inhibit a dominant response in order to make another response.

Cognitive Development

4. School-aged children are in Piaget's stage of **concrete operations**. They think more logically about their physical worlds because they are less influenced than preschoolers by the appearance of objects. However, it will be years before they will reason systematically about abstract concepts.

5. Working memory capacity expands during middle childhood as speed of processing increases, children learn to use memory strategies (**rehearsal**, **organization**, and **elaboration**), and cognitive inhibition improves (which keeps irrelevant information from popping into mind). These advances promote better problem-solving skills.

6. Children gradually improve their pronunciation, vocabularies, and knowledge of the rules for combining words. As **metalinguistic awareness** (awareness of language)

grows, they also appreciate a broader range of jokes and puns, are more likely to understand difficult sentences, can describe things more clearly, and can vary their speech to adjust to different social situations.

7. Piaget's theory suggests four educational principles: (a) avoid material that is far above a child's current developmental level, (b) do not rush learning, (c) use concrete demonstrations, and (d) plan activities that help children to discover inconsistencies between their current level of understanding and new concepts. Quality instruction promotes *transfer of training* to new situations. One way to encourage transfer of training is to build **desirable difficulties** into instruction, that is, conditions that slow initial learning but build conceptual understanding.

Emotional and Social Development

8. Emotional life becomes more complicated as children start to integrate positive and negative feelings ("I was happy to get a present but mad it wasn't what I wanted"), reflect on why they feel proud or ashamed, and attend to **cultural display rules** (conventions for when to express emotions). They gradually become less afraid of immediate dangers and more concerned about social comparison. Adults can help children develop their emotional intelligence by teaching them to label emotions and encouraging them to think about how their actions affect other people.

9. School-aged children use trait-like terms to describe themselves ("I'm smart but lazy"), realize they have opposite traits in different domains, and experience a general decline in self-esteem. Their **self-esteem** (global evaluation of their self-worth) and **self-concepts** (self-evaluations of specific competencies) develop by comparing themselves to other people. There is little evidence that early differences in self-esteem cause differences in achievement. Rather, accomplishments help children build high self-esteem.

10. Moral reasoning develops as children begin to consider multiple pieces of information simultaneously. Young children believe in treating everyone equally, whereas older children take people's productivity, needs, and circumstances into account. Altruistic behavior increases as children internalize expectations for cooperation and sharing.

11. As children grow, their friendships become based on shared values, interests, and the exchange of feelings.

Interactions with friends provide emotional support, motivate children to resolve conflicts, and create an atmosphere that encourages cooperation. **Rejected children**—those who are disliked by their peers—are at risk for many negative outcomes, including externalizing behavior, poor academic achievement, and loneliness.

12. Children sometimes say cruel things because they have difficulty considering their ideas and the effect their words will have on people at the same time. They often reserve their most hurtful comments for parents because they are not afraid that these relationships will end.

>>>KEY TERMS<<<

effortful control   (p. 309)
concrete operational thought   (p. 311)
rehearsal   (p. 317)
organization   (p. 317)
elaboration   (p. 317)
overlapping waves theory   (p. 318)
metalinguistic awareness   (p. 320)
desirable difficulties   (p. 322)
industry versus inferiority   (p. 324)
cultural display rules   (p. 325)

emotional intelligence (EI)   (p. 327)
self-esteem   (p. 328)
self-concept   (p. 328)
self-efficacy   (p. 329)
intrinsic motivation   (p. 330)
peer group   (p. 335)
popular children   (p. 336)
rejected children   (p. 336)
neglected children   (p. 336)
controversial children   (p. 336)

MILESTONES of middle and late childhood

6 to 8 Years Children refine the skills they built during early childhood.

- As they move into the specialized movement phase, children perfect and combine motor skills for use in demanding situations, like skipping rope and playing soccer.
- Effortful control and the ability to plan are not well developed, so 6- to 8-year-olds still require a lot of supervision.
- Having entered the period of concrete operational thought, children 6 and up are able to think more logically about information they can see and touch. Nevertheless, they will not deal systematically with abstract ideas until adolescence.
- Throughout middle and late childhood, children are in Erikson's phase of industry versus inferiority, when they learn about themselves by monitoring their successes and failures.

8 to 10 Years A period of relative calm emerges, when children enjoy many types of activities.

- Fine motor and spatial skills improve as the brain continues to mature. Now children find it easier to inhibit inappropriate actions.
- Improvements in speed of processing and response inhibition lead to gradual improvements in memory and reasoning.
- As children come to grasp cultural display rules, they understand that acting appropriately means not always expressing one's true feelings.
- Children's status in a peer group is determined by how quickly they tune into social norms and how well they control inappropriate behavior.

10 to 12 Years Family is the foundation of children's lives, but friends gradually become more important.

- Older children become more passionate about activities that suit their abilities and interests.
- They become more strategic about remembering information and more likely to follow through with plans.
- In late childhood, children communicate more clearly because they can take other people's needs into account. They also become more interested in helping others.
- By the end of late childhood, children hold onto emotional reactions for longer periods of time and expect friends to share interests and feelings. Many children identify with a peer group.

Preview: Middle and late childhood in **CONTEXT**

Health and Safety

Unintentional injury is the biggest risk to children's health during middle and late childhood. Asthma, overweight, and maltreatment are other frequent problems during this period of life.

Children, Schools, and Achievement

Cultures that require children to spend a lot of time mastering academic skills have high achievement scores. Within a culture, academic achievement is associated with numerous factors, including parents' educational levels and school characteristics. Schooling is adapted for children with special academic needs, such as those with mental retardation, English language learners, and children with special gifts and talents.

Family Life
Children experience stress reactions when there is instability at home, but the quality and consistency of caregiving are more important than the structure of their families. Children adapt to a wide variety of family situations, including single-parent households, households with stepparents and stepsiblings, and households headed by same-sex parents.

Individuality
Intelligence and achievement tests are used to assess how children's cognitive performance and knowledge compare with their peers. If children have problem behaviors, professionals look at characteristics of the children and their environments to predict the likelihood that problems will persist.

Boys and girls in late childhood show many interesting differences in social behavior, achievement test performance, and rates of school-related problems.

In this next chapter, you'll learn how developmental principles explain the pathways individuals take through middle and late childhood when we consider the question:
Do parents matter?

Do parents matter?

CHAPTER NINE

Pathways through Middle and Late Childhood

Stories of Our Lives

The Lost Boys of Sudan

Alepho and Benson's story illustrates how different individual childhoods can be. In 1983, the People's Liberation Army and the Sudanese government began a war that killed over 2 million people. Alepho and Benson were "collateral damage"—children ripped from their families when troops came and relatives urged them to run (Weddle, 2003). About 17,000 children, mostly boys, tried to reach refugee camps in 1987. Seven thousand died, weakened by hunger and disease.

Alepho was only 5 years old when the conflict started; older brother Benson was 7. But in Dinka culture, Benson was old enough to tend the family's cattle, which is why he was sleeping at his uncle's house when an explosion woke him. Journalist David Weddle later told the story of their journey with cousins Lino and Benjamin (Weddle, 2003):

> The day his parents had warned him about had arrived. Government troops were methodically destroying homes, livestock and stockpiles of food. A few of the Dinka men fought back with spears, but they were quickly cut down.
>
> Benson's parents had told him to run into the forest if the soldiers came. He did, along with about 25 others, fleeing through the night and eventually joining with

This group of over three thousand Sudanese boys, some as young as 6 years, was photographed during a thousand mile trek to safety after war separated them from their families. Their courage and ability to survive reveals strengths that are not typically associated with early and middle childhood.

hundreds of refugees on a months-long journey to the Ethiopian border. His life and those of his brother and cousins over the next 16 years is a hodgepodge of memories and impressions. Their recollections, from a series of interviews provide a narrative of their African experience.

As Benson fled toward Ethiopia, he wore only lice-infested underpants; his bare feet always sore. "I used to sit alone and I don't want to talk to anybody, because I am alone," Benson recalls. "Where is my mother? Where is my father? Where am I going? Am I going to die here by myself?"

He lived in an Ethiopian refugee camp for three years, subsisting on meager handouts from relief agencies. Boys at the camp formed their own support network, sitting around the fire at night, groups of youngsters 5, 7, 10 years old, imitating the tribal gatherings of their villages. "When one of us made a mistake, the others helped him see his mistake," Benjamin says. "We became our own parents." (p. 14)

After troops forced the boys back into Sudan, the survivors formed the 10,000 "Lost Boys of Sudan." Rebel leaders picked a safe destination near relief centers in northwestern Kenya. But to get there, the children had to walk. Their path stretched through "one of the driest, most disease-ridden and worn-torn corners of the globe" (Lyman, 1992, p. 5). The Red Cross issued each boy a week of food and followed their journey, nursing weakened boys.

The children arrived in surprisingly healthy condition and lived for a decade with only limited adult supervision until agencies resettled them abroad. Benson and Alepho were airlifted to one of the states that agreed to integrate over 3,000 Lost Boys into American life ("Sudan's 'Lost Boys' Find Chicago," 2001; Weddle, 2003). The children stayed in contact with each other by meetings, phone, and e-mail, forming a peer-support network that helped them adjust to their new culture. "Ya, it's good to talk about it," one boy told a researcher who was studying how children develop without their biological families. "Sometimes it takes the stinging away from my mind" (Luster et al., 2003, p. 3).

As one relocation worker remarked, "We thought it was going to be chaos when they got here. These men never had any parents. They're all going to get into drugs. They're going to be wild; it's going to be 'Lord of the Flies'!" (Weddle, 2003, p. 15). But the boys had good English skills and a determination to better themselves. They also had deep spiritual traditions, a commitment to care for one another, and a belief in the value of education. Alepho told Weddle that he wanted a degree in biology or literature; Benson fancied computer science or drawing. And while many of the children suffered from nightmares and depression, they continued to talk about their dream: to return to Sudan one day, to be Lost Boys no more.

A FREQUENT QUESTION about the Lost Boys in our opening story is, "Where were the girls?" In traditional Sudanese villages, only boys leave home to receive an education or work; their sisters stay home until marriage. Because boys are more often killed during war, families protected their children by keeping their girls and sending their boys away (Lyman, 1992).

Today's children grow up in many different environments, from war-torn countries where some children fend for themselves to wealthy communities where adults overschedule their children's time. Some families are headed by biological mothers and fathers, others by stepparents, grandparents, adoptive and foster parents. In this chapter, you will explore some of the pathways children follow on their way to adolescence, pathways influenced by their health, the structure of their families, the nature of their schools and communities, and their individual temperaments. After you read about some of the diversity that exists during middle and late childhood, you will revisit the developmental principles from Chapter 1 in this section's featured topic, "Do Parents Matter?"

Health and Safety

Close your eyes and picture a "childhood" scene. What are you imagining? If you are thinking about bright-eyed children who are bounding with energy, there is a good reason: For most people, the period from 6 to 12 years is the healthiest time of life. As you can see in Figure 9.1, this age bracket enjoys the lowest risk of death because medical conditions that plague older people, such as heart disease and cancer, are uncommon early in life. In this chapter, you'll learn about some of the most frequent health risks during the school years, including asthma, being overweight, and maltreatment. But first, let's explore the number-one killer of children in developed countries: unintentional injuries.

Preventing Injuries

In middle childhood, injuries take more lives in industrialized countries each year (7.3 per 100,000 in the United States) than the next three most frequent causes of death combined (cancer, congenital malformations, and assault). In addition to injuries that kill, each year about 25 percent of children experience an injury that requires them to miss school, stay in bed, or receive medical treatment (National Center for Injury Prevention and Control, 2003). As we saw in the previous chapter, middle to late childhood is a time when children gain exquisite control over their bodies, but their cognitive abilities—including the ability to make sound judgments about risk—lag behind their physical prowess. Therefore, it is not obvious to them that icy stairs on a slide might be slippery, or that slamming on a bicycle brake might throw them over the handlebars. As children begin spending more time on playgrounds and exploring their neighborhoods, an increasing number of injuries involve play equipment and bicycles.

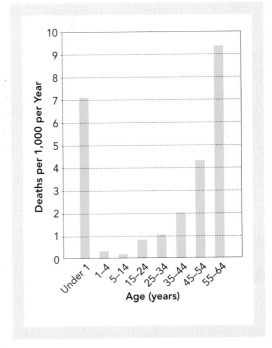

FIGURE 9.1 The healthiest time of life.

The risk of death is lower during middle childhood than in any other developmental period.

SOURCE: Hoyert et al. (2005).

PLAYGROUND SAFETY. More than 200,000 children in the United States are treated in hospital emergency rooms each year for playground-related injuries, many for serious conditions such as broken bones, damage to internal organs, and concussions (Tinsworth & McDonald, 2001). The National Program for Playground Safety (2004) recommends the following steps to make playgrounds safer:

▶ *Provide adequate adult supervision.* Poor supervision contributes to more than 40 percent of playground injuries. Adults should watch for dangerous situations and get involved when children are playing on wet equipment, pushing one another, or playing unsafely in other ways.

▶ *Direct children to age-appropriate equipment.* Equipment designed for one age group may be inappropriate for other age groups. For example, young children's hands are too small to grasp some overhead bars safely, and older children often play too roughly for younger ones. Areas designed for toddlers, 2- to 5-year-olds, and school-aged children should be marked with signs.

▶ *Keep play areas free from hazards.* Be alert for broken pieces of metal and damaged equipment that should be repaired.

▶ *Maintain the cushioned surfacing.* Falls contribute to more than 70 percent of playground injuries, so it is important that the fill material or rubberized padding around slides and swings is adequate for the height of the equipment. Loose fill needs to be repositioned under play equipment periodically.

BICYCLE SAFETY. If you have ever watched children playing on their bicycles, you may have wondered how any child escapes a broken bone or two. Boys and girls frequently ride in the middle of the road, perform stunts to test skills, and dart across intersections without looking. When an accident occurs, children under 10 years are more likely than older bikers to be seriously injured, yet only 25 percent of child cyclists wear helmets (Centers for Disease Control and Prevention, 2004). Clearly, all children should be required to put on a helmet as soon as they straddle their first bike.

Most cycling injuries happen while children are biking near home, on minor roads, and away from intersections—in other words, when caregivers think they are safe. Of course, this is partly due to the fact that children are most likely to be injured where they spend the most time. But accidents also occur in seemingly safe places because children find it hard to translate cycling knowledge into safe cycling behavior. For example, most 8-year-olds know that it is dangerous to dart across a street without looking both ways, yet most 8-year-olds will occasionally do just that when they spot a friend on the other side.

Carelessness is the main cause of some accidents, but Jodi Plumert and her colleagues have discovered another reason why children are at risk for cycling accidents. Plumert and her colleagues watched 10-year-olds, 12-year-olds, and adults ride bicycles in a "virtual environment" that simulated cycling across an intersection (Plumert, Kearney, & Cremer, 2004). Surprisingly, most children rarely bolted into traffic, and they selected gaps between themselves and oncoming traffic that were as large as the gaps adults selected. Children took longer to get their bikes moving, however, and they reached the roadway later than adults. Because there was little room to spare between themselves and oncoming traffic, virtual collisions occurred on 2 percent of children's crossings. In other words, the children simply overestimated how well they could ride.

Recall from Chapter 6 that perceptual development involves judging "affordances"—fits between the physical characteristics of an individual and properties of the environment. Young children overestimate their abilities because they have difficulty judging affordances. For example, children often misjudge when they can reach a toy on a shelf or step across two sticks (Plumert, 1995). Overconfidence has serious consequences in a wide range of situations—including traffic crossings. In one study, 5- to

This girl is cycling in a simulator that records how well she avoids traffic as she crosses computer-generated intersections. Virtual collisons occur 2 percent of the time when 10- and 12-year-old children attempt to cross.

Courtesy Jodi Plumert.

9-year-olds would have been hit 6 percent of the times they thought they could safely walk across a road (Lee, Young, & McLaughlin, 1984). But all children are not the same: It is the outgoing, impulsive toddlers who are most likely to grow into injury-prone children. Thus caregivers need to take personality and injury history into account before deciding that Shawna or Kevin is old enough to ride to the corner store (Schwebel & Plumert, 1999).

Asthma

Some children have their play disrupted by a chronic condition you can appreciate by trying the following demonstration: Take a drinking straw, hold your nose, and breathe through the narrow tube. Notice the panic that sets in as your body becomes starved for oxygen. Sit still and relax, trying to use as little oxygen as possible, until you have to gasp for air. This is what it feels like when children have an asthma attack.

Asthma (also called reactive airway disease) is a disease in which the airways of the lungs become inflamed and "twitchy." During an attack, muscles around the airways go into spasms and cells secrete mucus, narrowing the airways. People with asthma feel breathlessness and sometimes produce a high-pitched sound, called a *wheeze*, as they exhale. Exposure to *allergens* (substances our bodies detect as foreign) triggers some people's attacks, with frequent culprits including pollen, mold, feces from dust mites or cockroaches, and animal dander. Other asthma sufferers have labored breathing when they exercise or are exposed to cold air.

Currently, almost 1 out of every 8 children has been diagnosed with asthma, making it the most common chronic (long-lasting) childhood disease (Centers for Disease Control and Prevention, 2005b; Dey & Bloom, 2003). Children in all ethnic groups and communities are affected, but asthma is more prevalent in urban areas, especially among children who are poor, African American, or Puerto Rican. The higher incidence among these children reflects a variety of factors, including lower outdoor air quality, more indoor pollutants, and inadequate medical care.

Asthma is difficult for children and families: Children miss school days and endure frequent doctor or hospital visits, while families are burdened by lost work and medical expenses. These problems can be minimized by removing environmental triggers and using medication to prevent attacks. With proper precautions, even children with exercise-induced asthma often participate in sports, and over half of all children with asthma stop having attacks by the time they are grown (Cramer, 2001).

Scientists are still trying to identify the cause of this "modern epidemic." One hypothesis is that asthma is "the price we pay for cleaner living" (Prescott, 2003, p. 64). When children are exposed to bacteria and viruses, their bodies develop immune responses that inhibit unwanted allergic reactions. Children who are not exposed to a wide range of dirt and germs may develop "untrained" systems that have difficulty telling the difference between harmless substances and biological threats. This may be why the lowest rates of asthma are found where children have the most exposure to pets, farm animals, and a life of playing in dirt, mud, and ponds. An alternative hypothesis is that asthma rates are higher wherever children get relatively little exercise (Platts-Mills et al., 2005). Until more evidence is available, experts are advising caregivers to worry less about keeping children germ-free but more about keeping them active and strong.

asthma (also called reactive airway disease) A disease in which the airways of the lungs become inflamed, causing them to narrow. Asthma is the most common childhood chronic disease.

Which child is less likely to have asthma—and why? The girl above has two characteristics associated with a lower risk of asthma: contact with the germs associated with farm animals, which may prevent her immune system from overreacting to substances like pollen, and an active lifestyle.

Weight Control

Another risk to children's health is the skyrocketing weight problem. The percentage of overweight children in the United States nearly quadrupled during the last 40 years, from 4 percent in the mid-1960s to 16 percent today (National Center for Health Statistics, 2004, 2005b). Minority children are especially likely to be heavy. Currently, 20 percent of African American children and 22 percent of Mexican children are overweight.

People are getting fatter around the world, even in regions that were recently plagued by malnutrition. In fact, there are higher proportions of overweight people in some Middle Eastern and Pacific Island countries than there are in the United States. This rapid shift from undernutrition to overnutrition, which experts call the "nutrition transition," occurs because there is a fine line between a healthy diet and a diet that causes one to become overweight. Only 50 extra calories per day, either from increased food or decreased activity, is enough to add 5 pounds (2.3 kilograms) to your weight each year.

Being overweight increases a child's risk of developing numerous chronic diseases, including diabetes, sleep disturbances, asthma, and gallbladder disease. Excess weight is one reason why rates of childhood diabetes nearly doubled in the United States over a 20-year period, while breathing difficulties during sleep increased fivefold (Wang & Dietz, 2002). From a child's perspective, these physical problems may seem trivial compared to the social consequences of being heavy. As you read in Chapter 8, children become self-conscious during the school years and peers can be cruel. As a result, being chronically overweight also takes a toll on psychological health, increasing children's chances of suffering from depression, anxiety, and behavior problems (Lumeng et al., 2003; Mustillo et al., 2003; Vila et al., 2004).

Most children who have a high body mass index (BMI) (see Chapter 6) during the school years grow up to be overweight. When one research team followed children for over 8 years, only 5 percent of the boys and girls who were overweight at the start of the study dropped to a healthy weight by adolescence (Mustilla et al., 2003). One reason overweight children rarely take a healthy turn is that many parents fail to recognize weight problems. For example, a third of the mothers who had overweight children in one survey responded that their children were "about the right weight" (Maynard et al., 2003).

How can parents and schools prevent weight problems? One way is to expose children to a wide variety of healthy foods. In an award-winning demonstration, food educator Antonia Demas and her assistants repeatedly visited elementary school classrooms in Trumansburg, New York, to introduce children to healthy foods. Some children had fun preparing novel, low-fat snacks while they learned about the history and lore of the foods. When these items later appeared in the school cafeteria, students who were familiar with them selected the new foods more often (Demas, 1995). Demas suggests that children can become familiar with a new food like lentils by counting them in math class, sprouting them in science class, and talking about them when the class is learning about other cultures (Demas & Landis, 2001).

Activity level is another component of weight control. In one national survey, 20 percent of children exercised vigorously only two times or fewer per week, and more than 25 percent watched at least 4 hours of television per day (Anderson, Crespo, et al., 1998). When Dr. Richard Strauss fitted 100 children with beeper-size motion detectors, the results were astounding: "Three-quarters of their waking day the kids were barely moving at all," Strauss reported. "When they did move, it was mostly low-level activity such as slow walking" ("Weighty Problem," 2001, p. 66). It is not surprising that children who have a television in their bedroom and those who report watching a lot of television have higher BMIs than children who are not "glued to the tube." The solution is simple: Just get children moving again. One study found that children who changed their activity levels over the course of a year also changed their BMIs, and an intervention program trimmed children significantly just by restricting their television viewing (Berkey et al., 2003; Robinson, 1999).

In sum, three changes could reverse the 40-year trend of growing sizes and blossoming medical bills:

▶ Say "no" to unhealthy convenience foods—no matter what children's friends are eating.

▶ Expose children to a variety of nutritious foods in fun, relaxed settings. By experimenting with new recipes, parents, grandparents, and teachers can pass a rich and exciting food culture onto the next generation.

▶ Encourage children to run and play.

Children who shout "no fair!" in the fifth grade will be healthy and grateful adults 10 years later.

Maltreatment

Children everywhere need adults to provide them with a safe environment, health care, and nutritious food. But as the Lost Boys in our opening story illustrate, not all children receive these essentials. Even in politically stable communities, many children lack basic care or are the victims of violence. In the United States, for example, about 12 out of every 1,000 elementary school children are identified as abused or neglected each year (U.S. Department of Health and Human Services, 2005), and an unknown number of children suffer from undetected abuse or neglect.

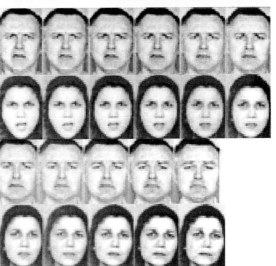

NEGLECT AND PHYSICAL ABUSE. Recall from Chapter 5 that the most frequent type of maltreatment, *neglect*, occurs when caregivers fail to provide basic food, shelter, medical care, or supervision. Neglected children may be left at home alone, fed inadequate food, or allowed to suffer from diseases that are left untreated. Children who suffer from *physical abuse* are repeatedly slapped, struck with objects, and violently thrown, shaken, or pulled. Neglected and physically abused children are more likely than other children to do poorly in school, have problems with peer relationships, and show aggressive, angry behavior (National Clearinghouse on Child Abuse and Neglect Information, 2001, 2005). These problems often survive into adulthood. Individuals who were maltreated as children are more likely to be arrested for violent crimes and to suffer from depression and other emotional problems (Kolko, 2002).

How does maltreatment interfere with social and emotional development? Neglectful and abusive households are more disorganized, with parents who are

Maltreated children believe that more of the faces shown here appear angry, and electrodes on their heads detect more than the typical amount of brain activity when they view angry faces. By affecting reactions to social information, maltreatment has a long-standing influence on children's social relationships.

intergenerational transmission of abuse The phenomenon of maltreated children growing up to abuse their own children. Across studies, only about 30 percent of abused children grow up to be abusers themselves.

less responsive and involved with their children. As a result, maltreated children may not learn how to maintain positive interactions with other people. But abuse also changes how children attend to social information. Compared to nonabused children, those who are physically abused pay more attention to angry faces and have difficulty turning away from anger-related information (Pollak & Kistler, 2002; Pollak & Tolley-Schell, 2003). They are also more likely to interpret routine situations as threatening. For instance, when a group of boys is poking at friends in good humor, most children assume that the next smiling boy will also poke playfully and run. In contrast, a child who is used to being hit may ignore the smile and try to defend himself. As one investigator explained, "If you're a child on the playground, and you think someone is going to harm you, you're going to respond as if you're being threatened. If the person *wasn't* trying to harm you, your behavior looks bizarre to everyone else, and you get in trouble, even though you're just doing what comes naturally—protecting yourself" (Reynolds, 2003, p. 32).

Are abused children doomed to abuse their own children? A history of abuse is a risk factor for parenting problems, but most abused children manage to treat their own children differently than they were treated themselves. Across many studies, the **intergenerational transmission of abuse**—the phenomenon of children repeating their parents' abusive behavior with their own children—is about 30 percent (Pears & Capaldi, 2001).

Violence and the threat of violence can affect children's adjustment even when they are not the immediate victims of abuse. Like the Lost Boys, many children who are growing up in countries like Iraq and Palestine or in violent urban communities face the threat of death every day. To learn about the impact of community violence on children, turn to the next *Solutions* feature, "Growing Up Scared."

Children growing up in the midst of violence cope better when their families spend time together, when they are allowed to help with daily chores and household activities, and when adults include them in discussions about the better future that awaits them.

GROWING UP SCARED

During the 1990s alone, wars killed more than 2 million children worldwide, injured 6 million others, and created more than 15 million displaced and refugee children like the Lost Boys in our opening story (Bellamy, 2000). Even in politically stable countries, some children are exposed to violence through terrorist attacks, school shootings, and neighborhood gunfire. Indeed, many surveys have found that the majority of inner-city children in the United States have been exposed to community violence (Buka et al., 2001; Osofsky et al., 1993).

Exposure to violence has widespread effects on children's emotional, behavioral, and moral development. Those who are repeatedly exposed to threatening situations often show the following reactions (Joshi & O'Donnell, 2003; Osofsky, 1995):

Signs of worry such as sleep disturbances, nightmares, and physical complaints. Obvious fearfulness and weeping are signs of worry, but young children also express fear by waking frequently, staying close to their parents, and complaining about stomachaches. In one study, for example, many third and fifth graders from New Orleans drew graphic pictures of shootings, stabbings, and funerals, and these children often reported being scared (Osofsky, 1995).

Regression. School-aged children who have been exposed to violence often *regress*, that is, show behavior that is typical of younger children. In a telling example, developmental psychologist James Garbarino (1999, p. 87) described 16-year-old Sharnell, a boy who had lived in juvenile detention since the age of 12 due to his violent behavior. When Garbarino asked this street-wise boy about fear, Sharnell answered, "Nah. I ain't afraid of nothing. Nothing," while he rocked back and forth, sucking his thumb. Exposure to violence can bring out a number of regressive behaviors, including clinging to parents and bed-wetting (American Psychological Association, 2005b).

Difficulty concentrating. It is difficult to concentrate when you are worried about safety. School grades suffer when children are exposed to violence because they have trouble focusing on what they should be trying to learn.

Casual aggressiveness. Children who frequently see aggressive behavior learn to act aggressively and become "desensitized" to violence. As a result, they are nonchalant about actions others consider unacceptable, such as pushing people out of the way rather than asking them to move.

In addition to these behavioral effects, violence also destroys children's hopes for the future (Margolin & Gordis, 2000). But it is possible for children to acquire a sense of purpose in the face of violence. Close relationships with others help. Children who rebound from trauma often have close-knit families with adults who look forward to a better future (Blakeney & Meyer, 1995; Joshi & O'Donnell, 2003). Whenever children's lives are touched by war or other trauma, the American Psychological Association (2003) recommends increasing the amount of time children spend in activities with their families or surrogate (substitute) families. It is also good to let children help with routine chores. For instance, expecting children to set the table or to help in other ways can make them feel more confident and in control. Finally, children have not had enough experience to know that wars end and situations improve. Therefore, talking about the good times everyone expects in the future can help them deal with the present.

SEXUAL ABUSE. As we discussed in Chapter 7, it is not unusual for children to explore their body parts or "play doctor" with other children. This is not sexual abuse. Sexual activity is abusive when an adult initiates the activity, the child is forced to participate, or an age, power, or size difference limits a child's ability to consent. Sexual abuse includes a wide range of behaviors, including watching pornography with children, exposing body parts to children or fondling them, and sexual penetration.

Although sexual abuse is largely a secret crime, it is far from rare. About 20 to 25 percent of women and 5 to 15 percent of men report childhood sexual abuse experiences, and about half of these individuals report multiple episodes of abuse (Finkelhor, 1994). In one study, 34 percent of the adults who reported childhood sexual abuse said they were abused before 9 years of age, and 44 percent were abused between 9 and 12 years (Finkelhor et al., 1990).

Adults who are sexually attracted to children often reduce their risk of detection by choosing victims who are socially isolated or lonely, because these children are more likely to respond to attention and are less likely to report their abuse. Consequently, children are at higher risk for sexual abuse if they live without biological parents, have unhappy home lives, or have a disability. Many offenders engage in a process called *grooming*, in which they gradually gain children's trust with attention and gifts while desensitizing them to sexual talk and behavior. During the grooming process, offenders lead children to believe they care about them more than other people do ("I understand you better than your parents") or that physical contact is just an educational activity or special game. Sometimes, offenders use threats to discourage children from disclosing.

Sexual abuse experiences vary widely, from one-time fondling by an unfamiliar baby-sitter to repeated intercourse by a father. Therefore, the immediate effects of sexual abuse also vary. About 40 percent of sexually abused children show few or no immediate symptoms, while the remaining children show signs of depression, externalizing (acting-out) behavior, sexual behavior, or other problems (Putnam, 2003). The following conclusions summarize findings on long-term outcomes (Kendler et al., 2000; Rind, Tromovitch, & Bauserman, 1998):

▶ Adults with a history of sexual abuse are less well-adjusted than nonabused adults, but differences between groups are small. Many victims report no lasting problems because people generally rebound from challenges that are not ongoing.

▶ Some abused individuals do experience long-term problems, including depression, alcohol and drug dependence, social anxiety, and sexual promiscuity. However, no set of symptoms is consistently associated with a history of sexual abuse.

▶ Males are less likely than females to feel angry or victimized by their experiences. Still, a minority of abused males say that early sexual experiences were unwanted and had a negative influence on their adjustment.

To keep children safe, caregivers should be cautious about teenagers or adults who are inappropriately interested in being alone with youngsters. Adults can also teach children that no one has the right to touch their bodies without permission and that children should tell an adult if someone's actions are making them feel uncomfortable.

>>> MEMORY MAKERS <<<

Match each term or phrase on the left with a phrase on the right:

1. the number-one killer of children   (a) asthma
2. the modern epidemic   (b) unintentional injuries
3. problems judging affordances   (c) a major cause of bicycle accidents

4. The rate of intergenerational transmission of physical abuse is about _____ percent.

   (a) 10   (b) 30   (c) 50   (d) 80

5. Regressive behavior, difficulty concentrating, signs of worry, and casual aggressiveness are associated with _____.

   (a) micronutrient deficiencies   (b) head trauma   (c) hearing loss
   (d) exposure to violence

[1-b; 2-a; 3-c; 4-b; 5-d]

Family Life

Anthropologist Mark Flinn learned how important family life is when he studied a village he calls "Bwa Mawego," a group of about 700 people on the Caribbean island of Dominica. Because daily events were rarely shielded from public view, it was easy for Flinn to record children's home lives, school activities, friends, and health. But there was another reason why Bwa Mawego was the perfect setting for research: Fathers often left the island during harvests and mothers worked at tourist resorts. As a result, about a third of the children's households changed composition each year, which allowed Flinn to study families with biological parents, stepparents, and other relatives (Small, 2000).

To measure the impact of family structure and family stability, Flinn and his assistants made an unusual request: They asked children to spit into a cup. Saliva samples contain *cortisol*, a stress hormone that is produced when people encounter uncertainty (Sapolsky, 1999). By monitoring children's lives and measuring their stress responses, Flinn learned what types of events were most upsetting to children (Flinn & England, 1995).

The results were intriguing. Children experienced a wide variety of stressors, but uncertainty from family life produced the most severe and long-lasting reactions. Relatives fighting, parents leaving and returning, and changes in residences raised cortisol levels and increased children's rates of illness (Flinn, 1999). In contrast, school demands, squabbles with peers, and competitive play did not. As shown in Figure 9.2, Bwa Mawega households that included a stepfather and half siblings, distant relatives, or a single mother without supportive relatives had highly stressed children. Children were better adjusted in households containing a **nuclear family** (a mother and father) or a mother living with relatives who could help.

Flinn's research underscores how important families are to children's security and well-being. After a brief look at what today's families look like, we'll explore how children's pathways through middle and late childhood are influenced by the structure of their families.

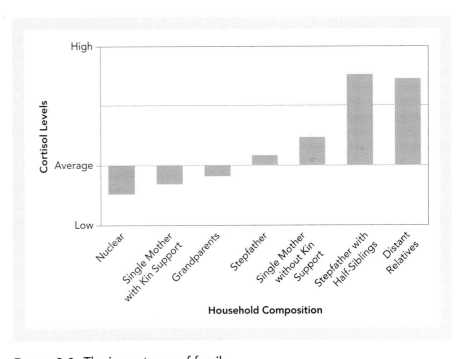

FIGURE 9.2 The importance of family.

Events such as teasing from friends and disappointments at school are not very stressful to children, but it is very upsetting when parents fight or leave home. As a result, children who live in a nuclear family or with a mother and a supportive relative feel less stress than children in less stable family environments.

SOURCE: Flinn & England (1995).

Children's Households

The so-called traditional family—a mother and father living with their children—is still the most common type of family. In the United States, about 69 percent of children live with both of their parents, and in 3 percent of these households a grandparent

nuclear family A family unit consisting of a mother, father, and their children.

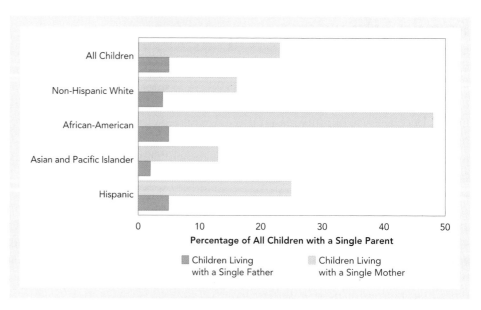

FIGURE 9.3 Children with single parents.

Many children in the United States live with a single parent, usually their mothers. Currently, over half of African American children live with a single mother or father.

SOURCE: Fields (2003).

is present as well. But other arrangements are not uncommon. As you can see in Figure 9.3, 23 percent of children live only with their mothers, and another 5 percent live only with their fathers. Among African American children, almost half live in a household without their biological father. When children do not live with either parent, about half of the time they are being raised by a grandparent (Fields, 2003). As you look at Figure 9.3, keep in mind that the term *single-parent household* is somewhat misleading because many of these households include another adult who helps care for the children. For example, one out of three single-father households includes a cohabitating partner, as do more than one out of 10 single-mother households.

The number of children living with a single parent rose during the last half of the 20th century due to an increasing divorce rate and an increase in births to single mothers. Only 24 percent of people born between 1925 and 1934 experienced divorce, whereas it is estimated that nearly half of the people who marry today will divorce (Kreider & Fields, 2002). Moreover, a third of current births are to unmarried women. Compared to earlier generations, today's parents view marriage as more optional and less of a permanent decision (Hetherington & Elmore, 2003). As a result, one in two children will spend at least some of their childhood years in a single-parent household (Children's Defense Fund, 2000).

Do these trends mean that today's children enjoy less family stability than children did in the past? Family historians say "no" because children have always coped with losing parents and changing residences. For example, at least one out of three children lost a parent during colonial times (often to illness), and children are more likely to be living with at least one parent today than they were in 1940 (Coontz, 1992; Fields, 2003). A major difference between the past and the present is that divorce has gradually replaced parental death as the major cause of family instability (Hernandez, 1994).

How are children coping with divorce? This is one of the questions scientists have answered by entering the fascinating world of family life.

Children of Divorce

In the opening line to *Anna Karenina*, Leo Tolstoy (1937, p. 1) wrote, "All happy families resemble one another, but each unhappy family is unhappy in its own way." Because children have different temperaments and there are so many reasons why marriages crumble, no two children have exactly the same experience with divorce. Nonetheless, scientists agree that the end of a marriage is usually a painful experience that can leave children stunned and confused (Hetherington & Kelly, 2002).

Clinicians who work with troubled families emphasize the heartbreak of divorce. In a popular book on children of divorce, therapist Judith Wallerstein and her colleagues (Wallerstein, Lewis, & Blakeslee, 2000) described divorce from a child's perspective in the following way:

> It's feeling sad, lonely, and angry during childhood. It's traveling on airplanes alone when you're seven to visit your parent. It's having no choice about how you spend your time and feeling like a second-class citizen compared with your friends in intact families who have some say about how they spend their weekends and their vacations. It's wondering whether you will have any financial help for college from your college-educated father, given that he has no legal obligation to pay. (p. xxxi)

But for every child who has experienced these problems, many have not. Divorce has different effects on different children because—as Tolstoy observed—every household is a unique place to grow and learn.

"Your father loves me very much, in his own way, and I love your father very much, in my own way, and that's why we're getting a divorce."

GROWING UP AFTER DIVORCE. Researchers estimate the overall effects of divorce by combining results from many studies using a statistical procedure called **meta-analysis**. Their findings show that children of divorce are less well-adjusted than children from never-divorced, two-parent families. Consistently, children of divorce have more conduct problems, higher rates of depression, lower scores on measures of school achievement, and poorer self-concepts and peer relationships (Amato, 2001a; Amato & Keith, 1991; Reifman et al., 2001). However, differences between groups are small on most measures, which means that most children of divorce have scores that overlap the scores of children who have not experienced divorce.

How well-adjusted are children of divorce years later? The majority of children who experienced parental divorce grow up to be well-adjusted adults, but divorce can take a toll on vulnerable children. In two large-scale studies, 20 to 25 percent of youths from divorced and remarried families were troubled compared to only 10 percent of children from intact families (Hetherington, Bridges, & Insabella, 1998). Children of divorce were also less likely to complete high school or college, so they earned less as adults (Amato, 1999). And as you might expect, children of divorce were more likely to divorce themselves.

Scientists agree that divorce is correlated with negative outcomes for children, but there are heated debates about why this is so. Differences between children of divorce and other children could be due to family characteristics that predated divorce, such as family conflict and financial difficulties. Moreover, divorce status and school achievement are more strongly correlated for biological children than for adoptive children, suggesting that genetically transmitted traits account for some of the outcomes associated with divorce (O'Connor et al.,

meta-analysis A statistical procedure that combines the results of many studies to determine the overall effect of a variable across samples.

It is easier for everyone when parents cooperate after a divorce.

2000). But when researchers control for predivorce factors, some of the differences between children of divorce and other children remain. This finding suggests that divorce does seem to increase the risk of emotional and behavioral problems (Amato & Keith, 1991; Amato & Sobolewski, 2001).

Divorce is experienced differently by different children because parents who divorce provide their children with different environments. Therefore, we have to look at specific factors associated with divorce if we want to understand divorce from a child's perspective.

THE ECOLOGY OF DIVORCE. When Chloe's parents divorced, her dad moved just down the block while Chloe and her mother stayed in the family home, close to where her mother worked as a university professor. Several blocks away, Matt was leaving town frequently to visit his divorced mother, who relied on a series of boyfriends to make ends meet. Two divorces, two children, two childhoods.

The "ecology of divorce" refers to the many factors that influence children's adjustment. Those who live with distressed mothers or move to more crowded schools after a divorce are more likely to show declines in adjustment and school performance. But for some, divorce is a chance to move from conflict-ridden homes into predictable homes run by a competent parent. In these cases, children have fewer problems than some of their peers who have experienced divorce (Amato, 2000). Each of the following factors is part of the ecology of divorce:

▸ *A child's age, gender, and temperament.* Children in elementary and high school generally have more difficulty than younger or older children accepting news of their parents' divorce (Amato & Keith, 1991). Sex differences and individual differences in temperaments also influence reactions. Divorce has more long-term economic consequences for girls because girls from divorced families are less likely than boys to complete high school and college. And as you might expect, children who responded poorly to challenges *before* divorce have the most problems *after* divorce. But some combinations of factors foster unusually competent behavior. For example, a subset of girls who are raised by competent, caring mothers after a divorce become resilient individuals who are unusually good at handling life's challenges (Hetherington, 1989, 1991).

▸ *Time since the divorce.* Children's immediate reaction to news of divorce is often a mix of anger and depression, but feelings usually become less intense over time. Experts tell families that life will probably settle down again after a 2-year period of adjustment unless remarriage or other family disruptions occur (Hetherington & Stanley-Hagan, 2002).

▸ *Parenting quality.* A common effect of divorce is *diminished parenting*: a breakdown in supervision and family routines. Children who are used to bedtime stories and balanced meals may find these activities displaced by more urgent needs, and many pick up additional chores or start caring for siblings. Some even nurture their parents. For example, one father said he described all of his business plans to a 7-year-old son who "understands everything" (Wallerstein et al., 2000). Overwhelmed parents like this father sometimes alternate between ignoring bad behavior and yelling at their children. Over time, however, most parents who had an authoritative parenting style (see Chapter 7) before a divorce eventually regain their warm, consistent behavior. Effective parenting is the most important buffer against negative outcomes, regardless of family circumstances (Dunn, 2004a, b; Hetherington & Elmore, 2003).

▶ ***The divorced parents' relationship.*** Children have fewer behavior problems, get along better with their siblings, and have better dating relationships during their teen years when the relationship between divorced parents is relatively harmonious. Conflict hurts children regardless of their family structure, so children from high-conflict, intact homes are less well adjusted than children of divorce are (Amato & Keith, 1991).

▶ ***A child's custody arrangements.*** Children's adjustment is also affected by the type of custody arrangements the parents work out. *Joint legal custody* refers to a situation in which both parents share responsibility for making decisions about medical treatment and other child-rearing issues, regardless of where the child lives. *Joint physical (residential) custody* refers to a joint living arrangement, one in which the child lives part-time (though not necessarily equal time) with each parent. Unless conflict between parents is extremely high, joint legal and physical custody is associated with somewhat fewer adjustment problems than sole custody, even when predivorce family characteristics are controlled (Bauserman, 2002; Gunnoe & Braver, 2001). Boys are especially likely to benefit from close relationships with fathers who are actively involved in homework and other daily activities (Amato & Gilbreth, 1999; Hetherington, 1993).

▶ ***Economic well-being.*** After a divorce, economic problems increase parental stress and can force families to move into more troubled neighborhoods. These are some of the reasons why children who receive child support payments show better school performance and fewer behavioral problems (Emery, 1999). Remarriage also increases resources, yet this route to financial stability is not immediately associated with improved adjustment because a second family transition is also stressful (Amato, 2001b).

▶ ***Positive life events.*** Families have different frequencies of negative events, such as fights, and different frequencies of positive events, such as special time with parents. Children who experience divorce show fewer problem behaviors when they also continue to experience many positive events. Positive events counteract the physiological changes produced by stressors, lead children to attend more broadly to their environments, and promote a greater sense of personal control (Doyle et al., 2003).

For many children, divorce is the first of many family transitions that include one or more moves and, often, the start of new families when parents remarry.

ADJUSTING TO STEPPARENTS Ask a group of college students what it is like adjusting to a stepparent and you'll probably hear answers like this one:

> It was just my mum and I for 9 years, so I was her world. So when she got remarried and there was a third person, you do get jealous of any time that she spends with him, and you kind of feel like you're not so important anymore. (Cartwright & Seymour, 2002, p. 129)

Remarriage threatens children's sense of security, and integrating them into the new marriage is challenging. As a result, it often takes 2 to 5 years for a family to stabilize after a stepparent enters the scene. Arguments over children are a common source of conflict in stepfamilies, and the presence of children increases the chance of a second marriage failing by 50 percent (Bray & Kelly, 1998; Hetherington & Kelly, 2002).

Why is it so difficult to build a harmonious stepfamily? Evolutionary psychologists believe that parents treat biological children and stepchildren differently because we are genetically programmed to invest in individuals who carry our genes. There is evidence for this view. Parents are more involved with their own children than their stepchildren, and partners disagree less when they discuss mutual children rather than children who are only related to one of them (Daly & Wilson, 1996; Hobart, 1991). But it is too simplistic to blame genes for all of the problems stepfamilies have. After all, new family members have not had years together to work out problems and establish routines. Whatever the reason for conflict, it is still the case that many children manage to develop close, productive relationships with stepparents. As one college student remarked, "Even though it's been tough and stressful there are a lot of people in my life now that I love and can't imagine my life without them" (Freisthler, Svare, & Harrison-Jay, 2003, p. 92).

The timing of remarriage influences how children react to stepparents. Young children usually accept new adults, and stepparents bond more easily to cute, affectionate youngsters. Older adolescents and young adults also tend to be cooperative, perhaps because they are busy building their own interests and lives. In contrast, children between the ages of 10 and 15 years are grappling with struggles for autonomy, which can make for a rocky adjustment. As you can see in Table 9.1, school-aged children tend to resent stepfathers who are physically affectionate too soon or who act as if the new family is just like a traditional family. Conflict is also worse when stepfathers act as disciplinarians before children are ready to accept their authority (American Psychological Association, 2005b).

After decades of research on how stepfamilies function, the most remarkable finding is how similar the dynamics are in biological and blended families. The same parenting qualities that promote harmony in nuclear families also promote harmony in stepfamilies: level-headed, authoritative parenting. Regardless of a family's structure, children who experience this style of parenting have fewer behavioral problems and more positive sibling relationships than those with highly coercive or permissive parents (Hetherington, 1999).

Table 9.1	Stepfamiles: Helping Children Adjust
Advice from Experts	**Explanation**
Avoid the nuclear family myth.	It is unrealistic to expect new family members to feel close right away. Parents should help children realize that a stepfamily can be happy even if it functions differently than their earlier family did.
Move slowly and let new roles develop gradually.	Children need time to develop trust in stepparents before they will accept them as mentors and limit-setters. Even affectionate behavior may seem "creepy" to children who still perceive a stepparent as just an acquaintance or a family friend.
Build a family identity by establishing new routines and traditions.	Mutually enjoyable routines, such special breakfasts every Saturday or volunteering for a church activity, give children a sense of belonging and stability. Celebrating the start of each school year or other milestones in a distinctive way establishes traditions that say, "We are a family."
Be patient and flexible.	Last-minute changes in plans are common when there are multiple sets of children, grandparents, and other relatives to accommodate. Children will be more relaxed if their parents are patient and flexible about unexpected interruptions to routines.

Sources: Bray & Kelly (1998); Hetherington & Kelly (2002).

Living with Gay and Lesbian Parents

Katie was only in the second grade when her mother asked the school principal to help with a sensitive situation: Katie's classmates were telling her she was lying when she said she had two mothers.

School-aged children are quick to realize when their families don't look like others in the neighborhood. For some children, this means being raised by at least one gay or lesbian parent. "Gaybies" arrive in a variety of ways. Many are born while their parents are in heterosexual marriages; others are adopted. A small percentage of gay fathers have biological children through a *surrogate mother* (a woman who agrees to become pregnant with his child), and many lesbian mothers become pregnant through *donor insemination*. Research on children raised by gay and lesbian parents has focused on the following three questions:

▶ *Are the children of gay and lesbian parents teased about their families?* Teasing does happen, so some children worry about other people's reactions to their families. Boys of lesbian mothers are especially likely to be teased about the possibility of being gay. Nevertheless, children from gay and lesbian families do not experience a lot more teasing than their peers, and serious harassment is rare (Anderssen, Amlie, & Ytterøy, 2002; Clarke, Kitzinger, & Potter, 2004).

▶ *How well-adjusted are children raised by gay and lesbian parents?* Children from gay or lesbian families are not more likely than other children to have emotional, behavioral, or cognitive problems (Golombok et al., 2003).

▶ *Are children from gay and lesbian families more likely to choose opposite-sex partners as adults?* Most studies have found no influence of family type on the percentage of teenagers or adults who identify themselves as gay or lesbian (Anderssen et al., 2002). However, one study did find that adults raised by lesbian mothers were more likely to have considered a same-sex relationship and more likely to have experienced same-gender sexual relations. Still, these individuals did not report more attraction to same-sex people than other adults. These findings suggest that exposure to a lesbian lifestyle increases openness to explore alternatives rather than one's final sexual orientation (Tasker & Golombok, 1997).

Children can thrive in all types of families, including traditional nuclear families, extended families, single-parent families, blended families, and, like the ones shown here, families headed by two lesbian or gay parents. In all cases, it is the quality of care and parenting the child receives that matters.

The conclusion is that children of gay and lesbian parents are very similar to children who are reared in other types of families (Lambert, 2005). For the outcomes scientists usually measure, such as children's general adjustment and achievement, the quality of family interactions is more important than the number and type of parents. Regardless of who raises children, they have fewer behavior problems and better well-being when caregivers are responsive, have loving relationships with other adults, and share the burdens of child rearing with a partner (Perrin & the Committee on Psychosocial Aspects of Child and Family Health, 2002). Children of gay and lesbian parents look similar to other children because parenting behavior is similar across parents with different sexual orientations (Flaks et al., 1995; Golombok et al., 2003).

Adopted Children

Only 2 percent of children in the United States are adopted, yet adoption touches most people's lives (Kreider & Fields, 2005). In one survey, 6 out of 10 adults were adopted, had a close friend or relative who was adopted, or had adopted or placed a child for adoption (Evan B. Donaldson Adoption Institute, 1997). It is no wonder, then, that scientists have been interested in children's understanding of adoption and the experience of being adopted.

Children's answers to questions about adoption reveal a range of levels of understanding depending on their age (Brodzinsky, Singer, & Braff, 1984). As shown in Table 9.2, 8- and 9-year-olds generally understand that adoption and birth are two routes to parenthood, but they do not yet understand that adoption is a permanent relationship based on a legal transfer of rights. Even many 8- to 11-year-olds think that biological parents might reclaim their children, and it is not until 12 to 13 years that the majority of children have a mature understanding of adoption. Whether they are adopted or not, children's understanding of adoption grows slowly (as it does about so many issues) as they come to understand reproduction and the legal process that authorizes adoption. Thus children are most likely to grasp the concept of adoption when their parents revisit the issue of adoption often, providing a little more information each time.

TABLE 9.2 Children's Understanding of Adoption

Level of Understanding	Example	Typical Ages
1. No understanding of adoption.		4–5 years
2. Knows the word *adoption* but confuses the concepts of birth and adoption.	Alan (5 years old): Adoption means you go to try to get a baby, and if you can't, you can't. [Where do you get the baby that you adopt?] From your vagina or your tummy.	4–5 years
3. Clearly differentiates between adoption and birth. Accepts that adoption is permanent but does not understand why.	Mary (6 years old): It's their baby now. [Why?] Cause it is. [Is the baby theirs forever?] Sure . . . no one can take it. [How come?] Cause that's the way it is when you are adopted . . . my mommy said so.	6–9 years
4. Differentiates between adoption and birth but is unsure about the permanence of the parent–child relationship.	Sara (7 years old): [Once the parents adopt the baby is it theirs forever?] I think so . . . unless maybe the other parents want it back. [Could they get the baby back if they wanted it?] Maybe, but they would have to want it back very much.	6–9 years
5. Has a vague understanding that some authority makes adoption permanent.	Amy (10 years old): After the people have the baby for some time, maybe a year or two years, they go to the court and see the judge. [What happens there?] Well they talk to him and signs (sic) lots of papers.	8–11 years
6. Understands that the adoption relationship involves a permanent legal transfer of rights.	Jimmy (13 years old): Well, they have it legally now. It's their baby and now they have to care for it . . . not other people. It's their baby forever . . . unless for some reason they find out that the parents are not responsible . . . the other parents don't have any right to the child now.	10–13 years

SOURCE: Brodzinsky et al. (1984, pp. 871–872)

These children are learning to play "mook chee bah" at one of the many camps for Korean-American adoptees that has sprung up throughout the United States. Learning about their country of origin helps adoptees develop a healthy sense of identity that combines their Asian and American roots.

Over 20,000 orphans from other countries are adopted by families in the United States each year. These children arrive from around the world, with the majority coming from China, Russia, Guatemala, and Korea (U.S. Department of State, 2006). Because adoptive parents are carefully screened and most children receive adequate care prior to adoption, it is not surprising that the majority of these children grow up well-adjusted. In fact, children from China have fewer internalizing and externalizing symptoms than their nonadopted peers who were born in the United States (Tan, 2004).

Children in mixed-race families face endless questions from peers about their family situation, and their ethnic identity is pulled in two directions as they become more aware of the physical differences between themselves and their parents (Borchers & AAP Committee on Early Childhood, Adoption, and Dependent Care, 2003). By 7 years, most Asian adoptees are aware that their ethnic appearance is permanent, and by 9 to 11 years they either accept their ethnicity or experience some ambivalence about their situation by disliking their appearance or rejecting an Asian identity. Typical 12- to 14-year-old adoptees have an integrated sense of themselves that includes knowledge of their Asian heritage along with their American identity (Huh & Reid, 2000). In general, Asian adoptees show fewer adjustment problems when their parents support their ethnic identity and expose them to the culture of their country of origin (Yoon, 2001).

>>> **MEMORY MAKERS** <<<

Match concepts on the left with corresponding concepts on the right:

1. meta-analysis
2. the ecology of divorce
3. diminished parenting
4. nuclear family
5. positive life events

(a) a breakdown in family supervision and routines

(b) a technique for combining results from many studies

(c) factors that counter the physiological changes produced by stressors

(d) environmental factors that influence children's reactions to divorce

(e) a mother, father, and their children

[1-b; 2-d; 3-a; 4-e; 5-c]

Children, Schools, and Achievement

What comes to mind when you think about your childhood? If you are like most people, some of your most vivid memories are about school. Perhaps you recall a favorite teacher, a year you were lonely during recess, or a class play. Scientists know that while you were making these memories, schooling was boosting your brain power. IQ scores rise during the school year and fall over summer vacation, when children are less likely to encounter academic work (Ceci & Williams, 1997; Hayes & Grether, 1983). And there is other evidence that children learn mental skills in school they would not learn at home. For example, children who delayed starting school due to World War II scored 7 points lower on intelligence tests than their peers who started on schedule, and test scores rose dramatically in an isolated region of Tennessee after educational opportunities increased (Ceci, 1996).

But it is not enough to know that school is important; educators want to know which practices do the best job of preparing children for a lifetime of learning. To explore what works for children with different talents and needs, scientists have observed classrooms in the inner city, the rural mountains of Appalachia, and around the world.

Culture and Achievement

Psychologist and education professor Howard Gardner (1989) watched the following art class during a visit to the People's Republic of China:

> The teacher, whom I'll call Mr. Wang, first drew a half-completed monkey on the board, using lines that suggested the body; this half-finished scheme was to be filled in or filled out. Then Mr. Wang drew three additional half-completed monkeys and asked for students to come to the board and finish them. Each monkey schema was drawn in a somewhat different orientation, thus making impossible slavish copying of a single solution. In effecting their completions, the children did nothing to the heads, but doubled the body lines and filled in missing parts.
>
> Mr. Wang praised the students' initial efforts (as Chinese teachers invariably do) but also pointed out missing features: an ear lacking in one, a tail missing in the second. He asked for volunteers to add these features. In one case, the tail was added but not in an acceptable manner. The teacher asked the class what was wrong, and several students responded that the tail was too short and lacked a curve. (pp. 237–238)

Gardner watched while the teacher strolled about, asking questions. What color should the monkey be? What would be appropriate for the eyes? After posting their drawings on a board, the children spilled onto the playground. Structured lessons such as these produce artwork that is stunning by American standards, as illustrated by the example in Figure 9.4.

Why do children from different cultures attain dramatically different levels of skill in art, mathematical reasoning, and other subjects? Let's explore some answers to this question.

EDUCATION AROUND THE WORLD. Sixty-three percent of Americans worry "a lot" about the quality of education (Gleick, 1995). Table 9.3 illustrates why. According to the Trends in International Mathematics and Science Study (TIMSS), U.S. eighth graders rank 15th in mathematics achievement, significantly behind students from several Asian and European countries (Mullis et al., 2004). Studies of these high-achieving countries have found four factors associated with excellence:

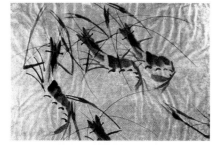

FIGURE 9.4 Teaching art in China.

Children in the People's Republic of China learn to paint highly stylized forms, resulting in artwork of unusual beauty from very young children. Here a painting of shrimp by an 8-year-old (top) is compared to a painting by a Chinese master (bottom).

SOURCE: Gardner (1989).

1. *Valuing effort.* Asian families generally believe that all children can do well if they try hard enough (Chen & Stevenson, 1995; Tsao, 2004). In contrast, Americans focus more on individual differences in ability ("I wasn't good in math either"), which can discourage children from trying when they encounter difficult problems.

2. *Setting high standards.* Asian parents set higher standards than American parents and are less satisfied with their children's performance (Whang & Hancock, 1994).

3. *More instructional time.* Teachers in high-performing countries spend more time on mathematics education and assign more home-work than American teachers do (Chen & Stevenson, 1989; Geary, 1996; Stevenson et al., 1986). Parents in high-achieving cultures also boost the amount of instruction their children receive. For example, Chinese American parents often give kindergarteners problems in math workbooks or ask them to practice writing, whereas European American parents more often interact with their children by cooking together or enjoying other joint activities (Huntsinger et al., 2000).

4. *Teaching for understanding.* U.S. education has been called a "mile wide and an inch deep" because students cover such a large number of topics (Vogel, 1996, p. 335). In contrast, high-achieving countries cover fewer topics but spend more time developing students' conceptual understanding (Zhang & Zhou, 2003).

TABLE 9.3 The Trends in International Mathematics and Science Study (TIMSS)	
Nation	**Average Score**
Singapore	605
Korea, Republic of	589
Hong Kong	586
Chinese Taipei	585
Japan	570
Belgium (Flemish)	537
Netherlands	536
Estonia	531
Hungary	529
Malaysia	508
Latvia	508
Russian Federation	508
Slovak Republic	508
Australia	505
United States	504
Lithuania	502
Sweden	499
Scotland	498
Israel	496
New Zealand	494

Red scores mean children scored significantly better than the U.S. average.
SOURCE: Mullis et al. (2004).

In addition to these factors, some psychologists believe that speaking an East Asian language might give children an advantage. This is because the Chinese words for 11, 12, and 13 translate as "ten one," "ten, two," and "ten three," which makes the base 10 number system more obvious. As a result, it is easier for East Asian children to count and solve simple arithmetic problems. But children around the world memorize answers to simple problems by the third grade, so it is unlikely that the structure of East Asian languages gives children an advantage on higher-level mathematical problems (Geary et al., 1996).

SOCIAL CLASS AND ACADEMIC ACHIEVEMENT. You don't have to travel to another country to find cultural differences that influence school achievement. On average, low-income parents—who are generally less educated than wealthier parents—provide their children with less exposure to the toys and experiences that build basic math and language skills. For example, adults in low-income households provide less language input to children, read to them less often, and buy fewer books and other educational materials. As a result, more low-income children start school without a basic understanding of letters and numbers. In one study, most of the variability in achievement was accounted for by literacy-related activities in the home (Serpell et al., 2002), and differences in family environment account for as much as one-third of the association between income and achievement (Duncan et al., 1998).

Because family income and parental education are strong predictors of school achievement, it is not surprising that U.S. African American and Hispanic children, who are more likely than white children to be poor, score lower on achievement tests. In fact, children from low-income households achieve lower scores than their peers even when comparisons are made within a single ethnic group (Lee & Burkam, 2002). Unfortunately, the lessons teachers provide in

In 2005, eighth grader Anurag Kashyap won the National Spelling Bee contest and $30,000 in prizes after spelling his final word, *appoggiatura* (a type of musical note). Youth with Indian heritage have been dominating the contest, partly because Indian Americans began holding spelling bees as a way to raise their children's scores on verbal achievement tests. The success of many recent immigrant groups illustrates how parents can improve their children's educational chances by providing academically oriented experiences throughout the school years.

school do not eliminate differences that exist when children begin school. For example, African American and Hispanic children enter kindergarten with lower average scores on math and reading tests than nonminority children, but the gap between groups becomes larger—not smaller—during kindergarten and first grade (Reardon, 2003).

The economic status of children's communities also influences their success. The least advantaged children have lower-quality schools regardless of whether school quality is defined by teacher qualifications, teacher attitudes, physical conditions, or student achievement (Tuerk, 2005; U.S. Department of Education, 1998). It is difficult for children to master challenging material when teachers are struggling with minimal resources and large numbers of students who are performing below grade level. Neighborhood resources also play a role by modeling standards for success. In a well-known study called the Gautreaux project, for example, low-income African American families were moved from public housing to private housing throughout the Chicago area. Children who moved to more affluent suburbs were more likely to stay in school and take college preparatory classes than their peers who remained in the city (Leventhal & Brooks-Gunn, 2000).

What does it take for children to succeed? One research team studied a group of over 5,000 economically disadvantaged third graders to find out how those who scored in the 95th to 98th percentiles on an achievement test differed from their peers. Like the other children, these high-achieving students lived with families that were near the poverty index. Unlike their peers, though, they had parents who were more educated and more likely to speak English in the home. Their families also had fewer challenges, such as caregiver health problems, and more family strengths, such as organized family routines (Robinson et al., 2002). In general, high-achieving children from low-income families tend to have supportive families that value education and provide more intellectual stimulation. And as you'll read next, characteristics of schools combine with characteristics of families to influence achievement.

Class Size

Small classes offer more individualized attention, more hands-on instruction, and fewer distractions from classmates. On the other hand, Hong Kong, Japan, Korea, and Singapore excelled in the TIMSS, yet the majority of students in these countries learn in classes with more than 32 students (Mullis et al., 2004). Does class size matter a lot, not at all, or only in some situations?

As you might have predicted, small classes sometimes—but not always—promote better learning. Researchers have found little benefit from having 25 rather than 35 students in a class, probably because teachers organize lessons similarly for both of these groups (Rutter & Maughan, 2002). However, smaller classes (under 20 or so) sometimes promote higher achievement. For example, a study in Tennessee randomly assigned students to complete their first four years of school in one of three conditions: a class of 13 to 17 students, a class of 22 to 26 students, or a class of 22 to 26 students with a full-time aide (Ehrenberg et al., 2001). Three findings have emerged from this and similar other studies (Finn, Gerber, & Boyd-Zaharias, 2005):

- ▶ Students who experience small classes, especially during the early grades, score higher on standardized achievement tests than students in larger classes do.
- ▶ The benefits of small classes persist into the upper grades after students have returned to larger classes.
- ▶ Low-income students benefit the most from small classes during their early grades.

Experts caution that large-scale decreases in class sizes could create space and teacher shortages that might hurt the quality of education. Moreover, it is possible that less costly interventions, such as providing computers for individualized instruction, could produce the same benefits (Ceci, Papierno, & Mueller-Johnson, 2002). So before you conclude that smaller classes are always the best solution for declining achievement, it is important to remember that *how* children are taught is just as important as how *many* children are taught.

Teaching Methods

Children need three things to be successful learners throughout life. First, they need to master fundamental skills and facts. For example, children must memorize answers to single-digit addition problems so they will not have to count on their fingers. Second, as discussed in Chapter 8, they need to understand concepts so they can transfer learning to new problems. For example, it is easier to answer subtraction problems like "21 minus 9" if you understand why you can "borrow" from the "tens" column. Finally, children need to maintain their desire to learn. This means they are curious, excited about learning, and confident about their ability to master new material.

Society continually changes its mind about how to accomplish these goals. Historically, schools emphasized the three "Rs"—reading, writing, and "aRithmetic." Then, in the 1960s and early 1970s, educators became worried that drilling children in basic skills would reduce their interest in learning, so **open education** become popular. Open education is a *constructivist* approach in which children direct their own learning by selecting hands-on experiences. (You read about constructivist preschools in Chapter 7.) At the elementary school level, open classrooms often include a broader range of ages than traditional classrooms, and learning is more personal and less competitive. By the mid-1980s, declining achievement test scores encouraged educators to combine approaches that teach fundamentals with approaches that emphasize enthusiasm for learning.

Today, most classrooms apply ideas from a variety of teaching philosophies. Some educators favor the more traditional approach in which students are offered *direct instruction* in various areas. In contrast, *immersion* approaches assume that children's natural ability to learn will lead them to absorb knowledge if they are exposed to interesting, meaningful activities.

Conflicts over how to teach reading—popularly called the "reading wars"—illustrate these two approaches. **Phonics** is a direct-instruction method in which children are taught the relationships between individual letters and sounds. In contrast, **whole-language instruction** (also called *literature-based instruction*) is an

open education An educational philosophy in which children direct their own learning by selecting hands-on experiences. At the elementary school level, open classrooms often include a broader range of ages than traditional classrooms, so learning is more personal and less competitive.

phonics A direct-instruction method that teaches children the relationship between individual letters and sounds so they can decode new words.

whole-language instruction (also called literature-based instruction) An approach to teaching reading that emphasizes meaningful activities, such as listening to literature and writing, more than phonics training.

evidence-based instruction In education, the practice of choosing instructional approaches that have produced the best achievement in scientific studies.

immersion approach. Teachers who practice whole-language instruction believe that children will learn to read as long as they are exposed to engaging language activities. These teachers often read interesting literature rather than books for early readers, and they emphasize activities that make reading fun. Although sound-letter correspondences might be taught in the context of writing or other meaningful activities, whole-language instruction does not emphasize phonics instruction.

In the 1990s, the reading wars collided with another educational movement: **evidence-based instruction**. Proponents of evidence–based instruction believe that schools should adopt instructional practices that produce the best outcomes in systematic studies. After research showed that some children failed to learn sound–letter correspondences on their own, many policy groups concluded that it had been a mistake to eliminate phonics instruction. A number of reports then swung the pendulum away from meaning-based instruction and reestablished the importance of basic skills for early reading (U.S. Department of Health and Human Services, 2000). To achieve the educational goals mentioned earlier, most educational experts now recommend a combination of direct instruction and meaningful, interesting projects (Klahr & Nigam, 2004).

Currently, there is a great deal of interest in using research to guide instructional development. To read some fascinating findings, turn to this chapter's *Don't Be Fooled!* feature entitled, "The Problem with Pop-Ups."

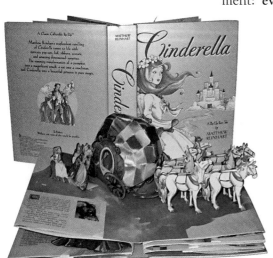

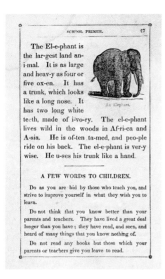

FIGURE 9.5 Children's books—then and now.

During the mid-1800s, children learned to read with no-frills primers (bottom). Today, early readers have lovely illustrations, and gift books, like Matthew Reinhart's *Cinderella*, are stunningly beautiful. Pop-up books delight children and develop a love of books, but it is easier to learn the basics from a more traditional book.

DON'T BE FOOLED

Children do not always learn better from instructional materials that are visually exciting. Scientific research—not intuition about what appeals to children—is the most reliable guide to what works best in the classroom.

THE PROBLEM WITH POP-UPS

Step into a children's bookstore and you know that learning has never been so much fun. In the 1800s, books like the one in Figure 9.5 were typical. In page after page, students found a simple black sketch, lines of text, and a charming dose of moral advice. ("Do not think that you know better than your parents and teachers. They have lived a good deal longer than you have.") In contrast, today's schoolbooks have stunning multicolor artwork. Gift books go even further, with scratch-and-sniffs, sound effects, and three-dimensional pop-ups.

Do children learn better from books with lively, engaging pictures? Not always. Poor readers who learn words without pictures actually perform *better* than readers who see pictures (Didden, Prinsen, & Sigafoos, 2000; Samuels, 1970). According to educational experts, there are many reasons why pictures make reading slower and less accurate. Children who know what a word means are sometimes distracted by adjacent pictures, but those who don't sometimes rely on the picture and fail to learn the word. Finally, pictures that are not closely related to the text may simply confuse early readers (Protheroe, 1993; Willows, 1978).

To illustrate the problem with distracting learning aids, graduate student Cynthia Chiong (2003) taught 30- to 36-month-olds letters in one of three ways: (a) with a plain book that had simple, black letters next to an illustration; (b) with a book that integrated letters into pictures in interesting ways (for example, the lines of an "H" formed the outline of a house); or (c) with a pop-up book that encouraged active manipulation. On a final test, children who learned from the plain book knew the most letters. Children's difficulty with *dual representation* might be partly responsible for these results. Recall from Chapter 6 that dual representation is the ability to think about something as an object and as a symbol. Because young children have difficulty building multiple mental representations of the same object, engaging illustrations of letters might impair their ability to think about letters as symbols.

Well into the elementary school years, children have trouble making the leap from concrete objects to abstract concepts. For example, children who work mathematics problems using manipulatives like blocks do not always mentally connect the blocks with the abstract concepts the blocks represent. In one study, third graders who performed the best on two- and three-digit subtraction problems when they manipulated blocks actually performed *the worst* on standard problems (Resnick & Omanson, 1987).

Scientists believe that concrete objects can help learning, but only when they are used appropriately (Uttal, Liu, & DeLoache, 1999). In Japan, for example, teachers believe that children are confused by changing manipulatives, which happens when teachers illustrate mathematical concepts with sticks, pennies, and an assortment of other items. Instead, Japanese teachers introduce tiles or other objects when children learn to add and use the same objects throughout the early grades (Stevenson & Stigler, 1992). Successful teachers also do not assume that children will learn merely by handling objects. Instead, these teachers explain the relationship between objects and concepts. As one teacher quipped, "understanding does not travel through the fingertips and up the arm" (Ball, 1992, p. 47). Teachers like this one also know that empirical studies—not intuitions about what appeals to children—are the most reliable guide to what works best in the classroom.

Educating Children with Disabilities

Two types of legislation guarantee all U.S. children a public education. Section 504 of the Rehabilitation Act of 1973 prohibits schools that receive federal funds from discriminating on the basis of handicapping conditions. This civil rights law ensures equal educational opportunities for students with physical and mental handicapping conditions, including children who are HIV positive. In addition, the Individuals with Disabilities Education Act (IDEA, Public Law 105-117) requires states to educate students in the *least restrictive environment*. This means that children with disabilities should have opportunities to socialize and learn with their nondisabled peers.

The practice of placing children with physical or cognitive disabilities in regular classrooms has long been called **mainstreaming**. Today, though, educators prefer the term **inclusion** to describe the practice of educating children with disabilities in regular educational environments. Sometimes this is accomplished by providing children with aides to assist them for some or all of the day. Other times, children spend some time in regular classrooms and part of their day in a *resource room*, a place where children receive instruction from teachers who are specially trained to deal with physical, emotional, or cognitive challenges.

mainstreaming The practice of educating children with disabilities in regular classrooms (now commonly called **inclusion**).

inclusion A newer term for educating children with disabilities in regular classrooms. Inclusion is an educational philosophy that values the contributions of all children and encourages all children to participate in their communities.

person-first language A way of talking about disabilities that mentions the person, rather than the disability, first. Person-first language indicates that a person *has* a disability but does not refer to the person *as* the disability. For example, "people who stutter" is preferable to "stutterers."

mental retardation A condition defined by significantly subaverage intelligence and problems with daily living skills that is evident during childhood.

specific learning disabilities Significant impairments in the domains of reading, mathematics, or language.

Inclusion philosophy recognizes that children with disabilities have differences that affect some aspects of their lives, but that these differences do not prevent them from benefiting from and enriching the lives of other children. To convey the idea that the disabilities do not define a person, many professionals use **person-first language** to talk about differences. Person-first language mentions *people* before a disability. For example, "people who stutter" is preferable to "stutterers," and "a child with mental retardation" is preferable to "a retarded child."

Mental retardation (also called *cognitive impairment*) is one category of disability that is protected under IDEA. Children with mental retardation have significantly subaverage intelligence and problems with daily living skills that impair their educational progress. There are hundreds of causes of mental retardation, including genetic conditions, prenatal insults, and problems resulting from early births. In many cases, however, the cause is unknown and the condition is not detected until it becomes clear that the child is not developing on schedule.

Unlike children with mental retardation, children with **specific learning disabilities** have difficulty mastering *a specific set* of skills due to information processing problems. Approximately 6 percent of public school children are identified as having a learning disability, with the majority showing a reading impairment (also called *dyslexia*) (Reschly, Hosp, & Schmied, 2003; Snowling, Gallagher, & Frith, 2003). Other children with learning disabilities have a mathematics or language impairment. Genetic problems cause some cases, whereas others are due to illnesses or early injuries that affected specific brain regions. As with mental retardation, however, the cause of most cases is unknown. The fact that many famous people have struggled with learning impairments—including Cher, Tom Cruise, and Danny Glover—proves that children with learning impairments can succeed by working hard and focusing on their strengths.

English-Language Learners

The majority of the world's population speaks more than one language, and most of the world's children receive at least some education in a later-acquired language. In New Guinea, for example, some children speak one language at home, another in the marketplace, learn *Tok Pisin* to communicate with children from other language backgrounds, and add English in school (Tucker, 1999).

Children can easily learn two languages (become *bilingual*) if they receive sufficient input from both languages early in life. The best situation is *additive bilingualism*, when learning the second language does not interfere with learning the first. In this case, proficiency in two languages enriches children's lives and produces some interesting cognitive advantages. Perhaps because bilingual children must shift back and forth between languages, they are especially good at attending to important information and inhibiting misleading information. These skills give bilingual children an advantage over other children when they need to reflect on language,

Is this a picture of Mexico, Spain, or somewhere else? Actually, these children are growing up in one of the many Spanish-speaking neighborhoods in the United States.

detect grammatical mistakes, and flexibly sort information on a number of different dimensions (Bialystok, 2001). The later in life a second language is introduced, however, the lower the proficiency tends to be in that language (Hakuta, Bialystok, & Wiley, 2003).

In the United States, about 18 percent of the public school enrollment speaks a language other than English (Figure 9.6), and English-language learners (children with limited proficiency in English) make up 10 percent of the public school enrollment (National Clearinghouse for English Language Acquisition, 2006). These school children speak over 400 languages, and Spanish-speaking students are by far the largest minority (Kindler, 2002).

Civil rights law requires U.S. schools to provide students from linguistic minorities with English-language training and subject-matter content. There are a number of ways to accomplish this goal. At one extreme is English-language *immersion*, in which classes are conducted only in English. With an *English as a second language approach*, children attend special classes to learn English and receive subject matter instruction in English. A popular approach is **transitional bilingual education**, where students receive instruction in their native language while they learn English, followed by a transition into English-language instruction.

Supporters of bilingual education point out that it takes about 2 years of exposure to English before students achieve *functional* use of the language. However, it takes about 4 to 7 years before they develop the skill to succeed when instruction is given only in the second language (Cummins, 1980; Thomas & Collier, 1996). The goal of bilingual programs is to prevent language-minority students from falling behind in reading and math while they are mastering English. On the other hand, defenders of immersion programs believe that children learn more rapidly in traditional classrooms and benefit from socializing with English-speaking peers.

Which type of program is most effective? Evaluations suggest that programs perform differently in different environments. In Canada, where native speakers of French make up 25 percent of the population, over 2,000 schools offer English-speaking children immersion in French-language instruction. In this environment, where parents speak the majority language and both languages are valued, children instructed in French score well on achievement tests (Bournot-Trites & Reeder, 2001; Lambert et al., 1993). In the United States, however, children in bilingual programs are often challenged by poverty and a dominant culture that doesn't value their native language. In this context, children in bilingual programs make the fastest academic strides (Hakuta, 1999). Indeed, bilingual education is an excellent example of the need to match educational strategies to the needs of students and their communities.

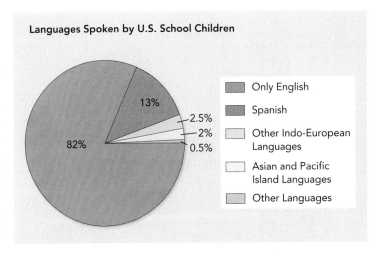

FIGURE 9.6 Bilingualism in the United States.

An increasing number of U.S. children speak a language other than English. Some of these children speak English well, but about 10 percent of the public school enrollment has limited proficiency in English.

SOURCE: Glimpse (2005).

Languages Spoken by U.S. School Children

- Only English — 82%
- Spanish — 13%
- Other Indo-European Languages — 2.5%
- Asian and Pacific Island Languages — 2%
- Other Languages — 0.5%

Gifted and Talented Children

David said his first words when he was 8 months old. By his second birthday, when most children are saying things like "Hi, Dada!", David said, "I saw a real ditch digger pick up real dirt and put in (sic) dump truck, and I saw pretend ditch

transitional bilingual education
An approach to educating English-language learners in which students receive instruction in their native language while they learn English, followed by a transition into English-language instruction.

Gifted children have unusual abilities, but they also spend a great deal of time developing their skills.

digger and sat in it and pulled the handles." According to Ellen Winner, who interviewed David's family, by 4 years David had read several volumes of the *Childcraft Encyclopedia*, and the gift he wanted most for his next birthday was an encyclopedia (Winner, 1996, p. 15).

Some children stand out because they have superior general intelligence; others have unusual aptitudes in art, music, or other specific abilities. Many scientists use the terms *gifts* and *talents* interchangeably when talking about these skills because they believe that all exceptional ability stems from a biological advantage. Others point out that *gifts* appear spontaneously but that *talents* are skills, such as playing the violin, that require specialized training (Gagné, 1997). Regardless of their theoretical approach, most researchers use the term *gifted* to talk about skills in academic subjects and *talent* to talk about artistic potential.

Like any group, gifted and talented individuals have different strengths, weaknesses, and dispositions. Children like David excel in language skills and mathematics. These "schoolhouse gifted" have a broad base of knowledge and score highly on intelligence tests. Other gifted children show more unevenness in performance. Many with exceptional artistic abilities are not outstanding students, and some even have learning disabilities (Winner, 2000). The most remarkable individuals are **prodigies**: children who perform a skill at a level that is rare even among trained professionals.

Despite their differences, many gifted children share three characteristics. First, they are *precocious*, which means they begin to master their domain earlier than most children and make more rapid progress. Second, they *learn in a qualitatively different way* because they need little help from adults to learn. Finally, they exhibit *intense interest* in their domain and are highly motivated to learn. For example, one study found that talented youths spend over 2 hours per day in activities that build skill in their domain of interest (Winner, 1996).

The most famous study of gifted children was launched by Lewis Terman in 1921. By asking teachers to nominate their smartest and youngest students, then administering IQ tests, Terman's team identified more than 1,500 gifted children (the "Termites") who were followed through adulthood. Terman found that many of the Termites spoke and read earlier than their peers, and they grew up to be enthusiastic readers who did well in school. They were also amazingly well-rounded. Compared to their peers, these high-IQ children were healthier and scored higher on measures of social adjustment. In short, Terman's work countered the idea that gifted children are all gangly nerds with poor social skills. Although some gifted children do feel uncomfortably different, others are valued for their wisdom and empathy. As one girl explained, "Everybody comes to me with their problems and I help them sort them out; in fact, I'm a bit like an agony aunt at school" (Freeman, 2001, p. 65).

One of Lewis Terman's main goals was to prove that a high IQ during childhood predicted achievement during adulthood. It does—but not as much as Terman had hoped. Although most of his sample grew up to become successful

prodigies Children who perform a skill at a level that is rare even among trained professionals.

professionals, none grew up to be creative geniuses. As Ellen Winner (1996) pointed out, two future Nobel laureates were actually rejected from the study because their IQ scores were not high enough! So although it may take intelligence to produce an Einstein or a Picasso, the vast majority of highly intelligent children will never become one (Dweck, 2002).

>>> MEMORY MAKERS <<<

1. Valuing effort, setting high standards, and teaching for understanding are _____.

   (a) characteristics of most American parents
   (b) characteristics that describe public schools more so than private schools
   (c) characteristics of cultures that show high performance in mathematics
   (d) none of the above

2. During the early grades, the gap in achievement between low-income and middle-class students _____.

   (a) stays the same   (b) becomes larger   (c) narrows

3. Small class sizes are most beneficial for _____.

   (a) high-income children in the upper grades
   (b) high-income children in the early grades
   (c) low-income children in the upper grades
   (d) low-income children in the early grades

4. The idea that schools should adopt instructional practices that produce the best outcomes in systematic studies is called _____.

   (a) evidence-based instruction   (b) open education
   (c) whole-language instruction   (d) immersion

[1-c; 2-b; 3-d; 4-a]

Individuality

In a perfect world, every child would be successful at school, cooperative at home, and popular with friends. In the real world, however, there are obvious differences in how children cope. Knowing about individual differences helps professionals decide which children are handling life well and which are drifting off course.

Measuring Cognitive Ability

Have you ever thought you could do better in classes than your grades show? If so, you know that most people draw a distinction between the *potential* to learn and what *has actually* been learned. In theory, psychologists also distinguish between **intelligence**, which is an individual's potential to learn and adapt to the environment (also called *aptitude*), and **achievement**, which is how much someone has actually learned about a specific subject. This distinction makes conceptual sense: A fourth grader might be capable of learning the material, yet still fail in school due to poor preparation or an undetected hearing loss. In practice, it is impossible to completely separate potential and achievement because scores on both types of tests are related to one's learning experiences (Ceci, 1991). But even if the distinction between intelligence and achievement is not as clear as scientists would like, tests that are designed to tap these concepts are popular ways of assessing cognitive differences among children.

intelligence An individual's potential to learn and adapt to the environment.

achievement How much someone has learned about a specific academic domain.

INTELLIGENCE TESTING. The best way to understand why intelligence tests contain the questions they do is to consider where they came from. Early attempts to design an intelligence test were launched by Sir Francis Galton (1822–1911), a half cousin of Charles Darwin. Galton collected data on a large number of people, recording such things as head size, visual and auditory sensitivity, and how fast people reacted to stimuli. Later, others experimented with different tasks, such as the speed of naming colors. But these early efforts to build an intelligence test failed because performance on simple skills does not correlate with an outcome that should be a consequence of intelligence: school performance.

The next attempt to create an intelligence test is one of the most famous stories in psychology. Between 1881 and 1886, a series of laws in France made school attendance free and compulsory.* By 1904, the French Ministry of Education was eager to have a procedure that would identify students with cognitive limitations who would benefit from special education classes. The Ministry decided against asking teachers to pick out these students, fearing they would pick the poor or troublesome children to be removed from their classes. Instead, French psychologist Alfred Binet (1857–1911) was commissioned to develop an objective screening test. In 1905, Binet and his colleague, Théodore Simon, published the first version of the *Binet-Simon Intelligence Test.*

Armed with his own research on intelligence as well as Galton's experiences, Binet had two insights that shaped the field of intelligence testing. First, he rejected the approach of looking at "elementary" sensations and reaction times. Instead, he assembled tasks that measured so-called higher-order abilities, such as problem solving, comprehension, and reasoning. Second, he noticed that slower learners performed much like younger children. Therefore, by administering items that children passed at different ages, he could compute each child's *mental age*, which is the age typically associated with that child's level of performance.

Lewis Terman (1877–1956), a psychologist at Stanford University, later modified Binet's test. Following an earlier suggestion, Terman reported results as an **IQ (intelligence quotient) score**, a number that indicated whether children scored below average, average, or above average. To compute IQ scores, a child's mental age (MA) was divided by his or her chronological age (CA), then multiplied by 100 (IQ = MA/CA × 100). Thus every child whose chronological age was the same as his or her mental age had an average IQ of 100. This formula was eventually abandoned in favor of computing IQ scores from tables. By convention, though, the average score is still 100.

Figure 9.7 shows you how to compare one child's IQ score with another's. Recall from Chapter 1 that many traits are distributed in the population as a bell-shaped (normal) curve, with many people clustering around the average and a few individuals having very high or very low scores. The distribution of IQ scores also approximates this pattern. Notice in Figure 9.7 that 100 is the mean score, and that roughly 68 percent of the population scores between 85 and 115. The distance between each vertical bar is a *standard deviation*, a measure of the degree to which scores vary from the mean. Most intelligence tests have a standard deviation of 15 points, so a score of 115 is 1 standard deviation above the mean and a score of 130 is 2 standard deviations above the mean. In a normal distribution, the percentage of people who fall between each pair of adjacent bars is fixed by definition. Therefore, if you know the mean and standard deviation for a test and

IQ (intelligence quotient) score
A number that indicates whether children have below average, average, or above average intelligence.

_____

*compulsory: Required, mandatory.

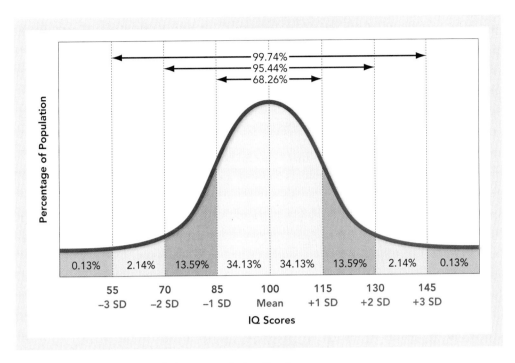

FIGURE 9.7 IQ scores and the normal distribution.

The distribution of IQ scores follows a normal, bell-shaped, distribution. Specific scores correspond to specific standard deviation units (shown across the bottom). By definition, "100" is the mean score. The percentage of individuals who score between the mean and each standard deviation unit is fixed by definition. For example, less than 3 percent of the population scores above 130 (more than 2 standard deviations above the mean).

a child's score, you know how well the child scored compared to other children. For example, Sammy scored 115 on a test with a standard deviation of 15 points scores, so he scored in the 84th percentile (better than 84 percent of his peers).

A modern version of Binet's test is the *Stanford-Binet Intelligence Scale*, an in-dividually administered test for people ages 2 years through adulthood. Another widely used test is the *Wechsler Intelligence Scale for Children* (WISC-IV), which was developed by psychologist David Wechsler. (The WISC-IV is used for chil-dren ages 6 through 16 years; other Wechsler tests are available for preschoolers and adults.) Items on the WISC are divided into four composites (sections) with multiple subtests in each composite: verbal comprehension (such as vocabulary and other measures of verbal understanding and reasoning), perceptual reasoning (such as the ability to reproduce patterns with colored blocks), working memory (the ability to hold information in mind and act on it to produce a result), and processing speed (such as the ability to search a list of symbols to find a target). Example items appear in Figure 9.8. Children receive separate scores on each composite as well as an overall (full-scale) IQ score.

IQ scores become fairly stable over time and, therefore, meaningful by age 5 (Brody, 1992; Weinert & Hany, 2003). (As you learned in Chapter 5, most tests for infants and toddlers tend not to be useful predictors of later intelligence, largely because the skills they tap are not highly correlated with later learning and reasoning ability.) Supporters of IQ tests argue that the tests provide the following useful information during the school years:

Children who are accustomed to showing off what they know in test situations score higher on intelligence tests than their peers who are more reserved about talking to an adult.

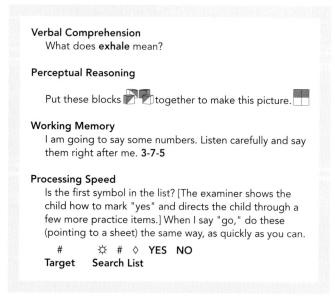

FIGURE 9.8 Typical intelligence test items.

These questions are similar to items that appear on intelligence tests for children. (Actual items are protected by copyright and cannot be reproduced.) Intelligence tests include more types of items than are shown here.

▶ *IQ scores predict academic success.* The correlation between IQ scores and grades is about .50, which means that 25 percent of the variability in grades can be accounted for by IQ. The remaining 75 percent is associated with other factors, including interest in school, ability to cooperate, and so forth (Neisser et al., 1996).

▶ *The testing process provides a sample of children's behavior.* One reason intelligence tests predict academic success is that behaviors that help children do well on tests—such as sitting still and listening, cooperating with the goals of the examiner, and inhibiting irrelevant behavior—are also important in school. Examiners gain insight into why a child might be having trouble in class by paying attention to children's language abilities, fine motor skills, and ability to attend.

▶ *IQ scores predict later adjustment and marital, job, and educational success (Wilk, Desmarais, & Sackett, 1995).* In fact, IQ scores often predict later adjustment better than other characteristics, including personality and mental health ratings (Kohlberg et al., 1972).

In sum, intelligence tests predict school performance, give examiners an opportunity to watch how children behave in a structured situation, and predict later success.

CRITICISMS OF INTELLIGENCE TESTS. Despite the fact that IQ scores correlate with so many outcomes, not everyone is enthusiastic about intelligence tests. One problem is that IQ scores are not pure measures of innate ability. For example, the average difference between a child's scores at ages 8 and 17 was 9 points in one study (Brody, 1992), and children whose scores increased in another study tended to come from families that valued academic success and monitored their progress (McCall, Appelbaum, & Hogarty, 1973). When one school closed during the 1960s to avoid integration, the IQ scores of black children dropped by about 6 points for every missed year of school compared to their peers who attended school (Green et al., 1964). These data suggest that IQ scores are the result of children's abilities interacting with environmental opportunities (Ceci, 1996).

Another criticism is that IQ tests are *culturally biased* because they ask for information that children from white, middle-class households are especially likely to know. It is true that the average score of African American children is about 10 to 15 points lower than the average of European American children, whereas Latinos and American Indians score between these two groups (Nisbett, 2005; Suzuki & Valencia, 1997). Do these findings mean the tests are unfair? There is no single answer to this question because there are several types of bias. *Predictive bias* occurs when test scores predict lower performance for a group than what that group actually achieves. IQ tests do not have predictive bias because they predict school performance equally well for African American and European American children (Neisser et al., 1996). But as Figure 9.8 illustrates, they are *culturally loaded,* meaning they contain items and procedures that reflect some cultures more than others. For example, some children may never have encountered specific vocabulary words or played with games or puzzles that give them practice manipulating shapes. Also, middle-class children are familiar with the ritual in which adults ask questions so children can show off what they know, but this type of language interaction is not universal (Heath, 1989). As a result, test situations that seem like enjoyable games to some children may be strange and uncomfortable situations that inhibit others from talking.

Because heritability estimates for intelligence range between .50 and .70, many authors have tried to counter criticism of IQ tests by looking for evidence that group differences in scores reflect underlying genetic differences rather than test bias (Gottfredson, 2005; Rushton & Jensen, 2005). (Recall from Chapter 2 that heritability estimates alone cannot tell us why there are differences between groups.) In a sophisticated study to test the biological hypothesis, Sandra Scarr and her colleagues (1977) gave an IQ test to dark-skinned individuals in the Philadelphia area and estimated each person's degree of African and European ancestry from blood samples. Their findings contradicted the claim that ethnic differences in average IQ have a biological basis: African Americans who had a large number of European ancestors scored no better or worse than those who had a large proportion of African ancestry. Similarly, the average IQ score of children fathered by African American servicemen who partnered with German women following World War II was almost identical to the average score of children with European American fathers (Eyferth, 1961). But despite such evidence, the origin of group differences in scores remains a hotly debated subject.

If intelligence tests are culturally loaded, why don't psychologists design a culture-free test? One reason is that performance on even seemingly simple tasks is influenced by culture (Kearins, 1981; Klich & Davidson, 1983; Miyamoto, Nisbett, & Masuda, 2006). But a culture-free test would also undermine the *purpose* of tests, which is to predict behavior in a specific environment (such as the culture of school). Given this state of affairs, the best solution is to understand the limitations of intelligence tests and guard against inappropriate uses of the scores.

ACHIEVEMENT TESTING. In contrast to intelligence tests, which try to predict future learning, achievement tests measure what children have already learned in specific areas, such as reading, mathematics, social science, and science. The assumption behind achievement tests is that a large number of items define a body of knowledge in a field, so we can estimate achievement by sampling from this set.

Achievement testing becomes controversial when schools are pressured to prove that their students are measuring up to expectations. One concern is *teaching to the test*, which is the practice of preparing children for the content of a specific test rather than helping them master the body of knowledge the items represent. Because emphasizing test material can cause teachers to sacrifice time they would have spent on other topics, achievement test scores can rise even though students are not learning more (and may be learning less).

At-Risk Children

Some children who take intelligence and achievement tests have been referred for mental health evaluations due to problems at home or in school. The typical client during middle childhood is an 8- to 10-year-old boy with externalizing behavior problems, such as bullying or failing to follow rules in class. Children are also evaluated in schools, clinics, and medical settings for poor academic performance and a host of other concerns.

Most of the time, adults complain about behaviors almost all children show from time to time, such as lying, disobedience, or reluctance to go to school.

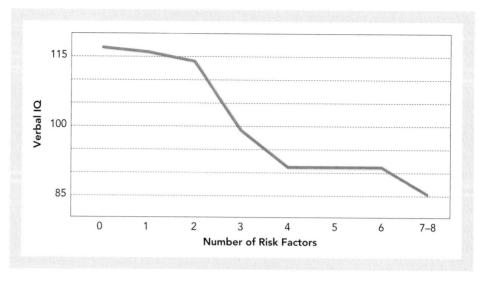

FIGURE 9.9 The cumulative stressor hypothesis.

Children's development suffers as a function of the number of risk factors in their environments. For example, there is a sharp decline in the verbal IQ scores of children who face three or more environmental stressors (such as poverty, low levels of maternal education, and single parenthood).

SOURCE: Sameroff et al. (1987).

When this is the case, the goal is to determine whether the child is showing *clinically significant* behavior. Symptoms are clinically significant when the behavior is extreme enough to need treatment or is one of several behaviors that define a particular syndrome, such as attention deficit disorder.

What are the differences between children who are likely to outgrow their problems and children who may not? Two sets of factors help predict how serious a child's problems are: characteristics of the child's behavior and characteristics of the child's environment (Stouthamer-Loeber et al., 2002). In general, children with externalizing problems are more likely to have continued problems if they have a high rate of troublesome behavior (Broidy et al., 2003; Lee & Hinshaw, 2004), if they behave badly in more than one environment (such as at home and at school) (Xue, Hodges, & Wotring, 2004), if they show a variety of antisocial behavior (such as stealing and lying rather than just lying), (Lahey, McBurnett, & Loeber, 2000), and if they were clearly more antisocial than other children early in life (Leve & Chamberlain, 2004; Loeber, 1982).

Children's environments also have a great deal to do with how long problems persist. For example, one famous study looked at a variety of risk factors or *stressors*, including maternal mental illness, poverty, low levels of parental education, and single parenthood (Sameroff et al., 1987). Figure 9.9 shows that children's average IQ scores dropped steeply once they accumulated three or more risks. Findings such as these have led to the **cumulative stressor hypothesis,** which is the idea that the sheer number of stressors in a child's life is the best predictor of long-term problems.

Cumulative stressor exposure helps explain why poverty takes such a devastating toll on children. As you can see in Figure 9.10, 8- to 10-year-olds from low-income environments face a large array of challenges, including more crowded housing, exposure to noise and violence, family turmoil, and separation from

cumulative stressor hypothesis
The hypothesis that the sheer number of environmental stressors in a child's life is a stronger predictor of developmental outcomes than the presence of any particular stressor. Stressors are such things as maternal mental illness, poverty, low levels of parental education, and single parenthood.

family members. Although any single stressor is not a good predictor of later adjustment, the *number* of stressors is an excellent predictor of children's mental health scores and their ability to control their actions (Evans & English, 2002). Research on the cumulative stressor model explains why many people skip happily through childhood even though they face one or two challenges: Children are "built" to absorb a little hardship. Beyond a certain level, however, hardship overwhelms their ability to cope and interferes with development. We will revisit the topic of stress and development in Chapter 11, when we look at the factors that help children cope in difficult environments. As you will see throughout this book, the risks people face are a function of many factors—including whether they are male or female.

Boys and Girls

The Lost Boys in our opening story show how sharply some cultures divide the roles of males and females. But how different are boys and girls during middle childhood? As you will read next, there are numerous average differences between the sexes, from very obvious differences in social behavior to subtle differences in cognitive skills.

SOCIAL BEHAVIOR AND ATTITUDES. This is what 9-year-old Shameka said when we spoke with her about boys and girls:

Interviewer: Do the girls play with the boys at school?

Shameka: For my school there's mostly girls hanging together and boys hanging together. The boys usually are at the field playing football and the girls are just, ah, doing something.

Interviewer: What do the girls do?

Shameka: I don't know (laugh). Like play house or tag or something like that.

Interviewer: How do the girls feel about the boys at school?

Shameka: They're obnoxious.

As we mentioned in Chapter 7, most children prefer playing with same-sex peers by the time they start school. The preference for same-sex playmates continues during the school years, when play groups become even more well-defined and less fluid.

Why are children more likely to socialize with same-sex friends? One possibility is that humans are programmed to affiliate with people who are members of the same group. Alternatively, children may simply gravitate to peers who play the way they do or people they think will share the same interests (Barbu et al., 2000; Hoffmann & Powlishta, 2001). But regardless of why children segregate, their groups display some interesting differences during middle childhood. Males tend to congregate in larger groups that are farther from adult supervision, where they quickly establish hierarchical pecking orders that are maintained by rougher styles of play. Often, boy's activities are focused on a project that has a clearly defined group goal. In contrast, girls play closer to adults in smaller groups, are

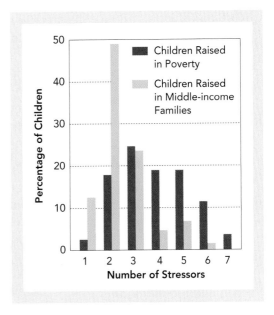

FIGURE 9.10 Growing up in poverty.

Eight- to ten-year olds raised in poverty are much more likely than their middle-income peers to face multiple stressors such as violence, family turmoil, child–family separation, crowding, noise, and poor housing quality.

SOURCE: Evans & English (2002).

Around the world, boys and girls spend a great deal of time playing in single-sex groups.

less competitive, and more often select play themes related to household and romantic scripts (Maccoby, 2002; Martin & Fabes, 2001).

Sometime around 11 or 12 years of age, children start to become more egalitarian about the activities they think are appropriate for males and females. Now girls start to be less enthusiastic about traditionally feminine characteristics, perhaps because they realize society is rather tolerant of females who have "masculine" interests (Liben & Bigler, 2002).

COGNITIVE SKILLS. It is difficult to pin down sex differences in cognitive skills because patterns change over time, geographic locations, and tasks. Boys and girls also favor different play materials, so we don't know to what extent sex differences in basic skills are caused by neurological differences, different experiences, or some combination of factors. Despite these complications, it is fascinating to look at what differences actually exist by middle to late childhood.

One research strategy is to track performance on standardized achievement tests. Data for 4th- and 8th-grade children are available from the National Assessment of Educational Progress ("the Nation's Report Card"), an assessment of what students know in eight subjects including reading, mathematics, geography, and science. Results show a female advantage for reading but a male advantage for mathematics, geography, and science. These differences show up early, at least by the 4th grade (National Center for Education Statistics, 2006).

But there is no reason to believe that achievement test differences are set in stone. By 2000, girls in Britain were outperforming boys in all public school examinations except for physical education. No one knows exactly why a performance shift occurred, but changes in test formats and peer cultures that ridicule boys for studying might be involved (Freeman, 2001, 2003). Other international data also show narrowing differences between girls and boys. Pooling across countries, there was no significant gender difference in mathematics achievement for eighth graders who participated in the 2003 TIMSS (Mullis et al., 2004), and data from the United States showed only a small difference, with boys averaging 507 points and girls averaging 502.

If gender differences in mathematics achievement are small, why is there so much talk about a gender gap in mathematics? One reason is that the number of boys and girls who achieve high scores can be very imbalanced even when the average difference between groups is not very large. Consider an example in which boys average 100 on a hypothetical test with a standard deviation of 15 points. If each boy with a score of 130 or above is admitted into a math enrichment program, 2.3 percent of the boys will be eligible. If girls average only 5 points lower, less than half as many will be eligible for math enrichment. Because future engineers and some scientists will be drawn from this top group, it is easy to see why women would be underrepresented in scientific careers.

Another reason people worry about sex differences is that the males score better than females on difficult mathematical reasoning tests even though females often score better on basic calculations. Why is this so? One hypothesis focuses on how fast children retrieve basic math facts. Math-fact retrieval is a strong predictor of mathematical reasoning, perhaps because students who retrieve information quickly have more time to perform operations before information fades from working memory (Royer et al., 1999). High-performing boys start retrieving basic math facts faster than high-performing girls in the 4th grade. During later grades, males become better than females at ignoring irrelevant information and at translating information into forms that can be solved numerically (Kimura, 1999; Low & Over, 1993).

It is also possible that gender differences in spatial reasoning account for the male advantage in mathematical reasoning. Figure 9.11 illustrates two spatial tasks that favor males: mental rotation and spatial visualization. Males score better on mental rotation as early as 4 to 5 years of age and are clearly superior by 9 to 12 years—at least in middle-class and upper-income families (Kimura, 1999; Levine et al., 2005). Because good spatial skills and good mathematical skills often occur together, some scientists believe that spatial reasoning causes the male superiority in mathematics (Geary et al., 2000). New evidence suggests that math-fact retrieval and spatial reasoning both contribute to the gender difference in mathematical reasoning: Good spatial abilities help children build a mental representation of mathematical problems while efficient math-fact retrieval helps them compute the answers (Royer & Garofoli, 2005).

SCHOOL-RELATED PROBLEMS. As you learned in Chapters 2 and 3, males are more likely than females to have a variety of genetically related disorders because they lack the "insurance policy" of an extra X chromosome. As a result, males are 50 percent more likely to have mental retardation (Sachs & Barrett, 2000). Males are also more than twice as likely to receive special education services for learning disabilities, although the reason is unclear (Coutinho, Oswald, & Best, 2002). It is possible that males and females suffer from learning disabilities at equal rates but that males have more severe cases. It is also possible that learning disabilities are overlooked in girls because they "play school" better, waiting patiently or finding ways to look busy rather than moving off task (Anderson, 1997).

Regardless of why boys are referred so often for evaluations, one thing is clear: Teachers *perceive* them as bigger nuisances than girls. Depending on the setting, boys are 2 to 9 times more likely to be identified has having attention deficit hyperactivity disorder during the school years and more likely to be diagnosed with a conduct disorder, a pattern of unacceptable behavior that can include getting into fights, destroying property or stealing, and breaking rules (American Psychiatric Association, 2000). In recent years, many parents have been pushing for schools to adjust to boys rather than always expecting boys to adjust to school. For some, this means finding out which teachers like boys and structure their classrooms so that boys can succeed, often by giving boys more time for physical activity between classes and tolerating louder, more energetic behavior in the classroom.

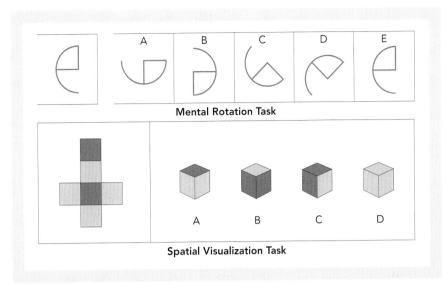

FIGURE 9.11 Two spatial tasks.

Males achieve higher average scores than females on spatial tasks such as mental rotation and spatial visualization. The largest differences are found on mental rotation, which requires people to imagine what a shape would look like in a different orientation. The male and female distributions of scores overlap, however, so on every task some females perform better than some males.

Some school districts are experimenting with single-sex classes to cope with the fact that boys are more active and distractible than girls during the elementary school years. Critics say that same-sex classrooms do not always improve learning and violate children's right to receive the same educational experience regardless of sex.

>>> MEMORY MAKERS <<<

1. In theory, intelligence tests try to measure _____ whereas achievement tests try to measure _____.

   (a) what an individual has already learned; potential to learn
   (b) potential to learn, what an individual has already learned

2. The idea that the sheer number of stressors in a child's life is the best predictor of long-term problems is called the _____ hypothesis.

   (a) clinically significant   (b) cumulative stressor
   (c) density   (d) variety and risk

3. Speed of math-fact retrieval and spatial reasoning are two explanations for why _____.

   (a) males score higher than females on basic calculations
   (b) females score higher than males on basic calculations
   (c) males score higher than females on challenging mathematics tests
   (d) females score higher than males on challenging mathematics tests

[1-b; 2-b; 3-c]

Revisiting Developmental Principles: Do Parents Matter?

Horizons expand during middle childhood, when a game of softball is suddenly more attractive than the dinner waiting at home. In addition to friends and teachers, school-aged children are influenced by the broader world as they are exposed to more varied television shows and a wider array of books. With all of these forces competing for time, do parents matter? More specifically, do interactions with parents mold children's personalities and interests?

Author Judith Harris rocked the country by answering "No." In *The Nurture Assumption* (1998), Harris attacked the widespread assumption that how parents raise children is the main reason why people turn out the way they do. Instead, Harris argued that children cast off early learning "as easily as the dorky sweater their mother made them wear" (p. 13). Harris believes that lessons from parents stay home while children acquire their adult personalities from interactions with other children.

Harris's **group socialization theory** starts with the idea that learning is context specific. Of course, children learn a lot from parents, including how to talk and how to act around family members. Still, Harris argues that these lessons tend not to transfer outside the home. For example, when parents speak a different language than the rest of the community, their children learn to speak the dominant language without an accent. And as many parents know, children who are wild and uninhibited at home can be cautious and inhibited at school.

Why do children so often abandon their "home" behavior when they step outside? According to Harris, people pay attention to relevant social groups, so children pay attention to the people they will be competing against as adults—other children. Successes and failures with peers then determine their subsequent personalities. As Harris explained, "Children would develop into the same sort of adults if we left their lives outside the home unchanged—left them in their schools and their neighborhoods—but switched all the parents around" (1998, p. 359).

Harris admits that parents influence children in contexts where they repeatedly interact. As a result, parents influence food preferences and how children act

group socialization theory A theory that states that children's personalities are constructed as they adopt the behaviors and attitudes of their peers and compare themselves to others in their social group. This theory assumes that one's status and role in the peer group build characteristics that carry into adult life.

around family members. But she objects to the tendency to assume that children's behavior resembles that of their parents because parents *cause* their children's behavior. Instead, parents who are doing well may have well-adjusted children simply due to shared genes and cultural settings—not because they are better parents. Harris poses an interesting question to make this point: If parents are children's primary socialization agents, then why are children reared in the same family so different? Group socialization theory says that genetic differences and different experiences with peers make sisters and brothers different from each other.

Many professionals welcomed *The Nurture Assumption* with open arms. Finally, they said, we can stop blaming parents and see that children play a role in their own development. On the other hand, critics accused Harris of selecting studies that proved her point (Gardner, 1998). For example, by emphasizing studies that correlated parenting behavior to children's behavior years later, Harris reduced the chances of finding significant relationships. In fact, parents' behavior does have an impact on children at the time it is measured (Lewis, 1999). As we discussed in Chapter 7, for example, children's aggressive behavior can be altered by changing parenting behavior.

The publicity sparked by Harris's book generated interesting discussions about how parents influence children and the limits of that influence. Although experts continue to argue about details, most agree that the developmental principles from Chapter 1 can help us understand both sides of this issue.

1. **Development is the joint product of nature and nurture.** Many forces influence children, including genetically transmitted traits, experiences in the home, and contact with peers. These experiences then lead to different outcomes depending on children's strengths and weaknesses. In general, variations in parenting behavior have smaller effects among children with easy temperaments (because these children tend to grow up well-adjusted regardless of their environment) and larger effects for children with difficult temperaments (Belsky, 1997).

2. **Physical, cognitive, and socioemotional development are interrelated.** Experiences can influence children indirectly. As we mentioned in this chapter, children who are exposed to harsh physical punishment tend to view other people's behavior negatively, which is associated with higher levels of aggression. In other words, parental control strategies lead to cognitive changes that influence children's social relationships (Weiss et al., 1992). Similarly, the eating habits parents establish can promote or deter obesity, which in turn influences children's peer relationships for years to come. So even though differences among parents may not have a big effect on whether individual children are outgoing or shy, parenting decisions do affect children's lives.

3. **Developmental outcomes vary over time and contexts.** Education professor Howard Gardner believes that parents and peers influence children in complementary ways (1998). Parents have more influence on children's educational achievement, sense of responsibility, orderliness, charitableness, and behavior toward authority figures. In contrast, peers are critical for learning cooperation and influencing how children interact with their friends. But these links between socializing experiences and individual behavior vary over time and contexts. For instance, parents who force their children to clean their rooms will temporarily have neater children, but personality often overwhelms training once children move to college.

4. **Development is characterized by continuity and discontinuity.** Some lessons from parents are carried into adulthood while others are stored on a shelf. In general, there is more continuity between childhood and adult behavior when people find themselves in similar cultures across these developmental periods. But when cultural circumstances differ, people adjust. This is why most college students reject their parents' taste in clothes, yet fights between college roommates often stem from family expectations that are difficult to change, such as attitudes about sharing personal belongings.

As always, then, the story of development is delightfully complicated.

The refugees in our opening story illustrate how multiple influences shape children's lives. Growing up without parents to guide them, the Lost Boys of Sudan formed supportive peer groups and later adapted to their new cultures. But they also clung to their families' values, creating new lives that were a blend of past, present, and hopes for the future. To a lesser extent, all children confront new challenges when they move into adolescence and prepare to choose careers, find partners, and start their own families. How children make this journey is the next chapter in the story of human development.

⟩⟩⟩ SUMMARY ⟨⟨⟨

Health and Safety

1. Each year, about 20 to 25 percent of children experience an injury that requires them to miss school, stay in bed, or receive medical treatment. Younger children are especially prone to injuries because they are more likely to overestimate their abilities.

2. **Asthma**, an inflammatory lung disease, affects 1 out of every 8 children. Children with asthma experience breathlessness when they are exposed to allergens, cold air, or exercise. Asthma is managed by eliminating environmental triggers and preventing attacks with medication.

3. Overweight children are at risk for numerous chronic diseases, including diabetes, sleep disturbances, and asthma. Interventions to prevent weight problems familiarize children with nutritious foods and increase their activity levels.

4. Children who are neglected or physically abused are more likely than their peers to do poorly in school and have problems with social relationships. About 40 percent of children who are sexually abused show few or no immediate symptoms, but some suffer from depression and other psychological problems.

Family Life

5. Children are exposed to stress hormones when there is fighting in the home or family instability. They show fewer stress reactions when their families are nurturant and when primary caregivers have access to social support from friends and relatives.

6. Children of divorce have more behavioral problems, lower school achievement, lower earnings as adults, and a higher rate of marital instability than their peers. The magnitude of the difference between children of divorce and other children is small for most outcomes, however, and many factors, such as the quality of parents' postdivorce relationship, influence how children adjust. Regardless of the structure of a family, authoritative parents have children with fewer behavioral problems and more positive relationships with siblings.

7. Children of gay or lesbian parents are as well-adjusted as children from other types of families, and they experience similar gender-role and sexual development.

8. Children's understanding of adoption develops gradually, so parents need to revisit the issue of adoption as children mature. By 12 to 13 years, the majority of children understand that adoption is a permanent arrangement based on a legal transfer or rights.

Children, Schools, and Achievement

9. Cultures that promote high mathematics achievement value effort, set high standards for children, allocate more instructional time for mathematics, and use teaching strategies that build conceptual knowledge.

Low-income and minority children often begin elementary school lacking basic academic skills because they encounter few academic activities at home.

10. Small classes in the early grades particularly benefit low-income students, and these benefits persist even after students return to larger classes.

11. Successful education helps students master fundamental skills, understand concepts, and maintain their desire to learn. Many educators support **evidence-based instruction**: instructional approaches that have produced the best achievement in scientific studies.

12. Educators in the United States favor **inclusion**, which is the practice of instructing children with **mental retardation** (significantly subaverage intelligence) or **specific learning disabilities** (problems mastering a specific set of skills) in regular classrooms whenever possible.

13. Popular instructional approaches for students who do not speak English are *immersion* and **transitional bilingual education** programs. Immersion is most successful when parents speak the majority language and both languages are valued.

14. As a group, gifted and talented children are healthier than their peers and score better on measures of social adjustment. However, most children who learn quickly or have special talent at a young age do not grow up to be creative geniuses.

Individuality

15. **Intelligence (IQ)** tests predict school performance and later adjustment. However, scores are not pure measures of ability because they are influenced by educational opportunities and the culture of children's homes. **Achievement** tests measure how much children have already learned about a specific knowledge domain.

16. Children who show externalizing behavior during middle childhood are more likely to have continued problems as they grow if their unwanted behavior occurs frequently, in multiple settings, is one of several deviant behaviors, and has an early age of onset. The **cumulative stressor hypothesis** says that the sheer number of environmental stressors in a child's life is a strong predictor of negative outcomes later in development.

17. School-aged children play predominantly in same-sex peer groups. Females score higher than males on reading tests, whereas males score higher on tests of mathematics, geography, science, and spatial processing. Males are more likely than girls to have mental retardation and to be referred for specific learning disabilities.

Revisiting Developmental Principles: Do Parents Matter?

18. **Group socialization theory** says children's personalities are molded by their experiences with peers, but critics say that this theory underestimates the importance of parental behavior. Four principles of development help explain why parenting choices influence some—but not all—aspects of development. (1) Nature and nurture are important, so parental behavior influences children differently depending on their temperaments. (2) It is easy to overlook parental influences because one domain of parenting (such as family diet influencing weight) can have an indirect influence on an area of development that seems unrelated (such as peer relationships). (3) Links between parental behavior and child outcomes are inconsistent across studies because developmental outcomes change over time and contexts. (4) Consequently, there is continuity from childhood experiences to adult behavior, but there is also discontinuity.

〉〉〉 KEY TERMS 〈〈〈

asthma (p. 351)
intergenerational transmission of abuse (p. 354)
nuclear family (p. 357)
meta-analysis (p. 359)
open education (p. 369)
phonics (p. 369)
whole-language instruction (p. 369)
evidence-based instruction (p. 370)
mainstreaming (p. 371)
inclusion (p. 371)

person-first language (p. 372)
mental retardation (p. 372)
specific learning disabilities (p. 372)
transitional bilingual education (p. 373)
prodigies (p. 374)
intelligence (p. 375)
achievement (p. 375)
IQ (intelligence quotient) score (p. 376)
cumulative stressor hypothesis (p. 380)
group socialization theory (p. 384)

CHAPTER TEN

Profile of Adolescence

Stories of Our Lives

An Extreme Teen

At a 1995 motorcycle race, Travis Pastrana lifted his hands and legs off his motorcycle at the peak of a jump to debut his "nothing" jump. At 16, he astounded fans at the San Francisco X Games Freestyle Motocross event by jumping 100 feet off course into the San Francisco Bay, completing a stunt that helped him win the event but also cost him a $10,000 fine. Two years later, the freestyle motocross champion fulfilled a dream when he executed his most famous feat, which a writer later described in a book for young motocross fans (Poolos, 2005):

> { The young are permanently in a state resembling intoxication; for youth is sweet and they are growing. }
>
> Aristotle

On November 14, [Travis Pastrana] jumped his Suzuki into the Grand Canyon. He had planned every last detail of the stunt—including extensive skydiving lessons—and he was confident he could do it safely. His mother and father accompanied him to Arizona, along with a small crew and cameramen from the television show *Ripley's Believe It or Not.* Travis first jumped the bike into the canyon in a practice run. He gave his parents a scare when he barely cleared the cliff after jumping off the ramp. For his second jump, he pinned the throttle in fourth gear, hit the ramp, pulled a backflip, then ditched the bike and parachuted into the 2,000-foot (610-m) gorge. When asked by a reporter at ESPN.com why he did a backflip into the Grand Canyon, Travis replied, "Heck, since I was about ten years old I wanted to jump it. Every motocrosser in the world thinks about it." (p. 46)

Today, Pastrana is one of the biggest names in action sports. But he was never just another reckless teen. The man who has been called "one of the most daring and entertaining motocross riders on the planet" finished high school 2 years early and enrolled in the University of Maryland—although he had already earned enough money to build his own track ("Motocross—Travis Pastrana," 2005). In a sport where piercings and tattoos are all the rage, Pastrana's clean-cut, apple-pie image has won the respect of his competitors and a mountain of endorsement opportunities.

Travis Pastrana's passion was celebrated by his close-knit, supportive family. As his mother explained, "We are in it 100 percent, I've been with him every step of the way" (Poolos, 2005, p. 15). Meanwhile, Travis has a simple way of summing up what makes him tick. "My strengths and weaknesses are the same," he explains. "I've got the willingness and stupidity to try anything. If I think it's even remotely possible, I'll do it" ("Travis Pastrana," 2005, para. 3).

DURING HIS ADOLESCENCE, Travis Pastrana (born 1983) had the love of novelty and enthusiasm for life that make the teenage years so exciting. Yet the respect he earned from his parents, fans, and friends shows how accomplished even the most "extreme" teen can be. Like Travis, all children begin to think and act differently as they move into their teen years. These changes influence how they make decisions, how they explore their identities, and how they interact with friends. Suddenly, boys and girls who used to collect trading cards and play handheld video games are wondering, "Should I drink alcohol at a party?", "Should I go to college?", and even "Should I do a backflip into the Grand Canyon on my motorcycle?" The increased freedom to make risky decisions—together with the ability to generate offbeat ideas—are due to transformations that will forever close the door on childhood.

The Wonder of Puberty

When Jessica started to develop breasts a few years before her friends, she hoped she'd end up looking just like her Aunt Theresa. "She had such a feminine body," Jessica told us when she was 22 years old. "I wanted to look exactly like her. But then the boys started teasing me and talking behind my back, and it wasn't so much fun anymore," she laughed.

Changing bodies are a source of anticipation and uncertainty for many teens. Some events, such as breast development in girls and facial hair in boys, are welcomed. Others, such as the increase in body odor and acne, cause embarrassment and worry. But regardless of whether a teen views these changes as positive or not, the end result of puberty is a mature face, a different body, and even a different brain.

Puberty is the period of rapid development during which individuals become capable of reproduction. In contrast, **adolescence** is the time between puberty and adulthood when children undergo the physical and psychological changes they need to assume adult roles. Unlike puberty, which is a universal phase of development, the concept of adolescence is socially constructed, with different cultures having different ideas about this time of life. In industrialized societies, puberty usually marks the beginning of a period of adolescence that lasts up to a decade.

puberty The period of rapid development during which individuals become capable of reproduction.

adolescence The time between puberty and adulthood when children undergo the physical and psychological changes they need to assume adult roles. In industrialized societies, puberty usually marks the beginning of a period of adolescence that may last up to a decade.

Hormones: The Puberty "Directors"

People usually think of puberty as a time when our hormones suddenly "kick in," but this image is not entirely accurate. Surprisingly, virtually everything needed to complete the pubertal process is present and functional at birth. It is more accurate to say that puberty is the time when "the heat gets turned up" on a system that has been in place for more than a decade. That heat comes from the **endocrine system**: a control system of glands that produce, store, and secrete **hormones**. Unlike chemicals that influence cells near their point of origin, hormones are molecules that travel through the bloodstream to affect distant cells.

You can see the major structures of the endocrine system in Figure 10.1. On the top is the hypothalamus, a structure in the brain that monitors and regulates the body's hormone levels. The main instructions from the hypothalamus are sent to the pituitary gland, a tiny gland below the brain and behind your eyes. The pituitary gland is often called the "master gland" because it receives messages from the hypothalamus, releases its own growth hormone, and tells other glands to produce hormones.

Hormones typically deliver their instructions to cells in the body that have receptors on the surface or inside the cells that can respond to that hormone. Some target cells stimulate the release of other hormones that promote the growth and development of our sexual organs, muscle and bones, and brain. This cascade of hormones must be constantly monitored to maintain a state of internal balance called *homeostasis*.

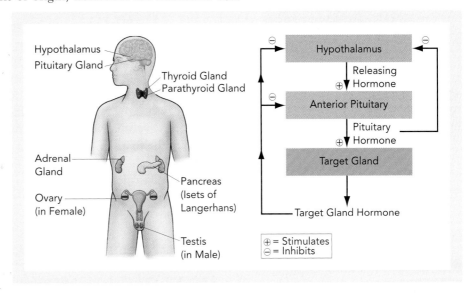

FIGURE 10.1 The endocrine system.

The major hormone-producing organs of the endocrine system are shown on the left. One way this system coordinates hormone levels is through a negative feedback loop, as shown on the right. Like a thermostat that turns off a furnace when the desired temperature is reached, the hypothalamus inhibits hormone production when levels are at or above a specific setting. When levels fall below that setting, the hypothalamus sends instructions to the pituitary to release more hormones. During puberty, this setting increases (like turning a thermostat up to a higher temperature) and more hormones are produced.

SOURCE: Adapted from Hiller-Sturmhöfel & Bartke (1998).

HORMONAL FEEDBACK. One of the ways the endocrine system monitors and coordinates hormonal levels is the *negative feedback loop*. In a simple loop, illustrated in Figure 10.1, the brain inhibits production of a hormone unless it receives information from the body that the hormone level is low. When a deficiency occurs, the brain sends instructions to the pituitary to release more hormones. In this way, hormonal levels are maintained through an elegant but simple feedback loop (Hiller-Sturmhöfel & Bartke, 1998).

Your hormonal feedback loop works much like the thermostat that regulates the heating and cooling of your home: If you want to feel warmer, you simply turn up the setting on the thermostat. This is exactly what happens at puberty. Your main pubertal thermostat—called a *gonadostat*—is sensitive to low levels of sex hormones during childhood, so it inhibits the release of hormones even when hormone levels are low (Finkelstein, 1992). At puberty, the sensitivity of the gonadostat decreases, so higher levels of hormones are needed to inhibit hormone production. The process is the same before and after puberty, but during puberty the setting is turned up.

endocrine system A control system of glands that produce, store, and secrete *hormones*.

hormones Molecules that can travel through the bloodstream and affect distant cells.

A changing body is fascinating—especially if it's your own. Most teens spend a good deal of time watching the events of puberty unfold.

adolescent growth spurt A period of rapid growth that begins at an average age of 9 years for girls and 11 years for boys.

peak height velocity (PHV) The time when growth is most rapid. The average age of PHV is 11½ years for girls and 13½ years for boys.

THE PROCESS OF PUBERTY. The collection of physical changes you experienced during adolescence was triggered by two largely independent processes: *andrenarche*, which occurs before puberty, and *gonadarche*, which signals the beginning of puberty.

Andrenarche begins when a feedback system between the hypothalamus, the pituitary, and the adrenal glands (the *HPA axis*) begins to reset around 6 to 8 years of age. The HPA axis is part of the body's stress response system, the same system that goes into overdrive when children lose their parents or suffer from frequent conflict in the home (Chapter 9). This system also regulates the release of *androgens*, a group of hormones that is more abundant in males than females. Androgen levels gradually rise from childhood until about 20 years of age. Because androgens change the composition of perspiration, children begin smelling more like adults by 10 years or so—long before parents are usually thinking about puberty. Once puberty begins, androgens from the adrenal glands are responsible for acne in girls and heavier growth of body hair. In boys, the small amount of androgen from the adrenals is eventually swamped by more significant production from the testes.

One of the first signs of puberty is a noticeable change in the rate of growth. Children who seem to be growing out of shoes and pants right before our eyes are experiencing the **adolescent growth spurt**. This process, which can add up to 0.4 millimeters of height a day, is often accompanied by a similar increase in appetite (Garn, 1992a; Malina, 1990). As you can see in Figure 10.2, the time of maximum growth, which is called **peak height velocity (PHV)**, is usually reached by midpuberty, roughly 11 to 13 years for girls and 13 to 15 years for boys (Finkelstein, 1992).

All skeletal and muscular features are affected by the growth spurt, but not all are on the same timetable. Reversing the direction of growth that occurred during infancy, the head, hands, and feet grow first, followed by the legs and arms and, finally, the body trunk (Tanner, 1998). Even individual facial features grow at the different rates, with the nose and ears typically growing before the rest of the face. This *asynchrony* (unevenness) in growth can be a source of embarrassment for teenagers who are temporarily "all ears" or "all feet."

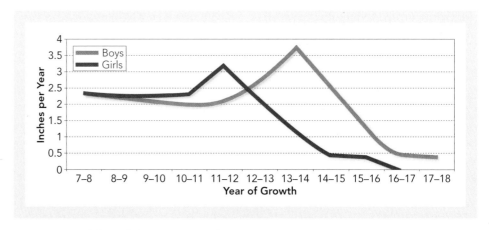

FIGURE 10.2 The adolescent growth spurt.

Children grow quickly as puberty approaches, with girls reaching the peak of their growth spurt earlier than boys. As appetites also increase, it is even more important that schools and parents provide a variety of healthy foods.

SOURCE: Abbassi (1998).

When growth ends, the average male is more than 5 inches taller than the average female (Rogol, Clark, & Roemmich, 2000). Males also experience about twice the increase in muscle mass as females do, and they develop larger muscle cells that are capable of more force per gram (Dyk, 1993). Boys and girls experience a decrease in fat accumulation and the development of localized fat pads. However, boys experience a greater overall loss of fat than girls and distribute fat differently (Malina, 1990; Tanner, 1998). Whereas boys accumulate fat in the stomach area, girls experience the familiar rounding of their breasts, arms, buttocks, and thighs (Garn, 1992a). By the end of puberty, boys have greater muscle mass than girls, a lower percentage of body weight as fat, and a squarer, more masculine appearance.

Two types of features develop during the adolescent growth spurt. **Primary sex characteristics** are structures that are directly involved in reproduction, including the uterus, ovaries, and vagina in girls and the penis and testes in boys. As these structures are becoming more prominent, **secondary sex characteristics** are also emerging, including breasts in girls and facial hair and a deeper voice in boys. Secondary sex characteristics help distinguish between males and females but are not necessary for reproduction.

Sexual maturation, which is called *gonadarche*, is regulated by a feedback loop among the hypothalamus, the pituitary, and the gonads (the *HPG axis*). Prompted by instruction from the hypothalamus, the pituitary gland releases two hormones that stimulate the *gonads* (the ovaries in females and the testes in males). These hormones prompt the gonads to release their own hormones (estrogens and androgens) and initiate the production of mature eggs (oocytes) or sperm (Weisfeld, 1999). Although estrogens are frequently called the "female" hormones and androgens the "male" hormones, both sexes produce both types of hormones. During puberty, there is an eightfold increase in estradiol (a type of estrogen) in females and more than an eightfold increase in testosterone in males (Nottlemann et al., 1987).

Girls usually begin puberty between 8 and 14 years of age, whereas boys begin puberty between 9 and 15 years (Kipke, 1999). (It is frequently said that males develop 2 years later than girls, but the 2-year difference applies only to the timing of the growth spurt, *not* pubertal development.) Due to normal variability in the process, 10-year-old girls who wear sports bras play softball with friends who are years away from retiring their little-girl clothes, and some boys begin shaving when others are still playing with action figures.

Under the influence of sex hormones, sexual development unfolds as described in Table 10.1. Girls usually begin their growth spurt around 9 years of age, followed at 10 to 11 years by the development of "breast buds," which is a swelling of the nipples (although some girls sprout a little pubic hair first). Next the breasts round out and pubic hair clearly appears. Prompted by hormones, the uterus,

primary sex characteristics
Structures that are directly involved in reproduction, including the uterus, ovaries, and vagina in girls and the penis and testes in boys.

secondary sex characteristics
Characteristics that help distinguish between males and females but are not necessary for reproduction, including breasts in girls and facial hair and a deeper voice in boys.

TABLE 10.1 Pubertal Development

Girls	Approximate Age	Boys
Beginning of the growth spurt	9–10	
Budding of the nipples	10–11	
Breasts begin to round	11–12	Testicular growth
Pubic hair appears		Pubic hair appears
Uterus, ovaries, and external genitalia enlarge		Beginning of the growth spurt
Peak height velocity		
Underarm hair		
Menarche	12–13	Penile growth
	13–14	Nocturnal emissions ("wet dreams")
		Peak height velocity
		Underarm hair
Mature oocyte production	14–15	Voice deepens
	15–16	Mature sperm production
End of skeletal growth	16–17	
	17–19	End of skeletal growth

SOURCE: Abbassi (1998); Gallahue & Ozmun (2006); Hammar (2002).

Teens in the same grade represent various levels of pubertal development. Those who develop early are more likely to spend time with older adolescents, whereas those who develop late may feel embarrassed and inadequate.

menarche First menstruation.

secular trend A trend that occurs across generations. A widely discussed secular trend is the decline in the age of pubertal onset that has occurred as nutrition and overall health have improved.

precocious puberty Pubertal onset at an age that is more than two standard deviations below the mean. There is debate about what age norms should be used to define precocious puberty and what secondary sex characteristics must be present. A conservative definition is pubertal onset before 8 years of age in girls and 10 years of age in boys.

delayed puberty Pubertal onset more than two standard deviations above the mean. For girls, puberty is considered delayed if there is an absence of breast development by 14 years and delayed menstruation. Boys are considered delayed if there are no signs of puberty by 14 years.

ovaries, and external genitalia increase in size. Girls usually reach the peak of their growth spurt around 11.5 years, followed by **menarche** (the onset of menstruation) at an average age of 12.3 years. But as you can see in Table 10.1, most girls do not have regular periods or ovulate (release eggs from the ovary) immediately after the onset of menstruation, and secondary sex characteristics continue to develop over the next 4 to 5 years.

In boys, the earliest marker of puberty is growth of the testes, the organs that produce most of the androgen needed to produce a masculine appearance. Males begin their pubertal changes about 6 months to 1 year later than girls, when sex hormones produced by the testes prompt the appearance of pubic hair and, about a year later, penile growth (Table 10.1). Under the influence of androgens, vocal folds grow larger and the voice drops suddenly, often changing around 14 years. During this time, it is not uncommon for boys to experience some breast development that usually resolves after a few years. Several months to a year later, facial hair typically appears. Over the next few years, boys become more muscular than girls and facial hair continues to sprout (at a rate that is too slow for some boys' liking).

EARLY AND LATE BLOOMERS. The age when you started puberty was partly determined by your genes (Eaves et al., 2004), but your environment also played a role. In poor countries, girls from high-income families mature several months to a year earlier than poor children do (Qamra, Mehta, & Deodhar, 1991), probably due to better nutrition, better health care, and less exposure to disease. Due to improved health over time, the average age of puberty has declined across generations. As you can see in Figure 10.3, the average age of a girl's first period in industrialized nations declined from about 17 years to 12.5 years over a 150-year period, and you'd see a similar line if we plotted the timing of other pubertal changes. Similar to the average increase in height (which you read about in Chapter 8), the **secular trend** (a change across generations) toward earlier puberty is probably due to improved health and nutrition (Dyk, 1993).

Children who have pubertal onsets that are more than two standard deviations above or below the mean are considered to have a *disordered puberty* (Palmert & Boepple, 2001). **Precocious (early) puberty** can be caused by a variety of medical problems, including infections, injuries to the central nervous system, and endocrine disorders. At the other extreme is **delayed puberty**, which is a pubertal onset more than two standard deviations *beyond* average. Girls with delayed puberty have no breast development by 14 years of age or have not menstruated within 5 years after initial breast development. Boys with delayed puberty may be 14 or 15 years of age and still not showing the expected growth spurt. Girls are more likely than boys to experience precocious puberty, whereas boys are more likely to experience delayed puberty.

In 1997, a landmark study found an alarming trend: Seven percent of Caucasian girls and 27 percent of African American girls were experiencing signs of puberty before 8 years (the traditional cutoff for precocious puberty) (Herman-Giddens et al., 1997). Nevertheless, the average age of menarche was similar to earlier samples, suggesting that breast development does not always signal the

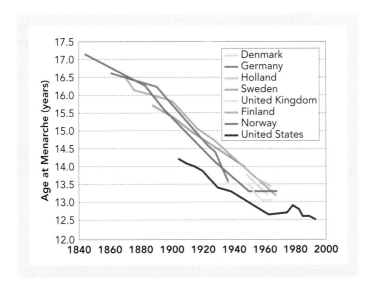

FIGURE 10.3 The declining age of menarche.

There has been a sharp decline in the average age of menarche over a 150-year period, probably due to improved health and nutrition.

SOURCES: Freedman et al. (2002); Tanner (1973).

beginning of puberty or that puberty is starting earlier but progressing more slowly than in the past (Lee, Kulin, & Guo, 2001).

What is causing some girls to develop so early? Scientists are looking at four possibilities:

▶ **Weight and obesity.** One hypothesis is that body weight or body fat proportion triggers the onset of puberty. This hypothesis fits the fact that African American girls (who are heavier on average than Caucasian girls) are especially likely to experience precocious puberty (Kaplowitz et al., 2001). But there is little evidence that being overweight is the sole cause of pubertal onset (Brooks-Gunn & Reiter, 1990; Garn, 1992b). For example, population shifts in BMI did not parallel shifts in the age of pubertal onset (Demerath et al., 2004). As a whole, the data suggest that body fat contributes to early pubertal signs but that other factors must be involved as well.

▶ **Environmental chemicals.** High levels of environmental chemicals have been found in the blood of some girls with early breast development (Colón et al., 2000; Krstevska-Konstantinova et al., 2001). Still, there is no evidence that *most* cases of precocious puberty are triggered by environmental chemicals.

▶ **Hormones in animal products.** Many beef and dairy farmers in the United States use hormones to improve growth and increase milk production. Critics have long blamed these hormones for a host of health problems, including increased rates of breast cancer and premature puberty. However, agricultural hormones have not been clearly linked to health problems (Partsch & Sippell, 2001).

▶ **Stress.** According to a hypothesis from the evolutionary perspective, childhood is extended when the social environment is favorable for development but shortened when the cost of delaying reproduction outweighs the benefits of a longer childhood (Ellis, 2004). This hypothesis may explain why family conflict and the absence of a father are associated with earlier onset of puberty (Belsky, Steinberg, & Draper, 1991). One limitation of this theory is that genetic characteristics of parents who provide less optimal environments may cause pubertal timing rather than the environments they provide (Comings et al., 2002).

While researchers continue to look for the reason why some girls are developing so early, physicians are debating how to treat them. Some medical experts do not believe it is necessary to evaluate every girl who experiences physical changes before age 8, but others worry that endocrine conditions will be overlooked if physicians lower the age that defines precocious puberty (Herman-Giddens et al., 2001; Kaplowitz & Oberfield, 1999; Midyett, Moore, & Jacobson, 2003). For now, the best course of action for parents is to seek medical advice for unexpected symptoms and reassure children that puberty occurs at different times.

What are the psychological consequences of being out of step with one's peers? To answer this question, researchers have looked at how puberty affects children who develop at different ages and in different environments.

Adjusting to Puberty

After her son grew up and left home, our friend Annette found a decade-old issue of *Playboy* magazine in his room. As much as she enjoyed teasing him about this, she was annoyed when he told her how he had gotten it: by trading his Nintendo system.

To an adult, a game system is a high price to pay for a magazine; to a 13-year-old boy, it may seem like a steal. During puberty, androgens—the so-called male hormones—are involved in sexual motivation in both sexes. Testosterone levels are associated with a number of sexual behaviors in boys, including the frequency of masturbation, time spent thinking about sex, and even whether they have had intercourse or not. Among girls, androgen levels predict individual differences in masturbation and sexual interest, including thinking about and planning to have sex (Udry et al., 1985; Udry, Talbert & Morrise, 1986). But sexual *motivation* and sexual *behavior* are not always linked. As you will read in the next chapter, for example, girls' sexual behavior is influenced by their future opportunities and community standards for sexual behavior—not just their physical maturity.

The effect of "raging" hormones on adolescents' psychological adjustment has fascinated researchers (and parents!) since the 1930s. But despite the volume of work on this topic, there is no simple story about the relationship between pubertal hormones and adjustment (Buchanan, Eccles, & Becker, 1992). One reason is that connections between hormones and behavior are complex: Hormone levels influence behavior, but behavior and environmental stressors also change hormone levels. As a result, it is too simplistic to blame most troublesome behavior on hormones (as in, "Oh, don't mind him/her, he/she is just being hormonal"). Also, hormones sometimes influence behavior *directly* (for example, when a hormone surge prompts a doe to respond to a buck's attention) and sometimes *indirectly* (for example, when adults grant more privileges to tall, maturely built teenagers because they look older) (Palmer et al., 2004). Indirect effects are difficult to pin down because they vary across children with different family circumstances. As a result of these complications, it is not uncommon for some studies to find relationships between hormone levels and adolescent problems while others do not. Despite these complexities, scientists generally agree on the following conclusions about adjustment during puberty.

IRRITABILITY AND AGGRESSION. The masculinizing hormone *testosterone* sometimes produces feelings of impatience and irritability that can trigger aggressive behavior. Boys with higher levels of testosterone are more likely to strike out when they are provoked, and boys with high hormone levels and a low tolerance for frustration show more unprovoked aggression (Maras et al., 2003; Susman & Rogol, 2004). Relationships between hormones and behavior are not as strong for girls, but high hormone levels are associated with emotionality and aggressive impulses among early-maturing girls and those who are receiving hormone treatments (Finkelstein et al., 1997; Graber, Brooks-Gunn, & Warren, in press).

MOODINESS AND DEPRESSION. It is well known that boys are slightly more likely to be clinically depressed before puberty whereas girls are twice as likely to be depressed afterward. The gender shift occurs during midpuberty, when girls with high levels of estrogen and testosterone (which the body easily converts into estrogen) are most likely to be depressed. Many scientists believe that hormones act on the brain by affecting the neurotransmitters that regulate mood. However, most girls with high hormone levels do not become depressed, so hormones alone rarely trigger depression. Vulnerable girls have a combination of high hormone levels, a family history of depression, and exposure to stressful life events (Angold et al., 1999; Angold, Costello, & Worthman, 1998; Angold, Worthman, & Costello, 2003).

THE TIMING OF PUBERTY AND ADJUSTMENT. Developing bodies that are more adult-like affects boys and girls differently. Boys who mature early tend to have a better self-image than their later-maturing peers, whereas late development is associated with a better self-image for girls (Connolly et al., 1996). To understand these findings, think for a minute about what it means when children mature before most of their same-sex peers. An early-maturing boy, though earlier than other boys, is probably in step with most of the girls. He is also experiencing physical changes that make him more popular because he is approaching the male ideal of being tall and muscular. In contrast, girls who mature early are out of sync with all of the boys and most of the girls. Though they may be more attractive to boys (particularly older boys!), this attention can be difficult to deal with—especially if they are only 9 or 10 years of age. Therefore, some of the impact of physical maturity on self-image is due to the comparisons adolescents make with others their age (Flaming & Morse, 1991).

By middle adolescence, children who are early maturers are more likely than on-time peers to have mental health problems (Kaltiala-Heino et al., 2003). Early-maturing girls are more likely to be depressed and to use illegal drugs, to engage in delinquent activity, and to show poorer academic performance. Across ethnic groups, early-maturing boys show more violent and nonviolent delinquency (Cota-Robles, Neiss, & Rowe, 2002). One reason mature-looking teens show more troublesome behavior is that they are likely to associate with older, higher-risk peers. In one study, for example, pubertal timing had no effect on girls' violent behavior unless they lived in neighborhoods where violent behavior was common (Obeidallah et al., 2004). Late maturation is not consistently related to undesirable outcomes, although late-maturing boys are somewhat more likely to show depressed moods (Susman & Rogol, 2004).

Angelica wants to wear pretty clothes like the ones she sees on older girls, but at only 13, her mother won't allow her to leave the house in an outfit like this. Young girls who look mature are more likely than their peers to date early and associate with older teens, which increases their chances of delinquent activity and poor school performance.

By adulthood, many boys and girls have discarded the disadvantages of off-time puberty. But for some, the timing of puberty directs them onto a life path that forever changes their journey. Early-maturing girls are more likely to become mothers and to marry earlier than their peers, and they are less likely than late-developing girls to stay in school and pursue a career. The timing of puberty is less important to males over the long run, although late bloomers are somewhat more likely to abuse alcohol or other drugs (perhaps because off-time puberty is associated with depression) (Graber et al., 2004; Weichold, Silbereisen, & Schmitt-Rodermund, 2003). But these findings are only trends. As you know from watching your friends pass through adolescence, individuals differ as a function of their temperaments and environments.

In sum, hormone levels are not good predictors of behavior. It is true that teens are more irritable when hormones are changing abruptly, but bodies and brains soon adjust. It is also true that teens are generally less happy than children, but this could be due to the fact that their lives are more demanding. In one study, neither age nor physical maturity predicted negative emotions, and hormone levels accounted for no more than 4 percent of the individual differences in mood. Instead, social factors (such as problems with friends or school) and interactions between social factors and pubertal status (such as the combination of early maturation and exposure to older, delinquent peers) are most related to sadness and aggression (Brooks-Gunn & Warren, 1989). Throughout life, negative feelings often erupt when specific physical events combine with specific personalities and experiences.

Physical Performance

In all societies, the transition from scrawny child to powerful adult occurs most rapidly between 12 and 18 years, when both sexes become more physically capable. Up to 12 or 13 years of age, boys are only slightly stronger than girls of the same height (depending on the skill). Over the next few years, however, boys develop greater *muscular endurance* (the ability to sustain force over time) than girls and greater *aerobic endurance* (the ability of the heart, lungs, and vascular system to deliver oxygen and fuel to muscles). But even though males have more muscle mass than females, larger hearts to deliver oxygen to muscles, and anatomical differences that influence the mechanics of running and jumping, sex differences in physical performance are reduced when girls train as hard as boys and believe they can be strong. For example, differences between boys and girls are sometimes smaller after repeated testing, perhaps because girls do not "go all out" at first (Shepard, 1982). And even though sex differences exist even among elite athletes, girls may be motivated to know that they are as strong as boys when muscle mass is taken into account (Gallahue & Ozmun, 2006).

The Teenage Brain

As the body is slowly remodeled during puberty, so, too, is the brain. This is evident if you think about driving behavior. Most 10-year-olds are cautious about getting hurt, but we don't let them drive cars because they have a limited ability to attend broadly and make fast decisions. Over time, though, young children grow into 17-year-olds who have the ability to drive safely, even though they often do not. Inept but cautious 10-year-olds develop into competent but risk-taking 17-year-olds due to a second brain spurt that occurs during the teenage years.

To understand how the brain is transformed during adolescence, think back to the discussion of early brain development from Chapters 2 and 3. Remember that brain development starts with a period of rapid growth when neural connections are made in an overabundant, haphazard fashion. Following this period, connections that are not strengthened by input from the environment are eliminated through the process of neural pruning. This brain spurt, which occurs from the third month of pregnancy to the second birthday, is followed by a second spurt during adolescence. At this time, new connections are again rapidly forged while others are eliminated. Unlike infants, however, adolescents choose their environments when they choose their activities and friends. As a result, teenagers, their personal worlds, and genetically controlled processes form a team that writes the script for the final stages of brain development.

[handwritten margin note: leading hypothesis is (TV, video, music etc.) what you use will be hard wired]

During the teenage brain spurt, it is the *timing* of developmental change that makes 17-year-olds such risky drivers (Steinberg, 2004). As Travis Pastrana's desire to jump into the Grand Canyon illustrates, the chemical changes that lead teens to seek stimulation and novelty occur early in adolescence, years before brain systems are fully mature. Let's look at each of these developments in turn.

TAKING RISKS. In many species, adolescence is a time of increased risk taking and novelty seeking, two tendencies that motivate youngsters to establish territories and families of their own. Humans are no exception. During early adolescence, our young experience changes in the levels of various *neurotransmitters*, the chemicals that transmit signals throughout the brain. For example, there is a marked increase in *dopamine* activity in the prefrontal cortex (the seat of rationality) and the limbic system (the seat of emotions). Dopamine is involved in novelty seeking and the pleasurable effects of many drugs. Under the influence of changing neurochemical levels, teenagers are increasingly drawn to novel situations, react more strongly to stressful situations, and are more prone to negative emotional reactions (Kelley, Schochet, & Landry, 2004; Spear, 2000).

GUT REACTIONS. But teenage brains are not always prepared to accurately assess the situations that tempt them. In one study, for example, researchers imaged brains while people reacted to a photograph of a fearful adult. Adults correctly labeled the emotion in the photograph 100 percent of the time whereas teenagers often saw a different emotion, such as anger or shock. The two age groups also showed different patterns of brain activation. Teenagers showed relatively more activation in a primitive brain area, the *amygdala*, that determines your "gut reaction" to situations. In contrast, adults relied more on the prefrontal cortex, which allows you to think rationally and plan a response. Because their emotional and rational centers are not fully coordinated, teenagers frequently misinterpret other people's reactions. As brain researcher Deborah Yurgelun-Todd explained (Frontline, 2002):

> The teenager is not going to take the information that is in the outside world, in using and organize it and understand it the same way [adults] do . . . Whatever conversation you have with them, if you're assuming they've understood everything you said—they may not have. Or they may have understood it differently . . . [But] they're not really trying to disappoint you or frustrate you.

BECOMING THOUGHTFUL AND EVALUATING MISTAKES. Problems evaluating other people's emotions are partly a consequence of the fact that the *frontal lobe* is so slow to mature (Rubia et al., 2000; Spear, 2000). Recall that the frontal

Teenagers often react first and think later, especially when they are being threatened.

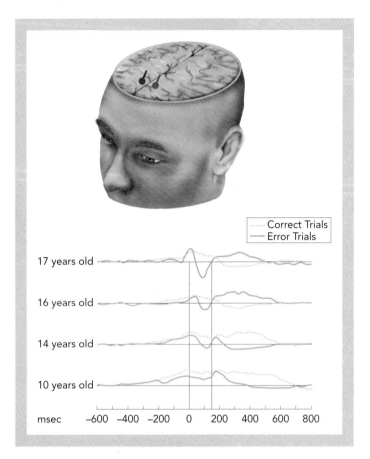

FIGURE 10.4 Error monitoring in the teenage brain.

What happens when we realize we have made a mistake? When adults make an error or realize they didn't make the best choice, centers in a part of the brain called the anterior cingulate cortex (one in each hemisphere, shown in the drawing at the top) generate a change in electrical activity. (The bar projecting from each generator indicates the direction of the signal, in this case almost straight up.) The bottom half of the Figure shows the electrical activity that occurs before and after a response (at 0). Note the different activity for a correct response (Correct Trial) and an error (Error Trial). As you can see in the shaded area, the brain activity characterizing adult-like responses does not emerge until mid to late adolescence.

lobe is involved in higher-order processing—planning, controlling emotions, maintaining attention, and weighing the consequences of decisions. Using functional magnetic resonance imaging (fMRI), scientists have found rapid growth in this region during adolescence (Paus et al., 1999; Thompson et al., 2000). As in infancy, this growth results in many more neural connections than we need, so a period of synaptic pruning eliminates large numbers of connections starting in the midteens and continuing through the midtwenties (Giedd, 2004; Sowell & Jernigan, 1998; Sowell et al., 2001).

The development of the frontal lobe influences behavior through connections with other brain regions. One system that is attracting the attention of scientists includes the *anterior cingulate cortex* (ACC), an area that connects the most advanced part of the frontal lobe, the *prefrontal cortex*, with the limbic system. The ACC becomes activated whenever complicated situations arise, and it appears to be especially important for *error monitoring*, the cognitive and emotional consequences of making a mistake or realizing that you didn't make the best choice. Using an electroencephalogram (EEG), scientists record how the brain responds to errors by monitoring electrical activity from the ACC while people perform tasks that produce errors (such as pressing a left button if they see one letter but a right button if they see another) (Pailing et al., 2002).

Figure 10.4 shows what happens in the brain when people know they are going to make an error but cannot stop. This "point of no return" sets in motion an interesting neurological event—an abrupt shift in brain wave response called the *error-related negativity* (ERN). The size of this response is related to concern about one's performance. For example, anxious adults show a larger ERN response (Hajcak & Simons, 2002), whereas people who are not as bothered by cheating or breaking the law show a small response (Dikman & Allen, 2000).

Adolescents are known for acting irresponsibly, but studies of the ERN show us that there are physiological reasons for their behavior: Young brains respond differently than older brains to mistakes. Starting at about 10 years of age for girls and 13 for boys, the size of the ERN gradually increases. But as you can see in Figure 10.4, it is not until 17 or 18 years that people achieve adult-like reactions. The transition after midadolescence marks a shift between the learning strategies of children and those of adults. As neuroscientist Sidney Segalowitz and his research team (2004) explained, persisting in the face of error helps younger children confront new social challenges, so it is adaptive for them not to react much to mistakes. With adolescence comes a new sense of self-consciousness that prompts children to care more about the quality of their work and feel disturbed by mistakes. But this shift is gradual, so even children in midadolescence do not monitor their actions the way a responsible adult does.

Studies of children's risk-taking behavior, interpretations of emotional expressions, and error monitoring prove that typical teenage behavior springs from changes that occur throughout the brain—not just developments in the "higher" brain centers. To learn about an annoying change that occurs deep inside the brain, turn to our special feature, "Sleepy Teens: Shouldn't They Just Go to Bed Earlier?"

Teenagers naturally feel like staying up later at night due to changes in their internal biological rhythms. Their tendency to give in to this urge often leaves them chronically sleepy, which can contribute to poor school grades and depressive symptoms. Teens can help their bodies get the 9 hours of sleep most adolescents need by sticking to a sleep schedule and avoiding stimulating activities near bedtime.

SLEEPY TEENS: SHOULDN'T THEY JUST GO TO BED EARLIER?

We phoned college roommates Shanna and Julie-Ann to ask them how they felt about getting up for classes during high school:

Shanna: UGHHH! It was the worst when it was dark outside! I just threw the blankets over my head and hid.

Julie-Ann: It was REALLY HARD to get up (laugh). I hit the snooze button at least twice. It got to the point where I'd be up at the last minute and wouldn't even eat breakfast, or sometimes I'd eat in the car.

Most teens have trouble getting out of bed in the morning. And once they are up, their teachers complain that they aren't very alert until noon. The most frequent advice is something you may have heard as a teenager: "If you'd just go to bed earlier, you could get up in the morning." Why is this advice so hard to follow?

People have long assumed that teenagers go to bed later because they want to spend time with friends or watch late-night television shows. Today, sleep researchers know that changes in the brain actually alter their sleep–wake cycles, causing a shift in early adolescence to a preference for a later bed time and later rising time (Carskadon, 1999a).

One culprit is the brain chemical *melatonin*, a hormone that helps regulate the sleep–wake cycle. Throughout life, increases in melatonin levels at night make us drowsy and help us experience deep, satisfying sleep. Levels of melatonin begin to drop after 5 years of age and show a distinct pattern of change during puberty, when the onset of nighttime levels shifts by an hour or more (Wurtman, 2000). This change may push adolescents to stay up later because they just don't feel sleepy until later (Carskadon, Acebo, & Jenni, 2004).

Most adolescents get less sleep than they need, but stealing a short nap during the day is not as refreshing as a good 9 hours of sleep at night.

Unfortunately, late bedtimes leave many teenagers chronically short of sleep. To assess how much sleep teenagers crave, Mary Carskadon and her colleagues evaluated 10- to 12-year-olds during a summer research project and then each year for 5 to 6 years. Because children slept 10 hours a night for a week before each session and were allowed to sleep as long as their bodies wanted during sessions, Carskadon measured how long well-rested children sleep when their brains—not alarm clocks—determine their wake-up time. The team was startled by the results: All age groups slept between $9\frac{1}{4}$ and 10 hours a night (Carskadon, 1999b). Experts now say that teenagers need at least 9 hours of sleep a night for optimal health and brain growth.

Are most teenagers getting the sleep they need? Not by a long shot. The average number of hours children sleep on school nights declines from just under 8 hours at 13 years to only 7 hours by 19, and about 13 percent of adolescents sleep 6 hours or less (Wolfson & Carskadon, 1998). According to Carskadon, inadequate sleep leaves teens in a "gray cloud" that leads them to view the world more negatively, increases the chance of illness and driving accidents, and interferes with their ability to learn (Grady, 2002). Insufficient sleep is also associated with struggling or failing in school, low self-esteem, and depressive symptoms (Fredriksen et al., 2004; Wolfson & Carskadon, 1998).

But teenagers shouldn't blame biology for all of their problems. Parents have become lenient about bedtimes (Wellbery, 2003), and television sets and computers in bedrooms encourage many teens to stay up late (Van den Bulck, 2004). Sleepiness is also associated with the transition to schools that have earlier start times and more homework (Carskadon et al., 1998). Other pressures that make it hard for teenagers to get enough sleep include after-school work and sports practices that pressure them to use evening hours for socializing.

To respond to adolescents' needs, some school districts have changed their high school start time—with positive results. In Minneapolis, for example, changing to an 8:40 start time improved attendance and increased the number of hours students slept (Wahlstrom, 2003). But many school districts resist making this change due to conflicts with teacher preferences and schedules for buses and after-school activities. Still, teenagers who need to rise early do not have to be foggy-headed because the timing of melatonin secretion can be shifted by keeping to a sleep schedule and wearing eye-shades to block out light (Carskadon, 1999b). And everyone—regardless of age—dozes off more easily when they follow these tips from the National Sleep Foundation (2005):

★   Don't drink coffee, tea, or caffeinated soft drinks after late afternoon.

★   Use light to communicate with your brain. Go into bright light as soon as you wake up and dim lights before bedtime.

★   Stick to a regular sleep schedule. Even on weekends, try not to vary your bedtime by more than an hour, and try not to wake up more than 1 to 2 hours later than your usual time.

★   Condition yourself to sleep when you hit the bed. Your brain will associate your bed with sleeping if you avoid reading, watching television, or talking on the phone from bed. A consistent bedtime routine, such as a hot shower, will relax you for sleep.

★   Avoid stimulating television shows, music, or activities before bedtime. Instead, record your favorite shows to watch at a better time.

Like many older teens, Shanna and Julie-Ann know they feel better when they follow this advice—but they don't. "There is so much pressure to stay up late with friends," Julie-Ann told us. "Everyone is downing coffee the next morning, trying to get to class. Sleep is just not a priority yet, I guess."

Cognitive Development

Allison had lined up baby-food jars on the counter to prepare for a visit from her sister and 7-month-old niece. As she entered the kitchen one day, she noticed her 16-year-old son, Chris, chatting on the phone with a friend. Absentmindedly, Chris was picking up jars one after the next, twisting the lids, breaking the vacuum seals that keep the contents fresh, and neatly replacing the jars.

Yet just when we think teenagers would poison babies if we didn't keep constant watch, we're confronted with evidence of their brilliance. Consider an article from *People* magazine about teens who became rich after starting businesses. There was Shazad Mohamed, who started GlobalTek Solutions from his Texas home at the age of 12 and eventually hired more than 20 employees to create programs that computerize medical records. And Rich Stachowski, who sold his underwater walkie-talkie idea for $1 million when he was still a high school student (Fields-Meyer et al., 2004).

It's hard to know what to expect from a 16-year-old who can explain Einstein's theory of relativity but is constantly misplacing her shoes. Describing the mental architecture that supports this uneven performance is the goal of cognitive scientists who study adolescence. Their understanding of why teenagers act so unpredictably comes from three lines of research: Piaget's account of cognitive development, studies of judgment and decision making, and age trends in basic information processing skills.

Piaget's Theory of Adolescent Thought

In previous chapters you learned about Piaget's theory of cognitive development. Recall that infants and toddlers develop the ability to manipulate mental symbols during the first 2 years of life (the *sensorimotor* period). During the preschool years (the *preoperational* period), children's cognitive limitations, such as a tendency to focus on one feature of a problem at a time, lead them to respond illogically to questions about their physical world. Children are ready for more formal instruction when they begin to think logically about materials they can see and handle during the school years (the *concrete operational* period). But even school-aged children have difficulty with situations that require them to imagine *possibilities* and test *hypotheses*, so they often fail problems that require scientific reasoning.

formal operational thought
In Piaget's theory, the capacity for increasingly abstract thought that emerges around 11 to 12 years of age (often described as an intellectual shift from "things" to "ideas"). Formal operational children can engage in *hypothetico-deductive reasoning* (the ability to generate and test hypotheses) and *formal propositional logic* (the ability to understand possible combinations of variables).

For example, in Chapter 8 you read about their haphazard approach to the *pendulum problem*, a task that asks them to figure out which factors determine the number of swings a pendulum makes in a fixed amount of time.

Children are ready for more challenging science education once they enter adolescence and become more capable of abstract thinking. This fact of life is made possible by the achievements described in the next stage of Piaget's theory.

FORMAL OPERATIONS. According to Piaget (Inhelder & Piaget, 1958), a type of thinking called **formal operational thought** emerges around 11 to 12 years of age and solidifies over the next 4 to 5 years. Whereas concrete operational children generally need to hear or see something before they begin to ruminate about it, formal operational children think about *abstract* ideas, that is, ideas that are not grounded in concrete reality. One way to think about this shift is to say that intelligence shifts from "things" to "ideas" during adolescence (Brainerd, 1978). Mentally, formal operational teens move beyond the here and now to consider "what is possible," and they generate new knowledge by internal reflection. Once thinking is no longer tied to concrete objects and events, individuals can speculate about the future and develop problem-solving strategies for planning future events. Thus concrete operational children focus on immediate reality, lack the ability to mentally draw inferences from disjointed information, and fail to design systematic problem-solving strategies. In contrast, formal operational children focus on possibilities, make inferences from data, and systematically experiment with their environments.

A central feature of formal operations is *formal propositional logic*: the ability to understand possible combinations and relations among variables (Gray, 1990). These ideas are easy to grasp by looking at the simple example. In their classic work on adolescence, Inhelder and Piaget (1958) presented children with four numbered bottles, each containing a different colorless, odorless liquid. A fifth bottle held another liquid labeled *g*. The children were shown that when an unknown combination of liquids from the numbered bottles was combined with *g*, the mixture formed a yellow liquid. The tester then asked them to determine which combination of liquids produced the yellow mixture. Take a moment to look at this problem, which is illustrated in Figure 10.5, and imagine how you would go about solving it.

As formal operational skills are emerging, adolescents become intrigued by the unknown and the world of science. These teens are participating in a science program affiliated with the National Science Olympiad, a nonprofit organization that provides opportunities for teens to explore science through summer programs and competitive events.

Concrete operational children get bogged down when they try to find the solution. They often combine liquids unsystematically, so they forget which combinations they have already tried. As a result, children who find the solution do so by accident, not by careful planning. In contrast, children who have achieved formal operational thinking envision all possible combinations of liquids and generate strategic ways to eliminate combinations that do not work. For example, they might combine Bottle 1 with *g*, then Bottle 2 with *g*, then Bottle 3 with *g*, and so forth. In other words, these children understand the *combinatorial structure* of the problem. (By the way, only one combination, Bottle 1 + Bottle 3 + *g*, created the yellow liquid.)

The ability to envision possible combinations and relationships among variables helps teenagers approach the pendulum problem with a newfound skill called **hypothetico-deductive reasoning**. Because they can imagine possibilities, teenagers can mentally generate hypotheses about what the answer *might* be. Then, for each set of ideas, they can figure out (deduce) how an experiment should come out if the premises are true. The ability to mentally generate hypotheses ("Maybe only the string length matters, not the weight") and deduce the appropriate conclusions ("So the long string will work the same with the heavy or light weight")—in other words, hypothetico-deductive reasoning—allows them to approach the problem as a scientist would.

Abstract thinking prompts adolescents to think about the world and themselves in new ways. For example, formal operational individuals can turn abstract thinking inward to think about their *ideal* rather than *real* selves, which leads to increased self-awareness and self-doubt. This ability to think abstractly can even be applied to their own thinking. As a result, teenagers are increasingly aware of their efforts to be rational and often think about their own thinking processes. In fact, these advances in **metacognition** (knowledge and awareness of one's own cognitive processes) may be the most significant advances of the formal operational period (Keating, 2004; Moshman, 1998). For example, metacognitive skills make children more aware of the need to write down things they might not remember and realize when randomly trying solutions might not be the best way to solve a problem.

LIMITATIONS OF PIAGET'S THEORY. Piaget's tasks capture some fascinating differences between young children's and teenagers' thinking. But Piaget's theory of formal operational thought is incomplete because cognitive development is not a simple evolution toward hypothetico-deductive reasoning. To illustrate, try this popular reasoning task. First, imagine that you are a teacher in a high school that has the following rule: "If a student is caught running in the school halls, then the student must be punished." You have four pieces of information that are represented by the four cards that follow. Each of these cards has a student's behavior in school on one side and information about whether or not the student has been punished for that behavior on the other.

running in school halls	punished	walking in school halls	not punished

Before you read further, select the card or cards you would definitely need to turn over to decide whether or not the rule stated previously is being broken.

The correct answer is to turn over "running in the school halls" (to verify that this student was punished) and "not punished" (to verify that this student wasn't running). It is irrelevant what happened to the student who was punished (because this information cannot tell you if the rule has been broken), and what happened to the walking student is also irrelevant (because the rule is about students who run).

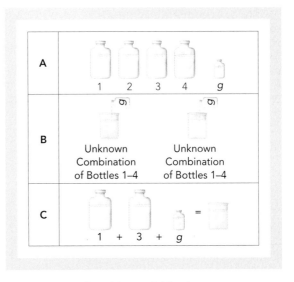

FIGURE 10.5 Combinatorial logic.

Can you solve Piaget's problem of colored and colorless liquids? Imagine four bottles filled with colorless liquid and a fifth bottle labeled *g* (A). In advance, the experimenter has prepared two glasses, each containing an unknown combination of the first four liquids. The experimenter shows you that when *g* is added to the first glass, the liquid turns yellow; the liquid remains colorless when *g* is added to the second glass (B). Your task is to figure out which liquid or liquids, when combined with *g*, makes the yellow mixture. Individuals who have achieved formal operational thought can mentally imagine all possible combinations and systematically test them to find the solution (C).

SOURCE: Inhelder & Piaget (1958).

hypothetico-deductive reasoning The ability to think like a scientist by mentally generating hypotheses, deducing how an experiment should come out if a hypothesis is true, and coordinating conclusions with evidence.

metacognition Knowledge and awareness of one's own cognitive processes.

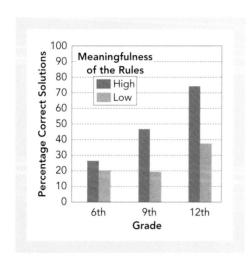

FIGURE 10.6 The growth of hypothetico-deductive reasoning.

In this study, children decided which cards to turn over to test meaningful rules (such as "If a student is caught running in the halls, then the student must be punished") and rules that did not make as much sense (such as "If a student is caught running in the halls then the student must be wearing sneakers"). The ability to test hypotheses improved from the sixth to twelfth grades, but all age groups had difficulty solving problems about rules that were not very meaningful.

SOURCE: Ward & Overton (1990).

heuristics Commonsense strategies or rules of thumb that are often useful but do not guarantee an optimal solution.

To study the development of this kind of thinking, psychologists Shawn Ward and Willis Overton (1990) asked 11-year-olds, 14-year-olds, and 17-year-olds to complete a series of "four card" problems. Half of the problems had information-rule pairs that were highly meaningful (such as getting punished for running), whereas the other problems had pairs that did not make as much sense (for example, "If a student is caught running in the school halls, then the student must be wearing sneakers"). Figure 10.6 shows the proportion of children who answered correctly in each age group. As Piaget predicted, older children did better on these tasks. But two findings pose problems for the concept of formal operations. First, even 17-year-olds frequently failed this problem. Second, the children found it easier to solve the meaningful problems even though the formal structure of both types of problems was the same.

Unfortunately, Piaget's theory cannot be stretched to fit findings like these simply by saying that development is more gradual than he claimed or that performance is more influenced by prior knowledge than he anticipated. Instead, scientists have discovered that formal reasoning is *just one type of reasoning* that people use to make decisions. Therefore, in addition to understanding Piaget's findings, we need to consider how people make decisions about real-world situations if we want to understand why adolescent behavior is so inconsistent.

Dual Processing: Two Ways People Reason

Today, scientists know that humans have two types of mental processes: a slow, conscious system that deliberately applies rules to solve problems (which is the type of problem solving Piaget studied), and a quick, largely unconscious system that rapidly interprets information in light of prior experiences. Understanding both of these systems is the key to understanding how teenagers can be brilliant one minute and frighteningly irresponsible the next.

ANALYTICAL AND EXPERIENTIAL REASONING. The following problem illustrates the two types of reasoning that develop during childhood and adolescence. First, imagine that you plan to sign up for one of several math classes. You overhear two teachers, Ken and Toni, arguing about whether students enjoy a new computer-based teaching method that is being used in some math classes (Klaczynski, 2001):

> Ken's argument is, "Each of the 3 years that we've had the computer-based learning class, about 60 students have taken it. At the end of each year, they have written essays on why they liked or didn't like the class. Over 85% of the students say that they have liked it. That's more than 130 out of 150 students who liked the computer class!"
>
> Toni's argument is, "I don't think you're right. Stephanie and John (the two best students in the school, both are high-honors students) have come to me and complained about how much they hate the computer-based learning class and how much more they like regular math classes. They say that a computer just can't replace a good teacher, who is a real person." (p. 859)

After hearing this conversation, what would you decide? Which argument was more intelligent?

This problem creates a conflict between two types of reasoning. A purely analytical approach to reasoning is one based on logical or mathematical rules. You used this approach if you reasoned that information based on 150 responses is better than two anecdotes (Ken's position). Another approach is to make a decision based on biases and **heuristics**, commonsense strategies or rules of thumb that allow you to make quick decisions but do not guarantee an optimal solution. You used this approach if you reasoned that opinions from top students will be more like your own. People often feel pulled in different directions by problems such as this one, and adolescents frequently choose an option they do *not* consider most intelligent. These inconsistent responders acknowledge the superiority of an analytical, quantitative approach, yet nonetheless choose their math class based on Toni's vivid, personal information (Klaczynski, 2001).

The **dual-processing model** says that decision making involves two cognitive systems. *Analytical processing* is formal, logical thought. The goal of analytical reasoning is to make accurate, precise inferences—regardless of the content of the problem. Analytical processing takes conscious effort, often places a large burden on mental resources (for example, by requiring you to hold a lot of information in memory), and is relatively slow. In contrast, *experiential processing* is the type of processing you use most often in everyday life. This type of reasoning uses judgment biases and heuristics to make decisions relatively quickly and automatically. Heuristic processing is useful because cognitive resources are not taken up by "easy" decisions. But unlike analytical processing, experiential processing is an intuitive system that is heavily influenced by people's prior knowledge and stereotypes. Therefore, experiential processing does not always produce an accurate result (Brainerd & Reyna, 2001; Jacobs & Klaczynski, 2002).

Adolescents have the mental power to make a rational purchase by combining information about performance and price. But like most older consumers, they probably rely on gut reactions most of the time to pick a product they love.

Justina's worry that she won't be selected for the lead in the school play illustrates the distinction between analytical and experiential processing. Justina could compute her chances analytically by using her knowledge that 12 people tried out for the play. Dividing 1 by 12 tells her that she has an 8.3 percent chance of being chosen. Alternatively, she could simply compare herself to the person who got the lead in the play the previous year. If she thinks she is similar to last year's actor, she might feel that her changes of getting the part are good (Jacobs & Potenza, 1991).

A complete view of cognitive development recognizes that analytical *and* experiential processing develop with age (Brainerd & Reyna, 2001; Klaczynski, 2001; Kokis et al., 2002). Adolescents are better than children at careful, logical thought (analytical thinking), but they also rely more on heuristics that are tied to specific types of problems (experiential processing) than young children do, partly because they have more experiences to rely on. On problems like the "Ken versus Toni" task, for example, early adolescents said that an opinion based on statistical information was more intelligent than one based on anecdotes only 23 percent of the time, whereas middle adolescents did so 45 percent of the time. Yet we know that even middle adolescents depend heavily on information from anecdotes because they chose the option suggested by the two honor students 58 percent of the time (Klaczynski, 2001).

Even though older teens are better than younger children at formal reasoning, their frequent preference for anecdotal, emotional data is one reason why their decisions are sometimes so puzzling to adults. Why is adolescent thinking prone to rely on emotion over logic? As you will read next, teenagers are simply using a type of reasoning that everyone relies on from time to time—only a little more often.

"HOT" COGNITION. If you are a careful observer of the world, you are probably aware that people's decisions and beliefs are influenced by their moods and motivations. Psychologists use the term **hot cognition** to describe the mental processes that occur when personal goals and emotions influence judgments (Kunda, 1999). As opposed to cold cognition, which is purely intellectual, hot cognition often recruits biases and heuristics. People are especially likely to rely

dual-processing model A model of decision making that includes two systems: an *analytical* processing system that solves problems using formal, logical thought, and an *experiential* processing system that uses mental shortcuts to make decisions quickly and automatically.

hot cognition The mental processes that occur when personal goals, moods, and prior stereotypes influence judgments.

on experiential processing when they will be personally affected by the decision, have prior beliefs about the issue, or the problem involves some uncertainty (Jacobs & Klaczyski, 2002). Therefore, experiential processing is especially common in situations that involve social interactions and risk because these are the situations that often involve powerful emotions.

Self-interest and emotions frequently lead to beliefs that cannot be defended on rational grounds. For example, investigator Kiva Kunda (1999) has always been fascinated that her mother, a heavy smoker, would not acknowledge the evidence that smoking during pregnancy was bad for babies. When Kunda pointed out that smoking is associated with smaller babies, her mother responded that *her babies* didn't grow up to be small. When Kunda pointed out that her brothers frequently suffered from bronchitis during childhood, her mother said that this point was based on only two children. As Kunda later wrote, "I have spent a considerable amount of effort trying to demonstrate that this kind of motivated reasoning is not restricted to my mother" (p. 212).

Teenagers and adults are better than children at realizing when evidence is necessary to form an opinion (Morris & Sloutsky, 2001), but self-interest can nonetheless lead them to ignore it. The concept of hot cognition is especially important when dealing with teenagers because many of our worries about this age group involve risk taking (such as reckless driving) and social behavior (such as letting friends pressure them to steal or do drugs)—the very situations in which analytical reasoning is often abandoned (Jacobs & Potenza, 1991).

Is there any evidence that teenagers are more likely than adults to make poor decisions in situations that evoke hot cognition? From the section on brain development, you probably guessed that the answer is "yes." To illustrate, one research team recruited troubled teens from an alternative high school, an agency that works with delinquent teenagers, and a juvenile detention center. Each volunteer watched a 5-minute movie clip in which four boys planned to steal hot dogs from a vendor but presumably ended up killing a man. Experimenters stopped the video at various points to ask questions about the boys' decisions, possible consequences, and the role of peer influence. Each teen also filled out questionnaires that tapped the ability to consider long-range consequences, resist peer influence, and assess the risk involved in activities such as smoking and stealing (Fried & Reppucci, 2001).

Middle adolescence is a time when children are prone to overlook the risks involved in following the crowd. In the heat of the moment, approval from friends is often more important than the opinions of adults.

When evaluating the video, middle adolescents thought that the boys' initial decisions were less risky than younger and older adolescents did, and they judged themselves less capable of resisting peer influence in their own lives (Figure 10.7). Vulnerability increased between 12 and 16 years on a number of measures, followed by a gradual return to more cautious, thoughtful behavior. For example, one questionnaire asked the children to rate their tendency to make long-term plans by reacting to statements such as, "When I want to achieve something, I set goals and consider specific means for reaching those goals." The 16-year-olds endorsed fewer of these statements than older or younger children did. Similarly, younger and older children were more likely than middle adolescents to think that the boys in the video should have known that someone might get hurt.

In sum, it can be challenging for adolescents to focus on long-range goals—especially when peers are pressuring them to pursue something that promises immediate pleasure. But does this mean that teenagers are too young to be held accountable for their actions? As you will see in our special feature entitled "A Law Divided," there is no simple answer to this question.

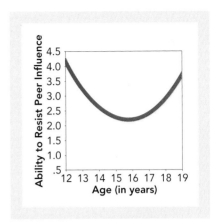

FIGURE 10.7 Teens at risk.

In this study, children with a history of behavior problems watched a videotape in which the characters planned to steal hot dogs but ended up harming an innocent man. Compared to younger and older adolescents, 15- and 16-year-olds thought the prank was not very risky. They also said they were less likely than younger or older teens to resist peer pressure in their own lives.

SOURCE: Fried & Reppucci (2001).

INNOVATIONS

Many countries have separate systems of justice for children and adults. But although the legal system in the United States recognizes that adolescents are not as mature as older individuals, laws frequently change due to debate about when to treat teenagers as adults. Based partly on new information about adolescent brain development, in 2005 the U.S. Supreme Court banned the execution of murderers who were less than 18 years of age at the time of their crimes.

A LAW DIVIDED

Consider the following cases from the files of forensic psychologist* Thomas Grisso (1996):

★ Depressed about his relationship with a girl, a boy decided to go to see her in order to say goodbye before killing himself.

★ A boy decided to go to the house of another boy who had been taunting him in school by making lewd comments about his mother; he was grieving his mother's death and thought the boy would stop if he explained.

★ A 15-year-old boy resisted recruitment efforts of a neighborhood gang, but gang members threatened harm to him if he did not join. He decided to avoid them as much as he could but to "play along" whenever they cornered him, which they did on a day when they later began harassing and eventually beating a young woman in a neighborhood park. (p. 232)

---

*forensic psychologist: A psychologist who does work in the legal system, such as evaluating people who have committed crimes or helping attorneys understand and evaluate evidence in a case.

What do these cases have in common? According to Grisso, each of these boys was charged with murder within hours of these decisions. Yet none began with an intention to harm someone, and none had a history of violent behavior.

Teens like these are judged by one of two systems of justice: a juvenile justice system that recognizes the special needs of youth or a system for adults that holds criminals fully accountable for their actions. In the United States, there has long been an option to prosecute juveniles as adults. The decision to transfer a case from juvenile to adult court is usually made through a hearing, when courts consider the severity of the crime, a child's maturity and criminal history, and testimony from experts like Thomas Grisso (Witt, 2003). However, some states automatically transfer juveniles if they are above a minimum age and have committed a serious crime. In the past, transfer could even result in *capital punishment*— the death penalty—for children who lived in a state that permitted such executions.

In 2004, the Supreme Court was asked to rule on the practice of executing juvenile offenders. Psychologists, legal experts, and family members of defendants and victims queued up on both sides of the debate. On one side were dozens of organizations that opposed the death penalty for juveniles, including the American Bar Association, the American Medical Association, and the United Methodist Church. In briefs submitted to the Supreme Court, these groups cited evidence that adolescents think differently than adults and are less capable of controlling their behavior (American Bar Association, 2005). According to this view, 14- and 15-year-olds seem as competent as adults when they answer simple questions about right and wrong—but they are not. For example, when children are questioned about their understanding of rights and courtroom procedures, one-fifth of 14- to 15-year-olds perform as poorly as seriously mentally ill adults who would probably be found incompetent (Steinberg et al., 2003). They are also less likely than adults to make good decisions when they confront emotionally charged situations. According to this view, youth who commit severe but isolated crimes are not likely to make decisions that lead to violence after they mature. In fact, in one sample of about 100 juvenile murder cases, only one individual committed a second murder after release (Grisso, 1996).

Others believe that children should not be released from responsibility just because they are less than 18 years of age. These people want juries to sort through the evidence and distinguish between crimes that erupted from immaturity and crimes committed by cold-blooded murderers. That is the position of Tim Carroll, whose parents were killed "execution style" by Robert Acuna when Acuna was 17 years old. As Carroll explained, "If you're going to make the argument that someone's cognitive reasoning is not developed at 17 years and 8 months but would be at 18, we should rethink whether they should be able to drive, and make split-second decisions in an 8,000-pound vehicle, or get married, or have children" (Liptak, 2005, para. 28).

On March 1, 2005, the Supreme Court sided with most countries in the world when it banned the execution of offenders under age 18. In its decision, the Court cited a "national consensus" that juveniles are less responsible for their actions than the average adult criminal. The decision was not unanimous, however. For example, Justice O'Connor argued that the difference in maturity between an adult and a juvenile was not significant enough to exclude adolescents from the death penalty. Debate about the juvenile death penalty is an excellent reminder that the path from scientific findings to innovations in public policy is not always clear.

Information Processing

The growth of formal reasoning during adolescence is at least partly due to improvements in basic information processing skills. Increases in response inhibition, mental speed, and working memory capacity give teenagers a cognitive edge over younger children. Along with increased knowledge, these improvements allow them to make routine decisions more automatically, which frees up cognitive resources so they can have more complicated thoughts about their physical and social worlds (Keating, 1990). For example, a teenager who is trying to solve Piaget's colorless liquids task has an advantage over her younger sister because she can inhibit herself from thinking irrelevant thoughts, which will cause her to lose track of what she intended to do next, and she can perform tests more quickly, which helps her find a solution before she forgets which liquids she has already combined.

Neuroscientist Beatriz Luna and her colleagues illustrated these trends by measuring the eye movements of 8- to 30-year-olds while they completed tasks that tap three basic processes (Luna et al., 2004):

▶ *Response inhibition.* As we described in Chapter 8, trying to look *away* from a light that suddenly appears on a screen tests the ability to inhibit a dominant response (in this case, the strong tendency to look *at* the light). Performance on this task improved dramatically until about 14 years of age, when it was essentially adult-like.

▶ *Speed of processing.* For a simple measure of mental speed, volunteers looked at a dot, waited for a light to appear on the left or right of the dot, and then looked at the target light as quickly as they could. Speed of responses improved until age 15.

▶ *Working memory.* To measure how well individuals could hold information in working memory, the volunteers completed a series of trials that began by looking at a center light. Soon a light flashed on one side, and after a short delay a signal instructed them to look to the exact location where the second light had appeared. The ability to remember location information showed mature performance by 19 years.

During middle and late adolescence, improvements in response inhibition, speed of processing, and working memory open the door for more sophisticated problem solving. Better problem-solving skills then feed back and enhance processing efficiency and working memory (Demetriou et al., 2002; Keating, 2004). As brain development gradually produces a more mature executive (planning) system, adolescents become better at drawing on prior learning to inhibit irrelevant information and select the best course of action.

>>> **M E M O R Y   M A K E R S** <<<

Which word in each pair best describes *formal operational thought*?

1. **(a)** abstract   **(b)** concrete

2. **(a)** thinking about the here and now   **(b)** thinking about what is possible

3. **(a)** thinking about "things"   **(b)** thinking about ideas

4. The ability to think like a scientist by mentally generating hypotheses and deducing how an experiment should come out if the hypothesis is true is called _____.

   (a) hypothetico-deductive reasoning   **(b)** hot cognition
   (c) heuristic reasoning   **(d)** concrete operational thought

5. According to the dual-processing model, the two types of mental processes are _____ reasoning (a quick and largely unconscious system that often relies on heuristics) and _____ reasoning (a slower system that deliberately applies rules to solve problems).

   (a) combinatorial; deductive   **(b)** deductive; combinatorial
   (c) experiential; analytical   **(d)** analytical; experiential

[1-a; 2-b; 3-b; 4-a; 5-c]

Emotional and Social Development

It is common to think of adolescence as a time of turmoil. In popular culture, the "terrible twos" are followed a decade later by the "terrible teens." In scientific literature, adolescence has long been described as a time of "storm and stress"—a period when emotions run strong and sour (Deutsch, 1944; Hall, 1904). News reports reinforce the idea that adolescents are vulnerable and unpleasant: In one analysis, nearly half of the stories about youth dealt with violent crime, accidents, or acts of victimization (Gilliam & Bales, 2001).

But most teenagers avoid the extremes that are so popular in characterizations of adolescence. In fact, about 80 percent of teenagers do not experience significant problems on their journey to adulthood (Offer & Schonert-Reichl, 1992). In recent polls, 97 percent of teens said they got along with their parents, and 83 percent said they completely trusted and could confide in a person close to their own age (Carroll, 2002, March 12; Ray, 2004). Also, today's teenagers are doing as well or better than their parents' generation on many social indicators, such as employment rates, SAT scores, and participation in volunteer activities (Youniss & Ruth, 2000).

Even though most children travel to adulthood without major trauma, adolescence is a time of transitions for nearly everyone. The emotional uncertainties we all remember are usually related to the two universal tasks of adolescence: developing an independent sense of self and developing close, intimate relationships with others.

Contrary to popular stereotypes, most teenagers get along well with their parents and like to spend time with them.

Emotions, Self, and the World

Cognitive growth during early adolescence helps children to be more tuned into what others are doing and thinking, so they often worry about what people are thinking about *them*. Teenagers compare themselves to other people and ideal standards—standards they absorb from the media or from other people that define how they should look and what traits define "success." But different children handle their new thoughts differently. Sensitive, anxious children are more troubled by their own and other peoples' shortfalls, whereas easygoing teens can turn their minds to more positive thoughts.

Psychologist David Elkind developed a theory that describes how adolescents think about the relationship between themselves and the rest of the world. Research on his ideas has helped us understand more about what characteristics make a well-adjusted teen.

ADOLESCENT EGOCENTRISM. According to Elkind, the major task of the adolescent period is the "conquest of thought" (1967, p. 1029). Compared to younger children, adolescents have a more solid understanding of their own and others' thinking process. However, they initially fail to distinguish between thoughts that are important to them and what others are likely to be thinking. As a result, teenagers construct an **imaginary audience**: a mistaken belief that other people are looking at them and are as preoccupied with their appearance and

imaginary audience The adolescent's false belief that other people are preoccupied with his or her appearance and behavior.

behavior as they are. Heightened self-consciousness is evident when a teenager begs to stay home from school because "EVERYONE will stare!" at her pimple. The imaginary audience is a type of egocentric thinking because, of course, teenagers are not really the center of other people's thoughts to such a degree.

At the same time teenagers are worrying about what other people are thinking, they also tend to assume that their feelings are unique to them alone. Teenagers often believe their emotional torments are unusual and so assume that no one else can understand them. This presumed "specialness" has another consequence: Teens tend to believe they are protected from the consequences of danger and perhaps even from death. Elkind calls this sense of uniqueness and invulnerability the **personal fable**. According to Elkind's theory of **adolescent egocentrism**, the imaginary audience and the personal fable are two types of egocentric thinking that develop after middle childhood.

Elkind initially proposed a straightforward reason for adolescent egocentrism: As formal operations emerge, children become capable of thinking about multiple possibilities and reflecting on their own thinking. According to this theory, adolescent egocentrism is the product of using mental skills that are not fully established. Elkind also thought that egocentrism explained the tendency to take risks, because teens who think they are different from everyone else may also think they will not get pregnant, have a driving accident, or die from an illegal drug.

EVALUATION OF ADOLESCENT EGOCENTRISM. Research on adolescent egocentrism suggests that teenagers might not be as different from adults as Elkind claimed. Contrary to Elkind's predictions, young adults do not always score lower than adolescents on measures of egocentrism (Frankenberger, 2000), and there is no clear relationship between egocentrism and formal operational reasoning (Vartanian, 2000). In addition, it is possible that teenagers are concerned about other people's opinions because these opinions have important consequences—not because it is irrational to do so. For example, two girls told one research team that "No fat people are popular" and their friends were "perpetually aware of people talking behind their backs" (Bell & Bromnick, 2003, p. 213). In other words, teens may be largely correct when they think other people are criticizing them. Finally, personal fable beliefs ("that can't/won't happen to me") are not good predictors of risk-taking behavior (Vartanian, 2000) and are associated with *lower* levels of depression (Goossens et al., 2002). Both of these findings suggest that the personal fable may be a healthy way to cope with life's uncertainties rather than a sign of immaturity.

Far from emotional and social development being the simple "slaves" of cognitive development, advances in each area may give a boost to development in the other. Consider the famous diary of Anne Frank. Anne kept her diary from the ages of 13 to 15 while hiding with her family from the Nazis. (She died in 1945 from typhus in the Bergen-Belsen concentration camp, at the age of 15.) Her notes are filled with the typical issues of a young girl: menarche, her desire for greater independence from her parents, and relations with peers. But it is also filled with the emotional consequences of adolescence and war. "As I've written you many times before," she entered in her diary one Christmas eve, "moods have a tendency to affect us quite a bit here, and in my case it's been getting worse lately. '*Himmelhoch jauchzend, zu Tode betrübt*' certainly applies to me" (Frank, 1995, p. 153). (Translation: "On top of the world, or in the depths of despair.")

Psychologists Jeannette Haviland and Deirdre Kramer (1991) analyzed Anne's writings to identify emotionally dense passages and passages that

personal fable The adolescent's sense of being unique and invulnerable. The personal fable involves the belief that one's emotions and insights are special and that no one is likely to understand them.

adolescent egocentrism A type of egocentrism, which emerges during adolescence, that involves creation of the *imaginary audience* and the *personal fable*.

represented shifts to higher levels of cognitive reasoning. Contrary to Elkind's prediction that emotional upheaval results from more complicated thoughts, emotional peaks came *before* advances in thinking. This finding raises the interesting possibility that emotional outbursts may encourage more complex thinking, which helps teenagers master the developmental tasks they face. These tasks—building an identity and building relationships—are the next topics of this story.

Identity Development

One of the important tasks of adolescence and young adulthood is to develop an *identity*, that is, a sense of yourself and how you fit into society, of where you are going in your life and who you want to become. As you figure out your place in society, you also define yourself by identifying your strengths and weaknesses. As Erik Erikson explained, your sense of yourself will continue to change throughout life, but your first serious thoughts about these issues probably started during adolescence.

ERIKSON'S THEORY OF THE ADOLESCENT IDENTITY CRISIS. As you read in previous chapters, Erikson (1950) proposed that children pass through four stages as they move from infancy through late childhood: trust versus mistrust (birth to 1 year), autonomy versus shame and doubt (1 to 3 years), initiative versus guilt (3 to 6 years), and industry versus inferiority (6 to 11 years). Although life thrusts people into the next developmental task whether they are ready or not, adjustment is assumed to be easier for individuals who have successfully resolved their earlier challenges.

According to Erikson, the primary conflict of adolescence is the *identity crisis*: a period of confusion as children explore who they are. Erikson thought that adolescents have to actively seek self-definition, and *role confusion* (or *identity diffusion*, as it's sometimes called) results when adolescents fail to develop a consistent definition. Some role confusion is to be expected during early adolescence, but Erikson believed that a failure to define one's identity was associated with a variety of adjustment problems during late adolescence and early adulthood, including difficulty establishing intimate relationships. Thus the outcome from this fifth stage of psychosocial development is **identity versus role confusion**. Although Erikson popularized the idea of an adolescent identity crisis, the finding that most adolescents are relatively well-adjusted has led scientists to recast this stage as a time of self-exploration rather than crisis.

EXPANSIONS ON ERIKSON'S WORK. Erikson's work was rich in description but short on scientific data and details. These problems left the next generation of psychologists to interpret his work and figure out ways to test his theory. Identity researcher James Marcia (1966, 1980) rose to the challenge by developing the most widely used assessment of the identity crisis. Marcia proposed that this crisis could be viewed as varying along two dimensions: whether people have actively explored identity issues and whether they have made a commitment. These dimensions result in four identity classifications.

As you can see in Table 10.2, adolescents who are currently in a state of exploration but have not made a commitment are in a stage of identity development that Marcia called *moratorium*. Those who have had a period of crisis or exploration and have made a commitment, such as by choosing a career, have reached *identity achievement*. Individuals who are in *foreclosure* have made commitments without actively exploring or undergoing an identity crisis. These people may

identity versus role confusion
In Erik Erikson's theory, the fifth stage of development in which adolescents explore who they are and how they fit into society.

TABLE 10.2 James Marcia's Identity Statuses

		Has the individual seriously explored alternative identities?	
		No	**Yes**
Has the individual committed to various roles and beliefs?	**No**	**Identity diffusion**: the individual is not committed to particular occupational roles or belief systems and is not exploring alternatives	**Moratorium**: The individual is experimenting with possible futures and personal beliefs but has not reached enough decisions to have an enduring sense of self.
	Yes	**Identity foreclosure**: The individual has committed to roles, values, and goals without seriously considering alternatives.	**Identity achievement**: The individual has an enduring sense of self that involves occupational and ideological choices.

have defined themselves in response to their parents' expectations or committed early to a peer group that kept them from exploring alternatives. Whatever the reason, foreclosure is viewed negatively by identity theorists because it is thought to produce an inflexible personality (Muuss, 1988). The final category in Marcia's classification is *identity diffusion*, which describes individuals who have made no commitments and are not actively exploring any. Though Marcia did not equate diffusion with adjustment problems, as Erikson did, he nevertheless viewed it as an undesirable outcome that was sometimes related to apathy* and social isolation (Marcia, 1966).

Critics have complained that Marcia's categories are mere descriptions rather than a developmental theory in which people progress in a systematic way. Even though the percentage of individuals in moratorium decreases after age 19, many people stay in a single category or move back and forth between categories (Meeus et al., 1999; Nurmi, 2004). In addition, there does not seem to be a single end point for development: Young adults who are in a state of foreclosure look as well-adjusted as their peers who are identity achieved, so it is difficult to argue that one is a less desirable or mature accomplishment (Meeus et al., 1999).

The process of identity development is also variable because different cultures provide adolescents with different opportunities for making choices (Ferrer-Wreder et al., 2002). For instance, American culture allows teenagers to spend unsupervised time with opposite-sex peers, so sexual decisions are part of the process of forming an identity. But in the Arab world, interactions with people outside the family are more limited, especially for girls (Brown, Larson, & Saraswathi, 2002). Similarly, American teens struggle with decisions about college whereas few teens in Cambodia do (where only 1 percent of youth attend college). Thus adolescence provides the cognitive equipment for children to begin thinking about their place in society, but there may be no universal process of identity formation.

It is easy to experiment with different values and identities during adolescence. Many teens simply change peer groups when they grow tired of a particular style of dress or music.

---

*apathy: Lack of interest, often characterized by a lack of emotion or feeling.

SELF-ESTEEM AND SELF-CONCEPTS. As you learned in Chapter 8, self-esteem refers to your overall view of yourself, whereas self-concept refers to evaluations of specific competencies (academic ability, social skills, physical appearance, etc.). Given all of the changes that adolescents face, it is not surprising that both of these self-assessments undergo some predictable changes.

Researchers often assess self-esteem with self-report measures that ask people to respond to statements such as, "On the whole, I am satisfied with myself." Self-esteem as measured in this way declines around 11 years of age and is at its lowest point between 12 and 13 years. This dip is probably due to a variety of factors, including bodily changes that trigger negative feelings (such as weight gain and acne) and pubertal status that is out of sync with the perceived norm (Eccles et al., 1993; Moneta, Schneider, & Csikszentmihalyi, 2001; Rosenberg, 1986).

Girls (especially Caucasian girls) tend to have lower self-esteem than boys, partly because they evaluate their attractiveness less favorably than boys do. And as you learned in Chapter 8, self-esteem is also heavily influenced by real accomplishments in school and other areas of life. As a result, there are differences among children based on their achievement in school, status with peers, and other important accomplishments (Harter, 1999; Quatman & Watson, 2001). And as we will discuss in Chapter 11, self-esteem sometimes drops when children transition into middle school, where work is harder and friendships often change (Seidman et al., 2003).

It is easier to feel good about yourself when you have a clear definition of who you are. As a result, adolescents who have strong ethnic identities score somewhat higher on self-esteem measures than those who identify less strongly with an ethnic tradition. African American adolescents often report higher self-esteem than whites or Asians. However, part–African American biracial teens tend to have less positive feelings about their ethnic backgrounds and slightly lower self-esteem (Bracey, Bámaca, & Umaña-Taylor, 2004; Herman, 2004).

Children's self-concepts become quite complicated by adolescence. For example, in response to the question, "What am I like as a person?", one 15-year-old girl wrote, "You're probably not going to understand. I'm complicated! With my really *close* friends, I am very tolerant. I mean I'm understanding and caring. With a *group* of friends, I'm rowdier. I'm also usually friendly and cheerful but I can get pretty obnoxious and intolerant if I don't like how they're acting. I'd *like* to be friendly and tolerant all of the time, that's the kind of person I *want* to be, and I'm disappointed in myself when I'm not" (Harter, 1999, p. 67).

How do adolescents' self-concepts differ from those of children? The most obvious difference is length: The first 86 words this girl wrote about herself were followed by another 600! Teenagers have more to write about when their self-concepts shift from concrete to more abstract descriptions as they grow. For example, an adolescent boy might integrate the fact that he feels dumb and uncreative in science class by calling himself an "airhead," while a girl might combine the traits of "quiet" and "shy" to decide she is an "introvert."

Children also begin to have more *differentiated* views of themselves around 12 to 13 years, which means that their self-perceptions include more categories of evaluation (Harter, 1999). For example, in one study adolescents' self-perceptions varied across at least eight domains, with perceptions of scholastic competence that were usually independent from perceptions of athletic competence, social acceptance, and so forth. Younger children, on the other hand, did not make so many distinctions about their strengths and weaknesses. According to developmental psychologist Susan Harter, increased differentiation is prompted by cognitive development along with social pressures to act differently in different situations. By about 14 or 15 years, children can become quite distressed by their different "selves." As one teen remarked, "I really don't understand how I can switch so fast from being cheerful with my friends, then coming home and feeling anxious, and then getting frustrated and sarcastic with my parents. Which one is the *real* me?" (Harter, 1999, p. 67).

Because it is confusing to think that we are different people in different times and places, we eventually integrate our multiple self-concepts into an integrated, consistent sense of self. This integration occurs later in adolescence, usually starting around 18 years of age and continuing into the early twenties (Elbogen, Carlo, & Spaulding, 2001). For example, a 19-year-old woman might describe herself as "moody" to reconcile the fact that she's sometimes happy and sometimes depressed. Similarly, a young man might say that he's shy on dates and outgoing with friends because he is "flexible" (Harter, 2003). Thus the development of self-concepts occurs through three processes: First, adolescents come to see themselves in terms of increasingly abstract traits, then they differentiate among broader traits, and finally they see how those traits are integrated into the whole that is their self. This developmental progression leads to a decrease in stress as early contradictions are explained and blended into a coherent sense of self.

Writing in a diary is a popular activity among teenage girls—and a way to explore their changing feelings about themselves. In a diary, a girl can be happy, depressed, in love, and angry—all in the same day! As they grow older, teenagers become more comfortable with conflicting traits and see these as part of an integrated whole that is "me."

Relationships

On January 6, 1944, Anne Frank (1995) made an entry into her diary about Peter, the son of a couple who was in hiding with her family. She had strolled into his room that day looking for conversation but worried about bothering him:

> It gave me a wonderful feeling when I looked into his dark blue eyes and saw how bashful my unexpected visit had made him. I could read his innermost thoughts, and in his face I saw a look of helplessness and uncertainty as to how to behave, and at the same time a flicker of awareness of his masculinity. I saw his shyness, and I melted. I wanted to say, "Tell me about yourself. Look beneath my chatty exterior." But I found that it was easier to think up questions than to ask them . . .
>
> You mustn't think I'm in love with Peter, because I'm not. If the van Daans had had a daughter instead of a son, I'd have tried to make friends with her. (pp. 162–163)

The budding sexual feelings revealed in Anne Frank's diary are a universal feature of adolescence. But opportunities for sexual relationships vary tremendously from culture to culture, so we will wait until the next chapter to discuss the consequences of early sexual behavior. Here we focus on the relationship issues in Anne's remarkable diary that affect nearly all adolescents.

FRIENDSHIP CHANGES DURING ADOLESCENCE. Friends are important throughout life. Children who enjoy positive relationships with friends are more involved in school and feel more accepted by their peers than children who have poor-quality friendships (Berndt, 2002), and people who have friends tend to feel good about themselves (Hartup & Stevens, 1999). As we saw in Chapter 8, being rejected by peers is related to a variety of negative outcomes, including trouble with the law, drug abuse, and poor academic performance. The relationship between friendship quality and social competence goes both ways: Socially competent children and adolescents have more friends, and friends provide an opportunity to practice social skills and become more competent. Throughout life, intimate relationships help buffer the stress of life transitions—and this is especially true during adolescence. For example, Berndt and Keefe (1992) found that transitions from grade to grade or school to school resulted in fewer problems when children moved with friends rather than without them.

Friends become more important to children around 10 to 13 years of age. In one study, for example, children rated how much companionship they experienced from various individuals in their lives by rating how often they played around and spent free time with mothers, fathers, same-sex friends, and so forth. Second graders said they received as much companionship from parents as they did from same-sex friends, and fifth graders rated parents *higher* on companionship than friends. But by the eighth grade, same-sex friends were the *greatest* source of companionship. Similarly, second and fifth graders said they were more intimate with parents than friends, whereas by the eighth grade boys were just as intimate with friends as parents while girls were more intimate with friends (Buhrmester & Furman, 1987).

As friends become central to their lives, what teens expect from friends also changes. When asked to talk about what makes someone a friend, adolescents are more likely than younger children to mention qualities that promote intimacy, such as mentioning personal details about oneself (self-disclosure) and providing emotional support. As you can see in Figure 10.8, intimate disclosure to parents decreases from the fifth grade on and is low throughout adolescence (although there is a rebound in intimacy with parents when individuals reach college age). The opposite pattern is found for friendships and romantic partnerships: Intimacy for these relationships rises throughout late childhood and early adolescence (Buhrmester, 1996).

But adolescent girls' and boys' friendships differ in the level and importance of intimacy. Girls are more motivated to maintain friendships (Richard & Schneider, 2005), are more likely than boys to think that self-disclosure and emotional support are important characteristics for friends to have, and report higher levels of self-disclosure and emotional support in their interactions with friends (Buhrmester, 1996; Buhrmester & Furman, 1987; Furman & Buhrmester, 1992; Jarvinen & Nicholls, 1996). As you might imagine, these differences can cause conflict between girls and boys. When teenagers form romantic attachments, girls assume they have a "new best friend" who will be even more intimate than their girlfriends were (Tannen, 1990). In contrast, boys expect interactions that are similar to the ones they are used to enjoying, so they try to connect with the opposite sex by teasing, engaging in harmless rough-and-tumble play, or just spending time with their crush, just as they would with their male friends (Pellegrini, 2003). Read on to hear more about other features of teens' relationship behavior.

FRIENDSHIP PATTERNS. In addition to wondering whether their friends will like their new haircut or invite them to a party, adolescents are also looking at their social lives and wondering, "Am I normal?" To answer this question, let's look at five key facts that characterize the teenage social system (Brown, 2004):

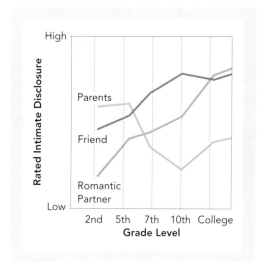

FIGURE 10.8 The targets of intimacy.

By the seventh grade, children have a clear preference to disclose personal information to friends rather than parents, but parental popularity rebounds somewhat by the college years.

SOURCE: Adapted from Buhrmester (1996).

▶ *Peer cultures vary across cultures and social contexts.* The size of a community and its cultural values influence the structure of teenagers' social worlds. Children who live in small communities do not tend to separate into different groups the way teenagers in larger communities do, and it is normal for children who are encouraged to socialize with extended family members to have smaller, less intense friendship networks. For example, a focus on family is common in traditionally oriented Mexican Americans families and numerous other groups.

▶ *Peer relationships are constantly changing.* Between one-third and one-half of all teen peer groups do not survive for an entire academic year. Even among pairs who consider themselves best friends, fewer than half still do after a year.

▶ *It is common to have multiple peer groups.* Teenagers often have different groups of friends for different activities—and they like to keep these groups separate. As one teen said, "I don't want my worlds colliding. When I'm here [at youth group] I don't have to be the same person that I am with my school friends; I don't want to mess that up" (Brown, 2004, p. 367). Separate social worlds help prepare teens for life in the adult world, where they will routinely shift from roles as they move between work, community activities, and home life.

▶ *One-on-one relations are influenced by interactions at other levels.* For example, best friends act differently among themselves than when they are with a group, and children tend to explore romantic relations at younger ages when their peer group contains a mix of boys and girls.

▶ *Peer status shows some stability and some instability.* As in childhood, *rejected* adolescents tend to stay rejected even after they transition to a new school. But peer *acceptance* is not as stable, particularly for girls. Instead, it is not uncommon for girls with many friends one year to have fewer the next, and vice versa (Hardy, Bukowski, & Sippola, 2002).

As you can see, many ways of socializing are "normal" during adolescence. Some children have a single, close-knit group of friends throughout their high school years, and these children may not experiment much with different ways of looking, acting, and thinking. Other children take advantage of changing friendships to experiment with a variety of beliefs and identities. For example, a conservative middle schooler may adopt the dark clothing and musical tastes of Goth culture for the first two years of high school and then cast off this persona in favor of something else.

Because different cultures provide different ways for adolescents to socialize, visitors from other countries often miss the types of social gatherings they are used to at home. For example, exchange students often come from urban areas where teens congregate at a wide variety of public events. This visitor from Korea is experiencing the U.S. tradition of just "hanging out."

CLIQUES AND CROWDS. Adolescents' identities and friendships are often related through their connections with larger social groups. One important group is the friendship *clique*. Cliques vary in size from 3 to 10 members, with the average clique containing about 5 members (Brown & Klute, 2003; Ennett & Bauman, 1996). By definition, cliques are tight-knit groups whose members socialize with one another both in and out of school.

Like friendships, cliques tend to be homogenous. Most clique members are the same age and gender and of similar ethnicity. As in all types of peer relationships, children model the attitudes and beliefs of friends in their clique. They also receive pressure to conform through conversations, gossip, and teasing, as well as more direct peer pressure. Often clique leaders enforce group norms by ridiculing individuals who are outside the group and encouraging clique members to engage in similar behaviors. Of course, many adolescents do not belong to a particular school clique. Some are *liaisons* who have friendships with members of two or more cliques, whereas others are more isolated, without clique ties but still having at least one friend (Adler & Adler, 1995; Brown & Klute, 2003; Ennett & Bauman, 1996).

There are benefits and costs to belonging in a clique. On the positive side, cliques provide clear guidelines that help children determine how to be successful in their social system. As a result, clique members have more close friends, more positive peer relationships, and fewer internalizing problems such as depression than do peers who are more isolated (Henrich et al., 2000). There is also a positive relationship between group membership and academic performance (Wentzel & Caldwell, 1997). On the negative side, membership in a clique with antisocial norms can encourage teens to model each other's undesirable behavior. For example, one study of a clique of five boys found they accounted for 7 percent of all disciplinary referrals at school (Henrich et al., 2000).

But *peer pressure*—encouragement from one's friends to act in particular ways—is not always the reason for bad behavior. Instead, teens who are prone to act in certain ways tend to select each other as friends (Simons-Morton et al., 2004), and teens who are especially interested in risky behavior are more likely than their peers to imitate harmful behavior (Henry, Slater, & Oetting, 2005). Furthermore, it is not the case that teens are more likely to be influenced by friends when the quality of friendship is high (Berndt, 2002). Thus teens are not blindly following the behavior of friends in their cliques. Instead, they are active participants in choosing who they will spend time with and how they will behave.

A group of people who do not necessarily know one another but are grouped together because they share certain characteristics is known as a *crowd*. Most secondary schools have crowds such as jocks (athletically oriented adolescents), populars or preps (a high-status elite group), burnouts (a group that promotes deviant behavior), brains (adolescents who do well in school and are academically oriented), and loners (adolescents without any affiliations). Another crowd that is often identified is the nonconformists, a group of individuals whose musical tastes and clothing styles do not fit in with the mainstream school culture. Although you may have attended schools with more or different crowds, these general types have been found in schools across the country (Prinstein & LaGreca, 2002). Crowds are another level of social structure that helps adolescents define themselves and helps them locate individuals with similar interests and characteristics (Urberg et al., 2000).

DATING AND ROMANTIC ATTACHMENTS. Wherever societies let people select their partners, dating is an important process that helps individuals preparing for choosing a mate. This process is a two-edged sword: a moderate amount of dating can be a positive socializing experience, but early dating and dating many different partners are associated with teen pregnancy, sexually transmitted diseases, and exposure to dating violence (Furman, 2002; Savin-Williams & Diamond, 2004).

Though dating is a common adolescent experience, a growing number of teenagers either do not date or date infrequently. As you can see in Figure 10.9, the percentage of students who report never dating has been rising steadily since 1991, and the number of twelfth graders who report dating at least once a week declined from 34 percent in 1991 to 29 percent in 2000 (Child Trends, 2003). The reasons for these trends are not exactly clear. Boys and girls' first interactions usually take place in mixed boy-girl groups, with one-on-one dating becoming more common later in adolescence (Furman, 2002). It may be that today's teens are just less likely to describe these early activities as "dating" than earlier generations were. Alternatively, "formal" dating patterns that were prevalent in the past may have been replaced by more casual interactions. For example, inviting a girl out for a hamburger and a movie on Saturday night is less common than a group of boys and girls deciding to watch a rented movie in someone's home.

For many years, it was commonly believed that adolescent romances were short-lived (by adult standards) and, therefore, were not to be taken too seriously. The popularity of the term *puppy love* conveys this dismissive attitude. To some degree, this response is justified: In one study, romantic attachments in mid-adolescence lasted an average of less than 4 months (Feiring, 1999). But averages do not convey the whole picture. When researchers studied students who were in dating relationships, approximately 20 percent of adolescents who were 14 years or younger, 35 percent of 15- and 16-year-olds, and almost 60 percent of 17- and 18-year-olds had been involved for 11 months or longer. Furthermore, romantic attachments involve a high degree of intimacy, and breaking up is a common trigger for a first episode of major depression. Thus it is a mistake for adults to trivialize these relationships (Collins, 2003). As you will read next, one reason some adolescents are deeply affected by how they are treated by friends and romantic partners has to do with their increasing sophistication when it comes to thinking about moral behavior and fairness.

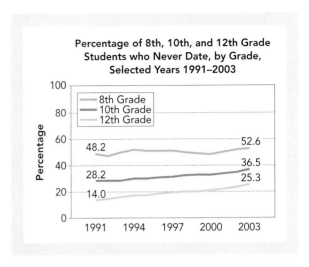

FIGURE 10.9 Trends in dating.

Dating is an important activity for many adolescents, but it is not uncommon not to date. In fact, the percentage of teenagers who report that they never date has been increasing over the past 15 years.

SOURCE:
http://www.childtrendsdatabank.org/indicators/73Dating.cfm

Moral Development

During the 2004 presidential debates, journalists watched eagerly as audiences reacted to issues like Iraq, abortion, and tax cuts. During one postdebate discussion, a viewer named Ally Rogers said the election was "like choosing the lesser of two evils." In response, Scott Cantonwine quipped, "When did evil become acceptable?" Cantonwine had hoped to hear more about border security and immigration, while Brooke Bell-Uribe was disappointed that the candidates hadn't mentioned *No Child Left Behind* and education. "They really don't talk enough about what they are planning to do for the school districts in the U.S.," she told a reporter (Evans, 2004).

This may sound like a room of middle-aged Democrats and Republicans, but it was actually a group of high school students, assembled to produce a story for Oregon's *Statesman Journal*. Recall from Chapter 8 that late childhood is the time when individuals develop what Piaget called a *morality of cooperation*: Now children understand that rules can be changed if people agree to do so, so they enjoy debating principles. During adolescence, the ability to contemplate abstract ideas increases the complexity of children's thinking about fairness, justice, and morality. At the same time, a heightened interest in relationships and increased emotional passion lead children to become more curious about political issues and their place in larger social systems. As these developments unfold, many teens become deep thinkers who are troubled by moral issues. As with younger children, they mostly get fired up when the target of injustice is themselves, but teenagers feel increasingly connected to distant concerns as well.

The thought processes and emotional passions that are involved in handling moral issues are the foundation of responsible behavior and even the democratic process. But to explore these thoughts and feelings, we need to look beyond the cognitive changes Piaget described to a theory developed by psychologist Lawrence Kohlberg.

KOHLBERG'S THEORY OF MORAL REASONING. To tap moral reasoning, Lawrence Kohlberg asked children and adults to react to *moral dilemmas*, stories that described a conflict between two moral values. One of his most famous dilemmas is the story of Heinz, which pits the desire to obey the law (by not stealing) against the desire to save a human life (by stealing) (Colby et al., 1983). Here is the dilemma:

> In Europe, a woman was near death from a special kind of cancer. There was one drug that the doctors thought might save her. It was a form of radium that a druggist in the same town had recently discovered. The drug was expensive to make, but the druggist was charging 10 times what the drug cost him to make. He paid $200 for the radium and charged $2,000 for a small dose of the drug. The sick woman's husband, Heinz, went to everyone he knew to borrow the money, but he could only get together about $1,000, which is half of what it cost. He told the druggist that his wife was dying and asked him to sell it cheaper or let him pay later. But the druggist said, "No, I discovered the drug and I'm going to make money from it." So Heinz gets desperate and considers breaking into the man's store to steal the drug for his wife. (p. 77)

Kohlberg asked children and adults "Should Heinz steal the drug?", "Why or why not?", as well as other questions to probe their thinking. Rather than focusing on their choices, he was interested in their reasoning and the moral issues that guided their choices. After analyzing people's responses, Kohlberg concluded that moral reasoning falls into three broad levels that emerge in a developmental sequence (Kohlberg, 1963, 1976):

▶ **Preconventional morality** (typical of children from 4 to 10). Consistent with Piaget's description of early moral reasoning, children in these stages view rules as absolute and judge actions by whether they lead to punishment or not. For example, children who vote to steal the drug might say that Heinz would get in trouble if he let her die. Children who vote against stealing might mention that it is illegal to steal ("It's against the law") or point out individual risks and interests ("He shouldn't steal because he can get arrested and punished").

preconventional morality In Lawrence Kohlberg's theory of moral development, the two stages of moral reasoning (typical of 4- to 10-year-olds) when children view rules as absolute and judge actions by whether or not they lead to punishment.

▶ **Conventional morality** (typical of most adolescents and adults). Children in these stages are concerned about pleasing others, being "good," or maintaining social order. Those who vote to steal might say "He should take the drug because he loves her and it's the right thing to do." Those who think that Heinz should not steal might say that society would break down if everybody stole.

▶ Postconventional morality (found only in some adolescents and adults) makes reference to protecting individual rights, the needs of the majority, or fundamental principles of fairness and justice ("A human life is more valuable than the cost of the drug").

Kohlberg initially divided these broad levels into six stages, with two stages per level, resulting in the sequences of stages in Table 10.3.

Kohlberg's methods have been attacked on several grounds. For example, his moral dilemmas do not tap issues teenagers face in everyday life, and his scoring system does not allow for cultural differences in which decisions are preferred. Nonetheless, research in several countries—including the United States, Israel, and Turkey—supports his claim that the first four stages describe a universal developmental sequence.

To get an idea of what responses are typical during adolescence, look at the results of a longitudinal study that appear in Figure 10.10 (Colby et al., 1983). Notice that 81 percent of 10-year-olds reasoned at stage 1 or 2, compared to only 13 percent of 16- to 18-year-olds. Most adolescents provided answers to moral dilemmas that represent conventional morality (stages 3 or 4), and none of the children showed postconventional reasoning. Results such as these suggest that development is slower than Kohlberg originally expected. You will read more

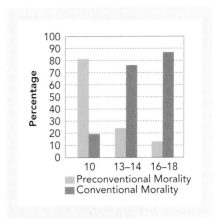

FIGURE 10.10 Moral development during adolescence.

Changes in moral reasoning are gradual. By 16 to 18 years, the majority of children give reasons to moral dilemmas that fit Kohlberg's level of conventional morality: They are concerned about pleasing others, being "good," or maintaining social order. These children have abandoned the focus on breaking rules that characterizes preconventional morality, but they are not yet focusing on moral principles.

SOURCE: Colby et al. (1983).

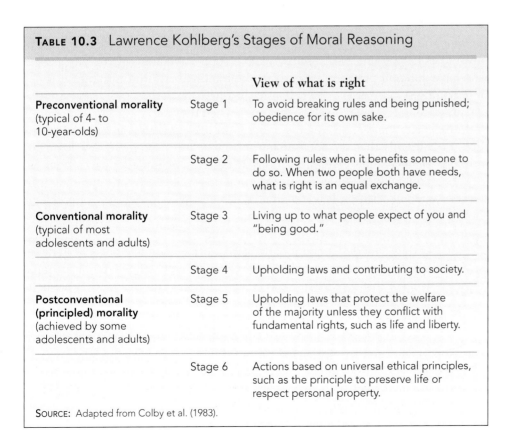

TABLE 10.3 Lawrence Kohlberg's Stages of Moral Reasoning		
		View of what is right
Preconventional morality (typical of 4- to 10-year-olds)	Stage 1	To avoid breaking rules and being punished; obedience for its own sake.
	Stage 2	Following rules when it benefits someone to do so. When two people both have needs, what is right is an equal exchange.
Conventional morality (typical of most adolescents and adults)	Stage 3	Living up to what people expect of you and "being good."
	Stage 4	Upholding laws and contributing to society.
Postconventional (principled) morality (achieved by some adolescents and adults)	Stage 5	Upholding laws that protect the welfare of the majority unless they conflict with fundamental rights, such as life and liberty.
	Stage 6	Actions based on universal ethical principles, such as the principle to preserve life or respect personal property.

SOURCE: Adapted from Colby et al. (1983).

conventional morality In Lawrence Kohlberg's theory of moral development, the two stages of moral reasoning that are typical of most adolescents and adults. At this stage, people are concerned about pleasing others, being a good person, and maintaining social order rather than making decisions based on universal ethical principles.

This teenage boy has agreed to let a jury of his peers determine his sentence for breaking the law, which might include writing a letter of apology (for vandalizing a neighbor's yard) or completing community service (for stealing). In some locations, first-time offenders who admit wrongdoing can be sentenced by a panel of teen volunteers who are chosen so that no teen hears a case involving someone they know. The teen jury process is made possible because adolescents have a growing ability to consider moral issues and are better able than younger children to make the punishment fit the crime.

about moral development in Chapter 13 when we discuss gender and cultural influences on moral decisions.

ENCOURAGING MORAL DEVELOPMENT. Kohlberg believed that giving people, including adolescents, opportunities to think about moral issues provides the motivation for moral development. Consistent with this prediction, numerous studies have found that discussions in a supportive atmosphere with people who have different perspectives on issues help individuals shift into higher levels of reasoning (Colby et al., 1977; Lapsley, Enright, & Serlin, 1989). As a result, parents encourage higher levels of reasoning when they are warm, encourage children to express views, and involve children in decision making. Similarly, conflicts with friends that do not become too heated also promote development, although highly competitive interactions do not (Eisenberg & Morris, 2004).

Regrettably, impressive moral reasoning does not necessarily translate into impressive moral *behavior*. It is true that adolescents who have behavior problems show lower levels of moral reasoning, whereas higher levels of reasoning are associated with social competence and helpful social behavior. But moral reasoning accounts for only a modest amount of the variability in moral behavior (Eisenberg & Morris, 2004). This makes sense because the *reason* for a choice is not the same as the choice. For instance, people can be helpful and kind because they are conventional and follow rules (which is an immature reason), or they can engage in antisocial behavior, such as letting the neighbor's rabbits out of their outdoor cages, because of a dearly held ethical principle (which is a high-level reason). The slippage between reasoning and behavior also makes sense because—as you learned earlier in this chapter—emotionally relevant behavior isn't usually the product of analytical thinking. Instead, such behavior is heavily influenced by group norms, immediate circumstances, and religious, spiritual, and cultural traditions that give our choices meaning and direction.

>>> **M E M O R Y   M A K E R S** <<<

Match each word on the left with a phrase on the right:

1. imaginary audience
2. personal fable
3. adolescent egocentrism
4. identity versus role confusion

(a) the idea that one is special and invulnerable

(b) Elkind's theory of adolescent thought

(c) Erikson's fifth stage of psychosocial development

(d) the idea that other people are preoccupied with one's appearance and behavior

5. Research on Kohlberg's theory of moral development has found that most teenagers are in the stage of _____ morality, when they are concerned about _____.

(a) postconventional morality; fundamental principles of fairness and justice

(b) postconventional morality; maintaining social order

(c) conventional morality; fundamental principles of fairness and justice

(d) conventional morality; maintaining social order

[1-d; 2-a; 3-b; 4-c; 5-d]

Working with Adolescents

Due to the developmental events we have been discussing, interacting with an adolescent is a different experience from interacting with younger children or adults. This is why many professions, including education and medicine, have special certifications or training programs for people who work primarily with this age group. If you are planning a career that involves adolescents—or if you just want to understand this time of life better—you will enjoy the following observations about living and working with teens.

There is no doubt that adolescents have expanding minds with increased potential for abstract thought and the ability to reason about future possibilities. But they also lack life experience, and their brains have not completed the circuitry that helps adults monitor errors, regulate emotions, and interrupt a first impression to think rationally. As a result, there is a widespread stereotype that some teenagers are—for lack of a kinder word—obnoxious. The following anecdotes from school psychologist Joan Newman (1985) illustrate three characteristics of adolescence that are the source of this stereotype:

▶ *Argumentativeness and a "know-it-all" attitude.* Sixteen-year-old Donald drove to school with his mother after missing the school bus. "As he got into

the car," Newman explained, "he said most belligerently, 'If *some* people hadn't forgotten to set their alarm clocks, I'd have gotten to school on time.' Not only is he rude and obnoxious, his remark is also inappropriate because it ignores his own responsibility and assumes his right to limitless help from his mother" (p. 635).

Most teenagers love to point out what other people don't know, blame them for failings, and initiate arguments occasionally. These traits stem from their ability to imagine possibilities, which encourages them to think about how things might have been different.

▶ *Unrestrained idealism.* A 13-year-old girl wanted her mother to drive her to a friend's house on a day school was closed due to snow. "Her mother refused," Newman recalled, "and suggested that her now angry daughter count the number of cars passing along the street to demonstrate that the roads were impassable. Not one car came by in a period of a half hour, but the teenager still protested, 'It's not fair! When I grow up and have a daughter, and she wants her best friend over, *I* won't refuse. I'll be a good mother. I'll at least try to drive and get her best friend.' By refusing to accept the reality of the situation, this teenager's behavior is inappropriate to the point of being ludicrous" (p. 642).

Teenagers can imagine a world that is free from hunger, violence, and the boredom of snow days. They believe that they will do better than their parents and teachers in the future, and they are frustrated by the inability of adults to build a better world. Lacking experience, they often fail to appreciate the practical constraints that produce hardships in life. On the bright side, their ability to think about things that are not physically present allows them to empathize with the victims of war and natural disasters, so they become interested in service activities and citizenship.

▶ *Flexing their ability to control.* If you have an older brother or sister, you will probably recognize the following story. "A younger brother is playing with playdough," Newman explains, "something that teenage sister has not done for years. Now, however, she develops an urgent need to play, demands a share, and when she gets it, complains that the younger child has more than she has. She suggests 'improvements' to the younger child's efforts, then makes her own superior model. Younger brother cries and the parent intervenes. The teenager's righteous response is truly obnoxious: 'I was only helping. Gosh, what do you have to do around here to please?'" (p. 638)

Teenage life can be stressful: School work is more difficult, social relationships are more challenging, and internal thoughts are more complicated. But, unlike adults, adolescents can't fall back on memories of past success to calm themselves. Instead, they sometimes deal with stress by trying to control people who are less capable than themselves. Of course, they also test their wits against adults, just to see where they stand.

As annoying as these behaviors are, most teenagers are delightful to be around. It is remarkable to listen to a group of 13-year-old friends spend time in the kitchen, having a heated discussion about infinity or the concept of God.

TABLE 10.4 Tips for Working with Adolescents		
Characteristic	Showing tolerance	Setting limits
Argumentativeness	Avoid arguments by ignoring insignificant challenges and obnoxious behavior.	Don't allow verbal comments or behavior that is hurtful to others or their property.
Pride in what they know and a "know-it-all" attitude	Teenagers have spent over a decade listening to adults; they want a turn to share their own feelings and ideas. Try to listen as much as you talk.	Let teenagers know that it is not acceptable to publicly embarrass people by "one-upping" them. Model appropriate behavior by reserving your own corrections and criticisms for a private time.
Unrestrained idealism	Adolescents are envisioning possible worlds and futures. Respond to their criticism by inviting them to talk about how they would act or how they would like their life to be when they grow up.	Let them know that you are a person who has feelings. Give them examples of how people can make suggestions without being hurtful.
Flexing their ability to control	Reinforce adolescents for working cooperatively with other people rather than punishing them when they don't. Give them increasing responsibilities so they take pride in their new stage of development and the contributions they can make to family and community life.	Teach children that life is not always easy or fair. Refuse to negotiate issues that are important to you.

SOURCES: National Clearinghouse on Families & Youth (2006); Newman (1988).

And it is gratifying to discuss history, science, and moral values with people who ask penetrating questions and bring up issues 2 days later, when they have had another idea. To help family members and professionals enjoy this exciting time of life, experts recommended the simple strategies outlined in Table 10.4 for dealing with the challenges teenagers create.

You can understand why we started this chapter with a story about motocross champion Travis Pastrana: He is an extreme version of many characteristics that make adults so worried about yet proud of adolescents. Pastrana's excellent mind allowed him to whiz through high school, his people skills helped him build a career, and his zeal for thrills and adventure regularly made the news. But, unlike most youngsters, the world watched closely while this teen consolidated an identity, made important choices, and—as we breathed sighs of relief—survived.

Adolescents are not usually as sure about their futures as Travis Pastrana was. Individuals take many pathways on the road to adulthood, paths that depend on their environments, talents, and personalities. These differences are the focus of the next chapter on adolescence.

⟩⟩⟩ SUMMARY ⟨⟨⟨

The Wonder of Puberty

1. The **endocrine system** (a system of glands that produce and secrete **hormones**) coordinates the unfolding of **puberty**, a period of rapid development during which individuals become capable of reproduction. Typically, girls begin puberty between 8 and 14 years of age, whereas boys begin between 9 and 15 years. **Adolescence** is the time between puberty and adulthood when children undergo the physical and psychological changes they need to assume adult roles.

2. During adolescence, the hormones that direct puberty can lead to increases in irritableness, aggressive behavior, moodiness, and depression. But hormones alone are rarely the only cause of difficult feelings or unreasonable behavior. Teenagers who go through puberty at the same time as most of their peers experience fewer problems than those who are extremely early or late.

3. Children develop greater muscular strength and aerobic endurance during puberty. Sex differences in fitness scores that emerge around 12 to 13 years of age are due to physical differences and differences in motivation to perform on physical tasks.

4. There is a second "brain spurt" during adolescence, a time of rapid synaptogenesis followed by synaptic pruning. The chemical changes that lead teens to seek stimulation and novelty occur early in adolescence, years before the brain systems that help them interpret other people's behavior, anticipate the consequences of their reactions, and react like adults to mistakes are fully mature.

Cognitive Development

5. Adolescence is the time when children transition into Piaget's stage of **formal operational thought**. Now they have the capacity for increasingly abstract thought, including the abilities to think about possibilities and systematically test hypotheses.

6. Piaget's theory describes the development of *analytical thinking*: the process of solving problems by deliberately applying logical or mathematical rules. But according to the **dual-processing model**, everyday thinking often relies on *experiential thinking*: commonsense strategies or rules of thumb that do not guarantee the best solution. Because both systems of thinking develop with age, adolescents can seem brilliant one moment and irrational the next.

7. Response inhibition, speed of processing, and working memory become more adult-like during adolescence.

Emotional and Social Development

8. David Elkind described two characteristics of **adolescent egocentrism**: the *imaginary audience* (the belief that people are preoccupied with one's appearance and behavior) and the *personal fable* (a belief in one's "specialness" and invulnerability). But contrary to what Elkind predicted, adolescent egocentrism is not strongly related to formal operational reasoning, does not always diminish after early adolescence, and is not always irrational.

9. Erik Erikson believed that adolescents were in the stage of **identity versus role confusion**. Research on James Marcia's model has found that *identity achievement* (forming an identity after exploration) and *foreclosure* (forming an identity without exploration) are both common during late adolescence. As children experiment with various identities, their concepts of themselves undergo predictable changes. Self-esteem reaches its lowest point around 12 to 13 years and then rebounds. With increasing age, self-concepts become more abstract ("I am an introvert"), more differentiated ("I am introverted in class but extroverted with my friends"), and more integrated into a consistent sense of self ("I am sometimes happy and sometimes depressed because I am moody").

10. Friends become the primary targets of intimacy during adolescence. The structure of teenage friendships varies across cultures, is constantly changing, involves multiple peer groups, and is influenced by interactions at social levels above the friendship pair. Two of these levels are the *clique* (a small group of children who frequently socialize) and the *crowd* (a group of children who share certain characteristics, such as the jocks and the brains). Romantic relationships are important to teenagers, and some individuals become seriously depressed when they end.

11. Most teenagers are in Kohlberg's stage of **conventional morality**, a period when children are more likely to be concerned with being "good" and maintaining social order than acting in ways that are consistent with fundamental ethical principles. Advanced moral reasoning is associated with exposure to a variety of opinions and parents who involve their children in decision making.

Working with Adolescents

12. Adolescents are often argumentative and act as if they "know it all." Their idealism can lead them to criticize others, and they often test boundaries by trying to control other people. Adults who work successfully with teenagers are tolerant about these tendencies but set limits on harmful or hurtful behavior.

>>>KEY TERMS<<<

puberty   (p. 390)
adolescence   (p. 390)
endocrine system   (p. 391)
hormones   (p. 391)
adolescent growth spurt   (p. 392)
peak height velocity (PHV)   (p. 392)
primary sex characteristics   (p. 393)
secondary sex characteristics   (p. 393)
menarche   (p. 394)
secular trend   (p. 394)
precocious (early) puberty   (p. 394)
delayed puberty   (p. 394)

formal operational thought   (p. 404)
hypothetico-deductive reasoning   (p. 405)
metacognition   (p. 405)
heuristics   (p. 406)
dual-processing model   (p. 407)
hot cognition   (p. 407)
imaginary audience   (p. 412)
personal fable   (p. 413)
adolescent egocentrism   (p. 413)
identity versus role confusion   (p. 414)
preconventional morality   (p. 422)
conventional morality   (p. 423)

MILESTONES of adolescence

12 to 14 Years The changes of puberty appear, with girls maturing about a year earlier than boys.

- By age 12, about half of girls have experienced the onset of menstruation, while many boys are noticing pubic hair and testicular growth.
- Chemical changes in the brain prompt teens to seek more stimulation and novelty than they did earlier in development.
- Improvements in basic information processing functions support the transition to formal operational thought. Teens begin to think more abstractly and spend more time thinking about possibilities.
- As they enter Erikson's phase of identity versus role confusion, children begin to experiment with different ways of dressing and acting.

14 to 17 Years Friends are important influences in adolescents' lives.

- Many brain regions are still developing and becoming integrated. As a result, adolescents are more likely than adults to misinterpret other people's emotions.
- As the sleep-wake cycle changes, teens tend to stay up later in the evening and have trouble getting up early in the morning.
- Adolescents often use analytical reasoning, but they tend to rely on experiential reasoning in highly emotional situations.
- Because self-concepts are becoming more differentiated, many adolescents feel troubled by their "different selves."

17 to about 20 Years Adolescents develop a more integrated, consistent sense of themselves.

- As skeletal growth ends, individual body sizes and shapes are revealed.
- Late maturation of higher brain centers improves self-monitoring and planning, but change will continue into the early 20s.
- An increasing number of adolescents form romantic attachments.
- Knowledge about their own behavior in different situations is integrated into a more coherent sense of self.

How do you build

Preview: Adolescence in **CONTEXT**

Communities, Schools, and Families
Adolescents' adjustment is influenced by numerous factors at the family, school, and community levels. Among the important influences are parents' expectations, parental monitoring, family involvement in important decisions, the academic standards that schools convey, and adolescents' perceptions of their economic opportunities.

Leisure and Work North American children have more discretionary time than children in Asian countries and those in unschooled populations.

Every activity, including time spent on the Internet, watching television, and working after-school jobs, has risks and benefits depending on what adolescents are doing, how much time they are spending doing it, and what other activities are being displaced.

Risky Choices
There are many threats to adolescents' health and well-being. Understanding the factors that contribute to reckless driving, substance use, sexual activity, delinquent behavior, eating disorders, and suicide help individuals and communities work more effectively to keep adolescents safe.

Gender Differences around the World In modern industrialized societies, boys and girls come back together during adolescence after years of mostly same-sex play. In traditional societies, girls and boys are often separated and encouraged to behave very differently.

In this next chapter, you'll learn how developmental principles explain the pathways individuals take through adolescence when we consider the question:
How do you build a resilient teen?

a resilient teen?

CHAPTER ELEVEN

Pathways through Adolescence

Stories of Our Lives
The Power of Books

{ Always remember that you are absolutely unique, just like everyone else. }

Margaret Mead

Our friend Rachel grew up in an 8-foot-wide trailer. Long after she had earned a Ph.D. in social psychology, she was speaking to a class about growing up poor when someone asked her an interesting question: "What made you think you could have a different life than the one your family lived?"

"Books," Rachel said softly. "I learned about the world through books."

We are struck by how often the answer is "books." A prison library transformed Malcolm X from a directionless criminal into one of the driving forces of the civil rights movement. Actor Tom Cruise felt he had mastered the world when he finally overcame his dyslexia and learned how to read. But the best example of how books change lives is one of the most famous women in the world: Oprah Winfrey. Like so many individuals, Oprah's relationship with words grew during her teenage years, when reading helped her escape from a troubled past.

Born poor to parents who never married, Oprah lived her first 6 years on a southern farm with her grandmother, Hattie Mae Lee. From 6 to 14 years of age, Oprah moved frequently between her father's home in Nashville and her mother's in Milwaukee, where she experienced beatings and sexual abuse. She escaped into books. When a seventh-grade teacher spotted her reading at the lunch table, arrangements were made for a scholarship so that Oprah could attend a better school. But she felt out of place in the white suburbs, was experimenting with sex and drugs, and was pregnant when she moved back into her father's house at age 14. (Her premature baby died shortly after birth.) A writer who interviewed her for *Life* magazine explained how Oprah's future brightened under the influence of her father's care and her growing relationship with books (Johnson, 1997):

> During these tumultuous years, books were her preferred reality. "I went back to school after the baby died, thinking that I had been given a second chance in life. I threw myself into books. I read books about troubled women, Helen Keller and Anne Frank. I read about Eleanor Roosevelt."
>
> The harsher the stories, the more she liked them. She empathized with any heroine going through hard times. In particular, she was drawn to Margaret Walker's *Jubilee*. The story of a slave fathered by her master, set in the Civil War era—"the Negro *Gone with the Wind*," it was called when it first came out in 1966—*Jubilee* is graphic and dramatic. Like most of the books Oprah likes, it is the coming-of-age narrative of a naïve, moral girl. The action is brutal; the end, redemptive. "Oprah is the realist who also has a sense of idealism," book club author Wally Lamb observes. What echoes after reading *Jubilee*, as well as all her other favorite books, are the voices—strong, rhythmic and often in dialect. Oprah loves writing that begs to be read out loud. (p. 53)

Oprah credits her father, her teachers, and books for giving her the support she desperately needed during her adolescent years. She won a scholarship to attend Tennessee State University and landed a job as Nashville's first African American TV news anchor when she was only 19 years old. Today, the girl who was a powerless teenager has become one of the richest and most influential women in the world. But her favorite activity is still connecting with people by reading and sharing books. "What a difference it makes in your world to go into some other life. It's what I love most. I'm reading always to leave myself, always to leave myself behind," Oprah explained. "That's what reading is. You get to leave" (Johnson, 1997, p. 60).

IN EVERY GENERATION, some people grow up in poverty, some in violence, and some in the warm security of protected childhoods. Yet in every generation, some children from all walks of life construct meaningful lives while others flounder. The story of Oprah Winfrey's childhood leads us to think about why teenagers head in one direction or the other. Television and radio were heavily censored when Oprah was young, movies were expensive, and the Internet didn't exist. Back then, a book was one of the few windows into the world.

But times have changed. Families, schools, and communities are still important influences, and some adolescents are avid readers. Increasingly, though, children are learning about the world from a range of electronic resources, including a more explicit media and the Internet. In this chapter, you will explore how all of these factors influence teens as they take different pathways through adolescence.

Communities, Schools, and Families

People assume the responsibilities of adulthood at different ages and with different degrees of fanfare, depending on where they live. Some societies abruptly change children's rights and responsibilities at times determined by an arbitrary age or a pubertal event (such as menarche). For example, a popular tradition in Mexico is the *quinceañera*, a celebration of a girl's fifteenth birthday. In the past, this ceremony marked the transition from childhood to adulthood and announced that a girl was eligible for marriage. (Today the event is more symbolic but may be followed by more dating privileges.) Teens in other societies are gradually given more responsibility with no formal recognition that childhood is over. For example, most U.S. and European adolescents enjoy increased driving privileges and more autonomy to come and go as they mature, but they are also expected to help out more with chores and pay for more of their nonessential expenses. Regardless of where they live, teens around the world are socialized by the forces you will read about next, including their communities, the schools that educate them, and their families.

rites of passage Ritual ceremonies that mark transitions from one phase of life to another. Traditionally, rites of passage marked events such as births, the end of childhood ("coming-of-age" initiations), marriage, and death.

Coming of Age around the World

Many societies mark transitions from one phase of life to another with ritual ceremonies called **rites of passage**. Rites of passage commemorate events such as births, formal recognition of the end of childhood ("coming-of-age" initiations), marriage, and death. Confirmation ceremonies, bar mitzvahs,* and the quinceañera are modern rites of passage. These formal ceremonies separate individuals from a previous identity, announce the new identity to the community, provide an opportunity to instruct individuals about their new roles, and reinforce cultural values (Markstrom & Iborra, 2003).

*bar mitzvah: A Jewish ceremony to recognize that a 13-year-old
 boy is now a member of the adult religious community. The
 ceremony for girls (bat mitzvah or bas mitzvah) is celebrated
 after the 12th birthday.

Celebrations like the Mexican quinceañera (left) and the Jewish bat mitzvah (right) publicly recognize the growing rights and responsibilities children assume as they approach adulthood.

Rites of passage that celebrate the end of childhood are often elaborate affairs. An example is the Navajo *Kinaaldá*, a 4-day-long ceremony that marks a girl's first or second menstrual period and her entering into adulthood (Markstrom & Iborra, 2003). The *Kinaaldá* involves rituals that symbolize the roles the girl will assume as an adult, the characteristics that are valued for women, and the girl's new responsibilities to family members. Three of these rituals are physically taxing: grinding corn for a cake that will be baked on the last night of the ceremony (and fed to everyone except the girl herself), running two or three times a day to prepare for the hardships of life, and an all-night sing. In some cases, the girl receives a new name to underscore her new identity. In these ways, the process of defining one's identity involves the entire community. Adolescents say that formal recognition of a new status is highly meaningful. In one study, for example, the majority of college students said they had received some type of "parental blessing" that recognized their grown-up status, and over half of those who did not *wished that they had* (Bjornsen, 2000).

What Matters for Success

Cultures with rites of passage have a number of characteristics that might smooth the transition to adulthood. The children in these cultures tend to have strong family ties, share responsibilities with a group of peers their own age, and have well-defined relationships with adults in the broader community. Are all of these influences equally important? To answer this question, Sociologist Thomas Cook and his colleagues studied over 12,000 seventh- and eighth-grade students from a large area to the south and east of Washington, DC (Cook et al., 2002). The region was racially diverse and included urban, suburban, and rural communities. For each adolescent, the research team measured a variety of environmental variables to see which best related to overall success, including family quality (such as whether parents discussed important issues with their teen), peer quality (such as the number of close friends), school quality (such as expectations for high achievement), and neighborhood quality (such as youth resources and adult involvement in community organizations).

The researchers then computed "overall success" by counting the number of domains (from a set of 9) that adolescents were doing well enough in to "get by" in American culture. These included a grade point average of C+ or better, a passing score on state competency testing, fewer than 10 school absences per school year, participation in fewer than 8 out of 11 misbehaviors (most of which were illegal), and spending at least half of their free time in "conventional" activities (such as homework, reading, music lessons, or organized recreation). The average seventh-grade student was getting by on over 70 percent of the success outcomes, but this figure dropped to just over 60 percent 19 months later as more students failed state competency testing, entered lower math tracks, experimented with drugs, and dropped out of conventional leisure activities. By relating changes in success with each of the environmental variables, the team made three important discoveries:

▶ *Each individual environmental variable had only a small effect on success.*

▶ *Specific environmental contexts affected specific outcomes.* For example, families had more influence on mental health, such as whether students felt positively about themselves, peers had more influence on drug use and other misbehavior, schools had more influence on academic performance, and neighborhoods had more influence on how children spent their leisure time.

▶ *The best predictor of overall success was the sum of scores across environmental contexts.* As you can see in Figure 11.1, eighth-grade success increased gradually as the quality of adolescents' environmental contexts increased.

Surprisingly, there was no evidence that any particular combination of contexts was especially important. As the authors explained, these results suggest that "there are no early adolescent 'silver bullets' that can radically transform young lives for the better" (Cook et al., 2002, p. 1306). Instead, development rests on the accumulation of myriad influences: *Everything matters a little.*

Schools

Oprah Winfrey has always expressed appreciation for teachers, so it didn't surprise fans when she showered gifts on an audience of teachers during a show she dedicated to "the most honorable profession" (Lowe, 2004, para. 4). Research on schools has confirmed that what happens inside classroom walls changes millions of lives each day.

SCHOOL TRANSITIONS. Students used to make only one transition during their school years, from elementary school to high school after the eighth grade. As crowding caused new schools to be built, the grade structure of schools also changed. By the 1960s most children attended elementary school for 6 or 7 years and then transitioned into a *junior high school* that was organized like high school. Later, by the mid-1980s, the majority of school districts had *middle schools* that typically included grades 7 and 8 or 6, 7, and 8. The term *middle school* refers to a particular age range and also implies a philosophy of teaching (Krouscas, 2005). This philosophy recognizes that young adolescents have a newfound ability to think abstractly and grapple with moral issues but still learn best when schools create strong ties to significant adults and encourage active, hands-on learning (National Middle School Association, 2003).

The transition to middle school and then high school is often associated with a drop in grades. There are many reasons for this. Academic requirements become more stringent as adolescents enter middle school and then high school, and the greater freedom in these schools provides more opportunities for students to fall behind in their work. This decline also appears to be due to the disruptive effects of a transition itself, because students who make two transitions by high school show larger declines than those who make one (Crockett et al., 1989). There are many reasons why adolescents would be troubled by transitions, including the fact that friendships are often interrupted by transitions and that children feel less connected to teachers after elementary school. In general, academic achievement is more negatively affected by school transitions for young adolescents, girls, and children from lower socioeconomic families (Mullins & Irvin, 2000).

Several studies have found declines in self-esteem across the transition to middle school or junior high school, especially for girls (Dusek & McIntyre, 2003; Seidman et al., 1996; Simmons & Blyth, 1987). But this is not a universal finding. Children who have many friends and few daily hassles in their families are less bothered by school transitions, and declines are not typically found in smaller communities (J. E. Newman, 2004; Seidman et al., 2003). These findings tell us that children may be more vulnerable to a drop in self-esteem when challenges accumulate during early adolescence and they lack social support.

Developmental psychologist Jacquelynne Eccles (2004) believes that children's motivation for school declines across the transition to middle school or junior

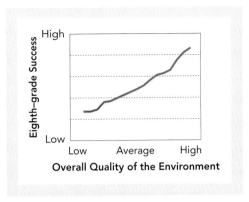

FIGURE 11.1 The recipe for success.

Successful children have passed more "thresholds" for what is needed to get by in society. Success increases gradually as the overall quality of children's environment increases, including positive characteristics of their family lives, peer relationships, schools, and neighborhoods.

SOURCE: Cook et al. (2002).

It can be stressful transitioning to a higher grade, especially in large schools where last year's friendships often dissolve.

high school when there is a poor *stage–environment fit*. That is, transitioning to middle school often disrupts friendships just when peers are becoming more important, school staff take a more disciplinarian approach just as children are seeking more independence, and teachers feel less responsibility for children's mental health and academic problems just as the frequency of problems increases. According to Eccles, academic and social problems are due to mismatches between children's needs and the characteristics of some schools.

SCHOOL SIZE. School size is an environmental characteristic that has attracted a lot of attention. On average, students who make the biggest gains in mathematics and reading attend middle-sized high schools, those with 600 to 900 students. Achievement gains are smaller for students in very small schools, but students in schools that are larger than 900 students also learn considerably less. School size is especially important for schools that enroll a high number of disadvantaged students (Lee & Smith, 1997).

School size influences students through the sense of connection that exists between children and school as well as the academic programs offered. Students in smaller schools report more emotional attachment to school as indicated by their responses to questions such as, "I feel like I am part of this school," and "I feel close to people at this school" (McNeely, Nonnemaker, & Blum, 2002). Probably as a result, they have better attitudes about school, fewer behavioral problems, greater involvement in extracurricular activities, and higher attendance rates than students in large high schools. In addition, teachers from smaller schools report more positive attitudes toward work (Cotton, 1996). However, if the school is so small that teachers must offer instruction outside their areas of expertise or the school offers only a limited number of honors and college-equivalent (AP) courses, then performance can suffer (Ready, Lee, & Welner, 2004).

Research on school size has encouraged some large high schools to reorganize into subunits, each with its own student body and teaching staff. Some benefits have been found from this *schools-within-schools* reorganization, including better social relationships, safer school atmospheres, and greater commitment to school (Ready et al., 2004).

DROPPING OUT OR GRADUATING. As a whole, teens who drop out of high school have poorer reading skills and a long history of disengagement from school (Christenson & Thurlow, 2004). But even though personal characteristics are important, psychologists and educators are increasingly emphasizing how the *ecology* surrounding children influences their achievement. Just as the ecology of an area can promote or deter the growth of plants, so too can social environments promote or hinder academic growth. The environmental factors that are most closely linked to academic success are *economic opportunities*, *school characteristics*, and *parental expectations*.

A powerful example of how economic opportunity influences achievement is the remarkable story of businessman Gene Lang. Lang was asked to speak in 1981 to a sixth-grade graduation class at New York City's P.S. 121—the same school he had attended years earlier. After hearing that three-fourths of the students would drop out before high school graduation, Lang made an unexpected announcement: He said he would provide the college tuition for *every student* who stayed in school and graduated. But Lang did more than make a promise of financial support. He also coordinated a project that provided mentoring during the years between the sixth grade and graduation. All of the students were still in school four years after his promise, and a year later Lang launched the I Have a

Dream® Foundation, an organization that continues to help cohorts of low-income students (I Have a Dream Foundation, 2005).

If academic performance were mainly due to personal characteristics, tuition promises would not avert failure. But this is not the case. Compared to control groups, "Dreamers" have better school attendance, less involvement in the juvenile justice system, higher graduation rates, and higher college attendance rates.

Some characteristics of schools also help adolescents succeed. We've already discussed the effect of school size, but dropout rates are also lower in schools that offer more academic courses and enjoy positive student–teacher relationships (Lee & Burkham, 2003). Such schools help children learn by setting high standards and expecting that most students will succeed.

Economic opportunities and high standards influence performance by influencing students' **self-efficacy**, that is, their beliefs about whether they can control important outcomes in their lives (Bandura, 2000). Individuals have a sense of self-efficacy in many different areas, such as their ability to succeed in math, in social situations, and so forth. Social learning theorist Albert Bandura believes that social influences, such as teachers' encouragements to apply to college, direct beliefs about our abilities. In turn, these beliefs influence our aspirations. In one study, for example, Bandura and his colleagues found that adolescents' ratings of which occupations they would be good at were more affected by perceptions of their *abilities* than their actual achievement in math and science (Bandura et al., 2001). Similarly, numerous studies have found that future plans are more dependent on self-efficacy than prior performance. This finding helps explain how children with troubled academic histories can reengage in learning when significant adults in their lives expect them to succeed.

Unfortunately, the opportunities, school characteristics, and expectations associated with academic success are not equally distributed. African American, Hispanic, and Native American teens in the United States are more likely than non-Hispanic white and Asian students to drop out of school before they receive a high school diploma. The quality of life for these teens has steadily declined over the past few years as the skills that are needed to secure a good job have increased. Fewer teens who do not graduate and attend college are moving out of their parents' homes, buying their own homes, and enjoying health insurance coverage. They also are experiencing longer periods of unemployment and relying more on part-time jobs (Halperin & Howe, 1998). As a result, there is considerable interest in programs that provide training for teens who are transitioning into the workforce after high school graduation.

HIGH-STAKES TESTS. More and more often, students' academic opportunities are determined in part by how well they do on **high-stakes tests**, that is, standardized tests that are tied to major consequences such as high school graduation, scholarship opportunities, or college admission. The most well known of these tests is the SAT, a college-admissions test. (This test was originally called the "Scholastic Aptitude Test" and then the "Scholastic Achievement Test," but these names have been dropped in favor of simply the "SAT.") The SAT is designed to measure mathematical reasoning, critical reading, and verbal skills that are necessary for college success (Camara, 2003). During the senior year of high school, SAT scores are one of several achievement measures that many colleges consider for admission, eligibility for college honors programs, and scholarship awards.

Is the SAT a fair measure of academic potential? Scores predict about 18 percent of the variability in first-year college grades (25 percent when combined with high school grade-point average), but there is concern that they measure

self-efficacy People's belief that they can control important outcomes by their actions (belief in the "power to make things happen").

high-stakes tests Tests that are tied to major consequences, such as retention in a grade, high school graduation, scholarship opportunities, or college admission.

economic opportunity as much as academic potential. For example, African American students received an average score on the SAT verbal of 430 in 2004, compared to 451 for Mexican American students and 528 for white students. Although the gap between whites and ethnic minorities has been closing, the differences that persist mean that minority adolescents will enjoy fewer educational opportunities unless policies are targeted specifically to help them (Chew, 2004).

There are three major reasons why minority students perform more poorly than other students on tests like the SAT. The first is academic achievement. For instance, only 13 percent of African American students and 18 percent of Mexican American students who took the SAT in 2004 had taken calculus in high school, compared to 27 percent of white students (Chew, 2004).

A second factor involves how questions are selected. Remarkably, ethnic differences are relatively large on some *easier* items because these items often contain language that is open to interpretation based on one's cultural background. But due to the characteristics test makers look for in items, items that favor African American students tend not to be selected (Freedle, 2003).

A third reason for group differences on tests involves students' reactions to testing situations. In numerous studies, psychologist Claude Steele and his colleagues have documented an interesting phenomenon: If there is a stereotype that a particular group performs poorly on a task, members of that group actually perform less well when they believe their ability is being tested. Steele coined the term **stereotype threat** to describe the anxiety produced when a situation threatens to confirm a negative stereotype. In one study, for example, African American and white students completed a test composed of verbal SAT questions (Steele & Aronson, 1995). Experimenters told half of the students in each group that scores would indicate their ability; the other half were told that the test was just a laboratory problem-solving task. Academically comparable African American and white students did equally well when they believed the task was unrelated to ability, but the African American students did worse when they thought they were taking an abilities test.

Surprisingly, decreased performance in the face of stereotype threat is not associated with becoming discouraged and giving up. On the contrary, students try *harder* when they think their ability is being measured. The problem is that anxiety and effort can actually bring down performance on difficult tasks (Aronson, 2002). Because anxiety hurts everyone's performance, stereotype threat has also been used to explain why women do more poorly on mathematical tests when they believe there is a gender difference in scores (Inzlicht & Ben-Zeev, 2000; Spencer, Steele, & Quinn, 1999).

Defenders of the SAT often point out that test scores do not predict lower grades than minorities actually achieve. Indeed, African American students' SAT scores often *overpredict* their college grades. According to Steele, this finding could result from the fact that African American students are less identified with academic pursuits due to negative stereotypes about their ability. To test this claim, Steele successfully improved the academic performance of minority students by implementing a program that emphasized their potential for challenging work (Steele, 1997). His findings underscore how important it is for adults in children's lives to believe in their abilities and to expect success. As we discuss next, this is especially true of the adults who live with teens.

stereotype threat The anxiety produced when a situation threatens to confirm a negative stereotype. For example, African Americans may experience stereotype threat when they take difficult achievement tests.

Adolescents and Their Families

Who is raising today's teenagers? In the United States, the majority live in two-parent households, but 1 out of every 3 lives with either a single mother, single father, grandparent, other relative, or nonrelative (Figure 11.2). In addition, many single parents have cohabitating partners, about 4 percent of all households with a parent include one or more grandparents (Fields, 2003), and many children who live most of the time with a single parent still see their other parent. Thus many people "parent" teenagers—not just their biological parents.

Adults who raise teenagers manage their relationships in many different ways. Some monitor their child's activities closely and try to make most of their important decisions, including decisions about which friends they can have and what classes they will take in school. Others give them more independence, guided by clear household rules. Still others act more like highly involved or distant friends. No specific type of relationship is best for every teen yet, as you'll read next, research shows that some types of relationships are associated with smoother journeys through this time of life.

PARENT–CHILD CONFLICT. Lara was tall, thin, and driving her parents to distraction when she was 13. One day her mother needed to pick her up from school and deliver her to a baby-sitting class while she was transporting Girl Scouts to a meeting. "Meet me at the front of the building at 4:00 SHARP," she told Lara and her friend. When the girls were missing, she checked the science room and Lara's locker before spotting them around the corner. "You always pick me up on the side," Lara said with annoyance, which started a heated exchange. Soon the embarrassed mother was fighting in front of a car full of Girl Scouts. "Oh, that's okay," one of the girls said reassuringly. "You should hear how my mom and sister fight!"

There are three reasons why this story is so typical of adolescence. First, Lara became snippier during early adolescence, when conflict between parents and children starts to increase. Conflict *frequency* is usually the greatest during early adolescence and declines across mid and late adolescence. In contrast, the *emotional intensity* of conflict generally peaks around mid-adolescence (Laursen, Coy, & Collins, 1998).

Second, Lara was bickering with the parent who generally absorbs the brunt of parent–adolescent conflict—mothers (Laursen, 1995). But, third, the two were only bickering. Most conflicts between teens and parents are minor spats over such things as dirty rooms and how teens dress—what experts call "garbage and galoshes" disputes (Hill, 1988). Parents get worn down not because these issues are so important but because they pop up so often. In one study, 11- and 14-year-olds typically had conflicts over 17 different issues during the course of a month, and 20 percent of the children said they had locked horns with their parents over 25 to 40 different issues (Allison & Schultz, 2004).

But conflict is not always a bad thing. Minor arguments strengthen communication between parents and teens, and the ensuing discussions give both parties a chance to revise their expectations in age-appropriate directions. Only a small proportion of families have a level of conflict

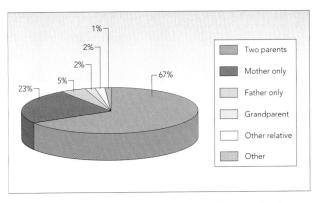

FIGURE 11.2 Living arrangements of teens in the United States.

One-third of American adolescents do not live with both of their parents, but only 5 percent do not live with at least one. Adolescents' households are diverse and often include a single parent's partner, a grandparent, or another relative.

SOURCE: Fields (2003).

A fight may darken the day, but squabbles over minor issues help parents and children renegotiate teenagers' rights and responsibilities.

©The New Yorker Collection 1999. Roz Chast from cartoonbank.com. All Rights Reserved.

that is so intense or unhealthy that it contributes to depression or encourages family members to avoid one another. And when these things occur, it is usually the case that the family had problems well before puberty (Collins & Laursen, 2004).

PARENTING QUALITIES. As you read in Chapter 7, the way parents handle minor issues generally has no impact on children's future adjustment. Whether a parent asks them to say "yes, sir" or allows them to speak more casually to adults, how many chores they are required to do, and whether or not they have a specific bedtime are largely matters of individual culture and choice. Nonetheless, four parenting characteristics influence the probability that adolescents will feel good about themselves and stay out of trouble:

1. *Parental expectations*. We already mentioned that adults' expectations influence children's academic performance, but parental expectations also predict a multitude of other behaviors. For example, one study found that children who were more likely to drink in the future had mothers and fathers who overestimated their likelihood of drinking (Madon et al., 2004), and parental predictions also affect future smoking (Simons-Morton, 2004). Of course, parental expectations might predict behavior simply because parents know their children's personalities. But it is also the case that parents who assume their child will drink, smoke, or try drugs probably do less to prevent these behaviors.

2. *Parental monitoring*. You were lucky if an adult asked you where you were going and when you'd be home when you were in high school. Caregivers who pay attention to their children's activities have teens who are less likely to drink alcohol in the future (Beck, Boyle, & Boekeloo, 2004), and careful monitoring is also associated with higher grades and lower levels of sexual activity, drug use, minor delinquency, and depression (Fletcher, Steinberg, & Williams-Wheeler, 2004; Jacobson & Crockett, 2000). Parents who set limits on behavior help adolescents build self-control, perhaps by giving them frequent chances to compare their impulses against rules and adjust their behavior accordingly (Finkenauer, Engels, & Baumeister, 2005). Results from studies of parental monitoring also help explain why boys engage in more risky behaviors than girls, and why problem behavior tends to increase with time: Parents monitor boys less carefully than girls, and parents tend to decrease the frequency of their checks as children grow older (Richards et al., 2004).

Although parental monitoring is important, research has not found that having a working mother increases the likelihood of adolescent problems. In fact, mothers who work longer hours often supervise their children slightly more closely than other mothers (Vander Ven et al., 2001), and employment can buffer children from risk by raising family income (Chase-Lansdale et al., 2003). What is important is setting rules: Parents with lax rules tend to experience more conflicts with their teens and monitor them less closely than parents who provide more guidance (Hayes, Hudson, & Matthews, 2004).

3. *Family decision making*. Teens are better adjusted when parents and teens share decision making rather than letting teens make most decisions on their own (Dornbusch et al., 1990; Lamborn, Dornbusch, & Steinberg, 1996). The optimal amount of parental involvement depends on the type of decision and changes as teens mature. Over time, most parents give their teens more control over personal issues, such as when to do homework or what books to read, with conflicts about what is a personal issue gradually giving adolescents more autonomy. In one study, teens who were well-adjusted generally had parents who granted increasing autonomy dur-

ing middle to late adolescence for personal issues but not for issues that had strong consequences for health and safety (Smetana, Campione-Barr, & Daddis, 2004).

4. Parental involvement. In addition to monitoring what their children do when they are not in school, parents and caregivers can also help their children by being involved in their lives, including their school lives. Compared to uninvolved parents, parents who communicate with teachers, help their children complete assignments at home, and attend school functions have children who perform better, have higher aspirations for the future, and have fewer behavioral problems. School involvement affects development by giving parents information that helps them assist their children, such as the expectations for assignments. Parental involvement also builds a consensus between parents and schools so that children receive consistent messages (Hill et al., 2004; Hill & Taylor, 2004). Parental involvement is another link in the chain of positive parenting that involves clearly defined standards, monitoring, and family decision making.

Unfortunately, there is no guidebook that tells parents exactly how high to set their expectations, how much to monitor behavior, or how involved they should be in school-related issues. The lucky children are those who have multiple people in their lives, so if one person is unavailable or overly annoying at a particular point in time, another adult will probably act in ways that are exactly what they need.

FATHERS IN AND OUT OF THE HOME. It is clear that many teenagers enjoy turning to Dad when Mom is getting on their nerves. And increasingly, researchers are asking how fathers' behavior and availability affect teenagers' choices and sense of well-being.

A father who lives with his children full time does not simply provide another dose of the mother's parenting behavior. Instead, parents often have different parenting styles (Winsler, Madigan, & Aquilino, 2005). Individual dads and moms come in all varieties, but it is most common for teens to say that their dads are more authoritarian than their moms (using terminology you learned in Chapter 7) and less authoritative (Shek, 2000; Smetana, 1995).

Relationships with fathers, like relationships with mothers, are correlated with measures of problem behavior. For example, girls who share more activities with their fathers and boys who feel closer to their fathers are less likely than other children to initiate or increase sexual activity during an 18-month period (Ream & Savin-Williams, 2005). Keep in mind, however, that difficult children complain more about their parents, so these findings probably reflect the influence of children on parents as well as the influence of parents on children.

The effects of growing up in a single-parent home on development are not clear. Statistically, adolescents in single-parent households are at higher risk for poor academic performance, delinquency, violent behavior, drinking, and risky sexual behavior. But these adolescents are also more likely to live in poverty and to have less educated mothers. When children with single mothers are compared to those from dual-parent households with similar characteristics, they show similar academic performance and rates of behavior problems (Ricciuti, 2004).

Children who have noncustodial fathers are generally better adjusted when their father provides financial assistance and engages in authoritative parenting that encourages a close emotional relationship (Amato & Gilbreth, 1999; Ellis et al., 2003). But it is the quality of fathers' (or mothers') involvement—not their mere presence—that matters. For example, a longitudinal study of twins found that 5-year-olds whose fathers were high on antisocial behavior (such as using physical violence

In many societies, fathers assume more responsibility for teaching important skills as boys reach adolescence. Whether these lessons are practical or just for fun, everyone enjoys this quality time.

or abusing drugs) showed more antisocial behavior the longer their fathers had lived with the family, whereas children whose fathers were low in antisocial behavior showed fewer antisocial behaviors the longer they lived with their fathers (Jaffee et al., 2003). The fact that contact with any adult can help or harm children, depending on what they learn, helps explain why the frequency of contact with fathers does not always predict children's adjustment (Amato & Gilbreth, 1999). Especially among minority families, family structure is not a good predictor of adjustment because single-parent households are common, extended family members provide emotional support, and fathers are often involved in children's lives even when parents are no longer together (Salem, Zimmerman, & Notaro, 1998).

> > > **MEMORY MAKERS** < < <

1. Confirmation ceremonies, the quinceañera, and a bar mitzvah are _____.

   (a) "secular" ceremonies
   (b) male initiation ceremonies
   (c) "promise" ceremonies
   (d) rites of passage

2. You are high in _____ if you believe you can control important outcomes in your life.

   (a) self-efficacy
   (b) self-actualization
   (c) external control
   (d) internalization

3. Studies of parent–child conflict reveal that conflict *frequency* is usually the highest during _____ adolescence, whereas the emotional *intensity* of conflict is usually highest during _____ adolescence.

   (a) early; early
   (b) early; mid
   (c) mid; mid
   (d) mid; late

[1-d; 2-a; 3-b]

Leisure and Work

One of our daughters was in middle school when she first began visiting Internet chat rooms. Her parents had heard about sexual predators in the electronic world, so the computer was in the center of the house where they could keep an eye on the screen. But even though they had been warned, they were still horrified when a man began writing to her about sex—after only 3 days.

Adolescence is a vulnerable period when children gain more control over what they do. Because there are so many possible activities in the modern world, knowing the benefits and risks of various choices can help families and teens make informed decisions about how teens should spend their time. After a brief look at what teens around the world are doing, we'll look at the influence of the Internet, television, and after-school jobs.

A Global Look at How Teens Spend Time

Researchers have clocked the daily habits of teens in rural villages in Nepal, urban slums in India, and numerous other communities around the world. Table 11.1 compares how much time adolescents in North America, East Asia, and nonindustrial,

TABLE 11.1 How Adolescents Spend Time Each Day

Activity	Nonindustrialized, unschooled population	North America	East Asia
Household labor	5–9 hr	20–40 min	10–20 min
Paid labor	0.5–8 hr	40–60 min	0–10 min
School work	—	3.0–4.5 hr	5.5–7.5 hr
Total work time	6–9 hr	4–6 hr	6–8 hr
TV viewing	*unknown*	1.5–2.5 hr	1.5–2.5 hr
Talking	*unknown*	2–3 hr	45–60 min
Sports	*unknown*	30–60 min	0–20 min
Other structured leisure activities	*unknown*	10–20 min	0–10 min
Total free time	4–7 hr	6.5–8.0 hr	4.0–5.5 hr

Note. Estimates are averaged across the week, including weekdays and weekends.
SOURCE: Larson & Verma (1999).

unschooled populations spend in work and leisure activities (Larson & Verma, 1999). As you can see, household chores make up a large chunk of a typical day of unschooled populations, whereas North American teens help their families only about 20 to 40 minutes per day. Teens in East Asia have even fewer chores, largely because household work is viewed as a distraction from school work. Patterns for paid employment are similar: Children in unschooled populations join the workforce at a young age, followed by children in North America and, rarely, teens in East Asia. Societies clearly trade off labor and school work, so teens in East Asia spend more time in school than their counterparts in North America. Children in North America have the most discretionary* time (up to 8 hours per day!), and these children spend more time than children in other societies simply socializing and talking with people.

---

*discretionary: Available to be used as one desires.

Each culture has its own ideas about how adolescents should spend their time. Many Asian families view studying as the road to success, whereas families in nonindustrialized societies expect everyone to help produce the goods they need to survive.

online victimization A variety of distressing events occurring via the Internet, including harassment, unwanted exposure to sexual images or sexual conversation, and sexual solicitation.

Is it more productive to do chores or study than to watch TV or talk with friends? Scientists do not answer this question the way your grandparents might. Most chores in traditional societies are repetitive and unchallenging, such as carrying water or herding animals (Whiting & Whiting, 1975), and there is no evidence that children derive much benefit from spending long hours on these activities (Goodnow, 1988). Only skilled activities that are directly related to adult work, such as trapping or producing pottery, provide valuable lessons for later life. But the number of hours children spend on school-related activities is associated with intelligence and future earnings (Larson, 2001b). Once again, though, an extreme amount of any one activity is not always desirable. For example, children who spend unusually long hours studying are more likely to be depressed and to lose interest in learning (Larson & Verma, 1999). Most experts agree that a balance of many activities is healthy, including those we will talk about next.

Interactive Media—Games and the Internet

There was a revolution during the end of the last century when interactive media became fixtures in our lives. By 2000, 68 percent of households in the United States with a 2- to 17-year-old owned video games, 70 percent owned computers, and 52 percent had online access (Woodard, 2000).

The impact of interactive media on children depends on the content of the activity more than the type of technology. For example, research on violent video games has arrived at the same conclusion that research on television violence has: In both cases, violent content is associated with increases in aggressive behavior and decreases in prosocial behavior, as discussed in Chapter 7 (Anderson & Bushman, 2001; Wartella, Caplovitz, & Lee, 2004).

Computer use increases as children grow. In the United States, about 75 percent of 5-year-olds and over 90 percent of teenagers use computers, and about 75 percent of 15- to 17-year-olds log onto the Internet. But access is not universal. Adolescents from two-parent households are more likely to use a computer than those from single-parent homes, and computer usage increases as parents' educational levels and income increase. Due to correlations between ethnicity and these family characteristics, minority adolescents are less likely to use computers at home. In 2001, for example, 77 percent of white adolescents used computers at home compared to only 41 percent of African American and Hispanic adolescents (DeBell, Chapman, & the National Center for Education Statistics, 2003).

Although few people would go back to life without the Internet, online victimization is a serious risk for most teens. **Online victimization** refers to unwanted exposure to sexual images, sexual conversation, and sexual solicitation as well as harassment, threats, and social attacks. For example, one 17-year-old girl reported that people posted a "hate page" about her, and a 14-year-old boy who was home alone was frightened after he received an instant message from someone who claimed to be hiding in his house (Finkelhor, Mitchell, & Wolak, 2000).

Online victimization is distressingly common. A national survey of 10- to 17-year-olds found that 1 in 4 children had received unwanted exposure to sexual pictures during the year preceding the survey, 1 in 5 had received a sexual solicitation, and 1 in 33 had received an aggressive solicitation by someone who sent regular mail, gifts, or tried to arrange a meeting (Finkelhor et al., 2000). As you can see in Figure 11.3, 14-, 15-, and 16-year-olds are at highest risk for sexual solicita-

FIGURE 11.3 Online victimization.

The majority of children who experience online sexual solicitation are 14, 15, or 16 years of age, but 22 percent of victims are 13 years or younger. It is never too soon to teach children about Internet safety.

SOURCE: Finkelhor et al. (2000).

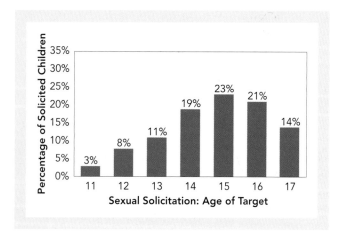

tions, but an alarming percentage of victims (over 22 percent) are younger children. And counter to the stereotype that sexual targets are usually girls, 34 percent of solicitations targeted boys. Most youths said they were not very bothered by these incidents, but they were disturbing to a significant number.

Some teens increase their chances of victimization by forming close relationships with people they meet online, and 3 percent of teenage Internet users form such a relationship with an adult. Although most of these incidents are harmless, some children have been assaulted and even killed by people who contacted them online. The FBI investigates incident reports and even hires teenagers to teach agents how to pose as youngsters online. Still, it is up to adults to talk to children about the dangers of giving out personal information and chatting with strangers. Adults should also ask questions when children are being secretive about their Internet use and report incidents to a relevant agency or the CyberTipline (through the toll-free number or Web-based form sponsored by the National Center for Missing and Exploited Children).

TV: It's Not All Bad

Parents are largely correct when they say that television rarely provides meaningful instruction (Larson, 2001a). But a closer look at research on television provides a more shaded picture. If television viewing occurs late in the day, when people are typically not productive anyway, it is less detrimental than an afternoon spent in front of the tube instead of studying. In addition, some shows do expose children to basic information about the world. For example, when teenagers were interviewed 4 weeks after the episode of *Friends* in which Rachel became pregnant after using a condom, those who had discussed the episode with an adult were twice as likely to say they had learned something new about condoms (Collins et al., 2003).

In summary, it is probably meaningless to ask "How much time should adolescents spend doing X?" Instead, it is more important to ask whether the activity builds a skill, satisfies an emotional need, or helps the community; what activities are being displaced by doing X; and whether X serves a function that is different from other activities during the course of a day. As one expert concluded in advice that is as true for adults as it is for teens, "Development is probably best served by combinations of complementary activities, including those that shape good habits, teach literacy, build interpersonal relationships, foster initiative, and provide relaxation" (Larson, 2001b, p. 163).

The biggest problem for modern adolescents is that 40 to 50 percent of their time is discretionary and not spent in activities that advance their academic or social development (Larson & Verma, 1998). Many teens would benefit from spending more time in structured activities that challenge them (to advance learning and responsibility), more time with adults (which is associated with lower rates of depression), and less time driving around or hanging out aimlessly with friends (which promotes delinquency) (McHale, Crouter, & Tucker, 2001; Osgood et al., 1996). Next we consider whether paid employment satisfies these criteria.

Earning Money

The parents in our neighborhoods disagree about whether teenagers should work. One family keeps framed copies of their children's first paychecks displayed in the kitchen, a symbol of their belief in the value of work. Across town, another family forbids their son to take jobs, believing it will waste valuable study time. Most of the adolescents in our towns drift in and out of jobs during high school, just like the majority of teens nationwide.

As with all activities, jobs are associated with developmental advances or risks, depending on what teenagers are actually doing on the job, how much time they are doing it, and what activities they would be involved in if they were not working. Three general conclusions summarize the research on teen employment:

▶ **The nature of the job matters.** Most jobs that are available to teens—such as working in a fast-food restaurant—are too simple to build significant work-related skills. The kinds of jobs that benefit teens the most (such as being an office clerk or a museum usher) teach real skills and keep teens away from delinquent peers (Staff & Uggen, 2003).

▶ **Time at work matters.** A moderate amount of time working an age-appropriate job can build responsibility, independence, and self-esteem. But spending more than 20 hours per week on a job is associated with poorer school performance and, for older adolescents, a decreased likelihood of graduating from college compared to a more balanced mix of work, school, and extracurricular activities (National Research Council Committee on the Health and Safety Implications of Child Labor, 1998; Staff, Mortimer, & Uggen, 2004).

▶ **The community context matters.** Whether work exposes children to good or bad influences depends on what they would be exposed to if they didn't work. For teens who live in low-risk neighborhoods, a heavy workload can interfere with extracurricular school activities, detract from family time, and place them in contact with delinquent peers. For children in poorer neighborhoods, work can be a place to meet people who value education and work more than their unemployed peers do. Intense work affects school performance regardless of ethnicity (Johnson, 2004; Weller et al., 2003), but some decline in grades may be justified if it increases the chances that poor children will be able to attend college.

In sum, decisions about working must be made on an individual basis. It is important to consider the people teens will associate with at work, how much a job will interfere with studying, and whether the experience and money earned have implications for a better future.

⟩⟩⟩ M E M O R Y   M A K E R S ⟨⟨⟨

1. Compared to adolescents who live in East Asia and nonindustrial societies, adolescents in North America_____.
   (a) spend more time in school
   (b) spend more time working or doing chores
   (c) spend more time socializing and talking with people

2. A survey of 10- to 17-year-olds found that one in _____ children experienced online victimization during the preceding year.
   (a) 20
   (b) 15
   (c) 4

3. School performance tends to suffer when adolescents spend more than _____ hours per week at a job.
   (a) 20
   (b) 10
   (c) 3

[1-c; 2-c; 3-a]

Risky Choices

Many teenagers hear "Be careful!" shouted as they leave the house. There is a good reason: Risky behavior is their biggest threat to health and well-being. According to the Centers for Disease Control and Prevention (2006b), six major health behaviors are the leading causes of death and disability among teens: injury and violence (including the three biggest killers of teens: accidental injuries, homicide, and suicide), sexual behavior, alcohol and drug use, tobacco use, nutrition, and physical activity. We'll explore homicide, nutrition, and physical activity in Chapter 13. Here we focus on motor vehicle accidents, sexual behavior, substance use, eating disorders, and suicide.

Teenage Drivers

Sierra was enjoying an hour of supervised driving with her mother a few months before she was scheduled to test for her driver's license. The two were having an animated discussion as they crossed an intersection just two blocks from home. Then Sierra did something that astounds her mother to this day: She let go of the steering wheel and continued talking while the car drifted into the right-most curb. "My daughter is getting her driver's license," her mother later remarked, "but she can't talk and hold onto the wheel at the same time."

Young drivers are responsible for more crashes than any other age group (Figure 11.4). The problems they have behind the wheel are clear from looking at their accident patterns. Teens are more likely than older drivers to die in single-vehicle accidents in which they roll over or collide with a tree or pole. This finding suggests that their basic driving skills are weak, not just their ability to maneuver in traffic. Young drivers also have difficulty keeping their attention focused on the road, so many accidents occur when they are distracted by music, conversation with passengers, or recent emotional events (Harré, 2000). And when teenagers are involved in fatal crashes, it is common to find that the driver was moving too fast for road conditions, which is a symptom of risk taking as well as inexperience (National Highway Traffic Safety Administration, 2006). Young men are especially prone to seek thrills just for the sake of a thrill. In one study of high school drivers, males said that "reckless intent" was involved the majority of the times they drove dangerously (Harré, 2000).

One measure that has reduced the number of accidents is *graduated driver licensing*. These laws require new drivers to pass through stages, with each stage giving them increased privileges in more risky driving situations. Sierra was in the learner's permit stage when she let go of the wheel, so she could drive only with a licensed adult. Depending on the location, the next phase may prohibit driving during late evening hours or with passengers. Crash rates have declined 9 to 31 percent in states where graduated licensing regulations are in effect (National Highway Traffic Safety Administration, 2000).

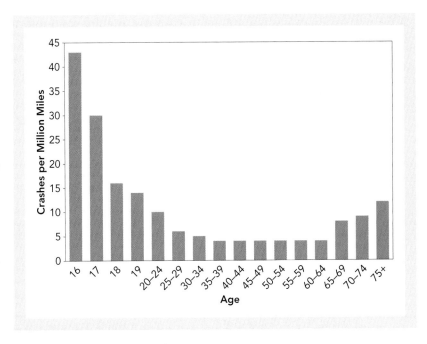

FIGURE 11.4 Dangerous drivers.

Young drivers are the most dangerous drivers, whether you look at the number of crashes per person or per mile driven.

SOURCE: National Highway Traffic Safety Administration (2006).

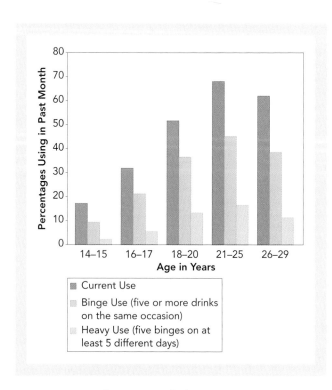

FIGURE 11.5 Lifetime trends for alcohol use.

Alcohol use increases during adolescence and peaks among the college-age population. By 18 to 20 years, over 10 percent of Americans report heavy alcohol use.

SOURCE: Substance Abuse and Mental Health Services Administration (2004).

psychoactive drugs Chemicals that influence perception, mood, or behavior. Alcohol, marijuana, and cocaine are examples of psychoactive drugs.

Alcohol is the most popular psychoactive drug—and the most deadly when mixed with driving.

Unfortunately, there is no graduated licensing for most of the behaviors that threaten an adolescent's future. Today, pressures to use drugs and engage in risky sexual behavior are two of their biggest temptations.

Substance Use

It was a typical party, like so many of the parties students organize when parents are gone overnight. But it was the last one for Sarkis George Nazarian, Jr., a 16-year-old who died after he drank alcohol and then drove his sport utility vehicle off a rain-washed road. George's death left parents wondering what had gone wrong in Montgomery County, Maryland, a community where 10 other teenagers had died that year alone in vehicle accidents (Snyder & Johnson, 2004).

Teens like Nazarian use alcohol and other drugs for the same reasons they sometimes drive too quickly or rearrange the neighbors' lawn ornaments: because they can, because it is interesting to see what will happen, and because it makes them feel part of a group of teens who are encouraging the behavior. Substances like alcohol, marijuana, and even the nicotine in tobacco have special appeal to curious teens because these are **psychoactive drugs**: chemicals that influence perception, mood, or behavior. Each psychoactive drug has different risks because each drug affects the body and mind somewhat differently.

ALCOHOL. Alcohol consumption increases dramatically during the high school years. Figure 11.5 shows the percentage of individuals in the United States who engage in three levels of drinking as a function of age. *Current use* refers to at least 1 drink in the past 30 days, *binge use* to 5 or more drinks on the same occasion in the past 30 days, and *heavy use* to at least 5 days of binge drinking. Notice that a third of 16- to 17-year-olds use alcohol regularly and over 10 percent of 18- to 20-year-olds are heavy users of alcohol (Substance Abuse and Mental Health Services Administration, 2004).

In one survey, 30 percent of adolescents said they had recently ridden in a car with a driver who had been drinking (Grunbaum et al., 2004). It is especially dangerous to mix alcohol with driving because alcohol is a central nervous system *depressant*. By slowing brain activity, alcohol impairs motor performance, particularly reaction time, reduces self-awareness, and lifts the inhibitions that prevent us from acting inappropriately. Because alcohol impairs judgment, it is also associated with homicides, suicides, and risky sexual behavior.

TOBACCO. Tobacco use, primarily in the form of cigarette smoking, is the leading preventable cause of death in the United States (Centers for Disease Control and Prevention, 2006b). Nicotine is a highly addictive substance, so teens who try it are often quickly hooked. In fact, nicotine addiction is the most frequent addiction to be established during the adolescent years. The percentage of children who have smoked cigarettes in the past month increases steadily from only 3 percent at age 13 to about 26 percent by age 17 (Substance Abuse and Mental Health Services Administration, 2004).

Cigarette smoking decreases the quality of life long before it encourages an early death. Adolescents who smoke have higher rates of respiratory illnesses, decreased physical endurance, and slower rates of lung growth and function; those who use smokeless tobacco and cigars have an increased risk of oral and esophageal cancer (Centers for Disease Control and Prevention, 2006b).

INHALANTS, PRESCRIPTION DRUGS, AND OTHER DRUGS. Today's teenagers have access to a wide array of dangerous drugs. An increasingly popular practice is "pharming": taking prescription-type drugs, such as painkillers or anti-anxiety medication, that have been stolen from relatives or purchased illegally. Many of these medications are deadly when taken in high doses or combined with alcohol or other drugs. An especially popular drug is anabolic steroids, male hormones that are taken to promote muscle growth. In a survey of high school students, 5 percent of girls and 7 percent of boys had tried steroids, which can cause impotence in males, reduced growth, and damage to the liver and cardiovascular systems (Grunbaum et al., 2004). As you can see in Figure 11.6, young teens are more likely to experiment with prescription-type drugs than marijuana.

Inhalants are also one of the first drugs teens experiment with because they are so readily available. Inhalants are breathable chemicals in household products, such as aerosol cans, that make people feel stimulated and uninhibited. Inhalant use ("huffing") can cause death from heart failure, lack of oxygen, and vomit-induced choking. They can also produce cognitive and motor difficulties by harming myelin, the fatty sheath that surrounds axons.

By 14 and 15 years, marijuana is the most frequently used drug after alcohol and tobacco. Its active ingredient, tetrahydrocannabinol (THC), has different effects on different individuals. Although THC is generally known for producing a sense of relaxation and mild silliness, it can also produce uncomfortable feelings of paranoia and even hallucinations. Marijuana affects coordination (and therefore driving), interferes with the body's ability to fight infection, and influences nerve cells that are involved in storing memories.

In addition to the drugs just mentioned, a small percentage of teens (1 percent or fewer) report recent use of LSD (a hallucinogen), Ecstasy (a so-called "rave" or club drug), cocaine, and methamphetamine (a stimulant drug), among other drugs. Altogether, almost one in five 16- and 17-year-olds in the United States has used an inhalant, prescription-type drug, or illegal drug such as marijuana or cocaine in the past month (Substance Abuse and Mental Health Services Administration, 2004). This statistic alone makes it clear that drug use is not confined to a few deviant teens.

THREE MYTHS ABOUT DRUG USERS. If you ask middle-aged adults to picture the typical drug user, they might imagine a person with body piercings, outrageous clothes, and a defiant attitude. This stereotype is inaccurate, but it is also dangerous because it can lead them to assume that teens who don't fit the

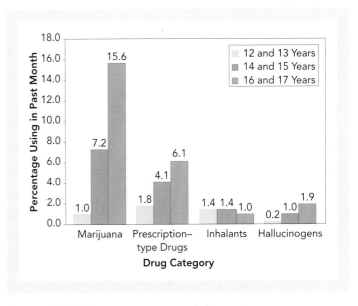

FIGURE 11.6 Drug use among adolescents.

In the United States, about 11 percent of children aged 12 to 17 have used an illegal substance in the past month. This graph shows the percentage who have used marijuana, prescription-type drugs, inhalants, and hallucinogens. Young teens are most likely to experiment with prescription-type drugs and inhalants because these drugs are easier to obtain.

SOURCE: Substance Abuse and Mental Health Services Administration (2004).

stereotype are safe. The reality is that patterns of drug use are quite different from popular stereotypes, as illustrated by the following three myths:

▶ *Myth 1: Minority teens are the most likely teens to use drugs.* *Fact:* The truth is that white adolescents are *more* likely than African American, Asian, or Hispanic/Latino teens to have used an illicit drug in the past month (Substance Abuse and Mental Health Services Administration, 2004).

▶ *Myth 2: Drug use is much more common in large urban areas.* *Fact:* Among children 12 years and over, rates of drug use during the past month are just as high in small metropolitan areas (8.6 percent in 2003) as large metropolitan areas (8.3 percent). And outside of major cities, less urbanized communities have rates that are almost as high as urbanized areas (Substance Abuse and Mental Health Services Administration, 2004).

▶ *Myth 3: Girls are much less likely than boys to experiment with drugs.* *Fact:* The numbers are roughly equal: About 11 percent of adolescent boys *and* girls have recently used illicit drugs.

It is clear that efforts to prevent drug abuse have to reach out to all adolescents. But as you will read next, it is only recently that experts have gotten a handle on what types of measures actually prevent this risky behavior.

PREVENTING DRUG ABUSE. In the past, communities took a straightforward approach to drug prevention: Assemble information on the dangers of drugs, teach that information to children, and hope that fewer children would take drugs. But, unfortunately, programs that simply provided factual information either had no impact on drug use or actually stimulated use by arousing curiosity (Botvin & Griffin, 1999).

Why is it so difficult to steer kids from drugs? Some critics blame prevention programs for exaggerating the dangers of drugs. Antidrug campaigns that portray drugs "frying" the brain are inconsistent with what children see in their everyday lives, so they tend to ignore the message completely (Martz, 1990). For example, adolescents are actually more likely to try anabolic steroids when adults fail to acknowledge the benefits people experience from taking them (National Institute on Drug Abuse, 2000).

But prevention efforts suffer from more than just a credibility problem. Drug abuse is a complicated problem that is influenced by a range of risk factors at the individual, family, peer, school, and community levels. Children are more likely to use drugs when they have aggressive behavior that isolates them from peers, when their parents fail to monitor their whereabouts, and when poverty leads them to be pessimistic about their futures. Therefore, effective prevention programs need to address many layers of children's lives. Successful programs teach information about the risks of drugs but also work with parents and the broader community to teach children the life skills they need to be successful and resist peer influence, such as goal setting, problem solving, and saying "no" to people who offer them drugs (Montoya, Atkinson, & McFaden, 2003; Robertson et al., 2003).

Sexual Behavior

Handling sexual decisions is another challenge for adolescents. They tell researchers that sexual health issues are "big concerns" for people their age, and nearly a third report being pressured to have sex. Both girls and boys are troubled by sexual issues. In fact, boys say they feel more pressure to have sex than girls (Henry J. Kaiser Family Foundation et al., 2003). Acting responsibly in the face of such pressure takes knowledge, but this is one area where many teens are lacking.

SEXUAL ACTIVITY AND KNOWLEDGE. One source of information about teenage sexual activity is the Youth Risk Behavior Surveillance System, a program that monitors the six health categories mentioned earlier in this chapter (Grunbaum et al., 2004). The data in Figure 11.7 show that the majority of boys and girls in the United States have had sexual intercourse by the time they graduate from high school. African American adolescents report the most sexual activity, followed by Hispanics and then whites. For example, 19 percent of African American high school students reported first intercourse before the age of 13 years, compared to 8 percent of Hispanic students and 4 percent of white students. Also, 29 percent of African American high school students reported more than four partners at the time of the survey, compared to 16 percent of Hispanic students and 11 percent of white students. These data show that many teens engage in sexual activity at a young age and/or experience sex with multiple partners. In addition, 34 percent had had sexual intercourse during the past 3 months.

As sexual exploration has become more common among young teens, the process of exploring sexuality has also changed. In the past, sexual intimacy usually started with "making out" (kissing), followed by petting and "heavy petting" (touching breasts and sometimes genital regions), then intercourse. Oral sex used to be an exotic behavior that some couples added only when they were sexually comfortable with one another. Today, oral sex often precedes intercourse, partly because it is falsely viewed as a safe practice and partly because teenagers see it as a way to be sexually active without losing their virginity. In one survey, almost 25 percent of sexually active 15- to 17-year-olds reported that they had had oral sex to avoid having sexual intercourse (Henry J. Kaiser Family Foundation et al., 2003).

Do most teens know the dangers associated with sexual activity? As you can see in Table 11.2, many do not. For example, 19 percent of 15- to 17-year-olds do not know that you can get a sexually transmitted disease through oral sex, and 22 percent believe that pulling out before ejaculation is "safer" sex. Lack of knowledge is not restricted to teens who are sexually inexperienced. For example, 22 percent of the teens who are not sexually active do not know that oral sex can spread disease, but 13 percent of sexually active teens are also unaware of this basic fact (Henry J. Kaiser Family Foundation et al., 2003).

It may seem surprising that so many teenagers are uninformed about sex. But like driving, sex is something with which they have had limited experience. Their

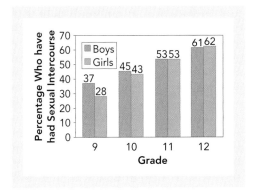

FIGURE 11.7 Adolescent sexual behavior.

The majority of American adolescents have had sexual intercourse by the time they graduate from high school. Still, a sizeable minority of high school seniors—38 percent—have decided to wait.

SOURCE: Grunbaum et al. (2004).

Teens in some parts of the world have limited opportunities to mingle with the opposite sex; in others, boys and girls are free to interact away from adult supervision. But even in locations where teenagers date from an early age, it is not unusual for many teens to have misconceptions about sex.

TABLE 11.2 American Adolescents' Attitudes and Knowledge about Sex

Percentage who does not know that—	15 to 17 years	18 to 24 years
You can get a sexually transmitted disease through oral sex.	19	9
Half of all new HIV infections that occur each year are among people under 25.	37	40
Sexually transmitted diseases can cause some kinds of cancer.	60	60
Sexually transmitted diseases can cause fertility problems when you want to have children.	24	17
Sexually transmitted diseases can be spread even when affected individuals do not have symptoms.	20	13
Percentage who consider the practice "safer" sex		
Oral sex	39	36
Pulling out before ejaculation	22	20

SOURCE: Henry J. Kaiser Family Foundation et al. (2003).

sources of information are also weak. Many get misleading sexual information from movies, where sex is usually free from consequences and unencumbered by conversations about sexual histories or birth control. At home, many adults are too embarrassed by conversations about sex to offer teenagers more useful information. Sex education in school does not always fill in the gaps. Most teens say they would like sex education to deal more with birth control, preventing sexually transmitted diseases (STDs), and getting tested for disease. Also, over 40 percent would like to learn strategies for talking about sexual issues with intimate partners and doctors (Henry J. Kaiser Family Foundation et al., 2003).

Often sex education is incomplete because adults fear that teens who learn about preventing pregnancy and disease will be more likely to become sexually active. However, research provides little support for this claim. Comprehensive sex education programs that discuss contraception (birth control), sexually transmitted diseases, and abstinence (avoiding sex) do not increase sexual activity and often decrease it (McElderry & Omar, 2003). Furthermore, countries that have more open policies about educating teens (including France, Australia, and especially the Netherlands) have lower rates of sexually transmitted diseases and pregnancy than the United States, where abstinence-based programs are popular (Weaver, Smith, & Kippax, 2005).

sexually transmitted diseases (STDs, formerly called *venereal diseases*, and also called *sexually transmitted infections*, or STIs) Diseases that are usually transmitted through sexual contact. These diseases pass from person to person by contact with infected body parts or the exchange of semen, blood, or other body fluids.

SEXUALLY TRANSMITTED DISEASES. As the AIDS crisis has made dramatically clear, the intimate nature of sexual contact can easily spread disease. **Sexually transmitted diseases (STDs,** formerly called *venereal diseases*) are infections that are *usually* transmitted through sexual contact. (STDs are also called *sexually transmitted infections*, or STIs.) It is estimated that there are about 19 million new cases of STDs each year in the United States alone, almost half of them among individuals 15 to 24 years of age (Centers for Disease Control and Prevention, 2005i). These infections can cause discomfort and embarrassment, infertility, cervical cancer, blindness, and even death (in the case of AIDS or untreated syphilis). Consequently, it is important that adolescents know the symptoms of STDs and how they spread as the first step toward preventing the following diseases. The number of STDs is too numerous to cover here, but we'll explain a few of the common ones.

Trichomoniasis is the most common curable STD among young women, with over 7 million new cases each year. It is caused by a single-celled protozoan parasite that finds a new host during penis-to-vagina intercourse or vulva-to-vulva contact. In females the disease usually infects the vagina, often causing a vaginal discharge. Untreated trichomoniasis increases their susceptibility to HIV infection (the virus that causes AIDS) and can cause pregnant women to have low-birth-weight babies. In males the disease affects the urethra (urine canal), often causing no or only mild irritation.

Gonorrhea is caused by a bacterium (a one-celled organism) that spreads by contact with the penis, vagina, mouth, or anus of an infected individual. Most infected females have no or only mild symptoms that are easily mistaken for a bladder infection. Untreated gonorrhea is a common cause of *pelvic inflammatory disease*, a condition that can lead to chronic pelvic pain and infertility, and pregnant women may pass the disease to their babies during childbirth, causing blindness or a blood infection in the newborn. Symptoms in males include a burning sensation while urinating and discharge from the penis.

Chlamydia is a common bacterial disease that is transmitted through oral, vaginal, or anal sex. It usually infects the cervix and urethra in females but can also infect the fallopian tubes, rectum, and throat. Untreated chlamydia can cause pelvic inflammatory disease and infertility in females, and it is the leading cause of infant pneumonia and pink eye in newborns. Males rarely have serious complications but can reinfect partners if they are not treated at the same time.

Genital herpes is caused by the herpes simplex viruses type 1 and 2. Most infected individuals are not aware they have the disease; others experience painful blisters around the genitals or rectum. People acquire genital herpes by direct contact with an infected partner, often from partners who have no visible symptoms. In the United States, about one out of four women and one out of five men are infected with genital herpes. Herpes can cause fatal infections in newborns and makes people more susceptible to HIV infection. There is no cure, but antiviral drugs reduce the frequency of outbreaks.

Syphilis is a bacterial disease that spreads when people have contact with a syphilis sore that is usually on the mouth, external genitals, vagina, anus, or rectum. Sores that appear early in the disease are followed by a skin rash and other symptoms, which may include fever, swollen lymph glands, and fatigue. Some people progress to the next stage, which involves damage to the heart and nervous system, or even a late stage in which blindness, mental illness, and death can occur. Syphilis is easily cured by administering an antibiotic drug.

Acquired immunodeficiency disease (AIDS) is a condition caused by HIV (human immunodeficiency virus). HIV invades cells in the body's immune system, reducing its ability to fight infections and cancers. The body continues to mount an effective immune response during early stages of infection. Individuals have AIDS when the number of critical immune cells falls below a specified value or serious infections or cancers appear. Death results from bacterial infections, tuberculosis, pneumonia, or other illnesses. HIV is transmitted when infected blood, semen, or vaginal secretions pass through mucous membranes or broken

TABLE 11.3 Strategies for Preventing Sexually Transmitted Diseases (STDs)

Strategy	Explanation
Delay sexual relations	Abstinence (not having sex) is the only fail-safe measure to avoid infection. By taking time to know your partner, you will learn more about his or her sexual and drug history, which helps you assess your risk of infection.
Have your partner and yourself tested for STDs	It is not uncommon for people to lie about their STD status. Taking time to develop trust with a prospective partner before you have sex makes it easier to suggest that you both get tested for STDs. Your local health department or college health service can provide information about testing options in your area.
Enjoy a monogamous relationship	Adults have less to worry about if they agree not to have sexual relations with other people. It is impossible to control your partner's behavior, however, so it makes sense to continue other precautions (such as a yearly medical exam).
Seek medical treatment if you or your partner develops symptoms that could stem from an STD	See a doctor if you develop any unusual pain, discharge, lesions, or rashes. Abstain from sex while you are being treated for an STD, and have your partner treated for diseases that can reinfect you.
Use condoms	Proper use of latex condoms reduces the risk of contracting an STD.
Avoid mixing alcohol and illegal drugs with sex	Alcohol and drugs impair judgment and increase your risk of making sexual decisions that you later regret.
Notify your sexual partners if you become aware that you have an STD	It is important to swallow your pride and notify partners you may have infected with an STD. This will alert them to seek treatment and stop the STD from spreading.

skin, or when pregnant mothers pass the virus to their baby during pregnancy, delivery, or breast-feeding. Globally, over 20 million people have died since AIDS statistics have been kept; 3 million died in 2003 alone.

The AIDS crisis has dramatically increased people's awareness of STDs. But in addition to knowing about these diseases, teenagers also need to know the options for preventing disease that are listed in Table 11.3.

CONTRACEPTION. One area in which adolescents seem to have reasonable knowledge about sex is birth control. But knowledge is one thing and behavior is another. Most adolescents are aware of their options for birth control, yet many teenagers use birth control inconsistently. In the United States, 30 percent of the sexually active teens in one sample reported that they sometimes have unprotected sex (Henry J. Kaiser Family Foundation et al., 2003), and only 25 percent of girls in another sample were taking birth control pills the last time they had intercourse (Grunbaum et al., 2004). Therefore, it not surprising that the United States has the highest teenage birthrate among the eight industrialized countries shown in Figure 11.8. Birthrates are actually lower in countries that are the most tolerant of adolescent sexuality. For example, health administrators in Sweden and the Netherlands believe that teens should be able to obtain contraceptives without embarrassing procedures such as pelvic examinations, which makes it more likely that they will seek out and use contraceptives (Cromer & McCarthy, 1999).

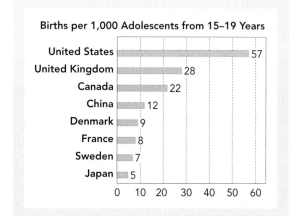

FIGURE 11.8 Births to teenage mothers.

The number of teenagers from 15 to 19 years of age who give birth each year is much higher in the United States than in other industrialized countries. One reason is that U.S. teenagers have a great deal of freedom but less ready access to contraceptive information and supplies compared to teenagers in other Western nations.

SOURCE: U.S Census Bureau (2004).

Five factors distinguish teens who use contraception reliably from those who do not:

▶ Adolescents are more likely to use contraception when their parents have comfortable, open discussions with them about sexuality and sexual risks (Whitaker et al., 1999).

▶ Adolescents who have more positive feelings about their sexuality are more likely to use contraceptives than teens who do not. Individuals who feel guilty about having sex find it difficult to admit they are thinking about having sex and are less likely to plan ahead (Gerrard, 1987).

▶ Couples who are involved in a steady relationship are more likely to use contraception, perhaps because they care about one another and feel comfortable discussing intimate issues (Herceg-Baron et al., 1990).

▶ Teens who do well in school and have higher aspirations for the future tend to use contraceptives (Herceg-Baron et al., 1990; Hogan, Astone, & Kitagawa, 1985; Scher, Emans, & Grace, 1982). And because highly educated parents generally expect their children to attend college, sexually active adolescents are more likely to use contraception if their parents attended college (B. C. Miller, 2002).

▶ Contraceptive use is influenced by cultural norms for the timing of pregnancy. Early pregnancies are not always accidents, even though these pregnancies are at odds with middle-class norms. As one urban teenager told a researcher, "Mr. Dash, will you please stop asking me about birth control? Girls out here know all about birth control . . . Girls out here get pregnant because they *want* to have babies!" (Dash, 1989, p. 11). In one study of over 400 nonpregnant African American girls, 24 percent expressed some desire to become pregnant, and these girls were more likely than their peers to use contraception inconsistently (Davies et al., 2004).

These characteristics tell a coherent story: Adolescents are more likely to prevent pregnancy when teenage pregnancy is uncommon in their community, when they have future plans that would be disrupted by pregnancy, and when they are comfortable enough with sexual issues to talk about pregnancy prevention.

PARENTS TOO SOON. Teenage pregnancy has always been common in the United States. For example, 90 out of every 1,000 girls between the ages of 15 and 19 gave birth in 1955, which is more than the rate of 57 per 1,000 in 2002 (U.S. Census Bureau, 2004). Teenage childbearing started to be viewed as a social problem in the early 1970s—not because teenagers were suddenly having babies, but because they were getting married less frequently (Furstenberg, Brooks-Gunn, & Morgan, 1987). There has actually been a gradual decline in the teenage birthrate since 1991 that is greatest among African American girls. This trend is the result of fewer pregnancies, so rates of abortion and miscarriages have also declined.

Pregnancy throws serious obstacles into young women's paths. Adolescent mothers experience more pregnancy complications than older mothers, including high blood pressure and gestational diabetes, and their newborns are more likely than the newborns of older mothers to be small and premature (Orvos et al., 1999). The children of teenage mothers are more likely to be victims of violent and unintentional injuries—even when factors associated with teen parenthood, such as socioeconomic status and substance abuse, are taken into account (Ekéus, Christensson, & Hjern,

Teenagers are less likely to use contraception consistently when they feel their future opportunities are limited and there are many teenage mothers in their community.

2004). These findings suggest that young mothers are less equipped to manage the realities of child rearing.

But what about the fathers? Teenage mothers are usually about 3 years younger than their partners, and girls between 17 and 19 years are the largest group of adolescents who give birth. As a result, many of the fathers are young adults, not teenagers. These fathers range from involved and financially responsible to absent. In one study of African American fathers, fewer than 58 percent believed that dads in their circumstances should attend the delivery, feed or play with the child, or take the child to clinic visits, and 27 percent never provided financial support or did so only on holidays. Despite these discouraging results, the majority did offer weekly financial and child-care assistance (Rhein et al., 1997). These results are similar to those from a study of white and African American men who fathered a child with a teenage mother: In both groups, only about one-third of the men maintained high levels of involvement with their children a year after the birth (Kalil, Ziol-Guest, & Coley, 2005).

Until recently, teenage pregnancy was viewed as the consequence of sheer immaturity (for middle-class teens) or hopelessness and academic failure (for poor, inner-city teens). Society's bleak view of teenage childbearing is captured by the famous quote, "When a 16-year-old girl has a child . . . 90 percent of her life's script is written for her" (Campbell, 1968, p. 242). This script usually is believed to include dropping out of school and living in poverty. But research has challenged these stereotypes. Many teenage mothers are strong, resilient individuals who find that the responsibilities of parenting motivate them to achieve. To read about the long-term consequences of becoming a teenage mother, turn to our special feature entitled "Teenage Moms Grown Up."

Once they are adults, the educational and financial circumstances of teenage mothers are not dramatically different from those of women with similar backgrounds and characteristics who delayed childbearing. It is important to set high goals for teenage mothers because many are motivated to continue their education, and they can make up for income losses after their children start school.

TEENAGE MOMS GROWN UP

The Internet is filled with testimonials from mothers who became pregnant when they were teenagers. This excerpt was written by a 29-year-old mom who became pregnant when she was 16 ("The Longest Nine Months of My Life," 2006):

Although it has been tough, I think I have made a good life for [my daughter]. As I will continue to do forever. I still get comments from time to time from passersby about how young I look and so on, but I have learned to ignore them. What matters is my daughter, and that I make it right for her. I will spend my life with that goal in mind, and

I will never stop. If I could turn back time, yes I would have waited to have a child, and I would tell anyone to take that advice, learn from my life. Live for yourself, and then for your children. Believe me there is time to do all you want to do, and your childhood can be the best time of your life, if you let it. Remember that the next time you are having unsafe sex, or you're sleeping with your boyfriend when you think you aren't really ready. Being an adult isn't all it's cracked up to be, don't make yourself one before you're ready. (para. 48)

This young woman pulled her life together. She reconciled with her parents, had a short marriage to the father, then remarried and had a son. But what is the fate of most teenage mothers? Is early motherhood usually a one-way ticket to a life of hardship?

Years ago, an award-winning book started to revise stereotypes about early parenting. In *Adolescent Mothers in Later Life*, a research team reported results from a longitudinal study of a group of girls in Baltimore, most of whom were poor and African American (Furstenberg et al., 1987). These women's lives looked bleak 5 years after childbirth: Just under half had completed high school, many had had another pregnancy, and almost a third were receiving public assistance. But their situations improved 12 years later. They still had about a year less of education than their peers, but a quarter had attended college and 5 percent had graduated. Also, they averaged only 2.3 children per mother, and less than a quarter had received public assistance during the previous year. As the authors concluded, "The popular belief that early childbearing is an almost certain route to dropping out of school, subsequent unwanted births, and economic dependency is greatly oversimplified, if not seriously distorted" (p. 46). Early motherhood does carry a price, but the price is not as high as many people had believed.

It is difficult to isolate the effects of an early pregnancy because young parents differ from their peers in many ways—not just the fact that they have given birth. For example, young mothers are more likely than other teens to be poor and to have lower academic motivation. In fact, one-third of the teenage mothers in one sample had dropped out of high school *before* they became pregnant, so dropping out of school is not always a consequence of pregnancy (Maynard, 1995). The real question is not whether these mothers have more problems than girls who delay parenting but whether they have more problems than teenagers *like themselves* who didn't give birth. When these two groups are compared, the long-term consequences of early childbearing are smaller in some studies and nonexistent in others. One analysis concluded that postponing childbirth increased average educational attainment only by .38 years (Hoffman, Foster, & Furstenberg, 1993), and another found no effect of early childbearing on educational level by the time women were in their late twenties (Holz, McElroy, L Sanders, 1999). Moreover, teenage mothers make up for early income losses several years down the line, when their children are in school (Coley & Chase-Lansdale, 1998). As one team of economists concluded, "While teen mothers are very likely to live in poverty and experience other forms of adversity . . . little of this would be changed just by getting teen mothers to delay their childbearing into adulthood" (Holz et al., 1999, p. 2).

We don't want to downplay the negative side of early pregnancies: Adolescent pregnancies cost society, disrupt opportunities for college, and reduce the chances that women will be married many years later (Coley & Chase-Lansdale, 1998; Furstenberg et al., 1987). But results from longitudinal studies suggest that teachers and other mentors should set high goals for young mothers because many are motivated to make a better life for their children. A case in point is Lianne, who finished a nursing program after she gave birth to her son. "Before [my son] was born . . . I used to cut school all of the time . . . I didn't care about nothing," she told a researcher. "But after I got pregnant . . . I started thinking about what I wanted to do . . . After I had him it just seemed like everything changed . . . That made me do a lot of thinking" (Schultz, 2001, pp. 595–596). ◆

SEXUAL IDENTITY AND SAME-SEX ATTRACTIONS. As you read in Chapter 5, children begin to have a gender identity—a sense of themselves as male or female—by 3 years of age. During preschool it is common to explore sex parts, and by elementary school many children are having their first crushes. The process of exploring *sexual orientation*—our preferences to interact sexually with opposite-sex partners, same-sex partners, or both sexes—can continue well into adulthood. Nonetheless, adolescence is an important time when children become more aware of their attractions and more worried about whether their feelings will be accepted by the people around them.

There is a difference between feeling attraction to one sex or the other, acting on that attraction by having sex, and labeling oneself heterosexual or gay, lesbian, or bisexual (GLB). These aspects of sexuality have fuzzy boundaries while adolescents are experimenting sexually and coming to terms with their feelings. It is not unusual for preteen or teenage boys who ultimately identify as heterosexual to engage in homosexual sex play, and some girls label themselves heterosexual even though they have same-sex crushes.

In a national survey of Swiss 16- to 20-year-olds, 95 percent of girls and 96 percent of boys defined themselves as predominantly heterosexual, about 1 percent of girls and 2 percent of boys described themselves as predominantly homosexual or bisexual, and 4 percent of girls and 2 percent of boys were unsure of their sexual orientation (Narring, Stronski Huwiler, & Michaud, 2003). These findings are similar to a U.S. sample of children, from the eighth through the twelfth grades, in which 3 percent of boys and girls reported same-sex sexual activity (Vermont Department of Health, 2003). Uncertainty about one's sexuality declines from early adolescence (when as many as one in four children express some uncertainty) to later adolescence, when no more than 5 percent do (Remafedi et al., 1992).

Gay, lesbian, and bisexual teenagers still face challenges from discrimination and harassment, but they are less likely than sexual minority teens from past generations to feel that sexual orientation defines who they are.

Most scientists believe that biological mechanisms operate early in life to determine whether individuals have heterosexual, same-sex, or bisexual attractions. This conclusion is based on evidence that sexual orientation is heritable (although the mechanisms may differ for women versus men) (Bailey et al., 1993; Kirk, Bailey, & Martin, 2000), that early exposure to sex hormones influences gender identification and sexual orientation (Meyer-Bahlburg et al., 1996; Zucker et al., 1996), and that GLB people show cross-gender behavior and interests more often than heterosexual people early in life (Bailey & Zucker, 1995). And as we will discuss in Chapter 13, patterns of attraction are highly stable even though how people act on their feelings is not. In other words, there is good evidence that biology is largely responsible for how much you are attracted to males or females even though your culture influences whom you choose to be with at any particular time.

The average age when girls begin to become aware of same-sex attractions is between 10 and 11 years; the average for boys is between 9 and 13. Thus most GLB youth are grappling with their sexual identity and feelings of being out of the mainstream throughout adolescence. These teens have a higher rate of suicide attempts than their peers, and they often live in fear of harassment and violence. In one sample, nearly 20 percent of GLB youth had been hit, kicked, or physically assaulted in other ways (Pilkington & D'Augelli, 1995), as were 7 percent of lesbian and bisexual female youth in another sample (D'Augelli, 2003).

A critical milestone for GLB youth is when (and if) they *come out*, that is, when they disclose their orientation to others. Most discuss their feelings with friends first, and only 10 percent disclose to a parent first (usually their mother) (Savin-Williams, 2001). Some parents react with shock, anger, and a sense of loss. As one mother explained (Saltzburg, 2004),

> I can't stop the thoughts I have about homosexuality. This is what I've learned and what I believe. And now these apply to my child. It's awful to have these thoughts about one of your children. And I think that's what the depression and drinking was about. I felt so torn by all the awful thoughts I had about the child I loved. And I shut down from her and felt so empty. (p. 113)

Should GLB youth be encouraged to come out to their parents—even if they might react as this mother did? Not necessarily, says Rich Savin-Williams (2001), a professor of human development at Cornell University. Coming out can put them at risk for being ordered out of the house, cut off financially, and isolated from sources of emotional support. Furthermore, adolescents who rely on their parents' approval for a sense of self-worth may not be ready to weather the consequences. On the other hand, coming out can be a relief for teens who have understanding parents, so it is best to make this important decision on a case-by-case basis.

Despite the challenges faced by teens who have same-sex attractions, some experts believe that stereotypes of the "suffering gay adolescent" are overblown because many do not experience significant problems with harassment or depression. As Savin-Williams (2005) explained, "It is clear to me that many youth who happen to have same-sex attractions live their lives in much the same way that those with heterosexual attractions do. They go to football games, try out for cheerleader, run for Student Council, argue with their parents, and wonder what to wear. Somehow we missed this, but we won't in the future if we listen to their lives" (p. 69). Increasingly, GLB teens are viewing sexuality as a side issue in their lives and are resisting the idea that sexual feelings define who they are. As one girl responded when asked how she "identified" sexually, "I don't. What's the need?" (Savin-Williams, 2005, p. 11).

Delinquency

When we interviewed Officer Don Sytsema, he was spending time at the local high school as a member of his police department's youth services team. Don intervened when fights broke out, assisted with crime investigation, and talked to classes about alcohol use, computer law, and other important issues. "I love interacting with the kids," he told us. "At this age, you can joke with them, talk about real life experiences. They are adults for all practical purposes."

It makes sense to have police officers in schools because crime rates soar during the high school years. As shown in Figure 11.9, arrest rates for assault and robbery increase steeply from age 10 until late adolescence or early adulthood, then gradually decline, and the pattern is similar for crimes against property: Individuals

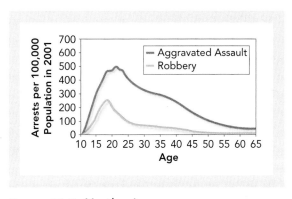

FIGURE 11.9 Youth crime.

Crime rates rise sharply after childhood and peak during late adolescence and early adulthood. Here you see arrest rates for aggravated assault and robbery. Age trends for property crimes (such as burglary, motor vehicle theft, and arson) follow the same pattern.

SOURCE: *OJJDP Statistical Briefing Book* (2004).

under age 18 account for 49 percent of all arson arrests, 38 percent of vandalism acts, and 30 percent of motor vehicle thefts and burglaries (*OJJDP Statistical Briefing Book*, 2004). Collectively, crimes committed by children and adolescents are called *delinquency*, and the criminals are called *juvenile delinquents*.

Of course, most crimes never result in an arrest. To gather more information about delinquency, social scientists ask teens to report their activities on anonymous questionnaires. The results show that most adolescents have committed at least one criminal offense. In one national survey, for example, 25 percent of girls and 41 percent of boys had been in a physical fight during the past year, and 3 percent of girls and 9 percent of boys had carried a weapon into school during the past 30 days (Grunbaum et al., 2004).

It is normal for adolescents to occasionally break rules or even violate the law, but it is important to distinguish between those teens who break the law largely because they are simply curious or swept away by the moment and those who break the law due to deeper problems in their lives or communities. In one study, psychologists Jonathan Shedler and Jack Block (1990) looked at three groups of 18-year-olds who had been involved in a longitudinal study: *abstainers* (who had never tried marijuana or any other drug), *experimenters* (who had used marijuana only occasionally and had tried no more than one other drug), and *frequent users* (who used marijuana once a week or more and had tried at least one other drug). Compared to the experimenters, the abstainers were fearful and anxious at age 11, not very curious or lively, and not self-reliant. At age 18, these youngsters were still anxious and socially unskilled. Frequent users were clearly maladjusted. They were inattentive at age 11, deviant from peers, and prone to overreact in the face of minor frustrations. At 18, frequent users were a distressed group who had poor self-control. But experimenters were the healthiest teens. As Shedler and Block (1990) explained, when an illegal act is prevalent and accepted by one's peer group, "psychologically healthy, sociable, and reasonably inquisitive individuals" are going to be tempted to try it (p. 625).

We're not suggesting that adults should overlook illegal behavior. On the contrary, detecting misbehavior is an opportunity to reinforce community values. However, there is no need to be seriously worried about a single act of petty theft or a few damaged mailboxes. In fact, many studies have found it useful to distinguish between two types of delinquents (Moffitt, 1993). **Adolescence-limited delinquents** show no particular pattern of risk factors before adolescence, do not begin engaging in frequent or serious illegal behavior until adolescence, and tend to commit crimes with peers. Most of these individuals stop their illegal behavior once they are older. In contrast, **life-course persistent delinquents** often have difficult temperaments, attentional problems, and learning difficulties as children, a history of engaging in solitary antisocial behavior, and family risk factors. As adolescents, these individuals are more likely to commit serious crimes, and they often continue criminal activity into adulthood.

Because delinquent behavior is common during the teen years, it is difficult to predict which children are at risk for becoming alcoholics, chronic drug abusers, or violent criminals. To learn about a common reasoning error that leads to faulty predictions, turn to our next "Don't Be Fooled!" feature entitled "Explain Backward, Predict Forward."

adolescence-limited delinquents
Teenagers who do not begin to engage in frequent or serious illegal behavior until adolescence and tend to commit crimes with peers. These individuals show no particular pattern of risk factors before adolescence and stop their illegal behavior once they are older.

life-course persistent delinquents
Teenagers who have a history of engaging in solitary antisocial behavior. These individuals often have a history of difficult temperaments, attentional problems, learning difficulties, and family risk factors. They are more likely than other adolescents to continue criminal activity into adulthood.

DON'T BE FOOLED

Single risk factors during adolescence are not usually strong predictors of adult mental health problems. For example, most adults who abuse alcohol skipped school when they were younger, but most adolescents who skip school will not grow up to abuse alcohol. The probability of X given Y (for example, the probability that an adult skipped school if he or she now abuses alcohol) is *not* the same as the probability of Y given X (that is, the probability that a teenager will become an alcoholic if he or she has been skipping school).

Explain Backward, Predict Forward

Raymond still laughs about the time his father, who was born in Southeast Asia, caught him smoking a cigar. This concerned dad, who lectured Raymond for an hour, was convinced that his son would grow up to use drugs. Why? He had heard that people who take "hard" drugs, like heroin, usually start out with "gateway" substances, like tobacco or marijuana. Due to the same type of reasoning, many parents worried after the media featured a study that reported that 86 percent of prisoners had experienced a childhood head injury (Barnfield & Leathem, 1998). These alarmed parents mistakenly thought that their teenagers' football and bicycle injuries would predispose them to a life of crime.

The findings that frightened these parents came from *follow-back* studies (also called "retrospective" studies). Follow-back studies start with adults who have a target condition (such as drug abuse or a prison record) and then explore their earlier environments and characteristics. Scientists use this strategy to generate hypotheses about the pathways that lead to alcoholism, drug addiction, and other conditions. But there is a problem with this strategy: The percentage of heroin users who first used tobacco or marijuana is *not the same* as the percentage of tobacco or marijuana users who become heroin users. Statements like, "If X, then this percent Y" are *conditional probabilities*, and these statements cannot be reversed. This fact is obvious if you simply replace "marijuana" with "milk." Clearly, the percentage of heroin users who have tried milk is NOT the same as the percentage of milk drinkers who become heroin users. Like milk, marijuana is a popular substance, so most heroin users have tried it. But in one study, only 1 percent of individuals who experimented with marijuana went on to try heroin (Johnson, 1973). Similarly, most children with head injuries never grow up to become criminals.

To predict a teen's *future* behavior, you need to look at *follow-up* data. Follow-up studies start with a group of children who have a risk factor and determine how this group fares as adults. The difference between follow-back and follow-up research is illustrated by a classic example from psychiatric researcher Lee Robins (1966). Robins found that 75 percent of the alcoholics in one sample were truants (had chronically skipped school) as juveniles, compared to only 26 percent of psychologically healthy people. This follow-back finding leads us to think that truancy is a powerful predictor of alcoholism. However, when she looked at the adult outcomes of children who had been seen in a mental health clinic, only 11 percent of truants became alcoholics compared to 8 percent of the group as a whole. In other words, truancy was not a strong predictor of alcoholism. Results like

anorexia nervosa A condition in which people starve themselves to stay thin. Most cases occur among young women and begin during mid-to-late adolescence.

these are common when the childhood symptom occurs much more frequently than the adult problem.

Adolescence is filled with pitfalls as teens experiment to expand the boundaries of their lives. Like the father who was devastated when his son smoked cigars, it is natural for parents to be worried about risky behavior. But the truth is that single risk factors are rarely strong predictors of future problems. With a few hours of lecturing, some monitoring, and some goals for the future, the vast majority of teens who get into minor trouble turn out just fine. ◆

Eating Disorders

 In the late 1880s, when girls thought that "good works" defined who they were, one teen made the following entry into her diary:

> Resolved, not to talk about myself or feelings. To think before speaking. To work seriously. To be self-restrained in conversations and actions. Not to let my thoughts wander. To be dignified. Interest myself more in others. (Brumberg, 1997, p. xxi)

By the 1920s, when girls thought that "good looks" defined who they were, diary entries sounded more like this one, which was written by a 15-year-old in 1929:

> I'm so tired of being fat! I'm going back to school weighing 119 pounds—I swear it. Three months in which to lose thirty pounds—but I'll do it—or die in the attempt. (pp. 102–103).

Historian Joan Brumberg (1997) made an interesting discovery by analyzing diaries: Girls began to organize their identities around perceptions of their bodies during the twentieth century. In fact, an obsession with weight is so common that it has long been called the " 'normative' worry" of American women (Rodin, Silberstein, & Striegle-Moore, 1985, p. 267). But even common obsessions can go too far. Teens who suffer from an eating disorder engage in behaviors that can seriously damage their health and, in some cases, even lead to death. Two forms of eating disorder are anorexia nervosa and bulimia nervosa.

ANOREXIA NERVOSA. People with **anorexia nervosa** (often simply called "anorexia") starve themselves to stay extremely thin. Medical doctors and therapists diagnose anorexia nervosa when the following symptoms are present (American Psychiatric Association, 2000):

▶ *Refusal to maintain a healthy weight for one's age and height.* An eating disorder is suspected when someone weighs less than 85 percent of their expected weight. Individuals with anorexia lose weight by eating very little but may also exercise excessively, induce vomiting, or use laxatives to lower their weight.

▶ *An intense fear of gaining weight.* These individuals are highly motivated to stay as small as possible. They may try to hide their emaciated bodies with loose clothes, lie about what they have been eating, or pretend they are eating more than they are.

▶ *Disturbed perceptions and thoughts about one's body.* Individuals with anorexia nervosa often perceive themselves as heavy even when they are not, and they are highly dissatisfied with their bodies (Cash & Deagle, 1997).

▶ *An absence of menstrual periods.* Girls stop menstruating when they do not have a sufficient amount of body fat. It is normal to miss periods occasionally, but *amenorrhea* is present when three consecutive periods have been missed.

Anorexia nervosa is not just a fad that some teenagers pass through—it is a serious disorder that can lead to permanent organ damage and death.

Contrary to what would seem to be the case, anorexics do not dislike food; in fact, they are often preoccupied with it, sometimes preparing elaborate meals for their friends and families but not eating them. Control over one's body and, by association, one's life, is often one of the motivating factors behind this eating disorder. But this control takes a severe toll on the body. Self-starvation leads to anemia and other nutritional imbalances that strain the body's vital organs, cause bone loss, and interfere with normal immune system functioning. Over 10 percent of patients who are admitted to hospitals eventually die from starvation, suicide, or organ damage (American Psychiatric Association, 2000).

Who is most at risk for anorexia nervosa? Over 90 percent of cases are females, with most cases beginning during mid-to-late adolescence. But there is little agreement about other demographic characteristics (Gard & Freeman, 1996). Anorexic girls are often high-achieving, perfectionist people who have problems managing anxiety. Their families exhibit more conflict and criticism than the families of teens who do not have unhealthy relationships with food. As one college student explained about her father, "It just seems like . . . I'm never good enough" (Murray, 2003, p. 278). Thus one view of anorexia suggests that it is often seen in girls who feel they don't measure up and wish to exert control over some aspect of their lives. But genetic factors are also involved, possibly because genes produce variability in levels of brain chemicals that are involved in the control of eating (Collier & Treasure, 2004). Thus anorexia nervosa is believed to be caused by a combination of individual, family, and genetic factors (Linscheid & Butz, 2003). This condition has existed throughout recorded history, but the current cultural emphasis on thinness seems to have produced a modest increase in rates (Keel & Klump, 2003).

BULIMIA NERVOSA. The eating disorder that is most strongly associated with Western culture is **bulimia nervosa** (Keel & Klump, 2003). Individuals with bulimia nervosa engage in *binge eating* (the rapid consumption of large amounts of food) followed by *purging*—vomiting, using laxatives, or other means to rid the body of calories. Most people eat excessively from time to time, but bulimia nervosa is present when the following symptoms occur in someone who does not have anorexia nervosa (American Psychiatric Association, 2000):

▶ *Repeated episodes of binge eating with a sense of lack of control.* Most people occasionally eat too much during holidays or when they are just acting silly with friends. However, individuals with bulimia nervosa eat large amounts of food in situations that are not typically associated with overeating. And instead of deciding to overeat, these individuals feel they cannot control their eating.

▶ *Using extreme efforts to purge the body of food or extra weight.* Vomiting, taking laxatives, excessive exercise, and fasting are some of the ways individuals with bulimia compensate for binging. (Notice that *binging,* not vomiting, is the defining feature of bulimia nervosa.)

▶ *Binging and purging at least twice a week for 3 months.*

▶ *Having an excessive preoccupation with body shape and weight.* People who suffer from bulimic symptoms evaluate their self-worth in terms of their body, which they would like to conform to an unrealistic ideal. But unlike people with anorexia nervosa, they usually are only slightly underweight, average, or slightly overweight.

Most cases of bulimia nervosa begin during late adolescence or early adulthood and, as with anorexia nervosa, 90 percent of sufferers are women. Bulimia

bulimia nervosa A condition in which people binge eat (take in large amounts of food) and then try to rid the body of calories by dieting, exercising, vomiting, or other means.

TABLE 11.4 Eating Disorders: Tips for Helping a Friend

Tip	Reason
Collect facts about eating disorders and identify some local treatment centers. College counseling centers are good resources for pamphlets and information about support groups.	Individuals with eating disorders are not motivated to stop destructive behavior because they want to lose weight. They often don't know about or minimize the health risks of starving or purging, but they probably will not look for this information themselves.
In a nonjudgmental way, tell your friend what behaviors or physical symptoms you have observed and explain that you care. Provide the information you have collected, including phone numbers where your friend can talk to a qualified professional. If you feel comfortable, you can offer to accompany your friend to a counseling or treatment center.	Your friend might deny there is a problem and be upset about your accusations. Avoid a battle by sticking to the facts and letting your friend know that you're available to listen.
Avoid shaming your friend with "you" statements, such as "You need to eat!" or "You are acting so immature!" Instead, use "I" statements, such as "I am concerned" and "I am afraid when I hear you throw up."	Making friends feel guilty and uncomfortable reduces your ability to help and increases the chances they will lie, avoid you, and try harder to conceal their behavior.
If your friend is a minor, discuss your concerns with his or her parent, teacher, or guidance counselor.	Eating disorders are unhealthy and potentially deadly, so an adult who has legal responsibility for your friend should be involved in making treatment decisions.
Once your friend is involved in treatment, act naturally but avoid commenting on your friend's weight or appearance. Support your friend by talking about other aspects of life, including relationships, school, and leisure activities.	Comments such as "You look so much better now that you are eating" can make individuals with an eating disorder feel as if everyone is noticing their weight gain. Talking about bodies and weight only reinforces an unhealthy obsession with these topics.

nervosa also causes numerous health problems, including eroded tooth enamel (from the acids in vomit), bowel problems, and a number of rare but potentially fatal conditions (Burns et al., 2003). To learn how to help a friend who may have an eating disorder, turn to the practical advice in Table 11.4.

Suicide

"I felt like jumping out the window," Holden Caulfield recalled in *The Catcher in the Rye* (Salinger, 1951, p. 136). "I probably would've done it, too, if I'd been sure somebody'd cover me up as soon as I landed. I didn't want a bunch of stupid rubbernecks looking at me when I was all gory."

Nearly everyone remembers a time during adolescence when they imagined other people's reactions to their death. In fact, it is common for adolescents to think about ending their lives. In one survey, 17 percent of high school students said they had seriously considered attempting suicide, and almost as many had made a suicide plan. These plans were not all harmless: Almost 3 percent of high school students say they have made a suicide attempt that required medical attention in the last year (Grunbaum et al., 2004).

Suicide rates vary tremendously across ethnic and national groups. In the United States, rates of completed suicides rise steeply during adolescence, plateau during middle adulthood, and then rise again during the elderly years. Notice in Figure 11.10 that white males have the highest suicide rate, followed by nonwhite males. Among 15-to 19-year-olds, five times as many males as females commit suicide (National Institute of Mental Health, 2003), although females make many more suicide attempts. Females more often survive suicide attempts because they use less lethal means, such as taking pills, whereas males more often hang themselves or use firearms.

Many teens who commit suicide suffer from depression that is triggered by the loss of a romantic relationship, legal or disciplinary problems, conflict with parents, or other life troubles (Brent et al., 1999). Others suffer from disruptive behavior disorders and substance abuse (Shaffer et al., 1996). But these findings do not explain why suicide rates are so much higher in Western nations than in Arabic and Latin American countries, or why suicide rates climbed rapidly during the last half of the 20th century in Brazil, India, and many other countries (Brown, 2001). To explain these trends, it is useful to think of suicide as a problem of self-concept or identity. For example, suicides are more common among college students than people of comparable age who are working (even though college students have rosier futures), and rates have risen as economic opportunities have risen. These findings suggest that high expectations, combined with feedback that one is somehow inadequate, play a role in **suicidal ideation** (thoughts or plans about suicide) (Baumeister, 1990).

Feeling part of a community or culture can help protect adolescents from suicide. For example, suicide rates drop during times of war, when people bond together for a common cause. Findings such as this one have led experts to suggest that the lack of a sense of community can make it difficult for some teens to establish an identity that allows them to feel good about themselves and envision a meaningful future. This hypothesis was tested in an ambitious study of completed suicides among Native Americans in British Columbia (Chandler et al., 2003). The investigators computed youth suicide rates in communities that were represented by various tribal councils. They also determined the "cultural continuity" of each community by measuring such things as land claims and whether communities controlled their own health care and other services. Figure 11.11 shows that suicide rates were dramatically lower in communities where a cultural identity provided youth with a sense of a shared past and a "collective future" (p. 75). This finding is consistent with the other information in this chapter, which showed that seemingly personal decisions—such as whether to use drugs or have sex—are often influenced by the relationships individuals have with their families and communities.

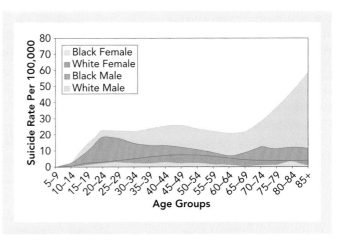

FIGURE 11.10 Suicide across the life span.

The rate of completed suicides increases rapidly during adolescence. According to the National Institute of Mental Health, there may be 8 to 25 suicide attempts for every completed suicide.

SOURCE: National Institute of Mental Health (2003).

suicidal ideation Thoughts or plans about suicide.

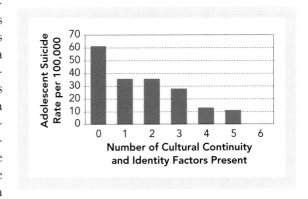

FIGURE 11.11 Cultural identity and suicide.

Adolescent suicide rates are dramatically lower in Native American communities that have more factors associated with cultural continuity and identity, such as a history of land claims and control over their own health care and other services. Strong community identities ease the transition through adolescence.

SOURCE: Chandler et al. (2003).

Native American youth who live in areas that enjoy a sense of community and a shared history have lower suicide rates than those who live in less cohesive communities. This lucky teen is celebrating community traditions and values in one of the many powwows that are held in the United States each year.

>>> **MEMORY MAKERS** <<<

True or false:

1. Drugs that influence perception, mood, or behavior are called *psychoactive* drugs. T
2. Adolescents are more likely to try drugs when adults discuss the benefits of a drug for some people. F
3. Boys are much more likely than girls to have recently used an illicit drug. F
4. Minority teens are more likely to experiment with drugs than white teens. F
5. Over 95 percent of today's teens know how STDs are transmitted. F
6. Teen couples who are involved in a steady relationship are more likely than other teens to use contraception reliably. T
7. Vomiting after meals is a defining feature of anorexia nervosa. F
8. Adolescents are less likely to commit suicide than older individuals. T

[1-true; 2-false; 3-false; 4-false; 5-false; 6-true; 7-false; 8-true]

Gender Differences around the World

It is impossible to talk about the different pathways children take through adolescence without talking about what it means to be male or female around the world. The differences in how societies treat boys and girls become more obvious during adolescence, as cultures step up their efforts to prepare children for adult roles, including gender roles.

Boys and Girls in Traditional Cultures

Men and women lead very different lives in tribal and peasant cultures, so adolescence in traditional cultures is a time when life pathways separate for boys and girls (Arnett, 2004). Typically, the world expands for adolescent boys as adults encourage them to develop skills for hunting, fishing, or other activities that will provide for their future families (Mensch, Bruce, & Greene, 1998). Teenage boys spend a lot of time socializing with other boys, learning from adult men, and expanding their responsibilities in the wider community. As they are increasingly encouraged to prove their bravery and self-reliance, boys are often ridiculed for socializing with women or staying too close to home.

In contrast, the world generally contracts for girls. Traditional cultures work diligently to protect girls from sexual attention, so they are supervised more than boys and encouraged to stay near home. It is typical for adolescent girls to work on domestic tasks under the watchful eyes of their mothers and other adult females. And unlike boys, who have to prove that they have become men, maturity for girls is viewed as a natural consequence of physical development (Arnett, 2004).

Wherever societies have clearly different work roles for men and women, the separate play worlds that boys and girls develop during childhood are reinforced and exaggerated as puberty approaches. By emphasizing that males and females have different traits, these societies work to increase gender differences during the reproductive years.

Gender in the Industrialized World

Industrialized societies tolerate a wider variety of roles for men and women, so gender relationships are more complicated than they are in traditional societies. Instead of separating socially, boys and girls begin to mingle in mixed-sex groups after years of predominantly same-sex play. Compared to traditional societies, there is less pressure for the sexes to have different skills because both males and females generally grow up to help out at home and be employed. But even in industrialized countries, budding sexuality prompts teens to focus on and exaggerate some differences between the sexes.

GENDER BECOMES MORE IMPORTANT. According to the **gender intensification hypothesis**, societies place increased pressure on teens to conform to cultural expectations for male and female behavior during adolescence (Hill & Lynch, 1983). As the changes of puberty collide with societal expectations, many girls shave body hair, emphasize feminine body features, and laugh in high-pitched voices while boys "bulk up" and talk tough. Meanwhile, teens who don't engage in these practices are often teased and socially excluded by peers.

There is some support for the idea that gender intensification occurs during adolescence. For example, teenage girls of all ages spend more time on feminine tasks (such as handicrafts and dance classes) than masculine tasks (such as sports or hunting), but activities are the least gender stereotyped at age 13 and the most stereotyped at 15 (McHale et al., 2004). Gender intensification also occurs for household tasks, such as doing laundry and mowing the lawn, particularly in families that adhere to traditional divisions of labor (Crouter, Manke, & McHale, 1995). These findings suggest that as teens move through adolescence, they are monitoring and conforming to sex-role behavior more than they were a few years earlier.

ACADEMIC PERFORMANCE. Even when girls are educated alongside boys, differences in cognitive skill emerge by the adolescent years. As in childhood, male adolescents are more likely than females to have a learning disability, and they are more likely to drop out of high school. But if males are more likely than females to perform extremely poorly, they are also more likely to perform extremely well on achievement tests. In 2004, for example, girls averaged 8 points lower than males on the SAT verbal section (out of 800 possible) and 36 points lower on math. On Advanced Placement tests, boys outperformed girls in physics, chemistry, calculus, economics, government, history, and biology, whereas girls outperform boys in Spanish, French, and English literatures and art history (Stumpf & Stanley, 1998).

gender intensification hypothesis The idea that behavioral and psychological differences between the sexes increase during adolescence as a result of social pressure to conform to stereotypical gender roles.

We know that social forces must contribute to how well males and females master academic material because the size of these differences changes over time. For instance, the gender difference favoring boys on the Advanced Placement computer science exam was much larger in 1984 than it was in 1996, when computer programming had caught on as an activity for girls (Stumpf & Stanley, 1998). Nevertheless, some scientists believe that fundamental differences in the brains of males and females may contribute to three sex differences in cognitive ability that are already in place by adolescence:

▶ *Spatial reasoning.* The sex differences in spatial reasoning that first appear in childhood become larger after puberty. Males are better at spatial rotation, whereas females are better at remembering the positions of objects (Kimura, 1999). But spatial skills develop from engaging in tasks that hone spatial skills, such as building three-dimensional models, so the size of the sex differences varies as a function of children's environments (Levine et al., 2005).

▶ *Mathematics.* Boys and girls show no difference on moderately easy mathematics tests, and girls generally perform better on school math tests. However, males perform better on difficult mathematical reasoning tests, such as solving word problems (Gallagher et al., 2000).

▶ *Verbal skills.* Females are better spellers than males and are better at remembering lists of words and other verbal material (Kimura, 1999). They perform better on reading and writing tests administered in school (Coley, 2001) but score lower than males on the verbal portion of the SAT ("SAT® Math Scores . . .," 2005).

According to educators, the best way to think about these sex differences in cognition is not to think much about them at all. This is because correlations between sex and mathematical skill, and sex and verbal skill, are trivial (about .1) (Campbell & Storo, 1994). Because knowing a student's sex tells you nothing about what his or her interests and abilities will be after high school, it makes sense to encourage every student to try to excel in all subjects.

> > > **MEMORY MAKERS** < < <

Which sex performs better on the following tasks during adolescence?

1. spatial rotation
2. difficult mathematics word problems
3. spelling
4. The size of correlations between sex and overall mathematical skill and sex and verbal skill is _____.

   (a) close to the maximum of 1.00
   (b) about .5
   (c) trivial

[1-males; 2-males; 3-females; 4-c]

Revisiting Developmental Principles: How Do You Build a Resilient Teen?

Troubled children often have multiple individual, family, and community risk factors. Yet even the harshest environments produce remarkable people like Oprah Winfrey. Scientists use the term **resilience** to refer to this ability to thrive in the

resilience The ability to thrive in the face of hardship or overcome the negative effects of hardship.

face of hardship. The assumption is that resilient children have a set of **protective factors**: characteristics that buffer them from negative outcomes. As long as social scientists have been studying development, they have wondered whether people like Oprah share a common set of protective factors.

An early investigation of resilience began in 1955, when a multidisciplinary team started a longitudinal study of 698 babies who were born on the Hawaiian island of Kauai (Werner, 1993). The team considered about one-third of the sample to be high risk because these children were born into poverty, had experienced birth stress, and lived in disordered families. As you might expect, two out of three developed serious learning or behavior problems. But amazingly, one out of three did not. What distinguished the resilient children from their vulnerable peers?

First, resilient children shared a number of personal attributes. They were affectionate, good-natured, and easy to care for in infancy. By the school years, the resilient children got along well with classmates, had a variety of interests and hobbies, and set high goals. Since this study was conducted, numerous others have found that resilient children have easy temperaments and are high in self-control and self-efficacy (Eisenberg et al., 2004; Kim-Cohen et al., 2004).

Relationships also helped buffer the resilient Kauai youngsters from stress. Resilient children had established a close bond with at least one caregiver, such as a parent, an older cousin, uncle, or another important nurturer and mentor. Other studies have found similar results. As one inner-city student from Chicago explained, "In elementary school I had a teacher, Ms. T., and she pretty much influenced me. She always knew I could do better than I did. Because of her I was always on the honor roll. I felt like if I didn't make the honor roll she would be disappointed or something" (Smokowski, Reynolds, & Bezruczko, 2000, p. 442). In other studies, warm adults who set limits and high expectations were important in the lives of resilient children (Masten & Coatsworth, 1998).

Initially, resilient children where considered extraordinary, the "superkids of the ghetto" (Buggie, 1995). But today, scientists view resilience as a common phenomenon that occurs when ordinary adaptive processes keep development on course. These processes fail when the foundational systems of development fail. For example, children find it difficult to rebound from abnormal brain development, a lack of early emotional attachments, or unpredictable interactions with caregivers that prevent them from learning self-control (Masten, 2001).

The phenomenon of resilience beautifully illustrates the four principles of human development:

1. *Development is the joint product of nature and nurture.* Resilient children are the product of innate temperamental and cognitive abilities along with positive qualities in their rearing environments.

2. *Physical, cognitive, and socioemotional development are interrelated.* The characteristics associated with resilience cut across all areas of development. Resilient teens tend to be healthy, intelligent individuals who have had opportunities to forge meaningful emotional attachments to other people.

3. *Developmental outcomes vary over time and contexts.* The variables that predict resilience change as children grow and are different for boys and girls. In the Kauai study, for example, the number of adults outside the household whom the child liked during middle childhood was a stronger predictor of future adjustment for boys than girls. For girls, one of the best predictors of success during early adulthood was whether the mother was steadily employed (Werner, 1993).

protective factors Characteristics that protect individuals against the negative outcomes that are usually associated with various risk factors.

4. Development is characterized by continuity and discontinuity. All but two of the resilient Kauai youngsters had positive outcomes in their 30s, proving the stability of resilient characteristics across time. But as many other studies have found, the lives of teenage mothers were actually better at age 32 than they had been at 18. In other words, an individual's adjustment is not fixed in stone at age 18.

In sum, the recipe for building a resilient teen contains the following ingredients: a healthy gestation and birth, consistent early parenting that builds self-control, meaningful bonds with one or more adults and—as children become adolescents—connections to positive influences outside the immediate family, such as community organizations and schools (Masten & Coatsworth, 1998).

Regardless of where teens have come from, by the end of adolescence they are heading in a thousand different directions. But whether they are entering the job market or heading to college, most have not yet decided what to do with their lives. Over the next few years, important changes will alter their brains, broaden their intellects, and influence the way they think about themselves and their futures. These changes are the next chapters in the story of human development.

> > > SUMMARY < < <

Communities, Schools, and Families

1. Many cultures recognize adolescents' new responsibilities and roles with **rites of passage**, rituals or celebrations that separate an individual from a previous identity and announce a new identity.

2. Family interactions (such as whether parents discuss important issues with their teen), peer interactions (such as the number of close friends), and neighborhood quality (such as adult involvement in community organizations) all have small effects on adolescent adjustment (that is, whether adolescents are performing satisfactorily in school, staying out of trouble, and using their free time productively). The best predictor of success is a measure that sums the quality of all of these environmental contexts.

3. It is not uncommon for academic performance and self-esteem to suffer when children transition into middle or junior high school. Academic achievement during adolescence is influenced by school size (with middle-sized schools showing the highest levels of achievement), students' economic opportunities for the future, and their beliefs in their own abilities. College opportunities are often partly determined by performance on **high-stakes tests** such as the SAT.

4. Parent–child conflict increases during adolescence but does not usually involve serious issues. Parental expectations and monitoring, parental involvement in decision making, and parental involvement in school work are all

associated with adolescents' well-being. The quality of a father's relationship with his children—rather than the amount of contact—also predicts teenagers' behavior.

Leisure and Work

5. There is no evidence that children learn best when they spend an extreme amount of time doing simple chores or studying. Instead, development is best served by a balance of activities that build different skills.

6. Interactive media can expose adolescents to violence and **online victimization**.

7. The influence of paid employment depends on the job, the amount of time teenagers spend at work, and what they would be doing if they were not working. School achievement is most likely to be compromised when adolescents work over 20 hours per week.

Risky Choices

8. Compared to older drivers, young drivers are more inexperienced, have more difficulty staying focused on driving, and take more driving risks.

9. Experimentation with alcohol, marijuana, and other **psychoactive** substances is common during adolescence. Successful prevention programs address drug risks, teach skills children need for success, and help them resist peer influence.

10. Deficient sexual knowledge and frequent sexual behavior put teens at risk for **sexually transmitted diseases** and pregnancy. Uncertainty about sexual orientation declines from early to late adolescence.

11. Teens who do not begin delinquent activity until adolescence (**adolescence-limited delinquents**) have better adult outcomes than those who engage in antisocial behavior from a young age (**life-course persistent delinquents**).

12. Individuals with **anorexia nervosa** starve themselves while those with **bulimia nervosa** eat large amounts of food and then try to eliminate calories by vomiting or other means. Eating disorders stress the body's vital organs, causing a host of medical problems and, sometimes, even death.

13. **Suicidal ideation** (thoughts or plans about suicide) and suicide attempts are not uncommon during adolescence. The most vulnerable teens have recently experienced negative feedback or live in communities that make it difficult for them to establish a healthy identity.

Gender Differences around the World

14. In traditional cultures, the lives of boys and girls separate as they prepare for different adult roles.

15. There is some **gender intensification** in industrialized societies as adolescents emphasize their feminine or masculine traits and interests, but biological sex is only weakly associated with performance on most cognitive tasks.

Revisiting Developmental Principles: How Do You Build a Resilient Teen?

16. Research on **resilience**—the ability to thrive in the face of hardship—illustrates the four principles of development. (1) Resilient individuals tend to be born with easy temperaments and are able to find some positive features in their environments; nature and nurture are important. (2) The characteristics associated with resilience cut across all areas of development. Resilient teens tend to be healthy, intelligent individuals who have had opportunities to forge meaningful emotional attachments to other people. (3) The variables that predict resilience change as individuals grow and are different for males and females. (4) Resilient children tend to grow into well-adjusted adults (showing continuity in development), but the life circumstances of other children sometimes change for the better with time (showing discontinuity).

>>>KEY TERMS<<<

rites of passage (p. 435)
self-efficacy (p. 439)
high-stakes tests (p. 439)
stereotype threat (p. 440)
online victimization (p. 446)
psychoactive drugs (p. 450)
sexually transmitted diseases (p. 454)
adolescence-limited delinquents (p. 462)

life-course persistent delinquents (p. 462)
anorexia nervosa (p. 464)
bulimia nervosa (p. 465)
suicidal ideation (p. 467)
gender intensification hypothesis (p. 469)
resilience (p. 470)
protective factors (p. 471)

CHAPTER TWELVE

Profile of Early to Middle Adulthood

Stories of Our Lives
Boarding the Flight to Adulthood

O ne spring Deb and her two children spent a few days on the tidal cove in Maine where the children's grandparents lived. At 19 and 22 years, Lin and Bret were treated as adults during their visit. Bret drove the rental car; Lin monitored arrangements. Bret helped his grandfather prepare the boat for fishing; Lin took pictures. Their grandparents watched them for a few days and then quietly rummaged through cupboards to pass down family belongings. No one said, "You are an adult now." They just were.

On the flight home, Deb found a paperback book nestled behind the flight magazine. Soon she was reading Cynthia Kaplan's memoir, *Why I'm Like This* (2003). After reflecting on summer camp, dating, and the quirks of her family members, Kaplan recounted a nearly universal experience that marks impending adulthood:

One of the hardest things about growing up is how one day it suddenly dawns on you that your parents are human. It hadn't occurred to you before. Why should it have? But then something happens, some *thing* happens, and the veil drops. It may have been totally insignificant, like the way your mother ran her finger around the lip of her wineglass at dinner parties as if she were one of those water-glass musicians, or how your father mixed Bosco straight into the milk carton and didn't tell

> "We have not passed that subtle line between childhood and adulthood until we move from the passive voice to the active voice—that is, until we have stopped saying 'It got lost,' and say, 'I lost it.'"
>
> Sidney J. Harris

anyone else. Or it could have been something huge, like the night not long ago when your mother told you she felt like her dad was the only person who ever loved her exactly as she was. Or the moment you realized your father was truly *incapable* of changing, even to save his own life. These are just moments, really, blips on the parental screen, during which they reveal their humanity, and that they are in the world, flailing about as helplessly as everyone else, everyone who is *not* your parents. Blowing it. Surviving. Hanging on by their nails. That they are at once more spectacularly resourceful and more deeply flawed than you might ever have imagined inspires scorn and admiration, two emotions you'd always reserved for nonrelatives. But, happily, between the blips, they are just the same as they have always been, annoying, yet impeccably dressed, and you breathe a sigh of relief. It is too painful for them to be human. (pp. 98–99)

Deb put the book in her lap, looked over at her children, and remembered when her view of her *own* parents began to change. She knew that Lin and Bret weren't adults because they were financially independent (they weren't) or because they'd become parents themselves (they hadn't). They were adults because they knew her weaknesses as well as she knew theirs—because they were just three people now, sharing this flight together.

WHEN DOES ADULTHOOD BEGIN? Most Americans say that graduating from high school or college, obtaining full-time employment, and supporting a family mark the transition to adulthood. According to survey results, people expect these events to occur between 21 and 25 years of age (Smith, 2003). Psychologists call the years between 18 and 25 **emerging adulthood**, a time when most people are too old to be adolescents yet not quite independent enough to be full-fledged adults (Arnett, 2000). Bret and Lin didn't suddenly become adults on their trip to Maine, but the trip did highlight their growing independence and changing relationship to their mother and grandparents. (Like so much else in development, becoming an adult is a process that occurs over time, with individual journeys occurring on somewhat different timetables.)

Emerging adulthood has been called a product of modern times, a stage that arose as more young people delayed financial independence to attend college. It is more accurate, though, to say that definitions of adulthood have fluctuated throughout history. In England, for example, a statute from 1563 established a 7-year period of apprenticeship on the grounds that "until a man grows unto 23 years, he for the most part, though not always, is wild, without judgement, and not of sufficient experience to govern himself" (Best, 2005). Even in the 1500s, a young man in his early 20s was not considered a full-fledged adult.

Is there something special about the early 20s that defines adulthood? Are the 30s and 40s a time of continued growth, continuity, or decline? As you will see in this two-chapter section, it is more accurate to think about the first 30 years of adulthood as a continuous journey rather than a series of separate stages. Most developmental changes are gradual throughout this period of life, so differences between a healthy 45-year-old and most 25-year-olds are subtle. Moreover, the transitions covered in the next chapter—including the challenges of starting new careers and new relationships—are challenges that are no longer tightly linked to specific ages. To begin, in this chapter we profile the "raw materials" of adulthood by reviewing the fundamental changes we experience between 20 and 50 years of age—a period that begins with the emergence of adulthood and ends after 30 years of learning, love, dreams, and disappointments.

emerging adulthood The time between 18 and 25 years when most people are too old to be adolescents, yet not independent enough to be full-fledged adults.

Our Bodies from 20 to 50

There is a reason why grandparents look at their adult grandchildren with pride and longing: Physical maturity and motor performance peak in the 20s, when most people are healthy, energetic, and eager to explore. Families around the world rely on young adults for jobs that require strength and stamina, such as launching boats and bringing in harvests. And if grandparents think back to their 20s and 30s, most smile about a time when they were also beautiful and strong.

But nature doesn't hold fast to the joys of youth. **Senescence,** the gradual physical decline that occurs with age, begins almost as soon as growth has ceased. Some physical abilities are already declining by 20, whereas others start their gradual descent by 30. Yet most young adults barely notice this aging process. Early aging is easy to overlook because changes are too small to affect routine activities. Also, genetic and lifestyle differences alter the timing of change, so some people are still improving functions that respond to practice even while others are showing signs of decline.

The physical consequences of early aging are easier to spot among elite* athletes, a small group of people who constantly push against limits and monitor performance. Because practice builds skill, "personal bests" usually occur after athletes have already reached their physical peaks (Ericsson, 1990). On average, peak performance occurs earlier for sports that require immediate strength and speed and later for sports that are won by accumulating small motor advantages over longer periods of time (Schulz & Curnow, 1988). As a result, 800- to 1500-meter runners peak around age 25 for males and 27 for females. But as distance increases, so does peak age—to 27 for males in a 3-kilometer race (29 for women) and 29 for males in a 10-kilometer race (31 for women) (Horwill, 2004). Similarly, many competitive cross-country skiers are in their 30s, and some celebrities—such as Martina Navratalova, Tiger Woods, and Lance Armstrong—enjoyed their greatest fame long after they had reached the physical peak set by nature.

Baseball statistics illustrate these principles. As you can see in Figure 12.1, stolen base percentage (which relies on speed) peaks between 25 and 27 years, whereas least walks per inning pitched (which reflects precision) improves through the late 30s. For all performance indicators, high-ability players (such as those elected into the Hall of Fame) peak later than average players do (Schulz et al., 1994).

Athletes are not the only individuals who reach their physical primes between 20 and 30 years. As you will read next, the human body starts to lose vigor at a surprisingly young age.

Growth, Strength, and Appearance

Most people reach their adult heights by late adolescence, typically by 17 years for girls and 19 for boys (Malina & Bouchard, 1991). Some late-maturing boys add noticeable height during their early 20s (Tanner, 1990), but height is generally

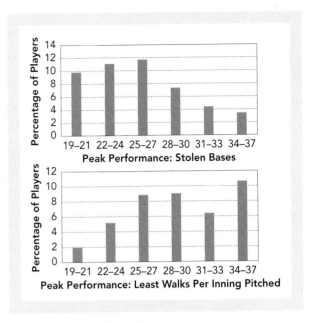

FIGURE 12.1 Peak performance.

In baseball, as in other sports, peak performance occurs earlier for skills that require explosive speed (such as stealing bases) than for skills that depend more on coordination and precision (such as pitching without walking batters). The mean age of peak performance is 27 to 30 across a set of ten baseball skills.

---

*Elite: A group of people who enjoy superior performance or status.

senescence The gradual physical decline that occurs with age (i.e., the process of getting old).

basal metabolism The number of calories a resting body needs to survive.

stable throughout early adulthood. Then, some time after 30, people begin to lose height as disks between the spinal vertebrae shrink and then the bones themselves. As a result, males lose about half an inch (1.3 centimeters) of height between 30 and 50 years, while females lose slightly more (Schulz & Salthouse, 1999).

The shape of the body also evolves during adulthood. The famous "freshman 15" refers to weight gain associated with residence hall food, but muscle and fat continue to accumulate in the early 20s even if people are healthy eaters. A young woman can expect her breasts and hips to reach adult size by the middle of the college years, while a young man can expect to develop more muscle in his upper body by this time.

Due to changes in muscle mass, physical strength peaks between 18 and 29 years and declines a little by 40 to 45 years (Aoyagi & Shephard, 1992; Bächman et al., 1995; Kallman, Plato, & Tobin, 1990). Afterward, there is about a 5 percent loss of strength per decade as fat gradually replaces muscle fiber. But throughout adulthood, people who maintain muscle mass by engaging in weight-bearing exercise appear younger than their softer-looking friends.

When muscle mass decreases, there is a corresponding decrease in **basal metabolism**, which is the number of calories a resting body needs to survive. Basal metabolism slows by about 3 percent every 10 years starting in early adulthood, so people usually require fewer calories to maintain weight as they age. As a result, adults who fail to adjust what they eat often start packing on pounds. However, there are no large declines in basal metabolism among physically active people, such as distance runners and swimmers, who can eat well and stay trim (van Pelt et al., 1997, 2001).

You have probably noticed that some adults look much younger or older than they really are. Genes play a role in this variation, but lifestyle is important as well. Consider wrinkles. Our first lines usually appear on the forehead by age 30, followed by the gradual appearance of "crow's feet" around the eyes and lines between the nostrils and lip corners. These creases are caused by a loss of fat cells from the inner layer of skin, deterioration of collagen and elastin (two protein fibers that provide support and elasticity for the skin), and decreases in the skin's ability to hold moisture. Wrinkling is inevitable, but smoking and sun exposure significantly speed up the process by damaging collagen fibers, as shown in Figure 12.2 (Contet-Audonneau, Jeanmaire, & Pauly, 1999; Lahmann et al., 2001). Because most significant sun damage occurs during adolescence and early adulthood, it is never too soon to prevent wrinkles—and skin cancer—by wearing a daily sunscreen.

While women are fretting about wrinkles, men are more often upset by early balding. About 95 percent of hair loss cases are *male pattern baldness*, a type of balding in which the hairline recedes at the temples and the top of the head. Baldness can begin anytime after puberty, but about 25 percent of men begin to bald by 30. Balding is largely determined by heredity, which explains why European Americans are four times more likely to bald than their African American neighbors. Many women also experience hair loss, although usually to a lesser extent and not until after age 40 (Hordinsky, 2003). Both sexes also lose cells that produce pigment in the hair follicles as they age. Some people sprout

FIGURE 12.2 Lifestyle and aging.

These identical wins shared their genes but not their lifestyles. After years of sun exposure and smoking, Gay (left) looks older than her sister Gwyn. According to researcher Nancy Segal, the twins were not aware that they looked different.

SOURCE: Segal (1999).

their first gray hairs in their 20s, whereas a few are virtually gray-free until their mid-70s. For most, however, the graying process speeds up noticeably between 40 and 50 years.

Basic Physical Functions

Most body systems reach peak performance between 25 and 30 years of age, then decline at a rate of about 1 percent per year. Specific trends vary as a function of the system and your lifestyle choices, such as the frequency and type of physical activity you enjoy (Gabbard, 2004). But although the early signs of aging are measurable, they are also subtle, so most people do not have to adjust their lifestyles to accommodate the declines that occur between 20 and 50 years.

VISION. Visual changes are one of the most noticeable consequences of the early stages of aging. Serious conditions are rare in early to middle adulthood, but there is a large increase from 20 to 50 in the number of people who rely on glasses or contact lenses to see well. Often people who developed myopia (a blurring of distant objects) as children experience a worsening of this condition during their 20s and 30s, while other people develop the condition for the first time (Goss et al., 1997; Kikukawa, Yagura, & Akamatsu, 1999).

By 40, the lens, the part of the eye that changes shape to bring objects into focus, begins to lose its ability to adjust. The lens is made of *epithelial tissue*—the same type of tissue found in skin, hair, and nails. Because this tissue grows throughout life, the lens becomes increasingly dense and inflexible as new cell layers form. Thus all adults eventually develop some degree of *presbyopia* (meaning "old eyes"), a condition in which close objects appear blurry. When presbyopia first becomes apparent (usually between 40 and 50 years of age), people adjust by holding reading material away from their bodies. After this strategy is no longer effective, most of those who already wear glasses for distance face the annoying task of adjusting to *bifocals*: glasses with one prescription on top for distant objects and another on the bottom for near work. Those who do not already use glasses end up buying reading glasses.

HEARING. The hearing losses that are so apparent in the elderly actually begin decades earlier. Figure 12.3 shows the change in hearing as a function of age for an easy task (understanding clear speech signals) and two difficult tasks (listening with voices in the background and listening to speech that is interrupted eight times per second). Most people still have good hearing for normal speech in their 40s, but many have minor difficulty when signals are unclear. This is why families are more likely to disagree about the television volume when the group includes young and older adults.

It used to be that people began to develop noise-related hearing loss between 40 and 50 years of age. But modern life is so noisy that many people now show diminished hearing by young adulthood. For example, one study found hearing losses among 18- to 24-year-old men who frequently listened to loud music or had worked in a noisy occupation for 6 months or more (Job, Raynal, & Rondet, 1999).

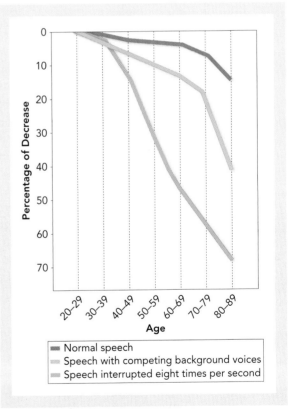

FIGURE 12.3 Understanding speech during adulthood.

The ability to interpret speech has already declined by the time people reach their 40s. Difficulties are greater in noisy environments and when signals are unclear. By midlife, some people are already setting phone and television volumes higher.

SOURCE: Bergman et al. (1976).

Permanent hearing loss can occur whenever you are exposed to noise at 110 decibels or higher for more than a minute or to prolonged exposure to any noise above 90 decibels (National Institute on Deafness and Other Communication Disorders, 2004). To evaluate your risk, think about how often you experience the following noises:

▶ Rock concerts and firecrackers: 140 decibels

▶ Loud bass in cars (when other cars can feel the vibration) and snowmobiles: 120 decibels

▶ A chainsaw: 110 decibels

▶ Lawn mowers and motorcycles: 90 decibels

Because the harmful effects of noise accumulate throughout life, even young adults should minimize their exposure to noise and regularly wear ear protection for noisy activities (American Hearing Research Foundation, 2004).

MANAGING PHYSICAL CHALLENGES. Distance bikers know how it feels when the body is challenged. The first 10 minutes of a ride feel surprisingly difficult as the body makes numerous adjustments to deliver more oxygen and nutrients to muscles. Then a state of homeostasis, or balance, is achieved, and the rider is "in the groove" until fatigue sets in. Afterward, there is a predictable period of recovery, followed by the urge to ride again.

As we leave young adulthood, everyone gradually reacts more slowly and less efficiently to all phases of this process. Older bodies take longer to achieve homeostasis, have difficulty maintaining a high state of performance, and recover more slowly afterward. As adulthood progresses, this package of changes is a major reason why people more often opt for going to bed early rather than partying all night.

A number of physical changes contribute to decreased stamina. Less air is taken into the lungs during strenuous exercise as we age, so a 50-year-old may breathe in the same volume of air as a 10- to 13-year-old child does (Gabbard, 2004). Over time, the amount of oxygen delivered to the blood decreases, the ability of the heart to move blood through the body declines, and the body becomes less efficient at clearing the by-products of metabolic activity. These changes do not interfere with the ability to perform routine tasks between 20 and 50 years, but we gradually feel more strain from challenging ones. For example, one measure of stamina is the number of pounds people can turn with a weighted crank and still have their heart rate return to normal after 2 minutes of rest; on this task, performance decreases about 15 percent between 30 and 50 (Schulz & Salthouse, 1999).

BONE HEALTH STARTS EARLY. After Sonya had a minor spill on her bike, she was startled to discover that bones in both of her arms had cracked. At 37 years of age, Sonya thought she was too young for her bones to be so fragile.

Bone health is a good reminder that the choices we make early in adulthood can influence our quality of life decades down the road. The body continuously removes old bone and creates new bone through *bone remodeling*, a process that replaces about 20 percent of our living bone tissue each year. Growth occurs during childhood and adolescence as new bone forms faster than old bone is removed (Monson et al., 2002). But after our bones have stopped growing larger, they continue to build mass by increasing density and, therefore, strength. Because peak densities are reached by 20 to 29 years of age, early adulthood is a final opportunity to build strong bones (Henry, Fatayerji, & Eastell, 2004; Nguyen et al., 2001). Then, after a long period of relative stability, declining hormone levels (around 45 years for women and later for men) cause the rate of bone loss to exceed the replacement rate ("Bone remodeling," 2004).

People who fail to build adequate bone density during early adulthood are at risk for **osteoporosis** later in life. Osteoporosis is a painful, crippling condition in which bones become fragile and prone to breaks. (*Osteoporosis* literally means "porous bones.") Women are eight times more likely than men to develop this condition, partly because they start out with smaller bones, but also because women's bodies rely on estrogen—a hormone that declines as they approach 50—to repair bone. In contrast, a higher level of the hormone testosterone protects men from rapid bone loss.

Three lifestyle factors in early and middle adulthood influence the risk of osteoporosis later in life:

▶ *Exercise.* Our bodies respond to weight-bearing exercise by making bones stronger. Weight-bearing exercise is any activity that makes us work against gravity, such as walking, dancing, playing tennis, mowing the lawn, and even bowling. Inactive women are at risk for fragile bones, and thin women (like Sonya) are also in danger because they place less stress on their bones during routine activities.

▶ *A healthy diet.* Calcium is essential for normal bone growth. Dairy products are rich in calcium, as is tofu (a curd made from soybeans), canned fish that contains small bones, dried beans, and some dark green vegetables (including broccoli and cabbage). Conversely, a high-protein diet leeches calcium out of the body (because the kidneys neutralize acidity from excess protein by pushing calcium into the urine). But the body needs many nutrients to absorb and use calcium, so it is important to eat a well-balanced diet during the bone-building years.

▶ *Maintaining a healthy weight.* Women dieters and athletes who train rigorously sometimes lose so much fat that they miss periods, which is a sign that estrogen production has dropped. Because this hormone is necessary for bone growth and replacement, women with a history of dieting or missed periods are at risk for osteoporosis later in life.

To determine how bone friendly your lifestyle is, turn to the short quiz in Table 12.1.

Sexual Function and Reproduction

Sexuality colors many corners of our lives. Desire bonds us to partners, inspires us to be the best we can be, and throws us into the depths of despair. Many adults say that involvement in sports or dance is sexy, whereas others describe career achievements as "sexual." Erotic words dominate the language we use to describe pleasurable experiences, and literature is populated by struggles for love.

Sexual attitudes and behavior are intertwined with relationships, spiritual traditions, and culture. Therefore, in this chapter we will describe only the capacity for sexual function and reproduction during our prime reproductive years; we will discuss the range of sexual behavior in the next chapter, when we focus on variability in development.

These young adults are doing more than just building attractive muscles—they are putting stress on their bones that will prompt their bodies to build denser, stronger bones.

osteoporosis A painful and often crippling condition in which bones become fragile and prone to breaks. (*Osteoporosis* literally means "porous bones.")

TABLE 12.1 Risk Factors for Osteoporosis in Women

A woman can determine her risk of osteoporosis by answering the following questions. The more "yes" responses she has, the higher her risk is.

Risk Factor	Explanation
Are you over 45, or have you experienced surgical menopause before the age of 45?	The risk of osteoporosis increases when hormone production declines prior to menopause.
Do you have fair skin?	Caucasian and Asian women have a higher risk of osteoporosis than African American and Hispanic women do. However, a significant percentage of African American and Hispanic women develop osteoporosis, so all women should take measures to prevent bone loss.
Has your mother or a sister been diagnosed with osteoporosis, or have any elderly females in your family developed an abnormal curve in the spine as they aged?	Genetic differences contribute to peak bone density and osteoporosis.
Are you small-boned or thin?	Gradual bone loss later in life has a greater impact on individuals who start out with smaller bones. Furthermore, thin individuals place less stress on their bones, so their bones are not stimulated to build density.
Do you engage in weight-bearing exercise several times per week?	Exercise stimulates increased bone density.
Do you have a low-calcium or high-protein diet?	Calcium is necessary for building bone, but excess protein causes the kidneys to spill calcium into the urine.
Are you a frequent dieter, or have you ever dieted so much that you skipped your period?	Stringent dieting reduces the nutrient intake and hormone production necessary for building bone.
Do you avoid spending time outdoors?	Vitamin D, which is produced when the skin is exposed to sunlight, is necessary for the body to absorb and utilize calcium.
Has your doctor ever told you that medications you have taken for an extended period of time may interfere with calcium absorption?	Certain medications, including insulin, diuretics, and anti-coagulants, can interfere with bone replacement.

SOURCES: Danielson et al. (1999); Geller, Graf, & Dyson-Washington (2003); Wilkins & Goldfeder (2004).

SEXUAL RESPONSIVENESS. The human sexual response occurs in the following predictable sequence (Masters & Johnson, 1966; Westheimer & Lopater, 2005):

▶ *The excitement phase.* Erotic feelings gradually build during the excitement phase as heart rate and blood pressure increase. In women, blood accumulates in vaginal blood vessels and secretions lubricate the vagina; in men, the penis becomes erect.

▶ *The plateau phase.* Sexual tension heightens during the plateau phase. The opening of the vagina tightens in women and the testes draw closer to the body in men.

▶ *The orgasm phase.* Both men and women experience orgasm as pleasurable muscular contractions. Women experience a series of contractions in the vagina, whereas men experience rhythmic contractions throughout the pelvic area as they ejaculate (expel semen).

▶ *The resolution phase.* As tissue swelling subsides, a return to the prearousal state occurs. Men enter a *refractory period*—a period of time that must elapse before they can experience another erection.

Although men and women share this common sexual process, the sexes differ in the timing of age-related change. If "sexual peak" is defined by the ability to copulate fast and often, then men reach their peaks around age 18 (Kinsey, Pomeroy, & Martin, 1948). Young men arouse rapidly and often experience erections just from thinking about sex or looking at erotic images. Beginning about age 30, testosterone levels decline at a rate of about 1 percent each year while the rate of physical conditions that interfere with sexual performance—including diabetes, obesity, and high cholesterol levels—increases (Fisch, 2005). As a result of normal changes and disease, men gradually experience fewer "unwanted" erections, arouse more slowly, and become more dependent on explicit stimuli or touch to achieve an erection. They also notice that the penis softens more quickly after ejaculation and the refractory period becomes longer. Among healthy men, sexual slowing is rarely dramatic even at 40 years, but these changes become more noticeable by 50 and beyond (Bullough & Bullough, 1994).

Women also take longer to arouse as they age, particularly after hormones decline in midlife. But unlike men, women say their sexuality peaks in the early to mid-30s, which is the age when they describe themselves as most lustful, seductive, and sexually active (Schmitt et al., 2002). One clue to why this famous sex difference exists is that men and women interpret "sexual peak" differently, with men focusing on sexual *performance* while women focus on desire and sexual *satisfaction* (Barr, Bryan, & Kenrick, 2002; Schmitt et al., 2002). There are many reasons why women's satisfaction might improve after age 18. Early experiences with heterosexual sex can be disappointing because women arouse more slowly than men and are less often satisfied by intercourse alone. As they gain experience, though, women learn more about how their bodies work, become less inhibited about sex, and learn to communicate their sexual needs. Correspondingly, their partners are also likely to be older, which means they are also more relaxed and knowledgeable about lovemaking.

FERTILITY. Age-related changes in *fertility*—the ability to conceive a child—are also different for men and women. Men bolt out of the reproductive gate with an abundant supply of sperm and stay in the race for a surprisingly long time. Only 2.5 percent of men are completely impotent by 45 to 49 years of age (meaning they cannot maintain an erection sufficient for intercourse), and many have sufficient sexual function and mobile sperm to father children well into their 60s and beyond. Nevertheless, it does take a man longer to impregnate a woman with each passing year. Sperms' ability to move forward quickly and efficiently, which is called *progressive motility*, declines by about 3 percent each year starting in the 20s, and sperm volume also declines (Eskenazi et al., 2003). As a result, the odds of conceiving within 6 months of trying decrease 2 percent for each year after a man is over 24 years of age, regardless of the age of his partner (Ford, 2000).

Unlike men, women rarely conceive naturally after 45 because they have a limited supply of sex cells in their ovaries. These cells begin to die even before a female is born, causing a population of 6 to 7 million cells in the embryo to drop to only 2 to 3 million by birth. At puberty, only 300,000 remain. Throughout young adulthood, 30 to 40 immature oocytes, each in a small sack called a follicle, compete to become dominant during each menstrual cycle. By the late 30s and 40s, the quality of aging oocytes has deteriorated markedly. To compensate, women's bodies increase the chance of finding a healthy follicle by stimulating more oocytes to compete, leading to rapid loss (Petrozza, 2004).

For most women, the reproductive changes that occur during their 20s and 30s make conception increasingly less likely during any given menstrual cycle—but not

perimenopause The 4 to 6 years before a woman's last menstrual period when she often fails to ovulate and the hormone levels necessary to support a pregnancy are declining. Symptoms of perimenopause include irregular menstrual cycles, heavier or lighter periods, and water retention.

menopause The end of menstruation and the ability to conceive a child. The average age of menopause is 51 years. However, some women experience menopause before they are 40, whereas others continue having periods until they are almost 60.

impossible. Therefore, the percentage of women who are completely unable to conceive stays about 1 percent during these decades of life. Nonetheless, the rate of *infertility*—which is the failure to achieve pregnancy after 1 year of unprotected intercourse—does increase. Only 8 percent of women between 19 and 26 years of age fail to conceive after 1 year of trying, compared to 18 percent of 35- to 39-year-olds (Dunson, Baird, & Colombo, 2004). Also, pregnancies that occur later in life are more likely to end with a miscarriage, largely due to poor quality oocytes that result in a higher number of zygotes with chromosomal abnormalities (Nybo Andersen et al., 2000).

In their late 30s or 40s, most women enter a reproductive phase called **perimenopause** (also called the "change of life" or the *climacteric*, a word that means "turning point"). Now they sometimes fail to ovulate and experience declines in the hormones that support a pregnancy. A variety of symptoms can occur during the 4- to 6-year transition before periods stop altogether, including irregular menstrual cycles, heavier or lighter periods, and water retention. Perimenopause ends with **menopause**, when pregnancy is impossible because ovulation and menstrual periods have ceased. (By definition, menopause has arrived if a woman has not had a menstrual period for 1 year.) The average age of menopause is 51 years, but some women enter menopause in their 30s whereas others menstruate throughout their 50s or, occasionally, beyond. (You'll read more about menopause in Chapter 14.)

Now that people are waiting longer to start families, an increasing number of couples are relying on medical technologies to help them conceive. Read about one couple's experience in our next special feature entitled "Beating the Odds: Making Babies in a High-Tech World."

INNOVATIONS

Assisted reproductive technology (ART) is responsible for about 1 percent of births in the United States. Couples who elect to use ART have decided to accept some risks, including a higher probability of twins and fetal malformations.

BEATING THE ODDS: MAKING BABIES IN A HIGH-TECH WORLD

At the age of 40, writer Judith Newman and her 66-year-old husband, John, welcomed Gus and Henry into the world—after 7 years of fertility treatment and $70,000 in medical bills. The diary of her experiences, published as a humor book, recounts the harrowing world of a Manhattan "momasaurus"—a world where older first-time mothers, often toting twins, vie for bragging rights and keys to private playgrounds (J. Newman, 2004).

Increasingly, people who want to be parents are turning to physicians to help them conceive. If couples are young, time is all they usually need. The majority of healthy young couples who failed to get pregnant after a year successfully conceive during the following year (Dunson et al., 2004), and most of the remaining cases can be treated by medical therapies that correct hormonal or structural problems. For instance, surgery can open blocked fallopian tubes (so that egg and sperm can meet) and repair varicose veins in the testes (which kill sperm by raising tissue temperature). Other problems, such as abnormal cervical mucus, can be bypassed simply by injecting processed semen from a partner or donor into the uterus.

A minority of would-be parents turn to *assisted reproductive technology* (ART). ART refers to a range of techniques for overcoming infertility by handling oocytes and sperm in the laboratory. Each year, more than 100,000 ART procedures are performed in the United States alone, resulting in about 1 percent of all births (Wright et al., 2005).

Judith and John conceived their twins during their fourth attempt at one form of ART: *in vitro fertilization* (IVF). Judith took a drug that caused multiple oocytes to mature, and then the eggs were surgically removed and mixed with sperm in a Petri dish. (*In vitro* is Latin for "in glass.") Some of the embryos that were dividing normally were then placed directly into her uterus. IVF results in a live delivery about 29 percent of the time—higher than the 20 percent chance that a reproductively healthy couple has of conceiving and carrying a pregnancy to term in any given month. But despite these optimistic chances, the high cost of IVF (about $12,400 a cycle in 2004) prevents many couples from taking advantage of this technique (American Society for Reproductive Medicine, 2004).

IVF is one of several related techniques. During a procedure called *gamete intrafallopian transfer* (GIFT), a physician surgically removes eggs and places them back into the fallopian tube with sperm. (This technique is preferred by religious and ethnic groups that oppose fertilization outside the woman's body.) Another, called *zygote intrafallopian transfer* (ZIFT), involves in vitro fertilization followed by embryo transfer into a fallopian tube. These two techniques initially had higher success rates than IVF, but improvements in IVF have increased its success and made it the most widely used of the three procedures. If the male has too few sperm, an individual sperm cell can be injected into the egg during *intracytoplasmic sperm injection* (VCSI). Thanks to this technique, one man who survived testicular cancer experienced the birth of his son 21 years after his sperm cells were frozen (Reaney, 2004).

The decision to attempt ART can be a difficult one. For example, about 35 percent of IVF pregnancies involve twins or higher order multiples, which substantially increase the risk of prematurity, low birth weight, and the medical problems associated with these conditions. In addition, babies produced by in vitro procedures have an increased rate of genetic modifications and fetal malformations (Hansen et al., 2002; Silver et al., 1999).

Judith and John faced this side of ART when doctors discovered that the blood supply to Baby A had slowed at 28 gestational weeks. The couple learned that the twins would live if doctors delivered them right away, but the early birth could leave them permanently damaged. Judith and John had a choice: They could give the twins more time to grow, but then one—or both—could die. "All I knew was, Let's roll the dice," Judith recalled about their decision to wait (J. Newman, 2004, p. 51). Happily, Henry and Gus were born healthier than expected, at 3 pounds, 2 ounces and 3 pounds, 11 ounces.

Not all ART-assisted births end so well, however. As we saw in Chapter 3, even premature infants who are carefully monitored are at risk for a variety of medical and developmental complications. But for parents who are struggling to conceive, the promise of ART and its potential rewards are often worth the financial burden and risks. ◆

The number of multiple births is increasing as more families are turning to assisted reproductive technologies.

Brain Development

During the trip described in this chapter's opening story, the rental car bill was twice as large as Deb and her family had expected. You might have encountered the reason yourself: a $7 per day fee to add a second driver and an additional *$25 per day* because Bret was less than 25 years of age. Bret could drive, vote, and drink, but—as far as the rental car company was concerned—he was 3 years away from adulthood.

Is there any reason for car rental companies to think that adulthood finally arrives around 25 years? According to neuroscientists, the answer is "yes." It is true that brain development during adulthood is less dramatic than earlier development was, but change continues. One trend is an increase in the proportion of white matter (the interior layer of the brain that houses the neurons that connect various parts of the brain) to gray matter (the outer layer that is responsible for information processing). White matter gets its color from myelin, the fatty sheath that coats axons. As fibers that interconnect brain regions continue to myelinate, information transmission gradually becomes more efficient (Sowell et al., 2003). Meanwhile, the pruning of cortical (higher brain center) gray matter that was occurring during adolescence continues at least into the early 20s (Pfefferbaum et al., 1994). Overall, increased white matter and decreased gray matter result in a faster, more efficient brain by young adulthood.

Because different brain regions show different courses of development, the brain does not suddenly "mature" at any specific age. Nevertheless, many scientists believe that brain development is basically complete by early adulthood, some time between 22 and 25 years of age (Bower, 2004). Young adults are more dependable than most adolescents because brain regions associated with mature behavior complete development so late. For example, in Chapter 10 we discussed the *anterior cingulate cortex* (ACC), an area that has tracts connecting the limbic system (the brain's emotional center) with the prefrontal cortex (the brain's center for planning and reasoning). Recall that the ACC, which continues to develop into early adulthood, is involved in handling conflicting response demands, detecting errors, and evaluating the emotional significance of events (Davies, Segalowitz, & Gavin, 2004; Luu et al., 2003). Clearly, these are critical abilities that help a 25-year-old manage difficult jobs, understand complex social interactions and, of course, drive.

How Important Is Age?

In a youth-oriented culture such as our own, it can be disturbing to learn that age-related declines begin in the 20s. But before you conclude that your best years will soon be behind you (or already are!), remember that information about average performance is just that—an average. One of the most striking conclusions from longitudinal studies is just how misleading these averages can be. In the Baltimore Longitudinal Studies of Aging, for example, relatively few individuals had patterns of aging that matched the trends produced by averaging over individuals (Shock, 1985).

The truth is that age is a poor predictor of performance. At any given age, genetic differences, the presence of medical conditions, and lifestyle factors create huge differences from person to person—differences we will be exploring in more

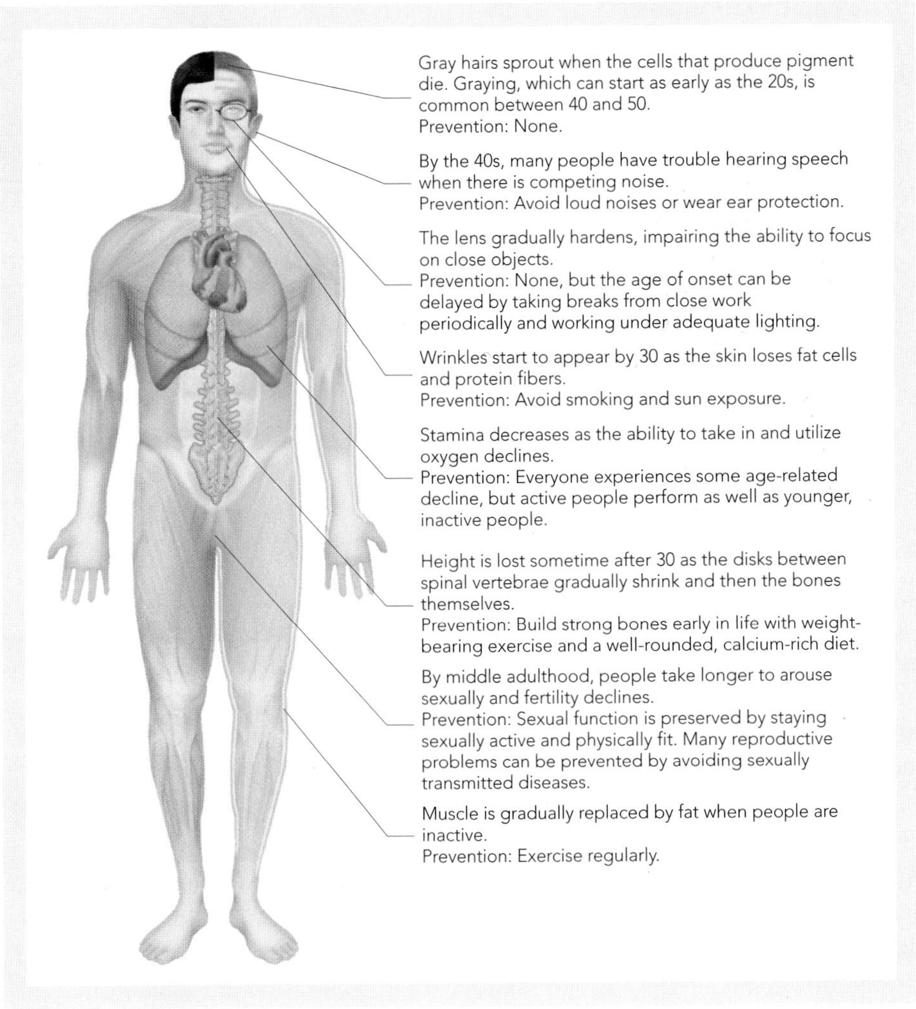

Gray hairs sprout when the cells that produce pigment die. Graying, which can start as early as the 20s, is common between 40 and 50.
Prevention: None.

By the 40s, many people have trouble hearing speech when there is competing noise.
Prevention: Avoid loud noises or wear ear protection.

The lens gradually hardens, impairing the ability to focus on close objects.
Prevention: None, but the age of onset can be delayed by taking breaks from close work periodically and working under adequate lighting.

Wrinkles start to appear by 30 as the skin loses fat cells and protein fibers.
Prevention: Avoid smoking and sun exposure.

Stamina decreases as the ability to take in and utilize oxygen declines.
Prevention: Everyone experiences some age-related decline, but active people perform as well as younger, inactive people.

Height is lost sometime after 30 as the disks between spinal vertebrae gradually shrink and then the bones themselves.
Prevention: Build strong bones early in life with weight-bearing exercise and a well-rounded, calcium-rich diet.

By middle adulthood, people take longer to arouse sexually and fertility declines.
Prevention: Sexual function is preserved by staying sexually active and physically fit. Many reproductive problems can be prevented by avoiding sexually transmitted diseases.

Muscle is gradually replaced by fat when people are inactive.
Prevention: Exercise regularly.

FIGURE 12.4 Early physical aging.

From top to toe, all adults are slowly aging.

[handwritten note: exercise & diet are the major ways to delay ageing]

detail in the next chapter. For example, active 50-year-olds score like inactive 35-year-olds when tested for their ability to take in and utilize oxygen (Fitzgerald et al., 1997). Similarly, sexual functioning inevitably declines with age, but men who remain healthy and sexually active are unlikely to be troubled by sexual problems (Meuleman, 2002). Other signs of aging, such as the decline in muscle mass, can actually be reversed (in this case, by starting a weight-training program) (Nelson et al., 1994).

To capture the fact that aging is caused by inevitable biological changes and lifestyle factors, scientists distinguish between two types of aging. **Primary aging** is the gradual process of bodily decline that is genetically programmed to occur in all humans. In contrast, **secondary aging** refers to bodily declines due to genetic defects and environmental factors, such as diseases, lack of physical and mental activity, and injuries. Turn to Figure 12.4 for a review of early physical aging and strategies for preventing secondary aging.

[handwritten note: aging & disease are not because of each other disease is from lifestyle & genetics]

primary aging The gradual process of bodily decline that is genetically programmed to occur in all humans.

secondary aging Bodily declines that are due to genetic defects and environmental factors, such as diseases, inactivity, and injuries.

>>> M E M O R Y   M A K E R S <<<

Match each term to the phrase that describes it:

1. primary aging
2. senescence
3. presbyopia
4. osteoporosis
5. perimenopause
6. emerging adulthood
7. secondary aging

(a) The 4 to 6 years before a woman's last menstrual period.

(b) A condition in which bones become fragile.

(c) Bodily declines due to genetic defects and environmental factors.

(d) The gradual physical decline that occurs with age.

(e) The time between 18 and 25 years.

(f) Bodily decline that is genetically programmed to occur.

(g) Difficulty seeing near objects due to age-related changes in the lens.

[1-f; 2-d; 3-g; 4-b; 5-a; 6-e; 7-c]

Expanding Minds

Elaine, who was in her 40s, approached one of us after the first day of class: She had just returned to college and was afraid she wouldn't be able to keep up with the younger students. Do people gradually lose their intellectual edge as they pass through adulthood, or does experience make them better thinkers and problem solvers? After reviewing cognitive development during early and middle adulthood, we will describe what a professor might tell students like Elaine.

Is There Room to Grow?

The Greek philosopher Plato (c. 427?–347 B.C.) believed that rationality was the key to virtue and happiness—but a key that few people attained. According to Plato, most adults are fundamentally irrational and the victims of passion; only natural talent, nurtured by a rigorous education, would liberate some from a lifetime of ignorance.

Generations of philosophers and cognitive psychologists have shared Plato's belief that rational thought is difficult to achieve. As we saw in Chapter 10, adolescents develop the capacity for logical reasoning, yet they often rely on mental shortcuts that lead to less than optimal conclusions. But how does the adult mind fare? Do we continue to grow mentally in adulthood? Or does mental development stall and then decline? Two types of research on thinking during adulthood address these questions: the Piagetian and human judgment perspectives.

PERFORMANCE ON PIAGET'S TASKS. As we saw in Chapter 10, Piaget proposed that people reached the stage of *formal operational thought* during their teenage years. Recall that this is the age when adolescents begin to think abstractly and consider multiple possibilities, so they can work through problems that mystified them just a few years earlier.

Piaget's ideas were so widely accepted that investigators were puzzled when they tested college students: Typically, about 20 to 40 percent of incoming freshmen either lacked formal operational reasoning altogether or failed to use this type of thinking consistently (Anderson, 2003; Schwebel, 1975). Those students who reasoned concretely tended to struggle in college, and on average they achieved poorer grades than students who were more cognitively advanced (Hudak & Anderson, 1990; Mwamwenda, 1993). But their disappointing grades were not simply the result of lower intelligence or lack of preparation for college because there was almost no relationship between level of reasoning, academic rank in high school, and SAT scores (Schwebel, 1975).

If research on college students failed to support Piaget's claim that formal operational thinking was almost always achieved by late adolescence, it did support Plato's belief in the power of education. At one college, for example, the percentage of concrete thinkers dropped from 22 percent in the freshman year to only 7 percent in the senior year (Anderson, 2003). Of course, the passage of time could account for some of this development, but it is unlikely that maturation alone explains these results because students do not express formal operational thinking across all types of problems. Instead, it is common for students to show an improved ability to think more abstractly and rationally about topic areas they have encountered more frequently. As a result, juniors and seniors perform best when the content of problems relates to their majors (de Lisi & Staudt, 1980).

In response to the question, "Is there room to grow during adulthood?", the answer from studies of formal operational reasoning is a resounding "Yes." And as you'll read next, scientists from another research tradition agree.

JUDGMENT AND DECISION MAKING. You learned in Chapter 10 that normal, educated adolescents do not always reason rationally (Griffin & Kahneman, 2003). Many cognitive scientists believe that systematic biases in thinking—such as a tendency to believe a few personal anecdotes more than data about many people's experiences—reflect the fact that humans often rely on a swifter experiential reasoning system rather than a slower analytical system. As we explained in Chapter 10, experiential reasoning is common when people make personally relevant decisions ("Which class should I take?") or think about complex social situations ("Can I trust him?").

But many of the decisions adults face, such as whether to change jobs or to buy a new home, are best given a more thoughtful approach. How people make medical decisions, invest their money, and estimate the probability of events are some of the day-to-day tasks that human judgment researchers study (Dawes, 2001). Their results reveal three characteristics of judgment and decision making during adulthood:

▸ **Adult reasoning is limited by systematic biases.** Human judgment deviates in predictable ways from mathematical and logical principles. For example, when people are asked to judge which pattern in Figure 12.5 depicts the more random placement of white and black squares, most erroneously say "B." (In fact, "A" is the random pattern.) People's tendency to think there must be a reason for clusters of events leads to some interesting errors in thinking. For example, basketball players are as likely to score after they have missed as they are after they have made a basket, yet many sports fans insist that a few baskets in a row is evidence of a "hot hand" that increases the probability a player will make another basket (Tversky & Gilovich, 2004). The tendency to look for causes that underlie random events is one of dozens of reasoning errors adults face as they try to understand their world (Myers, 2002).

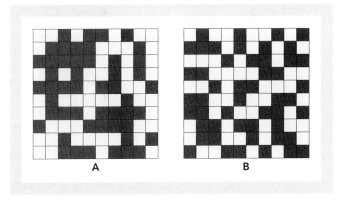

FIGURE 12.5 Everyday irrationality.

Which of these checkerboard patterns represents more random placement of black and white squares? Many people say "B," but the correct answer is "A." Everyday reasoning does not always lead to conclusions that are accurate or logical. Instead, adults have a number of biases in their thinking, including a tendency to think that there must be a reason whenever an event—including a black square, a basketball player making a basket, or the occurrence of a rare type of cancer—happens several times in a row.

SOURCE: Falk & Konold (1997).

▶ *Reasoning is domain specific.* Learning tends to be tied to specific knowledge domains, so people are usually better problem solvers in domains where they have extensive knowledge and experience. For example, experienced chess players are not especially likely to apply their strategies for planning ahead in a chess game to their holiday shopping or their choice of a new car (Ceci, 1996).

▶ *Experience does not always improve judgment.* Reasoning skills do not always improve with experience—even though adults become more confident about their abilities (Dawes, 1996; Garb, 1989). In fact, experience actually hinders performance when people let outcomes from isolated examples override reliable evidence. For example, one cancer specialist reported that he rarely chose a specific drug for ovarian cancer because it hadn't worked with several of his own patients, even though the drug had performed well in large clinical trials. "I think, 'The last time, that lady got *so* sick,'" the physician said. "Bias is very hard. It's easier when you're dealing with test tubes and experimental animals, but when it's real people looking you in the eye, you get wrapped up in their hopes and your hopes for their hopes, and it's *hard*" (Russo, 1999, p. 36). The tendency to base decisions on a small number of personal experiences is one of the systematic biases of thinking that leads people to make poor decisions.

Together with research on Piagetian tasks, these findings suggest how intellectual abilities can continue to blossom during adulthood: As we age, we pick up new information, learn to apply old strategies more efficiently to a broader range of situations, and discover new strategies for making decisions and solving problems. We can also become better at monitoring our decision processes to avoid using mental shortcuts (such as basing decisions on isolated examples) in situations where they might lead to errors.

Two Views of Adult Cognition

Views of intellectual development during adulthood fall into two broad categories: approaches that propose development beyond formal operational reasoning and approaches that view growth as the ability to apply formal operational skills to a wider variety of problems.

POSTFORMAL THOUGHT. The formal problems Piaget studied have a single correct answer that is best discovered by systematically applying rules or procedures. For example, you would certainly figure out what makes a pendulum swing faster (a problem discussed in Chapter 8) if you tested all possible combinations of factors (weight, string length and height, and force of releasing the pendulum). But unlike these sorts of problems, the practical tasks adults usually confront—such as which doctor to see or how to spend a gift of cash—involve opposing values, unknown facts, and social realities that constrain which solutions will work in which contexts. Therefore, some scientists prefer to learn about adult development by studying the types of problems adults grapple with in their everyday lives.

Unlike formal problems, decisions about practical affairs are often solved through **dialectical reasoning**, a process of critical thinking in which conflicting viewpoints are evaluated by considering the evidence for and against both sides. For example, suppose your doctor recommended a popular antidepressant medication to help you overcome symptoms of depression. The idea of taking medication might trouble you, yet the thought of feeling better would probably be appealing.

dialectical reasoning A process of critical thinking in which a person considers conflicting viewpoints by evaluating the evidence for and against both sides.

Faced with this decision, you might mentally list the pros and cons of antidepressants, including information about side effects, effectiveness, and the risk of withdrawal symptoms. Through the process of dialectical reasoning, you would consider the value of both sides of the argument and make a decision. You would also realize that the best decision right now may not be the best decision at some other time or the best decision for a friend of yours who is also depressed.

There is evidence that cognitive skills can grow beyond those that define formal operations into what has been called **postformal thought** (Sinnott, 1998). Postformal thought is not just an extension of formal operational reasoning; instead, it is a qualitatively different achievement. (Postformal thinkers realize that many questions lack a single correct answer, that the search for knowledge is never ending, and that there may be value in seemingly opposing positions.) Postformal thinkers make decisions about whether to take antidepressant drugs, but they also realize that other people might make informed decisions that differ from their own.

Two lines of research illustrate postformal thought. In a groundbreaking study, college counselor and education professor William Perry, Jr., found that students approach the intellectual challenges of college in one of three ways (Perry, 1970, 1981):

▶ **Dualism.** Dualist students reason mostly at the level of concrete operations. These students approach learning as the process of memorizing facts and spitting them back to the professor. The term *dualism*, which means "two elements," describes the either–or nature of their thinking: To the dualist, information is right or wrong, good or bad. Because these students have difficulty understanding how concepts and theories organize facts, their knowledge exists in bits and pieces. As a result, they find it difficult to distinguish main points from supportive information and are frequently overwhelmed by the amount of material. As one student explained, "If teachers would stick more to the facts and do less theorizing one could get more out of their classes" (Perry, 1970, p. 67).

▶ **Relativism.** Relativist students have developed formal operations: They think abstractly and have abandoned the idea that there are absolute truths that apply to every situation. (The term *relative* means "dependent on something else.") Because these students can organize information into concepts, they remember facts as they pertain to larger ideas and are no longer prisoners of rote memorization. As a result, the relativist student can manage the workload, compare different viewpoints, and understand that many ideas have merit. However, a downside to these accomplishments is the possibility of believing that "everything is relative" means "nothing matters." As one student lamented, "You know, in the past months . . . I really wasn't sure there was anything in particular to follow" (Perry, 1970, p. 116).

▶ **Commitments in relativism.** As students progress through college, many find peace in a world of possibilities. Those who have commitments in relativism believe they can make informed decisions even though new information may come along to change their opinion. Once students embrace the idea that different answers are correct in different contexts, they can begin to enjoy an "examined life," that is, the joy of analyzing situations and deciding for oneself. One student described this accomplishment as "grabbing hold of myself and saying, 'This I want, that I don't want, this I am, that I'm not, and I'll be solid about it . . .'" (Perry, 1970, p. 159).

Perry believed that gender, race, and culture influence how people approach learning in various contexts; he also thought that learners always approach knowledge from a variety of different standpoints. Therefore, a student might reason from one

Each day, jury members like these use dialectical reasoning—a type of reasoning that involves weighing information on both sides of an issue—to decide whether a peer was guilty or innocent of a crime.

postformal thought A way of thinking that develops after formal operational reasoning. Postformal thinkers realize that many questions lack a single answer, that the search for knowledge is never ending, and that there may be some value in seemingly opposing positions.

position in psychology class and another in philosophy class. Still, Perry found a general tendency for students' reasoning ability to evolve throughout college.

By interviewing students about controversial issues, educational psychologist Patricia King and her colleague, counselor Karen Kitchener (1994, 2002), also found that college seniors were more likely than freshmen to *evaluate* evidence rather than blindly accept the conclusion of an authority figure. Paralleling Perry's findings, the doctoral students who participated in their research were more likely than college seniors to show *reflective judgment*: the ability to reason dialectically and defend their choices. Perry's stage of commitments in relativism and the idea of reflective judgment are examples of postformal thought—a type of thinking that goes beyond the logical achievements of formal operations.

CRITIQUES OF POSTFORMAL THOUGHT. The concept of postformal thought has considerable appeal, but some researchers doubt whether there is a unified mode of thinking after adolescence. Postformal thought has been criticized for lacking a clear definition and for describing variations in thinking that stem from specific experiences rather than universal stages of development. As a result, one critic suggested abandoning the term *postformal* altogether and speaking simply of "adult cognition" or "adult thought" (Marchand, 2001). Life span researcher K. Warner Schaie agrees (Schaie, 1977-1978; Schaie & Willis, 2000). Schaie does not believe that adults progress beyond the "powerful methods of science" that characterize formal operational reasoning (Schaie & Willis, 2002, p. 347). Instead, what changes are people's priorities: Adults who are building families and careers are focused on using knowledge in ways that will secure long-term goals, middle-aged adults who find themselves in complex organizations develop skills for monitoring various levels of responsibility, and older adults who have few family or work responsibilities focus on problems that are personally meaningful.

Building Everyday Intelligence

The idea that intelligence is best understood by looking at what people actually do has encouraged some scientists to focus on **everyday intelligence** (also called *practical intelligence*), that is, how adults apply their cognitive resources in daily life. Everyday intelligence includes the ability to navigate basic life skills (such as reading medication labels) and skill at solving real-life dilemmas (such as deciding how to get a broken lawn mower fixed).

Performance on formal academic tasks, such as the ability to solve quadratic equations, often declines after young adulthood as people forget some of the material they learned in school (Karsenty, 2002). In contrast, the development of everyday intelligence shows a more complicated pattern of results:

▶ *A high IQ does not guarantee practical intelligence.* IQ scores correlate highly with scores on objective questions of knowledge, such as questions about how to read a map. But when tasks involve more open-ended problems, such as how to get a negligent landlord to make repairs, IQ scores correlate only modestly with performance or not at all (Cornelius & Caspi, 1987; Sternberg, Grigorenko, & Oh, 2001). In other words, adults who were high achievers in school are not always the best performers on the job, where "street smarts" often prevail.

▶ *Performance peaks earlier for traditional academic problems than for tasks involving real-life situations.* In an early demonstration, researchers asked 20- through 79-year-olds to complete a formal reasoning task (discovering which of 42 pictures was the target by asking the fewest number of yes–no questions) and tasks involving practical issues (such as what to do if you were stranded on the highway during a blizzard). Performance on the formal task declined after the 20s, but

everyday intelligence (also called "practical intelligence") The ability to use cognitive resources during daily life. Everyday intelligence includes the ability to navigate basic life skills (such as reading medication labels) and skill at solving real-life dilemmas (such as deciding how to get a broken lawn mower fixed).

performance on the practical tasks improved until the 40s to 50s (Denney & Palmer, 1981).

▶ *No one age group consistently outperforms other age groups.* The developmental course of practical intelligence varies depending on the task and how performance is scored (Berg, 2000; Marsiske & Willis, 1995). In the study we just mentioned, middle-aged adults generated safer and more effective solutions to problems than younger or older adults did. In contrast, performance improved steadily from 20 to 70 years of age on a battery of questions about practical issues in another study, such as how to encourage friends to visit more often (Cornelius & Caspi, 1987). One reason for discrepant results is that adults and children alike perform better on tasks that are familiar to them and problems that are relevant to their age group (Sebby & Papini, 1994; Sternberg et al., 2001).

The years of experience that middle-aged adults have can give them an edge over younger adults when it comes to finding useful solutions on the job.

Taken as a whole, these findings show that practical intelligence involves different skills that develop as a function of one's environment and personal experiences. There is a general trend for people to develop more flexible thinking and more tolerance for ambiguity as they pass through adulthood, but there is variability in problem-solving skill at all ages.

Isolating Mental Abilities

Scientists from the psychometric and information processing traditions try to break cognitive performance down into specific mental abilities. As you'll read next, their results provide even more evidence that patterns of change during adulthood are different for different cognitive skills.

THE PSYCHOMETRIC APPROACH. Psychometric research analyzes performance on standardized tests, including traditional IQ tests. (The term *psychometric* literally means "measuring the mind.") We will discuss individual differences in Chapter 13 when we explore approaches to defining intelligence. For now, let's look at what standardized tests reveal about cognitive development during early and middle adulthood.

Age trends on standardized tests differ depending on how investigators compare ages. The fastest way is a *cross-sectional study* (introduced in Chapter 1), one in which different age groups are tested at one point in time. For example, you can see in Figure 12.6 that cross-sectional scores for inductive reasoning—a type of reasoning in which people infer the general rule that underlies a set of specific examples—are high in the mid-20s and then decline markedly. (Choosing the number or letter that would logically come next in a series of numbers or letters is an example of inductive reasoning.) But before you conclude that reasoning skill peaks when physical abilities peak, read on.

Cross-sectional data are misleading because they are based on different *cohorts,* that is, groups of people who were educated in different historical times. Scores might drop with age because older individuals had less education or received education that was less relevant to the content of the test. In fact, intelligence tests must be renormed periodically because scores increase over time, which is a well-known phenomenon called the *Flynn effect* (Daley et al., 2003;

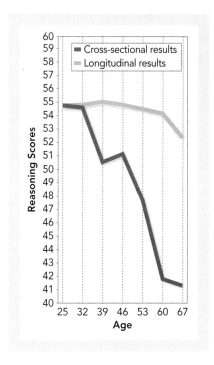

FIGURE 12.6 Cross-sectional versus longitudinal research.
- -
Scores on tests of mental ability drop dramatically with increasing age when cross-sectional results are plotted (scores from different age groups tested at one point in time). In contrast, longitudinal data (data based on following the *same* individuals over time) do not show large drops in performance during early to middle adulthood.

SOURCE: Schaie (1996).

Flynn, 1999). To compensate for performance gains by younger people, the difficulty of intelligence test items is increased periodically to reset the mean. Thus the early decline in Figure 12.6 could be due to *young people performing better* than people used to rather than older people performing worse.

A *longitudinal study*, one that repeatedly tests a single cohort over time, tells a different story. Unlike cross-sectional findings, the longitudinal data in Figure 12.6 suggest that inductive reasoning scores are stable until middle age and do not decline noticeably until 67 years of age. However, these results may be overly optimistic because the people who drop out of longitudinal studies tend to be less educated than those who remain (which inflates mean scores). Then repeated practice with the test might boost the scores of older individuals even more.

Both sets of results in Figure 12.6 are from the Seattle Longitudinal Study, an ambitious study of intellectual abilities that assessed more than 5,000 adults and followed some for as long as 35 years (Schaie, 1996b). The lead investigator, K. Warner Schaie, realized that cross-sectional and longitudinal approaches both have drawbacks. To compensate, he designed the study to include *cross-sequential* methodology (a research design described in Chapter 1): Cohorts of participants were retested over intervals ranging from 7 to 35 years, but new cohorts were continuously added. Therefore, the resulting data set had overlapping waves of longitudinal data. This type of data allowed Schaie to analyze the effects of cohort and time of measurement.

Figure 12.7 shows age trends for five mental abilities (adjusted for cohort and time-of-measurement effects). Notice that performance is stable on most

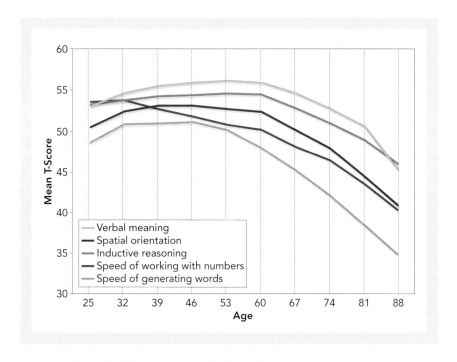

FIGURE 12.7 Mental abilities across adulthood.

These results are from the Seattle Longitudinal Study, an ambitious study that followed numerous groups of individuals longitudinally, from 7 to 35 years, adding new groups as time passed. This *cross-sequential design* allowed the research team to adjust results for unwanted factors that might influence developmental trends, including systematic differences from group to group that are not due to age differences. Notice that most mental abilities are stable during young to middle adulthood.

SOURCE: Schaie (1996b).

tasks until at least age 50. In contrast to cross-sectional findings, most abilities improve until age 40 and do not decline markedly until after 60. The two exceptions both involve declines in speed: how quickly and accurately people solve math problems and how quickly they generate words that fit a rule. These data suggest that normal aging does not seriously affect cognitive performance before 45 to 50 years except in circumstances where speed is critical.

Patterns of performance on standardized tests have led to the theory that mental skill is composed of two primary abilities. **Crystallized intelligence** involves knowledge and verbal skills that accumulate with age, and this type of intelligence grows with education and experience. From early to middle adulthood and even beyond, people's vocabularies and basic knowledge about the world continue to increase. In contrast, **fluid intelligence** is the ability to reason abstractly and solve new problems. As you'll read shortly, this type of intelligence is more dependent on the efficiency of the nervous system—especially how fast the mind can take in and compare information (Cattell, 1971; Geary, 2005; Horn, 1968). Challenging problems that require us to detect patterns and solve unfamiliar problems tap fluid intelligence, and performance on these tasks declines from the early 20s onward. In real-world situations, these two types of intelligence are often related. For example, people who are quick to notice information and make new connections (which involves fluid intelligence) will build a larger knowledge base (thereby augmenting their crystallized intelligence). And many tests, including timed tests of word meanings, tap both speed of processing (fluid intelligence) and knowledge (crystallized intelligence).

THE INFORMATION PROCESSING APPROACH. Information processing researchers identify age-related changes in the specific mental processes that underlie reasoning and decision making by isolating the steps involved in answering various types of questions. For example, consider a test of spatial ability described in Chapter 9: mental rotation. For each trial, people start by looking at a geometric shape (the "standard") and "encode" (develop a mental picture of) that shape. Next they scan a set of shapes that are drawn in different orientations until they find a match. This step requires people to mentally rotate either the standard or the response options. Finally, they respond by pressing a button, touching a screen, or simply saying the correct choice ("B"). By comparing performance when the correct choice is rotated a little versus a lot, the speed of mental rotation can be separated from other mental operations, such as encoding the standard and responding.

Mental rotation results mirror results from reasoning and memory tests: Older adults are slower than younger adults for each processing component, not just one (Salthouse, 1991). Because age differences are not localized in specific components, scientists believe that changes in a few basic processing abilities explain why age differences emerge by middle adulthood for a wide variety of fluid intelligence measures (Berg, 2000).

One candidate for explaining age-related decline is *speed of processing.* Beginning in the early 20s, there is a continuous decline in how fast people complete a wide variety of tasks, such as deciding whether pairs of letters are the same or different and drawing geometric shapes (Park et al., 2002). Slower processing impairs performance on complex reasoning problems because the products of early mental operations fade by the time later operations require them (Salthouse, 1996). Perhaps due to changes in speed of processing, *working memory capacity* also shows a steady decline beginning in the 20s (Salthouse et al., 1989). (Recall from Chapter 8 that working memory capacity refers to the amount you can store in the mental

crystallized intelligence The knowledge and verbal skills that accumulate as you age.

fluid intelligence The ability to reason abstractly and solve new problems.

Dan Sheahan and his son, Tanner, walked side by side for their graduations from Oregon State University. Dan, who returned to school after being laid off at work, joined the growing number of older adults who are attending college to make a new start. "It's been really great going to school with my dad," Tanner said. "We have become close friends."

"scratch pad" that holds the information you need to solve problems.). In fact, the rate of cognitive decline in basic information processing abilities is remarkably steady throughout life, with equivalent changes in speed of processing and working memory between 20 to 30 years and between 50 to 60 years.

What do these findings mean for healthy adults under age 50? For most of life's tasks, the answer is "not much." Although some parents lose when they play video games with their teenagers, success on most day-to-day chores is not affected by small differences in speed. Furthermore, older adults perform better than their young counterparts on tests that measure acquired experiences, such as verbal knowledge tests (Park et al., 2002). During the first half of adulthood, increases in knowledge and life experience often compensate for losses of speed and memory function, at least when people are engaged in practical tasks like planning a party or developing a financial portfolio.

The Total Picture: Elaine's Story

We don't know what Elaine did after she left class, but we can describe a typical series of events. She may have stopped by the financial aid office to fill out scholarship applications, taken a longer route home to avoid school buses, and served as a referee for her son and daughter (who were fighting over the last ice-cream bar when she arrived home). In a single hour, Elaine drew upon a vast array of intelligent behaviors, including cultural knowledge (such as knowing her social security number), spatial processing (to plan her route home), and social problem-solving skills (to deal with the orphaned ice-cream bar).

Because the range of intelligent behaviors is so broad, it is not surprising that there is not a single trend in cognitive performance across adulthood. As we are forgetting some of the "book learning" we gained in school, real-world experience is giving us an advantage when it comes to solving everyday problems. But practical tasks often rely on specialized knowledge, so whether we do well or poorly depends on how familiar we are with a problem's content. During adulthood, our experience in particular domains is a stronger predictor of practical success than our age.

What do these changes mean for students like Elaine? Adults forget some of the academic information they learned in school, so their confidence on academic tasks declines somewhat (Donaldson & Graham, 1999; Karsenty, 2002). Nonetheless, older students generally do well in their classes. On average, nontraditional students report more enthusiasm for learning than traditional students do (Dill & Henley, 1998), and they achieve grades that are equal to or better than younger students in most classes. In one study, for example, community college classes that enrolled a higher percentage of nontraditional students had higher average grades, and—with the exception of mathematics—this result was also true at a nearby public university (Darkenwald & Novak, 1997). Like these students, Elaine should do well in college because she has a lot of knowledge about the world and is a more dialectical thinker (capable of weighing the pros and cons of a decision) than she was in her 20s. The small decline in fluid intelligence that occurs between 20 and 40 could have a minor impact on her ability to learn, but Elaine can improve her success in classes that emphasize abstract problem solving by refreshing her memory for the fundamental material she learned in high school (such as basic mathematical knowledge).

Despite Elaine's worries, most of the challenges she faced in college did not involve cognitive skills. Instead, the most important changes in her life occurred in the emotional and social realms. We will visit Elaine once more after we sketch some typical adult transitions in these facets of life.

>>> **MEMORY MAKERS** <<<

1. Across studies, the percentage of college freshmen who fail tests of formal operational reasoning (or fail to use formal thinking consistently) is about _____ percent.

   (a) 1 to 3   **(b)** 10   **(c)** 20 to 40   **(d)** 70 to 80

2. Perry's stage of *commitments in relativism* and King and Kitchener's concept of *reflective judgment* both describe _____.

   (a) concrete thinking
   (b) formal operational thinking
   (c) postformal thought
   (d) crystallized intelligence

3. _____ intelligence depends on the efficiency of the nervous system, and this type of intelligence tends to _____ during young and middle adulthood.

   (a) Fluid; increase
   (b) Fluid; decrease
   (c) Crystallized; increase
   (d) Crystallized; decrease

[1-c; 2-c; 3-b]

Emotional and Social Development

In addition to worrying about her academic abilities, Elaine felt out of place when she realized she was the only student who had celebrated her 40th birthday. Why did Elaine think age was so important? Like many older students, she assumed her priorities were different than her classmates' priorities, and she was acutely aware of having grown up in a different world. After all, most of the other students had used computers since childhood, had researched their high school papers on the Internet, and had enjoyed more personal freedom than Elaine had been given when she was a young woman. From her vantage point, the rest of the class looked incredibly self-confident and carefree.

Does a person's fundamental outlook on life really change between early and middle adulthood? Was Elaine more similar to her classmates than she imagined, or is there really some psychological distance between generations? To answer these questions, we need to explore what it "feels" like to be an adult—in other words, what developmental issues consume our thoughts, how we view ourselves and our relationships, and how our values change over time.

Ways of Viewing Adulthood

Theories of adult development provide a broad overview of the transitions that occur as we travel through our 20s, 30s, and beyond. Some look at the psychological challenges of adult life, others at the events that punctuate the years of adulthood, and still others at the implications of marching in step or out of step with our culture's idea of what an adult should be doing. Each approach provides ideas that can help you understand the feelings and challenges you face in your own journey through adulthood.

ADULTHOOD AS SEEN THROUGH ERIK ERIKSON'S CRISES. It is common to view development as a series of stages that people pass through as they move from younger to older age groups. We introduced you to the most famous

intimacy versus isolation The sixth phase of life in Erikson's theory (roughly 19 to 40 years) when adults forge meaningful relationships or suffer from a lack of connection.

generativity versus self-absorption and stagnation The seventh phase of life in Erikson's theory when people in middle adulthood (about 40 to 65 years) either focus on production by nurturing, teaching, and leading or become self-absorbed and experience stagnation.

seasons of adulthood The idea that adult life consists of roughly 25-year eras with 5- to 8-year transitions between eras. According to the seasons of adulthood, development involves gains and losses as we progress through repeated periods of stability and change.

Erikson's theory issues

stage theory of life span development in earlier chapters: Erik Erikson's theory of psychosocial development (Erikson, 1950, 1959; Erikson, Erikson & Kivnick, 1986). Recall from Chapter 10 that adolescence is a time when people struggle with Erikson's fifth stage of development: *identity versus role confusion*. Teenagers question their parents' religious and political beliefs, and they experiment with forming their own opinions. As they search for a set of values to guide them throughout life, they also realize that their future "selves" will have occupations and sexual identities. The process of achieving self-identity is the process of identifying with specific values and people from the world of possible values and people.

Young adulthood poses the additional challenge of the sixth stage of psychosocial development: **intimacy versus isolation**. From roughly 19 to 40 years, adults forge meaningful relationships or suffer from a lack of connection. Erikson thought that men who have not achieved a workable sense of identity will shy away from intimacy and experience shallow relationships. In contrast, he believed that women's identities are more often connected to relationships, so they will complete their identities as their relationship networks expand. Although this distinction may sound a bit old fashioned, it does reflect the historical role of marriage in women's lives. Even today, many psychologists believe that women are more likely than men to consider relationships integral to their sense of self (Gilligan, 1993; Guimond et al., 2006).

The majority of the adult years—from about 40 to 65 years—is concerned with the seventh stage of psychosocial development: **generativity versus self-absorption and stagnation**. After defining themselves and forming intimate relationships, adults turn to nurturing others, teaching others what they have learned, and helping to lead society. Middle-aged adults are concerned with production, which can involve child rearing, being a role model to younger colleagues at work, and taking an interest in broader social issues. The key virtue that emerges during this stage is *caring*: the process of extending interests beyond oneself and becoming part of the broader society. To varying degrees, individuals who lack generativity become self-absorbed and feel a sense of stagnation.

Erikson's focus on age has some limitations. For example, his emphasis on work-related issues rather than stages of family life may make the theory less descriptive of women's lives, because a woman's focus is more likely than a man's to change if she enters, leaves, and reenters the workforce to accommodate family needs (Barnett & Baruch, 1978). Also, specific ages may not be strongly linked to specific life issues now that many people are marrying later, having children later, and retiring either earlier or later than they did when Erikson was writing.

Will Erikson's stages withstand cultural changes that are introducing more variability into the timing of major life events? Only time will tell. But his theory does seem to describe how life was patterned in the past. When one team of investigators asked elderly adults to recall three memories from each decade of their lives, the rise and fall of Erikson's themes followed the predicted pattern: Identity issues peaked during adolescence but continued to trouble young adults, stories about intimacy were most often associated with young adulthood, and issues regarding production dominated middle age. The results, plotted in Figure 12.8, not only show that life themes ebb and flow but also that people face multiple themes throughout their lives.

Daniel Levinson's seasons of life. Because it is possible to adjust to life circumstances without advancing from less mature to more mature behavior, adulthood could be described as a progression that involves gains and losses. This is exactly what psychologist Daniel Levinson proposed in his concept of **seasons of adulthood**. From the results of interviews with 35- to 45-year-old men, Levinson developed the idea of a *life structure*, which is the underlying design of an individual's life that is defined by

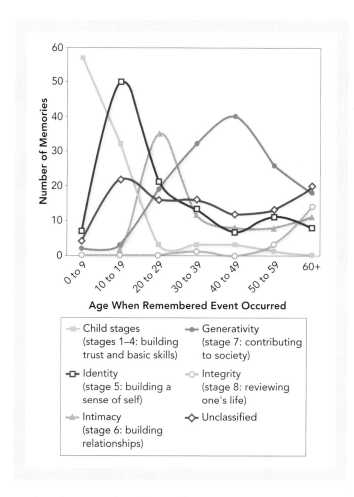

FIGURE 12.8 Autobiographical memories across Erikson's stages.

When older adults recalled memories from each decade of life, the peak frequency of various themes paralleled Erikson's stages of socioemotional development. Notice, however, that multiple themes were relevant at every stage of life.

SOURCE: Conway & Holmes (2004).

relationships with other people, jobs, and features of the physical environment (Levinson, 1990). Change is common during adulthood because age brings changes in our relationships, our work roles, and our physical surroundings. These changes inevitably lead to different life phases that Levinson explained in his book, *The Seasons of a Man's Life* (Levinson, 1978). Levinson described life in terms of roughly 25-year eras, with 5- to 8-year transitions between each era. Within eras, people experience less disruptive transitions as they periodically reassess their life structures and make adjustments. For example, early adulthood (roughly 17 to 45 years) ends with a midlife transition as people reflect back on what they have accomplished and reevaluate commitments to their current relationships, careers, and lifestyles.

Near the end of his life, Levinson expanded his findings by interviewing women. The results, published as *The Seasons of a Woman's Life* (Levinson, 1996), confirmed some of his previous findings but not all. Compared to men, the task of balancing family and work was more consuming for women throughout adulthood, and women were less likely to feel that life had settled down between 33 and 40 years of age.

One of the strengths of Levinson's approach is his emphasis on human diversity. "It is abundantly evident that, at the level of specific events, roles, or personality, individual lives evolve in myriad ways," he explained. "There is not much order in the concrete individual life course" (1990, p. 43). Still, Levinson believed that periods of stability and transitions are a defining feature of adulthood in all cultures.

Levinson's finding of a midlife transition is engrained in popular culture.

time-of-events model The idea that adults experience crises not from reaching particular ages but from events that are unpredictable or off schedule from society's expectations for the timing of events.

social clock Society's expectations for the timing of various life events, such as marriage, childbirth, and retirement.

life-span theory of control A theory that looks at how people select strategies for pursuing goals and coping with failure at different points in the life cycle.

primary control Control strategies that involve changing the external world to fit people's needs and desires. People are using primary control strategies when they study for an exam, argue a point with another individual, or put money into a retirement account.

secondary control Control strategies that involve turning inward by changing one's goals or beliefs to fit a situation. People are using secondary control strategies when they reason that they didn't want a goal very much or lack the ability to pursue a specific goal.

THE TIME-OF-EVENTS MODEL. We asked a fifth-year college student, Antonio, how he felt after his friends had graduated and found jobs. "You feel like you are being left behind," he replied. "You realize the world is spinning a little faster and they all got on the bus and you are sitting behind in the bus station all by yourself, and you don't even know when the next bus is coming."

This comment illustrates how much significant life events—such as college graduation or the birth of a child—influence perceptions of our own development. Because changing social roles propel people through life transitions, it makes sense to construct theories of adulthood around these events rather than age. Social psychologist Bernice Neugarten's **time-of-events model** does just that. Neugarten started with the idea that adults are different from children because they think about their pasts and futures, and they compare their lives to those of other individuals. Unlike children, adults are aware of a **social clock**: society's expectations for the timing of life events. According to this model, people experience crises not from reaching particular ages but from events that are *unpredictable* or *off schedule* (Neugarten, 1969, 1976). For example, we expect students to have a career plan by the time they are preparing to graduate from college, so students like Antonio feel "out of step" with their peers.

Stage theories such as Erikson's and Levinson's provide a nice overview of development, but they may seem oversimplified because, as mentioned earlier, the timing of life events has become less regular than it was in the past (Neugarten, 1979; Neugarten & Neugarten, 1987). Today, more people are building a career before marriage, having their first child after age 35, and starting over with new families and careers in midlife. As a result, many psychological concerns appear and reappear throughout our lives. In general, though, people who assume various roles "on time" with their social clock are more satisfied with their lives than people who are "off time" (Hurwicz et al., 1992).

One strength of the time-of-events model is the realization that people from different cohorts and cultures experience different expectations and, consequently, different life courses. For example, women from high SES backgrounds often delay childbearing until they have built a career, which may occur in their 30s, whereas women from low SES backgrounds more often have a first baby in their 20s or even earlier. As a result, the age of the mother does not by itself dictate whether a baby is "on time" or "off time."

LIFE-SPAN THEORY OF CONTROL. Another way of looking at adult development is to focus on the sometimes difficult choices adults make—the roads taken and not taken—and how these choices influence their course of development (Heckhausen, 1999; Lerner, 2002). Research psychologists Jutta Heckhausen's and Richard Schulz's **life-span theory of control** focuses on the fact that humans are highly motivated to master their environments—and feel terrible when they fail (Heckhausen & Schulz, 1993, 1995). The theory's goal is to explain how we select activities to pursue and deal with the consequences throughout our lives.

A central tenet of the life-span theory of control is that people in all cultures prefer **primary control**, which involves actions that change the world to fit their needs and desires. But it is a fact of life that we often fail to achieve our goals. Sometimes efforts fail, whereas other times we abandon goals because it is impossible to achieve everything in a single lifetime. People use **secondary control** to handle failure and justify one course of action over another. In contrast to primary control (which is behavior directed toward the external environment), people turn inward for secondary control by changing their goals or beliefs. For example, you use primary control when you study for an exam, but you use secondary control when you cope with a low grade by concluding that you had been too sick to study. People prefer primary control strategies for most of their lives, but secondary control strategies increase in late adulthood as people begin to cope with age-related declines and reduced opportunities to reinvent their lives (Schulz & Heckhausen, 1998). In other words, older adults are more likely than young adults to deal with disappointment by changing their goals and emotional reactions to situations rather than trying to influence the environment (Heckhausen & Schulz, 1995).

The life-span theory of control encourages scientists to study the essence of what it means to be an adult: how we make difficult choices and cope with the outcomes. This idea of choices raises an interesting question: What do older adults say they would do differently if they could live their lives over again? For an intriguing look at the mistakes that haunt adults, read our *Don't Be Fooled!* feature entitled "The Psychology of Regret."

DON'T BE FOOLED

The decisions people regret immediately are not always the ones they regret over the long run. When adults look back on their lives, they generally regret *failing to act* more than any mistakes or failures that stemmed from their actions. When you are faced with difficult life choices, ask yourself how you might feel many years from now—not how you might feel tomorrow.

THE PSYCHOLOGY OF REGRET

When you look back on your life, will you be more likely to regret your actions or your inactions? To help you think about this question, consider the following situations (Kahneman & Tversky, 1982):

> Paul owns shares in Company A. During the past year he considered switching to stock in Company B, but he decided against it. He now finds that he would have been better off by $1,200 if he had switched to the stock of Company B. George owned shares in Company B. During the past year he switched to stock in Company A. He now finds that he would have been better off by $1,200 if he had kept his stock in Company B. (p. 173)

Who feels more regret? Ninety-two percent of adults think that George, who lost money because he acted, will feel more regretful. They are probably right—in the short term. Immediately after a negative life event, people generally feel more regret if they did something to cause the situation (Gilovich & Medvec, 1994). But does this result hold up over the long run? Decision researchers Thomas Gilovich and Victoria Husted Medvec (1995) assembled data from a variety of sources to answer this question. The results were clear: Adults regret action more than inaction over the short run, but over the long run we generally feel more regret if we *failed to act*.

Consider a group of people we would expect to make excellent decisions—the intellectually gifted "Termites" described in Chapter 9. Researchers coded what male and female Termites said in response to the question

Adults who don't spend enough time nurturing their relationships may regret it years later. When people look back on their lives, a failure to emphasize relationships is one of the most frequently mentioned regrets.

"What would you do differently if you could live your life over again?" (Hattiangadi, Medvec, & Gilovich, 1995). Some responses weren't either actions or inactions, but over 80 percent of the remaining responses were things they *wished* they had done (Table 12.2). For example, these exceptional people wished they had gotten more education, worked harder to develop their careers, and taken more time for friends and family life—the very sorts of intimacy and generativity issues Erikson highlighted for this age group.

Many studies have found that people are more troubled by decisions to accept the status quo rather than work for change (Kinnier & Metha, 1989; Savitsky, Medvec, & Gilovich, 1997). Even in mainland China, where individual initiative is not emphasized as much as it is in America, adults were most likely to mention failures to act when investigators asked for their regrets. Similarly, adults in Japan and Russia gave responses that were remarkably close to reports from U.S. samples (Gilovich et al., 2003).

Do these results mean you should throw caution to the wind, seize the moment, and just "go for it"? Not necessarily. As Gilovich and Medvec (1995) pointed out, it can be adaptive to get stuck in a rut because—from an evolutionary perspective—at least the rut has kept you alive until now. For example, investing all of your money toward a new career would be disastrous if there were no jobs at the end of the line. But some risks have minimal consequences. For example, you will probably feel silly after you tell someone you like them if your feelings are not reciprocated, but life will go on. Over the long run, though, chances are that the pain of rejection will not last nearly as long as your regret over not expressing your feelings. Research on regret gives us a new question to ask ourselves whenever we face a difficult life decision: "How will I feel in 20 years if I don't try?" ◆

TABLE 12.2 What Terman's "Geniuses" Would Do Differently If They Could Live Their Lives Over: The Eight Most Frequent Regrets of Inaction and Action	Number (out of 720) who mentioned the regret
Regrets of Inaction	
Should have completed college or graduate school; not have interrupted education	39
Should have attended college; needed more education	21
Should have worked harder; not wasted college time; been more motivated	17
Should have pursued a career or a professional interest; aimed higher in career	16
Should have been more assertive; more selfish in developing own abilities	15
Should have emphasized social relationships	13
Should have prepared for a professional career or avocation	11
Should have tried harder to be married and/or have a family	10
Regrets of Action	
Shouldn't have married so early	12
Shouldn't have smoked; should have conquered alcoholism earlier	7
Shouldn't have stressed work so much	6
Shouldn't have participated in Terman study	4
Shouldn't have managed finances badly; made bad investments	3
Shouldn't have divorced	3
Shouldn't have made love and sex so important in choice of partner	2
Shouldn't have married	2

SOURCE: Hattiangadi et al. (1995).

ELDER'S LIFE-COURSE THEORY. The most sweeping theory of life-span development is sociologist Glen H. Elder, Jr.'s, **life-course theory**. Elder wants to explain *developmental trajectories*: the individual courses people take through life. (A *trajectory* is a path or progression.) He emphasizes that life events have different effects on people depending on the historical context of those events and their timing during the life cycle (Elder, 1998a).

Elder's most famous work compared people who were different ages during the Great Depression of the 1930s (Elder, 1998b, 1999). Children born in the late 1920s experienced the depression during the vulnerable years of childhood, and their adolescence coincided with World War II. In contrast, those born in the early 1920s were older during the depression, and economic circumstances had improved by the time they were mature enough to leave home. As a result, the first group was more negatively affected by the economic collapse. But not every child in the vulnerable group was affected equally because people experience historical events through their networks of relationships, including their parents' choices and reactions. For example, some parents built positive life courses for their children by moving into cheaper housing, finding work opportunities for mothers, and asking their children to assume more responsibilities at home.

Research on the timing of life events suggests the following four cornerstones of life-course theory (Elder, 1998b):

▶ The life course of individuals is shaped by the historical times and places they experience.

▶ The impact of life events depends on when they occur in a person's life.

▶ Social and historical influences are expressed through a network of shared relationships.

▶ Individuals construct their own life course through the choices and actions they take within the constraints of history and social circumstances.

As you can see, life-course theory combines elements of the other developmental theories, including the importance of developmental stage, the timing of life events, and the role of human agency in determining individual trajectories. What is unique about Elder's theory is the importance of historical and social influences in constraining individual lives. You can compare the major focus of each of the theories in this chapter by turning to Table 12.3.

Knowing Ourselves: Identity in Adulthood

A middle-aged man sought therapy for depression after losing his job and suffering from medical problems. A conversation with his therapist illustrates how central work had been for his sense of identity (Parry & Doan):

Therapist: Other than your job, what else gave meaning to your life? Was it religion, what it means to be a male, family tradition . . . any of those?

Client: No, not really. I've never been very religious, and the men's movement just doesn't interest me. The family tradition was all about work . . . that's all there was.

Therapist: How about what it means to be a good human being? Has that been important to you all along?

Client: Well, yeah, sure. I've always tried to be a good person.

Therapist: Since the doctors are telling you to take it easy, since it appears you won't be able to work professionally like you did in the past, would it be time to replace the work story with one about being a good person?

Client: Gosh, that would be hard. Being good involves working. (pp. 85–86).

life-course theory A theory of development, proposed by Glen H. Elder, Jr., that describes how development is influenced by the historical context, the timing of events in an individual's life, the impact of events on relationship networks, and the choices people in those networks make.

TABLE 12.3 Theories of Adult Development

Theory	Description	Major Contribution
Erik Erikson's psychosocial theory	People face different challenges as they pass through different phases of life. Adults progress toward more mature behavior as they find intimacy with others (during the stage of *intimacy vs. isolation*, when they are roughly 19 to 40 years old) and give back to their communities through their ideas and works (during the stage of *generativity vs. self-absorption and stagnation*, from roughly 40 to 65 years of age).	Summarizes the experiences, challenges, and goals that are typical as people age.
Daniel Levinson's seasons of life	Describes adulthood in terms of roughly 25-year eras that contain alternating periods of stability and change. Adult development is viewed as a process that involves both gains and losses.	The realization that change is common during adulthood because age brings changes in our relationships, our work roles, and our physical surroundings.
The time-of-events model	Proposes that major life events, such as graduating from college, will be experienced differently when they occur out of phase with society's norms rather than on schedule.	A recognition that people are aware of the *social clock* (society's expectations for when life transitions should occur).
Life-span theory of control	Describes the strategies people use to control their lives across the life span. *Primary control*, which is changing the environment to suit one's wishes, predominates throughout young and middle adulthood. As people grow older, they more often cope by using *secondary control*, which involves changing internal beliefs or goals.	A focus on two key tasks of adulthood: how people make choices to pursue some goals rather than others and how they adjust their goals in response to failure.
Elder's life-course theory	Encourages us to look at how individual lives are influenced by historical contexts, the age of occurrence of specific events, and how people and their social networks respond to challenges.	Descriptions of how lives are influenced by historical and social contexts.

Many adults experience unexpected life events that leave them searching for a new identity to provide a sense of meaning in their lives. Although most of these people already have a basic understanding of who they are, identities are not completely fixed during adulthood. For example, it is not uncommon to abandon a childhood religion during young adulthood, only to return to that faith after becoming a parent (Wilson & Sherkat, 1994). Similarly, many people change careers and periodically revise their political beliefs. Investigators who study identity during adulthood have looked at many issues, including how we organize information about ourselves, how we are motivated by our ability to envision possible lives, and how we cope with challenges to our identities.

DESCRIBING OURSELVES. Who are you? Around the world, adults mention a variety of characteristics when they answer this question, including physical attributes ("I am tall"), social memberships ("I am a member of a tennis club"), and psychological traits ("I am outgoing"). But culture influences how we think about the concept of "self." For example, adults in the United States are encouraged to act "themselves" in all situations, whereas those in Japan are encouraged to adapt to the demands of different situations. Accordingly, a study of Japanese and American women found that the Japanese women's self-descriptions varied more across situations. Specifically, Japanese women were more likely to mention the immediate situation ("I am in a psychology class") rather than psychological attributes when they were with a peer, reflecting their hesitancy to emphasize differences between themselves and other people. They were also less likely than U.S. women to mention psychological attributes (such as "I am friendly") and were more likely to mention physical traits, activities (such as "I have a part-time job"), and social memberships. Apparently, adults in the United States define themselves by characteristics that reflect their unique attributes *across* situations, whereas Japanese adults define themselves more in terms of characteristics that help them fit *into* various situations (Kanagawa, Cross, & Markus, 2001).

But identity is more than just a list of your physical characteristics, interests, and descriptions of how you behave in various situations. Instead, people develop a coherent sense of self by constructing *narrative identities*—stories about their lives, including causally linked events, that provide them with an overall sense of identity (Roser & Gazzaniga, 2004; Singer, 2004). For example, the renowned historian Drew Gilpin Faust lived in Virginia in 1957 when, at age 9, she sent a letter asking President Eisenhower to end segregation. Later she wrote, "I have always known that I became a southern historian because I grew up in that particular time and place . . . I developed a narrative about my childhood, about my identity as rebellious daughter, that I offered to all those who asked—and to some who didn't—a narrative that explained my redemption as a white southerner and my resurrection as civil-rights advocate and activist" (Faust, 2003, para. 6).

Once we have developed a story about our lives, we tend to recall new events that are consistent with the meaning of our story and ignore other information. Autobiographical memory and identity become intertwined because the themes we recall lead us to act in ways that are consistent with our identity stories. And as you will read next, these narratives also influence how we envision our futures.

POSSIBLE SELVES. A hallmark of adulthood is the ability to mentally connect the past and the present in order to plan for the future. As a result, our self-concepts include images of what we *might* be (Whitbourne, 1985). These **possible selves** motivate behavior because we are more likely to make choices that are compatible with our visions of the future (Markus & Nurius, 1986). For instance, a full-time homemaker who pictures herself running a small company after the children are in school will be more likely than other homemakers to brush up on her computer skills. In this case, the mental image of herself next to a thick book of clients is her *hoped-for self*. But people are also motivated by *feared selves*—the people they do not want to become. For example, a 35-year-old man with portly uncles may stick with an exercise regime due to his fear of becoming overweight.

Adults have no trouble generating hoped-for selves; in fact, 18- to 86-year-olds in one study generated between 1 and 23 hoped-for selves (Cross & Markus, 1991)! The number of hoped-for selves declines with age, though, and the content of people's dreams about their futures also changes over time. Family and occupational issues dominate the dreams of young adults, whereas older adults are more likely to think about their future physical states than their future careers. Even more interesting, a "settling down" occurs with age, as illustrated by the descriptions of hoped-for selves that appear in Table 12.4. In contrast to young adults, who often envision exciting and successful futures ("famous musician," "successful businessman"), middle-aged adults are less likely to envision dramatic changes and more likely to mention being good at their current roles ("a good husband and father," "more community oriented").

possible selves Visions of what an individual might be in the future.

TABLE 12.4 Possible Selves throughout Adulthood

Age	Themes	Sample Possible Selves
18–24 years	Young adults who are asked to list their hoped-for possible selves often mention choices they will soon be making, such as marriage, family, and careers. Many answers describe extremely positive possible selves.	"Famous musician, successful businessman, thin, good father/husband/friend, intelligent, both academically and socially, street smart, good psychologist, cultured, many interests, hobbies."
25–39 years	The hopes of this age group are more moderate. Instead of mentioning fabulous success, they often mention concrete achievements.	"A more loving person, to have enough money to live comfortably, a better nurse, to have a steady relationship with a warm, loving guy, to stay energetic until I die, a good guitar player, stay in good health and in good shape."
40–59 years	This age group mentions fewer dramatic changes and new beginnings. Instead, they often mention enjoying their current roles.	"Successful at work, a good husband and father, better tennis player, comfortably retired, put my children through the colleges of *their* choice, more community oriented."
60+ years	Self-development is still important to this age group. More so than the younger groups, they focus on development in their current roles.	"Being an 'active' old person, being able to continue to learn and grow, being useful and able to help others, being a loving and loved person, being independent, writing a publishable article."

SOURCE: Cross & Markus (1991).

Research has shown that adults are more motivated to achieve possible selves when examples come readily to mind, are rich in detail, and are believed to be under the individual's control. Thus you can promote new possible selves by imagining specific details of your dreams and identifying concrete ways to work toward them (Norman & Aron, 2003).

IDENTITY STYLES. How do people cope with unexpected challenges to their identities, such as losing a job or developing diabetes? A theoretical model by developmental psychologist Susan Krauss Whitbourne (1986, 1996) captures this process. Whitbourne sees identity as an organizing scheme through which the individual filters experience. Just as Piaget described how children continually change their schemes about the physical world, each new experience must be interpreted to fit into one's identity scheme, or the scheme must be adjusted to fit the experience. *Identity assimilation* is the process of adding new information into an existing scheme in a way that maintains continuity about our identities. *Identity accommodation* is the process of adjusting our identities in response to new experiences. For example, the man who sought therapy for depression had to replace an identity defined by work with one based on characteristics that had not been the focus of his attention.

These adults have what Whitbourne called a "balanced identity style": They adapted to a devastating injury by making changes to their lifestyles, but without sacrificing an identity as fun-loving, strong, and athletic individuals.

According to Whitbourne, each of us has an *identity style* that reflects our tendency to rely on assimilation versus accommodation (Sneed & Whitbourne, 2001; Whitbourne, 1996). People who rely too much on assimilation—by forcing every experience to fit their existing sense of self—will not make healthy adjustments as their lives change. For example, a person who is more prone to assimilation may continue to look for jobs in a dying industry rather than retraining for another vocation. Still, it is unhealthy to allow every life challenge to threaten your identity. For example, relying too much on accommodation as you age may lead you to accept losses of function ("I'm older and different now") even when an active lifestyle might keep you fit and strong. A *balanced identity style* is flexible enough to change when change is needed but not so unstable that every new experience undermines your sense of self. Whitbourne's model illustrates a growing interest in how adults assemble their identities and respond to transitions.

Relationships

Throughout life, our sense of who we are is influenced by our relationships. A strong desire to bond with others is part of our biological makeup, a quality that increases our chances of survival by converting relatively weak individuals into groups that cooperate to gather resources, defend its members, and raise children. Even in today's high-tech world—where information is more important than hunting partners—close relationships give us the reassurance and knowledge we need to cope with life's challenges.

People seek intimacy on many different levels throughout adulthood, including partnerships based on romantic love and sexual sharing, reciprocal relationships with family members, and trusting friendships. Because intimate relationships and family life have so many variations, we will discuss love, marriage, and families in the next chapter. Here we look at two aspects of adult life that are more universal: friendship and the experience of loneliness.

BONDING WITH FRIENDS. Between 1946 and 1947, 270 families moved into Westgate and Westgate West, a complex of single-family apartments that was built to accommodate married veterans at the Massachusetts Institute of Technology (MIT). Because couples moved in as their names rose to the top of the waiting list, most were strangers when the units filled. If you could earn $10 for each couple you predicted would become friends, and you could have one piece of information about each couple, what would you want to know?

Since the study of relationship patterns at Westgate was published in 1950 (Festinger, Schachter, & Back, 1950), social psychologists have designed hundreds of others to explore the forces that draw friends together. Three broad factors summarize the results:

▶ *Physical proximity.* Even among adults who live or work near each other, people who live or work *very* close by are most likely to become friends. At MIT, for example, friendships formed between 41 percent of the people who lived next door to each other but only between 22 percent of people who were separated by *a single* housing unit.

Physical proximity is important because we are designed to like and trust familiar things. Whether we are judging people, drawings, or new products, the amount of *repeated exposure* we have with a target influences how we feel about it (Moreland & Beach, 1992).

THE FAR SIDE® BY GARY LARSON

"Thanks for being my friend, Wayne."

In the modern world of instant messaging and online journals (where physical distance is not tightly linked to exposure), this result suggests that people who are out of step with the ways others are communicating might find it harder to strengthen their friendships.

▶ *Similarity.* Exposure is important, but it is still the case that we don't become friends with everyone we know. Generally, we prefer to be with people who are like ourselves in terms of physical attractiveness, gender-role attitudes, interests, and beliefs and values. And when the structure of the physical or social environment encourages people to interact, joint experiences make them more similar to one another over time (Festinger et al., 1950; Gibbons & Olk, 2003). Thus perceived similarity promotes friendship, but friendship also promotes increased similarity.

▶ *Emotional influences.* It is obvious that we are more attracted to people who like us and make us feel good about ourselves (Cramer, Helzer, & Mone, 1986), but we are also attracted to people who just happen to be around when we feel good (Clark & Waddell, 1983). In a related vein, a sudden, intense sense of connection often develops when we are in highly arousing situations, such as an unexpected medical crisis or an exciting experience away from home (Meston & Frohlich, 2003). Stressful situations increase our need to be with others, while the act of talking about shared mishaps helps us feel emotionally close.

Throughout life, having friends is associated with better health and subjective well-being (Eng et al., 2002; Lutgendorf et al., 2002; Taylor et al., 2001). Still, it is natural for the size of friendship circles to change as people age. During young adulthood, most people make a lot of friends and see their best friends frequently. As partners and work begin to take up more time, most adults restrict the number of people they consider close friends (Antonucci, Akiyama, & Merline, 2001; Carstensen, 1992). But friendships are still important during middle age and beyond. Indeed, middle-aged adults say that their current friendships are more stable and intimate than their earlier friendships were (Carstensen, 1992).

LONELINESS. Despite the fact that most adults see dozens of people each day, it is not unusual to feel lonely. Loneliness can be a fleeting feeling during a boring day, the temporary result of a life transition, or a more chronic condition. But you don't have to be lacking company to feel lonely. Loneliness is a complicated feeling that can stem from inadequacies in the number or the quality of your social relationships, distance from the people you love, or a sense of not belonging to your immediate environment (Austin, 1983; McWhirter, 1990). Therefore, it is perfectly natural to feel lonely even if you are socially active.

Studies conducted in Taiwan, Angola, Portugal, and numerous other countries prove that loneliness is a universal phenomenon (Neto & Barros, 2003; Yeh & Lo, 2004). The feeling of loneliness is most common among adolescents and adults in their early 20s, perhaps because friendships during this period are often short-lived, identity development is ongoing, and people frequently change schools and work environments. In fact, 30 percent of the student body at one university reported a problem with loneliness during the previous 12 months, and 6 percent said that loneliness was a major problem for them (Brigman & Roberts, 1986).

Individual differences in loneliness are associated with situational and individual factors. It is common for people to feel alone when transitions disrupt their social relationships, which occurs when they have recently moved, lost a partner, or experienced a death. But some people suffer from chronic loneliness due to unrealistic expectations about social interactions ("I'll never go back to her house after what SHE said to me") or poor social skills ("I just didn't feel comfortable talking to them"). Those who are too shy or self-conscious to initiate social contact make up some of the chronically lonely population (Jackson et al., 2002), but in other cases lonely adults are those who are hostile and insensitive to others (Furr & Funder, 1998).

Interventions for chronically lonely people try to change how they interpret social situations through *cognitive therapy*, a type of therapy that helps people interpret social interactions more realistically. For example, a serious 29-year-old man with a disappointing dating history might learn through cognitive therapy that mild criticism from a woman does not mean a relationship is doomed to fail. Therapy for this individual might also involve *social skills training*, in which he practices concrete behaviors such as small talk, asking questions, and reacting to unexpected comments (Curran, 1977; Gambrill, 1996). Then, by watching videos and role-playing, he would learn how to keep interactions upbeat and light for the first few dates.

Moral Growth and Spirituality

As identities and relationships evolve during adulthood, so, too, do moral values and spiritual concerns. Throughout life, moral and spiritual transitions trigger strong emotional reactions because humans are "meaning makers" (Fowler, 1981) who strive to understand what we should do and why we should do it. As you learned in earlier chapters, even children have strong moral reactions to situations (Chapter 8), and cognitive advances "rev up" thinking about moral issues during adolescence (Chapter 10). Nonetheless, early and middle adulthood is a time when morality and spirituality can deepen as experiences lead us to think more critically about practical problems, we become more aware of choosing certain paths and forgoing others, and concern for family members directs our attention away from selfish interests.

KOHLBERG'S THEORY OF MORAL REASONING. Earlier you read about Lawrence Kohlberg's theory of moral development as it pertained to the development of adolescents' moral compass. Recall that Kohlberg asked children and adults how they felt about hypothetical dilemmas, such as whether Heinz should steal a drug to save his dying wife. Individuals who show *preconventional morality* (which is typical of children from 4 to 10 years) mention external controls based on rewards or punishments ("He shouldn't steal because he can get arrested and punished"). Those who show *conventional morality* (which is typical of most adolescents and adults) focus on pleasing others, being "good," and maintaining social order ("The judge should punish Heinz because judges have accepted the responsibility to uphold the laws of society").

A minority of individuals eventually show **postconventional morality** (which is found only in some adolescents and adults) by mentioning fundamental principles of fairness and justice ("A human life is more valuable than the cost of the drug") (Kohlberg, 1963b, 1969). Kohlberg initially divided each level of reasoning into two stages, so stages 5 and 6 are two degrees of postconventional morality. The difference between them is subtle. Stage 5 is a *social contract orientation* in which individuals realize the benefits of democratically accepted laws yet

postconventional morality In Kohlberg's theory, the highest level of moral reasoning that makes reference to fundamental principles of fairness and justice.

realize that laws cannot take all situations into account. Laws should usually be upheld, but the stage 5 individual will side with larger principles if a law violates basic human rights (like the right to life). Stage 6 is a morality based on *universal ethical principles*, such as preserving life or respecting the personal property of others, regardless of social laws and conventions. The difference between these two stages is illustrated by people's reactions to civil disobedience: A stage 5 individual would feel more comfortable working to change an unjust law, whereas the stage 6 individual would freely engage in civil disobedience—as Martin Luther King, Jr., did—to promote justice (Crain, 2005).

Longitudinal studies conducted in the United States, Israel, and Turkey have found that moral reasoning scores increase from adolescence through the early 30s (Colby et al., 1983; Nisan & Kohlberg, 1982; Snarey, Reimer, & Kohlberg, 1985). It was quite common in these studies for people to shift from stage 3 to stage 4, and a few moved to stage 5. But few answers in a sample of Chicago males represented stage 5, and stage 6 was not found at all. There is other evidence that Kohlberg's highest levels of reasoning do not describe the way many people think about moral issues. For example, when Dutch researchers asked university students to order statements representing the first five stages from "most simplistic" to "wise," the students agreed with Kohlberg's order only up to stage 4 (Boom, Brugman, & van der Heijden, 2001).

Because it is rare for adults to show the highest stages of moral reasoning, critics have questioned whether reasoned justice is the essence of mature morality (Nicholson, 1983). Instead, postconventional reasoning may simply be a specific cultural view of morality—an individualistic, rights-oriented approach adopted by some educated adults from industrialized countries. Confirming this idea, a review of 45 studies found lower levels of reasoning the farther adults were from middle-class urban environments (Snarey, 1985). Kohlberg himself found that individuals from an Israeli kibbutz often described communal principles that were not represented in his scoring manual, suggesting that descriptions of postconventional thought fail to capture mature reasoning in all cultures (Snarey et al., 1985).

Civil rights activist Martin Luther King, Jr., attained postconventional morality—Kohlberg's highest level of moral reasoning. King believed in supporting the principle of equality for all people even if it meant nonviolent resistance to the law.

In sum, there appear to be two parts to Kohlberg's theory: The first four stages describe the early development of moral reasoning across cultures, whereas the last stages represent changes experienced by some adults in some cultures. Adults emphasize abstract principles over specific cultural values or laws when they have been exposed to cultures and opinions that are different from their own, which forces them to confront the relativity of moral standards. But adults do not reason consistently from situation to situation. Instead, it is common to consider justice the highest moral value for some situations but interpersonal caring the highest value in others (Boom et al., 2001). This tension between abstract principles of justice and caring for others is most evident in studies that have compared the moral reasoning of men and women.

GENDER, JUSTICE, AND CARING. Early research on moral reasoning found that many women scored at Kohlberg's stage 3, whereas men typically scored at stage 4 or 5. When social psychologist Carol Gilligan (1993) looked at the reasons for this, she found that women tended to favor an approach to working out the problem with others (such as bargaining with the pharmacist in the case of the Heinz dilemma) rather than breaking the law to uphold higher principles. Instead of interpreting this difference as evidence of women's deficient moral reasoning, Gilligan (1993) argued that Kohlberg's scoring system emphasized individualistic values characteristic of men in Western cultures and was insensitive to the females' more cooperative emphasis on caring and compassion for others. Gilligan's argument became popular because it represented a shift in thinking from "men and women are different so one must be better" to "men and women can be different yet equal" (Barlow, 1984; Tavris, 1992).

Gilligan-vs-Kohlberg

In her later writing, Gilligan (1990) emphasized that men *and* women develop a dialectical mode of reasoning that recognizes the contradictions in moral problems. In other words, men and women both consider issues of justice and caring when making moral judgments, but it can be difficult to capture these sometimes conflicting values when answers are assigned to a single stage. Therefore, new approaches to moral reasoning allow people to express caring- and justice-focused values without forcing them to choose between the two.

In a representative study, Mexican American and Anglo American men and women read vignettes that had no simple solution (Gump, Baker, & Roll, 2000). In one, for example, Susanna, a troublesome teenager, took the family car without permission and dented it; Julie, her older sister, had to decide whether to take the blame. The story detailed many reasons why Julie might choose to lie as well as reasons why she should not. Volunteers rated how important various reasons would be for their decision, including four caring-oriented reasons ("Julie didn't want to cause further strain on her parents' marriage") and four justice-oriented reasons ("Julie didn't want to have to lie about what happened, as she felt that lying was wrong").

Because Mexican culture places a high value on one's role in the family, it is not surprising that the Mexican American adults gave higher ratings to reasons involving the welfare of family members. However, both groups gave equal importance to justice-oriented reasons. Similarly, the women in both

Mexican Americans value family involvement and often mention the welfare of the family when they explain their decisions about moral dilemmas. For them, a morality based on caring is not incompatible with a morality based on justice principles.

TABLE 12.5 Religion around the World

"Independently of whether you go to church or not, would you say you are a religious person?" (% "yes")	
Iran	95
Nigeria	97
Poland	94
Brazil	85
Argentina	84
United States	83
Puerto Rico	82
Turkey	80
India	79
Mexico	77
Taiwan	75
Chile	71
Finland	67
Spain	61
Australia	59
Switzerland	57
Norway	47
Sweden	39
Japan	27

SOURCE: Inglehart et al. (2004).

FIGURE 12.9 Religious participation across adulthood.

Older adults in the U.S. are more likely than young adults to be active members of a church or synagogue. At all ages, females report more religious involvement than males.

SOURCE: Inglehart et al. (2004).

ethnic groups gave more weight than the men to care-oriented items but equal weight to justice-oriented items. These results illustrate that people do not view caring and justice as mutually exclusive values, although women sometimes focus on interpersonal concerns more than men.

In sum, conclusions about gender differences in moral reasoning have swung from emphasizing differences to emphasizing similarities and then to an intermediate position that recognizes differences in some situations. It is fair to say that there are no gender or cultural differences in people's potential for thinking about justice, but that some cultures are more likely than others to integrate relationship issues into their reasons for moral actions.

RELIGION AND SPIRITUALITY. Many adults explore moral issues and find purpose and meaning to their lives by connecting with specific religious or spiritual traditions—often the very traditions they experienced as children and questioned during adolescence. *Religions* are socially organized patterns of beliefs and practices that address the meaning of life and refer to the supernatural (forces beyond the material world as we usually experience it) (Stark, 2004). In contrast, "spirituality" often refers to a more personal journey to understand one's place in the universe, a journey that may be less tightly tied to a particular religious tradition.

Religion means different things to different people. Some believe that religion is an expression of ultimate truths. Others believe that humans construct religious ideas because we are intelligent enough to appreciate our own mortality (Gould, 1991), and still others pay little or no attention to religious questions. But as you can see in Table 12.5, the majority of adults in most countries consider themselves religious.

Religious participation generally increases from younger to older age groups, with the largest increase in church and synagogue attendance occurring between the 20s and 30s, when adults are establishing families and striving to pass religious traditions onto their children (Figure 12.9). It is common to find a small drop in active participation during the 40s, when people are busy with family life and career responsibilities. Another drop in the frequency of attending religious services occurs among elderly adults, but this reflects life circumstances (specifically, declining health and mobility) rather than a decline in spirituality per se (Blazer & Palmore, 1976; Chatters & Taylor, 1989).

It is obvious from Figure 12.9 that women are more involved in religion than men. Women report greater church attendance, are more likely to believe in life after death, pray more frequently, and have more denominational loyalty. One explanation—that females are socialized to be more religious and to take care of their families' religious needs—has found little support: The magnitude of the gender difference has not declined over time (even though traditional sex-role attitudes have declined), is not smaller among people with liberal political leanings, and is not predicted by sex-role attitudes (Miller & Stark, 2002). Currently, exactly why women are more involved with religion than men is an unanswered question.

Religious involvement also varies as a function of geographic region and ethnic/cultural background. In the United States, for example, African Americans are more likely than European Americans to say that faith is a cornerstone of their lives (Taylor et al., 1996): Over a third of African Americans surveyed report that they read religious material and monitor religious broadcasts at least once a week, 8 out of 10 say that religious beliefs are very important to them, and almost half (44 percent) say that they "almost always" seek spiritual comfort through religion.

Throughout adulthood, religious participation is associated with three factors that improve health and well-being (Hummer et al., 1999; Koenig, Larson, & Larson, 2001):

▶ *Health behaviors.* Many faith groups encourage their members to abstain from or exercise responsibility about alcohol, cigarettes, and risky sexual behavior.

▶ *Social ties.* Worship and religious celebrations provide people with opportunities for social interaction and support, which reduce stress and improve health.

▶ *Coping mechanisms.* Religious beliefs help people cope with illnesses and other life challenges by providing them with feelings of control, hope, and a sense of purpose to their lives.

In addition to these general findings, religious participation also influences how people deal with adult transitions. During emerging adulthood, religious background influences people's concepts of what defines an adult. For example, youth from Mormon universities consider the ability to care for a family more central to the definition of "adulthood" than youth from Catholic universities do, who in turn consider family capacities more important than youth from public universities do (Barry & Nelson, 2005). And once people have married and had children, religiousness is associated with somewhat lower divorce rates, greater marital satisfaction, higher ratings of affection for children, and greater parental consistency (Mahoney et al., 2001).

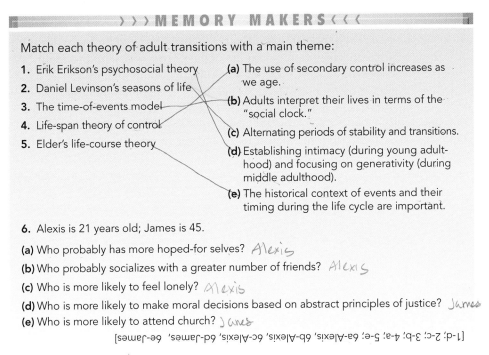

>>> **MEMORY MAKERS** <<<

Match each theory of adult transitions with a main theme:

1. Erik Erikson's psychosocial theory
2. Daniel Levinson's seasons of life
3. The time-of-events model
4. Life-span theory of control
5. Elder's life-course theory

(a) The use of secondary control increases as we age.
(b) Adults interpret their lives in terms of the "social clock."
(c) Alternating periods of stability and transitions.
(d) Establishing intimacy (during young adulthood) and focusing on generativity (during middle adulthood).
(e) The historical context of events and their timing during the life cycle are important.

6. Alexis is 21 years old; James is 45.

(a) Who probably has more hoped-for selves? Alexis
(b) Who probably socializes with a greater number of friends? Alexis
(c) Who is more likely to feel lonely? Alexis
(d) Who is more likely to make moral decisions based on abstract principles of justice? James
(e) Who is more likely to attend church? James

[1-d; 2-c; 3-b; 4-a; 5-e; 6a-Alexis, 6b-Alexis, 6c-Alexis, 6d-James, 6e-James]

The End of Elaine's Story

Remember Elaine, the 40-something college student who was concerned about fitting in with her classmates? Is her outlook on life really so different from that of a younger adult?

Because Elaine is older and has more family responsibilities, she may always feel a bit out of place in class. Indeed, many nontraditional students never come to identify with the label of "student" (Harrison, 2000). Unlike the typical college student, who is focused on establishing intimate relationships (in Erikson's sixth stage of development), Elaine is embarking on Erikson's seventh stage (generativity versus self-absorption and stagnation), when people think more about the meaning of their lives and how they will contribute back to society. With a family to support, Elaine has fewer opportunities to reinvent her life than a young adult has, and she draws on practical experience acquired over the last 20 years to define herself, solve problems, and think about moral issues.

But despite all of the differences between the typical 20-year-old and the typical 40+-year-old, adults of all ages continue to revise their identities and relationships—and this is especially true when they attend college. In one study, the majority of African American women who returned to college said that school had a positive influence on their lives, including improved relationships with their husbands ("I feel an increased sense of identity and ability to share problems with him"), children ("I am more able to help them by encouraging, advising, and supporting them"), and co-workers ("Since returning to school . . . people [at work] listened to me more") (Thomas, 2001, p. 149).

So when you meet people like Elaine, tell them we are all on a journey of constant change—whether we are 20 or 49. Like the family members in our opening story, adults can bridge the gap between generations by remembering that everyone within this broad age range is dealing with the same basic issues of adulthood—how to find intimacy, how to carve a place for themselves in society, and how to find meaning in their lives.

During young and middle adulthood, people's circumstances shape how they solve problems, whether they feel in step with life or out of step, and how they define relationships between themselves and the broader world. It makes sense to talk about age-related change during adulthood, but knowing something about an adult's life often tells you more about him or her than knowing an age does. You'll explore what some of those "somethings" are in the next chapter when you read about the contexts that frame individual lives.

>>>SUMMARY<<<

Our Bodies from 20 to 50

1. **Senescence**—the gradual physical decline that occurs with increasing age—begins during young adulthood. After 30, most people experience declines in physical strength and basal metabolism, and everyone eventually notices wrinkles and graying hair.

2. Most body systems reach peak performance between 25 and 30 years. There are gradual declines in visual acuity, hearing, and stamina for prolonged physical activity. Bones begin to lose density and strength by middle adulthood, especially for women.

3. Fertility gradually declines for both sexes, but only women experience the abrupt decline in hormones that cause **perimenopause** (a time of declining hormones) and **menopause** (the end of menstruation and the ability to conceive a child naturally) during middle adulthood.

4. The brain continues to mature at least until age 25, as the neurons that connect distant brain regions continue to myelinate. During the early 20s, there is improved efficiency in brain regions responsible for detecting errors and evaluating the emotional significance of events.

5. Age is often a poor predictor of physical abilities because medical conditions and lifestyle factors, including patterns of physical exercise, create differences from person to person. During young and middle adulthood, **primary aging** (the gradual process of bodily decline that all humans experience) has less of an impact on our lives than **secondary aging** (bodily decline due to genetic defects and environmental factors).

Expanding Minds

6. There is room for cognitive growth during adulthood. Individuals can improve their performance on tests of for-

mal operational thought and learn to overcome systematic biases that lead to errors in judgment.

7. Some theorists believe that adults can mature beyond formal operational reasoning into a stage of **postformal thought** when they think more flexibly and are more skilled at **dialectical reasoning** (integrating evidence from opposing sides of open-ended issues). Others believe that the basic structure of the mind stays the same during adulthood but that different age groups have different priorities for how to use their knowledge.

8. IQ scores correlate only modestly with **practical intelligence** (performance on everyday problems). During early and middle adulthood, no age group consistently outperforms other age groups on practical tasks.

9. Performance on measures of **crystallized intelligence** (tasks that rely on acquired knowledge) improves until at least age 40. In contrast, performance declines from the 20s onward when tasks tap **fluid intelligence** (the ability to reason abstractly and solve new problems) or sheer speed of responding.

10. The cognitive changes that occur from early to middle adulthood do not dramatically affect older college students' performance. Older students are enthusiastic learners who achieve grades that are equal to or better than traditional students in most classes.

Emotional and Social Development

11. Theories of adult transitions highlight different aspects of the adult experience. Erikson's psychosocial theory focuses on the goals of achieving **intimacy** (from 19 to 40) and **generativity** (from 40 to 65). Levinson's concept of **seasons of adulthood** describes alternating periods of stability and transition. According to the **time-of-events**

model, crises stem from transitions that do not occur at socially expected times in the life cycle. The **life-span theory of control** describes how people of various ages try to maintain a sense of mastery over their lives. Finally, Elder's **life-course theory** highlights how the impact of events is influenced by the historical context and the time in the life cycle when events occur.

12. People achieve a sense of personal unity and meaning by developing narratives about themselves that include casually linked events. Individual identities include past selves, present selves, and **possible selves**. Each person has an *identity style* that is determined by whether they tend to fit new information into their existing identities or react to feedback by adjusting their identities.

13. Friendships are most likely to develop among adults who interact frequently, are similar, and make one another feel good. The number of friends people have typically declines with age, but friendships become more stable and intimate over time. Young adults are more likely than those in middle adulthood to struggle with loneliness.

14. Some adults rely on **postconventional morality** (a type of moral reasoning that is based on fundamental principles of fairness and justice), but many adults consider both caring-oriented and justice-oriented reasons when they consider moral issues. Religious participation increases with age and is associated with good health, social ties, and positive coping mechanisms.

The End of Elaine's Story

15. Young and middle adulthood is a time of continual change—whether people are 20 or 49. Within this broad age range, everyone is dealing with the same basic issues of adulthood—how to find intimacy, carve a place in society, and find meaning in their lives.

>>> KEY TERMS <<<

emerging adulthood (p. 476)
senescence (p. 477)
basal metabolism (p. 478)
osteoporosis (p. 481)
perimenopause (p. 484)
menopause (p. 484)
primary aging (p. 487)
secondary aging (p. 487)
dialectical reasoning (p. 490)
postformal thought (p. 491)
everyday intelligence (p. 492)
crystallized intelligence (p. 495)

fluid intelligence (p. 495)
intimacy versus isolation (p. 498)
generativity versus self-absorption and stagnation (p. 498)
seasons of adulthood (p. 499)
time-of-events model (p. 500)
social clock (p. 500)
life-span theory of control (p. 500)
primary control (p. 500)
secondary control (p. 500)
life-course theory (p. 503)
possible selves (p. 505)
postconventional morality (p. 509)

MILESTONES of early to middle adulthood

20 to 30 Years Individuals enjoy the years of peak strength and stamina.

- Most body systems reach peak performance between 25 and 30 years of age.

- Adults learn to apply formal reasoning to a wider array of problems and begin to think more dialectically by considering evidence on multiple sides of issues.

- Fluid intelligence (the ability to solve new problems) peaks for tasks that rely on speed, but crystallized intelligence (an individual's reservoir of knowledge) will continue to expand throughout most of adulthood.

- During the 20s, many individuals transition from emerging adults who are still in school and/or economically dependent on parents to independent adults. Young adults are in Erikson's phase of intimacy versus isolation, when they focus on establishing close relationships with friends and romantic partners.

30 to 40 Years Life often focuses on nurturing growing families and careers.

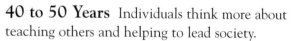

- An active, healthy lifestyle can compensate for the small physical declines that are typical during this time of life.

- Many adults make plans for children as reproductive capacities decline.

- Individuals are at different stages of their family and career lives.

- A settling down occurs that is revealed by the possible selves people report. Instead of mentioning hopes of fabulous success, as many people in their 20s do, adults in their 30s are more likely to mention moderate, attainable goals.

40 to 50 Years Individuals think more about teaching others and helping to lead society.

- Senescence becomes more noticeable as wrinkles appear, eyesight and hearing decline, and basal metabolism slows.

- Women experience perimenopause, and many reach menopause by age 50. Although men do not experience a sudden shift in reproductive capacity, their odds of conceiving a child gradually decline.

- Performance peaks on some types of practical problem-solving tasks.

- Middle-aged adults enter Erikson's phase of generativity versus self-absorption and stagnation, when they think more about what they are contributing to society.

Is every phase

Preview: Early to middle adulthood in **CONTEXT**

Health and Well-Being The leading causes of death and chronic illness during adulthood are all related to behavior. Unintentional injuries claim the most lives during early adulthood, but adults also suffer from violence, obesity, and stress-related illnesses. Many characteristics of individuals and their environments contribute to the perception that life is good.

Relationships Love is a complicated set of feelings that includes the chemical changes of romantic passion along with expressions of intimacy and commitment. In addition to romantic partners, the relationship landscape during adulthood often includes children and continued relationships with siblings. Many characteristics of individuals and families determine the quality of these relationships.

Earning a Living
In industrialized countries, an increasing number of jobs emphasize good communications skills, social skills, and the ability to work with people from a variety of backgrounds. Job changes are common during early to middle adulthood as individuals discover more about their abilities and seek to balance family life with their work outside the home.

Individuality Individual differences during adulthood include differences in personality, intelligence, and accomplishments. You would know very little about someone simply by knowing whether the individual is male or female, but as a group the sexes hold different types of jobs and have different rates of numerous medical and mental health conditions.

> **In this next chapter,** you'll learn how developmental principles explain the pathways individuals take through early to middle adulthood when we consider the question:
> *Is every phase a life crisis?*

a life crisis?

Pathways through Early to Middle Adulthood

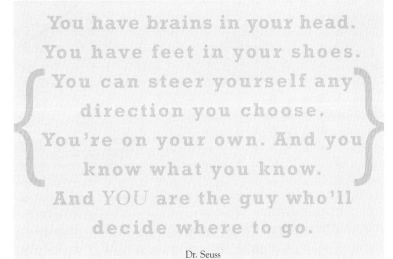

You have brains in your head.
You have feet in your shoes.
You can steer yourself any
direction you choose.
You're on your own. And you
know what you know.
And YOU are the guy who'll
decide where to go.

Dr. Seuss

Stories of Our Lives

A Boat and a Dream

Boat captains go to great lengths to protect their secret fishing spots. In 1991, a man called Skeets had been silent for years about a once-in-a-lifetime site about 60 miles off the New Jersey coast. He knew the oasis of marine life meant one thing: a shipwreck. But this site was different from the public wrecks; this site grabbed hold of his curiosity. As author Robert Kurson (2004) later explained, "Over a lifetime at sea, a fisherman develops a feel for what matters and what does not. To Skeets, this site mattered" (p. 14).

Skeets turned the coordinates over to Bill Nagle, the captain of a wreck-diving ship called the *Seeker*. Nagle and his friend, John Chatterton, gathered a group of divers who could make the 200-foot plunge. Chatterton's first dive revealed a cigar-shaped metal body and an intact torpedo—signs of a German U-boat from World War II.

Chatterton became obsessed with discovering the identity of the submarine the divers called the U-Who. After three divers lost their lives on

519

the wreck, Chatterton and his friend, Richie Kohler, continued to search for an artifact that would identify the ship. One day, Chatterton risked his life by removing his tank underwater so he could pass through a small opening into the submarine's motor room and grab a parts box he hoped would contain the U-boat number. Delayed by a tangle of cables, he was out of gas by the time he snaked his way out. As Robert Kurson (2004) later wrote:

> Chatterton spit the regulator from his mouth. His only remaining hope lay in reaching his stage bottles. But they were outside the compartment and on top of the wreck, a swim of at least fifty feet. He dared not risk buddy-breathing with Kohler, as even a slight delay or mix-up in communications could be deadly. Chatterton, his mouth now totally exposed to the ocean, kicked with force and equanimity. He had seen guys die flailing. He was near death. He would not flail.
>
> Chatterton torpedoed out of the diesel motor room and up toward the top of the wreck. Kohler, stunned by the sight of his friend without a regulator, gave chase behind him. Chatterton's lungs screamed as his stage bottles came into sight. He kicked harder. Every cell in his body shrieked for oxygen and pulled at his jaws to breathe. He clenched his mouth shut. He reached the stage bottles. In a single motion, he grabbed a regulator from one of the bottles, stuck it in his mouth, and turned the valve. Fresh gas flooded into his lungs. Chatterton had come down to this final breath.
>
> A few seconds later, Kohler arrived at his side. He looked Chatterton in the eye, then pointed to his chest, sign language for "You just gave me a heart attack—now I'm the one who's going to die instead of you." The divers began their long decompression hang. For nearly two hours, Chatterton thought only of the terrible risks he had taken during the dive. Often, he said aloud, "I can't ever let that happen again." He had long since forgotten the spare-parts box he had recovered, which Kohler had passed to another diver for tag inspection topside.
>
> Near the end of their decompressions, Chatterton and Kohler saw another diver, Will McBeth, swim down the anchor line. McBeth handed Chatterton a slate just like the one on which Chatterton had written "SUB" during the discovery trip six years earlier. This time, however, the slate said something different. This time, it read:
>
> The U-Who now has a name—it is U-869. Congratulations.
>
> In his younger days, Kohler might have jumped for joy and slapped Chatterton on the back. Chatterton might have pumped his fists in triumph. Today, they looked into each other's eyes. Then, simultaneously, neither one before the other, each extended his hand. The divers shook. Today, they had found something important. Today, they had their answers. (pp. 322–323)

ON THE SURFACE, people like the men in our opening tale seem to be larger than life, a different breed of human. But in *Shadow Divers*, author Robert Kurson (2004) described how the discovery of U-869 intersected lives that were filled with struggle and uncertainty. In November 2000—the same month PBS aired a special on the submarine—Chatterton was diagnosed with cancer. After 20 years as a commercial diver, he quit his career to pursue a history degree and teaching certification. Both Chatterton and Kohler suffered the loss of their marriages, and Kohler's new partner, 8 months pregnant with his child, was gunned down by a former boyfriend. But Chatterton found a new relationship, and Kohler realized his dream of meeting with relatives of the crewmen who had died on the submarine.

Early and middle adulthood is a time of discovery and productivity as people explore their worlds, build families, and establish themselves in careers. All remarkable stories about this developmental period explore the contexts that frame our lives, including our physical and mental frailties, how we find fulfilling work, and our searches for love and companionship. These themes, and the individual differences that give life texture, are the topics of this chapter.

Health and Well-Being

People are more likely to become involved in risky hobbies, dangerous jobs, and interpersonal conflicts as they pass from adolescence into early adulthood. Then, with each passing year, an increasing number of adults acquire serious medical conditions. As a result, the risk of death creeps up steadily with each passing decade. As shown in Figure 13.1, unintentional injuries cause the most deaths during early adulthood with vehicle accidents accounting for 73 percent of these fatalities. Accidents continue to claim the majority of lives during the next decade of life, but cancer and heart disease become greater threats as we age.

To identify major health risks, public health officials track **mortality rates** (rates of death), **morbidity rates** (rates of various diseases), and *disability* rates (physical and mental conditions that limit major life activities, such as hearing or walking). Collectively, these indicators reveal two basic facts. First, as discussed in Chapter 11, the leading causes of death and chronic (long-term) illness during adulthood are all related to *behavior*. For example, vehicle injuries often involve speeding and alcohol use, and heart disease is associated with smoking, poor diet, and lack of exercise (Marks et al., 2000). Second, some environments promote better health, so good health is not distributed equally across adults from different economic and cultural circumstances.

Due to these facts, medical professionals do not view wellness as a gift that nature bestows on lucky adults. Instead, good health is partly a consequence of choices: choices about how we live our lives and how society distributes the conditions associated with wellness. Read on to learn how your future could be affected by the choices you are making right now.

Behavior and Health

As you read in Chapter 11, six health-related behaviors contribute to the leading causes of death and disability among youth and young adults: injury and violence (including accidental injuries, homicide, and suicide), sexual behavior, alcohol and drug use, tobacco use, nutrition, and physical activity. Here we explore three of the major threats to health and safety during adulthood: violence and the two components of fitness, nutrition and physical activity (Centers for Disease Control and Prevention, 2006b).

VIOLENCE. The shock wave rippled through the scientific community when Jane Goodall reported what a field assistant had witnessed in the Gombe National Park in Africa: A small band of male chimpanzees had traveled out of their territory and attacked a male from another community. The victorious chimpanzees continued to wage war, shattering the myth that apes enjoy a peaceful life in the forest (Goodall, 1986b).

Out of more than 10 million animal species, only chimpanzees and humans have been seen joining forces to raid neighboring groups and kill members of their own species (Buss, 2004). Tragically, this behavior is especially common among

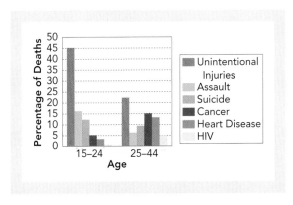

FIGURE 13.1 Age trends in the causes of death.

The six most frequent causes of death among 22- to 44-year-olds are unintentional injuries, assault, self-harm, cancer, heart disease, and HIV. Injury and violence are the greatest threats to life early in adulthood, but cancer and heart disease become greater threats as we age.

SOURCES: Hoyert, Kung, & Smith (2005); Federal Bureau of Investigation (2005).

mortality rates The rate of death in a population, often expressed as the number of deaths per 100,000 in a given year. By comparing mortality rates for different age groups and segments of the population, health officials can plan interventions and assess their effectiveness.

morbidity rates The frequency of various chronic diseases in a population. Health officials use changes in morbidity rates over time to evaluate the success of interventions and to identify emerging issues.

This sign in an Indianapolis suburb reminds residents that "there's no room for domestic violence in this community." Adults are less likely to resort to violence when their communities express strong disapproval of violence.

war

humans, who in one year alone waged war in over 35 countries (World Press Review, 2004). Like chimpanzees, who expand their feeding territory by killing, humans engage in organized conflict against other groups to obtain physical resources. Therefore, war is especially likely to erupt wherever a single group controls natural resources, there is marked social inequality, or rapid change has weakened a country's economy and government (Carnegie Commission on Preventing Deadly Conflict, 1997).

Like other animals, humans also increase their chances of survival by engaging in one-on-one (interpersonal) aggression, with males displaying more physical aggression than females. The trend for greater male aggressiveness is evident as early as 3 years of age and is found throughout the world. As in other species, our males use aggression to acquire material goods, defend against attack, compete for females, deter sexual partners from being unfaithful, and improve their social status (Buss, 2004). Competition for material and sexual resources is most severe when young men are striking out on their own. From an evolutionary perspective, this is the reason behind the *young male syndrome*: the increase in risky and aggressive behavior during late adolescence and early adulthood (Wilson & Daly, 1985).

Homicide statistics illustrate the young male syndrome. The majority of people who kill—about 88 percent—are male, and individuals from 18 to 25 years are more likely than any other age group both to kill and be killed (Fox & Zawitz, 2004). But rates of violence vary as a function of a group's economic status. In 2000, for example, African Americans in the United States were seven times more likely than European Americans to commit a homicide and six times more likely to be murdered, but racial differences disappear at upper income brackets (Reiss & Roth, 1994). These findings support the idea that competition for resources fuels the young male syndrome.

Although humans often act aggressively against individuals from other families and social groups, we are more peaceful than chimpanzees toward members of our immediate social group (Shermer, 2003). Nevertheless, within-group violence—including domestic partner violence—is disturbingly common. About 25 percent of women in the United States report that they have been physically assaulted, stalked, or raped by an intimate partner (Centers for Disease Control and Prevention, 2003b). Abuse by a husband is more common when men have lower economic status than their wives or believe they have less power (Pan, Neidig, & O'Leary, 1994; Sagrestano, Heavey, & Christensen, 1999). But a one-sided stereotype of crazed men abusing helpless women is far from accurate, because as many as one-fourth of the people arrested for domestic violence are women in some locations (Goldberg, 1999). Still, men aggress more often than women and show a different pattern of aggression. Specifically, men are less likely to injure in self-defense and are more likely to initiate physical fighting, stalk or injure a partner who has left them, inflict injuries that require medical treatment, and sexually assault their partners (Felson & Cares, 2005; Saunders, 2002). However, the fact that 12 percent of murderers are women shows that sex differences in violent behavior are matters of degree rather than absolutes (Fox & Zawitz, 2004).

Rates of violent behavior vary dramatically around the world because our biological potential for violence is just that: a potential that can be encouraged or discouraged by our environments. For example, the number of homicides each year per 100,000 residents is relatively low in Southeast Asia (6), higher in North and South America (19), and higher still in Africa (22) (Krug et al., 2002). Adults are more likely to inflict harm on others when aggression is tolerated by their culture, there is a high probability that others will harm them, and guns or

domestic Partner violence

other weapons are readily available (Cook & Moore, 1999; Hepburn & Hemenway, 2004). Therefore, one way to prevent violence is to promote a nonviolent culture by helping adults achieve the basic needs discussed in this chapter: a sense of wellness, productive work, and satisfying social relationships.

STAYING FIT. Excess weight is a health issue that only recently began to threaten a large number of adults. Currently, about 65 percent of American adults are overweight or obese, and obesity is increasingly a problem in other countries as well (Centers for Disease Control and Prevention, 2006c). (Recall that being overweight is defined as having a BMI greater than or equal to 25; obesity is a BMI greater than or equal to 30.) As in children, the obesity rate is especially high among Mexican American and African American adults. Nonetheless, the population as a whole has experienced a dramatic increase in weight that is illustrated by the maps in Figure 13.2.

Overweight adults are at risk for many chronic conditions, including high blood pressure and heart disease, diabetes, arthritis-related disabilities, and some cancers. Because obesity and a sedentary lifestyle go hand in hand, it is not surprising that more than 50 percent of American adults do not get enough exercise to prevent weight-related disease (Centers for Disease Control and Prevention, 2005f). One reason is that American culture places a high value on comforts, that is, spending money to make life easier. Microwave ovens, automatic garage door openers, and driving to visit the neighbor down the street make many people feel they are enjoying the "good life." In contrast, many cultures do not value spending to avoid exercise. For instance, the French, whose obesity rate is only 7 percent, prefer to spend money on "pleasures," which are experiences such as plays, flowers, and fine meals (Rozin, 2000).

How do the French enjoy food and wine yet stay so slim? When psychologist Paul Rozin and his colleagues compared restaurants in Paris and Philadelphia, they discovered that American portions were 25 percent larger than the ones offered abroad (Rozin et al., 2003). Unexpectedly, even food that is "standardized," such as the grilled chicken sandwich from McDonald's, weighed less in France. (Apparently, even the chickens are smaller in Europe.) These results help explain the *French paradox*: a low rate of heart disease in France despite a love of high-fat foods. In a nutshell, the French simply eat less.

The comparison of French and American diets illustrates an important point. Regardless of the amount of fat and carbohydrates in food, obesity results from a **positive energy balance**: consuming more energy than an individual expends. Nutritionists agree that adults should protect themselves from the perils of food by monitoring how much they eat; adding more complex grains, fruits, and vegetables to their diets; and exercising more.

Education and Health

The number of years of education an individual has is one of the best predictors of health. Compared to less educated adults, those who spend more years in school have lower death rates, lower disease rates, and lower disability rates. The association between education and health remains even after age, sex, race, marital status, and parental education are taken into account. Furthermore, it is the number of years of education—not the prestige of people's colleges or whether they actually completed

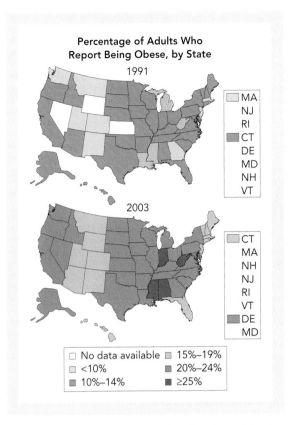

FIGURE 13.2 The obesity epidemic.

The percentage of adults with a body mass index of 30 or greater (about 30 pounds overweight for a person who is 5′ 4″ tall) increased dramatically during the 1990s. Currently, about 65 percent of adults in the United States are overweight or obese.

SOURCE: Centers for Disease Control and Prevention (2005f). *http://www.cdc.gov/nccdphp/ aag/aag_dnpa.htm* Retrieved November 21, 2005.

positive energy balance The consumption of more energy than an individual expends, which is the cause of weight gain.

a degree—that matters. These findings suggest that education is not related to health merely because people with college degrees are wealthier than other adults. Instead, the relationship between years of education and health is largely due to the fact that more educated people have more fulfilling work, a sense of personal control and social support, and a healthier lifestyle. For example, those who stay in school longer are more likely to exercise, refrain from smoking, and stay at a recommended weight (Mirowsky & Ross, 2003; Ross & Mirowsky, 1999).

Healthy behavior reduces your risk of *chronic diseases*, but diet, exercise patterns, smoking, and alcohol consumption do not account for very much of the variability in how often people suffer from *infectious diseases* (Marsland et al., 2001). To understand why some of us are more vulnerable to colds and flu, researchers have focused on the relationship between stress and health.

Stress and Health

Your world is teeming with bacteria and viruses, yet you usually feel well. Every day, your immune system fights off microorganisms that cause infectious disease. But something changes when you experience long-term stress. Chronic stress disrupts the delicate balance of hormones and proteins that regulates your immune system, causing immune responses that trigger inflammation to increase while responses that help fend off microscopic invaders decrease (Cohen, 2005; Robles, Glaser, & Kiecolt-Glaser, 2005). Therefore, it is one of the ironies of life that you are most likely to feel ill when you most need to be well.

Adults have lots of reasons to suffer from chronic stress, including job stress, marital conflict, natural disasters (such as earthquakes), and the loss of intimate relationships (Marsland et al., 2001). But how do we know that the illnesses that follow these events are not caused by the unhealthy behaviors that so often follow a crisis, such as lack of sleep or alcohol use? To determine whether stress directly affects illness, scientists expose people who have experienced different amounts of stress to a pathogen. (Often this involves giving volunteers a sizable sum of money for the right to administer a nasal drop containing a cold-producing virus.) Consistently, individuals who have experienced a larger number of stressful life events are the ones who become ill. Negative reactions to life events contribute to—but are not essential for—illness. That is, people who have recently experienced stressful events are more likely to eventually develop symptoms *even if they are not aware* of feeling unusually upset by those events (Cohen, 1996).

The older we are, the more likely it is that we have built up immunity to specific pathogens that cause minor illnesses. As a result, young and middle-aged adults are more likely to suffer from common colds (averaging two to four per year) than are people over the age of 60 (who average less than one per year) (Nordenberg, 1999). But younger adults may also be more likely to suffer from minor illnesses because they experience more social stress and react more intensely to stressful events. In one study, for example, young and middle-aged adults reported more arguments and other interpersonal tensions over the course of a day than adults ages 60 or over did, and these younger age groups were more bothered by negative interactions and more likely to argue (Birditt, Fingerman, & Almeida, 2005).

Even within an age group, individual immune systems respond very differently to stress. Adults who cope with stress without getting ill tend to have the following characteristics:

▶ *Sociability.* People who are extraverted, agreeable, and liked by others get sick less often than their peers. In one study, over 40 percent of the people who scored low on sociability became ill after exposure to a cold-producing virus, compared to only 20 percent of the highly sociable people (Cohen et al., 2003). Similarly, socially extroverted men who are infected with HIV respond to antiviral treatment better than inhibited men (Cole et al., 2003).

▶ *A strong social network.* It is comforting when friends help you through stressful times. The size of people's social networks predicts their immune response beyond what we know from measuring how sociable they are. Among college students, for instance, loneliness and small social networks are associated with poorer antibody response to a vaccination (Pressman et al., 2005).

▶ *Psychological hardiness.* Among people who are equally stressed, those with a history of depression and anxiety show poorer immune system functioning (Cohen, 2002; Locke et al., 1984). On the other hand, interventions that teach relaxation or other stress-management techniques improve immune responses (Marsland et al., 2001).

These findings prove that psychological health can influence physical health. But what factors are associated with a psychologically healthy adulthood? Why do some individuals celebrate life while others grumble and despair? Read on to see if you predicted some of the answers.

Well-Being in Adulthood

When we ask what makes for a psychologically healthy adulthood, we are asking what factors predict **well-being**: the perception that life is fulfilling, meaningful, and pleasant (Myers, 1992). Counter to what many people expect, income is a poor predictor of well-being once a community's standard of living reaches a comfortable level. For example, the Masai of Africa, who live without electricity in huts made from dung, are almost as satisfied as the richest Americans are. Furthermore, the mean life satisfaction in the United States has not changed over the past 50 years, despite the fact that houses have become larger and electronic devices more plentiful (Diener & Seligman, 2004).

There is also no strong relationship between well-being and age (Figure 13.3). Contrary to the stereotype that teenagers are miserable, middle-aged adults are pining for lost youth, and the elderly are sick and unhappy, the majority of people at all ages are rather pleased with their lives (Inglehart et al., 2004). What, then, makes for a good life? Five broad factors predict well-being:

▶ *"Happiness" traits.* Twin studies confirm that between 44 and 52 percent of the variability in well-being is associated with genetic differences (Lykken & Tellegen, 1996). Optimism (the belief that things usually turn out well) and extroversion (being outgoing) are examples of heritable traits associated with happiness (Bouchard & Hur, 1998; Schulman, Keith, & Seligman, 1993).

Because a person's biological makeup influences mood, there is an astonishing tendency for people to return to their usual level of happiness after a crisis. For example, many adults who are paralyzed by car accidents or other traumatic events say they experience happiness more often than depression or anger within weeks of their

well-being The perception that one's life is fulfilling, meaningful, and pleasant.

Individuals' sense of whether their economic well-being is good or poor is a function of what they have grown to expect. As a result, even people in societies with few material goods—such as this Masai villager—typically report that they are quite happy.

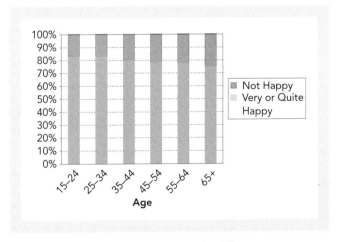

FIGURE 13.3 Satisfaction across the life span.

In a worldwide survey involving over 93,000 people, the percentage who said they were "very happy" or "quite happy" was remarkably stable—about 80 percent—from 15 to 64 years of age. Even from 64 to 101 years, 74 percent of people felt they were happy.

SOURCE: Prepared by the authors from the World Values Survey (Inglehart et al., 2004).

tragedies (Wortman & Silver, 1987). On the flip side, most people are *not* happier long after an episode of good fortune. As psychologist Dave Myers (1992) noted, "*Every* desirable experience—passionate love, a spiritual high, the pleasure of a new possession, the exhilaration of success—is transitory" (p. 53). These findings suggest that each of us has a typical happiness state or "set point" that is only temporarily shaken by crises. But there are exceptions. For example, most adults in one 15-year-long study eventually returned to their usual level of subjective well-being after losing a spouse, yet some people remained substantially less happy (Lucas et al., 2003).

▶ *Social relationships.* People need social contact in the form of committed relationships to feel good about life. It is easier to be happy when you live in a community where people trust one another, have high rates of volunteer activity, and frequently socialize (Diener & Seligman, 2002, 2004). And as a group, married adults report higher levels of well-being than singles do (Tepperman & Curtis, 1995).

▶ *Positive social comparison.* You can feel good or bad about your life depending on your frame of reference. In general, people feel better when they "compare downward" by thinking about others who are worse off than themselves. Unlike cranky people, happy people focus on social information that helps them feel satisfied (Lyubomirsky, 2001; Lyubomirsky & Ross, 1997).

▶ *Being productive.* Dozens of studies have found that people like to be doing something. For example, most people say they would continue working even if they inherited a large fortune, and unemployment usually breeds unhappiness (Myers, 1992). But it is not just busywork that makes people happy. Most people prefer moderately difficult tasks over those that are too easy, and they like to feel in control of the situation (Warr, 1999). One of the most pleasurable experiences is a state of *flow*: being so absorbed in an activity that you become unaware of yourself, the time, and your surroundings (Nakamura & Csikszentimihalyi, 2002).

▶ *Faith.* As discussed in Chapter 12, participation in religious activities gives people a sense of meaning, hope, and opportunities for social contact. So it is not surprising that those who are religious experience greater well-being as a group than those who are not (Diener et al., 1999; Ferriss, 2002).

These findings help explain why the rising standard of living has not dramatically changed people's perceptions of their lives: Material goods do little to improve your social relationships or your sense that life is meaningful. In fact, the choices made possible by modernization can actually impair your sense of well-being. Today, millions of potential partners are available through Internet dating, there are thousands of product brands, and career paths abound, yet rates of depression have risen as these options have expanded (Cross National Collaborative Group, 1992). Psychologist Barry Schwartz (2000, 2004) has found that—paradoxically—well-being declines as options increase. For example, shoppers who view 30 products are less likely to buy something than those who view 6, and college seniors who send out more job applications are less happy with the outcome than seniors who send out fewer. Instead of improving our lives, too much choice adds stress and increases feelings of regret. As a result, people who try to make "good enough" choices are happier than those who strive for the best possible result.

These basic ingredients for well-being are the same around the globe. For example, a study conducted in Pakistan, an Eastern Muslim culture, also found that happiness was associated with work satisfaction, social support, and marital status (Suhail & Chaudhry, 2004). Apparently, Sigmund Freud was right when he said that two of the most significant influences on quality of life are the ones you will read about next: work and love.

>>> **MEMORY MAKERS** <<<

1. During early and middle adulthood, the leading causes of death and chronic illness are all related to ____. For example, ____ claims the most lives throughout this period of life.

   (a) genetically transmitted diseases; cancer
   (b) genetically transmitted diseases; heart disease
   (c) behavior; smoking
   (d) behavior; accidental injury

2. A major reason why France has a lower obesity rate than the United States is that____.

   (a) the French dislike high-fat foods
   (b) most adults in France eat only two meals a day
   (c) portion sizes are smaller in France
   (d) French adults spend less time eating

3. Which of the following individuals is *least* likely to catch a cold?

   (a) Bill, who likes people and is very outgoing
   (b) Carl, who has very few friends
   (c) Juan, who has a history of depression
   (d) Jayden, who is unusually anxious

[1-d; 2-c; 3-a]

Earning a Living

Early and middle adulthood is a productive time because people generally like to work. Although a thesaurus says that *work* is synonymous with "the daily grind" and "drudgery," most people enjoy work more than they dread it, and most are satisfied with their jobs (Kiecolt, 2003). When people around the world were asked whether leisure or work makes life worth living, 85 percent either ranked these activities equally or voted for work (Inglehart et al., 2004). Moreover, 43 percent of Americans, 49 percent of the Japanese, and 80 percent of Brazilians agreed or strongly agreed with the statement, "I like work so much that I often stay up late at night to finish it" (World Values Survey, 2004). But regardless of how we feel about work, there is no doubt that it consumes a large part of our lives, helps define who we are, and structures our social relationships.

"I just want to go home, crawl into bed, and do some more work."

The Changing Workforce

Three revolutions have changed the way adults earn a living. For tens of thousands of years, humans were hunters and gatherers who lived in bands of 25 to 50 people. Social groups became larger and more complex after the *agricultural revolution* when farming freed people from having to travel for their meals. After technological advances sparked the *industrial revolution*, fewer people were needed to produce the food and goods society needed. As a result, more adults abandoned farming to work in factories, large urban centers developed, and work lives became more varied. Some people still farmed, but others owned factories, sold their labor to factory owners, distributed goods, or provided professional services.

The most recent change to restructure work is the *information revolution* (also called the *microchip revolution*). As computerization made it possible for fewer adults to produce needed food and other products, more people became involved in providing services and acquiring, storing, and sharing information. Personal shopping, investment consulting, and running travel Web sites are good examples of such jobs. A number of changes have accompanied this transition into the information age (National Research Council Committee on Techniques for the Enhancement of Human Performance, 1999). Today's workers need a higher level of skill to land desirable jobs, and there is more emphasis on communication and social skills rather than physical strength. The workforce is also increasingly diverse, with a higher proportion of older workers, women, and minorities than in the past. As a result, today's employees need to function effectively with people from a variety of ages and backgrounds. Finally, today's adults have less job stability than their grandparents did because jobs are created and eliminated at a faster pace.

What do these changes mean for life in a technologically advanced country? In a nutshell, change and flexibility are the rules of the game. One longitudinal study found that employees averaged almost 10 different jobs from ages 18 to 36, which is more than one job change every 2 years (U.S. Department of Labor, 2002). Changing financial circumstances often accompany these shifts—and not always for the better. In one sample, 35 percent of managers experienced a substantial salary change over a 2-year period, with 11 percent of men and 21 percent of women moving from a high-wage to a lower-wage position (Gabriel, 2003). But even people who do not change jobs are often under pressure to learn new skills, adjust to new ways of performing tasks, and adapt to co-workers who have values and experiences that are different from their own. In other words, adjusting to work is now a lifelong process.

Building a Career

One of the central features of adulthood is entering the workforce and building a career (or two or three over the course of a lifetime). Here we highlight some of the concerns adults have as they select their initial careers, adjust to work, and settle into midcareer.

SELECTING A CAREER. Career selection begins in childhood, when children learn about visible jobs such as fire fighting, teaching, and (sometimes) what their parents do. Knowledge of possible careers expands considerably during adolescence but is still incomplete.

An important and often stressful transition is the need to finalize plans for a first career. The possibility of choosing poorly and closing off options is frightening, so some young adults approach this task with a sense of dread. Three sets of findings suggest that many feel trapped in what one expert called a "self-perpetuating state of hesitancy and confusion" (Feldman, 2002a, p. 93):

▶ ***Procrastination.*** In the United States, about 33 percent of high school graduates delay starting college, and the number of years between high school and college graduation has increased dramatically. Many of these young adults are biding their time in temporary, low-paying jobs while they try to figure out the best course of action for the future.

▶ *Frequent switching of fields of study.* Compared to past generations, more of today's students are transferring colleges or changing majors late in the game. Remarkably, 12 percent of students attend three or more colleges before graduating, and one-third of students with a 4-year-degree leave graduate school without a degree.

▶ *Inability to identify early-career goals.* In an effort to find a career that satisfies all of their goals, some young adults collect so much information that they feel paralyzed about making a decision.

There are advantages and disadvantages to this leisurely approach. On the bright side, students who consider a range of options have a better chance of finding careers that match their interests and talents. But it is costly to delay graduation. Compared to people who are more certain of their future path, those who delay deciding on a career tend to be more introverted (and thus less likely to seek out information from other adults) (Caldwell & Burger, 1998) and more likely to have a broad range of interests (Rysiew, Shore, & Leeb, 1999).

ADJUSTING TO WORK LIFE. Finding an enjoyable job can be a long process. As many as one-third of young workers leave their jobs within 6 months, and one-half do so within the first year (Farber, 2003). There are many reasons why young workers are not very stable employees. An obvious one is that the match between interests, abilities, and jobs improves as people gain work experience and better understand themselves as workers. For example, some people like fast-paced, unpredictable jobs, whereas others find these pressures unpleasant. But many careers have both options, with employees changing jobs until they find a fit. Thus health workers who start out in critical care may move into home health care (and vice versa), just as writers who start out with newspaper deadlines sometimes move into book publishing (and vice versa). Mismatches between abilities and jobs are greater during early work life, when people are still discovering their talents and preferences (Wilk, Desmarais, & Sackett, 1995; Wilk & Sackett, 1996).

Another reason for early-career job changes is that young workers often have unrealistic expectations about work. In one survey, over a third of recent college graduates said that work was more difficult than they had expected. These young workers reported that they worked longer hours than they had anticipated, were more

Mike Judge's hysterical movie, *Office Space*, highlighted the dark side of work in the information age—and the discontent young workers often feel during their first jobs.

tired after work, and were paid less than they had hoped (Hatcher & Crook, 1988). Similarly, employers complain that recent graduates lack experience yet expect high starting salaries and rapid advancement (Davison, Brown, & Davison, 1993).

MIDCAREER. Regardless of how long someone has been involved in a particular line of work, there is a tendency for people's goals to change as they grow older. Many people in their 30s crave more challenge and autonomy from their work lives than they demanded in their 20s, and the 40s and 50s are times when workers become increasingly interested in taking on leadership roles and *mentoring* (advising less experienced employees) (Feldman, 2002b; Raabe & Beehr, 2003). As a consequence of boredom and changing goals, it is not uncommon for adults to revisit their commitment to a career. In fact, about half of the people who participated in one survey said they would be interested in changing careers (Miller & Hanson, 2000).

A major challenge for many adults is the difficulty of balancing family demands with the demands of a career. Work and family lives are less separate than they were in the past, as employees more often interrupt their workday to do family chores and bring work home to complete at night (Goad, 2002). Men and women report similar levels of conflict between work and family demands because both sexes feel pressure to excel in all of their life roles (Winslow, 2005).

Diversity in the Workplace

There is a good reason why many college students fret about picking a career: They know that their choices will influence more than just what they do for 40 hours each week. Indeed, the job you have very often affects your economic status and leisure activities, your children's neighborhood and school, and, in turn, your family life. Partly as a result of *social reproduction* (as discussed in Chapter 5), there are considerable differences in the typical work lives of different ethnic groups and those of men versus women.

WOMEN AT WORK. There is no doubt that women have gained a stronger foothold in the workforce. Only 33 percent of women were employed in the United States in 1950, compared to 61 percent in 2000. Similarly, only 47 percent of women with children under 6 years were employed in 1980, compared to 66 percent by 2000. But despite these trends, men are still more likely to be employed and to work full time. Indeed, over 73 percent of men were in the workforce during each year between 1970 and 2000 (Population Reference Bureau, 2004). Throughout adulthood, women are more likely than men to forgo paid employment in order to raise children and manage a household.

Few cultures value paid employment equally for men and women, but opinions differ even among industrialized countries. For example, one survey asked people from many countries to respond to the statement, "When jobs are scarce, men should have more right to a job than women" (Inglehart et al., 2004). Few adults in Sweden agreed with this statement, whereas 10 percent of Americans and nearly a third of the Japanese adults did. Worldwide, 30 percent of women and 39 percent of men believed that men had more rights to jobs.

Traditional sex-role attitudes continue to influence women's work lives. Women still earn less money than men, and there is an income disparity even when occupation, training, and years of experience are taken into account (Roos & Gatta, 1999; U.S. Census Bureau, 2003b). Women also face the *glass ceiling*, which refers to unofficial barriers that can block women from promotion into upper levels of management or responsibility at work. But if you ask a group of married working women what bothers them the most, you are sure to hear an earful about housework. Housework has long been called the "second shift," a job that awaits most women as they return home from work. For example, an Australian study found that husbands contributed fewer hours of housework even when their wives earned as much as they did (Bittman et al., 2003), and a U.S. study found that women's paid and unpaid work averaged 5 to 7 hours more per week than men's (Sayer, England, et al., 2004). It is easy to see why working women face a "time famine": If working/commuting (9 hours), sleeping (8 hours), and housework (3 hours) consume 20 hours per day, there is little time left for personal needs, family life, and fun.

ETHNICITY AND SOCIAL CLASS. There are many reasons why different ethnic groups earn different average incomes: These groups have different high school completion rates, different rates of attending and completing college, and different experiences during hiring and promotion. As a result of these and other factors, Asian and white adults enjoy a higher average income than Hispanic and African American adults. You can compare your assumptions about ethnic differences in income against the actual data in Figure 13.4.

People who continue their education past high school are more likely to hold jobs that have a lower accident risk and allow them to live in safer neighborhoods. But in addition to the obvious health benefits of education, as discussed earlier in this chapter, delaying entry into the workforce also tends to delay marriage and parenthood. As a result, our pathways into the workforce influence a more private part of our lives: our relationships.

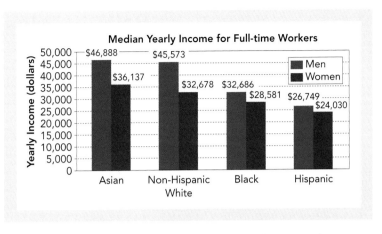

FIGURE 13.4 Ethnicity and income.

By adulthood, the various ethnic groups in the United States have accumulated different experiences that translate into large differences in income. The financial picture is two-tiered: Asian and non-Hispanic white adults are overrepresented at the higher income brackets, while African American and Hispanic adults are overrepresented in the lower income brackets.

SOURCE: Fronczek (2005).

›››MEMORY MAKERS‹‹‹

1. When people around the world were asked whether work or leisure make life worth living, ____ percent ranked these activities equally or voted for work.

   (a) 5   **(b)** 25   **(c)** 50   **(d)** 85

2. Which conclusion best describes the nature of work now that we have experienced the information revolution?

   (a) Jobs are more stable than they were in the past.

   (b) More jobs involve producing food and other goods.

   (c) Communication and social skills are less important than they were in the past.

   (d) Adjusting to work is a lifelong process.

3. Which of the following is *not* a concern for women in industrialized countries who have paid employment?

   (a) time famine

   (b) the "second shift"

   (c) the glass ceiling

   (d) all three are concerns

[1-d (most people value work and leisure equally or vote for work); 2-d (adjusting to work is a lifelong process because people change jobs so frequently and are constantly expected to change how they perform tasks); 3-d (employed women deal with balancing multiple roles, the time famine, doing household tasks after work, the "second shift", and informal barriers to advancement at work, the glass ceiling)]

Relationships

When Angela celebrated her 50th birthday, we asked her what she had learned about relationships since she was 20. "I used to think relationships would get easier as I grew older, but they didn't," she said. "They're a lot of work. But I learned to expect less from people. When I was younger, I wanted a man to be my lover, my best friend, and my father all rolled up in one. I wanted every girl friend to agree with me on every issue. That's unrealistic. Everyone has something to offer, but you can't expect one person to meet all of your needs." Now Angela enjoys what each person contributes to her life. "When my mom is driving me nuts, I call my sister," she explained. "When my son says something on the phone that upsets me, I visit John in the office next to me, because he always makes me laugh."

While Angela was building 30 years of relationship experience, scientists were busy exploring why relationships are so important yet so fragile. Their findings tell us about the neurochemistry of love, how happy couples relate, what people are doing in bed, how children change our lives, and who we turn to for lifelong support. Let's start our look at how relationships pave life pathways by introducing a new field that is helping us understand a universal and exhilarating phenomenon: romantic love.

INNOVATIONS

Using neuroimaging tools, studies of pair-bonding in animals and attraction in humans show that chemical changes in the brain "addict" us to romantic partners, causing us to crave them and feel highly motivated to be with them.

THE COLORS OF LOVE

How much time do you spend each day thinking about a special someone, wishing you had a special someone, or making choices that will help you attract a special someone? If you are like most 19- to 40-somethings, the answer is "a lot." Recently, scientists from a new field, *social neuroscience*, have discovered why: The urge to partner is embedded in our genes.

Social neuroscientists use neuroimaging tools and techniques for analyzing brain tissue to investigate complex social behavior—including the mysteries of love. Two types of field mice—prairie and montane voles—have helped these scientists understand how the genes that build a brain also influence the tendency to bond with social partners. When a male prairie vole mates, his brain releases *vasopressin*, a chemical that floods the reward regions of his brain, causing him to prefer her above all others. Meanwhile, both lovers produce *oxytocin*, a chemical that makes them feel calm and secure when they are together (Insel & Carter, 1995). As a result, prairie voles prefer **monogamy**: the practice of mating with only one partner. In contrast, sex feels good to the montane vole (thanks to a release of dopamine) but, lacking the brain circuits

monogamy The practice of mating with only one partner. Monogamous marriages are marriages to only one other person.

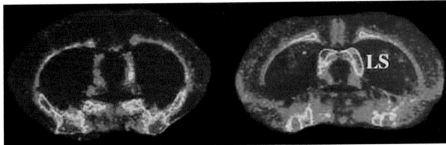

A devoted prairie vole dad mates only with one female and staunchly defends his territory against intruders. A scan of his brain (left) shows that receptors for the hormone vasopressin are distributed differently than they are in the non-monogamous montane vole (right).

that link this experience with information about specific partners, sex with anyone feels just as good. As one journalist explained, "If we could read the montane vole's thoughts, he or she would be thinking 'Gee, sex feels great!' Where the monogamous prairie vole would be thinking, 'Gee, sex with this particular partner feels great!'" (Mims, 2004, para. 24).

Three brain chemicals—dopamine, vasopressin, and oxytocin—are involved in pair-bonding and parenting behavior in humans as well as voles. Although humans may change partners more often than the devoted prairie vole, both species experience chemical changes that "addict" them to specific individuals, at least temporarily. The result is an eerie biochemical similarity between drug addiction and love, including feelings of tolerance (get a little of it and you feel you need more) and withdrawal (lose it and fall into a state of depression) (Fisher, 2004).

Anthropologist Helen Fisher has studied this process in humans. Working with a psychologist and a neuroscientist, she recruited college students who were hopelessly, madly in love. Each volunteer provided a photograph of their beloved and one of an emotionally neutral person. Then the fun began. As each student reclined in a scanning machine, the team recorded which brain areas were active as they gazed at the photographs. Pictures of their brains, with different hues showing how hard each region was working, revealed the colors of love (Aron et al., 2005).

One region that lit up the most among students who were passionately in love is a primitive area deep in the brain called the *caudate nucleus* (Figure 13.5). (You can determine if a current or past love was passionate by taking the quiz at the end of this feature.) The caudate nucleus is part of the brain's reward system, a network of connections that registers pleasure and motivates people to seek rewards. Other parts of the reward system also showed more activity when people thought about their beloved, including a collection of cells that distributes the chemical *dopamine*. Dopamine is involved in focused attention, addictive behavior, heightened energy, and intense motivation to obtain a reward—in short, the symptoms of romantic bliss. Dopamine also stimulates the release of testosterone, a hormone that increases sexual desire. Based on these findings, Fisher concluded that romantic love is not just a simple feeling. Instead, love is a *motivational system* that is wired into the brain—a "fundamental human mating drive" (Fisher, 2004, p. 74).

Studies of human relationships have also revealed a well-known kink in the bliss of love: As a relationship matures, our feelings—and how our brains respond—change. The surge of love that helps us overcome our fear of strangers eventually mellows into other feelings, good or bad, depending on the circumstances. Because the strength of our bond to particular partners hovers somewhere between the prairie and montane voles'—and

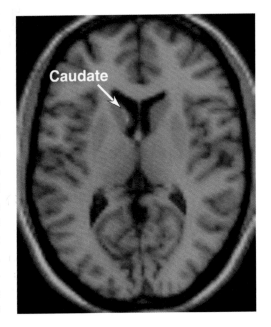

FIGURE 13.5 Passionate love in the brain.

Activation in a region of the brain called the anterior caudate nucleus (left side highlighted here) increases when people look at pictures of someone they love passionately.

Courtesy Lucy Brown.

different brains have different "devotion" tendencies—social neuroscience cannot yet tell us where an individual relationship will be 5, 10, or 20 years after our brains first light up with love.

THE PASSIONATE LOVE SCALE

To determine whether volunteers were passionately in love, Helen Fisher gave them a test devised by psychologist Elaine Hatfield of the University of Hawaii and sociologist Susan Sprecher of Illinois State University. You can take it yourself:

Think of the person you love most passionately now. If you are not in love, think of the last person you loved. If you have never been in love, think of the person you came closest to caring for in that way. Try to describe the way you felt when your feelings were most intense. Answers range from (1) not at all true to (9) definitely true.

1	2	3	4	5	6	7	8	9
Not at all true			Moderately true			Definitely true		

_9_ 1. I would feel deep despair if ____ left me.

_9_ 2. Sometimes I feel I can't control my thoughts; they are obsessively about____.

_9_ 3. I feel happy when I am doing something to make ____ happy.

_9_ 4. I would rather be with ____ than anyone else.

_9_ 5. I'd get jealous if I thought ____ were falling in love with someone else.

_7_ 6. I yearn to know all about ____.

_9_ 7. I want ____ physically, emotionally, and mentally.

_9_ 8. I have an endless appetite for affection from ____.

_9_ 9. For me, ____ is the perfect romantic partner.

_9_ 10. I sense my body responding when ____ touches me.

_7_ 11. ____ always seems to be on my mind.

_9_ 12. I want ____ to know me—my thoughts, my fears and my hopes.

_9_ 13. I eagerly look for signs indicating ____'s desire for me.

_9_ 14. I possess a powerful attraction for ____.

_9_ 15. I get extremely depressed when things don't go right in my relationship with ____.

_131_ **Total score**

Results:

★ 106–135 = Wildly, even recklessly, in love

★ 86–105 = Passionate, but less intense

★ 66–85 points = Occasional bursts of passion

★ 45–65 points = Tepid, infrequent passion

★ 15–44 = No thrill, never was ◆

The Feelings That Bind Us Together

What we call "love" is really a number of reactions, from the romantic passion Helen Fisher studied to the quiet peace you feel when you sit near a longtime partner. Psychologist Robert Sternberg's (1988, 1997a, 1998) **triangular theory of love** breaks these feelings down into three components:

▶ *Passion* is an intense longing for another person.

▶ *Intimacy* involves feelings that promote a sense of connectedness. People who are intimate enjoy being with one another, care about each other's welfare, and give and receive emotional support.

▶ *Decision and commitment* occur when we decide to love and commit to working through the ups and downs of a relationship. Commitment helps maintain a relationship by carrying us through periods of boredom and other challenges.

Adults experience different types of loving relationships because some relationships lack one or more of these components. If you unexpectedly run into someone and find yourself speechless, you probably have an "infatuation"—feelings of passion without intimacy or commitment. But if you often confide in someone you would never consider dating, you probably share "companionate love"—intimacy and commitment without passion. The presence or absence of each point in the triangle of love produces the types of relationships described in Table 13.1.

Because different brain circuits drive different feelings, romantic love is not always connected to feelings of lust or the desire for long-term commitment. We can feel romantic love for someone we would never commit to for a long-term relationship, feel lust for someone we do not love romantically, and be deeply attached to a partner yet still feel jolts of passion for other people. An evolutionary perspective sees this complicated system as an insurance policy that helps us gain resources from more than one suitor and attach to new partners if one partner dies. But conflicts over romantic issues disrupt communities and interfere with the teamwork needed to raise children in hostile environments. To establish more stability than the brain naturally provides, cultures around the world have adopted the practice of marriage.

triangular theory of love Robert Sternberg's theory that love consists of three components: passion, intimacy, and decision to love or make a commitment.

TABLE 13.1 Kinds of Love from the Triangular Theory of Love

Kind of Love	Intimacy	Passion	Decision/Commitment
Nonlove	−	−	−
Liking	+	−	−
Infatuated love	−	+	−
Empty love	−	−	+
Romantic love	+	+	−
Companionate love	+	−	+
Factuous love	−	+	+
Consummate love	+	+	+

Note. A + means the component is present; a − means the component is absent.
Adapted from Sternberg (1998).

Marriage

For many people, marriage is the rite of passage that most alerts them to the fact that they are now adults. But human behavior is flexible, so how marriage is organized—and how often people jump on and off the marriage wagon—varies tremendously from culture to culture.

MARRIAGE AROUND THE WORLD. Only about 5 percent of mammal species (including humans and voles) pair up with specific partners to rear young. In Western cultures, monogamy often means **serial monogamy** (one partner at a time) rather than one partner for life. But some societies permit other types of marriage partnerships. Many allow **polygamy**, the right of a man to take more than one wife. This strategy is common where resources are generally scarce, so a woman might prefer to be the second wife of a rich man rather than the only wife of a poor man. Other cultures allow **polyandry**, the right of a woman to marry more than one man. In some parts of Tibet, for example, a woman might marry the oldest son in a family and one or more of his brothers (Smith, 1998).

In contrast to the Western ideal, love is not the primary reason for marriage in most societies. Many cultures view marriage as a vehicle to provide economic security and to cement relationships between the families joined by marriage. The practice of arranged marriages reflects these values. In traditional Nepal, for example, a bride and groom might meet for the first time on their wedding day. And in some parts of the world, girls are married by 12 years of age or younger to reduce promiscuity and strengthen clan relationships. Today, most people throughout the world choose their spouses, but some marriages are still arranged in regions where extended families have long been critical for survival, including India, Pakistan, and parts of sub-Saharan Africa.

In the United States, three changes have created more variation in the family structure of individuals in early and middle adulthood:

▶ *People are waiting longer to marry.* In 1970, the median age of first marriage was 23 for men and 21 for women; by 2000, it had risen to nearly 27 for men and 25 for women. But there is little evidence that society is abandoning marriage. On the contrary, 74 percent of men and women marry by their 35th birthday, and 95 percent do so by age 65 (Fields & Casper, 2001). Thus many adults approach marriage as they approach an unheated swimming pool: They're skittish because the water is cold, but most eventually jump in.

▶ *More people are having children prior to marriage.* Increasingly, adults are jumping into parenting before marriage. In the United States, about 35 percent of births are to unmarried women, with women in their 20s showing the highest unmarried birthrate (Martin et al., 2003). This situation is not unique to the United States. In Sweden, a typical pattern of forming a family consists of *cohabitation* (living together before marriage) followed by one or more children and, in some cases, marriage. This process stems from a belief that unions should not have to involve the government or religious authorities (Andersson, 1999).

▶ *More people are divorcing.* In the United States, only about 75 percent of marriages currently make it to the tenth anniversary, and it is estimated that 50 percent eventually end in divorce (Kreider, 2005; Kreider & Fields, 2002).

It is clear that, unlike the lucky prairie vole, our marriages do not survive because brain chemicals keep us content. Instead, couples who stay together tend to share a set of characteristics that make marriages work.

serial monogamy The practice of having only one sexual partner/spouse at any given time but a series of partners/spouses over time.

polygamy The right of a man to take more than one wife.

polyandry The right of a woman to be married to more than one man.

SUCCESSFUL MARRIAGES. It is natural for marital happiness to change over time. As shown in Figure 13.6, satisfaction with marriage declines rapidly during the first 4 years, stabilizes for a number of years, and then declines again between the eighth and tenth years (Kurdek, 1999). The first period of challenge is captured by the popular phrase, "The honeymoon is over"; the second is often called the "the 7-year-itch."

Why do some marriages survive these crisis points while others fizzle? Four factors are important:

▶ **The characteristics of spouses.** Age is one of the strongest predictors of marital success: People who tie the knot before age 22 are more likely to divorce than those who wait (Heaton, 2004; Larson & Holman, 1994). Early marriages have a higher risk of failure even when education, income, and premarital pregnancy are taken into account, so it is likely that people's goals and tastes are not very stable early in life.

Intimate relationships are also more likely to be strained when individuals suffer from physical illness, depression, and poor impulse control. Furthermore, unrealistic beliefs—such as thinking that disagreements destroy a relationship—increase the chance of failure (Larson & Holman, 1994; Meredith & Holman, 2001).

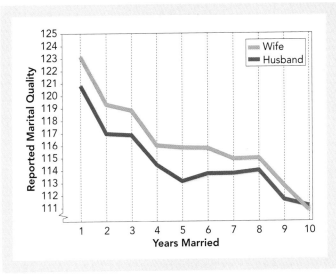

FIGURE 13.6 Marital quality over time.

It is common for satisfaction with marriage to decline a bit over time. Typically, there is a sharp decline during the first 4 years while couples adjust to the realities of living with a partner. Then, after a period of stability, there is another decline between 8 to 10 years.

SOURCE: Kurdek (1999).

How people react to intimacy is another important characteristic. Some adults bond easily, some find it difficult to trust others, and some frequently worry about their partner's love and commitment (Koski & Shaver, 1997). These "secure," "avoidant," and "anxious" attachment styles are the adult equivalents of the infant–mother styles described in Chapter 5. A secure attachment style during adulthood predicts a host of favorable outcomes, including good adjustment to college and high levels of satisfaction with intimate relationships. Couples that include at least one secure partner experience less conflict, partly because securely attached adults often have good communication skills (Cohn et al., 1992; Feeney, 1994).

▶ **Family histories.** The quality of our parents' marriages also predicts success. As mentioned in Chapter 9, children of divorce are more accepting of divorce and have more difficulty resolving conflicts (Amato, 1996; Amato & Keith, 1991). For example, adult children of divorce often make demands and then withdraw instead of negotiating solutions (Amato, 1996; Mullett & Stolberg, 2002).

▶ **Couples' interactions.** In general, happy couples agree on topics that are important to them, such as attitudes about money, and they construct a shared "philosophy of life" that includes beliefs about key relationship issues (Hojjat, 1997). They also say that a good relationship follows a *communal norm*, one in which people offer assistance when their partners need help without feeling the recipient owes them anything in return. Apparently, "keeping score" by trying to balance what each person contributes can make us feel that our partners don't really care about us. Comments such as "I make more money so I deserve a more expensive car" are warning signs that someone feels taken advantage of (Clark, Graham, & Grote, 2002).

To unravel the mysteries of how couples interact, relationship expert John Gottman videotapes pairs as they discuss problems in his research center at the University of Washington, popularly known as the "Love Lab." His research has discovered that many assumptions about what makes marriages strong are wrong, including the ideas that it is critical to avoid conflict, work to resolve every problem, and engage in "active listening" (that is, careful listening with feedback that proves you understood, such as "I hear how worried you are about money") (Gottman et al., 2002; Gottman & Silver, 1999). Instead, conflict often erupts in unhappy and happy couples, it is not uncommon for satisfied couples to ignore problems that cannot be solved, and even satisfied couples rarely use active listening. What happy couples do have is a high ratio of positive to negative interactions (Fincham, 2003) and a way of injecting *repair attempts*—such as humorous remarks or supportive comments—to defuse an argument (Gottman & Silver, 1999). Happy couples also know a lot about each other's hopes and dreams and allow themselves to be influenced by one another.

▶ ***Commitment to marriage.*** Another important predictor of marriage longevity is commitment to the relationship and the institution of marriage (Nock, 1995). As a group, people who live together before marriage have a divorce rate that is 50 percent higher than those who do not cohabitate, probably because people who put off marriage lack the commitment that makes for long-lasting unions. But two subgroups do not have an elevated risk of divorce: adults who waited until they were engaged to live together and those who have cohabitated only with their current spouse (Kline et al., 2004; Teachman, 2003). These results suggest that living together before marriage has become an accepted part of the normal courtship process for some people.

Of course, there is no crystal ball that can predict whether any individual relationship will survive. When marriages end, people's reactions to their changing lives are as different as their marriages were.

DIVORCE AND REMARRIAGE. Consider how two professors responded when we asked them how they felt about themselves and their lives shortly after a divorce:

Anna: Hopeless. I felt like I would spend the rest of my life without a partner. I was overwhelmed, stressed out, sad.

Gordon: I felt a great deal of relief. I felt like I was starting over in a lot of ways. I felt like I could be okay now.

Depending on the circumstances, divorce can be a devastating failure, a temporary inconvenience, or an exciting chance for a new and better life. But regardless of whether people wanted to divorce or not, dealing with divorce is usually stressful. It is unsettling to divide up belongings and, sometimes, friends. Many times, divorce forces people to move to unfamiliar surroundings and causes them to lose contact with their spouse's family. Even small issues, such as managing day-to-day decisions alone, cause considerable distress.

The stress of divorce disrupts the immune system and increases the chance of illness. During the first year after divorce, visits to doctors triple among women and double among men. The largest drop in immune system function occurs about 1 year after a divorce, when the strain of adjusting to a new life finally takes a toll on physical health (Hetherington & Kelly, 2002; Kiecolt-Glaser & Glaser, 1992).

Why is the first year after a divorce so stressful? Divorced men suffer the most from loneliness, problems managing a household by themselves, and the frustration of being separated from their children (Arendell, 1995; Frieman, 2002). A major concern for women is economic security, especially if they were previously homemakers or only worked part time outside of the home (Braver, 1999; Hope, Rodgers, & Power, 1999).

Divorce can also trigger an identity crisis. For example, Sue desperately wanted to be in a relationship and felt adrift without one. "I like being married," she told a researcher. "I don't know how I feel about not being married . . . I don't think on the day of the divorce I will suddenly see myself as a single person." Similarly, Donna said, "I just can't see myself as divorced, so I'm having a hard time with identity" (McDaniel & Coleman, 2003, pp. 120–121). Women with more education and those who work outside the home are most likely to report positive identity changes, such as feeling more in control of their lives and more competent (Rahav & Baum, 2002).

How do people fare several years after a divorce? Psychologist Mavis Hetherington found six styles of adjustment (Hetherington & Kelly, 2002). The largest group included the *good enoughs*: those who experienced some successes but also some setbacks. These adults started new projects and sought out new friends but often wished for a better life. The *enhancers* were people like Gordon who blossomed after divorce by creating interesting work lives and maintaining satisfying relationships with family members and friends. The *seekers* were eager to find new partners to structure their lives, but these adults often recreated the problems of their first marriage in new relationships. The *libertines* took advantage of their newfound freedom by "running wild" for a time, although most eventually sought a committed relationship. Finally, the *competent loners*, who made up only about 10 percent of the sample, had practical and social skills that made it easy for them to put together a new life. However, these adults were not interested in marrying again even though some maintained special relationships.

Despite these varied reactions, most people (about 86 percent of young, divorced men and 83 percent of young, divorced women) eventually remarry (Kreider & Fields, 2002). White non-Hispanic women are more likely to remarry within 10 years of a first divorce (79 percent) than Hispanic women (68 percent), and both of these groups are more likely to remarry within 10 years than African American women (49 percent) (Bramlett & Mosher, 2001). People who think love will be easier after a "practice" marriage are in for a surprise, though, because these marriages are even more likely than first marriages to end in divorce (Goldstein, 1999).

Living Single

Psychology professor Bella DePaulo always thought she would get married some day. When that day didn't come, she became fascinated by society's attitudes toward single adults. In contrast to the mountain of data on marriage, she noticed that there were no journals or academic conferences on single life, and she was especially irritated about the special treatment married couples enjoyed. For example, married workers often receive benefits from their employers that are worth more than what singles receive, and journalists often treat unmarried life as a problem that needs to be fixed. DePaulo, who enjoys friends and her close Italian family, abandoned her job to study her new passion—single life (Wilson, 2004).

Many types of people are considered "single" in government statistics. Some, like DePaulo, might marry if they found the right partner. Others are temporarily single due to divorce or the death of a spouse. Still others are gay or

Who is probably having more sex, college-aged students (shown here enjoying a night on the town) or married couples a few years older? According to surveys, married and cohabitating couples in their mid- to late 20s win because they have more of the opportunities that lead to an active sex life.

lesbian adults who are barred from marrying by law, although many are in a committed relationship (and, therefore, not "single" in the social sense). Only 9 percent of adults reach their middle years without having married, yet most people spend at least some of their adult life uncoupled. Thus the experience of living "single" is a feature of life for most adults.

Single adults face a number of negative stereotypes. Men are often viewed as commitment-phobic and irresponsible, whereas women are sometimes pitied or assumed to be "difficult." Moreover, family members sometimes devalue the significance of singles' friendships because they think only spousal relationships are important. Yet despite these attitudes, well-adjusted, single adults actually have the same characteristics that happily married couples have: close relationships with other people, work they enjoy, and a sense of purpose (Schwartzberg, Berliner, & Jacob, 1995).

Sexuality

Sexual motivation is universal: Most adults like to look at bodies and enjoy smelling, touching, and being touched. But as you'll read next, your biological code does not dictate what you will find attractive or how you will act on your sexual feelings.

SEXUALITY AROUND THE WORLD. One of our students, a handsome man from Africa, was smitten with an American student. To the amusement of everyone around him, he made no attempt to disguise his enjoyment as he watched her ample hips retreat into the distance. "It's so nice to find a man who isn't just interested in breasts," someone joked. "Why would I be interested in breasts?" he replied with annoyance. "Breasts are for babies."

Our African student belongs to an ethnic group that does not view breasts as sexual, and many cultures depart in other ways from Western sexual norms. Some cultures avoid sexual intercourse during menstruation; others do not. Some consider oral sex a routine part of sex; others consider it disgusting. Because sexual behavior varies across cultures and historical periods, keep in mind that the conclusions about sexual behavior you'll read about next are conclusions about sexual behavior in a particular context (Western, industrialized countries) at a particular point in time.

SEXUAL EXPRESSION. Programs such as *Sex in the City* create the impression that adults are having great sex—and lots of it. But sexual surveys tell a more boring story. One nationwide sample of 18- to 59-year-olds (Michael et al., 1994) revealed the following surprising—and highly publicized—findings:

▶ Only one-third of Americans have sex with a partner at least once a week. Another third have sex a few times a month, and the rest have sex less frequently or not at all.

▶ As you might expect, adults in their mid-to-late twenties have the most sex, with younger and older people having less. However, it is not unusual for adults to have little or no sex. For example, 36 percent of 18- to 24-year-old men had sex only a few times or not at all in the last year.

▶ Married and cohabitating people have more sex than single people do. About 40 percent of married people have sex two or more times per week, compared to fewer than 25 percent of single people.

▶ People's tastes are generally conservative. Apart from friendly touching and kissing, only vaginal sex and watching a partner undress are overwhelmingly popular among heterosexual couples. Forced sex, sex with strangers, and using drugs to enhance sex are some of the many practices most people rank as very unappealing.

One of the strongest predictors of sexual frequency is time with a partner. There is a large decline in sexual frequency after the so-called "honeymoon year" followed by a more gradual decline afterward (Call, Sprecher, & Schwartz, 1995). Also, lesbian couples have less sex than heterosexual couples, who in turn have less sex than homosexual couples. However, all of these types of couples are equally satisfied with their sexual lives and experience the same decline in sexual frequency as relationships mature (Christopher & Sprecher, 2000). The most reassuring finding is how satisfied most adults are: In one survey, 88 percent of married people said they were extremely pleased with their sex lives (Michael et al., 1994).

In contrast to these well-established findings, conclusions that compare men and women's sexual lives are riddled with inconsistencies. You may have read that men are more sexually driven than women, that the sexes have similar sex drives and behavior, and even that women are the winners of the sexual lottery (for their ability to have multiple orgasms). The truth is that all of these conclusions are correct. To explore how this can be, read our next *Don't Be Fooled!* feature entitled "Male and Female Sexualities: Why Small Differences Sometimes Seem Large."

DON'T BE FOOLED

Differences in the sexual attitudes and behaviors of men and women are sometimes large when researchers present mean scores (that is, scores based on the arithmetic average). However, large mean differences can result from a small number of individuals who have very atypical scores. When this is the case, *median* scores (that is, the scores that half of the people in a group score above and half score below) convey a more realistic picture of what men and women think about sexual issues and how they actually behave.

MALE AND FEMALE SEXUALITIES: WHY SMALL DIFFERENCES SOMETIMES SEEM LARGE

Books like *Men Are from Mars, Women Are from Venus* reinforce the idea that men and women are hopelessly different (Gray, 1992). Are the sexes really from different planets—or just different neighborhoods?

Compared to other mammals, human males and females are remarkably similar. Most mammals, such as your local house cat or dog, mate when the female goes into *estrus* ("heat"), a period of sexual responsiveness that is triggered by an increase in the hormone estrogen. (*Oestrus* is the Latin word for "frenzy.") In contrast, human females experience menstrual cycles rather than estrus. Like their male counterparts, they are sexually responsive throughout their cycles, and variations in their sex drives are heavily influenced by the hormone testosterone (Cameron & Braunstein, 2004). Human males and females both initiate sexual activity, experience similar physiological changes during arousal and orgasm (as discussed in Chapter 12), and have sexual lives that are heavily influenced by mental events.

The sex differences that do exist are large or small—depending on how you frame the data. One well-known difference involves the desire for sexual variety (Schmitt, 2003). For example, the men in one study said they would like 7.7 partners over the next 30-year period (on average), whereas the women desired only 2.8. But this difference is not as large as it seems because mean scores are heavily influenced by responses from a small group of atypical individuals. For example, if 47 men say they would like 1 sexual partner in the next month but 3 would like 20, the mean for the group is more than 2—twice the number preferred by most of the men. To reduce the influence of deviant scores, some investigators look at *median* scores instead. (The median is the score that half of the group falls below and half above.) Often sex differences that look dramatic when you look at means are small or nonexistent for median scores. In the study just mentioned, for example, there was no difference in the *median* number of partners that men and women desired (Figure 13.7), and only 1 male and 2 females out of 266 participants in a second study said they did not intend to settle down with one mutually exclusive sexual partner (Pedersen et al., 2002).

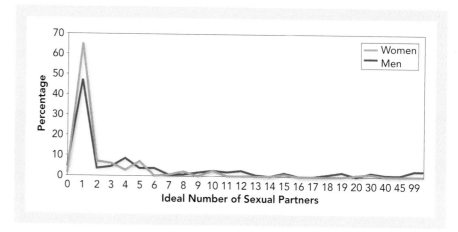

FIGURE 13.7 Gender and sexuality.

When men and women were asked what their ideal number of sexual partners would be over a 30-year period (the maximum value allowed was 99), the *mean* (average) for men was much higher (7.7) than the mean for women (2.8). But this difference was largely due to the fact that a small percentage of men indicated very high numbers. As the graph shows, women and men had similar preferences for variety, and there was no difference in the *median* number of sexual partners they listed: More than half of men *and* women wanted no more than 1 partner.

SOURCE: Pedersen et al. (2002).

So what do scientists conclude about male and female sexuality? Everyone agrees that the sexes are not identical: On average, men have higher rates of masturbation, more frequent sexual fantasies, greater interest in pornography, and a preference for more frequent sex (Baumeister, Catanese, & Vohs, 2001). Married men also report more affairs than married women do, although rates vary across samples (Blow & Harnett, 2005). In one survey, the rate of infidelity (sexual cheating) was the same for men and women under the age of 40, suggesting that cultural attitudes play a role in exaggerating sex differences (Wiederman, 1997). Because sexual behavior in humans is molded as much by culture as by hormones, it is impossible to know how large the sex differences we see today will be in the future. ◆

GAY AND LESBIAN ADULTS. In Chapter 11 you read about the challenges gay and lesbian teenagers face when they "come out" to the important people in their lives. During adulthood, some people are still exploring their sexualities, and many gay and lesbian adults come out over and over again as they change jobs, move, and meet new people.

What proportion of adults are gay or lesbian? Answers vary because there is no single definition of sexual orientation. In one survey, 4 percent of women and 6 percent of men said they were attracted to the same sex, and similar percentages said they had had sex with a same-sex partner since they turned 18. Yet only 1.4 percent of women and 2.8 percent of men considered themselves homosexual or bisexual. Among those who lived in large cities, about 2.5 percent of women and 9 percent of men identified themselves as homosexual or bisexual (Michael et al., 1994).

It is not uncommon for people to change how they act on their sexual feelings during adulthood. In one study, 27 percent of the women who identified themselves as nonheterosexual changed their identity to heterosexual or unlabeled over a 5-year period (Diamond, 2003). But although these women decided to *describe* themselves differently, the strength of their attraction to women was unchanged. Apparently, many women simply made their identity label consistent with their current choices. For instance, one woman told a researcher, "I think I still have the same orientation, but things are different because now I'm in a heterosexual relationship, and it's pretty serious and I guess that's what basically forms my identity" (Diamond, 2003, p. 361). Men are less likely than women to define sexuality based on current emotional attractions and, therefore, men who desire other men seldom change their sexual identity (Michael, 1994; Shidlo & Schroeder, 2002).

Gay and lesbian couples deal with day-to-day hassles, argue about who is doing more chores, and laugh over private jokes just as all couples do. Although they tend to divide housework chores more equitably than heterosexual couples, the same variables that predict relationship quality for heterosexual pairs (including personal characteristics and approaches to intimacy) predict relationship quality for gay and lesbian couples (Kurdek, 2005). And just like other couples, it is important for gay and lesbian couples to deal with the business side of life, such as planning for health insurance, setting money aside for retirement, and acting as legal representatives for their children. However, many of these activities are not routine for them due to *heterosexism*: laws and social customs that recognize only the heterosexual lifestyle. Depending on where they live, these couples may not be allowed to insure their partner through their work benefits, serve as legal parents to each other's children, or be recognized as their partner's closest relative during a medical crisis. In addition, fear of discrimination prevents many gay and lesbian adults from enjoying the simple pleasures most people take for granted, such as having a family picture on their desk at work or bringing their partner to a social event.

This gay couple held a marriage ceremony in 2004 after the major of San Francisco defied state law by issuing marriage licenses to same-sex couples. Their friends obviously enjoyed their public statement of love and commitment.

Parenting

Becoming a parent has been likened to falling off a cliff: It is an abrupt descent. One day you are taking care of yourself; the next, you have around-the-clock responsibility for an unfamiliar creature who is often irritable, sick, or demanding attention. In traditional cultures, an extensive network of family and friends assists by offering advice and helping hands. Sometimes those hands arrive even before the baby, as illustrated by the following description of childbirth in Yucatan, Mexico (Jordan, 1980):

> In Yucatan, the woman's husband is expected to be present during labor and birth. They say he should see "how a woman suffers." This rule is quite strong and explicit and we heard cases where the husband's absence was blamed for the stillbirth of a child. In addition to the husband, the woman's mother should also be there, and mothers sometimes travel considerable distances for their daughters' births. If the labor turns out to be long and difficult, other women will appear: mothers-in-law, godmothers, sisters, sisters-in-law, close friends and neighbors. This group of "helpers" substantially contributes to a successful birth. Jointly and by turns they give the woman the mental and physical support she needs. They encourage her, urge her on, scold her when necessary, always letting her know that she is not alone, that the business of getting this baby born will get done. It will take time and work and pain, to be sure, but "we have all done this before and this baby will arrive, soon now." (p. 24)

All communities value children, but societies have different ideas about what the ideal number of children is and who should help raise them. As a result, parenting is a different experience in different parts of the world.

RAISING CHILDREN. Today, the average woman in the least developed countries bears 5 children, compared to 2 in North America and 1.4 in Europe (Figure 13.8). The number of children adults have is influenced by many factors, including individual goals, cultural preferences, access to contraception, and even government policies. The highest fertility rates are in Africa, where inadequate medical care makes it difficult to distribute contraception. But in China, where an uncontrolled population could outstrip food supplies, the government has stepped in to regulate family size. Beginning in 1979, officials implemented a "one-child" policy that advocated delaying the age of marriage and having only one child per couple. In practice, this plan has always been enforced differently depending on community needs and the officials in charge. For example, policies are more lenient in rural areas, where farmers feel they need a son to help them work the land.

Mothers provide the majority of child care in most cultures (whether they work outside the home or not), yet most cultures assume they will recruit helpers, such as children, grandmothers, and other relatives. Expectations for fathers are more varied. When children are infants, fathers' contributions to direct care are often quite limited. For example, fathers never or rarely interacted with infants in 22 percent of the cultures in one sample, and they did so only occasionally in 38 percent. But it is common for fathers to take on more active roles as children grow. Among the Chimalteco of Mexico, for example, a boy of 10 years may spend most of his time learning skills with his dad (Broude, 1995).

Diary studies document how much time adults invest in raising children. In a study of American parents, married mothers spent 99

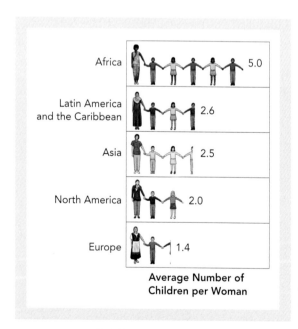

FIGURE 13.8 Childbearing around the world.

Around the world, a typical family has 2 to 3 children (world average = 2.7), but the average family size varies.

SOURCE: United Nations Population Division (2005).

minutes per day interacting directly with their children, and single mothers—who often have less help to run the household—averaged only 14 minutes less. In contrast, married fathers averaged 51 minutes per day caring for, teaching, and playing with children (Sayer, Bianchi, & Robinson, 2004). This figure is larger than it was in the past because fathers are taking a more active role in raising children (Figure 13.9).

The time-consuming nature of parenthood is behind the "time famine" complaint that we mentioned earlier. As one mother explained, "I was frantic to get out of the office so I could get home by 5:30 to relieve my babysitter. My husband and I would rush around making dinner, bathe my sons and read to them before bed. Then, I'd pull out my briefcase and work till midnight. I was exhausted" (Chisholm, 1994, p. 36). But despite the belief that modern families are pressed for time, there was no change from the 1960s through the 1990s in the amount of leisure time people reported (Sullivan & Gershuny, 2001), and there is no evidence that today's children are receiving less parental attention than children did in the past (Sayer et al., 2004). Apparently, the "time famine" is widespread only among a select group of adults: single parents and working couples with young children.

PARENTING AND WELL-BEING. Are adults who have children happier than those who don't? The answer is not a simple one. In order to control for inherited traits associated with partnering and having children, one research team compared levels of happiness between Danish adults who had children and their identical twins who did not (Kohler, Behrman, & Skytthe, 2005). For women, having a first child significantly increased subjective well-being ("How satisfied are you with your life, all things considered?"). But well-being declined for each additional child, and three more children canceled out the benefits from the first. A first child also improved well-being for men but, unlike women, men's well-being was not much affected by additional children.

Of course, parenting is more difficult when people are ill-prepared and lack resources. As a result, young parents and those with many children are more likely to show declines in well-being during the early years of family life. And because women bear the brunt of child rearing, their experiences are affected by the amount of support they receive from friends and family (Cairney et al., 2003; Graham et al., 2000). Overall, the recipe for maintaining sanity while raising children is clear: Avoid having children while you are young or lack financial resources, nurture your adult relationships to maintain a sense of community, and have reasonable expectations for life after children.

Other Special Adult Relationships

Siblings are lifelong relationships for most adults. About half of the adults who have a biological sibling speak with them at least once a month, a third would call a sibling first for emergency help, and about two-thirds consider a sibling to be one of their closest friends (White & Riedmann, 1992).

In American samples, the most common relationship among adult siblings is "casual," a pattern in which siblings "do their own thing" and socialize mostly with friends rather than each other. Other siblings describe themselves as "buddies" or report that one is the "caretaker" who comforts the other. Still others describe themselves as "loyal"—not particularly warm or cool but bound together

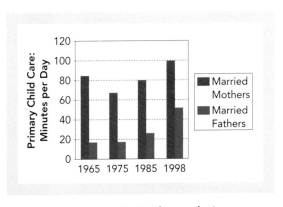

FIGURE 13.9 The evolution of fatherhood.

Compared to times past, today's fathers are taking a more active role in caring for children. In 1965, married mothers spent almost 5 hours in direct child-care activities (such as dressing children and driving them to school) for every hour their husbands spent. By 1998, mothers were spending just under 2 hours for every hour their spouses contributed. Regardless of who rears children, it is a time-consuming job that occupies about 2.5 hours of adult time per day.

SOURCE: Sayer et al. (2004).

Like many families around the world, this one is a close *extended family* that includes several generations and many types of relationships, such as relationships with parents, siblings, aunts, uncles, and cousins. These relationships are important sources of support during adulthood.

because they are siblings (Stewart, Verbrugge, & Beilfuss, 1998). These relationships often change as life transitions bring people closer or drive them apart. Marriage and the birth of children tend to pull siblings away from each other, whereas events during middle adulthood, such as the death of a parent, can bring them together again. When elderly individuals think back on their lives, 35 percent say there was no change in their sibling relationship over time, 46 percent say they grew closer, and 18 percent say they grew more distant (Gold, 1996).

Most adults also have regular contact with other family members. In traditional societies, interrelated families live nearby and rely on one another for physical and psychological support. For example, traditional African communities consist of extended family members who live in units called *compounds*. Here children of the same generation grow up interacting as brothers and sisters, and aunts and uncles often take on parenting responsibilities for nieces and nephews. Unlike modern suburbs, where the marital union is the focus of family life, family stability in these groups is based on a broader network of relatives. Today, many African American families (like families from so many ethnic groups) retain the values that bond extended family members together, including respect for older relatives, a sense of responsibility for a wide kinship network, and a belief in the importance of making peace with family members after a disagreement (Sudarkasa, 1997).

The importance of family is evident from the fascinating practice of **fictive kinship**. Fictive kin are people who are treated as relatives even though they are not related to a family by blood or marriage. These individuals may be called "auntie," "cousin," or another appropriate term, and they assume some rights and responsibilities that are usually reserved for family members. In one national survey, two out of three African Americans expanded their family networks with fictive kin (Chatters, Taylor, & Jayakody, 1994), and such relationships are found in numerous communities worldwide. Similarly, gay and lesbian adults frequently use the term *chosen families* to describe especially close, supportive relationships. As one gay man explained, "Some of my friends I've known for fifteen years. You get attached. You stay in one place long enough, you go through seasons and years together, it's like they're part of you, you're part of them" (Weston, 1991, p. 115).

fictive kinship The practice of treating people as relatives even though they are not related to us by blood or marriage. Fictive kin may be called "auntie," "cousin," or another appropriate term, and they assume some rights and responsibilities that are usually reserved for family members.

>>> **MEMORY MAKERS** <<<

1. Which type of marriage partnership involves a man marrying multiple women?

   (a) polyandry
   (b) polygamy

2. Which type of sharing in a relationship is associated with more successful marriages?

   (a) communal norm
   (b) keeping score

3. Which statistic will show the largest difference between groups when a few people in one group have very atypical scores?

   (a) a mean
   (b) a median

4. What are fictive kin?

   (a) extended family members
   (b) nonrelatives

[1-b; 2-a, a communal norm, which is giving without the expectation of return; 3-a, means (arithmetic averages) show larger group differences than median scores (the score that one-half of the group is above and one-half is below) when there are extreme scores; 4-b, fictive kin are nonrelatives who take on some of the privileges and responsibilities that are usually reserved for family members.]

Individuality

The divers in our opening story belong to a special class of people—those rare adults who explore the seas, the sky, and the outer recesses of space. Yet for every team who risks it all, many more people are quietly raising families, doing their jobs, and leading their communities at home. Read on to explore how our personalities, cognitive and creative skills, and experiences as men or women influence our life pathways through early and middle adulthood.

Personality

As you saw in earlier chapters, children come in many varieties, including quiet loners, social butterflies, and reckless risk takers who are often plastered with Band-Aids. By adulthood, these different temperaments have interacted with different experiences to form our *personalities*, that is, our characteristic patterns of thinking, feeling, and acting.

PERSONALITIES OVER TIME. Do personalities stay the same throughout early and middle adulthood? One way to explore this question is to measure the **Big Five** personality traits: neuroticism, extroversion, openness to experience, agreeableness, and conscientiousness. These are traits, described in Table 13.2, that frequently emerge from studies of individual differences. As you might expect, it is typical for some personality change to occur after adolescence just as part of growing up. Between late adolescence and older adulthood, scores on agreeableness (how cooperative and positive individuals are toward others) and conscientiousness (how disciplined and careful they are) increase, and scores on neuroticism (emotional instability) and extroversion (how outgoing people are) decline. Scores on openness to experience (how creative and unconventional people are) increase during adolescence and then decline (Costa & McCrae, 1997; McCrae & Costa, 2003; McCrae et al., 2002; Terracciano et al., 2005).

Big Five Five traits that frequently emerge from studies of individual differences: neuroticism (emotional instability), extroversion (how outgoing people are), openness to experience (how creative and unconventional people are), agreeableness (how cooperative and positive they are toward other people), and conscientiousness (how disciplined and careful they are).

TABLE 13.2 The Big Five Personality Traits

Trait	Sample Dimensions		Trend during Adulthood
	Low	High	
Neuroticism	calm	worrying	decreases
	even-tempered	temperamental	
	unemotional	emotional	
Extroversion	loner	joiner	decreases
	passive	active	
	reserved	affectionate	
Openness to experience	down-to-earth	imaginative	increases during adolescence and then decreases
	prefer routine	prefer variety	
	uncurious	curious	
Agreeableness	suspicious	trusting	increases slightly
	critical	lenient	
	irritable	good-natured	
Conscientiousness	lazy	hardworking	increases slightly
	disorganized	well-organized	
	quitting	persevering	

SOURCE: Adapted from McCrae & Costa (2003); McCrae et al. (2002); Terracciano et al. (2005).

There is a general pattern for greater personality change during a person's 20s, followed by a slower rate of change during each subsequent decade. But some traits don't follow this typical pattern. In one study, for example, increases in agreeableness were greatest during the 30s and 40s, perhaps because this is the time when most adults are struggling to get along with a broader social network that includes partners, children, and colleagues at work (Helson et al., 2002).

Because personality changes occur across cultures and are moderately heritable, some experts believe they are genetically programmed so that individuals can better adjust to the demands of each phase of life. The idea is that nature nudges young adults to strike out on their own and find mates by turning on genes that provide an extra dose of recklessness and extroversion and then settles us down when we need to raise families (McCrae et al., 1999). Others believe the realities of life can explain these changes. For example, people may become more agreeable over time because they learn that life goes more smoothly when they do (Helson et al., 2002). Also, adults juggle more social roles in their 40s than they did in their 20s, so a declining need for change and variety in life could stem from the fact that day-to-day life provides enough variety and change on its own (Helson & Soto, 2005).

PERSONALITY AND LIFE OUTCOMES. On average, people who score differently on the Big Five experience different life outcomes. Conscientious children grow up to be adults who adopt healthier lifestyles and live longer than their non-conscientious peers (Friedman et al., 1995), whereas adults who are high on neuroticism and low on agreeableness experience more conflicts and are less satisfied with their marriages. One study of men who were tested periodically for over 45 years found that neuroticism, extroversion, and openness were the traits that were most strongly related to life outcomes. Men who were more neurotic showed poorer overall adjustment, were more likely to be depressed and use drugs, and had lower incomes. In contrast, extroversion was associated with better incomes, and openness was associated with creativity and depression (Soldz & Vaillant, 1999).

Some characteristics that influence adult adjustment are not neatly captured by the Big Five. One is *self-control* (also called *self-regulation*): the ability to refrain from acting on impulses. People with good self-control can hold their tempers, inhibit the urge to gossip, and persist at work when more pleasant activities loom outside the door (Tangney, Baumeister, & Boone, 2004). Self-control has roots in early childhood, when children differ noticeably in their ability to inhibit a dominant response in order to make a more socially appropriate response. As we described in Chapter 8, psychologists often use the term *effortful control* to describe this ability to regulate one's behavior (Rothbart, Ahadi, & Evans, 2000).

Compared to their peers, adults who are high on self-control achieve better grades, are less likely to binge eat and abuse alcohol, and have fewer psychological problems such as obsessive-compulsive disorder, depression, anxiety, and inappropriate anger (Tangney et al., 2004). People with excellent self-control refrain from indulging themselves when it is beneficial to do so but can suspend control when other behavior is more appropriate. For example, these people can cancel a tennis game to study yet break a diet to eat a birthday cake their partners made. Flexibly matching behavior to the situation—rather than charging ahead with a rigid response—is the hallmark of happy children and happy adults.

Intelligence

The biographer of John Chatterton and Richie Kohler, the divers in our opening story, described them as two "ordinary men who . . . solved a historical mystery that even governments had not been able to budge" (Kurson, 2004, p. x). To discover the identity of the U-Who, these men became experts on U-boats, learned to conduct research in government archives, interviewed people abroad, and even mastered a bit of German. Are people like Chatterton and Kohler unusually intelligent, or do other qualities drive some individuals to become highly accomplished during early and middle adulthood? To explore the role of intelligence in life success, let's start by exploring what scientists have learned from traditional IQ tests.

TRADITIONAL MEASURES OF INTELLIGENCE. The most popular way to measure intelligence is to use adult versions of the standardized tests we described in Chapter 9. For example, the Weschler Adult Intelligence Scale (WAIS), like its child counterpart the WISC, also consists of a number of subtests that tap verbal and perceptual skills, working memory, and processing speed (Psychological Corporation, 1997). As with the WISC, the average IQ score is set at 100, with a standard deviation of 15.

Although tests like the WAIS represent just one way to define "intelligence," IQ scores do correlate with numerous outcomes. High scores during adulthood are associated with better job performance and mental health, higher incomes, and even lower divorce rates. Correlations between IQ and adult outcomes are often lower than correlations between IQ and school performance, but they are not trivial. For instance, typical correlations between IQ and job measures, such as supervisor ratings and work samples, are generally around .40, which means that about 16 percent of the variability in these outcomes is associated with intelligence (Neisser et al., 1996). Because scores on various sections of an intelligence test are highly correlated (that is, a high score in one area is often matched by a high score in another), some scientists believe that a single intellectual resource, called **g** (which is short for *general factor*), underlies intelligent behavior across a wide variety of tasks. According to this line of thought, g represents basic brain processes—such as speed of

g The hypothetical brain processes that produce variation in intelligent behavior across a wide variety of tasks. It is proposed that this "general factor" explains why scores on various sections of an intelligence test are highly correlated.

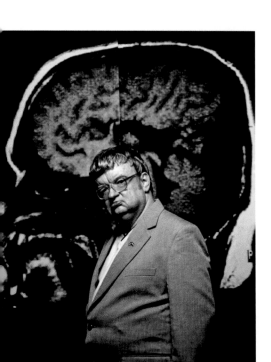

Kim Peek, shown here in front of a scan of his brain, inspired Barry Morrow to write the screenplay for *Rain Man*. The man his friends call "Kim-puter" has an astounding memory for information in at least 15 different topic areas, including sports, church history, and space programs. Savants like Kim, who excel on some mental tasks despite subaverage performance on others, provided motivation for the idea that intelligence is best thought of as a collection of different skills.

theory of multiple intelligences
A theory of intelligence by Howard Gardner that initially proposed the existence of seven types of intelligence: linguistic, logical-mathematical, spatial, musical, bodily-kinesthetic, interpersonal, and intrapersonal. Later he added naturalistic intelligence.

perceiving and manipulating information—that enable some people to learn and solve problems more efficiently than other people (Nyborg, 2003; Spearman, 1946).

But not everyone is convinced that traditional measures of intelligence explain why some people are better adjusted and more successful in their careers. One problem is an issue you read about in Chapter 9: Rather than being a fixed quality, IQ scores improve with education and other relevant experiences. Because IQ, education, and the socioeconomic status of people's parents are correlated, it is difficult to determine whether adults who have high IQs fare better in life because they are smarter or merely because they were born into environments that provided experiences—such as more education—that are associated with success. In fact, the predictive power of IQ scores was largely eliminated in one study when education and childhood social class were entered into an equation to predict income. But IQ did influence pathways to success. For example, people with high IQs and high social class tended to become lawyers, college professors, and other professionals, whereas those with low IQs and high social class tended to achieve by operating businesses (often making more money than their brighter siblings who entered the professions). Regardless of IQ, adults who came from lower social classes tended to enter skilled trades, such as carpentry and electrical work (Henderson & Ceci, 1992; Scullin et al., 2000).

Although scientists do not agree about why IQ scores predict adult outcomes, they do agree about this: If IQ correlates about .4 with job performance, most of the variability in job performance is due to characteristics other than IQ. Identifying those characteristics is the goal of scientists who study *multiple intelligences*.

MULTIPLE INTELLIGENCES. Brain research shows us that the human brain is highly *modularized*, which means it is constructed from a large number of interconnected processing units. (*Modules* are components that are put together to produce the whole.) This is most obvious among people who suffer from neurological conditions that harm some abilities while sparing others. For instance, individuals with *savant syndrome* have a severe mental disability, yet they are brilliant at a particular skill, such as music, art, or certain types of mathematical computations. Less dramatic examples are all around us. For example, every college residence hall has social geniuses who are bad at math along with social duds who are whizzes at calculus. To respond to these observations, some scientists have proposed that we stop thinking of intelligence as a single trait and think instead about multiple intelligences.

Two theories of multiple intelligence are summarized in Table 13.3. Developmental psychologist Howard Gardner's **theory of multiple intelligences** originally listed seven types of intelligence, including traditional academic abilities (linguistic, logical-mathematical, and spatial intelligence), some abilities that are not as highly valued by teachers (musical talent and athletic prowess), and the ability to understand people (interpersonal and intrapersonal intelligence). Later he added naturalistic intelligence, and other categories may follow in the future (Gardner, 1983, 1999, 2004).

Gardner's theory gained popularity among educators because it respects a variety of talents and learning styles. This upbeat approach is summed up by his comment, "The question is not how smart people are but in what ways people are smart" (Traub, 1998, p. 20). However, Gardner's theory has not been

TABLE 13.3 Theories of Multiple Intelligences

Howard Gardner's Theory of Multiple Intelligences

Linguistic intelligence	Ability to learn languages and skill using spoken and written language to accomplish goals.
Logical-mathematical intelligence	Ability to analyze information in ways that solve mathematical and scientific problems.
Spatial intelligence	The ability to recognize patterns in space.
Musical intelligence	Skill in recognizing, appreciating, and creating musical patterns.
Bodily-kinesthetic intelligence	The ability to coordinate bodily movement, such as a gymnast's or dancer's skill.
Interpersonal intelligence	The ability to understand other people's intentions, motivations, and needs.
Intrapersonal intelligence	The ability to reflect on one's own feelings and motivations.
Naturalistic intelligence	The ability to categorize features of the environment in order to recognize different species of plants and animals.

Robert Sternberg's Theory of Successful Intelligence

Analytical abilities	The ability to approach problems systematically. Analytical people are good at identifying the problem, setting up a strategy for solving it, and monitoring progress toward success.
Creative abilities	The ability to generate novel ideas. Creative people often gravitate toward ideas that are unpopular.
Practical abilities	The ability to apply intelligence in real-world settings. People with good practical abilities pick up on the unstated information and rules that are critical for success.

SOURCES: Gardner (1999, 2004); Sternberg (1997b).

accepted by all cognitive psychologists due to disagreement about whether the items in Table 13.3 reflect the performance of distinctly different cognitive structures.

An alternative is Robert Sternberg's **theory of successful intelligence** (also called the "triarchic theory" of intelligence). According to Sternberg, tests that focus only on analytical abilities fail to tap the creative and practical skills that are important in complex environments. For example, a department store manager with an IQ of 145 will be fired if he does not keep up with product trends and motivate his staff. Sternberg believes that productive people play up their strengths and compensate for their weaknesses using a balance of analytical, creative, and practical skills (Sternberg, 1997b; Sternberg & Williams, 1997).

An important concept in Sternberg's theory is an aspect of practical intelligence called **tacit knowledge**. (The word *tacit* means "not spoken.") Tacit knowledge is information you need to succeed in a specific environment that is not explicitly taught. As we mentioned in Chapter 8 when we discussed how popular children get a sense of a group before jumping in, people who are high on tacit knowledge have the ability to walk into a new situation and figure out the unspoken rules of the game. Measures of tacit knowledge sometimes predict job success better than IQ, and these measures improve predictions based only on IQ or personality (Sternberg, 2004).

Theories of multiple intelligences have not yet spawned a test that is widely used to evaluate adults. Nonetheless, research on multiple intelligences underscores the fact that IQ is just one of many traits that determine our pathways through adulthood. To read more about why adults succeed or fail, continue with our next *Solutions* feature entitled "Beliefs That Make Smart People Dumb."

theory of successful intelligence (also called the "triarchic theory" of intelligence) A theory of intelligence by Robert Sternberg that proposes the existence of three types of intelligence: analytical, creative, and practical.

tacit knowledge Knowledge you need to succeed in a specific environment that is not explicitly taught. (*Tacit* means "not spoken.")

Successful people consider intelligence something that can grow if they tackle complicated problems, believe that trying hard is as important as raw ability, and are willing to change strategies when old strategies fail.

Beliefs That Make Smart People Dumb

What is "intelligence"? For Westerners, a smart person is someone who was born with special abilities that help him or her learn quickly and solve problems. This view of intelligence is reinforced whenever children hear comments such as "Sally is better at math than her sister," "Jim is a born writer," or "languages just aren't my 'thing'." In China, though, people learn a different view of intelligence. Through stories that have been told for over 2,000 years, children hear about people who were brilliant because they *tried so hard*. As a famous Chinese philosopher once explained, "Intelligence means never being tired of learning" (Shi, 2004, p. 328). Thus people in China tend to view intelligence as *knowledge*, and enthusiastic effort is the road to knowledge.

Psychologist Carol Dweck (2002) believes that the difference between Western and Eastern views of intelligence holds the key to an important question: "Why do smart people sometimes act so dumb?" Dweck has found that people's ideas about intelligence determine whether they continue to grow intellectually or fall behind over time. Her research has identified four beliefs that can actually make you dumb:

⭐ *False belief 1: Intelligence is a fixed trait rather than a potential that can be developed.* Combined with the beliefs that follow, the idea that intelligence is fixed can lead you to avoid experiences that could make you smarter.

⭐ *False belief 2: Performance measures long-term potential.* When people with a fixed view of intelligence fail at a task, they often feel worthless and give up hope of success. In contrast, people with a malleable view assume they were unprepared and plan ways to reach their goal.

⭐ *False belief 3: Challenges are risky.* People with a fixed view of intelligence often avoid tasks they might fail. For example, when Dweck asked students what made them feel smart, people with a fixed view said they felt smart when they were doing something well or better than other people. In contrast, people who saw intelligence as something to be developed said they felt smart when they were trying to learn something new. In many studies, students with the fixed view preferred activities they excelled at rather than activities that would teach them something. Some even said, "If I knew I wasn't going to do well at a task, I probably wouldn't do it even if I might learn a lot from it" (Dweck, 2002, p. 30).

⭐ *False belief 4: Effort is only for incompetent people.* Some people believe that if you are really smart then you don't have to try. But as Dweck points out, most important tasks require a great deal of effort. In one study, people with a fixed view of intelligence were more likely than other people to not study enough for a test or to leave an important assignment until the last minute. Apparently, they hated to risk looking dumb by working hard and failing (Rhodewalt, 1994).

Regardless of the underlying nature of intelligence, you won't stay smart by sitting on your past accomplishments. As Dweck (2002, p. 39) explained, smart people are "in charge of their own intelligence"—they try, fail, and adjust their strategies and efforts to improve in the future. By envisioning intelligence as something that can grow, you will be more likely to master the challenges everyone faces during the march through adulthood. ◆

Outstanding Accomplishments

The 30s and early 40s are the years when people are most likely to influence the world—at least in terms of creative works and discoveries. (You will read about accomplishments that emerge later in life in Chapter 15.) For a study that became a classic, research psychologist Harvey Lehman (1953) compiled data from numerous sources to plot the ages when people made their notable contributions in chemistry, medicine, philosophy, music, educational theory, and other fields. The results were clear: The largest number of outstanding contributions were made by individuals in their mid-30s. Of course, many important contributions have been made by people 60 years of age or older, but it is still the case that young to middle adulthood is the age of achievement (Simonton, 1988).

Two characteristics are involved in discovering a chemical principle or patenting an invention: creativity and expertise. *Creativity*, one of three components of Sternberg's theory of successful intelligence (Sternberg, 1997b), is the ability to produce work that is original and unexpected, high in quality, and appropriate for its purpose (Sternberg, Kaufman, & Pretz, 2002). As with any group, creative people vary tremendously. For example, Charles Darwin, the father of evolutionary theory, was known for his wonderful social skills and gift for making friends (Howe, 1999). Conversely, Barbara McClintock, the first woman to win an unshared Nobel Prize for her work in genetics, lived an unusually solitary life. But despite a remarkable degree of variety, most creative people share the following characteristics:

Successful comedians like Dave Chappelle have the qualities that define creativity: an ability to rapidly find relationships among ideas along with the persistence to compete against thousands of aspiring comedians for a spot in the limelight.

▶ *A knack for divergent thinking.* When solving a problem, creative people are *divergent thinkers* who come up with many possibilities and look for relationships between ideas. (*Diverge* means "to extend in many directions.") In contrast, *convergent thinkers* try to find the one best answer by using rules that have worked for them in the past.

▶ *A motive for mastery.* Creative people are curious and derive great pleasure from mastering a problem (Henderson, 2004). They frequently enter the state of "flow" that was described earlier in this chapter.

▶ *Persistence.* Creative people often spend a great deal of time working in their domain of interest. For example, the young Isaac Newton would read a math book until he hit a point he didn't understand, then begin at the beginning, reading and rereading until he mastered the entire book (Howe, 1999).

▶ *Nonconformity.* Creative people persist even when they face criticism, partly because they are more concerned about their own goals than what other people think. After McClintock won the Nobel Prize, for example, a friend said she could "hardly bear" the attention. "To have her work understood and acknowledged was one thing," her friend explained. "But to make public appearances and submit to ceremonies was quite another" (Green, 2004, para. 4).

The traits associated with creativity usually do not translate into outstanding accomplishments unless an individual also has **expertise**: advanced skill or knowledge in a particular field. Studies of experts in chess, music, and other domains have uncovered an interesting rule of thumb: It usually takes at least 10 years of intense preparation to reach a high level of performance. This "10-year rule" testifies to the fact that unusual accomplishments are the product of hard work and persistence as much as they are the product of exceptional talent (Ericsson & Charness, 1994).

By asking experts and novices to solve similar sets of problems, scientists have described the core features of expert performance. Of course, experts possess a larger body of knowledge than novices, but there are more interesting differences. First, an

expertise Advanced skill or knowledge in a particular field.

expert's information is organized in terms of meaningful relationships. When confronted with a problem, they focus on "big ideas" and organizing principles. Perhaps as a result, experts notice different information than novices do and see patterns that novices don't see. Second, experts' knowledge is *conditionalized*, which means that experts know when specific information and strategies are relevant and when they are not. Finally, experts seem to retrieve relevant information effortlessly, which frees up mental resources for more complicated thinking (Bransford et al., 1999).

What is the best way to become an expert? Consider the task of becoming a professional tennis player or musician. People usually do not improve just by playing because the situations they need to work on do not occur often enough to help them increase their performance. Similarly, people do not improve during competitions because they are not at liberty to try different techniques. Unusual accomplishments result from **deliberate practice**: training, with individualized feedback, on tasks selected by a qualified teacher who can identify your weaknesses and plan practice sessions that will address specific skills (Ericsson, Krampe, & Tesch-Römer, 1993). In many fields, identifying a talented teacher or mentor is the fastest route to success.

Boy-land, Girl-land Grown Up

To what degree is your journey through adulthood influenced by whether you were born male or female? The answer depends on the society you grew up in and your time in history. Most cultures have different expectations for men and women while families are bearing and raising children. In traditional cultures, such as the Mayan village described in Chapter 7, a woman's work is close to home and planned around child-rearing responsibilities. But even in industrialized societies, there is an obvious difference in the presence of men and women in public versus private life.

Around the world, women hold only 10 percent of the positions in lawmaking branches of government and even fewer higher-level positions (United Nations Division for the Advancement of Women, 2004). They also hold few positions on corporate boards and are underrepresented in scientific and engineering fields. Men more often start on a path to power and economic security by selecting traditionally male majors in college (Thompson, 2003). After college, different career outcomes result from an accumulation of factors rather than any one factor (Sonnert & Holton, 1996). For example, women take more time off from work to launch families and spend more time managing family life. And as we mentioned earlier, women also face subtle barriers that make it harder for them to be promoted into top positions. Different choices, together with societal stereotypes and pressures, produce the differences we see in how men and women invest their time across cultures. But these differences are just averages, so individual lives include stay-at-home dads as well as women like Michaëlle Jean, the governor general of Canada who, among other duties, is commander in chief of the country's armed forces.

Regardless of where or when you live, the physical differences between men and women nudge them toward different activities and influence the risks they face. As mentioned in Chapter 12, men have greater physical power (Holden, 2004), but they also have faster reaction times due to nerve conduction velocities that are 4 percent faster than the female average (Reed, Vernon, & Johnson, 2004). These differences explain why men excel in sports where brute force and quick responses are critical.

The sexes also have different medical vulnerabilities. For example, women are almost three times as likely as men to be diagnosed with an **autoimmune disease**, one in which the immune system attacks the body's own cells. Autoimmune disorders include rheumatoid arthritis (a disease that destroys tissues that line bone joints), multiple sclerosis (a disease that affects the central nervous

deliberate practice Training with individualized feedback on tasks selected by a qualified teacher.

autoimmune disease A disease in which the immune system attacks the body's own cells. Rheumatoid arthritis (which destroys tissues that line bone joints), multiple sclerosis (which affects the central nervous system), and lupus (which can involve many types of tissue) are autoimmune diseases.

TABLE 13.4 Lifetime Risk of Death from Pregnancy and Childbirth

Around the world, a woman dies every minute from conditions related to pregnancy and birth. In 20 percent of cases, death is caused by diseases that are aggravated by pregnancy, such as malaria or tuberculosis.

Region	Lifetime Risk of Maternal Death: 1 in—
World total	74
Developed regions	2,800
Developing regions	61
Sub-Saharan Africa	16
Africa	20
Central and South Pacific Islands	83
Asia	94
Latin America and the Caribbean	160
Northern Africa	210

SOURCE: World Health Organization (2004).

system), and lupus (a disease that can involve many types of tissue). And, of course, women face illness and death due to complications from childbearing. As shown in Table 13.4, this risk is startlingly high in some regions of the world. In contrast, men are more likely than women to have their life cut short by violence or suicide (Centers for Disease Control and Prevention & National Center for Health Statistics, 2005). Neurological differences influence the mental health profiles of men and women. Continuing a trend that began during adolescence, women are two to three times more likely to develop depression, perhaps because they produce less of a brain chemical, serotonin, which is involved in mood regulation (Nishizawa et al., 1997). And although an equal number of men and women develop schizophrenia, their symptom profiles differ. On average, men experience schizophrenia at a younger age and have more severe symptoms than women.

These trends in social behavior, physical skill, and medical risks are just a few examples of numerous average differences between the sexes. But individual lives follow a single path, not an average path, so knowing someone's biological sex tells us little about what that path will be.

>>> MEMORY MAKERS <<<

Match each term to a related phrase:

1. the Big Five
2. *g*
3. theory of successful intelligence
4. theory of multiple intelligences
5. tacit knowledge
6. expertise
7. deliberate practice

(a) advanced knowledge or skill
(b) training on tasks selected to identify your weaknesses
(c) the intellectual resource that underlies intelligent behavior across a wide variety of tasks
(d) the primary personality traits
(e) a set of analytical, creative, and practical skills
(f) a theory that proposes over half a dozen types of intelligence
(g) information you need to succeed that is not taught

[1-d; 2-c; 3-e; 4-f; 5-g; 6-a; 7-b]

Revisiting Developmental Principles: Is Every Phase a Life Crisis?

As the world was celebrating a new century, writers Alexandra Robbins and Abby Wilner were putting the finishing touches on *Quarterlife Crisis: The Unique Challenges of Life in Your Twenties* (2001). Based on conversations with overwhelmed twentysomethings, they argued that college graduation is a time of self-doubt in a world that offers adults too many choices. "Welcome to the casino," they explained. "The confusion and helplessness that strike millions of twentysomethings soon after graduation is frequently the result of the feeling that they are about to gamble. Often. On their lives" (p. 8).

The quarterlife crisis joined a long list of crises that have populated books and movies for decades. In these forums, thirtysomethings are either mourning their youth or desperately trying to reproduce before it is too late. Then, by the 40s and early 50s, a "midlife crisis" kicks in. In this phase, men buy sports cars and ditch their wives for younger lovers while women face the "empty nest" syndrome as their children leave home. But if we are challenged by our 20s, mourning youth in our 30s, and having a midlife crisis in our 40s, is every phase a life crisis?

Scientists don't think so. Despair sells books, but studies of adulthood have not found crises that map neatly onto specific ages. The most widely studied myth, the midlife crisis, is a case in point. The idea of a rocky midlife gained authority from theorists like Daniel Levinson, whom you read about in Chapter 12. Levinson thought that most men experienced a transition in their 40s, when they began thinking about their own mortality and grappling with the possibility of changing their lives. But when researchers analyzed more representative samples of men, there was no tendency for the issues associated with midlife stereotypes to cluster within a single age bracket (Farrell & Rosenberg, 1981). Moreover, the challenges men and women label their "midlife crisis" often occur before age 40 or after 50, and they attribute these crises to major life events rather than age. Importantly, only 26 percent of adults feel they had experienced anything resembling a midlife crisis during this broad age range (Wethington, 2000).

The empty-nest syndrome is also more of an occasional or short-term problem than a universal experience. Yes, many parents grieve when children leave home, but most get over it. In fact, relationships between parents and children often improve when children move away, and parents generally enjoy their newfound freedom (Fingerman, 2000, 2003).

But some adults do feel overwhelmed in their 20s, old in their 30s, and trapped by their lives in their 40s. So how can we reconcile this with the lack of evidence for widespread crises? Thinking about developmental principles helps put challenges into perspective.

1. ***Development is the joint product of nature and nurture.*** Individuals sail smoothly through adulthood or hit rocky shores depending on their personalities and the skills they have learned. As described in this chapter, well-adjusted people tend to be low on neuroticism and high on extroversion, show good self-control, and enjoy a sense of purpose that helps them weather events such as losing a job or facing a health crisis.

2. *Physical, cognitive, and socioemotional development are interrelated*. At any age, it is easier for people to feel happy when they are healthy and have mastered the cognitive skills they need to navigate life. For example, a young adult who has not achieved postformal thought will have more difficulty than her classmates dealing with the ambiguities of life after college, and a fit 42-year-old man is less likely to worry about aging than a neighbor who has neglected his health. Throughout life, people who feel they are in crisis at every bend in the road often lack the physical, cognitive, and emotional resources they need to cope with challenges.

3. *Developmental outcomes vary over time and contexts*. It made sense to link crises to specific ages when most people started families in their 20s and consolidated careers in their 30s. But today, family life, career development, and even health status are not so tightly associated with age. As a result, adulthood is the process of periodically revisiting important themes—like intimacy versus freedom—throughout our lives.

4. *Development is characterized by continuity and discontinuity*. Some challenges follow us through most of adulthood, such as trying to be a good child to our parents, a good homemaker or employee, and a good friend or lover. But at any time, unexpected events such as the loss of a job or the end of a marriage can toss us onto a different life course. It is these unusual events—rather than the normal turning points of life—that cause the most distress (Neugarten, 1979).

In sum, some people experience a life crisis because their pathway through life hits challenges, not because development inevitably pushes us from one crisis to the next. In adulthood as in childhood, many individuals are resilient, others cope well enough, and some need periodic support and assistance.

We began this chapter with a tale of courage and discovery because early to middle adulthood is the time when people make history, advance culture, and start the next generation on its way. As this phase draws to a close, those who have lived well are reaping the rewards that come from family, friends, and pride in their accomplishments. But the transition into our 50s is not a time to rest and reflect. On the contrary, many people still have at least 30 more years to live, love, and learn. The tales of those years are the next chapters of our story.

〉〉〉 S U M M A R Y 〈〈〈

Health and Well-Being

1. **Mortality** (death) and **morbidity** (disease) rates show that the leading health risks during adulthood are all related to behavior. In addition to accidents, sexual behavior, and substance abuse, there are significant risks from violence, poor diets, and physical inactivity.

2. On average, people with more years of education are healthier than less educated people. Highly educated adults tend to have more fulfilling work, and they are more likely than less educated adults to exercise, refrain from smoking, and stay at a healthier weight.

3. Stress produces immune system changes that make people more susceptible to infectious diseases. People who respond well to stress tend to have sociable personalities, good support systems, and no history of depression or anxiety disorders.

4. **Well-being**—the perception that one's life is fulfilling, meaningful, and pleasant—is not strongly associated with wealth. People who are satisfied with life tend to have positive personalities and good social relationships. They also tend to compare themselves to people less fortunate than themselves, engage in productive work, and participate in religious activities.

Earning a Living

5. Due to the information (microchip) revolution, an increasing number of jobs involve providing services and acquiring, storing, and sharing information. Today's jobs emphasize high-level cognitive skills, good communication and social skills, and the ability to work with people from a variety of backgrounds.

6. Many young adults postpone choosing a first career due to feelings of hesitancy and confusion. During the adjustment to work, it is common for people to have unrealistic expectations and to shift jobs frequently. Satisfaction varies during midcareer, when about half of adults say they would be interested in changing careers.

7. Women are more likely than men to leave the workforce to attend to family needs, and they earn less money than men. In the United States, Asian workers earn the highest average salaries, followed by white workers, Hispanic workers, and African Americans workers.

Relationships

8. Romantic passion is a biologically based system that makes us highly motivated to pair with a mate. According to the **triangular theory of love**, the feelings we call "love" actually involve many different feelings, including passion, intimacy, and commitment.

9. Marriages have a higher chance of success when people do not marry young and are committed to the marriage. Happy couples have a pattern of interaction that includes a high ratio of positive to negative interactions, and they can turn the volume down on bad interactions by injecting humor or making supportive comments. When couples divorce, it often takes a year or more for them to adjust.

10. Well-adjusted singles have the same characteristics that happily married people have: close relationships, work they enjoy, and a sense of purpose.

11. Although culture influences what people consider "sexy," the sexual behavior of most adults is rather conservative. The desires and behaviors of males and females are more similar than popular culture leads us to believe. Gay and lesbian adults face the challenges of *heterosexism*—a world designed around heterosexual couples—and discrimination.

12. Well-being is more likely to decline after children are born if parents are young, have unrealistic expectations of the work involved in raising children, and receive little support from family members or friends.

13. Siblings and extended family members are important sources of support during adulthood. Many cultures expand their social networks with **fictive kin** who assume some of the rights and responsibilities that are usually reserved for family members.

Individuality

14. Studies of the **Big Five** personality characteristics (neuroticism, extroversion, openness to experience, agreeableness, and conscientiousness) show that personality changes are greater during young adulthood and more gradual afterward. Better life outcomes are associated with conscientiousness, extraversion, and low scores on neuroticism. People who have good self-control (self-regulation) also tend to be happier and more successful than their peers.

15. IQ is associated with success during adulthood, but many other factors, such as socioeconomic status and motivation, also contribute. The **theory of multiple intelligences** and the **theory of successful intelligence** try to capture skills associated with success during adulthood that are not represented on traditional IQ tests.

16. The majority of creative works and discoveries are made by people in their 30s to mid-40s. Creative people show *divergent thinking*, a type of thinking that involves coming up with many possibilities and looking for relationships between ideas. They are also highly motivated to solve problems, persistent, and nonconforming. It usually takes at least 10 years of experience to develop **expertise** (advanced skill or knowledge in a particular field).

17. More men than women hold positions of power, and there are also sex differences in athletic performance and rates of many medical and psychological conditions.

Revisiting Developmental Principles: Is Every Phase a Life Crisis?

18. Life crises do not map neatly onto specific developmental periods. Whether adults fall apart in the face of life's challenges or respond productively is largely a function of their individual personalities and learning histories, their current resources and skills, and the social context. Adulthood includes some challenges that are ongoing as well as periods of upheaval that are caused by unexpected events.

>>>KEY TERMS<<<

mortality rates (p. 521)

morbidity rates (p. 521)

positive energy balance (p. 523)

well-being (p. 525)

monogamy (p. 532)

triangular theory of love (p. 535)

serial monogamy (p. 536)

polygamy (p. 536)

polyandry (p. 536)

fictive kinship (p. 546)

Big Five (p. 547)

g (p. 549)

theory of multiple intelligences (p. 550)

theory of successful intelligence (p. 551)

tacit knowledge (p. 551)

expertise (p. 553)

deliberate practice (p. 554)

autoimmune disease (p. 554)

CHAPTER FOURTEEN

Profile of Middle to Late Adulthood

Stories of Our Lives
How Old Is Old?

Richard Alpert is better known as Ram Dass, the name his guru (spiritual teacher) gave him when he studied in India. Now a guru himself, the former psychology professor encourages others to achieve inner peace by living fully in the present moment. But even Dass's emotional balance was thrown off when he discovered he was "old" at age 62. His moment of realization is an amusing story in one of his books, *Still Here: Embracing Aging, Changing, and Dying* (Dass, 2000):

On a soft autumn evening in 1993, I was on a train between Connecticut and New York admiring the brilliant New England foliage after a day spent hiking with a dear friend in the woodlands surrounding her home. I was deeply contented there on the coach, reflecting on the colors of the day, when a conductor came down the aisle, collecting tickets.

"I'll have to buy mine from you," I said.

"What kind will it be?" he asked.

"Do I have a choice?"

"Regular or senior citizen?"

> "The great secret that all old people share is that you really haven't changed in seventy or eighty years. Your body changes, but you don't change at all. And that, of course, causes great confusion."
>
> Doris Lessing

Now, although I was bald, covered with age spots and battling high blood pressure and gout, it had never ever occurred to me—not once—that I could be called a senior citizen! I remembered the time when I was eighteen and tried to buy a beer legally in a bar, and was astounded that they'd sell one to *me*. But this conductor hadn't asked for ID; he'd taken one look and thought, "Discount." Offended, amused, confused, I said in a squeaky-sounding voice, "Senior Citizen?"

"That'll be four and a half dollars," he said.

"How much would the regular ticket be?"

"Seven dollars."

Well, I was pleased with that, of course, but the satisfaction of saving the money quickly faded. What identity had I taken on with the discount of senior citizen? As the coach rattled on, I felt troubled and anxious, weighed down by the baggage of my new label. Was the saving worth the cost? The role itself seemed so constricting—senior citizen! Old fogey! . . .

That very evening, on a train from Hartford to New York City, I began to seriously question where my ideas about aging had come from, why being old felt like such a stigma, and whether or not I could transform this process, with all the fears, losses, and uncertainties that came with it, from a necessary evil into an opportunity for spiritual and emotional growth. (pp. 10–12)

Ram Dass was indeed able to transform his aging process, partly by spending time in cultures where views of aging are quite different from those in North America. During one of his returns to India, for example, he was greeted with "Ram Dass, you are looking so old!" But far from being a tactless insult, the remark was meant as high praise. Imagine how different our views of ourselves would be if we grew up in a society where it was desirable to be—and even *look*—old!

IN OUR OPENING STORY, Ram Dass didn't feel old until someone else thought he was old. We're not surprised. According to one survey, there is little agreement about who is "old." Young adults think that 58 is old, but for people over 65, old age does not begin until 75 (Takeuchi & Groeneman, 1999). In the United States, adults who manage to make it through their 40s without thinking about growing old are sure to do so shortly after their 50th birthdays—when they become eligible for membership in the AARP (formerly called the American Association for Retired Persons). As one of our friends jokes, you know you are old the minute you find an AARP membership card in your mailbox!

Regardless of *who* you think is old, there is no doubt that the world is graying. The population over 65 years of age (our so-called senior citizens) is projected to more than triple between 2002 and 2050 while the population of children under 15 increases slowly (U.S. Census Bureau, 2004). These trends are changing the **age dependency ratio**: the number of nonworking citizens per 100 people ages 15 to 64. This ratio is important because the taxes working adults pay support services for children and the elderly. As a result, the economic burden on young adults increases as the age dependency ratio increases. By the last U.S. census, there were only two working-age adults for every dependent and only five for every elderly adult (McDevitt & Rowe, 2002). As the number of older adults continues to grow, so do two fields that study aging: **gerontology** (the study of biological, psychological, and sociological phenomena associated with aging) and **geriatrics** (the branch of medicine that deals with diseases and problems of the elderly).

age dependency ratio The number of nonworking citizens (under age 15 or 65 and older) per 100 people ages 15 to 64.

gerontology The study of biological, psychological, and sociological phenomena associated with aging.

geriatrics The branch of medicine that deals with diseases and problems of the elderly.

How will this "age wave" affect our lives? There will probably be a greater market for products targeted for adults in the last decade of middle age (those from 50 to 60 years), including wrinkle creams, easy-open packages, and remakes of hit songs from the 1960s. In addition, electronic equipment and buildings will probably become more elderly-friendly, with larger buttons and wheelchair ramps for ease of use by the *young-old* (from 61 to 74 years), the *old-old* (from 75 to 84 years), and the *oldest-old* (85 and older). You can also expect more research dollars to be spent on aging issues because the well-being of older adults will determine their quality of life, the peace of mind their families enjoy, and the economic stress they place on society. In this chapter, you will explore the fundamental changes that occur as people embark on life after 50—changes that will increasingly affect your world and your life.

You will be seeing more products and physical spaces designed with older people in mind as the population of the world grows older.

The Mystery of Aging

Aging—those gradual changes in the structure and function of our bodies over time that are not due to disease or accidents—is a universal phenomenon: People age, cars age, plants age. But aging does not occur on the same timetable for all creatures. Unlike humans, for example, the asexual sea anemone, which reproduces by sprouting an identical organism out of its side, can live for decades without losing the glow of youth. According to biologist Michael Rose (2004), sexual species are the ones that age—not because aging serves a useful purpose but because there is no selection pressure *not* to age. That is, traits that strike us down early in life prevent us from reproducing, so these traits are removed from the gene pool. But late-acting traits—those that cause us to deteriorate *after* reproduction—have already been passed onto our children. In turn, our children reproduce before the unfortunate genes work their mysteries again, passing aging on from generation to generation.

Evolutionary theory makes an interesting prediction about the relationship between reproduction and aging: If we delayed reproduction, more harmful genes would be eliminated from the gene pool and individuals would eventually live longer. This is exactly what happens—at least in the lowly fruit fly. By delaying reproduction and breeding only robust survivors, scientists have produced stocks of flies that live two to three times longer than normal. According to Rose, these elderly parents are "surprisingly perky" (2004, p. 27). "What they can do when normal flies are long dead is absolutely amazing," Rose explained. "They're just dynamic and vigorous while normal flies are barely moving around" (*"Discover Dialog: Michael Rose,"* 2001, p. 16).

But, alas, those of us who are alive today are stuck with a life span that has been passed down for generations. Measuring this span and discovering what sets its clock are two goals of scientists who study the aging process.

Life Span and Life Expectancy

When Frenchwoman Jeanne Calment died in 1997 at the age of 122 years, she earned a place in history as the oldest person of documented age. Scientists are not sure whether anyone has ever lived longer than Calment because birth records were infrequent prior to the middle of the 20th century. Nonetheless, they estimate that your **life span**—the maximum amount of time you can live—is about 120 years.

Your **life expectancy** is the average amount of time someone in your place and time *actually* lives. The human life span has not changed much

aging Gradual changes in the structure and function of our bodies over time that are not due to diseases or accidents.

life span The maximum amount of time that any human can live, which is estimated to be approximately 120 years.

life expectancy The average amount of time a person in a given place and time will live. For example, a life expectancy of 80 years means that 50 percent of newborns will survive until 80 years of age.

FIGURE 14.1 Historical fall in the death rate.

As these examples illustrate, standard death rates from infectious diseases dropped sharply after 1900, but health had already improved *before* innoculations and drug treatments were introduced. Scientists credit our growing life expectancy to improved nutrition, sanitation, and the sense of hope for the future that comes with modernization.

SOURCE: McKinlay & McKinlay (1981).

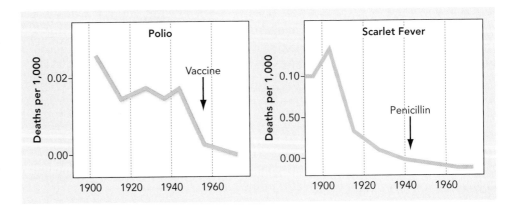

FIGURE 14.2 Life expectancy at birth: 1900 to 2002

In the United States, life expectancy at birth has risen 30 years since 1900. Most of this improvement is due to reduced mortality during infancy and early childhood.

SOURCE: National Center for Health Statistics (2004).

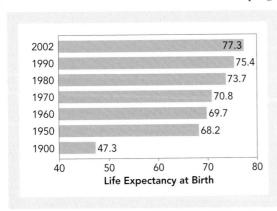

since the beginning of recorded history, but life expectancy has quadrupled since the height of early Greek and Roman civilizations, when it averaged only 18 to 22 years. Of course, this doesn't mean that ancient Grecians never lived past 18 (or few would have borne and raised children). Rather, it means that only half of all Grecian babies born at that time reached adulthood (Hayflick, 1996).

Today, life expectancy varies widely. A baby girl born in Japan can expect to live 85 years, whereas a girl born on the same day in the West African country of Sierra Leone has a life expectancy of only 36 years (World Health Organization, 2003). In the United States, life expectancy at birth is 80 years for females and 75 years for males (National Center for Health Statistics, 2005a). The female advantage leads to a noticeable gender imbalance later in life, when 71 percent of persons ages 85 and older are female (Gist & Hetzel, 2004).

What explains the historical increase in life expectancy? Most people guess that vaccinations and medicines played a role, but these were only minor pieces of the puzzle. As you can see in Figure 14.1, death rates from many diseases dropped sharply after 1900, well before these medical advances. Most of the increase in life expectancy is the result of more sanitary birthing conditions, public health measures (such as cleaner water) that reduced infant and child mortality, and better nutrition (Ray, 2004). Improved health in the United States has added 30 years to life expectancy from birth since 1900 (Figure 14.2). But people today who have already reached 65 can expect to live only 6.5 years longer than their forerunners from 1900 (Bell & Miller, 2005; U.S. Census Bureau, 2004). In other words, we have been much more successful in helping children survive to adulthood than in helping middle-aged adults reach old age.

Experts believe that even if scientists eliminated all the leading causes of death, life expectancy probably would not increase past 120 years because the human body is simply not designed to last forever. Other causes of death would emerge, and 100-year-olds would eventually die of these so-called natural causes (Hayflick, 2004; Olshansky, Hayflick, & Carnes, 2002).

If you plan to use Figure 14.2 to determine how many years *you* have left to live, don't bother. Life expectancy changes as people age, so the number at birth is *not* the same as the number at age 20, 30, or later. The reason this is true has fascinating implications for elderly adults. To explore this issue, turn to our last *Don't Be Fooled!* feature entitled, "If You're older, You're Better!"

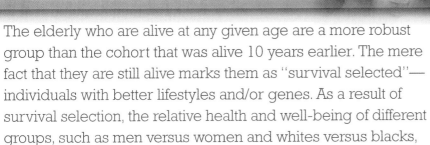

The elderly who are alive at any given age are a more robust group than the cohort that was alive 10 years earlier. The mere fact that they are still alive marks them as "survival selected"— individuals with better lifestyles and/or genes. As a result of survival selection, the relative health and well-being of different groups, such as men versus women and whites versus blacks, changes with age.

IF YOU'RE OLDER, YOU'RE BETTER!

How long will you live? That depends on many factors, including your sex (females live longer, on average), race (Caucasians live longer, on average), and economic status (the higher, the better). Other important factors are where you live (Hawaiians currently enjoy the longest life expectancy in the United States) as well as your current health, lifestyle, genetic susceptibility to disease, and degree of exposure to environmental hazards. Many Web sites help you calculate your life expectancy. (You can find a variety by searching for "life expectancy calculator.") These programs start with an assumption of an average life expectancy for your birth year, then add and subtract years depending on your answers to questions about factors correlated with longer and shorter longevity.

Let's take an example. If you were 20 years old in 2005, you were born in 1985. That year, life expectancy at birth was 74.7. So at 20, you might expect to live another 54.7 years, right? Wrong. Most likely, you'll live longer. How can this be?

The answer is that an individual's life expectancy changes with age. Life expectancy at birth factors in early mortality, including deaths from accidents, childhood diseases, and so forth. But if you have survived this far without succumbing to accidents and diseases, your life expectancy is actually somewhat *higher* than it was when you were born. To illustrate, the following table below shows life expectancy for selected ages (Aries, 2004). As you can see, 60-year-old males can expect to live another 20 years on average. But once they survive 20 more years, they have improved their chances again and can expect to live almost 8 years more.

	Years Left to Live	
Age	Females	Males
birth	79.9	74.5
5	75.4	70.2
10	70.5	65.3
20	60.7	55.6
30	51.0	46.3
40	41.4	37.0
50	32.2	28.3
60	23.5	20.3
70	15.8	13.2
80	9.4	7.8
90	5.0	4.2
100	2.8	2.5

So each time you find yourself 5 years older, you do not necessarily take 5 years off your life expectancy. The older you become, the more you have proven your ability to avoid risk and the longer you can expect to live! The idea that nature weeds out unhealthy or maladapted organisms is called *survival selection,* and this process has an interesting implication: As a group, the people who are alive at one age are not necessarily like the people who were alive at an earlier age. Instead, survival selection causes interesting *cross-over effects,* in which the relative health of various groups changes with age.

Some well-known crossover effects involve ethnic differences. For example, black adults have a greater risk than white adults of dying before age 80, but after age 80 it is the black adults who are more likely to survive (Corti et al., 1999). This crossover is mostly due to changing death rates from heart disease: Blacks are more vulnerable to heart disease, but those who survive to age 80 are especially robust. Similarly, men typically die earlier than women, but those who live to at least 90 have *better* mental function than their female counterparts do. According to geriatrician Thomas Perls (2004), men are more likely than women to die from problems that cause cognitive skills to deteriorate, so those who survive into very old age are unexpectedly sharp. Due to survival selection, if you're older, you're better! ◆

Why We Age

Why do we age and die? Do we simply wear out, like cars that have been driven for hundreds of thousands of miles? Or is there an ever-ticking alarm clock inside us that rings periodically no matter what? The answer to this question has preoccupied people throughout history. If we could determine why we age, we could perhaps discover the "fountain of youth"—the key to slowing, stopping, or even reversing the aging process. This would have enormous implications, both positive (you would live longer) and negative (everyone else who lived longer would compete with you and your family for food and other resources).

All theories of aging start with the assumption that aging is a *normal biological process* (Strehler, 1986). Some theories assume that this process has been programmed or built into our genetic code (Skulachev & Longo, 2005). But if death is programmed, why do we usually die after a long period of decline instead of suddenly, as some salmon do? And why can't we be like sea turtles and reproduce in old age? Because of such unresolved issues, other theories build on the idea that aging is a *random* process that results from accidental events. These accidents include losses due to wear and tear as well as buildups of genetic errors or harmful substances (Cristofalo et al., 1999). The theories of aging you will read about next all describe bodily changes that are known to occur as we age, but what scientists debate is *which* of these changes is a fundamental cause of aging and, subsequently, death. Let's look at some of these ideas.

AGING AS THE RESULT OF PREPROGRAMMED CHANGES. *Programmed aging theories* describe the nature of the internal alarm clock that regulates aging. One example is *immunological theory,* a theory of aging that focuses on normal declines in immune system function that occur after adolescence. According to this theory, a weakened ability to fight infections makes us more susceptible to disease over time. In addition, our immune systems begin to produce antibodies against normal body proteins, leading to autoimmune diseases (such as some forms of arthritis). Although it is clear that these changes occur, is not yet clear if these immune system changes are centrally involved in normal aging.

Endocrine theories blame aging on declining levels of hormones that regulate growth, metabolism, protein synthesis, and reproduction (Hertoghe, 2005). The fact that women who give birth late in life or reach menopause later actually live longer (on average) seems to support this view (Perls, Lauerman & Silver, 1999; Snowdon, 2001). But as you will read in the next chapter, findings on the protective effects of reproductive hormones have been disappointing. Other hormones that might play a role in aging, such as human growth hormone and melatonin, are currently under investigation (Bartke, 2005; Leon et al., 2004).

According to *genetic theories*, aging results from a sequence of genes that switch on and switch off during our lives. Some genetic theories of aging take the view that "death genes" switch on at certain points in time, causing massive cell death; others assume that helpful genes switch off after midlife, just as those that produce hair pigments do.

An important concept for understanding genetic theories of aging is the **Hayflick limit**. The Hayflick limit refers to the fact that many cells are programmed to die after a fixed number of divisions. In the laboratory, for example, cells taken from human fetuses divide about 50 times, but cells from adults usually divide only 20 times (Hayflick, 1965). In addition, the older the cell donor, the fewer times their cells will divide. The number of possible cell divisions is related to the length of the tip of the chromosome known as the **telomere**. This tip, which you can see in Figure 14.3, is made up of subunits of DNA sequences repeated thousands of times. With each cell division, the repeated sequence is reduced, until the telomere becomes too short to allow further divisions and the Hayflick limit has been reached (Figueroa et al., 2000). The telomeres of normal cells behave this way, but cancer cells have an enzyme that produces more telomeres, allowing them to keep dividing past the usual limit (Marx, 2002).

Research on telomeres and how to keep them from shortening is an exciting area of exploration in the antiaging field. Nonetheless, cell division does not provide a simple answer to the riddle of aging. This is because the cells of even the oldest human donors still have a few divisions left in them, and changes in cells that do not divide much (if at all)—such as most brain cells—produce some of the biggest and most important age-related changes. Finally, telomere shortening isn't involved in many of the other maladies of age, such as vascular disease and thinning bones. As one telomere researcher concluded, "Telomere shortening is not the cause of overall aging as we know it" (Hopkin, 2004, p. 15).

AGING AS RANDOM OR ACCIDENTAL EVENTS. Other theories of aging focus on the gradual accumulation of biological damage that occurs over the life span. According to *DNA damage theory*, for example, mutations and radiation damage the DNA until cells no longer divide properly. *Cross-linkage theory* focuses on the bonds (or cross-links) that develop over time between parts of the same molecule or between different molecules. Some proteins, such as collagen, develop more cross-links over time, making tissue less soft and pliable. Cross-links may have serious consequences for our bodies if they occur in important molecules, such as the nucleic acids that make up our genes (National Institute on Aging, 2005a).

One explanation of biological damage that is receiving a lot of attention is **free radical theory**. Free radicals are atoms or molecules that lose an electron. Free radicals are highly reactive because they try to replace the missing electron by "stealing" from nearby molecules, causing harm to cells in the body. Of special interest to aging researchers are oxygen-free radicals, a type of free radical that is produced by normal metabolism inside your cells when oxygen combines with

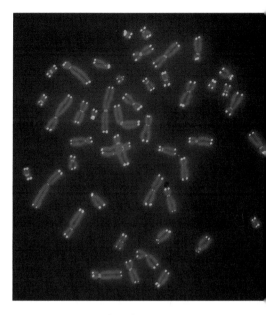

FIGURE 14.3 Molecular timekeepers.

Telomeres—the ends of chromosomes—light up like fireflies in this photograph. Each time a cell divides, its telomeres get a little shorter. Once a cell's telomeres reach a critically short length, that cell can no longer divide.

SOURCE: From "Making Methuselah," by K. Hopkin, 2004, *Scientific American 14* (3), p.14. Reprinted with permission.

[handwritten note: as we age we have less reserve in our organs. Genes limit our maximum life span.]

Hayflick limit The number of cell divisions that occurs before a cell dies.

telomere The tip of the chromosome, which gets shorter with each cell division.

free radical theory A theory that says that aging occurs when oxygen-free radicals, a highly reactive form of oxygen, are produced inside cells. Free radicals damage cell molecules by "stealing" electrons from them.

caloric restriction Severely limiting the number of calories consumed each day.

other substances. Much of the daily assault on your body from free radicals is mopped up by antioxidant chemicals and proteins that safely provide the missing electrons, but the repair process isn't perfect. As one writer explained, "the house is always getting dirty, and we're always trying to clean it up. But eventually . . . our tired cells get less efficient at repelling free radicals and mopping up oxidative messes, and the damage accumulates" (Brown, 2004, p. 31).

Extending Life

Each of the theories of aging summarized in Table 14.1 suggests ways to extend the life span. But despite claims you may see in the popular media, scientists doubt there will ever be a "quick fix" for the loss of function that eventually accompanies aging. For example, exercise can improve your quality of life and possibly forestall heart problems, but there is no evidence that staying fit alters the basic limits of the human life span. And as you will read in the next chapter, efforts to boost hormone levels have had unintended side effects, so scientists consider this approach to slowing or preventing aging too risky. Another approach is to prevent free radicals from forming by loading your diet with fruits and vegetables, which are rich in antioxidants such as vitamins C and E. There is some evidence that animals fed large amounts of antioxidants live longer and develop cancer and cardiovascular disease later, but there is no convincing evidence that antioxidants extend the human life span (Rose, 2004).

Another approach for conquering aging is to reduce the formation of free radicals by reducing metabolic activity (Roth, Lane, & Ingram, 2005). It is well known that cold-blooded animals that spend more time in colder temperatures, such as some types of sea turtles, have reduced metabolism and long lives. Furthermore, severely restricting the calorie intake of rats (without producing malnutrition) decreases their metabolic activity and extends life expectancy (Cristofalo et al., 1999). **Caloric restriction** is also being studied in primates and some human volunteers. For example, Roy Walford, a UCLA scientist who conducted some of the original research on rats, started on his own calorie-restricted diet in the late 1980s. His typical daily regime contained about 1,600 calories—far below the 2,300 calories that is typical for a man of his height: a milk shake with yeast and fruit for breakfast; salad for lunch; and fish, a sweet potato, and

---

TABLE 14.1 Some Theories of Aging

Theory	Explanation
Programmed Theories	Aging is built into our bodies; it is a product of heredity and maturation, not experience.
immunological theory	A programmed decline in immune system functions leads to an increased vulnerability to infectious disease and, thus, aging and death.
endocrine theory	Biological clocks act through hormones to control the pace of aging.
genetic theory	Aging results from the switching on and off of certain genes.
Random or Accidental (Biological Damage) Theories	Environmental assaults and random biological events gradually cause things to go wrong.
DNA damage	Mutations and radiation damage the DNA until cells no longer divide properly.
cross-linkage theory	Bonds (cross-links) develop between parts of a molecule or between different molecules. An increase over time in the cross links between protein molecules causes tissues to age.
free radical theory	Highly reactive oxygen radicals are produced when energy is released inside cells. Free radicals damage protein, DNA, and other essential molecules. The accumulated damage causes cells and eventually organs to stop functioning.

some vegetables for dinner (Maugh, 2004). At 5 feet 9 inches tall, Walford kept his weight near 130 pounds—about 20 pounds less than what he carried as a 25-year-old (O'Connor, 2004; Scientific American Frontiers Archives, 2005).

In humans, a calorie-restricted diet has been shown to lower blood pressure, blood sugar, and cholesterol levels and to increase resistance to colds and flu—benefits that led to the establishment of the Calorie Restriction Society (2006). But, unfortunately, Walford's diet could not prevent his death at 79 from ALS (Lou Gehrig's disease), an inherited, incurable illness. However, he did credit his unique diet with slowing down the disease and allowing him to live a longer and more productive life. If you are tempted to try his diet at home, you should know that it is difficult to achieve a well-balanced diet with caloric restriction, and some evidence links extreme thinness to a *shorter* life expectancy (Gaesser, 1999; Troiano et al., 1996)! Until future research resolves this contradictory evidence, most developmentalists continue to enjoy their food (Prentice, 2005).

It is clear that scientists will need to put many pieces of information together and discover a few more before they will successfully extend the human life span (or understand why this is impossible). So before you turn a minute older, let's shift your attention from *why* you age to explore *what* aging is.

Could you eat this for lunch every day? Roy Walford, a UCLA scientist, stuck to a daily regime of about 1,600 calories a day in an effort to extend his life. Despite evidence that caloric restriction helps other species live longer, evidence for humans is inconclusive.

> > > **MEMORY MAKERS** < < <

Place the terms on the left of each sentence into the correct blanks:

1. gerontology, geriatrics
1. The branch of medicine that deals with diseases and problems of the elderly is called _____; the study of biological, psychological, and sociological phenomena associated with aging is called _____.

2. life span, life expectancy
2. The maximum amount of time a human can live is his or her _____; the average amount of time someone in your place and time actually lives is that person's _____.

3. Hayflick limit, telomere
3. The _____ is the maximum number of times a cell can divide, which is determined by the length of the tip of the chromosome called a _____.

[1-geriatrics, gerontology; 2-life span, life expectancy; 3-Hayflick limit, telomere]

Physical Aging after 50

Nothing fully prepares us for the moment we glance at the flesh of our aging arms and see our mother's or father's arms. "Oh my," we think, remembering back to our fascination with these arms during childhood, when we thought there was too much skin for the amount of arm that needed to be covered. Our arms are part of a package of aging surprises that arrive within a few years of each other, including changing eyeglass prescriptions, new aches in the morning, and a different face in the mirror.

One of America's longest-running studies of the changes associated with aging is the **Baltimore Longitudinal Study of Aging (BLSA)**, which began in 1958 (National Institute on Aging, 2005b). Currently, more than 1,400 study volunteers receive free physical exams and medical screening tests every 2 years to help researchers separate the changes that result from disease from those that represent normal aging. Because longitudinal studies follow the same people over time, projects like this one can also separate cohort effects from the effects of biological aging. For example, improved nutrition has made recent generations taller and heavier, so today's 70-year-olds look especially short and thin. If we just compared them to 20-year-olds, we might come to the conclusion that aging causes us to become much shorter and thinner. But, of course, those 70-year-olds were never particularly tall or heavy to begin with. Clearly, it is only by watching individuals age *over time* that scientists can determine how much height is lost due to aging. In the sections that follow, you will learn some key findings from this and other studies, starting with the physical changes you see on the outside and then exploring the changes that are unfolding within.

What Over 50 Looks Like

People of the same age look very different after midlife. Those who avoided the sun have fewer wrinkles than their sun-worshiping friends, those who took care of their teeth have healthy gums, and those who ate well and stayed active can still wear the clothes they wore after college graduation. But even the healthiest 50- or 60-year-old has a look of maturity that will never be mistaken for a 30-year-old.

SKIN, HAIR, TEETH, AND FACIAL FEATURES. Changes in skin, hair, and teeth are the main features we use to judge how old people are. For this reason, these are the changes more people try to minimize, with treatments ranging from the inexpensive and safe (hair dye and teeth bleaching) to the costly and risky (cosmetic surgery).

After 50, further loss of the protein *collagen* and an excess of the protein *elastin* reduce the elasticity of our skin and speed wrinkle formation. If you are 45 or younger, you can pinch the skin on the back of your hand and watch it return to its original state in about 2 seconds. By age 75, it may take 50 seconds—25 times longer (Kligman, Grove, & Balin, 1985)!

Next to wrinkles, changing hair is the most obvious sign of aging. Individual hairs become gray as pigment-producing cells in the hair bulbs die at an age and rate that depend on heredity. The hair on our heads also becomes thinner due to fewer hairs and thinner strands, especially after age 65. Male-pattern baldness, which begins earlier in life in genetically susceptible men, continues into midlife and old age. By age 70, fewer than 15 percent of men have experienced little or no balding (Sinclair & Thai, 2004). And due to hormonal shifts after menopause, baldness also begins to show up in some women. Many middle aged people joke that their hair is "migrating" because they lose hair in some areas (most notably, the underarms) and see increased growth in others. To the dismay of many women, facial hair becomes thicker and darker, and older men see more hair in their ears, noses, and eyebrows.

We almost automatically judge age by the appearance of people's teeth. Teeth yellow over time, and older people are more likely to have tooth decay

Baltimore Longitudinal Study of Aging (BLSA) One of America's longest-running studies of human aging, which began in 1958. The BLSA is funded by the National Institute on Aging.

and gum disease. These problems, rather than normal aging, are the reasons for tooth loss. Happily, the addition of fluoride to toothpastes and public water supplies has reduced tooth decay over the last 30 years, so the majority of older people in the United States still have their own teeth (Federal Interagency Forum on Aging Related Statistics, 2004). As our skin, hair, and teeth are changing, more subtle changes are occurring to our noses and ears, which become longer and wider with age.

HEIGHT, WEIGHT, AND BODY APPEARANCE. As we mentioned in Chapter 12, most people lose about half an inch of height by age 50 as the disks in the spine, and then the bones themselves, deteriorate. Women usually start out shorter and shrink faster than men because they are more likely to develop *osteoporosis* (severe loss of bone density), especially in the 10 years after menopause. On average, men lose approximately 17 percent of the bone they had as young adults while women lose 30 percent. As a result, roughly half of all women over age 50 experience a fracture due to brittle bones, compared to only 1 out of 8 men (Amin, 2003; Spirduso, 1995; Wei & Levkoff, 2000).

Body proportions and muscle tone change as we age, but this is no reason to forgo a day of sun and fun. Walking on the beach is a good way to strengthen muscles and build stamina.

During the second half of life, metabolism continues to slow at a rate that began during young adulthood: about 3 percent every 10 years. As the number of calories needed to sustain weight declines, we need to eat less to maintain weight. Men generally gain weight until their mid 40s and women until their mid 50s, after which both sexes gradually lose weight due to the losses of muscle mass, water, bone, and lean tissue (Ogden et al., 2004). As muscle mass declines and body fat increases, arms and legs become thinner and torsos thicken. Men generally tend to accumulate fat in their abdomens, whereas women more often develop a "pear shape" as fat is deposited on hips and thighs.

Until age 60, declines in muscle size, weight, strength, and endurance are mostly caused by lack of use rather than aging, so declines can be offset by exercise and weight training. But muscle decline speeds up after 60, even among those who are physically fit. Muscle fiber is slowly replaced by fat and connective tissue, leading to stiffer muscles that take longer to recover from injuries. As a result of changes in metabolism and muscle mass, it is hard for older individuals to look fit and athletic. In Figure 14.4 you can review some changes that age our reflections in the mirror and get a preview of other changes that are occurring inside the body.

Age-Related Changes in Sensory Systems

A particular episode of the television show, *Everybody Loves Raymond*, is a favorite among the middle-aged crowd. Forty-something Robert just watched his younger girlfriend storm out of a restaurant after learning his age, much to the relief of his table companions, Ray and Debra. Talk turns to antacids, their problems with drinking coffee too late in the day, and the fact that Robert didn't even have enough "phone stamina" for his crush. By the end of the episode, you felt there was only one way to face aging: with humor, grace, and companionship.

Although there are many changes to face after 50, declines in vision and hearing are among the most common and troublesome aspects of aging. Most people have some visual or hearing deficits after age 75, with many adjusting to the problems you will read about next (Fozard & Gordon-Salant, 2001).

VISION. About 1 in 28 individuals age 40 and older are blind or have low vision, and 7 percent of adults 80 and older are blind (National Eye Institute,

FIGURE 14.4 The physical changes of aging.

Aging produces many visible changes and even more changes inside the body. The consequences of normal aging are widespread.

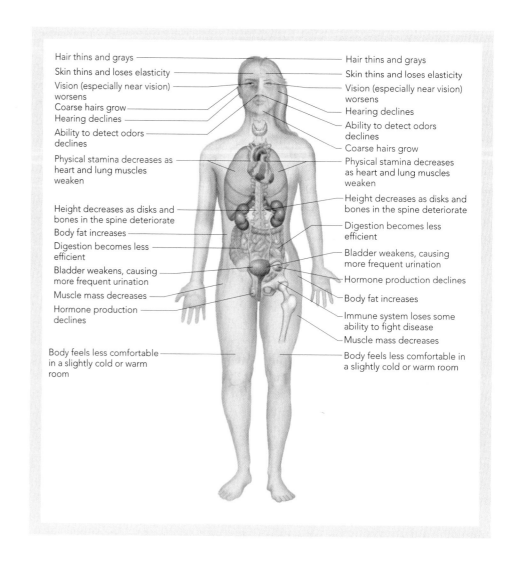

Hair thins and grays

Skin thins and loses elasticity

Vision (especially near vision) worsens

Coarse hairs grow

Hearing declines

Ability to detect odors declines

Physical stamina decreases as heart and lung muscles weaken

Height decreases as disks and bones in the spine deteriorate

Body fat increases

Digestion becomes less efficient

Bladder weakens, causing more frequent urination

Muscle mass decreases

Hormone production declines

Body feels less comfortable in a slightly cold or warm room

Hair thins and grays

Skin thins and loses elasticity

Vision (especially near vision) worsens

Hearing declines

Ability to detect odors declines

Coarse hairs grow

Physical stamina decreases as heart and lung muscles weaken

Height decreases as disks and bones in the spine deteriorate

Digestion becomes less efficient

Bladder weakens, causing more frequent urination

Hormone production declines

Body fat increases

Immune system loses some ability to fight disease

Muscle mass decreases

Body feels less comfortable in a slightly cold or warm room

2005). Even among healthy adults, the following visual changes are common during the second half of life (Jackson & Owsley, 2003; Kline & Scialfa, 1996):

▶ *Reduced acuity.* As we age, the lens in the eye continues to grow larger, thicker, less flexible, and more yellow. At the same time, the ciliary muscles lose their power to control lens thickness. These events reduce our ability to adjust focus, and *presbyopia*—the difficulty with near vision we described in Chapter 12—worsens. Significant presbyopia occurs in about 42 percent of people between 52 and 64 years, 73 percent between 65 and 74, and 92 percent over age 75.

▶ *Problems seeing in low-light conditions.* The pupil gets smaller with age, so less light reaches the retina and it becomes more difficult to see under low light conditions. The ability of the pupil to constrict in bright light and expand in low light also slows, so seniors adapt to changing light levels less effectively and are more bothered by glare.

▶ *Impaired color perception.* Older individuals have a harder time distinguishing colors, especially those in the green/blue range.

▶ *Annoying "floaters."* As time goes on, the fluid that fills the eye sometimes produces fairly harmless but annoying "floaters," debris that appears as little white specks in the field of view.

Although these changes are all part of the normal aging process, their extent can be influenced by environmental factors. For example, sun exposure damages the lens and smoking increases the risk of several eye diseases, including *cataracts* (cloudy spots on the lens). Cataracts are so common (affecting 1 in 2 people over age 80) that some experts believe they should be considered part of the normal aging process rather than a disease. This condition can be treated by surgery once it becomes severe enough to interfere with daily living.

Older adults often avoid busy restaurants where background noise makes it hard for them to follow the conversation. As people grow older, smaller gatherings help everyone feel part of the group.

HEARING. The deterioration of hearing associated with aging is called **presbycusis**. Numerous changes in the auditory system contribute to this condition, including stiffening of the eardrum and the bones that vibrate to transmit sound, a loss of hair cells that detect sound, and neurological changes (including increased "background noise" in the auditory cortex). These changes produce the following problems (Fozard & Gordon-Salant, 2001; Kline & Scialfa, 1996):

▶ *Difficulty detecting sounds.* Some hearing loss occurs in all adult age groups, but the rate of loss is about three times faster after age 55 than it was before (Kline & Scialfa, 1996). People usually have trouble hearing high-pitched sounds first, with men losing their hearing sooner and faster than women (Pearson et al., 1995).

▶ *Difficulty locating sounds.* Aging causes problems in the ability to locate the sources of sounds, such as where a siren or a horn is coming from (Willott, Hnath Chisolm, & Lister, 2001).

▶ *Problems understanding speech.* Impaired communication is the most troubling aspect of hearing loss. Older people have more problems understanding speech, especially when the environment is noisy or conversation is very fast (Kline & Scialfa, 1996). As a result, they sometimes avoid social events where several conversations will occur at the same time or they anticipate background noise, like music or dishes clinking. Seniors can compensate somewhat by using contextual cues, such as what people are most likely to be saying about a certain topic. Hearing aids also help, but only about 20 percent of older people have hearing aids and consistently use them, partly because of their high cost. Also, understanding speech requires more mental effort than some older people have or are willing to use, even with the help of hearing aids (Fozard & Gordon-Salant, 2001).

TASTE AND SMELL. Food (at least good food) remains a pleasure throughout life. Nevertheless, older adults do have slightly more difficulty detecting all of the primary taste sensations (sweet, sour, salty, and bitter) (Mojet, Christ-Hazelhof, & Heidema, 2001; Receputo et al., 1996; Schiffman, 1997). Our sense of smell is another story. The ability to detect odors drops sharply after 70 (Doty, 2001), with rates of impairment basically doubling every decade as people move through their 60s to their 70s and on to their 80s (Murphy et al., 2002). The declining ability to detect odors can decrease people's enjoyment of food so much that their nutrition suffers.

THE SKIN SENSES. The *somatosensory system* tells us about body contact (are you touching anything?) as well as temperature and pain. Due to age-related changes in this system, older people find it more difficult to tell whether they are being poked by two distinct prongs or just one (Spirduso, 1995). They also become more sensitive to cold environments and have a greater risk of hypothermia (below-normal body temperatures) due to reduced blood circulation in the skin and less fat. On average, older people prefer room temperatures that are 10 or 15 degrees higher than what younger people find comfortable, which is why your

presbycusis The deterioration of hearing associated with aging.

grandparents always keep the heat turned up so high. And because of fewer and less effective sweat glands, the risk of heat stroke is also higher among the elderly.

DIMINISHING MOTOR CONTROL Watch older people in a grocery store and it is clear they are living in a different temporal world: They are slow to move out of the way once they notice they are blocking you and take a long time to put items in the cart (Ketcham & Stelmach, 2001; Seidler & Stelmach, 1996). Indeed, *simple reaction time*, the time it takes to respond to a single stimulus, slows by about 25 percent from young to older adulthood. There are even larger declines in *choice reaction time*, which is the ability to respond quickly to one of several different stimuli (such as stopping for a yellow light but speeding up for a green light). *Movement time* refers to the time from the start to the end of a movement. Older adults have about 30 percent slower movement times than younger adults on a large variety of tasks, including grasping and reaching.

Balance is another area of physical decline. Compared to younger adults, older adults sway more, lose their balance more quickly, and need more time to recover their balance. This delay in responding means that older people do not always adjust quickly enough to prevent falls (Roos et al., 1999). Aging brings about numerous problems that cause walking difficulties and an increased risk of falling, including vision impairments, reductions in leg strength, and neurologic changes that cause dizziness and slow reaction times (Fuller, 2000). In fact, about one-third of people over 65 fall each year, and between 10 and 15 percent of these falls cause serious injury or death (Braun, 1998). Even when injuries are minor, many older people develop a fear of falling that causes them to restrict their activities (Vellas et al., 1997).

Changes in Organ Systems and Health

The changes aging works on the body do not arise from any single cause. Instead, numerous events combine to decrease physical stamina, reduce the ability to process food and fight illness, and end our reproductive lives.

PHYSICAL STAMINA. Your physical stamina is affected by the health of two systems: your respiratory system, which takes in oxygen and transfers it into the bloodstream, and your cardiovascular system, which pumps blood to deliver oxygen to cells (Spirduso, 1995; Wei & Levkoff, 2000). Sometime after age 50, the muscles that operate the lungs weaken and tissues in the chest wall stiffen, making the lungs less effective. As a result, breathing and even talking require more effort. Heart muscles also weaken with age. Between 20 and 70 years, the time it takes our hearts to fill with blood doubles, and blood is not transported as efficiently to the rest of the body. Although resting heart rate (how fast your heart beats when you are not active) remains about the same throughout adulthood, the maximum heart rate during exercise declines. Together with narrowing arteries and changes in the respiratory system, these developments gradually cause older individuals to lose stamina for physical activity.

PROCESSING FOOD AND WATER. The muscles of the entire digestive system become weaker and less effective as we age, so it takes longer for food and waste to move through the body. Our stomachs also produce less acid, decreasing our ability to digest protein, fat, and carbohydrates. Changes in the small intestine make it more difficult to absorb some nutrients, and the large intestine absorbs more water. Along with the weaker muscle contractions in the colon and large intestine, this can lead to constipation, which is a common problem among the elderly.

By age 70, the typical kidney is only half as fast at filtering waste out of the blood as it was at 30. The bladder's holding capacity, ability to delay urination, and rate of emptying all decline with age, causing more frequent and urgent urination. Complicating the matter, our sense of thirst declines, so we are at risk for dehydration (Kleiner, 1999).

FIGHTING ILLNESS. Not surprisingly, aging also affects our ability to fend off illness. Older immune systems generate fewer antibodies to detect foreign substances (such as viruses, bacteria, and cancer cells), and the immune cells produced are less able to recognize and kill invaders. As a result, our susceptibility to various diseases, including cancer, increases dramatically. Older people take longer to recover from illness and are more likely to have serious complications, even for common illnesses such as the flu. But aging does bring one noticeable health benefit: As we mentioned in Chapter 13, people become less likely to catch the common cold because they have already encountered and built immunity to so many different viruses that cause routine colds.

CHANGING HORMONE LEVELS. Hormone changes affect us in numerous ways as we age. A decline in growth hormone contributes to the loss of muscle mass that impairs strength, and the pancreas often becomes less effective in secreting hormones that allow the body to convert glucose into energy. When this is combined with increased weight, decreased physical activity, and dietary changes, reduced efficiency of the pancreas can lead to diabetes, an unhealthy rise in blood sugar levels. The thyroid gland may also develop scar tissue and nodules that reduce its effectiveness. Rates of *hypothyroidism* (underactive thyroid) increase with age, with the condition affecting 5 to 20 percent of elderly women and 3 to 8 percent of elderly men (Laurberg et al., 2005). Hypothyroidism leads to a loss of energy, dry skin, depression, and a variety of other symptoms. Instead of dismissing these problems as part of normal aging, older people should have a simple blood test to rule out this easily treated disorder.

For women, the most obvious consequence of an aging endocrine system is *menopause*. As described in Chapter 12, a woman has experienced menopause if she has had 12 months without menstrual bleeding. Menopause signals the end of her natural ability to conceive a child, but even postmenopausal women can give birth with assisted reproductive technology. In fact, Arceli Keh of California gave birth to her daughter, Cynthia, at the age of 63!

The age of menopause varies widely (usually between 35 and 55), with the average age being 51 years. As menopause approaches, reproductive organs and genitalia begin to shrink and the breasts become smaller, less dense, and more fatty. The symptoms associated with estrogen loss—hot flashes, night sweats, and vaginal dryness—also increase. But women differ greatly in terms of how many of these symptoms they have, how severe these symptoms are, and how long they last. Rates of problems also vary around the world. For example, few Japanese women report hot flashes (about 12 to 20 percent), whereas 33 to 75 percent of American women do. There is no simple pattern to geographic differences, and the reason for variability is currently unknown (Obermeyer, 2000; Robinson, 1996). Whether and how symptoms should be treated with hormone replacement therapy is a hotly debated question that you will read about in the next chapter.

Other symptoms and fears also differ as a function of cultural expectations. For example, menopausal Japanese women often report stiffness and dizziness but rarely depression, whereas European women are often depressed. The greatest

Some physical consequences of aging are experienced differently in different parts of the world. A well-known example involves menopause: Women from Asia are less likely than those from the United States to report hot flashes and depression during middle adulthood.

differences involve the social significance of menopause. In many traditional cultures, such as the Navajo of North America, women assume greater leadership roles after menopause, so menopause in these cultures can be viewed as a positive event. In contrast, women in industrialized societies more often feel a sense of loss as they leave their youth and childbearing years behind. But despite different reactions to menopause, most women worldwide pass through this normal transition rather easily (Obermeyer, 2000; Robinson, 1996).

Although there is no true male equivalent to menopause, the term **andropause** describes an age-related decrease in testosterone levels. Men do not experience a sudden or large reduction that ends their reproductive abilities, but their sex drive decreases with age and their need to release sexual tension through orgasm decreases. Ejaculations also become less forceful and contain less fluid. About one-quarter to one-half of 65-year-old men and up to two-thirds of 80-year-old men are impotent, meaning they are not able to achieve and maintain an erection when desired. Rather than being a natural consequence of aging, impotence is usually caused by disease, medicine, surgery, smoking, or psychological factors such as depression. Another common age-related change for men is an enlarged *prostate*, the gland that produces most of the fluid contained in semen. More than half of 60-year-old men have this condition, which increases the urge to urinate (because the enlarged prostate puts pressure on the bladder) and makes it more difficult to urinate.

If this list of age-related changes is affecting your mood, you might be due for a break from a team of well-known aging experts. For some humorous relief, turn to our *Innovations* feature entitled "The 150-Year-Old Man (and Woman)."

andropause The gradual decrease in testosterone levels that occurs among older males. Although men do not experience a sharp drop in sex hormones during middle adulthood, andropause is often referred to in popular culture as "male menopause."

INNOVATIONS

Our bodies have numerous design flaws, so it is unlikely that a single discovery will allow us to function well for much more than 100 years. If very old individuals are more active in the future, it will probably be due to scores of technological innovations that solve scores of specific complaints.

THE 150-YEAR-OLD MAN (AND WOMAN)

What kind of body should humans have if we want to live longer, healthier lives? Not just a "buff" version of our current selves, according to gerontologists S. Jay Olshansky, Bruce A. Carnes, and Robert N. Butler (2001). Instead, these aging researchers say we would look very different if we had been designed to function well for a century or more, rather than only long enough to mate and rear children. As they explain, "It is grossly unfair to blame people for the health consequences of inheriting a body that lacks perfect maintenance and repair systems and was not built for extended use or perpetual health. We would still wear out over time even if some mythical, ideal lifestyle could be identified and adopted" (p. 51). The reason is simple: The maladies of aging—from brittle bones to urination problems—result from countess design flaws.

Their solution to this design challenge is a body like the one shown in Figure 14.5. We would have bigger ears to collect sound more efficiently, equipped with more numerous and durable "hair cells" that relay sound information to the brain. (Our current hair cells are too susceptible to damage from loud noises.) Our eyes would require changes, too. The currently fragile connections between our retinas (the part of the eye that receives visual stimulation) and our optic nerves (that carry visual signals to the brain) would be "rewired" to prevent retinal detachments and resulting blindness.

But some of the biggest design changes would improve upon flaws that arise from the way we walk—upright, on two feet. Every step puts pressure on our feet, ankles, knees, and backs. Over the years, our spinal disks can slip, rupture, or bulge, while the lubricants in our joints thin and our bones begin to grind against each other. Meanwhile, our leg veins become enlarged and twisted as small valves malfunction and cause blood to pool.

Our redesigned bodies would be shorter with a lower center of gravity to prevent falls. The torso would tilt forward to relieve pressure on vertebrae and disks, and the disks themselves would be thicker. Our necks would be curved to counterbalance the tilted torso and allow our heads to stay up and face forward. We would have thicker bones and extra muscles and fat to cushion and protect against breaks. Our leg veins would have more valves to prevent malfunctions, and we would have larger hamstrings and tendons to better support our legs and hips. Finally, our knees would bend backwards, so they would not "lock in," and bones would be less likely to grind and deteriorate. (Unfortunately, this would result in difficulty standing for long periods, so further modifications would be needed, according to Olshansky and his colleagues.)

The final product is functional yet ugly by today's standards. Robert Butler, the first director of the National Institute on Aging, explained that while the body redesign project "was intended to be fun, it was also intended to be a serious reminder to people that you really should make good use of what you presently have" (*Morning Edition*, para. 8). The project is also a reminder that no single discovery will fix the myriad flaws that appear with age. The 100+-year-olds of the future will be more comfortable than today's centenarians only if numerous technological advances solve numerous specific design flaws. Hopefully, advances in genetics and pharmaceuticals will keep diseases at bay and stimulate the body's own self-repair mechanisms, while improved replacement parts—like artificial cartilage for the knees—will fill in for worn-out originals. Meanwhile, you can help your body last by avoiding the loud noises that harm your hearing, seeing an eye doctor once a year to catch problems early, and exercising regularly in well-fitting shoes to keep muscles strong and joints flexible. ◆

FIGURE 14.5 A person designed for a healthy old age.

The loss of function and discomfort that many people experience in their later years stem from design problems throughout the body. This picture shows how humans might look if we were designed with joints, bones, and veins that lasted 150 years.

SOURCE: From "If Humans Were Built to Last," by S. J. Olshansky, B. A. Carnes, and R. N. Butler, 2001, *Scientific American*, *284* (3), p. 50, copyright 2004, by Scientific American, Inc. Adapted with permission.

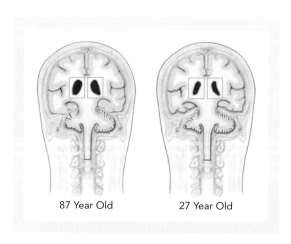

87 Year Old   27 Year Old

FIGURE 14.6 The Aging Brain.

As the brain shrinks with age, the hollow spaces fill with fluid. Notice the enlarged central spaces, called the ventricles, in the 87-year-old brain.

SOURCE: Oregon Brain Aging Study

The Aging Brain

Biologist Marion Diamond gets stares from passersby as she walks to her office at the University of California, Berkeley. While most people are trying not to attract attention, Diamond is walking on the 6-inch-wide curb and swinging her arms over her head to test her balance. "It's good for the cerebellum," she explains, citing research showing that walking on curbs can stimulate a part of the brain that controls physical coordination (American Society on Aging, 1998, para. 1).

Diamond knows that the brain ages differently in healthy, active people than it does in sick or inactive people. The changes that finally occur in all of us are found throughout the brain, from structures deep inside its tiny cells to the gross appearance of the brain as a whole (Raz, 2005). But early changes do not immediately change our behavior. The aging that occurs between 30 and 60 has little effect on how we perform because it does not influence neural processing or is compensated for by corresponding changes in how we approach tasks. Eventually, though, aging exceeds our ability to adjust, causing performance declines on nearly every complex motor and cognitive task. And as you will read shortly, the aging brain can frustrate us even when we close our eyes to rest for the night.

HOW THE BRAIN CHANGES. Six major changes unfold inside our aging brains:

▶ *Reduced size.* Brains begin shrinking as early as age 30 and more clearly after the age of 50 (Raz, et al. 2005, Resnick et al., 2003). Scientists used to think this shrinkage was due to massive cell loss, but recent evidence suggests that neuronal loss is less dramatic in normal aging than previously thought. Moreover, we actually generate *new* neurons well into our 70s. Instead of a large reduction in the *number* of neurons, much of the loss of size is due to shrinking neurons themselves. As brain tissue shrinks, the gaps between the folds of the cortex (sulci) widen and the large spaces (ventricles) inside the brain get bigger, as shown in Figure 14.6. Even over only a 4-year-period, there is significant loss of both gray matter (the outer layer of cell bodies) and white matter (the layer of myelinated axons that connect various parts of the brain).

▶ *Fewer dendritic connections.* When brain cells die, "connected" cells respond by releasing chemicals that stimulate surviving cells to make new connections. In healthy older people, this process of branching away from dying cells is more extensive than in middle-aged adults, but we gradually lose this capacity to respond to cell loss after age 70 (Whalley, 2001). Thus one reason neurons shrink as we age is that we lose synapses (connections between neurons) and become less likely to form new ones (Raz, 2000; Reuter-Lorenz, 2000).

▶ *Declining neurotransmitter activity.* Two of the neurotransmitters that wane with age are *dopamine* (which is important for frontal lobe function) and *acetylcholine* (which is important for learning and memory) (Reuter-Lorenz, 2000; Volkow et al., 2000). For example, the amount of dopamine that is produced and the number of receptors that respond to dopamine decrease by 5 to 10 percent each decade (Kaasinen et al., 2000). Declining neurotransmitters may be responsible for the mild cognitive declines that occur with normal aging (Li, 2002).

▶ *Buildup of unwanted debris.* For example, *lipofuscin*, a yellowish-brown pigment, is deposited in neurons in the cerebellum and cerebral cortex (Raz, 2000). We'll describe other unwanted debris when we discuss Alzheimer's disease in Chapter 15.

▶ *Broader activation patterns.* Compared to younger adults, older adults use more areas of the brain to complete certain tasks. Apparently, the brain compensates for decreased efficiency in some areas by recruiting other areas to help. As a result, the performance of younger and older adults sometimes looks the same even though underlying brain processes have changed or "moved around" (Reuter-Lorenz, 2002).

Due to a phenomenon known as "last in, first out," age-related declines are most noticeable in areas of the brain that developed last (Raz, 2000). As a result, the prefrontal cortex (responsible for controlled attention and planning) is especially vulnerable to aging. But many brain areas are affected by aging, including the hippocampus (responsible for memory) and the cerebellum (the seat of coordinated movement and a contributor to many cognitive skills, including verbal fluency and attentional control). When you read about cognitive development in late adulthood next, you will see how these changes affect how the brain handles information.

ADJUSTING TO CHANGING SLEEP PATTERNS. Recently, one of us meant to phone her mother but had been too distracted to think about it all day. When she finally looked at a clock she muttered, "Aw, no, it's eight-thirty in the evening—probably too late to call." Then she jokingly thought, "That's okay, I can call at four o'clock in the morning if I want!"

Our retired parents have already experienced brain changes that have shifted their biological clocks. During adulthood, most people establish a pattern of wanting to fall asleep between 10:00 and 11:00 at night and sleeping for 7 to 9 hours. As they grow older, the *amount* of sleep they need stays the same, but their *pattern* of sleeping changes in the ways summarized in Table 14.2 (National Sleep Foundation, 2002).

TABLE 14.2 Sleeping in Later Life

Change	Explanation	Associated Problems
Earlier bedtime	Daily rhythm shifts, so individuals become sleepy as early as 7:00 or 8:00 at night.	Some people try to delay sleep by taking a long afternoon nap. A short nap is an effective way to stay alert, but lengthy naps can make it harder to doze off in the evening.
Earlier final wake time	Due to an early bedtime but a continued need for about 8 hours of sleep, the elderly often rise as early as 3:00 or 4:00 in the morning.	Individuals who delay bedtime may still wake up in the early morning as body temperature rises. As a result, they will not get the amount of sleep they need to be alert during the day.
Poorer-quality sleep with more awakenings	Elderly people spend less time in deep (non-rem) phases of sleep and more time in lighter stages of sleep.	People who experience less deep sleep wake more frequently during the night and experience fewer total hours of sleep. These changes dramatically increase complaints about sleep.
An increase in sleep disorders	Elderly adults are more likely to suffer from sleep apnea (a condition in which breathing stops and people startle awake), insomnia (difficulty falling asleep), restless legs syndrome (unpleasant sensations in the legs), and periodic limb movements (a condition in which the legs jerk at regular intervals).	Sleep disorders result in daytime sleepiness, negative moods, and an increased risk of falls.

SOURCES: Campbell, Murphy, & Stauble (2005); Kryger et al. (2004); Vitiello, Larsen, & Moe (2004).

The elderly often have more difficulty falling asleep, spend less time in deep sleep, and are more likely to wake after they go to sleep as they age (Vitiello, Larsen, & Moe, 2004). Some people easily adjust to these changes whereas others are greatly bothered by them. Those in the second group sometimes turn to medications to induce sleep, but this practice has a number of unwanted side effects, including a higher risk of nighttime falls. It is better to cope with routine sleep problems by taking simple steps to improve sleep and trying to accept the inevitable changes.

Sleep problems increase dramatically as health decreases. For example, about 5 percent of elderly individuals experience new sleep problems compared to only 2 percent of the healthiest elderly (Foley et al., 1999). Sleep is hampered by bladder problems, aching joints, and lung disease, as well as some drugs that are used to treat medical and psychiatric problems. Because physical health and mental health are tightly connected, a healthy lifestyle that involves adequate exercise, good nutrition, and avoidance of smoking and other health hazards will help you stay alert during day and sleep like a baby (albeit a frequently waking baby) at night.

>>> **MEMORY MAKERS** <<<

1. Which of the following problems increase with age?
   (a) difficulty detecting sounds
   (b) problems understanding speech
   (c) difficulty locating sounds
   (d) a and b
   (e) all of the above

2. The age-related decrease in testosterone levels in men is called ____.
   (a) menopause   **(b)** testopause   **(c)** andropause   **(d)** the masculine shift

3. Which of the following describe changes in the brain that occur among the very old? (Pick all that apply.)
   (a) buildup of unwanted debris
   (b) broader activation patterns
   (c) increased neurotransmitter activity
   (d) increased dendritic connections

[1-e; 2-c; 3-a and b (neurotransmitter activity and dendritic connections decrease)]

The Aging Mind

Our friend Bill takes his little dog on a walk around the block each morning. As he passes his mailbox on the other side of the street, he often thinks, "I'll grab those letters on my way back." By the time he turned 50, though, Bill was usually back in the house before he had thought about the mail again. He was also having more trouble recalling names and sometimes walked into a room but temporarily forgot why he had gone there.

Like many middle-aged adults, Bill developed a secret fear that he was in the early stages of **dementia** (pronounced "de-**MEN**-sha"), a permanent loss of mental ability that is serious enough to impair daily living tasks. People who have one of the many conditions that produce dementia experience problems in memory, reasoning, and planning that dramatically affect their behavior. Bill knew that dementia is often preceded by *mild cognitive impairment*, which is a noticeable

dementia A permanent loss of mental ability that is serious enough to impair daily living tasks. People who have one of the many conditions that produce dementia experience problems in memory, reasoning, and planning that dramatically affect their behavior.

Many older adults become concerned when the normal cognitive changes associated with aging—such as difficulty recalling names—first appear. A visit to the doctor can rule out physical problems and provide some peace of mind.

[handwritten notes in right margin: 10 to 20 yrs progression; progressive → total loss of cognition → death]

change in attention, language, and critical thinking. About 10 to 15 percent of people who develop mild cognitive impairment will progress into *Alzheimer's disease*—the leading cause of dementia—each year (Petersen, 2000).

We suspect that Bill is one of the people physician Ronald Petersen calls the "worried well"—individuals who are aware of their forgetfulness but have no reason to be alarmed (Schmiedskamp, 2004). What are the differences between "normal" aging and the problems caused by special medical conditions? After reviewing the cognitive changes most people experience after age 50, we'll explain why Bill probably doesn't need to worry.

What Fades?

The human brain can be thought of as an integrated system of modules or programs that accomplish different tasks, such as understanding language and recognizing faces (Pinker, 1997, 2005). When we ride a bike, recall someone's name, and come to a decision about which car to buy, we are using specific brain circuits that have their own ways of manipulating information. Just as we develop these circuits at different ages, we lose skill unevenly as we age. For example, Bill usually forgot to pick up his mail, but he was just as efficient as ever at designing and crafting renovations for his house. The two approaches for separating mental skills that we described in Chapter 12 tell us a lot about how mental abilities change as we age. The psychometric approach describes our performance on standardized paper-and-pencil tests across the life span, and the information processing approach digs deeper to learn how our performance is affected by age-related changes in specific skills, such as attention, memory, and language.

INTELLIGENCE TEST PERFORMANCE IN LATER LIFE. As you read in Chapter 12, patterns of performance on standardized tests suggest there is a difference between *crystallized intelligence* (knowledge and verbal skills that accumulate with age) and *fluid intelligence* (the ability to reason abstractly and solve new problems). Scores on tests of crystallized intelligence are generally steady or increase, at least up to age 60. When people are not required to respond quickly, scores on

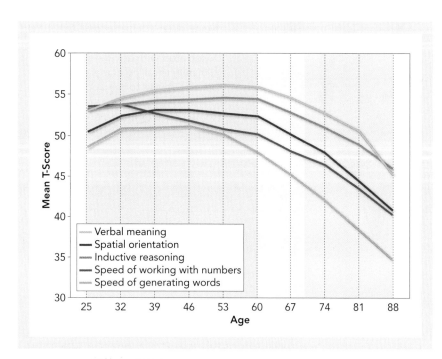

FIGURE 14.7 Mental abilities across adulthood.

The ambitious Seattle Longitudinal Study followed numerous cohorts longitudinally, from 7 to 35 years, adding new cohorts as time passed. With this *cross-sequential design*, mental declines for a variety of cognitive tasks become obvious at age 60 and occur more steeply after age 70.

SOURCE: *From Intellectual Development in Adulthood: The Seattle Longitudinal Study.* (p. 168), by K. W. Schaie, 1996, New York: Cambridge University Press. Copyright 1996 by Cambridge University Press. Adapted with permission.

measures of fluid intelligence also do not show substantial drops until age 60 (at least in longitudinal studies). In contrast, our speed of performing some tasks, such as solving mathematical problems, is already dropping by age 30 (Salthouse, 2004; Schaie, 1994).

These trends influence scores on the Weschler Adult Intelligence Scale (WAIS), a test that you read about in Chapter 13, and other standardized tests (Ackerman, 2000; McArdle et al., 2002). Verbal subtests of the WAIS place heavier demands on crystallized abilities, whereas perceptual subtests emphasize fluid abilities. As expected, verbal subtest scores are fairly stable until about age 70 and do not decline dramatically until the end of life. In contrast, perceptual scores decline from early to middle adulthood and ultimately reach a much lower endpoint (Schulz & Salthouse, 1999). Fluid abilities continue to decline at a faster rate than crystallized abilities even into the 80s and 90s (Smith & Baltes, 1999).

Declines in performance become steeper after age 70 for a large variety of intellectual tasks. To illustrate, take a second look at Figure 14.7, which appeared in Chapter 12, but this time focus on results from the 53- to 88-year-olds. These data, from the Seattle Longitudinal Study, found excellent performance before age 50. But notice that scores on all tasks started to decline by age 60, and the rate of decline picked up speed by 70.

Average changes like the trends in Figure 14.7 do not represent what any *individual* is likely to experience as he or she ages. For example, most individuals studied in the Seattle Longitudinal Study had declined somewhat by age 60 on at least one of the five mental abilities tested, but few had declined on all five—even by age 88! (Schaie, 1993). Also, in the Berlin Aging Study, some of the oldest people tested (including one 103-year-old) were among the best performers, and some of the 70- to 74-year-olds were among the worst (Smith & Baltes, 1999). As Schaie (1996a) explained, " . . . even at advanced ages, competent behavior can be expected by many persons in familiar circumstances. Much of the observed loss occurs in highly challenging, complex, or stressful situations . . . " (p. 273). In other words, some of the poor performance of the elderly on certain types of tests of mental abilities may be due to the stress of being tested on unfamiliar tasks.

Aging specialist Timothy Salthouse has an interesting example of what can happen when the right people are matched with the right task. In a series of studies, Salthouse and his colleagues (2004) asked adults who regularly worked crossword puzzles to solve a puzzle from the *New York Times*. As you can see in Figure 14.8, the best average performance was *always* achieved by the 60- to 70-year-olds. It is clear that older adults are resources for information they have spent a lifetime accumulating. But they are also resources in situations that occur so rarely that most young people are unfamiliar with them. During an extended power outage in Maine, for example, one of our elderly relatives endeared himself to the neighborhood by installing generators, teaching his neighbors how to keep their pipes from freezing, and showing them how they could cook and stay in their homes. Of course, it is unusual for a community to lose power for a week, experience a flood, or suffer from an invasion of opossums that manage to avoid traps. When these infrequent events occur, however, local grandpas and grandmas are in great demand!

ATTENTION. Questions on standardized tests activate many mental processes, so age differences in performance could reflect age differences in a number of skills. For example, if we ask 75-year-old Benny to pick which of four words is a synonym of *weary*, he might pick the wrong answer because he is still attending to the previous word, because he doesn't remember *weary* after reading the first two options, or because he doesn't know the meaning of *weary*. Scientists who use an information processing approach design tasks that isolate these specific cognitive processes. By asking people to perform tasks that make different demands on attention, information processing researchers have pinpointed the following changes in attention that occur with age.

Elderly people are good at focusing on one thing and ignoring distracting information (*focused attention*)—as long as the target is easy to distinguish from the distractions. If their hearing is good, for example, they do well in movie theaters because they know where to look for the target (the movie) and the movie is different (louder, about different subjects) than popcorn crunching and background talking. When they have to look selectively for something (which is called *selective attention*), performance declines. For example, your grandfather may be slow to find you in a crowd of similar-looking people at the airport even though he is skilled at a task that is very familiar to him, such as finding an unwanted weed in the garden (Rogers, 2000).

Another difficult situation is *divided attention*, which is processing two or more kinds of information at the same time ("multitasking"). You engage in divided attention when you drive while listening to music or talking on the phone. Of course, some tasks require more attention (talking on the phone) than others (listening to music). Generally, the greater the effort that is required, the greater is the decline in performance with age. Once again, though, older adults can improve their performance with practice (though we are not recommending the elderly practice driving around making and taking phone calls) (Rogers, 2000; Rogers & Fisk, 2001). As an activity such as driving becomes routine, it moves down the scale from *effortful* to *automatic*. Tasks that are learned and automated earlier in life tend to remain automatic in older adulthood, but older people have more difficulty than younger people automating newly learned skills (Fisk & Rogers, 1991).

In sum, older adults are more attentionally challenged in many—but not all—situations. Their performance suffers the most when the task is perceptually demanding or confusing, when they are trying to juggle many ideas at once, or when they are trying to automate a new skill.

MEMORY. Comedian George Burns once said, "By the time you're eighty years old you've learned everything. You only have to remember it." His comment

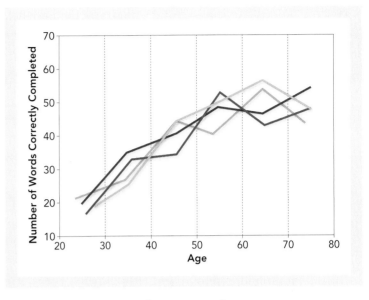

FIGURE 14.8 Expert performance and age.

In four studies, cognitive psychologist Timothy Salthouse and his colleagues asked adults who were experienced at solving crossword puzzles to complete a puzzle from the *New York Times*. As you can see, adults between 60 and 70 years old always had the highest average performance. In many societies, elderly adults are highly respected for their expert knowledge.

SOURCE: Salthouse (2004).

This Aboriginal man from Western Australia is discussing tribal law with other elders. (The pencil through his nose is a sign of seniority.) In many communities, older adults are highly respected for their knowledge.

illustrates the long-held ideas that knowledge increases with age while memory declines. In fact, memory problems are among the biggest complaints and fears of older people. They forget names, appointments, and when they last took their medicine. Anticipating the kinds of memory slips that are most likely to occur is the first step toward adopting strategies to compensate for these annoyances.

As discussed in Chapter 6, your *implicit memory* system stores skills and other kinds of knowledge that are not directly or consciously retrieved. *Procedural skills*, like solving a jigsaw puzzle or riding a bike, are not much influenced by age: Once you are skilled at a task that involves a sequence of steps or procedures, you rarely forget how to do it. Implicit memory is also involved in unintentional learning. For instance, a *priming task* might ask you to see a list of words containing BOOT and count the number of vowels in each word. A week later, you try to complete word fragments, such as B _ _ T. Although the list from the previous week is never mentioned, you are more likely to say "boot" than "boat" or "beet." Using tasks like this one, most studies of implicit memory find either no age differences at all or only very small advantages for younger adults. So when people are not asked to deliberately remember information, older adults perform about as well as young adults do (Bäckman, Small, & Wahlin, 2001; Fleischman et al., 2004).

Healthy older adults also have little difficulty keeping information in mind for very short periods, such as when they need to ask for a phone number and copy it down (Craik, 2000). But they perform worse when the task involves more active processing, such as trying to remember the results of several calculations in order to add them together (Park, 2000; Park et al., 2002). Cognitive psychologists describe these findings by saying that *short-term memory* (the passive storage of information) does not show age-related decline but *working memory* (the ability to hold information in mind while working with it) does.

Bill, whose concern about his forgetfulness was mentioned earlier, was mainly worried about his *prospective memory*: remembering to do something in the future, such as taking medicine or picking up the mail. Prospective memory is involved whenever you are interrupted by other activities and need to reactivate your intentions at the right time and place. Older adults often forget their earlier goals—unless they are allowed to use external reminders, such as writing a note or setting a timer. One reason for this is that it takes older adults longer to think back to previous thoughts, and revisiting ideas fails to strengthen memories as much as it does for younger adults. Compared to younger adults, a specific area of the prefrontal cortex is less active in older adults who are trying to "refresh" information stored earlier (Johnson et al., 2004; Johnson et al., 2002). Problems refreshing just-activated information account for a variety of difficulties later in life, including Bill's mailbox problem.

A number of long-term memory skills also decline with age. Older adults usually remember as much *semantic* information (basic facts and word meanings) as young adults do, but they have more difficulty retrieving it when needed. An especially frustrating event is the **tip of the tongue phenomenon (TOT)**. While writing this paragraph, for example, one of us came across the following question, "What word means to formally renounce a throne?" She *knew* that she knew the answer but could not come up with it. She struggled and struggled ("*excommunicate*, no, *denounce*, no") until she finally called a friend for the answer (*abdicate*) to avoid an afternoon of mental discomfort. (Look at Table 14.3 to see whether some of these definitions create TOTs for you.) Older adults experience TOTs more often and are slower to name common objects because of the retrieval problems outlined previously (Bäckman, et al., 2001; Burke & Shafto, 2004). Although word-finding errors become more common over time, differences between

tip of the tongue phenomenon (TOT) The frustrating feeling of knowing a word or name but not being able to retrieve it from memory. Older adults have more frequent TOT experiences than younger adults.

> **TABLE 14.3** Definitions That Often Produce Tip of the Tongue (TOT) States
>
> How many of these words can you retrieve easily? See page 586 to check yourself.
>
> 1. A metal or metal-tipped spear used in contests of distance throwing
> 2. A yarn-dyed cotton fabric woven in stripes, checks, plaids, or solid colors
> 3. A mild or hot red condiment often used on deviled eggs
> 4. An inscription on a tomb or tombstone
> 5. An incombustible, chemical-resistant material used for fireproofing
> 6. A place where one abides or dwells; house or home
> 7. A tough, elastic tissue forming part of the skeleton
> 8. A heavy, broad-bladed knife or hatchet used especially by butchers
> 9. A soft, black form of carbon used in pencils; not lead
> 10. A bittersweet longing for things, persons, or situations of the past
>
> **SOURCE:** Vigliocco et al. (1999).

younger and older adults on semantic memory tasks are usually only small to modest (Dixon & Cohen, 2003).

Other long-term memory skills also suffer over time. Recall from Chapter 6 that *episodic memory* is your ability to remember distinct episodes from your past, such as a list of words from a few minutes earlier or a conversation you heard months ago. What these kinds of episodes have in common is that you must deliberately remember the content (the list of words) along with the situation in which you learned it (the specific list you made in the kitchen). The ability to recall specific episodes begins to decline as early as the 30s and continues to steadily decline across the rest of adulthood (Dixon & Cohen, 2003; Park et al., 2002; Salthouse, 2004).

Problems linking an idea to a specific context—that is, remembering *where* and *when* something happened—create *source-monitoring* problems for the elderly (problems remembering the source of their memories). As a result, they often tell a story repeatedly to the same person (because they do not recall telling it previously to that person). And when information is coming from several different sources, they are more susceptible than younger adults to false memories. For example, adults over age 60 are more likely than young adults to say they actually *remember* learning or saying something that was just mentioned. Scam artists capitalize on this weakness by telling elderly people that they previously agreed to buy services at specific prices ("I told you that it would cost X [a much higher price than was originally quoted], and you agreed to pay"), which leads victims to falsely remember that they *did* agree to pay (Jacoby et al., 2005, p. 131). As Mark Twain quipped, "When I was younger, I could remember anything, whether it had happened or not; but my faculties are decaying now, and soon I shall be so I cannot remember any but the things that never happened" (Twain, 1924, p. 96).

It is mostly a myth that older people remember events that occurred long ago better than recent events. They do have vivid memories of some long-ago events, but these events are typically more distinctive and emotional (the time Dad took me to the World Series) than most of their recent events (my trip to Wal-Mart last week). In general, people over age 30 seem to recall more events from their teens and their 20s than from any other time period, possibly because more exciting or life-changing events happen then (e.g., going to college, getting married). Otherwise, the general pattern is that the longer ago something occurred, the *less* likely it is to be recalled (Rubin, 2000). This is true even for

Answers for Table 14.3

1. javelin
2. gingham
3. paprika
4. epitaph
5. asbestos
6. abode
7. cartilage
8. cleaver
9. graphite
10. nostalgia

elderspeak A type of slow, simplified speech that people sometimes use when they are speaking to elderly adults.

very emotional, historic events. For example, older adults recall hearing about the September 11 attacks better than they recall hearing about the assassination of President John F. Kennedy in 1963 or the bombing of Pearl Harbor in 1941, even though all three events were surprising, emotional, and had a significant impact on their lives (Denver, Warren, & Mathis, 2005).

The findings reviewed in Table 14.4 are consistent with what we know about the aging brain. The prefrontal cortex is especially affected by aging, which explains why older people have more trouble with memory tasks that require conscious effort, juggling ideas, and other executive functions. Neurological changes also make it harder to lay down new memories as we age, although even very old people benefit from special strategies and practice. As a result, older people often perform well once they have spent enough time learning material or practicing a new skill.

LANGUAGE AND AGING. As the speed of mental processing slows, elderly people find it more challenging to engage in rapid-fire conversation. They take longer to plan what they want to say and make more speech errors, such as false starts, sentence fragments, and unclear statements (Kemper, Kynette, & Norman, 1992; MacKay & Abrams, 1996). These problems are usually just an annoyance, but they can cause a loss of confidence that prompts some individuals to withdraw from challenging social interactions, such as going to parties or taking outings to the theater (Burke & Shafto, 2004). As working memory suffers, older adults also have a harder time understanding and remembering grammatically complex sentences. Everyday conversations, television shows, and the writing in newspapers and magazine articles usually don't pose much of a problem, but those in late adulthood may have trouble following instructions in product manuals and on medication labels (Morrell & Park, 1993; Morrow & Leirer, 1999). Therefore, information that will be used by the elderly should be written clearly, with fewer ideas per sentence (Kemper, 2001; Wingfield & Stine-Morrow, 2000).

Because older people often have hearing impairments and process things more slowly, other people often speak to them in a simpler, slower form of language known as **elderspeak**. Some features of elderspeak do make it easier for older people to understand, but overly simplified speech and exaggerated, sing-song intonation (like in baby

TABLE 14.4	Changes in Memory in Later Adulthood		
Memory type	**Example**	**Change with age**	
Implicit memory	Procedural: Put this familiar puzzle together.	Minimal	
	Priming: How many vowels are in each word? Boot, Lucky, Simple. (At a later time): Complete this word: b __ t.	Minimal	
Short-term memory	Digit span: Repeat after me, 6, 3, 7, 1, 5, 9, 8, 2.	Minimal	
Working memory	Remember a word sequence while solving a series of math problems.	Large decline	
Prospective memory	Remember to take your medicine at lunchtime.	Declines without external reminders	
Semantic memory	Name the kitchen tool you use to flip objects in a frying pan.	Slower retrieval	
Episodic memory	Recall a list of words after 10 minutes.	Large decline	
Source memory	Where did you learn this information?	Large decline	
Autobiographical memory (meaningful events)	What do you remember about your high school prom?	Minimal	

talk) make seniors feel less competent and give them less practice with sophisticated conversation. For example, caregivers in nursing homes often use terms of endearment and collective nouns that reinforce dependency (saying, for example, "Hi, *sweetie*. It's time for *our* exercise today" rather than "Hi, *Mrs. Smith*. It's time for *your* exercise today"). Young people should speak in ways that boost understanding while maintaining respect for the elderly and a mentally challenging environment (Kemper & Harden, 1999; Kemper, 2001; Williams, Kemper, & Hummert, 2003).

If you worry that there is nothing to look forward to when you grow older, here is a bright side of language and aging: Older adults are often terrific story tellers because they have had years to make connections among a variety of ideas. In fact, the stories told by older people are actually rated more favorably, are remembered better, and are preferred over the stories younger adults tell (James et al., 1998; Kemper et al., 1990; Ryan et al., 1992).

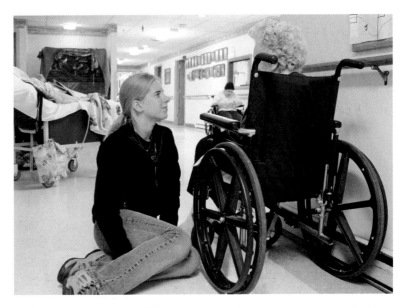

Most older adults get a great deal of enjoyment from talking with interested listeners. Like most elderly adults, this woman has a collection of wonderful stories she can share.

There is another interesting twist on language and aging: The complexity of people's stories when they are young predicts their mental sharpness in old age. Evidence comes from the Nun Study, an intriguing study of elderly nuns who donated their brains to science. Because most of the sisters had written autobiographies before taking their vows between 1931 and 1939, researchers could score their early writing for language complexity, such as how many ideas were contained in each sentence (idea density) and grammatical complexity (Snowdon et al., 1996). Consider the first sentence by Sister Helen, the nun who had the lowest idea density:

> I was born in Eau Claire, Wis., on May 24, 1913, and was baptized in St. James Church. (Snowdon, 2001, p.110)

In contrast, Sister Emma's narrative was bursting with details:

> It was about a half hour before midnight between February twenty-eighth and twenty-ninth of the leap year nineteen-hundred-twelve when I began to live and to die as the third child of my mother, whose maiden name is Hilda Hoffman, and my father, Otto Schmitt. (Snowdon, 2001, p.110)

Remarkably, the women's language complexity predicted their cognitive functioning more than 50 years later! The autobiographies of nuns who wound up healthy in old age had a much higher idea density than those who would later have cognitive problems—even though most of the nuns had worked as teachers and shared a similar lifestyle. (Sister Helen had the lowest score in the group on the Mini-Mental State Exam; Sister Emma had a perfect score.) As we'll discuss more in the next chapter, this finding suggests that some people are better able to handle the inevitable changes associated with aging because they start out at a higher level of mental functioning. So even though your dense writing may be causing your professors to lose their minds now, it may keep you from losing yours later!

Theories of Cognitive Decline

The theories of cognitive aging in Table 14.5 try to identify the mechanisms that explain patterns of strengths and weaknesses as people age. You are familiar with the first three from reading about cognitive development during early and middle childhood. The first theory emphasizes *speed of processing* (Salthouse, 1996):

as a person ages, they become slower in processing new information.

TABLE 14.5 Theories of Cognitive Aging

Theory	Description
Speed of processing	Central nervous system processing slows down, affecting all tasks.
Working memory	The ability to hold information in mind and process information at the same time declines.
Interference	Sorting out relevant from irrelevant information declines and disrupts processing.
Neurological fidelity	Important neuronal signals do not stand out as much from random activity in the brain. In other words, neurons lose the ability to reproduce incoming signals cleanly and consistently.

According to this viewpoint, older adults perform even the simplest of cognitive tasks more slowly than young adults, which affects later stages of processing (especially for complex tasks). The second theory focuses on *reduced working memory* capacity: Older adults can passively hold information but have trouble storing and actively processing information at the same time (Craik & Byrd, 1982). Speed of processing is highly related to working memory performance, but speed alone does not fully account for the differences we see between various age groups on complex tasks (Span, Ridderinkhof, & van der Molen, 2004).

Interference theory says that we lose the ability to efficiently ignore irrelevant information as we age (Hasher, Zachs, & May, 1999). When we "clog up" our working memories with unimportant information, we are unable to efficiently process and store important information. A weakened ability to control thoughts and responses may also explain the distractibility of older adults and their tendency to say whatever pops into their minds (Park, 2000). However, problems inhibiting irrelevant information show up only in some situations.

The final entry in Table 14.5 is really a class of theories that links cognitive performance to underlying brain function. According to *neurological fidelity* theories, the problems seniors experience cannot be explained by reversing the mechanisms that led to improvements during childhood. This is because widespread declines in brain function have implications that cannot be reduced to specific cognitive processes such as processing speed or inhibition. In the Berlin Aging Study, for example, people with better vision and hearing performed better on intelligence tests, and sensory functioning was more highly correlated with cognitive performance than speed of processing was (Lindenberger & Baltes, 1994; Smith & Baltes, 1999). The most likely explanation for this result is that sensory function is a marker for the overall health of the brain.

For an example of a neurological theory, consider the decline in neurotransmitter activity that occurs as we age. According to cognitive scientist Shu-Chen Li (2002), this causes our brains to lose their ability to balance the intensity of important neuronal signals relative to random activity in the brain. In other words, our neurons lose *fidelity*: the ability to respond distinctly to different stimuli. Computer models that simulate aging neural networks reproduce a number of age-related cognitive changes: They take longer to learn new material, reach a lower level of final learning, and are more affected by interference. The idea of an increasingly "noisy" system fits the widespread complaint among the elderly about "senior moments"—the experience of losing an idea just moments after having it.

Maximizing and Compensating

As you learned in Chapter 3, preschoolers act maturely and logically when problems do not tax their mental resources, but their answers are irrational (and often amusing) when task demands increase. In a classroom of little ones, brilliance is a "now you see it, now you don't" phenomenon. As resources diminish later in life, inconsistent performance reappears in a new form. Now the college professor who skillfully writes an e-mail while talking on the phone may flounder in front of a new ATM machine. The following factors influence whether seniors appear to be sharp as a tack or in need of a little help:

▶ **Task "fit."** Some activities, such as confronting a new ATM machine, place high demands on attentional resources, working memory, or other processes. Differences in performance between seniors and younger adults are smaller when the task burden is low.

▶ **Expectations.** Everyone assumes that memory declines with age, so older people feel anxious when they are told they are going to be in a memory study. As a result, young adults perform better than older adults if they are told they will take a "memory test," but age differences sometimes disappear when adults are simply told to "learn" the material (Rahhal, Hasher, & Colcombe, 2001). In an especially telling demonstration, older people who read fake newspaper articles that presented a negative view of memory and aging remembered 20 to 30 percent fewer words than those who read more positive information (Hess et al., 2003).

▶ **Relevance of the task to daily life.** People perform better when the material they are asked to remember is relevant to their lives. In our later years, for example, we are more likely to remember advertisements that mention emotions (e.g., "Capture those special moments" for a camera ad) rather than new experiences ("Capture the unexplored world") (Fung & Carstensen, 2003). Similarly, older adults have difficulty remembering whether a male or female voice made a particular statement, but they do a good job recalling whether a statement came from a truthful or unreliable source (Rahhal, May, & Hasher, 2002).

▶ **Time of day.** About three-fourths of older people say they are "morning people," and people score better on tasks that require conscious effort when they are tested during their "peak" time (May, Hasher, & Foong, 2005). Therefore, age differences on many memory tasks are smaller when people are tested in the morning rather than the afternoon, when most research is conducted (Yoon, May, & Hasher, 2000).

▶ **Availability of compensatory strategies.** In their everyday environments, older people find ways to maximize strengths and minimize weaknesses (Salthouse, 2004). For instance, by looking further ahead in the text as they are typing, older typists maintain their typing speeds despite slower key tapping (Salthouse, 1984). Seniors are also *more* likely than college students are to remember an appointment because they are more likely to write it down. Finally, older married couples who are working on memory tasks do better when they work together, whereas younger couples don't usually benefit from joint effort. Apparently, older couples have developed strategies and communication skills that make the most out of their collaboration (Dixon & Cohen, 2003).

In daily life, most people work when they feel most alert and choose tasks that match their abilities. As a result, most older people function well in their

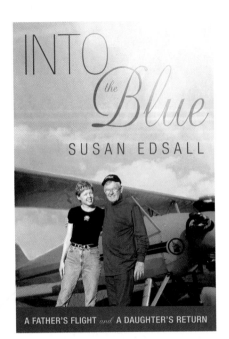

INTO
the Blue
SUSAN EDSALL

A FATHER'S FLIGHT *and* A DAUGHTER'S RETURN

After he suffered from a stroke, Wayne Edsall couldn't face life without flying the antique airplanes he loved. Instead of asking him to adjust his goals, his daughter, Susan, researched stroke rehabilitation and helped him regain function and his pilot's license. Wayne and Susan's determination illustrate "optimization," the process of working hard and finding ways to overcome limitations.

adjusting their lifestyle
↓
SOC model (selective optimization with compensation) A model by Paul Baltes that describes how people adjust to the opportunities and limitations they face throughout life. The SOC model proposes that well-adjusted individuals invest in some activities at the expense of others (selection), pursue these goals effectively (optimization), and develop different strategies when usual methods stop working (compensation).

wisdom The ability to understand and solve ambiguous problems and make good judgments and decisions in everyday contexts.

everyday environments, and senior citizens serve as political leaders, CEOs of corporations, and experts in virtually every field (Salthouse, 1990). Professor of psychology Paul Baltes (1997) believed that the people who adjust best to aging manage their lives by *selection, optimization,* and *compensation.* In his **SOC model (selective optimization with compensation)**, selection refers to one's choice of goals: If a goal becomes unreachable due to a physical or cognitive limitation, then you can choose a different goal. Selection involves making the most of life by investing in activities that fit with your abilities, interests, and life circumstances. Optimization involves pursuing these goals effectively, such as by practicing harder or finding a skilled mentor. Compensation involves developing different methods or strategies when the usual methods stop working. For example, an aging researcher might move from a technical position that requires cognitive speed into a management position (selection), work on more difficult tasks during the morning (optimization), and rely more on notes for reminders (compensation).

Everyday Intelligence, Wisdom, and Creativity

As we mentioned in Chapter 12, people who do not score highly on traditional IQ tests sometimes do well on measures of *everyday (practical) intelligence* (Baltes, 1997; Sternberg et al., 2001). Everyday intelligence is important because the problems adults solve often involve complicated interpersonal matters, such as what to do after you mistakenly made two appointments for the same time, rather than the formal problems we encounter in educational settings.

Does practical intelligence decline in our elderly years? The answer depends on the task (Sternberg et al., 2001). Performance improves from the 20s to the 70s on tests about real-life situations, such as how to encourage friends to visit more often or how to find out why you were passed over for a promotion (Cornelius & Caspi, 1987). But compared to middle-aged adults, both young and older adults provide fewer safe and effective solutions to unusual problems, such as what to do if you are stranded on a highway during a blizzard (Denney & Palmer, 1981; Denney & Pearce, 1989). As people advance from the late 60s into their late 80s, they also become less capable of carrying out household tasks, such as checking local numbers on a phone bill (Diehl, Willis, & Schaie, 1995) or comparing nutrition labels (Allaire & Marsiske, 1999). It is fair to say that older adults perform better, the same, or worse than younger adults depending on the type of problem (Smith & Baltes, 1990).

One type of cognition that is assumed to peak in old age is **wisdom**. As Ram Dass discovered when he traveled to India, older people are highly respected in many societies for the knowledge they have gained. But wisdom means more than just knowing specific words, facts, or procedures. It also involves the ability to understand and solve ambiguous problems and make good judgments and decisions in everyday contexts (Sternberg, 2005; Sternberg & Lubart, 2001).

Psychologist Robert Sternberg (1990) believes that wisdom involves some *cognitive* components, such as understanding the limits of one's knowledge, and some components related to *personality traits* or *motives,* such as being tolerant of ambiguity in life (Sternberg & Lubart, 2001). Using Sternberg's broad definition, it is not clear that wisdom should automatically increase with age. Older adults certainly should have greater knowledge of the world and how it works, but they may not use their knowledge in ways we consider "wise" if they don't have the motivation or personality to do so. Consistent with this prediction, life span researcher Paul Baltes and his colleague, Ursula Staudinger, have found no in-

A 15-year-old girl wants to get married right away. What should one/she consider and do?

Low Wisdom Score

A 15-year-old girl wants to get married? No, no way, marrying at age 15 would be utterly wrong. One has to tell the girl that marriage is not possible. (After further probing) It would be irresponsible to support such an idea. No, this is just a crazy idea.

High Wisdom Score

Well, on the surface, this seems like an easy problem. On average, marriage for 15-year-old girls is not a good thing. But there are situations where the average case does not fit. Perhaps in this instance, special life circumstances are involved, such that the girl has a terminal illness. Or the girl had just lost her parents. And also, this girl may live in another culture or historical period. Perhaps she was raised with a value system different from ours. In addition, one has to think about adequate ways of talking with the girl and to consider her emotional state.

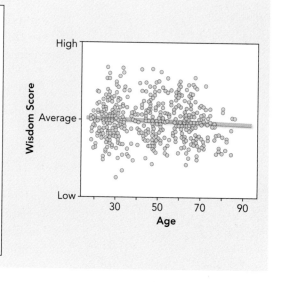

FIGURE 14.9 The stability of wisdom across adulthood.

As the examples on the left illustrate, psychologists believe that "wise" decisions demonstrate knowledge about life, acknowledge that situations have different implications in different contexts, and recognize that people have diverse values. When these criteria are used to score people's decisions, wisdom is remarkably stable across the life span (right).

SOURCE: Baltes & Staudinger (2000).

crease or decrease in scores on a measure of wisdom between 20 and 80 years of age (although more elderly people did score in the top 20 percent) (Baltes & Staudinger, 2000; Staudinger, 1999). But their findings, which appear in Figure 14.9, show that wisdom is *maintained* over time even as traditional measures of cognitive performance decline.

Apparently, living longer is no guarantee that people will develop better judgment. Still, there are trends for adults to experience improvements in their overall judgment in the following situations:

▶ *The problem is relevant to their lives.* Older adults show greater wisdom than younger adults when the issue is important to older people's lives, such as deciding whether to move into assisted living or in with adult children (Staudinger, 1999).

▶ *Experience with the problem builds skill.* Older adults can be more insightful in areas where experience is a good teacher. For example, the 70-year-olds in one study were better than 20-year-olds at explaining how to deal with such issues as criticism from someone and a landlord who won't make repairs (Cornelius & Caspi, 1987).

▶ *The situation requires social sensitivity.* Older people sometimes demonstrate greater social sensitivity than younger people do. For example, one investigator found that older people were more sensitive to the social and interpersonal features of problems, such as how to assign a limited number of beds to a number of visiting relatives (Sinnott, 1989). It is interesting that the younger people focused more on the sheer logic of the situation, such as how many beds and how many people there were, regardless of whether or not the people could get along! So when wisdom is defined as social/emotional skills combined with practical intelligence, then older people may indeed be wiser (Sternberg & Lubart, 2001).

In contrast to wisdom, it is widely believed that creativity decreases with age. Again, whether this is true or false depends on how we define creativity. If creativity is defined as thinking flexibly and quickly, then creativity declines with age. But if creativity is defined as the ability to redefine problems or see unique connections between different sets of information, then creativity sometimes increases with age (Sternberg & Lubart, 2001). Seniors are also less creative if you count the *number* of works produced, but quality does not change (Simonton, 1990). Of course, there are exceptions to any trend. Consider Nobel laureate and Pulitzer Prize–winning author Toni Morrison (one of Oprah Winfrey's favorite authors). While working as an editor and raising two children, she published her first novel at age 39. Since then she has continued to produce novels about every 5 years, although her pace picked up in her late 60s.

Aging or Dementia?

Earlier we told you about Bill, our friend who worried about his forgetfulness. He is not alone; declining memory is one of the changes older people complain about the most. But Bill shouldn't worry just yet. He is an intellectually active 50-year-old who is simply annoyed by his less-than-perfect memory. Like most people approaching late adulthood, Bill finds it a little more difficult than he wishes to attend to several things at once (such as multiple instant message conversations). He also needs more repetition to learn new names and occasionally has word-finding problems. And, of course, his prospective memory (such as remembering to take in the mail after his walk) is not what it used to be. These fleeting problems are typical of busy people his age.

When *should* Bill become concerned? Table 14.6 lists some of the differences between normal cognitive change and the changes associated with dementia. As you can see, normal memory loss involves minor lapses, such as misplacing your glasses or forgetting to return a library book. In contrast, early dementia involves an inability to recall very recent events and general confusion that rapidly becomes worse. Dr. Richard Mohs has a wonderful description of the difference: "[Dementia is] not that you misplaced your keys," he explains. "It's that you can't figure out what you would do to get them back" (Schmiedeskamp, 2004, p. 896).

In this chapter, we have been focusing on the experiences most people face as they pass through later life. Therefore, we will wait until the next chapter to tell you more about dementia and the special problems of the very old. For now, read on to learn some surprising findings about the impact of aging on people's emotional and social lives.

>>> MEMORY MAKERS <<<

1. A permanent loss of mental ability that is serious enough to impair daily living tasks is called _____.
   (a) mild cognitive impairment
   (b) fluid decline
   (c) atypical aging
   (d) dementia

2. Which of the following types of memory show the *largest* decline with age?
   (a) implicit memory (such as putting a puzzle together)
   (b) working memory (such as remembering words while solving math problems)
   (c) short-term memory (such as remembering a list of digits)
   (d) autobiographical memory (such as remembering your high school prom)

3. Interference, speed of processing, reduced working memory, and neurological fidelity are theories of___.
   (a) why the body ages
   (b) dementia
   (c) cognitive aging
   (d) why the elderly often fall

[1-d; 2-b; 3-c]

TABLE 14.6 Normal and Abnormal Memory Loss

Type of Memory	Healthy Older Person	Person with Dementia
Recent events	Memory for details may be vague.	May forget part or all of the event.
Words or names of things	Sometimes forgets a word or feels it is on the "tip of the tongue."	Forgets with increasing frequency.
Ability to follow written and verbal directions	Able to follow.	Increasingly unable to follow.
Ability to follow stories on TV, in movies, or in books	Able to follow.	Gradually losing the ability to follow.
Stored facts	Recall may be slower, but information is essentially retained.	Gradually loses information such as historical or political information learned in the past.
Ability to complete everyday skills	Retains ability, unless physically impaired.	Gradually loses the ability to perform tasks such as cooking and handling money.

SOURCE: Adapted from Alzheimer's Australia (2005).

Emotional and Social Development

Most discussions of aging focus on *decline*: Older individuals are weaker, more prone to major illnesses, slower, and more forgetful than they used to be. As a result, young people often assume that seniors must feel bad about their lives. Like George Costanza's father on *Seinfeld,* this stereotype of older individuals as cranky and negative is a familiar character in television sitcoms. But science is a wonderful corrective for false ideas, and there is no better example than what we have learned about emotional and social development later in life. Instead of feeling "washed up" and unhappy, most older adults feel as good about life as the typical graduate who has just snatched a diploma from the hands of a college president.

Emotions in Later Life

Worldwide, most adults rate themselves as "pretty" or "very" happy, and between 64 and 97 percent of older adults have a "positive subjective well-being," meaning they generally feel good (Bertrand & Lachman, 2003; Diener & Diener, 1996). In a recent study of men 33 years of age and older who reported their life satisfaction multiple times during a 22-year period, satisfaction peaked at 65—not at 40, as you might expect (Mroczek & Spiro, 2005). Psychologists use the phrase the **paradox of aging** to refer to the fact that seniors suffer physical and cognitive losses yet generally feel satisfied with their lives. Why is this so?

An old explanation is that elderly people simply don't expect much from life. Indeed, research on the SOC model shows that seniors adjust to losses by investing time in activities that are likely to yield success, such as long-time hobbies and spending time with valued friends. But adjusting goals is only part of the story. There is also evidence that emotional control and social functioning actually *improve* with age. Specifically, you can expect these enjoyable developments as you grow into your later years:

▶ *Fewer negative emotional reactions.* The frequency and duration of negative emotions, such as anger, fear, shame, and boredom, decline from young adulthood to age 60. After age 60, the trend is for stable or only slightly increasing rates of negative emotions (Carstensen et al., 2000; Diener & Suh, 1997).

paradox of aging The finding that seniors generally feel satisfied with their lives despite the fact that they suffer physical and cognitive losses.

socioemotional selectivity theory
A theory by Laura Carstensen that says that people respond to approaching endings by shifting to emotionally meaningful goals. As a result, older people attend to emotionally satisfying information more so than emotionally negative information, and they choose to spend time with people who matter the most to them.

▶ *A more positive outlook on the past.* Seniors are less likely than younger adults to attend to and remember negative information (Mather & Carstensen, 2003). This *positivity bias* has a neurological component. The amygdala, a part of the brain that processes emotional information, is less active when seniors process emotionally negative pictures than when they process emotionally positive pictures. In contrast, younger adults show similar activation patterns regardless of the emotional content of the pictures (Mather et al., 2004). Older people also enhance perceptions of their lives by forgetting sad events more than happy events and distorting memories of choices they have made to emphasize the positive (Kennedy, Mather, & Carstensen, 2004; Mather & Johnson, 2000).

▶ *More positive approaches to difficult interpersonal situations.* Seniors are more likely than younger adults to consider how individuals' personalities and contexts contributed to situations, more likely to control their impulses in difficult social situations, and more likely to interpret situations more positively (Charles & Carstensen, 2004). Thus a grandfather is more likely than his young adult son to keep his cool when a neighbor complains that the leaves on his lawn came from their trees. The ability to capture complex dynamics while focusing on the positive may be reasons why older adults are the best storytellers.

One explanation for the rosy outlook many seniors have is that they are more focused on making the most of the time they have left. According to psychologist Laura Carstensen's **socioemotional selectivity theory**, a critical difference between older and younger adults is *time left in life.* As our focus shifts to making the most of our remaining years, our interests shift to emotionally meaningful goals. We are more likely to emphasize emotional issues rather than other issues when choosing social partners, and we choose to spend our time with people who matter the most to us. Usually, these are close friends and family members whom we feel good around rather than new acquaintances. These choices help us maintain and sometimes even improve our emotional well-being and self-concepts (Carstensen, Fung, & Charles, 2003). In other words, a sense of having limited time leads us to focus on information and situations that are emotionally gratifying (Mather & Carstensen, 2003).

The idea that goals shift as we age has been replicated in numerous cultures, including the United States, Hong Kong, Taiwan, and Mainland China. Around the world, it is common for elderly individuals to become more interested in teaching, guiding, and helping others. For example, older individuals help maintain social groups by resolving disputes, and they play a key role in transmitting cultural values through storytelling and other ritual activities (Carstensen & Löckenhoff, 2003).

Additional support for socioemotional selectivity theory stems from the fact that people of all ages have a tendency to shift goals when they are facing an endpoint of one kind or another. For example, young gay men who are HIV-positive give emotional reasons for their choices of social contacts, just as elderly adults do (Carstensen & Fredrickson, 1998). Similarly, graduating seniors are more likely than other students to restrict their social activities to close friends (Fredrickson, 1995).

Around the world, children are more likely to survive when grandparents provide some food and child care. As we age, it is normal to focus more on important people in our lives.

Young and old adults alike make different choices about how and with whom to spend time when confronted with situations that are neutral (you have a half hour of free time) compared to situations that are focused on the end (you will soon be moving far away). In one study, emphasizing endings prompted people to want to be with someone who was emotionally meaningful to them (Fung & Carstensen, 2004).

Erik Erikson on Aging

In earlier chapters you read about Erik Erikson's psychosocial theory of development. Recall that the central issue for young adults is *intimacy versus isolation* (Stage 6), that is, learning to establish meaningful relationships or, if they fail, feeling lonely and isolated. Most of adult life is spent in the stage of *generativity versus self-absorption and stagnation* (Stage 7): After establishing friends and families of their own, adults turn to nurturing, teaching, and leading. The critical developmental task of this stage is *caring*—the activity emphasized by socioemotional selectivity theory.

The final stage of Erikson's theory (Stage 8) is **integrity versus despair**. This stage is the last life crisis when retirement or other experiences prompt people to dwell on their own mortality. Because they are reviewing their lives, successful resolution of this stage hinges on people's responses to all of the earlier stages. As developmentalist Richard Lerner (2002) explained:

> If the person has successfully progressed through his or her previous stages of development—if he or she has experienced more trust than mistrust, more autonomy than shame and doubt, more initiative than guilt, more industry than inferiority, and if he or she has had an identity, an intimate relationship, and has been a productive, generative person—then the individual will face the final years of life with enthusiasm and eagerness. The person will be childlike, said Erikson, in his or her enthusiasm for life. Thus Erikson argued that he or she will feel a *sense of ego integrity*. The person will feel that he or she has led a full and complete life. (p. 428, italics in the original)

People who have not been as fortunate or have not made the best choices—who have experienced more mistrust, shame, isolation and self-absorption—will be bitter that time is running out before they can live to the fullest. These are the minority of people who end life with a fear of death and a sense of despair.

Middle-aged people score higher on measures of generativity and ego integrity than college students do, which confirms Erikson's prediction that these issues aren't of much concern until at least midlife (Whitbourne et al., 1992). But in one study that compared women in their 60s to those in their 80s, the older women were not more likely to have successfully resolved generativity/self-absorption or integrity/despair issues, possibly because they were more likely to be dealing with the identity issues that arise after the death of a husband (Norman, McCluskey-Fawcett, & Ashcraft, 2002). For example, these older women said that phrases such as "wide gap between the person I am and who I want to be" and "haven't found my place in life" described them. They also had issues with trust/mistrust, as they felt more suspicious and questioned their ability to successfully cope with everyday life. These findings confirm Erikson's assumption that people grapple with identity and other basic issues throughout life. They also highlight the major criticism of stage approaches: that developmental issues are as much a function of life circumstances as they are a function of age per se.

Despite the limitations of stage approaches, there is remarkable agreement about the characteristics associated with successful aging. For example, George

integrity versus despair The eighth and final stage of Erik Erikson's theory of psychosocial development in which people review their lives and either feel satisfied with how they have lived (integrity) or feel they have not lived life to the fullest (despair).

Older adults dominate society as business and political leaders. U.S. Supreme Court justices are an example of how older individuals serve society in their role as wise, impartial judges.

Vaillant (2002) added a stage after generativity that he called "keepers of the meaning versus rigidity." Being a keeper of the meaning refers to sharing wisdom and passing down the culture. These activities involve caring about what happens in society as a whole rather than just what happens within our own families, workplaces, or communities. Vaillant compares "keeping the meaning" to being a wise, impartial judge. A perfect example is a Supreme Court justice, who must consider the "big picture" when making a ruling, including what has happened in past cases, what might happen in the future, and what the impact will be on the entire country.

Connecting and Pulling Away

Georgina and Lois, who are both in their 70s, live very different lives. Georgina is redoing the landscaping around her home, attending aerobics classes, and planning a neighborhood barbecue. Meanwhile, Lois leaves her house only to shop and has decided not to attend any neighborhood events. Is it more typical for older people to stay active or to restrict their interests later in life?

There are two views on this issue. According to the **disengagement theory of aging**, it is natural for seniors and societies to mutually withdraw (disengage) from one other. Sometimes people voluntarily restrict their roles, but sometimes they do so because societal pressures operate to replace them with more talented workers and leaders (Cumming & Henry, 1961). In contrast, **activity theory** says that seniors desire and benefit from continued involvement with friends, family members, and community activities (Cavan et al., 1949; Lemon, Bengtson, & Peterson, 1972). According to this view, disengagement is the unfortunate result of health problems, depression, or discrimination against the elderly—not a natural consequence of aging.

Which view is correct? Today, gerontologists acknowledge that people do withdraw from *specific* activities as they lose function. However, disengagement is not a typical consequence of aging. For example, one research team analyzed interviews with Swedish adults who were questioned about their activities when they were 66 to 75 years of age and again 11 years later (Silverstein & Parker, 2002). Each person's level of activity was measured across several domains, including culture-entertainment, outdoor-physical, friendship, and social groups. Across domains, 45 percent of these seniors reported a net loss of activity, 36 percent reported

[handwritten note: Older adults have smaller social groups]

disengagement theory of aging The idea that it is normal and beneficial for elderly individuals and society to mutually withdraw from each other as elderly individuals' abilities decline. See *activity theory.*

activity theory A theory proposing that it is normal and desirable for elderly individuals to maintain a variety of interests and activities and to stay involved with friends and family members. See *disengagement theory.*

a net gain, and 19 percent reported no change. The researchers concluded that a large percentage of very old people downsized their activities, but a fair percentage remained active even into their 80s. Most important, over one-third added more activity domains than they dropped.

Older adults with higher levels of social contact and activity are happier and healthier. In the Swedish study, people who increased their leisure activities reported more positive change in their lives over the past decade, and widening their range of activities helped compensate for the negative impact associated with declining health and losing a spouse. Positive relationships between level of social contacts, leisure activities, and life satisfaction have also been found in other countries, including England (Knapp, 1977), the United States (Rowe & Kahn, 1998), and Spain (Garcia-Martín, Gómez-Jacinto, & Matimportugués-Goyenechea, 2004). As a result, many gerontologists consider engagement in life to be one of the three components of *successful aging*, along with avoiding disease and maintaining high physical and cognitive functioning. Figure 14.10 depicts these components as overlapping to emphasize their interconnectedness: The absence of disease promotes better functioning, which in turn makes it easier and more rewarding to stay involved in leisure and productive activities (Rowe & Kahn, 1998).

Seniors need a variety of social relationships because different relationships satisfy different needs. Friends seem to be better than family members at boosting morale and one's sense of self-worth (Arling, 1976; Felton & Berry, 1992). Adults, particularly the elderly, select their friends because they share a common perspective, have similar interests, and can relate to each other's problems and concerns. For *instrumental needs*, such as providing help when they are ill, older adults tend to turn to their children and partners (Friedman, 1993). In a study of over a thousand older men, those who had a high level of support from both sources were in better health and had fewer depressive symptoms than those who had high support only from family members or not at all (DuPertuis, Aldwin, & Bossé, 2001).

But social contacts are not just about *getting* support. People also need to be needed, and this is especially true for seniors. One 5-year study of older couples found that *giving* emotional or instrumental support to neighbors, friends, and family members was associated with a lower risk of death—even after health, personality, and other factors were taken into account (Brown et al., 2003). Apparently, the adage "it is better to give than to receive" is true during our golden years. Important exceptions are people who are heavily burdened with responsibility, such as those who are primary caregivers for frail or dying relatives. In this case, helping takes a toll on physical and mental health (Burton et al., 2003).

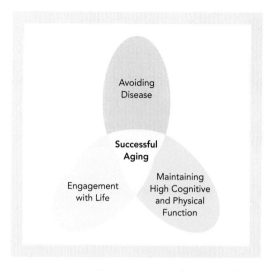

FIGURE 14.10 Components of successful aging.

Three goals that nearly everyone has as they age are to avoid disease, maintain a high level of physical and cognitive functioning, and stay engaged with life. Gerontologists consider these three the core of "successful aging."

SOURCE: Rowe & Kahn (1998).

Meaning and Spirituality in Later Life

Amy told a team of researchers how she had dealt with her husband's death. "I just can't sit back and become an invalid, or let life pass me by," she thought. "I have to do what I can do." Amy subsequently sold her house and her RV, and she remembers feeling that God was "watching" her (Fiori, Hays, & Meador, 2004 p. 411). Amy responded to the crisis of her husband's death the way many people do: by analyzing what it means to make the right choices and thinking more about spiritual issues.

As people grow older, it is common for religion to take a more important place in their search for meaning. In American surveys, 73 percent of individuals ages 65 to 74 say that religion is "very important" to them, compared to 61 percent of all adults (Newport, 2003). Similarly, 73 percent of people age 61 and older say that they pray once or more each day, compared to 58 percent of 41- to 60-year-olds and 43 percent of younger adults (Levin & Taylor, 1997). Older adults score higher on virtually every question about religiousness or spirituality, including attendance at religious services, meditative practice, a sense of working with God as a partner, feeling touched by the beauty of creation, and believing in life after death (Idler et al., 2003).

Although religiousness and spirituality generally increase with age, the pattern varies depending on when you were born. In a cohort born during the late 1920s, spirituality decreased from young to middle adulthood, then rose again. In a younger cohort, spirituality increased throughout adulthood. In both cohorts, however, spirituality increased after people reached their mid-50s, with steeper increases for women than for men (Wink & Dillon, 2002).

Religiousness and spirituality are not identical concepts. *Religiousness* refers to traditional forms of religious beliefs based on established authority, whereas *spirituality* encompasses more individual approaches to meaning and one's relationship to the universe that borrow from a variety of religious and philosophical approaches. During our later years, religiousness is related to positive relations with others and involvement in the community, whereas spirituality is related to personal growth, creative and knowledge-building activities, and wisdom (Wink & Dillon, 2003). A high score on either religiousness or spirituality is associated with Erikson's concept of *generativity*, defined as caring for others and being concerned about the welfare of others (Dillon, Wink, & Fay, 2003).

Like marriage, religiousness is also associated with better health and longer life spans (Hummer et al., 1999; Plante & Sherman, 2001), a greater sense of well-being, and a shorter time to recover from episodes of depression (Koenig, George, & Peterson, 1998). However, many studies have found no relationship between religiousness and positive outcomes once other variables that are associated with health are taken into account. Because people who are religious often have healthier lifestyles (drinking less, for example) than those of nonreligious people, it is premature to say that religiousness *causes* positive outcomes, or that promoting an increase in religiousness late in life will improve seniors' health and well-being (Sloan, Bagiella, & Powell, 2001).

⟩⟩⟩ MEMORY MAKERS ⟨⟨⟨

Match each item on the left with a description on the right:

1. paradox of aging	**(a)** Erikson's last stage of psychosocial development
2. socioemotional selectivity theory	**(b)** the idea that engagement in life benefits the elderly
3. integrity versus despair	**(c)** the fact that seniors suffer losses yet are satisfied with their lives
4. activity theory	**(d)** a theory that focuses on how our goals shift as a function of time left in life
5. spirituality	**(e)** approaches to meaning and one's relationship to the universe that borrow from a variety of religious and philosophical approaches

[1-c; 2-d; 3-a; 4-b; 5-e]

Aging-Friendly Spaces

As more of the population grapples with aging issues, there is a greater need to design a world that is aging friendly. A good way to review the profile of mid-to-later adulthood in this chapter is to consider how our world would change if it were designed with older people in mind.

Try the following exercise to test your understanding of aging. Look at the diagram of an office reception area in Figure 14.11a. This is a simple but typical space that you might find in a medical facility or business, with functional chairs, some magazines, a receptionist area, and posted instructions. Write down some changes that would make this space a better fit for the needs of our aging population. Then turn the page to see how many of our recommended changes you considered.

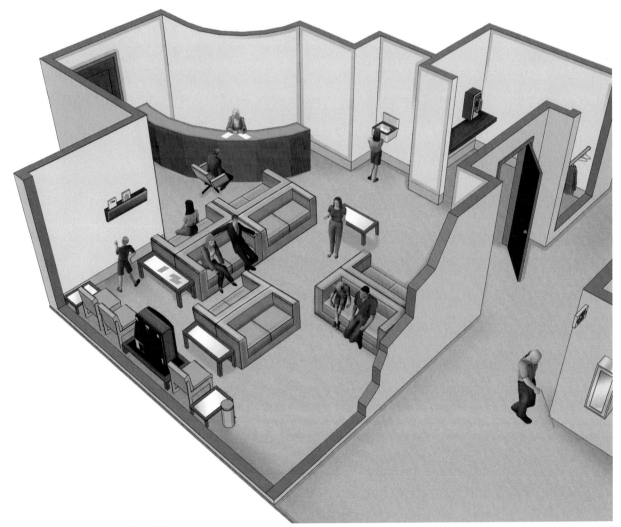

FIGURE 14.11a Redesign this!

What modifications would you make to this typical office reception area to make it a friendlier place for the elderly? Compare your ideas to the suggestions in Figure 14.11b on page 600.

Of course, many of the changes in Figure 14.11b are not at all crucial for healthy 50- to 60-year-olds, but most would be highly welcomed by the fastest-growing segment of the population: the active 80 or older crowd.

Psychiatrist and researcher George Vaillant (2002) posed the following question about growing old:

Aging means:

a. Decay (e.g., after age twenty we lose millions of brain cells a year)

b. Seasonal change (e.g., the maiden's alluring blond curls become the grandmother's beloved white bun)

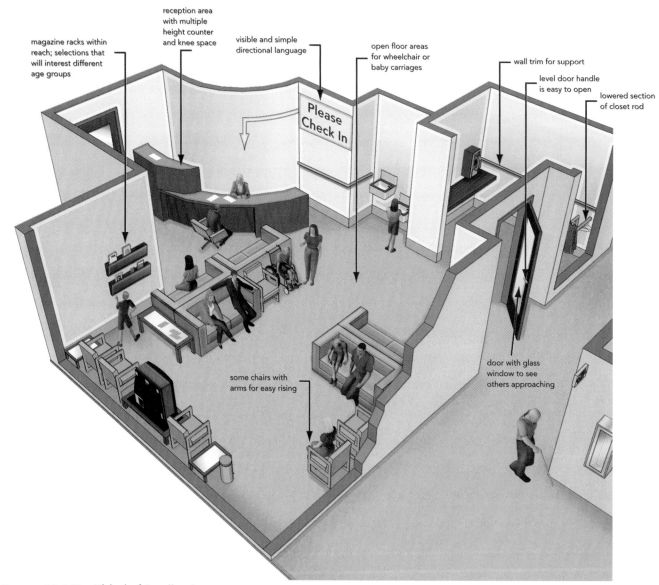

FIGURE 14.11b Elderly friendly places.

The high-contrast color scheme in this reception area helps older and visually impaired people see transitions between walls, floors, and doors. In addition to the labeled modifications, this space has nonskid flooring, adequate lighting, and informational fliers that encourage people to take written instructions home.

SOURCE: Adapted from *Removing Barriers to Health Care*, an online resource from the Center for Universal Design (2005).

c. Continued development right up to the moment of death (e.g., an oak tree or a fine Château Margaux wine)

d. All of the above (p. 39)

Of course, the answer is, "All of the above." Aging involves loss, but it also involves growing into wisdom, focusing more on the positive, and contributing to the community. Vaillant captured the spirit of older individuals when he described the volunteers from one longitudinal study (2002):

> As they surmount the inevitable crises of aging, the Study members seem constantly to be reinventing their lives. They surprise us even as they surprise themselves. In moments of sorrow, loss, and defeat many still convince us that they find their lives eminently worthwhile. They do not flinch from acknowledging how hard life is, but they also never lose sight of why one might want to keep on living it. (p. 5)

But individual circumstances vary tremendously. What proportion of people from middle to older adulthood *are* healthy, active, and joyful? How does the experience of growing old differ across individuals and cultures? The various pathways we take after age 50 are the next chapter of our story.

〉〉〉 SUMMARY 〈〈〈

The Mystery of Aging

1. As the number of older adults continues to grow, there is increasing interest in **gerontology** (the study of biological, psychological, and sociological phenomena associated with aging) and **geriatrics** (the branch of medicine that deals with diseases and problems of the elderly). The science of aging tries to understand why the maximum **life span** of a human is about 120 years, what factors influence an individual's **life expectancy**, and how our physical, cognitive, and emotional selves change as we age.

2. No single theory of aging accounts for all of the changes that occur as people age. *Programmed theories of aging* focus on genetically determined declines in key functions, whereas *random (accidental) theories* focus on the gradual accumulation of errors or biological by-products.

3. Due to the lack of evidence that aging can be prevented, the scientific community does not endorse any specific recommendations for extending the life span.

Physical Aging after 50

4. Individuals can maintain a youthful appearance longer by avoiding the sun, taking care of their teeth and gums, and exercising to maintain muscle mass.

5. With increasing age, vision declines, people become aware of **presbycusis** (the deterioration of hearing asso-

ciated with aging), the sense of smell fades, and the body more often feels overly cold or hot.

6. Aging slows reaction time and makes it harder to regain balance, which contribute to falls.

7. Aging also decreases physical stamina. Seniors process food and water differently than when they were young and fight illness less effectively. Women experience *menopause*, the end of their reproductive lives, but healthy older men can still father children despite **andropause** (the gradual decrease in testosterone levels that occurs among older males).

8. The brain shrinks as we age, loses connections between neurons, experiences reductions in neurotransmitter activity, and accumulates unwanted substances. Older individuals recruit more areas of the brain to accomplish tasks than younger adults. They also experience changing sleep patterns that cause them to tire earlier in the day and wake more frequently at night.

The Aging Mind

9. Many older adults confuse the typical cognitive changes that occur as we age with signs of **dementia**. Among healthy older adults, it is common for crystallized and fluid abilities to decline during the second half of life, but fluid abilities decline earlier and more steeply. Most

older individuals retain their skills at simple attentional tasks, nondeliberate memory tasks (implicit tasks), and basic verbal skills. However, they have more difficulty than younger adults when they have to attend to or remember several things at once, and they often experience the **tip of the tongue phenomenon** when they need to recall specific words.

10. Theories of cognitive aging focus on declines in processing speed, working memory capacity, the ability to ignore irrelevant information, and the fidelity of signal transmission in the brain.

11. The performance of older adults is influenced by the fit between their processing abilities and task demands, their expectations for success, the relevance of the task to their lives, the time of day, and the availability of strategies to compensate for cognitive decline. The **SOC (selective optimization with compensation)** model says that well-adjusted individuals *select* goals they can achieve, make choices that *optimize* their performance (such as practicing harder), and use new strategies to *compensate* for losses.

12. Depending on the task, older individuals do better, the same, or worse than younger adults on practical problems and daily living tasks. Older individuals perform better in some situations that require social sensitivity and special knowledge.

13. Normal memory decline consists of word-finding problems and other minor annoyances. In contrast, people with dementia forget important events and have difficulty completing routine tasks.

Emotional and Social Development

14. Most older adults experience the **paradox of aging**: a sense of well-being despite age-related declines in physical and cognitive functioning. **Socioemotional selectivity theory** proposes that emotional functioning actually improves with age because older people focus more on caring for others and spending time with people who are meaningful to them.

15. Individuals enter the final stage of Erikson's psychosocial theory—**integrity versus despair**—when retirement or other events prompt them to review their lives. Those who successfully resolved earlier developmental issues will be satisfied and have a sense of integrity; those who failed to achieve positive outcomes will end their lives in despair.

16. Although seniors withdraw from specific activities as they age, about half show no decline in overall activities. A variety of social contacts and leisure activities is associated with lower rates of depression and better health.

17. Religion and spirituality become more important to many people as they age.

Aging-Friendly Spaces

18. Aging-friendly places use contrasting colors to make door openings and other transitions stand out, provide nonskid surfaces and ledges for support, and have adequate lighting and features that reduce background noise. Older individuals enjoy places where the selection of art, magazines, and fliers makes them feel welcomed.

>>>KEY TERMS<<<

age dependency ratio   (p. 562)

gerontology   (p. 562)

geriatrics   (p. 562)

aging   (p. 563)

life span   (p. 563)

life expectancy   (p. 563)

Hayflick limit   (p. 567)

telomere   (p. 567)

free radical theory   (p. 567)

caloric restriction   (p. 568)

Baltimore Longitudinal Study of Aging (BLSA)   (p. 570)

presbycusis   (p. 573)

andropause   (p. 576)

dementia   (p. 580)

tip of the tongue phenomenon (TOT)   (p. 584)

elderspeak   (p. 586)

SOC model (selective optimization with compensation)   (p. 590)

wisdom   (p. 590)

paradox of aging   (p. 593)

socioemotional selectivity theory   (p. 594)

integrity versus despair   (p. 595)

disengagement theory of aging   (p. 596)

activity theory   (p. 596)

MILESTONES of middle to late adulthood

50 to 60 Years Most adults are active and working during the last decade of middle age.

- Toward the end of middle age, adults begin to adjust to an aging appearance that includes more noticeable wrinkles, thinning hair, and a decrease in muscle mass.

- An increasing number of people wear glasses for presbyopia and rates of hearing loss increase markedly.

- Women who did not complete menopause earlier do so now, and men experience andropause, a gradual decrease in testosterone.

- Difficulty retrieving words and minor lapses of memory are common, but few people have serious memory impairments and most perform well on practical problems.

61 to 84 Years The majority of young-old adults (61 to 74 years) and old-old adults (75 to 84 years) feel positively about life despite declining physical functions.

- Individuals lose strength more rapidly as fat and connective tissue replace muscle fiber. Now it takes longer to recover from injuries.

- Performance on many cognitive tasks starts to decline by age 60, with sharper declines after age 70.

- Individuals adjust to aging by selecting attainable goals, working harder to achieve goals, and developing ways to compensate for declining abilities.

- Elderly adults are more likely than younger adults to view things positively, and they want to spend time with people who mean the most to them.

85+ The oldest old (85 and older) are a diverse group that includes healthy, cognitively alert individuals and some with serious health problems and activity limitations.

- Physical declines are more rapid and an increasing number of the oldest old suffer from sleep problems.

- Aging affects many regions of the brain, including areas responsible for planning, memory, and coordinated movement.

- It is increasingly difficult for individuals to keep information in mind while they work with it, but they are still able to learn new skills when given enough practice.

- According to Erikson, individuals enter a phase of life called integrity versus despair, when they review their lives and feel satisfied or disheartened.

Do childhood experiences

Preview: Middle to late adulthood in **CONTEXT**

Living with an Aging Body

Chronic conditions such as high blood pressure, diabetes, and arthritis are common during middle to late adulthood, and nearly half of adults over 85 years have Alzheimer's disease. Individual genetic makeups and lifestyles influence the chances of developing a condition that limits the ability to live independently.

Work and Retirement

Older workers tend to be satisfied, committed, and motivated to do well on the job. Today, retirement is less abrupt and final than it used to be because many workers return to the workforce after they have left a career. Individual, family, and job-related factors influence the decision to retire.

Family Life after 50

Family situations vary greatly in later adulthood and include people who are single, married, divorced and recently divorced, and an increasing number who experienced the death of a spouse or partner. Relationships and sexuality continue to be important to most people. Many elderly adults help their now-adult children, have active roles as grandparents, and care for ill spouses or parents.

Individual Differences across Time

Individual personality profiles are relatively stable during late adulthood even though some people show significant changes. It is not unusual for men and women to step outside traditional gender roles and act more androgynously as they age.

In this next chapter, you'll learn how developmental principles explain the pathways individuals take through middle to late adulthood when we consider the question:
Do childhood experiences influence old age?

influence old age?

CHAPTER FIFTEEN

Pathways through Middle to Late Adulthood

{ "Outwardly I am 83, but inwardly I am every age, with the emotions and experience of each period." }

Elizabeth Coatsworth

Stories of Our Lives
Aging Gracefully

Y ou don't have to attend Catholic school to learn a lot from nuns.

That's what Dr. David Snowdon discovered when he began studying a group of 678 nuns known as the Notre Dame sisters. These remarkable women allowed Snowdon and his colleagues to test their physical and intellectual health every few years, record their diets and daily activities, and—most incredibly—examine their brains after death. Snowdon explained why in his book, *Aging with Grace: What the Nun Study Teaches Us about Leading Longer, Healthier, and More Meaningful Lives* (2001):

It's been a sweltering day in the horse-farm and bluegrass country of central Kentucky, and many of my colleagues at the Sanders-Brown Center on Aging have gone home, while I've stayed on in the air-conditioned building to try to finish a grant proposal that is due next week.

After a couple of hours, I decide it's time for a break and head downstairs to [Bill] Markesbery's laboratory. Cecil Runyons, his research assistant, is also working late. We're chatting when I spot a large UPS box on the black Formica counter near the door. Judging from the size of the box, I already know what is inside. Brains.

607

These shipments make for an unusual office routine. *Any mail today? Not much. The usual junk mail . . . a couple of scientific journals. Oh, and a UPS box containing human brains.*

By now we have received several hundred brains, coming from all seven Notre Dame provinces in the United States, but the arrival of these shipments has never become routine for me. I ask Cecil if it's okay to open the box to see how many new brains we have. Four. I lift the gallon-sized plastic tubs out of the box, one by one, and read the label taped to each lid.

Name: Sister Cecilia   Age at death: 97   Weight in grams: 1,040
Name: Sister Wilhelmina   Age at death: 94   Weight in grams: 1,070
Name: Sister Frances   Age at death: 92   Weight in grams: 920
Name: Sister Elizabeth   Age at death: 82   Weight in grams: 1,190

I'm both curious and cautious. I've never forgotten Dave Wekstein's lesson: "Remember, somebody died." I know that every brain comes to us at a cost. Sometimes a sister who is ailing will say to me—always cheerfully—"Dr. Snowdon, you'll be getting my brain soon." And I always reply, "Hang in there, Sister. We're in no hurry."

Now I lift one container to the light and see the outline of the brain resting in the cloudy yellow formalin solution. . . As unscientific as it sounds, I feel my own sort of reverence toward this brain; what I hold in my hand is sacred. Its weight reminds me of my responsibility as the director of the Nun Study. Each brain represents a rich, vibrant life, and each brain offers a unique legacy to those who probe its mysteries.

Before the Nun Study, I had never seen a human brain. Amazing as the organ is, with its winding mountains of gray and white matter, the sight at first spooked me a bit. As I learned more about the intricacies of brains and saw ever more of them, my initial discomfort gave way to wonder and awe. . .

I find it fascinating to sit at the second eyepiece as Bill guides me through the maze of the brain. Even as he examines its tissue millimeter by millimeter, pinpointing abnormalities and tracing the characteristic signs of Alzheimer's, the brain maintains some of its secrets. Most of the brains neatly fit our expectations, with little or no evidence of disease in a tack-sharp sister and abundant damage seen in a sister who had dementia. But sometimes Markesbery finds little evidence of Alzheimer's in a sister who had the classic symptoms of the disease. And sometimes brains from other sisters who appeared mentally intact when alive show extensive evidence of Alzheimer's. Illuminating the relationship between the symptoms of the disease—the progressive, devastating loss of function—and the damage to the brain that causes those symptoms is a central focus of the Nun Study (pp. 84–85).

David Snowdon is an unlikely person to be looking at a brain; he is an epidemiologist, someone who examines health statistics and trends. But today, teams that study development include statisticians, neuroscientists, psychologists, and other professionals, all joined by a deep curiosity about what it takes to have a healthy, meaningful life.

DAVID SNOWDON DRIVES TO work each day to answer the following questions: Why do some people age gracefully, assisting the people around them, continuing to work, and retaining their mental sharpness well into their 80s and 90s? And why do others seem to disappear into aging, losing themselves and their connections with others?

Surprisingly, the answers are *not* answers about the last years of life. Instead, the riddle of aging begins years earlier in medical events during middle adulthood, choices made during youth, and even the distant circumstances of childhood. In this chapter, you will read how we traverse the longest segment of our lives, a period that begins decades before most people retire and ends in a million different ways. Periodically, we will revisit the Nun Study to look at the clues about aging that were left by Sister Cecilia, Sister Wilhelmina, and the other sisters of Notre Dame.

These men are having their blood pressure and heart rate monitored while they watch the Super Bowl in a men's health center. They have volunteered for a study that is trying to understand why men develop some chronic diseases earlier than women.

Living with an Aging Body

Brian King, 52, was transported to an emergency room after a young rugby player threw him to the ground. "At 40, you know you're not as young as you used to be," the coach later remarked. "At 50, you realize it almost every day" (Brink, 2002, p. 62).

The period from 50 to 60 has been called the "Do or Die Decade"—a time when people either embrace a healthy lifestyle or face the possibility of developing conditions that can lead to disability and death (Brink, 2002). But for every adult who believes that aging knocks the wind out of our sails, another is feeling healthy and strong. Why?

One reason people feel differently about growing old traces back to our ancestors. For most of human history, adults worked hard to forage for food, track animals, and move from one place to another. Those who survived had bodies designed for physical activity, and they passed down genes that work best with an active lifestyle. Daily exercise builds skeletal muscle that burns more calories, keeps the heart healthy, and triggers a series of physiological changes that helps the hormone *insulin* move fuel into muscles. When humans became more sedentary,* some of the genes that helped us survive in the past began making us ill. For example, one gene in the body conserves energy by initiating the transfer of blood glucose to muscles only when muscles are working. When individuals are generally inactive, blood glucose and insulin levels rise, leading to diabetes. Through this and other physiological pathways, more than 20 medical conditions became more common as people started living longer but less active lives, including coronary artery disease and stroke (Booth & Neufer, 2005).

Today, adults who are enjoying their later years tend to have forgiving genes and health-related habits that keep them feeling on top of the world. Their less fortunate neighbors either have different genetic profiles or earlier lifestyles that failed to prepare them for the inevitable changes that occur after 50. Knowing what health problems arise as we age—and what we can do to prevent them—is crucial for understanding why people take such different pathways through middle and late adulthood.

Physical Challenges after 50

With all of the negative stereotypes about aging, it is important to realize that most people—even old people—perceive themselves as healthy. Seventy-three percent of adults 65 and over say their health is good to excellent, and 65 percent of the 85-and-older crowd still consider themselves to be fairly healthy (Federal Interagency Forum on Aging Related Statistics, 2004). One reason people generally feel good

---

*sedentary: Involving a lot of sitting or little activity.

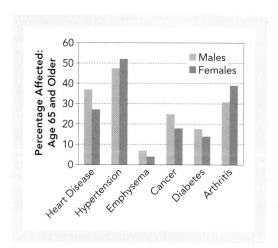

FIGURE 15.1 Chronic health conditions.
- -
Many older adults are coping with a chronic health condition. The first five conditions in this figure contribute to the leading causes of death: heart disease, hypertension (a risk factor for cerebral vascular diease and stroke), cancer, diabetes, and emphysema (one of several chronic respiratory diseases). Arthritis can increase the chances of developing a life-threatening condition by limiting people's ability to exercise and to live independently.

SOURCE: Federal Interagency Forum on Aging Related Statistics (2004).

about their health is that they compare themselves to others their own age. But as you will read next, the percentage of people who actually have various diseases or disabilities paints a less optimistic picture of aging.

CHRONIC DISEASES. Most diseases that trouble us as we age are **chronic diseases**: medical conditions that develop slowly and are long-lasting. During late adulthood, six of the seven leading causes of death involve chronic conditions: heart disease, cancers, cerebrovascular diseases (conditions affecting the arteries in the brain that result in tissue damage), respiratory diseases (such as emphysema), Alzheimer's disease (which you'll read about shortly), and diabetes (an abnormality in the body's ability to use sugar). The remaining cause of death is infections that overwhelm the body when the immune system is weakened by age or disease (Hoyert et al., 2005).

Figure 15.1 reports the percentage of older adults in the United States who live with one of six common chronic diseases. (Keep in mind that this figure reports only *diagnosed* illness, so actual rates are undoubtedly higher.) Your risk of acquiring one of these conditions is influenced by the following factors:

▸ *Age.* The prevalence of chronic diseases increases with age. For example, only 8 percent of adults under 35 years of age report high blood pressure compared to 51 percent of 55- to 64-year-olds. Among adults ages 75 and older, 76 percent have high blood pressure (American Heart Association, 2005a).

▸ *Ethnicity.* Some ethnic groups are more likely to develop a chronic disease. For example, elderly African American and Hispanic adults are more likely than white adults to have diabetes (Federal Interagency Forum on Aging Related Statistics, 2004), and elderly African Americans are more likely to have high blood pressure than white or Hispanic adults (American Heart Association, 2005a). A variety of factors probably contribute to the greater frequency of chronic diseases among minorities, including genetic differences, neighborhood factors (such as exposure to lead, which is a risk factor for high blood pressure), higher stress levels due to higher poverty rates (which dysregulates the immune system, as mentioned in Chapter 13), dietary differences (such as less consumption of fruits and vegetables), and higher obesity rates (He et al., 2006; Lohmeuller et al., 2006; Martin et al., 2006; Rosenberg et al., 1999).

▸ *Socioeconomic status.* In Chapter 12 you read that the number of years of education is one of the best predictors of health because adults who have more education (and the higher earnings more education often brings) tend to have more fulfilling work, a sense of personal control, and a healthier lifestyle. Even within ethnic groups, adults with higher socioeconomic status tend to have better health after age 50. For example, adults with the fewest years of formal education have the highest rates of high blood pressure, diabetes, and even arthritis. And as you can see in Figure 15.2, the advantage associated with additional years of education is substantial (Centers for Disease Control and Prevention, 2005a).

▸ *Sex differences.* The risk profiles for women and men change as they age. For example, men are more likely than women to have high blood pressure until 55 years, but women are more likely than men to have this condition after menopause (American Heart Association, 2005a). Even though sex differences are only a matter of degree, associations between sex and specific diseases often lead health professionals to overlook illness in the group that is

chronic diseases Medical conditions like diabetes and arthritis that develop slowly and are long-lasting.

less affected. Thus cardiovascular disease is the leading cause of death for women *and* men, but women are less likely than men to receive adequate care and aggressive treatment because the stereotype of a cardiac patient is an older man (Stoney, 2003).

As people succumb to chronic disease, there is a corresponding decrease in the number of days each month when they feel healthy. In the United States, young adults average just under 2 unhealthy days per month, but this figure more than doubles (to just over 5 days) by 65 and older. Because unhealthy men tend to die younger than unhealthy women do (as discussed in Chapter 14), older women report about 1 more unhealthy day per month than men (Merck Institute of Aging & Health, 2005).

METABOLIC SYNDROME. A condition that greatly increases your chances of serious heart disease and diabetes is **metabolic syndrome** (also called Syndrome X) (American Heart Association, 2005b). As summarized in Table 15.1, this collection of symptoms includes obesity, high blood pressure, unhealthy blood fat levels, and insulin resistance (a condition in which cells lose their ability to use insulin to convert glucose—a type of sugar—into energy). Over time, the biochemical changes associated with metabolic syndrome raise blood levels of insulin and glucose, damaging arteries and increasing the risk of blood clots that can cause heart attacks and strokes. Some people eventually develop diabetes, a condition in which the cells in the body cannot absorb glucose. As you can see in Figure 15.3, rates of diabetes have increased markedly over the past few decades, but people who are just beginning to show signs of metabolic syndrome can reduce their risk of serious disease by losing weight and increasing their physical activity.

VISION DISORDERS. As discussed in Chapter 14, sensory impairments also increase with age. Eighteen percent of the population is having trouble seeing by 65, and this number jumps to 33 percent among people aged 85 and older (Federal Interagency Forum on Aging Related Statistics, 2004).

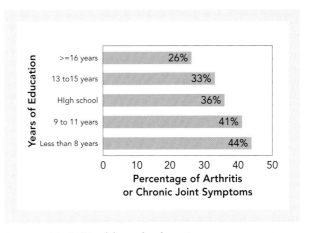

FIGURE 15.2 Health and education.

The more education adults have, the less likely they are to suffer from a chronic health condition. In this figure, every few years of additional education is associated with a large drop in the risk of suffering from arthritis or chronic joint symptoms. On average, people who have more education began life in wealthier circumstances that promoted health. As adults, education helps them land safe jobs and buys better housing, food, and relaxing leisure activities.

SOURCE: Centers for Disease Control and Prevention (2005a).

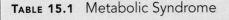

TABLE 15.1 Metabolic Syndrome

There is no single definition of metabolic syndrome. According to one expert panel, an individual who has three or more of the following has metabolic syndrome:

▸ Obesity with significant fat in the waist and abdomen (often called "central obesity"). A waist measurement greater than 40 inches (102 centimeters) for a man or 35 inches (88 centimeters) for a woman is indicative of central obesity.

▸ A high level of blood triglycerides (a type of fat), measured after fasting (consuming nothing but water from the evening before the test until the test the next morning).

▸ A high level of HDL ("good") cholesterol in the blood (another type of fat).

▸ High blood pressure.

▸ Elevated fasting blood sugar level.

SOURCE: National Institutes of Health (2002).

metabolic syndrome (also called Syndrome X). A collection of symptoms that includes obesity, high blood pressure, unhealthy blood fat levels, and insulin resistance (a condition in which cells lose their ability to use insulin to convert glucose into energy).

FIGURE 15.3 The price of inactivity.

In recent years, the decline in physical activity and the resulting increase in obsesity has produced an alarming increase in the rate of adult-onset diabetes. Today, 17 percent of individuals ages 65 to 74 have diabetes, which is 14 times the rate for people less than 45 years of age.

SOURCE: Centers for Disease Control and Prevention (2005g, h).

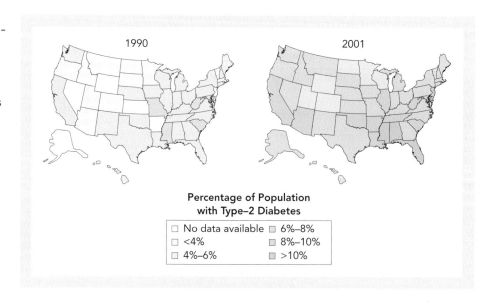

Percentage of Population
with Type–2 Diabetes

☐ No data available	☐ 6%–8%
☐ <4%	☐ 8%–10%
☐ 4%–6%	☐ >10%

You read about a frequent cause of vision loss, cataracts, in Chapter 14. Another is **glaucoma**, a group of conditions in which fluid pressure in the eye is too high, causing damage to the optic nerve. Glaucoma is the leading *preventable* cause of blindness in the United States, and it is especially frequent among African Americans. (Prompt diagnosis and treatment with eye drops usually prevent blindness.) A more serious disorder is **macular degeneration**, in which there is damage to the central part of the retina that allows us to read, causing blurred vision and a dark spot in the center of the visual field. Macular degeneration is the leading cause of blindness among older adults, affecting more than 1.6 million people over age 50 in the United States alone. No cure exists, but laser surgery to destroy leaking blood vessels under the retina may treat the most serious form of the disease (Prevent Blindness America & National Eye Institute, 2002). A complication of diabetes is **diabetic retinopathy**, in which elevated blood sugar levels harm tiny blood vessels in the retina. Due to this condition, individuals with diabetes are 25 times more likely than the general population to become blind (Centers for Disease Control and Prevention 1993a).

Dementia

Anne Simpson remembers when her husband's behavior first started to aggravate her. Bob was disorderly, failed to finish projects, and didn't seem to be listening to her. "He was retired, after all; I expected him to help me!" she later explained. "Bob was trying harder and harder to hang on to the tasks he had always done (balance the checkbook, make household repairs, service the cars, help when the grandchildren visited. . .), but he got tired and forgetful and discouraged. I felt letdown because he didn't do a task he said he would do, and he got defensive, accusing me of attacking him—as I probably was" (Simpson & Simpson, 1999, pp. 26-27). When doctors confirmed that Bob had Alzheimer's disease, the couple settled into the difficult task of coping.

In Chapter 14 we mentioned *dementia*, a loss of mental ability serious enough to impair a person's ability to handle daily activities. The health of our brains is dependent on the health of our bodies, so dozens of conditions can lead to dementia. In the past, physicians used a general term, *senile dementia*, to describe severe cognitive dysfunction among the elderly. (The word *senile* means "related to old age.") Today, the term *senile* is used most often in popular culture to describe a state of memory loss and confusion (as in, "I must be getting *senile*!"). In its place, medical professionals usually use more specific terms to describe the dementias.

glaucoma A group of conditions in which pressure from fluid in the eye is too high, causing damage to the optic nerve.

macular degeneration A condition in which the part of the retina that gives us sharp central vision (for reading) degrades. Macular degeneration causes blurred vision and a dark spot in the center of the visual field. It is the leading cause of blindness in older individuals.

diabetic retinopathy An eye disease that develops when an elevated blood sugar level harms blood vessels in the retina.

ALZHEIMER'S DISEASE. The most common cause of dementia is **Alzheimer's disease** (AD). As described in Table 15.2, this disease begins with mild cognitive impairment, especially memory loss for recent activities and information. Patients soon develop more serious memory failure, confusion, and personality changes. As Bob wrote in his journal, "I can make change. But writing checks?! I can't do it! I'm exhausted. I don't mind that it takes me so long, really—I just mind that I don't know how any more. Things that I did all the time. . . Now nothing is familiar" (Simpson & Simpson, 1999, p. 50). Patients who are in late stages of the disease no longer recognize their family members and are unable to care for themselves. Alzheimer's patients are challenging to care for because they behave in socially inappropriate ways, such as swearing or making insulting comments, are often agitated, and will wander off unless they are watched closely or confined. Death usually occurs within 3 to 10 years after diagnosis.

The incidence of Alzheimer's disease rises as we age. About 3 percent of 65- to 74-year-olds have the disease, compared to 19 percent of 75- to 84-year-olds and nearly 50 percent of adults over 85 years (Hebert et al., 2003). To diagnose the disease, physicians take the patient's history (including when and how symptoms developed), interview family members (to explore personality changes), consider results from physical and neurological tests (to rule out other disorders and evaluate cognitive functioning), and sometimes order a brain scan.

Alzheimer's disease interferes with three key neural processes: the ability of neurons to communicate with other neurons, to generate the energy needed to survive, and to engage in normal cell cleanup and repair (National Institute on Aging, 2002). As brain

Alzheimer's disease (**AD**). The most common form of dementia, characterized by beta-amyloid plaques and neurofibrillary tangles in the brain. Symptoms begin with mild cognitive impairment, especially memory loss for recent activities and information, and then progress to severe confusion, personality changes, and death.

In facilities for patients with Alzaimer's disease, staff members are trained to offer activities that stimulate individuals without overwhelming them.

TABLE 15.2	The Progression of Alzheimer's Disease
Preclinical	Brain changes begin as much as 10 to 20 years before visible symptoms appear. A brain area near the hippocampus (a critical structure for memory), and then the hippocampus itself, begin to shrink.
	Mild memory problems begin to appear.
Mild	The disease begins to affect the cerebral cortex, causing shrinkage. An increased number of plaques and tangles affect areas of the brain that are responsible for memory, language, and reasoning.
	Symptoms include memory loss, confusion about the location of familiar places, problems accomplishing daily tasks (such as handling money and paying bills), and increased anxiety and other personality and mood changes.
Moderate	Brain damage spreads further and includes areas responsible for sensory processing.
	More supervision is necessary as agitation and disorientation become more severe. Individuals have short attention spans, difficulty recognizing friends and family members, and problems reading and writing. Motor problems occur, such as problems getting out of chairs, hallucinations and suspiciousness can appear, and socially inappropriate behavior becomes more common.
Severe	Plaques and tangles appear throughout the brain.
	Patients are completely dependent on others for care. They lose bladder and bowel control and experience weight loss, difficulty swallowing, and increased sleeping. The immediate cause of death is often pneumonia from inhaling food or beverages into the lungs.

SOURCE: National Institute on Aging (2002).

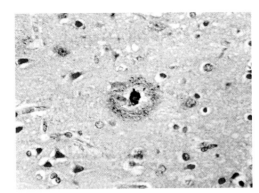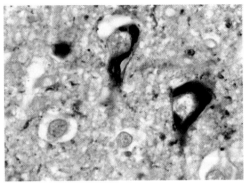

FIGURE 15.4 Anatomical signatures of Alzheimer's disease.

Brain tissues of individuals with Alzheimer's disease contain an abundance of two abnormal structures. Beta-amyloid plaques (on the left) contain protein fragments mixed with other molecules and brain cells. Neurofibrillary tangles (on the right) are produced when long protein fibers inside neurons twist and neurons die.

beta-amyloid plaques Debris in the brain that contains fragments of protein mixed with other molecules and brain cells. Beta-amyloid plaques are a signature feature of Alzheimer's disease, but they occur to a lesser extent in some normal elderly brains.

neurofibrillary tangles Structures produced in the brain when long protein fibers inside neurons twist and the neurons die. Neurofibrillary tangles are a signature feature of Alzheimer's disease, but they occur to a lesser extent in normal aging brains.

cells lose connections with each other and die, two anatomical "signatures" of the disease appear (Figure 15.4). One is an abnormal number of **beta-amyloid plaques**, debris that contains fragments of protein mixed with other molecules and brain cells. The second is **neurofibrillary tangles**, which are structures produced when long protein fibers inside neurons twist and neurons die. Researchers are still exploring whether plaques or tangles come first and the role each plays in Alzheimer's disease (Adlard & Cummings, 2004; Schönheit, Zarski, & Ohm, 2004). Changes at the cellular level produce the changes in brain function and structure that you can see in Figure 15.5: dramatic shrinkage of the brain and a corresponding decrease in neural activity.

Most of what we know about Alzheimer's disease has been learned fairly recently. Scientists have identified genetic mutations for early-onset Alzheimer's, a

FIGURE 15.5 Brain changes in Alzheimer's disease.

A computer graphic of a vertical slice through the brain of a patient with Alzheimer's disease (left) and a normal older adult (right) show profound shrinkage caused by the disease. Numerous changes inside tissues cause the characteristic symptoms of Alzheimer's disease: memory loss, problems completing routine tasks of daily living, and personality changes.

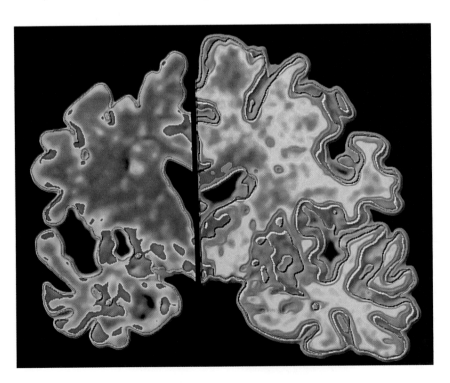

form of the disease that appears in the 30s, 40s, or 50s, and they have also found genes that increase an individual's risk of having the common form of Alzheimer's disease. In addition, research on *acetylcholine*, a neurotransmitter that is rapidly depleted in people with Alzheimer's disease, has led to the development of new medications that can improve functioning during early stages of the disease.

But the full story of Alzheimer's disease will not be a simple one. One interesting finding is that the amount of tangling and plaques does not always match up with the degree of cognitive decline. In the Nun Study, for example, the research team found healthy-looking brains in nuns who had very poor cognitive functioning, along with brains full of plaques and tangles from nuns who had functioned well (Snowdon, 2001). Clues to this mystery were obtained from brain tissue and the nuns' life histories. Some brains had pits of dead tissue, called *infarcts*, caused by damaged blood vessels, and these brains came from individuals who had been more disabled than one would expect from the distribution of plaques and tangles. This finding suggests that people with some damage from Alzheimer's may function fairly normally until they get "pushed over the edge" by strokes or head injuries (Corey-Bloom, 2000; Honig et al., 2003). On the other hand, nuns who had more education or more "idea dense" writing, as described in Chapter 14, had less disability than one would expect from their brain tissue. This finding led to the **cerebral reserve hypothesis**, which is the idea that intellectual challenges build a brain that can compensate better for the physical assaults of aging (Staff et al., 2004).

OTHER DEMENTIAS. When mental confusion first appears, it may be impossible to know whether an individual will develop Alzheimer's disease or one of several related conditions. For example, some seniors have abnormal deposits in their brainstem and cortical regions called *Lewy bodies*. Like Alzheimer's patients, these individuals show numerous plagues but fewer tangles. Some scientists have argued that this type of dementia should be considered a subtype of Alzheimer's, whereas others call it the second most common type of dementia, **dementia with Lewy bodies.** Dementia with Lewy bodies produces memory disturbances just as Alzheimer's disease does, but with motor and sensory symptoms (such as visual hallucinations) as well (Baskys, 2004).

Vascular dementia is a collection of medical syndromes that interferes with the brain's blood supply. A common cause of vascular dementia is one or more *strokes*, a sudden interruption of blood flow to the brain due to a ruptured blood vessel or blockage. Unlike Alzheimer's disease, which causes a gradually progressing dementia, the behavioral effects of a stroke can be sudden and severe. Many patients improve somewhat after a stroke and then have stable functioning unless they experience further strokes. A diagnosis of "mixed dementia" is given when Alzheimer's and vascular disease coexist, and these patients generally have more severe memory and planning problems than patients who do not have vascular disease. The risk factors for vascular dementia are the same as the risk factors for cardiovascular disease: high blood pressure, high cholesterol levels, diabetes, and smoking. Vascular dementia is involved in about 20 percent of dementia cases in the United States but 50 percent in Japan and China, where lifestyle factors, including an extremely low-fat diet among some individuals, increase the risk of stroke (Román, 2004; Taubes, 2001).

Numerous less frequent conditions also produce dementia. For example, some individuals with Parkinson's disease eventually develop Lewy bodies and dementia, and those with a rare disease called *frontotemporal dementia* experience sudden and bizarre changes in personality and interests.

cerebral reserve hypothesis The idea that intellectual challenges build a brain that can better compensate for the physical assaults of aging.

dementia with Lewy bodies The second most common form of dementia, characterized by disturbances in memory, language, and motor behavior, often with visual hallucinations and personality disturbances.

vascular dementia A collection of syndromes that lead to cognitive impairment when the blood supply is cut off to brain cells, causing them to die.

Artist William Utermohlen painted a series of self-portraits during the 4 years after he was diagnosed with Alzheimer's disease. Alzheimer's disease impairs people's ability to perform tasks that involve spatial relationships and completing a series of steps in order. As a result, patients gradually lose the ability to dress and, in this case, to paint.

WHEN MENTAL CONFUSION ISN'T DEMENTIA. Physicians who suspect dementia begin a patient evaluation by ruling out illnesses and drug reactions that can masquerade as dementia. Here are some of the most common causes of non-dementia-related memory problems and sudden changes in behavior:

▶ *Water balance and nutrition.* Older adults are prone to dehydration as feelings of thirst diminish, which can reduce their alertness and ability to concentrate (Maughan, 2003). Inadequate nutrition can also cause older minds to become foggy. For example, a diet of refined carbohydrates can lead to a magnesium deficiency, which is associated with confusion, and laxatives and some blood pressure medications deplete potassium, which can lead to depression and mental impairment.

▶ *Depression.* Healthy older adults are no more likely than younger adults to feel depressed (Roberts et al., 1997). Nevertheless, depression is relatively common among some groups of seniors, including heart disease patients and nursing home residents (Frasure-Smith & Lespérance, 2005; Jongenelis et al., 2004). Depressed people function more slowly on cognitive tasks and often show working memory problems (Harvey et al., 2004). But unlike younger patients, who usually improve after their depression lifts, older patients do not always experience a rebound in mental functioning over time (Nebes et al., 2000).

▶ *Reactions to medication and drug interactions.* Old organs eliminate drugs more slowly and experience more side effects from medications, yet half of our elderly population is regularly taking three or more prescription medications (Moxey et al., 2003). Regrettably, many elderly are taking drugs that are not recommended for older adults (Curtis et al., 2004), including drugs that have memory impairment and hostility as potential side effects (Howard et al., 2004).

▶ *Medical conditions.* Numerous medical conditions cause temporary cognitive symptoms (Brands et al., 2005). For example, poorly controlled diabetes leads to mental slowing that can increase the time it takes people to subtract numbers and respond to visual information.

▶ *Alcohol abuse.* Heavy alcohol use is associated with lower scores on memory tests (Galanis et al., 2000), and chronic alcoholism can cause a pattern of learning and memory problems called *alcohol dementia*. In addition, many prescription drugs should not be taken with alcohol because they compound its effects, slowing reaction times and interfering with balance and thinking. On the other hand, occasional to moderate drinking by healthy individuals can help the brain by raising levels of "good" cholesterol, reducing the risk of blood clots, and slowing the declines in cognitive functioning that occur as we age (Ganguli et al., 2005; Letenneur, 2004). (Moderate use is generally considered a drink a day for women or two drinks for men.)

It is clear that good thinking starts with good health. But good health buys us more than just a clear mind as we grow older—it also buys us the gift we turn to next: our independence.

Living in a Senior World

Losses of function due to normal aging and disease have widespread implications on how—and where—we live. As we grow older, more of us develop conditions that require us to change how we accomplish the various tasks of daily life, such as cleaning, doing laundry, and preparing meals. As shown in Figure 15.6, aching joints, weakness in the hands or legs, memory impairment, and other conditions cause 35 percent of elderly, noninstitutionalized adults to have difficulty performing at least one routine activity (National Center for Health Statistics, 2005).

But despite some physical limitations, most seniors want to live in their own homes, surrounded by memories and personal belongings in the same communities where they raised their families (Sichelman, 2001). One way to help more people achieve this goal is **universal design** (also called "aging in place"), a philosophy of building homes that meet the needs of as many people as possible, from childhood through old age. (Think of it as "This Old House" meets "This Old Homeowner.") We built some universal design features into the office space activity in Chapter 14, such as low counter spaces and lever door handles. Other modifications that promote independence for all age groups include furniture that is difficult to knock over and emergency buttons in areas where falls might occur (AARP, 2005c; Null & Cherry, 1998).

But even the best-designed home cannot shop, cook, or maintain the yard. When these tasks become too burdensome, some seniors make the transition into senior apartments or assisted living facilities. *Senior apartments* are complexes that often have 24-hour emergency call systems, optional meals in a common dining room, weekly housecleaning, and sometimes an on-site nurse to help with medications. Residents in these facilities can keep their own schedules and choose their activities while enjoying some help with transportation and maintenance. *Assisted living* provides a higher level of support, including 24-hour supervision with help for bathing, getting dressed, and getting to and from meals. Senior apartments and assisted living facilities are expensive, and most insurance programs do not cover costs. In 2005, for example, a typical assisted living facility cost an older individual over $34,000 a year (MetLife Mature Market Institute, 2005). This is one reason why only 5 percent of elderly adults in the United States live in some type of senior housing rather than in their own homes, with relatives, or in nursing homes (U.S. Department of Health and Human Services, Administration on Aging 2004).

Nursing homes are medical settings that offer the highest degree of care for people who cannot live on their own, often because they cannot walk or need ongoing medical attention. Residents have very little privacy and little control over their lives, so this expensive option is usually considered a "last resort" for those who are very ill and frail. It is estimated that 4.5 percent of the elderly population lives in nursing homes, although this figure increases to 18 percent among individuals 85 and older.

Regardless of where people live, the best quality of care is usually the *least amount of help* that each person needs. Too often, staff members in senior facilities "train" residents to become even more dependent through a pattern of behavior called a *dependency-support script*. This is a pattern in which staff members ignore independent behavior but reinforce dependent behaviors, such as looking at a food tray without eating, by giving attention ("Come on, Ruthie, you can eat by yourself"). Over time, such interactions foster *learned helplessness*, behavior in which seniors act dependent to satisfy their need for social interactions. By reinforcing independent behavior and giving nursing home residents opportunities for responsibility, such as letting them care for a plant, researchers have improved the well-being of elderly adults and reinstated independent eating, dressing, and other activities of daily living (Baltes, 1995; Langer & Rodin, 2004).

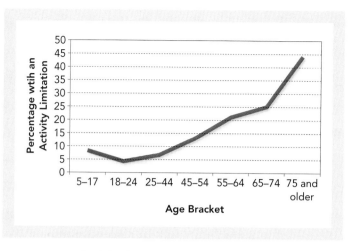

FIGURE 15.6 Activity limitations and age.

Beginning in the mid-40s, an increasing number of people experience one or more limitations of daily activity due to poor physical health. Notice the large increase in the number of people who have limitations after age 75.

SOURCE: National Center for Health Statistics (2005).

universal design (or aging in place) A philosophy of building homes to meet the needs of as many people as possible from childhood to old age.

FIGURE 15.7 Our independent seniors.

Today's older adults are remarkably active and independent. Only 4.5 percent of people ages 65 and older live in an institution, and only a minority of the remaining population needs help with one or more complicated tasks that are critical for independent living, such as preparing meals or managing money. This optimistic picture reflects the health of today's seniors, and also the fact that only 12 percent of the elderly population is 85 years of age or older.

SOURCES: National Center for Health Statistics (2005); U.S. Department of Health and Human Services (2004).

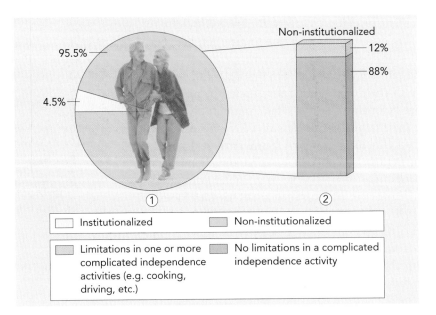

FIGURE 15.7 Our independent seniors.

95.5%

4.5%

Non-institutionalized

12%

88%

① ②

| Institutionalized | Non-institutionalized |

| Limitations in one or more complicated independence activities (e.g. cooking, driving, etc.) | No limitations in a complicated independence activity |

Happily, most seniors do not need the assistance offered by senior housing or nursing homes. For example, only 12 percent of the noninstitutionalized population needs help with complicated tasks that are critical for independent living, such as grocery shopping, money management, or meal preparation (Figure 15.7). And due to improved health, the percentage of older people with limitations has *decreased* over the past decade. So even though there are now more older people in the United States, we do not have that many more *disabled* seniors (Federal Interagency Forum on Aging Related Statistics, 2004).

But even active people face challenges to established routines as they move from their 60s into their 70s and beyond. One of the most emotionally charged symbols of independence is parked in the garage. For many adults, dignity means driving—and drive they do, even after their skills are obviously failing. Should policy makers do more to get elderly drivers off the road? To explore this issue, turn to our special feature, "Aging behind the Wheel."

Older drivers are involved in fewer accidents than younger drivers because they avoid risk and drive less often; however, they have more accidents per mile driven than younger drivers do. Driver skills training, safer cars, "age smart" roads and signage, and senior transportation programs can help seniors maintain their independence safely.

AGING BEHIND THE WHEEL

In July, 87-year-old Marie Wyman crashed her car into a restaurant in Winslow, Maine, sending panicked patrons diving out of the way; 28 had minor injuries. There was a more disastrous outcome in June when Albertinah Mkhize, 72, made a wildly wide turn through a San Francisco crosswalk: a 10-month-old boy being pushed in a stroller by his mother was struck and killed. Just hours before, the driver had flunked a road test and lost her license. (Shapiro, 1999, p. 61)

Stories like these fuel stereotypes that older drivers are confused and dangerous. There is reason to be concerned. Adjusted for miles driven, elderly drivers have twice the accident rate of their younger counterparts (Owsley et al., 1998), and they are far more likely to be involved in fatal crashes (partly because they are more likely than younger drivers to die from their injuries) (Insurance Institute for Highway Safety, 2001). These findings are of concern due to the sheer number of older drivers who will be on the road in the future. By 2030, for example, it is estimated that 18 percent of drivers will be 70 and older (Insurance Institute for Highway Safety, 2003).

Why don't licensing offices take incompetent drivers off the road? The answer is that it isn't easy to identify dangerous drivers. Simple vision tests don't capture the complicated demands of driving, and most older drivers who are involved in crashes have good vision. Performance on a test that detects dementia predicts driving ability a little better, but not well enough to screen seniors who are just beginning to have problems (Ball et al., 1993; Ball & Rebok, 1994). To do a better job, screening tests have to evaluate three skills that are related to driving performance: speed of mental processing, the ability to divide attention, and the ability to ignore distractions.

A procedure that taps these processes is the useful field of view test (UFOV®), a set of tasks that looks at a driver's ability to rapidly identify information and divide attention between various places in the visual field (Roenker et al., 2003). Scores on the UFOV predict performance on road tests and can identify the majority of drivers who have recently had a vehicle crash (Ball, Wadley, & Edwards, 2002; Goode et al., 1998). But screening tests do not predict perfectly and crashes are rare events, so their usefulness in

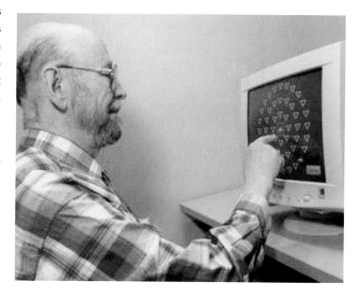

saving lives is limited. According to one estimate, over 500 drivers would need to lose their licenses to prevent a single crash (Insurance Institute for Highway Safety, 2001). As a result, don't look for early screening tests to have widespread support any time soon.

Advocates for elderly drivers cite a host of other reasons why driving privileges should not be tied to age. Older drivers are more likely to wear seatbelts, less likely to speed or follow other vehicles too closely, and less likely to drink and drive (Insurance Institute for Highway Safety, 2001; Straight & Jackson, 1999). And because they avoid risk and drive less often, elderly adults (age 65 and older) are involved in only 8 percent of crashes even though they represent 14 percent of all licensed drivers. In comparison, 16- to 24-year-olds, who also make up 14 percent of licensed drivers, account for 28 percent of crashes (Lyman et al., 2002). Older drivers also kill fewer motorists and pedestrians than do younger drivers (Insurance Institute for Highway Safety, 2001). But despite these optimistic statistics, the fact that the average 70- to 74-year-old will be driving for another 11 years has policy makers looking for ways to make them safer behind the wheel (Foley et al., 2002). The following four approaches can help:

★ *Driver training.* The frequency of turning into the wrong lane and improper signaling is reduced when older drivers attend training classes that review safe driving practices with a driving simulator. Another approach is speed-of-processing training, a procedure in which drivers

Skilled drivers have a larger useful field of vision (shown on the top left), a greater area in which they can divide attention between multiple objects and successfully ignore distracting objects. Older drivers can expand their useful field of vision by performing a series of increasingly difficult visual tasks on a computer.

SOURCE: Courtesy of Daniel Roenker.

learn to detect information more rapidly by gradually decreasing the length of time critical information appears on a screen. Speed of processing training improves people's useful field of view, reduces dangerous on-the-road maneuvers (Roenker et al., 2003), and produces performance improvements that generalize to other tasks, such as finding directions on a medicine container and locating phone numbers in a directory (Edwards et al., 2005).

★ *"Smarter" cars.* In the future, new products may improve visibility at night, keep cars at a safer distance from one another, and warn drivers about possible collisions and intersections (McKnight, 2000/2001).

★ *Safer roads and signage.* Special lanes for left turns, larger fonts on traffic signs, and longer periods at intersections when lights in all directions are red help seniors navigate tricky situations.

★ *Senior transportation.* Innovative transportation programs are a lifesaver for seniors who need to put down their keys. For example, one program allows older adults to trade in their cars for "mileage credits" on a taxi-like service that will take them anywhere they need to go, including on dates or to do volunteer work (Insurance Institute for Highway Safety, 2001).

These initiatives delay the depression that often arrives when people lose their ability to drive. But sadly, many seniors live in communities that lack such programs. An example is Roy Leahy, an 81-year-old whose wife lives in a nursing home. Giving up his car key meant that he was dependent on friends for transportation and couldn't see her very often. As Leahy explained sadly, "I can't get out much less, unless I was in a coffin" (Shapiro, 1999, p. 61).

The Oldest Old

What will your life be like if you live to be 100? If you are lucky, you will be like Harold Stilson, Sr. This remarkable man drove to and from his golf club every day and to his daughter's house for dinner on Sunday evenings. He played golf every Monday, Wednesday, and Friday and practiced on Sundays. He also played pool, gin rummy, and got on the computer occasionally. Mr. Stilson was 101 years old when he shot his 6th hole in one, setting a record for the oldest known person to do so (National Public Radio, 2001)!

Harold Stilson was a **centenarian**, a person who has lived for a century or more. There were at least 50,000 centenarians in the United States in 2000, and this number is expected to double in 10 years, making this age group the fastest growing segment of the population (U.S. Census Bureau, 2000, 2003a).

Around the world, researchers are discovering some surprises about life after 100. If you consider the declines that occur while people are in their 80s, as described in Chapter 14, and then project ahead to what you think people should be like at 100, the picture is grim. But due to *survival selection*, people with serious health issues usually die well before their 100th birthday. As a result, many centenarians are clear-minded and active. In the New England Centenarian Study (Boston University School of Medicine, 2005), between one-quarter and one-third of the individuals studied did not show signs of Alzheimer's disease, and 90 percent were mostly independent until an average age of 92. Instead of enduring a lengthy period of disability, these robust survivors had a period of decline that was limited to the last few years of their lives. For example, Harold Stilson hit his record-breaking hole in one in May 2001 and died less than a year later after complications from a viral illness.

But despite the fact that some centenarians are mentally sharp, longevity does come at a cost. In an Italian sample, only 1 out of 5 centenarians was still in good health, and only 6 percent of these healthy adults were independent in all of the routine activities the study team evaluated (Motta et al., 2005). Similarly, the majority of the oldest old in a German sample had signs of dementia, and at least 83 percent were dependent on nursing care (Heidelberg Centenarian Study, 2005).

Adelaide Kruger, age 101, is part of the New England Centenarian Study—a study of people who have lived for 100 years or more. Here you see Adelaide tending her garden.

centenarian A person who has lived for a century or more.

Why do some people turn out like Harold Stilson while others suffer in poor health for years? Centenarians differ widely in their ethnic, educational, and religious backgrounds as well as their dietary habits (some are strictly vegetarian and some eat high-saturated-fat foods). Nevertheless, the oldest old tend to share the following characteristics (Boston University School of Medicine, 2005; Heidelberg Centenarian Study, 2005):

▶ **A genetic advantage.** There is little doubt that genes help some people live to blow out 100 candles. Eighty percent of centenarians are women, and more than half have family members who also reached very old age. In addition, the oldest old are much less likely than younger individuals to have a genetic profile associated with Alzheimer's disease.

▶ **A healthy lifestyle.** Very few centenarians have ever smoked (although Jeanne Calment smoked until she was 117!), and few are obese.

▶ **Psychological resilience.** The oldest old tend to handle stress well and have beliefs that promote well-being, such as extroverted personalities and a sense of self-efficacy.

You have a good chance of living to 100 if you have these characteristics—but would you want to? Most adults say "no," although they want to come pretty close (about 91 years, on average) (Takeuchi & Groeneman, 1999). Their main concerns are a fear of poor health and not having enough money to be self-sufficient, while other worries include losing mental abilities, being dependent on others, feeling alone, and living in a nursing home. Clearly, most adults want to preserve their quality of life more than they want to add a few extra years onto their lives. Read on for suggestions about how you can do just that.

Protecting Your Health

In the past, conditions like heart disease were thought to be due to aging itself, part of "nature's script for human beings" (Snowdon, 2001, p. 26). But that was before epidemiologists learned how rates of chronic conditions varied across places, occupations, and lifestyles. For example, London bus conductors who walked up and down bus aisles had lower rates of heart disease than bus drivers did, and people with office jobs who enjoyed vigorous exercise had fewer heart attacks than their colleagues who merely puttered in the yard to relax (Paffenberger, 2000). After subsequent studies explored the associations between lifestyles and health more systematically, scientists became convinced that you can improve your odds of aging well by making good choices and sticking to them throughout life.

DIET ("YOU ARE WHAT YOU EAT"). The longest-living people in the world (86 years old for women and 78 for men) live on the islands of Okinawa, Japan. This population has the lowest rates of stroke, heart disease, and cancer in the world, and lower rates of Alzheimer's disease than people from the United States and European countries. One of the striking features of their lifestyle is what they eat. Okinawans eat less salt, less fat, and take in fewer calories than the typical Westerner. They also eat nutrition-dense food, including lots of leafy green vegetables, seafood, and unrefined carbohydrates (Willcox, Willcox, & Suzuki, 2001).

But you don't have to eat seaweed to stay healthy. The most celebrated "longevity" diet is the so-called Mediterranean diet, a daily fare of fruits, vegetables, and nuts, with little saturated fat. The olive oil in this cuisine is a source of healthy monounsaturated fat, and fish provides omega-3 fatty acids that protect the cardiovascular system and brain. Seniors who combine this diet with physical activity, moderate alcohol use, and nonsmoking cut their risk of death from heart disease, cardiovascular disease, and cancer *in half* (Knoops et al., 2004).

It's never too late to start! Kozo Haraguchi took up running when he was 65 years old; 30 years later he set a world record for the 95–99 age group by finishing a 100-meter sprint in 22.04 seconds. Exercise keeps Kozo's muscles strong and stimulates the production of a brain chemical that helps the neurons in his brain stay healthy.

PHYSICAL AND MENTAL ACTIVITY ("USE IT OR LOSE IT").

Activities such as walking, jogging, dancing, and hiking increase heart and lung fitness, flexibility, and endurance. In fact, older people who get regular aerobic exercise are more fit than middle-aged people who are inactive. Exercise also cuts the risk of heart disease, high blood pressure, colon cancer, and diabetes, and it relieves some of the pain from arthritis (Rowe & Kahn, 1998). Adding strength training improves balance, which reduces falls and injuries. The benefits from weight-bearing exercise are noticeable after only a few months, even among very frail nursing home residents (Fiatarone, et al., 1990; Fiatarone et al., 1994).

Physical activity also reduces depression and improves cognitive function. Indeed, the simple act of walking several miles each day reduces the risk of developing dementia (Abbott et al., 2004). Exercise has the most effect on executive-control aspects of cognition, such as decision making, planning, and multitasking—the very skills that show the most age-related declines (Kramer & Willis, 2002). In addition to improving blood flow and reducing the risk of stroke, exercise helps our brains by increasing levels of *brain-derived neurotrophic factor*, a chemical that stimulates the formation of new neurons, promotes the formation of new connections, and keeps neurons healthy (Asdlard & Cotman, 2004; Cotman & Berchtold, 2002). It is no wonder that people who exercise have more positive emotions, say their lives are more meaningful, and have a longer life expectancy (d'Epinay & Bickel, 2003; Fukukawa et al., 2004; Kahana et al., 2002).

Mental activity is equally important. Older adults who enjoy board games, play musical instruments, or read more have a lower risk of developing Alzheimer's disease (Hultsch et al., 1999; Verghese et al., 2003; Wilson & Bennett, 2003), and active people who have already developed signs of the disease experience fewer cognitive problems than less active people with the same level of brain damage (Scarmeas & Stern, 2003).

EDUCATION ("BE COOL, STAY IN SCHOOL").

Education and a characteristic that grows with more education—intelligence—are associated with better physical and mental health. In a series of studies conducted in Scotland, for example, lower intelligence at age 11 was related to increased rates of alcoholism, smoking, obesity, cardiovascular disease, and cancer before age 76 (Gottfredson & Deary, 2004). On the flip side, higher intelligence is associated with physical fitness, better diets, and greater longevity (Deary et al., 2004).

One way education improves our lives is by giving us the skills to make informed choices. For instance, many people smoked during the first half of the 1990s, but people who were more intelligent were more likely to quit smoking after the health risks became known (Taylor et al., 2003). And once health problems arise, people with more education are better equipped to deal with them by effectively monitoring their conditions (Gottfredson & Deary, 2004). Education also promotes health by encouraging people to assume more stimulating jobs and leisure activities (Smyth et al., 2004). Finally, well-educated people may be better off simply because they begin their later years with a higher level of cognitive skill.

MANAGING STRESS ("DON'T WORRY, BE HAPPY").

When she was asked about the key to a long life, one Guinness record holder for longevity responded, "not to worry too much" (Guinness World Records, 2003). Scientists agree. Stress has long been associated with our biggest killers, including strokes and heart attacks. More recently, researchers have discovered that chronic stress actually speeds up aging of the DNA itself.

In Chapter 14 we discussed *telomeres*, the end pieces of chromosomes that become shorter each time a cell divides. Remember that older cells have shorter telomeres and fewer times left to replicate before their telomeres "run out." That is exactly what happens to women who spend years caring for children with severe disabilities. Compared to women of the same age who were not as stressed, the telomeres of their white blood cells are significantly shorter. In addition, the longer they have cared for a disabled child, the more their telomeres have shrunk. The good news is that women who feel more relaxed and in control have longer telomeres (Epel et al., 2004). Because your perception of stress is so important, techniques for managing stress, such as relaxation training and meditation, may help you age well.

Because the way we respond to stress is so important, personality also predicts health and well-being. In one sample, for example, cognitive decline was 30 percent faster among people who had a tendency to be negative (Wilson et al., 2005). Negativity could harm the body and brain directly (through the production of stress hormones) or indirectly (because people who feel more control over their lives are more likely to take positive steps to improve their health). Even our attitudes about aging make a difference (Levy & Myers, 2004). In one study, for example, some people showed negative views of aging when they were younger by endorsing statements such as "As you get older, you are less useful." On average, these individuals died 7.5 years earlier than those who viewed aging more positively. What is important is that these individuals formed these views of aging many years earlier, before they had fully experienced aging for themselves (Levy et al., 2002).

))) MEMORY MAKERS (((

Choose the correct term for each sentence:

1. Most diseases that trouble older adults are _____ diseases—diseases that develop slowly and are long-lasting.
   (a) infectious
   (b) acute
   (c) chronic

2. A condition that increases your chances of serious heart disease and diabetes is _____ (also called "Syndrome X").
   (a) metabolic syndrome
   (b) Alzheimer's disease
   (c) glaucoma

3. The most common cause of dementia is _____, a condition that causes plaques and tangles to form in the brain.
   (a) dementia with Lewy bodies
   (b) Alzheimer's disease
   (c) vascular dementia

4. These terms describe a philosophy of building homes and other structures to meet the needs of as many people as possible. (Select all that apply).
   (a) universal design
   (b) aging in place
   (c) assisted design

[1-c; 2-a; 3-b; 4-a and b]

With all of the ages and personalities that populate families, no two older adults have exactly the same roles and experiences. Throughout our lives, the only constant in family life is constant change.

Family Life after 50

We once exchanged birthing stories with a British woman who had her first child during her late 30s. With a good deal of laughter, she recalled how startled she was when a nurse referred to her as a "geriatric mother." Although the term suggested that our friend was a maternal oddball, "geriatric mothers" have never been uncommon. In the early 1900s, almost half of the women in one settlement had a child after age 40, as have many of our friends today (Greksa, 2002). The fathers of these children are no youngsters either. Men tend to marry women younger than themselves, and many remarry and start second families. As a result, a 45- or 55-year-old dad with an infant may be adorable, but he is not a news story.

People are in all stages of family life during middle and late adulthood. A gathering of three older sisters and their husbands might include a pair who is enjoying 14-year-old twin boys, a recently married couple who have grown children from their first marriages, and a third couple who are busy with two young grandchildren. And, of course, the number of single people grows during this time as divorce and deaths disrupt lives. During all of this adjusting and readjusting, many adults are caring for parents or ill partners, and many older adults are learning how to let others care for *them*. More than any other time of life, the 50 and older crowd has varied and interesting domestic lives.

Marriage and Divorce

Sometime after 50, most married couples face a series of adjustments as children leave home, one or both spouses retires, and health issues crop up. Each pair adjusts to these changes in different ways. Mr. Kenny, who was interviewed for a study of how couples adjust to retirement, described how his marriage got stronger over time. "I think we got a lot closer, me and Janet," he told the research team. "We just didn't have time for each other when we were running the business, doing 15 hours a day. . . [Now] we can go where we want, do what we want, and we find it very nice!" In contrast, Mrs. Sampson and her husband liked a lot more privacy. "We don't like to live in each other's pockets," she explained. "We do things together, and we go out a lot, you know, but it's nice to have our own space…I wouldn't get anything done if he was under my feet all day!" (Barnes & Parry, 2004, p. 225).

The Kennys and the Sampsons are part of the "married majority." As you can see in Figure 15.8, most people over 50 live with a spouse, although older men are more likely than older women to be married. This gender difference is largely due to a higher rate of widowhood for women, especially after 65.

Most newlyweds wonder how satisfied couples are after many years of marriage. Cross-sectional research shows one pattern: New couples are highly satisfied, satisfaction declines among those who have been living together for several years and reaches a low point for couples with teenagers, and then increases among couples whose children have left home (Glenn, 1995). But cross-sectional comparisons may find that young couples and those with lengthy marriages are more satisfied simply because fewer people in these groups are on the brink of divorce. When the *same* couples are followed over time in longitudinal samples, research finds that marital satisfaction declines sharply during the first 10 years, and then the decline slows and is very gradual thereafter (Glenn, 1998; Kupperbusch, 2003; Vaillant & Vaillant, 1993).

But "decline" does not mean "unhappy." Indeed, most older adults say their marriages are happy or very happy (Huyck, 1996; Lauer, Lauer, & Kerr, 1990), and most long-term marriages (more than 45 years) either show a stable level of satisfaction or an up-and-down pattern rather than continual decline (Weishaus & Field, 1988). When one team compared middle-aged couples (married at least 15 years) and older couples (married at least 35 years), they found that the marriage "veterans" disagreed less than middle-aged couples about money, religion, recreation, and children, and these long-term partners got more enjoyment than younger couples did from talking about children and activities they had recently shared (Levenson, Carstensen, & Gottman, 1993).

Research on long-term couples tells us a lot about what it takes to stay married for 35 years, 50 years, or longer. Long-time spouses tend to agree on family finances, life goals, religion, sexual relations, career decisions, and more. When asked what they think makes marriages last, husbands and wives give very similar answers: Both like their spouses as people and consider them their best friends, think it is important to agree on goals, are committed to marriage, and have a sense of humor. More than 70 percent of happy, longtime couples say that they kiss every day, laugh together at least once a day, and confide in their spouse most or all the time (Lauer et al., 1990).

Most couples who stay together long enough eventually face the need to readjust their routines after retirement. As Mrs. Sampson's comment suggests, retirement strains some marriages—at least for a while. Spouses who were career oriented may feel restless when they start spending so much free time at home, and those who ran the household feel annoyed when a retired spouse interferes with established routines (Barnes & Parry, 2004). Over time, though, most couples adjust well to retirement, and retired couples are more satisfied in the long run than couples who have a spouse still working (Kim & Moen, 2001; Pruchno & Rosenbaum, 2003).

Of course, not all late-life marriages are happy. Although the divorce rate declines after a peak during our 30s and 40s, over 5 percent of divorces occur among 55- to 64-year-olds (Kreider, 2005). Furthermore, the number of post-50

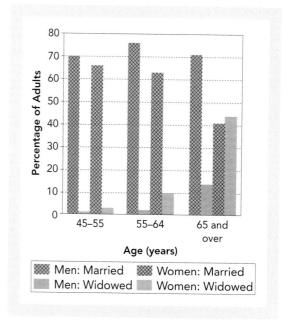

FIGURE 15.8 The marital gender gap.

Older men are more likely than women to be living with a married partner, especially after 65 years of age. Many older women build satisfying social networks around other family members and friends.

SOURCE: Fields (2004).

divorces may be on the rise, possibly because the current generation views divorce as more acceptable than their parents did. Another factor is the increasing life expectancy. As one man who divorced after 38 years of marriage explained, "I am sure that people 50 years ago who wanted to get divorced at the age I was just stuck it out... They probably weren't going to live much longer, were they?" (Kuczynski, 2004, para. 10). Today, even 70-year-olds realize they may have many years left to live, so many are unwilling to spend them in an unhappy relationship.

Divorce in later life can be liberating or colored by financial strain, loneliness, and depression. Older women are more likely than those who divorced earlier to have low incomes, and they are less likely to live in their own home (Davies & Denton, 2002). Men and women alike often have difficulty forming new relationships, although this problem is especially acute for heterosexual women who outnumber eligible men (partly because there are fewer men than women in upper age brackets, but also because older men are more likely than older women to choose a younger partner). And no matter when a divorce occurs, the pain can affect the entire family. As one marriage counselor explained, "Even adult children need a home to go to" (Kuczynski, 2004, p. 1).

Losing a Spouse

Although late-life divorces do occur, it is more common for elderly adults to become single due to the death of a spouse. As shown in Figure 15.8, the chances of becoming a widow or widower increase dramatically by 60 to 65 years of age, particularly for women. Losing a spouse is extremely stressful, even when it is expected. The survivor must deal with the tremendous loss of social and emotional support, often some loss of financial support, and help with everyday household tasks and decisions. It is not surprising, then, that widowed people are more likely to be depressed, lonely, and less satisfied with life—even years after their spouse's death (Pruchno & Rosenbaum, 2003). But people are resilient throughout life, so those who lose a spouse generally become less depressed and more social after an initially difficult time (Wilcox et al., 2003).

Men and women report somewhat different challenges from widowhood. Because losing a spouse's earnings tends to leave women in worse financial shape than men, financial stress is a common source of anxiety for new widows. In contrast, men tend to be the group that is more affected emotionally. Men's life satisfaction declines more after a spouse dies and they suffer more from depression than women (Chipperfield & Havens, 2001; G. R. Lee et al., 2001). This is partly because married men are happier than married women to begin with (so they have more to lose). But it is also the case that widowed women often have larger social networks to turn to for comfort and company, whereas widowed men sometimes lose their only close friend when they lose their spouse.

Sexuality in Later Life

If you think older people lose interest in sex, pick up a book by the Kensington Ladies' Erotica Society. The society began in the 1970s, when a librarian at the University of California, Berkeley, gathered a group of women at a party and started a reading group. Soon they were penning and publishing their own erotic stories. Most of the women, who were in their 40s at the start of the club, were still kicking—and writing—30 years later. In 2002 they unveiled *Sex, Death, & Other Distractions*, a book one member of the club called a "bridge between the ridiculous unrealistic romanticism of our mothers and this generation" (Ganahl, 2002, para. 29).

From literary matrons to wrinkled couples holding hands in the park, older adults are sending a loud message: "We are sensual (and sexual, thank you very much)." In the following ways, our sex lives during middle and late adulthood are influenced by the biology of aging, our attitudes about sex, our health, and our cultures:

▶ *Sexual activity and interest gradually wane (but not as much as you might predict).* It is natural for sexual interest to decline with age due to the normal bodily changes you read about in Chapter 12. Our drive for sexual release decreases as androgen levels ("male" sex hormones, including testosterone) decrease, causing us to become slower to respond to stimulation. We require more direct stimulation to stay aroused as we come to the end of our reproductive lives, and we have shorter and less intense orgasms. After menopause, some women also experience discomfort during intercourse due to vaginal dryness, which is a problem that can be remedied by using a lubricant.

Older couples who clearly enjoy life and each other are a reminder that people crave companionship and closeness throughout their lives.

But older adults are still sexy creatures. In the famous *Sex in America* survey that we mentioned in Chapter 13, men in their 50s said they were almost as sexually active as men who were a decade younger: 66 percent of the older group were having sex a few times a month or more, compared to 73 percent of the 40- to 49-year-olds. Women's sex lives slowed more over time, which is to be expected. (After all, women tend to marry men older than themselves and are more likely to be widowed.) Still, 49 percent of the 50- to 59-year-olds were having sex a few times a month or more, compared to 69 percent of women in their 40s. A better index of sexual desire is the frequency of masturbation, because this behavior measures interest rather than opportunity. There is a noticeable decline in this activity during the mid to late 50s, showing that sexual urgency starts to diminish later in life (Michael et al., 1994).

▶ *Older men express more interest in sex than older women do.* During every decade of life, men focus on sex more than women. In the AARP survey reported in Table 15.3, for example, 35 percent of men in the oldest age group (aged 75 and older) said

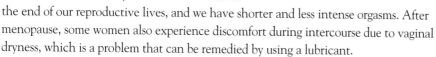

TABLE 15.3 Senior Sex

Item	Percentage "Yes" (Men / Women)		
	45–59 YEARS	60–74 YEARS	75 YEARS +
Sexual activity is important to my overall quality of life (strongly agree or agree).	71/48	51/25	35/13
I would be happy never having sex again.	1/9	5/28	5/36
Never feel sexual desire.	2/7	6/35	17/60
Sexual touching occurs at least once a week.	69/61	61/37	45/15
Kiss or hug occurs at least once a week.	77/72	73/49	63/28
Intercourse occurs at least once a week.	55/50	31/24	19/7

SOURCE: NFO Research, Inc. (1999).

that sexual activity was important to their overall quality of life compared to only 13 percent of women, and 7 times as many women as men said they "would be happy never having sex again." Still, these senior citizens were far from sexless: 83 percent of men aged 75 and older still felt sexual desire, as did 40 percent of the women.

▶ *The frequency of sexual union during late adulthood is largely a matter of having a willing partner, prior interest in sex, and a healthy body.* Older adults who have a potential sexual partner (which is usually a spouse) report higher levels of sexual desire than their peers (DeLamater & Sill, 2005). Thus some adults—especially women, who are more likely to be widowed—think about sex less often than they used to simply because there is no one stirring up their thoughts.

But opportunity is not the entire story. People who stay sexually active tend to have been more sexually active when they were younger (Avis et al., 2000), and these people have more positive attitudes about sex, more sexual knowledge, and better overall psychological well-being (Zeiss & Kasl-Godley, 2001). Perhaps this is why the phrase "use it or lose it" is most often spoken about sex. Health also matters (Avis et al., 2000). Many conditions, including depression, diabetes, hypertension, and stroke, decrease the sex drive and, in men, contribute to impotence (Lau et al., 2005). As important as health is, though, people attitudes about sex and the availability of a partner are stronger predictors of sexual desire than the number of illnesses they have been diagnosed with or the number of medications they take (DeLamater & Sill, 2005).

▶ *Older people still value cuddles and other expressions of intimacy.* Many seniors say that kisses, hugs, and sexual touching have replaced passionate sex as a way of expressing love and feeling connected. In the AARP survey, many people enjoyed sexual touching at least once a week even though they did not have frequent intercourse.

▶ *Social attitudes about the elderly can interfere with sexual expression.* Many younger people view sex in old age as funny, disgusting, or nonexistent. As a result, older couples may be embarrassed to discuss sexual issues with their doctors, and doctors sometimes brush off their shy descriptions of sexual problems as normal consequences of aging. In nursing homes, workers sometimes react with disgust when they discover residents engaging in sexual activity, and even married couples can have difficulty being sexual if they are housed in separate facilities or have little privacy (Kessel, 2001).

There is evidence that the current generation is less likely than their parents were to accept declines in sexual performance. Today, drugs like Viagra (to help men with erection problems) and hormone supplements (to help women feel younger and to increase sex drive) are part of a booming industry to purchase youth. However, recent evidence is questioning the idea that pills can safely slow aging. For a closer look at this issue, turn to our *Innovations* feature, "Is the Fountain of Youth Filled with Hormones?"

INNOVATIONS

Hormone replacement therapy has helped millions of women find relief from menopausal symptoms. However, women and their doctors must weigh the benefits of hormone treatment against the risks of long-term side effects, which include higher rates of heart attacks and strokes.

IS THE FOUNTAIN OF YOUTH FILLED WITH HORMONES?

In a former British colony, most healers believed the conventional wisdom that a distillation of fluids extracted from the urine of horses, if dried to a powder and fed to aging women, could act as a general tonic, preserve youth, and ward off a variety of diseases. The preparation became enormously popular throughout the culture and was used widely by older women in all strata of society. Many years later modern scientific studies revealed that long-term ingestion of the horse-urine extract was useless for most of its intended purposes, and that it caused tumors, blood clots, heart disease, and perhaps brain damage (Avorn, 2004, p. 23).

Did you guess the former colony, the time, and the medicine? They are (a) the United States, (b) today, and (c) estrogen products such as Premarin (whose name comes from "pregnant" "mares'" "urine"). Why was estrogen replacement so widely used, and why is it now considered dangerous for longtime use?

Scientists have long known that some uncomfortable symptoms of menopause, such as hot flashes, insomnia, and vaginal dryness, were caused by a reduction in estrogen levels. Later they discovered that pregnant mares could mass-produce estrogen, which could be converted into pill form. Then, in 1966, a gynecologist named Robert Wilson suggested that long-term hormone replacement therapy (HRT) might prevent the "personality" problems and loss of sex appeal that are associated with menopause. In Wilson's words, "Every woman has the right—indeed, the duty—to counteract the chemical castration that befalls her during her middle years" (Avorn, 2004, p. 25).

Although the Federal Drug Administration never approved long-term HRT, most women and their doctors came to believe that it had antiaging properties. In studies that compared HRT users with nonusers, HRT users had lower rates of heart disease, Alzheimer's disease, depression, and bone loss (osteoporosis). Prescriptions for HRT soared, and by 2002 at least 13 million women in the United States were on HRT (Avorn, 2004; Cowley & Springen, 2002).

As with most medications, HRT came with some problems. It was known that women who chose HRT had an increased risk of uterine and breast cancer, so those who were already at risk for these diseases were advised against HRT. However, heart disease kills far more women than uterine or breast cancer, so HRT still seemed well worth the risks. Then came even worse news. A study funded by the maker of Premarin found that women taking supplementary estrogen had significantly more heart attacks, blood clots, and gallbladder disease than women taking placebos. But what about women who didn't have heart disease to begin with? Would they benefit from taking estrogen or estrogen plus progestin?

The public had an answer in 2002—a resounding "No." In fact, women taking HRT were more likely than other women to have heart attacks, strokes, blood clots, and breast cancer. A year later, research showed that women over 65 who were taking HRT developed dementia at *double the rate* of those taking placebos (Avorn, 2004; Shumaker et al., 2003; Yaffe, 2003).

How could the medical profession have been so wrong? Studies that supported HRT were correlational studies; the discouraging results came from controlled experiments (Bromley et al., 2005; Marriott & Wenk, 2004). Remember that people are not randomly assigned to treatment and control groups in correlational research, so we don't know when differences between groups are due to the treatment versus other factors. As it turned out, women who chose to use HRT for many years were better educated, wealthier, and had better access to health care than other women. These women not only stuck with HRT, but they also stuck with other health regimens (diet, physical activity, not smoking) that lowered their risk of chronic disease. It was only when similar women were randomly given HRT or placebos that the risks of HRT became clear.

But HRT is not going to be shelved any time soon. It is effective for easing menopausal symptoms, which in a minority of women are severe. And timing matters. Estrogen may improve cognitive functions during and just after menopause even though it impairs functions when taken over long periods (Dunkin et al., 2005; Marriott & Wenk, 2004). Therefore, the American Medical Association currently endorses HRT for temporary (less than 5 years) treatment of menopausal symptoms (Yaffe, 2003).

All this controversy has left millions of women wondering whether they should start—or discontinue—HRT. Meanwhile, TRT (testosterone replacement therapy) is on the rise among men to improve sex drive, mood, and energy levels. Will TRT turn out to be a fountain of youth or only another promise that increases the risk of cancer and heart disease? Only future experiments will tell.

Relations among the Generations

Deb burst into tears in front of a class the week her daughter left for college. Clipped to a microphone and standing in front of 150 students, she tried to repair the embarrassing situation by mumbling, "Go home and call your mother . . . you have no idea how much your mother loves you."

This high-strung professor would never have cried if she knew that her children were not going to disappear from her life just because they had left home. Years later, they are keeping her as busy as ever, and their partners and little ones are expanding the size of her family. Like many adults, this one has slipped happily into the warmth of family life after 50.

PARENTS AND THEIR ADULT CHILDREN. Most older parents and their adult children feel the way Deb and her children do: They have a positive relationship, want to live near one another (but not in the same household), and stay in close contact even when they live far apart. Older parents generally are satisfied with their role as parents and feel good about how their children have turned out, while adult children generally feel loved and supported by their parents (Pruchno & Rosenbaum, 2003; Umberson, 1992).

Older parents and children are often involved in extensive "exchange" networks, providing different kinds of resources and support to one another. Although we usually hear about adult children taking care of their aging parents, research shows that as long as they are healthy enough, older adults are more likely to give help than to get help. For example, when older people and their young adult children live together, it is usually in the parents' home and often because of the grown child's needs (Pruchno & Rosenbaum, 2003).

Relationships with their adult children face new challenges when parents' health starts to fail. Older adults want to remain independent but hope that their children will help if needed—because the children want to, not because they have to. Although parents appreciate their children's concern, older parents don't want to feel controlled, overprotected, or babied. In fact, some parents are so ambivalent about their children's help that they deliberately minimize or even hide evidence of problems (Spitze & Gallant, 2004).

But whether out of duty or love, adult children frequently do help aging parents. Unmarried children are more likely than those who are coupled to help (Laditka & Laditka, 2001), and daughters are far more likely to help than are sons (especially in terms of "hands-on" domestic care, such as housecleaning, chores, and meal preparation). Both sons and daughters tend to help with finances, paperwork (such as filling out insurance forms), and providing emotional support (Pruchno & Rosenbaum, 2003; Starrels et al., 1995).

In the past, African American families were described as especially close and likely to offer assistance to family members, and this is somewhat true. For example, African American adults describe stronger emotional ties to their mothers than white adults do, and African American daughters spend more time assisting parents. But differences are small and depend on people's circumstances. One study found that African American daughters who were part of a couple helped more than other coupled daughters, but there was no ethnic difference among single daughters. Furthermore, African American sons were less likely than white sons to help their parents, regardless of whether they had a partner or not (Laditka & Laditka, 2001). You will read more about family assistance later in this chapter when we explore the lives of people who are taking care of ill spouses or parents.

It's hard to tell who enjoys a day at the library more, Grandpa or his special girl. Around the world, it is common for grandparents to be highly involved in children's lives.

GRANDPARENTING. When you think about grandparents, do you think about gray-haired women in rocking chairs or bald men talking endlessly about the "good old days"? These stereotypes are changing as baby boomers are becoming grandparents at a record pace (Hayslip, Henderson, & Shore, 2003). Today, the average age of first-time grandparents is around 50—definitely not old by today's standards (AARP, 2002b)—and one-third of all grandparents are under 55 (Mills, Wakeman, & Fea, 2001). As a group, today's grandparents are healthier and more active than their forerunners, and they have fewer grandchildren, higher incomes, and more education (Hayslip et al., 2003).

What this often means is that grandparents are very much involved in their grandchildren's lives. More than two-thirds say they are "extremely close" with their grandchildren, and 80 percent say that the grandparent role is extremely important to their sense of self (Silverstein & Marenco, 2001). About two-thirds of grandparents talk with a grandchild at least once a week, and 78 percent have seen a grandchild in the past month. Many grandparents also help out financially. More than half of those surveyed by the AARP (2002b) said that they helped pay for their grandchildren's education, and 45 percent helped with living expenses. Grandparents provide even more assistance in cultures such as rural China, where grandmothers often assume domestic chores so younger women can work outside the home (Chen, 2003). But even in industrialized societies, grandparents are important resources for their families.

Many factors influence whether grandparents are highly involved, warm but only somewhat involved, or part of the 28 percent of grandparents who are emotionally detached. Grandparents who are supportive tend to be more educated, live closer to their grandchildren, and have fewer grandchildren, whereas detached grandparents tend to be on the father's side of the family, live farther away, and have more grandchildren (Mueller, Wilhelm, & Elder, 2002).

The ultimate level of involvement is when grandparents live with their grandchildren. In the last U.S. census, 5.8 million grandparents were living with at least one grandchild, and 42 percent of these "co-resident" grandparents had primary responsibility for their grandchildren. The frequency of these multigenerational arrangements differs across ethnic groups. African American, Native American, Asian, and Hispanic households are more likely than white households to include a grandparent, but minority families are not all alike. Only 20 percent of Asian grandparents who live with their grandchildren have primary responsibility for their care, compared to 35 percent of Hispanic co-resident grandparents and over half of African American and Native American co-resident

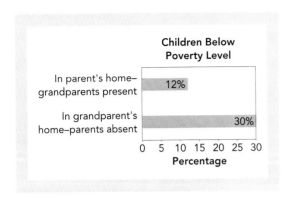

FIGURE 15.9 Life with Grandma and Grandpa.

In the United States, children who are being raised solely by their grandparents are more than twice as likely as children who reside with parents *and* grandparents to live in poverty. Many grandparents who assume responsibility for their grandchildren struggle with their own health issues as well as the special needs of their grandchildren, who sometimes relocated as a result of parental drug use or neglect.

SOURCE: Fields (2003).

grandparents (Simmons & Dye, 2003). In other words, Asian and Hispanic grandparents are more likely to be getting help from their children's families than providing help.

Many grandparents act as safety nets in the midst of troubled communities and families. In one study, over 40 percent of grandparents who had assumed responsibility for their grandchildren did so because the children's mothers were drug users or had neglected their children (Goodman et al., 2004). Many of these grandparents struggle to provide the care their grandchildren need. As Figure 15.9 shows, 30 percent of children in grandparent care are living in poverty (Fields, 2003), and their grandparents are often contending with their own health problems and strained relationships with absent children (the parents of the grandchildren they are rearing). In addition, many are coping with their grandchildren's emotional, intellectual, or physical disabilities (that stem from their parents' neglect, drug use, or physical abuse), and some face legal/custody issues, including problems arranging medical care for uninsured children. As one step-grandfather lamented, "I'm making more money now than ever before in my life. And I'm scraping. . . We went through long periods of time where Tommy wasn't covered on our insurance and so you take him to the doctor anyway, you know. A kid has an earache; a kid has an earache. You don't sit there and look at your checkbook balance and decide how bad his earache is" (Waldrop & Weber, 2001, p. 467).

A small number of grandparents become isolated from their families when they are denied visits after their children die or divorce. Many heartbroken grandparents endorse the *grandparents' rights movement*, a movement seeking legislation that allows grandparents to sue for visitation. The most visible case involved Jenifer and Gary Troxel, the grandparents of two girls whose father had committed suicide. These determined grandparents asked their state to award them two overnight visits per month and 2 weeks' visitation in the summer. After receiving half that much, the mother of the girls protested, claiming it was inappropriate to award overnight visits with children who were only 3-years-old and 18-months-old at the time. Also, the ruling contrasted sharply with the established belief that parents should have the ultimate say in how their children are raised. In 2000, the U.S. Supreme Court agreed with the mother, although the justices could not agree on the principle that guided their judgments (Newman, 2003/2004). Today, statutes do exist that allow grandparents in some states to appeal to the courts for visitation under some circumstances, and the issue of grandparents' "rights" remarks controversial.

Caregiving

You've seen that older adults are usually actively involved with their families and often provide assistance to their adult children and grandchildren. As the older population grows, an increasing number of middle-aged and older adults are also helping their families by taking care of disabled spouses and parents. Many care recipients have Alzheimer's disease or other conditions that require caregivers to make rather drastic changes to their lives. There are losses and rewards in this transition, as illustrated by Anne Simpson's remarks about caring for her husband, Bob (Simpson & Simpson, 1999):

> The process of watching my beloved husband deteriorate is painful, lonely, and immensely sad. I cannot deny it; I have spells of depression and self-pity. I have days when I am so frustrated that I go into the garage and sit in the car with all the windows rolled up, so I can scream without being overheard. (p. 154)

Our life seems perfectly normal until I talk to friends who are making independent plans to travel, attend workshops, visit grandchildren, or serve on boards and committees. I know that I did those things, too, once upon a short time ago, but I cannot imagine such freedom now. (p. 153)

The job of caring for a sick or frail relative takes a toll on caregivers' mental and physical health. Caregivers are often depressed and anxious, so they take more medications for psychological problems than their peers (Schulz et al., 1995; Wisniewski et al., 2003). As mentioned earlier, the stress of caregiving also compromises immune system function, increasing the chances of health problems and leading to increased mortality (Kiecolt-Glaser & Glaser, 2001; Schulz & Beach, 1999; Vitaliano, Young, & Zhang, 2004). But people's expectations about family issues influence how they react. On average, African American caregivers report less depression and feel less burdened by caregiving responsibilities than do white or Hispanic caregivers (Connell & Gibson, 1997), perhaps because they expect to frequently lend assistance to family members.

Programs that offer information and emotional support for caregivers produce only small to modest benefits, probably because they cannot significantly change the sacrifices that accompany caregiving or the tragedy of watching a loved one deteriorate. However, caregivers do benefit from learning behavior modification techniques, such as granting requests only when care recipients ask appropriately, so they will not unintentionally reinforce patients for being aggressive, making loud sounds repeatedly, or other annoying behaviors (Gitlin et al., 2003). Also, the information and emotional support that programs provide can reduce depression and improve people's general sense of well-being (Schulz et al., 2002).

>>> MEMORY MAKERS <<<

1. Which statement best describes the trend in marital satisfaction when couples are studied over time?
   (a) Marital satisfaction increases for the first three years of marriage and then remains rather stable over time.
   (b) Marital satisfaction decreases sharply for the first year and then stabilizes.
   (c) Marital satisfaction stays largely constant after the first year of marriage.
   (d) Marital satisfaction declines sharply during the first 10 years and then very gradually thereafter.

2. Which of the following is NOT one of the three major factors associated with having an active sex life during later adulthood?
   (a) having a willing partner
   (b) prior interest in sex
   (c) good health
   (d) early age of menopause for the female of the couple

3. Today, the average age of first-time grandparents is about_____.
   (a) 45
   (b) 50
   (c) 65
   (d) 70

[1-d; 2-d; 3-b]

Work and Retirement

Our friend Melanie is a remarkable woman. Soon after losing her husband and undergoing treatment for cancer, she discovered that her job would end in a few years. Because she was already in her 50s, we assumed that Melanie would look for an easygoing job to tic-off the years before retirement. We were wrong. Although she could find a job like the one she had had for most of her career, this choice was not challenging enough for her. "You know how it is," she told us matter-of-factly. "I've been there, done that." And instead of feeling discouraged from all of her troubles, Melanie was shopping for clothes, meeting new people, and attending conferences to broaden her knowledge.

Around the world, industrialized countries are experiencing a "graying of the workforce" as the number of older adults increases and more of these people (especially women) are working (Henretta, 2001; Yearta & Warr, 1995). In the United States, almost 20 million people ages 55 years and older are working now, making up almost 16 percent of the workforce (U.S. Department of Labor, Bureau of Labor Statistics, 2005). More than ever, researchers who study aging are interested in older people's attitudes about work, the quality of their performance, and how they decide when to retire.

Work Satisfaction and Performance

As Melanie's situation reminds us, older adults generally enjoy working. In fact, more than four-fifths of workers ages 45 to 74 say they would keep working even if they were financially secure. About a third of these people say they would keep their current jobs, whereas a quarter say they would prefer to work part-time (AARP, 2002a).

Research has found several average differences between older and younger workers:

▶ **Commitment and motivation.** Older workers are more satisfied with, more committed to, and more motivated about their jobs and organizations than younger workers are.

▶ **Work ethics.** Older workers also tend to have better *work ethics* than younger workers—that is, beliefs that are important for being a good employee, such as the desire to be on time, to work hard, and to respect others in the workplace. Some of the age difference in commitment, motivation, and work ethics probably reflects generational values, because older workers grew up in times when loyalty between organizations and employees was valued more than it is now. But another factor is *job tenure* (length of time at a job): People who have been in their jobs longer happen to be older, and these workers may have been more motivated and satisfied with their jobs to begin with (Beehr & Bowling, 2002). In contrast, many younger workers are still looking for jobs that are the best match for their interests and values (Ostroff, Shin, & Feinberg, 2002).

▶ **Job turnover.** Older workers are less likely than younger workers to leave jobs voluntarily, perhaps because they are more satisfied with their jobs or perhaps because they anticipate difficulty finding new jobs. They are also less likely than younger workers to be absent from work by choice (although they are more likely to be absent due to illness or family problems).

▶ **Accidents.** Finally, older workers have fewer accidents on the job, possibly because of their greater job experience, but perhaps because their jobs are less

Regardless of whether they are meeting in a conference room or at a construction site, today's work teams often include a mix of young and older adults.

physically demanding and dangerous. But the job-related accidents that older people have are generally more serious and cause them to miss work for longer periods of time (Beehr & Bowling, 2002).

Bosses appreciate older workers' motivation, but how do these workers actually perform? As we saw in Chapter 14, many sensory and cognitive skills decline with age, including vision and hearing, working memory, reaction time, and fluid intelligence. Because cognitive ability is one of the best predictors of job performance, it would make sense if age-related declines translated into worse job performance. Surprisingly, it does not: Numerous studies have found virtually no differences in performance between older and younger workers (Beehr & Bowling, 2002; Salthouse & Maurer, 1996).

There are many reasons why older workers continue to perform well despite some cognitive and physical declines. One is that the changes you read about in Chapter 14 often do not become obvious until many workers are ready to retire. Another is that older and younger workers often perform different jobs, with workers selecting into jobs that fit their abilities (Warr, 1994). It is also the case that some older workers have been promoted into more challenging jobs that call on their expertise, which may help them stay sharp (Staff et al., 2004). Finally, as discussed in Chapter 14, older workers have greater knowledge and experience that help offset declines in basic physical and cognitive skills (Warr, 1994). For example, older workers can solve many problems by remembering how they solved similar problems in the past (thereby making use of their crystallized intelligence) whereas younger workers more often have to work out new solutions (thereby relying on fluid intelligence) (Salthouse & Maurer, 1996).

In sum, older and younger workers have different jobs and may do them in different ways. As people age and skills change, many workers move into different jobs that fit with their strengths and weaknesses or find different ways of doing their jobs to use their talents and avoid their weaknesses.

Developing Skills

One way older workers maintain their ability to compete with younger workers is through training. Unfortunately, though, older workers do not participate in training and development activities as much as their younger colleagues do. There are many reasons for this state of affairs. In some cases older workers don't see the value of the information being offered to them, but other times employers do not encourage them to attend training because they believe these workers are less likely than younger employees to catch on to new ideas (Maurer, Weiss, & Barbeite, 2003; Salthouse & Maurer, 1996; Wrenn & Maurer, 2004). Finally, older workers sometimes lack confidence in their ability to learn. Indeed, one research team discovered that how workers *feel* about their age—not age *per se*—predicts their involvement in training. That is, people who feel older than their coworkers may mistakenly believe that they lack the potential to acquire new skills (Cleveland & Shore, 1992).

When older workers do receive training, how much do they learn from it? In general, older employees learn new skills as well as younger people, although training often takes somewhat longer and may need to be adapted for older learners. For examples of adaptations, turn to our *Solutions* feature, "Aging and Technology: Surfing Seniors."

Seniors are more likely to use technology when they have appropriate training and electronic devices are designed with their needs in mind. For example, recommendations for making Web sites "senior friendly" help everyone—regardless of age—surf the Web without frustration.

AGING AND TECHNOLOGY: SURFING SENIORS

On a typical day, many of us use computers at work, then come home and sign on to the Internet to pay bills, track our finances, get news and information online, and stay in touch with our friends and family members. How are older adults faring in this technology revolution?

A common stereotype is that older people are resistant to "newfangled" devices. But this is not always the case. Recently, the largest increases in computer and Internet appliance purchases have been among people over 55 years, and one-half of older Internet subscribers surf the Net every day (Kaiser Family Foundations, 2005). The Internet is a welcomed addition to their lives, a place where older adults find useful health information, order clothing, and reduce feelings of isolation through e-mail and other communication features. Moreover, older adults who don't use computers typically say that they would if they had training (Morrell, Mayhorn, & Bennett, 2000).

Unfortunately, skills training is not always suited for the older mind. Seniors (and most people!) learn faster and retain more information when instructions are simple and concrete, but many instructors present extraneous information that makes learning more difficult. For example, talking about how a piece of equipment was invented can distract older people and make it harder for them to think about the task at hand (Morrell, Park, et al., 2000). Older individuals also learn better when training includes illustrations and practice opportunities. Finally, it may be best to train different age groups separately. Seniors sometimes get frustrated when younger people are "getting it" faster than they are, and younger people feel bored by slow-paced instruction. In general, though, older adults do just as well as younger people once they have learned how to use technology (Rogers, Campbell, & Pak, 2001).

Another way to increase computer use is to develop more senior-friendly equipment, software, and Web sites. For example, using a mouse for long periods is challenging for people who have stiff joints, and reading the screen can be difficult if the font is too small or lacks contrast. When searching the Web, older people find it harder to keep track of where they are and to remember previously visited links. With research on physical and cognitive aging in mind, the National Institute on Aging and the National Library of Medicine (2001) developed a checklist for "Making Your Web Site Senior Friendly," including the commonsense suggestions for font sizes, colors, and backgrounds that are listed in Table 15.4. As technology developers become more aware of older adults' needs and desires, we should see even more people "surfing" into the information age (Spiezle & Moulton, 2001).

The look of concentration on this couple illustrates two findings: Older adults sometimes require more effort than younger adults to master computer tasks, but they are highly motivated to learn.

TABLE 15.4 Senior Friendly Web Sites

Feature	Use	Avoid
Printed material	Helvetica or Arial font, upper and lower case, in at least 12 to 14 font.	Times New Roman or novelty fonts; fonts that are less than 12 point, all caps, or printed in pale colors.
Spacing	Double space.	Single space.
Color	Red, yellow, and orange.	Blue, green, and yellow close together.
Background	Dark with white letters or light with dark letters.	Patterned backgrounds.
Organization	More short sections.	A few long sections.
Pictures	Text-relevant only.	Many unnecessary pictures.
Buttons and mouse clicks	Large buttons; single clicks.	Small buttons that require precise mouse aiming; double clicks.
Menus	Few pull down.	Many pull down.

SOURCE: National Institute on Aging and the National Library of Medicine (2001).

Age Bias and Discrimination

All of the research we have reviewed so far shows that older workers often perform as well as younger workers do. But supervisors and organizations may not think so. Supervisors perceive older workers as less qualified, slower, less productive, less motivated, less efficient, less creative, less flexible, more resistant to change, and more accident-prone and likely to be ill (Bird & Fisher, 1986; Finkelstein, Burke, & Raju, 1995). It is not just young supervisors who have these biases. Older managers actually evaluate older workers' performance lower than younger managers do, perhaps because stereotypes about the elderly were more negative when older managers were working their way up the ranks (Shore, Cleveland, & Goldberg, 2003).

Negative stereotypes about the elderly can lead to **age discrimination**, a situation that occurs when competent, qualified older workers are not hired or promoted, are fired or forced to retire, or are not given development opportunities solely because of their ages. In the United States, the Age Discrimination in Employment Act (ADEA) protects people over age 40 against discrimination in hiring, firing, wages, and benefits (Henretta, 2001), yet human resource managers report that age discrimination is fairly common (Yearta & Warr, 1995).

Most ADEA lawsuits are filed by former employees who feel they were unfairly terminated. For example, in a typical case filed after a 51-year-old was replaced with a younger employee, company memos documented that they planned to "thin the ranks" of older sales people, claiming the company "needed racehorses, not plow horses" (*Palasota v. Haggar Clothing Co.*, 342 F.3d 569, 5th Cir., 2003). Failures to hire older applicants are also common (Yearta & Warr, 1995), but people are less likely to sue over hiring decisions because it is difficult to prove that age was the reason (Issacharoff & Harris, 1997).

Despite legal protection, older workers are somewhat more likely than younger workers to be "displaced," that is, to lose their jobs due to downsizing, plant closings, and reorganizations, and they have more difficulty finding new

age discrimination Differential treatment of competent older workers solely because of their age. Age discrimination occurs when qualified older workers are not hired or not promoted or when they are fired, forced to retire, or not given development opportunities because of their age.

"Have you given much thought to what kind of job you want after you retire?"

jobs (Hipple, 1999). Older employees are often the ones chosen to leave because they typically have higher salaries and are viewed as less likely to keep up with new technologies (Puri, 2003). Many laid-off workers over 65 retire, but middle-aged workers usually don't have enough benefits or eligibility for Social Security. Many of these workers spend a long time without work, and they usually make less money if they do find new jobs. Losing a job can be devastating—economically and personally. But as you'll read next, transitions out of the workforce can be welcomed events for individuals who choose to retire.

Retirement

Many of us will do paid work for 50 years, which is more than three-fourths of our adulthood. How do we transition out of the biggest portion of our lives?

Although mandatory (forced) retirement was abolished in the United States in 1986 (except for some public safety jobs such as police officers, firefighters, and airline pilots), an increasing number of people are choosing to retire early, making retirement increasingly a midlife event. At the same time, changes to Social Security (increasing the age of eligibility for full benefits) and organizational benefit plans (reducing pensions and health benefits) are encouraging others to work longer. As a result, retirement has become more of an individualized experience instead of a mandatory rite of passage into "old age."

In addition to being more of a personal choice, retirement is less abrupt and final than it used to be. Today, people often retire from career jobs and take "bridge" jobs, which are part- or full-time jobs that fill the gap until they retire permanently (Beehr et al., 2000; Schulz, 2003). For example, in a study of 800 men and women from a North Carolina metropolitan area, 33 percent of men and 28 percent of women had returned to some type of work for pay by 6 months postretirement, and these figures jumped to 51 percent and 43 percent 2 years after retirement (Reitzes & Mutran, 2004).

What influences when people decide to retire? Individual factors, family factors, and institutional factors all play a role (Adams & Beehr, 2003; Beehr et al., 2000):

▶ *Individual factors* include financial well-being and health, which are the strongest and most obvious predictors of retirement. In general, you are more likely to retire if you have enough money and resources to live fairly well or have poor physical or mental health. Also, being older, tired of working, or believing you have already reached your career goals encourages retirement (Adams, 1999).

▶ *Family factors* include marital status and number of dependents. Men who have more dependents retire later, and married people usually retire earlier than unmarried workers do, especially if they have a spouse who is retired (Kim & Feldman, 1998; Talaga & Beehr, 1995).

▶ *Organizational factors* also influence the decision to retire. People retire earlier when cutbacks and layoffs are occurring, but positive factors, such as good benefits after retirement, also encourage earlier retirement (Beehr, et al. 2000).

Once people choose to retire, their adjustment depends on many factors. People who adjust poorly to retirement tend to be those who are older and have poorer health, a history of low-status jobs, and greater decreases in income after retiring. In contrast, those who adjust better tend to have more education and higher prestige jobs before retirement, personal identities that are not solely tied to work, good financial planning for retirement, a marriage or other close interpersonal relationship, and involvement in leisure activities, volunteering, or bridge work (Beehr & Bowling, 2002; Kim & Moen, 2001).

Contrary to the stereotype of retirement as a highly stressful transition, there is a trend for both men and women who have been retired for a few years to be more satisfied with their lives than those who are still working or those who retired more recently (Kim & Moen, 2001; Moen, Kim, & Hofmeister, 2001). Adjustment to retirement is usually a gradual process that often involves a happy "honeymoon" period followed by disenchantment and then a period of reorientation when retirees reexamine their situations and develop satisfying daily routines. This period of stability usually lasts as long as one's health or that of one's spouse holds up (Atchley, 1976). In the sample from North Carolina that we mentioned earlier, for example, positive attitudes about retirement rose shortly after retirement, dipped by 12 months afterward, then rebounded by 2 years postretirement to a level that was higher than ever (Reitzes & Mutran, 2004). (You can compare the results for men and women in Figure 15.10.) Other longitudinal studies have confirmed that retirement is not a crisis for most people, partly because a continuation of their basic values and activity patterns tends to create a smooth transition (Atchley, 2003).

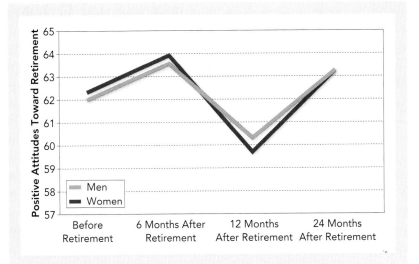

FIGURE 15.10 Adjusting to retirement.

In this study, people saw the phrase "I think retirement means being . . . " followed by 14 adjective pairs, such as sad/happy and full/empty. For each pair, people expressed their feelings by selecting a number from 1 to 5, with 1 anchoring the negative pole (sad) and 5 anchoring the positive pole (happy). Ratings collected before and after retirement showed highs and lows during the adjustment process. But retirement was not a crisis for most individuals: At all time points, ratings were close to the maximum value of 70. Also, attitudes were more positive 2 years after retirement than they had been beforehand.

SOURCE: Reitzes & Mutran (2004).

>>> **MEMORY MAKERS** <<<

1. Is a younger worker or an older worker more likely to experience each of the following?

   (a) job turnover
   (b) missed days from work due to illness
   (c) missed days from work by choice
   (d) accidents

2. In each pair, which characteristic of training is better suited for the mind of an older adult?

   (a) keeping instructions simple and concrete; presenting engaging stories to elaborate on the material
   (b) training younger and older adults together to motivate older students; training various age groups separately
   (c) building in illustrations and practice opportunities; avoiding interruptions in the presentation

3. On average, men and women who have been retired for a few years are (select: more, less) satisfied with their lives than those who are still working or are recently retired.

[1a-younger, 1b-older, 1c-younger, 1d-younger; 2a-keeping instructions simple, 2b-training various age groups separately, 2c-building in illustrations and practice opportunities; 3-more satisfied]

Individual Differences across Time

David Snowdon, the researcher in our opening story, was intrigued by the diversity of personalities that existed among nuns even though their values and lifestyles were so similar (2001). For example, Sister Dolores and Sister Maria were both rambunctious* as children, earning names like "whirlwind" and "tomboy." Yet as adults, Sister Dolores was active and upbeat while Sister Maria was, in her friend's words, "controlled," "private," and "sedate." How enduring are the traits we associate with personality and gender once people reach their later years? Although the Nun Study was not designed to provide an answer to this question, thousands of others have been conducted with just that question in mind.

Personality

"We are living proof that you don't change one bit from cradle to grave," Bessie Delany said about herself and her sister, Sarah, when they were both over 100 years old (Delany, & Delany, 1993, p. xiii). But the stereotype of older people is that they *do* change. It is common to think of seniors as grouchier, more worried and unhappy, and more rigid in their opinions and behavior patterns than younger adults. Does personality really change in these ways, or do we stay basically the same way once our personalities have been established?

From the personality research described in Chapter 13, you have probably guessed that both stability and change characterize our later years. Some people change and some don't. Some traits change and some don't. And some traits change more at some points in adulthood than others do (Bertrand & Lachman, 2003).

Much of what we know about personality and aging comes from studies that used the Big Five perspective discussed in Chapter 13. (Recall that this perspective has identified five core characteristics of personality: neuroticism, extroversion, openness to experience, agreeableness, and conscientiousness). When individuals are tested over time, researchers do not see much change in their scores between the ages of 50 and 70 (Martin, Long, & Poon, 2002; Roberts & DelVecchio, 2000). According to McCrae and Costa (2003), "No matter how you view it, the only consistent evidence points to predominant stability. With age, adults as a group neither increase nor decrease much in any of the traits identified by major personality instruments" (p. 78).

But some individuals *do* change. For example, one study looked at levels of neuroticism from 55 to 85 years of age, tracking people within this age range for as long as 7 years. Neuroticism items on self-report questionnaires measure a range of negative moods, including fear, sadness, and dissatisfaction with oneself ("I often hate myself"). People who score highly on this scale tend to handle stress poorly and are uncomfortable in social situations. Results countered the stereotype that people become more negative as they age. Instead, neuroticism declined until the age of 70, and then increased only slightly. On average, changes with age were too small to have much effect on people's everyday functioning. However, 12 percent of the sample showed changes that were large enough to be "clinically significant": 5 percent showed a large

---

*rambunctious: Noisy, lacking in restraint, and unruly.

decrease in neuroticism, whereas 7 percent showed a large *increase* (Steunenberg et al., 2005). These results confirm earlier conclusions about personality: As a group, people change very little during their later years, although a few people change a lot.

Other changes emerge when researchers compare *average* levels of traits across age groups. Compared to younger adults, older adults frequently report lower levels of extraversion and openness to experience. On the other hand, older adults report *higher* levels of agreeableness and conscientiousness (Caprara, Caprara, & Steca, 2003; Field & Millsap, 1991; Helson & Kwan, 2000; Helson, Jones, & Kwan, 2002; McCrae & Costa, 1994). Put another way, older adults are better at controlling their impulses, are more morally responsible, and do not seek thrills as much as adolescents or young adults do. However, this shunning of thrills sometimes also translates into being less willing to try new things. So the evidence confirms our stereotype of older people in some ways and contradicts it in others. On average, older adults may be better adjusted and more easygoing within their own lives but also more rigid than they were during their younger years (Bertrand & Lachman, 2003; Helson et al., 2002).

One research team tested women once at about age 74 and again around 80 to explore why some individuals experience late-life changes in personality (Maiden et al., 2003). When women had less social support and more needs that were not fulfilled, measures of neuroticism increased. And not surprisingly, extraversion decreased when health declined. In another study, scores on dominance and independence increased during early adulthood, were highest in middle age, and then declined (Helson et al., 2002). This pattern may reflect career stages, because middle-aged people usually have more independence and power at work than younger adults do. As age advances, many adults start to lose some of their power at work, and they feel less dominant and independent after they give up their careers. Findings like these suggest that aspects of personality may change as life circumstances and roles change.

Men and Women Growing Old

You have already read about some ways in which older men and women differ. Women go through menopause whereas men have a smaller and slower decline in their reproductive abilities. Men typically spend more years in the workforce, earn more money, and get better benefits, so they are more financially prepared for old age than women. Women, however, tend to be more closely involved with friends and family members, including their children and grandchildren. They are more likely to have a large social support network to provide help but are also far more likely to give help to others, caring for children, grandchildren, and sick or disabled spouses, relatives, and friends. Women generally live longer, are more likely to be widowed, and are less likely to remarry after becoming widowed or divorced, so they are more likely to live alone in their old age.

The gender difference in longevity produces what is called the **feminization of old age**. Women make up 58 percent of the U.S. population after age 65 and 69 percent of the population after age 85, making the ratio of women to men about 2 to 1 among the oldest-old. But although men are less likely to make it to old age, those who do are often especially hardy. As a result, men have better self-rated health and lower rates of many chronic health conditions that produce disabilities

feminization of old age The increasing proportion of females in a population from younger to older age brackets.

In Western cultures, men and women often grow more comfortable about crossing traditional gender roles as they age. But cultural expectations have a strong influence on gender-typed behavior, so the men in some societies—especially older men—would not be found cooking for their wives.

after age 70, including high blood pressure and arthritis (Baltes, Freund, & Horgas, 1999; Perls, 2004). Better health translates into greater independence. For example, 31 percent of female Medicare enrollees age 65 and over are unable to perform at least one of five physical activities related to independent living, such as lifting 10 pounds or walking two to three blocks, compared to only 18 percent of men (Federal Interagency Forum on Aging Related Statistics, 2004).

Clinical psychologist David Gutmann (1987, 1997) described an age-related change that has dominated discussions about gender and aging for decades: According to Gutmann, men's personalities become more feminine over time as they develop more passivity and nurturance, whereas women become more masculine as they develop more independence and assertiveness. To understand this observation, it is important to think of femininity and masculinity as two different dimensions, not opposite sides of the same coin. Therefore, a person can be mostly feminine (high on feminine traits and low on masculine traits), mostly masculine (low on feminine traits and high on masculine traits), or *androgynous* (high on feminine *and* masculine traits that are highly valued). Gutmann believed that women suppress their competitive and aggressive urges to patiently nurture their children during young adulthood, whereas men suppress their passive, nurturing sides in order to provide for their families. When parenting responsibilities diminish, sex roles in many cultures blur as women and men become more androgynous.

Consistent with Gutmann's hypothesis, some studies have found that men's emotional sensitivity increases with age while women's decreases, men's independence (sense of self-determination and control over life) decreases while women's increases, and women become more confident and assertive in middle age (Caprara et al., 2003; Helson, 1993; Helson et al., 2002). These findings support the idea that differences in personality are most obvious when people are first pairing up to start families during late adolescence and early adulthood. On the other hand, there are fewer gender differences between the ages of 70 and 100, and those that have been found are small (Baltes et al., 1999; Costa, Terracciano, & McCrae, 2001).

But these trends may not describe what occurs in all cultures and historical periods. For example, women who build careers outside the home during young adulthood (which encourages them to adopt masculine values early on) may become less masculine during later phases of life, just as men do (Sowles, 2004). And in Japan, where young women are rejecting traditional roles, elderly women score higher on femininity than younger age groups, contrary to what many researchers have found in American samples (Shimonaka et al., 1997).

Findings like these have led some scientists to believe that gender roles become more complex over time rather than more balanced: Instead of seeing characteristics as simply masculine or feminine, older adults may see them as neither (Sinnott & Shifren, 2001). But sex differences in personality depend on time and place—in one generation and culture women and men are expected to play "traditional" roles throughout life, whereas in other generations and cultures these roles become more flexible after the reproductive years (Helson et al., 2002).

⟩⟩⟩ MEMORY MAKERS ⟨⟨⟨

1. Which conclusion best captures trends in personality across middle to late adulthood?
   (a) Most people show dramatic personality shifts after age 50.
   (b) Most people show dramatic personality shifts after age 70.
   (c) Personality profiles rarely change after age 50 or 60.
   (d) Most people change little during their later years, although a few people change a lot.

2. The fact that the percentage of women increases from younger to older age groups is called the ____.
   (a) gender shift　(b) androgyny factor　(c) feminization of old age　(d) survival factor

3. During what developmental period are gender differences in personality usually most obvious?
   (a) adolescence and young adulthood　(b) middle adulthood　(c) late adulthood

[1-d; 2-c; 3-a]

Revisiting Developmental Principles: Do Childhood Experiences Influence Old Age?

Do early experiences "expire" as we age? One place to look for the answer is in the lives of the "Termites," the group of more than 1,000 intellectually gifted children whom you read about in Chapter 9. Sociologists Robert Crosnoe and Glen Elder examined what happened to a group of male Termites who survived into their 60s (Crosnoe & Elder, 2002, 2004; Elder & Crosnoe, 2002). The Termites are a wonderful group to study because there is so much information about their childhoods, and they frequently filled out questionnaires as adults. Based on their answers to questions about life satisfaction, energy, family engagement, occupational success, and involvement in community and other organizations, Crosnoe and Elder identified four distinct "styles of aging":

▶ *Less adjusted* men scored low on life satisfaction, vitality, family engagement, occupational success, and civic involvement.

▶ *Career-focused but socially disengaged* men scored low in all areas except for occupational success.

▶ *Family-focused* men scored low in all areas except for family engagement.

▶ *Well-rounded* men scored high in all areas.

Crosnoe and Elder then looked for clues that might predict who ended up in each of these categories. The early family factors they examined included parents' socioeconomic status, how closely the men had been attached to their parents, and whether or not their parents had divorced. Early adulthood experiences included whether the Termites had a long-term marriage and educational attainment (years of schooling and degrees earned). Finally, current circumstances included retirement status, physical health, emotional health, and marital status.

Which factors do you think predicted aging styles? As you might have guessed, current life circumstances played a big role. For instance, better physical health was associated with being well-rounded, whereas a lower income was related to being less adjusted. But earlier adult experiences also factored into the picture. Specifically, more educated men had a greater likelihood of being well-rounded, and a long-term marriage predicted membership in the family-focused and well-rounded categories.

The surprising finding was that childhood experiences predicted aging styles *over and beyond* adulthood experiences and circumstances. In other words, knowing what people's lives are like *now* is important, but knowing what their lives were like *earlier* is also important. In fact, all three of the early childhood experiences measured predicted aging profiles. Regardless of what happened during adulthood, men who came from homes with more educated parents were more likely to be career focused than family focused, men whose parents had gotten a divorce were more likely to be well-rounded than family focused, and men who had been more attached to their parents early in life were more likely to end up well-rounded or family focused. These findings support a view of human development as a lifelong, interconnected process, with functioning in later years building on events that occur during earlier stages (Elder & Johnson, 2002).

The study of gifted children by Lewis Terman illustrates how basic developmental principles operate across the life span:

1. ***Development is the joint product of nature and nurture.*** Many studies have found that genetic influences grow stronger from childhood to adulthood because adults have more autonomy to choose environments consistent with their genetically influenced personalities and interests (Scarr & McCartney, 1983). For example, identical twins become *more* similar in basic personality traits as they age, whereas fraternal twins become *less* similar. Yet, as the study of the Termites shows, childhood experiences also influence who we are

in later life. Separating what is a genetic influence from what is environmental is tricky, especially by old age. Some early experiences arise partly from genetic influences, as when parents who value education pass the potential for intelligence on to their children. But potentials are not achieved without the right experiences. As physicist and science historian Evelyn Fox Keller remarked about efforts to separate nature versus nurture, "It is rarely clear where to draw the line, and where to draw the line is rarely stable. What a mess! What a mess all our efforts to sort nature from nurture get us into" (Dean, 2005 para. 24).

2. *Physical, cognitive, and socioemotional development are interrelated.* As adults, the Termites who were the healthiest physically and emotionally were also the most successful in their careers. During our later years, physical health, cognitive ability, achievement, and emotional well-being are so intertwined that it is meaningless to try to separate them.

3. *Developmental outcomes vary over time and contexts.* For example, men who had weak ties to parents and poor social skills during childhood began their careers less successfully than the other Termites, but these men tended to catch up during midlife. As a result, group differences were not very large at this point in life. By their 60s, though, the men who had poor self-images during early adulthood were less satisfied with their achievements than their peers, even if these achievements were impressive. In other words, early mental health is important, but it is more important at particular times in life when specific contexts force people to grapple with specific types of challenges.

4. *Development is characterized by continuity and discontinuity.* Parents' education levels, parental divorce during early life, and attachment to parents during childhood predicted outcomes in older adulthood even after current circumstances were taken into account. So there certainly was some continuity in the lives of the Termite men. But even with all the information scientists have about the Termites, they could not have predicted individual outcomes with 100 percent certainty because there are also discontinuities in development. As Crosnoe and Elder (2002) explained, "A good start in life might be followed by misfortune or greater vulnerability as advantages are squandered in later years through drug use, family dysfunction, or health crises. Conversely, a bad start in life may be turned around by hard work, supportive relationships, or even by chance opportunities" (pp. 157–158). Your future is written in the choices you make.

In some ways, the second half of life is the more varied part of life. Some people are moving adult children out of their homes while others are walking little ones to kindergarten; some are enjoying the pinnacle of their careers while others are starting new careers or retiring. Even the nuns in our opening story, who lived very similar lives, traveled their last decades with different capabilities and ended their lives at different ages. But despite all of these differences, the people who greet each day as a gift have a few simple things in common: They nurture their social relationships and help others, they enjoy playing, they create, and they continue to learn throughout life (Vaillant, 2002).

>>> SUMMARY <<<

Living with an Aging Body

1. During late adulthood, six of the seven leading causes of death are **chronic diseases**—diseases that develop slowly and are long-lasting. Rates of chronic diseases increase with age and vary as a function of ethnicity, socioeconomic status, and sex. **Metabolic syndrome** greatly increases the chances of serious heart disease and diabetes (a common cause of vision loss).

2. The most frequent cause of dementia is **Alzheimer's disease**, a condition in which **plaques** and **tangles** in the brain produce profound memory loss, confusion, and personality changes. Other common causes of dementia are **dementia with Lewy bodies** and **vascular dementia**. A number of medical conditions, including drug reactions, can mimic the early symptoms of dementia.

3. About 35 percent of the elderly have difficulty performing at least one routine activity of daily living. Still, most seniors are remarkably independent. When disabilities prevent people from staying in their own homes, progressively more assistance can be provided by senior apartments, assisted living facilities, and nursing homes.

4. **Centenarians**—people who live to 100—tend to have a family history of longevity, suggesting a genetic advantage. But they also are unlikely to smoke or be obese, and they tend to have positive personalities that lead them to handle stress well.

5. You have a better chance of aging in good health if you maintain a healthy diet, engage in regular physical and mental activity, pursue your education, and learn how to manage stress.

Family Life after 50

6. Despite some decline in marital satisfaction over time, most older adults are happy with their marriages. Older couples who enjoy long-lasting marriages experience less conflict and more shared enjoyment than younger couples do.

7. Widowed people are more likely than those who are married to be depressed and lonely, even years after the spouse's death. Widowhood leaves women in worse financial shape than men, but men are more emotionally affected because they tend to have smaller social support networks.

8. Sexual desire and activity decrease with age, yet many older adults are sexually active well into their advanced years. Long-term hormone replacement therapy is associated with a higher rate of heart attacks, strokes, and breast cancer.

9. Older parents tend to have good relationships with their adult children and are more likely to give help than to receive help. Most grandparents stay in contact with their grandchildren, and more than half provide some financial support. In the United States, children who are being raised by a grandparent are more likely than other children to be living in poverty.

10. Older adults who take care of ill relatives and spouses have higher levels of depressive symptoms, use more medications for psychological problems, and have more health problems.

Work and Retirement

11. The average age of the workforce is increasing around the world. Older workers are generally dedicated, satisfied, and knowledgeable employees who usually perform just as well as younger workers.

12. Older workers are not given as much job training as younger workers. When older workers are given training, they usually take longer to learn but learn as much as younger workers do.

13. Older workers frequently encounter **age discrimination** in hiring, layoffs, and firing.

14. Retirement is no longer as sudden or final as it used to be because more people are phasing into retirement and returning to work after leaving a job. Financial well-being and health are the strongest predictors of when people retire, but family issues, organizational characteristics, and other factors are also involved. People who have been retired for a few years are generally more satisfied with their lives than those who are still working or are recently retired.

Individual Differences across Time

15. People's personalities generally change very little during their later years, although a few people change a lot. Compared to younger adults, older adults are less neurotic, less extroverted, and less open to new experiences but more agreeable and conscientious.

16. Gender differences often become smaller during late adulthood as both sexes move away from traditional sex roles. Often men become more emotionally sensitive and less independent whereas women become less emotionally sensitive, more independent, and more assertive.

Revisiting Developmental Principles: Do Childhood Experiences Influence Old Age?

17. A long-term study of the gifted children initially seen by Lewis Terman illustrates four principles of development.

(a) Development is the joint product of nature and nurture because nature influences the environments people experience, but experiences influence how genetic potentials translate into observable characteristics and behaviors. Childhood experiences and genes both influence our later lives. (b) Physical, cognitive, and socioemotional development are interrelated. Throughout life, people who do well in one area of development tend to do well in others. (c) Developmental outcomes vary over time and contexts, so the individual factors that predict adjustment at one point in time may not predict adjustment at another point in time or in another context. (d) People experience both continuity and unexpected change in the course of their lives.

>>> KEY TERMS <<<

chronic diseases   (p. 610)

metabolic syndrome (also called Syndrome X)   (p. 611)

glaucoma   (p. 612)

macular degeneration   (p. 612)

diabetic retinopathy   (p. 612)

Alzheimer's disease   (p. 613)

beta-amyloid plaques   (p. 614)

neurofibrillary tangles   (p. 614)

cerebral reserve hypothesis   (p. 615)

dementia with Lewy bodies   (p. 615)

vascular dementia   (p. 615)

universal design (or aging in place)   (p. 617)

centenarian   (p. 620)

age discrimination   (p. 637)

feminization of old age   (p. 641)

The End of Life

Stories of Our Lives

A Daughter's Love

Naturalist Terry Tempest Williams and her family have deep roots in the Utah soil. They also have a relationship with cancer. Her mother, grandmothers, and six aunts all had mastectomies; seven were dead when she published *Refuge: An Unnatural History of Family and Place* in 2001. Terry's mother, Diane, was only 38 years old when she had her first surgery. In the years that followed, Terry and her family enjoyed a period of hope, followed by crushing weight when the cancer returned. Diane spent the last weeks of her life at home, a morphine drip fighting the pain while her daughter grappled with the reality of losing her mother. Williams's journal from that time offers a portrait of the end of one life and its effect on the people left behind:

January 15, 1987. It is 2:00 P.M. The wind continues. The large bedroom windows rattle with each gust. I fear they will shatter. The house is cold. I am alone with Mother as she is dying. And for the first time in weeks, I am afraid. The child in me, which lives as long as she does, wishes that the doorbell would ring, that Mimi or Grandmother or my aunts or anyone, would be there to help me.

TEXT BOX

SOLUTIONS
Death in the Media: Helping Children Cope

Mother is restless. As she breathes, her throat rattles. Her neck is swollen. I worry that she is uncomfortable. I moisten her lips with a pink sponge swab. She appears to be talking with someone in this room, someone I cannot see. All at once she rises and says, "I'm ready to go," and begins walking out the door. The morphine pump wavers, ready to tip over, as the morphine line threatens to snap.

I leap to my feet and grab her waist before she collapses on the floor. I lay her gently back on the bed and pull the covers around her. She looks to the corner of the room and points. "Can't you see?"

I look but see nothing.

Mother falls back into a deep sleep, and silence returns to the room.

I am left trembling, frightened by all I don't know, all I can't see. I leave Mother, close the door, and escape into the living room. Through the windows, my eyes focus on Great Salt Lake. It's still there, mirroring the sky. I collapse under the weight of grief and cry. I curl up on the floor in a fetal position. I am sick of death. I want life. I want to surround myself with flocks of white pelicans in full summer sun. I want to dance naked on sand dunes. I yearn to have someone hold me and save me from this pain.

And then it hits me—I still have a mother. She is in the room next door and deserves to know how I feel, to see the underside of my heart. Dad keeps telling me she no longer understands what we are saying, that she is in a coma. I don't believe him.

I walk back into her room, kneel at her bedside, and with bowed head and folded arms, I sob. I tell her I can no longer be strong in her presence. I tell her how agonizing this has been, how helpless I have felt, how much I hurt for her, for all that she has had to endure. I tell her how much I love her and how desperately I will miss her, that she has not only given me a reverence for life, but a reverence for death.

I cry out from my soul, burying my head in the quilt that covers her.

I feel my mother's hand gently stroking the top of my head. (pp. 225–226)

IN *REFUGE*, TERRY TEMPEST WILLIAMS (2001) reminds us that death is the end of a life, but it is also a part of life. Death enters our childhood worlds when we ponder a dead animal for the first time. By adolescence, the thought of death leads us to question our place in the universe. We can be any age when we face the grief of losing a loved one, and any age when we cope with our own impending death. As psychologist Robert Kastenbaum (2004) explained, "Life cannot be fully appreciated or understood without somehow taking death and loss into account" (p. 20).

Kastenbaum is a **thanatologist**: an individual who studies death and dying. The field of thanatology studies the process of dying, but it also explores how we prepare for our own deaths and how we cope with loss. In the same way, this epilogue looks at the many ways death touches us throughout our lives.

Early Learning about Death

Our struggle to accept the inevitability of death begins in childhood when we feel the pain of a pet dying, attend a family member's funeral, or view events on television that caused individuals to die. By the time we approach young adulthood, our understanding of death includes basic biological facts along with ideas about death that we have absorbed from our individual cultures and faith communities. Regardless of whether we are 3 or 90 years old, we are bound together by a common struggle to grasp the limits of life.

thanatologist an individual who studies death and dying.

Young Children's Ideas about Death

Malon was 6 years old when his toad, Firestone Sam-Sam, died. The toad's demise triggered a revelation about death that sent the boy into a mental tailspin for months. Malon frequently asked about death and became afraid of activities, such as flying in an airplane, that could cause death. The toad's death was so significant that, 15 years later, Malon still kept a portrait of the toad that his mother had painted to console him.

Children are not unaware of death. They see when Mother kills a spider and realize that opossums in the street are dead. Even 16- and 18-month-olds make comments such as, "No more! No more!" when they see a crushed caterpillar, or point out "A bird; a dead bird" (Kastenbaum, 2004, p. 314). But early ideas about death are incomplete. Children 2 and 3 years old sometimes say that dead people can feel or breathe, that going to the hospital might "fix" death, and that specific people, such as their teachers and themselves, will not die (Speece & Brent, 1984). These spontaneous comments suggest that many preschoolers fail to grasp the four core concepts of death: *nonfunctionality* (that life functions stop with death), *irreversibility* (that death is irreversible and permanent), *universality* (that all living things eventually die), and finally, *personal mortality* (the realization that "I will die too," which demonstrates a full understanding of universality) (Kenyon, 2001).

Between 5 and 7 years, the majority of children develop some understanding that life functions stop with death, and that death is irreversible and universal. By 10, most have a mature concept of death. In one study, for example, only 53 percent of kindergartners said "yes" to the question "Does everyone die?" whereas 77 percent of the third graders and all but one of the sixth graders (99 percent) did (Atwood, 1984). Many factors influence how quickly individual children grasp death. As you might expect, experiencing the death of a friend or close relative often accelerates understanding. Another important influence is religious culture. For instance, children from Unitarian homes typically say that death cannot be reversed, whereas Muslim children, who are taught that God will recreate their decayed bodies on the Day of Judgment, often say the opposite (Kenyon, 2001).

Malon's story shows us that even young children can be very disturbed by the concept of death. After an experience has led them to contemplate death, it is not uncommon for children to become afraid of sleeping by themselves or to talk repeatedly about dying. Years later, when adults describe their earliest experiences with the death of a pet or a grandparent, many report vivid memories of their reactions to these losses, and anger is a frequently reported emotion (Dickinson, 1992). We'll revisit children's reactions to loss later in this epilogue, when we discuss the types of grief that accompany highly personal losses, such as the loss of a parent.

How Older Children and Adolescents Understand Death

Because older minds juggle several ideas at once, school-aged children and adults often mix biological and religious themes into their dialogues about death. As a result, high school and college students sometimes give answers to questions about death that look less mature than those that children provide. For example, only 55 percent of the college students in one sample responded "No" to the question "Can a dead person become alive again?", whereas 93 percent of the children did. Their thoughtful explanations mentioned a wide variety of medical reasons ("Proper medical help that is fast enough") and spiritual ideas ("I believe in reincarnation") (Brent & Speece, 1993).

Six-year-old Alexis drew this picture of her dead guinea pig, Squeaker, which she depicted lying in a cage as she and her mother frown in bed on either side. Despite the fact that Alexis drew sad faces, she was not very concerned that the animal had died. Neither the event itself—nor the request to draw a picture—prompted any discussion or questions about death. Unlike some 6-year-olds, who are deeply troubled by the reality of death, it may be years before this child thinks about the fact that she and her mother will also die.

Adults often try to satisfy children's fears of death with vague comments, such as the oft-said, "Don't worry, I won't die for a long, long time." But older children are likely to want more substantial discussion about the topic. Their questions can be unsettling to adults who are unprepared to talk about the issue and may not have completely resolved the meaning of death for themselves. Teachers and parents are sure to face this problem when public disasters, such as terrorist events and natural disasters, expose children to the possibility of unexpected death. Our special feature on death in the media provides suggestions for helping children participate in public tragedies without feeling overwhelmed.

It is not uncommon for children to become anxious, fearful, or aggressive after terrorist attacks or natural disasters expose them to images of death. Parents and teachers can help children cope by acting calm, maintaining routines, and limiting television viewing. It is also helpful to remind children that trustworthy people are in charge and to answer their questions simply and honestly.

DEATH IN THE MEDIA: HELPING CHILDREN COPE

Most adults will never forget the moment they learned about the terrorist attacks on the World Trade Center that occurred on September 11, 2001. Time seemed suspended as people crowded near television sets, repeatedly watching footage of the events that ended over 2,000 lives. Meanwhile, hospital personnel in Manhattan waited for patients who never arrived as rescue workers realized that few people would survive the swift collapse of the buildings. One minute, it was a typical September morning; the next, the entire nation was struck with disbelief and grief.

Acts of terrorism and natural disasters, such as the Asian tsunami of 2004 and the flooding of New Orleans in 2005, are powerful threats to our sense of safety. In the aftermath of such events, children share their communities' feelings of disorientation, anger, fear, and sadness. One survey found that 85 percent of children who did not live near New York City had seen coverage of the September 11 attacks within hours or days of the event, and only 15 percent never saw footage of the airplanes hitting the World Trade Center, people fleeing the scene in fear, or injured and dying people (Saylor et al., 2003).

Adults often underestimated the impact of this coverage on children. In one study, nearly half of the third to fifth graders were afraid that a friend or family member might have died, yet only 18 percent of their parents knew about these fears. Similarly, almost half were afraid *they* might be hurt or killed, and these children were more likely than their peers to experience symptoms associated with trauma, such as acting anxious, fearful, or aggressive. On average, children who had more exposure to negative and graphic images, such as footage of death and injury, also experienced more behavioral changes (Saylor et al., 2003). Moreover, fully one-fourth of the children who lived in New York City showed signs of major mental disorder in the aftermath of the disaster, including depression and separation anxiety (Hoven, Mandell, & Duarte, 2003).

How can parents and teachers help children regain a sense of safety and control? First, children's responses are strongly influenced by the reactions of those around them. They are less likely to be troubled when adults act calmly and provide ongoing, consistent routines (Fremont, 2004). And while it is unrealistic (and possibly upsetting) to prevent children from watching the news, adults can limit exposure and help children interpret events in ways that maintain optimism about the future. The following list summarizes these guidelines and other suggestions from school psychologists and pediatricians (National Association of School Psychologists, 2002; Schonfeld, 2003):

- *Model being calm and in control.* Avoid appearing anxious or frightened.

- *Maintain a normal routine.* Try to stick to the family's dinner and homework times, but don't be inflexible.

- *Limit television viewing.* Avoid watching disaster coverage over and over.

- *Reassure children that they and (if true) their families are safe.* Point out specific factors that ensure their safety, such as their distance from the disaster or the presence of police.

- *Remind them that trustworthy people are in charge.* Explain that emergency workers and federal officials are working to keep people safe.

Children who had more exposure to images of the attack on the World Trade Center were also more likely than their peers to suffer from anxiety and depression.

- *Let children know that it is okay to feel upset.* Letting children talk about their feelings will reveal specific fears that can be addressed.

- *Tell children the truth.* Children may inflate the situation in their minds if they believe you are shielding them from what is really happening.

- *Stick to the facts.* Don't speculate about what might happen or dwell on the scope of the tragedy, especially with young children.

- *Spend time reading or playing quiet games with children before bed.* This will foster a sense of security.

- *Offer to discuss the events with older children and adolescents.* Periodic invitations to talk about events, but without forcing a conversation, will give mature children a chance to explore their questions and concerns.

>>> **MEMORY MAKERS** <<<

1. The majority of children develop some understanding that life functions stop with death and that death is irreversible and universal between ___ years of age.
   (a) 2 and 3   (b) 4 and 5   (c) 5 and 7   (d) 9 and 10

2. College students are more likely than children to say that a dead person can become alive again because ____.
   (a) they understand that they will die too and need to control their anxiety
   (b) they are more likely than children to believe in ghosts
   (c) they tend to answer any question about possibilities by acknowledging multiple possibilities.
   (d) they consider issues such as medical resuscitation and spiritual (afterlife) issues

[1-c (children younger than 5 often believe that only some people die, but by 10 most understand that they, too, will die); 2-d (college students sometimes mention that heroic medical efforts can restore function or that an individual's essence may be reborn)]

Death and Dying

Long after we first learn about death, details about the death process and how society deals with death may still be a mystery. This was true for Ron, a businessman who was in his 30s when he placed his frail, confused father in a nursing home. Ron was relieved that the facility was clean, cheerful, and next to a hospital. Like many adults in his situation, he counted on the professional staff to make all of the day-to-day decisions about Ronald Senior's care.

One evening, a nurse called to say that Ronald was slipping away. "Are you taking him to the hospital?" Ron asked, assuming he would drive there instead of to the nursing home. "Do you want us to?" the nurse replied. Ron was confused. "Aren't they required to take him to the hospital?" he thought. Ron was unprepared to make a decision—in the next few minutes—that might keep his father alive for a few more weeks.

Like Ron, many people think as little as possible about death. Some purposely avoid thinking about death, but others assume that when the time comes, decisions about when and how to die will be out of their hands. Increasingly, though, adults are learning about death so they can make choices about the end of life—choices that are influenced by their conditions, their spiritual beliefs, and their options for care.

Defining Death

Dying is a process that takes place over time, so the definition of death is subject to debate and revision. In the past, people assumed that death occurred when heart function and breathing ceased. However, the discovery of cardiopulmonary resuscitation (CPR) and defibrillation (the process of delivering electric shocks to the heart to restart contractions) prompted more complex distinctions. Today, we say that **somatic death** has occurred when the heart and respiratory systems malfunction. Without intervention, these events will cause all cells in the body to die from lack of oxygen within about 6 minutes. It is during these minutes (a period called *clinical death*) when people who have no major organ damage are sometimes resuscitated.

Legally, death has occurred when respiration and circulation have irreversibly stopped or there is **brain death** (an absence of brain function). Specific criteria for brain death differ around the world, but typical laws require physicians to document a lack of brain activity throughout the brain on more than one occasion, including lower brainstem functions that control our pupils and other reflexes.

Brain death is often confused with two other conditions. Patients who are in a *coma* appear asleep but are actually in a prolonged state of unconsciousness. A coma usually results from injury or pressure to multiple parts of the brain, including the brainstem. These patients have no sleep–wake cycle, show no awareness of themselves or their surroundings, and cannot be awakened by stimulating them. Some coma patients eventually enter a *persistent vegetative state*. These individuals have lost most higher brain functions, such as the ability to recognize others, but appear awake due to behavior regulated by lower brain regions. People in a persistent vegetative state show sleep–wake cycles and may groan, turn toward sound, and even smile.

The most famous case of vegetative function is Karen Ann Quinlan, a 21-year-old who sank into a vegetative state in 1975 after ingesting several drugs and drinking alcohol. Her case launched the "right-to-die" movement after her parents won a legal battle to take her off a respirator. (Remarkably, Karen breathed

somatic death When the heart and respiratory systems malfunction, which causes all cells in the body to die from lack of oxygen.

brain death An absence of brain function. Definitions and criteria for brain death vary around the world. Typical laws require physicians to document a lack of brain activity throughout the brain on more than one occasion, including lower (brainstem) functions.

on her own and continued to live for almost 10 years.) Cases such as Karen's illustrate that the brains of patients in vegetative states continue to maintain some vital functions. As a result, they are alive according to definitions of brain death that consider brainstem activity a sign of life.

The definition of brain death is highly controversial. Some ethicists* hope that the criteria for legal death will be changed to allow physicians to harvest organs from patients who have brainstem activity but no evidence of consciousness or thinking (Veatch, 2004). People who support a relaxed definition point out that this change would save lives by relieving the shortage of donor organs. Others, however, worry that brain death cannot be diagnosed reliably enough to avoid errors (Sundin-Huard & Fahy, 2004). Moreover, many spiritual traditions oppose transplantation from individuals who still have brain function. For example, people in a persistent vegetative state are alive according to Jewish law, and the concept of brain death has not garnered widespread support in Japan, where many people believe that a living body is part of the essence of who we are (Breitowitz, 2004; Morioka, 2001).

End-of-Life-Care

It used to be common for people to die in their homes after brief illnesses, so death in the past was generally swift and public. To illustrate how past generations of children encountered death firsthand, renowned psychiatrist and thanatologist Elisabeth Kübler-Ross (1969) related a memory from her own childhood:

> He fell from a tree and was not expected to live. He asked simply to die at home, a wish that was granted without questioning. He called his daughters into the bedroom and spoke with each one of them alone for a few minutes . . . He asked his friends to visit him once more, to bid good-bye to them. Although I was a small child at the time, he did not exclude me or my siblings. We were allowed to share in the preparations of the family just as we were permitted to grieve with them until he died. (p. 5)

By the middle of the 20th century, death was often a prolonged event, a story with many chapters, that took place in hospitals. As dying became more of a private affair, people grew more uncomfortable talking about or planning for death. During the past 30 years, medical and mental health professionals have been advocating a return to more open discussions about death. Increasingly, we are encouraged to think about the care we would choose for our final days, weeks, or months, and we are asked to talk more openly with sick or elderly relatives about their own wishes.

WHEN DEATH IS NEAR. Some people quietly die in their sleep, some die quickly from massive heart attacks or strokes, and others die slowly from cancer or other conditions. It is difficult to predict when an individual will die until death is near. There is some evidence that the rate of decline accelerates for certain cognitive functions, such as the ability to recall specific experiences, during the months or years before death. But a marked change in cognitive performance, which is called **terminal decline** (or "terminal drop"), has not been found in all studies and is at best only subtle (Hassing et al., 2002; Kliegel, Moor, & Rott, 2004).

When an individual is seriously ill, a number of signs that are collectively called the **syndrome of imminent death** may signal that death is near (National Cancer Institute, 2002; Weissman, 2005). As you read about this syndrome in

terminal decline (or terminal drop) An unexpected change in the rate of cognitive decline during the months or years before death.

syndrome of imminent death A collection of signs associated with impending death, including mental confusion, sleepiness, decreased urine volume, and heart rate changes.

---

*ethicists: Individuals who specialize in ethics, the study of behavioral standards, morals, and moral choices.

TABLE E.1   Syndrome of Imminent Death

Symptom	Response
Drowsiness, sleepiness, and unresponsiveness	Many patients can hear even when they are unresponsive, so it is important for visitors to always assume that the dying person can hear what is said.
Confusion about where they are or who loved ones are, pulling at bed linens, and reporting visions of people who are not present (often called *terminal delirium*)	Speak calmly and remind the patient of where the patient is and who is in the room.
Decreased interest in socializing	Speak to the patient directly and reassure the patient that you are there.
Lack of interest in food and fluids	Respect the patient's choices about eating. Keep the patient's lips moist with a lip balm.
Loss of bladder or bowel control	Change disposable pads underneath the patient to keep the patient comfortable.
Darkened urine or decreased urine volume	Consult a member of the patient's health team in the event a catheter is needed to avoid blockage.
Cool skin	Use blankets to warm the patient if the patient desires.
Noisy or altered pace of breathing	Labored breathing is not usually uncomfortable to the patient but can be relieved by a change of position, oxygen, or a cool mist humidifier.
Increasing pain	Explore options with the patient's health team.
Involuntary movements and a changing heart rate	Do not be alarmed by these signs that death is near.

SOURCE: Adapted from the National Cancer Institute (2002).

Table E.1, keep in mind that any one sign can be caused by numerous factors and does not always forecast death. For example, reactions to medication and low sodium levels can cause mental confusion, and depression causes people to withdraw socially. When this syndrome is truly present, death usually occurs within the next 2 weeks. As Terry Tempest Williams expressed in our opening story, uncertainty about how long this process will take is distressing to friends and family members who must watch their loved one lose functions and mental clarity.

HOSPITAL, HOME, AND HOSPICE CARE.   With the exception of sudden, accidental deaths, the majority of deaths among adults in the United States occur in hospitals or nursing homes (Teno et al., 2004). Many of these deaths happen while people are being cared for in intensive care units (ICU), which are facilities for seriously ill patients that offer the highest level of care and treatment. The first goal of an ICU is to protect patients from disease and closely monitor their physical status—not to provide a relaxed environment. Typically, visiting hours are restricted, there is little privacy, and patients are not allowed to receive flowers or other gifts that might introduce germs into the area. Due to monitors, respirators, and other equipment, the ICU is especially uncomfortable for patients who are fearful of high-tech equipment, and the environment is noisy enough to interfere with nearly everyone's sleep (Gabor, Cooper, & Hanly, 2001).

Despite the fact that hospitals can be frightening places, there has been a trend for increasingly aggressive medical care during the last year of life. One analysis of Medicare claims for elderly patients who died of cancer during a 4-year period in the mid-1990s found that an increasing proportion were experiencing more than one emergency department visit, multiple hospitalizations, and admission to an ICU unit during the last month of life. Among those who received chemotherapy, 18 percent were still being treated within 2 weeks of death, and a growing number were starting a new chemotherapy regimen within 30 days of death (Earle et al., 2004).

It is difficult to improve the quality of life for dying patients as long as people hold onto hope that aggressive treatment might prolong their lives. There are many reasons why dying patients often suffer unnecessarily in hospitals, including a medical culture that instructs physicians to treat aggressively and a "wide gap between what the public believes technology is capable of doing and what technology actually accomplishes" (Feinberg, 1997, p. 164).

Once it is clear that more treatment is not going to be effective in preventing death, the task for patients and family members is to focus on making the process of dying as comfortable and meaningful as possible. One alternative is to die at home. Among people who choose this option, 38 percent die without any nursing services, 12 percent have home nursing, and 50 percent have **hospice care** (Teno et al., 2004). Hospice is a philosophy of care that is committed to maintaining the quality of life for terminally ill patients by keeping them as alert, pain free, and engaged with their families as possible during their final days. The term, which comes from the tradition of offering "hospitality" (lodging and food) to tired travelers, has been used to refer to humane end-of-life care since 1967.

The focus of hospice care is the *person* and *family* rather than the illness. Because curing the illness is no longer an option, medical intervention consists of **palliative care** (also called *comfort care*), which is care to relieve pain and other distressing symptoms of illness, such as nausea and breathing problems. Hospice care also addresses emotional and spiritual needs by providing 24-hour assistance and after-death emotional support for family members. This philosophy of care can be implemented in a special facility, nursing home, or individual homes. Currently, home hospice care is the most common option, with family members providing the majority of care when possible. Other members of the hospice team may include nurses, chaplains, social workers or counselors, physicians, and volunteers. The team designs an individualized care plan, arranges for special equipment, provides necessary medications, and answers questions about arrangements that need to be made before and after death.

What are people's experiences with various end-of-life options? By contacting survivors who were listed on death certificates, one research team assembled data that were representative of 1.97 million deaths that occurred in the United States in 2000 (Teno et al., 2004). As you can see in Table E.2, families rated hospice care more favorably than the other alternatives for level of patient comfort, patient respect, and attending to the needs of the family. But keep in mind that

hospice care A philosophy of end-of-life care that is committed to maintaining quality of life for terminally ill patients by keeping them as alert, pain free, and engaged with their families as possible.

palliative care (also called comfort care) Measures to relieve pain and other distressing symptoms of illness when there is no possibility of curing an illness.

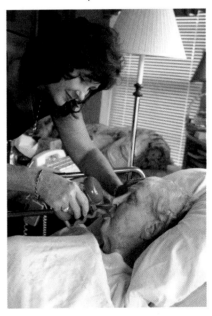

This woman has chosen to spend her final weeks at home. She is relying on hospice staff members to keep her as comfortable as possible.

TABLE E.2	Satisfaction with the Last Place of Care			
	Home with Home Care Nursing Services	Home Hospice Care	Nursing Home	Hospital
Patient did not receive enough help with pain	43%	18%	32%	19%
Family member or friend wanted but did not have contact with physician	23%	14%	31%	51%
Patient not always treated with respect	16%	4%	32%	20%
Concern(s) about emotional support	45%	21%	36%	38%
Concern(s) about information regarding what to expect while patient was dying	32%	29%	44%	50%

SOURCE: Adapted from Teno et al. (2004).

patients who choose hospice care probably differed from other patients in a number of ways. As a group, hospice patients may have had more lingering illnesses that provided time to develop relationships with staff members, and they probably had supportive, involved families. In addition, hospice patients had opted for treatment that maximized comfort instead of treatment aimed at prolonging life. Because of these factors, we cannot conclude that hospitals and nursing homes do a poorer job of managing the dying process. What we *can* conclude is that clients are highly satisfied with home hospice care.

Terminally Ill Children

It used to be considered humane to avoid telling terminally ill children they were dying. In part, this practice was based on the false assumption that children were too unsophisticated about death to realize they were dying or to understand the significance of dying. Experts changed their position on this issue after they discovered that dying children often learn about their conditions by overhearing comments and watching the reactions of those around them. Subsequently, studies found that terminally ill children show better adjustment and compliance with treatment regimes when there is open dialogue about death, and this is true even among children who are less than 6 years old (O'Halloran & Altmaier, 1996). For example, children who are informed about their HIV status have higher self-esteem and fewer behavior problems than uninformed children, perhaps because they are less confused about their medical treatment and their family members' distress (Armstrong, Willen, & Sorgen, 2003). As a result of these findings, the American Academy of Pediatrics (1999) encourages families to disclose HIV status to school-aged victims.

Parents also benefit from an atmosphere of openness about death. In one survey of 429 parents who had lost a child to cancer, no one who had talked about death with their child regretted that decision, but 27 percent of the parents who were *not* open with their children wished that they had been (Kreicbergs et al., 2004). As you'll read next, the shift in our culture toward more open dialogue about death has also increased discussion about end-of-life choices and the possibility of planning for death.

Euthanasia and Physician-Assisted Suicide

Dr. Mike Martineau and his wife Connie were delighted when she became pregnant. (We changed the couple's names to protect their privacy.) But hopes turned to a nightmare when their infant son was born extremely premature. The couple agonized when medical staff placed the tiny infant on mechanical life support despite their instructions to withhold aggressive medical aid. Mike and Connie knew there was a 60 percent chance their son would die—and if he lived, he could suffer severe brain damage. After Dr. Martineau removed his child from a ventilator in the neonatal ICU, his state charged him with manslaughter. In 1995, a jury returned a verdict of not guilty, confirming parents' rights to determine whether their children will receive aggressive medical intervention.

A man who is often called "Doctor Death" repeatedly challenged the law at the other end of the life span. Dr. Jack Kevorkian attended his first suicide in 1990, when he helped 54-year-old Janet Adkins, an Alzheimer's patient, hook up to a machine that induced sleep and then delivered drugs to stop her heart. Determined to fight for what he called the "right to die," Kevorkian helped over 100 patients with diseases such as multiple sclerosis, cancer, and emphysema commit suicide. But he lost his fight in April 1999, when a Michigan court convicted him of murder for injecting the drugs that killed Thomas Youk, a patient with Lou Gehrig's disease. (The legal system ruled again in November 2001 when the Michigan Court of Appeals upheld his conviction.)

These examples illustrate debates over *euthanasia*, the practice of ending the life of people with incurable illnesses or terminal diseases. The majority of the public supports individuals like Dr. Martineau, who engaged in **passive euthanasia** when he withheld life-sustaining treatment so his son could die naturally. In fact, it has always been common and legal for medical professionals to rely on their own judgment—along with patient and family wishes—to end aggressive treatment when there is little hope for a successful outcome.

In contrast, Dr. Kevorkian was convicted of **active euthanasia**, the practice of triggering death by lethal drugs, carbon monoxide inhalation, or other means. In contrast to passive euthanasia, active euthanasia is illegal throughout the United States. In earlier cases, Kevorkian was charged with **physician-assisted suicide**: arranging the means for death, which patients then initiated themselves. By repeatedly being charged with crimes and encouraging publicity, Kevorkian hoped that attention to the plight of terminally ill patients would facilitate the passage of laws to permit assisted suicide. (In the United States, only Oregon allows doctors to prescribe a lethal drug dose when terminally ill patients wish to end their lives.)

Individuals on both sides of the debate over euthanasia and physician-assisted suicide find it difficult to understand the other side. Some people oppose these practices for religious reasons; for them, it is simply not an option for humans to decide a fate that should be reserved for a higher power. Others are wary of these practices for nonreligious reasons. For example, critics who analyzed Kevorkian's cases have claimed that many of his patients were not terminally ill, that some showed no sign of disease at autopsy or any physical basis for pain, and that some had difficulty dealing with their disabilities due to depression rather than advanced stages of illness (Kaplan, Lachenmeier, et al., 1999–2000; Kaplan, O'Dell et al., 1999–2000; Roscoe et al., 2001). These findings fuel concern that physicians who are allowed to terminate lives will make errors in assessing the mental competence of patients or the severity and course of their conditions.

On the other side of the issue are people who believe it is unethical to let patients with excruciating pain or limitations suffer. According to this view, medical errors can be minimized by establishing strict guidelines and overseeing physician behavior. This philosophy guides practice in the Netherlands, where euthanasia is not punishable if (1) the patient is suffering with no hope of improvement; (2) the patient consistently makes a voluntary, informed request to die; (3) two physicians agree that it is justified to help the patient die; and (4) there is a careful medical assessment of the patient. Belgium passed similar controls when its parliament legalized active euthanasia, including the requirement that a second physician be consulted.

But law and practice are not the same. A study commissioned by the Dutch Ministers of Health and Justice found that 5 percent of all deaths in the Netherlands during 2001 had been intentionally and actively caused by physicians. However, many of these cases were never reported, did not occur at the request of the patient, and did not involve debilitating illness. For example, 3 percent of physicians admitted to helping people commit suicide who were merely "tired of life," and in 77 percent of cases, family members claimed that physicians promised assistance *before* consulting with the second physician (Fenigsen, 2004). These findings suggest that legal controls do not override the established tradition of deciding a course of action based on individual professional ethics and judgment.

passive euthanasia The practice of withholding life-sustaining treatment so that patients with incurable illness or terminal disease will die.

active euthanasia The practice of triggering death in an individual with an incurable illness or terminal disease by lethal drugs, carbon monoxide inhalation, or other means.

physician-assisted suicide Arranging the means for someone to commit suicide, which the person who desires death initiates.

advance medical directive A document that specifies wishes for health care in the event an individual is too ill to make those decisions.

durable power of attorney for health care (often called **durable power**) A document that appoints another person to make health care decisions for an individual who is unable to do so.

living will A document that specifies the type of medical treatment individuals want to receive and the treatment they refuse in the event they are too ill to make their wishes known.

Making Decisions about the End of Life

Imagine that you are involved in a devastating car accident. One day later, you are unconscious and your condition is rapidly deteriorating. Would you want physicians to determine your treatment, or would you want people you know to be involved in making decisions on your behalf? Would you want these decision makers to have the final say over everything that needs to be arranged, or do you have some wishes you would like observed? For example, would you want enough pain medication to stay comfortable even if this would hasten death by a few days, or would you rather not receive medication that will strain vital organs?

If you would like input into these decisions, you should prepare an **advance medical directive**. Advance directives specify your wishes for health care if you are too ill to speak for yourself. One type of advance directive, the **durable power of attorney for health care** (often simply called "durable power"), appoints another person to make decisions on your behalf if you are unable to do so yourself. The Karen Quinlan case, which you read about earlier, paved the way for legislation to recognize durable power when Karen's father won the right to make medical decisions on behalf of his daughter.

A second type of advance directive is a **living will**. This document specifies the medical treatment you would want if you had a serious condition but could not speak for yourself. By filling out a form, you can specify such things as whether you want to prolong life by receiving nutrition through a tube and whether medical staff should attempt to resuscitate you when you die. Not all U.S. states formally recognize living wills, but the information in a living will can be used as evidence of your wishes even in locations where it is not considered a legal document. Many states have forms to help you draft an advance directive by guiding you through the most common decisions. These forms, which are available online and through many health-care offices, are valid whether you fill them out yourself or with the assistance of a health professional or attorney. (Because different states have different requirements for signatures and witnesses, it is best to use state-specific rather than generic forms.)

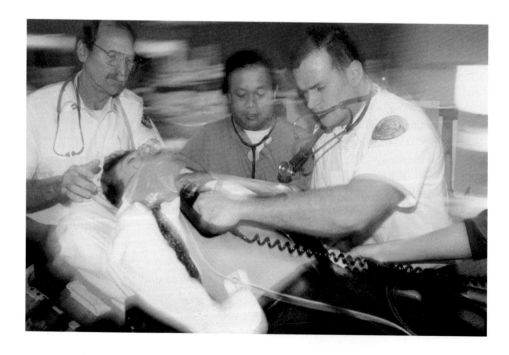

Most adults hope that emergency medical staff will resuscitate them in the event of a tragic accident or an unexpected medical crisis. Those who are terminally ill can express their wish to decline life-saving measures by preparing a living will.

It can be comforting to family members and friends when a patient has a living will. One woman expressed the sentiments of many wives when she wrote about Five Wishes, an advance directive form distributed by the nonprofit agency, Aging with Dignity (2005):

> My husband was diagnosed with Leukemia. . . . Near the end I found it necessary to invoke the responsibilities given to me under the terms of the Five Wishes living will and, although nothing can adequately prepare you for the pain of losing a loved one, at least I knew that I was doing what he wanted. Of all the painful and emotional issues I was going though, I didn't have the anxiety and agony wondering if I did the right things for him. I had it spelled out in black and white. . . . I knew to bring his favorite afghan and teddy bear to the hospital, as well as some of his granddaughter's drawings . . . this document, when properly executed, is a gift for them to give their loved ones, so that the survivors never have to agonize over any decisions they may have to make.

But not everyone believes that living wills are the best way to plan for death. The circumstances and options surrounding the end of life are not always predictable, so preferences laid out in living wills are often overly general or based on misinformation. And even over periods as short as 2 years, adults change almost one-third of their earlier decisions about life-sustaining medical treatment. Based on problems like these, some critics believe that living wills are appropriate only for a minority of adults who are near death from predictable medical conditions. For the others, these experts suggest using durable powers of attorney to appoint trusted individuals to make end-of-life decisions on their behalf (Fagerlin & Schneider, 2004). This recommendation is consistent with most people's wishes: In two large-scale studies, over 70 percent of patients preferred to let family members and physicians make end-of-life decisions (Puchalski et al., 2000). This finding introduces our next topics—the difficulty of facing death and the emotional burden on the friends and family members left behind.

>>> **MEMORY MAKERS** <<<

1. Which type of death occurs when the heart and respiratory systems malfunction?
   (a) somatic death   (b) brain death

2. What is the name for a number of signs that indicate death is near?
   (a) terminal decline   (b) syndrome of imminent death

3. Which term refers *specifically* to practices for relieving pain and distressing symptoms of disease?
   (a) hospice care   (b) palliative care

4. Which type of euthanasia refers to withholding life-sustaining treatment so that natural death occurs?
   (a) passive euthanasia   (b) active euthanasia

5. Which type of advance medical directive appoints another person to make decisions on your behalf?
   (a) living will   (b) durable power of attorney

[1-a (brain death refers to an absence of brain function); 2-b (terminal decline refers to declines in cognitive function that begin months or years before death); 3-b (hospice care is an entire philosophy of maintaining quality of life for the dying); 4-a (active euthanasia triggers death by lethal drugs or other means); 5-b (a living will specifies the medical treatment you would want if you could not speak for yourself)]

Coping with Death

There is no "right way" to react to death because every person who dies has a unique history and leaves different relationships behind. For example, Terry Tempest Williams and her mother, whom you met in our opening story, had months to prepare. When death arrived, an extended family and a set of comforting Mormon rituals directed everyone's behavior. Accompanied by her grandmother, Mimi, Terry prepared her mother's body with oils and perfumes, and she fought with a funeral director over the unnatural makeup on her mother's face. Later, she would have flashbacks of these rituals. "Some haunt. Some heal," she explained (Williams, 2001, p. 236).

In contrast, death blindsided writer Joan Didion and her husband John, who collapsed suddenly in their New York City apartment. Joan called the next year "a year of magical thinking," which is the title she gave to a book about her experiences. "I was going mad," she said. "I realized that I had not been entirely sane for most of the year" (Donadio, 2005, para. 4).

How we face our own deaths and experience the death of our loved ones is a function of many factors, including our personal circumstances and the sense of community our culture provides to heal us. The range of reactions to death you will read about here may help you accept your own reactions as normal, even if they are not the reactions you wanted or expected.

Facing Death

In her most famous work, *On Death and Dying* (1969), Kübler-Ross (1926–2004) summarized interviews with over 200 dying individuals. She concluded that terminally ill people often progress through five stages as they face death:

▶ *Denial and isolation.* Most patients react to news of their terminal illness with thoughts such as, "No, not me, it cannot be true" (p. 34). This initial reaction is a state of shock and numbness at the thought of facing death. Although this is usually a temporary state, some people maintain their denial for prolonged periods.

▶ *Anger.* It is not uncommon for people to react with anger and resentment after the reality of their situation sinks in. This stage is difficult for family members and health professionals because anger is so unpredictable and is often aimed in so many different directions.

▶ *Bargaining.* This stage is similar to a child who makes an angry demand, only to soften her voice and ask again nicely. Some patients ask God for "an extension" or bargain with health professionals to fulfill a wish, as one patient did when she worked with doctors to attend her son's wedding. Bargaining is an attempt to postpone death and feel in control one last time.

▶ *Depression.* The reality of illness and impending death often breeds depression. Thoughts about past losses, regrets, and life failures can fuel this feeling of unbearable sadness.

▶ *Acceptance.* Some patients reach a stage in which they are *not* angry or depressed. This stage is not a feeling of happiness but a time when psychological pain and struggle have ceased—a time when the fight is over.

Kübler-Ross qualified her descriptions of these stages by pointing out that "most" or only "some" patients reacted in the prescribed ways. And later, she said that people could show signs of two or three stages simultaneously or in rapid succession (Kübler-Ross, 1974). Nevertheless, discussions of her work often portrayed her list as a fixed sequence that people were expected to progress through in a step-by-step fashion. This led to criticism that her work was merely a set of individual stories about death and that only depression was a consistent reaction to impending death (Schulz & Aderman, 1974). Critics were also concerned that her list would lead family members and friends to dismiss patients' reactions ("Oh, it's just a temporary stage") or criticize those who were not dying "properly." Today, Kübler-Ross's observations are viewed as a list of possible reactions as the end of life grows near, not as a "stage theory" of dying. Experts recognize that people fluctuate among various emotional states and express needs that are not part of the five-stage model (Kastenbaum, 2000; Shneidman, 1982).

While dying individuals are coping, their need to belong to a community remains. But sadly, it is common for us to distance ourselves from people who are dying to avoid our own pain or the embarrassment of not knowing what to say. As one cancer patient explained, "I weigh my words to avoid burdening my friends, and they stay away because they think they don't know what words to use" (Johns, 2005, para. 3). Although no advice is best for everyone or every circumstance, the suggestions in Table E.3, such as avoiding criticism and enjoying the moment, can make it easier to support a dying friend or family member.

After death arrives, the attention of friends and family members shifts from the needs of the dying to the needs of the living. As we discuss next, ways of handling these needs are as varied as people's reactions to death are.

Funerals and Remembrance Rituals around the World

"I don't know if you can understand this, because you have never had a child die," Jimon Maram said quietly. "But for a parent, when your child dies, it's a sad thing to put his body in the earth."

. . . "It's cold in the earth," Jimon continued, and Quimoin's [his wife] shoulders trembled. "We keep remembering our child, lying there, cold. We remember, and we are sad." He learned forward, searching my eyes as if to see whether I could comprehend what he was trying to explain, then he concluded:

"It was better in the old days, when the others ate the body. Then we did not think about our child's body much. We did not remember our child as much, and we were not so sad." (Conklin, 2001, p. xv)

TABLE E.3	Visiting a Terminally Ill Individual
Suggestion	**Explanation**
Respect the individual's culture	Some cultures believe that talking about dying can speed its arrival or convey lack of hope. If you are unsure about a person's beliefs, consult with a knowledgeable family member or friend.
Avoid dismissing the person's concerns	Comments such as "I know you are going to get better" sound hopeful but discourage the person from talking about his or her concerns. Open-ended questions (such as "Tell me what you are thinking about right now" or "Is there something I can do for you?") encourage the person to talk.
Don't criticize or give advice	People who are expressing private thoughts often say things that sound ridiculous or illogical. Usually they want to share their feelings with you, not hear your opinions about them.
Enjoy the moment	Remember how you used to interact with this person and talk about things you usually discussed. Remember that the person who is dying is alive today.
Don't feel pressured to talk	Be a good listener. Your company is important; you don't need to keep the conversation going.
Tell the person you care	A hug or "I love you" is always appreciated.

SOURCE: Gallagher (2006).

In her book, *Consuming Grief*, anthropologist Beth Conklin illustrates the emotional ties that bind humans together by exploring a ritual that proves our separateness. Among the Wari' Indians of western Brazil, older members of the community remember a time when the dead were roasted, then tasted by those who were not close relatives of the deceased before the remains and belongings of the dead were burned. The Wari' considered the ritual a meaningful and humane practice that distanced them from thoughts of their loved one and helped them move on with their lives. By comparison, the modern practice of burial seems cruel and disrespectful to elders, who were taught that soil is cold and polluting. As one respondent explained, "When the body was eaten, we did not remember or long for the dead person much."

Today, the Wari' know that cannibalism is viewed with disdain, so they mourn death with other traditions. Now grieving begins with several days of public crying, *keening* (a high-pitched, stylized wailing), and discussing the deceased in songs. As in most cultures, the Wari' realize that people can be consumed by grief, so they try to prevent unhealthy reactions by using traditions to mark a transformation in their relationship with the person who has died (Miller, 2001). When survivors are in the throes of mourning, cultural rules for how to behave lighten the burden of decision and help them move on with their lives by drawing attention to their ongoing relationships.

All cultures have funeral rituals that specify how the body is to be handled, how loved ones are expected to behave, and how the community should assist those who are grief stricken. The term **mourning** refers to these culturally prescribed ways of behaving and expressing feelings after the death of a loved one. In traditional Southern culture, for example, African Americans were expected to be highly emotional following a death, so loud wailing, sobbing, and singing were appropriate responses at a funeral. As one informant explained, "Sometimes it's expected that the family should just give in to wailing. That shows how much they care. And if they don't do that. . . . [they say] 'That was quite a funeral wasn't it? . . . they certainly didn't care for 'em'" (Perry, 1993, p. 57). Muslims also believe that one should cry openly to achieve peace, and tea and sugar may be available during a funeral to assist people who faint (Gilanshah, 1993). In contrast, it is assumed that some people will cry at Christian and Jewish funerals, but in most cases people try to control themselves and avoid drawing attention to themselves. In Bali, on the other hand, friends joke with and distract mourners to keep them calm because emotional displays are viewed as bad for one's health (Rosenblatt, 1993).

Many death rituals occur in stages. For example, some Christian denominations host a wake, when the body (or a picture of the deceased) is displayed and the mourning family receives visitors, followed by a funeral (the church service) and burial at a cemetery. (If the family chooses, the body can be cremated—burned to reduce it to ashes—before a funeral service.)

To recognize the fact that individuals often grieve for a year or more, some cultures have expectations and obligations that encompass the period after burial or cremation. For example, traditional Jewish mourning consists of five clearly defined stages: (1) an intense period of mourning before burial, when individuals are not expected to fulfill normal religious duties; (2) a private time for the 3 days after burial, when mourners are highly distressed and visitors are discouraged; (3) the last four days of *shiva* (the first week of mourning), when visitors offer comfort; (4) 30 days of gradual reentry into the routine activities of life; and (5) the year after shiva, when normal life is expected to resume except in the case of a parent's death, when entertainments may be limited. After this year, mourning is reserved for memorial services that are held on Jewish Holy Days and for the yearly

mourning Culturally prescribed ways of behaving and expressing feelings after the death of a loved one.

There are many ways to grieve, and different cultural traditions encourage different behavior.

anniversary of the person's death on which a candle, the *yahrzeit*, is lit and allowed to burn itself out (Getzel, 1995; Lamm, 1969).

By setting aside certain times of the year for public remembrance of the dead, some societies provide an outlet for continued feelings of loss and reaffirm the sense of community that helps people live more joyfully. A well-known remembrance celebration is the Mexican *Day of the Dead*, a ceremony that occurs on the first and second of November, when souls of the departed are believed to return to visit the living. In a blend of Indian and Spanish customs and beliefs, families set up offerings for the comfort of their departed relatives, often including a washbasin and clean towel, food, and even cigarettes and toys, which are laid out on an altar with burning incense and candles. They also spruce up grave sites, and some even enjoy a festive reunion at a cemetery, complete with food, liquor, and music. These spirited celebrations seem strange to people who were raised to be secretive and somber about death, but they are consistent with the Mexican tradition of openness and joking about *La Muerte* (death).

Death rituals in multicultural societies often last only a few days or less, and there are few guidelines to help people feel confident that they are acting appropriately toward friends who have experienced a loss. As a result, it is easy to understand why people might feel uncomfortable around or even avoid people who are mourning. These reactions are justified because there is more opportunity to offend people when there is a lack of shared traditions. If you have friends who come from a different cultural tradition than your own, you might ask them to explain their traditions and feelings about various issues. For example, some cultures discourage talking about the deceased except on days set aside for remembrance, whereas others find it comforting. Some people even like to joke about their loved one's habits and quirks, which surprises people who consider this behavior disrespectful. Sometimes, simply saying, "I feel confused about how to act . . . what do you need from me?" is a good way to build understanding. Asking individuals what they need is helpful because, as we discuss next, there is no universal reaction to the death of a loved one.

Bereavement and Grief

At 11:00 at night, Jan and Kent Koppelman got a call from the Houston County Sheriff to tell them that their 19-year-old son, Jason, had been in a car accident. Jan believed Jason was dead as soon as they arrived at the hospital, but Kent didn't jump to conclusions. When the doctor finally told them that Jason "didn't make it," Kent was overwhelmed with agony while Jan, who had been preparing herself for the moment, was calmer (Koppelman, 2001).

Bereavement refers to the loss of a significant person by death; **grief** is the combination of emotional, behavioral, and physiological reactions to loss. The duration and extent of grief vary enormously, depending on our relationship with the departed, whether death followed a long life or cut life short, and the meaning of death in our culture or faith community. But despite a great deal of variability, all grief reactions have four components (Stroebe et al., 2001):

Emotional. Individuals who are grieving are often sad or depressed, but they may also feel anxious, guilty, angry, or hostile.

Cognitive. People who have lost a loved one are often preoccupied with thoughts of the deceased and experience problems with memory and concentration.

Behavioral. Grieving individuals often cry, but it is also common to be agitated, extremely tired, or socially withdrawn.

Physical. The body responds to loss by increasing production of stress hormones that increase vulnerability to disease. Individuals who are grieving are likely to experience a loss of appetite, sleep disturbances, and a variety of nonspecific physical symptoms.

Kent Koppelman experienced many of the reactions associated with sudden bereavement. Initially, he cried uncontrollably yet felt numb. "The pain was so intense," he later wrote, "I don't know how I could have tolerated it had it not been for the numbness. My entire body was numb" (2001, p. 86). He was also extremely tired and had trouble sleeping. But he was surprised when he didn't have many of the reactions we are led to expect. For example, he wasn't angry at Jason for driving recklessly, his work didn't suffer, and his relationship with Jan remained strong.

Grief responses can significantly impair functioning. For example, bereaved individuals have higher mortality rates than comparison samples, higher rates of depression, and poorer health (Archer, 2001). These consequences have piqued psychologists' interest in the following questions: If grief has such detrimental effects, why has it survived as a reaction to loss? How much variability is there in individual responses to loss? Can interventions speed the return to normal functioning? Let's look at each of these questions in turn.

THE FUNCTION OF GRIEF. Given how painful and debilitating grieving can be, what purpose could it serve? Evolutionary psychologists point out that all social animals, such as dogs, cats, and humans, show the behaviors associated with grief. In these species, individuals separate frequently, such as when small groups leave to hunt, but then reassemble to function as a team. Some scientists have speculated that sad reactions to an individual leaving prevent social networks from being "rapidly rearranged to accommodate their absence" (Archer, 2001, p. 268). According to this perspective, grief is part of an attachment system that maintains bonds during brief separations, a system that includes mental models of loved ones as well as emotional reactions to their absence. The idea is that temporary separations are vastly more common than permanent loss, so the benefits from "shutting down" after a separation outweigh the problems that can occur after a death.

If grief is a consequence of an attachment system that helps us maintain relationships, it follows that we will not feel the same about every death that touches

bereavement The loss of a significant person by death.

grief The emotional, behavioral, and physiological reactions to loss.

our lives because our relationships are not equally strong. Let's turn now to the range of reactions that occur after loss.

MYTHS AND FACTS ABOUT LOSS. Resources for grieving families detail three phases of grief: a first phase of shock, disbelief, and numbness; a second phase of "confrontation" with the reality of loss, when people struggle to cope with the life changes produced by the loss; and a third phase of acceptance and adjustment. Many discussions of grief mention that it often takes a year or so for people to travel through the first two phases (American Cancer Society, 2001). These "grief-in-a-nutshell" descriptions are helpful if they validate your reaction to loss and offer hope that things will improve in the future. Unfortunately, though, they can also lead you to worry that you are not reacting "correctly" if they fail to capture how you feel. As a result, grief researchers currently emphasize the diversity of people's reactions to loss. Specifically, they have challenged each of the following myths (Wortman & Silver, 2001):

▶ *Myth 1: Intense distress is the "normal" reaction to bereavement.* It is true that it is not uncommon to experience severe depression after a loss. In a study of caregivers of gay men, for instance, 76 percent had high depression scores 1 month after losing someone to AIDS (Folkman et al., 1996). But many people are not greatly distressed by bereavement. Only 20 to 35 percent of people who had lost a spouse in one group of studies were clinically depressed in the months following death (Wortman & Silver, 1989), and 40 percent of respondents in another study did not experience even a 2-week period of sadness that was sufficient to cause loss of interest in pleasurable things or activities (Bruce et al., 1990). Typically, people who show little obvious distress have good coping skills, have grieved for their loved one before the death, or experienced death as a relief from the burdens of illness.

▶ *Myth 2: The absence of grief is unhealthy over the long run.* There is no evidence that people who fail to grieve immediately after a death will experience problems with "delayed grief" down the road. In fact, mental health can improve when death relieves individuals from the stress of a difficult health situation or a bad marriage.

▶ *Myth 3: It is important to "work through" grief.* Many therapists believe that it helps the recovery process to think about events surrounding the death, review memories of the deceased, and think about one's feelings. Certainly, some individuals find these activities helpful. For example, Jan and Kent Koppelman (2001) wrote down their thoughts and feelings, Jan went through Jason's report cards and memorabilia to recall shared times, and Kent collected his writings into a book. But there is no evidence that people who engage in such behaviors are generally healthier a year later than those who choose to avoid reminders (Stroebe & Stroebe, 1991).

▶ *Myth 4: It is unhealthy to maintain strong emotional attachments to the deceased.* Some authors have said that it is important to detach emotionally from the deceased in order to form new attachments. On the other hand, many cultures assume that spirits of the dead continue to influence the family, and these cultures *encourage* continued involvement of the dead in the lives of the living (Klass & Walter, 2001). In fact, it is common everywhere for people to continue to talk to their loved ones and to think about them often. Instead of harming the living, research has found that emotional ties can be associated with good adjustment (Genevro, Marshall, & Miller, 2004).

▶ *Myth 5: People should "get over" their grief in about a year.* Well-meaning family members and friends sometimes expect that bereaved individuals will eventually recover from the loss. Bereaved individuals do show improved psychological health over time, but there is no discrete state of "recovery" at the end of grief. Instead, people often have difficult times even years after loss, and painful memories can reoccur throughout life. In one study of people who had lost spouses, most said that painful thoughts never faded completely, even though the frequency of such thoughts declined over time (Wortman & Silver, 2001).

As these myths were being dismantled, experts were constructing a new consensus about grief. The most important finding was that responses to loss are variable, so "there is no one clearly defined course or process of bereavement or grieving" (Genevro et al., 2004, p. 501). Still, the following patterns exist:

▶ *Children grieve differently from adults.* As discussed at the start of this chapter, children think differently about death depending on their age and, therefore, their reactions to death also change as they grow. Young children who have experienced a loss may show helpless behavior and act like an even younger child (such as by bed-wetting), whereas older children often become angry and show behavioral problems, such as disobeying rules and acting aggressively. Children who act out may be confused about their feelings and unable to express their concerns. As a result, it is important for adults to address the topic of death clearly and calmly. Experts suggest giving children time to think and respond after raising the issue, avoiding vague language that has no meaning to children (such as "He's *passed on*"), assuring children that they did not cause the death, and respecting their varied reactions (Willis, 2002). Adolescents often describe significant losses as life-changing experiences yet are reluctant to discuss their grief with friends.

Family dynamics influence how individual children adjust to a significant loss. Just under half of the 8- to 16-year-olds who had lost a biological parent or parent figure in one study were resilient and well-adjusted, but the remaining children received at least one unusually high score on measures of externalizing and internalizing behavior problems. Well-adjusted children tended to have warm caregivers who maintained discipline and had few mental health problems themselves. Apparently, an atmosphere of love with structure helps children maintain a feeling of personal control in the face of stress and leaves them feeling less threatened by negative life events (Lin et al., 2004).

▶ *People strive to give meaning to loss.* Those who are able to make sense of their loss within 6 months of the death, either through religious beliefs or other means, are more likely to be well-adjusted over time. As a result, people who believe in an afterlife and the continued presence of a loved one adjust more easily to a death, experience less helplessness, and use the experience to strengthen their values (Benore & Park, 2004).

▶ *People perceive some types of deaths as especially tragic.* Distress tends to be greater when the deceased was young, the death was sudden and traumatic, and the grieving individual believes the death was preventable. As former English professor Donald Murray (2003) explained about the death of his 20-year-old child, "There will be no healing, but I will become familiar with this new life, always having at my side the daughter no one else can see" (p. 105).

▶ *Some people experience complicated grief (also called pathological grief).* These individuals seem to get "stuck" in prolonged grief that significantly interferes with their ability to function. Compared to others who have experienced loss, individuals with complicated grief tend to have less social support to help them rebuild their lives.

It can be useful to think of the grieving mind as healing much as the body heals from a broken leg (Murray, 2002). A broken leg can heal rapidly and without much pain, or there can be complications. You will recover from the immediate trauma of the break, but there may always be reminders, such as a scar or an ache during cold weather. In the same way, some grieving individuals rebound quickly whereas others experience complications, yet few people are ever exactly the same as they were before the loss. And just as a broken leg ultimately heals due to the body's natural healing powers, individuals must also come to terms with their own grief. As grief expert Judith Murray explained, "Grieving can be seen to follow a pattern that takes a person from a state of disorganization and preoccupation with the loss, to a state of being able to participate in life again, although often with a changed perspective" (p. 53).

GRIEF INTERVENTIONS. Many programs have sprung up to assist grieving individuals, including crisis teams that visit shortly after a death, self-help groups, educational programs on grief, and group psychotherapy. Unfortunately, some of the assumptions these programs are based on have not been supported by research, so it is not surprising that most interventions have a poor track record in terms of effectiveness. One analysis of various types of grief therapy found no positive effect on any outcome variable for people who were experiencing normal grief, and there was evidence that some clients got worse as a result of treatment (Neimeyer, 2000). Based on findings such as these, numerous experts have concluded that interventions are unnecessary and unproductive for most people (Jordan & Neimeyer, 2003). However, those who are experiencing complicated grief may benefit from the same therapies that help depressed clients in general. For example, cognitive behavioral therapies can challenge unhealthy ideas, such as feelings of guilt, and encourage survivors to stay engaged with life (Jacobs & Prigerson, 2000).

Grieving friends and family members can search for the names of soldiers who lost their lives during the Vietnam War at a memorial in Washington, DC. People often touch and create pencil tracings of the engraved names to feel closer to their loved ones.

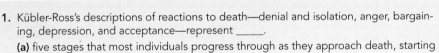

>>> MEMORY MAKERS <<<

1. Kübler-Ross's descriptions of reactions to death—denial and isolation, anger, bargaining, depression, and acceptance—represent _____.
   (a) five stages that most individuals progress through as they approach death, starting with the first stage and ending with the last
   (b) five "styles" of reacting to death, with each individual showing mostly one of these styles
   (c) a list of possible reactions to death

2. The loss of a significant person by death is called _____.
   (a) mourning   (b) grief   (c) bereavement

3. Which of the following is true?
   (a) Intense distress is the normal reaction to bereavement.
   (b) It is important to "work through" grief.
   (c) It is unhealthy to maintain strong emotional attachments to the deceased.
   (d) none of the above.

[1-c (experts no longer think of these as a "stage theory" of dying; 2-c; 3-d (see pages 667–668)]

Contemplating the end of life opens us up to experience life. As Terry Tempest Williams once said, "We are vulnerable, we are teachable once again. Call it a humility in the deepest sense. We allow ourselves to be touched" ("A Conversation," 2005, para. 27).

We hope the stories of life and death in this book will have a positive impact on your journey through the life span. Findings from the field of human development can help you appreciate the wonder of life, but they can also help you make choices that will enrich your life and offer solutions to the inevitable challenges of life. It is comforting to know that even though our individual pathways are unique, we are all part of a world community that shares the basic joys and sorrows that come from the universal cycle of birth, death, and constant change.

⟩⟩⟩ SUMMARY ⟨⟨⟨

Early Learning about Death

1. Most children between 5 and 7 years have some understanding that biological processes cease with death and that death is irreversible and universal; most have a mature concept of death by 10 years when they have a firm understanding that they, too, will die.

2. When school-aged children and adolescents talk about death, they often mix information about the biological reality of death with religious notions of life after death. Adults can help children cope with media coverage about terrorism and natural disasters by staying calm, maintaining normal routines, and limiting the amount of time they spend watching disaster coverage.

Death and Dying

3. Death is a process, so there is no single definition of death. **Somatic death** occurs when the heart and respiratory systems malfunction. In contrast, **brain death** is defined by the absence of specified brain function (often including brainstem function) when measured on more than one occasion.

4. The **syndrome of imminent death** is a set of symptoms that is present shortly before death. Unless death is sudden, people usually die in a hospital or nursing home, at home without nursing care, at home with nursing care, or at home with **hospice care**. Hospice care is a philosophy of care that works to keep patients as alert, pain free, and engaged with their families as possible during their final days. The hospice approach is an interdisciplinary approach to care that offers **palliative care** (measures to relieve pain and discomfort), emotional support, and counseling and information to family members.

5. Terminally ill children show better adjustment and compliance with treatment regimes when there is an open dialogue about death. Parents who discuss the impending death with their children are less likely to regret their decision than parents who withhold this information.

6. Three controversial practices are **passive euthanasia** (withholding life-sustaining treatment so that people can die naturally), **active euthanasia** (triggering another individual's death by lethal drugs or other means), and **physician-assisted suicide** (arranging for the means of death, which patients initiative themselves). Passive euthanasia is a common practice, but there is a great deal of debate about active euthanasia and physician-assisted suicide.

7. You can have a say in your own end-of-life care by preparing an **advance medical directive**. This document may contain a **durable power of attorney for health care** (which appoints another person to make decisions on your behalf) and a **living will** (which specifies the types of end-of-life care you desire or refuse).

Coping with Death

8. Elisabeth Kübler-Ross identified five reactions that dying individuals often experience: denial and isolation, anger, bargaining, depression, and acceptance. These reactions may or may not occur in any individual case, and people sometimes experience more than one feeling at a time or shift back and forth among feelings.

9. Funeral rituals are universal aspects of **mourning**: culturally prescribed ways of behaving and expressing feelings after the death of a loved one. Many cultures hold remembrance ceremonies for the dead at specified times of the year.

10. Many studies have charted how individuals react after **bereavement** (the loss of a significant person by death) when many people are in a state of **grief** (the emotional, behavioral, and physiological reactions to loss). A significant percentage of people are not greatly distressed by bereavement, and there is no evidence that people who fail to grieve immediately will experience emotional problems later on, that recovery is helped by dwelling on memories of the deceased, or that it is useful to sever emotional attachments to the decreased. There is also no evidence that grief interventions are helpful for most people who are experiencing normal grief.

>>>KEY TERMS<<<

thanatologist   (p. 650)
somatic death   (p. 654)
brain death   (p. 654)
terminal decline   (p. 655)
syndrome of imminent death   (p. 655)
hospice care   (p. 657)
palliative care   (p. 657)
passive euthanasia   (p. 659)

active euthanasia   (p. 659)
physician-assisted suicide   (p. 659)
advance medical directive   (p. 660)
durable power of attorney for health care   (p. 660)
living will   (p. 660)
mourning   (p. 664)
bereavement   (p. 666)
grief   (p. 666)

Glossary

A

accommodation In Piaget's theory of cognitive development, modifying a scheme, or way of understanding the world, to adjust to a new experience.

achievement How much someone has learned about a specific academic domain.

active euthanasia The practice of triggering death in an individual with an incurable illness or terminal disease by lethal drugs, carbon monoxide inhalation, or other means.

activity theory A theory proposing that it is normal and desirable for elderly individuals to maintain a variety of interests and activities and to stay involved with friends and family members. See *disengagement theory*.

acute otitis media (AOM) An ear infection in which fluid accumulates behind the eardrum causing fever, pain, and temporary hearing loss. AOM is the most frequently diagnosed disease in childhood.

adaptation In Piaget's theory of cognitive development, the ability to adapt to the environment by integrating new experiences into existing schemes (assimilation) and modifying existing schemes to reflect discrepant experiences (accommodation).

adolescence The time between puberty and adulthood when children undergo the physical and psychological changes they need to assume adult roles. In industrialized societies, puberty usually marks the beginning of a period of adolescence that may last up to a decade.

adolescence-limited delinquents Teenagers who do not begin to engage in frequent or serious illegal behavior until adolescence and tend to commit crimes with peers. These individuals show no particular pattern of risk factors before adolescence and stop their illegal behavior once they are older.

adolescent egocentrism A type of egocentrism, which emerges during adolescence, that involves creation of the *imaginary audience* and the *personal fable*.

adolescent growth spurt A period of rapid growth that begins at an average age of 9 years for girls and 11 years for boys.

affordances Fits between characteristics of the environment and opportunities for action. For example, chairs afford sitting and balls afford throwing.

advance medical directive A document that specifies wishes for health care in the event an individual is too ill to make those decisions.

age dependency ratio The number of nonworking citizens (under age 15 or 65 and older) per 100 people ages 15 to 64.

age discrimination Differential treatment of competent older workers solely because of their age. Age discrimination occurs when qualified older workers are not hired or not promoted or when they are fired, forced to retire, or not given development opportunities because of their age.

aging Gradual changes in the structure and function of our bodies over time that are not due to diseases or accidents.

alleles Alternative forms of single genes. For example, a parent may carry an allele for normal skin pigmentation and an allele for albinism, the absence of pigment.

Alzheimer's disease (AD). The most common form of dementia, characterized by beta-amyloid plaques and neurofibrillary tangles in the brain. Symptoms begin with mild cognitive impairment, especially memory loss for recent activities and information, and then progress to severe confusion, personality changes, and death.

amniocentesis A procedure in which a fine needle is passed through the mother's abdominal wall to draw off a sample of amniotic fluid. Fetal cells in the fluid provide material for genetic testing, and substances in the fluid predict lung development and other conditions.

andropause The gradual decrease in testosterone levels that occurs among older males. Although men do not experience a sharp drop in sex hormones during middle adulthood, andropause is often referred to in popular culture as "male menopause."

anorexia nervosa A condition in which people starve themselves to stay thin. Most cases occur among young women and begin during mid-to-late adolescence.

A-not-B error The tendency infants have to search for objects where they found them earlier (A) rather than their current location (B).

Apgar score A score given to newborns at 1 and 5 minutes after birth to indicate their general condition.

archival data Information in existing records such as school files, police reports, and government documents.

assimilation In Piaget's theory of cognitive development, integrating a new experience into an existing scheme or way of understanding the world.

asthma (also called **reactive airway disease**) A disease in which the airways of the lungs become inflamed, causing them to narrow. Asthma is the most common childhood chronic disease.

attention The process of focusing on particular information in the environment.

attention deficit hyperactivity disorder (ADHD) A condition associated with age-inappropriate patterns of inattention and impulsivity, often with hyperactivity.

authoritarian parents Parents who set high standards and expect their children to obey without question.

authoritative parents Supportive, nurturant parents who set standards, have high expectations, and explain the reasons for rules and restrictions.

autistic disorder (autism) A condition characterized by marked impairments in social interactions, deficits in language and imaginative activity, and a restricted scope of interests.

autoimmune disease A disease in which the immune system attacks the body's own cells. Rheumatoid arthritis (which destroys tissues that line bone joints), multiple sclerosis (which affects the central nervous system), and lupus (which can involve many types of tissue) are autoimmune diseases.

autonomy versus shame and doubt The second stage of Erik Erikson's psychosocial theory, when children from 18 months to 3 years of age react to feedback about their successes and failures by developing confidence in their abilities (autonomy) or feeling shame and doubt.

B

Baltimore Longitudinal Study of Aging (BLSA) One of America's longest-running studies of human aging, which began in 1958. The BLSA is funded by the National Institute on Aging.

basal metabolism The number of calories a resting body needs to survive.

basic trust versus mistrust The first stage of Erik Erikson's psychosocial theory, when sensitive caregiving gives infants from birth to 18 months of age a basic sense of trust in the world. Unresponsive or unpredictable caregiving leads infants to be mistrustful.

behavioral genetics The field that studies how much nature and nurture contribute to individual differences in human behavior.

behaviorism A movement in psychology that encouraged scientists to study the relationship between observable events and observable behavior, especially as described by the principles of conditioning.

bereavement The loss of a significant person by death.

beta-amyloid plaques Debris in the brain that contains fragments of protein mixed with other molecules and brain cells. Beta-amyloid plaques are a signature feature of Alzheimer's disease, but they occur to a lesser extent in some normal elderly brains.

Big Five Five traits that frequently emerge from studies of individual differences: neuroticism (emotional instability), extroversion (how outgoing people are), openness to experience (how creative and unconventional people are), agreeableness (how cooperative and positive they are toward other people), and conscientiousness (how disciplined and careful they are).

biological risk The risk of developmental problems stemming from harmful biological events during the prenatal, perinatal, and postnatal periods.

body mass index (BMI) A formula for determining how heavy someone is adjusted for height. BMI is calculated by dividing weight in kilograms by the square of height in meters (weight $\div$ height^2), or [weight(lb) $\div$ height(inches)^2 $\times$ 703].

brain lateralization The tendency for the left and right cerebral hemispheres to be specialized for different tasks.

brain death An absence of brain function. Definitions and criteria for brain death vary around the world. Typical laws require physicians to document a lack of brain activity throughout the brain on more than one occasion, including lower (brainstem) functions.

brain spurt The period of rapid synaptogenesis that occurs between 6 months after fertilization and 18 months postnatal.

bulimia nervosa A condition in which people binge eat (take in large amounts of food) and then try to rid the body of calories by dieting, exercising, vomiting, or other means.

C

caloric restriction Severely limiting the number of calories consumed each day.

canalization The extent to which a trait develops normally across a range of environments. Highly canalized traits are difficult to deflect from their expected tracks.

case study An in-depth study of a particular person.

centenarian A person who has lived for a century or more.

cephalocaudal development A pattern in which growth and development start at the head and proceed downward.

cerebral reserve hypothesis The idea that intellectual challenges build a brain

that can better compensate for the physical assaults of aging.

cesarean section (C-section) Surgery to remove a fetus through an incision in the mother's abdomen.

child maltreatment Actions (or failures to act) by caregivers that put children at risk of harm. Maltreatment includes physical abuse, sexual abuse, neglect, and emotional abuse.

child-centered preschool Preschool in which children learn by playing with everyday objects and participating in meaningful projects and interactions with other children.

child-directed speech The speech older children and adults use with young children, which is often simpler and more predictable than speech directed at adults.

chorionic villus sampling A procedure for collecting fetal cells from the chorion, a membrane surrounding the fetus.

chromosomal abnormality An abnormality caused by the loss of chromosomal material, duplication of chromosomal material, or the transfer of chromosomal material from one location to another. Down syndrome is an example.

chromosomes Threadlike structures in the nuclei of cells, constructed from DNA, that contain the genetic code. Humans typically have 46 chromosomes arranged in 23 pairs.

chronic diseases Medical conditions like diabetes and arthritis that develop slowly and are long-lasting.

cognitive perspective A theoretical perspective that analyzes how we think, that is, how we acquire knowledge and use it to solve problems, make decisions, and guide behavior.

cohort effects Systematic differences between age groups that are due to cultural changes over time.

concrete operational thought A mode of thinking, lasting roughly from 7 to 12 years of age, when children begin to think more logically and flexibly about concrete materials (materials they can see and touch). Concrete operational children have difficulty handling abstract concepts, that is, reasoning about possibilities that do not physically exist.

contextual perspective An approach to development that looks at mutual influences between children and their environments.

controversial children Children who receive many positive nominations but also many negative nominations when their peers indicate whom they like and dislike. (See *popular*, *rejected*, and *neglected* children.)

conventional morality In Lawrence Kohlberg's theory of moral development, the

two stages of moral reasoning that are typical of most adolescents and adults. At this stage, people are concerned about pleasing others, being a good person, and maintaining social order rather than making decisions based on universal ethical principles.

correlation coefficient A statistic that describes the strength and direction of the relationship between two variables.

correlational study A study that looks for a relationship between *naturally occurring variables*—physical traits, behaviors, and attitudes as these things naturally exist in the world.

cross-sectional study A research design in which investigators test individuals from several different age groups at one point in time.

cross-sequential study A combination of cross-sectional and longitudinal designs, in which several age groups are identified at one point in time and then retested at regular intervals.

crystallized intelligence The knowledge and verbal skills that accumulate as you age.

cultural display rules Social conventions for expressing feelings, such as the rule that we should act happy about receiving a gift we do not want.

culture Features of the environment that are learned, including the technology, art, morals, laws, customs, and beliefs of individual societies.

cumulative stressor hypothesis The hypothesis that the sheer number of environmental stressors in a child's life is a stronger predictor of developmental outcomes than the presence of any particular stressor. Stressors are such things as maternal mental illness, poverty, low levels of parental education, and single parenthood.

D

delayed puberty Pubertal onset more than two standard deviations above the mean. For girls, puberty is considered delayed if there is an absence of breast development by 14 years and delayed menstruation. Boys are considered delayed if there are no signs of puberty by 14 years.

deliberate practice Training with individualized feedback on tasks selected by a qualified teacher.

dementia A permanent loss of mental ability that is serious enough to impair daily living tasks. People who have one of the many conditions that produce dementia experience problems in memory, reasoning, and planning that dramatically affect their behavior.

dementia with Lewy bodies The second most common form of dementia, characterized by disturbances in memory, language, and motor behavior, often with visual hallucinations and personality disturbances.

dependent variable The variable a researcher measures in an experiment to determine the influence of the independent (manipulated) variable.

desirable difficulties Instructional conditions that make initial learning more difficult but improve long-term memory and transfer of learning to new situations.

developmental coordination disorder A condition in which motor clumsiness significantly impairs daily self-help skills or achievement.

developmental psychopathology The field that studies problem behavior from a developmental perspective.

developmental risk The risk of developmental problems stemming from harmful biological events or environmental factors during the prenatal, perinatal, and postnatal periods.

developmentally appropriate practice Educational practices that recognize and accommodate children's developmental levels and interests. An appropriate curriculum promotes development of the whole child by considering physical, emotional, social, and cognitive needs.

diabetic retinopathy An eye disease that develops when an elevated blood sugar level harms blood vessels in the retina.

dialectical reasoning A process of critical thinking in which a person considers conflicting viewpoints by evaluating the evidence for and against both sides.

discrepancy principle The idea that individuals pay more attention to information that differs somewhat—but not too much—from their existing schemes.

disengagement theory of aging The idea that it is normal and beneficial for elderly individuals and society to mutually withdraw from each other as the elderly individual's abilities decline. See *activity theory*.

dizygotic twins Twins produced from two fertilized eggs, commonly called fraternal twins.

DNA Deozyribonucleic acid, a molecule that contains the genetic code.

dominant allele An allele (form of a gene) that masks the influence of other alleles and is, therefore, expressed.

doula A lay person who is trained to serve as a labor coach.

Down syndrome A condition characterized by a distinctive physical appearance and moderate to severe mental retardation, often accompanied by defects that produce medical complications. It is caused by an extra copy or portion of chromosome 21; also called **trisomy 21**.

dual representation The ability to mentally represent a model as an object in its own right and, at the same time, as a symbol that stands for something else.

dual-processing model A model of decision making that includes two systems: an *analytical* processing system that solves problems using formal, logical thought, and an *experiential* processing system that uses mental shortcuts to make decisions quickly and automatically.

durable power of attorney for health care A document that appoints another person to make health care decisions for an individual who is unable to do so.

E

effortful control The ability to inhibit a dominant response in order to perform another response. Effortful control develops gradually during middle childhood as distant brain regions become integrated into functional circuits.

egocentrism A tendency to see things from one's own perspective. Egocentric people are unaware of other people's perceptions, ideas, or feelings.

elaboration A strategy for remembering that involves using information from existing knowledge to give meaning to to-be-remembered information. For example, making a mental picture of items on a grocery list and relating a new word to one that is already familiar are examples of elaboration.

elderspeak A type of slow, simplified speech that people sometimes use when they are speaking to elderly adults.

embryo The developing organism from 2 weeks after fertilization through the eighth week.

embryonic period Prenatal development from the beginning of the third week through the eighth week.

emerging adulthood The time between 18 and 25 years when most people are too old to be adolescents, yet not independent enough to be full-fledged adults.

emotional intelligence Skills that help people manage their emotions and respond to other people's emotional needs.

endocrine system A control system of glands that produce, store, and secrete *hormones*.

environment Nonheritable influences. The environment includes biological influences, such as exposure to diseases, as well as social influences.

episodic memories Memories of events that are stored as specific episodes by including information about the context in which the events occurred.

ethnicity Membership in a group defined by a common history, nationality, or culture. For example, Korean and Hispanic are ethnic terms.

ethnocentrism The belief that one's ethnic group is superior to other groups.

ethnography An in-depth description of a group's daily activities, generally developed by participant observation.

ethology The study of animal behavior, especially in natural habitats.

evaluation research Research to evaluate the effectiveness of programs or interventions.

everyday intelligence (also called **practical intelligence**) The ability to use cognitive resources during daily life. Everyday intelligence includes the ability to navigate basic life skills (such as reading medication labels) and skill at solving real-life dilemmas (such as deciding how to get a broken lawn mower fixed).

evidence-based instruction In education, the practice of choosing instructional approaches that have produced the best achievement in scientific studies.

evolutionary perspective A theoretical perspective that asks how patterns of growth and behavior reflect a species' adaptation to past environments.

executive processes The processes involved in monitoring and controlling individuals' attention and behavior, planning, and performing multiple tasks at once.

experience-dependent brain development Changes that occur in the brain when we adapt to specific environments, such as when we learn vocabulary words or how to ride a bicycle. (In contrast, *experience-expectant brain development* involves changes that occur when we acquire universal skills, such as vision or locomotion. Experience-expectant brain development occurs as long as basic stimulation is adequate.)

experience-expectant brain development Changes in the brain that require stimulation available in virtually all human environments, such as visual patterns.

experiment A research method for discovering cause–effect relationships that involves manipulating one variable to discover its effect on another variable.

expertise Advanced skill or knowledge in a particular field.

explicit memories Memories represented as words or mental pictures. Semantic and episodic memories are explicit memories.

externalizing behaviors A cluster of behaviors that includes disobedience, temper tantrums, irritability, and jealousy.

F

false-belief problem A test of whether people can set aside what they know to appreciate that other people may have different beliefs.

fast mapping The process of assigning meaning to a new word by quickly linking the word onto concepts that are already known.

feminization of old age The increasing proportion of females in a population from younger to older age brackets.

fertilization The process by which sperm and egg fuse to form the first cell of a new individual (also called *conception*).

fetal alcohol syndrome (FAS) A condition characterized by facial deformities, growth retardation, and central nervous system impairment that is caused by exposure to alcohol during gestation. Disruptions to the developing brain can lead to poor coordination, attentional problems, and mental retardation.

fetal monitoring Continuous monitoring of fetal heart rate either externally (by strapping a unit across the mother's abdomen) or internally (by attaching an electrode to the scalp of the fetus).

fetal period Prenatal development from the beginning of the ninth week until birth.

fetus The developing organism from the beginning of the ninth week after fertilization until birth.

fictive kinship The practice of treating people as relatives even though they are not related to us by blood or marriage. Fictive kin may be called "auntie," "cousin," or another appropriate term, and they assume some rights and responsibilities that are usually reserved for family members.

fluid intelligence The ability to reason abstractly and solve new problems.

folic acid (or **folate**) A B-complex vitamin. Folic acid is the synthetic form of folate, but both forms function the same once they are absorbed by the body. Women deficient in folic acid have a higher risk of delivering children with neural tube defects.

food insecurity Fear of not having access to safe, nutritious food.

food neophobia A fear of new foods, used to describe the tendency young children have to avoid unfamiliar foods.

formal operational thought In Piaget's theory, the capacity for increasingly abstract thought that emerges around 11 to 12 years of age (often described as an intellectual shift from "things" to "ideas"). Formal operational children can engage in *hypothetico-deductive reasoning* (the ability to generate and test hypotheses) and *formal propositional logic* (the ability to understand possible combinations of variables).

fragile X syndrome The most frequent inherited cause of mental retardation. This syndrome results from an abnormal number of copies of three bases of genetic code on the X chromosome.

free radical theory A theory that says that aging occurs when oxygen-free radicals, a highly reactive form of oxygen, are produced inside cells. Free radicals damage cell molecules by "stealing" electrons from them.

G

g The hypothetical brain processes that produce variation in intelligent behavior across a wide variety of tasks. It is proposed that this "general factor" explains why scores on various sections of an intelligence test are highly correlated.

gametes Reproductive cells. A new organism is produced when gametes from a male and a female combine.

gender constancy (sex-category constancy) An awareness that gender is a permanent characteristic based on one's genitals.

gender dysphoria A condition in which an individual's gender identity does not match his or her biological sex.

gender identity Our fundamental sense of being male or female.

gender intensification hypothesis The idea that behavioral and psychological differences between the sexes increase during adolescence as a result of social pressure to conform to stereotypical gender roles.

gender typing (also called **sex typing**) The process of adopting behaviors and preferences that are associated with males or females.

gender-role behaviors Behaviors consistent with cultural norms for how males and females should act.

generativity versus self-absorption and stagnation The seventh phase of life in Erikson's theory when people in middle adulthood (about 40 to 65 years) either focus on production by nurturing, teaching, and leading or become self-absorbed and experience stagnation.

genes Segments of DNA molecules that are the functional units of heredity.

genetic counseling Evaluation and counseling by a genetic care provider or other professional to calculate the risk of bearing a child with a genetic defect, provide prevention information, or diagnose a genetic condition.

genetic imprinting (also called **genomic** or **parental imprinting**) When expression of a trait depends on whether it was inherited from the mother or the father.

genotype An organism's genetic makeup.

gene–environment (G–E) correlations (also called **genotype–environment correlations**). Ways in which genetic mechanisms influence individuals' environments and experiences.

geriatrics The branch of medicine that deals with diseases and problems of the elderly.

germinal period The first 2 weeks of development after fertilization.

gerontology The study of biological, psychological, and sociological phenomena associated with aging.

glaucoma A group of conditions in which pressure from fluid in the eye is too high, causing damage to the optic nerve.

glial cells Cells in the nervous system that insulate neurons, provide them with nutrients, and remove cellular waste.

grief The emotional, behavioral, and physiological reactions to loss.

group socialization theory A theory that states that children's personalities are constructed as they adopt the behaviors and attitudes of their peers and compare themselves to others in their social group. This theory assumes that one's status and role in the peer group build characteristics that carry into adult life.

H

Hayflick limit The number of cell divisions that occurs before a cell dies.

heredity The genetic mechanisms by which parents pass traits on to their children.

heritability (h^2) For a particular trait, heritability is the proportion of observed variability among individuals in a group that is attributed to genetic variability. Heritability estimates range from 0 (no influence of genetic variability) to 1.0 (all of the observed variability is due to genetic variability).

heuristics Commonsense strategies or rules of thumb that are often useful but do not guarantee an optimal solution.

high-stakes tests Tests that are tied to major consequences, such as retention in a grade, high school graduation, scholarship opportunities, or college admission.

Home Observation for Measurement of the Environment (HOME) An inventory for measuring the quality of a child's home environment by direct observation and an interview with the child's primary caregiver.

Homo sapiens Latin for "wise human being" and the name of the human species.

hormones Molecules that can travel through the bloodstream and affect distant cells.

hospice care A philosophy of end-of-life care that is committed to maintaining quality of life for terminally ill patients by keeping them as alert, pain free, and engaged with their families as possible.

hot cognition The mental processes that occur when personal goals, moods, and prior stereotypes influence judgments.

human development The scientific study of patterns of change and stability that occur as we move from conception to death.

human genome The entire set of genes that defines our species.

Human Genome Project An international effort to map the human genetic code. The project was officially completed in 2003.

hypothetico-deductive reasoning The ability to think like a scientist by mentally generating hypotheses, deducing how an experiment should come out if a hypothesis is true, and coordinating conclusions with evidence.

I

identity versus role confusion In Erik Erikson's theory, the fifth stage of development in which adolescents explore who they are and how they fit into society.

imaginary audience The adolescent's false belief that other people are preoccupied with his or her appearance and behavior.

implicit memories Conditioned responses, habits, and learned procedures that can influence behavior without being voluntarily called to mind.

inclusion A newer term for educating children with disabilities in regular classrooms. Inclusion is an educational philosophy that values the contributions of all children and encourages all children to participate in their communities.

independent variable The variable a researcher manipulates in an experiment. Independent variables consist of two or more groups or conditions.

induction A strategy for correcting children that involves modeling empathy while explaining how children's behavior affects themselves or other people.

industry versus inferiority Erikson's fourth stage of psychosocial development, from roughly 6 years of age to puberty, when children are intrigued with the world of knowledge and work, try to master the technologies of their cultures, and monitor the success of their efforts. Children who succeed develop a sense of mastery and competence; those who fail feel inadequate and inferior.

infant determinism The belief that early events influence the rest of our lives.

infant states Changes in consciousness from deep sleep to alert behavior, fussing, and crying.

infantile amnesia The phenomenon that older children and adults typically have no memories of events that occurred before 2 to 3 years of age.

information processing approach An approach to studying thinking that analyzes how our brains manipulate information during the processes of perception, attention, memory storage and retrieval, and decision making.

inhibition Processes that decrease the probability of neural activity. Cognitive inhibition reduces interference from distracting events, suppresses irrelevant items in memory, and blocks previous responses from occurring again.

initiative versus guilt Erikson's third stage of psychosocial development, from roughly 3 to 6 years of age, when children compare themselves to others and want to master what other people have mastered. During this stage, the feedback they receive determines whether they feel worthy or bogged down by guilt because their behavior seems inadequate.

integrity versus despair The eighth and final stage of Erik Erikson's theory of psychosocial development in which people review their lives and either feel satisfied with how they have lived (integrity) or feel they have not lived life to the fullest (despair).

intelligence An individual's potential to learn and adapt to the environment.

intergenerational transmission of abuse The phenomenon of maltreated children growing up to abuse their own children. Across studies, only about 30 percent of abused children grow up to be abusers themselves.

internalizing behaviors A cluster of behaviors that includes sadness, shyness, anxiety, and physical complaints.

intimacy versus isolation The sixth phase of life in Erikson's theory (roughly 19 to 40 years) when adults forge meaningful relationships or suffer from a lack of connection.

intrinsic motivation The desire to do something because you want to, not because you are encouraged or forced to.

IQ (intelligence quotient) score A number that indicates whether children have below average, average, or above average intelligence.

L

language acquisition device (LAD) A hypothetical mental structure, including innate assumptions about the nature of language, that allows children to learn language.

lead poisoning Damage to the brain, nerves, and other body systems caused by swallowing or inhaling lead.

learning Relatively permanent changes in behavior that result from experience.

learning perspective A theoretical perspective that focuses on how people learn by describing observable relationships between environmental events and behavior.

life expectancy The average amount of time a person in a given place and time will live. For example, a life expectancy of 80 years means that 50 percent of newborns will survive until 80 years of age.

life span The maximum amount of time that any human can live, which is estimated to be approximately 120 years.

life span approach to development An approach to studying development that emphasizes the potential for change that exists throughout life.

life-course persistent delinquents Teenagers who have a history of engaging in solitary antisocial behavior. These individuals often have a history of difficult temperaments, attentional problems, learning difficulties, and family risk factors. They are more likely than other adolescents to continue criminal activity into adulthood.

life-course theory A theory of development, proposed by Glen H. Elder, Jr., that describes how development is influenced by the historical context, the timing of events in an individual's life, the impact of events on relationship networks, and the choices people in those networks make.

life-span theory of control A theory that looks at how people select strategies for pursuing goals and coping with failure at different points in the life cycle.

living will A document that specifies the type of medical treatment individuals want to receive and the treatment they refuse in the event they are too ill to make their wishes known.

longitudinal study A research design in which investigators follow a group of individuals over a period of time.

long-term memory A memory store that records experiences for hours, weeks, or years.

low birth weight A birth weight of less than 2,500 grams (5.5 pounds).

M

macular degeneration A condition in which the part of the retina that gives us sharp central vision (for reading) degrades. Macular degeneration causes blurred vision and a dark spot in the center of the visual field. It is the leading cause of blindness in older individuals.

mainstreaming The practice of educating children with disabilities in regular classrooms (now commonly called **inclusion**).

maturation The genetically determined unfolding of physical and behavioral changes over time.

menarche First menstruation.

menopause The end of menstruation and the ability to conceive a child. The average age of menopause is 51 years. However, some women experience menopause before they are 40, whereas others continue having periods until they are almost 60.

mental retardation A condition defined by significantly subaverage intelligence and problems with daily living skills that is evident during childhood.

meta-analysis A statistical procedure that combines the results of many studies to determine the overall effect of a variable across samples.

metabolic syndrome (also called **Syndrome X**). A collection of symptoms that includes obesity, high blood pressure, unhealthy blood fat levels, and insulin resistance (a condition in which cells lose their ability to use insulin to convert glucose into energy).

metacognition Knowledge and awareness of one's own cognitive processes.

metalinguistic awareness The ability to reflect on language as an object. Children show metalinguistic awareness when they appreciate nonliteral uses of language, such as when they understand puns or use sarcasm (saying "Nice catch" to someone who has just dropped a ball).

metamemory Knowledge about memory. Metamemory includes such things as knowing how much information you can learn in a specific amount of time and which of two lists will be easier to learn.

metamodels Guiding assumptions about the nature of development that characterize various theoretical perspectives.

midwife A medical professional who provides birthing assistance to mothers who do not have serious illness or complications.

modeling (also called **imitation** and **observational learning**) The processes involved in observing and copying other people's behavior.

monogamy The practice of mating with only one partner. Monogamous marriages are marriages to only one other person.

monozygotic twins Twins produced from one fertilized egg that divides between the first and fourteenth postfertilization day, commonly called identical twins.

Montessori preschool An approach to preschool education in which children are allowed to choose from a number of skill-building activities.

morality of constraint A stage of moral development when children respect rules but see them as absolute and unchangeable. In Piagetian theory, this type of thinking is most common between the ages of 5 and 7 years.

morality of cooperation A stage of moral development when people understand that social rules are arbitrary agreements that can be changed. In Piagetian theory, this type of thinking can begin as early as 7 years but is more common by 10 or 11 years.

morbidity rates The frequency of various chronic diseases in a population. Health officials use changes in morbidity rates over time to evaluate the success of interventions and to identify emerging issues.

mortality rates The rate of death in a population, often expressed as the number of deaths per 100,000 in a given year. By comparing mortality rates for different age groups and segments of the population, health officials can plan interventions and assess their effectiveness.

motor milestones Gross and fine motor behaviors that emerge according to a predictable timetable.

mourning Culturally prescribed ways of behaving and expressing feelings after the death of a loved one.

mutations Changes in genes that occur due to spontaneous internal processes or environmental influences.

myelination The production of a fatty substance around axons to insulate fibers and speed transmission.

N

naturalistic observation Observation in real-world settings that does not interfere with or influence people's ongoing activities.

nature–nurture controversy The debate about whether development is directed primarily by heredity or the environment.

neglected children Children who receive few positive *or* negative nominations when their peers indicate whom they like and dislike.(See *popular*, *rejected*, and *controversial children*.)

neonatal period The first 4 weeks after birth.

neonates Newborn babies.

neural migration The migration of neurons from the location where they are produced to their final locations in the brain.

neural plasticity The brain's ability to change from experience.

neural tube defects Defects caused by failure of the neural tube to close completely. Fusion failure at the top of the tube causes an absence of brain tissue called anencephaly; fusion failure farther down causes spina bifida, in which parts of the spinal cord develop outside the vertebrae.

neurofibrillary tangles Structures produced in the brain when long protein fibers inside neurons twist and the neurons die. Neurofibrillary tangles are a signature feature of Alzheimer's disease, but they occur to a lesser extent in normal aging brains.

neurogenesis The production of neurons in the brain.

neurons Cells in the nervous system that are designed to receive and send information.

neurulation The process of forming the neural tube, which will become the brain and spinal cord.

niche-picking The tendency of individuals to choose activities and environments that match their personalities and interests.

night terrors A type of partial arousal in which children scream, thrash about, and act incoherently.

nocturnal enuresis The loss of bladder control during sleep.

normative approach to development An approach to understanding development that describes average or typical development at various ages. Results are often summarized in charts that are called *developmental norms*.

norm-referenced tests Tests that have been administered to large and representative samples of children so the performance of individual children can be compared against the performance of children as a whole.

norms of reaction The idea that genetically influenced traits develop differently in different environments.

nuclear family A family unit consisting of a mother, father, and their children.

O

object permanence The ability to understand that objects continue to exist in space and time even when they are not currently being perceived.

online victimization A variety of distressing events occurring via the Internet, including harassment, unwanted exposure to sexual images or sexual conversation, and sexual solicitation.

open education An educational philosophy in which children direct their own learning by selecting hands-on experiences. At the elementary school level, open classrooms often include a broader range of ages than traditional classrooms, so learning is more personal and less competitive.

organization The tendency to integrate psychological structures (schemes) into more complex systems.

organization A strategy for remembering that involves clustering items into related groups, such as remembering all animals together and all flowers together.

osteoporosis A painful and often crippling condition in which bones become fragile and prone to breaks. (*Osteoporosis* literally means "porous bones.")

overlapping waves theory A theory that says that children and adults typically use a variety of strategies to solve problems. People retain multiple strategies as they mature, but the probability they will use any given strategy changes as they gain knowledge and experience.

overregularization The use of a linguistic rule in a situation in which it doesn't apply, such as when children say "mouses" or "I putted it away."

P

palliative care (also called **comfort care**) Measures to relieve pain and other distressing symptoms of illness when there is no possibility of curing an illness.

paradox of aging The finding that seniors generally feel satisfied with their lives despite the fact that they suffer physical and cognitive losses.

partial arousals Behaviors such as talking, sleepwalking, or night terrors that occur during the transition out of deep (delta) sleep.

participant observation Observation by a researcher who is actively participating in a group's activities.

passive euthanasia The practice of withholding life-sustaining treatment so that patients with incurable illness or terminal disease will die.

peak height velocity (PHV) The time when growth is most rapid. The average age of PHV is 11 1/2 years for girls and 13 1/2 years for boys.

peer group A social unit, often consisting of leaders and followers, that generates shared values and standards of behavior.

perceptual invariants Features that remain the same in the changing flow of perceptual information. These features help us distinguish one object from another.

perceptual learning The process by which people learn to attend to, process, or interpret perceptual information.

perimenopause The 4 to 6 years before a woman's last menstrual period when she often fails to ovulate and the hormone levels necessary to support a pregnancy are declining. Symptoms of perimenopause include irregular menstrual cycles, heavier or lighter periods, and water retention.

permissive parents Parents who demand little from their children and do little to train them to be more independent.

personal fable The adolescent's sense of being unique and invulnerable. The personal fable involves the belief that one's emotions and insights are special and that no one is likely to understand them.

person-first language A way of talking about disabilities that mentions the person, rather than the disability, first. Person-first language indicates that a person *has* a disability but does not refer to the person *as* the disability. For example, "people who stutter" is preferable to "stutterers."

phenotype An organism's actual physical and biochemical characteristics, which are the result of an underlying genetic code (*genotype*) interacting with the environment.

phenylketonuria (PKU) A condition in which individuals lack normal levels of an enzyme needed to metabolize phenylalanine, an amino acid that is present in large quantities in high-protein foods. Mental retardation is prevented by placing affected children on a special diet.

phonics A direct-instruction method that teaches children the relationship between individual letters and sounds so they can decode new words.

phonological awareness (phonemic awareness) Knowledge of the sound structure of spoken words. Children demonstrate phonological awareness when they decide if two words rhyme or start with the same sound.

physician-assisted suicide Arranging the means for someone to commit suicide, which the person who desires death initiates.

placenta A fleshy disk of cells that keeps the mother's bloodstream separate from the bloodstream of the developing embryo. The placenta sustains the life of the embryo by transferring oxygen and nutrients, removing waste products, and after the initial months of gestation, secreting hormones that sustain the pregnancy.

polyandry The right of a woman to be married to more than one man.

polygamy The right of a man to take more than one wife.

polygenic inheritance When trait inheritance is determined by more than one gene.

popular children Children who receive many positive nominations and few negative nominations when their peers indicate whom they like and dislike. (See *rejected*, *neglected*, and *controversial* children.)

positive energy balance The consumption of more energy than an individual expends, which is the cause of weight gain.

possible selves Visions of what an individual might be in the future.

postconventional morality In Kohlberg's theory, the highest level of moral reasoning that makes reference to fundamental principles of fairness and justice.

postformal thought A way of thinking that develops after formal operational reasoning. Postformal thinkers realize that many questions lack a single answer, that the search for knowledge is never ending, and that there may be some value in seemingly opposing positions.

power assertion A strategy for controlling children that appeals to one's status and right to set the rules. Power assertion often involves demands, threats, and punishments.

pragmatics The social uses of language, such as how to take turns at appropriate times, how to interpret intended meanings, and how to modify one's speech for different listeners.

precocious puberty Pubertal onset at an age that is more than two standard deviations below the mean. There is debate about what age norms should be used to define precocious puberty and what secondary sex characteristics must be present. A conservative definition is pubertal onset before 8 years of age in girls and 10 years of age in boys.

preconventional morality In Lawrence Kohlberg's theory of moral development, the two stages of moral reasoning (typical of 4- to 10-year-olds) when children view rules as absolute and judge actions by whether or not they lead to punishment.

predictive validity The ability of tests to predict later behaviors, skills, or academic achievement.

premature (preterm) infants Infants born 3 or more weeks before their due dates.

premoral stage A stage of moral development when children show little concern about rules. In Piagetian theory, this stage lasts from birth to about 5 years.

prenatal (antenatal) classes Classes that prepare parents for the experience of childbirth. Common topics include the stages of labor and techniques for managing pain.

preoperational stage Piaget's second stage of cognitive development (roughly from 2 to 7 years), when children are illogical because their thinking is centered (focused on only one aspect of a problem), appearance-bound (focused on what is perceptually obvious), static (considering only the current state of affairs), and irreversible (not capable of reversing a prior change).

presbycusis The deterioration of hearing associated with aging.

primary aging The gradual process of bodily decline that is genetically programmed to occur in all humans.

primary control Control strategies that involve changing the external world to fit people's needs and desires. People are using primary control strategies when they study for an exam, argue a point with another individual, or put money into a retirement account.

primary prevention Efforts to prevent a hazard from occurring.

primary sex characteristics Structures that are directly involved in reproduction, including the uterus, ovaries, and vagina in girls and the penis and testes in boys.

prodigies Children who perform a skill at a level that is rare even among trained professionals.

protective factors Characteristics that protect individuals against the negative outcomes that are usually associated with various risk factors.

protein-energy malnutrition (PEM) A type of malnutrition that occurs when the intake of energy or protein is too low to sustain the body.

proximodistal development A pattern in which growth and development begin in the center of the body and radiate outward.

psychoactive drugs Chemicals that influence perception, mood, or behavior. Alcohol, marijuana, and cocaine are examples of psychoactive drugs.

psychodynamic perspective A group of theories, inspired by Sigmund Freud and his followers, that emphasizes how biological forces and developmental experiences combine to produce behavior and personality.

puberty The period of rapid development during which individuals become capable of reproduction.

R

recessive allele An allele (form of a gene) that is not expressed unless both alleles in a pair are recessive.

redshirting Delaying a child's entrance into kindergarten. (This term, borrowed from collegiate sports, refers to the red jerseys athletes wear when they are kept out of varsity competition for a year.)

reflexes Involuntary, unlearned movements that occur in response to specific stimuli.

regulatory sequences (sometimes called **genetic switches**) Segments of DNA that influence when and where other genes are expressed.

rehearsal A strategy for remembering that involves mentally repeating items over and over again.

rejected children Children who receive many negative nominations and few positive nominations when their peers indicate

whom they like and dislike. (See *popular, neglected,* and *controversial* children.)

resilience The ability to thrive in the face of hardship or overcome the negative effects of hardship.

Rh disease A condition produced when antibodies from an Rh- mother, whose blood lacks a protein called Rh factor, attacks the blood system of an Rh− infant. Because commingling of blood is necessary to trigger antibody production, the mother's first child is usually unaffected. An injection given after childbirth prevents antibody production.

rites of passage Ritual ceremonies that mark transitions from one phase of life to another. Traditionally, rites of passage marked events such as births, the end of childhood ("coming-of-age" initiations), marriage, and death.

rough-and-tumble play A type of play that involves chasing, pushing, and play fighting.

S

scaffolding The process whereby competent mentors encourage development by providing clues, prompting, or modeling a skill.

scheme A psychological structure that contains the knowledge, rules, and strategies children use to understand and explore the world.

seasons of adulthood The idea that adult life consists of roughly 25-year eras with 5- to 8-year transitions between eras. According to the seasons of adulthood, development involves gains and losses as we progress through repeated periods of stability and change.

secondary aging Bodily declines that are due to genetic defects and environmental factors, such as diseases, inactivity, and injuries.

secondary control Control strategies that involve turning inward by changing one's goals or beliefs to fit a situation. People are using secondary control strategies when they reason that they didn't want a goal very much or lack the ability to pursue a specific goal.

secondary prevention Efforts to respond to the first symptoms of a hazard, so the problem will not become worse.

secondary sex characteristics Characteristics that help distinguish between males and females but are not necessary for reproduction, including breasts in girls and facial hair and a deeper voice in boys.

secular trend A trend that occurs across generations. A widely discussed secular trend is the decline in the age of pubertal onset that has occurred as nutrition and overall health have improved.

self concept Individuals' evaluation of their worth in specific domains, such as physical appearance, academic ability, or social skill.

self-efficacy The belief that one has the skill to achieve specific goals. (*Efficacy* means "having the power to produce a desired effect.")

self-efficacy People's belief that they can control important outcomes by their actions (belief in the "power to make things happen").

self-esteem Individuals' global (overall) evaluation of their self-worth.

self-regulation The skills involved in monitoring and controlling one's thoughts, emotions, and behavior.

self-reports People's descriptions of their own life events, behaviors, feelings, or attitudes. Self-reports include diary records and responses to interviews and questionnaires.

semantic development The part of language development that deals with understanding word meanings.

semantic memories Memories for general knowledge, like the meaning of words and facts about the world.

senescence The gradual physical decline that occurs with age (i.e., the process of getting old).

sensitive periods Times in development when specific experiences produce stronger effects than at other times.

sensorimotor stage The stage in Piaget's theory, from birth until approximately 2 years of age, when infants coordinate sensory systems, learn to keep mental representations of objects in mind, and begin to think through the results of actions before performing them.

serial monogamy The practice of having only one sexual partner/spouse at any given time but a series of partners/spouses over time.

sex-influenced inheritance When the expression of a trait is influenced by individual hormone levels and is, therefore, expressed differently in males than in females.

sexual orientation The preference to interact sexually with opposite-sex partners, same-sex partners, or both sexes.

sexually transmitted diseases (STDs, formerly called *venereal diseases,* and also called *sexually transmitted infections,* or **STIs)** Diseases that are usually transmitted through sexual contact. These diseases pass from person to person by contact with infected body parts or the exchange of semen, blood, or other body fluids.

shaken baby syndrome Retinal and neurological injuries caused by shaking a baby or violently throwing him or her against a surface.

sleeper effect When a condition or event that has no detectable effect at one point in development begins to have consequences later in development.

small-for-gestational-age Birth weight less than 90 percent of what infants born the same gestational age weigh.

SOC model (selective optimization with compensation) A model by Paul Baltes that describes how people adjust to the opportunities and limitations they face throughout life. The SOC model proposes that well-adjusted individuals invest in some activities at the expense of others (selection), pursue these goals effectively (optimization), and develop different strategies when usual methods stop working (compensation).

social clock Society's expectations for the timing of various life events, such as marriage, childbirth, and retirement.

social learning theory An aspect of the learning perspective that emphasizes how individuals learn through imitation (also called **modeling**).

social referencing A strategy for deciding how to react by watching how other people are reacting.

social reproduction The tendency for children to grow up to occupy the same social class level their parents occupy.

socioeconomic status (SES) A measure of economic status. Low SES is associated with low incomes, less formal education, and less prestigious occupations.

socioemotional selectivity theory A theory by Laura Carstensen that says that people respond to approaching endings by shifting to emotionally meaningful goals. As a result, older people attend to emotionally satisfying information more so than emotionally negative information, and they choose to spend time with people who matter the most to them.

somatic death When the heart and respiratory systems malfunction, which causes all cells in the body to die from lack of oxygen.

specific learning disabilities Significant impairments in the domains of reading, mathematics, or language.

stereotype threat The anxiety produced when a situation threatens to confirm a negative stereotype. For example, African Americans may experience stereotype threat when they take difficult achievement tests.

Strange Situation A sequence of events staged in the laboratory to measure infants' attachment behaviors.

structured observation Observations of behavior in situations or settings that are created by the investigator.

sudden infant death syndrome (SIDS) A label for the unexplained death of a sleeping infant less than 1year of age. SIDS occurs most often between 2 and 4 months.

suicidal ideation Thoughts or plans about suicide.

symbolic artifacts Objects or printed symbols that represent something else, such as models and maps.

synaptic pruning The elimination of synaptic connections. The synaptic pruning that occurs throughout childhood is essential for intellectual growth.

synaptogenesis The process of developing interconnections between neurons.

syndrome of imminent death A collection of signs associated with impending death, including mental confusion, sleepiness, decreased urine volume, and heart rate changes.

syntax The rules for combining words and other meaningful units (such as "s" and "ed").

T

tabula rasa A blank slate. Used by philosopher John Locke to convey his idea that children are neither good nor bad at birth; rather, they are the product of their subsequent experiences.

tacit knowledge Knowledge you need to succeed in a specific environment that is not explicitly taught. (*Tacit* means "not spoken.")

teacher-directed preschool Preschool that emphasizes teacher-directed instruction in basic academic skills, such as letters and numbers.

telegraphic speech Early word combinations that lack prepositions, articles, and other function words.

telomere The tip of the chromosome, which gets shorter with each cell division.

temperament Individuals' characteristic moods, ways of reacting to situations, and styles of self-regulation.

temporally extended self A rich view of the self that connects information about the self over time.

teratogen Any nongenetic agent that produces birth defects at exposures that commonly occur; derived from the Greek word *teras*, meaning "monster" or "marvel."

terminal decline (or **terminal drop**) An unexpected change in the rate of cognitive decline during the months or years before death.

thanatologist an individual who studies death and dying.

theory A set of concepts that organizes and explains data. Theories generate hypotheses (predictions) that can be tested.

theory of mind One's grasp of mental concepts, including one's understanding that other people have thoughts, desires, and intentions.

theory of multiple intelligences A theory of intelligence by Howard Gardner that initially proposed the existence of seven types of intelligence: linguistic, logical-mathematical, spatial, musical, bodily-kinesthetic, interpersonal, and intrapersonal. Later he added naturalistic intelligence.

theory of successful intelligence (also called the "triarchic theory" of intelligence) A theory of intelligence by Robert Sternberg that proposes the existence of three types of intelligence: analytical, creative, and practical.

third variable problem The problem that exists when two variables are correlated because they are both associated with a third variable, not because one causes the other. The possibility of unmeasured "third variables" makes it impossible to make causal influences from a single correlation coefficient.

time-of-events model The idea that adults experience crises not from reaching particular ages but from events that are unpredictable or off schedule from society's expectations for the timing of events.

time-out A procedure for punishing children by making them sit alone in a quiet, unstimulating place for a few minutes.

tip of the tongue phenomenon (TOT) The frustrating feeling of knowing a word or name but not being able to retrieve it from memory. Older adults have more frequent TOT experiences than younger adults.

transitional bilingual education An approach to educating English-language learners in which students receive instruction in their native language while they learn English, followed by a transition into English-language instruction.

triangular theory of love Robert Sternberg's theory that love consists of three components: passion, intimacy, and decision to love or make a commitment.

U

ultrasonography The use of high-frequency sound waves to produce a two-dimensional picture (a sonogram) of an embryo or fetus.

universal design (or **aging in place**) A philosophy of building homes to meet the needs of as many people as possible from childhood to old age.

V

variables Characteristics, events, or behaviors that take more than one value, such as weight, number of hospitalizations, and so forth. The factors scientists manipulate or measure when they conduct a study are the *variables* in the study.

vascular dementia A collection of syndromes that lead to cognitive impairment when the blood supply is cut off to brain cells, causing them to die.

viability The ability of a fetus to survive outside the uterus with expert care. The chance of survival is low at 22 weeks and increases with increasing gestational age.

visual preference method A method of determining what infants can discriminate by measuring whether they look longer at one of two visual stimuli.

W

washout effect When a condition or event has an effect on development at one point in time but not at a later point in time (the effect "washes out").

well-being The perception that one's life is fulfilling, meaningful, and pleasant.

whole-language instruction (also called **literature-based instruction**) An approach to teaching reading that emphasizes meaningful activities, such as listening to literature and writing, more than phonics training.

wisdom The ability to understand and solve ambiguous problems and make good judgments and decisions in everyday contexts.

working memory A memory store for holding and manipulating the mental information individuals are thinking about at any particular time.

X

X-linked traits Traits transmitted on the X chromosome. Such traits are more likely to be expressed in males than in females because females have a second X chromosome that often carries a dominant version of the trait.

Z

zone of proximal development In Vygotsky's sociocultural theory, the distance between what children can currently do and their potential when they collaborate with more competent individuals.

zygote A one-celled organism formed by the union of the male and female reproductive cells (gametes).

References

AARP. (2002a). *Staying ahead of the curve: The AARP Work and Career Study*. Washington, DC: Author. Retrieved June 24, 2006, from http://research.aarp.org/econ/multiwork.html

AARP. (2002b). *The Grandparent Study 2002 report*. Washington, DC: Author. Retrieved May 8, 2005, from http://assets.aarp.org/rgcenter/general/gp_2002.pdf

AARP. (2005). *What is universal design?* Washington, DC: Author. Retrieved May 8, 2005, from http://www.aarp.org/life/homedesign/Articles/a2004-03-23-whatis_univdesign.html

Abbassi, V. (1998). Growth and normal puberty. *Pediatrics, 102,* 507–511.

Abbott, R. D., White, L. R., Ross, G. W., Masaki, K. H., Curb, J. D., & Petrovitch, H. (2004). Walking and dementia in physically capable elderly men. *Journal of the American Medical Association, 292,* 1447–1453.

Abbott, S. (1992). Holding on and pushing away: Comparative perspectives on an eastern Kentucky child-rearing practice. *Ethos, 20,* 33–65.

Abe, J. A. A., & Izard, C. E. (1999). The developmental functions of emotions: An analysis in terms of differential emotions theory. *Cognition and Emotion, 13,* 523–549.

Abecassis, M., Hartup, W. W., Haselager, G. J. T., Scholte, R. H. J., & van Lieshout, C. F. M. (2002). Mutual antipathies and their significance in middle childhood and adolescence. *Child Development, 73,* 1543–1556.

Abu-Heija, A. T., Jallad, M. F., & Abukteish, F. (2000). Maternal and perinatal outcome of pregnancies after the age of 45. *Journal of Obstetrics and Gynaecology Research, 26,* 27–30.

Acker, M. M., & O'Leary, S. G. (1996). Inconsistency of mothers' feedback and toddlers' misbehavior and negative affect. *Journal of Abnormal Child Psychology, 24,* 703–714.

Ackerman, P. L. (2000). Domain-specific knowledge as the "dark matter" of adult intelligence: Gf/Gc, personality and interest correlates. *Journals of Gerontology: Psychological Sciences and Social Sciences, 55B,* P69–P84.

Acs, G., & Ng, M. W. (2002). Early childhood caries and well being. *Pediatric Dentistry, 24,* 288.

Adair, L. S. (1999). Filipino children exhibit catch-up growth from age 2 to 12 years. *Journal of Nutrition, 129,* 1140–1148.

Adam, E. K. (2004). Beyond quality: Parental and residential stability and children's adjustment. *Current Directions in Psychological Science, 13,* 210–213.

Adams, G. A. (1999). Career-related variables and planned retirement age: An extension of Beehr's model. *Journal of Vocational Behavior, 55,* 221–235.

Adams, G. A., & Beehr, T. A. (Eds.). (2003). *Retirement: Reasons, processes, and results*. New York: Springer.

Adams, R. J., & Courage, M. L. (1998). Human newborn color vision: Measurement with chromatic stimuli varying in excitation purity. *Journal of Experimental Child Psychology, 68,* 22–34.

Adams, R. J., Courage, M. L., & Mercer, M. E. (1994). Systematic measurement of human neonatal color vision. *Vision Research, 34,* 1691–1701.

Adamson, L. B., & Frick, J. E. (2003). The still face: A history of a shared experimental paradigm. *Infancy, 4,* 451–473.

Adlard, P. A., & Cotman, C. W. (2004). Voluntary exercise protects against stress-induced decreases in brain-derived neurotrophic factor protein expression. *Neuroscience, 124,* 985–992.

Adlard, P. A., & Cummings, B. J. (2004). Alzheimer's disease: A sum greater than its parts? *Neurobiology of Aging, 25,* 725–733.

Adler, P. A., & Adler, P. (1995). Dynamics of inclusion and exclusion in preadolescent cliques. *Social Psychology Quarterly, 58,* 145–162.

Adolph, K. E. (1997). Learning in the development of infant locomotion. *Monographs of the Society for Research in Child Development, 62*(3, Serial No. 251).

Adolph, K. E. (2000). Specificity of learning: Why infants fall over a veritable cliff. *Psychological Science, 11,* 290–295.

Aging with Dignity. (2005). *Five wishes*. Retrieved February 17, 2005, from http://www.agingwithdignity.org/feedback.html

Ahnert, L., Rickert, H., & Lamb, M. E. (2000). Shared caregiving: Comparisons between home and child-care settings. *Developmental Psychology, 36,* 339–351.

Ainsworth, M. D. S., & Bell, S. M. (1977). Infant crying and maternal responsiveness: A rejoinder to Gewirtz and Boyd. *Child Development, 48,* 1208–1216.

Ainsworth, M. D. S., Blehar, M. C., Waters, E., & Wall, S. (1978). *Patterns of attachment: A psychological study of the Strange Situation*. Hillsdale, NJ: Erlbaum.

Ainsworth, M. D. S., & Marvin, R. S. (1995). On the shaping of attachment theory and research: An interview with Mary D. S. Ainsworth (Fall 1994). In E. Waters, B. E. Vaughn, G. Posada, & K. Kondo-Ikemura (Eds.), Caregiving, cultural, and cognitive perspectives on secure-base behavior and working models: New growing points of attachment theory and research. *Monographs of the Society for Research in Child Development, 60*(2–3, Serial No. 244), 3–21.

Alexander, G. M., & Hines, M. (2002). Sex differences in responses to children's toys in nonhuman primates (*Cercopithecus aethiops sabaeus*). *Evolution and Human Behavior, 23,* 467–479.

Alexander, R. T., & Radisch, D. (2005). Sudden infant death syndrome risk factors with regards to sleep position, sleep surface, and co-sleeping. *Journal of Forensic Sciences, 50,* 147–151.

Alfirevic, Z., Gosden, C. M., & Neilson, J. P. (2000). Chorion villus sampling versus amniocentesis for prenatal diagnosis. *Cochrane Database of Systematic Reviews, 2,* CD000055.

Alfirevic, Z., Sundberg, K., & Brigham, S. (2003). Amniocentesis and chorionic villus sampling for prenatal diagnosis. *Cochrane Database of Systematic Reviews, 3,* CD003252.

Alger, L. S. (2000). Common viral infections. In W. R. Cohen, S. H. Sheldon, & I. R. Merkatz (Eds.), *Cherry and Merkatz's complications of pregnancy* (5th ed., pp. 709–745). Philadelphia: Lippincott Williams & Wilkins.

Allaire, J. C., & Marsiske, M. (1999). Everyday cognition: Age and intellectual ability correlates. *Psychology and Aging, 14,* 627–644.

Allen, L. S., Richey, M. F., Chai, Y. M., & Gorski, R. A. (1991). Sex differences in the corpus callosum of the living human being. *Journal of Neuroscience, 11,* 933–942.

Alley, T. R. (1981). Head shape and the perception of cuteness. *Developmental Psychology, 17,* 650–654.

Allison, B. N., & Schultz, J. B. (2004). Parent-adolescent conflict in early adolescence. *Adolescence, 39,* 101–119.

Alzheimer's Australia. (2005). *Memory changes*. Retrieved May 31, 2006, from http://www.alzheimers.org.au/content.cfm?infopageid=398&CFID=3617114&CFTOKEN=89176838

Amato, P. R. (1996). Explaining the intergenerational transmission of divorce. *Journal of Marriage and the Family, 58,* 628–640.

Amato, P. R. (1999). Children of divorced parents as young adults. In E. M. Hetherington (Ed.), *Coping with divorce, single parenting, and remarriage: A risk and resiliency perspective* (pp. 147–163). Mahwah, NJ: Erlbaum.

Amato, P. R. (2000). The consequences of divorce for adults and children. *Journal of Marriage and the Family, 62,* 1269–1287.

Amato, P. R. (2001a). Children of divorce in the 1990s: An update of the Amato and Keith (1991) meta-analysis. *Journal of Family Psychology, 15,* 355–370.

Amato, P. R. (2001b). The consequences of divorce for adults and children. In R. M. Milardo (Ed.), *Understanding families into the new millennium: A decade in review* (pp. 488–506). Minneapolis, MN: National Council on Family Relations.

Amato, P. R., & Gilbreth, J. G. (1999). Nonresident fathers and children's well-being: A meta-analysis. *Journal of Marriage and the Family, 61,* 557–573.

Amato, P. R., & Keith, B. (1991). Parental divorce and the well-being of children: A meta-analysis. *Psychological Bulletin, 110,* 26–46.

Amato, P. R., & Sobolewski, J. M. (2001). The effects of divorce and marital discord on adult children's psychological well-being. *American Sociological Review, 66,* 900–921.

American Academy of Audiology. (2005). *How's your hearing? Ask an audiologist! Technical topics: Newborn hearing screening.* Retrieved July 19, 2005, from http://www.audiology.org/professional/tech/eihbrochure.php

American Academy of Pediatrics Committee on Child Abuse and Neglect. (1993). Shaken baby syndrome: Inflicted cerebral trauma. *Pediatrics, 92,* 872–875.

American Academy of Pediatrics Committee on Fetus and Newborn. (2002). Postnatal corticosteroids to treat or prevent chronic lung disease in preterm infants. *Pediatrics, 109,* 330–338.

American Academy of Pediatrics Committee on Pediatric AIDS. (1999). Disclosure of illness status to children and adolescents with HIV infection. *Pediatrics, 103,* 164–166.

American Academy of Pediatrics Committee on Public Education. (1999). Media education. *Pediatrics, 104,* 341–343.

American Academy of Pediatrics Committee on Public Education. (2001). Children, adolescents, and television. *Pediatrics, 107,* 423–426.

American Academy of Pediatrics Committee on Sports Medicine and Fitness. (2000a). Climatic heat stress and the exercising child and adolescent. *Pediatrics, 106,* 158–159.

American Academy of Pediatrics Committee on Sports Medicine and Fitness. (2000b). Intensive training and sports specialization in young athletes. *Pediatrics, 106,* 154–157.

American Academy of Pediatrics Committee on Sports Medicine and Fitness. (2001). Strength training by children and adolescents. *Pediatrics, 107,* 1470–1472.

American Academy of Pediatrics Committee on Sports Medicine and Fitness & Committee on Injury and Poison Prevention. (2000). Swimming programs for infants and toddlers. *Pediatrics, 105,* 868–870.

American Academy of Pediatrics Committee on Sport Medicine and Fitness & Committee on School Health. (2001). Organized sports for children and preadolescents. *Pediatrics, 107,* 1459–1462.

American Academy of Pediatrics Task Force on Sudden Infant Death Syndrome. (2005). The changing concept of sudden infant death syndrome: Diagnostic coding shifts, controversies regarding the sleeping environment, and new variables to consider in reducing risk. *Pediatrics, 116,* 1245–1255.

American Academy of Pediatrics Work Group on Breastfeeding. (1997). Breastfeeding and the use of human milk. *Pediatrics, 100,* 1035–1039.

American Bar Association. (2005). *Juvenile death penalty amicus briefs.* Retrieved January 10, 2005, from http://www.abanet.org/crimjust/juvjus/simmons/simmonsamicus.html

American Cancer Society. (2001). *Coping with physical and emotional changes.* Retrieved February 20, 2005, from http://www.cancer.org/docroot/MBC/content/MBC_4_1X_Phases_of_Grief.asp?sitearea=MBC

American College of Obstetricians and Gynecologists & Committee on Obstetric Practice. (2001). Committee opinion: Circumcision. *Obstetrics and Gynecology, 98,* 707–708.

American Hearing Research Foundation. (2004). *Noise induced hearing loss.* Retrieved October 19, 2005, from www.american-hearing.org/name/noise_induced.html

American Heart Association. (2005a). *Heart disease and stroke statistics—2005 update.* Dallas, TX: American Heart Association.

American Heart Association. (2005b). *Metabolic syndrome.* Retrieved March 27, 2005, from http://www.americanheart.org/presenter.jhtml?identifier=4756

American Optometric Association. (1997). *Impact of computer use on children's vision.* Retrieved May 9, 2006, from http://www.tifaq.com/kids/aoa-children_vision.html

American Optometric Association. (2006a). *Children's vision.* Retrieved May 12, 2006, from http://www.aoa.org/x770.xml

American Optometric Association. (2006b). *Eye conditions and concerns.* Retrieved May 9, 2006, from http://www.aoa.org/x775.xml

American Psychiatric Association. (2000). *Diagnostic and statistical manual of mental disorders: DSM-IV-TR* (4th ed., text revision). Washington, DC: Author.

American Psychological Association. (2002). *Ethical principles of psychologists and code of conduct.* Retrieved April 27, 2006, from http://www.apa.org/ethics/code2002.html

American Psychological Association. (2003). *Resilience in a time of war: Tips for parents and teachers of middle school children.* Washington, DC: Author. Retrieved June 5, 2005, from http://www.apahelpcenter.org/dl/resilience_in_a_time_of_war-tips_for_parents_and_teachers_of_middle_school_children.pdf

American Psychological Association. (2005a). *Making stepfamilies work.* Retrieved June 5, 2005, from http://www.apahelpcenter.org/articles/article.php?id=41

American Psychological Association. (2005b). *Managing traumatic stress: Tips for recovering from natural disasters.* Retrieved June 5, 2005, from http://www.apahelpcenter.org/articles/article.php?id=69

American Psychological Association Council of Representatives. (2002). *Guidelines on multicultural education, training, research, practice, and organizational change for psychologists.* Retrieved April 24, 2006, from ww.apa.org/pi/multicultural-guidelines.pdf

American Society for Reproductive Medicine. (2004). *Frequently asked questions about infertility.* Retrieved May 30, 2004, from www.asrm.org/Patients/faqs.html

American Society on Aging. (1998, May/June). Marian Diamond's optimism about the aging brain. *Aging Today.* Retrieved May 31, 2006, from http://www.asaging.org/at/at-193/diamond.html

American students respond. (2005). *Scholastic.* Retrieved May 11, 2006, from http://teacher.scholastic.com/scholasticnews/indepth/tsunami/kidshelp/index.asphttp://teacher.scholastic.com/scholasticnews/indepth/tsunami/kidshelp/index.asp

Ames, L. B., & Haber, C. C. (1985). *Your seven year old: Life in a minor key.* New York: Dell Publishing.

Amin, S. (2003). Male osteoporosis: Epidemiology and pathophysiology. *Current Osteoporosis Reports, 1,* 71–77.

Ammerman, R. T. (1991). The role of the child in physical abuse: A reappraisal. *Violence and Victims, 6,* 87–101.

Anders, T., Goodlin-Jones, B., & Sadeh, A. (2000). Sleep disorders. In C. H. Zeanah, Jr. (Ed.), *Handbook of infant mental health* (2nd ed., pp. 326–338). New York: Guilford.

Anderson, C. A., Berkowitz, L., Donnerstein, E., et al. (2003). The influence of media violence on youth. *Psychological Science in the Public Interest, 4,* 81–110.

Anderson, C. A., & Bushman, B. J. (2001). Effects of violent video games on aggressive behavior, aggressive cognition, physiological arousal, and prosocial behavior: A meta-analytic review of the scientific literature. *Psychological Science, 12,* 353–359.

Anderson, D. E. (2003). *Longitudinal study of the development and consequences of formal operations and intellectual flexibility*. Meadville, PA: Allegheny College. (ERIC Document Reproduction Service No. ED481115)

Anderson, D. R., Field, D. E., Collins, P. A., Lorch, E. P., & Nathan, J. G. (1985). Estimates of young children's time with television: A methodological comparison of parent reports with time-lapse video home observation. *Child Development, 56,* 1345–1357.

Anderson, D. R., Huston, A. C., Schmitt, K. L., Linebarger, D. L., & Wright, J. C. (2001). Early childhood television viewing and adolescent behavior: The recontact study. *Monographs of the Society for Research in Child Development, 66*(1, Serial No. 264).

Anderson, D. R., & Levin, S. R. (1976). Young children's attention to "Sesame Street." *Child Development, 47,* 806–811.

Anderson, D. R., Lorch, E. P., Field, D. E., & Sanders, J. (1981). The effects of TV program comprehensibility on preschool children's visual attention to television. *Child Development, 52,* 151–157.

Anderson, G. C., Marks, E. A., & Wahlberg, V. (1986). Kangaroo care for premature infants. *American Journal of Nursing, 86,* 807–809.

Anderson, J. W., Johnstone, B. M., & Remley, D. T. (1999). Breast-feeding and cognitive development: A meta-analysis. *American Journal of Clinical Nutrition, 70,* 525–535.

Anderson, K., Anderson, L. E., & Glanze, W. D. (Eds.). (1998). *Mosby's medical, nursing, and allied health dictionary.* St. Louis, MO: Mosby.

Anderson, K. G. (1997). Gender bias and special education referrals. *Annals of Dyslexia, 47,* 151–162.

Anderson, R. E., Crespo, C. J., Bartlett, S. J., Cheskin, L. J., & Pratt, M. (1998). Relationship of physical activity and television watching with body weight and level of fatness among children: Results from the Third National Health and Nutrition Examination Survey. *Journal of the American Medical Association, 279,* 938–942.

Anderson, V., Northam, E., Hendy, J., & Wrennall, J. (2001). *Developmental neuropsychology: A clinical approach.* Hove, England: Psychology Press.

Anderson, W. F. (1995). Gene therapy. *Scientific American, 273*(3), 124–128.

Anderson, W. F. (1998). Human gene therapy. *Nature, 392,* 25–30.

Anderssen, M., Amlie, C., & Ytterøy, E. A. (2002). Outcomes for children with lesbian or gay parents: A review of studies from 1978 to 2000. *Scandinavian Journal of Psychology, 43,* 335–351.

Andersson, G. (1999, March). *Trends in childbearing and nuptiality in Sweden, 1961(71)–1997.* Paper presented at the meeting of the Population Association of America, New York.

Angier, N. (2001, February 13). Genome shows evolution has an eye for hyperbole. *New York Times,* pp. D1, D5.

Anglin, J. M. (1993). Vocabulary development: A morphological analysis. *Monographs of the Society for Research in Child Development, 58*(10 Serial No. 238).

Angold, A., Costello, E. J., Erkanli, A., & Worthman, C. M. (1999). Pubertal changes in hormone levels and depression in girls. *Psychological Medicine, 29,* 1043–1053.

Angold, A., Costello, E. J., & Worthman, C. (1998). Puberty and depression: The roles of age, pubertal status, and pubertal timing. *Psychological Medicine, 28,* 51–61.

Angold, A., Erkanli, A., Costello, J. E., & Rutter, M. (1996). Precision, reliability and accuracy in the dating of symptom onsets in child and adolescent psychopathology. *Journal of Child Psychology and Psychiatry and Allied Disciplines, 37,* 657–664.

Angold, A., Worthman, C., & Costello, E. J. (2003). Puberty and depression. In C. Hayward (Ed.), *Gender differences at puberty* (pp. 137–164). New York: Cambridge University Press.

Anthony, J. L., & Lonigan, C. J. (2004). The nature of phonological awareness: Converging evidence from four studies of preschool and early grade school children. *Journal of Educational Psychology, 96,* 43–55.

Antonucci, T. C., Akiyama, H., & Merline, A. (2001). Dynamics of social relationships in midlife. In M. E. Lachman (Ed.), *Handbook of midlife development* (pp. 571–598). New York: Wiley.

Aoyagi, Y., & Shephard, R. J. (1992). Aging and muscle function. *Sports Medicine, 14,* 376–396.

Archer, J. (2001). Grief from an evolutionary perspective. In M. S. Stroebe, R. O. Hansson, W. Stroebe, & H. Schut (Eds.), *Handbook of bereavement research: Consequences, coping, and care* (pp. 263–283). Washington, DC: American Psychological Association.

Arendell, T. (1995). *Fathers and divorce.* Thousand Oaks, CA: Sage.

Aries, E. (2004). United States life tables, 2002. *National Vital Statistics Reports, 53*(6).

Arling, G. (1976). The elderly widow and her family, neighbors, and friends. *Journal of Marriage and the Family, 38,* 757–768.

Armsby, R. E. (1971). A reexamination of the development of moral judgments in children. *Child Development, 42,* 1241–1248.

Armstrong, E. M. (1998). Diagnosing moral disorder: The discovery and evolution of fetal alcohol syndrome. *Social Science and Medicine, 47,* 2025–2042.

Armstrong, F. D., Willen, E. J., & Sorgen, K. (2003). HIV/AIDS in children and adolescents. In M. C. Roberts (Ed.), *Handbook of pediatric psychology* (3rd ed., pp. 359–374). New York: Guilford.

Armstrong, P., & Feldman, S. (1986). *A midwife's story.* New York: Ivy Books.

Arnett, J. J. (2000). Emerging adulthood: A theory of development from the late teens through the twenties. *American Psychologist, 55,* 469–480.

Arnett, J. J. (2004). *Adolescence and emerging adulthood: A cultural approach* (2nd ed.). Upper Saddle River, NJ: Prentice Hall.

Arnold, A. P., & Gorski, R. A. (1984). Gonadal steroid induction of structural sex differences in the central nervous system. *Annual Review of Neuroscience, 7,* 413–442.

Aron, A., Fisher, H., Mashek, D. J., Strong, G., Li, H., & Brown, L. L. (2005). Reward, motivation, and emotion systems associated with early-stage intense romantic love. *Journal of Neurophysiology, 94,* 327–337.

Aronson, J. (2002). Stereotype threat: Contending and coping with unnerving expectations. In J. Aronson (Ed.), *Improving academic achievement* (pp. 279–301). San Diego, CA: Academic Press.

Arseneault, L., Tremblay, R. E., Boulerice, B., & Saucier, J.-F. (2002). Obstetrical complications and violent delinquency: Testing two developmental pathways. *Child Development, 73,* 496–508.

Asbury, K., Dunn, J. F., Pike, A., & Plomin, R. (2003). Nonshared environmental influences on individual differences in early behavioral development: A monozygotic twin differences study. *Child Development, 74,* 933–943.

Asidao, C. S., Vion, S., & Espelage, D. L. (1999, August). *Interviews with middle school students: Bullying, victimization, and contextual factors.* Paper presented at the meeting of the American Psychological Association, Boston.

Associated Press State and Local Wire. (2002, July 28). Judge: Mother hasn't learned how to feed child. *Morning Sun,* p. A3.

Atchley, R. C. (1976). *The sociology of retirement.* Cambridge, MA: Schenkman.

Atchley, R. C. (2003). Why most people cope well with retirement. In J. L. Ronch & J. A. Goldfield (Eds.), *Mental wellness in aging: Strengths-based approaches* (pp. 123–138). Baltimore: Health Professions Press.

Atwood, V. A. (1984). Children's concepts of death: A descriptive study. *Child Study Journal, 14,* 11–29.

Austin, B. A. (1983). Factorial structure of the UCLA Loneliness Scale. *Psychological Reports, 53,* 883–889.

Avis, N. E., Stellato, R., Crawford, S., Johannes, C., & Longcope, C. (2000). Is there an association between menopause status and sexual functioning? *Menopause, 7*, 297–309.

Avorn, J. (2004). *Powerful medicines: The benefits, risks, and costs of prescription drugs.* New York: Knopf.

Bäckman, E., Johansson, V., Häger, B., Sjöblom, P., & Henriksson, K. G. (1995). Isometric muscle strength and muscular endurance in normal persons aged between 17 and 70 years. *Scandinavian Journal of Rehabilitation Medicine, 27*, 109–117.

Bäckman, L., Small, B. J., & Wahlin, Å. (2001). Aging and memory: Cognitive and biological perspectives. In J. E. Birren & K. W. Schaie (Eds.), *Handbook of the psychology of aging* (5th ed., pp. 349–377). San Diego, CA: Academic Press.

Baddeley, A. (2000). The episodic buffer: A new component of working memory? *Trends in Cognitive Sciences, 4*, 417–423.

Bahl, R., Frost, C., Kirkwood, B. R., et al. (2005). Infant feeding patterns and risks of death and hospitalization in the first half of infancy: Multicentre cohort study. *Bulletin of the World Health Organization, 83*, 418–426.

Bailey, J. M., Pillard, R. C., Neale, M. C., & Agyei, Y. (1993). Heritable factors influence sexual orientation in women. *Archives of General Psychiatry, 50*, 217–223.

Bailey, J. M., & Zucker, K. J. (1995). Childhood sex-typed behavior and sexual orientation: A conceptual analysis and quantitative review. *Developmental Psychology, 31*, 43–55.

Baillargeon, R. (2004). Infants' physical world. *Current Directions in Psychological Science, 13*, 89–94.

Bakermans-Kranenburg, M. J., van IJzendoorn, M. H., & Juffer, F. (2005). Disorganized infant attachment and preventive interventions: A review and meta-analysis. *Infant Mental Health Journal, 26*, 191–216.

Baldwin, A. L. (1980). *Theories of child development* (2nd ed.). New York: Wiley.

Baldwin, D. A. (1991). Infants' contribution to the achievement of joint reference. *Child Development, 62*, 875–890.

Ball, D. L. (1992). Magical hopes: Manipulatives and the reform of math education. *American Educator, 16*, 14–18.

Ball, K. K., Wadley, V. G., & Edwards, J. D. (2002). Advances in technology used to assess and retrain older drivers. *Gerontechnology, 1*(4), 251–261.

Ball, K., Owsley, C., Sloane, M. E., Roenker, D. L., & Bruni, J. R. (1993). Visual attention problems as a predictor of vehicle crashes in older drivers. *Investigative Ophthalmology and Visual Science, 34*, 3110–3123.

Ball, K., & Rebok, G. (1994). Evaluating the driving ability of older adults. *Journal of Applied Gerontology, 13*, 20–38.

Baltes, M. M. (1995). Dependency in old age: Gains and losses. *Current Directions in Psychological Science, 4*, 14–19.

Baltes, M. M., Freund, A. M., & Horgas, A. L. (1999). Men and women in the Berlin Aging Study. In P. B. Baltes & K. U. Mayer (Eds.), *The Berlin Aging Study: Aging from 70 to 100* (pp. 259–281). New York: Cambridge University Press.

Baltes, P. B. (1997). On the incomplete architecture of human ontogeny: Selection, optimization, and compensation as foundation of developmental theory. *American Psychologist, 52*, 366–380.

Baltes, P. B., & Staudinger, U. M. (2000). Wisdom: A metaheuristic (pragmatic) to orchestrate mind and virtue toward excellence. *American Psychologist, 55*, 122–136.

Bandura, A. (1965). Influence of models' reinforcement contingencies on the acquisition of imitative responses. *Journal of Personality and Social Psychology, 1*, 589–595.

Bandura, A. (1977). *Social learning theory.* Englewood Cliffs, NJ: Prentice Hall.

Bandura, A. (1995). Exercise of personal and collective efficacy in changing societies. In A. Bandura (Ed.), *Self-efficacy in changing societies* (pp. 1–45). New York: Cambridge University Press.

Bandura, A. (1999). Social cognitive theory of personality. In L. A. Pervin & O. P. John (Eds.), *Handbook of personality: Theory and research* (pp. 154–196). New York: Guilford.

Bandura, A. (2000). Self-efficacy: The foundation of agency. In W. J. Perrig & A. Grob (Eds.), *Control of human behavior, mental processes, and consciousness: Essays in honor the 60th birthday of August Flammer* (pp. 17–33). Mahwah, NJ: Lawrence Erlbaum.

Bandura, A., Barbaranelli, C., Caprana, G. V., & Pastorelli, C. (2001). Self-efficacy beliefs as shapers of children's aspirations and career trajectories. *Child Development, 72*, 187–206.

Banfield, J. F., Wyland, C. L., Macrae, C. N., Münte, T. F., & Heatherton, T. F. (2004). The cognitive neuroscience of self-regulation. In R. F. Baumeister & K. D. Vohs (Eds.), *Handbook of self-regulation: Research, theory, and applications* (pp. 62–83). New York: Guilford.

Barbu, S., Le Maner-Idrissi, G., & Jouanjean, A. (2000). The emergence of gender segregation: Towards an integrative perspective. *Current Psychology Letters: Behaviour, Brain, and Cognition, 3*, 7–18.

Barinaga, M. (2000). Fetal neuron grafts pave the way for stem cell therapies. *Science, 287*, 1421–1422.

Barker, G. P., & Graham, S. (1987). Developmental study of praise and blame as attributional cues. *Journal of Educational Psychology, 79*, 62–66.

Barkley, R. A., Cook, E. H., Dulcan, M., et al. (2002). Consensus statement on ADHD. *European Child and Adolescent Psychiatry, 11*, 96–98.

Barlow, J. M. (1984). Carol and the beanstalk. *Psychoanalytic Psychology, 1*, 85–88.

Barlow, K., Thompson, E., Johnson, D., & Minns, R. A. (2004). The neurological outcome of non-accidental head injury. *Pediatric Rehabilitation, 7*, 195–203.

Barnard, K. E., & Bee, H. L. (1983). The impact of temporally patterned stimulation on the development of preterm infants. *Child Development, 54*, 1156–1167.

Barnes, H., & Parry, J. (2004). Renegotiating identity and relationships: Men and women's adjustments to retirement. *Ageing and Society, 24*, 213–233.

Barnett, C. R., Leiderman, P. H., Grobstein, R., & Klaus, M. (1970). Neonatal separation: The maternal side of interactional deprivation. *Pediatrics, 45*, 197–205.

Barnett, R. C., & Baruch, G. K. (1978). Women in the middle years: A critique of research and theory. *Psychology of Women Quarterly, 3*, 187–197.

Barnett, W. S. (1998). Long-term cognitive and academic effects of early childhood education on children in poverty. *Preventive Medicine, 27*, 204–207.

Barnfield, T. V., & Leathem, J. M. (1998). Incidence and outcomes of traumatic brain injury and substance abuse in a New Zealand prison population. *Brain Injury, 12*, 455–466.

Barr, A., Bryan, A., & Kenrick, D. T. (2002). Sexual peak: Socially shared cognitions about desire, frequency, and satisfaction in men and women. *Personal Relationships, 9*, 287–299.

Barr, H. M., & Streissguth, A. P. (2001). Identifying maternal self-reported alcohol use associated with fetal alcohol spectrum disorders. *Alcoholism: Clinical and Experimental Research, 25*, 283–287.

Barr, R., Dowden, A., & Hayne, H. (1996). Developmental changes in deferred imitation by 6- to 24-month-old infants. *Infant Behavior and Development, 19*, 159–170.

Barr, R. G. (1990). The normal crying curve: What do we really know? *Developmental Medicine and Child Neurology, 32*, 356–362.

Barr, R. G. (2001). "Colic" is something infants do, rather than a condition they "have": A developmental approach to crying phenomena, patterns, pacification and (patho)genesis. In R. G. Barr, I. St. James-Roberts, & M. R. Keefe (Eds.), *New evidence on unexplained early infant crying: Its origins, nature, and management* (pp. 87–104). Skillman, NJ: Johnson & Johnson Pediatric Institute.

Barr, R. G., Paterson, J. A., MacMartin, L. M., Lehtonen, L., & Young, S. N. (2005). Prolonged and unsoothable crying bouts in infants with and without colic. *Journal of Developmental and Behavioral Pediatrics, 26*, 14–23.

Barr, R. G., St. James-Roberts, I., & Keefe, M. R. (Eds.) (2001). *New evidence on unexplained early infant crying: Its origins, nature, and management.* Skillman, NJ: Johnson & Johnson Pediatric Institute.

Barry, C. M., & Nelson, L. J. (2005). The role of religion in the transition to adulthood for young emerging adults. *Journal of Youth and Adolescence, 34*, 245–255.

Bartke, A. (2005). Minireview: Role of the growth hormone/insulin-like growth factor system in mammalian aging. *Endocrinology, 146,* 3718–3723.

Baskys, A. (2004). Lewy body dementia: The litmus test for neuroleptic sensitivity and extrapyramidal symptoms. *Journal of Clinical Psychiatry, 65*(Suppl. 11), 16–22.

Bates, E., Reilly, J., Wulfeck, B., et al. (2001). Differential effects of unilateral lesions on language production in children and adults. *Brain and Language, 79*, 223–265.

Bates, J. E., Viken, R. J., Alexander, D. B., Beyers, J., & Stockton, L. (2002). Sleep and adjustment in preschool children: Sleep diary reports by mothers relate to behavior reports by teachers. *Child Development, 73*, 62–74.

Bauer, P. J. (2005). Developments in declarative memory: Decreasing susceptibility to storage failure over the second year of life. *Psychological Science, 16*, 41–47.

Bauer, P. J., Wenner, J. A., Dropik, P. L., & Wewerka, S. S. (2000). Parameters of remembering and forgetting in the transition from infancy to early childhood. *Monographs for the Society for Research in Child Development, 65*(4, Serial No. 263).

Bauer, P. J., & Wewerka, S. S. (1995). One- to two-year-olds' recall of events: The more expressed, the more impressed. *Journal of Experimental Child Psychology, 59*, 475–496.

Baumeister, A. A., & Bacharach, V. R. (2000). Early generic educational intervention has no enduring effect on intelligence and does not prevent mental retardation: The Infant Health and Development Program. *Intelligence, 28*, 161–192.

Baumeister, R. F. (1990). Suicide as escape from self. *Psychological Bulletin, 97*, 90–113.

Baumeister, R. F., Campbell, J. D., Krueger, J. I., & Vohs, K. D. (2003). Does high self-esteem cause better performance, interpersonal success, happiness, or healthier lifestyles? *Psychological Science in the Public Interest, 4*, 1–44.

Baumeister, R. F., Catanese, K. R., & Vohs, K. D. (2001). Is there a gender difference in strength of sex drive? Theoretical views, conceptual distinctions, and a review of relevant evidence. *Personality and Social Psychology Review, 5*, 242–273.

Baumrind, D. (1966). Effects of authoritative control on child behavior. *Child Development, 37*, 887–907.

Baumrind, D. (1967). Child care practices anteceding three patterns of preschool behavior. *Genetic Psychology Monographs, 75*, 43–88.

Baumrind, D. (1971). Current patterns of parental authority. *Developmental Psychology, 4*, 1–103.

Baumrind, D. (1993). The average expectable environment is not good enough: A response to Scarr. *Child Development, 64*, 1299–1317.

Baumrind, D., & Black, A. E. (1967). Socialization practices associated with dimensions of competence in preschool boys and girls. *Child Development, 38*, 291–327.

Baumrind, D., Larzelere, R. E., & Cowan, P. A. (2002). Ordinary physical punishment: Is it harmful? Comment on Gershoff (2002). *Psychological Bulletin, 128*, 580–589.

Bauserman, R. (2002). Child adjustment in joint-custody versus sole-custody arrangements: A meta-analytic review. *Journal of Family Psychology, 16*, 91–102.

Bayley, N. (1993). *Bayley Scales of Infant Development* (2nd ed.). New York: Psychological Corporation.

Bayley, N. (2006). *Bayley Scales of Infant and Toddler Development* (3rd ed). New York: Psychological Corporation.

Beard, A. S., & Blaser, M. J. (2002). The ecology of height: The effect of microbial transmission on human height. *Perspectives in Biology and Medicine, 45*, 475–498.

Beck, K. H., Boyle, J. R., & Boekeloo, B. O. (2004). Parental monitoring and adolescent drinking: Results of a 12–month follow-up. *American Journal of Health Behavior, 28*, 272–279.

Becker, J. (1986). Bossy and nice requests: Children's production and interpretation. *Merrill-Palmer Quarterly, 32*, 393–413.

Becker, J. A. (1988). The success of parents' indirect techniques for teaching their preschoolers pragmatic skills. *First Language, 8*, 173–182.

Beckerman, S., & Valentine, P. (2002). *Cultures of multiple fathers: The theory and practice of partible paternity in lowland South America.* Gainesville, FL: University Press of Florida.

Bee, H. L., Barnard, K. E., Eyres, S. J., et al. (1982). Prediction of IQ and language skill from perinatal status, child performance, family characteristics, and mother-infant interaction. *Child Development, 53*, 1134–1156.

Beehr, T. A., & Bowling, N. A. (2002). Career issues facing older workers. In D. C. Feldman (Ed.), *Work careers: A developmental perspective* (pp. 214–241). San Francisco: Jossey-Bass.

Beehr, T. A., Glazer, S., Nielson, N. L., & Farmer, S. J. (2000). Work and nonwork predictors of employees' retirement ages. *Journal of Vocational Behavior, 57*, 206–225.

Beischer, N. A., Mackay, E. V., & Colditz, P. (1997). *Obstetrics and the newborn: An illustrated textbook* (3rd ed.). Philadelphia: Saunders.

Bell, A. D., & Variend, S. (1985). Failure to demonstrate sexual dimorphism of the corpus callosum in childhood. *Journal of Anatomy, 143*, 143–147.

Bell, F. C., & Miller, M. L. (2005). *Life tables for the United States Social Security area 1990–2100: Actuarial study No. 116.* Retrieved September 3, 2005, from **http://www.ssa.gov/OACT/NOTES/ as116/as116_V.htmlhttp://www.ssa.gov/OAC T/NOTES/as116/as116_V.html**

Bell, J. H., & Bromnick, R. D. (2003). The social reality of the imaginary audience: A grounded theory approach. *Adolescence, 38*, 205–219.

Bell, S. M., & Ainsworth, M. D. (1972). Infant crying and maternal responsiveness. *Child Development, 43*, 1171–1190.

Bellamy, C. (1998). *State of the world's children 1998.* New York: Oxford University Press.

Bellamy, C. (2000). *State of the world's children 2000.* New York: UNICEF.

Belsky, J. (1997). Theory testing, effect-size evaluation, and differential susceptibility to rearing influence: The case of mothering and attachment. *Child Development, 68*, 598–600.

Belsky, J., Steinberg, L., & Draper, P. (1991). Childhood experience, interpersonal development, and reproductive strategy: An evolutionary theory of socialization. *Child Development, 62*, 647–670.

Bem, S. L. (1989). Genital knowledge and gender constancy in preschool children. *Child Development, 60*, 649–662.

Benbow, M. (2002). Hand skills and handwriting. In S. A. Cermak & D. Larkin (Eds.), *Developmental coordination disorder* (pp. 248–279). Albany, NY: Delmar.

Benedict, H. (1979). Early lexical development: Comprehension and production. *Journal of Child Language, 6*, 183–200.

Benore, E. R., & Park, C. L. (2004). Death-specific religious beliefs and bereavement: Belief in an afterlife and continued attachment. *The International Journal for the Psychology of Religion, 14*, 1–22.

Berg, C. A. (2000). Intellectual development in adulthood. In R. J. Sternberg (Ed.), *Handbook of intelligence.* New York: Cambridge University Press.

Bergamasco, N. H., & Beraldo, K. E. (1990). Facial expressions of neonate infants in response to gustatory stimuli. *Brazilian Journal of Medical and Biological Research, 23*, 245–249.

Bergman, M., Blumenfeld, V. G., Cascardo, D., Dash, B., Levitt, H., & Margulies, M. K. (1976). Age-related decrement in hearing for speech: Sampling and longitudinal studies. *Journal of Gerontology, 31*, 533–538.

Berkey, C. S., Rockett, H. R., Gillman, M. W., & Colditz, G. A. (2003). One-year changes in activity and in inactivity among 10– to 15–year-old boys and girls: Relationship to change in body mass index. *Pediatrics, 111*, 836–843.

Berndt, T. J. (1996). Transitions in friendship and friends' influence. In J. A. Graber, J. Brooks-Gunn, & A. C. Petersen (Eds.), *Transitions through adolescence: Interpersonal domains and context* (pp. 57–84). Mahwah, NJ: Erlbaum.

Berndt, T. J. (2002). Friendship quality and social development. *Current Directions in Psychological Science, 11*, 7–10.

Berndt, T. J., & Keefe, K. (1992). Friends' influence on adolescents' perceptions of themselves at school. In D. H. Schunk & J. L. Meece (Eds.), *Student perceptions in the classroom* (pp. 51–73). Hillsdale, NJ: Erlbaum.

Bernstein, J., Zimmerman, T. S., Werner-Wilson, R. J., & Vosburg, J. (2000). Preschool children's classification skills and a multicultural education intervention to promote acceptance of ethnic diversity. *Journal of Research in Childhood Education, 14*, 181–192.

Bernstein, P. S., Harrison, E. S., & Merkatz, I. R. (2000). Preconceptual and prenatal care. In W. R. Cohen, S. H. Sheldon, & I. R. Merkatz (Eds.), *Cherry and Merkatz's complications of pregnancy* (5th ed., pp. 1–15). Philadelphia: Lippincott Williams & Wilkins.

Berthenthal, B. I., & Campos, J. J. (1984). A reexamination of fear and its determinants on the visual cliff. *Psychophysiology, 21*, 413–417.

Bertollini, R., Pagano, M., & Mastroiacovo, P. (1993). What is a human teratogen? Clinical and epidemiological criteria. *Annali dell'Istituto Superiore de Sanità, 29*, 97–104.

Bertrand, R. M., & Lachman, M. E. (2003). Personality development in adulthood and old age. In B. Weiner (Series Ed.), R. M. Lerner, M. A. Easterbrooks, & J. Mistry (Vol. Eds.), *Handbook of psychology* (Vol. 6, pp. 463–485). New York: Wiley.

Best, J. (2001). *Damned lies and statistics: Untangling numbers from the media, politicians, and activists.* Berkeley, CA: University of California Press.

Best, M. (2005). *Shakespeare's life and times.* Victoria, BC: University of Victoria. Retrieved May 27, 2006, from http://ise.uvic.ca/Library/SLT/intro/introsubj.html

Bhatnager, S., & Taneja, S. (2001). Zinc and cognitive development. *The British Journal of Nutrition, 85*(Suppl. 2), S139–S145.

Bialystok, E. (2001). *Bilingualism in development: Language, literacy, and cognition.* New York: Cambridge University Press.

Bierman, J. M., Siegel, E., French, F. E., & Simonian, K. (1965). Analysis of the outcome of all pregnancies in a community: Kauai Pregnancy Study. *American Journal of Obstetrics and Gynecology, 91*, 37–45.

Bijou, S. W., & Baer, D. M. (1961). *Child development* (Vol. 1). New York: Appleton-Century-Crofts.

Birch, L. L. (1990). The control of food intake by young children: The role of learning. In E. D. Capaldi & T. L. Powley (Eds.), *Taste, experience, and feeding* (pp. 116–135). Washington, DC: American Psychological Association.

Birch, L. L., Marlin, D. W., & Rotter, J. (1984). Eating as the "means" activity in a contingency: Effects on young children's food preference. *Child Development, 55*, 431–439.

Birch, M. (1999). Psychological issues and infant-parent psychotherapy. In D. B. Kessler & P. Dawson (Eds.), *Failure to thrive and pediatric undernutrition: A transdisciplinary approach* (pp. 395–410). Baltimore: Paul H. Brookes.

Birch, S. A. J. (2005). When knowledge is a curse: Children's and adults' reasoning about mental states. *Current Directions in Psychological Science, 14*, 25–29.

Bird, C. P., & Fisher, T. D. (1986). Thirty years later: Attitudes toward the employment of older workers. *Journal of Applied Psychology, 71*, 515–517.

Birditt, K. S., Fingerman, K. L., & Almeida, D. A. (2005). Age differences in exposure and reactions to interpersonal tensions: A daily diary study. *Psychology and Aging, 20*, 330–340.

Bittman, M., England, P., Sayer, L., Folbre, N., & Matheson, G. (2003). When does gender trump money? Bargaining and time in household work. *American Journal of Sociology, 109*, 186–214.

Bjork, R. A. (1994). Memory and metamemory considerations in the training of human beings. In J. Metcalfe & A. Shimamura (Eds.), *Metacognition: Knowing about knowing* (pp. 185–205). Cambridge, MA: MIT Press.

Bjork, R. A. (1999). Assessing our own competence: Heuristics and illusions. In D. Gopher & A. Koriat (Eds.), *Attention and performance XVII: Cognitive regulation of performance: Interaction of theory and application* (pp. 435–459). Cambridge, MA: MIT Press.

Bjork, R. A. (2006). *IDDEAS: Introducing desirable difficulties for educational applications in science.* Retrieved February 4, 2006, from http://iddeas.psych.ucla.edu

Bjorklund, D. F., & Blasi, C. H. (2005). Evolutionary developmental psychology. In D. M. Buss (Ed.), *The handbook of evolutionary psychology* (pp. 828–850). Hoboken, NJ: Wiley.

Bjornsen, C. A. (2000). The blessing as a rite of passage in adolescence. *Adolescence, 35*, 357–363.

Black, H. (2005). Newborn screening report sparks debate in USA. *Lancet, 365*, 1453–1454.

Black, M. M., Dubowitz, H., & Starr, R. H., Jr. (1999). African American fathers in low income, urban families: Development, behavior, and home environment of their three-year-old children. *Child Development, 70*, 967–978.

Blair, C. (2002). School readiness: Integrating cognition and emotion in a neurobiological conceptualization of children's functioning at school entry. *American Psychologist, 57*, 111–127.

Blair, C., & Wahlsten, D. (2002). Why early intervention works: A reply to Baumeister and Bacharach. *Intelligence, 30*, 129–140.

Blakemore, C., & Cooper, G. F. (1970). Development of the brain depends on the visual environment. *Nature, 228*, 477–478.

Blakeney, P., & Meyer, W. (1995). Psychosocial recovery of burned patients and reintegration into society. In D. N. Herndon (Ed.), *Total burn care* (pp. 556–563). London: Saunders.

Blazer, D., & Palmore, E. (1976). Religion and aging in a longitudinal panel. *Gerontologist, 16*, 82–85.

Block, G., & Abrams, B. (1993). Vitamin and mineral status of women of childbearing potential. *Annuals of the New York Academy of Sciences, 678*, 244–254.

Bloom, L., & Tinker, E. (2001). The intentionality model and language acquisition: Engagement, effort, and the essential tension in development. *Society for Research in Child Development, 66*(4, Serial No. 267).

Blow, A. J., & Harnett, K. (2005). Infidelity in committed relationships II: A substantive review. *Journal of Marital and Family Therapy, 31*, 217–233.

Blum, N. J., Taubman, B., & Nemeth, N. (2004). Why is toilet training occurring at older ages? A study of factors associated with later training. *Journal of Pediatrics, 145*, 107–111.

Bogner, E., & Rafal, R. B. (2005). Failure to thrive. *Clinical Pediatrics, 44*, 185–188.

Bohannon, J. N., & Bonvillian, J. D. (2001). Theoretical approaches to language acquisition. In J. B. Gleason (Ed.), *The development of language* (pp. 254–314). New York: Allyn & Bacon.

Bone remodeling. (2004). Retrieved August 9, 2006, from http://www.medes.fr/home_fr/applications_sante/osteoporose/eristo/osteoporosis/Bone_Remodeling.html

Boom, J., Brugman, D., & Heijden, P. G. M. van der. (2001). Hierarchical structure of moral stages assessed by a sorting task. *Child Development, 72*, 535–548.

Booth, F. W., & Neufer, P. D. (2005). Exercise controls gene expression. *American Scientist, 93*(1), 28–35.

Borchers, D., & American Academy of Pediatrics Committee on Early Childhood, Adoption, and Dependent Care. (2003). Families and adoption: The pediatrician's role in supporting communication. *Pediatrics, 112*, 1437–1441.

Borke, H. (1975). Piaget's mountains revisited: Changes in the egocentric landscape. *Developmental Psychology, 11*, 240–243.

Bornstein, M. H. (1975). Qualities of color vision in infancy. *Journal of Experimental Child Psychology, 19*, 401–419.

Bornstein, M. H., & Arterberry, M. E. (1999). Perceptual development. In M. H. Bornstein & M. E. Lamb (Eds.), *Developmental psychology: An advanced textbook* (4th ed., pp. 231–274). Mahwah, NJ: Erlbaum.

Bortfeld, H., Morgan, J. L., Golinkoff, R. M., & Rathbun, K. (2005). Mommy and me: Familiar names help launch babies into speech-stream segmentation. *Psychological Science, 16*, 298–304.

Boston University School of Medicine. (2005). *The New England Centenarian Study*. Retrieved May 8, 2005, from **http://www.bumc.bu.edu/Dept/ Content.aspx?DepartmentID=361&PageID= 5924**

Botto, L. D., Moore, C. A., Khoury, M. J., & Erickson, J. D. (1999). Neural-tube defects. *The New England Journal of Medicine, 341*, 1509–1519.

Botvin, G. J., & Griffin, K. W. (1999). Preventing drug abuse. In A. J. Reynolds, H. J. Walberg, & R. P. Weissberg (Eds.), *Promoting positive outcomes* (pp. 197–228). Washington, DC: Child Welfare League of America.

Bouchard, T. J., Jr. (2004). Genetic influence on human psychological traits: A survey. *Current Directions in Psychological Science, 13*, 148–151.

Bouchard, T. J., Jr., & Hur, Y.-M. (1998). Genetic and environmental influences on the continuous scales of the Myers-Briggs Type indicator: An analysis based on twins reared apart. *Journal of Personality, 66*, 135–149.

Bouchard, T. J., Jr., & McGue, M. (2003). Genetic and environmental influences on human psychological differences. *Journal of Neurobiology, 54*, 4–45.

Bournot-Trites, M., & Reeder, K. (2001). Interdependence revisited: Mathematics achievement in an intensified French immersion program. *The Canadian Modern Language Review, 58*, 27–43.

Bower, B. (2004). Teen brains on trial. *Science News, 165*, 299–301.

Bowlby, J. (1944). Forty-four juvenile thieves: Their characters and home-life. *International Journal of Psycho-Analysis, 25*, 19–53.

Bowlby, J. (1969–1980). *Attachment and loss* (Vols. 1–3). New York: Basic Books.

Bowlby, J. (1980). By ethology out of psycho-analysis: An experiment in interbreeding. *Animal Behavior, 28*, 649–656.

Bowlby, J. (1982). *Attachment and loss: Vol. 1. Attachment* (2nd ed.). New York: Basic Books.

Bowlby, J. (1988). *A secure base: Parent-child attachment and healthy human development*. New York: Basic Books.

Boyce, W. T., & Ellis, B. J. (2005). Biological sensitivity to context: I. An evolutionary-developmental theory of the origins and functions of stress reactivity. *Development and Psychopathology, 17*, 271–301.

Brace, C. L. (1964). A nonracial approach towards the understanding of human diversity. In A. Montagu (Ed.), *The concept of race* (pp. 103–152). London: Collier-Macmillan.

Brace, C. L. (1996). The resurrection of race: The concept of race in physical anthropology in the 1990s. In L. T. Reynolds & L. Lieberman (Eds.), *Race and other misadventures: Essays in honor of Ashley Montagu in his ninetieth year* (pp. 174–186). Dix Hills, NY: General Hall.

Bracey, J. R., Bámaca, M. Y., & Umaña-Taylor, A. J. (2004). Examining ethnic identity and self-esteem among biracial and monoracial adolescents. *Journal of Youth and Adolescence, 33*, 123–132.

Bradley, R. H., Caldwell, B. M., & Corwyn, R. F. (2003). The Child Care HOME Inventories: Assessing the quality of family child care homes. *Early Childhood Research Quarterly, 18*, 294–309.

Bradley, R. H., Corwyn, R. F., Burshinal, M., McAdoo, H. P., & García Coll, C. (2001). The home environments of children in the Unites States Part II: Relations with behavioral development through age thirteen. *Child Development, 72*, 1868–1886.

Bradley-Johnson, S. (2001). Cognitive assessment for the youngest children: A critical review of tests. *Journal of Psychoeducational Assessment, 19*, 19–44.

Bradley-Johnson, S., & Johnson, C. M. (2001). *Cognitive Abilities Scale (CAS-2)*. Austin, TX: Pro-Ed.

Brady, M. S., Poole, D. A., Warren, A. R., & Jones, H. R. (1999). Young children's responses to yes-no questions: Patterns and problems. *Applied Developmental Science, 3*, 47–57.

Brainerd, C. J. (1978). *Piaget's theory of intelligence*. Englewood Cliffs, NJ: Prentice Hall.

Brainerd, C. J., & Mojardin, A. H. (1998). Children's and adults' spontaneous false memories: Long-term persistence and mere-testing effects. *Child Development, 69*, 1361–1377.

Brainerd, C. J., & Poole, D. A. (1997). Long-term survival of children's false memories: A review. *Learning and Individual Differences, 9*, 125–151.

Brainerd, C. J., & Reyna, V. F. (2001). Fuzzy-trace theory: Dual processes in memory, reasoning, and cognitive neuroscience. In H. W. Reese & R. Kail (Eds.), *Advances in child development and behavior* (Vol. 28, pp. 41–100). San Diego, CA: Academic Press.

Brainerd, C. J., & Reyna, V. F. (2004). Fuzzy-trace theory and memory development. *Developmental Review, 24*, 396–439.

Brainerd, C. J., Reyna, V. F., & Poole, D. A. (2000). Fuzzy-trace theory and false memory: Memory theory in the courtroom. In D. F. Bjorklund (Ed.), *False-memory creation in children and adults: Theory, research, and implications* (pp. 93–127). Mahwah, NJ: Erlbaum.

Bramlett, M. D., & Mosher, W. D. (2001, May 31). First marriage dissolution, divorce, and remarriage: United States. *Advance Data From Vital and Health Statistics, No. 323*. Hyattsville, MD: National Center for Health Statistics.

Branden, N. (1984, August-September). In defense of self. *Association for Humanistic Psychology*, pp. 12–13.

Brands, A. M., Biessels, G. J., de Haan, E. H., Kappelle, L. J., & Kessels, R. P. (2005). The effects of Type 1 diabetes on cognitive performance: A meta-analysis. *Diabetes Care, 28*, 726–735.

Bransford, J. D., Brown, A. L., & Cocking, R. R. (Eds.). (1999). *How people learn: Brain, mind, experience, and school*. Washington, DC: National Academy Press.

Braun, B. L. (1998). Knowledge and perception of fall-related risk factors and fall-reduction techniques among community-dwelling elderly individuals. *Physical Therapy, 78*, 1262–1276.

Braver, S. L. (1999). The gender gap in standard of living after divorce: Vanishingly small? *Family Law Quarterly, 33*, 111–134.

Bray, J. H., & Kelly, J. (1998). *Stepfamilies: Love, marriage, and parenting in the first decade*. New York: Broadway Books.

Brazelton, T. B. (1992). *Touchpoints: Your child's emotional and behavioral development*. Reading, MA: Perseus.

Breitowitz, Y. A. (2004). The brain death controversy in Jewish law. *Jewish Law Articles*. Retrieved December 24, 2004, from **http:// www.jlaw.com/Articles/brain.html**

Brennan, M. B. (1999). Neuroscience: The ultimate moon walk. *Chemical and Engineering News, 77*, 91–99.

Brent, D. A., Baugher, M., Bridge, J., Chen, T., & Chiappetta, L. (1999). Age- and sex-related risk factors for adolescent suicide. *Journal of the American Academy of Child and Adolescent Psychiatry, 38*, 1497–1505.

Brent, S. B., & Speece, M. W. (1993). "Adult" conceptualization of irreversibility: Implications for the development of the concept of death. *Death Studies, 17,* 203–224.

Breslau, N., & Chilcoat, H. D. (2000). Psychiatric sequelae of low birth weight at 11 years of age. *Biological Psychiatry, 47,* 1005–1011.

Breslau, N., Johnson, E. O., & Lucia, V. C. (2001). Academic achievement of low birthweight children at age 11: The role of cognitive abilities at school entry. *Journal of Abnormal Child Psychology, 29,* 273–279.

Brestan, E. V., Eyberg, S. M., Boggs, S. R., & Algina, J. (1997). Parent-Child Interaction Therapy: Parents' perceptions of untreated siblings. *Child and Family Behavior Therapy, 19,* 13–28.

Breuer, J., & Freud, S. (1893–95/1955). Studies on hysteria. In J. Strachey (Ed. and Trans.), *The standard edition of the complete psychological works of Sigmund Freud* (Vol. 2, pp. 1–305). London: Hogarth Press.

Brigance, A. H. (1991). *Brigance Diagnostic Inventory of Early Development (Revised).* North Billerica, MA: Curriculum Associates.

Brigman, S. L., & Roberts, B. A. (1986). *Opinions, attitudes, and needs of Arizona State University students, Fall 1985.* Tempe, AZ: Research and Evaluation Program in Student Affairs, Arizona State University.

Brink, S. (2002, March 11). The do or die decade: Men plummet into poor health when they hit their 50s. They don't have to. *U.S. News and World Report, 132,* 60–73.

Brody, N. (1992). *Intelligence* (2nd ed.). San Diego, CA: Academic Press.

Brodzinsky, D. M., Singer, L. M., & Braff, A. M. (1984). Children's understanding of adoption. *Child Development, 55,* 869–878.

Broidy, L. M., Nagin, D. S., Tremblay, R. E., et al. (2003). Developmental trajectories of childhood disruptive behaviors and adolescent delinquency: A six-site, cross-national study. *Developmental Psychology, 39,* 222–245.

Bromley, S. E., de Vries, C. S., Thomas, D., & Farmer, R, D. (2005). Hormone replacement therapy and risk of acute myocardial infarction: A review of the literature. *Drug Safety, 28,* 473–493.

Bronfenbrenner, U. (1977). Toward an experimental ecology of human development. *American Psychologist, 32,* 513–531.

Bronfenbrenner, U. (1979). *The ecology of human development: Experiments by nature and design.* Cambridge, MA: Harvard University Press.

Bronfenbrenner, U. (1999). Environments in developmental perspective: Theoretical and operational models. In S. L. Friedman & T. D. Wachs (Eds.), *Measuring environment across the life span: Emerging methods and concepts* (pp. 3–28). Washington, DC: American Psychological Association.

Bronfenbrenner, U., & Ceci, S. J. (1994). Nature-nurture reconceptualized in developmental perspective: A bioecological model. *Psychological Review, 101,* 568–586.

Bronfenbrenner, U., & Morris, P. A. (1998). The ecology of developmental processes. In W. Damon (Series Ed.) & R. M. Lerner (Vol. Ed.), *Handbook of child psychology: Vol. 1. Theoretical models of human development* (5th ed., pp. 993–1028). New York: Wiley.

Brook, J. S., Brook, D. W., & Whiteman, M. (1999). Older sibling correlates of younger sibling drug use in the context of parent-child relations. *Genetic, Social, and General Psychology Monographs, 125,* 451–468.

Brook, J. S., Whiteman, M., Finch, S., & Cohen, P. (1998). Mutual attachment, personality, and drug use: Pathways from childhood to young adulthood. *Genetic, Social, and General Psychology Monographs, 124,* 492–510.

Brooks-Gunn, J. (2001). What are the components of successful early childhood programs? *Social Policy Report, 15*(2), 9.

Brooks-Gunn, J. (2003). Do you believe in magic? What we can expect from early childhood intervention programs. *Social Policy Report, 17*(1).

Brooks-Gunn, J., Han, W.-J., & Waldfogel, J. (2002). Maternal employment and child cognitive outcomes in the first three years of life: The NICHD Study of Early Child Care. *Child Development, 73,* 1052–1072.

Brooks-Gunn, J., & Reiter, E. O. (1990). The role of pubertal processes. In S. S. Feldman & G. R. Elliott (Eds.), *At the threshold: The developing adolescent* (pp. 16–53). Cambridge, MA: Harvard University Press.

Brooks-Gunn, J., & Warren, M. P. (1989). Biological and social contributions to negative affect in young adolescent girls. *Child Development, 60,* 40–55.

Broude, G. J. (1995). *Growing up: A cross-cultural encyclopedia.* Santa Barbara, CA: ABC-CLIO.

Brouillette, R. T., & Nixon, G. (2001). Risk factors for SIDS as targets for public health campaigns. *Journal of Pediatrics, 139,* 759–761.

Brown, B. B. (2004). Adolescents' relationships with peers. In R. M. Lerner & L. D. Steinberg (Eds.), *Handbook of adolescent psychology* (2nd ed., pp. 363–394). Hoboken, NJ: Wiley.

Brown, B. B., & Klute, C. (2003). Friendships, cliques, and crowds. In G. R. Adams & M. D. Berzonsky (Eds.), *Blackwell handbook of adolescence* (pp. 330–348). Malden, MA: Blackwell.

Brown, B. B., Larson, R. W., & Saraswathi, T. S. (Eds.). (2002). *The world's youth: Adolescence in eight regions of the globe.* New York: Cambridge University Press.

Brown, J. D., Steele, J. R., & Walsh-Childers, K. (Eds.). (2002). *Sexual teens, sexual media: Investigating media's influence on adolescent sexuality.* Mahwah, NJ: Erlbaum.

Brown, K. (2004). A radical proposal. *Scientific American, 14*(3), 30–35.

Brown, M., Keynes, R., & Lumsden, A. (2001). *The developing brain.* New York: Oxford University Press.

Brown, P. (2001). Choosing to die: A growing epidemic among the young. *Bulletin of the World Health Organization, 79,* 1175–1177.

Brown, S. L., Nesse, R. M., Vinokur, A. D., & Smith, D. M. (2003). Providing social support may be more beneficial than receiving it: Results from a prospective study of mortality. *Psychological Science, 14,* 320–327.

Browne, K. D., & Hamilton-Giachritsis, C. (2005). The influence of violent media on children and adolescents: A public-health approach. *Lancet, 365,* 702–710.

Brownell, C. A. (1990). Peer social skills in toddlers: Competencies and constraints illustrated by same-age and mixed-age interaction. *Child Development, 61,* 838–848.

Bruce, M. L., Kim, K., Leaf, P. J., & Jacobs, S. (1990). Depressive episodes and dysphoria resulting from conjugal bereavement in a prospective community sample. *American Journal of Psychiatry, 147,* 608–611.

Bruer, J. T. (1999). *The myth of the first three years: A new understanding of early brain development and lifelong learning.* New York: Free Press.

Brumberg, J. J. (1997). *The body project: An intimate history of American girls.* New York: Random House.

Brumfield, B. D., & Roberts, M. W. (1998). A comparison of two measurements of child compliance with normal preschool children. *Journal of Clinical Child Psychology, 27,* 109–116.

Bryant, J. B. (2001). Language in social contexts: Communicative competence in the preschool years. In J. B. Gleason (Ed.), *The development of language* (5th ed., pp. 213–253). Boston: Allyn & Bacon.

Bryden, P. J., Pryde, K. M., & Roy, E. A. (2000). A developmental analysis of the relationship between hand preference and performance: II: A performance-based method of measuring hand preference in children. *Brain and Cognition, 43,* 60–64.

Buchanan, C. M., Eccles, J. S., & Becker, J. B. (1992). Are adolescents the victims of raging hormones? Evidence for activational effects of hormones on moods and behavior at adolescence. *Psychological Bulletin, 111,* 62–107.

Buggie, S. E. (1995). Superkids of the ghetto. *Contemporary Psychology, 40,* 1164–1165.

Buhrmester, D. (1996). Need fulfillment, interpersonal competence, and the developmental contexts of early adolescent friendship. In W. M. Bukowski, A. F. Newcomb, & W. W. Hartup (Eds.), *The company they keep: Friendship in childhood and adolescence.* (pp. 158–163). New York: Cambridge University Press.

Buhrmester, D., & Furman, W. (1987). The development of companionship and intimacy. *Child Development, 58,* 1101–1113.

Buhs, E. S., & Ladd, G. W. (2001). Peer rejection as antecedent of young children's school adjustment: An examination of mediating processes. *Developmental Psychology, 37,* 550–560.

Buka, S. L., Stichick, T. L., Birdthistle, I., & Earls, F. J. (2001). Youth exposure to violence: Prevalence, risks, and consequences. *American Journal of Orthopsychiatry, 71,* 298–310.

Bullough, V. L., & Bullough, B. (Eds.). (1994). *Human sexuality: An encyclopedia.* New York: Garland.

Burke, D. M., & Shafto, M. A. (2004). Aging and language production. *Current Directions in Psychological Science, 13,* 21–24.

Burns, J. J., Stanton, B., Perkins, K., Pack, R., & Hobby-Burns, L. (2003). Eating disorders in adolescents. *The West Virginia Medical Journal, 99,* 60–66.

Burton, L. C., Zdaniuk, B., Schulz, R., Jackson, S., & Hirsch, C. (2003). Transitions in spousal caregiving. *Gerontologist, 43,* 230–241.

Burts, D., Hart, C. H., Charlesworth, R., & Kirk, L. (1990). A comparison of frequencies of stress behaviors observed in kindergarten children in classrooms with developmentally appropriate versus developmentally inappropriate instructional practices. *Early Childhood Research Quarterly, 5,* 407–423.

Bush, G., Valera, E. M., & Seidman, L. J. (2005). Functional neuroimaging of attention-deficit hyperactivity disorder: A review and suggested future directions. *Biological Psychiatry, 57,* 1273–1284.

Bushman, B. J., & Baumeister, R. F. (1998). Threatened egotism, narcissism, self-esteem, and direct and displaced aggression: Does self-love or self-hate lead to violence? *Journal of Personality and Social Psychology, 75,* 219–229.

Buss, D. M. (1994). *The evolution of desire: Strategies of human mating.* New York: Basic Books.

Buss, D. M. (2004). *Evolutionary psychology: The new science of the mind* (2nd ed.). Boston: Allyn & Bacon.

Buss, D. M. (Ed.) (2005). *The handbook of evolutionary psychology.* Hoboken, NJ: Wiley.

Buss, D. M., Haselton, M. G., Shackelford, T. K., Belske, A. L., & Wakefield, J. C. (1998). Adaptations, exaptations, and spandrels. *American Psychologist, 53,* 533–548.

Bussey, K., & Bandura, A. (1999). Social cognitive theory of gender development and differentiation. *Psychological Review, 106,* 676–713.

Butler, R. J. (2004). Childhood nocturnal enuresis: Developing a conceptual framework. *Clinical Psychology Review, 24,* 909–931.

Butterfield, E. L., & Siperstein, G. N. (1972). Influence of contingent auditory stimulation on nonnutritional sucking. In J. F. Bosma (Ed.), *Third symposium on oral sensation and perception: The mouth of the infant* (pp. 313–334). Springfield, IL: Thomas.

Butterworth, G. (1998). What is special about pointing in babies? In F. Simion & G. Butterworth (Eds.), *The development of sensory, motor and cognitive capacities in early infancy: From perception to cognition* (pp. 171–190). Hove, England: Psychology Press.

Cairney, J., Boyle, M., Offord, D. R., & Racine, Y. (2003). Stress, social support and depression in single and married mothers. *Social Psychiatry and Psychiatric Epidemiology, 38,* 442–449.

Cairns, R. B., & Ornstein, P. A. (1979). Developmental psychology. In E. Hearst (Ed.), *The first century of experimental psychology* (pp. 459–512). Hillsdale, NJ: Erlbaum.

Caldwell, D. F., & Burger, J. M. (1998). Personality characteristics of job applicants and success in screening interviews. *Personnel Psychology, 51,* 119–136.

Call, V., Sprecher, S. S., & Schwartz, P. (1995). The incidence and frequency of marital sex in a national sample. *Journal of Marriage and the Family, 57,* 639–652.

Callaghan, T., Rochat, P., Lillard, A., et al. (2005). Synchrony in the onset of mental-state reasoning: Evidence from five cultures. *Psychological Science, 16,* 378–384.

Calorie Restriction Society. (2006). Retrieved April 15, 2006, from **http://www.calorierestriction.org**

Camara, W. (2003). More time unnecessary. *USA Today.* Retrieved February 8, 2005, from **http://www.usatoday.com/news/opinion/editorials/2003–10–09–oppose_x.htm**

Cameron, D. R., & Braunstein, G. D. (2004). Androgen replacement therapy in women. *Fertility and Sterility, 82,* 273–289.

Campbell, A. A. (1968). The role of family planning in the reduction of poverty. *Journal of Marriage and the Family, 30,* 236–245.

Campbell, D. T. (1987). Problems for the experimenting society in the interface between evaluation and service providers. In S. L. Kagan, D. R. Powell, B. Weissbourd, & E. F. Zigler (Eds.), *America's family support programs* (pp. 345–351). New Haven, CT: Yale University Press.

Campbell, P. B., & Storo, J. N. (1994). *Girls are . . . boys are . . . : Myths, stereotypes and gender differences.* Washington, DC: U.S. Department of Education, Office of Educational Research and Improvement.

Campbell, S. B., Shaw, D. S., & Gilliom, M. (2000). Early externalizing behavior problems: Toddlers and preschoolers at risk for later maladjustment. *Development and Psychopathology, 12,* 467–488.

Campbell, S. M. (2000). Attention-deficit/hyperactivity disorder: A developmental view. In A. J. Sameroff, M. Lewis, & S. M. Miller (Eds.), *Handbook of developmental psychopathology* (2nd ed., pp. 383–401). New York: Kluwer Academic/Plenum.

Campbell, S. S., Murphy, P. J., & Stauble, T. N. (2005). Effects of a nap on nighttime sleep and waking function in older subjects. *Journal of the American Geriatrics Society, 53,* 48–53.

Campos, J. J., Frankel, C. B., & Camras, L. (2004). On the nature of emotion regulation. *Child Development, 75,* 377–394.

Campos, J. J., Langer, A., & Krowitz, A. (1970). Cardiac responses on the visual cliff in prelocomotor human infants. *Science, 170,* 196–197.

Cantor-Graae, E., Ismail, B., & McNeil, T. F. (2000). Are neurological abnormalities in schizophrenic patients and their siblings the result of perinatal trauma? *Acta Psychiatrica Scandinavica, 101,* 142–147.

Caplan, P. J., & Hall-McCorquodale, I. (1985). Mother-blaming in major clinical journals. *American Journal of Orthopsychiatry, 55,* 345–353.

Caprara, G. V., Caprara, M., & Steca, P. (2003). Personality's correlates of adult development and aging. *European Psychologist, 8,* 131–147.

Capron, C., & Duyme, M. (1991). Children's IQs and SES of biological and adoptive parents in a balanced cross-fostering study. *Current Psychology of Cognition, 11,* 323–348.

Carey, S. (1978). The child as a word learner. In M. Halle, J. Brenan, & G. A. Miller (Eds.), *Linguistic theory and psychological reality* (pp. 264–293). Cambridge, MA: MIT Press.

Carey, W. B. (1985). Interactions of temperament and clinical conditions. *Advances in Development and Behavioral Pediatrics, 6,* 83–115.

Carlson, B. M. (1999). *Human embryology and developmental biology* (2nd ed.). St. Louis, MO: Mosby.

Carlson, S. J., Andrews, M. S., & Bickel, G. W. (1999). Measuring food insecurity and hunger in the United States: Development of a national benchmark measure and prevalence estimates. *Journal of Nutrition, 129*(Suppl. 2), 510S–516S.

Carlson, S. M., & Taylor, M. (2005). Imaginary companions and impersonated characters: Sex differences in children's fantasy play. *Merrill-Palmer Quarterly, 51,* 93–118.

Carnegie Commission on Preventing Deadly Conflict. (1997). *Preventing deadly conflict: Final report with executive summary.* Washington, DC: The Commission.

Carroll, J. (2002, March 12). Parent/teen relations: Where's the grief? *The Gallup Poll.* Retrieved January 10, 2005, from **http://poll.gallup.com**

Carroll, S. B. (2005). *Endless forms most beautiful: The new science of evo devo and the making of the animal kingdom.* New York: Norton.

Carroll-Pankhurst, C., & Mortimer, E. A., Jr. (2001). Sudden infant death syndrome, bed-sharing, parental weight, and age at death. *Pediatrics, 107,* 530–536.

Carskadon, M. A. (1999a). Sleepy students fight the school clock. *The Education Digest, 64*(9), 12–14.

Carskadon, M. A. (1999b). When worlds collide: Adolescent need for sleep versus societal demands. *Phi Delta Kappan, 80,* 348–353.

Carskadon, M. A., Acebo, C., & Jenni, O. G. (2004). Regulation of adolescent sleep: Implications for behavior. In R. E. Dahl & L. P. Spear (Eds.), *Annals of the New York Academy of Sciences: Vol. 1021. Adolescent brain development: Vulnerabilities and opportunities* (pp. 276–291). New York: New York Academy of Sciences.

Carskadon, M. A., Wolfson, A. R., Acebo, C., Tzischinsky, O., & Seifer, R. (1998). Adolescent sleep patterns, circadian timing, and sleepiness at a transition to early school days. *Sleep, 21,* 871–881.

Carson-DeWitt, R. (2001). Otitis media. In J. L. Longe & D. S. Blanchfield (Eds.), *The Gale encyclopedia of medicine* (2nd ed.). Retrieved July 1, 2002, from http://0–infotrac.galegroup.com

Carstensen, L. L. (1992). Social and emotional patterns in adulthood: Support for socioemotional selectivity theory. *Psychology and Aging, 7,* 331–338.

Carstensen, L. L., & Fredrickson, B. (1998). Influence of HIV status and age on cognitive representations of others. *Health Psychology, 17,* 494–503.

Carstensen, L. L., Fung, H. H., & Charles, S. T. (2003). Socioemotional selectivity theory and the regulation of emotion in the second half of life. *Motivation and Emotion, 27,* 103–123.

Carstensen, L. L., & Löckenhoff, C. E. (2003). Aging, emotion, and evolution: The bigger picture. In P. Ekman (Ed.), *Annals of the New York Academy of Sciences: Vol. 1000. Emotions inside out: 130 years after Darwin's The Expression of the Emotions in Man and Animals* (pp. 152–179). New York: New York Academy of Sciences.

Cartstensen, L. L., Pasupathi, M., Mayr, U., & Nesselroade, J. R. (2000). Emotional experience in everyday life across the adult life span. *Journal of Personality and Social Psychology, 79,* 644–655.

Cartwright, C., & Seymour, F. (2002). Young adults' perceptions of parents' responses in step-families: What hurts? What helps? *Journal of Divorce and Remarriage, 37*(3–4), 123–141.

Cash, T. F., & Deagle, E. A., III. (1997). The nature and extent of body-image disturbances in anorexia nervosa and bulimia nervosa: A meta-analysis. *International Journal of Eating Disorders, 22,* 107–125.

Casper, M. J. (1998). *The making of the unborn patient: A social anatomy of fetal surgery.* New Brunswick, NJ: Rutgers University Press.

Castejon, H. V., Ortega, P., Amaya, D., Gomez, G., Leal, J., & Castejon, O. J. (2004). Co-existence of anemia, vitamin A deficiency and growth retardation among children 24–84 months old in Maracaibo, Venezuela. *Nutritional Neuroscience, 7,* 113–119.

Castle, J., Groothues, C., Bredenkamp, D., et al. (1999). Effects of qualities of early institutional care on cognitive attainment. *American Journal of Orthopsychiatry, 69,* 424–437.

Cattell, R. B. (1971). *Abilities: Their structure, growth, and action.* Boston: Houghton Mifflin.

Caudill, W., & Weinstein, H. (1969). Maternal care and infant behavior in Japan and America. *Psychiatry: Journal for the Study of Interpersonal Processes, 32,* 12–43.

Cavan, R. S., Burgess, E. W., Havighurst, R. J., & Goldhamer, H. (1949). *Personal adjustment in old age.* Oxford, England: Science Research Associates.

Ceci, S. J. (1991). How much does schooling influence general intelligence and its cognitive components? A reassessment of the evidence. *Developmental Psychology, 27,* 703–722.

Ceci, S. J. (1996). *On intelligence: A bioecological treatise on intellectual development.* Cambridge, MA: Harvard University Press.

Ceci, S. J., & Bruck, M. (1995). *Jeopardy in the courtroom: A scientific analysis of children's testimony.* Washington, DC: American Psychological Association.

Ceci, S. J., Leichtman, M. D., & Putnick, M. (Eds.) (1992). *Cognitive and social factors in early deception.* Hillsdale, NJ: Erlbaum.

Ceci, S. J., Papierno, P. B., & Mueller-Johnson, K. U. (2002). The twisted relationship between school spending and academic outputs: In search of a new metaphor. *Journal of School Psychology, 40,* 477–484.

Ceci, S. J., & Williams, W. M. (1997). Schooling, intelligence, and income. *American Psychologist, 52,* 1051–1058.

Centers for Disease Control and Prevention. (1993a). Public health focus: Prevention of blindness associated with diabetic retinopathy. *Morbidity and Mortality Weekly Report, 42*(10), 191–195.

Centers for Disease Control and Prevention. (1993b). Rates of cesarean delivery—United States, 1993. *Morbidity and Mortality Weekly Report, 44*(15), 285.

Centers for Disease Control and Prevention. (2000). *2000 CDC growth charts: United States.* Retrieved January 30, 2006, from http://www.cdc.gov/growthcharts

Centers for Disease Control and Prevention. (2003a). *Childhood lead poisoning.* Retrieved November 3, 2003, from www.cdc.gov/nceh/lead/factsheets/childhoodlead.htm

Centers for Disease Control and Prevention. (2003b). *Costs of intimate partner violence against women in the United States.* Retrieved June 10, 2006, from http://www.cdc.gov/ncipc/pub-res/ipv_cost/ipv.htm

Centers for Disease Control and Prevention. (2004). *Bike/helmet: Why kids are at risk.* Retrieved September 12, 2004, from http://www.safekids.org/tier3_cd.cfm?content_item_id=306&folder_id=169

Centers for Disease Control and Prevention. (2005a). *Arthritis.* Retrieved March 30, 2005, from http://www.cdc.gov/nccdphp/arthritis/index.htm

Centers for Disease Control and Prevention. (2005b). *Basic facts about asthma.* Retrieved June 5, 2005, from http://www.cdc.gov/asthma.faqs.htm

Centers for Disease Control and Prevention. (2005c). *Birth defects: Frequently asked questions (FAQs).* Retrieved April 27, 2006, from http://www.cdc.gov/ncbddd/bd/faq2.htm#causeofBD

Centers for Disease Control and Prevention. (2005d). Blood lead levels—United States, 1999–2002. *Morbidity and Mortality Weekly Report, 54*(20), 513–516.

Centers for Disease Control and Prevention. (2005e). *Breastfeeding: Data and statistics: Practices—Results from the 2004 National Immunization Survey.* Retrieved April 25, 2006, from http://www.cdc.gov/breastfeeding/data/NIS_data/data_2004.htm

Centers for Disease Control and Prevention. (2005f). *Chronic disease prevention: Physical activity and nutrition: Essential elements to prevent chronic diseases and obesity.* Retrieved May 29, 2006, from http://www.cdc.gov/nccdphp/publications/aag/dnpa.htm

Centers for Disease Control and Prevention. (2005g). *Data and trends: National diabetes surveillance system.* Retrieved April 23, 2006, from http://www.cdc.gov/diabetes/statistics/prev/national/figbyage.htm

Centers for Disease Control and Prevention. (2005h). *Diabetes maps.* Retrieved April 23, 2006, from http://www.cdc.gov/diabetes/statistics/maps/map1.htm

Centers for Disease Control and Prevention. (2005i). *Sexually transmitted diseases.* Retrieved April 27, 2006, from http://www.cdc.gov/node.do/id/0900f3ec80009a98

Centers for Disease Control and Prevention. (2005j). *Trends in reportable sexually transmitted diseases in the United States, 2004.* Retrieved March 7, 2006, from http://www.cdc.gov/std/stats/04pdf/trends2004.pdf

Centers for Disease Control and Prevention. (2006a). *About DES: Known health effects for DES sons.* Retrieved April 27, 2006, from **http://www.cdc.gov/DES/consumers/about/effects_sons.html**

Centers for Disease Control and Prevention. (2006b). *Health topics.* Retrieved March, 2006, from **http://www.cdc.gov/HealthyYouth/healthtopics**

Centers for Disease Control and Prevention. (2006c). *Overweight and obesity: Frequently asked questions (FAQs).* Retrieved April 2, 2006, from **http://www.cdc.gov/nccdphp/dnpa/obesity/faq.htm**

Centers for Disease Control and Prevention. (2006d). *Poliomyelitis.* Retrieved January 8, 2006, from **http://www.cdc.gov/doc.do/id/0900f3ec802286ba**

Centers for Disease Control and Prevention & National Center for Health Statistics. (2005). *Deaths, percent of total deaths, and death rates for the 15 leading causes of death in 5-year age groups, by Hispanic origin, race for non-Hispanic population and sex: United States, 2002.* Retrieved November 7, 2005, from **http://www.cdc.gov/nchs/data/dvs/LCWK4_2002_3.pdf**

Centers for Disease Control and Prevention, National Immunization Program. (2002). *Six common misconceptions about vaccinations and how to respond to them.* Retrieved May 3, 2006, from www.cdc.gov/nip/publications/6mishome.htm

Cermak, S. A., Gubbay, S. S., & Larkin, D. (2002). What is developmental coordination disorder? In S. A. Cermak & D. Larkin (Eds.), *Developmental coordination disorder* (pp. 2–22). Albany, NY: Delmar.

Cermak, S. A., & Larkin, D. (Eds.). (2002). *Developmental coordination disorder.* Albany, NY: Delmar.

Certain, L. K., & Kahn, R. S. (2002). Prevalence, correlates, and trajectory of television viewing among infants and toddlers. *Pediatrics, 109,* 634–642.

Chamberlain, P., & Patterson, G. R. (1985). Aggressive behavior in middle childhood. In D. Shaffer, A. A. Ehrhardt, & L. L. Greenhill (Eds.), *The clinical guide to child psychiatry* (pp. 229–250). New York: Free Press.

Chan, B. C., & Lao, T. T. (1999). Influence of parity on the obstetric performance of mothers aged 40 years and above. *Human Reproduction, 14,* 833–837.

Chandler, M. J., Lalonde, C. E., Sokol, B. W., & Hallett, D. (2003). Personal persistence, identity development, and suicide. *Monographs of the Society for Research in Child Development, 68*(2, Serial No. 273).

Chao, R. K. (1994). Beyond parental control and authoritarian parenting style: Understanding Chinese parenting through the cultural notion of training. *Child Development, 65,* 1111–1119.

Chao, R. K. (2001). Extending research on the consequences of parenting style for Chinese Americans and European Americans. *Child Development, 72,* 1832–1843.

Charles, D. H., Ness, A. R., Campbell, D., Smith, G. D., Whitley, E., & Hall, M. H. (2005). Folic acid supplements in pregnancy and birth outcome: Re-analysis of a large randomised controlled trial and update of Cochrane review. *Paediatric and Perinatal Epidemiology, 19,* 112–124.

Charles, S. T., & Carstensen, L. L. (2004). A life span view of emotional functioning in adulthood and old age. In M. P. Mattson (Series Ed.) & P. Costa & L. Siegler (Vol. Eds.), *Advances in cell aging and gerontology: Vol. 15. Recent advances in psychology and aging* (pp. 133–162). Amsterdam: Elsevier.

Charlesworth, W. R., & Dzur, C. (1987). Gender comparison of preschoolers' behavior and resource utilization in group problem solving. *Child Development, 58,* 191–200.

Charlesworth, W. R., & La Freniere, P. (1983). Dominance, friendship, and resource utilization in preschool children's groups. *Ethology and Sociobiology, 4,* 175–186.

Chase, A. (1975). The great pellagra cover-up. *Psychology Today, 8*(9), 82–86.

Chase-Lansdale, P. L., Moffitt, R. A., Lohman, B. J., et al. (2003). Mothers' transitions from welfare to work and the well-being of preschoolers and adolescents. *Science, 299,* 1548–1552.

Chatkupt, S., Antonowicz, M., & Johnson, W. G. (1995). Parents do matter: Genomic imprinting and parental sex effects in neurological disorders. *Journal of the Neurological Sciences, 130,* 1–10.

Chatters, L. M., & Taylor, R. J. (1989). Age differences in religious participation among Black adults. *Journals of Gerontology: Psychological Sciences and Social Sciences, 44B,* S183–S189.

Chatters, L. M., Taylor, R. J., & Jayakody, R. (1994). Fictive kinship relations in Black extended families. *Journal of Comparative Family Studies, 25,* 297–312.

Chen, C., & Stevenson, H. W. (1989). Homework: A cross-cultural examination. *Child Development, 60,* 551–561.

Chen, C., & Stevenson, H. W. (1995). Motivation and mathematics achievement: A comparative study of Asian-American, Caucasian-American, and East Asian high school students. *Child Development, 66,* 1215–1234.

Chen, F. (2003). The division of labor between generations of women in rural China. *Social Science Research, 33,* 557–580.

Chen, X., Chang, L., He, Y., & Liu, H. (2005). The peer group as a context: Moderating effects on relations between maternal parenting and social and school adjustment in Chinese children. *Child Development, 76,* 417–434.

Chen, X., Dong, Q., & Zhou, H. (1997). Authoritative and authoritarian parenting practices and social and school performance in Chinese children. *International Journal of Behavioral Development, 21,* 855–873.

Chen, X., Hastings, P. D., Rubin, K. H., et al. (1998). Child-rearing attitudes and behavioral inhibition in Chinese and Canadian toddlers: A cross-cultural study. *Developmental Psychology, 34,* 677–686.

Chervenak, F. A., McCullough, L. B., & Birnbach, D. J. (2004). Ethical issues in fetal surgery research. *Best Practice and Research: Clinical Anaesthesiology, 18,* 221–230.

Chess, S., & Hassibi, M. (1986). *Principles and practice of child psychiatry* (2nd ed.). New York: Plenum Press.

Chess, S., & Whitbread, J. (1978). *Daughters: From infancy to independence.* Garden City, NY: Doubleday.

Chew, C. (2004). Minority test takers make significant gains on SAT. *Black Issues in Higher Education, 21,* 8, 10.

Chi, M. T. H. (1978). Knowledge structures and memory development. In R. S. Siegler (Ed.), *Children's thinking: What develops?* (pp. 73–96). Hillsdale, NJ: Erlbaum.

Chien, Y.-c., & Wexler, K. (1990). Children's knowledge of locality conditions in binding as evidence for the modularity of syntax and pragmatics. *Language Acquisition, 1,* 225–295.

Child Trends. (2003, February 13). *Will there be fewer teenage valentines this year? New data show a decline in teen dating.* Retrieved February 26, 2006, from **http://www.childtrends.org/_mediarelease_page.cfm?LID=20C71C8D-F98D-4CD9-ADADC9AC8281512B**

Children's Defense Fund. (2000). *The state of America's children yearbook 2000.* Washington, DC: Author.

Children's Health Care Collaborative Study Group. (1992). Romanian health and social care system for children and families: Future directions in health care reform. *British Medical Journal, 304,* 556–559.

Children's higher IQ is linked to breast milk. (1992, January 31). *The Washington Post,* p. A4.

Chiong, C. (2003, October). *Learning the ABC's: Do some kinds of picture books help or hinder young children's learning?* Poster presented at the meeting of the Cognitive Development Society, Park City, UT.

Chipperfield, J. G., & Havens, B. (2001). Gender differences in the relationship between marital status transitions and life satisfaction in later life. *Journals of Gerontology: Psychological Sciences and Social Sciences, 56B,* P176–P186.

Chisholm, P. (with Webb, A.). (1994, June 20). The time crunch. *Maclean's, 107,* 36–37.

Chiriboga, C. A. (1998). Neurological correlates of fetal cocaine exposure. In J. A. Harvey & B. E. Kosofsky (Eds.), *Annals of the New York Academy of Sciences: Vol. 846. Cocaine: Effects on the developing brain* (pp. 109–125). New York: New York Academy of Sciences.

Chomsky, N. (1957). A review of B. F. Skinner's *Verbal Behavior*. *Language, 35*, 26–58.

Chomsky, N. (1965). *Aspects of the theory of syntax*. Cambridge, MA: MIT Press.

Chong, D. S., Yip, P. S., & Karlberg J. (2004). Maternal smoking: An increasing unique risk factor for sudden infant death syndrome in Sweden. *Acta Paediatrica, 93*, 471–478.

Christenson, S. L., & Thurlow, M. L. (2004). School dropouts: Prevention considerations, interventions, and challenges. *Current Directions in Psychological Science, 13*, 36–39.

Christopher, F. S., & Sprecher, S. (2000). Sexuality in marriage, dating, and other relationships: A decade review. *Journal of Marriage and the Family, 62*, 999–1017.

Chuang, H. Y., Schwartz, J., Gonzales-Cossio, T., et al. (2001). Interrelations of lead levels in bone, venous blood, and umbilical cord blood with exogenous lead exposure through maternal plasma lead in peripartum women. *Environmental Health Perspectives, 109*, 527–532.

Cicchetti, D., Toth, S. L., & Maughan, A. (2000). An ecological-transactional model of child maltreatment. In A. J. Sameroff, M. Lewis, & S. M. Miller (Eds.), *Handbook of developmental psychopathology* (2nd ed., pp. 689–722). New York: Kluwer Academic/Plenum.

Cifuentes, J., Bronstein, J., Phibbs, C. S., Phibbs, R. H., Schmitt, S. K., & Carlo, W. A. (2002). Mortality in low birth weight infants according to level of neonatal care at hospital of birth. *Pediatrics, 109*, 745–751.

Cillessen, A. H., van IJzendoorn, H. W., van Lieshout, C, F., & Hartup, W. W. (1992). Heterogeneity among peer-rejected boys: Subtypes and stabilities. *Child Development, 63*, 893–905.

Cillessen, A. H. N., & Mayeux, L. (2004). Sociometric status and peer group behavior: Previous findings and current directions. In J. B. Kupersmidt & K. A. Dodge (Eds.), *Children's peer relations: From development to intervention* (pp. 3–20). Washington, DC: American Psychological Association.

Clark, M. S., Graham, S., & Grote, N. (2002). Bases for giving benefits in marriage: What is ideal? What is realistic? What really happens? In P. Noller & J. A. Feeney (Eds.), *Understanding marriage: Developments in the study of couple interaction* (pp. 150–176). New York: Cambridge University Press.

Clark, M. S., & Waddell, B. A. (1983). Effects of moods on thoughts about helping, attraction and information acquisition. *Social Psychology Quarterly, 46*, 31–35.

Clarke, V., Kitzinger, C., & Potter, J. (2004). "Kids are just cruel anyway": Lesbian and gay parents' talk about homophobic bullying. *British Journal of Social Psychology, 43*, 531–550.

Clearfield, M. W., & Thelen, E. (2001). Stability and flexibility in the acquisition of skilled movement. In C. A. Nelson & M. Luciana (Eds.), *Handbook of developmental cognitive neuroscience* (pp. 253–266). Cambridge, MA: MIT Press.

Clemmer, S. C., Klifman, T. J., & Bradley-Johnson, S. (1992). Long-term predictive validity of the Cognitive Ability Scales. *Journal of Psychoeducational Assessment, 10*, 265–275.

Cleveland, J. N., & Shore, L. M. (1992). Self- and supervisory perspectives on age and work attitudes and performance. *Journal of Applied Psychology, 77*, 469–484.

Clinical reference systems. (2000). Health reference center academic [Electronic database]: Thomson Gale.

Cohen, S. (1996). Psychological stress, immunity, and upper respiratory infections. *Current Directions in Psychological Science, 5*, 86–90.

Cohen, S. (2002). Psychosocial stress, social networks, and susceptibility to infection. In H. G. Koenig & H. J. Cohen, (Eds.), *The link between religion and health: Psychoneuroimmunology and the faith factor* (pp. 101–123). New York: Oxford University Press.

Cohen, S. (2005). Keynote presentation at the Eighth International Congress of Behavioral Medicine: The Pittsburgh Common Cold Studies: Psychosocial predictors of susceptibility to respiratory infectious illness. *International Journal of Behavioral Medicine, 12*, 123–131.

Cohen, S., Doyle, W. J., Turner, R., Alper, C. M., & Skoner, D. P. (2003). Sociability and susceptibility to the common cold. *Psychological Science, 14*, 389–395.

Cohn, D. A., Silver, D. H., Cowan, C. P., Cowan, P. A., & Pearson, J. (1992). Working models of childhood attachment and couple relationships. *Journal of Family Issues, 13*, 434–449.

Coie, J. D., & Kupersmidt, J. B. (1983). A behavioral analysis of emerging social status in boys' groups. *Child Development, 54*, 1400–1416.

Colby, A., Kohlberg, L., Fenton, E., Speicher-Dubin, B., & Lieberman, M. (1977). Secondary school moral discussion programs led by social studies teachers. *Journal of Moral Education, 6*, 90–111.

Colby, A., Kohlberg, L., Gibbs, J., & Lieberman, M. (1983). A longitudinal study of moral judgment. *Monographs of the Society for Research in Child Development, 48*(1–2, Serial No. 200).

Cole, D. A., Maxwell, S. E., Martin, J. M., et al. (2001). The development of multiple domains of child and adolescent self-concept: A cohort sequential longitudinal design. *Child Development, 72*, 1723–1746.

Cole, M. (1990). Cognitive development and formal schooling: The evidence from cross-cultural research. In L. C. Moll (Ed.), *Vygotsky and education: Instructional implications and applications of sociohistorical psychology* (pp. 89–110). New York: Cambridge University Press.

Cole, M. (1999). Culture in development. In M. H. Bornstein & M. E. Lamb (Eds.), *Developmental psychology: An advanced textbook* (4th ed., pp. 73–123). Mahwah, NJ: Erlbaum.

Cole, M., & Cole, S. (1989). *The development of children*. New York: Scientific American Books.

Cole, P. M., Bruschi, C. J., & Tamang, B. L. (2002). Cultural differences in children's emotional reactions to difficult situations. *Child Development, 73*, 983–996.

Cole, R. E., Grolnick, W. S., Laurenitis, L. R., McAndrews, M. M., Matkoski, K. M., & Schwartzman, P. (1986). *Children and fire: Rochester Fire Related Youth Project progress report (2)*. Albany, NY: New York State Office of Fire Prevention and Control.

Cole, S. W., Kemeny, M. E., Fahey, J. L., Zack, J. A., & Naliboff, B. D. (2003). Psychological risk factors for HIV pathogenesis: Mediation by the autonomic nervous system. *Biological Psychiatry, 15*, 1444–1456.

Coles, R. (1970). *Erik H. Erikson: The growth of his work*. Boston: Little, Brown & Company.

Coles, R. (1997). *The moral intelligence of children*. New York: Random House.

Coley, R. J. (2001). *Differences in the gender gap: Comparisons across racial/ethnic groups in education and work*. Princeton, NJ: Educational Testing Service.

Coley, R. L., & Chase-Lansdale, P. L. (1998). Adolescent pregnancy and parenthood: Recent evidence and future directions. *American Psychologist, 53*, 152–166.

Collier, D. A., & Treasure, J. L. (2004). The aetiology of eating disorders. *British Journal of Psychiatry, 185*, 363–365.

Collins, R. L., Elliott, M. N., Berry, S. H., Kanhouse, D. E., & Hunter, S. B. (2003). Entertainment television as a healthy sex educator: The impact of condom-efficacy information in an episode of *Friends*. *Pediatrics, 112*, 1115–1121.

Collins, W. A. (2003). More than myth: The developmental significance of romantic relationships during adolescence. *Journal of Research on Adolescence, 13*, 1–24.

Collins, W. A., & Laursen, B. (2004). Parent-adolescent relationships and influences. In R. M. Lerner & L. D. Steinberg (Eds.), *Handbook of adolescent psychology* (2nd ed., pp. 331–361). Hoboken, NJ: Wiley.

Colón, I., Caro, D., Bourdony, C. J., & Rosario, O. (2000). Identification of phthalate esters in the serum of young Puerto Rican girls with premature breast development. *Environmental Health Perspectives, 108*, 895–900.

Colvin, M. K., Funnell, M. G., & Gazzaniga, M. S. (2005). Numerical processing in the two hemispheres: Studies of a split-brain patient. *Brain and Cognition, 57,* 43–52.

Comings, D. E., Muhleman, D., Johnson, J. P., & MacMurray, J. P. (2002). Parent-daughter transmission of the androgen receptor gene as an explanation of the effect of father absence on age of menarche. *Child Development, 73,* 1046–1051.

Committee on Ethical Guidelines for Forensic Psychologists. (1991). Specialty guidelines for forensic psychologists. *Law and Human Behavior, 15,* 655–665.

Condon, W. S., & Sander, L. W. (1974). Synchrony demonstrated between movements of the neonate and adult speech. *Child Development, 45,* 465–472.

Conduct Problems Prevention Research Group. (2004). The effects of the Fast Track program on serious problem outcomes at the end of elementary school. *Journal of Clinical Child and Adolescent Psychology, 33,* 650–661.

Conklin, B. A. (2001). *Consuming grief: Compassionate cannibalism in an Amazonian society.* Austin, TX: University of Texas Press.

Connell, C. M., & Gibson, G. D. (1997). Racial, ethnic, and cultural differences in dementia caregiving: Review and analysis. *Gerontologist, 37,* 355–364.

Connolly, S. D., Paikoff, R. L., & Buchanan, C. M. (1996). Puberty: The interplay of biological and psychosocial processes in adolescence. In G. R. Adams, R. Montemayor, & T. P. Gullotta (Eds.), *Psychosocial development during adolescence* (Vol. 8, pp. 259–299). Thousand Oaks, CA: Sage.

Contet-Audonneau, J. L., Jeanmaire, C., & Pauly, G. (1999). A histological study of human wrinkle structures: Comparison between sun-exposed areas of the face, with or without wrinkles, and sun-protected areas. *British Journal of Dermatology, 140,* 1038–1047.

A conversation with Terry Tempest Williams. (2006). Retrieved May 13, 2006, from **http://www.randomhouse.com/vintage/catalog/display.pperl?isbn=9780679752578&view=qa**

Conway, M. A., & Holmes, A. (2004). Psychosocial stages and the accessibility of autobiographical memories across the life cycle. *Journal of Personality, 72,* 461–480.

Cook, P. J., & Moore, M. H. (1999). Guns, gun control, and homicide: A review of research and public policy. In M. D. Smith & M. A. Zahn (Eds.), *Homicide: A sourcebook of social research* (pp. 277–296). Thousand Oaks, CA: Sage.

Cook, T. D., Herman, M. R., Phillips, M., & Settersten, R. A., Jr. (2002). Some ways in which neighborhood, nuclear families, friendship groups, and schools jointly affect changes in early adolescent development. *Child Development, 73,* 1283–1309.

Coontz, S. (1992). *The way we never were: American families and the nostalgia trap.* New York: Basic Books.

Corah, N. L., Anthony, E. J., Painter, P., Stern, J. A., & Thurston, D. L. (1965). Effects of perinatal anoxia after seven years. *Psychological Monographs: General and Applied, 79* (3, No. 596).

Corey-Bloom, J. (2000). Dementia. In S. K. Whitbourne (Ed.), *Psychopathology in later adulthood* (pp. 217–243). New York: Wiley.

Cornelius, S. W., & Caspi, A. (1987). Everyday problem solving in adulthood and old age. *Psychology and Aging, 2,* 144–153.

Cornell, A. H. (2004). The contribution of parenting styles and behavioral inhibition to the development of conscience in preschool children. *Dissertation Abstracts International, 65* (04), 2124B.

Corti, M.-C., Guralnik, J. M., Ferrucci, L., et al. (1999). Evidence for a black-white crossover in all-cause and coronary heart disease mortality in an older population: The North Carolina EPESE. *American Journal of Public Health, 89,* 308–314.

Costa, P. T., Jr., & McRae, R. R. (1997). Longitudinal stability of adult personality. In R. Hogan, J. A. Johnson, & S. R. Briggs (Eds.), *Handbook of personality psychology* (pp. 269–290). San Diego, CA: Academic Press.

Costa, P. T., Jr., Terracciano, A., & McCrae, R. R. (2001). Gender differences in personality traits across cultures: Robust and surprising findings. *Journal of Personality and Social Psychology, 81,* 322–331.

Cota-Robles, S., Neiss, M., & Rowe, D. C. (2002). The role of puberty in violent and nonviolent delinquency among Anglo American, Mexican American, and African American boys. *Journal of Adolescent Research, 17,* 364–376.

Cotman, C. W., & Berchtold, N. C. (2002). Exercise: A behavioral intervention to enhance brain health and plasticity. *Trends in Neurosciences, 25,* 295–301.

Cotton, K. (1996). *School size, school climate, and student performance.* Portland, OR: NW Regional Educational Laboratory. Retrieved May 15, 2006, from **http://www.nwrel.org/scpd/sirs/10/c020.html**

Coutinho, M. J., Oswald, D. P., Best, A. M., & Forness, S. R. (2002). Gender and sociodemographic factors and the disproportionate identification of culturally and linguistically diverse students with emotional disturbance. *Behavioral Disorders, 27,* 109–125.

Cowan, N., Chen, Z., & Rouder, J. N. (2004). Constant capacity in an immediate serial-recall task: A logical sequel to Miller (1956). *Psychological Science, 15,* 634–640.

Cowley, G., & Springen, K. (2002, July 22). The end of the age of estrogen? *Newsweek, 140,* 38–41.

Crabb, M. K. (1992). An epidemic of pride: Pellagra and the culture of the American south. *Anthropologica, 34,* 89–103.

Craik, F. I. M. (2000). Age-related changes in human memory. In D. C. Park & N. Schwarz (Eds.), *Cognitive aging: A primer* (pp. 75–92). Hove, England: Psychology Press.

Craik, F. I. M., & Byrd, M. (1982). Aging and cognitive deficits: The role of attentional resources. In F. I. M. Craik & S. Trehub (Eds.), *Aging and cognitive processes* (pp. 191–211). New York: Plenum Press.

Crain, W. (2005). *Theories of development: Concepts and applications* (5th ed.). Upper Saddle River, NJ: Prentice Hall.

Cramer, D. A. (2001). Asthma. In J. L. Longe & D. S. Blanchfield (Eds.), *The Gale encyclopedia of medicine* (2nd ed.). Retrieved June 2, 2002, from **http://0–infotrac.galegroup.com**

Cramer, R. E., Helzer, K., & Mone, R. (1986). Variations in the conditions of reinforcement and the attribution of liking. *Journal of General Psychology, 113,* 341–349.

Crews, F. (1985, January 21). The future of an illusion. *New Republic, 192,* 28–33.

Crick, N. R., Casas, J. F., & Nelson, D. A. (2002). Toward a more comprehensive understanding of peer maltreatment: Studies of relational victimization. *Current Directions in Psychological Science, 11,* 98–101.

Cristofalo, V. J., Tresini, M., Francis, M. K., & Volker, C. (1999). Biological theories of senescence. In V. L. Bengtson & K. W. Schaie (Eds.), *Handbook of theories of aging* (pp. 98–112). New York: Springer.

Crockett, L. J., Petersen, A. C., Graber, J. A., Schulenberg, J. E., & Ebata. A. (1989). School transitions and adjustment during early adolescence. *Journal of Early Adolescence, 9,* 181–210.

Cromer, B. A., & McCarthy, M. (1999). Family planning services in adolescent pregnancy prevention: The views of key informants in four countries. *Family Planning Perspectives, 31,* 287–293.

Crone, D., & Whitehurst, G. J. (1999). Age and schooling effects on emergent literacy and early reading skills. *Journal of Educational Psychology, 91,* 604–614.

Cronk, L. (1993). Parental favoritism toward daughters. *American Scientist, 81*(3), 272–279.

Crosnoe, R., & Elder, G. H., Jr. (2002). Successful adaptation in the later years: A life course approach to aging. *Social Psychology Quarterly, 65*, 309–328.

Crosnoe, R., & Elder, G. H., Jr. (2004). From childhood to the later years: Pathways of human development. *Research on Aging, 26*, 623–654.

Cross National Collaborative Group. (1992). The changing rate of major depression: Cross national comparisons. *Journal of the American Medication Association, 268*, 3098–3105.

Cross, S., & Markus, H. (1991). Possible selves across the life span. *Human Development, 34*, 230–255.

Crouter, A. C., Manke, B. A., & McHale, S. M. (1995). The family context of gender intensification in early adolescence. *Child Development, 66*, 317–329.

Cumming, E., & Henry, W. E. (1961). *Growing old: The process of disengagement.* New York: Basic Books.

Cummins, J. (1980). Psychological assessment of immigrant children: Logic or intuition. *Journal of Multilingual and Multicultural Development, 1*, 97–111.

Cunningham, C. E., & Boyle, M. H. (2002). Preschoolers at risk for attention-deficit hyperactivity disorder and oppositional defiant disorder: Family, parenting, and behavioral correlates. *Journal of Abnormal Child Psychology, 30*, 555–569.

Curran, J. P. (1977). Skills training as an approach to the treatment of heterosexual-social anxiety: A review. *Psychological Bulletin, 84*, 140–157.

Curtis, L. H., Østbye, T., Sendersky, V., et al. (2004). Inappropriate prescribing for elderly Americans in a large outpatient population. *Archives of Internal Medicine, 164*, 1621–1625.

Curtis, M. A., Penney, E. B., Pearson, J., Dragunow, M., Connor, B., & Faull, R. L. (2005). The distribution of progenitor cells in the subependymal layer of the lateral ventricle in the normal and Huntington's disease human brain. *Neuroscience, 132*, 777–788.

Daily, D. K., & Ellison, P. H. (2005). The premieneuro: A clinical neurologic examination of premature infants. *Neonatal Network, 24*, 15–22.

Daley, K. C. (2004). Update on sudden infant death syndrome. *Current Opinion in Pediatrics, 16*, 227–232.

Daley, T. C., Whaley, S. E., Sigman, M. D., Espinosa, M. P., & Neumann, C. (2003). IQ on the rise: The Flynn effect in rural Kenyan children. *Psychological Science, 14*, 215–219.

Dalton, T. C., & Bergenn, V. W. (1995). *Beyond heredity and environment: Myrtle McGraw and the maturation controversy.* Boulder, CO: Westview Press.

Daly, M., & Wilson, M. (1996). Evolutionary psychology and marital conflict: The relevance of stepchildren. In D. M. Buss & N. M. Malamuth (Eds.), *Sex, power, conflict: Evolutionary and feminist perspectives* (pp. 9–28). New York: Oxford University Press.

Daly, M., & Wilson, M. (2000). Not quite right. *American Psychologist, 55*, 679–680.

Damon, W. (1977). *The social world of the child.* San Francisco: Jossey-Bass.

Damon, W. (1988). *The moral child: Nurturing children's natural moral growth.* New York: Free Press.

Damsgaard, R., Bencke, J., Matthiesen, G., Petersen, J. H., & Müller, J. (2000). Is prepubertal growth adversely affected by sport? *Medicine and Science in Sports and Exercise, 32*, 1698–1703.

Danielson, M. E., Cauley, J. A., Baker, C. E., et al. (1999). Familial resemblance of bone mineral density (BMD) and calcaneal ultrasound attenuation: The BMD in Mothers and Daughters Study. *Journal of Bone and Mineral Research, 14*, 102–110.

Dannemiller, J. L. (2001). Brain-behavior relationships in early visual development. In C. A. Nelson & M. Luciana (Eds.), *Handbook of developmental cognitive neuroscience* (pp. 221–235). Cambridge, MA: MIT Press.

Darkenwald, G. G., & Novak, R. J. (1997). Classroom age composition and academic achievement in college. *Adult Educational Quarterly, 47*, 108–116.

Darlington, C. D. (1953). *The facts of life.* London: Allen & Unwin.

da Rocha, S. T., & Ferguson-Smith, A. C. (2004). Genomic imprinting. *Current Biology, 14*, R646–R649.

Darwin, C. (1859). *On the origin of species by means of natural selection.* London: J. Murray.

Dash, L. (1989). *When children want children: The urban crisis of teenage childbearing.* New York: William Morrow and company.

Dass, R. (with Matousek, M., & Roeder, M., Eds.). (2000). *Still here: Embracing aging, changing, and dying.* New York: Riverhead Books.

D'Augelli, A. R., (2003). Lesbian and bisexual female youths ages 14 to 21: Developmental challenges and victimization experiences. *Journal of Lesbian Studies, 7*, 9–29.

Davenport, C. B. (1910). *Eugenics: The science of human improvement by better breeding.* New York: Holt.

Davies, P. L., Segalowitz, S. J., & Gavin, W. J. (2004). Development of response-monitoring ERPs in 7- to 25-year-olds. *Developmental Neuropsychology, 25*, 355–376.

Davies, S., & Denton, M. (2002). The economic well-being of older women who become divorced or separated in mid- or later life. *Canadian Journal on Aging, 21*, 477–493.

Davies, S. L., DiClemente, R. J., Wingood, G. M., et al. (2004). Relationship characteristics and sexual practices of African American adolescent girls who desire pregnancy. *Health Education and Behavior, 31*, 85S–96S.

Davis, B. E., Moon, R. Y., Sachs, H. C., & Ottolini, M. C. (1998). Effects of sleep position on infant motor development. *Pediatrics, 102*, 1135–1140.

Davison, L. J., Brown, J. M., & Davison, M. L. (1993). Employer satisfaction ratings of recent business graduates. *Human Resource Development Quarterly, 4*, 391–399.

Dawes, R. M. (1996). *House of cards: Psychology and psychotherapy built on myth.* New York: Free Press.

Dawes, R. M. (2001). *Everyday irrationality: How pseudo-scientists, lunatics, and the rest of us systematically fail to think rationally.* Boulder, CO: Westview Press.

Dean, C. (2005, April 12). Theorist drawn into debate "that will not go away." *New York Times.* Retrieved April 17, 2005, from http://www.nytimes.com/2005/04/12/science/12prof.html

Dearing, E., McCartney, K., & Taylor, B. A. (2001). Change in family income-to-needs matters more for children with less. *Child Development, 72*, 1779–1793.

Deary, I. J., Whiteman, M. C., Starr, J. M., Whalley, L. J., & Fox, H. C. (2004). The impact of childhood intelligence on later life: Following up the Scottish Mental Surveys of 1932 and 1947. *Journal of Personality and Social Psychology, 86*, 130–147.

DeBell, M., Chapman, C., & National Center for Education Statistics. (2003). *Computer and Internet use by children and adolescents in 2001.* Washington, DC: National Center for Education Statistics.

DeCasper, A. J., & Spence, M. J. (1986). Prenatal maternal speech influences newborns' perception of speech sounds. *Infant Behavior and Development, 9*, 133–150.

de Hann, M., & Johnson, M. H. (2003). Mechanisms and theories of brain development. In M. de Haan & M. H. Johnson (Eds.), *The cognitive neuroscience of development* (pp. 1–18). Hove, England: Psychology Press.

de Jong, H. L. (2002). Levels of explanation in biological psychology. *Philosophical Psychology, 15*, 441–462.

DeLamater, J. D., & Sill, M. (2005). Sexual desire in later life. *Journal of Sex Research, 42*, 138–149.

Delany, S. L., & Delany, A. E. (with Hearth, A. H.). (1993). *Having our say: The Delany sisters' first 100 years.* New York: Kodansha America.

de Lisi, R., & Staudt, J. (1980). Individual differences in college students' performance on formal operations tasks. *Journal of Applied Developmental Psychology, 1*, 201–208.

DeLoache, J. S. (1995). Early understanding and use of symbols: The model model. *Current Directions in Psychological Science, 4,* 109–113.

DeLoache, J. S. (2005). Mindful of symbols. *Scientific American, 293*(2), 72–77.

DeLoache, J. S., Miller, K. F., & Rosengren, K. S. (1997). The credible shrinking room: Very young children's performance with symbolic and nonsymbolic relations. *Psychological Science, 8,* 308–313.

DeMarie, D., Miller, P. H., Ferron, J., & Cunningham, W. R. (2004). Path analysis tests of theoretical models of children's memory performance. *Journal of Cognition and Development, 5,* 461–492.

Demas, A. (1995). Food education in the elementary classroom as a means of gaining acceptance of diverse, low-fat foods in the school lunch program. *Dissertation Abstracts International, 55* (12), 3717A.

Demas, A., & Landis, C. P. (2001). *Food is elementary: A hands on curriculum for young students.* Trumansburg, NY: Food Studies Institute.

Demerath, E. W., Li, J., Sun, S. S., et al. (2004). Fifty-year trends in serial body mass index during adolescence in girls: The Fels Longitudinal Study. *The American Journal of Clinical Nutrition, 80,* 441–446.

Demetriou, A., Christou, C., Spandoudis, G., & Platsidou, M. (2002). The development of mental processing: Efficiency, working memory, and thinking. *Monographs of the Society for Research in Child Development, 67*(1, Serial No. 268).

Dempster, F. N. (1981). Memory span: Sources of individual and developmental differences. *Psychological Bulletin, 89,* 63–100.

Denney, N. W., & Palmer, A. M. (1981). Adult age differences on traditional and practical problem-solving measures. *Journal of Gerontology, 36,* 323–328.

Denney, N. W., & Pearce, K. A. (1989). A developmental study of practical problem solving in adults. *Psychology and Aging, 4,* 438–442.

Denver, J., Warren, A. R., & Mathis, K. (2005, January). *Bumps and declines in flashbulb memory.* Paper presented at the meeting of the Society for Applied Research in Memory and Cognition, Wellington, New Zealand.

d'Epinay, C. J., & Bickel, J.-F. (2003). Do "young-old" exercisers feel better than sedentary persons? A cohort study in Switzerland. *Canadian Journal on Aging, 22,* 155–165.

DeRosier, M. E., & Marcus, S. R. (2005). Building friendships and combating bullying: Effectiveness of S.S.GRIN at one-year follow-up. *Journal of Clinical Child and Adolescent Psychology, 34,* 140–150.

Deutsch, H. (1944). *The psychology of women* (Vol. 1). New York: Grune & Stratton.

de Villiers, J. G., & de Villiers, P. A. (1978). *Language acquisition.* Cambridge, MA: Harvard University Press.

deVries, M. W. (1984). Temperament and infant mortality among the Masai of East Africa. *American Journal of Psychiatry, 141,* 1189–1194.

de Vries, P. (2005). Lessons from home: Scaffolding vocal improvisation and song acquisition with a 2-year-old. *Early Childhood Education Journal, 32,* 307–312.

DeVries, R., & Goncu, A. (1990). Interpersonal relations in four-year-old dyads from Constructivist and Montessori programs. In A. S. Honig (Ed.), *Optimizing early child care and education* (pp. 11–27). New York: Gordon and Breach.

de Wolff, M., & van IJzendoorn, M. H. (1997). Sensitivity and attachment: A meta-analysis on parental antecedents of infant attachment. *Child Development, 68,* 571–591.

Dey, A. N., & Bloom, B. (2003, March). Summary health statistics for U.S. children: National Health Interview Survey, 2003. *Vital and Health Statistics, Series 10*(223), 1–78.

Diamond, A. (2001). A model system for studying the role of dopamine in the prefrontal cortex during early development in humans: Early and continuously treated phenylketonuria. In C. A. Nelson & M. Luciana (Eds.), *Handbook of developmental cognitive neuroscience* (pp. 433–472). Cambridge, MA: MIT Press.

Diamond, L. M. (2003). Was it a phase? Young women's relinquishment of lesbian/bisexual identities over a 5-year period. *Journal of Personality and Social Psychology, 84,* 352–364.

Diaz, R. M., & Berndt, T. J. (1982). Children's knowledge of a best friend: Fact or fancy? *Developmental Psychology, 18,* 787–794.

Dickinson, G. E. (1992). First childhood death experiences. *Omega, 25,* 169–182.

Dickinson, J. J., Poole, D. A., & Laimon, R. L. (2005). Children's recall and testimony. In N. Brewer & K. D. Williams (Eds.), *Psychology and law: An empirical perspective* (pp. 151–176). New York: Guilford.

Didden, R., Prinsen, H., & Sigafoos, J, (2000). The blocking effect of pictorial prompts on sight-word reading. *Journal of Applied Behavior Analysis, 33,* 317–320.

Diehl, M., Willis, S. L., & Schaie, K. W. (1995). Everyday problem solving in older adults: Observational assessment and cognitive correlates. *Psychology and Aging, 10,* 478–491.

Diener, E., & Diener, C. (1996). Most people are happy. *Psychological Science, 7,* 181–185.

Diener, E., & Seligman, M. E. P. (2002). Very happy people. *Psychological Science, 13,* 81–84.

Diener, E., & Selgiman, M. E. P. (2004). Beyond money: Toward an economy of well-being. *Psychological Science in the Public Interest, 5,* 1–31.

Diener, E., & Suh, M. E. (1997). Subjective well-being and age: An international analysis. *Annual Review of Gerontology and Geriatrics, 17,* 304–324.

Diener, E., Suh, E. M., Lucas, R. E., & Smith, H. L. (1999). Subjective well-being: Three decades of progress. *Psychological Bulletin, 125,* 276–302.

Dikman, Z. V., & Allen, J. J. B. (2000). Error monitoring during reward and avoidance learning in high- and low-socialized individuals. *Psychophysiology, 37,* 43–54.

Dill, P. L., & Henley, T. B. (1998). Stressors of college: A comparison of traditional and nontraditional students. *Journal of Psychology, 132,* 25–32.

Dillon, M., Wink, P., & Fay, K. (2003). Is spirituality detrimental to generativity? *Journal for the Scientific Study of Religion, 42,* 427–442.

Dion, K. K. (1973). Young children's stereotyping of facial attractiveness. *Developmental Psychology, 9,* 183–188.

Discover dialog: Michael Rose. (2001, May). *Discover, 22,* 16.

Dixon, R. A., & Cohen, A.-L. (2003). Cognitive development in adulthood. In R. M. Lerner, M. A. Easterbrooks, & J. Mistry (Eds.), *Handbook of psychology* (Vol. 6, pp. 443–461). Hoboken, NJ: Wiley.

Dixon, R. A., & Lerner, R. M. (1999). History and systems in developmental psychology. In M. H. Bornstein & M. E. Lamb (Eds.), *Developmental psychology: An advanced textbook* (4th ed., pp. 3–45). Mahwah, NJ: Erlbaum.

Dodge, K. A. (1983). Behavioral antecedents of peer social status. *Child Development, 54,* 1386–1399.

Dodman, N., & Natale, R. (2004). Birth can be a hazardous journey: Electronic fetal monitoring does not help. *Journal of Obstetrics and Gynaecology Canada, 26,* 327–328.

Doman, G, & Delacato, C. H. (1965, March). Train your baby to be a genius. *McCall's,* 65.

Doman, G. J., Doman, J., & Aisen, S. (2001). *How to give your baby encyclopedic knowledge.* Towson, MD: Gentle Revolution Press.

Donadio, R. (2005, October 9). Every day is all there is. *New York Times.* Retrieved May 13, 2006, from http://www.nytimes.com/2005/10/09/books/review/09donadio.html?ex=1147665600&en=6542336025ff1b54&ei=5070

Donaldson, J. F., & Graham, S. (1999). A model of college outcomes for adults. *Adult Education Quarterly, 50,* 24–40.

Dornbusch, S. M., Ritter, P. L., Mont-Reynaud, R., & Chen, Z.-y. (1990). Family decision-making and academic performance in a diverse high school population. *Journal of Adolescent Research, 5,* 143–160.

Doty, R. L. (2001). Olfaction. *Annual Review of Psychology, 52,* 423–452.

Douglass, F. (1989). *Narrative of the life of Frederick Douglass, an American slave.* New York: Anchor Books.

Doyle, K. W., Wolchik, S. A., Dawson-McClure, S. R., & Sandler, I. N. (2003). Positive events as a stress buffer for children and adolescents in families in transition. *Journal of Clinical Child and Adolescent Psychology, 32,* 536–545.

Doyle, L. W., & Anderson, P. J. (2005). Improved neurosensory outcome at 8 years of age of extremely low birthweight children born in Victoria over three distinct eras. *Archives of Disease in Childhood: Fetal and Neonatal Edition, 90,* F484–F488.

Draghi-Lorenz, R., Reddy, V., & Costall, A. (2001). Rethinking the development of "nonbasic" emotions: A critical review of existing theories. *Developmental Review, 21,* 263–304.

Drillien, C. M. (1957). The social and economic factors affecting the incidence of premature birth. *Journal of Obstetrical Gynecology, 64,* 161–184.

Drillien, C. M. (1964). *Growth and development of the prematurely born infant.* Baltimore: Williams & Wilkins.

Driscoll, A., & Nagel, N. G. (2002). *Early childhood education, birth-8: The world of children, families, and educators.* Boston: Allyn & Bacon.

Drotar, D., & Robinson, J. (2000). Developmental psychopathology of failure to thrive. In A. J. Sameroff, M. Lewis, & S. Miller (Eds.), *Handbook of developmental psychopathology* (2nd ed., pp. 351–364). New York: Kluwer Academic/Plenum.

Dube, R., Dube, R., & Bhatnagar, R. (1999). Women without choice: Female infanticide and the rhetoric of overpopulation in postcolonial India. *Women's Studies Quarterly, 27,* 73–86.

Dunbar, G., Hill, R., & Lewis, V. (2001). Children's attentional skills and road behavior. *Journal of Experimental Psychology: Applied, 7,* 227–234.

Duncan, G. J., & Brooks-Gunn, J. (2000). Family poverty, welfare reform, and child development. *Child Development, 71,* 188–196.

Duncan, G. J., & Magnuson, K. A. (2003). Off with Hollingshead: Socioeconomic resources, parenting, and child development. In M. H. Bornstein & R. H. Bradley (Eds.), *Socioeconomic status, parenting, and child development* (pp. 83–106). Mahwah, NJ: Erlbaum.

Duncan, G. J., Yeung, W. J., Brooks-Gunn, J., & Smith, J. R. (1998). How much does childhood poverty affect the life chances of children? *American Sociological Review, 63,* 406–423.

Duncan, S., Mercho, S., Lopes-Cendes, I., et al. (2001). Repeated neural tube defects and valproate monotherapy suggests a pharmacogenetic abnormality. *Epilepsia, 42,* 750–753.

Dunkin, J., Rasgon, N., Wagner-Steh, K., David, S., Altshuler, L, & Rapkin, A. (2005). Reproductive events modify the effects of estrogen replacement therapy on cognition in healthy postmenopausal women. *Psychoneuroendocrinology, 30,* 284–296.

Dunn, J. (1996). Arguing with siblings, friends, and mothers: Developments in relationships and understanding. In D. I. Slobin, J. Gerhardt, A. Kyratzis, & J. Guo (Eds.), *Social interaction, social context, and language: Essays in honor of Susan Ervin-Tripp* (pp. 191–204). Mahwah, NJ: Erlbaum.

Dunn, J. (2004a). Annotation: Children's relationships with their nonresident fathers. *Journal of Child Psychology and Psychiatry, 45,* 659–671.

Dunn, J. (2004b). *Children's friendships: The beginning of intimacy.* Malden, MA: Blackwell.

Dunn, J. (2004c). Understanding children's family worlds: Family transitions and children's outcome. *Merrill-Palmer Quarterly, 50,* 224–235.

Dunn, J. & Hughes, C. (1998). Young children's understanding of emotions within close relationships. *Cognition and Emotion, 12,* 171–190.

Dunn, J., Kendrick, C., & MacNamee, R. (1981). The reaction of first-born children to the birth of a sibling: Mothers' reports. *Journal of Child Psychology and Psychiatry, 22,* 1–18.

Dunn, J., & Munn, P. (1986). Sibling quarrels and maternal intervention: Individual differences in understanding and aggression. *Journal of Child Psychology and Psychiatry, 27,* 583–595.

Dunn, J., & Plomin, R. (1990). *Separate lives: Why siblings are so different.* New York: Basic Books.

Dunson, D. B., Baird, D. D., & Colombo, B. (2004). Increased infertility with age in men and women. *Obstetrics and Gynecology, 103,* 51–56.

DuPertuis, L. L., Aldwin, C. M., & Bossé, R. (2001). Does the source of support matter for different health outcomes? Findings from the Normative Aging Study. *Journal of Aging and Health, 13,* 494–510.

Dusek, J. B., & McIntyre, J. G. (2003). Self-concept and self-esteem development. In G. Adams & M. D. Berzonsky (Eds.), *Blackwell handbook of adolescence* (pp. 290–309). Malden, MA: Blackwell.

Dweck, C. S. (2002). Beliefs that make smart people dumb. In R. J. Sternberg (Ed.), *Why smart people can be so stupid* (pp. 24–41). New Haven, CT: Yale University Press.

Dyk, P. H. (1993). Anatomy, physiology, and gender issues in adolescence. In T. P. Gullotta, G. R. Adams, & R. Montemayor (Eds.), *Adolescent sexuality* (pp. 35–56). Thousand Oaks, CA: Sage.

Earle, C. C., Neville, B. A., Landrum, M. B., Ayanian, J. Z., Block, S. D., & Weeks, J. C. (2004). Trends in aggressiveness of cancer care near the end of life. *Journal of Clinical Oncology, 22,* 315–231.

East, P. L., & Felice, M. E. (1996). *Adolescent pregnancy and parenting: Findings from a racially diverse sample.* Mahwah, NY: Erlbaum.

Eaves, L., Silberg, J., Foley, D., et al. (2004). Genetic and environmental influences on the relative timing of pubertal change. *Twin Research, 7,* 471–481.

Eccles, J. S. (2004). Schools, academic motivation, and stage-environment fit. In R. M Lerner & L. D. Steinberg (Eds.), *Handbook of adolescent psychology* (2nd ed., pp. 125–153). Hoboken, NJ: Wiley.

Eccles, J. S., Midgley, C., Wigfield, A., et al. (1993). Development during adolescence: The impact of stage-environment fit on young adolescents' experiences in schools and in families. *American Psychologist, 48,* 90–101.

Edgren, A. R. (1999). Prematurity. In D. Olendorf, C. Jeryan, & K. Boyden (Eds.), *The Gale encyclopedia of medicine* (Vol. 4, p. 2348). Detroit, MI: Thompson Gale.

Edwards, A. W. F. (2003). Human genetic diversity: Lewontin's fallacy. *BioEssays, 25,* 798–801.

Edwards, J. D., Wadley, V. G., Vance, D. E., Wood, K., Roenker, D. L., & Ball, K. K. (2005). The impact of speed of processing training on cognitive and everyday performance. *Aging and Mental Health, 9,* 262–271.

Eggan, D. (1997). Instruction and affect in Hopi cultural continuity. In G. D. Spindler (Ed.), *Education and cultural process: Anthropological approaches* (3rd ed., pp. 339–361). Prospect Heights, IL: Waveland Press.

Ehrenberg, R. G., Brewer, D. J., Gamoran, A., & Willms, J. D. (2001). Class size and student achievement. *Psychological Science in the Public Interest, 2,* 1–30.

Eimas, P. D., Siqueland, E. R., Jusczyk, P., & Vigorito, J. (1971). Speech perception in infants. *Science, 171* 303–306.

Eisenberg, M. E., & Aalsma, M. C. (2005). Bullying and peer victimization: Position paper of the Society for Adolescent Medicine. *Journal of Adolescent Health, 36,* 88–91.

Eisenberg, N., & Morris, A. S. (2004). Moral cognitions and prosocial responding in adolescence. In R. M. Lerner & L. D. Steinberg (Eds.), *Handbook of adolescent psychology* (2nd ed., pp. 155–188). Hoboken, NJ: Wiley.

Eisenberg, N., & Mussen, P. H. (1989). *The roots of prosocial behavior in children.* New York: Cambridge University Press.

Eisenberg, N., Spinrad, T. L., Fabes, R. A., et al. (2004). The relations of effortful control and impulsivity to children's resiliency and adjustment. *Child Development, 75,* 25–46.

Eisenberg, N., & Valiente, C. (2002). Parenting and children's prosocial and moral development. In M. H. Bornstein (Ed.), *Handbook of parenting* (Vol. 5, pp. 111–142). Mahwah, NJ: Erlbaum.

Ekéus, C., Christensson, K., & Hjern, A. (2004). Unintentional and violent injuries among preschool children of teenage mothers in Sweden: A national cohort study. *Journal of Epidemiology and Community Health, 58,* 680–685.

Elardo, R., Solomons, H. C., & Snider, B. C. (1987). An analysis of accidents at a day care center. *American Journal of Orthopsychiatry, 57,* 60–65.

Elbogen, E. B., Carlo, G., & Spaulding, W. (2001). Hierarchical classification and the integration of self-structure in late adolescence. *Journal of Adolescence, 24,* 657–670.

Elder, G. H., Jr. (1998a). The life course and human development. In W. Damon (Series Ed.) & R. M. Lerner (Vol. Ed.), *Handbook of child psychology: Vol. 1. Theoretical models of human development* (5th ed., pp. 939–991). New York: Wiley.

Elder, G. H., Jr. (1998b). The life course as developmental theory. *Child Development, 69,* 1–12.

Elder, G. H., Jr. (1999). *Children of the Great Depression: Social change in life experience* (Rev. ed.). Boulder, CO: Westview Press.

Elder, G. H., Jr., & Crosnoe, R. (2002). The influence of early behavior patterns on later life. In L. Pulkkinen & A. Caspi (Eds.), *Paths to successful development: Personality in the life course* (pp. 157–176). New York: Cambridge University Press.

Elder, G. H., Jr., & Johnson, M. K. (2002). Perspectives on human development in context. In C. von Hofsten & L. Bäckman (Eds.), *Psychology at the turn of the millennium* (Vol. 2, pp. 153–172). Hove, England: Psychology Press.

Elkind, D. (1967). Egocentrism in adolescence. *Child Development, 38,* 1025–1034.

Ellis, B. J. (2004). Timing of pubertal maturation in girls: An integrated life history approach. *Psychological Bulletin, 130,* 920–958.

Ellis, B. J., Bates, J. E., Dodge, K. A., et al. (2003). Does father absence place daughters at special risk for early sexual activity and teenage pregnancy? *Child Development, 74,* 801–821.

Ely, R. (2001). Language and literacy in the school years. In J. B. Gleason (Ed.), *The development of language* (5th ed., pp. 409–454). Boston: Allyn & Bacon.

Emery, R. E. (1999). Postdivorce family life for children: An overview of research and some implications for policy. In R. A. Thompson & P. R. Amato (Eds.), *The postdivorce family: Children, parenting, and society* (pp. 3–27). Thousand Oaks, CA: Sage.

Eng, P. M., Rimm, E. B., Fitzmaurice, G., & Kawachi, I. (2002). Social ties and change in social ties in relation to subsequent total and cause-specific mortality and coronary heart disease incidence in men. *American Journal of Epidemiology, 155,* 700–708.

Enkin, M., Keirse, M. J. N. C., Neilson, J., et al. (2000). *A guide to effective care in pregnancy and childbirth* (3rd ed.). New York: Oxford University Press.

Ennett, S. T., & Bauman, K. E. (1996). Adolescent social networks: School, demographic, and longitudinal considerations. *Journal of Adolescent Research, 11,* 194–215.

Epel, E. S., Blackburn, E. H., Lin, J., et al. (2004). Accelerated telomere shortening in response to life stress. *Proceedings of the National Academy of Sciences of the United States of America, 101,* 17312–17315.

Epstein, A. S., Schweinhart, L. J., & McAdoo, L. (1996). *Models of early childhood education.* Ypsilanti, MI: High/Scope Press.

Ericson, K. (2006). *Health A to Z: Birth defects.* Retrieved May 9, 2006, from http://www.healthatoz.com/healthatoz/Atoz/ency/birth_defects.jsp

Ericsson, K. A. (1990). Peak performance and age: An examination of peak performance in sports. In P. B. Baltes & M. M. Baltes (Eds.), *Successful aging: Perspectives from the behavioral sciences* (pp. 164–196). New York: Cambridge University Press.

Ericsson, K. A., & Charness, N. (1994). Expert performance: Its structure and acquisition. *American Psychologist, 49,* 725–747.

Ericsson, K. A., Krampe, R. T., & Tesch-Römer, C. (1993). The role of deliberate practice in the acquisition of expert performance. *Psychological Review, 100,* 363–406.

Erikson, E. H. (1950). *Childhood and society.* New York: Norton.

Erikson, E. H. (1959). Identity and the life cycle: Selected papers. *Psychological Issues, 1*(1). New York: International Universities Press.

Erikson, E. H., Erikson, J. M., & Kivnick, H. Q. (1986). *Vital involvement in old age.* New York: Norton.

ESHRE Capri Workshop Group. (2000). Multiple gestation pregnancy. *Human Reproduction, 15,* 1856–1864.

Eskenazi, B., Wyrobek, A. J., Sloter, E., et al. (2003). The association of age and semen quality in healthy men. *Human Reproduction, 18,* 447–454.

Estil, L.-B., & Whiting, H. T. A. (2002). Motor/language impairment syndrome—Direct or indirect foundations? In S. A. Cermak & D. Larkin (Eds.), *Developmental coordination disorder* (pp. 54–84). Albany, NY: Delmar.

Etheridge, E. W. (1972). *The butterfly cast: A social history of pellagra in the south.* Westport, CT: Greenwood Publishing Company.

Etzel, R. A., Balk, S. J., & American Academy of Pediatrics Committee on Environmental Health. (1999). *Handbook of pediatric environmental health.* Elk Grove Village, IL: American Academy of Pediatrics.

Evan B. Donaldson Adoption Institute. (1997). *Benchmark Adoption Survey: Report on the findings.* New York: Author.

Evans, G. W., & English, K. (2002). The environment of poverty: Multiple stressor exposure, psychophysiological stress, and socioemotional adjustment. *Child Development, 73,* 1238–1248.

Evans, R. I. (1973). *Jean Piaget, the man and his ideas.* New York: E. P. Dutton.

Evans, S. (2004, October 9). Area teens split on debate, candidates. *Statesman Journal.* Retrieved January 18, 2005, from http://news.statesmanjournal.com/article.cfm?i=88034

Eyer, D. E. (1992). *Mother-infant bonding: A science fiction.* New Haven, CT: Yale University Press.

Eyferth, K. (1961). Leistungen verschiedener Gruppen von Besatzungskindern in Hamburg-Wechsler Intelligenztest für Kinder (HAWIK). *Archiv für die gesamte Psychologie, 113,* 222–241.

Fabes, R. A., Martin, C. L., & Hanish, L. D. (2003). Young children's play qualities in same-, other-, and mixed-sex peer groups. *Child Development, 74,* 921–932.

Fabris, C., Prandi, G., Perathoner, C., & Soldi, A. (1998). Neonatal drug addiction. *Panminerva Medica, 40,* 239–243.

Fagerlin, A., & Schneider, C. E. (2004). Enough: The failure of the living will. *Hastings Center Report, 34*(2), 30–42.

Falk, D. (2000). *Primate diversity.* New York: Norton.

Falk, R., & Konold, C. (1997). Making sense of randomness: Implicit encoding as a basis for judgment. *Psychological Review, 104,* 301–318.

Fantz, R. L. (1963). Pattern vision in newborn infants. *Science, 140,* 296–297.

Faraone, S. V., Perlis, R. H., Doyle, A. E., et al. (2005). Molecular genetics of attention-deficit/hyperactivity disorder. *Biological Psychiatry, 57,* 1313–1323.

Farber, H. S. (2003, July 9). Evaluating competing theories of worker mobility. *NLS Discussion Paper, Report NLS 92–95.* Retrieved December 17, 2004, from http://stats.bls.gov/nls/nlsdis5.htm

Farkas, G., & Beron, K. (2001, March 31). *Family linguistic culture and social reproduction: Verbal skill from parent to child in the preschool and school years.* Paper presented at the meeting of the Population Association of America, Washington, D.C.

Farran, D. C. (2000). Another decade of intervention for children who are low income or disabled: What do we know now? In J. P. Shonkoff & S. J. Meisels (Eds.), *Handbook of early childhood intervention* (2nd ed., pp. 510–548). New York: Cambridge University Press.

Farrell, M. P., & Rosenberg, S. D. (1981). *Men at midlife.* Boston: Auburn House.

Faust, D. G. (2003, May-June). Living history: A schoolgirl's letter to "Mr. Eisenhower" illuminates a childhood in the segregated South. *Harvard Magazine.* Retrieved June 27, 2004, from www.harvardmagazine.com/on-line/050333.html

Federal Bureau of Investigation. (2005). *Crime in the United States—2003.* Retrieved November 21, 2005, from **http://www.fbi.gov/ucr/03cius.htm**

Federal Interagency Forum on Aging Related Statistics. (2004). *Older Americans 2004: Key indicators of well-being.* Washington, DC: U.S. Government Printing Office.

Feeney, J. A. (1994). Attachment style, communication patterns, and satisfaction across the life cycle of marriage. *Personal Relationships, 1,* 333–348.

Feinberg, A. W. (1997). The care of dying patients. *Annals of Internal Medicine, 126,* 164–165.

Feinstein, N. F. (2000). Fetal heart rate auscultation: Current and future practice. *Journal of Obstetric, Gynecologic, and Neonatal Nursing, 29,* 306–315.

Feiring, C. (1999). Other-sex friendship networks and the development of romantic relationships in adolescence. *Journal of Youth and Adolescence, 28,* 495–512.

Feldman, D. C. (2002a). Stability in the midst of change: A developmental perspective on the study of careers. In D. C. Feldman (Ed.), *Work careers: A developmental perspective* (pp. 3–26). San Francisco: Jossey-Bass.

Feldman, D. C. (2002b). When you come to a fork in the road, take it: Career indecision and vocational choices of teenagers and young adults. In D. C. Feldman (Ed.), *Work careers: A developmental perspective* (pp. 93–125). San Francisco: Jossey-Bass.

Felson, R. B., & Cares, A. C. (2005). Gender and the seriousness of assaults on intimate partners and other victims. *Journal of Marriage and Family, 67,* 1182–1195.

Felton, B. J., & Berry, C. A. (1992). Do the sources of the urban elderly's social support determine its psychological consequences? *Psychology and Aging, 7,* 89–97.

Fen, X., Weixing, W., & Wenjing, Z. (2005). Kindergartners acts of lying and its relation to theory of mind. *Acta Psychologica Sinica, 37,* 73–78.

Fenigsen, R. (2004). Dutch euthanasia: The new government ordered study. *Issues in Law and Medicine, 20,* 73–79.

Fenson, L. (2002). BMDP outputs from the data set reported in Fenson, L., Dale, P. S., Reznick, J. S., Bates, E., Thal, D. J., & Pethick, S. J. (1994). Variability in early communicative development. *Monographs of the Society for Research in Child Development, 59*(5, Serial No. 242). Courtesy L. Fenson.

Fenson, L., Dale, P. S., Reznick, J. S., Bates, E., Thal, D. J., & Pethick, S. J. (1994). Variability in early communicative development. *Monographs of the Society for Research in Child Development, 59*(5, Serial No. 242).

Ferber, R. (1985). *Solve your child's sleep problems.* New York: Simon & Schuster.

Ferrer-Wreder, L., Lorente, C. C., Kurtines, W., et al. (2002). Promoting identity development in marginalized youth. *Journal of Adolescent Research, 17,* 168–186.

Ferriss, A. L. (2002). Religion and the quality of life. *Journal of Happiness Studies, 3,* 199–215.

Festinger, L., Schachter, S., & Back, K. W. (1950). *Social pressures in informal groups: A study of human factors in housing.* Stanford, CA: Stanford University Press.

Fiatarone, M. A., Marks, E. C., Ryan, N. D., Meredith, C. N., Lipsitz, L. A., & Evans, W. J. (1990). High intensity strength training in nonagenarians: Effects on skeletal muscle. *Journal of the American Medical Association, 263,* 3029–3034.

Fiatarone, M. A., O'Neill, E. F., Ryan, N. D., et al. (1994). Exercise training and nutritional supplementation for physical frailty in very elderly people. *New England Journal of Medicine, 330,* 1769–1775.

Fido, A., & Al-Saad, S. (2005). Toxic trace elements in the hair of children with autism. *Autism, 9,* 290–298.

Field, D., & Millsap, R. E. (1991). Personality in advanced old age: Continuity or change? *Journals of Gerontology: Psychological Sciences and Social Sciences, 46B,* P299–P308.

Field, T. (2000). Infant massage therapy. In C. H. Zeanah, Jr. (Ed.), *Handbook of infant mental health* (2nd ed., pp. 494–500). New York: Guilford.

Field, T., Diego, M., Hernandez-Reif, M., Schanberg, S., & Kuhn, C. (2003). Depressed mothers who are "good interaction" partners versus those who are withdrawn or intrusive. *Infant Behavior and Development, 26,* 238–252.

Field, T., Healy, B., Goldstein, S., & Guthertz, M. (1990). Behavior-state matching and synchrony in mother-infant interactions of nondepressed versus depressed dyads. *Developmental Psychology, 26,* 7–14.

Field, T. M. (1998). Massage theory effects. *American Psychologist, 53,* 1270–1281.

Fields, J. (2003). Children's living arrangements and characteristics: March 2002. *Current Population Reports, P20–547.* Washington, DC: U.S. Census Bureau.

Fields, J. (2004). America's families and living arrangements: 2003. *Current Population Reports, P20–553.* Washington, DC: U.S. Census Bureau.

Fields, J., & Casper, L. M. (2001). America's families and living arrangements: 2000. *Current Population Reports, P20–537.* Washington, DC: U.S. Census Bureau.

Fields-Meyer, T., Aguayo, A., Arias, R., et al. (2004, November 8). Teen titans. *People, 62,* 127–128, 131.

Figueroa, R., Lindenmaier, H., Hergenhahn, M., Nielson, K. V., & Boukamp, P. (2000). Telomere erosion varies during in vitro aging of normal human fibroblasts from young and adult donors. *Cancer Research, 60,* 2770–2774.

Fincham, F. D. (2003). Marital conflict: Correlates, structure, and context. *Current Directions in Psychological Science, 12,* 23–27.

Finckh-Krämer, U., Spormann-Lagodzinski, M., & Gross, M. (2000). German registry for hearing loss in children: Results after 4 years. *International Journal of Pediatric Otorhinolaryngology, 56,* 113–127.

Fingerhut, L. A., Cox, C. S., & Warner, M. (1998). International comparative analysis of injury mortality: Finding from the ICE on injury statistics. *Advance Data From Vital and Health Statistics, No. 303.* Hyattsville, MD: National Center for Health Statistics.

Fingerman, K. L. (2000). "We had a nice little chat": Age and generational differences in mothers' and daughters' descriptions of enjoyable visits. *Journals of Gerontology: Psychological Sciences and Social Sciences, 55B,* P95–P106.

Fingerman, K. L. (2003). *Mothers and their adult daughters: Mixed emotions, enduring bonds.* Amherst, NY: Prometheus.

Finkelhor, D. (1994). Current information on the scope and nature of child sexual abuse. *Future of Children, 4,* 31–53.

Finkelhor, D., Hotaling, G., Lewis, I. A., & Smith, C. (1990). Sexual abuse in a national survey of adult men and women: Prevalence, characteristics, and risk factors. *Child Abuse and Neglect, 14,* 19–28.

Finkelhor, D., Mitchell, K. J., & Wolak, J. (2000, June). *Online victimization: A report on the nation's youth.* National Center for Missing and Exploited Children. Retrieved February 7, 2005, from **http://www.missingkids.com/missingkids/servlet/ResourceServlet?LanguageCountry=en_US&PageId=869**

Finkelstein, J. W. (1992). Endocrine physiology at puberty. In S. B. Friedman, M. Fisher, & S. K. Schonberg (Eds.), *Comprehensive adolescent health care* (pp. 12–17). St. Louis, MO: Quality Medical Publishing.

Finkelstein, J. W., Susman, E. J., Chinchilli, V., et al. (1997). Estrogen or testosterone increases self-reported aggressive behaviors in hypogonadal adolescents. *Journal of Clinical Endocrinology and Metabolism, 82,* 2433–2438.

Finkelstein, L. M., Burke, M. J., & Raju, N. S. (1995). Age discrimination in simulated employment contexts: An integrative analysis. *Journal of Applied Psychology, 80,* 652–663.

Finkenauer, C., Engels, R. C. M. E., & Baumeister, R. F. (2005). Parenting behavior and adolescent behavioural and emotional problems: The role of self-control. *International Journal of Behavioral Development, 29,* 58–69.

Finn, J. D., Gerber, S. B., & Boyd-Zaharias, J. (2005). Small classes in the early grades, academic achievement, and graduating from high school. *Journal of Educational Psychology, 97,* 214–223.

Fiori, K. L., Hays, J. C., & Meador, K. G. (2004). Spiritual turning points and perceived control of the life course. *International Journal of Aging and Human Development, 59,* 391–420.

First Candle/SIDS Alliance. (2006). *Tips for parents and caregivers.* Retrieved May 9, 2006, from http://www.sidsalliance.org/newparents/np_reduce_tips.html

Fisch, H. (with Braun, S.). (2005). *The male biological clock: The startling news about aging, sexuality, and fertility in men.* New York: Free Press.

Fish, J. M. (1995). Mixed blood: The myth of racial classifications. *Psychology Today, 28*(6), 55–62.

Fisher, H. E. (2004). *Why we love: The nature and chemistry of romantic love.* New York: Holt.

Fisk, A. D., & Rogers, W. A. (1991). Toward an understanding of age-related memory and visual search effects. *Journal of Experimental Psychology: General, 120,* 131–149.

Fitzgerald, M. D., Tanaka, H., Tran, Z. V., & Seals, D. R. (1997). Age-related declines in maximal aerobic capacity in regularly exercising vs. sedentary women: A meta-analysis. *Journal of Applied Physiology, 83,* 160–165.

Fitzgibbon, M. L., Stolley, M. R., Dyer, A. R., Van Horn, L., & KauferChristoffel, K. (2002). A community-based obesity prevention program for minority children: Rationale and study design for Hip-Hop to Health Jr. *Preventive Medicine, 34,* 289–297.

Fitzgibbon, M. L., Stolley, M. R., Schiffer, L., Van Horn, L., KauferChristoffel, K., & Dyer, A. (2005). Two-year- follow-up results for Hip-Hop to Health Jr.: A randomized controlled trial for overweight prevention in preschool minority children. *Journal of Pediatrics, 146,* 618–625.

Fivush, R. (2001). Owning experience: Developing subjective perspective in autobiographical narratives. In C. Moore & K. Lemmon (Eds.), *The self in time: Developmental perspectives* (pp. 35–52). Mahwah, NJ: Erlbaum.

Fivush, R., & Nelson, K. (2004). Culture and language in the emergence of autobiographical memory. *Psychological Science, 15,* 573–577.

Flaks, D., Ficher, I., Masterpasqua, F., & Joseph, G. (1995). Lesbians choosing motherhood: A comparative study of lesbian and heterosexual parents and their children. *Developmental Psychology, 31,* 105–114.

Flaming, D., & Morse, J. M. (1991). Minimizing embarrassment: Boys' experiences of pubertal changes. *Issues in Comprehensive Pediatric Nursing, 14,* 211–230.

Flannery, D. J., Vazsonyi, A. T., Liau, A. K., et al. (2003). Initial behavior outcomes for the PeaceBuilders universal school-based violence prevention program. *Developmental Psychology, 39,* 292–308.

Flavell, J. H. (1975). *The development of role-taking and communication skills in children.* Huntington, NY: Krieger.

Flavell, J. H. (1980, Fall). A tribute to Piaget. *Society for Research in Child Development Newsletter,* p. 1.

Flavell, J. H., Beach, D. R., & Chinsky, J. M. (1966). Spontaneous verbal rehearsal in a memory task as a function of age. *Child Development, 37,* 283–299.

Fleischman, D. A., Wilson, R. S., Gabrieli, J. D. E., Bienias, J. L., & Bennett, D. A. (2004). A longitudinal study of implicit and explicit memory in old persons. *Psychology and Aging, 19,* 617–625.

Fletcher, A. C., Steinberg, L., & Williams-Wheeler, M. (2004). Parental influences on adolescent problem behavior: Revisiting Stattin and Kerr. *Child Development, 75,* 781–796.

Flinn, M. V. (1999). Family environment, stress, and health during childhood. In C. Panter-Brick & C. M. Worthman (Eds.), *Hormones, health, and behavior: A socio-ecological and lifespan perspective* (pp. 105–138). New York: Cambridge University Press.

Flinn, M. V., & England, B. G. (1995). Childhood stress and family environment. *Current Anthropology, 36,* 854–866.

Flouri, E., & Buchanan, A. (2003). The role of mother involvement and father involvement in adolescent bullying behavior. *Journal of Interpersonal Violence, 18,* 634–644.

Flynn, J. R. (1999). Searching for justice: The discovery of IQ gains over time. *American Psychologist, 54,* 5–20.

Fogel, A. (2001). *Infancy: Infant, family, and society* (4th ed.). Belmont, CA: Wadsworth.

Fogel, A., & Melson, L. G. (1988). *Child development: Individual, family, and society.* St. Paul, MN: West.

Foley, D. J., Helmovitz, H. K., Guralnik, J. M., & Brock, D. B. (2002). Driving life expectancy of persons aged 70 years and older in the United States. *American Journal of Public Health, 92,* 1284–1289.

Foley, D. J., Monjan, A., Simonsick, E. M., Wallace, R. B., & Blazer, D. G. (1999). Incidence and remission of insomnia among elderly adults: An epidemiologic study of 6,800 persons over three years. *Sleep, 22*(Suppl. 2), S366–S372.

Folkman, S., Chesney, M., Collette, L., Boccellari, A., & Cooke, M. (1996). Postbereavement depressive mood and its prebereavement predictors in HIV+ and HIV– gay men. *Journal of Personality and Social Psychology, 70,* 336–348.

Ford, D. H., & Lerner, R. M. (1992). *Developmental systems theory: An integrative approach.* Newbury Park, CA: Sage.

Ford, W. C. L., North, K., Taylor, H., et al. (2000). Increasing paternal age is associated with delayed conception in a large population of fertile couples: Evidence for declining fecundity in older men. *Human Reproduction, 15,* 1703–1708.

Fowler, J. W. (1981). *Stages of faith: The psychology of human development and the quest for meaning.* San Francisco: Harper & Row.

Fox, B., & Routh, D. K. (1984). Phonemic analysis and synthesis as word attack skills: Revisited. *Journal of Educational Psychology, 76,* 1059–1064.

Fox, J. A., & Zawitz, M. W. (2004). *Homicide trends in the United States.* U.S. Department of Justice, Bureau of Justice Statistics. Retrieved November 21, 2005, from http://www.ojp.usdoj.gov/bjs/homicide/homtrnd.htm

Fox, N. A., Henderson, H. A. Rubin, K. H., Calkins, S. D., & Schmidt, L. A. (2001). Continuity and discontinuity of behavioral inhibition and exuberance: Psychophysiological and behavioral influences across the first four years of life. *Child Development, 72,* 1–21.

Fox, N. A., Nichols, K. E., Henderson, H. A., et al. (2005). Evidence for a gene-environment interaction in predicting behavioral inhibition in middle childhood. *Psychological Science, 16,* 921–926.

Fozard, J. L., & Gordon-Salant, S. (2001). Changes in vision and hearing with aging. In J. E. Birren & K. W. Schaie (Eds.), *Handbook of the psychology of aging* (5th ed., pp. 241–266). San Diego, CA: Academic Press.

Fraga, M. F., Ballestar, E., Paz, M. F., et al. (2005). Epigenetic differences arise during the lifetime of monozygotic twins. *Proceedings of the National Academy of Sciences of the United States of America, 102,* 10604–10609.

Francis, D., Diorio, J., Liu, D., & Meaney, M. J. (1999). Nongenomic transmission across generations of maternal behavior and stress responses in the rat. *Science, 286,* 1155–1158.

Frank, A. (1995). *The diary of a young girl: The definitive edition* (O. H. Frank & M. Pressler, Eds.). New York: Doubleday.

Frankenberger, K. D. (2000). Adolescent egocentrism: A comparison among adolescents and adults. *Journal of Adolescence, 23,* 343–354.

Franz, C. E., McClelland, D. C., & Weinberger, J. (1991). Childhood antecedents of conventional social accomplishment in midlife adults: A 36–year prospective study. *Journal of Personality and Social Psychology, 60*, 586–595.

Frascarolo, F. (2004). Paternal involvement in child caregiving and infant sociability. *Infant Mental Health Journal, 25*, 509–521.

Frasure-Smith, N., & Lespérance, F. (2005). Depression and coronary heart disease: Complex synergism of mind, body, and environment. *Current Directions in Psychological Science, 14*, 39–43.

Fredrickson, B. L. (1995). Socioemotional behavior at the end of college life. *Journal of Social and Personal Relationships, 12*, 261–276.

Fredriksen, K., Rhodes, J., Reddy, R., & Way, N. (2004). Sleepless in Chicago: Tracking the effects of adolescent sleep loss during the middle school years. *Child Development, 75*, 84–95.

Freedle, R. O. (2003). Correcting the SAT's ethnic and social-class bias: A method for reestimating SAT scores. *Harvard Educational Review, 73*, 1–43.

Freedman, D. S., Khan, L. K., Serdula, M. K., Dietz, W. H., Srinivasan, S. R., & Berenson, G. S. (2002). Relation of age at menarche to race, time period, and anthropometric dimensions: The Bogalusa Heart Study. *Pediatrics, 110*, e43.

Freeman, J. (2001). *Gifted children grown up.* London: David Fulton.

Freeman, J. (2003). Gender differences in gifted achievement in Britain and the U.S. *Gifted Child Quarterly, 47*, 202–211.

Freisthler, B., Svare, G. M., & Harrison-Jay, S. (2003). It was the best of times, it was the worst of times: Young adult stepchildren talk about growing up in a stepfamily. *Journal of Divorce and Remarriage, 38*(3–4), 83–102.

Fremont, W. P. (2004). Childhood reactions to terrorism-induced trauma: A review of the past 10 years. *Journal of the American Academy of Child and Adolescent Psychiatry, 43*, 381–392.

Freud, S. (1905/1953). Three essays on the theory of sexuality. In J. Strachey (Ed. and Trans.), *The standard edition of the complete psychological works of Sigmund Freud* (Vol. 7, pp. 123–243). London: Hogarth Press.

Freud, S. (1923–25/1961). The ego and the id and other works. In J. Strachey (Ed. and Trans.), *The standard edition of the complete psychological works of Sigmund Freud* (Vol. 19). London: Hogarth Press.

Freud, S. (1932–36/1964). New introductory lectures on psycho-analysis and other works. In J. Strachey (Ed. and Trans.), *The standard edition of the complete psychological works of Sigmund Freud* (Vol. 22). London: Hogarth Press.

Frick, P. J., Christian, R. E., & Wooton, J. M. (1999). Age trends in association between parenting practices and conduct problems. *Behavior Modification, 23*, 106–128.

Fried, C. S., & Reppucci, N. D. (2001). Criminal decision making: The development of adolescent judgment, criminal responsibility, and culpability. *Law and Human Behavior, 25*, 45–61.

Friedman, H. S., Tucker, J. S., Schwartz, J. E., et al. (1995). Childhood conscientiousness and longevity: Health behaviors and cause of death. *Journal of Personality and Social Psychology, 68*, 696–703.

Friedman, M. M. (1993). Social support sources and psychological well-being in older women with heart disease. *Research in Nursing and Health, 16*, 405–413.

Frieman, B. B. (2002). Challenges faced by fathers in a divorce support group. *Journal of Divorce and Remarriage, 37*(1–2), 163–173.

Fronczek, P. (2005). *Income, earnings, and poverty from the 2004 American Community Survey* (American Community Survey Reports No. ACS-01). U.S. Census Bureau. Retrieved May 29, 2006, from **http://blueprod.ssd.census.gov/ prod/2005pubs/acs-01.pdf**

Frontline. (2002). *Inside the teenage brain: Interview with Deborah Yurgelun-Todd.* Retrieved January 17, 2005, from **http://www.pbs.org/wgbh/ pages/frontline/shows/teenbrain/interviews/todd. html**

Fry, A. F., & Hale, S. (1996). Processing speed, working memory, and fluid intelligence: Evidence for a developmental cascade. *Psychological Science, 7*, 237–241.

Fry, A. F., & Hale, S. (2000). Relationships among processing speed, working memory and fluid intelligence in children. *Biological Psychology, 54*, 1–34.

Fuentez-Afflick, E., Hessol, N. A., & Pérez-Stable, E. J. (1999). Testing the epidemiologic paradox of low birth weight in Latinos. *Archives of Pediatrics and Adolescent Medicine, 153*, 147–153.

Fuentes-Afflick, E., & Lurie, P. (1997). Low birth weight and Latino ethnicity: Examining the epidemiologic paradox. *Archives of Pediatrics and Adolescent Medicine, 151*, 665–674.

Fukukawa, Y., Nakashima, C., Tsuboi, S., et al. (2004). Age differences in the effect of physical activity on depressive symptoms. *Psychology and Aging, 19*, 346–351.

Fuller, G. F. (2000). Falls in the elderly. *American Family Physician, 61*, 2159–2168, 2173–2174.

Funderburg, L. (2000, June). Saving Jason. *Life, 23*, 48–62.

Fung, H. H., & Carstensen, L. L. (2003). Sending memorable messages to the old: Age differences in preferences and memory for advertisements. *Journal of Personality and Social Psychology, 85*, 163–178.

Fung, H. H., & Carstensen, L. L. (2004). Motivational changes in response to blocked goals and foreshortened time: Testing alternatives to socioemotional selectivity theory. *Psychology and Aging, 19*, 68–78.

Furman, W. (2002). The emerging field of adolescent romantic relationships. *Current Directions in Psychological Science, 11*, 117–180.

Furman, W., & Buhrmester, D. (1992). Age and sex differences in perceptions of networks of personal relationships. *Child Development, 63*, 103–115.

Furr, R. M., & Funder, D. C. (1998). A multimodal analysis of personal negativity. *Journal of Personality and Social Psychology, 74*, 1580–1591.

Furstenberg, F. F., Brooks-Gunn, J., & Morgan, S. P. (1987). *Adolescent mothers in later life.* New York: Cambridge University Press.

Gabbard, C. P. (2004). *Lifelong motor development* (4th ed.). San Francisco: Benjamin Cummings.

Gabor, J. Y., Cooper, A. B., & Hanly, P. J. (2001). Sleep disruption in the intensive care unit. *Current Opinion in Critical Care, 7*, 21–27.

Gabriel, P. E. (2003). An examination of occupational mobility among full-time workers. *Monthly Labor Review, 126*(9), 32–36.

Gaesser, G. A. (1999). Thinness and weight loss: Beneficial or detrimental to longevity? *Medicine and Science in Sports and Exercise, 31*, 1118–1128.

Gagné, F. (1997). Critique of Morelock's (1996) definitions of giftedness and talent. *Roeper Review, 20*, 76–85.

Galanis, D. J., Joseph, C., Masaki, K. H., Petrovitch, H., Ross, G. W., & White, L. (2000). A longitudinal study of drinking and cognitive performance in elderly Japanese American men: The Honolulu-Asia Aging Study. *American Journal of Public Health, 90*, 1254–1259.

Gallagher, A. M., De Lisi, R., Holst, P. C., McGillicuddy-De Lisi, A. V., Morely, M., & Cahalan, C. (2000). Gender differences in advanced mathematical problem solving. *Journal of Experimental Child Psychology, 75*, 165–190.

Gallagher, R. (2006). *Talking about death and dying.* Retrieved May 14, 2006, from **http://www. medbroadcast.com/channel_section_details.asp? text_id=1046&channel_id=1012&relation_ id=6976**

Gallahue, D. L., & Ozmun, J. C. (2006). *Understanding motor development: Infants, children, adolescents, adults* (6th ed.). Boston: McGraw Hill.

Galton, F. (1883). *Inquiries into human faculty and its development.* London: Macmillan.

Gambrill, E. (1996). Loneliness, social isolation and social anxiety. In M. A. Mattaini & B. A. Thyer (Eds.), *Finding solutions to social problems: Behavioral strategies for change* (pp. 345–371). Washington, DC: American Psychological Association.

Ganahl, J. (2002, June 23). Ladies first: Pioneering erotica writers club still at it after 26 years. *San Francisco Chronicle*. Retrieved April 14, 2005, from http://www.sfgate.com/cgi-bin/article.cgi%3Ffile%3D/chronicle/archive/2002/06/23/LV187.DTL

Ganguli, M., Vander Bilt, J., Saxton, J. A., Shen, C., & Dodge, H. H. (2005). Alcohol consumption and cognitive function in late life: A longitudinal community study. *Neurology*, 65, 1210–1217.

Ganske, M. G. (2001). Winning bedtime battles. *Parenting*, 15, 84–88.

Garb, H. N. (1989). Clinical judgment, clinical training, and professional experience. *Psychological Bulletin*, 105, 387–396.

Garbarino, J. (1988). Preventing childhood injury: Developmental and mental health issues. *American Journal of Orthopsychiatry*, 58, 25–45.

Garbarino, J. (1999). *Lost boys: Why our sons turn violent and how we can save them*. New York: The Free Press.

Garbarino, J., & Ganzel, B. (2000). The human ecology of early risk. In J. P. Shonkoff & S. J. Meisels (Eds.), *Handbook of early childhood intervention* (2nd ed., pp. 76–93). New York: Cambridge University Press.

Garber, K. (2000). High stakes for gene therapy. *Technology Review*, 103(2), 58–60, 62, 64.

Garces, E., Thomas, D., & Currie, J. (2002). Longer-term effects of Head Start. *American Economic Review*, 92, 999–1012.

García-Martín, M. Á., Gómez-Jacinto, L., & Martim-portugués-Goyenechea, C. (2004). A structural model of the effects of organized leisure activities on the well-being of elder adults in Spain. *Activities, Adaptation, and Aging*, 28(3), 19–34.

Gard, M. C., & Freeman, C. P. (1996). The dismantling of a myth: A review of eating disorders and socioeconomic status. *International Journal of Eating Disorders*, 2, 1–12.

Gardner, H. (1983). *Frames of mind: The theory of multiple intelligences*. New York: Basic Books.

Gardner, H. (1989). *To open minds: Chinese clues to the dilemma of contemporary education*. New York: Basic Books.

Gardner, H. (1998). Do parents count? *New York Review of Books*, 45(17), 19–22.

Gardner, H. (1999). *Intelligence reframed: Multiple intelligences for the 21st century*. New York: Basic Books.

Gardner, H. (2004). *Frames of mind: The theory of multiple intelligences* (Rev. ed.). New York: Basic Books.

Garn, S. M. (1992a). Growth and development. In S. B. Friedman, M. Fisher, & S. K. Schonberg (Eds.), *Comprehensive adolescent health care* (pp. 18–23). St. Louis, MO: Quality Medical Publishing.

Garn, S. M. (1992b). Physical growth and development. In S. B. Friedman, M. Fisher, & S. K. Schonberg (Eds.), *Comprehensive adolescent health care* (pp. 18–23). St. Louis: Quality Medical Publishing.

Gartstein, M. A., & Rothbart, M. K. (2003). Studying infant temperament via the Revised Infant Behavior Questionnaire. *Infant Behavior and Development*, 26, 64–86.

Gaskins, S. (2000). Children's daily activities in a Mayan village: A culturally grounded description. *Journal of Cross-Cultural Research*, 34, 375–389.

Geary, D. C. (1996). International differences in mathematical achievement: Their nature, causes, and consequences. *Current Directions in Psychological Science*, 5, 133–137.

Geary, D. C. (1999). Evolution and developmental sex differences. *Current Directions in Psychological Science*, 8, 115–120.

Geary, D. C. (2005). Evolution of general intelligence. In D. C. Geary (Ed.), *The origin of mind: Evolution of brain, cognition, and general intelligence* (pp. 253–305). Washington, DC: American Psychological Association.

Geary, D. C., Bow-Thomas, C. C., Liu, F., & Siegler, R. S. (1996). Development of arithmetical competencies in Chinese and American children: Influence of age, language, and schooling. *Child Development*, 67, 2022–2044.

Geary, D. C., Saults, S. J., Liu, F., & Hoard, M. K. (2000). Sex differences in spatial cognition, computational fluency, and arithmetical reasoning. *Journal of Experimental Child Psychology*, 77, 337–353.

Geary, D. C., & Wiley, J. G. (1991). Cognitive addition: Strategy choice and speed-of-processing differences in young and elderly adults. *Psychology and Aging*, 6, 474–483.

Geertz, C. (1973). *The interpretation of cultures*. New York: Basic Books.

Geller, P. A., Graf, M. C., & Dyson-Washington, F. (2003). Women's health psychology. In I. B. Weiner (Series Ed.) & A. M. Nezu, C. M. Nezu, & P. A. Geller (Vol. Eds.), *Handbook of psychology: Health psychology* (Vol. 9, pp. 513–544). New York: Wiley.

Gelman, S. A., Taylor, M. G., & Nguyen, S. P. (2004). Mother-child conversations about gender. *Monographs of the Society for Research in Child Development*, 69(1, Serial No. 275).

GeneTests. (2001). *About genetic services: Who should have a genetics consultation?* Retrieved August 4, 2006, from http://www.genetests.org/servlet/access?id=8888891&key=dZoY3QCkLrJqk&fcn=y&fw=wZpQ&filename=/concepts/primer/primerwhoshould.html

Genevro, J. L., Marshall, T., & Miller, T. (2004). Report on bereavement and grief research. *Death Studies*, 28, 491–575.

Georgieff, M. K., & Rao, R. (2001). The role of nutrition in cognitive development. In C. A. Nelson & M. Luciana (Eds.), *Handbook of developmental cognitive neuroscience* (pp. 491–504). Cambridge, MA: MIT Press.

Gerardi-Caulton, G. (2000). Sensitivity to spatial conflict and the development of self-regulation in children 24–36 months of age. *Developmental Science*, 3, 397–404.

Gerrard, M. (1987). Sex, sex guilt, and contraceptive use revisited: The 1980s. *Journal of Personality and Social Psychology*, 52, 975–980.

Gershoff, E. T. (2002). Corporal punishment by parents and associated child behaviors and experiences: A meta-analytic and theoretical review. *Psychological Bulletin*, 128, 539–579.

Gerstadt, C. L., Hong, Y. J., & Diamond, A. (1994). The relationship between cognition and action: Performance of children 3 1/2–7 years old on a Stroop-like day-night test. *Cognition*, 53, 129–153.

Getzel, G. S. (1995). Judaism and death: Practice implications. In J. K. Parry & A. S. Ryan (Eds.), *A cross-cultural look at death, dying, and religion* (pp. 18–31). Chicago: Nelson-Hall.

Gewirtz, J. L., & Boyd, E. F. (1977). Does maternal responding imply reduced infant crying? A critique of the 1972 Bell and Ainsworth Report. *Child Development*, 48, 1200–1207.

Gibbons, D., & Olk, P. M. (2003). Individual and structural origins of friendship and social position among professionals. *Journal of Personality and Social Psychology*, 84, 340–351.

Gibbs, R. S. (2001). The relationship between infections and adverse pregnancy outcomes: An overview. *Annals of Periodontology*, 6, 153–163.

Gibson, E. J. (1969). *Principles of perceptual learning and development*. New York: Appleton-Century-Crofts.

Gibson, E. J., Gibson, J. J., Pick, A. D., & Osser, H. (1962). A developmental study of the discrimination of letter-like forms. *Journal of Comparative and Physiological Psychology*, 55, 897–906.

Gibson, E. J., & Pick, A. D. (2000). *An ecological approach to perceptual learning and development*. New York: Oxford University Press.

Gibson, E. J., & Walk, R. D. (1960). The "visual cliff." *Scientific American*, 202(4), 64–71.

Gibson, J. J. (1979). *The ecological approach to visual perception*. Boston: Houghton-Mifflin.

Giedd, J. N. (2004). Structural magnetic resonance imaging of the adolescent brain. In R. E. Dahl & L. P. Spear (Eds.), *Annals of the New York Academy of Sciences: Vol. 1021. Adolescent brain development: Vulnerabilities and opportunities* (pp. 77–85). New York: New York Academy of Sciences.

Giedd, J. N., Blumenthal, J., Jeffries, N. O., et al. (1999). Brain development during childhood and adolescence: A longitudinal MRI study. *Nature Neuroscience*, 2, 861–863.

Giedd, J. N., Castellanos, F. X., Rajapakse, J. C., Vaituzis, A. C., & Rapoport, J. L. (1997). Sexual dimorphism of the developing human brain. *Progress in Neuro-Psychopharmacology and Biological Psychiatry, 21,* 1185–1201.

Giedd, J. N., Vaituzis, A. C., Hamburger, S. C., et al. (1996). Quantitative MRI of the temporal lobe, amygdala, and hippocampus in normal human development: Ages 4–18 years. *Journal of Comparative Neurology, 366,* 223–230.

Gilanshah, F. (1993). Islamic customs regarding death. In D. P. Irish, K. F. Lundquist, & V. J. Nelsen (Eds.), *Ethnic variations in dying, death, and grief: Diversity in universality* (pp. 137–145). Philadelphia: Taylor & Francis.

Gilbert, S. F. (2000). *Developmental biology* (6th ed.). Sunderland, MA: Sinauer Associates.

Gill, G. W. (2005). Does race exist? A proponent's perspective. *Nova online.* Retrieved April 23, 2006, from http://www.pbs.org/wgbh/nova/first/gill.html

Gilliam, F. D., Jr., & Bales, S. N. (2001). Strategic frame analysis: Reframing America's youth. *Social Policy Report, 15*(3).

Gilligan, C. (1990). Remapping the moral domain: New images of the self in relationship. In C. Zanardi (Ed.), *Essential papers on the psychology of women* (pp. 480–495). New York: New York University Press.

Gilligan, C. (1993). *In a different voice: Psychology theory and women's development.* Cambridge, MA: Harvard University Press.

Gilmour, J., & Skuse, D. (1999). Peer and self perception of children with short stature—The role of recognition. In U. Eiholzer, F. Haverkamp, & L. D. Voss (Eds.), *Growth, stature, and psychosocial well-being* (pp. 37–46). Seattle, WA: Hogrefe & Huber.

Gilovich, T., & Medvec, V. H. (1994). The temporal pattern to the experience of regret. *Journal of Personality and Social Psychology, 67,* 357–365.

Gilovich, T., & Medvec, V. H. (1995). The experience of regret: What, when, and why. *Psychological Review, 102,* 379–395.

Gilovich, T., Wang, R. F., Regan, D., & Nishina, S. (2003). Regrets of action and inaction across cultures. *Journal of Cross-Cultural Psychology, 34,* 61–71.

Ginsburg, H., & Opper, S. (1988). *Piaget's theory of intellectual development* (3rd ed.). Englewood Cliffs, NJ: Prentice Hall.

Gist, Y. J., & Hetzel, L. I. (2004). We the people: Aging in the United States. *Census 2000 Special Reports.* Retrieved May 31, 2006, from http://www.census.gov/prod/2004pubs/censr-19.pdf

Gitlin, L. N., Belle, S. H., Burgio, L. D., et al. (2003). Effect of multicomponent interventions on caregiver burden and depression: The REACH multisite initiative at 6–month follow-up. *Psychology and Aging, 18,* 361–374.

Glantz, J. C., & Guzick, D. S. (2004). Can differences in labor induction rates be explained by case mix? *Journal of Reproductive Medicine, 49,* 175–181.

Gleason, T. R. (2002). Social provisions of real and imaginary relationships in early childhood. *Developmental Psychology, 38,* 979–992.

Gleason, T. R., Sebanc, A. M., & Hartup, W. W. (2000). Imaginary companions of preschool children. *Developmental Psychology, 36,* 419–428.

Gleick, E. (1995, January 30). The costly crisis in our schools. *Time, 145,* 67–68.

Glenn, N. D. (1995). Marital quality. In D. Levinson (Ed.), *Encyclopedia of marriage and the family* (pp. 448–455). New York: Macmillan.

Glenn, N. D. (1998). The course of marital success and failure in five American 10–year marriage cohorts. *Journal of Marriage and the Family, 60,* 569–576.

Glimpse, W. (2005). *Assessing English language proficiency.* Retrieved June 4, 2005, from http://www.proximityone.com/elp/htm

Goad, T. W. (2002). *Information literacy and workplace performance.* Westport, CT: Quorum Books.

Gogate, L. J., Bahrick, L. E., & Watson, J. D. (2000). A study of multimodal motherese: The role of temporal synchrony between verbal labels and gestures. *Child Development, 71,* 878–894.

Goin-Kochel, R. P., & Myers, B. J. (2005). Parental report of early autistic symptoms: Differences in ages of detection and frequencies of characteristics among three autism-spectrum disorders. *Journal on Developmental Disabilities, 11,* 21–39.

Gold, D. T. (1996). Continuities and discontinuities in sibling relationships across the life span. In V. L. Bengtson (Ed.), *Adulthood and aging: Research on continuities and discontinuities* (pp. 228–243). New York: Springer.

Goldberg, C. (1999, November 23). Spouse abuse crackdown, surprisingly, nets many women. *New York Times,* p. A16.

Goldberg, S., & DiVitto, B. (1995). Parenting children born preterm. In M. H. Bornstein (Ed.), *Handbook of parenting* (Vol. 1, pp. 209–231). Mahwah, NJ: Erbaum.

Goldberg, S., & DiVitto, B. A. (1983). *Born too soon: Preterm birth and early development.* San Francisco: W. H. Freeman.

Goldberger, J., & Wheeler, G. A. (1920). The experimental production of pellagra in human subjects by means of diet. *Hygienic Laboratory Bulletin, 120,* 7–116.

Goldschmidt, L., Day, N. L., & Richardson, G. A. (2000). Effects of prenatal marijuana exposure on child behavior problems at age 10. *Neurotoxicology and Teratology, 22,* 325–336.

Goldstein, J. R. (1999). The leveling of divorce in the United States. *Demography, 36,* 409–414.

Goleman, D. (1995). *Emotional intelligence.* New York: Bantam Books.

Golombok, S., & Fivush, R. (1994). *Gender development.* New York: Cambridge University Press.

Golombok, S., Perry, B., Burston, A., et al. (2003). Children with lesbian parents: A community study. *Developmental Psychology, 39,* 20–33.

Goodall, J. (1986). *The chimpanzees of Gombe: Patterns of behavior.* Cambridge, MA: Harvard University Press.

Goode, K. T., Ball, K. K., Sloane, M., et al. (1998). Useful field of view and other neurocognitive indicators of crash risk in older adults. *Journal of Clinical Psychology in Medical Settings, 5,* 425–440.

Goodlin-Jones, B. L., Burnham, M. M., & Anders, T. F. (2000). Sleep and sleep disturbances: Regulatory processes in infancy. In A. J. Sameroff, M. Lewis, & S. M. Miller (Eds.), *Handbook of developmental psychopathology* (2nd ed., pp. 309–325). New York: Kluwer Academic/Plenum.

Goodman, C. C., Potts, M., Pasztor, E. M., & Scorzo, D. (2004). Grandmothers as kinship caregivers: Private arrangements compared to public child welfare oversight. *Children and Youth Services Review, 26,* 287–305.

Goodnow, J. J. (1988). Children's household work: Its nature and functions. *Psychological Bulletin, 103,* 5–26.

Goossens, L., Beyers, W., Emmen, M., & van Aken, M. A. G. (2002). The imaginary audience and personal fable: Factor analyses and concurrent validity of the "New Look" measures. *Journal of Research on Adolescence, 12,* 193–215.

Gootman, E. (2003, March 3). Separated at birth in Mexico, reunited at campuses on L. I. *New York Times,* p. A1.

Gopnik, A., Meltzoff, A. N., & Kuhl, P. K. (2001). *The scientist in the crib: What early learning tells us about the mind.* New York: HarperCollins.

Gordon, A. M. (2001). Development of hand motor control. In A. F. Kalverboer & A. Gramsbergen (Eds.), *Handbook of brain and behavior in human development* (pp. 513–537). London: Kluwer.

Goss, D. A., Grosvenor, T. P., Keller, J. T., Marsh-Tootle, W., Norton, T. T., & Zadnik, K. (1997). *Care of the patient with myopia: Reference guide for clinicians.* St. Louis, MO: American Optometric Association. Retrieved May 27, 2006, from http://www.aoa.org/documents/CPG-15.pdf

Gottfredson, L. S. (2005). What if the hereditarian hypothesis is true? *Psychology, Public Policy, and Law, 11,* 311–319.

Gottfredson, L. S., & Deary, I. J. (2004). Intelligence predicts health and longevity, but why? *Current Directions in Psychological Science, 13,* 1–4.

Gottfried, A. W., Gottfried, A. E., Bathurst, K., Guerin, D. W., & Parramore, M. M. (2003). Socioeconomic status in children's development and family environment: Infancy through adolescence. In M. H. Bornstein & R. H. Bradley (Eds.), *Socioeconomic status, parenting, and child development* (pp. 189–207). Mahwah, NJ: Erlbaum.

Gottlieb, S. (2001). Methylphenidate works by increasing dopamine levels. *British Medical Journal, 322,* 259.

Gottman, J. M., Murray, J. D., Swanson, C., Tyson, R., & Swanson, K. R. (2002). *The mathematics of marriage: Dynamic nonlinear models.* Cambridge, MA: MIT Press.

Gottman, J. M., & Silver, N. (1999). *Seven principles for making marriage work.* New York: Three Rivers Press.

Gould, S. J. (1991). Exaptation: A crucial tool for an evolutionary psychology. *Journal of Social Issues, 47*(3), 43–65.

Gould, S. J. (1996). *The mismeasure of man.* New York: Norton.

Goyal, R., Sharma, P., Kaur, I., Aggarwal, N., & Talwar, V. (2004). Bacterial vaginosis and vaginal anaerobes in preterm labour. *Journal of the Indian Medical Association, 102,* 548–550, 553.

Graber, J. A., Brooks-Gunn, J., & Warren, M. P. (in press). Pubertal effects on adjustment in girls: Moving from demonstrating effects to identifying pathways. *Journal of Youth and Adolescence.*

Graber, J. A., Seeley, J. R., Brooks-Gunn, J., & Lewinsohn, P. M. (2004). Is pubertal timing associated with psychopathology in young adulthood? *Journal of the American Academy of Adolescent Psychiatry, 43,* 718–726.

Grady, D. (2002, November 5). Sleep is one thing missing in busy teenage lives. *New York Times,* p. F5.

Graham, C. W., Fischer, J. L., Crawford, D., Fitzpatrick, J., & Bina, K. (2000). Parental status, social support, and marital adjustment. *Journal of Family Issues, 21,* 888–905.

Graham, F. K., Ernhart, C. B., Thurston, D., & Craft, M. (1962). Development three years after perinatal anoxia and other potentially damaging newborn experiences. *Psychological Monographs, 76* (3, No. 522).

Granados, C. (2000, December). "Hispanic" vs "Latino." *Hispanic Magazine.* Retrieved April 23, 2006, from http://www.hispanicmagazine.com/2000/dec/Features/latino.html

Gray, J. (1992). *Men are from Mars, women are from Venus: A practical guide for improving communication and getting what you want in your relationships.* New York: HarperCollins.

Gray, W. (1990). Formal operational thought. In W. F. Overton (Ed.), *Reasoning, necessity, and logic: Developmental perspectives* (pp. 227–253). Hillsdale, NJ: Erlbaum.

Graziano, A. M. (2002). *Developmental disabilities: Introduction to a diverse field.* Boston: Allyn & Bacon.

Green, H. (2004). *In memorium-Barbara McClintock.* Retrieved December 21, 2004, from http://nobelprize.org/medicine/articles/green

Green, R. L., Hoffman, L. T., Morse, R., Hayes, M. E., & Morgan, R. F. (1964). *The educational status of children in a district without public schools* (Co-Operative Research Project No. 2321). Washington, DC: Office of Education, U.S. Department of Health, Education, and Welfare.

Greenberg, M. T., & Kusché, C. A. (2006). Building social and emotional competence: The PATHS curriculum. In S. R. Jimerson & M. Furlong (Eds.), *Handbook of school violence and school safety: From research to practice* (pp. 395–412). Mahwah, NJ: Erlbaum.

Greene, M. F. (2000, May). Surprising news about self-esteem. *Good Housekeeping, 231,* 79–80.

Greenhalgh, S., & Li, J. (1995). Engendering reproductive policy and practice in peasant China: For a feminist demography of reproduction. *Signs, 20,* 601–641.

Greksa, L. P. (2002). Population growth and fertility patterns in an Old Order Amish settlement. *Annals of Human Biology, 29,* 192–201.

Greulich, W. W. (1957). A comparison of the physical growth and development of American-born and native Japanese children. *American Journal of Physical Anthropology, 15,* 489–515.

Griffin, D., & Kahneman, D. (2003). Judgmental heuristics: Human strengths or human weaknesses? In L. G. Aspinwall & U. M. Staudinger (Eds.), *A psychology of human strengths: Fundamental questions and future directions for a positive psychology* (pp. 165–178). Washington, DC: American Psychological Association.

Griffiths, A. J. F., Miller, J. H., Suzuki, D. T., Lewontin, R. C., & Gelbart, W. M. (1996). *An introduction to genetic analysis* (6th ed.). New York: Freeman.Grisso, T. (1996). Society's retributive response to juvenile violence: A developmental perspective. *Law and Human Behavior, 20,* 229–247.

Grolnick, W., Cole, R., Laurenitis, L., & Schwartzman, P. (1990). Playing with fire: A developmental assessment of children's fire understanding and experience. *Journal of Clinical Child Psychology, 19,* 128–135.

Gross, T. F. (1997). Children's perception of faces of varied immaturity. *Journal of Experimental Child Psychology, 66,* 42–63.

Groswasser, J., Simon, T., Scaillet, S., Franco, P., & Kahn, A. (2001). Reduced arousals following obstructive apneas in infants sleeping prone. *Pediatric Research, 49,* 402–406.

Groves, R. M., Fowler, F. J., Couper, M. P., Lepkowski, J. M., Singer, E., & Tourangeau, R. (2004). *Survey methodology.* Hoboken, NJ: Wiley.

Gruenwald, P. (1966). Growth of the human fetus. I. Normal growth and its variation *American Journal of Obstetrics and Gynecology, 94,* 1112–1119.

Grunbaum, J. A., Kann, L., Kinchen, S., et al. (2004). Youth Risk Behavior Surveillance—United States, 2003. *Morbidity and Mortality Weekly Report, 53*(2), 1–96.

Guerri, C., Pascual, M., & Renau-Piqueras, J. (2001). Glia and fetal alcohol syndrome *Neurotoxicology, 22,* 593–599.

Guesry, P. (1998). The role of nutrition in brain development. *Preventive Medicine, 27,* 189–194.

Guest, E. (2001). *Children of AIDS: Africa's orphan crisis.* London: Pluto Press.

Guimond, S., Chatard, A., Martinot, D., Crisp, R. J., & Redersdorff, S. (2006). Social comparison, self-stereotyping, and gender differences in self-construals. *Journal of Personality and Social Psychology, 90,* 221–242.

Guinness world records. (2003). *Oldest woman—Living.* Retrieved May 20, 2003, from http://www.guinnessworldrecords.com/sides.html

Gullone, E., & King, N. J. (1997). Three-year follow-up of normal fear in children and adolescents aged 7 to 18 years. *British Journal of Developmental Psychology, 15,* 97–111.

Gulotta, C. S., & Finney, J. W. (2000). Intervention models for mothers and children at risk for injuries. *Clinical Child and Family Psychology Review, 3,* 25–36.

Gump, L. S., Baker, R. C., & Roll, S. (2000). Cultural and gender differences in moral judgment: A study of Mexican Americans and Anglo-Americans. *Hispanic Journal of Behavioral Sciences, 22,* 78–93.

Gunnar, M. R. (2001). Effects of early deprivation: Findings from orphanage-reared infants and children. In C. A. Nelson & M. Luciana (Eds.), *Handbook of developmental neuroscience* (pp. 617–629). Cambridge, MA: MIT Press.

Gunnar, M. R., & Donzella, B. (2002). Social regulation of the cortisol levels in early human development. *Psychoneuroendocrinology, 27,* 199–220.

Gunnar, M. R., Larson, M. C., Hertsgaard, L., Harris, M. L., & Brodersen, L. (1992). The stressfulness of separation among 9–month-old infants: Effects of social context variables and infant temperament. *Child Development, 63,* 290–303.

Gunnoe, M. L., & Braver, S. L. (2001). The effects of joint legal custody on mothers, fathers, and children controlling for factors that predispose a sole maternal versus joint legal award. *Law and Human Behavior, 25,* 25–43.

Gutmann, D. (1987). *Reclaimed powers: Toward a new psychology of men and women in later life.* New York: Basic Books.

Gutmann, D. (1997). *The human elder in nature, culture, and society.* Boulder, CO: Westview Press.

Hack, M., & Fanaroff, A. A. (2000). Outcomes of children of extremely low birthweight and gestational age in the 1990s. *Seminars in Neonatology, 5,* 89–106.

Hack, M., Flannery, D. J., Schluchter, M., Cartar, L., Borawski, E., & Klein, N. (2002). Outcomes in young adulthood for very-low-birth-weight infants. *The New England Journal of Medicine, 346,* 149–157.

Hack, M., Taylor, H. G., Drotar, D., et al. (2005). Chronic conditions, functional limitations, and special health care needs of school-aged children born with extremely-low-birth-weight in the 1990s. *Journal of the American Medical Association, 294,* 318–325.

Haishi, K., & Kokubun, M. (1995). Developmental trends in pursuit eye movements among preschool children. *Perceptual and Motor Skills, 81,* 1131–1137.

Haith, M. M. (1998). Who put the cog in infant cognition? Is rich interpretation too costly? *Infant Behavior and Development, 21,* 167–179.

Haith, M. M., & Sameroff, A. J. (1996). The 5 to 7 year shift: Retrospect and prospect. In A. J. Sameroff & M. M. Haith (Eds.), *The five to seven year shift* (pp. 435–449). Chicago: University of Chicago Press.

Hajcak, G., & Simons, R. F. (2002). Error-related brain activity in obsessive-compulsive undergraduates. *Psychiatry Research, 110,* 63–72.

Hakuta, K. (1999). The debate on bilingual education. *Journal of Developmental and Behavioral Pediatrics, 20,* 36–37.

Hakuta, K., Bialystok, E., & Wiley, E. (2003). Critical evidence: A test of the critical-period hypothesis for second-language acquisition. *Psychological Science, 14,* 31–38.

Hale, S. (1990). A global developmental trend in cognitive processing speed. *Child Development, 61,* 653–663.

Hall, G. S. (1904). *Adolescence: Its psychology and its relations to physiology, anthropology, sociology, sex, crime, religion and education* (Vols. 1–2). New York: Appleton.

Hall, G. S. (1922). *Senescence: The last half of life.* New York: Appleton.

Halperin, S., & Howe, H. (1998). *The forgotten half revisited: American youth and young families, 1988–2008.* Washington, DC: American Youth Policy Forum.

Hamer, D. (1997). The search for personality genes: Adventures of a molecular biologist. *Current Directions in Psychological Science, 6,* 111–114.

Hamilton, B. E., Ventura, S. J., Martin, J. A., & Sutton, P. D. (2005). Preliminary births for 2004. *Health E-Stats.* National Center for Health Statistics, Centers for Disease Control and Prevention. Retrieved May 7, 2006, from **http://www.cdc.gov/nchs/products/pubs/pubd/hestats/prelim_births/prelim_births04.htm**

Hamilton, W. D. (1971). The genetical evolution of social behavior. In G. C. Williams (Ed.), *Group selection* (pp. 23–43). Chicago: Aldine. (Reprinted from *Journal of Theoretical Biology,* 1964, *7,* 1–16.)

Hammar, S. L. (2002). Puberty. In L. G. Yamamoto, A. S. Inaba, J. K. Okamoto, M. E. Patrinos, & V. K. Yamashiroya (Eds.), *Case based pediatrics for medical students and residents.* An online textbook from the University of Hawaii John A. Burns School of Medicine. Retrieved May 15, 2006, from **http://www.hawaii.edu/medicine/pediatrics/pedtext/s20c01.html**

Handley, S. J., Capon, A., Beveridge, M., Dennis, I., & Evants, J. St. B. T. (2004). Working memory, inhibitory control and the development of children's reasoning. *Thinking and Reasoning, 10,* 175–195.

Hankin, B. L., Fraley, R. C., & Abela, J. R. Z. (2005). Daily depression and cognitions about stress: Evidence for a traitlike depressogenic cognitive style and the prediction of depressive symptoms in a prospective daily diary study. *Journal of Personality and Social Psychology, 88,* 673–685.

Hansen, K. K. (1998). Folk remedies and child abuse: A review with emphasis on caida de mollera and its relationship to shaken baby syndrome. *Child Abuse and Neglect, 22,* 117–127.

Hansen, M., Kurinczuk, J. J., Bower, C., & Webb, S. (2002). The risk of major birth defects after intracytoplasmic sperm injection and in vitro fertilization. *The New England Journal of Medicine, 346,* 725–730.

Harada, M. (1995). Minamata disease: Methylmercury poisoning in Japan caused by environmental pollution. *Critical Reviews in Toxicology, 25,* 1–24.

Hardy, C. L., Bukowski, W. M., & Sippola, L. K. (2002). Stability and change in peer relationships during the transition to middle-level school. *Journal of Early Adolescence, 22,* 117–142.

Harlow, H. F. (1959). Love in infant monkeys. *Scientific American, 200*(6), 68–74.

Harlow, H. F., & Zimmermann, R. R. (1959). Affectional responses in the infant monkey: Orphaned baby monkeys develop a strong and persistent attachment to inanimate surrogate mothers. *Science, 130,* 421–432.

Harnishfeger, K. K., & Bjorklund, D. F. (1993). The ontogeny of inhibition mechanisms: A renewed approach to cognitive development. In M. L. Howe & R. Pasnak (Eds.), *Emerging themes in cognitive development* (Vol. 1, pp. 28–49). New York: Springer-Verlag.

Harnishfeger, K. K., & Bjorklund, D. F. (1994). A developmental perspective on individual differences in inhibition. *Learning and Individual Differences, 6,* 331–355.

Harré, N. (2000). Risk evaluation, driving, and adolescents: A typology. *Developmental Review, 20,* 206–226.

Harris, B. (1979). Whatever happened to little Albert? *American Psychologist, 34,* 151–160.

Harris, J. R. (1998). *The nurture assumption: Why children turn out the way they do.* New York: The Free Press.

Harrison, C. H. (2000). The adult learner: Not a student yet. *Dissertation Abstracts International, 61* (04), 1254A.

Harrison, K. A. (1985). Child-bearing, health and social priorities: A survey of 22,774 consecutive hospital births in Zaria, Northern Nigeria. *British Journal of Obstetrics and Gynaecology, 92*(Suppl. 5), 1–119.

Harrison, M. R. (2004). The University of California at San Francisco Fetal Treatment Center: A personal perspective. *Fetal Diagnosis and Therapy, 19,* 513–524.

Harrison, M. R., Keller, R. L., Hawgood, S. B., et al. (2003). A randomized trial of fetal endoscopic tracheal occlusion for severe fetal congenital diaphragmatic hernia. *The New England Journal of Medicine, 349,* 1916–1924.

Hart, B., & Risley, T. R. (1995). *Meaningful differences in the everyday experiences of young American children.* Baltimore: P. H. Brookes.

Harter, S. (1999). *The construction of the self: A developmental perspective.* New York: Guilford.

Harter, S. (2003). The development of self-representations during childhood and adolescence. In M. R. Leary & J. P. Tangney (Eds.), *Handbook of self and identity* (pp. 610–642). New York: Guilford.

Harter, S., & Whitesell, N. R. (1989). Developmental changes in children's understanding of single, multiple and blended emotion concepts. In C. Saarni & P. L. Harris (Eds.), *Children's understanding of emotion* (pp. 81–116). New York: Cambridge University Press.

Hartup, W. W. (1996). The company they keep: Friendships and their developmental significance. *Child Development, 67,* 1–13.

Hartup, W. W., & Stevens, N. (1999). Friendships and adaptation across the life span. *Current Directions in Psychological Science, 8,* 76–79.

Harvey, J. A., & Kosofsky, B. E. (Eds.). (1998). *Annals of the New York Academy of Sciences: Vol. 846. Cocaine: Effects on the developing brain.* New York: New York Academy of Sciences.

Harvey, P. H., Martin, R. D., & Clutton-Brock, T. H. (1987). Life histories in comparative perspective. In B. B. Smuts, D. L. Cheney, R. M. Seyfarth, R. W. Wrangham, & T. T. Struhsaker (Eds.), *Primate societies* (pp. 181–196). Chicago: University of Chicago Press.

Harvey, P. O., Le Bastard, G., Pochon, J. B., et al. (2004). Executive functions and updating of the contents of working memory in unipolar depression. *Journal of Psychiatric Research, 38,* 567–576.

Hasher, L., Zacks, R. T., & May, C. P. (1999). Inhibitory control, circadian arousal, and age. In D. Gopher & A. Koriat (Eds.), *Attention and performance XVII: Cognitive regulation of performance: Interaction of theory and application* (pp. 653–675). Cambridge, MA: MIT Press.

Hassing, L. B., Johansson, B., Berg, S., et al. (2002). Terminal decline and markers of cerebro- and cardiovascular disease: Findings from a longitudinal study of the oldest old. *Journals of Gerontology: Psychological Sciences and Social Sciences, 57B,* P268–P276.

Hatch, E. E., Palmer, J. R., Titus-Ernstoff, L., et al. (1998). Cancer risk in women exposed to diethylstilbestrol in utero. *Journal of the American Medical Association, 280,* 630–634.

Hatcher, L., & Crook, J. C. (1988). First-job surprises for college graduates: An exploratory investigation. *Journal of College Student Development, 29,* 441–448.

Hattiangadi, N., Medvec, V. H., & Gilovich, T. (1995). Failing to act: Regrets of Terman's geniuses. *International Journal of Aging and Human Development, 40,* 175–185.

Haustein, K. O. (1999). Cigarette smoking, nicotine, and pregnancy. *International Journal of Clinical Pharmacology and Therapeutics, 37,* 417–427.

Havighurst, R. J., & Neugarten, B. L. (1955). *American Indian and white children: A sociopsychological investigation.* Chicago: University of Chicago Press.

Haviland, J. M., & Kramer, D. A. (1991). Affect-cognition relationships in adolescent diaries: The case of Anne Frank. *Human Development, 34,* 143–159.

Hawkins, J. L., Koonin, L. M., Palmer, S. K., & Gibbs, C. P. (1997). Anesthesia-related deaths during obstetric delivery in the United States, 1979–1990. *Anesthesiology, 86,* 277–284.

Hayes, B. K., & Hennessy, R. (1996). The nature and development of nonverbal implicit memory. *Journal of Experimental Child Psychology, 63,* 22–43.

Hayes, D. P., & Grether, J. (1983). The school year and vacations: When do students learn? *Cornell Journal of Social Relations, 17,* 56–71.

Hayes, L., Hudson, A., & Matthews, J. (2004). Parental monitoring behaviors: A model of rules, supervision, and conflict. *Behavior Therapy, 35,* 587–604.

Hayflick, L. (1965). The limited *in vitro* lifetime of human diploid cell strains. *Experimental Cell Research, 37,* 614–636.

Hayflick, L. (1996). *How and why we age.* New York: Ballantine Books.

Hayflick, L. (2004). "Anti-aging" is an oxymoron. *Journals of Gerontology: Biological Sciences and Medical Sciences, 59A,* B573–B578.

Hayslip, B., Jr., Henderson, C. E., & Shore, R. J. (2003). The structure of grandparental role meaning. *Journal of Adult Development, 10,* 1–11.

He, K., Liu, K., Daviglus, M. L., et al. (2006). Magnesium intake and incidence of metabolic syndrome among young adults. *Circulation, 113,* 1675–1682.

Head Start Bureau. (2006). *About Head Start.* Retrieved January 23, 2006, from **http://www2.acf.dhhs.gov/programs/hsb/about**

Heath, S. B. (1989). Oral and literate traditions among Black Americans living in poverty. *American Psychologist, 44,* 367–373.

Heaton, T. (2004). *Marriage over age 22 increases marital stability.* Brigham Young University Family Studies Center. Retrieved September 9, 2004, from **http://familycenter.byu.edu/columns.aspx?id=17**

Hebert, L. E., Scherr, P. A., Bienias, J. L., Bennett, D. A., & Evans, D. A. (2003). Alzheimer disease in the U.S. population: Prevalence estimates using the 2000 Census. *Archives of Neurology, 60,* 1119–1122.

Hechtman, L., Abikoff, H. B., & Jensen, P. S. (2005). Multimodal therapy and stimulants in the treatment of children with attention-deficit/hyperactivity disorder. In E. D. Hibbs & P. S. Jensen (Eds.), *Psychosocial treatments for child and adolescent disorders: Empirically based strategies for clinical practice* (2nd ed., pp. 411–437). Washington, DC: American Psychological Association.

Heckhausen, J. (1999). *Developmental regulation in adulthood: Age-normative and sociocultural constraints as adaptive challenges.* New York: Cambridge University Press.

Heckhausen, J., & Schulz, R. (1993). Optimization by selection and compensation: Balancing primary and secondary control in life span development. *International Journal of Behavioral Development, 16,* 287–303.

Heckhausen, J., & Schulz, R. (1995). A life-span theory of control. *Psychological Review, 102,* 284–304.

Heidelberg Centenarian Study. (2005). *Adult development.* Retrieved June 1, 2006, from **http://www.dzfa.uni-heidelberg.de/english_version/safe/projekte_HD100.html**

Hein, H. A., & Pettit, S. F. (2001). Back to sleep: Good advice for parents but not for hospitals? *Pediatrics, 107,* 537–539.

Helson, R. (1993). Comparing longitudinal studies of adult development: Toward a paradigm of tension between stability and change. In D. C. Funder, R. D. Parke, C. Tomlinson-Keasey, & K. Widaman (Eds.), *Studying lives through time: Personality and development* (pp. 93–119). Washington, DC: American Psychological Association.

Helson, R., Jones, C., & Kwan, V. S. Y. (2002). Personality change over 40 years of adulthood: Hierarchical linear modeling analyses of two longitudinal samples. *Journal of Personality and Social Psychology, 83,* 752–766.

Helson, R., & Kwan, V. S. Y. (2000). Personality development in adulthood: The broad picture and processes in one longitudinal sample. In S. E. Hampson (Ed.), *Advances in personality psychology* (Vol. 1, pp. 77–106). Hove, England: Psychology Press.

Helson, R., Kwan, V. S. Y., John, O. P., & Jones, C. (2002). The growing evidence for personality change in adulthood: Findings from research with personality inventories. *Journal of Research in Personality, 36,* 287–306.

Helson, R., & Soto, C. J. (2005). Up and down in middle age: Monotonic and nonmonotonic changes in roles, status, and personality. *Journal of Personality and Social Psychology, 89,* 194–204.

Henderlong, J., & Lepper, M. R. (2002). The effects of praise on children's intrinsic motivation: A review and synthesis. *Psychological Bulletin, 128,* 774–795.

Henderson, C. R., & Ceci, S. J. (1992). Is it better to be born rich or smart? A bioecological analysis of the contributions of IQ and socioeconomic status to adult income. In K. R. Billingsley, H. U. Brown, III, & E. Derohanes (Eds.), *Scientific excellence in supercomputing: The 1990 IBM Contest prize papers* (pp. 705–751). Athens, GA: Baldwin Press.

Henderson, S. J. (2004). Inventors: The ordinary genius next door. In R. J. Sternberg, E. L. Grigorenko, & J. L. Singer (Eds.), *Creativity: From potential to realization* (pp. 103–125). Washington, DC: American Psychological Association.

Hendricks, K. A., Nuno, O. M., Suarez, L., & Larsen, R. (2001). Effects of hyperinsulinemia and obesity on risk of neural tube defects among Mexican Americans. *Epidemiology, 12,* 630–635.

Hendricks, M. (2000, September). Into the hands of babes. *Johns Hopkins Magazine.* Retrieved January 10, 2006, from **http://www.jhu.edu/~jhumag/0900web/babes.html**

Henretta, J. C. (2001). Work and retirement. In R. H. Binstock & L. K. George (Eds.), *Handbook of aging and the social sciences* (5th ed., pp. 255–271). San Diego, CA: Academic Press.

Henrich, C. C., Kuperminc, G. P., Sack, A., Blatt, S. J., & Leadbeater, B. J. (2000). Characteristics and homogeneity of early adolescent friendship groups: A comparison of male and female clique and nonclique members. *Applied Developmental Science, 4,* 15–26.

Henry J. Kaiser Family Foundation. (2005). *e-Health and the elderly: How seniors use the Internet for health information: Key findings from a national survey of older Americans.* Retrieved June 29, 2006, from **http://www.kff.org/entmedia/7223.cfm**

Henry J. Kaiser Family Foundation, Hoff, T., Greene, L., & Davis, J. (2003). *National survey of adolescents and young adults: Sexual knowledge, attitudes and experiences.* Menlo Park, CA: Henry J. Kaiser Family Foundation.

Henry, K. L., Slater, M. D., & Oetting, E. R. (2005). Alcohol use in early adolescence: The effect of changes in risk taking, perceived harm and friends' alcohol use. *Journal of Studies on Alcohol, 66,* 275–283.

Henry, Y. M., Fatayerji, D., & Eastell, R. (2004). Attainment of peak bone mass at the lumbar spine, femoral neck and radius in men and women: Relative contributions of bone size and volumetric bone mineral density. *Osteoporosis International, 15,* 263–273.

Hepburn, L. M., & Hemenway, D. (2004). Firearm availability and homicide: A review of the literature. *Aggression and Violent Behavior, 9,* 417–440.

Hepper, P. G., Wells, D. L., & Lynch, C. (2005). Prenatal thumb sucking is related to postnatal handedness. *Neuropsychologia, 43,* 313–315.

Herceg-Baron, R., Harris, K. M., Armstrong, K., Furstenberg, F. F., & Shea, J. (1990). Factors differentiating effective use of contraception among adolescents. In A. R. Stiffman & R. A. Feldman (Eds.), *Contraception, pregnancy, and parenting* (pp. 37–50). London: Jessica Kingsley Publishers.

Herman, M. (2004). Forced to choose: Some determinants of racial identification in multiracial adolescents. *Child Development, 75,* 730–748.

Herman-Giddens, M., Bourdony, C., Slora, E., & Wasserman, R. (2001). Early puberty: A cautionary tale. *Pediatrics, 107,* 609–610.

Herman-Giddens, M., Slora, E. J., Wasserman, R. C., et al. (1997). Secondary sexual characteristics and menses in young girls seen in office practice: A study from the Pediatric Research in Office Settings network. *Pediatrics, 99,* 505–512.

Hernandez, B., Uphold, C. R., Graham, M. V., & Singer, L. (1998). Prevalence and correlates of obesity in preschool children. *Journal of Pediatric Nursing, 13,* 68–76.

Hernandez, D. J. (1994). Children's changing access to resources: A historical perspective. *Social Policy Report, 8*(1).

Herrnstein, R. J., & Murray, C. (1994). *The bell curve: Intelligence and class structure in American life.* New York: Free Press.

Herschell, A. D., Calzada, E. J., Eyberg, S. M., & McNeil, C. B. (2002). Parent-child interaction therapy: New directions in research. *Cognitive and Behavioral Practice, 9,* 9–16.

Herschell, A. D., & McNeil, C. B. (2005). Parent-child interaction therapy for children experiencing externalizing behavior problems. In L. A. Reddy, T. M. Files-Hall, & C. E. Schaefer (Eds.), *Empirically based play interventions for children* (pp. 169–190). Washington, DC: American Psychological Association.

Herschkowitz, N. (2000). Neurological bases of behavioral development in infancy. *Brain and Development, 22,* 411–416.

Herskovits, E. H., Megalooikonomou, V., Davatzikos, C., Chen, A., Bryan, R. N., & Gerring, J. P. (1999). Is the spatial distribution of brain lesions associated with closed-head injury predictive of subsequent development of attention-deficit/hyperactivity disorder? Analysis with brain-image database. *Radiology, 213,* 389–394.

Hertoghe, T. (2005). The "multiple hormone deficiency" theory of aging: Is human senescence caused mainly by multiple hormone deficiencies? In W. Pierpaoli (Ed.), *Annals of the New York Academy of Sciences: Vol. 1057. Reversal of aging: Resetting the pineal clock* (pp. 448–465). New York: New York Academy of Sciences.

Hertz-Pannier, L., Chiron, C., Jambaqué, I., et al. (2002). Late plasticity for language in a child's non-dominant hemisphere: A pre- and post-surgery fMRI study. *Brain, 125,* 361–372.

Hess, T. M., Auman, C., Colcombe, S. J., & Rahhal, T. A. (2003). The impact of stereotype threat on age differences in memory performance. *Journals of Gerontology: Psychological Sciences and Social Sciences, 58B,* P3–P11.

Hetherington, E. M. (1989). Coping with family transitions: Winners, losers, and survivors. *Child Development, 60,* 1–14.

Hetherington, E. M. (1991). The role of individual differences and family relationships in children coping with divorce and remarriage. In P. Cowan & E. M. Hetherington (Eds.), *Family transitions* (pp. 165–194). Hillsdale, NJ: Erlbaum.

Hetherington, E. M. (1993). An overview of the Virginia Longitudinal Study of Divorce and Remarriage with a focus on early adolescence. *Journal of Family Psychology, 7,* 39–56.

Hetherington, E. M. (1999). Adolescent siblings in stepfamilies: Family functioning and adolescent adjustment. *Monographs of the Society for Research in Child Development, 64*(4, Serial No. 259).

Hetherington, E. M., Bridges, M., & Insabella, G. M. (1998). What matters? What does not? Five perspectives on the association between marital transitions and children's adjustment. *American Psychologist, 53,* 167–184.

Hetherington, E. M., & Elmore, A. M. (2003). Risk and resilience in children coping with their parents' divorce and remarriage. In S. S. Luthar (Ed.), *Resilience and vulnerability: Adaptation in the context of childhood adversities* (pp. 182–212). New York: Cambridge University Press.

Hetherington, E. M., & Kelly, J. (2002). *For better or for worse: Divorce reconsidered.* New York: Norton.

Hetherington, E. M., Reiss, D., & Plomin, R. (1994). *Separate social worlds of siblings: The impact of nonshared environment on development.* Hillsdale, NJ: Erlbaum.

Hetherington, E. M., & Stanley-Hagan, M. (2002). Parenting in divorced and remarried families. In M. H. Bornstein (Ed.), *Handbook of parenting* (2nd ed., Vol. 3, pp. 287–315). Mahwah, NJ: Erlbaum.

Heyman, J. W. (1996). Sensory dominance in infant perception of dynamic expressions of emotion. *Dissertation Abstracts International, 56* (09), 5195B.

High, P. (2001). Section 4 discussion: Empirically based approaches to management: Behavioral strategies. In R. G. Barr, I. St. James-Roberts, & M. R. Keefe (Eds.), *New evidence on unexplained early infant crying: Its origins, nature and management* (pp. 245–254). Skillman, NJ: Johnson & Johnson Pediatric Institute.

Hill, J. P. (1988). Adapting to menarche: Familial control and conflict. In M. R. Gunnar & W. A. Collins (Eds.), *Minnesota Symposia on Child Psychology: Vol. 21. Development during the transition to adolescence* (pp. 43–77). Hillsdale, NJ: Erlbaum.

Hill, J. P., & Lynch, M. E. (1983). The intensification of gender-related role expectations during early adolescence. In J. Brooks-Gunn & A. C. Petersen (Eds.), *Girls at puberty: Biological and psychosocial perspectives* (pp. 156–182). New York: Plenum Press.

Hill, N. E., Castellino, D. R., Lansford, J. E., et al. (2004). Parent academic involvement as related to school behavior, achievement, and aspirations: Demographic variations across adolescence. *Child Development, 75,* 1491–1509.

Hill, N. E., & Taylor, L. C. (2004). Parental school involvement and children's academic achievement: Pragmatics and issues. *Current Directions in Psychological Science, 13,* 161–164.

Hiller-Sturmhöfel, S., & Bartke, A. (1998). The endocrine system: An overview. *Alcohol Health and Research World, 22,* 153–164.

Hinde, R. A., & Stevenson-Hinde, J. (Eds.). (1973). *Constraints on learning: Limitations and predispositions.* New York: Academic Press.

Hines, M. (2004). Androgen, estrogen, and gender: Contributions of the early hormone environment to gender-related behavior. In A. H. Eagly, A. E. Beall, & R. J. Sternberg (Eds.), *The psychology of gender* (2nd ed., pp. 9–37). New York: Guilford.

Hines, M., Golombok, S., Rust, J., Johnston, K. J., Golding, J., & Avon Longitudinal Study of Parents and Children Study Team. (2002). Testosterone during pregnancy and gender role behavior of preschool children: A longitudinal, population study. *Child Development, 73,* 1678–1687.

Hipple, S. (1999). Worker displacement in the mid-1990s. *Monthly Labor Review, 122,* 15–32.

Hirsch, E., & Wang, H. (2005). The molecular pathophysiology of bacterially induced preterm labor: Insights from the murine model. *Journal of the Society for Gynecologic Investigation, 12,* 145–155.

Hitch, G. J., Towse, J. N., & Hutton, U. (2001). What limits children's working memory span? Theoretical accounts and applications for scholastic development. *Journal of Experimental Psychology: General, 130,* 184–198.

Hobart, C. (1991). Conflict in remarriages. *Journal of Divorce and Remarriage, 15*(3–4), 69–86.

Hockberg, J. (1979). Sensation and perception. In E. Hearst (Ed.), *The first century of experimental psychology* (pp. 89–145). New York: Erlbaum.

Hodges, J., & Tizard, B. (1989). Social and family relationships of ex-institutional adolescents. *Journal of Child Psychology and Psychiatry, 30,* 77–97.

Hodnett, E. D. (2000). Caregiver support for women during childbirth. *Cochrane Database of Systematic Reviews, 2,* CD000199.

Hoff, E. (2001). *Language development.* Belmont, CA: Wadsworth/Thomson.

Hoffman, D. R., Birch, E, E., Castañeda, Y. S., et al. (2003). Visual function in breast-fed term infants weaned to formula with or without long-chain polyunsaturates at 4 to 6 months: A randomized clinical trial. *Journal of Pediatrics, 142,* 669–677.

Hoffmann, M. L., & Powlishta, K. K. (2001). Gender segregation in childhood: A test of the interaction style theory. *Journal of Genetic Psychology, 162,* 298–313.

Hoffman, M. L., & Saltzstein, H. D. (1967). Parent discipline and the child's moral development. *Journal of Personality and Social Psychology, 5,* 45–57.

Hoffman, S. D., Foster, E. M., & Furstenberg, F. F., Jr. (1993). Reevaluating the costs of teenage childbearing. *Demography, 30,* 1–13.

Hogan, D. P., Astone, N. M., & Kitagawa, E. M. (1985). Social and environmental factors influencing contraceptive use among black adolescents. *Family Planning Perspectives, 17,* 165–169.

Högberg, U., & Broström, G. (1985). The demography of maternal mortality—Seven Swedish parishes in the 19th century. *International Journal of Gynaecology and Obstetrics, 23,* 489–497.

Högberg, U., & Joelsson, I. (1985). The decline in maternal mortality in Sweden, 1931–1980. *Acta Obstetricia et Gynecologica Scandinavica, 64,* 583–592.

Hojjat, M. (1997). Philosophy of life as a model of relationship satisfaction. R. J. Sternberg & M. Hojjat (Eds.), *Satisfaction in close relationships* (pp. 102–126). New York: Guilford.

Holden, C. (2004). An everlasting gender gap? *Science, 305,* 639–640.

Holden, G. W. (1983). Avoiding conflict: Mothers as tacticians in the supermarket. *Child Development, 54,* 233–240.

Holden, G. W. (2002). Perspectives on the effects of corporal punishment: Comment on Gershoff (2002). *Psychological Bulletin, 128,* 590–595.

Holland, A. J., Hon, J., Huppert, F. A., & Stevens, F. (2000). Incidence and course of dementia in people with Down's syndrome: Findings from a population-based study. *Journal of Intellectual Disability Research, 44,* 138–146.

Hollo, O., Rautava, P., Korhonen, T., Helenius, H., Kero, P., & Sillanpää, M. (2002). Academic achievement of small-for-gestational-age children at age 10 years. *Archives of Pediatrics and Adolescent Medicine, 156,* 179–187.

Holloway, S. D. (2000). *Contested childhood: Diversity and change in Japanese preschools.* New York: Routledge.

Holt, L. E. (1894). *The care and feeding of children: A catechism for the use of mothers and children's nurses.* New York: D. Appleton.

Holz, V. J., McElroy, S. W., & Sanders, S. G. (1999). *Teenage childbearing and its life cycle consequences: Exploiting a natural experiment.* Cambridge, MA: National Bureau of Economic Research. Retrieved June 7, 2006, from **http://www. jcpr.org/wp/wpdownload.cfm?pdflink=wpfiles/ HOTZ_WPoriginal2–7–2000.pdf**

Honig, L. S., Tang, M. X., Albert, S., et al. (2003). Stroke and the risk of Alzheimer disease. *Archives of Neurology, 60,* 1707–1712.

Hood, M. Y., Moore, L. L., Sundarajan-Ramamurti, A., Singer, M., Cupples, L. A., & Ellison, R. C. (2000). Parental eating attitudes and the development of obesity in children: The Framingham Children's Study. *International Journal of Obesity and Related Metabolic Disorders, 24,* 1319–1325.

Hope, S., Rodgers, B., & Power, C. (1999). Marital status transitions and psychological distress: Longitudinal evidence from a national population sample. *Psychological Medicine, 29,* 381–389.

Hopkin, K. (2004). Making Methuselah. *Scientific American, 14*(3), 12–17.

Hordinsky, M. (2003). *Hair loss.* Retrieved July 28, 2004, from **http://merck.praxis.md/index.asp? page=bpm_author&article_id=BPM01DE12 &author=1**

Horn, J. L. (1968). Organization of abilities and the development of intelligence. *Psychological Review, 75,* 242–259.

Hörster, F., Surtees, R., & Hoffmann, G. F. (2005). Disorders of intermediary metabolism: Toxic leukoencephalopathies. *Journal of Inherited Metabolic Disease, 28,* 345–356.

Horwill, F. (2004). *Act your age.* Retrieved July 27, 2004, from www.serpentine.org.uk/advice/coach/fh32.php

Horwood, L. J., & Fergusson, D. M. (1998). Breast-feeding and later cognitive and academic outcomes. *Pediatrics, 101,* e9.

Houck, G. M., & Lecuyer-Maus, E. A. (2004). Maternal limit setting during toddlerhood, delay of gratification, and behavior problems at age five. *Infant Mental Health Journal, 25,* 28–46.

Hoven, C. W., Mandell, D. J., & Duarte, C. S. (2003). Mental health of New York City public school children after 9/11: An epidemiologic investigation. In S. W. Coates, J. L. Rosenthal, & D. S. Schechter (Eds.), *September 11: Trauma and human bonds* (pp. 51–74). Hillsdale, NJ: Analytic Press.

Howard, M., Dolovich, L., Kaczorowski, J., Sellors, C., & Sellors, J. (2004). Prescribing of potentially inappropriate medications to elderly people. *Family Practice, 21,* 244–247.

Howe, M. J. A. (1999). *Genius explained.* New York: Cambridge University Press.

Howe, M. L. (2000). *The fate of early memories: Developmental science and the retention of childhood experiences.* Washington, DC: American Psychological Association.

Howe, M. L. (2003). Memories from the cradle. *Current Directions in Psychological Science, 12,* 62–65.

Howe, M. L., & Courage, M. L. (1993). On resolving the enigma of infantile amnesia. *Psychological Bulletin, 113,* 305–326.

Howes, C., Hamilton, C. E., & Phillipsen, L. C. (1998). Stability and continuity of child-caregiver and child-peer relationships. *Child Development, 69,* 418–426.

Howes, C., & Matheson, C. C. (1992). Sequences in the development of competent play with peers: Social and social pretend play. *Developmental Psychology, 28,* 961–974.

Howes, C., & Phillipsen, L. (1992). Gender and friendship: Relationships within peer groups of young children. *Social Development, 1,* 230–242.

Howes, C., & Tonyan, H. (1999). Peer relations. In L. Balter & C. S. Tamis-Lemonda (Eds.), *Child psychology: A handbook of contemporary issues.* Hove, England: Psychology Press.

Hoyert, D. L., Kung, H. C., & Smith, B. L. (2005). Deaths: Preliminary data for 2003. *National Vital Statistics Reports, 53*(15).

Hrdlicka, M., Dudova, I., Beranova, I., et al. (2005). Subtypes of autism by cluster analysis based on structural MRI data. *European Child and Adolescent Psychiatry, 14,* 138–144.

Hubbard, F. O., & van IJzendoorn, M. H. (1991). Maternal unresponsiveness and infant crying across the first 9 months: A naturalistic longitudinal study. *Infant Behavior and Development, 14,* 299–312.

Hubbard, J. A., & Dearing, K. F. (2004). Children's understanding and regulation of emotion in the context of their peer relations. In J. B. Kupersmidt & K. A. Dodge (Eds.), *Children's peer relations: From development to intervention* (pp. 81–99). Washington, DC: American Psychological Association.

Hudak, M. A., & Anderson, D. E. (1990). Formal operations and learning style predict success in statistics and computer science courses. *Teaching of Psychology, 17,* 231–234.

Hudson, I. J. (2003). *Age progression: Keeping special photos current.* Internet Broadcasting Systems, Inc. Retrieved July 30, 2003, from **http://nbc4.com/technology/1936516/detail.html&**

Hudson, J. A., Fivush, R., & Kuebli, J. (1992). Scripts and episodes: The development of event memory. *Applied Cognitive Psychology, 6,* 483–505.

Hueppchen, N. A., Anderson, J. R., & Fox, H. E. (2000). Human immunodeficiency virus infection. In W. R. Cohen, S. H. Sheldon, & I. R. Merkatz (Eds.), *Cherry and Merkatz's complications of pregnancy* (5th ed., pp. 677–691). Philadelpha: Lippincott Williams & Wilkins.

Huesmann, L. R., & Eron, L. D. (1986). *Television and the aggressive child: A cross-national comparison.* Hillsdale, NJ: Erlbaum.

Huh, N. S., & Reid, W. M. (2000). Intercountry, transracial adoption and ethnic identity: A Korean example. *International Social Work, 43,* 75–87.

Hultsch, D. F., Hertzog, C., Small, B. J., & Dixon, R. A. (1999). Use it or lose it: Engaged lifestyle as a buffer of cognitive decline in aging? *Psychology and Aging, 14,* 245–263.

Human Genome Project Information. (2004, October 27). *How many genes are in the human genome?* Retrieved April 24, 2006, from **http://www.ornl.gov/sci/techresources/Human_Genome/faq/genenumber.shtml**

Hummer, R. A., Rogers, R. G., Nam, C. B., & Ellison, C. G. (1999). Religious involvement and U.S. adult mortality. *Demography, 36,* 273–285.

Humphreys, A. P., & Smith, P. K. (1987). Rough and tumble, friendship, and dominance in schoolchildren: Evidence of continuity and change with age. *Child Development, 58,* 201–212.

Hunt, C. E. (2005). Gene-environment interactions: Implications for sudden unexpected deaths in infancy. *Archives of Disease in Childhood, 90,* 48–53.

Hunt, C. E., Lesko, S. M., Vezina, R. M., et al. (2003). Infant sleep position and associated health outcomes. *Archives of Pediatrics and Adolescent Medicine, 157,* 469–474.

Hunt, K. (1991, March 24). The Romanian baby bazaar. *New York Times Magazine,* pp. 24–29.

Huntsinger, C. S., Jose, P. E., Larson, S. L., Balsink, K. D., & Shaligram, C. (2000). Mathematics, vocabulary, and reading development in Chinese American and European American children over the primary school years. *Journal of Educational Psychology, 92,* 745–760.

Hunziker, U. A., & Barr, R. G. (1986). Increased carrying reduces infant crying: A randomized controlled trial. *Pediatrics, 77,* 641–648.

Hur, Y.-M., & Bouchard, T. J., Jr. (1995). Genetic influences on perceptions of childhood family environment: A reared apart twin study. *Child Development, 66,* 330–345.

Hurd, Y. L., Wang, X., Anderson, V., Beck, O., Minkoff, H., & Dow-Edwards, D. (2005). Marijuana impairs growth in mid-gestation fetuses. *Neurotoxicology and Teratology, 27,* 221–229.

Hurst, C. E. (1995). *Social inequality: Forms, causes, and consequences* (2nd ed.). Boston: Allyn & Bacon.

Hurwicz, M.-L., Durham, C. C., Boyd-Davs, S. L., Gatz, M., & Bengtson, V. L. (1992). Salient life events in three-generation families. *Journals of Gerontology: Psychological Sciences and Social Sciences, 47B,* P11–P13.

Huttenlocher, P. R. (1999). Dendritic and synaptic development in human cerebral cortex: Time course and critical periods. *Developmental Neuropsychology, 16,* 347–349.

Huyck, M. H. (1996). Continuities and discontinuities in gender identity. In V. L. Bengtson (Ed.), *Adulthood and aging: Research on continuities and discontinuities* (pp. 98–121). New York: Springer.

Hyde, J. S., & Linn, M. C. (1988). Gender differences in verbal ability: A meta-analysis. *Psychological Bulletin, 104,* 53–69.

Idler, E. L., Musick, M. A., Ellison, C. G., et al. (2003). Measuring multiple dimensions of religion and spirituality for health research: Conceptual background and findings from the 1998 General Social Survey. *Research on Aging, 25,* 327–365.

I Have a Dream Foundation. (2005). *The I Have a Dream Foundation.* Retrieved August 3, 2005, from **http://www.ihad.org**

Inciardi, J. A., Surratt, H. L., & Saum, C. A. (1997). *Cocaine-exposed infants: Social, legal, and public health issues.* Thousand Oaks, CA: Sage.

Ing, M. R., & Okino, L. M. (2002). Outcome study of stereopsis in relation to duration of misalignment in congenital esotropia. *Journal of the American Association for Pediatric Ophthalmology and Strabismus, 6,* 3–8.

Inglehart, R., Basáñez, M., Díez-Mendrano, J., Halman, L., & Luijkx, R. (Eds.). (2004). *Human beliefs and values: A cross-cultural sourcebook based on the 1999–2002 values surveys.* Mexico: Siglo XXI.

Inhelder, B., & Piaget, J. (1958). *The growth of logical thinking from childhood to adolescence.* New York: Basic Books.

Inhelder, B., & Piaget, J. (1964). *The early growth of logic in the child: Classification and seriation.* London: Routledge.

Inhelder, B., & Sinclair, H. (1969). Learning cognitive structures. In P. H. Mussen, J. Langer, & M. Covington (Eds.), *Trends and issues in developmental psychology* (pp. 2–21). New York: Holt, Rinehart & Winston.

Insel, T. R., & Carter, C. S. (1995). The monogamous brain: Prairie voles and the chemistry of mammalian love. *Natural History, 104*(8), 12–14.

Insurance Institute for Highway Safety. (2001). Special issue: Older drivers. *Status Report, 36*(8), 1–8.

Insurance Institute for Highway Safety. (2003). *Fatality facts 2003: Older people.* Arlington, VA: Author.

International Human Genome Sequencing Consortium. (2001). Initial sequencing and analysis of the human genome. *Nature, 409,* 860–921.

Inzlicht, M., & Ben-Zeev, T. (2000). A threatening intellectual environment: Why females are susceptible to experiencing problem-solving deficits in the presence of males. *Psychological Science, 11,* 365–371.

Issacharoff, S., & Harris, E. W. (1997). Is age discrimination really age discrimination? The ADEA's unnatural solution. *New York University Law Review, 72,* 780–840.

Iverson, J. M., & Goldin-Meadow, S. (2005). Gesture paves the way for language development. *Psychological Science, 16,* 367–371.

Jackson, F. (1999). A slightly radical neuron doctrine. *Behavioral and Brain Sciences, 22,* 840–841.

Jackson, G. R., & Owsley, C. (2003). Visual dysfunction, neurodegenerative diseases, and aging. *Neurologic Clinics, 21,* 709–728.

Jackson, T., Fritch, A., Nagasaka, T., & Gunderson, J. (2002). Towards explaining the association between shyness and loneliness: A path analysis with American college students. *Social Behavior and Personality, 30,* 263–270.

Jacobs, J. E., & Klaczynski, P. A. (2002). The development of judgment and decision making during childhood and adolescence. *Current Directions in Psychological Science, 11,* 145–149.

Jacobs, J. E., & Potenza, M. (1991). The use of judgment heuristics to make social and object decisions: A developmental perspective. *Child Development, 62,* 166–178.

Jacobs, S., & Prigerson, H. (2000). Psychotherapy of traumatic grief: A review of evidence for psychotherapeutic treatments. *Death Studies, 24,* 479–495.

Jacobson, K. C., & Crockett, L. J. (2000). Parental monitoring and adolescent adjustment: An ecological perspective. *Journal of Research on Adolescence, 10,* 65–97.

Jacobson, S. W., Chiodo, L. M., & Jacobson, J. L. (1999). Breastfeeding effects on intelligence quotient in 4– and 11–year-old children. *Pediatrics, 103,* e71.

Jacoby, L. L., Bishara, A. J., Hessels, S., & Toth, J. P. (2005). Aging, subjective experience, and cognitive control: Dramatic false remembering by older adults. *Journal of Experimental Psychology: General, 134,* 131–148.

Jacques, S., & Zelazo, P. D. (2001). The Flexible Item Selection Task (FIST): A measure of executive function in preschoolers. *Developmental Neuropsychology, 20,* 573–591.

Jaffe, J., Beebe, B., Felstein, S., Crown, C. L., & Jasnow, M. D. (2001). Rhythms of dialogue in infancy: Coordinated timing in development. *Monographs of the Society for Research in Child Development, 66*(2, Serial No. 265).

Jaffee, S. R., Moffitt, T. E., Caspi, A., & Taylor, A. (2003). Life with (or without) father: The benefits of living with two biological parents depend on the father's antisocial behavior. *Child Development, 74,* 109–126.

Jain, A., Concato, J., & Leventhal, J. M. (2002). How good is the evidence linking breastfeeding and intelligence? *Pediatrics, 109,* 1044–1053.

Jain, A., Sherman, S. N., Chamberlin, L. A., Carter, Y., Powers, S. W., & Whitaker, R. C. (2001). Why don't low-income mothers worry about their preschoolers being overweight? *Pediatrics, 107,* 1138–1146.

Jalkut, M. W., Lerman, S. E., & Churchill, B. M. (2001). Enuresis. *Pediatric Urology, 48,* 1461–1488.

James, D. C., Dobson, B., & American Dietetic Association. (2005). Position of the American Dietetic Association: Promoting and supporting breastfeeding. *Journal of the American Dietetic Association, 105,* 810–818.

James, L. E., Burke, D. M., Austin, A., & Hulme, E. (1998). Production and perception of "verbosity" in younger and older adults. *Psychology and Aging, 13,* 355–367.

James, S. A. (1993). Racial and ethnic differences in infant mortality and low birth weight. *Annals of Epidemiology, 3,* 130–136.

James, W. (1890). *The principles of psychology.* New York: Holt.

Jamison, K. R. (1995). *An unquiet mind.* New York: Knopf.

Jansson, U. B., Hanson, M., Sillén, U., & Hellström, A. L. (2005). Voiding pattern and acquisition of bladder control from birth to age 6 years—A longitudinal study. *Journal of Urology, 174,* 289–293.

Jarvinen, D. W., & Nicholls, J. G. (1996). Adolescents' social goals, beliefs about the causes of social success, and satisfaction in peer relations. *Developmental Psychology, 32,* 435–441.

Jeffcoat, M. K., Geurs, N. C., Reddy, M. S., Cliver, S. P., Goldenberg, R. L., & Hauth, J. C. (2001). Periodontal infection and preterm birth: Results of a prospective study. *Journal of the American Dental Association, 132,* 875–880.

Jensen, A. R. (1969). How much can we boost IQ and scholastic achievement? *Harvard Educational Review, 39,* 1–123.

Job, A., Raynal, M., & Rondet, P. (1999). Hearing loss and use of personal stereos in young adults with antecedents of otitis media. *Lancet, 353*(9146), 35.

Jobe, A. H. (2001). What do home monitors contribute to the SIDS problem? *Journal of the American Medical Association, 285,* 2244–2245.

Johns, F. M. (2005). *But I don't know what to say.* Retrieved February 15, 2005, from **http://www.beliefnet.com/story/128/story_12871.html**

Johnson, B. D. (1973). *Marihuana users and drug subcultures.* New York: Wiley.

Johnson, C. M. (1991). Infant and toddler sleep: A telephone survey of parents in one community. *Journal of Developmental and Behavioral Pediatrics, 12,* 108–114.

Johnson, C. M., & Bradley-Johnson, S. (2002). Construct stability of the Cognitive Abilities Scale-Second Edition for infants and toddlers. *Journal of Psychoeducational Assessment, 20,* 144–151.

Johnson & Johnson Consumer Companies. (2001). *Early infant crying: A parent's guide.* Skillman, NJ: Author.

Johnson, L. A., Safranek, S., & Friemoth, J. (2005). Clinical inquiries. What is the most effective treatment for ADHD in children? *Journal of Family Practice, 54,* 166–168.

Johnson, M. (1997, September). Oprah Winfrey: A life in books. *Life, 20,* 44–52.

Johnson, M. H. (1998). The neural basis of cognitive development. In W. Damon (Series Ed.) & D. Kuhn & R. S. Siegler (Vol. Eds.), *Handbook of child psychology: Vol. 2. Cognition, perception, and language* (5th ed., pp. 1–49). New York: Wiley.

Johnson, M. H. (1999). Developmental neuroscience. In M. H. Bornstein & M. E. Lamb (Eds.), *Developmental psychology: An advanced textbook* (4th ed., pp. 199–230). Mahwah, NJ: Erlbaum.

Johnson, M. K. (2004). Further evidence on adolescent employment and substance use: Differences by race and ethnicity. *Journal of Health and Social Behavior, 45,* 187–197.

Johnson, M. K., Mitchell, K. J., Raye, C. L., & Greene, E. J. (2004). An age-related deficit in prefrontal cortical function associated with refreshing information. *Psychological Science, 15,* 127–132.

Johnson, M. K., Reeder, J. A., Raye, C. L., & Mitchell, K. J. (2002). Second thoughts versus second looks: An age-related deficit in reflectively refreshing just-activated information. *Psychological Science, 13,* 64–67.

Johnson, S. L. (2002). Children's food acceptance patterns: The interface of ontogeny and nutrition needs. *Nutrition Reviews, 60,* S91–S94.

Joint United Nations Programme on HIV/AIDS. (2004). *2004 report on the global AIDS epidemic.* Retrieved May 5, 2006, from **http://www.unaids.org/bangkok2004/GAR2004_html/GAR2004_00_en.htm**

Jones, D. C., Abbey, B. B., & Cumberland, A. (1998). The development of display rule knowledge: Linkages with family expressiveness and social competence. *Child Development, 69,* 1209–1222.

Jones, K. L., Smith, D. W., Ulleland, C. N., & Streissguth, P. (1973). Pattern of malformation in offspring of chronic alcoholic mothers. *Lancet, 301,* 1267–1271.

Jones, P. H., & Ryan, B. P. (2001). Experimental analysis of the relationship between speaking rate and stuttering during mother-child conversation. *Journal of Developmental and Physical Disabilities, 13,* 279–305.

Jongenelis, K., Pot, A. M., Eisses, A. M. H., Beekman, A. T. F., Kluiter, H., & Ribbe, M. W. (2004). Prevalence and risk indicators of depression in elderly nursing home patients: The AGED Study. *Journal of Affective Disorders, 83,* 135–142.

Jordan, B. (1980). *Birth in four cultures: A crosscultural investigation of childbirth in Yucatan, Holland, Sweden, and the United States* (2nd ed.). Montréal, Canada: Eden Press Women's Publications.

Jordan, B. T., & Jordan, S. G. (1990). Jordan Left-Right Reversal Test: An analysis of visual reversals in children and significance for reading problems. *Child Psychiatry and Human Development, 21,* 65–73.

Jordan, J., & Neimeyer, R. (2003). Does grief counseling work? *Death Studies, 27,* 765–786.

Jorgensen, D. L. (1989). *Participant observation: A methodology for human studies.* Newbury Park, CA: Sage.

Joseph, R. (2000). Fetal brain behavior and cognitive development. *Developmental Review, 20,* 81–98.

Joshi, P. T., & O'Donnell, D. A. (2003). Consequences of child exposure to war and terrorism. *Clinical Child and Family Psychology Review, 6,* 275–291.

Jusczyk, P. W. (2002). How infants adapt speech-processing capacities to native-language structure. *Current Directions in Psychological Science, 11,* 15–18.

Kaasinen, V., Vilkman, H., Hietala, J., et al. (2000). Age-related dopamine D2/D3 receptor loss in extrastriatal regions of human brain. *Neurobiology of Aging, 21,* 683–688.

Kagan, J. (1994). *The nature of the child* (10th anniversary ed.). New York: Basic Books.

Kagan, J. (1998). *Three seductive ideas.* Cambridge, MA: Harvard University Press.

Kagan, J., & Gall, S. B. (Eds.). (1998). *The Gale encyclopedia of childhood and adolescence.* Detroit, MI: Thompson Gale.

Kahana, E., Lawrence, R. H., Kahana, B., et al. (2002). Long-term impact of preventive proactivity on quality of life of the old-old. *Psychosomatic Medicine, 64,* 382–394.

Kahneman, D., & Tversky, A. (1982). The psychology of preferences. *Scientific American, 246*(1), 160–173.

Kaiser, L. L., Melgar-Quinonez, H. R., Lamp, C. L., Johns, M. C., Sutherland, J. M., & Harwood, J. O. (2002). Food security and nutritional outcomes of preschool-age Mexican-American children. *Journal of the American Dietetic Association, 102,* 924–929.

Kalat, J. W. (2004). *Biological psychology* (4th ed.). Belmont, CA: Thomson/Wadsworth.

Kalb, L. M., & Loeber, R. (2003). Child disobedience and noncompliance: A review. *Pediatrics, 111,* 641–652.

Kalil, A., Ziol-Guest, K. M., & Coley, R. L. (2005). Perceptions of father involvement patterns in teenage-mother families: Predictors and links to mothers' psychological adjustment. *Family Relations: Interdisciplinary Journal of Applied Family Studies, 54,* 197–211.

Kallman, D. A., Plato, C. C., & Tobin, J. D. (1990). The role of muscle loss in the age-related decline of grip strength: Cross-sectional and longitudinal perspectives. *Journals of Gerontology: Biological Sciences and Medical Sciences, 45A,* M82–M88.

Kalter, H. (2000). Folic acid and human malformations: A summary and evaluation. *Reproductive Toxicology, 14,* 463–476.

Kaltiala-Heino, R., Marttunen, M., Rantanen, P., & Rimpelä, M. (2003). Early puberty is associated with mental health problems in middle adolescence. *Social Science and Medicine, 57,* 1055–1064.

Kanagawa, C., Cross, S. E., & Markus, H. R. (2001). "Who am I?" The cultural psychology of the conceptual self. *Personality and Social Psychology Bulletin, 27,* 90–103.

Kantrowitz, B. (1997, Spring-Summer). Off to a good start: Why the first three years are so crucial to a child's development. *Newsweek, 129,* 6–9.

Kaplan, C. (2003). *Why I'm like this.* New York: Perennial.

Kaplan, K. J., Lachenmeier, F., Harrow, M., et al. (1999–2000). Psychosocial versus biomedical risk factors in Kevorkian's first forty-seven physician-assisted deaths. *Omega, 40,* 109–163.

Kaplan, K. J., O'Dell, J., Dragovic, L. J., McKeon, M. C., Bentley, E., & Telmet, K. L. (1999–2000). An update on the Kevorkian-Reding 93 physician-assisted deaths in Michigan: Is Kevorkian a savior, serial-killer or suicidal martyr? *Omega, 40,* 209–229.

Kaplan, P. S., Bachorowski, J.-A., Smoski, M. J., & Hudenko, W. J. (2002). Infants of depressed mothers, although competent learners, fail to learn in response to their own mothers' infant-directed speech. *Psychological Science, 13,* 268–271.

Kaplowitz, P. B., & Oberfield, S. E. (1999). Reexamination of the age limit for defining when puberty is precocious in girls in the United States: Implications for evaluation and treatment. *Pediatrics, 104,* 936–941.

Kaplowitz, P. B., Slora, E. J., Wasserman, R. C., Pedlow, S. E., & Herman-Giddens, M. E. (2001). Earlier onset of puberty in girls: Relation to increased body mass index and race. *Pediatrics, 108,* 347–353.

Karmiloff-Smith, A. (1996, Fall). The connectionist infant: Would Piaget turn in his grave? *SRCD Newsletter,* 1–3, 10.

Karraker, K. H., Vogel, D. A., & Lake, M. A. (1995). Parents' gender-stereotyped perceptions of newborns: The eye of the beholder revisited. *Sex Roles, 33,* 687–701.

Karsenty, R. (2002). What do adults remember from their high school mathematics? The case of linear functions. *Educational Studies in Mathematics, 51,* 117–144.

Kastenbaum, R. (2000). *The psychology of death* (3rd ed.). New York: Springer.

Kastenbaum, R. (2004). *Death, society, and human experience* (8th ed.). Boston: Allyn & Bacon.

Kaufman, J., & Henrich, C. (2000). Exposure to violence and early childhood trauma. In C. H. Zeanah, Jr. (Ed.), *Handbook of infant mental health* (2nd ed., pp. 195–207). New York: Guilford.

Kazdin, A. E., & Benjet, C. (2003). Spanking children: Evidence and issues. *Current Directions in Psychological Science, 12,* 99–103.

Kearins, J. M. (1981). Visual spatial memory in Australian Aboriginal children of desert regions. *Cognitive Psychology, 13,* 434–460.

Keating, D. (2004). Cognitive and brain development. In R. M. Lerner & L. D. Steinberg (Eds.), *Handbook of adolescent psychology* (2nd ed., pp. 45–84). Hoboken, NJ: Wiley.

Keating, D. P. (1990). Adolescent thinking. In S. S. Feldman & G. R. Elliot (Eds.), *At the threshold: The developing adolescent* (pp. 54–89). Cambridge, MA: Harvard University Press.

Keel, P. K., & Klump, K. L. (2003). Are eating disorders culture-bound syndromes? Implications for conceptualizing their etiology. *Psychological Bulletin, 129,* 747–769.

Kelley, A. E., Schochet, T., & Landry, C. F. (2004). Risk taking and novelty seeking in adolescence: Introduction to part I. In R. E. Dahl & L. P. Spear (Eds.), *Annals of the New York Academy of Sciences: Vol. 1021. Adolescent brain development: Vulnerabilities and opportunities* (pp. 27–32). New York: New York Academy of Sciences.

Kellman, P. J., & Banks, M. S. (1998). Infant visual perception. In W. Damon (Series Ed.) & D. Kuhn & R. S. Siegler (Vol. Eds.), *Handbook of child psychology: Vol. 2. Cognition, perception, and language* (5th ed., pp. 103–146). New York: Wiley.

Kellogg, W. N., & Kellogg, L. A. (1933/1967). *The ape and the child: A study of environmental influence upon early behavior.* New York: Hafner Publishing Company.

Kelly, J. A., & Hansen, D. J. (1987). Social interactions and adjustment. In V. B. van Hasselt & M. Hersen (Eds.), *Handbook of adolescent psychology* (pp. 131–167). New York: Pergamon Press.

Kemper, S. (2001). Over-accommodations and under-accommodations to aging. In N. Charness, D. C. Parks, & B. A. Sabel (Eds.), *Communication, technology, and aging: Opportunities and challenges for the future* (pp. 30–46). New York: Springer.

Kemper, S., & Harden, T. (1999). Experimentally disentangling what's beneficial about elderspeak from what's not. *Psychology and Aging, 14,* 656–670.

Kemper, S., Kynette, D., & Norman, S. (1992). Age differences in spoken language. In R. L. West & J. D. Sinnott (Eds.), *Everyday memory and aging* (pp. 138–152). New York: Springer-Verlag.

Kemper, S., Rash, S., Kynette, D., & Norman, S. (1990). Telling stories: The structure of adults' narratives. *European Journal of Cognitive Psychology, 2,* 205–228.

Kendler, K. S., Bulik, C. M., Silberg, J., Hettema, J. M., Myers, J., & Prescott, C. A. (2000). Childhood sexual abuse and adult psychiatric and substance abuse disorders in women: An epidemiological and cotwin control analysis. *Archives of General Psychiatry, 57,* 953–959.

Kennedy, Q., Mather, M., & Carstensen, L. L. (2004). The role of motivation in the age-related positivity effect in autobiographical memory. *Psychological Science, 15,* 208–214.

Kensington Ladies' Erotica Society. (2002). *Sex, death, and other distractions.* Berkeley, CA: Ten Speed Press.

Kenyon, B. L. (2001). Current research in children's conceptions of death: A critical review. *Omega, 43,* 63–91.

Kessel, B. (2001). Sexuality in the older person. *Age and Ageing, 30,* 121–124.

Kessen, W. (1965). *The child.* New York: Wiley.

Kessler, S. J. (1998). *Lessons from the intersexed.* New Brunswick, NJ: Rutgers University Press.

Ketcham, C. J., & Stelmach, G. E. (2001). Age-related declines in motor control. In J. E. Birren & K. W. Schaie (Eds.), *Handbook of the psychology of aging* (5th ed., pp. 313–348). San Diego, CA: Academic Press.

Ketelaar, T., & Ellis, B. J. (2000). Are evolutionary explanations unfalsifiable? Evolutionary psychology and the Lakatosian philosophy of science. *Psychological Inquiry, 11,* 1–21.

Keysar, B., & Henly, A. S. (2002). Speakers' overestimation of their effectiveness. *Psychological Science, 13,* 207–212.

Kiecolt, K. J. (2003). Satisfaction with work and family life: No evidence of a cultural reversal. *Journal of Marriage and Family, 65,* 23–35.

Kiecolt-Glaser, J. K., & Glaser, R. (1992). Stress and the immune system: Human studies. *American Psychiatric Press Review of Psychiatry, 11,* 169–180.

Kiecolt-Glaser, J. K., & Glaser, R. (2001). Stress and immunity: Age enhances the risks. *Current Directions in Psychological Science, 10*, 18–21.

Kieras, J. E., Tobin, R. M., Graziano, W. G., & Rothbart, M. K. (2005). You can't always get what you want: Effortful control and children's responses to undesirable gifts. *Psychological Science, 16*, 391–396.

Kihlstrom, J. F. (1998). Exhumed memory. In S. J. Lynn & K. M. McConkey (Eds.), *Truth in memory* (pp. 3–31). New York: Guilford.

Kikukawa, A., Yagura, S., & Akamatsu, T. (1999). A 25–year prospective study of visual acuity in the Japan Air Self Defense Force personnel. *Aviation, Space, and Environmental Medicine, 70*, 447–450.

Killen, M., Park, Yoonjung, Lee-Kim, J., & Shin, Y. (2005). Evaluations of children's gender stereotypic activities by Korean parents and non-parental adults residing in the United States. *Parenting: Science and Practice, 5*, 57–89.

Kim, J. E., & Moen, P. (2001). Is retirement good or bad for subjective well-being? *Current Directions in Psychological Science, 10*, 83–86.

Kim, S. (1996). The effects of parenting style, cultural conflict, and peer relations on academic achievement and psychosocial adjustment among Korean immigrant adolescents. *Dissertation Abstracts International, 57* (02), 0578A.

Kim, S., & Feldman, D. C. (1998). Healthy, wealthy, or wise: Predicting actual acceptance of early retirement incentives at three points in time. *Personnel Psychology, 51*, 623–642.

Kim-Cohen, J., Moffitt, T. E., Caspi, A., & Taylor, A. (2004). Genetic and environmental processes in young children's resilience and vulnerability to socioeconomic deprivation. *Child Development, 75*, 651–668.

Kimura, D. (1999). *Sex and cognition.* Cambridge, MA: MIT Press.

Kindler, A. L. (2002). *Survey of the States' limited proficient students and available educational programs and services 2000–2001 summary report.* Washington, DC: National Clearinghouse for English Language Acquisition and Language Instruction Educational Programs.

King, P. M., & Kitchener, K. S. (1994). *Developing reflective judgment: Understanding and promoting intellectual growth and critical thinking in adolescents and adults.* San Francisco: Jossey-Bass.

King, P. M., & Kitchener, K. S. (2002). The Reflective Judgment Model: Twenty years of research on epistemic cognition. In B. K. Hofer & P. R. Pintrich (Eds.), *Personal epistemology: The psychology of beliefs about knowledge and knowing* (pp. 37–61). Mahwah, NJ: Erlbaum.

King, T. (1997). Epidural anesthesia in labor: Benefits versus risks. *Journal of Nurse-Midwifery, 42*, 377–388.

Kinnier, R. T., & Metha, A. T. (1989). Regrets and priorities at three stages of life. *Counseling and Values, 33*, 182–193.

Kinsey, A. C., Pomeroy, W. B., & Martin, C. E. (1948). *Sexual behavior in the human male.* Philadelphia: Saunders.

Kipke, M. D. (Ed.) (1999). *Adolescent development and the biology of puberty: Summary of a workshop on new research.* Washington, D.C.: National Academy Press.

Kirk, K. M., Bailey, J. M., & Martin, N. G. (2000). Etiology of male sexual orientation in an Australian twin sample. *Psychology, Evolution, and Gender, 2*, 301–311.

Kisilevsky, B. S., Hains, S. M. J., Lee, K., et al. (2003). Effects of experience on fetal voice recognition. *Psychological Science, 14*, 220–224.

Klaczynski, P. (2001). Analytic and heuristic processing influences on adolescent reasoning and decision-making. *Child Development, 72*, 844–861.

Klahr, D., & Nigam, M. (2004). The equivalence of learning paths in early science instruction: Effects of direct instruction and discovery learning. *Psychological Science, 15*, 661–667.

Klahr, D., & Wallace, J. G. (1976). *Cognitive development: An information-processing view.* Hillsdale, NJ: Erlbaum.

Klass, D., & Walter, T. (2001). Process of grieving: How bonds are continued. In M. S. Stroebe, R. O. Hansson, W. Stroebe, & H. Schut (Eds.), *Handbook of bereavement research: Consequences, coping, and care* (pp. 431–448). Washington, DC: American Psychological Association.

Klaus, M. H., & Kennell, J. H. (1976). *Maternal-infant bonding: The impact of early separation or loss on family development.* St. Louis, MO: Mosby.

Kleiner, S. M. (1999). Water: An essential but overlooked nutrient. *Journal of the American Dietetic Association, 99*, 200–206.

Kleinman, R. E., & American Academy of Pediatrics Committee on Nutrition. (1998). *Pediatric nutrition handbook* (4th ed.). Elk Grove Village, IL: American Academy of Pediatrics.

Kleinman, R. E., Murphy, J. M., Little, M., et al. (1998). Hunger in children in the United States: Potential behavioral and emotional correlates. *Pediatrics, 101*, e3.

Klesges, R. C., Shelton, M. L., & Klesges, L. M. (1993). Effects of television on metabolic rate: Potential implications for childhood obesity. *Pediatrics, 91*, 281–286.

Klich, L. Z., & Davidson, G. R. (1983). A cultural difference in visual memory: On le voit, on ne le voit plus. *International Journal of Psychology, 18*, 189–201.

Kliegel, M., Moor, C., & Rott, C. (2004). Cognitive status and development in the oldest old: A longitudinal analysis from the Heidelberg Centenarian Study. *Archives of Gerontology and Geriatrics, 39*, 143–156.

Kligman, A. M., Grove, G. L., & Balin, A. (1985). Aging of human skin. In C. E. Finch & E. L. Schneider (Eds.), *Handbook of the biology of aging* (2nd ed., pp. 820–841). New York: Van Nostrand Reinhold.

Kline, D. W., & Scialfa, C. T. (1996). Visual and auditory aging. In J. E. Birren & K. W. Schaie (Eds.), *Handbook of the psychology of aging* (4th ed., pp. 181–203). San Diego, CA: Academic Press.

Kline, G. H., Stanley, S. M., Markman, H. J., et al. (2004). Timing is everything: Pre-engagement cohabitation and increased risk for poor marital outcomes. *Journal of Family Psychology, 18*, 311–318.

Kluckhohn, C. (1951). The study of culture. In D. Lerner & H. D. Lasswell (Eds.), *The policy sciences* (pp. 86–101). Standford, CA: Stanford University Press.

Klug, W. S., Cummings, M. R., & Spencer, C. A. (2006). *Concepts of genetics* (8th ed.). Upper Saddle River, NJ: Prentice Hall.

Klurfeld, D. M. (1999). Nutritional regulation of gastrointestinal growth. *Frontiers in Bioscience, 4*, D299–302.

Knapp, M. R. (1977). The activity theory of aging: An examination in the English context. *Gerontologist, 17*, 553–559.

Knoops, K. T., de Groot, L. C., Kromhout, D., et al. (2004). Mediterranean diet, lifestyle factors, and 10–year mortality in elderly European men and women: The HALE project. *Journal of the American Medical Association, 292*, 1433–1439.

Kochanska, G., & Aksan, N. (2004). Conscience in childhood: Past, present, and future. *Merrill-Palmer Quarterly, 50*, 299–310.

Kochanska, G., Coy, K. C., & Murray, K. T. (2001). The development of self-regulation in the first four years of life. *Child Development, 72*, 1091–1111.

Kochanska, G., Gross, J. N., Lin, M.-H., & Nichols, K. E. (2002). Guilt in young children: Development, determinants, and relations with a broader system of standards. *Child Development, 73*, 461–482.

Kochanska, G., Padavich, D. L., & Koenig, A. L. (1996). Children's narratives about hypothetical moral dilemmas and objective measure of their conscience: Mutual relations and socialization antecedents. *Child Development, 67*, 1420–1436.

Koenig, H. G., George, L. K., & Peterson, B. L. (1998). Religiosity and remission of depression in medically ill older patients. *American Journal of Psychiatry, 155*, 536–542.

Koenig, H. G., Larson, D. B., & Larson, S. S. (2001). Religion and coping with serious medical illness. *The Annals of Pharmacotherapy, 35,* 352–359.

Kohlberg, L. (1963a). Moral development and identification. In H. W. Stevenson (Ed.), *Child psychology: The 62ⁿᵈ yearbook of the National Society for the Study of Education* (pp. 232–277). Chicago: University of Chicago Press.

Kohlberg, L. (1963b). The development of children's orientations toward a moral order: I. Sequence in the development of moral thought. *Vita Humana, 6,* 11–33.

Kohlberg, L. (1969). Stage and sequence: The cognitive-developmental approach to socialization. In D. A. Goslin (Ed.), *Handbook of socialization theory and research* (pp. 347–480). Chicago: Rand McNally.

Kohlberg, L. (1976). Moral stages and moralization: The cognitive developmental approach. In T. Lickona (Ed.), *Moral development and behavior: Theory, research, and social issues* (pp. 31–53). New York: Holt, Rinehart & Winston.

Kohlberg, L., LaCrosse, J., & Ricks, D. (1972). The predictability of adult mental health from childhood behavior. In B. B. Wolman (Ed.), *Manual of child psychopathology* (pp. 1217–1284). New York: McGraw Hill.

Kohler, H.-P., Behrman, J. R., & Skytthe, A. (2005). Partner + children = happiness? The effects of partnerships and fertility on well-being. *Population and Development Review, 31,* 407–446.

Kokis, J. V., Macpherson, R., Toplak, M. E., West, R. F., & Stanovich, K. E. (2002). Heuristic and analytic processing: Age trends and associations with cognitive ability and cognitive styles. *Journal of Experimental Child Psychology, 83,* 26–52.

Kolb, B., & Whishaw, I. Q. (1998). Brain plasticity and behavior. *Annual Review of Psychology, 49,* 43–64.

Kolko, D. J. (2002). Child physical abuse. In J. E. B. Myers, L. Berliner, J. Briere, C. T. Hendrix, & C. Jenny (Eds.), *The APSAC handbook on child maltreatment* (2ⁿᵈ ed., pp. 21–54). Thousand Oaks, CA: Sage.

Kopp, C. B., & Krakow, J. B. (1983). The developmentalist and the study of biological risk: A view of the past with an eye toward the future. *Child Development, 54,* 1086–1108.

Koppelman, K. (2001). Emerging from the anguish: A father's experience with loss and grief. In D. A. Lund (Ed.), *Men coping with grief* (pp. 85–95). Amityville, NY: Baywood.

Koren, G., Bologa, M., & Pastuszak, A. (1993). How women perceive teratogenic risk and what they do about it. In C. L. Keen & C. C. Willhite (Eds.), *Annals of the New York Academy of Science: Vol. 678. Maternal nutrition and pregnancy outcome* (pp. 317–324). New York: New York Academy of Sciences.

Koren, G., Nulman, I., Rovet, J., Greenbaum, R., Loebstein, M., & Einarson, T. (1998). Long-term neurodevelopmental risks in children exposed in utero to cocaine: The Toronto Adoption Study. In J. A. Harvey & B. E. Kosofsky (Eds.), *Annals of the New York Academy of Sciences: Vol 846. Cocaine: Effects on the developing brain* (pp. 306–313). New York: New York Academy of Sciences.

Koski, L. R., & Shaver, P. R. (1997). Attachment and relationship satisfaction across the lifespan. In R. J. Sternberg & M. Hojjat (Eds.), *Satisfaction in close relationships* (pp. 26–55). New York: Guilford.

Kramer, A. F., & Willis, S. L. (2002). Enhancing the cognitive vitality of older adults. *Current Directions in Psychological Science, 11,* 173–177.

Kranz, S., & Siega-Riz, A. M. (2002). Sociodemographic determinants of added sugar intake in preschoolers 2 to 5 years old. *Journal of Pediatrics, 140,* 667–672.

Kreicbergs, U., Valdimarsdóttir, U., Onelöv, E., Henter, J. I., & Steineck, G. (2004). Talking about death with children who have severe malignant disease. *New England Journal of Medicine, 351,* 1175–1186.

Kreider, R. M. (2005). Number, timing, and duration of marriages and divorces: 2001. *Current Population Reports, P70–97.* Washington, DC: U.S. Census Bureau.

Kreider, R. M., & Fields, J. (2005). Living arrangements of children: 2001. *Current Population Reports, P70–104.* Washington, DC: U.S. Census Bureau.

Kreider, R. M., & Fields, J. M. (2002). Number, timing, and duration of marriages and divorces: 1996. *Current Population Reports, P70–80.* Washington, DC: U.S. Census Bureau.

Kreutzer, M. A., Leonard, C., & Flavell, J. H. (1975). An interview study of children's knowledge about memory. *Monographs of the Society for Research in Child Development, 40*(1, Serial No. 159).

Kristensen, P., Irgens, L. M., Daltveit, A. K., & Anderson, A. (1993). Perinatal outcome among children of men exposed to lead and organic solvents in the printing industry. *American Journal of Epidemiology, 137,* 134–144.

Krouscas, J. (2005). *The history of middle schools.* Retrieved February 13, 2005, from **http://www.vmsa.org/VMCENT/history.html**

Krstevska-Konstantinova, M., Charlier, C., Craen, M., et al. (2001). Sexual precocity after immigration from developing countries to Belgium: Evidence of previous exposure to organochlorine pesticides. *Human Reproduction, 16,* 1020–1026.

Krug, E. G., Dahlberg, L. L., Mercy, J. A., Zwi, A. B., & Lozano, R. (2002). *World report on violence and health.* Geneva, Switzerland: World Health Organization.

Kryger, M., Monjan, A., Bliwise, D., & Ancoli-Israel, S. (2004). Sleep, health, and aging: Bridging the gap between science and clinical practice. *Geriatrics, 59,* 24–26, 29–30.

Kübler-Ross, E. (1969). *On death and dying.* New York: Macmillan.

Kübler-Ross, E. (1974). *Questions and answers on death and dying.* New York: Macmillan.

Kuczynski, A. (2004, August 8). The 37–year itch. *New York Times,* Sunday Late Edition-Final, Section 9, p. 1.

Kuhl, P. K. (2001). Speech, language, and developmental change. In F. Lacerda, C. von Hofsten, & M. Heimann (Eds.), *Emerging cognitive abilities in early infancy* (pp. 111–133). Mahwah, NJ: Erlbaum.

Kunda, Z. (1999). *Social cognition: Making sense of people.* Cambridge, MA: MIT Press.

Kunkel, D., Cope-Farrar, K., Farinola, W., Biely, E., Rollin, E., & Donnerstein, E. (2001). *Sex on TV: II. A biennial report to the Kaiser Family Foundation.* Menlo Park, CA: Kaiser Family Foundation.

Kunnanatt, J. T. (2004). Emotional intelligence: The new science of interpersonal effectiveness. *Human Resource Development Quarterly, 15,* 489–495.

Kupperbusch, C. S. (2003). Change in marital satisfaction and change in health in middle-aged and older long-term married couples. *Dissertation Abstracts International, 63* (09), 4419B.

Kurdek, L. A. (1999). The nature and predictors of the trajectory of change in marital quality for husbands and wives over the first 10 years of marriage. *Developmental Psychology, 35,* 1283–1296.

Kurdek, L. A. (2005). What do we know about gay and lesbian couples? *Current Directions in Psychological Science, 14,* 251–254.

Kurson, R. (2004). *Shadow divers.* New York: Random House.

Kyriakou, C., Thomson, K., D'Sa, S., et al. (2005). Low-dose thalidomide in combination with oral weekly cyclophosphamide and pulsed dexamethasone is a well tolerated and effective regimen in patients with relapsed and refractory multiple myeloma. *British Journal of Haematology, 129,* 763–770.

Laditka, J. N., & Laditka, S. B. (2001). Adult children helping older parents: Variations in likelihood and hours by gender, race, and family role. *Research on Aging, 23,* 429–456.

Laguna, K. D., & Babcock, R. (2000). Computer testing of memory across the adult life span. *Experimental Aging Research, 26,* 229–243.

Lahey, B. B., McBurnett, K., & Loeber, R. (2000). Are attention-deficit/hyperactivity disorder and oppositional defiant disorder developmental precursors to conduct disorder? In A. J. Sameroff, M. Lewis, & S. M. Miller (Eds.), *Handbook of developmental psychopathology* (2ⁿᵈ ed., pp. 431–446). New York: Kluwer Academic/Plenum.

Lahmann, C., Bergemann, J., Harrison, G., & Young, A. R. (2001). Matrix metalloproteinase-1 and skin ageing in smokers. *Lancet, 357,* 935–936.

Laidlaw, M. A., Mielke, H. W., Filippelli, G. M., Johnson, D. L., & Gonazales, C. R. (2005). Seasonality and children's blood lead levels: Developing a predictive model using climatic variables and blood lead data from Indianapolis, Indiana, Syracuse, New York, and New Orleans, Lousiana (USA). *Environmental Health Perspectives, 113,* 793–800.

Lamb, M. E. (1998). Fatherhood then and now. In A. Booth & A. C. Crouter (Eds.), *Men in families: When do they get involved? What difference does it make?* (pp. 47–52). Mahwah, NJ: Erlbaum.

Lamb, M. E. (2000). The history of research on father involvement: An overview. *Marriage and Family Review, 29,* 23–42.

Lambert, S. (2005). Gay and lesbian families: What we know and where to go from here. *Family Journal: Counseling and Therapy for Couples and Families, 13,* 43–51.

Lambert, W. E., Genesee, F., Holobow, N., & Chartrand, L. (1993). Bilingual education for majority English-speaking children. *European Journal of Psychology of Education, 8,* 3–22.

Lamborn, S. D., Dornbusch, S. M., & Steinberg, L. (1996). Ethnicity and community context as moderators of the relations between family decision making and adolescent adjustment. *Child Development, 67,* 283–301.

Lamm, M. (1969). *The Jewish way in death and mourning.* New York: J. David.

Lampl, L., Ashizawa, K., Kawabata, M., & Johnson, M. L. (1998). An example of variation and pattern in saltation and stasis growth dynamics. *Annals of Human Biology, 25,* 203–219.

Lampl, L., Veldhuis, J. D., & Johnson, M. L. (1992). Saltation and stasis: A model of human growth. *Science, 258,* 801–803.

Lanes, R., & Gunczler, P. (1998). Final height after combined growth hormone and gonadotrophin-releasing hormone analogue therapy in short healthy children entering into normally timed puberty. *Clinical Endocrinology, 49,* 197–202.

Langaas, T., Mon-Williams, M., Wann, J. P., Pascal, E., & Thompson, C. (1998). Eye movements, prematurity, and developmental co-ordination disorder. *Vision Research, 38,* 1817–1826.

Langer, E. J., & Rodin, J. (2004). The effects of choice and enhanced personal responsibility for the aged: A field experiment in an institutional setting. In R. M. Kowalski & M. R. Leary (Eds.), *The interface of social and clinical psychology: Key readings* (pp. 339–348). New York: Psychology Press.

Lantos, J. (2001, July 20). Life and death in neonatal intensive care. *The Chronicle of Higher Education,* pp. B12–B13.

La Paro, K. M., & Pianta, R. C. (2000). Predicting children's competence in the early school years: A meta-analytic review. *Review of Educational Research, 70,* 443–484.

Lapsley, D. K., Enright, R. D., & Serlin, R. C. (1989). Moral and social education. In J. Worrell & F. Danner (Eds.), *The adolescent as decision-maker: Applications to development and education* (pp. 111–141). San Diego, CA: Academic Press.

Larson, J. H., & Holman, T. B. (1994). Premarital predictors of marital quality and stability. *Family Relations, 43,* 228–237.

Larson, R. (2001a). Children and adolescents in a changing media world. *Monographs of the Society for Research in Child Development, 66*(1, Serial No. 264), 148–154.

Larson, R. W. (2001b). How U.S. children and adolescents spend time: What it does (and doesn't) tell us about their development. *Current Directions in Psychological Science, 10,* 160–164.

Larson, R. W., & Verma, S. (1999). How children and adolescents spend time across the world: Work, play, and developmental opportunities. *Psychological Bulletin, 125,* 701–736.

Larsson, I., & Svedin, C.-G. (2002). Teachers' and parents' reports on 3- to 6-year-old children's sexual behavior—A comparison. *Child Abuse and Neglect, 26,* 247–266.

Larsson, I., Svedin, C.-G., & Friedrich, W. N. (2000). Differences and similarities in sexual behaviour among pre-schoolers in Sweden and USA. *Nordic Journal of Psychiatry, 54,* 251–257.

Lary, J. M., & Paulozzi, L. J. (2001). Sex differences in the prevalence of human birth defects: A population-based study. *Teratology, 64,* 237–251.

Lasky, R. E., Klein, R. E., Yarbrough, C., & Kallio, K. D. (1981). The predictive validity of infant assessments in rural Guatemala. *Child Development, 52,* 847–856.

Lau, D. H., Kommu, S., Mikhailidis, D. P., et al. (2005). The prevalence of hypertension, hyperlipidemia, diabetes mellitus and depression in men with erectile dysfunction. *Journal of Urology, 173,* 1050.

Laucht, M., Essser, G., Baving, L., et al. (2000). Behavioral sequelae of perinatal insults and early family adversity at 8 years of age. *Journal of the American Academy of Child and Adolescent Psychiatry, 39,* 1229–1237.

Lauer, R. H., Lauer, J. C., & Kerr, S. T. (1990). The long-term marriage: Perceptions of stability and satisfaction. *International Journal of Aging and Human Development, 31,* 189–195.

Laurberg, P., Andersen, S., Bülow Pedersen, I., & Carlé, A. (2005). Hypothyroidism in the elderly: Pathophysiology, diagnosis and treatment. *Drugs and Aging, 22,* 23–38.

Laursen, B. (1995). Conflict and social interaction in adolescent relationships. *Journal of Research on Adolescence, 5,* 55–70.

Laursen, B., Coy, K. C., & Collins, W. A. (1998). Reconsidering changes in parent-child conflict across adolescence: A meta-analysis. *Child Development, 69,* 817–832.

Lazar, I., & Darlington, R. B. (1982). Lasting effects of early education: A report from the Consortium for Longitudinal Studies. *Monographs of the Society for Research in Child Development, 47*(2–3, Serial No. 195).

Lee, D. N., & Aronson, E. (1974). Visual proprioceptive control of standing in human infants. *Perception and Psychophysics, 15,* 529–532.

Lee, D. N., Young, D. S., & McLaughlin, C. M. (1984). A roadside simulation of road crossing for children. *Ergonomics, 27,* 1271–1281.

Lee, G. R., DeMaris, A., Bavin, S., & Sullivan, R. (2001). Gender differences in the depressive effect of widowhood in later life. *Journals of Gerontology: Psychological Sciences and Social Sciences, 56B,* S56–S61.

Lee, L., Brittingham, A., Tourangeau, R., et al. (1999). Are reporting errors due to encoding limitations or retrieval failure? Surveys of child vaccination as a case study. *Applied Cognitive Psychology, 13,* 43–63.

Lee, P. A., Kulin, H. E., & Guo, S. S. (2001). Age of puberty among girls and the diagnosis of precocious puberty. *Pediatrics, 107,* 1493.

Lee, S. S., & Hinshaw, S. P. (2004). Severity of adolescent delinquency among boys with and without attention deficit hyperactivity disorder: Predictions from early antisocial behavior and peer status. *Journal of Clinical Child and Adolescent Psychology, 33,* 705–716.

Lee, V. E., & Burkam, D. T. (2002). *Inequality at the starting gate: Social background differences in achievement as children begin school.* Washington, DC: Economic Policy Institute.

Lee, V. E., & Burkam, D. T. (2003). Dropping out of high school: The role of school organization and structure. *American Educational Research Journal, 40,* 353–393.

Lee, V. E., & Smith, J. B. (1997). High school size: Which works best, and for whom? *Educational Evaluation and Policy Analysis, 19,* 205–227.

LeFevre, J.-A., Sadesky, G. S., & Bisanz, J. (1996). Selection of procedures in mental addition: Reassessing the problem-size effect in adults. *Journal of Experimental Psychology: Learning, Memory, and Cognition, 22,* 216–230.

Lehman, H. C. (1953). *Age and achievement.* Princeton, NJ: Princeton University Press.

Lemon, B. W., Bengtson, V. L., & Peterson, J. A. (1972). An exploration of the activity theory of aging: Activity types and life satisfaction among in-movers to a retirement community. *Journal of Gerontology, 27,* 511–523.

Lempers, J. D., & Clark-Lempers, D. S. (1992). Young, middle, and late adolescents' comparisons of the functional importance of five significant relationships. *Journal of Youth and Adolescence, 21*, 53–96.

Lenneberg, E. H. (1967). *Biological foundations of language.* New York: Wiley.

Leon, J., Acuña-Castroviejo, D., Sainz, R. M., Mayo, J. C., Tan, D. X., & Reiter, R. J. (2004). Melatonin and mitochondrial function. *Life Sciences, 75*, 765–790.

Lerner, R. M. (2002). *Concepts and theories of human development* (3rd ed.). Mahwah, NJ: Erlbaum.

Lerner, R. M., Castellino, D. R., Terry, P. A., Villarruel, F. A., & McKinney, M. H. (1995). Developmental contextual perspective on parenting. In M. H. Bornstein (Ed.), *Handbook of parenting* (Vol. 2, pp. 285–309). Mahwah, NJ: Erlbaum.

Lerner, R. M., & Lerner, J. V. (1977). Effects of age, sex, and physical attractiveness on child-peer relations, academic performance, and elementary school adjustment. *Developmental Psychology, 13*, 585–590.

Leroi, A. M. (2005, March 14). A family tree in every gene. *New York Times*, p. A23.

Leshner, A. I. (1998). Foreward. In J. A. Harvey & B. E. Kosofsky (Eds.), *Annals of the New York Academy of Sciences: Vol 846. Cocaine: Effects on the developing brain* (pp. xv–xvii). New York: New York Academy of Sciences.

Lester, B. M., LaGasse, L. L., & Seifer, R. (1998). Cocaine exposure and children: The meaning of subtle effects. *Science, 282*, 633–634.

Letenneur, L. (2004). Risk of dementia and alcohol and wine consumption: A review of recent results. *Biological Research, 37*, 189–193.

Leve, L. D., & Chamberlain, P. (2004). Female juvenile offenders: Defining an early-onset pathway for delinquency. *Journal of Child and Family Studies, 13*, 439–452.

Levenson, R. W., Carstensen, L. L., & Gottman, J. M. (1993). Long-term marriage: Age, gender, and satisfaction. *Psychology and Aging, 8*, 301–313.

Leventhal, T., & Brooks-Gunn, J. (2000). The neighborhoods they live in: The effects of neighborhood residence on child and adolescent outcomes. *Psychological Bulletin, 126*, 309–337.

Leventhal, T., Martin, A., & Brooks-Gunn, J. (2004). The EC-HOME across five national data sets in the 3rd to 5th year of life. *Parenting: Science and Practice, 4*, 161–188.

Levin, J. S., & Taylor, R. J. (1997). Age differences in patterns and correlates of the frequency of prayer. *Gerontologist, 37*, 75–88.

Levine, S. C., Vasilyeva, M., Lourenco, S. F., Newcombe, N. S., & Huttenlocher, J. (2005). Socioeconomic status modifies the sex difference in spatial skill. *Psychological Science, 16*, 841–845.

Levinson, D. J. (1990). A theory of life structure development in adulthood. In C. N. Alexander & E. J. Langer (Eds.), *Higher stages of human development: Perspectives on adult growth* (pp. 35–54). New York: Oxford University Press.

Levinson, D. J. (with Darrow, C. N., Klein, E. B., Levinson, M. H., & McKee, B.). (1978). *The seasons of a man's life.* New York: Knopf.

Levinson, D. J. (with Levinson, M. H.). (1996). *The seasons of a woman's life.* New York: Knopf.

Levy, B. R., & Myers, L. M. (2004). Preventive health behaviors influenced by self-perceptions of aging. *Preventive Medicine, 39*, 625–629.

Levy, B. R., Slade, M. D., Kunkel, S. R., & Kasl, S. V. (2002). Longevity increased by positive self-perceptions of aging. *Journal of Personality and Social Psychology, 83*, 261–270.

Levy, G. D., Barth, J. M., & Zimmerman, B. J. (1998). Associations among cognitive and behavioral aspects of preschoolers' gender role development. *Journal of Genetic Psychology, 159*, 121–126.

Lewis, M. (1999). The nurture assumption. *Social Policy, 29*, 34–43.

Lewis, P. D. (1985). Neuropathological effects of alcohol on the developing nervous system. *Alcohol and Alcoholism, 20*, 195–200.

Lewkowicz, D. J. (1988). Sensory dominance in infants: II. Ten-month-old infants' response to auditory-visual compounds. *Developmental Psychology, 24*, 172–182.

Lewontin, R. (1972). The apportionment of human diversity. *Evolutionary Biology, 6*, 381–398.

Lewontin, R. (2000). *The triple helix: Gene, organism, environment.* Cambridge, MA: Harvard University Press.

Li, S.-C. (2002). Connecting the many levels and facets of cognitive aging. *Current Directions in Psychological Science, 11*, 38–43.

Liaw, F.-r., & Brooks-Gunn, J. (1994). Cumulative familial risks and low-birthweight children's cognitive and behavioral development. *Journal of Clinical Child Psychology, 23*, 360–372.

Libbey, J. E., Sweeten, T. L., McMahon, W. M., & Fujinami, R. S. (2005). Autistic disorder and viral infections. *Journal of Neurovirology, 11*, 1–10.

Liben, L. S., & Bigler, R. S. (2002). The developmental course of gender differentiation: Conceptualizing, measuring, and evaluating constructs and pathways. *Monographs of the Society for Research in Child Development, 67*(2, Serial No. 269).

Lidsky, T. I., & Schneider, J. S. (2003). Lead neurotoxicity in children: Basic mechanisms and clinical correlates. *Brain, 126*, 5–19.

Lieberman, L. (1997). Gender and deconstruction of the race concept. *American Anthropology, 97*, 231–242.

Lieberman, L., & Jackson, F. L. C. (1995). Race and three models of human origin. *American Anthropologist, 97*, 231–242.

Liebert, R., Sprafkin, J. N., & Davidson, E. S. (1982). *The early window: Effects of television on children and youth.* New York: Pergamon Press.

Lillard, A. S., & Witherington, D. C. (2004). Mothers' behavior modifications during pretense and their possible signal value for toddlers. *Developmental Psychology, 40*, 95–113.

Lin, K. K., Sandler, I. N., Ayers, T. S., Wolchik, S. A., & Luecken, L. J. (2004). Resilience in parentally bereaved children and adolescents seeking preventive services. *Journal of Clinical Child and Adolescent Psychology, 33*, 673–683.

Lindenberger, U., & Baltes, P. B. (1994). Sensory functioning and intelligence in old age: A strong connection. *Psychology and Aging, 9*, 339–355.

Linscheid, T. R., & Butz, C. (2003). Anorexia nervosa and bulimia nervosa. In M. C. Roberts (Ed.), *Handbook of pediatric psychology* (3rd ed., pp. 636–651). New York: Guilford.

Liptak, A. (2005, January 4). Ruling is awaited on death penalty for young killers. *New York Times*, p. A1.

Liston, R., Crane, J., Hughes, O., et al. (2002). Fetal health surveillance in labour. *Journal of Obstetrics and Gynaecology Canada, 24*, 342–355.

Litt, J., Taylor, H. G., Klein, N., & Hack, M. (2005). Learning disabilities in children with very low birthweight: Prevalence, neuropsychological correlates, and educational interventions. *Journal of Learning Disabilities, 38*, 130–141.

Livingstone, F. B. (1962). On the non-existence of human races. *Current Anthropology, 3*, 279–281.

Locke, S. E., Kraus, L., Leserman, J., Hurst, M. W., Heisel, J. S., & Williams, R. M. (1984). Life change stress, psychiatric symptoms, and natural killer cell activity. *Psychosomatic Medicine, 46*, 411–453.

Lockhart, K. L., Chang, B., & Story, T. (2002). Young children's beliefs about the stability of traits: Protective optimism? *Child Development, 73*, 1408–1430.

Lockwood, C. J., & Paidas, M. J. (2000). Preeclampsia and hypertensive disorders. In W. R. Cohen, S. H. Sheldon, & I. R. Merkatz (Eds.), *Cherry and Merkatz's complications of pregnancy* (5th ed., pp. 207–231). Philadelphia: Lippincott Williams & Wilkins.

Loeber, R. (1982). The stability of antisocial and delinquent child behavior: A review. *Child Development, 53*, 1431–1446.

Lohmueller, K. E., Wong, L. J., Mauney, M. M., et al. (2006). Patterns of genetic variation in the hypertension candidate gene GRK4: Ethnic variation and haplotype structure. *Annals of Human Genetics, 70*, 27–41.

Lomax, E. M. R., Kagan, J., & Rosenkrantz, B. G. (1978). *Science and patterns of child care*. San Francisco: W. H. Freeman.

Londerville, S., & Main, M. (1981). Security of attachment, compliance, and maternal training methods in the second year of life. *Developmental Psychology, 17*, 289–299.

The longest nine months of my life. (2006). Retrieved March 7, 2006, from http://www.angelfire.com/ny4/justforteenmoms/My

Louis, J. M., Ehrenberg, H. M., Collin, M. F., & Mercer, B. M. (2004). Perinatal intervention and neonatal outcomes near the limit of viability. *American Journal of Obstetrics and Gynecology, 191*, 1398–1402.

Love, C. B., Thomson, E. J., & Royal, C. D. (1999). Ethical issues in research involving human participants. *Current Bibliographies in Medicine 99–3.* Retrieved April 24, 2006, from www.nlm.nih.gov/pubs/cbm/hum_exp.html

Love, J. M., Harrison, L., Sagi-Schwartz, A., et al. (2003). Child care quality matters: How conclusions may vary with context. *Child Development, 74*, 1021–1033.

Low, B. S. (1998). The evolution of human life histories. In C. Crawford & D. L. Krebs (Eds.), *Handbook of evolutionary psychology* (pp. 131–161). Mahwah, NJ: Erlbaum.

Low, R., & Over, R. (1993). Gender differences in solution of algebraic word problems containing irrelevant information. *Journal of Educational Psychology, 85*, 331–339.

Lowe, A. (2004, December 1). *Oprah showers teachers with gifts.* Retrieved February 13, 2005, from http://www.post-gazette.com/pg/04336/419580.stm

Lucas, A., & Cole, T. J. (1992). Reply to letters to the editor. *Lancet, 339*, 613.

Lucas, A., Morley, R., Cole, T. J., Lister, G., & Leeson-Payne, C. (1992). Breast milk and subsequent intelligence quotient in children born preterm. *The Lancet, 339*, 261–264.

Lucas, R. E., Clark, A. E., Georgellis, Y., & Diener, E. (2003). Reexamining adaptation and the set point model of happiness: Reactions to changes in marital status. *Journal of Personality and Social Psychology, 84*, 527–539.

Lumeng, J. C., Gannon, K., Cabral, H. J., Frank, D. A., & Zuckerman, B. (2003). Association between clinically meaningful behavior problems and overweight in children. *Pediatrics, 112*, 1138–1145.

Luna, B., Garver, K. E., Urban, T. A., Lazar, N. A., & Sweeney, J. A. (2004). Maturation of cognitive processes from late childhood to adulthood. *Child Development, 75*, 1357–1372.

Luna, B., & Sweeney, J. A. (2004). The emergence of collaborative brain function: fMRI studies of the development of response inhibition. In R. E. Dahl & L. P. Spear (Eds.), *Annals of the New York Academy of Sciences: Vol. 1021. Adolescent brain development: Vulnerabilities and opportunities* (pp. 296–309). New York: New York Academy of Sciences.

Luna, B., Thulborn, K. R., Munoz, D. P., et al. (2001). Maturation of widely distributed brain function subserves cognitive development. *NeuroImage, 13*, 786–793.

Lundqvist, C., & Sabel, K. G. (2000). Brief report: The Brazelton Neonatal Behavioral Assessment Scale detects differences among newborn infants of optimal health. *Journal of Pediatric Psychology, 25*, 577–582.

Luster, T., Johnson, D. J., Martin, A., Lee, R. E., Lambert, M. C., Bates, L., & Abrams, L. A. (2003, April). *The "Lost Boys" of Sudan: Adapting to life in the U.S.* Paper presented at the meeting of the Society for Research in Child Development, Tampa, FL.

Lutgendorf, S. K., Johnsen, E. L., Cooper, B., et al. (2002). Vascular endothelial growth factor and social support in patients with ovarian carcinoma. *Cancer, 95*, 808–815.

Luu, P., Tucker, D. M., Derryberry, D., Reed, M., & Poulsen, C. (2003). Electrophysiological responses to errors and feedback in the process of action regulation. *Psychological Science, 14*, 47–53.

Lykken, D., & Tellegen, A. (1996). Happiness is a stochastic phenomenon. *Psychological Science, 7*, 186–189.

Lykken, D. T., McGue, M., Tellegen, A., & Bouchard, T. J., Jr. (1992). Emergenesis: Genetic traits that may not run in families. *American Psychologist, 47*, 1565–1577.

Lyman, R. (1992, May 17). "Lost boys of Sudan" find future at end of epic trek. *Chicago Tribune.* Section 1, p. 5.

Lyman, S., Ferguson, S. A., Braver, E. R., & Williams, A. F. (2002). Older driver involvements in police reported crashes and fatal crashes: Trends and projections. *Injury Prevention, 8*, 116–120.

Lynch, E., & Braithwaite, R. (2005). A review of the clinical and toxicological aspects of "traditional" (herbal) medicines adulterated with heavy metals. *Expert Opinion on Drug Safety, 4*, 769–778.

Lyubomirsky, S. (2001). Why are some people happier than others? The role of cognitive and motivational processes in well-being. *American Psychologist, 56*, 239–249.

Lyubomirsky, S., & Ross, L. (1997). Hedonic consequences of social comparison: A contrast of happy and unhappy people. *Journal of Personality and Social Psychology, 73*, 1141–1157.

Maccoby, E. E. (1988). Gender as a social category. *Developmental Psychology, 24*, 755–765.

Maccoby, E. E. (2002). Gender and group process: A developmental perspective. *Current Directions in Psychological Science, 11*, 54–58.

MacKay, D. G., & Abrams, L. (1996). Language, memory, and aging: Distributed deficits and the structure of new-versus-old connections. In J. E. Birren & K. W. Schaie (Eds.), *Handbook of the psychology of aging* (4th ed., pp. 251–265). San Diego, CA: Academic Press.

Madon, S., Guyll, M., Spoth, R., & Willard, J. (2004). Self-fulfilling prophecies: The synergistic accumulative effect of parents' beliefs on children's drinking behavior. *Psychological Science, 15*, 837–845.

Maestripieri, D. (2001). Is there mother-infant bonding in primates? *Developmental Review, 21*, 93–120.

Mahoney, A., Pargament, K. I., Tarakeshwar, N., & Swank, A. B. (2001). Religion in the home in the 1980s and 1990s: A meta-analytic review and conceptual analysis of links between religion, marriage, and parenting. *Journal of Family Psychology, 15*, 559–596.

Maiden, R. J., Peterson, S. A., Caya, M., & Bert, H., Jr. (2003). Personality changes in the old-old: A longitudinal study. *Journal of Adult Development, 10*, 31–39.

Main, M., & George, C. (1985). Responses of abused and disadvantaged toddlers to distress in agemates: A study in the day care setting. *Developmental Psychology, 21*, 407–412.

Main, M., & Solomon, J. (1990). Procedures for identifying infants as disorganized/disoriented during the Ainsworth Strange Situation. In M. T. Greenberg, D. Cicchetti, & E. M. Cummings (Eds.), *Attachment in the preschool years: Theory, research, and intervention* (pp. 121–160). Chicago: University of Chicago Press.

Malina, R. M. (1990). Physical growth and performance during the transitional years (9–16). In R. Montemayor, G. R. Adams, & T. P. Gullotta (Eds.), *From childhood to adolescence: A transitional period?* (Vol. 2, pp. 41–62). Thousand Oaks, CA: Sage.

Malina, R. M., & Bouchard, C. (1991). *Growth, maturation, and physical activity*. Champaign, IL: Human Kinetics Academic.

Malloy, M. H., & Berendes, H. (1998). Does breast-feeding influence intelligence quotients at 9 and 10 years of age? *Early Human Development, 50*, 209–217.

Malloy, M. H., & Freeman, D. H., Jr. (2000). Birth weight- and gestational age-specific sudden infant death syndrome mortality: United States, 1991 versus 1995. *Pediatrics, 105*, 1227–1231.

Mao, A., Burnham, M. M., Goodlin-Jones, B. L., Gaylor, E. E., & Anders, T. F. (2004). A comparison of the sleep-wake patterns of cosleeping and solitary-sleeping infants. *Child Psychiatry and Human Development, 35*, 95–105.

Marable, M. (2000, February 25). We need new and critical study of race and ethnicity. *The Chronicle of Higher Education*, pp. B4–B7.

Maras, A., Laucht, M., Gerdes, D., et al. (2003). Association of testosterone and dihydrotestosterone with externalizing behavior in adolescent boys and girls. *Psychoneuroendocrinology, 28*, 932–940.

March of Dimes. (2002). *United States: Prenatal care*. Retrieved June 26, 2005, from **http://www.marchofdimes.com/peristats/level1.aspx?dv=ms&reg=99&top=5&stop=24&lev=1&slev=1&obj=1**

March of Dimes. (2005). *Spina bifida*. Retrieved December 31, 2005, from **http://www.marchofdimes.com/professionals/681_1224.asp**

March of Dimes Perinatal Data Center. (2000). *Leading categories of birth defects*. Retrieved May 31, 2001, from **http://www.modimes.org/HealthLibrary2/InfantHealthStatistics/bdtable.htm**

March of Dimes Perinatal Data Center. (2005). *PeriStats*. Retrieved December 31, 2005, from **http://www.marchofdimes.com/peristats**

Marchand, H. (2001). Some reflections on postformal thought. *The Genetic Epistemologist, 29*(3). Retrieved June 7, 2004, from **http://www.piaget.org/GE/2001/GE-29-3.html#item2**

Marcia, J. E. (1966). Development and validation of ego-identity status. *Journal of Personality and Social Psychology, 3*, 551–558.

Marcia, J. E. (1980). Ego identity development. In J. Adelson (Ed.), *Handbook of adolescent psychology* (pp. 159–186). New York: Wiley.

Marcus, G. F. (2000). Pabiku and Ga Ti Ga: Two mechanisms infants use to learn about the world. *Current Directions in Psychological Science, 9*, 145–147.

Margaritis, P., Arruda, V. R., Aljamali, M., Camire, R. M., Schlachterman, A., & High, K. A. (2004). Novel therapeutic approach for hemophilia using gene delivery of an engineered secreted activated Factor VII. *Journal of Clinical Investigation, 113*, 1025–1031.

Margolin, G., & Gordis, E. B. (2000). The effects of family and community violence on children. *Annual Review of Psychology, 51*, 445–479.

Markestad, T., Kaaresen, P. I., Rønnestad, A., et al. (2005). Early death, morbidity, and need of treatment among extremely premature infants. *Pediatrics, 115*, 1289–1298.

Markman, E. M., & Seibert, J. (1976). Classes and collections: Internal organization and resulting holistic properties. *Cognitive Psychology, 8*, 561–577.

Marks, D. F., Murray, M., Evans, B., & Willig, C. (2000). *Health psychology: Theory research and practice*. Thousand Oaks, CA: Sage.

Markstrom, C. A., & Iborra, A. (2003). Adolescent identity formation and rites of passage: The Navajo Kinaaldá ceremony for girls. *Journal of Research on Adolescence, 13*, 399–425.

Markus, H., & Nurius, P. (1986). Possible selves. *American Psychologist, 41*, 954–969.

Marmion, S., & Lundberg-Love, P. (2004). Learning masculinity and femininity: Gender socialization from parents and peers across the life span. In M. A. Paludi (Ed.), *Praeger guide to the psychology of gender* (pp. 1–26). Westport, CT: Praeger Publishers.

Marriott, L. K., & Wenk, G. L. (2004). Neurobiological consequences of long-term estrogen therapy. *Current Directions in Psychological Science, 13*, 173–176.

Marshall, E. (2000). The business of stem cells. *Science, 287*, 1419–1421.

Marsiske, M., & Willis, S. L. (1995). Dimensionality of everyday problem solving in older adults. *Psychology and Aging, 10*, 269–283.

Marsland, A. L., Bachen, E. A., Cohen, S., & Manuck, S. B. (2001). Stress, immunity and susceptibility to infectious disease. In A. Baum, T. A. Revenson, & J. E. Singer (Eds.), *Handbook of health psychology* (pp. 683–695). Mahwah, NJ: Erlbaum.

Martensen, R. L., & Jones, D. S. (1997). Male reproductive science when Darwin ruled and Victoria reigned. *Journal of the American Medical Association, 277*, 1325.

Martin, C. L., Eisenbud, L., & Rose, H. (1995). Children's gender-based reasoning about toys. *Child Development, 66*, 1453–1471.

Martin, C. L., & Fabes, R. A. (2001). The stability and consequences of young children's same-sex peer interactions. *Developmental Psychology, 37*, 431–446.

Martin, C. L., & Ruble, D. (2004). Children's search for gender cues: Cognitive perspectives on gender development. *Current Directions in Psychological Science, 13*, 67–70.

Martin, C. L., Ruble, D. N., & Szkrybalo, J. (2002). Cognitive theories of early gender development. *Psychological Bulletin, 128*, 903–933.

Martin, D., Glass, T. A., Bandeen-Roche, K., Todd, A. C., Shi, W., & Schwartz, B. S. (2006). Association of blood lead and tibia lead with blood pressure and hypertension in a community sample of older adults. *American Journal of Epidemiology, 163*, 467–478.

Martin, J. A., Hamilton, B. E., Sutton, P. D., Ventura, S. J., Menacher, F., & Munson, M. L. (2003). Births: Final data for 2002. *National Vital Statistics Reports, 52*(10).

Martin, P., Long, M. V., & Poon, L. W. (2002). Age changes and differences in personality traits and states of the old and very old. *Journals of Gerontology: Psychological Sciences and Social Sciences, 57B*, P144–P152.

Martini, M., & Kirkpatrick, J. (1992). Parenting in Polynesia: A view from the Marquesas. In I. E. Sigel (Series Ed.) & J. L. Roopnarine & D. B. Carter (Vol. Eds.), *Advances in applied developmental psychology: Vol. 5. Parent-child socialization in diverse cultures* (pp. 199–222). Norwood, NJ: Ablex.

Martinson, F. M. (1994). *The sexual life of children*. Westport, CT: Bergin & Garvey.

Martz, L. (1990, February 19). A dirty drug secret. *Newsweek, 115*, 74–77.

Marx, J. (2002). Tackling cancer at the telomeres. *Science, 295*, 2350.

Mascolo, M. F., & Li, J. (Eds.). (2004). *Culture and developing selves: Beyond dichotomization*. San Francisco: Jossey-Bass.

Masland, T., & Nordland, R. (2000, January 17). 10 million orphans. *Newsweek, 135*, 42–45.

Mason, M. K. (1942). Learning to speak after six and a half years of silence. *Journal of Speech Disorders, 7*, 295–304.

Massart, F., Harrell, J. C., Federico, G., & Saggese, G. (2005). Human breast milk and xenoestrogen exposure: A possible impact on human health. *Journal of Perinatology, 25*, 282–288.

Masten, A. S. (2001). Ordinary magic: Resilience processes in development. *American Psychologist, 56*, 227–238.

Masten, A. S., & Coatsworth, J. D. (1998). The development of competence in favorable and unfavorable environments: Lessons from research on successful children. *American Psychologist, 53*, 205–220.

Masters, W. H., & Johnson, V. E. (1966). *Human sexual response*. Boston: Little, Brown & Company.

Matheny, A. P., Jr. (1988). Accidental injuries. In D. K. Routh (Ed.), *Handbook of pediatric psychology* (pp. 108–134). New York: Guilford.

Mather, M., Canli, T., English, T., et al. (2004). Amygdala response to emotionally valenced stimuli in older and younger adults. *Psychological Science, 15*, 259–263.

Mather, M., & Carstensen, L. L. (2003). Aging and attentional biases for emotional faces. *Psychological Science, 14*, 409–415.

Mather, M., & Johnson, M. K. (2000). Choice-supportive source monitoring: Do our decisions seem better to us as we age? *Psychology and Aging, 15*, 596–606.

Mathews, T. J., MacDorman, M. F., & Menacker, F. (2002). Infant mortality statistics from the 1999 period linked birth/infant death data set. *National Vital Statistics Reports, 50*(4).

Matsumoto, A. (1991). Synaptogenic action of sex steroids in developing and adult neuroendocrine brain. *Psychoneuroendocrinology, 16*, 25–40.

Mauer, D., & Lewis, T. L. (2001). Visual acuity and spatial contrast sensitivity: Normal development and underlying mechanisms. In C. A. Nelson & M. Luciana (Eds.), *Handbook of developmental cognitive neuroscience* (pp. 237–251). Cambridge, MA: MIT Press.

Maugh, T., II. (2004). *Obituary: Roy Walford, 79; eccentric UCLA scientist touted food restriction.* Retrieved May 31, 2006, from **http://www. grg.org/RWalford.htm**

Maughan, R. J. (2003). Impact of mild dehydration on wellness and on exercise performance. *European Journal of Clinical Nutrition, 57*(Suppl. 2), S19–23.

Maunsell, C., Smith, H. V., & Stevenson, C. (2000). What happens in court? The development of understanding of the legal system in a sample of Irish children and adults. *Irish Journal of Psychology, 21*(3–4), 215–226.

Maurer, T. J., Weiss, E. M., & Barbeite, F. G. (2003). A model of involvement in work-related learning and development activity: The effects of individual, situational, motivational, and age variables. *Journal of Applied Psychology, 88,* 707–724.

May, C. P., Hasher, L., & Foong, N. (2005). Implicit memory, age, and time of day: Paradoxical priming effects. *Psychological Science, 16,* 96–100.

May-Benson, T., Ingolia, P., & Koomar, J. (2002). Daily living skills and developmental coordination disorder. In S. A. Cermak & D. Larkin (Eds.), *Developmental coordination disorder* (pp. 140–156). Albany, NY: Delmar.

Mayer, J. D., Salovey, P., & Caruso, D. R. (2000). Emotional intelligence as zeitgeist, as personality, and as a mental ability. In R. Bar-On & J. D. A. Parker (Eds.), *The handbook of emotional intelligence* (pp. 92–117). San Francisco: Jossey-Bass.

Mayer, R. E. (2004). Should there be a three-strikes rule against pure discovery learning? *American Psychologist, 59,* 14–19.

Maynard, A. E., & Greenfield, P. M. (2003). Implicit cognitive development in cultural tools and children: Lessons from Maya Mexico. *Cognitive Development, 18,* 489–510.

Maynard, L. M., Galuska, D. A., Blanck, H. M., & Serdula, M. K. (2003). Maternal perceptions of weight status of children. *Pediatrics, 111,* 1226–1231.

Maynard, R. (1995). Teenage childbearing and welfare reform: Lessons from a decade of demonstration and evaluation research. *Children and Youth Services Review, 17,* 309–332.

McArdle, J. J., Ferrer-Caja, E., Hamagami, F., & Woodcock, R. W. (2002). Comparative longitudinal structural analyses of the growth and decline of multiple intellectual abilities over the life span. *Developmental Psychology, 38,* 115–142.

McCabe, L. A., Cunnington, M., & Brooks-Gunn, J. (2004). The development of self-regulation in young children: Individual characteristics and environmental contexts. In R. F. Baumeister & K. D. Vohs (Eds.), *Handbook of self-regulation: Research, theory, and applications* (pp. 340–356). New York: Guilford.

McCall, R. B., Appelbaum, M. I., & Hogarty, P. S. (1973). Developmental changes in mental performance. *Monographs of the Society for Research in Child Development, 38*(3, Serial No. 150).

McClain, C. (1982). Toward a comparative framework for the study of childbirth: A review of the literature. In M. A. Kay (Ed.), *Anthropology of human birth* (pp. 25–59). Philadelphia: F. A. Davis.

McClelland, D. C., Constantian, C. A., Regalado, D., & Stone, C. (1978). Making it to maturity. *Psychology Today, 12*(6), 42–46.

McClure, E. B. (2000). A meta-analytic review of sex differences in facial expression processing and their development in infants, children, and adolescents. *Psychological Bulletin, 126,* 424–453.

McColm, J. R., & Fleck, B. W. (2001). Retinopathy of prematurity: Causation. *Seminars in Neonatology, 6,* 453–460.

McCormick, D. P., Baldwin, C. D., Klecan-Aker, J. S., Swank, P. R., & Johnson, D. L. (2001). Association of early bilateral middle ear effusion with language at age 5 years. *Ambulatory Pediatrics, 1,* 87–90.

McCrae, R. R., & Costa, P. T., Jr. (1994). The stability of personality: Observation and evaluations. *Current Directions in Psychological Science, 3,* 173–175.

McCrae, R. R., & Costa, P. T., Jr. (2003). *Personality in adulthood: A five-factor theory perspective.* New York: Guilford.

McCrae, R. R., Costa, P. T., Jr., de Lima, M. P., et al. (1999). Age differences in personality across the adult life span: Parallels in five cultures. *Developmental Psychology, 35,* 466–477.

McCrae, R. R., Costa, P. T., Jr., Terracciano, A., et al. (2002). Personality trait development from age 12 to age 18: Longitudinal, cross-sectional and cross-cultural analyses. *Journal of Personality and Social Psychology, 83,* 1456–1468.

McDaniel, A. K., & Coleman, M. (2003). Women's experiences of midlife divorce following long-term marriage. *Journal of Divorce and Remarriage, 38*(3–4), 103–128.

McDevitt, T. M., & Rowe, P. M. (2002). *The United States in international context: 2000.* Washington, DC: U.S. Census Bureau. Retrieved April 21, 2006, from **http://www.census.gov/prod/ 2002pubs/c2kbr01-11.pdf**

McDonald, K. A. (1999, April 9). Shared paternity in South American tribes confounds biologists and anthropologists. *The Chronicle of Higher Education,* pp. A19–A20.

McElderry, D. H., & Omar, H. A. (2003). Sex education in the schools: What role does it play? *International Journal of Adolescent Medicine and Health, 15,* 3–9.

McEwen, B. S. (1999). Stress and hippocampal plasticity. *Annual Review of Neuroscience, 22,* 105–122.

McGillicuddy-De Lisi, A. V., Watkins, C., & Vinchur, A. J. (1994). The effect of relationship on children's distributive justice reasoning. *Child Development, 65,* 1694–1700.

McGrath, J. (1999). Hypothesis: Is low prenatal vitamin D a risk-modifying factor for schizophrenia? *Schizophrenia Research, 40,* 173–177.

McGraw, M. B. (1935). *Growth: A study of Johnny and Jimmy.* New York: Appleton-Century.

McGraw, M. B. (1981). Challenges for students of infancy. In L. P. Lipsitt, C. K. Rovee-Collier, & H. Harlene (Eds.), *Advances in infancy research* (Vol. 1, pp. xv-xxii). Norwood, NJ: Ablex.

McGraw, M. B. (1985). Professional and personal blunders in child development. *The Psychological Record, 35,* 165–170.

McHale, K., & Cermak, S. A. (1992). Fine motor activities in elementary school: Preliminary findings and provisional implications for children with fine motor problems. *American Journal of Occupational Therapy, 46,* 898–903.

McHale, S. M., Crouter, A. C., & Tucker, C. J. (2001). Free-time activities in middle childhood: Links with adjustment in early adolescence. *Child Development, 72,* 1764–1778.

McHale, S. M., Shanahan, L., Updegraff, K. A., Crouter, A. C., & Booth, A. (2004). Developmental and individual differences in girls' sex-typed activities in middle childhood and adolescence. *Child Development, 75,* 1575–1593.

McKey, R. H., Condelli, L., Ganson, H., Barrett, B., McConkey, C., & Plantz, M. (1985). *The impact of Head Start on children, family, and communities: Final report of the Head Start Evaluation, Synthesis and Utilization Project (DHHS Pub. No. OHDS 85–31193).* Washington, DC: U.S. Government Printing Office.

McKinlay, J. B., & McKinlay, M. (1981). Medical measures and the decline of mortality. In P. Conrad & R. Kern (Eds.), *The sociology of health and illness: Critical perspectives* (pp. 12–30). New York: St. Martin's Press.

McKinney, M. L. (1998). The juvenilized ape myth—our "overdeveloped" brain. *BioScience, 48,* 109–116.

McKnight, A. J. (2000/2001). Too old to drive? *Issues in Science and Technology, 17*(2), 63–69.

McNeely, C. A., Nonnemaker, J. M., & Blum, R. W. (2002). Promoting school connectedness: Evidence from the National Longitudinal Study of Adolescent Health. *Journal of School Health, 72,* 138–146.

McNeil, C. B., Capage, L. C., Bahl, A., & Blanc, H. (1999). Importance of early intervention for disruptive behavior problems: Comparison of treatment and waitlist-control groups. *Early Education and Development, 10*, 445–454.

McWhirter, B. T. (1990). Loneliness: A review of current literature, with implications for counseling and research. *Journal of Counseling and Development, 68*, 417–422.

Mednick, S. A., Huttunen, M. O., & Machón, R. A. (1994). Prenatal influenza infections and adult schizophrenia. *Schizophrenia Bulletin, 20*, 263–267.

Meeus, W., Iedema, J., Helsen, M., & Vollebergh, W. (1999). Patterns of adolescent identity development: Review of literature and longitudinal analysis. *Developmental Review, 19*, 419–461.

Meier, J. (2003, June 20). *Kindergarten Readiness Study: Head Start success. Interim report.* Preschool Services Department of San Bernardino County.

xMeisels, S. J., & Shonkoff, J. P. (2000). Early childhood intervention: A continuing evolution. In J. P. Shonkoff & S. J. Meisels (Eds.), *Handbook of early childhood intervention* (2nd ed., pp. 3–31). New York: Cambridge University Press.

Meltzer, H. Y. (2000). Genetics and etiology of schizophrenia and bipolar disorder. *Biological Psychiatry, 47*, 171–173.

Menn, L., & Ratner, N. B. (Eds.). (2000). *Methods for studying language production.* Mahwah, NJ: Erlbaum.

Mensch, B. S., Bruce, J., & Greene, M. E. (1998). *The uncharted passage: Girls' adolescence in the developing world.* New York: Population Council.

Merck Institute of Aging and Health. (2005). *The state of aging and health in America 2004.* Washington, DC: Merck Institute of Aging and Health & Centers for Disease Control and Prevention. Retrieved April 23, 2006, from **http://www.cdc.gov/aging/pdf/State_of_Aging _and_Health_in_America_2004.pdf**

Meredith, D. B., & Holman, T. B. (2001). Breaking up before and after marriage. In T. B. Holman (Ed.), *Premarital prediction of marital quality or breakup: Research, theory, and practice* (pp. 47–77). New York: Kluwer.

Mesibov, G. B., Schroeder, C. S., & Wesson, L. (1977). Parental concerns about their children. *Journal of Pediatric Psychology, 2*, 13–17.

Mesman, J., & Koot, H. M. (2001). Early preschool predictors of preadolescent internalizing and externalizing DSM-IV diagnoses. *Journal of the American Academy of Child and Adolescent Psychiatry, 40*, 1029–1036.

Meston, C. M., & Frohlich, P. F. (2003). Love at first fright: Partner salience moderates roller-coaster-induced excitation transfer. *Archives of Sexual Behavior, 32*, 537–544.

MetLife Mature Market Institute. (2005, October). *The MetLife market survey of assisted living costs.* New York: MetLife. Retrieved April 22, 2006, from **http://www.metlife.com/WPSAssets/ 17307883101138293602V1F2005Assisted LivingSurvey.pdf**

Meuleman, E. J. (2002). Prevalence of erectile dysfunction: Need for treatment? *International Journal of Impotence Research, 14*(Suppl. 1), S22–S28.

Meyer-Bahlburg, H. F., Gruen, R. S., New, M. I., et al. (1996). Gender change from female to male in classical congenital adrenal hyperplasia. *Hormones and Behavior, 30*, 319–332.

Michael, R. T., Gagnon, J. H., Laumann, E. O., & Kolata, G. (1994). *Sex in America: A definitive survey.* Boston: Little, Brown & Company.

Midyett, L. K., Moore, W. V., & Jacobson, J. D. (2003). Are pubertal changes in girls before age 8 benign? *Pediatrics, 111*, 47–51.

Mielke, H. W. (1999). Lead in the inner cites. *American Scientist, 87*(1), 62–73.

Milgrom, J., Westley, D. T., & Gemmill, A. W. (2004). The mediating role of maternal responsiveness in some longer term effects of postnatal depression on infant development. *Infant Behavior and Development, 27*, 443–454.

Miller, A. F., Jr., & Hanson, M. (2000). Mismatches. *Across the Board, 37*(6), 25–29.

Miller, A. S., & Stark, R. (2002). Gender and religiousness: Can socialization explanations be saved? *American Journal of Sociology, 107*, 1399–1423.

Miller, B. C. (2002). Family influences on adolescent sexual and contraceptive behavior. *Journal of Sex Research, 39*, 22–26.

Miller, D. W. (2001, August 10). Love me, miss me, eat me. *The Chronicle of Higher Education.* Retrieved February 17, 2005, from **http:// chronicle.com/prm/weekly/v47/i48/48a01501. htm**

Miller, E., Cradock-Watson, J. E., & Pollack, T. M. (1982). Consequences of confirmed maternal rubella at successive stages of pregnancy. *Lancet, 320*, 781–784.

Miller, G. A. (1956). The magical number seven, plus or minus two: Some limits on our capacity for processing information. *Psychological Review, 63*, 81–97.

Miller, G. A., & Keller, J. (2000). Psychology and neuroscience: Making peace. *Current Directions in Psychological Science, 9*, 212–215.

Miller, P. H. (2002). *Theories of developmental psychology* (4th ed.). New York: Worth.

Mills, T. L., Wakeman, M. A., & Fea, C. B. (2001). Adult grandchildren's perceptions of emotional closeness and consensus with their maternal and paternal grandparents. *Journal of Family Issues, 22*, 427–455.

Mims, C. (2004, May/June). Addicted to love. *Zoogoer.* Retrieved December 19, 2004, from **http://nationalzoo.si.edu/Publications/ZooGoer/ 2004/3/monogamy.cfm**

Mindell, J. A. (1999). Empirically supported treatments in pediatric psychology: Bedtime refusal and night wakings in young children. *Journal of Pediatric Psychology, 24*, 465–481.

Mindell, J. A., & Dahl, R. E. (1998). Sleep. In R. T. Ammerman & J. V. Campo (Eds.), *Handbook of pediatric psychology and psychiatry* (Vol. 1, pp. 162–181). Needham Heights, MA: Allyn & Bacon.

Mirowsky, J., & Ross, C. E. (2003). *Education, social status, and health.* New York: A. de Gruyter.

Miyamoto, Y., Nisbett, R. E., & Masuda, T. (2006). Culture and the physical environment: Holistic versus analytic perceptual affordances. *Psychological Science, 17*, 113–119.

Mize, J., & Ladd, G. W. (1990). Toward the development of successful social skills training for preschool children. In S. R. Asher & J. D. Coie (Eds.), *Peer rejection in childhood* (pp. 338–361). New York: Cambridge University Press.

Moe, V., & Slinning, K. (2002). Prenatal drug exposure and the conceptualization of long-term effects. *Scandinavian Journal of Psychology, 43*, 41–47.

Moen, P. K., Kim, J. E., & Hofmeister, H. (2001). Couples' work/retirement transitions, gender, and marital quality. *Social Psychology Quarterly, 64*, 55–71.

Moffitt, T. E. (1993). Adolescence-limited and life-course persistent antisocial behavior: A developmental taxonomy. *Psychological Review, 100*, 674–701.

Mojet, J., Christ-Hazelhof, E., & Heidema, J. (2001). Taste perception with age: Generic or specific losses in threshold sensitivity to the five basic tastes? *Chemical Senses, 26*, 845–860.

Monastersky, R. (2001, July 6). New research shows babies employ many tricks to pick up language. *The Chronicle of Higher Education*, p. A14.

Mondschein, E. R., Adolph, K. E., & Tamis-LeMonda, C. S. (2000). Gender bias in mothers' expectations about infant crawling. *Journal of Experimental Child Psychology, 77*, 304–316.

Moneta, G. B., Schneider, B., & Csikszentmihalyi, M. (2001). A longitudinal study of the self-concept and experiential components of self-worth and affect across adolescence. *Applied Developmental Science, 5*, 125–142.

Money, J., & Ehrhardt, A. A. (1972). *Man and woman, boy and girl.* Baltimore, MD: John Hopkins University Press.

Monobe, H., Ishibashi, T., Fujishiro, Y., Shinogami, M., & Yano, J. (2003). Factors associated with poor outcome in children with acute otitis media. *Acta Oto-laryngologica, 123*, 564–568.

Monson, J. P., Drake, W. M., Carroll, P. V., Weaver, J. U., Rodriguez-Arnao, J., & Savage, M. O. (2002). Influence of growth hormone on accretion of bone mass. *Hormone Research, 58*(Suppl. 1), 52–56.

Montagu, A. (1989). *Growing young* (2nd ed.). Granby, MA: Bergin & Garvey.

Montemayor, R., & Eisen, M. (1977). The development of self-conceptions from childhood to adolescence. *Developmental Psychology, 13*, 314–319.

Montoya, I. D., Atkinson, J., & McFaden, W. C. (2003). Best characteristics of adolescent gateway drug prevention programs. *Journal of Addictions Nursing, 14*, 75–83.

Moore, C., & Lemmon, K. (2001). The nature and utility of the temporally extended self. In C. Moore & K. Lemmon (Eds.), *The self in time: Developmental perspectives* (pp. 1–13). Mahwah, NJ: Erlbaum.

Moore, K. L., & Persaud, T. V. N. (2003). *The developing human: Clinically oriented embryology* (7th ed.). Philadelphia: Saunders.

Moore, M. K., Borton, R., & Darby, B. L. (1978). Visual tracking in young infants: Evidence for object identity or object permanence? *Journal of Experimental Child Psychology, 25*, 183–198.

Moore, M. K., & Meltzoff, A. N. (1999). New findings on object permanence: A developmental difference between two types of occlusion. *British Journal of Developmental Psychology, 17*, 623–644.

Moreland, R. L., & Beach, S. R. (1992). Exposure effects in the classroom: The development of affinity among students. *Journal of Experimental Social Psychology, 28*, 255–276.

Morioka, M. (2001). Reconsidering brain death: A lesson from Japan's fifteen years of experience. *Hastings Center Report, 31*(4), 41–46.

Morison, P., & Masten, A. S. (1991). Peer reputation in middle childhood as a predictor of adaptation in adolescence: A seven-year follow-up. *Child Development, 62*, 991–1007.

Morning edition. (2001, April 2). *Interview: Dr. Robert N. Butler discusses what the human body would look like if it was built to last for 200 years or more.* Transcript available from http://www.npr.org

Morrell, R. W., Mayhorn, C. B., & Bennett, J. (2000). A survey of World Wide Web use in middle-aged and older adults. *Human Factors, 42*, 175–182.

Morrell, R. W., & Park, D. C. (1993). The effects of age, illustrations, and task variables on the performance of procedural assembly tasks. *Psychology and Aging, 8*, 389–399.

Morrell, R. W., Park, D. C., Mayhorn, C. B., & Kelley, C. L. (2000). Effects of age and instructions on teaching older adults to use ELDERCOMM, an electronic bulletin board system. *Educational Gerontology, 26*, 221–235.

Morris, B. J., & Sloutsky, V. (2001). Children's solutions of logical versus empirical problems: What's missing and what develops? *Cognitive Development, 16*, 907–928.

Morrongiello, B. A., Fenwick, K. D., Hillier, L., & Chance, G. (1994). Sound localization in newborn human infants. *Developmental Psychobiology, 27*, 519–538.

Morrow, D., & Leirer, V. O. (1999). Designing medication instructions for older adults. In D. C. Park, R. W. Morrell, & K. Shifren (Eds.), *Processing of medical information in aging patients: Cognitive and human factors perspectives* (pp. 249–265). Mahwah, NJ: Erlbaum.

Morsy, S. (1982). Childbirth in an Egyptian village. In M. A. Kay (Ed.), *Anthropology of human birth* (pp. 147–174). Philadelphia: F. A. Davis.

Mortensen, E. L., Michaelsen, K. F., Sanders, S. A., & Reinisch, J. M. (2002). The association between duration of breastfeeding and adult intelligence. *Journal of the American Medical Association, 287*, 2365–2371.

Moshman, D. (1998). Cognitive development beyond childhood. In W. Damon (Series Ed.) & D. Kuhn & R. S. Siegler (Vol. Eds.), *Handbook of child psychology: Vol. 2. Cognition, perception, and language* (5th ed., pp. 947–978). New York: Wiley.

Mosko, S., Richard, C., & McKenna, J. (1997). Infant arousals during mother-infant bed sharing: Implications for infant sleep and sudden infant death syndrome research. *Pediatrics, 100*, 841–849.

Motocross—Travis Pastrana. (2005). Retrieved April 22, 2005, from www.kidzworld.com/site/p1739.htm

Motta, M., Bennati, E., Ferlito, L., Malaguarnera, M., & Motta, L. (2005). Successful aging in centenarians: Myths and reality. *Archives of Gerontology and Geriatrics, 40*, 241–251.

Moxey, E. D., O'Connor, J. P., Novielli, K. D., Teutsch, S., & Nash, D. B. (2003). Prescription drug use in the elderly: A descriptive analysis. *Health Care Financing Review, 24*, 127–141.

Moyers, S., & Bailey, L. B. (2001). Fetal malformations and folate metabolism: Review of recent evidence. *Nutrition Reviews, 59*, 215–224.

Mroczek, D. K., & Spiro, A., III. (2005). Change in life satisfaction during adulthood: Findings from the Veterans Affairs Normative Aging Study. *Journal of Personality and Social Psychology, 88*, 189–202.

Mueller, C. M., & Dweck, C. S. (1998). Praise for intelligence can undermine children's motivation and performance. *Journal of Personality and Social Psychology, 75*, 33–52.

Mueller, M. M., Wilhelm, B., & Elder, G. H., Jr. (2002). Variations in grandparenting. *Research on Aging, 24*, 360–388.

Müller, O., & Krawinkel, M. (2005). Malnutrition and health in developing countries. *Canadian Medical Association Journal, 173*, 279–286.

Mullett, E., & Stolberg, A. L. (2002). Divorce and its impact on the intimate relationships of young adults. *Journal of Divorce and Remarriage, 38*(1–2), 39–60.

Mulligan, G. M., Brimhall, D., & West, J. (2005). *Child care and early education arrangements of infants, toddlers, and preschoolers: 2001* (NCES Publication No. 2006–039). U.S. Department of Education, National Center for Education Statistics, Washington, DC: U.S. Government Printing Office.

Mullins, E. R., & Irvin, J. L. (2000). Transition into middle school. *Middle School Journal, 31*, 57–60.

Mullis, I. V. S., Martin, M. O., Gonzalez, E. J., & Chrostowski, S. J. (2004). *TIMSS 2003 International Mathematics Report.* Boston: TIMSS & PIRLS International Study Center, Lynch School of Education, Boston College.

Munn, P., & Dunn, J. (1989). Temperament and the developing relationship between siblings. *International Journal of Behavioral Development, 12*, 433–451.

Muraskas, J. K., Myers, T. F., Lambert, G. H., & Anderson, C. L. (1992). Intact survival of a 280–g infant: An extreme case of growth retardation with normal cognitive development at two years of age. *Acta Paediatrica, 382*(Suppl.), 16–20.

Murata, M. (2000). Secular trends in growth and changes in eating patterns of Japanese children. *The American Journal of Clinical Nutrition, 72*, 1379S–1383S.

Murphy, C., Schubert, C. R., Cruickshanks, K. J., Klein, B. E., Klein, R., & Nondahl, D. M. (2002). Prevalence of olfactory impairment in older adults. *Journal of the American Medical Association, 288*, 2307–2312.

Murray, D. M. (2003). *The lively shadow: Living with the death of a child.* New York: Ballantine Books.

Murray, J. A. (2002). Communicating with the community about grieving: A description and review of the foundations of a broken leg analogy of grieving. *Journal of Loss and Trauma, 7*, 47–69.

Murray, T. (2003). Wait not, want not: Factors contributing to the development of anorexia nervosa and bulimia nervosa. *The Family Journal, 11*, 276–280.

Mustillo, S., Worthman, C., Erkanli, A., Keeler, G., Angold, A., & Costello, E. J. (2003). Obesity and psychiatric disorder: Developmental trajectories. *Pediatrics, 111*, 851–859.

Muuss, R. E. H. (1988). *Theories of adolescence.* New York: Random House.

Mwamwenda, T. S. (1993). Formal operations and academic achievement. *Journal of Psychology, 127*, 99–103.

Myers, D. G. (1992). *The pursuit of happiness.* New York: Avon Books.

Myers, D. G. (2002). *Intuition: Its powers and perils.* New Haven, CT: Yale University Press.

Nagel, J. (1994). Constructing ethnicity: Creating and recreating ethnic identity and culture. *Social Problems, 41,* 152–176.

Nainar, S. M., & Crall, J. J. (1997). Caries experience in inner-city preschoolers at the time of their initial dental visit. *ASDC Journal of Dentistry for Children, 64,* 421–424.

Nakamura, J., & Csikszentmihalyi, M. (2002). The concept of flow. In C. R. Snyder & S. J. Lopez (Eds.), *Handbook of positive psychology* (pp. 89–105). New York: Oxford University Press.

Napolitano, A. C., & Sloutsky, V. M. (2004). Is a picture worth a thousand words? The flexible nature of modality dominance in young children. *Child Development, 75,* 1850–1870.

Narring, F., Stronski Huwiler, S. M., & Michaud, P. A. (2003). Prevalence and dimensions of sexual orientation in Swiss adolescents: A cross-sectional survey of 16 to 20–year-old students. *Acta Paediatrica, 92,* 233–239.

Nathan, R. (2005). *My freshman year: What a professor learned by becoming a student.* Ithaca, NY: Cornell University Press.

Nathanielsz, P. W. (1996). The timing of birth. *American Scientist, 84*(6), 562–569.

Nathwani, A. C., Davidoff, A. M, & Linch, D. C. (2005). A review of gene therapy for haematological disorders. *British Journal of Haematology, 128,* 3–17.

National Association for the Education of Young Children. (1997). *Developmentally appropriate practice in early childhood programs serving children from birth through age 8.* Retrieved May 9, 2006, from **http://www.naeyc.org/about/positions/pdf/PSDAP98.PDF**

National Association for the Education of Young Children. (1998). *Accreditation criteria.* Retrieved May 9, 2006, from **http://www.naeyc.org/accreditation/criteria98.asp**

National Association of Early Childhood Specialists in State Departments of Education. (2000). *STILL unacceptable trends in kindergarten entry and placement.* Retrieved January 28, 2006, from **http://www.naeyc.org/about/positions/pdf/Psunacc.pdf**

National Association of School Psychologists. (2002). *Helping children cope with violence and terror: Tips for parents and teachers.* Retrieved May 14, 2006, from **http://www.nasponline.org/pdf/ViolenceTerrorHO.pdf**

National Association of State Fire Marshals. (2000). *Juvenile Firesetter Intervention Research Project: Final report.* Author.

National Cancer Institute. (2002). *End-of-life care: Questions and answers.* Retrieved February 25, 2005, from **http://www.cancer.gov/cancertopics/factsheet/support/end-of-life-care**

National Center for Education Statistics. (2006). *National Assessment of Educational Progress: The Nation's Report Card.* Retrieved February 13, 2006, from **http://nces.ed.gov/nationsreportcard**

National Center for Health Statistics. (2004). *Health, United States, 2004: With chartbook on trends in the health of Americans.* Hyattsville, MD: U.S. Government Printing Office. Retrieved May 13, 2006, from **http://www.cdc.gov/nchs/data/hus/hus04acc.pdf**

National Center for Health Statistics. (2005a). *Health, United States, 2005: With chartbook on trends in the health of Americans.* Hyattsville, MD: U.S. Government Printing Office. Retrieved June 23, 2006, from **http://www.cdc.gov/nchs/data/hus/hus05.pdf**

National Center for Health Statistics. (2005b). *Overweight among U.S. children and adolescents.* Retrieved June 5, 2005, from **http://www.cdc.gov/nchs/data/nhanes/databriefs/overwght.pdf**

National Center for Injury Prevention and Control. (2003). *Childhood injury fact sheet.* Retrieved December 2, 2003, from www.cdc.gov.ncipc/factsheets/childh.htm

National Center for Injury Prevention and Control. (2005). *National child passenger safety week, February 13–19, 2005.* Retrieved July 30, 2005, from **http://www.cdc.gov/ncipc/duip/spotlite/chldseat.htm**

National Center for Injury Prevention and Control. (2006). *Child passenger safety: Fact sheet.* Retrieved May 9, 2006, from **http://www.cdc.gov/ncipc/factsheets/childpas.htm**

National Center on Birth Defects and Developmental Disabilities. (2005a). *Fetal alcohol information.* Retrieved January 2, 2006, from **http://www.cdc.gov/ncbddd**

National Center on Birth Defects and Developmental Disabilities. (2005b). *Having a healthy pregnancy: ABC's . . . Pregnancy Tips (A-Z).* Retrieved January 1, 2006, from **http://www.cdc.gov/ncbddd/bd/abc.htm**

National Clearinghouse for English Language Acquisition and Language Instruction Educational Programs. (2006). *NCELA FAQ No. 1.* Retrieved February 13, 2006, from **http://www.ncela.gwu.edu/expert/faq/01leps.htm**

National Clearinghouse on Child Abuse and Neglect Information. (2001). *In focus: Acts of omission: An overview of child neglect.* Retrieved February 13, 2006, from **http://nccanch.acf.hhs.gov/pubs/focus/acts/index.cfm**

National Clearinghouse on Child Abuse and Neglect Information. (2005). *Long-term consequences of child abuse and neglect.* Retrieved February 13, 2006, from **http://nccanch.acf.hhs.gov/pubs/factsheets/long_term_consequences.cfm**

National Clearinghouse on Families and Youth. (2006). *Supporting your adolescent: Tips for parents.* Retrieved June 13, 2006, from **http://www.ncfy.com/supporti.htmhttp://www.ncfy.com/supporti.htm**

National Eye Institute. (2005). *Prevalence and causes of visual impairment and blindness among adults 40 years and older in the United States.* Retrieved March 21, 2005, from http://www.nei.nih.gov

National Highway Traffic Safety Administration. (2000, January). *State legislative fact sheet: Graduated driver licensing system.* Washington, DC: U.S. Department of Transportation.

National Highway Traffic Safety Administration. (2003, February). *Research note: The use of child restraints in 2002.* Washington, DC: U.S. Department of Transportation.

National Highway Traffic Safety Administration. (2006). *Saving teenage lives, Section 1: Introduction: The need for graduated driver licensing.* Retrieved May 27, 2006, from **http://www.nhtsa.dot.gov/people/injury/newdriver/SaveTeens/sect1.htmlhttp://www.nhtsa.dot.gov/people/injury/newdriver/SaveTeens/sect1.html**

National Institute of Mental Health. (2003). *In harm's way: Suicide in America.* Retrieved June 14, 2006, from **http://www.nimh.nih.gov/publicat/harmaway.cfm**

National Institute on Aging. (2002). *Alzheimer's disease: Unraveling the mystery.* (NIH Publication No. 02–3782). Bethesda, MD: National Institutes of Health.

National Institute on Aging. (2005a). *Aging under the microscope: A biological quest (Ch. 3).* Retrieved May 31, 2006, from **http://www.nia.nih.gov/HealthInformation/Publications/AgingUndertheMicroscope/chapter03.htm**

National Institute on Aging. (2005b). *Welcome to the BLSA.* Retrieved May 31, 2006, from **http://www.grc.nia.nih.gov/branches/blsa/blsanew.htm**

National Institute on Aging & National Library of Medicine. (2001). *Making your Web site senior friendly: A checklist.* Retrieved April 22, 2006, from **http://www.nih.gov/icd/od/ocpl/resources/wag/documents/checklist.pdf**

National Institute on Deafness and Other Communication Disorders. (2004). *Protect your ears.* Retrieved July 20, 2004, from www.nidcd.nih.gov/health/hearing/ruler.asp

National Institute on Drug Abuse. (2000, April). *NIDA Community Drug Alert Bulletin—Anabolic steroids.* Retrieved February 13, 2005, from www.drugabuse.gov/SteroidAlert/SteroidAlert.html

National Institutes of Health. (2000). Phenylketonuria (PKU): Screening and management. *NIH Consensus Statement, 17*(3), 1–33.

National Institutes of Health. (2002). *Third report of the National Cholesterol Education Program (NCEP) expert panel on detection, evaluation, and treatment of high blood cholesterol in adults (Adult Treatment Panel III): Final report* (NIH Publication No. 02–5215). Retrieved March 30, 2005, from http://www.nhlbi.nih.gov/guidelines/cholesterol

National Middle School Association. (2003). *This we believe: Successful schools for young adolescents.* Westerville, OH: Author.

National Program for Playground Safety. (2004). *National Program for Playground Safety.* Retrieved February 6, 2006, from www.uni.edu/playground

National Public Radio. (2001, May 18). *All things considered: Harold Stilson discusses hitting a hole in one at the age of 101.*

National Research Council Committee on Techniques for the Enhancement of Human Performance. (1999). *The changing nature of work: Implications for occupational analysis.* Washington, DC: National Academy Press.

National Research Council Committee on the Health and Safety Implications of Child Labor. (1998). *Protecting youth at work: Health, safety, and development of working children and adolescents in the United States.* Washington, DC: National Academy Press.

National Safe Kids Campaign. (2006). *Welcome to Safe Kids Worldwide.* Retrieved May 9, 2006, from http://www.safekids.org

National Sleep Foundation. (2002). *Sleep and aging.* Retrieved March 7, 2005, from http://www.sleepfoundation.org/publications/sleeppage.cfm

National Sleep Foundation. (2005). *Healthy sleep tips.* Retrieved January 5, 2005, from http://www.sleepfoundation.org/sleeptips.cfm

National Statistics. (2001). *Health statistics quarterly: Spring 2001.* Retrieved May 7, 2006, from http://www.statistics.gov.uk/products/p6725.asp

Nebes, R. D., Butters, M. A., Mulsant, B. H., et al. (2000). Decreased working memory and processing speed mediate cognitive impairment in geriatric depression. *Psychological Medicine, 30,* 679–691.

Needleman, H. L., & Bellinger, D. (Eds.). (1994). *Prenatal exposure to toxicants: Developmental consequences.* Baltimore: Johns Hopkins University Press.

Neiger, B. L. (2000). The re-emergence of Thalidomide: Results of a scientific conference. *Teratology, 62,* 432–435.

Neimeyer, R. A. (2000). Searching for the meaning of meaning: Grief therapy and the process of reconstruction. *Death Studies, 24,* 541–558.

Neiss, M., & Rowe, D. C. (2000). Parental education and child's verbal IQ in adoptive and biological families in the National Longitudinal Study of Adolescent Health. *Behavior Genetics, 30,* 487–495.

Neisser, U. (1997). Rising scores on intelligence tests. *American Scientist, 85*(5), 440–447.

Neisser, U., Boodoo, G., Bouchard, T. J., Jr., et al. (1996). Intelligence: Knowns and unknowns. *American Psychologist, 51,* 77–101.

Nelson, C. A. (1999). How important are the first 3 years of life? *Applied Developmental Science, 3,* 235–238.

Nelson, C. A. (2000). The neurological bases of early intervention. In J. P. Shonkoff & S. J. Meisels (Eds.), *Handbook of early childhood intervention* (2nd ed., pp. 204–227). New York: Cambridge University Press.

Nelson, C. A. (2004). Brain development during puberty and adolescence: Comments on part II. In R. E. Dahl & L. P. Spear (Eds.), *Annals of the New York Academy of Sciences: Vol. 1021. Adolescent brain development: Vulnerabilities and opportunities* (pp. 105–109). New York: New York Academy of Sciences.

Nelson, C. A., & Horowitz, F. D. (1987). Visual motion perception in infancy: A review and synthesis. In P. Salapatek & L. B. Cohen (Eds.), *Handbook of infant perception: From perception to cognition* (Vol. 2, pp. 123–153). New York: Academic Press.

Nelson, C. A., Thomas, K., & de Haan, M. (2006). Neural bases of cognitive development. In W. Damon & R. M. Lerner (Series Eds.) & D. Kuhn & R. Siegler (Vol. Eds.), *Handbook of child psychology: Vol. 2. Cognition, perception, and language* (6th ed., pp. 3–57). Hoboken, NJ: Wiley.

Nelson, K. (1988). The ontogeny of memory for real events. In U. Neisser & E. Winograd (Eds.), *Remembering reconsidered: Ecological and traditional approaches to the study of memory* (pp. 244–276). New York: Cambridge University Press.

Nelson, M. E., Fiatarone, M. A., Morganti, C. M., Trice, I., Greenberg, R. A., & Evans, W. J. (1994). Effects of high-intensity strength training on multiple risk factors for osteoporotic fractures: A randomized controlled trial. *Journal of the American Medical Association, 272,* 1090–1914.

Neto, F., & Barros, J. (2003). Predictors of loneliness among students and nuns in Angola and Portugal. *Journal of Psychology, 137,* 351–362.

Neugarten, B. L. (1969). Continuities and discontinuities of psychological issues into adult life. *Human Development, 12,* 121–130.

Neugarten, B. L. (1976). Adaptation and the life cycle. *The Counseling Psychologist, 6,* 16–20.

Neugarten, B. L. (1979). Time, age, and the life cycle. *American Journal of Psychiatry, 136,* 887–894.

Neugarten, B. L., & Neugarten, D. A. (1987). The changing meanings of age. *Psychology Today, 21*(5), 29–33.

New Jersey Department of Health and Senior Services. (2005). *New Jersey health statistics, 2003: Births.* Retrieved January 1, 2006, from http://www.state.nj.us/health/chs/stats03/natality.shtml

Newcomb, A. F., & Bagwell, C. L. (1995). Children's friendship relations: A meta-analytic review. *Psychological Bulletin, 117,* 306–347.

Newcomb, A. F., Bukowski, W. M., & Pattee, L. (1993). Children's peer relations: A meta-analytic review of popular, rejected, neglected, controversial, and average sociometric status. *Psychological Bulletin, 113,* 99–128.

Newcombe, N. S., Drummey, A. B., Fox, N. A., Lie, E., & Ottinger-Alberts, W. (2000). Remembering early childhood: How much, how, and why (or why not). *Current Directions in Psychological Science, 9,* 55–58.

Newman, J. (1985). Adolescents: Why they can be so obnoxious. *Adolescence, 20,* 635–646.

Newman, J. (2004). *You make me feel like an unnatural woman: Diary of a new (older) mother.* New York: Miramax Books.

Newman, J. E. (2004). Exploring early adolescents' adjustment across the middle school transition: The role of peer experiences and social-cognitive factors. *Dissertation Abstracts International, 64*(09), 4655B.

Newman, S. A. (2003/2004). Five critical issues in New York's grandparent visitation law after *Troxel v. Granville. New York Law School Law Review, 48,* 489–535.

Newport, F. (2003). *A look at Americans and religion today.* The Gallup Poll. Retrieved May 31, 2006, from http://speakingoffaith.publicradio.org/programs/godsofbusiness/galluppoll.shtml

NFO Research, Inc. (1999). *AARP/Modern Maturity Sexuality Study.* Washington, DC: AARP.

Ngianga-Bakwin, K., & Stones, R. W. (2005). Birth intervals and injectable contraception in sub-Saharan Africa. *Contraception, 71,* 353–356.

Nguyen, T. V., Maynard, L. M., Towne, B., et al. (2001). Sex differences in bone mass acquisition during growth: The Fels Longitudinal Study. *Journal of Clinical Densitometry, 4,* 147–157.

NICHD Center for Research for Mothers and Children. (2000). The relation of child care to cognitive and language development. *Child Development, 71,* 960–980.

NICHD Early Child Care Research Network. (1997). The effects of infant child care on infant-mother attachment security: Results of the NICHD Study of Early Child Care. *Child Development, 68,* 860–879.

NICHD Early Child Care Research Network. (2001). Child care and children's peer interaction at 24 and 36 months: The NICHD Study of Early Child Care. *Child Development, 72,* 1478–1500.

NICHD Early Child Care Research Network. (2002). Child-care structure ? process ? outcome: Direct and indirect effects of child-care quality on young children's development. *Psychological Science, 13,* 199–206.

NICHD Early Child Care Research Network. (2003). Does quality of child care affect child outcomes at age 4 1/2? *Developmental Psychology, 39,* 451–469.

NICHD Early Child Care Research Network. (2004). Trajectories of physical aggression from toddlerhood to middle childhood. *Monographs of the Society for Research in Child Development, 69*(4, Serial No. 278).

NICHD Early Child Care Research Network & Duncan, G. J. (2003). Modeling the impacts of child care quality on children's preschool cognitive development. *Child Development, 74,* 1454–1475.

Nicholson, L. J. (1983). Women, morality, and history. *Social Research, 50,* 514–536.

Niec, L. N., Hemme, J. M., Yopp, J. M., & Brestan, E. V. (2005). Parent-child interaction therapy: The rewards and challenges of a group format. *Cognitive and Behavioral Practice, 12,* 113–125.

Nisan, M., & Kohlberg, L. (1982). Universality and variation in moral judgment: A longitudinal and cross-sectional study in Turkey. *Child Development, 53,* 865–876.

Nisbett, R. E. (2005). Heredity, environment, and race differences in IQ: A commentary on Rushton and Jensen (2005). *Psychology, Public Policy, and Law, 11,* 302–310.

Nishina, A., & Juvonen, J. (2005). Daily reports of witnessing and experiencing peer harassment in middle school. *Child Development, 76,* 435–450.

Nishizawa, S., Benkelfat, C., Young, S. N., et al. (1997). Differences between males and females in rates of serotonin synthesis in human brain. *Proceedings of the National Academy of Sciences of the United States of America, 94*(10), 5308–5313.

Nock, S. L. (1995). Commitment and dependency in marriage. *Journal of Marriage and the Family, 57,* 503–514.

Nolan, J. J., III, McDevitt, J., Cronin, S., & Farrell, A. (2004). Learning to *see* hate crimes: A framework for understanding and clarifying ambiguities in bias crime classification. *Criminal Justice Studies, 17,* 91–105.

Nordenberg, T. (1999). *Colds and flu: Time only sure cure.* Retrieved October 30, 2005, from **http://www.fda.gov/fdac/features/896_flu.html**

Norman, C. C., & Aron, A. (2003). Aspects of possible self that predict motivation to achieve or avoid it. *Journal of Experimental Social Psychology, 39,* 500–507.

Norman, S. M., McCluskey-Fawcett, K., & Ashcraft, L. (2002). Older women's development: A comparison of women in their 60s and 80s on a measure of Erikson's developmental tasks. *International Journal of Aging and Human Development, 54,* 31–42.

Nottlemann, E. D., Susman, E. J., Blue, J. H., et al. (1987). Gonadal and adrenal hormone correlates of adjustment in early adolescence. In R. M. Lerner & T. T. Foch (Eds.), *Biological-psychosocial interactions in early adolescence.* Hillsdale, NJ: Erlbaum.

Null, R. L., & Cherry, K. F. (1998). *Universal design: Creative solutions for ADA compliance.* Belmont, CA: Professional Publications.

Nurmi, J. (2004). Socialization and self-development: Channeling, selection, adjustment, and reflection. In R. M. Lerner & L. D. Steinberg (Eds.), *Handbook of adolescent psychology* (2nd ed., pp. 85–124). Hoboken, NJ: Wiley.

Nybo Andersen, A. M., Wohlfahrt, J., Christens, P., Olsen, J., & Melbye, M. (2000). Maternal age and fetal loss: Population based register linkage study. *British Medical Journal, 320,* 1708–1712.

Nyborg, H. (Ed.). (2003). *The scientific study of general intelligence: Tribute to Arthur R. Jensen.* Oxford, England: Pergamon/Elsevier.

Obeidallah, D., Brennan, R. T., Brooks-Gunn, J., & Earls, F. (2004). Links between pubertal timing and neighborhood contexts: Implications for girls' violent behavior. *Journal of the American Academy of Child and Adolescent Psychiatry, 43,* 1460–1468.

Obermeyer, C. M. (2000). Menopause across cultures: A review of the evidence. *Menopause, 7,* 184–192.

Obihara, C. C., Marais, B. J., Gie, R. P., et al. (2005). The association of prolonged breastfeeding and allergic disease in poor urban children. *The European Respiratory Journal, 25,* 970–977.

O'Connor, A. (2004, May 4). Roy Walford, 79, researcher who linked diet to longevity, is dead. *New York Times,* p. C15.

O'Connor, A. M. (2003). "I found my long-lost twin." *Latina, 7,* 106.

O'Connor, S., Vietze, P. M., Sherrod, K. B., Sandler, H. M., & Altemeier, W. A. (1980). Reduced incidence of parenting inadequacy following rooming-in. *Pediatrics, 66,* 176–182.

O'Connor, T. G., Caspi, A., DeFries, J. C., & Plomin, R. (2000). Are associations between parental divorce and children's adjustment genetically mediated? An adoption study. *Developmental Psychology, 36,* 429–437.

Offer, D., & Schonert-Reichl, K. A. (1992). Debunking the myths of adolescence: Findings from recent research. *Journal of the American Academy of Child and Adolescent Psychiatry, 31,* 1003–1014.

Ogden, C. L., Fryar, C. D., Carroll, M. D., & Flegal, K. M. (2004). Mean body weight, height, and body mass index, United States 1960–2002. *Advance Data From Vital and Health Statistics, No. 347.* Hyattsville, MD: National Center for Health Statistics.

Ogden, C. L., Kuczmarski, R. J., Flegal, K. M., et al. (2002). Centers for Disease Control and Prevention 2000 growth charts for the United States: Improvements to the 1977 National Center for Health Statistics Version. *Pediatrics, 109,* 45–60.

O'Halloran, C. M., & Altmaier, E. M. (1996). Awareness of death among children: Does a life-threatening illness alter the process of discovery? *Journal of Counseling and Development, 74,* 259–262.

Ohgi, S., Takahashi, T., Nugent, J. K., Arisawa, K., & Akiyama., T. (2003). Neonatal behavioral characteristics and later behavioral problems. *Clinical Pediatrics, 42,* 679–686.

OJJDP statistical briefing book. (2004, August 1). Age-specific arrest rate trends. Retrieved February 2, 2005, from **http://ojjdp.ncjrs.org/ojstatbb/crime/qa05301.asp?qaDate-20040801**

Olds, D., Henderson, C., Kitzman, H., et al. (1998). Prenatal and infancy home visitation by nurses: A program of research. *Advances in Infancy Research, 12,* 79–130.

Olejnik, A. B. (1980). Adults' moral reasoning with children. *Child Development, 51,* 1285–1288.

Olshansky, S. J., Carnes, B. A., & Butler, R. N. (2001). If humans were built to last. *Scientific American, 284*(3), 50–55.

Olshansky, S. J., Hayflick, L., & Carnes, B. A. (2002). No truth to the fountain of youth. *Scientific American, 286*(6), 92–95.

Olweus Bullying Prevention Program. (2005). Retrieved May 16, 2005, from **http://www.clemson.edu/olweus**

O'Mara, P. (1999, January 1). We've come a long way, babies. *Mothering.* Retrieved January 3, 2006, from **http://findarticles.com/p/articles/mi_m0838/is_1999_Jan/ai_54308839**

Oneida advertisement. (2001, March). *Better Homes and Gardens, 79,* 47.

Online Mendelian inheritance in man, OMIM (TM). (2005). McKusick-Nathans Institute for Genetic Medicine, Johns Hopkins University (Baltimore, MD) and National Center for Biotechnology Information, National Library of Medicine (Bethesda, MD). Retrieved April 27, 2006, from **http://www.ncbi.nlm.nih.gov/omim**

O'Rahilly, R., & Müller, F. (2001). *Human embryology and teratology* (3rd ed.). New York: Wiley-Liss.

Orel, V. (1996). *Gregor Mendel: The first geneticist.* New York: Oxford University Press.

Orvos, H., Nyirati, I., Hajdú, J., Pál, A., Nyári, T., & Kovács, L. (1999). Is adolescent pregnancy associated with adverse perinatal outcome? *Journal of Perinatal Medicine, 27,* 199–203.

Osgood, D. W., Wilson, J. K., O'Malley, P. M., Bachman, J. G., & Johnston, L. D. (1996). Routine activities and individual deviant behavior. *American Sociological Review, 61,* 635–655.

Osofsky, J. D. (1995). The effects of exposure to violence on young children. *American Psychologist, 50,* 782–788.

Osofsky, J. D., & Thompson, M. D. (2000). Adaptive and maladaptive parenting: Perspectives on risk and protective factors. In J. P. Shonkoff & S. J. Meisels (Eds.), *Handbook of early childhood intervention* (2nd ed., pp. 54–75). New York: Cambridge University Press.

Osofsky, J. D., Wewers, S., Hann, D. M., & Fick, A. C. (1993). Chronic community violence: What is happening to our children? *Psychiatry, 56,* 36–45.

Ostroff, C., Shin, Y., & Feinberg, B. (2002). Skill acquisition and person-environment fit. In D. C. Feldman (Ed.), *Work careers: A developmental perspective* (pp. 63–90). San Francisco: Jossey-Bass.

Owsley, C., Ball, K., McGwin, G., Jr., et al. (1998). Visual processing impairment and risk of motor vehicle crash among older adults. *Journal of the American Medical Association, 279,* 1083–1088.

Paerregaard, A., Hjelt, K., Christiansen, L., & Krasilnikoff, P. A. (1990). Postenteritis enteropathy in infancy: A prospective study of 10 patients with special reference to growth pattern, long-term outcome and incidence. *Acta Paediatrica Scandinavica, 79,* 1045–1051.

Paffenbarger, R. S., Jr. (2000). Jerry Morris: Pathfinder for health through an active and fit way of life. *British Journal of Sports Medicine, 34,* 217.

Pagel, J. F. (2000). Nightmares and disorders of dreaming. *American Family Physician, 61,* 2037–2044.

Pailing, P. E., Segalowitz, S. J., Dywan, J., & Davies, P. L. (2002). Error negativity and response control. *Psychophysiology, 39,* 198–206.

Palasota v. Haggar Clothing Co., 342 F.3d 569, 5th Cir., 2003.

Palmer, D. L., Berg, C. A., Wiebe, D. J., et al. (2004). The role of autonomy and pubertal status in understanding age differences in maternal involvement in diabetes responsibility across adolescence. *Journal of Pediatric Psychology, 29,* 35–46.

Palmert, M. R., & Boepple, P. A. (2001). Variation in the timing of puberty: Clinical spectrum and genetic investigation. *Journal of Clinical Endocrinology and Metabolism, 86,* 2364–2368.

Pan, B. A., & Gleason, J. B. (2001). Semantic development: Learning the meanings of words. In J. B. Gleason (Ed.), *The development of language* (5th ed., pp. 125–161). Boston: Allyn & Bacon.

Pan, H. S., Neidig, P. H., & O'Leary, K. D. (1994). Predicting mild and severe husband-to-wife physical aggression. *Journal of Consulting and Clinical Psychology, 62,* 975–981.

Paneth, N., Bommarito, M., & Stricker, J. (1993). Electronic fetal monitoring and later outcome. *Clinical and Investigative Medicine, 16,* 159–165.

Papousek, M., & Hofacker, N. von. (1998). Persistent crying in early infancy: A non-trivial condition of risk for the developing mother-infant relationship. *Child: Care, Health, and Development, 24,* 395–424.

A parent speaks out. (2002). *Pediatrics, 109,* 249.

Paris, C. A., Remler, R., & Daling, J. R. (2001). Risk factors for sudden infant death syndrome: Changes associated with sleep position recommendations. *Journal of Pediatrics, 139,* 771–777.

Park, D. C. (2000). The basic mechanisms accounting for age-related decline in cognitive function. In D. C. Park & N. Schwarz (Eds.), *Cognitive aging: A primer* (pp. 3–21). Hove, England: Psychology Press.

Park, D. C., Lautenschlager, G., Hedden, T., Davidson, N. S., Smith, A. D., & Smith, P. K. (2002). Models of visuospatial and verbal memory across the adult life span. *Psychology and Aging, 17,* 299–320.

Park, Y. K., Sempos, C. T., Barton, C. N., Vanderveen, J. E., & Yetley, E. A. (2000). Effectiveness of food fortification in the United States: The case of pellagra. *American Journal of Public Health, 90,* 727–738.

Parke, R. D. (1995). Fathers and families. In M. H. Bornstein (Ed.), *Handbook of parenting* (Vol. 3, pp. 27–63). Mahwah, NJ: Erlbaum.

Parke, R. D. (2004). Fathers, families, and the future: A plethora of plausible predictions. *Merrill-Palmer Quarterly, 50,* 456–470.

Parry, A., & Doan, R. E. (1994). *Story re-visions: Narrative therapy in the postmodern world.* New York: Guilford.

Parten, M. B. (1932). Social participation among preschool children. *Journal of Abnormal and Social Psychology, 27,* 243–269.

Partsch, C. J., & Sippell, W. G. (2001). Pathogenesis and epidemiology of precocious puberty: Effects of exogenous oestrogens. *Human Reproductive Update, 7,* 292–302.

Pascalis, O., de Hann, M., Nelson, C. A., & de Schonen, S. (1998). Long-term recognition memory for faces assessed by visual paired comparison in 3– and 6–month-old infants. *Journal of Experimental Psychology: Learning, Memory, and Cognition, 24,* 249–260.

Patterson, G. R. (1982). *Coercive family process.* Eugene, OR: Castalia.

Paulk, D. L., Swearer, S. M., Song, S., & Carey, P. T. (1999, August 21). *Teacher-, peer-, and self-nominations of bullies and victims of bullying.* Paper presented at the meeting of the American Psychological Association, Boston.

Paus, T., Zijdenbos, A., Worsley, K., et al. (1999). Structural maturation of neural pathways in children and adolescents: In vivo study. *Science, 283,* 1908–1911.

Pearlin, L. I. (1982). Discontinuities in the study of aging. In T. Haraven & K. J. Adams (Eds.), *Aging and life course transitions: An interdisciplinary perspective* (pp. 55–74). New York: Guilford.

Pears, K. C., & Capaldi, D. M. (2001). Intergenerational transmission of abuse: A two-generational prospective study of an at-risk sample. *Child Abuse and Neglect, 25,* 1439–1461.

Pearson, J. D., Morrell, C. H., Gordon-Salant, S., et al. (1995). Gender differences in a longitudinal study of age-associated hearing loss. *Journal of the Acoustical Society of America, 97,* 1196–1205.

Pedersen, W. C., Miller, L. C., Putcha-Bhagavatula, A. D., & Yang, Y. (2002). Evolved sex differences in the number of partners desired? The long and short of it. *Psychological Science, 13,* 157–161.

Pedlow, R., Sanson, A., & Wales, R. (2004). Children's production and comprehension of politeness in requests: Relationships to behavioural adjustment, temperament and empathy. *First Language, 24,* 347–367.

Pellegrini, A. D. (2003). Perceptions and functions of play and real fighting in early adolescence. *Child Development, 74,* 1522–1533.

Pellegrini, A. D., & Long, J. D. (2002). A longitudinal study of bullying, dominance, and victimization during the transition from primary school through secondary school. *British Journal of Developmental Psychology, 20,* 259–280.

Pepler, D., Craig, W., Yuile, A., & Connolly, J. (2004). Girls who bully: A developmental and relational perspective. In M. Putallaz & K. L. Bierman (Eds.), *Aggression, antisocial behavior, and violence among girls: A developmental perspective* (pp. 90–109). New York: Guilford.

Perlman, J. M. (2001). Neurobehavioral deficits in premature graduates of intensive care—Potential medical and neonatal environmental risk factors. *Pediatrics, 108,* 1339–1348.

Perls, T. T. (2004). The oldest old. *Scientific American, 14*(3), 6–11.

Perls, T. T., Silver, M. H., & Lauerman, J. F. (1999). *Living to 100: Lessons in living to your maximum potential at any age.* New York: Basic Books.

Perrin, E. C., & Committee on Psychosocial Aspects of Child and Family Health. (2002). Technical report: Coparent or second-parent adoption by same-sex parents. *Pediatrics, 109,* 341–344.

Perry, H. L. (1993). Mourning and funeral customs of African Americans. In D. P. Irish, K. F. Lundquist, & V. J. Nelsen (Eds.), *Ethnic variations in dying, death, and grief: Diversity in universality* (pp. 51–65). Philadelphia: Taylor & Francis.

Perry, W. G., Jr. (1970). *Forms of intellectual and ethical development in the college years: A scheme.* New York: Holt, Rinehart & Winston.

Perry, W. G., Jr. (1981). Cognitive and ethical growth: The making of meaning. In A. W. Chickering (Ed.), *The modern American college* (pp. 76–116). San Francisco: Jossey-Bass.

Pérusse, L., & Bouchard, C. (1999). Role of genetic factors in childhood obesity and in susceptibility to dietary variations. *Annals of Medicine, 31*(Suppl. 1), 19–25.

Petersen, R. C. (2000). Mild cognitive impairment: Transition between aging and Alzheimer's disease. *Neurologia, 15,* 93–101.

Peterson, C. (2002). Children's long-term memory for autobiographical events. *Developmental Review, 22,* 370–402.

Peterson, C. C., Peterson, J. L., & Seeto, D. (1983). Developmental changes in ideas about lying. *Child Development, 54,* 1529–1535.

Petrozza, J. C. (2004). Assisted reproduction technology. *eMedicine.* Retrieved May 30, 2004, from www.emedicine.com/med/topic3288.htm

Petterson, S. M., & Albers, A. B. (2001). Effects of poverty and maternal depression on early child development. *Child Development, 72,* 1794–1813.

Pettit, G. S., Bates, J. E., & Dodge, K. A. (1997). Supportive parenting, ecological context, and children's adjustment: A seven-year longitudinal study. *Child Development, 68,* 908–923.

Pezdek, K., & Hartman, E. F. (1983). Children's television viewing: Attention and comprehension of auditory versus visual information. *Child Development, 54,* 1015–1023.

Pfefferbaum, A., Mathalon, D. H., Sullivan, E. V., Rawles, J. M., Zipursky, R. B., & Lim, K. O. (1994). A quantitative magnetic resonance imaging study of changes in brain morphology from infancy to late adulthood. *Archives of Neurology, 51,* 874–887.

Philippi, A., Roschmann, E., Tores, F., et al. (2005). Haplotypes in the gene encoding protein kinase c-beta (PRKCB1) on chromosome 16 are associated with autism. *Molecular Psychiatry, 10,* 950–960.

Piaget, J. (1936/52). *The origins of intelligence in children.* New York: International Universities Press.

Piaget, J. (1951). *Play, dreams, and imitation in childhood.* New York: Norton.

Piaget, J. (1952). *The child's conception of number.* London: Routledge.

Piaget, J. (1954). *The construction of reality in the child.* New York: Basic Books.

Piaget, J. (1965/1997). *The moral judgment of the child.* New York: Free Press.

Piaget, J. (1968). *On the development of memory and identity.* Worcester, MA: Clark University Press.

Piaget, J., & Inhelder, B. (1956). *The child's conception of space.* London: Routledge.

Pickering, S. J. (2001). The development of visuo-spatial working memory. *Memory, 9,* 423–432.

Pilkington, N. W., & D'Augelli, A. R. (1995). Victimization of lesbian, gay, and bisexual youth in community settings. *Journal of Community Psychology, 23,* 34–57.

Pinker, S. (1994). *The language instinct.* New York: William Morrow and Company.

Pinker, S. (1997). *How the mind works.* New York: Norton.

Pinker, S. (2002). *The blank slate: The modern denial of human nature.* New York: Viking.

Pinker, S. (2005). So how does the mind work? *Mind and Language, 20,* 1–24.

Pinto-Correia, C. (1997). *The ovary of Eve: Egg and sperm and preformation.* Chicago: University of Chicago Press.

Place, K. S., & Becker, J. A. (1991). The influence of pragmatic competence on the likeability of grade-school children. *Discourse Processes, 14,* 227–241.

Plante, T. G., & Sherman, A. C. (Eds.). (2001). *Faith and health: Psychological perspectives.* New York: Guilford.

Platts-Mills, T. A., Erwin, E., Heymann, P., & Woodfolk, J. (2005). Is the hygiene hypothesis still a viable explanation for the increased prevalence of asthma? *Allergy, 60*(Suppl. 79), 25–31.

Plomin, R. (1994). *Genetics and experience: The interplay between nature and nurture.* Thousand Oaks, CA: Sage.

Plomin, R., DeFries, J. C., Craig, I. W., & McGuffin, P. (Eds.). (2003). *Behavioral genetics in the postgenomic era.* Washington, DC: American Psychological Association.

Plomin, R., DeFries, J. C., McClearn, G. E., & McGuffin, P. (2001). *Behavioral genetics* (4th ed.). New York: Worth.

Plumert, J. M. (1995). Relations between children's overestimation of their physical abilities and accident proneness. *Developmental Psychology, 31,* 866–876.

Plumert, J. M., Kearney, J. K., & Cremer, J. F. (2004). Children's perception of gap affordances: Bicycling across traffic-filled intersections in an immersive virtual environment. *Child Development, 75,* 1243–1253.

Pollak, S. D., & Kistler, D. J. (2002). Early experience is associated with the development of categorical representations for facial expressions of emotion. *Proceedings of the National Academy of Science of the United States of America, 99,* 9072–9076.

Pollak, S. D., & Tolley-Schell, S. A. (2003). Selective attention to facial emotion in physically abused children. *Journal of Abnormal Psychology, 112,* 323–338.

Poole, D. A. (1995). The two bell curves. *American Behavioral Scientist, 39,* 35–43.

Poole, D. A., & Lamb, M. E. (1998). *Investigative interviews of children: A guide for helping professionals.* Washington, DC: American Psychological Association.

Poole, D. A., & Lindsay, D. S. (2001). Children's eyewitness reports after exposure to misinformation from parents. *Journal of Experimental Psychology: Applied, 7,* 27–50.

Poole, D. A, & Lindsay, D. S. (2002). Reducing child witnesses' false reports of misinformation from parents. *Journal of Experimental Child Psychology, 81,* 117–140.

Poole, D. A., Lindsay, D. S., Memon, A., & Bull, R. (1995). Psychotherapy and the recovery of memories of childhood sexual abuse: U.S. and British practitioners' opinions, practices, and experiences. *Journal of Consulting and Clinical Psychology, 63,* 426–437.

Poole, D. A., & White, L. T. (1993). Two years later: Effect of question repetition and retention interval on the eyewitness testimony of children and adults. *Developmental Psychology, 29,* 844–853.

Poolos, J. (2005). *Travis Pastrana: Motocross superstar.* New York: The Rosen Publishing Group.

Poortinga, Y. H., & van de Vijver, F. J. R. (2004). Cultures and cognition: Performance differences and invariant structures. In R. J. Sternberg & E. L. Grigorenko (Eds.), *Culture and competence: Contexts of life success* (pp. 139–162). Washington, DC: American Psychological Association.

Population Reference Bureau. (2004). *Record number of women in the U.S. labor force.* Retrieved August 24, 2004, from **http://www.prb.org/ AmeristatTemplate.cfm?Section=Labor__ Employment&template=/ContentManagement/ ContentDisplay.cfm&ContentID=7880**

Povinelli, D. J. (2001). The self: Elevated in consciousness and extended in time. In C. Moore & K. Lemmon (Eds.), *The self in time: Developmental perspectives* (pp. 75–95). Mahwah, NJ: Erlbaum.

Prentice, A. M. (2005). Starvation in humans: Evolutionary background and contemporary implications. *Mechanisms of Ageing and Development, 126,* 976–981.

Prentice, D. A. (2004). Adult stem cells. *Issues in Law and Medicine, 19,* 265–294.

Prescott, S. L. (2003). Allergy: The price we pay for cleaner living? *Annals of Allergy, Asthma, and Immunology, 90*(Suppl. 3), 64–70.

Preslan, M. W., & Novak, A. (1998). Baltimore Vision Screening Project: Phase 2. *Ophthalmology, 105,* 150–153.

Pressman, S. D., Cohen, S., Miller, G. E., et al. (2005). Loneliness, social network size, and immune response to influenza vaccination in college freshmen. *Health Psychology, 24,* 297–306.

Prevent Blindness America & National Eye Institute. (2002). *Vision problems in the U.S.* Schaumberg, IL: Prevent Blindness America. Retrieved April 18, 2005, from **http://www. nei.nih.gov/eyedata/pdf/VPUS.polf**

Principe, G. F., & Ceci, S. J. (2002). "I saw it with my own ears": The effects of peer conversations on preschoolers' reports of nonexperienced events. *Journal of Experimental Child Psychology, 83*, 1–25.

Prinstein, M. J., & LaGreca, A. M. (2002). Peer crowd affiliation and internalizing distress in childhood and adolescence: A longitudinal follow-back study. *Journal of Research on Adolescence, 12*, 325–351.

Prior, M., Smart, D., Sanson, A., & Oberklaid, F. (2000). Does shy-inhibited temperament in childhood lead to anxiety problems in adolescence? *Journal of the American Academy of Child and Adolescent Psychiatry, 39*, 461–468.

Protheroe, P. (1993). Are picture books harmful? *New Scientist, 1878*, 44–45.

Pruchno, R., & Rosenbaum, J. (2003). Social relationships in adulthood and old age. In R. M. Lerner, M. A. Easterbrooks, & J. Mistry (Eds.), *Handbook of psychology* (Vol. 6, pp. 487–509). Hoboken, NJ: Wiley.

Pschirrer, E. R., & Yeomans, E. R. (2000). Does asphyxia cause cerebral palsy? *Seminars in Perinatology, 24*, 215–220.

Psychological Corporation. (1997). *WAIS-III-WMS-III technical manual*. San Antonio, TX: Harcourt Brace.

Puchalski, C. M., Zhong, Z., Jacobs, M. M., et al. (2000). Patients who want their family and physician to make resuscitation decisions for them: Observations from SUPPORT and HELP. *Journal of the American Geriatrics Society, 48*, S84–S90.

Puri, S. (2003, March 18). As layoffs rise, so do age-discrimination charges. *New York Times*, p. E4.

Putallaz, M. (1983). Predicting children's sociometric status from their behavior. *Child Development, 54*, 1417–1426.

Putallaz, M., & Bierman, K. L. (Eds.). (2004). *Aggression, antisocial behavior, and violence among girls: A developmental perspective*. New York: Guilford.

Putallaz, M., & Wasserman, A. (1990). Children's entry behavior. In S. R. Asher & J. D. Coie (Eds.), *Peer rejection in childhood* (pp. 60–89). New York: Cambridge University Press.

Putnam, F. W. (2003). Ten-year research update review: Child sexual abuse. *Journal of the American Academy of Child and Adolescent Psychiatry, 42*, 269–278.

Putnam, S. P., Spritz, B. L., & Stifter, C. A. (2002). Mother-child coregulation during delay of gratification at 30 months. *Infancy, 3*, 209–225.

Qamra, S. R., Mehta, S., & Deodhar, S. D. (1991). A mixed-longitudinal study on the pattern of pubertal growth: Relationship to socioeconomic status and caloric-intake—IV. *Indian Pediatrics, 28*, 145–156.

Quas, J. A., Goodman, G. S., Bidrose, S., Pipe, M.-E., Craw, S., & Ablin, D. S. (1999). Emotion and memory: Children's long-term remembering, forgetting, and suggestibility. *Journal of Experimental Child Psychology, 72*, 235–270.

Quatman, T., & Watson, C. M. (2001). Gender differences in adolescent self-esteem: An exploration of domains. *Journal of Genetic Psychology, 162*, 93–117.

Querido, J. G., Warner, T. D., & Eyberg, S. M. (2002). Parenting styles and child behavior in African American families of preschool children. *Journal of Clinical Child and Adolescent Psychology, 31*, 272–277.

Raabe, B., & Beehr, T. A. (2003). Formal mentoring, versus supervisor and coworker relationships: Differences in perceptions and impact. *Journal of Organizational Behavior, 24*, 271–293.

Raffaelli, M., Crockett, L. J., & Shen, Y.-L. (2005). Developmental stability and change in self-regulation from childhood to adolescence. *Journal of Genetic Psychology, 166*, 54–75.

Rahav, G., & Baum, N. (2002). Divorced women: Factors contributing to self-identity change. *Journal of Divorce and Remarriage, 37*(3–4), 41–59.

Rahhal, T. A., Hasher, L., & Colcombe, S. J. (2001). Instructional manipulations and age differences in memory: Now you see them, now you don't. *Psychology and Aging, 16*, 697–706.

Rahhal, T. A., May, C. P., & Hasher, L. (2002). Truth and character: Sources that older adults can remember. *Psychological Science, 13*, 101–105.

Rajah, M. N., & McIntosh, A. R. (2005). Overlap in the functional neural systems involved in semantic and episodic memory retrieval. *Journal of Cognitive Neuroscience, 17*, 470–482.

Ram, A., & Ross, H. S. (2001). Problem-solving, contention, and struggle: How siblings resolve a conflict of interest. *Child Development, 72*, 1710–1722.

Ramey, C. T., & Ramey, S. L. (1998). Prevention of intellectual disabilities: Early interventions to improve cognitive development. *Preventive Medicine, 27*, 224–232.

Ramey, C. T., Ramey, S. L., Lanzi, R. G., & Cotton, J. N. (2002). Early educational interventions for high-risk children: How center-based treatment can augment and improve parenting effectiveness. In J. G. Borkowski, S. L. Ramye, & M. Bristol-Power (Eds.), *Parenting and the child's world: Influences on academic, intellectual, and social-emotional development*. Mahwah, NJ: Erlbaum.

Rattaz, C., Goubet, N., & Bullinger, A. (2005). The calming effect of a familiar odor on full-term newborns. *Journal of Developmental and Behavioral Pediatrics, 26*, 86–92.

Ravicz, M. E., Rosowski, J. J., & Merchant, S. N. (2004). Mechanisms of hearing loss resulting from middle-ear fluid. *Hearing Research, 195*, 103–130.

Ray, J. (2004, May 25). Teens seek confidants in adults, peers. *The Gallup Poll*. Retrieved January 10, 2005, from http://poll.gallup.com

Ray, O. (2004). How the mind hurts and heals the body. *American Psychologist, 59*, 29–40.

Raymond, L. W., Ford, M. D., Porter, W. G., Saxe, J. S., & Ullrich, C. G. (2002). Maternal-fetal lead poisoning from a 15–year-old bullet. *Journal of Maternal-Fetal and Neonatal Medicine, 11*, 63–66.

Rayner, K., Foorman, B. R., Perfetti, C. A., Pesetsky, D., & Seidenberg, M. S. (2001). How psychological science informs the teaching of reading. *Psychological Science in the Public Interest, 2*, 31–74.

Raz, N. (2000). Aging of the brain and its impact on cognitive performance: Integration of structural and functional findings. In F. I. M. Craik & T. A. Salthouse (Eds.), *The handbook of aging and cognition* (2nd ed., pp. 1–90). Mahwah, NJ: Erlbaum.

Raz, N. (2005). The aging brain observed in vivo: Differential changes and their modifiers. In R. Cabeza, L. Nyberg, & D. Park (Eds.), *Cognitive neuroscience of aging: Linking cognitive and cerebral aging* (pp. 19–57). New York: Oxford University Press.

Raz, N., Lindenberger, U., Rodrigue, K. M., et al. (2005). Regional brain changes in aging healthy adults: General trends, individual differences and modifiers. *Cerebral Cortex, 15*, 1676–1689.

Readdick, C. A., & Chapman, P. L. (2001). Young children's perception of time out. *Journal of Research in Childhood Education, 15*, 81–87.

Ready, D. D., Lee, V. E., & Welner, K. G. (2004). Educational equity and school structure: School size, overcrowding, and schools-within-schools. *Teachers College Record, 106*, 1989–2014.

Ream, G. L., & Savin-Williams, R. C. (2005). Reciprocal associations between adolescent sexual activity and quality of youth-parent interactions. *Journal of Family Psychology, 19*, 171–179.

Reaney, P. (2004, May 25). Baby boy born from sperm frozen record 21 years. *Medline Plus*. Retrieved May 30, 2004, from www.nlm.nih.gov/medlineplus/news/fullstory_17965.html

Reardon, S. F. (2003). *Sources of educational inequality: The growth of racial/ethnic and socioeconomic test score gaps in kindergarten and first grade*. Population Research Institute, Pennsylvania State University. Retrieved June 5, 2005, from http://www.pop.psu.edu/general/pubs/working_papers/psu-pri/wp0305R.pdf

Receputo, G., Mazzoleni, G., Di Fazio, I., et al. (1996). Study on the sense of taste in a group of Sicilian centenarians. *Archives of Gerontology and Geriatrics, 22*(Suppl. 1), 411–414.

Reed, T. E., Vernon, P. A., & Johnson, A. M. (2004). Sex difference in brain nerve conduction velocity in normal humans. *Neuropsychologia, 42*, 1709–1714.

Reese, E. (1999). What children say when they talk about the past. *Narrative Inquiry, 9,* 215–241.

Reich, P. A. (1986). *Language development.* Englewood Cliffs, NJ: Prentice Hall.

Reifman, A., Villa, L. C., Amans, J. A., Rethinam, V., & Telesca, T. Y. (2001). Children of divorce in the 1990s: A meta-analysis. *Journal of Divorce and Remarriage, 36*(1–2), 27–36.

Reijneveld, S. A., Wal, M. F. van der, Brugman, E., Sing, R. A., & Verloove-Vanhorick, S. P. (2004). Infant crying and abuse. *Lancet, 364,* 1340–1342.

Reiss, A. J., Jr., & Roth, J. A. (Eds.) (1994). *Understanding and preventing violence: Vol. 3. Social influences.* Washington, DC: National Academy Press.

Reiss, A. L., Abrams, M. T., Singer, H. S., Ross, J. L., & Denckla, M. B. (1996). Brain development, gender and IQ in children: A volumetric imaging study. *Brain, 119,* 1763–1774.

Reitzes, D. C., & Mutran, E. J. (2004). The transition to retirement: Stages and factors that influence retirement adjustment. *International Journal of Aging and Human Development, 59,* 63–84.

Remafedi, G., Resnick, M., Blum, R., & Harris, L. (1992). Demography of sexual orientation in adolescents. *Pediatrics, 89,* 714–721.

Renshaw, D. C. (1999). Lessons from the intersexed. *Journal of the American Medical Association, 281,* 1137.

Reschly, D. J., Hosp, J. L., & Schmied, C. M. (2003). *And miles to go . . . State SLD requirements and authoritative recommendations.* Retrieved July 19, 2006, from http://www.nrcld.org/research/states/index.shtml

Resnick, L. B., & Omanson, S. F. (1987). Learning to understand arithmetic. In R. Glaser (Ed.), *Advances in instructional psychology* (Vol. 3, pp. 41–95). Hillsdale, NJ: Erlbaum.

Resnick, S. M., Pham, D. L., Kraut, M. A., Zonderman, A. B., & Davatzikos, C. (2003). Longitudinal magnetic resonance imaging studies of older adults: A shrinking brain. *Journal of Neuroscience, 23,* 3295–3301.

Reuter-Lorenz, P. A. (2000). Cognitive neuropsychology of the aging brain. In D. C. Park & N. Schwartz (Eds.), *Cognitive aging: A primer* (pp. 93–114). Hove, England: Psychology Press.

Reuter-Lorenz, P. A. (2002). New visions of the aging mind and brain. *Trends in Cognitive Sciences, 6,* 394–400.

Reynolds, T. (2003). Understanding emotion in abused children. *APS Observor, 16*(10), 1, 31–33.

Rhein, L. M., Ginsburg, K. R., Schwarz, D. F., et al. (1997). Teen father participation in child rearing: Family perspectives. *Journal of Adolescent Health, 21,* 244–252.

Rhodewalt, F. (1994). Conceptions of ability, achievement goals, and individual differences in self-handicapping behavior: On the application of implicit theories. *Journal of Personality, 62,* 67–85.

Ricciuti, H. N. (2004). Single parenthood, achievement, and problem behavior in white, black, and Hispanic children. *Journal of Educational Research, 97,* 196–206.

Rich, S. S., DiMarco, N. M., Huettig, C., Essery, E. V., Andersson, E., & Sanborn, C. F. (2005). Perceptions of health status and play activities in parents of overweight Hispanic toddlers and preschoolers. *Family and Community Health, 28,* 130–141.

Richard, J. F., & Schneider, B. H. (2005). Assessing friendship motivation during preadolescence and early adolescence. *Journal of Early Adolescence, 25,* 367–385.

Richards, M. H., Miller, B. V., O'Donnell, P. C., Wasserman, M. S., & Craig, C. (2004). Parental monitoring mediates the effects of age and sex on problem behaviors among African American urban young adolescents. *Journal of Youth and Adolescence, 33,* 221–233.

Rickert, V. I., & Johnson, C. M. (1988). Reducing nocturnal awakening and crying episodes in infants and young children: A comparison between scheduled awakenings and systematic ignoring. *Pediatrics, 81,* 203–212.

Rigby, K. (2005). Why do some children bully at school? The contributions of negative attitudes towards victims and the perceived expectations of friends, parents and teachers. *School Psychology International, 26,* 147–161.

Riley, E. P., & McGee, C. L. (2005). Fetal alcohol spectrum disorders: An overview with emphasis on changes in brain and behavior. *Experimental Biology and Medicine, 230,* 357–365.

Rind, B., Tromovitch, P., & Bauserman, R. (1998). A meta-analytic examination of assumed properties of child sexual abuse using college samples. *Psychological Bulletin, 124,* 22–53.

Robbins, A., & Wilner, A. (2001). *Quarterlife crisis: The unique challenges of life in your twenties.* New York: Tarcher/Putnam.

Roberts, B. W., & DelVecchio, W. F. (2000). The rank-order consistency of personality traits from childhood to old age: A quantitative review of longitudinal studies. *Psychological Bulletin, 126,* 3–25.

Roberts, K. P., & Lamb, M. E. (1999). Children's responses when interviewers distort details during investigative interviews. *Legal and Criminological Psychology, 4,* 23–31.

Roberts, L. (2000, January 3). The gene hunters: Unlocking the secrets of DNA to cure disease, slow aging. *U.S. News and World Report, 128,* 34–38.

Roberts, R. E., Kaplan, G. A., Shema, S. J., & Strawbridge, W. J. (1997). Prevalence and correlates of depression in an aging cohort: The Alameda County Study. *Journals of Gerontology: Psychological Sciences and Social Sciences, 52B,* S252–S258.

Robertson, E. B., David, S. L., Rao, S. A., & National Institute on Drug Abuse. (2003). *Preventing drug use among children and adolescents: A research-based guide for parents, educators, and community leaders* (2nd ed.). Bethesda, MD: National Institute on Drug Abuse.

Robins, L. N. (1966). *Deviant children grown up: A sociological and psychiatric study of sociopathic personality.* Baltimore: Williams & Wilkins.

Robinson, G. (1996). Cross-cultural perspectives on menopause. *Journal of Nervous and Mental Disease, 184,* 453–458.

Robinson, J. L., Kagan, J., Reznick, J. S., & Corley, R. (1992). The heritability of inhibited and uninhibited behavior: A twin study. *Developmental Psychology, 28,* 1030–1037.

Robinson, N. M., Lanzi, R. G., Weinberg, R. A., Ramey, S. L., & Ramey, C. T. (2002). Family factors associated with high academic competence in former Head Start children at third grade. *Gifted Child Quarterly, 46,* 278–290.

Robinson, T. N. (1999). Reducing children's television viewing to prevent obesity: A randomized controlled trial. *Journal of the American Medical Association, 282,* 1561–1567.

Robles, T. F., Glaser, R., & Kiecolt-Glaser, J. K. (2005). Out of balance: A new look at chronic stress, depression, and immunity. *Current Directions in Psychological Science, 14,* 111–115.

Rochat, P., & Striano, T. (2002). Who's in the mirror: Self-other discrimination in specular images by four- and nine-month-old infants. *Child Development, 73,* 35–46.

Rodin, J., Silberstein, L., & Striegel-Moore, R. (1985). Women and weight: A normative discontent. In R. A. Dienstbier (Series Ed.) & T. B. Sonderegger (Vol. Ed.), *Nebraska symposium on motivation, 1984: Vol. 32. Psychology and gender* (pp. 267–307). Lincoln, NE: University of Nebraska Press.

Roe, D. A. (1973). *A plague of corn: The social history of pellagra.* Ithaca, NY: Cornell University Press.

Roenker, D. L., Cissell, G. M., Ball, K. K., Wadley, V. G., & Edwards, J. D. (2003). Speed-of-processing and driver simulator training result in improved driving performance. *Human Factors, 45,* 218–233.

Roffwarg, H. P., Muzio, J. N., & Dement, W. C. (1966). Ontogenetic development of the human sleep-dream cycle. *Science, 152,* 604–619.

Rogers, W. A. (2000). Attention and aging. In D. C. Park & N. Schwarz (Eds.), *Cognitive aging: A primer* (pp. 57–73). Hove, England: Psychology Press.

Rogers, W. A., Campbell, R. H., & Pak, R. (2001). A systems approach for training older adults to use technology. In N. Charness, D. C. Parks, & B. A. Sabel (Eds.), *Communication, technology, and aging: Opportunities and challenges for the future* (pp.187–208). New York: Springer.

Rogers, W. A., & Fisk, A. D. (2001). Understanding the role of attention in cognitive aging research. In J. E. Birren & K. W. Schaie (Eds.), *Handbook of the psychology of aging* (5th ed., pp. 267–287). San Diego, CA: Academic Press.

Rogoff, B. (2003). *The cultural nature of human development.* New York: Oxford University Press.

Rogoff, B., & Chavajay, P. (1995). What's become of research on the cultural basis of cognitive development? *American Psychologist, 50,* 859–877.

Rogoff, B., Sellers, M. J., Pirotta, S., Fox, N., & White, S. H. (1975). Age of assignment of roles and responsibilities to children: A cross-cultural survey. *Human Development, 18,* 353–369.

Rogol, A. D., Clark, P. A., & Roemmich, J. N. (2000). Growth and pubertal development in children and adolescents: Effects of diet and physical activity. *American Journal of Clinical Nutrition, 72*(Suppl.), 521S–528S.

Rohde, L. A., Szobot, C., Polanczyk, G., Schmitz, M., Martins, S., & Tramontina, S. (2005). Attention-deficit/hyperactivity disorder in a diverse culture: Do research and clinical findings support the notion of a cultural construct for the disorder? *Biological Psychiatry, 57,* 1436–1441.

Rolls, B. J., Engell, D., & Birch, L. L. (2000). Serving portion size influences 5–year-old but not 3–year-old children's food intakes. *Journal of the American Dietetic Association, 100,* 232–234.

Román, G. C. (2004). Facts, myths, and controversies in vascular dementia. *Journal of the Neurological Sciences, 226,* 49–52.

Roos, M. R., Rice, C. L., Connelly, D. M., & Vandervoort, A. A. (1999). Quadriceps muscle strength, contractile properties, and motor unit firing rates in young and old men. *Muscle and Nerve, 22,* 1094–1103.

Roos, P. A., & Gatta, M. L. (1999). The gender gap in earnings: Trends, explanations, and prospects. In G. N. Powell (Ed.), *Handbook of gender and work* (pp. 95–123). Thousand Oaks, CA: Sage.

Roscoe, L. A., Malphurs, J. E., Dragovic, L. J., & Cohen, D. (2001). A comparison of characteristics of Kevorkian euthanasia cases and physician-assisted suicides in Oregon. *Gerontologist, 41,* 439–446.

Rose, M. R. (2004). Will human aging be postponed? *Scientific American, 14*(3), 24–29.

Rose, R. J., Viken, R. J., Dick, D. M., Bates, J. E., Pulkkinen, L., & Kaprio, J. (2003). It does take a village: Nonfamilial environments and children's behavior. *Psychological Science, 14,* 273–277.

Rose, S. A., & Feldman, J. F. (1995). Prediction of IQ and specific cognitive abilities at 11 years from infancy measures. *Developmental Psychology, 31,* 685–696.

Rose, S. A., & Feldman, J. F. (2000). The relation of very low birthweight to basic cognitive skills in infancy and childhood. In C. A. Nelson (Ed.), *Minnesota Symposia on Child Psychology: Vol. 31. The effects of early adversity on neurobehavioral development* (pp. 31–59). Mahwah, NJ: Erlbaum.

Rosen, M. G., & Dickinson, J. C. (1993). The paradox of electronic fetal monitoring: More data may not enable us to predict or prevent infant neurologic morbidity. *American Journal of Obstetrics and Gynecology, 168,* 745–751.

Rosenberg, L., Palmer, J. R., Rao, R. S., & Adams-Campbell, L. L. (1999). Risk factors for coronary heart disease in African American women. *American Journal of Epidemiology, 150,* 904–909.

Rosenberg, L. E., & Schechter, A. N. (2000). Gene therapist, heal thyself. *Science, 287,* 1751.

Rosenberg, M. (1986). Self-concept from middle childhood through adolescence. In J. M. Suls & A. G. Greenwald (Eds.), *Psychological perspectives on the self* (pp. 182–205). Hillsdale, NJ: Erlbaum.

Rosenblatt, P. C. (1993). Cross-cultural variation in the experience, expression, and understanding of grief. In D. P. Irish, K. F. Lundquist, & V. J. Nelsen (Eds.), *Ethnic variations in dying, death, and grief: Diversity in universality* (pp. 13–19). Philadelphia: Taylor & Francis.

Rosenfield, A. (1997). The history of the Safe Motherhood Initiative. *International Journal of Gynaecology and Obstetrics, 59*(Suppl. 2), S7–S9.

Rosenthal, R. (1995). *State of New Jersey v. Margaret Kelly Michaels:* An overview. *Psychology, Public Policy, and Law, 1,* 246–271.

Roser, M., & Gazzaniga, M. S. (2004). Automatic brains-Interpretive minds. *Current Directions in Psychological Science, 13,* 56–59.

Ross, C. E., & Mirowsky, J. (1999). Refining the association between education and health: The effects of quantity, credential, and selectivity. *Demography, 36,* 445–460.

Ross, G. (2003). Hyperbilirubinemia in the 2000s: What should we do next? *American Journal of Perinatology, 20,* 415–424.

Ross, H. S., Filyer, R. E., Lollis, S. P., Perman, M., & Martin, J. L. (1994). Administering justice in the family. *Journal of Family Psychology, 8,* 254–273.

Rossiter, C. E., Chong, H., Lister, U. G., et al. (1985). The influence of maternal age and parity on child-bearing with special reference to primigravidae aged 15 years and under. *British Journal of Obstetrics and Gynaecology, 92*(Suppl. 5), 23–31.

Rosso, I. M., Young, A. D., Femia, L. A., & Yurgelun-Todd, D. A. (2004). Cognitive and emotional components of frontal lobe functioning in childhood and adolescence. In R. E. Dahl & L. P. Spear (Eds.), *Annals of the New York Academy of Sciences: Vol. 1021. Adolescent brain development: Vulnerabilities and opportunities* (pp. 355–362). New York: New York Academy of Sciences.

Roth, A. (2001, September 6). *Williams harbors hope of someday being released.* Copley News Service.

Roth, G. S., Lane, M. A., & Ingram, D. K. (2005). Caloric restriction mimetics: The next phase. In W. Pierpaoli (Ed.), *Annals of the New York Academy of Sciences: Vol. 1057. Reversal of aging: Resetting the pineal clock* (pp. 365–371). New York: New York Academy of Sciences.

Rothbart, M. K. (2004a). Commentary: Differentiated measures of temperament and multiple pathways to childhood disorders. *Journal of Clinical Child and Adolescent Psychology, 33,* 82–87.

Rothbart, M. K. (2004b). Temperament and the pursuit of an integrated developmental psychology. *Merrill-Palmer Quarterly, 50,* 492–505.

Rothbart, M. K., Ahadi, S. A., & Evans, D. E. (2000). Temperament and personality: Origins and outcomes. *Journal of Personality and Social Psychology, 78,* 122–135.

Rothbart, M. K., Chew, K. H., & Gartstein, M. A. (2001). Assessment of temperament in early development. In L. T. Singer & P. S. Zeskind (Eds.), *Biobehavioral assessment of the infant* (pp. 190–208). New York: Guilford.

Rothbart, M. K., Ellis, L. K., & Posner, M. I. (2005). Temperament and self-regulation. In R. F. Baumeister & K. D. Vohs (Eds.), *Handbook of self-regulation: Research, theory, and applications* (pp. 357–370). New York: Guilford.

Rothbart, M. K., & Mauro, J. A. (1990). Questionnaire approaches to the study of infant temperament. In J. Colombo & J. W. Fagen (Eds.), *Individual differences in infancy: Reliability, stability and prediction* (pp. 411–429). Hillsdale, NJ: Erlbaum.

Rothbart, M. K., & Posner, M. I. (2001). Mechanism and variation in the development of attentional networks. In C. A. Nelson & M. Luciana (Eds.), *Handbook of developmental cognitive neuroscience* (pp. 353–363). Cambridge, MA: MIT Press.

Rothbart, M. K., & Posner, M. I. (2006). Temperament, attention, and developmental psychopathology. In D. Cicchetti & D. J. Cohen (Eds.), *Handbook of developmental psychopathology* (2nd ed., pp. 99–166). Hoboken, NJ: Wiley.

Rothbart, M. L., & Rueda, M. R. (2005). The development of effortful control. In U. Mayr, E. Awh, & S. W. Keele (Eds.), *Developing individuality in the human brain: A tribute to Michael I. Posner* (pp. 167–188). Washington, DC: American Psychological Association.

Roush, W. (1996). Guarding against premature birth. *Science, 271*, 139–140.

Routh, D. K., & Fox, B. (1984). "MM . . . is a little bit of May": Phonemes, reading and spelling. *Advances in Learning and Behavioral Disabilities, 3*, 95–124.

Rovee-Collier, C. (1996). Shifting the focus from what to why. *Infant Behavior and Development, 19*, 385–400.

Rovee-Collier, C., Hayne, H., & Colombo, M. (2001). *The development of implicit and explicit memory.* Philadelphia: John Benjamins.

Rowe, J. W., & Kahn, R. L. (1998). *Successful aging.* New York: Dell.

Roy, P., Rutter, M., & Pickles, A. (2004). Institutional care: Associations between overactivity and lack of selectivity in social relationships. *Journal of Child Psychology and Psychiatry, 45*, 866–873.

Royer, J. M., & Garofoli, L. M. (2005). Cognitive contributions to sex differences in math performance. In A. M. Gallagher & J. C. Kaufman (Eds.), *Gender differences in mathematics: An integrative psychological approach* (pp. 99–120). New York: Cambridge University Press.

Royer, J. M., Tronsky, L. N., Chan, Y., Jackson, S. J., & Marchant, H., III. (1999). Math-fact retrieval as the cognitive mechanism underlying gender differences in math test performance. *Contemporary Educational Psychology, 24*, 181–266.

Rozin, P. (2000). Why we're so fat (and the French are not). *Psychology Today, 33*(6), 64–68.

Rozin, P., Kabnick, K., Pete, E., Fischler, C., & Shields, C. (2003). The ecology of eating: Smaller portion sizes in France than in the United States help explain the French paradox. *Psychological Science, 14*, 450–454.

Rubia, K., Overmeyer, S., Taylor, E., et al. (2000). Functional frontalisation with age: Mapping neurodevelopmental trajectories with fMRI. *Neuroscience and Biobehavioral Reviews, 24*, 13–19.

Rubin, D. C. (2000). Autobiographical memory and aging. In D. C. Park & N. Schwarz (Eds.), *Cognitive aging: A primer* (pp. 131–149). Hove, England: Psychology Press.

Rubin, J. Z., Provenzano, F., & Luria, Z. (1974). The eye of the beholder: Parents' views on sex of newborns. *American Journal of Orthopsychiatry, 44*, 512–519.

Rubin, K. H., Burgess, K. B., & Hastings, P. D. (2002). Stability and social-behavioral consequences of toddlers' inhibited temperament and parenting behaviors. *Child Development, 73*, 483–495.

Rubin, K. H., Coplan, R. J., Nelson, L. J., Cheah, C. S. L., & Lagace-Seguin, D. G. (1999). Peer relationships in childhood. In M. H. Bornstein & M. E. Lamb (Eds.), *Developmental psychology: An advanced textbook* (4th ed., pp. 451–501). Mahwah, NJ: Erbaum.

Ruff, H. A., Capozzoli, M., & Weissberg, R. (1998). Age, individuality, and context as factors in sustained visual attention during the preschool years. *Developmental Psychology, 34*, 454–464.

Ruffman, T. (1999). Children's understanding of logical inconsistency. *Child Development, 70*, 872–886.

Ruffman, T., Slade, L., & Crowe, E. (2002). The relation between children's and mothers' mental state language and theory-of-mind understanding. *Child Development, 73*, 734–751.

Rupa, D. S., Reddy, P. P., & Reddi, O. S. (1991). Reproductive performance in population exposed to pesticides in cotton fields in India. *Environmental Research, 55*, 123–128.

Rushton, J. P. (1996). Race differences in brain size. *American Psychologist, 51*, 556.

Rushton, J. P., & Jensen, A. R. (2005). Wanted: More race realism, less moralistic fallacy. *Psychology, Public Policy, and Law, 11*, 328–336.

Rushton, J. P., & Rushton, E. W. (2003). Brain size, IQ, and racial-group differences: Evidence from musculoskeletal traits. *Intelligence, 31*, 139–155.

Russell, R. (2000). The effects of regional analgesia on the progress of labour and delivery. *British Journal of Anaesthesia, 84*, 709–712.

Russo, F. (1999). The clinical-trials bottleneck. *Atlantic Monthly, 283*(5), 30–34.

Rutter, M., & Maughan, B. (2002). School effectiveness findings 1979–2002. *Journal of School Psychology, 40*, 451–475.

Rutter, M., O'Connor, T. G., & English and Romanian Adoptees (ERA) Study Team. (2004). Are there biological programming effects for psychological development? Findings from a study of Romanian adoptees. *Developmental Psychology, 40*, 81–94.

Rvachew, S., Slawinski, E. B., Williams, M., & Green, C. L. (1999). The impact of early onset otitis media on babbling and early language development. *Journal of the Acoustical Society of America, 105*, 467–475.

Ryan, E. B., See, S. K., Meneer, W. B., & Trovato, D. (1992). Age-based perceptions of language performance among younger and older adults. *Communication Research, 19*, 423–443.

Rysiew, K. J., Shore, B. M., & Leeb, R. T. (1999). Multipotentiality, giftedness, and career choice: A review. *Journal of Counseling and Development, 77*, 423–430.

Sachs, H. T., & Barrett, R. P. (2000). Psychopathology in individuals with mental retardation. In A. J. Sameroff & M. Lewis (Eds.), *Handbook of developmental psychopathology* (2nd ed., pp. 657–670). New York: Kluwer Academic/Plenum.

Sachs, J. (2001). Communication development in infancy. In J. B. Gleason (Ed.), *The development of language* (pp. 40–69). Boston: Allyn & Bacon.

Saffran, J. R. (2003). Statistical language learning: Mechanisms and constraints. *Current Directions in Psychological Science, 12*, 110–114.

Saffran, J. R., Aslin, R. N., & Newport, E. L. (1996). Statistical learning by 8–month-old infants. *Science, 274*, 1926–1928.

Sagrestano, L. M., Heavey, C. L., & Christensen, A. (1999). Perceived power and physical violence in marital conflict. *Journal of Social Issues, 55*(1), 65–79.

Salem, D. A., Zimmerman, M. A., & Notaro, P. C. (1998). Effects of family structure, family process, and father involvement on psychosocial outcomes among African American adolescents. *Family Relations, 47*, 331–341.

Salili, F. (1996). Learning and motivation: An Asian perspective. *Psychology and Developing Societies, 8*, 55–81.

Salinger, J. D. (1951). *The catcher in the rye.* New York: Bantam Books.

Salk, L. (1974). *Preparing for parenthood: Understanding your feelings about pregnancy, childbirth and your baby.* New York: Bantam Books.

Salthouse, T. A. (1984). Effects of age and skill in typing. *Journal of Experimental Psychology: General, 113*, 345–371.

Salthouse, T. A. (1990). Cognitive competence and expertise in aging. In J. E. Birren & K. W. Schaie (Eds.), *Handbook of the psychology of aging* (3rd ed., pp. 310–319). San Diego, CA: Academic Press.

Salthouse, T. A. (1991). Age and experience effects on the interpretation of orthographic drawings of three-dimensional objects. *Psychology and Aging, 6*, 426–433.

Salthouse, T. A. (1996). The processing-speed theory of adult age differences in cognition. *Psychological Review, 103*, 403–428.

Salthouse, T. A. (2004). What and when of cognitive aging. *Current Directions in Psychological Science, 13*, 140–144.

Salthouse, T. A., & Maurer, T. J. (1996). Aging, job performance, and career development. In J. E. Birren & K. W. Schaie (Eds.), *Handbook of the psychology of aging* (4th ed., pp. 353–364). San Diego, CA: Academic Press.

Salthouse, T. A., Mitchell, D. R., Skovronek, E., & Babcock, R. L. (1989). Effects of adult age and working memory on reasoning and spatial abilities. *Journal of Experimental Psychology: Learning, Memory, and Cognition, 15*, 507–516.

Saltzburg, S. (2004). Learning that an adolescent child is gay or lesbian: The parent experience. *Social Work, 49*, 109–118.

Sameroff, A. J., & Haith, M. M. (1996). Interpreting developmental transitions. In A. J. Sameroff & M. M. Haith (Eds.), *The five to seven year shift: The age of reason and responsibility* (pp. 3–15). Chicago: University of Chicago Press.

Sameroff, A. J., Seifer, R., Barocas, R., Zax. M., & Greenspan, S. (1987). Intelligence quotient scores of 4–year-old children: Social-environmental risk factors. *Pediatrics, 79,* 343–350.

Sampson, P. D., Streissguth, A. P., Bookstein, F. L., & Barr, H. M. (2000). On categorizations in analyses of alcohol teratogenesis. *Environmental Health Perspectives, 108*(Suppl. 3), 421–428.

Samuels, S. J. (1970). Effects of pictures on learning to read, comprehension, and attitudes. *Review of Educational Research, 40,* 397–407.

Sandberg, D. E. (1999). Experiences of being short: Should we expect problems of psychosocial adjustment? In U. Eiholzer, F. Haverkamp, & L. D. Voss (Eds.), *Growth, stature, and psychosocial well-being* (pp. 15–26). Seattle, WA: Hogrefe & Huber.

Sandberg, D. E., & Barrick, C. (1995). Endocrine disorders in childhood: A selective survey of intellectual and educational sequelae. *School Psychology Review, 24,* 146–170.

Sandberg, D. E., Brooke, A. E., & Campos, S. P. (1994). Short stature: A psychosocial burden requiring growth hormone therapy? *Pediatrics, 94,* 832–840.

Sapolsky, R. M. (1999). Hormonal correlates of personality and social contexts: From non-human to human primates. In C. Panter-Brick & C. M. Worthman (Eds.), *Hormones, health, and behavior: A socio-ecological and lifespan perspective* (pp. 18–46). New York: Cambridge University Press.

SAT[(r)] math scores for 2005 highest on record. (2005). Retrieved September 9, 2005, from **http://www.collegeboard.com/press/article/0,, 46851,00html**

Satz, P. (2001). Mild head injury in children and adolescents. *Current Directions in Psychological Science, 10,* 106–109.

Saunders, D. G. (2002). Are physical assaults by wives and girlfriends a major social problem? A review of the literature. *Violence Against Women, 8,* 1424–1448.

Savin-Williams, R. C. (2001). *Mom, Dad, I'm gay: How families negotiate coming out.* Washington, DC: American Psychological Association.

Savin-Williams, R. C. (2005). *The new gay teenager.* Cambridge, MA: Harvard University Press.

Savin-Williams, R. C., & Diamond, L. M. (2004). Sex. In R. M. Lerner & L. D. Steinberg (Eds.), *Handbook of adolescent psychology* (2nd ed., pp. 189–231). Hoboken, NJ: Wiley.

Savitsky, K., Medvec, V. H., & Gilovich, T. (1997). Remembering and regretting: The Zeigarnik effect and the cognitive availability of regrettable actions and inactions. *Personality and Social Psychology Bulletin, 23,* 248–257.

Sayer, L. C., Bianchi, S. M., & Robinson, J. P. (2004). Are parents investing less in children? Trends in mothers' and fathers' time with children. *American Journal of Sociology, 110,* 1–43.

Sayer, L. C., England, P., Bittman, M., & Bianchi, S. M. (2004, April). *How long is the second (plus first) shift? Gender differences in paid, unpaid, and total work time in Australia and the United States.* Paper presented at the meeting of the Population Association of America, Boston.

Saylor, C. F., Cowart, B. L., Lipovsky, J. A., Jackson, C., & Finch, A. J., Jr. (2003). Media exposure to September 11: Elementary school students' experiences and posttraumatic symptoms. *American Behavioral Scientist, 46,* 1622–1642.

Scannapieco, F. A., Bush, R. B., & Paju, S. (2003). Periodontal disease as a risk factor for adverse pregnancy outcomes: A systematic review. *Annals of Periodontology, 8,* 70–78.

Scarmeas, N., & Stern, Y. (2003). Cognitive reserve and lifestyle. *Journal of Clinical and Experimental Neuropsychology, 25,* 625–633.

Scarr, S. (1993). Biological and cultural diversity: The legacy of Darwin for development. *Child Development, 64,* 1333–1353.

Scarr, S. (1997). Why child care has little impact on most children's development. *Current Directions in Psychological Science, 6,* 143–148.

Scarr, S., & McCartney, K. (1983). How people make their own environments: A theory of genotype ⟶ environment effects. *Child Development, 54,* 424–435.

Scarr, S., Pakstis, A. J., Katz, S. H., & Barker, W. B. (1977). Absence of a relationship between degree of White ancestry and intellectual skills within a Black population. *Human Genetics, 39,* 69–86.

Schaie, K. W. (1965). A general model for the study of developmental problems. *Psychological Bulletin, 64,* 92–107.

Schaie, K. W. (1977–1978). Toward a stage theory of adult cognitive development. *International Journal of Aging and Human Development, 8,* 129–138.

Schaie, K. W. (1993). The organization of cognitive function in old age: Predictions based on cohort-sequential and longitudinal data. In P. B. Baltes & M. M. Baltes (Eds.), *Successful aging* (pp. 94–117). New York: Cambridge University Press.

Schaie, K. W. (1994). The course of adult intellectual development. *American Psychologist, 49,* 304–313.

Schaie, K. W. (1996a). Intellectual development in adulthood. J. E. Birren, K. W. Schaie, R. P. Abeles, M. Gatz, & T. A. Salthouse (Eds.), *Handbook of the psychology of aging* (4th ed., pp. 266–286). San Diego, CA: Academic Press.

Schaie, K. W. (1996b). *Intellectual development in adulthood: The Seattle Longitudinal Study.* New York: Cambridge University Press.

Schaie, K. W., & Willis, S. L. (2000). A stage theory model of adult cognitive development revisited. In R. L. Rubinstein, M. Moss, and M. H. Kleban (Eds.), *The many dimensions of aging* (pp. 175–193). New York: Springer.

Schaie, K. W., & Willis, S. L. (2002). *Adult development and aging* (5th ed.). Upper Saddle River, NJ: Prentice Hall.

Scher, P. W., Emans, S. J., & Grace, E. M. (1982). Factors associated with compliance to oral contraceptive use in an adolescent population. *Journal of Adolescent Health Care, 3,* 120–123.

Schiffman, S. S. (1997). Taste and smell losses in normal aging and disease. *Journal of the American Medical Association, 278,* 1357–1362.

Schmiedeskamp, M. (2004). Preventing good brains from going bad. *Scientific American, 14*(3), 85–92.

Schmitt, D. P. (2003). Universal sex differences in the desire for sexual variety: Tests from 52 nations, 6 continents, and 13 islands. *Journal of Personality and Social Psychology, 85,* 85–104.

Schmitt, D. P., Shackleford, T. K., Duntley, J., et al. (2002). Is there an early-30s peak in female sexual desire? Cross-sectional evidence from the United States and Canada. *Canadian Journal of Human Sexuality, 11,* 1–18.

Schneider, B. A., & Trehub, S. E. (1992). Sources of developmental change in auditory sensitivity. In L. A. Werner & E. W. Rubel (Eds.), *Developmental psychoacoustics* (pp. 3–46). Washington, DC: American Psychological Association.

Schneider, B. H., Atkinson, L., & Tardif, C. (2001). Child-parent attachment and children's peer relations: A quantitative review. *Developmental Psychology, 37,* 86–100.

Schneider, W. (1998). Performance prediction in young children: Effects of skill, metacognition and wishful thinking. *Developmental Science, 1,* 291–297.

Schneider, W., & Pressley, M. (1997). *Memory development between two and twenty* (2nd ed.). Mahwah, NJ: Erlbaum.

Scholz, H. S., Haas, J., & Petru, E. (1999). Do primiparas aged 40 years or older carry an increased obstetric risk? *Preventive Medicine, 29,* 263–266.

Schonfeld, D. J. (2003). Supporting children after terrorist events: Potential roles for pediatricians. *Pediatric Annals, 32,* 182–187.

Schönheit, B., Zarski, R., & Ohm, T. G. (2004). Spatial and temporal relationships between plaques and tangles in Alzheimer pathology. *Neurobiology of Aging, 25,* 607–711.

Schrauf, M., Wist, E. R., & Ehrenstein, W. H. (1999). Development of dynamic vision based on motion contrast. *Experimental Brain Research, 124,* 469–473.

Schuhmann, E. M., Foote, R. C., Eyberg, S. M., Boggs, S. R., & Algina, J. (1998). Efficacy of parent-child interaction therapy: Interim report of a randomized trial with short-term maintenance. *Journal of Clinical Child Psychology, 27,* 34–45.

Schulman, P., Keith, D., & Seligman, M. E. (1993). Is optimism heritable? A study of twins. *Behaviour Research and Therapy, 31,* 569–574.

Schultz, K. (2001). Constructing failure, narrating success: Rethinking the "problem" of teen pregnancy. *Teachers College Record, 103,* 582–607.

Schulz, K. S. (2003). Bridge employment: Work after retirement. In G. A. Adams & T. A. Beehr (Eds.), *Retirement: Reasons, processes, and results* (pp. 214–241). New York: Springer.

Schulz, R., & Aderman, D. (1974). Clinical research and the stages of dying. *Omega, 5,* 137–144.

Schulz, R., & Beach, S. R. (1999). Caregiving as a risk factor for mortality: The Caregiver Health Effects Study. *Journal of the American Medical Association, 282,* 2215–2219.

Schulz, R., & Curnow, C. (1988). Peak performance and age among superathletes: Track and field, swimming, baseball, tennis, and golf. *Journals of Gerontology: Psychological Sciences and Social Sciences, 43B,* P113–P120.

Schulz, R., & Heckhausen, J. (1998). Emotion and control: A life-span perspective. In K. W. Schaie & M. P. Lawton (Eds.), *Annual review of gerontology and geriatrics* (Vol. 17, pp. 185–205). New York: Springer.

Schulz, R., Musa, D., Staszewski, J., & Siegler, R. S. (1994). The relationship between age and major league baseball performance: Implications for development. *Psychology and Aging, 9,* 274–286.

Schulz, R., O'Brien, A., Czaja, S., et al. (2002). Dementia caregiver intervention research: In search of clinical significance. *Gerontologist, 42,* 589–602.

Schulz, R., O'Brien, A. T., Bookwala, J., & Fleissner, K. (1995). Psychiatric and physical morbidity effects of dementia caregiving: Prevalence, correlates, and causes. *Gerontologist, 35,* 771–791.

Schulz, R., & Salthouse, T. A. (1999). *Adult development and aging: Myths and emerging realities* (3rd ed.). Upper Saddle River, NJ: Prentice Hall.

Schum, T. R., Kolb, T. M., McAuliffe, T. L., Simms, M. D., Underhill, R. L., & Lewis, M. (2002). Sequential acquisition of toilet-training skills: A descriptive study of gender and age differences in normal children. *Pediatrics, 109,* e48.

Schutte, A. R., & Spencer, J. P. (2002). Generalizing the dynamic field theory of the A-not-B error beyond infancy: Three-year-olds' delay- and experience-dependent location memory biases. *Child Development, 73,* 377–404.

Schwartz, B. (2000). Self-determination: The tyranny of freedom. *American Psychologist, 55,* 79–88.

Schwartz, B. (2004). *The paradox of choice: Why more is less.* New York: Ecco.

Schwartz, B. B., & Reznick, S. (1999). Measuring infant spatial working memory using a modified delayed-response procedure. *Memory, 7,* 1–17.

Schwartz, D., Dodge, K. A., Pettit, G. S., & Bates, J. E. (1997). The early socialization of aggressive victims of bullying. *Child Development, 68,* 665–675.

Schwartzberg, N., Berliner, K., & Jacob, D. (1995). *Single in a married world: A life cycle framework for working with the unmarried adult.* New York: Norton.

Schwebel, D. C., & Plumert, J. M. (1999). Longitudinal and concurrent relations among temperament, ability estimation, and injury proneness. *Child Development, 70,* 700–712.

Schwebel, M. (1975). Formal operations in first-year college students. *Journal of Psychology, 91,* 133–141.

Scientific American frontiers archives. (2005). *Ask the scientists: Roy Walford as seen on Never Say Die: Eat Less—Live Longer.* Retrieved September 3, 2005, from www.pbs.org/safarchive/3_ask/archive/qna/32103_walford.html

Scott, K. D., Klaus, P. H., & Klaus, M. H. (1999). The obstetrical and postpartum benefits of continuous support during childbirth. *Journal of Women's Health and Gender-Based Medicine, 8,* 1257–1264.

Scullin, M. H., Peters, E., Williams, W. M., & Ceci, S. J. (2000). The role of IQ and education in predicting later labor market outcomes: Implications for affirmative action. *Psychology, Public Policy, and Law, 6,* 63–89.

Sears, R. R. (1975). *Your ancients revisited: A history of child development.* Chicago: University of Chicago Press.

Sears, R. R., Maccoby, E. E., & Levin, H. (1957). *Patterns of child rearing.* Evanston, IL: Row & Peterson.

Sebby, R. A., & Papini, D. R. (1994). Postformal reasoning during adolescence and young adulthood: The influence of problem relevancy. *Adolescence, 29,* 389–400.

Secondi, G. S. (2002). Biased childhood sex ratios and the economic status of the family in rural China. *Journal of Comparative Family Studies, 33,* 215–234.

Segal, N. L. (1999). *Entwined lives: Twins and what they tell us about human behavior.* New York: Dutton.

Segalowitz, S. J., Davies, P. L., Santesso, D., Gavin, W. J., & Schmidt, L. A. (2004). The development of the error negativity in children and adolescents. In M. Ullsperger & M. Falkenstein (Eds.), *Errors, conflicts, and the brain: Current opinions on performance monitoring* (pp. 177–184). Leipzig, Germany: Max Planck Institute for Cognition and Brain Sciences.

Seidel, H. M., Rosenstein, B. J., & Pathak, A. (Eds.). (2001). *Primary care of the newborn* (3rd ed.). St. Louis, MO: Mosby.

Seidler, R., & Stelmach, G. (1996). Motor control. In J. E. Birren (Ed.), *Encyclopedia of gerontology: Age, aging, and the aged* (pp. 177–185). San Diego, CA: Academic Press.

Seidman, E., Aber, J. L., Allen, L., & French, S. E. (1996). The impact of the transition to high school on the self-esteem and perceived social context of poor urban youth. *American Journal of Community Psychology, 24,* 489–515.

Seidman, E., Lambert, L. E., Allen, L., & Aber, J. (2003). Urban adolescents' transition to junior high school and protective family transactions. *Journal of Early Adolescence, 23,* 166–193.

Seifer, R. (2000). Temperament and goodness of fit: Implications for developmental psychopathology. In A. J. Sameroff, M. Lewis, & S. M. Miller (Eds.), *Handbook of developmental psychopathology* (2nd ed., pp. 257–276). New York: Kluwer Academic/Plenum.

Seligman, M. E. (1970). On the generality of the laws of learning. *Psychological Review, 77,* 406–418.

Senior, K. (1999). Is the case for fetal surgery for spina bifida proven? *The Lancet, 354,* 1795.

Serbin, L. A., Poulin-Dubois, D., Colburne, K. A., Sen, M. G., & Eichstedt, J. A. (2001). Gender stereotyping in infancy: Visual preferences for and knowledge of gender-stereotyped toys in the second year. *International Journal of Behavioral Development, 25,* 7–15.

Serketich, W. J., & Dumas, J. E. (1997). Adults' perceptions of the behavior of competent and dysfunctional children based on the children's physical appearance. *Behavior Modification, 21,* 457–469.

Serpell, R., Sonnenschein, S., Baker, L., & Ganapathy, H. (2002). Intimate culture of families in the early socialization of literacy. *Journal of Family Psychology, 16,* 391–405.

Shaffer, D., Gould, M. S., Fisher, P., et al. (1996). Psychiatric diagnosis in child and adolescent suicide. *Archives of General Psychiatry, 53,* 339–348.

Shalidullah, S., & Hepper, P. G. (1994). Frequency discrimination by the fetus. *Early Human Development, 36*, 13–26.

Shannon, J. D., Tamis-LeMonda, C. S., London, K., & Natasha, C. (2002). Beyond rough and tumble: Low-income fathers' interactions and children's cognitive development at 24 months. *Parenting: Science and Practice, 2*, 77–104.

Shantz, C. U. (1975). *The development of social cognition*. Chicago: University of Chicago Press.

Shapiro, J. (1999, October 25). Off the road: Deciding if someone is too old to get behind the wheel. *U.S. News and World Report, 127*, 60–64.

Shapiro, J. P. (2000, January 3). Many benefits, many perils: Genetic testing. *U.S. News and World Report, 128*(1), 38.

Shatz, M., & Gelman, R. (1973). The development of communication skills: Modifications in the speech of young children as a function of the listener. *Monographs of the Society for Research in Child Development, 38*(5, Serial No. 152).

Shawky, S., & Milaat, W. (2001). Cumulative impact of early maternal marital age during the childbearing period. *Paediatric and Perinatal Epidemiology, 15*, 27–33.

Shedler, J., & Block, J. (1990). Adolescent drug use and psychological health: A longitudinal inquiry. *American Psychologist, 45*, 612–630.

Shek, D. T. L. (2000). Differences between fathers and mothers in the treatment of, and relationship with, their teenage children: Perceptions of Chinese adolescents. *Adolescence, 35*, 135–146.

Shelov, S. P. (Ed.) (2004). *Caring for your baby and young child: Birth to age 5*. New York: Bantam Books.

Shephard, R. J. (1982). *Physical activity and growth*. Chicago: Year Book Medical Publishers.

Shermer, M. (2003). The domesticated savage. *Scientific American, 289*(3), 40.

Shi, J. (2004). Diligence makes people smart. In R. J. Sternberg (Ed.), *International handbook of intelligence*. New York: Cambridge University Press.

Shidlo, A., & Schroeder, M. (2002). Changing sexual orientation? A consumers' report. *Professional Psychology: Research and Practice, 33*, 249–259.

Shimizo, H., & Levine, R. A. (2001). *Japanese frames of mind: Cultural perspectives on human development*. New York: Cambridge University Press.

Shimonaka, Y., Nakazato, K., Kawaai, C., & Sato, S. (1997). Androgyny and successful adaptation across the life span among Japanese adults. *Journal of Genetic Psychology, 158*, 389–400.

Shneidman, E. S. (1982). *Voices of death*. New York: Bantam Books.

Shock, N. W. (1985). Longitudinal studies of aging in humans. In C. E. Finch & E. L. Schneider (Eds.), *Handbook of the biology of aging* (2nd ed., pp. 721–743). New York: Van Nostrand Reinhold.

Shonkoff, J. P., & Marshall, P. C. (2000). The biology of developmental vulnerability. In J. P. Shonkoff & S. J. Meisels (Eds.), *Handbook of early childhood intervention* (2nd ed., pp. 31–53). New York: Cambridge University Press.

Shore, L. M., Cleveland, J. N., & Goldberg, C. B. (2003). Work attitudes and decisions as a function of manager age and employee age. *Journal of Applied Psychology, 88*, 529–537.

Shumaker, S. A., Legault, C., Rapp, S. R., et al. (2003). Estrogen plus progestin and the incidence of dementia and mild cognitive impairment in postmenopausal women: The Women's Health Initiative Memory Study: A randomized controlled trial. *Journal of the American Medical Association, 289*, 2651–2662.

Shumway-Cook, A., & Woollacott, M. H. (1985). The growth of stability: Postural control from a developmental perspective. *Journal of Motor Behavior, 17*, 131–147.

Shute, B., & Wheldall, K. (1999). Fundamental frequency and temporal modifications in the speech of British fathers to their children. *Educational Psychology, 19*, 221–233.

Shute, B., & Wheldall, K. (2001). How do grandmothers speak to their grandchildren? Fundamental frequency and temporal modifications in the speech of British grandmothers to their grandchildren. *Educational Psychology, 21*, 493–503.

Shute, M. (2003, January 20). The human factor. *U.S. News and World Report, 134*, 62–63.

Sichelman, L. (2001, May 21). Design competition looks at aging in place. *Nation's Building News, 17*, p. 5.

Siddiqui, A. A., & Ross, H. S. (1999). How do sibling conflicts end? *Early Education and Development, 10*, 315–332.

Siegel, L. (1994). Working memory and reading: A life-span perspective. *International Journal of Behavioral Development, 17*, 109–124.

Siegal, M. (1997). *Knowing children: Experiments in conversation and cognition*. Hove, England: Psychology Press.

Siegal, M., & Peterson, C. C. (1996). Breaking the mold: A fresh look at children's understanding of questions about lies and mistakes. *Developmental Psychology, 32*, 322–334.

Siegel, A. C., & Burton, R. V. (1999). Effects of baby walkers on motor and mental development in human infants. *Journal of Developmental and Behavioral Pediatrics, 20*, 355–361.

Siegel, L. S. (1981). Infant tests as predictors of cognitive and language development at two years. *Child Development, 52*, 545–557.

Siegel, R. M., Kiely, M., Bien, J. P., et al. (2003). Treatment of otitis media with observation and a safety-net antibiotic prescription. *Pediatrics, 112*, 527–531.

Siegler, R. S. (1996). *Emerging minds: The process of change in children's thinking*. New York: Oxford University Press.

Siegler, R. S. (2006). Microgenetic analyses of learning. In W. Damon & R. M. Lerner (Series Eds.) & D. Kuhn & R. Siegler (Vol. Eds.), *Handbook of child psychology: Vol. 2. Cognition, perception, and language* (6th ed., pp. 464–510). Hoboken, NJ: Wiley.

Siegler, R. S., & Alibali, M. W. (2005). *Children's thinking* (4th ed.). Upper Saddle River, NJ: Prentice Hall.

Sigelman, C. K., & Waitzman, K. A. (1991). The development of distributive justice orientations: Contextual influences on children's resource allocations. *Child Development, 62*, 1367–1378.

Sigman, M., Cohen, S. E., & Beckwith, L. (1997). Why does infant attention predict adolescent intelligence? *Infant Behavior and Development, 20*, 133–140.

Silventoinen, K., Sammalisto, S., Perola, M., et al. (2002). Heritability of adult body height: A comparative study of twin cohorts in eight countries. *Twin Research, 6*, 399–408.

Silver, R. I., Rodriguez, R., Chang, T. S., & Gearhart, J. P. (1999). In vitro fertilization is associated with an increased risk of hypospadias. *Journal of Urology, 161*, 1954–1957.

Silverstein, M., & Marenco, A. (2001). How Americans enact the grandparent role across the family life course. *Journal of Family Issues, 22*, 493–522.

Silverstein, M., & Parker, M. G. (2002). Leisure activities and quality of life among the oldest old in Sweden. *Research on Aging, 24*, 528–547.

Simcock, G., & Hayne, H. (2002). Breaking the barrier? Children fail to translate their preverbal memories into language. *Psychological Science, 13*, 225–231.

Simmons, R. G., & Blyth, D. A. (1987). *Moving into adolescence: The impact of pubertal change and school context*. New York: A. de Gruyter.

Simmons, T., & Dye, J. L. (2003, October). *Grandparents living with grandchildren: 2000.* (U.S. Census 2000 Brief No. C2KBR-31). Retrieved July 19, 2006, from http://www.census.gov/prod/2003pubs/c2kbr-31.pdf

Simons-Morton, B., Chen, R., Abroms, L., & Haynie, D. L. (2004). Latent growth curve analyses of peer and parent influences on smoking progression among early adolescents. *Health Psychology, 23*, 612–621.

Simons-Morton, B. G. (2004). The protective effect of parental expectations against early adolescent smoking initiation. *Health Education Research, 19*, 561–569.

Simonton, D. K. (1988). Age and outstanding achievement: What do we know after a century of research? *Psychological Bulletin, 104*, 251–267.

Simonton, D. K. (1990). Creativity and wisdom in aging. In J. E. Birren & K. W. Schaie (Eds.), *Handbook of the psychology of aging* (3rd ed., pp. 320–329). San Diego, CA: Academic Press.

Simpson, R., & Simpson, A. (1999). *Through the wilderness of Alzheimer's: A guide in two voices.* Minneapolis, MN: Augsburg.

Sinclair, R. D., & Thai, K. E. (2004). *Male androgenetic alopecia.* Retrieved April 18, 2005, from http://www.endotext.org/male/male18/male18.htm

Singer, J. A. (2004). Narrative identity and meaning making across the adult lifespan: An introduction. *Journal of Personality, 72,* 437–459.

Sinnott, J. D. (1989). Life-span relativistic postformal thought: Methodology and data from everyday problem-solving studies. M. L. Commons et al. (Eds.), *Adult development* (Vol. 1, pp. 239–278). New York: Praeger.

Sinnott, J. D. (1998). *The development of logic in adulthood: Postformal thought and its applications.* New York: Plenum Press.

Sinnott, J. D., & Shifren, K. (2001). Gender and aging: Gender differences and gender roles. In J. E. Birren & K. W. Schaie (Eds.), *Handbook of the psychology of aging* (5th ed., pp. 454–476). San Diego, CA: Academic Press.

Skaalvik, E. M., & Hagtvet, K. A. (1990). Academic achievement and self-concept: An analysis of causal predominance in a developmental perspective. *Journal of Personality and Social Psychology, 58,* 292–307.

Skinner, B. F. (1957). *Verbal behavior.* New York: Appleton-Century-Crofts.

Skinner, B. F. (1969). *Contingencies of reinforcement: A theoretical analysis.* New York: Appleton-Century-Crofts.

Skinner, B. F. (1974). *About behaviorism.* New York: Knopf.

Skoczenski, A. M., & Norcia, A. M. (2002). Late maturation of visual hyperacuity. *Psychological Science, 13,* 537–541.

Skranes, J. S., Nilsen, G., Smevik, O., Vik, T., & Brukakk, A. M. (1998). Cerebral MRI of very low birth weight children at 6 years of age compared with the findings at 1 year. *Pediatric Radiology, 28,* 471–475.

Skranes, J. S., Vik, T., Nilsen, G., Smevik, O., Andersson, H. W., & Brubakk, A. M. (1997). Cerebral magnetic resonance imaging and mental and motor function of very low birth weight children at six years of age. *Neuropediatrics, 28,* 149–154.

Skulachev, V. P., & Longo, V. D. (2005). Aging as mitochondria-mediated atavistic program: Can aging be switched off? In W. Pierpaoli (Ed.), *Annals of the New York Academy of Sciences: Vol. 1057. Reversal of aging: Resetting the pineal clock* (pp. 145–164). New York: New York Academy of Sciences.

Slater, A. (2000). Visual perception in the young infant: Early organization and rapid learning. In D. Muir & A. Slater (Eds.), *Infant development: The essential readings* (pp. 95–116). Malden, MA: Blackwell.

Slee, P. T. (1994). Situational and interpersonal correlates of anxiety associated with peer victimization. *Child Psychiatry and Human Development, 25,* 97–107.

Sloan, R. P., Bagiella, E., & Powell, T. (2001). Without a prayer: Methodological problems, ethical challenges, and misrepresentations in the study of religion, spirituality, and medicine. In T. G. Plante & A. C. Sherman (Eds.), *Faith and healing: Psychological perspectives* (pp. 339–354). New York: Guilford.

Slobin, D. I. (1979). *Psycholinguistics* (2nd ed.). Glenview, IL: Scott, Foresman.

Smail, P. J., Reyes, F. I., Winter, J. S. D., & Faiman, C. (1981). The fetal hormone environment and its effect on the morphogenesis of the genital system. In S. J. Kogan & E. S. E. Hafez (Eds.), *Pediatric andrology* (pp. 9–20). Boston: M. Nijhoff.

Small, M. F. (1997). Making connections. *American Scientist, 85*(6), 502–504.

Small, M. F. (1998). *Our babies, ourselves.* New York: Anchor Books.

Small, M. F. (2000, August). Family matters. *Discover, 21,* 66–71.

Smetana, J. G. (1995). Parenting styles and conceptions of parental authority during adolescence. *Child Development, 66,* 299–316.

Smetana, J. G., Campione-Barr, N., & Daddis, C. (2004). Longitudinal development of family decision making: Defining healthy behavioral autonomy for middle-class African American adolescents. *Child Development, 75,* 1418–1434.

Smiciklas-Wright, H., Mitchell, D. C., Mickle, S. J., Cook, A. J., & Goldman, J. D. (2002). Foods commonly eaten in the United States: Quantities consumed per eating occasion and in a day, 1994–1996. *U.S. Department of Agriculture NFS Report No. 96–5, pre-publication version.* Retrieved May 29, 2006, from http://www.ars.usda.gov/SP2UserFiles/Place/12355000/pdf/Portion.pdf

Smith, E. A. (1998). Is Tibetan polyandry adaptive? Methodological and metatheoretical analyses. *Human Nature, 9,* 225–261.

Smith, E. A., & Smith, S. A. (1994). Inuit sex-ratio variation: Population control, ethnographic error, or parental manipulation? *Current Anthropology, 35,* 595–624.

Smith, J., & Baltes, P. B. (1990). Wisdom-related knowledge: Age/cohort differences in response to life-planning problems. *Developmental Psychology, 26,* 494–505.

Smith, J., & Baltes, P. B. (1999). Trends and profiles of psychological functioning in very old age. In P. B. Baltes & K. U. Mayer (Eds.), *The Berlin Aging Study: Aging from 70 to 100* (pp. 197–226). New York: Cambridge University Press.

Smith, L. W. (2001). Lead poisoning. In J. L. Longe & D. S. Blanchfield (Eds.), *The Gale encyclopedia of medicine* (2nd ed.). Retrieved May 30, 2006, from *Health Reference Center Academic* database.

Smith, P. K. (2005). Play: Types and functions in human development. In B. Ellis & D. F. Bjorklund (Eds.), *Origins of the social mind: Evolutionary psychology and child development* (pp. 271–291). New York: Guilford.

Smith, P. K., Pepler, D., & Rigby, K. (Eds.). (2004). *Bullying in schools: How successful can interventions be?* New York: Cambridge University Press.

Smith, T. W. (2003). Coming of age in 21st century America: Public attitudes towards the importance of timing of transitions to adulthood. *GSS Topical Report No. 35.* Chicago: National Opinion Research Center, University of Chicago.

Smokowski, P. R., Reynolds, A. J., & Bezruczko, M. (2000). Resilience and protective factors in adolescence: An autobiographical perspective from disadvantaged youth. *Journal of School Psychology, 37,* 425–448.

Smyth, K. A., Fritsch, T., Cook, T. B., McClendon, M. J., Santillan, C. E., & Friedland, R. P. (2004). Worker functions and traits associated with occupations and the development of AD. *Neurology, 63,* 498–503.

Snarey, J. R. (1985). Cross-cultural universality of social-moral development: A critical review of Kohlbergian research. *Psychological Bulletin, 97,* 202–232.

Snarey, J. R., Reimer, J., & Kohlberg, L. (1985). Development of social-moral reasoning among Kibbutz adolescents: A longitudinal cross-cultural study. *Developmental Psychology, 21,* 3–17.

Sneed, J. R., & Whitbourne, S. K. (2001). Identity processing styles and the need for self-esteem in middle-aged and older adults. *International Journal of Aging and Human Development, 52,* 311–321.

Snow, C. W. (1998). *Infant development.* Upper Saddle River, NJ: Prentice Hall.

Snowdon, D. (2001). *Aging with grace: What the Nun Study teaches us about leading longer, healthier, and more meaningful lives.* New York: Bantam Books.

Snowdon, D. A., Kemper, S. J., Mortimer, J. A., Greiner, L. H., Wekstein, D. R., & Markesbery, W. R. (1996). Linguistic ability in early life and cognitive function and Alzheimer's disease in late life: Findings from the Nun Study. *Journal of the American Medical Association, 275,* 528–532.

Snowling, M. J., Gallagher, A., & Frith, U. (2003). Family risk of dyslexia is continuous: Individual differences in the precursors of reading skill. *Child Development, 74,* 358–373.

Snyder, D., & Johnson, D. (2004, November 16). Teens' beer party raided after Montgomery crash. *Washington Post,* p. B1.

Society for Research in Child Development. (2005). *Ethical standards for research with children.* Retrieved August 1, 2006, from http://www.srcd.org/ethicalstandards.html

Soejima, H., & Wagstaff, J. (2005). Imprinting centers, chromatin structure, and disease. *Journal of Cellular Biochemistry, 95,* 226–233.

Sohmer, H., Perez, R., Sichel, J. Y., Priner, R., & Freeman, S. (2001). The pathway enabling external sounds to reach and excite the fetal inner ear. *Audiology and Neuro-otology, 6,* 109–116.

Soldz, S., & Vaillant, G. E. (1999). The Big Five personality traits and the life course: A 45-year longitudinal study. *Journal of Research in Personality, 33,* 208–232.

Solomon, J., & George, C. (Eds.). (1999). *Attachment disorganization.* New York: Guilford.

Sonnert, G., & Holton, G. (1996). Career patterns of women and men in the sciences. *American Scientist, 84*(1), 63–71.

Sonuga-Barke, E. J. S., Dalen, L., Daley, D., & Remington, B. (2002). Are planning, working memory, and inhibition associated with individual differences in preschool ADHD symptoms? *Developmental Neuropsychology, 21,* 255–272.

Soong, W. T., Chao, K. Y., Jang, C. S., & Wang, J. D. (1999). Long-term effect of increased lead absorption on intelligence of children. *Archives of Environmental Health, 54,* 297–301.

Sorce, J. F., Emde, R. N., Campos, J., & Klinnert, M. D. (2000). Maternal emotional signaling: Its effect on the visual cliff behavior of 1-year-olds. In D. Muir & A. Slater (Eds.), *Infant development: The essential readings* (pp. 282–292). Malden, MA: Blackwell.

Sowell, E. R., & Jernigan, T. L. (1998). Further MRI evidence of late brain maturation: Limbic volume increases and changing asymmetries during childhood and adolescence. *Developmental Neuropsychology, 14,* 599–617.

Sowell, E. R., Peterson, B. S., Thompson, P. M., Welcome, S. E., Henkenius, A. L., & Toga, A. W. (2003). Mapping cortical change across the human life span. *Nature Neuroscience, 6,* 309–315.

Sowell, E. R., Thompson, P. M., Tessner, K. D., & Toga, A. W. (2001). Mapping continued brain growth and gray matter density reduction in dorsal frontal cortex: Inverse relationships during postadolescent brain maturation. *Journal of Neuroscience, 21,* 8819–8829.

Sowles, C. B. (2004). Adult development of women: Changes and constancy in the gender-role orientation of homemakers, women in female-dominated, and male dominated-professions. *Dissertation Abstracts International, 64* (10), 5235B.

Span, M. M., Ridderinkhof, K. R., & Molen, M. W. van der. (2004). Age-related changes in the efficiency of cognitive processing across the life span. *Acta Psychologica, 117,* 155–183.

Spear, L. P. (2000). The adolescent brain and age-related behavioral manifestations. *Neuroscience and Biobehavioral Reviews, 24,* 417–463.

Spearman, C. (1946). Theory of general factor. *British Journal of Psychology, 36,* 117–131.

Speece, M. W., & Brent, S. B. (1984). Children's understanding of death: A review of three components of a death concept. *Child Development, 55,* 1671–1686.

Spelke, E. S. (2000). Core knowledge. *American Psychologist, 55,* 1233–1243.

Spencer, J. P., & Schutte, A. R. (2004). Unifying representations and responses: Perseverative biases arise from a single behavioral system. *Psychological Science, 15,* 187–193.

Spencer, J. P., Smith, L. B., & Thelen, E. (2001). Tests of a dynamic systems account of the A-not-B error: The influence of prior experience on the spatial memory abilities of two-year-olds. *Child Development, 72,* 1327–1346.

Spencer, S. J., Steele, C. M., & Quinn, D. M. (1999). Stereotype threat and women's math performance. *Journal of Experimental Social Psychology, 35,* 4–28.

Spiezle, C., & Moulton, G. (2001). Design challenges associated with longevity: The view from industry. In N. Charness, D. C. Parks, & B. A. Sabel (Eds.), *Communication, technology, and aging: Opportunities and challenges for the future* (pp. 47–59). New York: Springer.

Spirduso, W. W. (1995). *Physical dimensions of aging.* Champaign, IL: Human Kinetics.

Spitz, H. H. (1986). *The raising of intelligence: A selected history of attempts to raise retarded intelligence.* Hillsdale, NJ: Erlbaum.

Spitze, G., & Gallant, M. P. (2004). "The bitter with the sweet": Older adults' strategies for handling ambivalence in relations with their adult children. *Research on Aging, 26,* 387–412.

Spitzer, M. C. (1995). Birth centers: Economy, safety, and empowerment. *Journal of Nurse-Midwifery, 40,* 371–375.

Spivak, H., & Prothrow-Stith, D. (2001). The need to address bullying—An important component of violence prevention. *Journal of the American Medical Association, 285,* 2131–2132.

Spooner, C. (1999). Causes and correlates of adolescent drug abuse and implications for treatment. *Drug and Alcohol Review, 18,* 453–475.

Staff, J., Mortimer, J. T., & Uggen, C. (2004). Work and leisure in adolescence. In R. M. Lerner & L. D. Steinberg (Eds.), *Handbook of adolescent psychology* (2nd ed., pp. 429–450). Hoboken, NJ: Wiley.

Staff, J., & Uggen, C. (2003). The fruits of good work: Early work experiences and adolescent deviance. *Journal of Research in Crime and Delinquency, 40,* 263–290.

Staff, R. T., Murray, A. D., Deary, I. J., & Whalley, L. J. (2004). What provides cerebral reserve? *Brain, 127,* 1191–1199.

Stanton, M. T., & Therolf, W. (1990). *Our children are dying: Recognizing the dangers and knowing what to do.* Buffalo, NY: Prometheus Books.

Stanwood, G. D., & Levitt, P. (2001). The effects of cocaine on the developing nervous system. In C. A. Nelson & M. Luciana (Eds.), *Handbook of developmental cognitive neuroscience* (pp. 519–536). Cambridge, MA: MIT Press.

Stark, R. (2004). *Sociology* (9th ed.). Belmont, CA: Wadsworth.

Starrels, M. E., Ingersoll-Dayton, B., Neal, M. B., & Yamada, H. (1995). Intergenerational solidarity and the workplace: Employees' caregiving for their parents. *Journal of Marriage and the Family, 57,* 751–762.

Staudinger, U. M. (1999). Older and wiser? Integrating results on the relationship between age and wisdom-related performance. *International Journal of Behavioral Development, 23,* 641–664.

Steele, C. M. (1997). A threat in the air: How stereotypes shape intellectual identity and performance. *American Psychologist, 52,* 613–629.

Steele, C. M., & Aronson, J. (1995). Stereotype threat and the intellectual test performance of African Americans. *Journal of Personality and Social Psychology, 69,* 797–811.

Stein, N. L. (2002). Memories for emotional, stressful, and traumatic events. In J. M. Mandler, N. L. Stein, P. J. Bauer, & M. Rabinowitz (Eds.), *Representation, memory, and development: Essays in honor of Jean Mandler* (pp. 247–265). Mahwah, NJ: Erlbaum.

Steinberg, L. (2004). Risk taking in adolescence: What changes, and why? In R. E. Dahl & L. P. Spear (Eds.), *Annals of the New York Academy of Sciences: Vol. 1021. Adolescent brain development: Vulnerabilities and opportunities* (pp. 51–58). New York: New York Academy of Sciences.

Steinberg, L., Grisso, T., Woolard, J., et al. (2003). Juveniles' competence to stand trial as adults. *Social Policy Report, 17*(4).

Sternberg, R. J. (1988). *The triangle of love: Intimacy, passion, commitment.* New York: Basic Books.

Sternberg, R. J. (Ed.). (1990). *Wisdom: Its nature, origins, and development.* New York: Cambridge University Press.

Sternberg, R. J. (1997a). Construct validation of a triangular love scale. *European Journal of Social Psychology, 27,* 313–335.

Sternberg, R. J. (1997b). *Successful intelligence: How practical and creative intelligence determine success in life.* New York: Plume.

Sternberg, R. J. (1998). *Cupid's arrow: The course of love through time.* New York: Cambridge University Press.

Sternberg, R. J. (2004). North American approaches to intelligence. In R. J. Sternberg (Ed.), *International handbook of intelligence* (pp. 411–444). New York: Cambridge University Press.

Sternberg, R. J. (2005). The WICS model of giftedness. In R. J. Sternberg & J. E. Davidson (Eds.), *Conceptions of giftedness* (2nd ed., pp. 327–342). New York: Cambridge University Press.

Sternberg, R. J., Grigorenko, E. L., & Oh, S. (2001). The development of intelligence at midlife. In M. E. Lachman (Ed.), *Handbook of midlife development* (pp. 217–247). New York: Wiley.

Sternberg, R. J., Kaufman, J. C., & Pretz, J. E. (2002). *The creativity conundrum.* Hove, England: Psychology Press.

Sternberg, R. J., & Lubart, T. I. (2001). Wisdom and creativity. In J. E. Birren & K. W. Schaie (Eds.), *Handbook of the psychology of aging* (5th ed., pp. 500–522). San Diego, CA: Academic Press.

Sternberg, R. J., & Williams, W. M. (1997). Does the Graduate Record Examination predict meaningful success in the graduate training of psychologists? A case study. *American Psychologist, 52,* 630–641.

Steunenberg, B., Twisk, J. W. R., Beekman, A. T. F., Deeg, D. J. H., & Kerkhof, A. J. F. M. (2005). Stability and change of neuroticism in aging. *Journals of Gerontology: Psychological Sciences and Social Sciences, 60B,* P27–P33.

Stevens, E., Blake, J., Vitale, G., & MacDonald, S. (1998). Mother-infant object involvement at 9 and 15 months: Relation to infant cognition and early vocabulary. *First Language, 18,* 203–222.

Stevens, M., Golombok. S., Beveridge, M., & Study Team, APSPAC. (2002). Does father absence influence children's gender development? Findings from a general population of preschool children. *Parenting: Science and Practice, 2,* 47–60.

Stevenson, H. W., & Stigler, J. W. (1992). *The learning gap: Why our schools are failing and what we can learn from Japanese and Chinese education.* New York: Summit Books.

Stevenson, H. W., Stigler, J. W., Lee, S.-y., Kitamura, S., Kimura, S., & Kato, T. (1986). Achievement in mathematics. In H. W. Stevenson, H. Azuma, & K. Hakuta (Eds.), *Child development and education in Japan* (pp. 201–216). New York: W. H. Freeman.

Stewart, R. B., Verbrugge, K. M., & Beilfuss, M. C. (1998). Sibling relationships in early adulthood: A typology. *Personal Relationships, 5,* 59–74.

Stipek, D. (2001). Classroom context effects on young children's motivation. In F. Salili, C.-y. Chiu, & Y.-y. Hong (Eds.), *Student motivation: The culture and context of learning* (pp. 273–292). New York: Kluwer Academic/Plenum.

Stipek, D. (2002). At what age should children enter kindergarten? A question for policy makers and parents. *Social Policy Report, 16*(2).

Stipek, D., & Byler, P. (2001). Academic achievement and social behaviors associated with age of entry into kindergarten. *Journal of Applied Developmental Psychology, 22,* 175–189.

Stipek, D., & Greene, J. K. (2001). Achievement motivation in early childhood: Cause for concern or celebration? In S. L. Golbeck (Ed.), *Psychological perspectives on early childhood education: Reframing dilemmas in research and practice* (pp. 64–91). Mahwah, NJ: Erlbaum.

St. James-Roberts, I. (2001). Infant crying and its impact on parents. In R. G. Barr, I. St. James-Roberts, & M. R. Keefe (Eds.), *New evidence on unexplained early infant crying: Its origins, nature, and management* (pp. 5–24). Skillman, NJ: Johnson & Johnson Pediatric Institute.

Stolley, K. S. (1993). Statistics on adoption in the United States. *The Future of Children, 3,* 26–42.

Stolzer, J. (2005). ADHD in America: A bioecological analysis. *Ethical Human Psychology and Psychiatry, 7,* 65–75.

Stone, C. A. (1998). The metaphor of scaffolding: Its utility for the field of learning disabilities. *Journal of Learning Disabilities, 31,* 344–364.

Stoney, C. M. (2003). Gender and cardiovascular disease: A psychobiological and integrative approach. *Current Directions in Psychological Science, 12,* 129–133.

Stouthamer-Loeber, M. (1987, April). *Mothers' perceptions of children's lying and its relationship to behavior problems.* Paper presented at the meeting of the Society for Research in Child Development, Baltimore.

Stouthamer-Loeber, M., Loeber, R., Wei, E., Farrington, D. P., & Wikström, P.-O. H. (2002). Risk and promotive effects in the explanation of persistent serious delinquency in boys. *Journal of Consulting and Clinical Psychology, 70,* 111–123.

St. Pierre, R. G., & Layzer, J. I. (1998). Improving the life chances of children in poverty: Assumptions and what we have learned. *Social Policy Report, 12*(4).

Straight, A., & Jackson, A. M. (1999). *Older drivers fact sheet.* Washington, DC: AARP. Retrieved May 8, 2005, from **http://www.aarp.org/research/housing-mobility/transportation/aresearchimport191–FS51R.html**

Stray-Pedersen, B. (2000). Parasitic infections. In W. R. Cohen, S. H. Sheldon, & I. R. Merkatz (Eds.), *Cherry and Merkatz's complications of pregnancy* (5th ed., pp. 693–707). Philadelphia: Lippincott Williams & Wilkins.

Strehler, B. L. (1986). Genetic instability as the primary cause of human aging. *Experimental Gerontology, 21,* 283–319.

Streissguth, A. P., & Connor, P. D. (2001). Fetal alcohol syndrome and other effects of prenatal alcohol: Developmental cognitive neuroscience implications. In C. A. Nelson & M. Luciana (Eds.), *Handbook of developmental cognitive neuroscience* (pp. 505–518). Cambridge, MA: MIT Press.

Stroebe, M. S., Hansson, R. O., Stroebe, W., & Schut, H. (2001). Introduction: Concepts and issues in contemporary research on bereavement. In M. S. Stroebe, R. O. Hansson, W. Stroebe, & H. Schut (Eds.), *Handbook of bereavement research: Consequences, coping, and care* (pp. 3–22). Washington, DC: American Psychological Association.

Stroebe, M., & Stroebe, W. (1991). Does "grief work" work? *Journal of Consulting and Clinical Psychology, 59,* 479–482.

Stumpf, H., & Stanley, J. C. (1998). Stability and change in gender-related differences on the College Board Advanced Placement and Achievement Tests. *Current Directions in Psychological Science, 7,* 192–196.

Substance Abuse and Mental Health Services Administration. (2004). *Results from the 2003 National Survey on Drug Use and Health: National findings* (Office of Applied Studies, NSDUH Series H-25, DHHS Publication No. SMA 04-3964). Retrieved July 20, 2006, from **http://www.drugabusestatistics.samhsa.gov/NHSDA/2k3NSDUH/2k3Results.htm**

Sudan's "Lost Boys" find Chicago. (2001, July 5). Editorials. *Chicago Tribune,* Section 1, p. 12.

Sudarkasa, N. (1997). African American families and family values. In H. P. McAdoo (Ed.), *Black families* (3rd ed., pp. 9–40). Thousand Oaks, CA: Sage.

Suhail, K., & Chaudhry, H. R. (2004). Predictors of subjective well-being in an eastern Muslim culture. *Journal of Social and Clinical Psychology, 23,* 359–376.

Sullivan, F. M., & Barlow, S. M. (2001). Review of risk factors for sudden infant death syndrome. *Paediatric and Perinatal Epidemiology, 15,* 144–200.

Sullivan, O., & Gershuny, J. (2001). Cross-national changes in time-use: Some sociological (hi)stories re-examined. *The British Journal of Sociology, 52,* 331–347.

Sundin-Huard, D., & Fahy, K. (2004). The problems with the validity of the diagnosis of brain death. *Nursing in Critical Care, 9,* 64–71.

Surbey, M. K. (1998). Developmental psychology and modern Darwinism. In C. B. Crawford & D. L. Krebs (Eds.), *Handbook of evolutionary psychology: Ideas, issues, and applications* (pp. 369–403). Mahwah, NJ: Erlbaum.

Susman, E. J., & Rogol, A. (2004). Puberty and psychological development. In R. M. Lerner & L. D. Steinberg (Eds.), *Handbook of adolescent psychology* (2nd ed., pp. 15–44). Hoboken, NJ: Wiley.

Suzuki, L. A., & Valencia, R. R. (1997). Race-ethnicity and measured intelligence: Educational implications. *American Psychologist, 52,* 1103–1114.

Tager-Flusberg, H. (2001). Putting words together: Morphology and syntax in the preschool years. In J. B. Gleason (Ed.), *The development of language* (pp. 162–212). Boston: Allyn & Bacon.

Takeuchi, A. H., & Hulse, S. H. (1993). Absolute pitch. *Psychological Bulletin, 113,* 345–361.

Takeuchi, J., & Groeneman, S. (1999). *PBS special "Stealing Time" Study: A summary of findings.* Washington, DC: AARP. Retrieved June 1, 2006, from http://www.aarp.org/...rch/reference/agingtrends/ aresearch-import-79

Talaga, J. A., & Beehr, T. A. (1995). Are there gender differences in predicting retirement decisions? *Journal of Applied Psychology, 80,* 16–28.

Tamis-Lemonda, C. S., & Cabrera, N. (1999). Perspectives on father involvement: Research and policy. *Social Policy Report, 13*(2).

Tan, T. X. (2004). A quantitative study of Chinese adoptees' post-adoption socio-emotional adjustment and social competence. *Dissertation Abstracts International, 65* (05), 2671B.

Tangney, J. P., Baumeister, R. F., & Boone, A. L. (2004). High self-control predicts good adjustment, less pathology, better grades, and interpersonal success. *Journal of Personality, 72,* 271–322.

Tannen, D. (1990). *You just don't understand: Women and men in conversation.* New York: Ballantine Books.

Tanner, J. M. (1973). Growing up. *Scientific American, 229*(3), 34–43.

Tanner, J. M. (1990). *Foetus into man: Physical growth from conception to maturity* (Rev. ed.). Cambridge, MA: Harvard University Press.

Tanner, J. M. (1998). Sequence, tempo and individual variation in growth and development of boys and girls aged twelve to sixteen. In R. E. Muuss & H. D. Porton (Eds.), *Adolescent behavior and society: A book of readings* (5th ed., pp. 34–46). New York: McGraw Hill.

Tasker, F. L., & Golombok, S. (1997). *Growing up in a lesbian family: Effects on child development.* New York: Guilford.

Taubes, G. (2001). Nutrition: The soft science of dietary fat. *Science, 291,* 2536–2545.

Tavris, C. (1992). *The mismeasure of woman.* New York: Simon & Schuster.

Taylor, H. G., Klein, N., Minich, N. M., & Hack, M. (2000). Middle-school-age outcomes in children with very low birthweight. *Child Development, 71,* 1495–1511.

Taylor, M. (1999). *Imaginary companions and the children who create them.* New York: Oxford University Press.

Taylor, M., & Carlson, S. (1997). The relation between individual differences in fantasy and theory of mind. *Child Development, 68,* 436–455.

Taylor, M. D., Hart, C. I., Davey Smith, G., et al. (2003). Childhood mental ability and smoking cessation in adulthood. *Journal of Epidemiology and Community Health, 57,* 464–465.

Taylor, R. J., Chatters, L. M., Hardison, C. B., & Riley, A. (2001). Informal social support networks and subjective well-being among African Americans. *Journal of Black Psychology, 27,* 439–463.

Taylor, R. J., Chatters, L. M., Jayakody, R., & Levin, J. S. (1996). Black and White differences in religious participation: A multisample comparison. *Journal for the Scientific Study of Religion, 35,* 403–410.

Taylor, W. C., Blair, S. N., Cummings, S. S., Wun, C. C., & Malina, R. M. (1999). Childhood and adolescent physical activity patterns and adult physical activity. *Medicine and Science in Sports and Exercise, 31,* 118–123.

Teachman, J. (2003). Premarital sex, premarital cohabitation and the risk of subsequent marital dissolution among women. *Journal of Marriage and Family, 65,* 444–455.

Teno, J. M., Clarridge, B. R., Casey, V., et al. (2004). Family perspectives on end-of-life care at the last place of care. *Journal of the American Medical Association, 291,* 88–93.

Tepperman, L., & Curtis, J. (1995). A life satisfaction scale for use with national adult samples from the USA, Canada and Mexico. *Social Indicators Research, 35,* 255–270.

Terracciano, A., McCrae, R. R., Brant, L. J., & Costa, P. T., Jr. (2005). Hierarchical linear modeling analysis of the NEO-PI-R Scales in the Baltimore Longitudinal Study of Aging. *Psychology and Aging, 20,* 493–506.

Thacker, S. B., Stroup, D., & Chang, M. (2001). Continuous electronic heart rate monitoring for fetal assessment during labor. *Cochrane Database of Systematic Reviews, 2,* CD000063.

Thalidomide Victims Association of Canada. (2005). *What is Thalidomide?* Retrieved April 30, 2006, from http://www.thalidomide.ca/en/information/what_is_thalidomide.html

Thatcher, R. W., Walker, R. A., & Giudice, S. (1987). Human cerebral hemispheres develop at different rates and ages. *Science, 236,* 1110–1113.

Thelen, E., Schöner, G., Scheier, C., & Smith, L. B. (2001). The dynamics of embodiment: A field theory of infant perseverative reaching. *Behavioral and Brain Sciences, 24,* 1–86.

Thoman, E. B. (2001). Sleep-wake states as context for assessment, as components of assessment, and as assessment. In L. T. Singer & P. S. Zeskind (Eds.), *Biobehavioral assessment of the infant* (pp. 125–148). New York: Guilford.

Thoman, E. B., Hammond, K., Affleck, G., & Desilva, H. N. (1995). The breathing bear with preterm infants: Effects on sleep, respiration, and affect. *Infant Mental Health Journal, 16,* 160–168.

Thomas, A., Chess, S., & Birch, H. G. (1968). *Temperament and behavior disorders in children.* New York: New York University Press.

Thomas, K. M., Drevets, W. C., Whalen, P. J., et al. (2001). Amygdala response to facial expressions in children and adults. *Biological Psychiatry, 49,* 309–316.

Thomas, K. M., & Nelson, C. A. (2001). Serial reaction time learning in preschool- and school-aged children. *Journal of Experimental Child Psychology, 79,* 364–387.

Thomas, R. M. (2005). *Comparing theories of child development.* Belmont, CA: Wadsworth.

Thomas, V. G. (2001). Educational experiences and transitions of reentry college women: Special considerations for African American female students. *Journal of Negro Education, 70,* 139–155.

Thomas, W. P., & Collier, V. (1996). Language-minority student achievement and program effectiveness. *NABE News, 19,* 33–35.

Thompson, J. S. (2003). The effects of college major on work outcomes: Gender differences and change over time, 1960s/1970s–1980s/1990s. *Dissertation Abstracts International, 63* (11), 4110–4111A.

Thompson, P. M., Giedd, J. N., Woods, R. P., MacDonald, D., Evans, A. C., & Toga, A. W. (2000). Growth patterns in the developing brain detected by using continuum mechanical tensor maps. *Nature, 404,* 190–193.

Thompson, R. A. (1999). The individual child: Temperament, emotion, self, and personality. In M. H. Bornstein & M. E. Lamb (Eds.), *Developmental psychology: An advanced textbook* (4th ed., pp. 377–409). Mahwah, NJ: Erlbaum.

Tideman, E. (2000). Longitudinal follow-up of children born preterm: Cognitive development at age 19. *Early Human Development, 58,* 81–90.

Tinsworth, D., & McDonald, J. (2001). *Special study: Injuries and deaths associated with children's playground equipment.* Washington, DC: U.S. Consumer Product Safety Commission.

Tissot, S. A. D. (1758). Onania, or a treatise upon the disorders produced by masturbation. Cited in V. L. Bullough & B. Bullough (1994, p. 383), *Human sexuality: An encyclopedia.* New York: Garland.

Tobin, J. J., Wu, D. Y. H., & Davidson, D. H. (1989). *Preschool in three cultures: Japan, China, and the United States.* New Haven, CT: Yale University Press.

Tolstóy, L. (1937). *Anna Karénina* (L. Maude & A. Maude, Trans.). London: Oxford University Press.

Tong, S., Meagher, S., & Vollenhoven, B. (2002). Sonography: Dizygotic twin survival in early pregnancy. *Nature, 416,* 142.

Tong, S., Shirnding, Y. E. von, & Prapamontol, T. (2000). Environmental lead exposure: A public health problem of global dimensions. *Bulletin of the World Health Organization, 78,* 1068–1077.

Topping, K., Holmes, E. A., & Bremner, W. (2000). The effectiveness of school-based programs for the promotion of social competence. In R. Bar-On & J. D. A. Parker (Eds.), *The handbook of emotional intelligence* (pp. 411–458). San Francisco: Jossey-Bass.

Traub, J. (1998, October 26). Multiple intelligence disorder. *New Republic, 219,* 20–23.

Trautner, H. M., Gervai, J., & Németh, R. (2003). Appearance-reality distinction and development of gender constancy understanding in children. *International Journal of Behavioral Development, 27,* 275–283.

Travis, J. (1999). *Modus operandi* of an infamous drug. *Science News, 155,* 124–126.

Travis Pastrana. (2005). Retrieved February 23, 2006, from **http://expn.go.com/athletes/bios/ PASTRANA_TRAVIS.html**

Trinidad, D. R., Unger, J. B., Chou, C.-P., & Johnson, C. A. (2004). The protective association of emotional intelligence with psychosocial smoking risk factors for adolescents. *Personality and Individual Differences, 36,* 945–954.

Trivers, R. L. (1974). Parent-offspring conflict. *American Zoologist, 14,* 249–264.

Troiano, R. P., Frongillo, E. A., Jr., Sobal, J., & Levitsky, D. A. (1996). The relationship between body weight and mortality: A quantitative analysis of combined information from existing studies. *International Journal of Obesity and Related Metabolic Disorders, 20,* 63–75.

True, M. M., Pisani, L., & Oumar, F. (2001). Infant-mother attachment among the Dogon of Mali. *Child Development, 72,* 1451–1466.

Tsao, F.-M., Liu, H.-M., & Kuhl, P. K. (2004). Speech perception in infancy predicts language development in the second year of life: A longitudinal study. *Child Development, 75,* 1067–1084.

Tsao, Y.-L. (2004). A comparison of American and Taiwanese Students: Their math perception. *Journal of Instructional Psychology, 31,* 206–213.

Tucker, G. R. (1999). *A global perspective on bilingualism and bilingual education.* Washington, DC: ERIC Clearinghouse on Languages and Linguistics. (ERIC Document Reproduction Service No. ED435168)

Tuerk, P. W. (2005). Research in the high-stakes era: Achievement, resources, and No Child Left Behind. *Psychological Science, 16,* 419–425.

Tuhy, C. (1984). The care, feeding and funding of super babies. *Money, 13*(11), 88–91.

Turati, C. (2004). Why faces are not special to newborns: An alternative account of the face preference. *Current Directions in Psychological Science, 13,* 5–8.

Turkheimer, E., Haley, A., Waldron, M., D'Onofrio, B., & Gottesman, I. I. (2003). Socioeconomic status modifies heritability of IQ in young children. *Psychological Science, 14,* 623–628.

Turkheimer, E., & Waldron, M. (2000). Nonshared environment: A theoretical, methodological, and quantitative review. *Psychological Bulletin, 126,* 78–108.

Tversky, A., & Gilovich, T. (2004). The "hot hand": Statistical reality or cognitive illusion? In E. Shafir (Ed.), *Preference, belief, and similarity: Selected writings by Amos Tversky* (pp. 269–273). Cambridge, MA: MIT Press.

Twain, M. (1924). *Mark Twain's autobiography, with an introduction by Albert Bigelow Paine* (Vol. 1). New York: Harper & Brothers.

Uauy, R., & Peirano, P. (1999). Breast is best: Human milk is the optimal food for brain development. *American Journal of Clinical Nutrition, 70,* 433–444.

Udry, J. R., Billy, J. O., Morris, N. M., Groff, T. R., & Raj, M. H. (1985). Serum androgenic hormones motivate sexual behavior in adolescent boys. *Fertility and Sterility, 43,* 90–94.

Udry, J. R., Talbert, L. M., & Morris, N. M. (1986). Biosocial foundations for adolescent female sexuality. *Demography, 23,* 217–230.

Umberson, D. (1992). Relationships between adult children and their parents: Psychological consequences for both generations. *Journal of Marriage and the Family, 54,* 664–674.

Underwood, M. K., & Hurley, J. C. (1999). Emotion regulation in peer relationships during middle childhood. In L. Balter & C. S. Tamis-LeMonda (Eds.), *Child psychology: A handbook of contemporary issues* (pp. 237–258). Hove, England: Psychology Press.

Underwood, M. K., Kupersmidt, J. B., & Coie, J. D. (1996). Childhood peer sociometric status and aggression as predictors of adolescent childbearing. *Journal of Research on Adolescence, 6,* 201–223.

UNICEF. (2000, June). A league table of child poverty in rich nations. *Innocenti Report Card, 1.* Florence, Italy: UNICEF Innocenti Research Center.

UNICEF. (2001). *Infant and under-five mortality.* Retrieved June 30, 2005, from **http://www. unicef.org/specialsession/about/sgreport-pdf/01_ InfantAndUnder-FiveMortality_D7341Insert_ English.pdfUNICEF.**

UNICEF (2006). *Nutrition: The big picture.* Retrieved January 8, 2006, from **http:// www.unicef.org/nutrition/ index_bigpicture.html**

United Nations. (2001, September). *We the children: Meeting the promises of the World Summit for Children.* New York: UNICEF. Retrieved December 4, 2002, from **http://www. unicef.org/specialsession/about/sg-report.htm**

United Nations Division for the Advancement of Women. (2004). *FWCW platform for action: Women in power and decision-making diagnosis.* Retrieved November 27, 2004, from **http:// www.un.org/womenwatch/daw/beijing/platform/ decision.htm**

United Nations Population Division. (2005). *World population prospects: The 2004 revision.* New York: United Nations.

University of Michigan Health System. (2003, September 2). Help your overweight child have a healthy future through simple food and exercise tips, U-M expert says. *University of Michigan Health Minute Update.* Retrieved January 21, 2006, from **http://www.med.umich.edu/opm/ newspage/2003/childobesity.htm**

Unnever, J. D. (2005). Bullies, aggressive victims, and victims: Are they distinct groups? *Aggressive Behavior, 31,* 153–171.

Urberg, K. A., De[eth]irmencio[eth]lu, S., Tolson, J. M., & Halliday-Scher, K. (2000). Adolescent social crowds: Measurement and relationships to friendships. *Journal of Adolescent Research, 15,* 427–445.

U.S. Census Bureau. (2000, January 13). *(NP-T3-C) Projections of the total resident population by 5–year age groups, and sex with special age categories: Middle series, 2006 to 2010.* Retrieved May 8, 2005, from **http://www.census.gov/population/ projections/nation/summary/np-t3-c.txt**

U.S. Census Bureau. (2003a). *Annual estimates of the population by sex and five-year age groups for the United States: April 1, 2000 to July 1, 2003.* Retrieved May 8, 2005, from **http://www.census.gov/ popest/national/asrh/NC-EST2003–as.html**

U.S. Census Bureau. (2003b). *Historical income tables—People: Table P-40.* Retrieved May 29, 2006, from **http://census.gov/hhes/income/ histinc/p40.html**

U.S. Census Bureau. (2004, April 29). Father's Day: June 20. *Facts for Features* (U.S.Census Bureau Publication No. CB04–FF.09).

U.S. Census Bureau. (2004a). *Global population profile: 2002.* Retrieved February 13, 2005, from www.census.gov/ipc/www/wp02.html

U.S. Census Bureau. (2004b). *International population reports WP/02, Global population profile: 2002.* Washington, DC: U.S. Government Printing Office.

U.S. Consumer Product Safety Commission. (2006). *Safety tips.* Retrieved May 9, 2006, from www.cpsc.gov

U.S. Department of Education, Office of Educational Research and Improvement. (1998, January). First-graders' achievement in top and bottom schools. *Issue Brief.* Retrieved July 22, 2006, from **http://nces.ed.gov/pubsearch/ pubsinfo.asp?pubid=98041**

U.S. Department of Health and Human Services. (1978; reprinted 1985, 1992). *Plain talk about dealing with the angry child* (HHS Publication No. [ADM] 92–0781). Washington, DC: U.S. Government Printing Office.

U.S. Department of Health and Human Services. (2000). *Report of the National Reading Panel: Teaching children to read* (NIH Publication No. 00–4769). Retrieved July 20, 2006, from http://www.nichd.nih.gov/publications/nrp/smallbook.htm

U.S. Department of Health and Human Services. (2005). *Code of federal regulations: Title 45, part 46: Protection of human subjects.* Retrieved August 1, 2006, from http://www.hhs.gov/ohrp/humansubjects/guidance/45cfr46.htmhttp://www.nichd.nih.gov/publications/nrp/smallbook.htm

U.S. Department of Health and Human Services, Administration on Aging. (2004). *A profile of older Americans: 2004.* Author.

U.S. Department of Health and Human Services, Administration on Children, Youth and Families. (2005). *Child Maltreatment 2003.* Retrieved July 20, 2006, from http://www.acf.hhs.gov/programs/cb/pubs/cm03/index.htm

U.S. Department of Labor, Bureau of Labor Statistics. (2002). *Number of jobs held, labor market activity, and earnings growth among younger baby boomers: Results from more than two decades of a longitudinal survey.* Retrieved December 19, 2004, from http://www.bls.gov/nls/nlsy79r19.pdf

U.S. Department of Labor, Bureau of Labor Statistics. (2005, March). *Household data, not seasonally adjusted.* Retrieved April 16, 2005, from http://www.bls.gov/web/cpseea18.pdf

U.S. Department of State. (2006). *Immigrant visas issued to orphans coming to the U.S.* Retrieved February 13, 2006, from http://travel.state.gov/family/adoption/stats/stats_451.html

U.S. Food and Drug Administration. (2001). *Thalidomoide: Potential benefits and risks, and open public scientific workshop.* September 9, 1997. Retrieved March 10, 2001, from www.fda.gov/oashi/patrip/nih99.html

Uttal, D. H., Liu, L. L., & DeLoache, J. S. (1999). Taking a hard look at concreteness: Do concrete objects help young children learn symbolic relations? In L. Balter & C. S. Tamis-LeMonda (Eds.), *Child psychology: A handbook of contemporary issues* (pp. 177–192). Hove, England: Psychology Press.

Vaillant, C. O., & Vaillant, G. E. (1993). Is the U-curve of marital satisfaction an illusion? A 40–year study of marriage. *Journal of Marriage and the Family, 55,* 230–239.

Vaillant, G. E. (2002). *Aging well: Surprising guideposts to a happier life from the landmark Harvard Study of Adult Development.* Boston: Little, Brown & Company.

Valdivia, R. (1999). *The implications of culture on developmental delay* (ERIC Digest No. E589). Reston, VA: ERIC Clearinghouse on Disabilities and Gifted Education. (ERIC Document Reproduction Service No. ED438663)

Valenstein, E. S. (1998). *Blaming the brain: The truth about drugs and mental health.* New York: Free Press.

Van Ausdale, D., & Feagin, J. R. (2001). *The first R: How children learn race and racism.* Lanham, MD: Rowman & Littlefield.

Vandell, D. L., & Bailey, M. D. (1992). Conflicts between siblings. In C. U. Shantz & W. W. Hartup (Eds.), *Conflict in child and adolescent development* (pp. 242–269). New York: Cambridge University Press.

van den Boom, D. C. (2001). Behavioral management of early infant crying in irritable babies. In R. G. Barr, I. St. James-Roberts, & M. R. Keefe (Eds.), *New evidence on unexplained early infant crying: Its origins, nature, and management* (pp. 209–228). Skillman, NJ: Johnson & Johnson Pediatric Institute.

Van den Bulck, J. (2004). Television viewing, computer game playing, and Internet use and self-reported time to bed and time out of bed in secondary-school children. *Sleep, 27,* 101–104.

Vander Ven, T. M., Cullen, F. T., Carrozza, M. A., & Wright, J. P. (2001). Home alone: The impact of maternal employment on delinquency. *Social Problems, 48,* 236–257.

Van Horn, M. L., Karlin, E. O., Ramey, S. L., Aldridge, J., & Snyder, S. W. (2005). Effects of developmentally appropriate practices on children's development: A review of research and discussion of methodological and analytic issues. *Elementary School Journal, 105,* 325–351.

van IJzendoorn, M. H., & Sagi, A. (1999). Cross-cultural patterns of attachment: Universal and contextual dimensions. In J. Cassidy & P. R. Shaver (Eds.), *Handbook of attachment: Theory, research, and clinical applications* (pp. 713–734). New York: Guilford.

van Pelt, R. E., Dinneno, F. A., Seals, D. R., & Jones, P. P. (2001). Age-related decline in RMR in physically active men: Relation to exercise volume and energy intake. *American Journal of Physiology: Endocrinology and Metabolism, 281,* E633–E639.

van Pelt, R. E., Jones, P. P., Davy, K. P., et al. (1997). Regular exercise and the age-related decline in resting metabolic rate in women. *Journal of Clinical Endocrinology and Metabolism, 82,* 3208–3212.

Vargha-Khadem, F., Isaacs, E., & Muter, V. (1994). A review of cognitive outcome after unilateral lesions sustained during childhood. *Journal of Child Neurology, 9*(Suppl. 2), 67–73.

Vartanian, L. R. (2000). Revisiting the imaginary audience and personal fable constructs of adolescent egocentrism: A conceptual review. *Adolescence, 35,* 639–661.

Vasey, M. W., & Ollendick, T. H. (2000). Anxiety. In A. J. Sameroff, M. Lewis, & S. M. Miller (Eds.), *Handbook of developmental psychopathology* (2nd ed., pp. 511–529). New York: Kluwer Academic/Plenum.

Vaughan, C. C. (1996). *How life begins: The science of life in the womb.* New York: Times Books.

Veatch, R. M. (2004). Abandon the dead donor rule or change the definition of death? *Kennedy Institute of Ethics Journal, 14,* 261–276.

Vellas, B. J., Wayne, S. J., Romero, L. J., Baumgartner, R. N., & Garry, P. J. (1997). Fear of falling and restriction of mobility in elderly fallers. *Age and Ageing, 26,* 189–193.

Vendola, N., Passani, N., Zambello, A., & Fonzo, R. (2001). Low concentration Ropivacaine in labor epidural analgesia. A prospective study on obstetric and neonatal outcome. *Minerva Ginecologica, 53,* 397–403.

Venter, J. C., Adams, M. D., Myers, E. W., et al. (2001). The sequence of the human genome. *Science, 291,* 1304–1351.

Verghese, J., Lipton, R. B., Katz, M. J., et al. (2003). Leisure activities and the risk of dementia in the elderly. *New England Journal of Medicine, 348,* 2508–2516.

Vermont Department of Health. (2003). *Vermont Youth Risk Behavior Survey.* Retrieved May 26, 2006, from http://healthvermont.gov/adap/clearinghouse/yrbs_2003_report.pdf

Vigliocco, G., Vinson, D. P., Martin, R. C., & Garrett, M. F. (1999). Is "count" and "mass" information available when the noun is not? An investigation of tip of the tongue states and anomia. *Journal of Memory and Language, 40,* 534–558.

Vila, G., Zipper, E., Dabbas, M., et al. (2004). Mental disorders in obese children and adolescents. *Psychosomatic Medicine, 66,* 387–394.

Vinceti, M., Rovesti, S., Bergomi, M., et al. (2001). Risk of birth defects in a population exposed to environmental lead pollution. *The Science of the Total Environment, 278,* 23–30.

Vinter, A., & Perruchet, P. (2002). Implicit motor learning through observational training in adults and children. *Memory and Cognition, 30,* 256–261.

Vitaliano, P. P., Young, H. M., & Zhang, J. (2004). Is caregiving a risk factor for illness? *Current Directions in Psychological Science, 13,* 13–16.

Vitiello, M. V., Larsen, L. H., & Moe, K. E. (2004). Age-related sleep change: Gender and estrogen effects on the subjective-objective sleep quality relationships of healthy, noncomplaining older men and women. *Journal of Psychosomatic Research, 56,* 503–510.

Vogel, G. (1996). Global review faults U.S. curricula. *Science, 274,* 335.

Vogel, G. (2000). Can old cells learn new tricks? *Science, 287,* 1418–1419.

Volkow, N. D., Logan, J., Fowler, J. S., et al. (2000). Association between age-related decline in brain dopamine activity and impairment in frontal and cingulate metabolism. *American Journal of Psychiatry, 157,* 75–80.

Volling, B. L., McElwain, N. L., & Miller, A. L. (2002). Emotion regulation in context: The jealousy complex between young siblings and its relations with child and family characteristics. *Child Development, 73,* 581–600.

Voss, L. (1999). Short stature: Does it matter? A review of the evidence. In U. Eiholzer, F. Haverkamp, & L. D. Voss (Eds.), *Growth, stature, and psychosocial well-being* (pp. 7–14). Seattle, WA: Hogrefe & Huber.

Vurpillot, E. (1968). The development of scanning strategies and their relation to visual differentiation. *Journal of Experimental Child Psychology, 6,* 632–650.

Vygotsky, L. S. (1962). *Thought and language.* Cambridge, MA: MIT Press.

Vygotsky, L. S. (1978). *Mind in society: The development of higher psychological processes* (M. Cole, V. John-Steiner, S. Scribner, & E. Souberman, Eds.). Cambridge, MA: Harvard University Press.

Wahlstrom, K. (2003). Later high-school start times still working. *Education Digest, 68*(6), 49–53.

Walch, C., Anderhuber, W., Köle, W., & Berghold, A. (2000). Bilateral sensorineural hearing disorders in children: Etiology of deafness and evaluation of hearing tests. *International Journal of Pediatric Otorhinolaryngology, 53,* 31–38.

Waldrop, D. P., & Weber, J. A. (2001). From grandparent to caregiver: The stress and satisfaction of raising grandchildren. *Families in Society, 82,* 461–472.

Walker, A., Rosenberg, M., & Balaban-Gil, K. (1999). Neurodevelopmental and neurobehavioral sequelae of selected substances of abuse and psychiatric medications in utero. *Child and Adolescent Psychiatric Clinics of North America, 8,* 845–867.

Walker, A. G. (1999). *Handbook on questioning children: A linguistic perspective.* Washington, DC: ABA Center on Children and the Law.

Walker, S., Irving, K., & Berthelsen, D. (2002). Gender influences on preschool children's social problem-solving strategies. *Journal of Genetic Psychology, 16,* 197–210.

Wallace, D. C. (2005). A mitochondrial paradigm of metabolic and degenerative diseases, aging, and cancer: A dawn for evolutionary medicine. *Annual Review of Genetics, 39,* 359–407.

Wallerstein, J. S., Lewis, J. M., & Blakeslee, S. (2000). *The unexpected legacy of divorce: A 35 year landmark study.* New York: Hyperion.

Wang, G., & Dietz, W. H. (2002). Economic burden of obesity in youths aged 6 to 17 years: 1979–1999. *Pediatrics, 109,* e81.

Ward, S. L., & Overton, W. F. (1990). Semantic familiarity, relevance, and the development of deductive reasoning. *Developmental Psychology, 26,* 488–493.

Warr, P. (1994). Age and employment. In M. D. Dunnette, H. C. Triandis, & L. M. Hough (Eds.), *Handbook of industrial and organizational psychology* (2nd ed., Vol. 4, pp. 485–550). Palo Alto, CA: Consulting Psychologists Press.

Warr, P. (1999). Well-being and the workplace. In D. Kahneman, E. Diener, & N. Schwarz (Eds.), *Well-being: The foundations of hedonic psychology* (pp. 392–412). New York: Russell Sage Foundation.

Warren, A. R., & McCloskey, L. A. (1997). Language in social contexts. In J. B. Gleason (Ed.), *The development of language* (4th ed., pp. 210–258). Boston: Allyn & Bacon.

Warren-Leubecker, A., Tate, C. S., Hinton, I. D., & Ozbek, I. N. (1989). What do children know about the legal system and when do they know it? First steps down a less traveled path in child witness research. In S. J. Ceci, D. F. Ross, & M. P. Toglia (Eds.), *Perspectives on children's testimony* (pp. 158–183). New York: Springer-Verlag.

Wartella, E., Caplovitz, A. G., & Lee, J. H. (2004). From baby Einstein to Leapfrog, from Doom to Sims, from instant messaging to Internet chat rooms: Public interest in the role of interactive media in children's lives. *Social Policy Report, 18*(4).

Wassink, T. H., Piven, J., Vieland, V. J., et al. (2005). Evaluation of the chromosome 2q37.3 gene CENTG2 as an autism susceptibility gene. *American Journal of Medical Genetics, 136,* 36–44.

Watkins, R. V., Yairi, E., & Ambrose, N. G. (1999). Early childhood stuttering III: Initial status of expressive language abilities. *Journal of Speech, Language, and Hearing Research, 42,* 1125–1135.

Watson, J. B. (1913). Psychology as the behaviorist views it. *Psychological Review, 20,* 158–177.

Watson, J. B. (1924/1966). *Behaviorism.* Chicago: University of Chicago Press.

Watson, J. B. (1928). *Psychological care of infant and child.* New York: Norton.

Watson, J. B., & Rayner, R. (1920). Conditioned emotional reactions. *Journal of Experimental Psychology, 3,* 1–14.

Watson, J. D. (1999). *The double helix: A personal account of the discovery of the structure of DNA* (Rev. ed.). London: Penguin.

Weaver, H., Smith, G., & Kippax, S. (2005). School-based sex education policies and indicators of sexual health among young people: A comparison of the Netherlands, France, Australia and the United States. *Sex Education, 5,* 171–188.

Weddle, D. (2003, January 5). What the Lost Boys of Sudan found in America. *Los Angeles Times Magazine,* Section 1, pp. 12–17, 31.

Wei, J., & Levkoff, S. (2000). *Aging well: The complete guide to physical and emotional health.* New York: Wiley.

Weichold, K., Silbereisen, R. K., & Schmitt-Rodermund, E. (2003). Short-term and long-term consequences of early versus late physical maturation in adolescents. In C. Hayward (Ed.), *Gender differences at puberty* (pp. 241–276). New York: Cambridge University Press.

Weighty problem. (2001). *People Weekly, 55*(7), 65–66.

Weinert, F. E., & Hany, E. A. (2003). The stability of individual differences in intellectual development: Empirical evidence, theoretical problems, and new research questions. In R. J. Sternberg & J. Lautrey (Eds.), *Models of intelligence: International perspectives* (pp. 169–181). Washington, DC: American Psychological Association.

Weisfeld, G. E. (1999). *Evolutionary principles of human adolescence.* New York: Basic Books.

Weishaus, S., & Field, D. (1988). A half century of marriage: Continuity or change? *Journal of Marriage and the Family, 50,* 763–774.

Weiss, B., Dodge, K. A., Bates, J. E., & Pettit, G. S. (1992). Some consequences of early harsh discipline: Child aggression and a maladaptive social information processing style. *Child Development, 63,* 1321–1335.

Weiss, B., & Landrigan, P. J. (2000). The developing brain and the environment: An introduction. *Environmental Health Perspectives, 108*(Suppl. 3), 373–374.

Weissman, D. (2005). *Fast fact and concept #3: Syndrome of imminent death.* End of Life/Palliative Education Resource Center. Retrieved February 25, 2005, from **http://www.eperc.mcw.edu**

Wellbery, C. (2003). Sleep patterns in infants, children, and adolescents. *American Family Physician, 67,* 2397–2398.

Weller, N. F., Kelder, S. H., Cooper, S. P., Basen-Engquist, K., & Tortolero, S. R. (2003). School-year employment among high school students: Effects on academic, social, and physical functioning. *Adolescence, 38,* 441–458.

Wellman, H. M. (1992). *The child's theory of mind.* Cambridge, MA: MIT Press.

Wellman, H. M., Cross, D., & Watson, J. (2001). Meta-analysis of theory-of-mind development: The truth about false belief. *Child Development, 72,* 655–684.

Wellman, H. M., & Gelman, S. A. (1998). Knowledge acquisition in foundational domains. In W. Damon (Series Ed.) & D. Kuhn & R. S. Siegler (Vol. Eds.), *Handbook of child psychology: Volume 2. Cognition, perception, and language* (5th ed., pp. 523–573). New York: Wiley.

Wellman, H. M., & Woolley, J. D. (1990). From simple desires to ordinary beliefs: The early development of everyday psychology. *Cognition, 35,* 245–275.

Wells, K. C., & Forehand, R. (1985). Conduct and oppositional disorders. In P. H. Bornstein & A. E. Kazdin (Eds.), *Handbook of clinical behavior therapy with children* (pp. 218–265). Homewood, IL: Dorsey Press.

Wentzel, K. R. (2003). Sociometric status and adjustment in middle school: A longitudinal study. *Journal of Early Adolescence, 23,* 5–28.

Wentzel, K. R., & Caldwell, K. (1997). Friendships, peer acceptance, and group membership: Relations to academic achievement in middle school. *Child Development, 68,* 1198–1209.

Werler, M. M., Hayes, C., Louik, C., Shapiro, S., & Mitchell, A. A. (1999). Multivitamin supplementation and risk of birth defects. *American Journal of Epidemiology, 150,* 675–682.

Werner, E. E. (1993). Risk, resilience, and recovery: Perspectives from the Kauai Longitudinal Study. *Development and Psychopathology, 5,* 503–515.

Werner, E. E., Bierman, J. M., & French, F. E. (1971). *The children of Kauai: A longitudinal study from the prenatal period to age ten.* Honolulu, HI: University of Hawaii Press.

Werner, L. A., & Marean, G. C. (1996). *Human auditory development.* Madison, WI: Brown & Benchmark.

Westen, D., & Gabbard, G. O. (1999). Psychoanalytic approaches to personality. In L. A. Pervin & O. P. John (Eds.), *Handbook of personality: Theory and research* (2nd ed., pp. 57–101). New York: Guilford.

Westheimer, R. K., & Lopater, S. (2005). *Human sexuality: A psychosocial perspective* (2nd ed.). Baltimore: Lippincott Williams & Wilkins.

Weston, K. (1991). *Families we choose: Lesbians, gays, kinship.* New York: Columbia University Press.

Wethington, E. (2000). Expecting stress: Americans and the "midlife crisis." *Motivation and Emotion, 24,* 85–103.

Wetzler, M. J., Rubenstein, D., Gillespie, M. J., Schenck, R. C., Jr., & Gloystein, D. (2002). Shoulder injuries in swimmers: Why they develop, how to treat them; guidelines for preventing—and managing—swimmer's shoulder. *Journal of Musculoskeletal Medicine, 19,* 365–369.

Whaley, A. L. (2000). Sociocultural differences in the developmental consequences of the use of physical discipline during childhood for African Americans. *Cultural Diversity and Ethnic Minority Psychology, 6,* 5–12.

Whalley, L. (2001). *The aging brain.* New York: Columbia University Press.

Whang, P. A., & Hancock, G. R. (1994). Motivation and mathematics achievement: Comparisons between Asian-American and non-Asian students. *Contemporary Educational Psychology, 19,* 302–322.

Wheelwright, S., & Baron-Cohen, S. (2001). The link between autism and skills such as engineering, maths, physics and computing: A reply to Jarrold and Routh. *Autism, 5,* 223–227.

Whitaker, D. J., Miller, K. S., May, D. C., & Levin, M. L. (1999). Teenage partners' communication about sexual risk and condom use: The importance of parent-teenager discussions. *Family Planning Perspectives, 31,* 117–121.

Whitbourne, S. K. (1985). The psychological construction of the life span. In J. E. Birren & K. W. Schaie (Eds.), *Handbook of the psychology of aging* (2nd ed., pp. 594–618). New York: Van Nostrand Reinhold.

Whitbourne, S. K. (1986). *The me I know: A study of adult identity.* New York: Springer-Verlag.

Whitbourne, S. K. (1996). *The aging individual: Physical and psychological perspectives.* New York: Springer.

Whitbourne, S. K., Zuschlag, M. K., Elliot, L. B., & Waterman, A. S. (1992). Psychosocial development in adulthood: A 22-year sequential study. *Journal of Personality and Social Psychology, 63,* 260–271.

White, L. K., & Riedmann, A. (1992). Ties among adult siblings. *Social Forces, 71,* 85–102.

White, S. H. (1965). Evidence for a hierarchical arrangement of learning processes. In L. P. Lipsitt & C. C. Spiker (Eds.), *Advances in child development and behavior* (pp. 187–220). New York: Academic Press.

Whiting, B. B., & Whiting, J. W. M. (with Longabaugh, R.). (1975). *Children of six cultures: A psycho-cultural analysis.* Cambridge, MA: Harvard University Press.

Wiederman, M. W. (1997). Extramarital sex: Prevalence and correlates in a national survey. *Journal of Sex Research, 34,* 167–174.

Wigg, N. R., Tong, S., McMichael, A. J., Baghurst, P. A., Vimpani, G., & Roberts, R. (1998). Does breastfeeding at six months predict cognitive development? *Australian and New Zealand Journal of Public Health, 22,* 232–236.

Wigglesworth, G. (1990). Children's narrative acquisition: A study of some aspects of reference and anaphora. *First Language, 10,* 105–125.

Wilcox, S., Evenson, K. R., Aragaki, A., Wassertheil-Smoller, S., Mouton, C. P., & Loevinger, B. L. (2003). The effects of widowhood on physical and mental health, health behaviors, and health outcomes: The Women's Health Initiative. *Health Psychology, 22,* 513–522.

Wiley, E. W., Bialystok, E., & Hakuta, K. (2005). New approaches to using census data to test the critical-period hypothesis for second-language acquisition. *Psychological Science, 16,* 341–343.

Wilk, S. L., Desmarais, L. B., Sackett, P. R. (1995). Gravitation to jobs commensurate with ability: Longitudinal and cross-sectional tests. *Journal of Applied Psychology, 80,* 79–85.

Wilk, S. L., & Sackett, P. R. (1996). Longitudinal analysis of ability-job complexity fit and job change. *Personnel Psychology, 49,* 937–967.

Wilkins, C. H., & Goldfeder, J. S. (2004). Osteoporosis screening is unjustifiably low in older African-American women. *Journal of the National Medical Association, 96,* 461–467.

Willcox, B. J., Willcox, D. C., & Suzuki, M. (2001). *The Okinawa Program: How the world's longest-lived people achieve everlasting health-And how you can too.* New York: Three Rivers Press.

Willcutt, E. G., DeFries, J. C., Pennington, B. F., Smith, S. D., Cardon, L. R., & Olson, R. K. (2003). Genetic etiology of comorbid reading difficulties and ADHD. In R. Plomin, J. C. DeFries, I. W. Craig, & P. McGuffin (Eds.), *Behavioral genetics in the postgenomic era* (pp. 227–246). Washington, DC: American Psychological Association.

Williams, K., Kemper, S., & Hummert, M. L. (2003). Improving nursing home communication: An intervention to reduce elderspeak. *Gerontologist, 43,* 242–247.

Williams, P. A., Haertel, E. H., Haertel, G. D., & Walberg, H. J. (1982). The impact of leisure-time television on school learning: A research synthesis. *American Educational Research Journal, 19,* 19–50.

Williams, T. T. (2001). *Refuge: An unnatural history of family and place* (Rev. ed.). New York: Vintage Books.

Willis, C. A. (2002). The grieving process in children: Strategies for understanding, educating, and reconciling children's perceptions of death. *Early Childhood Education Journal, 29,* 221–226.

Willott, J. A., Hnath Chisolm, T., & Lister, J. J. (2001). Modulation of presbycusis: Current status and future directions. *Audiology and Neuro-Otology, 6,* 231–249.

Willows, D. M. (1978). A picture is not always worth a thousand words: Pictures as distracters in reading. *Journal of Educational Psychology, 70,* 255–262.

Wilson, B., Smith, S. L., Potter, W. J., et al. (2002). Violence in children's television programming: Assessing the risks. *Journal of Communication, 52,* 5–35.

Wilson, J., & Sherkat, D. E. (1994). Returning to the fold. *Journal for the Scientific Study of Religion, 33,* 148–161.

Wilson, M., & Daly, M. (1985). Competitiveness, risk taking, and violence: The young male syndrome. *Ethology and Sociobiology, 6,* 59–73.

Wilson, R. (2004, April 23). Singular mistreatment. *The Chronicle of Higher Education,* pp. A10–A12.

Wilson, R. D. (2000). Amniocentesis and chorionic villus sampling. *Current Opinion in Obstetrics and Gynecology, 12,* 81–86.

Wilson, R. S., & Bennett, D. A. (2003). Cognitive activity and risk of Alzheimer's disease. *Current Directions in Psychological Science, 12,* 87–91.

Wilson, R. S., Bennett, D. A., Mendes de Leon, C. F., Bienias, J. L., Morris, M. C., & Evans, D. A. (2005). Distress proneness and cognitive decline in a population of older persons. *Psychoneuroendocrinology, 30,* 11–17.

Winer, G. A., & Falkner, R. A. (1984). The effects of linguistic factors on class inclusion performance in adults and children. *Journal of Genetic Psychology, 145,* 251–265.

Wing, L. (1997). The history of ideas on autism. *Autism, 1,* 13–23.

Wingfield, A., & Stine-Morrow, E. A. (2000). Language and speech. In F. I. M. Craik & T. A. Salthouse (Eds.), *The handbook of aging and cognition* (2nd ed., pp. 359–415). Mahwah, NJ: Erlbaum.

Wink, P., & Dillon, M. (2002). Spiritual development across the adult life course: Findings from a longitudinal study. *Journal of Adult Development, 9,* 79–94.

Wink, P., & Dillon, M. (2003). Religiousness, spirituality, and psychosocial functioning in late adulthood: Findings from a longitudinal study. *Psychology and Aging, 18,* 916–924.

Winner, E. (1996). *Gifted children: Myths and realities.* New York: Basic Books.

Winner, E. (2000). Giftedness: Current theory and research. *Current Directions in Psychological Science, 9,* 153–156.

Winsler, A., Madigan, A. L., & Aquilino, S. A. (2005). Correspondence between maternal and paternal parenting styles in early childhood. *Early Childhood Research Quarterly, 20,* 1–12.

Winslow, S. (2005). Work-family conflict, gender, and parenthood, 1977–1997. *Journal of Family Issues, 26,* 727–755.

Wisniewski, A. B., Migeon, C. J., Meyer-Bahlburg, H. F., et al. (2000). Complete androgen insensitivity syndrome: Long-term medical, surgical, and psychosexual outcome. *Journal of Clinical Endocrinology and Metabolism, 85,* 2664–2669.

Wisniewski, S. R., Belle, S. H., Coon, D. W., et al. (2003). The Resources for Enhancing Alzheimer's Caregiver Health (REACH): Project design and baseline characteristics. *Psychology and Aging, 18,* 375–384.

Wissow, L. S. (2001). Ethnicity, income, and parenting contexts of physical punishment in a national sample of families with young children. *Child Maltreatment, 6,* 118–129.

Witt, P. H. (2003). Transfer of juveniles to adult court: The case of H. H. *Psychology, Public Policy, and Law, 9,* 361–380.

Wolf, A. W., Lozoff, B., Latz, S., & Paludetto, R. (1996). Parental theories in the management of young children's sleep in Japan, Italy, and the United States. In S. Harkness & C. M. Super (Eds.), *Parents' cultural belief systems* (pp. 364–384). New York: Guilford.

Wolfson, A. R., & Carskadon, M. A. (1998). Sleep schedules and daytime functioning in adolescents. *Child Development, 69,* 875–887.

Woll, S. (2002). *Everyday thinking: Memory, reasoning, and judgment in the real world.* Mahwah, NJ: Erlbaum.

Wong, A. M.-Y., & Johnston, J. R. (2004). The development of discourse referencing in Cantonese-speaking children. *Journal of Child Language, 31,* 633–660.

Wong, C. A., Scavone, B. M., Peaceman, A. M., et al. (2005). The risk of cesarean delivery with neuraxial analgesia given early versus late in labor. *The New England Journal of Medicine, 352,* 655–665.

Wood, J. N., & Spelke, E. S. (2005). Infants' enumeration of actions: Numerical discrimination and its signature limits. *Developmental Science, 8,* 173–181.

Woodard, E. H., IV (with Gridina, N.). (2000). *Media in the home 2000: The fifth annual survey of parents and children.* Philadelphia: University of Pennsylvania, Annenberg Public Policy Center.

World Bank Group. (2001). *Governments unite to save women's lives* (Press Release No. 2001/117/HD). Retrieved July 20, 2006, from http://web.worldbank.org/WBSITE/EXTERNAL/COUNTRIES/AFRICAEXT/EXTAFRREGTOPGENDER/0,,contentMDK:20012384~menuPK:502376~pagePK:34004173~piPK:34003707~theSitePK:502360,00.html

World Health Organization. (1997). *Reducing mortality from major childhood killer diseases* (Fact Sheet No. 180). Retrieved January 10, 2006, from http://www.who.int/child-adolescent-health/New_Publications/IMCI/fs_180.htm

World Health Organization. (1998). *Reducing mortality from major killers of children* (Fact Sheet No. 178). Retrieved June 10, 2006, from http://www.who.int/mediacentre/factsheets/fs178/en

World Health Organization. (2000–2004). *Nutrition: Infant and young child.* Retrieved January 8, 2006, from http://www.who.int/child-adolescent-health/NUTRITION/infant_exclusive.htm

World Health Organization. (2003). *Facts and figures: The World Health Report 2003—Shaping the future.* Retrieved March 1, 2005, from http://www.who.int/entity/whr/2003/en/Facts_and_Figures-en.pdf

World Health Organization. (2004). *Making pregnancy safer* (Fact Sheet No. 276). Retrieved November 27, 2004, from http://www.who.int/mediacentre/factsheets/fs276/en/

World Health Organization, UNICEF, & United Nations Population Fund. (2004). *Maternal mortality in 2000: Estimates developed by WHO, UNICEF, UNIFPA.* Retrieved http://www.who.int/reproductive-health/publications/maternal_mortality_2000/index.html

World Health Organization, United Nations Population Fund, United Nations Children's Fund, & World Bank. (2001). *UN, WHO, and World Bank partner to combat maternal mortality.* Retrieved February 2, 2002, from www.worldbank.org/html/extdr/extme/080.htm

World Press Review. (2004). *Armed conflict around the world.* Retrieved December 20, 2004, from https://worldpress.org//signup.cfm?promotype=wallmap

World Values Survey. (2004). *1995 data.* Retrieved December 11, 2004, from http://www.worldvaluessurvey.org

Worthington-Roberts, B. S. (2000). Nutrition. In W. R. Cohen, S. H. Sheldon, & I. R. Merkatz (Eds.), *Cherry and Merkatz's complications of pregnancy* (5th ed., pp. 17–48). Philadelphia: Lippincott Williams & Wilkins.

Wortman, C. B., & Silver, R. C. (1987). Coping with irrevocable loss. In A. Baum, G. R. VandenBos, & B. K. Bryant (Eds.), *Cataclysms, crises, and catastrophes: Psychology in action* (pp. 185–235). Washington, DC: American Psychological Association.

Wortman, C. B., & Silver, R. C. (1989). The myths of coping with loss. *Journal of Consulting and Clinical Psychology, 57,* 349–357.

Wortman, C. B., & Silver, R. C. (2001). The myths of coping with loss revisited. In M. S. Stroebe, R. O. Hansson, W. Stroebe, & H. Schut (Eds.), *Handbook of bereavement research: Consequences, coping, and care* (pp. 405–429). Washington, DC: American Psychological Association.

Woteki, C. E. (2001). Dietitians can prevent listeriosis. *Journal of the American Dietetic Association, 101,* 285–286.

Wrenn, K. A., & Maurer, T. J. (2004). Beliefs about older workers' learning and development behavior in relation to beliefs about malleability of skills, age-related decline, and control. *Journal of Applied Social Psychology, 34,* 223–242.

Wright, J. C., Huston, A. C., Murphy, K. C., et al. (2001). The relations of early television viewing to school readiness and vocabulary of children from low-income families: The early window project. *Child Development, 72,* 1347–1366.

Wright, R. O., Tsaih, S. W., Schwartz, J., Wright, R. J., & Hu, H. (2003). Association between iron deficiency and blood lead level in a longitudinal analysis of children followed in an urban primary care clinic. *Journal of Pediatrics, 142,* 9–14.

Wright, V. C., Schieve, L. A., Reynolds, M. A., & Jeng, G. (2005). Surveillance Summaries: Assisted reproductive technology surveillance—United States, 2002. *Morbidity and Mortality Weekly Report, 54*(SS-2), 1–24.

Wurtman, R. J. (2000). Age-related decreases in melatonin secretion—Clinical consequences. *Journal of Clinical Endocrinology and Metabolism, 85,* 2135–2136.

Wynbrandt, J., & Ludman, M. D. (2000). *The encyclopedia of genetic disorders and birth defects* (2nd ed.). New York: Facts on File.

Xue, Y., Hodges, K., & Wotring, J. (2004). Predictors of outcome for children with behavior problems served in public mental health. *Journal of Clinical Child and Adolescent Psychology, 33,* 516–523.

Yaffe, K. (2003). Hormone therapy and the brain: Déjà vu all over again? *Journal of the American Medical Association, 289,* 2717–2719.

Yearta, S. K., & Warr, P. (1995). Does age matter? *Journal of Management Development, 14*(7), 28–35.

Yeh, S.-C. J., & Lo, S. K. (2004). Living alone, social support, and feeling lonely among the elderly. *Social Behavior and Personality, 32,* 129–138.

Yeni-Komshian, G. H., Flege, J. E., & Liu, S. (2000). Pronunciation proficiency in the first and second languages of Korean-English bilinguals. *Bilingualism: Language and Cognition, 3,* 131–149.

Yoon, C., May, C. P., & Hasher, L. (2000). Aging, circadian arousal patterns, and cognition. In D. C. Park & N. Schwarz (Eds.), *Cognitive aging: A primer* (pp. 151–171). Hove, England: Psychology Press.

Yoon, D. P. (2001). Causal modeling predicting psychological adjustment of Korean-born adolescent adoptees. *Journal of Human Behavior in the Social Environment, 3,* 65–82.

Young, T. J., & French, L. A. (1998). Heights of U.S. presidents: A trend analysis for 1948–1996. *Perceptual and Motor Skills, 87,* 321–322.

Youniss, J., & Ruth, A. (2000). *Interim report: Positive indicators of youth development.* Unpublished manuscript, The Catholic University of America, Washington, DC. Cited in Gilliam, F. D., & Bales, S. N. (2001). *Strategic frame analysis: Reframing America's youth.* Ann Arbor, MI: Society for Research in Child Development.

Zadnik, K., Manny, R. E., Yu, J. A., et al. (2003). Ocular component data in schoolchildren as a function of age and gender. *Optometry and Vision Science, 80,* 226–236.

Zajac, R. J., & Hartup, W. W. (1997). Friends as coworkers: Research review and classroom implications. *Elementary School Journal, 98,* 3–13.

Zeidner, M., Matthews, G., Roberts, R. D., & MacCann, C. (2003). Development of emotional intelligence: Towards a multi-level investment model. *Human Development, 46,* 69–96.

Zeiss, A. M., & Kasl-Godley, J. (2001). Sexuality in older adults' relationships. *Generations, 25*(2), 18–26.

Zelazo, P. D., & Reznick, J. S. (1991). Age-related asynchrony of knowledge and action. *Child Development, 62,* 719–735.

Zhang, H., & Zhou, Y. (2003). The teaching of mathematics in Chinese elementary schools. *International Journal of Psychology, 38,* 286–298.

Zigler, E. F., & Finn-Stevenson, M. (1999). Applied developmental psychology. In M. H. Bornstein & M. E. Lamb (Eds.), *Developmental psychology: An advanced textbook* (4th ed., pp. 555–598). Mahwah, NJ: Erlbaum.

Zigler, E., & Styfco, S. J. (1993). Using research and theory to justify and inform Head Start expansion. *Social Policy Report, 7*(2).

Zimet, G. D., Owens, R., Dahms, W., Cutler, M., Litvene, M., & Cuttler, L. (1999). The psychosocial functioning of adults who were short as children. In U. Eiholzer, F. Haverkamp, & L. D. Voss (Eds.), *Growth, stature, and psychosocial well-being* (pp. 47–55). Seattle, WA: Hogrefe & Huber.

Zornberg, G. L., Buka, S. L., & Tsuang, M. T. (2000). Hypoxic-ischemia-related fetal/neonatal complications and risk of schizophrenia and other nonaffective psychoses: A 19-year longitudinal study. *America Journal of Psychiatry, 157,* 196–202.

Zucker, K. J., & Bradley, S. J. (2000). Gender identity disorder. In C. H. Zeanah, Jr. (Ed.), *Handbook of infant mental health* (2nd ed., pp. 412–424). New York: Guilford.

Zucker, K. J., Bradley, S. J., Oliver, G., Blake, J., Fleming, S., & Hood, J. (1996). Psychosexual development of women with congenital adrenal hyperplasia. *Hormones and Behavior, 30,* 300–318.

Credits

Photo Credits

Chapter 1 p. 2 PhotoDisc/Getty Images; p. 6 ©Lewis Wickes Hine/CORBIS All Rights Reserved; p. 9 Johnny Crawford/The Image Works; p. 11 PhotoAlto/Superstock Royalty Free; p. 18 (top) ©Jack Moebes/CORBIS All Rights Reserved; p. 18 (bottom), Steve Kohls/Brainerd Daily Dispatch/AP Wide World Photos; p. 19 Corbis/Sygma; p. 21 top Getty Images, Inc.; p. 21 (bottom) Sigmund Freud Museum/AP Wide World Photos; p. 23 ScienceCartoonsPlus.com; p. 25 Professor Ben Harris, University of New Hampshire; p. 26 Albert Bandura, D. Ross & S.A. Ross, Imitation of film-mediated aggressive models. "Journal of Abnormal and Social Psychology", 1963, 66. P. 8; p. 28 Nina Leen/Time Life Pictures/Getty Images/Time Life Pictures; p. 29 (left) ©Kazuyoshi Nomachi/CORBIS All Rights Reserved; p. 29 (center) ©Rick Gomez/CORBIS All Rights Reserved; p. 29 (right) Jean-Léo DUGAST/Peter Arnold, Inc.; p. 32 Corbis/Bettmann; p. 34 (top) Bill Wittman; p. 34 (bottom) ©Novosti/Sovfoto; p. 38 Charles A. Nelson III, Ph.D.

Chapter 2 p. 44 Getty Images, Inc.; p. 47 (top) Masterfile Stock Image Library; p. 47 (center) Mark Downey/Masterfile Stock Image Library; p. 47 (bottom) Rudi Von Briel/PhotoEdit Inc.; p. 48 (left) Photodisc/Getty Images; p.48 (right) Hartsoeker, N. Essay de dioptrique, Paris, 1694, p. 230. National Library of Medicine; p. 51 ©Jason Moore/CORBIS All Rights Reserved; p. 52 CNRI/Photo Researchers, Inc.; p. 54 Joel Gordon/Joel Gordon Photography; p. 55 Matt Davies; p. 57 Thomas Wanstall/The Image Works; p. 59 (left and right) National Cancer Centre (CNIO); p. 62 Hays Daily News, Adam Gerik/AP Wide World Photos; p. 69 ©Michael S. Lewis/CORBIS All Rights Reserved; p. 72 Stuart Franklin/Magnum Photos, Inc.; p. 74 (top and bottom) Rutgers Department of Anthropology; p. 80 Grey Villet/Getty Images/Time Life Pictures.

Chapter 3 p. 84 Purestock/Alamy Images; p. 88 Dennis Kinkel/Phototake USA/Alamy Images; p. 90 (left) Anatomical Travelogue/Photo Researchers, Inc.; p. 90 (center) Petit Format/Nestle/Science Source/Photo Researchers, Inc.; p. 90 (right) Steve Allen/Getty Images Inc.-Image Bank; p. 91 Photo Lennart Nilsson/Albert Bonniers Forlag AB; p. 92 Chuch Nacke/Woodfin Camp & Associates; p. 99 Joe Epstein/Design Conceptions; p. 102 ©David H. Wells/CORBIS All Rights Reserved; p. 105 David Young Wolff/PhotoEdit Inc.; p. 108 Jose Luis Pelaez, Inc./Blend Images/Alamy Images Royalty Free; p. 109 Max Aquilera-Hellweg; p. 110 Sachs/Corbis/Sygma; p. 115 (left) Joel Gordon/Joel Gordon Photography; p. 115 (right) ©Danny Lehman/CORBIS All Rights Reserved; p. 118 ©Eastcott/Momatiuk/The Image Works; p. 120, Shehzad Noorani/Woodfin Camp & Associates; p. 123 ©2007 Massachusetts Medical Society. All rights reserved.

Chapter 4 C-1p. 126 mediacolor's/Alamy Images; p. 129 ©Hironao NUMABE, M.D., Ph.D.; p. 131 Photo Researchers, Inc.; p. 134 (top left) ©Laura Dwight/CORBIS All Rights Reserved; p. 134 (right) Bubbles Photolibrary/Alamy Images; p. 134 (bottom left) ASTIER/Photo Researchers, Inc.; p. 145 (top) Carolyn Rovee-Collier; p. (157) Alamy Images; p. 159 Martin Rogers/Woodfin Camp & Associates; p. 162 ©Rick Gomez/CORBIS All Rights Reserved; p. 133 (all) Anthony Young; p. 139 Mark Richards/PHOTOEDIT; p. 140 (left) Don H. Johnson; p. 140 (right) Science Magazine.

Chapter 5 p. 170 Reality Stock/Alamy Images; p. 174 (top) Mark Richards/PhotoEdit Inc.; p. 174 (bottom) Michael Newman/PhotoEdit Inc.; p. 176 Daniel Morel/AP Wide World Photos; p. 180 ©CORBIS All Rights Reserved; p. 183 Victor Englebert/Time & Life Pictures/Getty Images/Time Life Pictures; p. 184 Hansel Mieth/Time Life Pictures/Getty Images/Time Life Pictures; p. 187 John T. Fowler/Alamy Images; p. 189 Alamy Images; p. 191 Getty Images, Inc.; p. 192 Robert Fried/robertfriedphotography.com; p. 195 plainpicture GmbH & Co. KG/Alamy Images; p. 199 Alan Evrard/Robert Harding World Imagery; p. 201 (all) Bradley-Johnson & Johnson (2001). Used with permission from Pro-Ed.; p. 206 Tony Freeman/PhotoEdit Inc.; p. 207 Alexis Rosenfeld/Photo Researchers, Inc.

Chapter 6 p. 212 Ryan McVay/Getty Images, Inc.- Photodisc; p. 214 Mike Derer/AP Wide World Photos; p. 218 Bob Daemmrich/The Image Works; p. 219 Douglas & Martin/Photo Researchers, Inc.; p. 221 Getty Images, Inc.; p. 222 (top left) Cavallini James/BSIP/Phototake NYC; p. 222 (center left) Poultry Science Association; p. 222 (bottom center) Debra Poole; p. 222 (right) Debra Poole; p. 223 David Young-Wolff/PhotoEdit Inc.; p. 229 Superstock Royalty Free; p. 231 Esbin-Anderson/The Image Works; p. 233 Brand X/Superstock Royalty Free; p. 237 Laura Dwight Photography; p. 242 Richard Lord/The Image Works; p. 244 Jeff Greenberg/Peter Arnold, Inc.; p. 248 Shehzad Nooran/Peter Arnold, Inc.

Chapter 7 p. 256 Sean Sprague/Sean Sprague; p. 260 The Enterprise-Journal, Aaron Rhoads/AP Wide World Photos; p. 262 Spencer Grant/PhotoEdit Inc.; p. 271 Tony Freeman/PhotoEdit Inc.; p. 272 Michael Newman/PhotoEdit Inc.; p. 275 Esbin/Anderson/The Image Works; p. 276 J. Pat Carter/AP Wide World Photos; p. 277 Susan Lapides/Design Conceptions; p. 279 Suzanne Gaskins; p. 281 Tony Freeman/PhotoEdit Inc.; p. 284 ©Purestock/Alamy; p. 285 Larissa Niec; p. 287 Frank Pedrick/The Image Works; p. 291 ©Solid Photo/Alamy; p. 295 Bill Wittman.

Chapter 8 p. 300 Larry Kolvoord/The Image Works; p. 302 Corbis/Bettmann; p. 303 Getty Images, Inc.; p. 305 (left and right) AP Wide World Photos; p. 306 Keith Brofsky/Getty Images, Inc-Photodisc; p. 309 Sedalia Democrat, Sydney Brin/AP Wide World Photos; p. 314 David Longstreath/AP Wide World Photos; p. 317 Nancy Richmond/The Image Works; p. 322 Laura Dwight Photography; p. 326 ©Lew Robertson/CORBIS All Rights Reserved; p. 328 Don Smetzer/PhotoEdit Inc.; p. 329 Richard Hutchings/PhotoEdit Inc.; p. 333 Lincoln Journal Star, Eric Gregory/AP Wide World Photos; p. 335 ullstein-JOKER/Ausserhofer/Peter Arnold, Inc.; p. 338 Superstock Royalty Free.

Chapter 9 p. 346 Gideon Mendel/CORBIS All Rights Reserved; p. 348 ©Wendy Stone/CORBIS All Rights Reserved; p. 350 Jodie Plumert, Ph.D.; p. 351 (top) Getty Images/Digital Vision; p. 351 (bottom) Robert Brenner/PhotoEdit Inc.; p. 353 (top) Jeff Miller/University of Wisconsin-Madison/Pollak, S.D., and Kistler, D. (2002). Early experience alters the development of categorical representations for facial expressions of emotion. Proceedings of the National Academy of Sciences, USA, 99, 9072–907; p. 353 (bottom) PNAS/Pollak, S.D., and Kistler, D. (2002). Early experience alters the development of categorical representations for facial expressions of emotion. Proceedings of the National Academy of Sciences, USA, 99, 9072–9076; p. 360 Bob Daemmrich/Stock Boston; p. 363 (top) S. Gazin/The Image Works; p. 363 (bottom) Rudi Von Briel/PhotoEdit Inc.; p. 365 Mike Derer/AP Wide World Photos; p. 368 Ason Reed/Reuters/Corbis/Reuters America LLC; p. 370 (top) Imagination Photo Design; p. 370 (bottom) Source not on Image; p. 372 ©Paul Fusco/Magnum Photos; p. 374 Frank Siteman/Index Stock Imagery, Inc.; p. 377 Bob Daemmirich/The Image Works; p. 381 ©LuckyPix/LuckyPix/Masterfile; p. 383 Stock Connection/Alamy Images.

Chapter 10 p. 388 Henry Romero/Corbis/Reuters America LLC; p. 392 Phanie/Photo Researchers, Inc.; p. 394 Bill Aron/PhotoEdit Inc.; p. 397 Lauren Greenfield/VII; p. 399 Michael Newman/PhotoEdit Inc.; p. 401 ©David Woolley/Getty Images, Inc.; p. 404 Jason Painter/U of North Carolina Chapel Hill; p. 407 Corbis Royalty Free; p. 408 Robert Brenner/PhotoEdit Inc.; p. 412 Getty Images/Digital Vision; p. 415 ©Alison Wright/CORBIS All Rights Reserved; p. 417 David Young-Wolff/PhotoEdit Inc.; p. 419 Alamy Images Royalty Free; p. 424 Sally Guiney/Investigative Services; p. 425 Zits-Zits Partnership. KING FEATURES SYNDICATE.

Chapter 11 p. 432 Tannen H. Maury/The Image Works; p. 435 (left) Jennifer Grimes/East Valley Tribune/AP Wide World Photos; p. 435 (right) Joel Gordon/Joel Gordon Photography; p. 437 Spencer Grant/PhotoEdit Inc.; p. 443 Thinkstock/Alamy Images Royalty Free; p. 445 (left) Elizabeth Dalziel/AP Wide World Photos; p. 445 (right) Robert Harding Picture Library Ltd./Alamy Images; p. 450 Image Source/Alamy Images; p. 453 (left) Brennan Linsley/AP Wide World Photos; p. 453 (right) Tony Freeman/PhotoEdit Inc.; p. 457 Shepad Sherbell/Corbis/SABA Press Photos, Inc.; p. 460 Marilyn Humphries/The Image Works; p. 464 Tony Freeman/PhotoEdit Inc.; p. 468 Traverse City Reord-Eagle, Meegan M. Reid/AP Wide World Photos.

Chapter 12 p. 474 Sergio Pitamitz/Robert Harding World Imagery; p. 478 (left and right) Photos courtesy of New York plastic surgeon, Dr. Darrick E. Antell. www.Antell-MD.com; p. 481 It Stock Free/AGE Fotostock America, Inc.; p. 485 John Birdsall/AGE Fotostock America, Inc.; p. 491 Jim Pickerell/The Stock Connection; p. 493 ©Ram Singh Bir/STSimages.com; p. 496 Margaret Herring/Oregon State University/Oregon's Argicultural Progress Magazine; p. 499 Walt Handelsman/2005,Newsday/TMS/MCT Reprints; p. 501 ©Corbis. All rights reserved; p. 506 Bob Daemmrich/PhotoEdit Inc.; p. 510 Popperfoto/Alamy Images; p. 511 Bill Aron/PhotoEdit Inc.

Chapter 13 p. 518 ©Natalie Fobes/CORBIS All Rights Reserved; p. 522 Jim West/The Image Works; p. 523 (top left and top right) Zuoxin Wang, Ph.D/Florida State University; p. 523 (bottom) Dr. Lucy Brown/Albert Einstein College of Medicine; p. 525 Joe Vogan/Joe Vogan Photography; p. 529 Redin, Van/20th Century Fox/Picture Desk, Inc./Kobal Collection; p. 540 (top) Minika Graff/The Image Works; p. 540 (bottom) ©Tom Stewart/CORBIS All Rights Reserved; p. 543 Norbert von der Groeben/The Image Works; p. 546 Big Cheese/AGE Fotostock America, Inc; p. 550 ©2002 ethan hill; p. 553 ©Jeff Moore/ZUMA/CORBIS All Rights Reserved.

Chapter 14 p. 560 Kevin Fleming/CORBIS All Rights Reserved; p. 563 Susan Van Etten/PhotoEdit Inc.; p. 569 Peter Menzel Photography; p. 573 ©John Henley/CORBIS All Rights Reserved; p. 571 Corbis Royalty Free; p. 576 Mark Downey/Mark Downey/Lucid Images; p. 581 Pixtal/AGE Fotostock America, Inc; p. 583 Will Burgess/Corbis/Reuters America LLC; p. 587 James Marshall/The Image Works; p. 590 Susan Edsall, author, Into The Blue: A Father's Flight and a Daughter's Return; p. 594 Judith Blake; p. 596 Getty Images, Inc.; p. 507 ECR International; p. 577 Patricia J. Wynne.

Chapter 15 p. 606 Walter/Peter Arnold, Inc.; p. 613 Tony Freeman/PhotoEdit Inc.; p. 609 Scott Goldsmith Photography; p. 615 Joseph Kaczmarek/AP Wide World Photos; p. 619 (top and bottom) Daniel Roenker/University of Kentucky; p. 620, Courtesy of New England Centenarian Study/Boston University Medical Center; p. 622 AFP/AFP/Getty Images; p. 624 ©Ariel Skelley/CORBIS All Rights Reserved; p. 627 Michael Goldman/Masterfile Stock Image Library; p. 631 Blend Images/Superstock Royalty Free; p. 634 ©Jim Pickerell/The Image Works; p. 636 Corbis Royalty Free; p. 642 Digital vision/Superstock Royalty Free; p. 614 (top left and top right) Pr. J.J. Hauw/Phototake NYC; p. 614 (bottom) Photo Researchers, Inc.

Epilogue p. 648 Bill Wittman; p. 651 Debra Poole; p. 653 Moshe Bursuker/AP Wide World Photos; p. 657 Jim Whitmer Photography; p. 660 Jim Arbogast/SuperStock, Inc.; p. 665 (left) ©David Alan Harvey/Magnum Photos; p. 665 (right) ©Andrew Lichenstein/CORBIS All Rights Reserved; p. 669 Rachel Epstein/PhotoEdit Inc.

Text and Figure Credits

Chapter 1   p. 17, Figure 1–4 *The New York Times;* p. 35, Figure 1–7 From *Development in the Social Context* by C. B. Kopp, J. B. Krakow. © 1982 by Addison Wesley Publishing Company, Inc. Reprinted by permission of Pearson Education, Inc.; p. 35, Figure 1–8 "Nature-nurture reconceptualized in the developmental perspective: A bioecological model" by U. Bronfenbrenner & S.J. Ceci, *Psychological Review,* 101, p. 575, 1994. © American Psychological Association, reprinted with permission.

Chapter 2   p. 42, From "Separated at Birth in Mexico, Reunited at Campuses on L.I" by Elissa Gootman, *The New York Times,* March 3, 2003; p. 52, Figure 2–4 ; p. 56, Ad Reprinted by permission of Oneida; p. 64, Figure 2–7 Reprinted by permission of the publisher from *The Postnatal Development of the Human Cerebral Cortex, Vols. I-VII* by Jesse LeRoy Conel, Cambridge, Mass.: Harvard University Press, Copyright © 1939, 1975 by the President and Fellows of Harvard College; p. 67, Figure 2–9 From *Racial Adaptations* by Carleton Stevens Coon, (Nelson-Hall, 1982).

Chapter 3   p. 85, Armstrong, Penny and Sheryl Feldman, A Midwife's Story, New York: Arbor House, 1986, pp. 59–60; p. 98, Figure 3–7 encarta.msn.com; p. 99, Figure 3–8 ; p. 106, Figure 3–10 From *Our Sexuality, 8E* by Robert Crooks and Karla Baur, 2002. Reprinted with permission of Wadsworth, a division of Thomson Learning, www.thomsonrights.com. Fax 800-730-2215; p. 116, Figure 3–12 Reprinted from *The Developing Human: Clinically Oriented Embryology, 6E* by K.L. Moore & T.V.N. Persaud, p. 118, © 1998 with permission of Elsevier; p. 103, From *Treating Drug Abusers Effectively* by Egertson, Fox & Leshner, 1998. Reproduced by permission of Blackwell Publishing; p. 119, Best, Joel, *Damned Lies and Statistics: Untangling Numbers from Media, Politicians and Activities,* Berkeley: University of California Press, 2001, pp. 2–3.

Chapter 4   p. 139, Figure 4–2 From *Life Span Development, 7E* by John E. Santrock. Reprinted with permission of The McGraw-Hill Companies; p. 127, From "10 Million Orphans" by Tom Masland and Rod Nordland. From *Newsweek,* January 17, 2000, © 2000 Newsweek, Inc. All rights reserved. Reprinted by permission. www.newsweek.com; p. 152, Figure 4–8 From "I Have A Dream" by Martin Luther King Jr. Reprinted by arrangement with the Estate of Martin Luther King Jr., c/o Writers House as agent for the proprietor New York, NY. Copyright © 1963 Martin Luther King Jr., copyright renewed 1991 Coretta Scott King; p. 164, Figure 4–10 "Are there biological programming effects for psychological development? Findings from a study of Romanian adoptees" by M. Rutter, T.G. O'Connor and the English and Romanian Adoptees Study Team, *Developmental Psychology,* 2004, 40, 81–94. © American Psychological Association, reprinted with permission of the APA and Thomas G. O'Conner.

Chapter 5   p. 178, Figure 5–2 From "The normal crying curve" What do we really know" by R.G. Barr from *Developmental Medicine and Child Neurology,* April 1990, 32, 356–362. Reproduced with permission of Mac Keith Press; p. 203, Figure 5–8 From "Change in family-to-needs matters more for children with less" by E. Dearing, K. McCartney and B.A. Taylor, *Child Development,* 2001, 72, 1779–1793. Reproduced with permission from Blackwell Publishing; p. 207, Figure 5–9 From "Early educational interventions for high-risk children" by C.T. Ramey, et. al. from *Parenting and the Child's World: Influences on academic, intellectual, and social-emotional development* edited by John G. Borkowski, et. al., 2002. Reproduced with permission of Lawrence Erlbaum Associates Inc. and Craig T. Ramey.

Chapter 6   p. 234, Figure 6–9 From "The Flexible Item Selection Task (FIST): A measure of executive function in preschoolers by S. Jacques and P.D. Zelazo, *Developmental Neuropsychology,* 2001, #20, pp. 573–591. Reproduced with permission of Lawrence Erlbaum Associates Inc. and Sophie Jacques.

Chapter 7   p. 262, Figure 7–3 From "Lead in the Inner Cities" by Howard W. Mielke, *American Scientist,* 1999, Vol. 87. Reproduced with permission of Howard W. Mielke, Ph.D.; p. 269, Figure 7–5 From "A comparison of two measurements of child compliance with normal preschool children" by B.D. Brumfield and M.W. Roberts, *Journal of Clinical Child Psychology,* 1998, 27, p. 114. Reprinted with permission of Lawrence Erlbaum Associates Inc., B.D. Brumfield and M.W. Roberts; p. 295, Figure 7–8 From "Prevalence, correlates, and trajectory of television viewing among infants and toddlers" by Laura K. Certain and Robert S. Kahn, *Pediatrics,* April 2002, 109, 634–642. Reprinted by permission of the American Academy of Pediatrics.

Chapter 8   p. 309, Figure 8–4 Reprinted from *NeuroImage,* 13, B. Luna, K. R. Thulborn, D. R. Munoz et al., "Maturation of widely distributed brain function subserves cognitive development," p. 788, © 2001, with permission from Elsevier; p. 316, Figure 8–7 Reprinted from *Biological Psychology,* 54, A. Fry and S. Hale, "Relationships Among Processing Speed, Working Memory and Fluid Intelligence in Children," p. 6, © 2000, with permission from Elsevier.

Chapter 9   p. 383, Figure 9–11a From the *PMA Spatial Relations Test in 1962 Manual of the Primary Mental Abilities, Spatial Relations Test;* Figure 9–11b "Spatial Visualization" based on *Differential Aptitude Test, Form L.*

Chapter 10   p. 409, Figure 10–7 "Criminal decision making: the development of adolescent judgment, criminal responsibility, and culpability" by C.S. Fried and N.D. Reppucci, *Law & Human Behavior,* 2001, 25, 45–61. © American Psychological Association, reprinted with permission; p. 418, Figure 10–8 From " Need fulfillment, interpersonal competence, and the developmental contexts of early adolescent friendship" by D. Buhrmester in *The Company They Keep: Friendship in Childhood and Adolescence* edited by W.M. Bukowski, A.F. Newcomb and W.W. Hartup, 1996. Reprinted with the permission of Cambridge University Press; p. 421, Figure 10–9 From Child Trends website, www.childtrendsdatabank.org. Reproduced with permission of Child Trends.

Chapter 12   p. 477, Figure 12–1 "The Relationship between age an major league baseball performance: Implications for development" by R. Schulz, D. Musa, J. Staszewski and R.S. Siegler, 1994, *Psychology and Aging,* 9, pp. 278–279. © American Psychological Association, reprinted with permission; p. 479, Figure 12–3 From "Age-related Decrement in Hearing for Speech: sampling and longitudinal studies" by M. Bergman, V.G. Blumenfeld, D. Casardo, B. Dash, H. Levitt, an M.K. Margulies, *Journal of Gerontology,* 1976, 31, p. 534; p. 494, Figure 12–7 From *Intellectual Development in Adulthood: The Seattle Longitudinal Study* by K.W. Schaie, 1996, p. 168. Reprinted with the permission of Cambridge University Press; p. 499, Figure 12–8 From "Psychosocial stages and the accessibility of autobiographical memories across the life cycle" by M.A. Conway and A. Holmes, *Journal of Personality,* 2004, 72, 461–480. Reproduced by permission of Blackwell Publishing Ltd.

Chapter 13   p. 519, From *Oh, the Places You'll Go!* by Dr. Seuss, copyright TM & copyright © by Dr. Seuss Enterprises L.P. 1990. Used by permission of Random House Children's Books, a division of Random House, Inc. and ICM; p. 607, From *Aging With Grace* by Dr. David Snowdon, copyright © 2001 by David A Snowdon. Used by permission of Bantam Books, a division of Random House, Inc. and David Snowdon; p. 537, Figure 13–6 "The nature and predictors of the trajectory of change in marital quality for husbands and wives over the first 10 years of marriage" by L.A. Kurdek, *Developmental Psychology,* 1999, 35, 1282–1296. © American Psychological Association, reprinted with permission; p. 542, Figure 13–7 From "Evolved sex differences in the number of partners desired? The long and short of it" by W.C. Pedersen, L.C. Miller, A.D. Putcha-Bhagavatula and Y. Yang, *Psychological Science,* 2002, 13, 157–16. Reproduced by permission of Blackwell Publishing Ltd.; p. 534, "Passionate Love Scale," from *Love and Sex: Cross-Cultural Perspectives* by E. Hatfield and R.L. Rapson, 2005. Lanham, MD: University Press of America. Reprinted by permission of E. Hatfield.

Name Index

Individuals featured in stories and research discussions are listed here; see the References for a complete list of cited authors and sources.

Subject Index